2011/12

THE GUIDE TO

GRANTS FOR
INDIVIDUALS
IN NEED

TWELFTH EDITION

Catriona Chronnell

Additional research by:
Anna Adams, Jessica Carver & Jonny Morris

Contributions from:
Ashley Wood

DIRECTORY OF SOCIAL CHANGE

Published by
Directory of Social Change
24 Stephenson Way
London NW1 2DP
Tel: 08450 77 77 07; Fax: 020 7391 4804
email: publications@dsc.org.uk
www.dsc.org.uk
from whom further copies and a full publications catalogue are available.

Directory of Social Change Northern Office
Federation House, Hope Street, Liverpool L1 9BW
Policy & Research 0151 708 0136; email: research@dsc.org.uk

Directory of Social Change is a Registered Charity no. 800517

First published 1987
Second edition 1990
Third edition 1992
Fourth edition 1994
Fifth edition 1996
Sixth edition 1998
Seventh edition 2000
Eighth edition 2002
Ninth edition 2004
Tenth edition 2006
Eleventh edition 2009
Twelfth edition 2011

ISBN 978 1 906294 48 9

British Library Cataloguing in Publication Data
A catalogue record for this book is available from the British Library

Cover design by Kate Bass
Original text design by Gabriel Kerne
Typeset by Marlinzo Services, Frome
Printed and bound by Page Bros, Norwich

CONTENTS

Introduction   5

How to use this guide   11

How to make an application   13

General charities   17

Illness and disability charities   43

Occupational charities   57

Service and ex-service charities   107

Religious charities   123

Local charities   133

Advice organisations   349

Index   365

INTRODUCTION

Welcome to the twelfth edition of *The Guide to Grants for Individuals in Need*. The main focus of the book is to list sources of non-statutory help for people in financial need. This edition details 2,060 trusts with £264 million available in grant awards, compared with 1,400 trusts giving £66 million in the first edition (1987).

Grants made by charities in this guide range from £10 food vouchers to larger contributions such as grants for domestic items such as washing machines, wheelchairs and house adaptations, although few will cover the whole cost of these. This kind of help does not overcome long-term financial problems, but it can be extremely valuable in helping to meet immediate needs which the state does not currently cover.

This introduction looks at the trusts included in this guide and how to locate them, before discussing what help is available from them and how the trusts can improve their roles. It looks briefly at other funding sources for individuals, highlighting the need to explore all statutory sources available. Ashley Wood of the Gaddum Centre has again provided a helpful section explaining how to make your application once the relevant trusts have been identified (see 'How to make an application' on page 13). We have also tried to highlight some of the key themes that have emerged from this research process in relation to the impact of the recession on grantmakers and how this may affect those wishing to apply.

About this guide

We aim to include all publicly registered charities (including those in Scotland and Northern Ireland) which give at least £500 a year to individuals in need, although most give considerably more than this.

With a few exceptions, we do not include:

- organisations which give grants solely for educational purposes
- organisations which give grants to members only and not to dependants
- individual employer or company welfare funds
- Friendly Societies
- local branches of national charities, although they may raise money locally for cases of need

- organisations only providing services (such as home visiting) rather than cash (or in kind) grants.

Many of the trusts support individuals for educational causes as well. These are all included in the sister guide to this book, *The Guide to Educational Grants*, which includes details for funding opportunities for all forms of education up to the end of a first degree, including apprenticeships, personal development and expeditions. Some trusts support organisations such as community groups, others have large financial commitments (often providing housing). The entries in this guide concentrate solely on the trusts' social welfare grants to individuals in need.

How trusts are ordered in this guide

The trusts are separated into six sections: five UK-wide sections followed by a local section, broken down into nine countries/ regions. The flow chart on page 12 shows how the guide works.

UK-wide trusts

The majority of the money in this book is given by the UK-wide trusts which are divided into five sections:

General charities (page 17)

This section includes charities which operate UK-wide (or at least in more than one country or more than two regions of England) and which are not tied to a particular trade, occupation or disability. These range from those which have very wide objectives, such as 'people in need', 'older people' or 'children and young people', to members of particular ethnic groups. General charities are among the best known and tend to be heavily oversubscribed.

Illness and disability charities (page 43)

These charities give grants to people with specific illnesses or disabilities. These trusts can help people (and often their families/ carers) who are in financial need as a result of a particular illness or disability. Many of these also give advisory and other support, although for a fuller list of organisations providing these functions please see 'Advice organisations' starting on page 349.

Occupational charities (page 57)

This section contains trusts that benefit not only the people who worked in the particular trade but also, in many cases,

their widows/widowers and dependent children. Membership or previous membership of the particular institute can be required, but many are open to non-members. Length of service can sometimes be taken into account. Many of these trusts are members of the Occupational Benevolent Fund Alliance, an umbrella organisation which represents this area of the sector. There are some occupations which have a number of funds covering the industry, and others which have none.

Service and ex-service charities (page 107)

This section contains exceptionally thorough charitable provision for people who have served in the forces, whether as a regular or during national service. This funding is different to the other occupational funds as they support a large percentage of the male population over retirement age (many of them would have undertaken national service). Again, these usually also provide for the widows, widowers and dependent children of the core beneficiaries. Many of these funds have local voluntary workers who provide advice and practical help, and who in turn are backed up by professional staff and substantial resources. Soldiers, Sailors, Airmen and Families Association (SSAFA) Forces Help is an influential member of this sector, providing the well-used model, and often the initial contact and application form, for many of the regimental funds.

Religious charities (page 123)

This section deals with trusts that support religious workers, such as members of the clergy, missionaries and so on. Often this support extends to dependants of these workers. Support for people connected to particular faiths (Christian, Christian Science and Jewish) are also detailed.

Local charities (page 133)

Included in this section are those trusts which only support individuals in Northern Ireland, Scotland or Wales, or just one region of England. Trusts which are eligible for two of these chapters have generally been given a full entry in one chapter and a cross reference in the other; trusts relevant to three or more of the chapters have generally been included in the national section. Charitable help is unequally distributed across the UK, often with more money available in London and the south east of England than the rest of the UK. However, many of the main cities have at least one large trust able to give more than £50,000 a year.

The local section starts with details on how to use this section.

Charities in Northern Ireland

Unfortunately the section for Northern Ireland is very limited, as very little information is available on charities based there at present. Despite the passing of the *Charities Act (Northern Ireland)* in September 2008, the Charity Commission for Northern Ireland has yet to begin the process of registering all of Northern Ireland's charitable organisations. However, this process is expected to start soon and will hopefully be well underway by the time the next edition of this guide is researched. In the meantime, up-to-date information on the current situation can be found on the Charity Commission for Northern Ireland's new website: www.charitycommissionni.org.uk.

How trusts can help

Some trusts lament the fact that the people they wish to support may refuse to accept charity and wish to maintain their independence. A charitable trust is public money being held for the benefit of a specific group of people; just as people are encouraged to access any statutory funds they can, they should also be encouraged to accept all charitable money which has been set aside for them.

However, it is not just people who are classified as 'poor' who are eligible for support from trusts. Formerly known as the 'relief of sickness', this charitable purpose has been re-defined under the provisions of the Charities Act 2006, and now comes under the purpose, 'the advancement of health or the saving of lives'.

The Charity Commission guidance on the 'advancement of health or the saving of lives' has broadened the scope of the previous guidance, *Charities for the Relief of Sickness* (CC6), meaning a wider range of activities has been deemed charitable. The following extract has been taken from the Charity Commission guidance:

The advancement of health includes the prevention or relief of sickness, disease or human suffering, as well as the promotion of health. It includes conventional methods as well as complementary, alternative or holistic methods which are concerned with healing mind, body and spirit in the alleviation of symptoms and the cure of illness.

The relief of sickness extends beyond the treatment or provision of care, such as a hospital, to the provision of items, services and facilities to ease the suffering or assist the recovery of people who are sick, convalescent, disabled or infirm or to provide comforts for patients.

The saving of lives includes a range of charitable activity directed towards saving people whose lives are in danger and protecting life and property.

The guidance goes on to provide examples of the sorts of charities and charitable purposes which fall within this description, such as:

- *charities that provide comforts, items, services and facilities for people who are sick, convalescent, disabled or infirm;*

- *charities that promote activities that have a proven beneficial effect on health;*

- *charities set up to assist the victims of natural disasters or war.*

These examples focus mainly on the physical aspect of 'relief' rather than on the financial position of people who are living with an illness or disability. This is not because grants for the advancement of health are not means-tested, but simply because these trusts exist to relieve a physical need rather than a financial one. There are charitable trusts that exist to carry out either or both charitable purposes, they may either deal exclusively with the financial impact that an illness or disability can have on an individual's life or concentrate on the physical aspect of 'relief', or they may address both.

Many trusts believe that people should not lose their life savings and standard of living to buy an essential item that they could afford but would leave them financially vulnerable for the future. Charity Commission guidance differentiates between organisations which attempt to relieve sickness, and organisations for the relief of the sick poor, which can only support people who are both sick and poor.

Although these are the areas trusts *may* support, it would be wrong to believe that any given trust will support all of these needs. Each trust in this guide has a governing document, stating who can and cannot be supported. As mentioned earlier, we have broken down the trusts in this guide to aid the reader in identifying those which might be of relevance to them, and we would strongly advise that individuals do not approach a trust for which they are not eligible.

Many trusts have complained to us that they receive applications outside their scope which they would like to support but their governing document prevents them from doing so. These applicants have no chance of being supported and only serve to be a drain on valuable resources. Please be aware that it is not the number of trusts you apply to which affects your chance of support but the relevance of them.

What types of help can be given?

Charity Commission guidance

The Charity Commission's 2008 guidance, *The Prevention or Relief of Poverty for the Public Benefit*, lists what type of help can be given. (Please note that this list should not be seen as comprehensive.) The list is given as follows:

Examples of ways in which charities might relieve poverty include:

Grants of money in the form of:

- *weekly allowances for a limited period;*

- *payments to meet a particular need;*

- *one-off payments in a crisis or disaster;*

- *payment of travelling expenses for visiting people, for example in a hospital, convalescent home, children's home, prison or other similar place, particularly where more frequent visits are desirable than payments from public funds will allow;*

- *payments to meet expenses associated with visiting people (as mentioned above) for example, child-minding, accommodation, refreshments etc;*

- *payments to assist in meeting energy and water bills.*

The provision of items *(either outright or, if expensive but appropriate, on loan), such as:*

- *furniture, bedding, clothing, food, fuel, heating appliances;*

- *washing machines and fridges.*

Payment for services, *such as:*

- *essential house decorating;*

- *insulation and repairs;*

- *laundering;*

- *meals on wheels;*

- *outings and entertainment;*

- *child-minding;*

- *telephone line, rates and utilities.*

The provision of facilities, *such as:*

- *the supply of tools or books;*

- *payments of fees for instruction, examination, or other expenses connected with vocational training, language, literacy, numerical or technical skills;*

- *travelling expenses to help the recipients to earn their living; or*

- *equipment and funds for recreational pursuits or training intended to bring the quality of life of the beneficiaries to a reasonable standard.*

*Charities for the relief of financial hardship might give extra help to people in poverty who are also **sick, convalescent, infirm, or*** *with disabilities*, whether physical or mental. This might include:

Grants of money in the form of:

- *special payments to relieve sickness or infirmity;*
- *payment of travelling expenses on entering or leaving hospitals, convalescent homes, or similar institutions, or for out-patient consultations;*
- *payment towards the cost of adaptations to the homes of people with disabilities; or*
- *payment of telephone installation charges and rentals.*

One-off grants

Some trusts will only give one-off cash payments. This means that they will award a single lump sum (say £50) which is paid by cheque or postal order either direct to the applicant, to the welfare agency applying on the person's behalf, or to another suitable third party. No more help will be considered until the applicant has submitted a new application, and trusts are usually unwilling to give more than one such grant per person per year.

Recurrent grants

Other trusts will only pay recurrent grants, usually weekly allowances, often of up to the current 'disregard' level. (The disregard level is the maximum income a person on income support can receive in addition to their state benefit before it affects their income support calculations.)

Weekly payments can be higher than this, particularly if the applicant requires expensive treatment or medicine on a regular basis, or has some other high ongoing cost.

Some trusts will give either one-off or recurrent payments according to what is more appropriate for the applicant.

Grants in kind

Occasionally grants are given in the form of vouchers or are paid directly to a shop or store in the form of credit to enable the applicant to obtain food, clothing or other prearranged items. Some charities still deliver coal.

More commonly, especially with disability aids or other technical equipment, the charity will either give the equipment itself to the applicant (rather than the money) or loan it free of charge or at a low rental for as long as the applicant needs it. More common items, such as telephones and televisions, can also be given as equipment because the charity can get better trade terms than the individual.

Statutory funding

Whilst there is a wide range of types of grants that can be given and a variety of reasons why they can be made, there is one area trusts cannot support. No charitable trust is allowed to provide funds which replace statutory funding. The reason for this is that if a trust gives £100, say, to an individual who could have received those funds from statutory sources, then it is the state rather than the individual who is benefiting from the grant.

The effectiveness of grant-making trusts

While some trusts, particularly national ones, produce clear guidelines, others (especially local trusts) do not. Based on our experience of researching this publication over the past 20 years, we would like to make some suggestions as to ways in which trusts giving grants to individuals, particularly local trusts, could seek to encourage greater fairness in funding:

- Local trusts could seek to expand their resources to meet new or more widespread needs.

- If trustees can only meet twice a year, they should aim to cover the peak periods. Although welfare needs arise throughout the year, there are obvious peak times; for example, for fuel needs this is around early winter.

- Trusts should also aim to ensure that needs can be met as rapidly as possible, for example by empowering the clerk or a small number of trustees to make payments up to a certain limit (such as £100).

- Trusts should ensure they are very well known in their area of benefit. We recommend that each trust (depending on its eligibility restrictions) writes to at least the following places: all welfare agencies (especially Citizens Advice); all community centres and other public meeting points; and the offices of the relevant education authority.

Over the years DSC has campaigned on a number of fronts for better grantmaking. We believe that grantmakers have a responsibility that extends far beyond providing funding. The way funders operate has a huge impact on the beneficiaries which their funding supports, as well as on the wider voluntary sector.

Our Great Giving campaign has grown out of these long-established beliefs. The campaign encompasses four areas: (1) a clear picture of the funding environment; (2) accessible funding for campaigning; (3) an end to hidden small print; and (4) no ineligible applications.

Although the campaign relates mainly to grant-making trusts that support organisations, the four principles of the campaign extend to the trusts covered in this guide. We believe that funders have a responsibility to understand the environment in which they are operating. At present there is little information about where money is going and what is being supported. Providing a clearer picture will enable better planning and decision-making from funders and policy makers, as well as contributing to the growing body of knowledge about the sector.

We know that most grantmakers receive more applications for funding than they can award. We also know that a significant proportion of those applications are ineligible. In some cases the fault lies with the information provided by the funder, and in some cases the fault lies with the interpretation of that information by the applicant. In our 2010 report, *Ineligible Applications*, we made some recommendations on what grantmakers can do to try and avoid receiving large numbers of ineligible applications:

- Provide comprehensive and accessible information: state what you do and what you want to fund, preferably online if you have a website.

- Ensure your application guidance is clear, concise and as jargon-free as possible: encourage prospective applicants to read it.

- Explain the application procedure clearly: what information will be required, by when and in what form.

- Providing constructive feedback, especially if the application is rejected; this should make it less likely that the applicant submits the same ineligible bid again and again.

- Provide a clear contact point for any queries, and instructions on how you prefer to be contacted.

- Keep track of ineligible applications and analyse them periodically to see if there are any patterns. Consider how the information you provide could be changed to reduce their number.

In the current financial climate (which we will touch upon more in the next section) where many grantmakers have experienced a rise in demand for their services, these recommendations are particularly important. Advertising clearly what you do and how you do it will not only empower individuals to make informed decisions about their applications, it should also limit the number of ineligible applications received and free up vital resources, which will ensure more time can be spent on those individuals the trust exists to support.

Further information on our research into ineligible applications and the Great Giving campaign itself can be found on our website (www.dsc.org.uk/GreatGiving).

The impact of the recession

In the last edition of this guide, individuals were beginning to experience the first consequences of the global economic recession. In the two years since then the UK has inched out of that recession, but rising unemployment, falling consumer spending and government cuts mean that economic recovery has been slow and we are likely to feel the effects for some time to come.

The research process for this guide has provided an opportunity, through analysis of annual reports and accounts and contact with grant-making trusts and beneficiaries, to assess how grantmakers are dealing with the changes and the implications this may have for individuals looking for funding.

Pressures in the funding environment

Grant-making trusts are currently struggling with three broad concerns: rising demand, financial difficulties and cuts to statutory funding – issues which will continue to shape their activities at least in the medium term.

The economic downturn has pushed many individuals into a position of financial hardship as a combination of cuts to local services, rising unemployment and higher costs of living have really begun to have an effect on household incomes.

A report by the Joseph Rowntree Foundation (*A minimum income standard for the UK in 2010*, Donald Hirsch et al, 2010) illustrates the growing financial pressures faced by individuals, particularly those on low incomes:

The cost of a minimum [household] budget is estimated to have risen by 38% in the past ten years, due to steep rises in the price of food (up 37%), bus fares (up 59%), council tax (up 67%) and some other essentials. But official inflation has only been 23% in total over the same period. This is the measure that will now be used to uprate all benefits, meaning that people out of work, who have already seen a fall in the value of their basic benefits, could fall further behind.

As a result, more people are finding themselves in need of extra help and are looking to the charitable sector for support. Occupational trusts, in particular, have seen an increase in demand for their services. For example, in 2008/09 the Royal College of Nursing Benevolent Fund experienced a 60% rise in applications due to redundancies and partner redundancies compared with the previous year (*Consolidated annual report and accounts*, Royal College of Nursing of the United Kingdom, 2009, p. 28).

Rising demand has been coupled with financial pressure as many trusts have seen the value of their assets fall – a particular problem for trusts which are heavily reliant on investment income. The Timber Trades' Benevolent Society (TTBS), for example, experienced a significant fall in both its asset value and income:

Most charities have suffered as a result of the economic problems which befell the world in 2008 and TTBS was no exception. Our investment income during 2009 fell by some £20,000 while income from fundraising, donations and subscriptions also suffered. Although the paper value of our investments increased in 2009 this was after a large fall in the previous year and stock prices have a long way to go before we are back to the pre 'crash' values. Overall income was down by 15% and the society ran at a deficit of £35,000.

Annual Report and Accounts 2009, Timber Trades' Benevolent Society, 2009, p. 2

In addition, some trusts have been reporting a reduction in the statutory contribution to some items and services, particularly at a local level. Trish Pickford, Head of Welfare at the Royal Agricultural Benevolent Institution explains their experience:

We have seen over the last few years, more requests for help with disability aids and adaptations and towards the cost of home helps and care home top-ups. I believe this is mainly down to local authority budgeting and cuts. As the elderly population increases, we see more people trying to struggle on in their own homes, many of whom are unable to obtain the help and support they need from the local authority as they are not deemed to be 'critical'. There are long waits of up to a year for occupational therapist assessments and so our charity is being approached for help with things that in the past would have been provided through public funding.

Correspondence with Trish Pickford, Head of Welfare at the Royal Agricultural Benevolent Institution, October 2010

This trend is likely to become increasingly prominent over the next few years as the budget cuts and welfare reforms detailed in the Emergency Budget (June 2010) and Spending Review (October 2010) begin to take effect.

Impact on grant-making trusts

The response of grantmakers to these pressures has varied depending on the extent by which they have been affected, and indeed, some have felt little detrimental impact. However, many have had to reassess, and in some cases amend, their grant-making strategy – something individuals applying for funding need to bear in mind.

The response can be broadly categorised into two fields, financial changes (i.e.

reduced grant levels lower average grants and savings on administration costs) and non-financial changes (i.e. tightening up of eligibility criteria, prioritising the type of grants given and reviewing the position of existing beneficiaries). Many trusts have employed a mixture of measures.

Compared with the last edition of the guide, published in 2009, there has been a fall of 12% in the level of grantmaking. Family Action (formerly Family Welfare Association), for example, gave £800,000 in 2006/07 but only £624,000 in 2008/09, a drop of 22%, largely due to the impact of low interest rates on their income (*Annual Report and Accounts 2006/07*, p. 8 and *Annual Report and Accounts 2008/09*, p. 11, Family Action). As this is the first edition of the guide to fully take account of the recession it will be interesting to compare these figures to those in the next guide, which is due out in 2013, to see if welfare provision recovers to its previous levels.

Falling average grants have also been a reoccurring theme. The Yorkshire Water Community Trust, for example, received over 2,200 applications in 2008/09, 1,900 of which were successful, compared with just under 1,500 applications in 2006/07, of which 1,100 were successful. The trust's grant expenditure has not kept up with this demand and consequently the average grant dropped from £352 in 2006/07 to £310 in 2008/09 (*Annual Report and Accounts 2007*, p. 10 and *Annual Report and Accounts 2009*, p. 8, The Yorkshire Water Community Trust).

This level may also be less in relative terms due to a rise in what is deemed to be an *effective* grant level; i.e. rising living costs and decreasing statutory support mean trusts will have to give more to make the same impact.

Consequently, while some trusts which have been affected by rising demand may allow their average grant level to fall, it is likely that many will turn to other non-financial measures to ensure that they can continue to strike a balance between helping as many people as possible while maintaining the effectiveness of their grantmaking.

The Greggs Foundation, for example, has witnessed a significant increase in the number of applications to the hardship fund. The foundation was not badly affected by the recession and managed to maintain its level of giving. However, due to the increase in demand it decided to prioritise applications which benefited dependent children within family units and warned that funding was highly unlikely to be given unless the item was essential. As a result, the success rate for applications to the hardship fund dipped from around 60% in 2008 to 40% in 2009 but the average grant given actually increased (Correspondence with David

Carnaffan, Greggs Foundation Assistant Manager, October 2010).

It is also inspiring to see how some grantmakers have tried to shield the worst of the impact from their beneficiaries, at least in the short term, either by utilising their reserves, saving in other areas or running a finer margin on income and expenditure. The Timber Trades' Benevolent Society, mentioned before for having experienced a fall in asset value and income, was still able to maintain the value of its main benefits and increase its payments for TV licences, telephone costs and winter fuel by dipping into its reserves (*Annual Report and Accounts 2009*, The Timber Trades' Benevolent Society, p. 2).

Another excellent example is the Northern Ladies Annuity Society, which endeavoured in 2009 to soften the impact of the financial downturn on its beneficiaries.

In a year that has seen the country go from 'credit crunch' to full blown recession, the Society has increased its endeavours to cushion our annuitants from the worst of the economic gloom. While inflation as a whole has been falling, food and fuel prices remain high and this, coupled with low returns on savings, has meant that many of our annuitants have felt the chill wind of recession more than most. As a result the decision was taken to increase the annuities by five pounds per week from the 1 November 2008. This means that each annuitant now receives a quarterly cheque of £325, up from £260. In addition fuel grants of £50 were paid out on 1 December and 1 January to help with the particularly high cost of fuel that was prevalent last autumn and winter. Fortunately this extra expenditure has not prevented the Society from awarding other grants. 15 holiday grants were paid out this year totalling £3,750 and there were 13 general grants totalling £3,900.

Advice for applicants

It is difficult to assess how the economic downturn will affect the funding environment over the next few years. Grant-making trusts have been affected differently depending on the area they work in and their financial position, and all will respond differently to these pressures. There will be more competition for funding but despite the fall in the level of grantmaking, trusts are trying to do all they can to help their beneficiaries and there is still a vast amount of money available to those in need.

For those individuals applying for funding the same basic principles apply (see 'How to make an application' on page 13 for Ashley Wood's excellent step-by-step guide). However, in the current climate it is worth bearing a few extra things in mind.

- **Check the latest criteria**: Financial pressures and rising applications have led many trusts to tighten up their eligibility criteria or limit the things for which they will give. Make sure you have the latest guidelines and read them carefully to check that you are eligible to apply and the trust can help with your specific need. If in doubt, a quick phone call is usually welcomed and can save time in the long run.

- **Be open and honest when applying**: Take care to fill in any application form as fully as possible and try to be as clear and open as you can. The same applies if you need to write a letter of application. It will help grantmakers to assess your needs quickly and advise you on any other benefits or potential sources of funding for which you may be eligible.

- **Don't just apply to large, well-known trusts**: They are likely to be the most oversubscribed, leaving you with less chance of success. Take the time to look for others you may also be eligible to apply for.

- **Apply to all appropriate trusts**: Falling average grants may mean that one trust cannot offer enough to cover the full cost of the item or service you need. You may have to consider applying to several trusts and ask for a small contribution from each. If it has not been indicated already in this guide, a quick phone call is usually enough to establish how much a trust is likely to give for an individual grant.

Other sources of support

Whilst there are many situations in which approaching a trust might be the best option, there is of course a limit to the support that they can provide, individually or collectively. There are a number of alternative sources of support that should be considered in conjunction with looking at grant-making trusts (note that these are beyond the direct scope of this publication).

Statutory sources

There are a lot of funding opportunities available to individuals from the state. The exact details of these sources vary in different countries in the UK, and in some instances among different local authorities. This area is likely to become ever more confusing in the light of recent budget cuts and welfare reforms. Consequently, comprehensive details are beyond the scope of this guide.

However, full details should be available from government departments such as benefits agencies and social services, as well as many of the welfare agencies listed on pages 349 to 354. The Direct Gov website (www.direct.gov.uk) and the Department for Work and Pensions' website (www.dwp.gov.uk) also have a wealth of information on what is available and how to apply.

There are a number of advice organisations that may also be able to offer advice and support to people who are unsure of their benefit entitlement or who are looking for extra support in the form of a grant. It may prove useful to visit websites such as Turn2Us (www.turn2us.org.uk) and Benevolence Today (www.benevolencetoday.org), which was a campaign set up by and for more than 35 coalition partners across the UK. These websites can offer advice on both statutory and non-statutory sources of funding to charities working on behalf of individuals and to individuals themselves. Note that Benevolence Today's project lifecycle has come to an end, but there remains a wealth of information on the website.

Citizens Advice also provide an online advice service called Adviceguide (www.adviceguide.org.uk) which offers useful information on issues relating to statutory benefits and individual entitlement. Local branches of Citizens Advice can also offer people more assistance in this area.

Disaster appeals

If there has been a large unexpected hardship which is beyond the scope of being relieved from statutory or charitable sources, then one possibility is to establish a disaster appeal. These are commonly established as a public response to a well-publicised disaster, such as the London Bombings in July 2005 or the South Yorkshire Floods in 2007, where the public wish to show their support. They can also be established in response to a personal misfortune. The Mark Davies Injured Riders Fund, for instance, was established by the parents of a talented rider killed during the Burghley Horse Trials to support injured riders. Appeals can also be established to aid a particular individual if they have needs which gain high levels of public sympathy and little time to apply for statutory or charitable sources. Disaster Appeals can be to relieve an epidemic rather than an individual case, or to leave a lasting legacy. The Charity Commission leaflet *Disaster Appeals* (CC40) provides further information.

Companies

Many employers are unhappy to see former members of staff or their dependants living in need or distress. Few have formal arrangements but a letter or telephone call to the personnel manager should establish if help is possible.

Most large companies give charitable grants, although most have a policy of only funding organisations (possibly because charities have more ways of publicising this support than individuals do). Many that will support individuals have their own charitable trusts, and therefore are included in this guide.

There has been a growing trend for many prominent utility companies to establish charitable trusts which give to individuals who are struggling to pay their utility bills. These charitable companies have continued to grow and have for a number of years provided much relief to the individuals involved, lessening the financial burden upon them and ensuring that no legal action will be taken against them for non-payment.

Community foundations

Over recent years, community foundations have established themselves as key community actors. According to the Community Foundation Network website: 'more than 95% of the population live in the area of benefit of a community foundation. It is one of the largest funders of community organisations in the UK (making grants of over £70 million a year).'

Community foundations are charities located throughout the UK. These foundations aim to be 'cause-neutral' and manage funds donated to them by both individuals and organisations, which are then distributed to the local communities in which they serve.

While most community foundations only support organisations, many of them also have funds available for individuals and are therefore included in this guide. The Community Foundation Network has a list of existing and emerging foundations on its website: (www.communityfoundations.org.uk).

Please note that, like most sources of financial support, funding for individuals is subject to frequent change. Even if your local community foundation is included in this guide it is worth checking the availability on your local community foundation website.

Vicars, priests and ministers of religion

There may be informal arrangements within a church, mosque, etc. to help people in need. Church of England vicars are often trustees of local charities which are too small to be included in the guide or which we have missed.

Hospitals

Most hospitals have patient welfare funds, but they are little known about even within the hospitals and so are little used. It may take some time to locate an appropriate contact. Start with the trust fund administrator or the treasurer's department of the health authority.

Local organisations

Rotary Clubs, Lions Clubs, Round Tables and so on are active in welfare provision. Usually they support groups rather than individuals and policies vary in different towns, but some welfare agencies (such as Citizens Advice) have a working relationship with these organisations and keep up-to-date lists of contacts. All enquiries should be made on behalf of the individual by a recognised agency.

Orders

Masonic and buffalo lodges and other organisations exist for the mutual benefit of their members and the wider community. Spouses and children of members (or deceased members) may also benefit, but people unconnected with these orders are unlikely to. Applications should be made to the lodge where the parent or spouse is or was a member.

Hobbies and interests

People with a particular hobby or interest should find out whether this offers any opportunities for funding. Included in this guide are a number of sporting associations which exist to help people who are in need, but there may be many more which are not registered with the Charity Commission or have less than £500 a year to give but are of great value to the people they can help. It is likely that other sports and interests have similar governing bodies wishing to help their members.

Educational support

This guide only deals with grants for the relief of need, ignoring trusts which can support individuals for educational purposes. However, many educational trusts are prepared to give grants to school children for uniforms, for instance. Receiving financial support for the cost of uniforms would obviously enable parents to spend the money budgeted for that purpose on other needs, so people with children of school age should check for any educational grants available to them. For information on statutory funds, contact your local educational authority or enquire for information at the office of the individual's school. For charitable funding, this guide's sister publication, *The Guide to Educational Grants*, should provide the relevant information.

Charity shops

Some charity shops will provide clothing if the applicant has a letter of referral from a recognised welfare agency.

Getting help

Unfortunately, none of these methods can offer a quick fix. Applying for grants can be a daunting experience, especially if you are unfamiliar with the process; it is probably worth starting with the help of a sympathetic advisor. Most branches of Citizens Advice have money advice workers or volunteers trained in basic money advice work. If you find that you are in financial need try going to the nearest Citizens Advice branch and talk to them about your financial difficulties. They may be able to help write an application to an appropriate charity, know of a welfare benefit you could claim or be able to renegotiate some of your debt repayments on your behalf. They will certainly be able to help you minimise your expenditure and budget effectively.

Acknowledgements

Throughout this introduction, we have commented on the Charity Commission for England and Wales's guidelines and advice. While we are aware that the Charity Commission only has rule over England and Wales, readers in Northern Ireland and Scotland (as well as the Isle of Man and the Channel Islands) should note that although the exact nature of charitable law differs in these countries, the spirit and guidance remains the same throughout the UK and the Charity Commission's advice should be seen as just as relevant.

We are extremely grateful to the many people, trust officers and others who have helped to compile this guide. To name them all individually would be impossible.

Request for further information

The research for this book was done as carefully as we were able, but there will be relevant charities that we have missed and some of the information may be incomplete or will become out of date. If you come across omissions or mistakes in this guide, please let us know by calling or emailing the Directory of Social Change's research department (0151 708 0136; email: research@dsc.org.uk) so that we can rectify them in future.

We are also always looking for ways to improve our guides and would appreciate any comments, positive or negative, about this guide, or suggestions on what other information would be useful for inclusion when we research the next edition.

How to use this GUIDE

Below is a typical trust entry, showing the format we have used to present the information obtained from each of the trusts.

On the following page is a flowchart. We recommend that you follow the order indicated on the flow chart to look at each section of the guide and find which trusts are relevant to you.

Individuals should therefore initially look at the charities that give nationally, firstly in the section classified by occupation of parent. Once you have found any charities in that section we advise you to look in the section classified by subject, followed by the section classified by need. Individuals should then look in the local section of the guide, which relates to where they live, or at any other areas with which they have a connection.

Eligibility

This states who is eligible to apply for a grant. It can include restrictions on age, family circumstances, occupation of parent, subject to be studied, ethnic origin, or place of residence.

Exclusions

This field gives information on what the trust will not fund.

Annual grant total

This indicates the total amount of money given in grants to individuals in the last financial year for which figures were available. Other financial information may be given where relevant.

Correspondent

This is the main person to contact, nominated by the trustees. Often the correspondent is the trust's solicitors or accountants, who may just pass applications on to the trustees and therefore will not be able to help with telephone enquiries.

The Fictitious Trust

Eligibility: Children or young people up to 25 years of age who are in need. Preference is given to children of single parent families and/or those who come from a disadvantaged or unstable family background.

Types of grants: Small one-off grants, to assist in cases of short-term need. The trust gives grants for a wide range of needs, including payment of utility bills, furniture, TV licence fees and medical equipment. The maximum grant is £250.

Exclusions: No grants for rent arrears.

Annual grant total: 140 grants totalled £25,000 in 2009/10.

Applications: On a form available from the correspondent, submitted either directly by the individual or by the parent or guardian for those under 18. Applications are considered in January, April, July and October.

Correspondent: Mrs I M Helpful, Charities Administrator, 7 Pleasant Road, London SN0 0ZZ (tel: 020 7123 4567; fax: 020 7123 4568).

Other information: The trust also gives educational grants to individuals.

Types of grants

Specifies whether the trust gives one-off or recurrent grants, or pensions, the size of grants given and for what grants are actually given, such as utility bills, furniture, TV licence fees and medical equipment.

Applications

This includes how to apply, who should make the application (i.e. the individual or a third party) and when to submit an application.

Other information

This contains miscellaneous further information about the trust.

How to identify sources of help – Quick reference flowchart

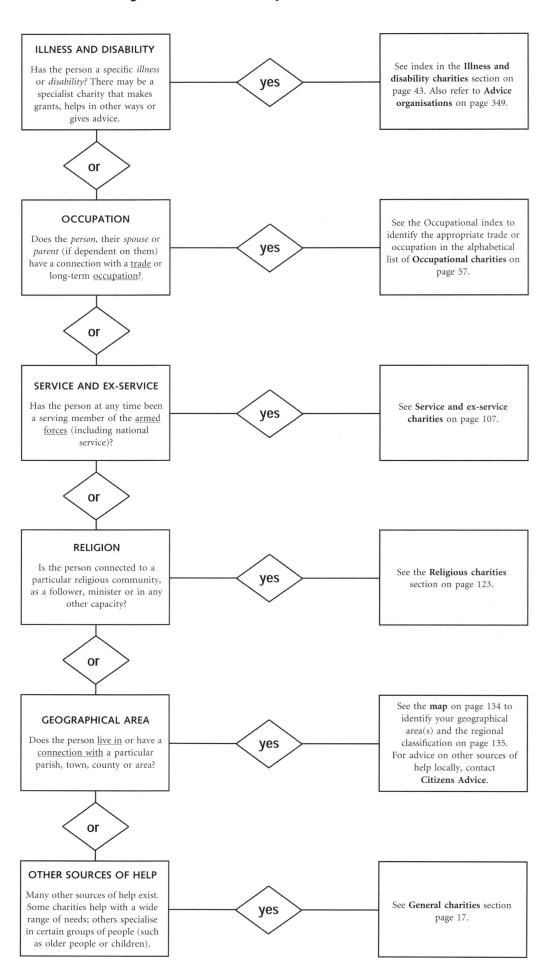

ILLNESS AND DISABILITY

Has the person a specific *illness* or *disability?* There may be a specialist charity that makes grants, helps in other ways or gives advice.

yes → See index in the **Illness and disability charities** section on page 43. Also refer to **Advice organisations** on page 349.

or

OCCUPATION

Does the *person*, their *spouse* or *parent* (if dependent on them) have a connection with a trade or long-term occupation?

yes → See the Occupational index to identify the appropriate trade or occupation in the alphabetical list of **Occupational charities** on page 57.

or

SERVICE AND EX-SERVICE

Has the person at any time been a serving member of the armed forces (including national service)?

yes → See **Service and ex-service charities** on page 107.

or

RELIGION

Is the person connected to a particular religious community, as a follower, minister or in any other capacity?

yes → See the **Religious charities** section on page 123.

or

GEOGRAPHICAL AREA

Does the person live in or have a connection with a particular parish, town, county or area?

yes → See the **map** on page 134 to identify your geographical area(s) and the regional classification on page 135. For advice on other sources of help locally, contact **Citizens Advice**.

or

OTHER SOURCES OF HELP

Many other sources of help exist. Some charities help with a wide range of needs; others specialise in certain groups of people (such as older people or children).

yes → See **General charities** section page 17.

How to make an Application

Once the appropriate charities have been identified, the next stage is the application itself. People often find making applications difficult and those who might benefit sometimes fail to do so because of the quality of the application submitted.

This article gives guidelines both to individuals applying directly and to welfare agencies applying on behalf of individuals on how to make good, clear and relevant applications.

The application form

The first stage in submitting an application is the question of application forms.

Applications on agency letter headings or personal letters direct from the applicant, no matter how well presented, are fairly pointless if the charity being approached has a specific application form which must be completed. This obvious point is often overlooked. It is frustrating when the application is returned with a blank form requesting substantially the same information as has already been submitted. The resulting delay may mean missing a committee meeting where the application would have been considered and a considerable wait until the next one.

Trust entries in this guide usually indicate when a particular application form is needed, but if there is any doubt the applicant should make a preliminary telephone call to the trust.

Who submits the application?

Again, it is important that an appropriate person sends the application. The guide usually indicates whether an individual in need can apply on his/her own behalf, or whether a third party (professional or otherwise) must apply for them.

In recognition of 'empowerment' of service users, advisory bodies sometimes simply advise families of funds they can approach themselves. However, most charities require applications and forms where appropriate to be completed by, for example, a professional person who is sponsoring the application. Therefore, the individual in need may have to press the agency to make an application on his/her behalf.

The questions

When application forms are used, the questions asked sometimes cause problems, often because they don't appear relevant. Applicants sometimes fail to realise all charities are governed by criteria laid down in their trust deeds and usually specific questions are designed to ensure these criteria are met.

For example, questions concerning date and place of birth are often answered very vaguely. 'Date of birth' is sometimes answered with 'late 50's' or, even worse, 'elderly'. Such a reply reflects the appearance of the person in question and not their age! If the charity can only consider applications for those below a pensionable age, and the request was on behalf of a woman, then the above answers would be too imprecise.

Equally 'Place of birth' is sometimes answered with 'Great Britain' which is not precise enough for funds whose area of benefit is regional or local. It is always better to state the place of birth as well as town and county, even if they are different from the current home address.

Where application forms are not requested, it is essential to prepare clear, concise applications that provide:

1. A description of the person or family and the need which exists

Although applications should be concise, they must provide sufficient detail, such as:

(a) the applicant's name, address, place and date of birth

(b) the applicant's family circumstances (i.e. married/partners, separated/divorced/single parent, widow/widower, the number and ages of dependent children)

(c) the applicant's financial position (i.e. breakdown of weekly income and expenditure and, where appropriate, DWP/housing benefit awarded/refused, savings, credit debts, rent/gas/electricity arrears, etc.)

(d) other relevant information, such as how the need arose (e.g. illness, loss of job, marital separation, etc.) and why other sources (especially DWP/housing departments) have not helped. If applying to a disability charity, applicants should include details of the nature and effects of the disability (although see Medical information below); if applying to a local charity, how long have they lived in the locality.

The application, which says 'this is a poor family who need their gas reconnecting', is unlikely to receive proper consideration. It is also worth mentioning that applications are dealt with in the strictest of confidence, so applicants should aim to provide as much information as is relevant. The form printed after this article may serve as a useful checklist to ensure that all relevant information is included for the particular application.

2. How much money is requested and what it will be used for

This second point appears to cause the most difficulty. Applications are often received without any indication of the amount required or without sufficient explanation as to the desired use of the money.

For example, an applicant may have multiple debts totalling over £1,000. A grant of £100 would clear one of the debts and free much-needed weekly income. So the applicant approaches a suitable charity for a grant of £100. If the applicant explains the situation clearly, trustees can see that a £100 grant in this instance would be an effective use of their charities resources. However, if it is not made clear, trustees can only guess at the possible benefits of the grant. Because they are unwilling to take undue risks with charitable money, trustees may either turn down an incomplete application or refer it for more information, which inevitably means delays.

Charity and the State

Charities are not supposed to give grants for items that are covered by statutory sources. However, the Big Lottery and other changes have made it much more difficult to say where statutory provision ends and charitable provision begins.

Similarly, means testing under some state provision such as Disabled Facilities Grants regulations can create shortfalls between the amount that statutory sources can and will pay, and the full costs of equipment and adaptations to properties. Sometimes, because of what can and cannot be taken into account, assessments of what families can pay appear unrealistic. Where this is the case it should be stated.

Changes arising from tightening of eligibility criteria and Community Care legislation are creating new areas of unmet need. If individuals are applying to charity because statutory provision is clearly no longer adequate, they should make it clear in the application that they have exhausted all possible statutory sources of funding but they are still left with a shortfall. A supporting reference from a knowledgeable agency may be helpful

Where the identified need is not met, following any assessment process, applications for alternative or complementary finance should make the reasons clear.

The way that social and health care services are provided is changing. Traditionally, the state assessed an individual's need, and then provided, or arranged for those assessed services to be provided. The change gives those assessed as eligible for services, the money to purchase them themselves by way of an Individual Budget. The aim is to give more independence and choice of services purchased. It is accepted that this is a radical change for many people. Applications to charities, particularly those with social care needs may well have to reflect the services already being purchased from an individual budget, with a cogent argument as to how what is now being applied for is needed and improves quality of life.

Realism

It helps to be realistic. Sometimes families have contributed to their own situation. The applicant who admits this and seems not to expect miracles but rather seeks to plan afresh – even if with fingers crossed – will often be considered more positively than the applicant who philosophises about deprivation and the imperfections of the political regime of the day.

Likewise, the application, which tries to make the trustees feel guilty and responsible for the impending doom which is predicted for the most vulnerable members of the family unless money is given, is unlikely to impress experienced trustees, however sympathetic.

In general, be clear and factual, not moralising and emotional. In effect, a good application attempts to identify the need and promote possible resolutions.

Applications to more than one charity

Where large amounts are being sought, it can take months to send applications one at a time and wait for the outcome of each before applying to another. However, if a number of applications are being sent out together, a paragraph explaining that other charities are being approached should be included together with a commitment to return any surplus money raised. It is also worth saying if any other applications have been successful in contributing to the whole–nothing succeeds like success!

The same application should not be sent off indiscriminately. For example, if somebody is applying to a trade charity on behalf of a child whose deceased father had lengthy service in that particular trade, then a detailed description of the deceased father's service would be highly relevant. If an application for the same child was being made to a local charity, it would not.

Sometimes people who are trustees of more than one charity receive three or four identical letters, none tailored to that particular trust and none indicating that other trusts have been approached. The omission of such details and the neglect of explanations raise questions in the minds of trustees, which in the end can result in delays or even refusal.

Timing

When applying to charities, remember the time factor, particularly in cases of urgent need. Committees often sit monthly, or even quarterly. Without knowledge but with 'luck', an application can be received the day before the meeting – but if Murphy's Law operates it will always arrive the day after. For the lack of a little homework, applications may not be considered in time.

From experience, few organisations object to a telephone call being made to clarify criteria, dates of meetings or requests for application forms. So often it seems that applicants leave the whole process to chance, which leads to disillusionment, frustration and wasted time for all concerned.

Savings

When awarding a grant, most trustees take the applicant's savings into account. Some applicants may think this unnecessarily intrusive, but openness and honesty make for a better presented application and save time. However, sometimes savings may not need to affect trustees' calculations.

For example, if a woman has a motor accident in which she was not at fault but which leaves her permanently disabled, she will receive compensation (often a one-off lump sum) through the guilty party's insurance company based on medical prognoses at the time. If her condition deteriorates faster and further than anticipated, requiring her to obtain an expensive item of equipment, it could well be argued that this should not be paid for out of the compensation awarded. The compensation was paid to cover factors such as loss of earnings potential, a reduced quality of life, reduced ability to easily fulfil basic household tasks and a general loss of future security, not to pay for unexpected and expensive pieces of equipment.

In such circumstances, the applicant should include a paragraph in the application to explain why his/her savings are not relevant to grant calculations.

In conclusion

Two final points should be borne in mind.

1. Be clear

Firstly, social care & health care professionals often resort to the use of jargon when plain English would be more effective. There appears to be two extremes; one to present a report on the basis that the trustees are not very intelligent lay people who need to be educated, or alternatively that they are all psychotherapists who need to be impressed. Usually, this only causes confusion.

2. Medical information

Secondly, medical information should not be presented without an accurate medical diagnosis to support it. Applicants' or social workers' presumptions on medical matters are not relevant. Often what is necessary is to explain why a financial need arises from a particular condition. This may be because of the rarity of the condition or the fluctuating nature of it.

The medical information should be presented by a professional in that field. The task of the applicant or the sponsor is to explain the implications of the condition.

Using the model application form for financial assistance

Over the page is a general-purpose application form. It has been compiled with the help of Gaddum Centre. It can be photocopied and used whenever convenient and should enable applicants (and welfare agencies applying on behalf of individuals) to state clearly the basic information required by most trusts.

Alternatively, applicants can use it as a checklist of points to include in the letter. Applicants using this form should note the following things in particular:

1. It is worth sending a short letter setting out the request in brief, even when using this application form.

2. Because this form is designed to be useful to a wide range of people in need, not all the information asked for in the form will be relevant to every application. For example, not all applicants are in receipt of state benefits, nor do all applicants have HP commitments. In such cases, applicants should write N/A (not applicable) in the box or on the line in question.

3. Filling out the weekly income and expenditure parts of the form can be worrying or even distressing. Expenditure when itemised in this way is usually far higher than people expect. It is probably worth filling out this form with the help of a trained welfare rights worker.

4. You should always keep a copy of the completed form in case the trust has a specific query.

5. This form should not be used where the trust has its own form, which must be completed.

Ashley Wood
Assistant Chief Executive,
Gaddum Centre

A model application form for financial assistance

PURPOSE FOR WHICH GRANT IS SOUGHT	AMOUNT SOUGHT FROM £ THIS APPLICATION
APPLICANT (Name)	Occupation/School
Address	
Tel. no	

Date of birth	Age	Place of birth

Nationality	Religion (if any)

☐ Single　　☐ Married　　☐ Divorced　　☐ Partnered　　☐ Separated　　☐ Widow/er

FAMILY DETAILS:

Name	Age	Occupation/School
Husband/ Wife	....	....
Partner	....	....
Children	....	....
....	....	....
Others (specify)...............................	....	....

INCOME (weekly)	£	p	EXPENDITURE (weekly)	£	p
Father/husband's wage	....		Rent/mortgage	....	
Mother/wife's wage	....		Council tax	....	
Partner's wage	....		Water rates	....	
Income Support	....		Electricity	....	
Jobseeker's Allowance	....		Gas	....	
Sickness/incapacity benefit	....		Coal	....	
Child benefit	....		Insurance	....	
Pension credit	....		Fares/travel	....	
Attendance allowance	....		Household expenses (food,		
Disability living allowance	....		laundry etc.)	....	
Housing benefit	....		Clothing	....	
Maintenance payments	....		Maintenance	....	
Retirement pension	....		Childcare fees	....	
Occupational pension	....		HP commitments	....	
Other income (specify)...........................	....		Telephone	....	
....	....		TV rental	....	
....	....		TV licence	....	
....	....		Other expenditure (specify)...................	....	
			....	....	
			....	....	
			....	....	

TOTAL WEEKLY INCOME	£	TOTAL WEEKLY EXPENDITURE	£

SAVINGS	£

DEBTS/ARREARS		Has applicant received help from any other source?

DEBTS/ARREARS
Rent, fuels, loans, HP etc.

Has applicant received help from any other source?
YES/NO
(If YES, please include details below)

Specify in detail	Amount owed	Sources of grant obtained	Amount
....	£	....	£ ....
....	£	....	£ ....
....	£	Other sources approached	
....	£	....	
....	£	....	
TOTAL	£	TOTAL STILL REQUIRED	£

Has applicant ever received previous financial help from this trust? YES/NO   If so, when?

REASON FOR THE APPLICATION

Continue on a separate sheet if necessary

FOR APPLICATIONS BEING SUBMITTED THROUGH A WELFARE AGENCY

Name of agency ....

Case worker ....

Address ....

....

Telephone ....

How long has the applicant been known to your department/organisation? ....

FOR ALL APPLICATIONS

Signature: Date:

GENERAL CHARITIES

This section includes all the entries which could not be tied to a particular occupation, disability or locality. It starts with 'Index of general charities' (including, for example, 'Children and young people', and 'Older people') with a separate category for trusts that specifically give grants for holidays. 'Children and young people' contains trusts for people aged 25 or under while 'Older people' contains trusts for people aged 50 or over. This reflects the criteria of some of the trusts in the guide, although not every trust will use these exact limits. We have included refugees and asylum seekers under the 'Ethnic and national minorities in the UK' sections.

The entries under each category are arranged alphabetically, with those trusts which do not fit into any particular category listed at the start of the chapter under 'General'. These charities are listed under 'General' because they can give to a wide range of people, so if individuals are unable to find help from other sources in the guide then they should be able to approach one or more of these. However, note that most of these charities still have restrictions on who they can help. Applicants should not simply send off indiscriminate applications to any charity under the 'General' heading; rather, they should first consider carefully whether they are eligible.

Similarly, within the alphabetically arranged categories following 'General', older people should not apply to all the trusts in the 'Older people' section, for instance, as there may be criteria that will makes them ineligible for support.

Index of general charities

General 17

Asylum seekers 26

Carers & volunteers 26

Children & young people 26

Divorced/separated people 29

Ethnic & national minorities in the UK 29

    Armenians 30

    Assyrians 30

    Belgians 30

    Dutch 30

    Egyptians 30

    Germans 31

    Indians 31

    Swiss 31

    Zimbabweans 31

Holidays 31

Homelessness 32

Older people 32

Orders 36

Politics 37

Prisoners/ex-offenders 37

Quakers 38

Vegetarian 38

Victims of crime or injustice 39

Women 39

General

The Alchemy Foundation

Eligibility: Individuals in need in the UK.

Types of grants: One-off and recurrent grants according to need. Recent grants have been given for holidays for children and respite for carers.

Annual grant total: In 2008/09 the trust had assets of £2.1 million and an income of £435,000. Approximately £16,000 was given in grants to individuals for relief-in-need and educational purposes, distributed through other charities.

Applications: In writing to the correspondent.

Correspondent: R Stilgoe, Trevereux Manor, Limpsfield Chart, Oxted, Surrey RH8 0TL (01883 730600; fax: 01883 730800)

Other information: The trust gives grants mostly to organisations, namely overseas development, social welfare and disability projects.

Al-Mizan Charitable Trust

Eligibility: British citizens, those granted indefinite leave to remain in the UK and asylum seekers who are living in a condition of social or economic deprivation. Preference is given to the following groups:

- orphans (a child who has lost either both parents or one parent who was the main bread-winner in the family)
- children and young people under the age of 19 years (particularly those in care or who are carers themselves)
- individuals who are disabled, incapacitated or terminally ill (particularly those who are severely mentally disabled)
- single parents (particularly divorcees and widows/widowers with children)
- estranged or isolated senior citizens
- individuals with severe medical conditions or their families
- ex-offenders or reformed drug addicts or alcoholics

- victims of domestic violence and/or physical or sexual abuse
- victims of crime, anti-social behaviour and/or terrorism.

Types of grants: Mainly one-off grants ranging from £200–£250, though in some cases up to £500 may be awarded. Grants are available both for subsistence costs and those which help break the cycle of poverty by encouraging educational attainment and employability.

Exclusions: No grants for: general appeals; applicants who are not claiming all available benefits; retrospective funding; expenses relating to the practice or promotion of religion; debt, including council tax arrears; fines or criminal penalties; university tuition fees; gap year trips; building work or construction projects; funeral expenses; gifts (including birthdays and festivals); vehicles; and, holidays or recreational outings, unless they serve a medical, social or educational need. No support is given to those who have received a grant in the last twelve months.

Annual grant total: This trust was only registered with the Charity Commission in April 2010 and has not submitted a set of annual report and accounts.

Applications: The trust expects to begin processing applications in early 2011 when its online grants system is introduced.

Correspondent: Mohammed Sadiq Mamdani, 2 Burlington Gardens, London W3 6BA (email: admin@almizantrust.org.uk; website: www.almizantrust.org.uk)

Anglian Water Assistance Fund (formerly The Anglian Water Trust Fund)

Eligibility: Customers of Anglian Water and Hartlepool Water who are in debt with their water and sewerage charges.

Types of grants: Gift vouchers ranging from £50 to £3,000 to clear or reduce arrears of domestic water/sewerage charges. On average, 1,700 grants are made each year.

Exclusions: No grants are given towards: fines for criminal offences; education or training needs; medical equipment, aids and adaptations; holidays; debts to central government departments such as tax and national insurance; business debts; overpayment of benefits; accommodation deposits; or catalogue, credit card, personal loan or other forms of unsecured lending. The trust cannot give loans, make payments towards bills, or make any grants in arrears.

Annual grant total: About £1 million each year.

Applications: On a form available from the correspondent or local welfare agencies such as Citizens Advice. The fund accepts applications made directly from the individual or family member, or from a third party organisation. Alternatively, forms can be downloaded from the trust's website and applications can also be made online. All applications must be sent with proof of income.

Individuals who receive an award from the trust can apply again after two years. Those who do not receive an award are eligible to re-apply after six months.

Correspondent: The Trustees, Anglian Water Assistance Fund, PO Box 42, Peterborough PE3 8XH (For application forms: 01733 421060; website: www.anglianwater.co.uk/awaf)

Other information: The Anglian Water Assistance Fund is administered by Charis Grants Ltd which also manages the British Gas Energy Trust, EDF Energy Trust, Eos Foundation and Veolia Water Three Valleys Trust.

The Attlee Foundation

Eligibility: People with disabilities or who are disadvantaged living anywhere in the UK. Priority will be given to applications involving children and young people when funds are low.

Types of grants: One-off grants up to £100 through the 'Tickets Please' programme towards travelling costs for therapeutic journeys. For example, to attend specialist treatment centres or to maintain family contacts with children or close relatives in hospital, prison or rehabilitation a long way from home within the UK.

Exclusions: No grants are given towards funerals, holidays, travel outside the UK, medical equipment, wheelchairs or mobility adaptations.

Annual grant total: In 2008/09 the foundation had assets of £3.6 million and an income of £261,000. Grants made to individuals through the 'Tickets Please' programme totalled £2,900.

Applications: On an form available from the correspondent or to download from the website. Applications must be made through a social worker, Citizens Advice or other welfare agency, to which the cheque will be payable on behalf of the individual. A stamped addressed envelope must be enclosed. Covering letters should be kept to one page. There are no deadlines.

Correspondent: Tickets Please Administrator, c/o Attlee Youth & Community Centre, 5 Thrawl Street, London E1 6RT (020 7183 0093; email: info@attlee.org.uk; website: www.attlee.org.uk)

Other information: The foundation also manages a youth centre in the Spitalfields area of East London, which provides open access and inclusive facilities for children, young people and the local community.

The Bagri Foundation

Eligibility: People in need worldwide.

Types of grants: One-off and recurrent grants according to need.

Annual grant total: In 2008/09 the foundation had assets of £2.1 million and an income of £69,000. Grants were made totalling £129,000, the majority of which was given in institutional grants.

Applications: In writing to the correspondent.

Correspondent: M C Thompson, 80 Cannon Street, London EC4N 6EJ (020 7280 0089)

Barony Charitable Trust

Eligibility: People in need through age, ill health or disablement who live in Edinburgh and Central Scotland.

Types of grants: One-off grants of around £100, possibly up to £250 in exceptional circumstances. Recent grants have included support for people trying to make a fresh start, the purchase of disability aids such as wheelchairs or hoists and contributions towards the cost of a carer to accompany an individual on holiday.

Annual grant total: Grants usually total around £5,000 per year.

Applications: On a form available from the correspondent, submitted preferably through a recognised referral agency such as a GP, health visitor, priest or minister, social worker or care worker. Details of what the money is for, how it will help and any other funding applied for should also be included in the application.

Correspondent: Agnes H Cunningham, Secretary, Barony Housing Association, 8 Balcarres Street, Morningside, Edinburgh EH10 5JB (0871 700 7777)

Other information: Please note, this trust is linked to the Barony Housing Association and applications from their area of activity receive priority.

Big Chance Good Causes Ltd

Eligibility: People with special needs who live in the operational areas of the Big Chance Good Causes lottery – the Midlands, the North West and the North East.

Types of grants: Grants towards items which improve quality of life and future development. For example, specialist wheelchairs, sensory equipment for children with delayed development, ceiling hoists, chair lifts, therapy treatment and medical equipment not available on the NHS.

Annual grant total: In 2008 the company had assets of £207,000 and an income of £93,000. Grants were made to individuals totalling £460.

Applications: Application forms are available to download from the website.

Correspondent: James Baxter, 1 Church Street, Eccles, Manchester M30 0DF

(0161 707 9776; email: info@big-chance.org.uk; website: www.big-chance.org.uk)

The Boston Green Trust

Eligibility: People who are in need in the UK.

Types of grants: One-off and recurrent grants according to need.

Annual grant total: In 2009/10 the trust had both an income and expenditure of £31,000.

Applications: In writing to the correspondent.

Correspondent: The Secretary, Bede Thomas Feechan, 1 Bloomesley Close, Newton Aycliffe, County Durham DL5 4XQ (01325 308823)

Other information: The trust also makes grants to organisations.

British Gas Energy Trust

Eligibility: Domestic customers of British Gas or Scottish Gas.

Types of grants: Grants to cover arrears of domestic gas/electricity charges and other essential domestic bills, white goods, bankruptcy deposits, debt relief orders and funeral expenses.

Exclusions: The trust cannot give loans or help with bills or items that have already been paid for. Nor can it help with the following: any household item that is not a 'white good'; fines for criminal offences; overpayments of benefits; educational or training needs; business debts; debts to central government departments, for example, tax and national insurance; catalogues, credit cards, personal loans and other forms of non-secured lending; medical equipment, aids and adaptations; deposits to secure accommodation; and holidays.

Annual grant total: In 2009 the trust had assets of £430,000 and an income of £3.3 million. Payments for British Gas energy debts were made totalling £2.3 million. Further assistance grants totalled £149,000.

Applications: On a form available from the correspondent or to download from the website. The trust also has an online application facility. A local money advice centre such as a Citizens Advice may be able to provide help in completing the form. Applicants may receive letters, emails, telephone calls or a home visit as part of the assessment process.

Those in receipt of an award from the trust cannot reapply for two years. Applicants who do not receive an award can apply again after six months.

Correspondent: Grants Officer, Freepost RRZJ-XBSY-GYRG, British Gas Energy Trust, PO Box 42, Peterborough PE3 8XH (01733 421021; fax: 01733 421020; email: bget@charisgrants.com; website: www.britishgasenergytrust.org.uk)

Other information: Grants are also made to voluntary organisations working in the fields of money advice, debt counselling or energy efficiency advice.

The Carnegie Hero Fund Trust

Eligibility: Heroes and their families (that is people who have suffered financial loss or have been injured – or the families of people who have been killed – in performing acts of heroism in saving human life in the UK, Eire, Channel Islands and territorial waters). About three to four new cases are recognised each year.

Types of grants: One-off and recurrent grants to help towards, for example, household bills and medical equipment.

Exclusions: Heroic acts performed in the saving of property are not recognised by the trust.

Annual grant total: In 2009 the trust had an income of £143,000. Grants are usually made totalling about £100,000.

Applications: Attention to potential cases for consideration is brought to the trustees' notice by a press cutting agency. Follow-up information is received from police, fire service and coroners.

Correspondent: Chief Executive, Andrew Carnegie House, Pittencrieff Street, Dunfermline, Fife KY12 8AW (01383 723638; fax: 01383 721862; email: herofund@carnegietrust.com; website: www.carnegietrust.org.uk)

Other information: The trust was established in 1908 by Andrew Carnegie, who made a great fortune from steel. His Birthplace Museum in Dunfermline displays the Roll of Honour of the Hero Fund Trust, now containing the names of over 6,000 heroes and heroines.

Catholic Clothing Guild

Eligibility: People in need of clothing regardless of denomination in England.

Types of grants: The guild is a small charity which distributes new donated clothing (mainly to children). It may give small money grants when this is not possible, however this is in exceptional circumstances as funding is limited.

Annual grant total: In 2008 the trust had both an income and total expenditure of £700.

Applications: Applications should be made by letter or email. Telephone calls are not welcomed. Applications must be made through a welfare agency or social services who will also receive the grants. Under no circumstances will applications be accepted by individuals.

Correspondent: Mrs C Edwards, Hon Treasurer, 5 Dark Lane, Shrewsbury, Shropshire SY2 5LP (email: carmel.edwards@btinternet.com)

Other information: Please note: the trust is only able to assist with up to six grants per month due to limited funding.

The Coffey Charitable Trust

Eligibility: People in need in the UK.

Types of grants: Occasional one-off and recurrent grants according to need.

Annual grant total: In 2008/09 the trust had an income of £15,000 and a total expenditure of £12,000.

Applications: In writing to the correspondent.

Correspondent: C H Green, 24 Portman Gardens, Uxbridge, Middlesex UB10 9NT

Other information: This trust mainly provides grants to Christian organisations and events.

The Cordwainers' Company Common Investment Fund

Eligibility: The company administers a number of small trusts, the eligibility of which varies. Specific trusts exist for people who are blind, people who are deaf and dumb, widows of clergymen, unmarried women in the Church of England, ex-servicemen and widows of those who served in the merchant or armed forces.

Types of grants: Small annual grants depending on the trust and the circumstances.

Annual grant total: In 2008/09 the trust had assets of £2.6 million and an income of £52,000. Grants were made to 80 individuals totalling £15,000.

Applications: In writing to the correspondent supported, if possible, by referrals from welfare or other charitable bodies.

Correspondent: The Clerk, Clothworkers Hall, Dunster Court, Mincing Lane, London EC3R 7AH (020 7929 1121; fax: 020 7929 1124; email: office@cordwainers.org; website: www.cordwainers.org)

Other information: The trust also makes grants to organisations (£68,000 in 2008/09).

The Gillian Diamond Charitable Fund

Eligibility: People in need in the UK, though in practice very strong preference is given to people living in Greater London.

Types of grants: Small one-off grants and loans.

Exclusions: Grants are not paid for fees or debts. No loans are made.

Annual grant total: In 2008/09 the fund had an income of £8,700 and a total expenditure of £13,000.

Applications: In writing to the correspondent to be submitted either directly by the individual or a family member, through an organisation such as Citizens Advice or school or through a third party such as a social worker or teacher. Applications are considered on an ongoing basis.

Correspondent: Gillian Diamond, PO Box 49849, London NW5 9AJ

East Africa Women's League (UK) Benevolent Fund

Eligibility: People of UK origin who have previously lived and worked in East Africa.

Types of grants: One-off and recurrent grants according to need.

Annual grant total: In 2008 the fund had assets of £155,000 and an income of £19,000. There were 29 grants made in necessitous circumstances and two grants made as special one-off payments, combined these grants totalled £20,000.

Applications: In writing to the correspondent. Members of a fund sub-committee may visit applicants. The trust does not accept any unsolicited applications.

Correspondent: Mrs Joan Considine, 13 Benenden Green, Alresford, Hampshire SO24 9PE (email: honsec@eawl.org.uk; website: www.eawl.org.uk)

EDF Energy Trust

Eligibility: Domestic customers of one of the EDF Energy brands. These are London Energy, Seeboard Energy, SWEB Energy and EDF Energy. People who live in a home which is supplied by EDF Energy but are not the account holder, for example, a lodger who pays gas or electricity as part of their rent, can still apply to the trust (evidence will be required that the household receives its energy from EDF Energy).

Types of grants: Grants to cover the payment of energy bills and other essential household bills or costs.

Exclusions: The trust cannot help with the following: fines for criminal offences; overpayments of benefits; educational or training needs; debts to central government departments e.g. tax and national insurance; catalogues, credit cards, personal loans and other forms of non-secured lending; medical equipment, aids and adaptations; deposits to secure accommodation; or holidays.

Annual grant total: In 2009 the trust had assets of £1.4 million and an income of £3.6 million. Grants made to individuals totalled £2.3 million, broken down as follows:

Between the four energy brands:

London Energy	£1,411,000
Seeboard Energy	£429,000
SWEB Energy	£322,000
EDF Energy	£77,000

In respect of further assistance payments:

Gas	£6,400
Electricity	£1,500
Telephone	£1,500
Household needs	£4,300
Rent	£960
Bankruptcy	£11,000
Council tax arrears	£1,200
Coal and oil	£440
Water	£550
Other	£5,700
Argos Ltd	£20,000
Comet Group plc	£14,000

Applications: Application forms are available on request or can be downloaded from the website. The website also supports an online application process. A local money advice centre such as a Citizens Advice may be able to provide help in completing the form.

Those in receipt of an award from the trust cannot reapply for two years. Applicants who do not receive an award can apply again after six months.

Correspondent: Grant Administrator, Freepost RLXG-RBYJ-USXE, PO Box 42, Peterborough PE3 8XH (01733 421060; fax: 01733 421020; email: edfet@ charisgrants.com; website: www. edfenergytrust.org.uk)

Other information: Grants are also made to voluntary organisations working in the field of money advice, debt counselling or energy efficiency advice (£282,000 in 2009).

Family Action (formerly Family Welfare Association)

Eligibility: Assistance from Family Welfare Association (FWA) is primarily targeted at families and individuals living on low incomes, particularly those living on benefits.

FWA's grants service distributes funds from over 70 trusts that have very diverse eligibility criteria allowing them to meet a wide variety of need.

FWA's priority areas for funding are: (i) Mental health – support to improve the quality of life and reduce isolation for families and individuals (over the age of 18) with mental health problems or learning difficulties; (ii) Domestic violence – support for those leaving a violent relationship to help rebuild their lives; (iii) Refugees and asylum seekers – support to promote the stability of families and integration into life in the UK; (iv) Older people – support to promote independence, improve the quality of life and reduce isolation for those aged 60 and over; and (v) Young people (aged 19 to 25) – support for vulnerable young people to help to establish a stable and independent life.

Types of grants: Clothing, fuel bills, household needs such as beds and cookers and so on are most commonly requested. Help can also be given for more varied needs.

Exclusions: Funds are not available for council tax arrears, debts (except utility bills), fines, funeral expenses, gifts, items already covered by statutory funds, private school fees, rent arrears, or repayment of Social Fund or other loans.

Annual grant total: In 2008/09 the charity disbursed grants to 3,296 individuals totalling £624,000.

Applications: Initial applications must be made by a professional person such a social worker, health visitor or by a voluntary agency using the association's application form. This form can be obtained by sending an sae marked 'GRANTS' to the address shown below. It can also be downloaded from the association's website. Please note that the information requested must be provided on the form, appended documentation will not be accepted.

Based on the completed application, an initial assessment will be made. A written response will be sent to the referrer within five working days of the receipt of the form. Should the applicant appear to be eligible for funding and sufficient funds are available, further information will be requested from the professional.

Where a grant is made the cheque will be made payable to the referring agency or service/utility provider. Under no circumstances are cheques made to individuals.

Correspondent: Grants Service, 501–505 Kingsland Road, Dalston, London E8 4AU (020 7241 7459 – Tuesday, Wednesday and Thursday only between 2pm and 4pm; website: www.family-action.org.uk)

Elizabeth Finn Care

Eligibility: People who are British or Irish and have a professional or similar background or connection, and their dependants.

Types of grants: Recurrent grants are made towards daily living expenses. One-off grants are also available towards needs such as car expenses, household items, house repairs and adaptations, specialist equipment and help with nursing/residential fees. All grants are means-tested.

Exclusions: The trust will not give grants for healthcare costs, computer equipment, educational costs, respite care, debts or funeral expenses.

Annual grant total: In 2008/09 the charity had assets of £43 million and an income of £25 million. Grants and allowances totalled £3.8 million.

Applications: On a form available from the correspondent to be submitted either directly by the individual, through a third party such as a social worker or through an organisation such as a Citizens Advice or other welfare agency. Applications are considered once a month.

Correspondent: Director of Casework, Hythe House, 200 Shepherds Bush Road, London W6 7NL (020 8834 9200; email: info@elizabethfinn.org.uk; website: www.elizabethfinncare.org.uk)

Other information: In April 2011 the association is due to take over the administration of a number of funds from City of Edinburgh Council and plans to open a new office in the city.

The association also manages its own residential and nursing homes.

The David Fogwill Charitable Trust

Eligibility: People in need who are involved in Christian outreach projects or ministry.

Types of grants: One-off and recurrent grants ranging from £50 to £1,000. Support costs are usually paid to the organisations for whom the Christian outreach worker is contracted to.

Annual grant total: In 2008/09 the trust had an income of £24,000 and a total expenditure of £35,000.

Applications: In writing to the correspondent. Applications can be submitted directly by the individual or family member and should include details of the Christian activity and the organisation involved. Applications are considered in January and July.

Correspondent: Alex Fogwill, 53 Brook Drive, Corsham, Wiltshire SN13 9AX (01249 713408)

Other information: The trust also makes grants to organisations.

Clan Forsyth Family Trust

Eligibility: People with the surname Forsyth, and their dependants, who are in need or disadvantaged.

Types of grants: One-off and recurrent grants according to need.

Annual grant total: Grants total about £1,000 each year.

Applications: In writing to the correspondent.

Correspondent: Bob Forsyth, The Cottage, Knock Farm, Bathgate, EH48 4NP (01506 676877; website: www. clanforsythsociety.net)

The Stanley Foster Charitable Trust

Eligibility: People in need in south east England.

Types of grants: One-off grants up to £1,000 mainly for medical support.

Annual grant total: About £1,000.

Applications: Grants are only made to individuals known to the trustees. The majority of grants are made to organisations.

Correspondent: The Trustees, 4 Meadowcroft, Bromley BR1 2JD (020 8402 1341)

The Ernest and Marjorie Fudge Trust for Warminster

Eligibility: People in need who live in Warminster and surrounding areas, with a preference for people who have a mentally illness.

Types of grants: One-off and recurrent grants according to need.

Annual grant total: In 2008/09 the trust had assets of £806,000 and an income of £47,000. Grants were made to 30 individuals totalling around £5,000.

Applications: In writing to the correspondent.

Correspondent: W A C Knowles, 69 Kingston Deverill, Warminster, Wiltshire BA12 7HG (01985 844476; email: knowles69@btinternet.com)

Other information: Grants are also made to organisations.

Fund for Human Need

Eligibility: Grants are available to refugees, asylum seekers, people who are homeless and anybody attempting to get over a short-term hurdle.

Types of grants: One-off and recurrent grants of up to £100 each.

Annual grant total: In 2008/09 grants were made to 23 individuals totalling £2,700.

Applications: In writing to the correspondent, including details of financial circumstances. In recent years the fund has received quite a large volume of applications and regrets that it cannot always reply to unsuccessful applicants.

Correspondent: S H Platt, 50 Leeds Road, Selby, North Yorkshire YO8 4HX (01757 706040; fax: 07006 024 004)

Other information: Grants are also made to organisations.

The R L Glasspool Charity Trust

Eligibility: People in need who are on a low income.

Types of grants: One-off grants ranging from £50 to £5,000, though in practice they rarely exceed £750. Recent grants have been made for white goods, clothing, holidays, furniture and disability equipment. The trust provides some of these items in kind.

Where appropriate, applications should always be made to statutory sources and any relevant specialist charities.

Exclusions: No grants for loans, debts, bursaries, project funding, research, educational grants, rents in advance/deposits, funeral costs/headstones. The following are not generally within the scope of the trust: children's toys, computers for general use, subsistence, building works, driving lessons/tests.

Annual grant total: In 2008/09 the trust made grants to 3,365 individuals totalling £778,000.

Applications: On a form available from the correspondent, to be submitted through an eligible agency such as social services, any Council-run service, Surestart, Connexions, youth offending teams, NHS agencies, probation service, Citizens Advice, Family Service Units, hospices or a relevant welfare agency such as Age Concern, Shelter or MIND.

The following details should be included: full name, age and address of applicant including names and ages of children; full breakdown of all income and expenditure and any debts; information on family circumstances; details of the need; if requesting a holiday, please provide an outline of the proposed holiday including date, type, location, duration and breakdown of costs; names of other charities approached and responses received; whether the Social Fund/Social Services have been approached and with what result; the name of the payee for any grant (which should normally be the referring agency). Cheques cannot be made payable to individuals.

The trust aims to reply within two weeks of receipt of applications. Please make any enquiries as to the progress of your application by post rather than telephone.

Correspondent: Frances Moore, Charity Administrator, Second Floor, Saxon House, 182 Hoe Street, Walthamstow, London EH17 4QH (020 8520 4354; fax: 020 8520 9040)

Other information: The trust is one of the few national charities that has no restrictions on the type of beneficiary it can support and as such it is usually heavily oversubscribed.

Gurunanak

Eligibility: People in financial need who live in the UK or overseas.

Types of grants: One-off grants according to need.

Annual grant total: In 2008/09 the trust had assets of £6,400 and an income of £240,000. Grants were made to both organisations and individuals totalling £246,000. Around £20,000 per year is given in grants to individuals.

Applications: In writing to the correspondent at any time.

Correspondent: Jill Prendergast, 12 Sherborne Street, Manchester M3 1ED (0161 831 7879)

The Margaret Jeannie Hindley Charitable Trust

Eligibility: Relief of poverty and distress among people in 'reduced or destitute circumstances'. In practice priority is given to people living in the Godalming area.

Types of grants: Some recurrent grants of £40 to £50 each month are made. One-off grants up to £750 are more usual.

Annual grant total: In 2009/10 the trust had an income of £14,000 and a total expenditure of £18,000. Grants totalled around £15,000, most of which was given to organisations.

Applications: In writing to the correspondent. The trustees meet regularly throughout the year to consider applications.

Correspondent: The Trustees, Marshalls Solicitors, 102 High Street, Godalming, Surrey GU7 1DS (01483 416101)

The Hoper-Dixon Trust

Eligibility: People in need connected with, or resident in, any house or pastoral centre under the direction of the Dominicans of the English Province Order of Preachers.

Types of grants: One-off and recurrent grants according to need ranging from £100 to £1,000.

Annual grant total: In 2008/09 the trust had an income of £16,000 and a total expenditure of £9,000. Grants were made to 14 individuals totalling £8,900.

Applications: In writing to the correspondent through a local Dominican house.

Correspondent: The Provincial Bursar, The Dominican Council, Blackfriars, St Giles, Oxford OX1 3LY (01865 288231; email: enquiries@hoperdixon.org.uk; website: www.hoperdixon.org.uk)

The Houston Charitable Trust

Eligibility: People in need worldwide.

Types of grants: One-off and recurrent grants according to need.

Annual grant total: In 2009/10 the trust had assets of £527,000 and an income of £256,000. Grants were made totalling £101,000 and were broken down as follows:

Advancement of the Christian faith	£61,000
Charities for the relief in poverty and those in need	£40,000

Grants to individuals usually total around £16,000 each year.

Applications: In writing to the correspondent. 'Unsolicited applications are not supported as the funds are already committed for the foreseeable future.'

Correspondent: G A Houston, Pednor Chase, Pednor, Nr Chesham, Buckinghamshire HP5 2SY

The Johnston Family Fund

Eligibility: 'Members of the upper and middle classes (and widows and daughters of such people) who, through no fault of their own, have fallen into impoverished circumstances.'

Types of grants: Recurrent grants of £650 a year and one-off grants of around £100 each for TV licences and birthday gifts.

Exclusions: The fund does not distribute grants to men under 50 or women under 40 years of age.

Annual grant total: In 2009 the trust had an income of £13,000 and a total expenditure of £19,000.

Applications: In writing to the correspondent. Applications are considered throughout the year.

Correspondent: Karen Owen Jones, Rathbones, Port of Liverpool Building, Liverpool L3 1NW (0151 243 7635; fax: 0151 243 7001)

The William Johnston Trust Fund

Eligibility: Older people in need who live in the UK.

Types of grants: Recurrent grants ranging from £250 to £2,000 and one-off grants for TV licences and birthdays.

Annual grant total: In 2008 the fund had assets of £764,000 and an income of £38,000. Grants were made to 43 individuals totalling £27,000.

Applications: In writing to the correspondent. Applications can be submitted directly by the individual or family member and are considered throughout the year.

Correspondent: Trust Administrator, Rathbone Trust Company Ltd, Port Of Liverpool Building, Pier Head, Liverpool L3 1NW (0151 236 6666)

St Jude's Trust

Eligibility: People in need through disability or disadvantage.

Types of grants: One-off and recurrent grants according to need.

Annual grant total: In 2008/09 the trust had assets of £726,000 and an income of £38,000. Grants to organisations totalled £26,000. No grants were made to individuals during the year.

Applications: In writing to the correspondent. They are considered twice a year. Acknowledgements are not given.

Correspondent: R G Millman, Arnold Fooks Chadwick, 15 Bolton Street, Piccadilly, London W1J 8AR (020 7499 3007)

Kilcreggan Trust

Eligibility: People in need in England and Wales.

Types of grants: One off and recurrent grants according to need.

Annual grant total: In 2008/09 the trust had an income of £6,200 and a total expenditure of £5,900.

Applications: In writing to the correspondent.

Correspondent: The Secretary, Manton Grange, Preshute Lane, Manton, Marlborough, Wiltshire SN8 4HQ (01672 514050)

The McKenna Charitable Trust

Eligibility: People in need in England and Wales, with a preference for children and people with disabilities.

Types of grants: One-off grants are occasionally made to individuals, according to need.

Annual grant total: In 2008/09 the trust had assets of £7,700 and an income of £157,000. Grants were made to organisations totalling £216,000. There were no grants made to individuals during the year.

Applications: In writing to the correspondent at any time.

Correspondent: The Trustees, c/o Buzzacott LLP, 12 New Fetter Lane, London EC4A 1AG (020 7556 1200)

Motability

Eligibility: People who receive one of the following benefits: Higher Rate Mobility Component of Disability Living Allowance; War Pensioners' Mobility Supplement (WPMS); or a government vehicle, trike or mini.

Types of grants: Grants can be given towards 'the best value suitable solution that meets basic mobility needs'. These are usually: vehicle advance payments; supplying and fitting adaptations, for instance hand controls to enable somebody with a lower body disability to drive an automatic car or hoists to load electric wheelchairs into estate cars; or driving lessons for people who are disabled, or whose children or spouses are disabled, especially people aged 16 to 24.

Annual grant total: In 2008/09 the trust had assets of £8.7 million, an income of £27 million and made grants totalling £1.3 million

Applications: Potential applicants should contact the customer services team on 0845 456 4566 and have the following information to hand: national insurance number; details of current motability car (if applicable); make, model and dimensions of your wheelchair or scooter; and details of any benefits, allowance or pensions. Applicants may be asked to visit a centre for assessment of transfer ability, give permission for third parties such as doctors to be contacted, and may receive a home visit.

Please note: All applicants are expected to contribute a minimum of £200 towards their vehicle and/or adaptations. This amount could increase depending on the applicant's individual circumstances.

Correspondent: Grants Directorate, Warwick House, Roydon Road, Harlow, Essex CM19 5PX (01279 635999; fax: 01279 632000; website: www. motability.co.uk)

Other information: Some of Motability's funds are administered on behalf of the government.

Municipal General Charities for the Poor

Eligibility: People in need who live in the borough of Newark.

Types of grants: One-off grants up to £300 are mainly given towards household items such as cookers, washing machines and furniture. Christmas gifts of £50 are also made.

Annual grant total: In 2009 the trust had assets of £957,000 and an income of £30,000. Grants to individuals totalled around £6,000.

Applications: On a form available from the correspondent submitted through a social worker, Citizens Advice or other welfare agency. Applications are considered in February, May, August and November and must include details of the particular need.

Correspondent: Michael Gamage, Clerk, Payne and Gamage Solicitors, 48 Lombard Street, Newark, Nottinghamshire NG24 IXP (01636 640649; fax: 01636 640627)

Other information: The trust also makes grants to organisations.

The Natlas Trust

Eligibility: People in need living in the UK or the State of Israel.

Types of grants: One-off and recurrent grants according to need.

Annual grant total: In 2008/09 the trust had assets of £608,000 and an income of £202,000. Grants were made totalling £243,000, the majority of which was given in grants to organisations.

Applications: In writing to the correspondent.

Correspondent: Joel Adler, 32 Brampton Grove, London NW4 4AQ

Newby Trust Ltd

Eligibility: People in the UK with welfare or medical needs. Beneficiaries are generally in receipt of welfare benefits, such as Income Support and Disability Living Allowance or living on a low wage.

Types of grants: One-off grants of £10 to £200, for items such as mobility aids, household essentials, furnishings, clothing, school uniforms and footwear.

Exclusions: The trust does not provide full funding for larger items, such as washing machines, but can make a contribution to the overall costs.

Annual grant total: In 2008/09 the trust had assets of £10 million and an income of £347,000. Grants were made to 389 individuals totalling £65,000, of which £56,000 was given for welfare purposes and £9,400 in medical grants.

Applications: Social services, NHS Trusts or registered charities may apply online on behalf of individuals in need. Applications made directly by the individual are not accepted. Cheques are payable to the sponsoring organisation. Full guidelines are available on the website.

Correspondent: Wendy Gillam, Secretary, Hill Farm, Froxfield, Petersfield, Hampshire GU32 1BQ (01730 827557; email: info@newby-trust.org.uk; website: www.newby-trust.org.uk)

Other information: Grants are mostly given to organisations and for research purposes.

The Osborne Charitable Trust

Eligibility: People in need in the UK and overseas.

Types of grants: One-off and recurrent grants according to need and one-off grants in kind.

Exclusions: No grants for religious or political purposes.

Annual grant total: In 2008/09 the trust had an income of £7,600 and a total expenditure of £71,000. Grants are made to organisations and individuals.

Applications: This trust does not respond to unsolicited applications.

Correspondent: John Eaton, 57 Osborne Villas, Hove, East Sussex BN3 2RA (01273 732500; email: john@eaton207.fsnet.co.uk)

Professional Classes' Aid Council

Eligibility: People with a professional background, and their dependants, who are not eligible for assistance from their own trade or professional fund, or who have no specific fund to turn to.

Types of grants: One-off and recurrent grants according to need.

Exclusions: No grants for bankruptcy fees, utility bills, funeral expenses and medical costs.

Annual grant total: In 2008 the trust had assets of £2.1 million and an income of £144,000. Grants made through the general welfare fund totalled £103,000.

Applications: On a form available from the correspondent, to be submitted either by the individual, or via a third party such as a social worker, Citizens Advice or other welfare agency.

Correspondent: Miss Nerina Inkson, 10 St Christopher's Place, London W1U 1HZ (020 7935 0641)

Other information: The trust ensures applicants are receiving all the state benefits they are entitled to before awarding any grant. Grants are also made for educational purposes.

The Rhona Reid Charitable Trust

Eligibility: People who are blind or partially sighted and people with disabilities to allow them to experience water activities and travel.

Types of grants: One-off grants according to need.

Annual grant total: In 2008/09 the trust had an income of £16,000 and a total expenditure of £21,000.

Applications: In writing to the correspondent.

Correspondent: Miss K Clayton, c/o Rathbone Taxation Services, Port of Liverpool Buildings, Pier Head, Liverpool L3 1NW (0151 236 6666)

Other information: Grants are also made to organisations and students involved in the study and advancement of ophthalmic work and music.

The J C Robinson Trust No. 3

Eligibility: People in need in England, with a preference for the elderly, people with disabilities and those living in East Sussex, Bristol and south Gloucester.

Types of grants: Grants range from £50 to £1,000 according to need.

Annual grant total: In 2008/09 the trust had assets of £465,000, which generated an income of £31,000. Grants were made to nearly 100 individuals totalling £25,000.

Applications: In writing to the correspondent, including supporting documents giving evidence of need, such as a letter from a doctor or social worker. Applications should usually be made through an organisation such as Citizens Advice or through a third party such as a social worker.

Correspondent: Christine Howe, Barnett Wood Bungalow, Blackboys, Uckfield, East Sussex TN22 5JL

Other information: A small number of grants are also made to organisations.

Mrs L D Rope's Second Charitable Settlement

Eligibility: People in need, with a preference for people who are resident in Suffolk.

Types of grants: One-off and recurrent grants ranging from £50 to £10,000. Grants are given for the relief of poverty and for the support of religion and education. Almost all grants are made to charities or organisations with which the trust has long-term connections or at the recommendation of members of the late founders' families.

Annual grant total: In 2008/09 the trust made 68 grants totalling £56,000, 31 of which were made to individuals (around £11,000).

Applications: The trust does not invite unsolicited applications.

Correspondent: Crispin Rope, Trustee, Crag Farm, Boyton, Near Woodbridge, Suffolk IP12 3LH

Mr William Saunders Charity for the Relief of Indigent Gentry and Others

Eligibility: 'Indigent gentry, tutors, governesses, merchants and others'; and their dependants, who are in need.

Types of grants: One-off and recurrent grants according to need.

Annual grant total: No recent financial information was available. In previous years grants have totalled about £6,000.

Applications: In writing to the correspondent.

Correspondent: Richard Kirby, 6 St Andrew Street, London EC4A 3LX (020 7427 6400)

Other information: Grants are also made to local organisations caring for people in need.

The Severn Trent Water Charitable Trust Fund

Eligibility: People with water or sewage services by Severn Trent Water or by companies or organisations which operate on behalf of Severn Trent, who are in financial difficulty and unable to pay their water charges.

Types of grants: One-off grants are given to clear or reduce water and/or sewage debt. Further assistance can be given through the purchase of essential household items or by the payment of other priority bills and debts. These grants are limited and will normally only be given if an application shows either that it will help the individual maintain a future sustainable weekly budget, or it will make an important and significant difference to the individual's quality of life.

Exclusions: No grants are made for court fines, personal debts, social fund loans or benefit overpayments. No retrospective grants are given. Grants are usually one-off and applicants cannot reapply within two years of receipt.

Annual grant total: In 2008/09 the fund had assets of £1 million and an income of £5.6 million. During the year the fund received 12,000 applications for help. Grants were made to over 7,000 individuals totalling £4.5 million and distributed as follows:

Water and sewage charges	£4,200,000
Council tax	£2,200
Rent	£5,800
Gas	£19,000
Electricity	£53,000
Telephone	£1,100
Other household needs	£156,000
Bankruptcy orders	£37,000

Applications: On a form available from the correspondent or to download from the website. Applications can be submitted at any time by the individual or through a money advice centre, Citizens Advice or similar third party, to: Severn Trent Trust Fund, FREEPOST RLZE-EABT-SHSA, Sutton Coldfield B72 1TJ.

Applicants may receive a telephone call or visit as part of the application process. Unsuccessful applicants may reapply after six months.

Correspondent: Grants Officer, 12–14 Mill Street, Sutton Coldfield, West Midlands B72 1TJ (0121 355 7766; email: office@sttf. org.uk; website: www.sttf.org.uk)

Other information: The fund also makes grants to organisations which provide free debt advice and debt counselling services (£335,000 in 2008/09).

The Skinners' Benevolent Trust (formerly the Hunt & Almshouse Charities)

Eligibility: People in England, with a preference for those living in Camden, City of London, Enfield, Hackney, Hounslow, Tonbridge and Malling and Tunbridge Wells, who are living on a very low income and have been cut off in some way from society and who are trying to re-build their lives.

The trust particularly welcomes applications from people living with mental health issues; those in recovery from substance/alcohol use; victims of domestic violence; people in receipt of a state retirement pension; and, people with a disability or chronic illness. Applicants must live on their own or with dependent children and be in receipt of a means-tested benefit. They should also have applied to the Social Fund (or, where applicable, for a Community Care Grant) and received a decision.

Types of grants: One-off grants of up to £250 towards essential household items.

Exclusions: No grants for: people who have received a grant from the charity in the previous two years; individuals or organisations providing 'one-off' support or advice; general financial assistance, including debt and utility costs; items that are available from the Social Fund (or Community Care Grant); mobility or computer equipment; and, items that have already been purchased.

Annual grant total: In 2008/09 pensions were paid to residents totalling £34,000 and grants were made totalling £16,000.

Applications: On a form available from the correspondent. Applications must be supported by a medical professional or someone working within a recognised social care agency, such as social services, disability information and support organisations, housing support agencies or local charities. This person should have a personal and ongoing knowledge of the applicant's circumstances and the ability to receive and monitor any grant. Applications are normally processed within six weeks, though urgent cases can be considered more quickly.

Correspondent: Deborah French, Skinners' Hall, 8 Dowgate Hill, London EC4R 2SP (020 7236 5629; fax: 020 7236 6590; email: charitiesadmin@ skinners.org.uk; website: www. skinnershall.co.uk)

Other information: In recent years the Hunt and Almshouse Charities have been trying to improve the effectiveness of their twin activities of almshouse provision and welfare relief. In 2009 the almshouse branch split away from the pensions branch to form a new charity: the Skinners' Almshouse Charity. The former pensions branch, renamed the Skinners' Benevolent Trust, was merged with the various subsidiary charities to create a specialist grant-making trust. This trust is a part of the Skinners' Company.

The Henry Smith Charity (UK)
see entry on page 128

The Speranza Trust

Eligibility: People in need in the UK or overseas.

Types of grants: Grants for items, services or facilities.

Annual grant total: In 2009 the trust had an income of £6,000 and a total expenditure of £7,000.

Applications: In writing to the correspondent.

Correspondent: Andrew Foster, Banbury House, 32 West End Road, Bradninch, Exeter, Devon EX5 4QW

Other information: The majority of grants are made to organisations.

The St Martin-in-the-Fields' Vicar's Appeal Charity

Eligibility: People in need or hardship. Priority is given to those who are in danger of becoming homeless, those who are currently homeless, destitute and/or vulnerable, and those attempting to establish or maintain a tenancy.

Types of grants: One-off grants of up to £250 to have a positive impact and help alleviate distress or avert a crisis. Grants have been given towards a range of needs, including furniture, child and adult clothing, domestic appliances, equipment for babies and toddlers, utility bills and household maintenance and repair.

Only one grant is usually made to an individual/family within 12 months.

Exclusions: No grants for holidays, course fees, recurring costs, holidays, respite breaks, school trips, IT equipment, medical treatment, TV's and TV licences, childcare expenses, toys, books and play equipment, administrative charges, fines and professional fees, structural renovations or specialist equipment such as wheelchairs.

Annual grant total: In 2008/09 the charity made grants to 1,376 individuals amounting to £228,000.

Applications: On a form available from the administrator. Applications should not be made directly by the individual but through agencies such as social services, probation, Citizens Advice or other welfare agencies. If applying in writing, applicants are asked to print on letterhead. Applications should include the name and address of the individual/family in need, current circumstances, amount required and the name of the organisation the cheque will be payable to. When applying for repayment of arrears or for the cost of a bankruptcy petition, please describe how the debts incurred. Requests for funds can usually be considered within four days.

Correspondent: The Administrator, St Martin-in-the-Fields, 6 St Martin's Place, London WC2N 4JJ (020 7766 1125; fax: 020 7839 5163; email: craig.norman@ smitf.org; website: www2.stmartin-in-the-fields.org/)

Other information: Grants are also made to organisations and parishes to provide relief grants in their area.

The St Vincent de Paul Society (England & Wales)

Eligibility: Anyone in need in England and Wales. Although predominantly a Catholic charity, it is completely non-denominational in its operation. Grants are only offered following a visit from a member of the society.

Types of grants: Small one-off grants are available through the befriending process. Material assistance is given in the provision of furniture, food, appliances, clothes and fuel. Friendship to anyone in need is a fundamental principle of the society; financial relief is incidental to this. During the year over 560,000 visits were made to 86,000 individuals and families across England and Wales.

Exclusions: There are no grants available for education.

Annual grant total: In 2008/09 grants were made to individuals and families amounting to around £50,000.

Applications: In writing to the correspondent at any time. Applications can be submitted directly by the individual

or through any third party, such as advice centres or probation services.

Correspondent: Elizabeth Palmer, 5th Floor, 291–299 Borough Hill Street, London SE1 1JG (020 7407 4644; fax: 020 7407 4634; email: info@svp.org.uk; website: www.svp.org.uk)

Other information: There are about 1,600 parish groups in England and Wales, with around 10,000 members. Most of the income is raised locally by members and distributed by them. The society runs several children's camps, holiday caravans and so on and a number of hostels, shops and furniture stores. Prison visitations take place in some areas, and a 'Catholic Cassette' for the blind and partially sighted is available. Considerable support is given to the developing world and Romania.

Mary Strand Charitable Trust

Eligibility: People who are in need due to poverty, sickness or old age.

Types of grants: One-off and recurrent grants, towards items like household goods and clothing.

Annual grant total: In 2008 the trust had assets of £567,000 and an income of £108,000. Grants totalling £85,000 were made during the year.

Applications: In writing to the correspondent, to be submitted either directly by the individual or through a local priest, charity or welfare agency.

Correspondent: Lynda Walker, Gabriel Communications Ltd, Landmark House, Station Road, Cheadle Hulme, Cheadle SK8 7JH (0161 4881700; email: lynda. walker@totalcatholic.com)

Other information: The trustees publish a column in each edition of The Universe, a weekly Catholic newspaper. The column contains details of deserving causes with names changed to preserve anonymity, and appeals are made for specific requirements. Donations from readers are received in answer to these appeals and then distributed.

Sir John Sumner's Trust

Eligibility: People in need who are resident in the UK, with strong preference for the Midlands.

Types of grants: One-off grants ranging between £30 and £70. The trust will sometimes give an amount towards larger requests if other charities make up the rest.

Exclusions: No grants towards religious or political causes.

Annual grant total: In 2009/10 the trust had assets of £706,000 and an income of £33,000. Grants made to institutions totalled £49,000; it appears that no grants were made to individuals during the year.

Applications: On a form available from the correspondent, supported by an appropriate welfare agency. Applications can be considered at any time.

Correspondent: The Secretary to the Trustees, No. 1 Colmore Square, Birmingham B4 6AA

The Talisman Charitable Trust

Eligibility: People in the UK who are living on a very low income.

Types of grants: One-off and recurrent grants according to need.

Annual grant total: In 2008/09 the trust had assets of £6.1 million and an income of £168,000. Nearly 1,000 applications for assistance were received. Grants were made to 117 individuals totalling £121,000 and were distributed as follows:

Child poverty	14	£12,000
Disablement or disability	27	£44,000
Educational	6	£3,400
Health	2	£2,000
Housing	61	£56,000
Small means or hardship	7	£3,000

Grants were also made to organisations totalling £45,000.

Applications: In writing to the correspondent through a social worker, Citizens Advice or similar third party.

Applications should be on headed paper and include the individual's full name and address, a summary of their financial circumstances, what is needed and how much it will cost. A brief history of the case and a list of any other charities approached should be included as well. Supporting evidence such as medical documentation, a letter from the applicant's school and written quotations would also be helpful. Applications are considered throughout the year. Only successful applications will receive a reply.

Please note: applications should not be sent by recorded delivery or any 'signed for' services.

Correspondent: Philip Denman, Lower Ground Floor Office, 354 Kennington Road, London SE11 4LD (020 7820 0254; website: www.talismancharity.org)

Other information: This trust was previously called The Late Baron F A D'Erlanger's Charitable Trust.

The Three Oaks Trust

Eligibility: People and families in need who live in West Sussex. There is a particular focus on people with a physical or mental disability (including learning difficulties), and on low-income families, single parents and the long-term sick.

Types of grants: One-off grants of up to £150 towards basic furnishings, clothing, washing machines, fridges, telephone connections and so on.

Annual grant total: In 2008/09 grants were made to individuals totalling £68,000.

Applications: On a form available from the correspondent or to download from the website. Applications can only be made through Crawley and Horsham Social

Services and Citizens Advice Bureaux and other invited local agencies. Details of the agency to which any cheque should be made payable should be included in the application.

Correspondent: The Trustees, The Three Oaks Family Trust Co. Ltd, PO Box 893, Horsham, West Sussex RH12 9JD (email: contact@thethreeoakstrust.co.uk; website: www.thethreeoakstrust.co.uk)

The Vardy Foundation

Eligibility: People in need in who live in the UK.

Types of grants: One-off and recurrent grants according to need.

Exclusions: The trust states that it 'does not accept unsolicited grants from individuals for educational or hardship grants. Grants are given to charitable organisations and individuals at the discretion of the trustees'.

Annual grant total: In 2008/09 the foundation had assets of £22 million and an income of £4 million. Grants were made to 41 individuals totalling £118,000, for both welfare and educational purposes.

Applications: In writing to the correspondent.

Correspondent: The Chair of the Trustees, Venture House, Aykley Heads, Durham DH1 5TS (0191 374 4744; website: www.vardyfoundation.com)

Other information: Grants are also made to organisations (£1.5 million in 2008/09).

Mrs Wingfield's Charitable Trust

Eligibility: People who are in need. Individuals in Shropshire have priority over the rest of the country.

Types of grants: One-off grants and recurrent grants according to need.

Annual grant total: In 2008/09 the trust had assets of £730,000, which generated an income of £38,000. Charitable expenditure totalled £14,000.

Applications: In writing to the correspondent, directly by the individual. Cases are considered at regular meetings of the trustees. Refusals are not always acknowledged due to the cost involved. If a reply is required, please enclose an sae.

Correspondent: Helen Thomas, Dyke Yaxley, 39 Chesholm Road, London N16 0DS (01743 241281; email: mwctrust@googlemail.com)

Other information: The trust also makes grants to organisations and to individuals for educational purposes.

Asylum seekers

Asylum Seeker Support Initiative – Short Term (ASSIST)

Eligibility: Asylum seekers who live in Sheffield.

Types of grants: Small weekly grants for food and basic living expenses, usually £20 per person.

Annual grant total: In 2008/09 the charity had assets of £53,000 and an income of £164,000. Grants were made totalling just over £75,000.

Applications: Preliminary contact should be made with the charity.

Correspondent: Welfare Payments Team, c/o Victoria Hall Methodist Church, 60 Norfolk Street, Sheffield, South Yorkshire S1 2JB (0114 275 4960; email: admin@assistsheffield.org.uk; website: www.assistsheffield.org.uk)

Other information: This charity is also provides advice and information and runs awareness-raising activities.

Carers & volunteers

The Andrew Anderson Trust

Eligibility: People who are, or were, involved in charitable activities, and their dependants, who are in need.

Types of grants: One-off and recurrent grants according to need.

Annual grant total: In 2008/09 the trust had assets of £7.7 million and an income of £289,000. Grants were made totalling £274,000, of which £67,000 was given to individuals for educational and welfare purposes. The remaining £207,000 was given to organisations.

Applications: The trust states that it rarely gives to people who are not known to the trustees or who have not been personally recommended by people known to the trustees. Unsolicited applications are therefore unlikely to be successful.

Correspondent: The Trustees, 84 Uphill Road, Mill Hill, London NW7 4QE (020 8959 2145)

The Margaret Champney Rest & Holiday Fund

Eligibility: Carers, particularly those caring for a severely disabled relative, who need a break away from the person they are caring for. Occasionally, grants may be made to couples or adult family members where one is the primary carer for the other and they wish to holiday together.

Types of grants: Generally one-off grants of between £75 and £250.

Exclusions: Grants are not available towards 'normal' family holidays.

Annual grant total: In 2009 the trust had an income of £14,000 and a total expenditure of £11,000. Grants were made totalling around £9,000.

Applications: In writing to the correspondent, through a social worker, community nurse or similar professional agency. Applications can be considered at any time, and should include full details of weekly income and expenditure, details of other agencies being approached for funding and details of the holiday break and who will care for the person while the break is being taken.

Correspondent: Gillian Galvan, General Manager, The Gate House, 9 Burkitt Road, Woodbridge, Suffolk IP12 4JJ (01394 388746; fax: 01394 388746; email: ogilviecharities@btconnect.com; website: theogilvietrust.org.uk)

The Princess Royal Trust for Carers

Eligibility: Unpaid carers in the UK, especially those who live near a Princess Royal Trust for Carers Centre.

Types of grants: One-off grants, for example towards driving lessons or domestic items.

Annual grant total: About 650 grants are made to individuals totalling about £2,000 each year.

Applications: Applications are made via your local Princess Royal Trust for Carers Centre.

Correspondent: The Clerk, Unit 14, Bourne Court, Southend Road, Woodford Green, Essex IG8 8HD (0844 800 4361; email: info@carers.org; website: www.carers.org)

Children & young people

Active Foundation

Eligibility: Children, people who are disadvantaged and people with disabilities.

Types of grants: One-off and recurrent grants according to need. Grants made have included those towards the purchase of equipment, wheelchairs, hoists and so on, activity holidays for children and adolescents being treated for various chronic illnesses and hospital transportation costs for a girl who had a kidney transplant.

Annual grant total: In 2008/09 the foundation had an income of £597 and a total expenditure of £670.

Applications: In writing to the correspondent.

Correspondent: The Secretary, Unit G, 41 Warwick Road, Solihull B92 7HS (0121 440 5855)

Other information: Grants are also made to organisations.

The Frank Buttle Trust

Eligibility: Children and young people with acute needs, including those living with any kind of disability; children suffering from illness, distress, abuse or neglect; children with behavioural or psychological problems; and, those living in severe poverty and deprivation.

The following groups are eligible to apply: adopted children; children cared for by grandparents, other relatives or friends; children and young people who are aged 18 years and under, cared for by single or two parents; and, estranged, orphaned and vulnerable young people under 21 who are living independently.

Types of grants: One-off grants for essential items or services which are critical to the well-being of the child. For example, beds, bedding, clothing (if there is very urgent need), essential items of furniture and household equipment, and, occasionally, short-term therapy costs.

Exclusions: The trust cannot help children and young people who are: in care, being rehabilitated home, subject to a Child Protection Plan, or where there is any other clear statutory responsibility; aged 19–20 and do not have full refugee status or exceptional or indefinite leave to remain in the UK, or who are normally resident abroad; living outside the UK. There are no grants towards payment of debts, holiday and child care costs, computers or adaptations to houses and cars. No repeat grants are made.

Annual grant total: In 2008/09 the trust made 9,852 grants to individuals under the Child Support Grants Scheme totalling £2 million.

Applications: On a form available from the correspondent, through a statutory agency or voluntary organisation that is capable of assessing the needs of the child and that can also administer a grant on behalf of the trust; where no such organisation exists, the trust will discuss alternative arrangements. Applications can be made by email (preferred) or post. For full details please refer to the trust's website.

Correspondent: Casework Manager, Audley House, 13 Palace Street, London SW1E 5HX (020 7828 7311; email: info@buttletrust.org; website: www.buttletrust.org)

Other information: The trust was founded by the Rev W F Buttle in 1953.

Grants are also given for educational purposes to school children and university students (see the *Guide's* sister publication, *The Guide to Educational Grants* for further information).

Children Today Charitable Trust

Eligibility: Children and young people under 25 who have a disability.

Types of grants: Grants of up to £1,000 to provide vital, life-changing specialist equipment, such as wheelchairs, walking aids, trikes, educational toys, communication aids, lifting and posturepaedic sleep equipment and specially designed sensory equipment like fibre optic sprays.

Annual grant total: In 2008/09 the trust distributed money for special aids and equipment totalling £124,000.

Applications: Application forms are available from the correspondent. Grants are only given for specialised pieces of equipment for individual children (not groups or schools), and applications must be made by the individual applying, their parent, or legal guardian. The charity aims to deal with all applications within 28 days of receipt.

Correspondent: A Dodd, The Moorings, Rowton Bridge, Christleton, Chester CH3 7AE (01244 335622; fax: 01244 335473; email: info@children-today.org.uk; website: www.children-today.org.uk)

Other information: If you wish to apply for computer equipment, the charity works in partnership with the Aidis Trust, and encourages applicants to contact them directly.

The J I Colvile Charitable Trust

Eligibility: People in need who are resident in Gloucestershire, west Oxfordshire and south Warwickshire. Help is regularly given to ex-servicemen and their families via, for example, SSAFA.

Types of grants: One-off grants ranging from £250 to £500.

Annual grant total: Grants usually total around £3,000 per year.

Applications: In writing to the correspondent. Applications can be submitted directly by the individual or family member, or by an organisation such as Citizens Advice. They are considered as necessary.

Correspondent: John Hankey, 4 Park Lane, Appleton, Abingdon, Oxfordshire OX13 5JT (01865 862668)

Other information: Grants are also made to youth training projects.

The Family Fund Trust

Eligibility: Families who are caring at home for a child under 17 who is severely disabled. Eligible families must have a gross income of no more than £25,000 a year for those living in England or £27,000 year for those living in Scotland, Northern Ireland and Wales. (This is the total amount received from benefits and tax credits from working and other sources of income e.g. maintenance or rental income. The trust does not count Disability Living Allowance or Child Benefit).

Types of grants: The help given must be related to the child's care needs. It may include help with a holiday, leisure activities, laundry equipment, bedding and clothing, transport, play equipment and other items.

Exclusions: The trust cannot provide items which are the responsibility of statutory agencies, such as medical or educational equipment or small items for daily living, such as bath aids, which are the responsibility of social services. No funding is given for general household bills, utility bills, mortgage or rent payments or household repairs.

Annual grant total: In 2008/09 the trust made grants to 49,357 individual families totalling £31 million.

Applications: Applications can be made by parents or carers or, with parental consent, by a professional worker. An application form is available from the trust or applications can be by letter giving the child's full name and date of birth, and parent's name, address and telephone number. Brief details about the child's disability and how this affects daily life are also needed. Tell the trust what kind of help is being requested and whether an application has been made before (if so, quote the Family Fund Trust number if possible).

Correspondent: Claire White, Unit 4, Alpha Court, Monks Cross Drive, Huntington, York YO32 9WN (0845 130 4542 or 01904 621115; fax: 01904 652625; email: info@familyfund.org.uk; website: www.familyfund.org.uk)

Other information: The trust is funded entirely by the government administrations of England, Northern Ireland, Scotland and Wales, and works within guidelines agreed by the trustees. More information about the Family Fund Trust and a publications list are available from the Information Officer at the above address. This includes 'Introducing the Family Fund Trust' which outlines how the trust works and the guidelines used.

Each family's application is looked at individually. If it is the first time a family has applied to the Family Fund Trust it is likely that a local visitor will arrange to call and discuss the request. The visitor will then report back to York, where a decision will be made about whether the trust can help.

The trust decides whether a child is 'severely disabled' by considering the child's age, how much his or her abilities are affected and how much care the child needs. The trust will ask for details of diagnosis, treatment and expected outcomes of the child's condition. However, it is the effects of these on the family rather than the actual diagnosis that is taken into account.

The Family Fund Trust also produces a number of information sheets: adaptations to housing, bedding and clothing, benefits checklist, equipment for daily living, hearing impairment, holidays, behaviour and attention difficulties and transport and a guide to the opportunities available to young disabled people over sixteen called 'After 16 – What's New?' is available free to young disabled people and their carers (£10 to professional workers). 'Taking Care' is a book for parents and carers based on parents' own experiences of caring for a child with a disability. It is available free to parents and carers (£4 to professional workers) from the address above.

The Glebe Charitable Trust

Eligibility: Children and young people up to the age of 18 who have a disability or are disadvantaged in addition to being in financial need. Please note that financial need alone is not sufficient.

Types of grants: One-off grants in the range of £250 to £2,000. Although some grants are made for individual children, the trust prefers to give to registered charities and organisations which give practical help to children living with disabilities or other disadvantages.

Exclusions: Grants are not made for UK school or university fees, building programmes, gap year activities or for dyslexia.

Annual grant total: In 2009 the trust had assets of £370,000 and an income of £20,000. Grants were made totalling £15,000, of which £3,000 was given in grants to individuals.

Applications: The trust has previously stated that it receives applications beyond its capacities both administrative and financial. The trustees have therefore taken the reluctant decision that they can no longer consider unsolicited applications from either charities or individuals. Its current policy is to make grants to organisations known to the trustees, which give practical help to children with disabilities or who are disadvantaged in some way.

Small grants are given to known schools and other organisations in Zimbabwe for individual children but the trustees have continued with their policy of not assisting any UK individuals with school fees.

Correspondent: The Secretary, PO Box 38078, London SW19

Grizzles Foundation *see entry on page 278*

Happy Days Children's Charity

Eligibility: Children and young people aged 3 to 17 years (inclusive) who are disadvantaged, have ongoing chronic health conditions, have experienced trauma or abuse, have emotional behavioural difficulties or have special needs. The charity can only assist families that earn less than £25,000 a year.

Types of grants: One-off grants ranging from £25 to £1,250 for respite break family holidays in the UK (occasionally children who are terminally ill are funded for an overseas holiday). All funding is paid directly to the providers, such as venue/resort, transport provider and so on. All trips are organised and funded directly by the charity, therefore cheques are not normally given directly to the family. Essential key carers who are necessary to support the needs of the children on the holiday are also funded.

Exclusions: No extra adults are funded.

Annual grant total: In 2008/09 the charity had assets of £209,000 and an income of £923,000. Grants towards holidays and leisure activities amounted to £524,000.

Applications: On a form available from the correspondent or to download from the website. Applications are considered year round and should include a supporting letter from a doctor or healthcare professional to confirm the applicant meets the criteria. A telephone call is welcome for advice and guidance.

Please note: the charity can take between 9–12 months to consider grant applications.

Correspondent: Angela Dearmer, Clody house, 90–100 Collingdon Street, Luton, Bedfordshire LU1 1RX (01582 755999; email: enquiries@happydayscharity.org; website: www.happydayscharity.org)

Other information: Grants are also made to groups of children and young people who have special needs for day trips and holidays.

Lifeline 4 Kids

Eligibility: Disabled people under the age of 19.

Types of grants: Cash grants are not given: rather, specific items are purchased and delivered on behalf of the individual in need.

The trust's website explains: 'For the individual child we provide the full spectrum of specialised equipment such as electric wheelchairs, mobility aids and varying items including specialised computers. We are also one of the only UK charities prepared to help a special needs child from a low-income family with essential smaller items such as shoes, clothing, bedding and specialist toys. We are able to give emergency and welfare appeals immediate approval within the authorised limits of our welfare sub-

committee. No appeal is too large or too small for us to consider.'

Annual grant total: In 2008 the trust had assets of £398,000 and an income of £94,000. Charitable expenditure came to £215,000

Applications: Initially, in writing (via email or post) to the correspondent, indicating any specific requirements and including brief factual information i.e. the child's name, date of birth and health condition. If appropriate, an application form will then be sent out. The form contains questions relating to the child's medical condition and requires backup information from health professionals together with a financial statement of the applicant.

Applications are considered monthly, although urgent cases can be dealt with more quickly.

Correspondent: Roger Adelman, 215 West End Lane, West Hampstead, London NW6 1XJ (020 7794 1661; fax: 020 8459 8826; email: appeals@lifeline4kids.org; website: www.lifeline4kids.org)

Other information: The trust also supplies equipment and so on for schools, hospitals and clubs for children who are disabled or underprivileged.

This trust was previously called *The Handicapped Children's Aid Committee.*

Eliza Shepherd Charitable Trust

Eligibility: Children and young people who are in need.

Types of grants: Grants given according to need.

Annual grant total: In 2008/09 the trust had an income of £4,000 and a total expenditure of £6,000.

Applications: In writing to the correspondent.

Correspondent: Carol Presley, Trustee, 7 Garden House Lane, East Grinstead RH19 4JT

Other information: Grants are also made to organisations.

Miss Doreen Stanford Charitable Trust

Eligibility: People who are disabled, deaf or blind and in need. Also, children whose families are in financial need.

Types of grants: One-off and recurrent grants ranging between £500 and £1,500, mainly for equipment related to sickness or disability.

Exclusions: No grants for holidays or items such as washing machines, clothes or repairs.

Annual grant total: About £25,000 a year.

Applications: Applications must be made through a charity, containing details of the individual's income and expenditure. The trustees meet once a year, in March, and applications must be submitted by the end of January. A sae is required if the applicant would like a reply.

Correspondent: Mrs G M B Borner, Secretary, 26 The Mead, Beckenham, Kent BR3 5PE (020 8650 3368)

S C Witting Trust

Eligibility: Individuals in need, ordinarily resident in England, and who are under 15 or over 60 years old.

Types of grants: One-off grants for specific items such as electric appliances, furniture, clothing, toys pushchairs, bedding and so on.

Exclusions: No grants towards debts or loans.

Annual grant total: In 2009 the trust made grants in England totalling £8,500 to individuals for welfare purposes. On average there are six successful grants per month (about one in ten of applications received).

Applications: In writing to the correspondent, at any time, through a social worker, Citizens Advice or other welfare agency, including a short case history, reason for need and the amount required. Unsuccessful applications are not acknowledged unless an sae is provided.

Correspondent: The Administrator, Friends House, 173 Euston Road, London NW1 2BJ

Other information: Grants are also made to individuals for educational purposes.

Divorced/ separated people

NCDS (National Council for the Divorced & Separated Trust)

Eligibility: People in need in the UK. All applications are considered regardless of marital status.

Types of grants: One-off grants according to need.

Annual grant total: In 2008 the trust had an income of £3,000 and a total expenditure of £4,000.

Applications: On a form available from the correspondent. Applications can be submitted directly by the individual or through a social worker, Citizens Advice or other welfare agency. Applications are considered every six to eight weeks, although urgent cases can be considered between meetings.

Correspondent: Joan Barbara Parnell-Raw, PO Box 6, Kingswinford, West Midlands BY6 8YS (020 8529 8778; fax: 020 8524 7822; email: info@ncds.org. uk; website: www.ncds.org.uk)

Ethnic & national minorities in the UK

The Ibero-American Benevolent Society

Eligibility: Spanish, Portuguese and Latin American nationals who are in need and live in the UK.

Types of grants: One-off grants of up to £300 for a wide range of needs. Recent grants have been made for washing machines, cookers and telephone installation.

Exclusions: No educational grants are made.

Annual grant total: Grants usually total around £5,000 per year.

Applications: In writing to the correspondent, including details of the individual's nationality, current circumstances and the amount needed. Applications should be submitted through a social worker, Citizens Advice, or similar welfare agency.

Correspondent: Lucia Martinez, 108 Cannon Street, London EC4N 6EU (020 7623 3060)

Prisoners of Conscience Appeal Fund

Eligibility: Prisoners of conscience and/or their families, who have suffered persecution for their beliefs. The fact that the person is seeking asylum or has been a victim of civil war is not sufficient grounds in itself.

Types of grants: One-off grants ranging from £350 to £500 for the provision of food, clothing, toiletries, travel costs, basic furniture, counselling/therapy sessions, family reunion costs, medical needs which are not supplied by the NHS such as orthopaedic beds or repairs to wheelchairs and PLAB or some vocational conversion courses.

Exclusions: No support is given to people who have used or advocated violence or supported a violent organisation.

Annual grant total: In 2009 relief payments amounted to £20,000, this included the following:

- Bursaries fund – £11,000
- UK relief grants to asylum seekers – £8,000
- Refugees Liverpool Fund – £1,000

Applications: Application forms are available from the correspondent and should be submitted through an approved agency on behalf of the individual. Applications should include evidence of identification of the applicant and of costs.

Correspondent: The Grants Officer, PO Box 61044, London SE1 1UP (020 7407 6644; email: grantsofficer@ prisonersofconscience.org; website: www. prisonersofconscience.org)

Other information: The fund was initially established in 1962 as the relief arm of Amnesty International, but is now a charity in its own right.

The Pusinelli Convalescent & Holiday Home

Eligibility: People who are or were German citizens and their dependants. Applicants must live in Greater London, Essex, Hertfordshire, Kent or Surrey.

Types of grants: Grants of up to £500 for families who would not otherwise be able to have a holiday.

Annual grant total: In 2008/09 the home had an income of £6,200 and a total expenditure of £2,700.

Applications: Applications should be made to the correspondent directly from the individual or from any welfare agency on their behalf.

Correspondent: David Leigh, Leigh Saxton Green, 4–7 Manchester Street, London W1U 3AE (020 7486 5553; email: enquiries@lsg-ca.co.uk)

The Society of Friends of Foreigners in Distress

Eligibility: People living in London or its surrounding area who are from countries not in the Commonwealth, the USA or which were once part of the British Empire.

Types of grants: Grants can be given for electrical goods, clothing, living costs, household bills, food, travel expenses, furniture and disabled equipment.

Annual grant total: In 2008/09 the trust had an income of £9,900 and a total expenditure of £21,000. Grants were made totalling around £12,000.

Applications: In writing to the correspondent at any time. Applications should be submitted by a social worker, Citizens Advice or other welfare agency.

Correspondent: Mrs Valerie Goodhart, 68 Burhill Road, Hersham, Walton-on-Thames, Surrey KT12 4JF (01932 244916)

Tollard Trust

Eligibility:
- People living in Bournemouth, Poole and elsewhere in Dorset who are older or disabled, who live in their own homes and are affected by hardship and sickness. Applicants should be, or have been: chemists; members of the clergy; ex-services and service people; farmers; legal professionals; masons; medical professionals; musicians; research

workers; seafarers and fishermen; and textile workers and designers.

● Older people from Asia and Africa who are disabled or in financial need.

Types of grants: Recurrent grants of about £100, towards items, services or facilities.

Exclusions: No grants are made for education and training, including expeditions or scholarships.

Annual grant total: In 2008/09 the trust had an income of £9,300 and a total expenditure of £13,000.

Applications: Grants are made once a year, usually in November. Most grants are in answer to requests from charities, for example, Salvation Army, Pramacare, RUKBA, Greenhill, McDougall and other local charities. Very occasionally grants are made directly to individuals in need who live locally.

Correspondent: R J Carlyle-Clarke, Tollard Green Farm, Tollard Royal, Salisbury, Wiltshire SP5 5PX (01725 516323)

Ethnic & national minorities in the UK – Armenians

The Armenian Relief Society of Great Britain Trust

Eligibility: Poor, sick or bereaved Armenians, worldwide.

Types of grants: One-off and recurrent grants of £150 are available.

Annual grant total: The majority of grants are usually made to organisations, although the trust does have the capacity to make grants to individuals.

Applications: In writing to the correspondent.

Correspondent: Mrs Matilda Megerdichian, 180 Great West Road, Hounslow TW5 9AR (020 8570 2268; fax: 020 8723 8948)

Ethnic & national minorities in the UK – Assyrians

The Assyrian Charity and Relief Fund of UK

Eligibility: People of Assyrian descent living in UK or worldwide who are in need, hardship or distress.

Types of grants: The fund offers food, medicine and temporary shelter to people in need. One-off and recurrent grants are made usually ranging between £10 and £400.

Exclusions: No grants are available for business people, political organisations, those already settled in Europe, America, Australia and Canada or those financially secure.

Annual grant total: No grants were made in the last financial year. Previously, grants have totalled around £1,000.

Applications: In writing to the correspondent, submitted through a social worker, Citizens Advice, welfare agency or other charity.

Correspondent: Revd Henry Shaheen, 277 Rush Green Road, Romford RM7 0JL (01708 730122)

Ethnic & national minorities in the UK – Belgians

The Royal Belgian Benevolent Society

Eligibility: Belgians who live in Britain, and their close dependants, who are in need.

Types of grants: Regular grants of £300 to £2,000.

Annual grant total: In 2009 the society had an income of £1,700 and a total expenditure of £15,000. The trust has stated that after a period of increased funding commitments in 2010, no scholarships will be awarded in 2011. Applications will continue to be received in 2012.

Applications: On a form available from the correspondent, submitted either directly by the individual, or via a social worker, Citizens Advice or other welfare agency.

Correspondent: Patrick Bresnan, 5 Hartley Close, Bromley BR1 2TP (020 8467 8442)

Ethnic & national minorities in the UK – Dutch

The Netherlands' Benevolent Society

Eligibility: People in need who are Dutch nationals or of Dutch extraction and living in the UK.

Types of grants: One-off grants ranging between £100 to £1,000 and regular allowances of £80 per month for each individual. In the past grants have included payments for: debts to allow someone to make a 'clean start'; essential home repairs; clothing; basic living items; the costs of a training course.

Exclusions: Beneficiaries must not have access to financial help from other sources.

Annual grant total: In 2009 the trust had assets of £706,000 and an income of £38,000. Grants were made totalling £35,000.

Applications: On a form available from the society administrator. Applications are usually made through churches, the Netherlands Embassy, the Netherlands Consulates, the Department of Work and Pensions regional offices or welfare charities. They are considered every month, except in August, at the trustees' monthly meeting. Information of the individual's financial situation, including details of any social security benefits, should be included.

Correspondent: Loesje Roele-Van Hellenberg Hubar, PO Box 36, Etchingham TN19 7WR (01932 355885; fax: 01932 355885; email: info@ koningwillemfonds.org.uk)

Ethnic & national minorities in the UK – Egyptians

Egyptian Community Association in the United Kingdom

Eligibility: People in need who are Egyptian or of Egyptian origin and are living in or visiting the UK.

Types of grants: Grants towards a broad range of needs, for example, help with the costs of medical treatment and gas bills.

Annual grant total: Grants usually total around £500 per year.

Applications: In writing to the correspondent.

Correspondent: Dr Wafik Moustafa, Chair, 100 Redcliffe Gardens, London SW10 9HH (020 7244 8925)

Other information: The association arranges seminars and national and religious celebrations, as well as offering other services. It also gives grants to individuals for educational purposes.

Ethnic & national minorities in the UK – Germans

The German Society of Benevolence

Eligibility: Older people in need who are, or were, citizens of Germany, and their dependants. Applicants must live in Greater London, Essex, Hertfordshire, Kent or Surrey.

Types of grants: Small one-off and recurrent grants for heating, clothing and other needs.

Annual grant total: In 2009 the society had an income of £7,200 and a total expenditure of £7,900.

Applications: Applications are considered from individuals or from agencies acting on their behalf.

Correspondent: David Leigh, Leigh Saxton Green, 4–7 Manchester Street, London W1U 3AE (020 7486 5553)

Ethnic & national minorities in the UK – Indians

India Welfare Society

Eligibility: Members of the Indian community, who have membership with the society and are in need.

Types of grants: One-off and recurrent grants according to need for hardship and welfare purposes only.

Annual grant total: About £1,000.

Applications: In writing to the correspondent.

Correspondent: S K Gupta, President, 11 Middle Row, London W10 5AT (020 8969 9493; email: iwslondon@hotmail.com; website: www.indiawelfaresociety.org)

Ethnic & national minorities in the UK – Swiss

The Swiss Benevolent Society

Eligibility: Swiss citizens who are experiencing hardship and are temporarily or permanently resident in the consular district of London. In special cases, those living in other parts of the UK may also receive assistance.

Types of grants: One-off and recurrent grants towards holidays, heating costs, travel to and from day centres, therapies, household equipment, telephone and TV licences and so on.

Annual grant total: In 2008/09 the society had assets of £1.1 million and an income of £56,000. Grants were made totalling about £45,000.

Applications: In writing to the correspondent, including proof of nationality. Applications can be submitted directly by the individual, through an organisation such as Citizens Advice or via any third party. They are considered at any time.

Correspondent: Petra Kehr Cocks, Welfare Officer, 79 Endell Street, London WC2H 9DY (020 7836 9119; fax: 020 7379 1096; email: info@swissbenevolent.org.uk; website: www.swissbenevolent.org.uk)

Other information: The trust also provides emotional support and counselling where necessary.

Ethnic & national minorities in the UK – Zimbabweans

The Rhodesians Worldwide Assistance Fund

Eligibility: People formerly resident in Zimbabwe (previously Rhodesia) who are in need, and their widows and dependants.

Types of grants: One-off grants are given to meet short term needs.

Exclusions: No grants are given for education, debts, business expenditure, house repairs, motor vehicles, legal expenses, foreign travel or medical expenses.

Annual grant total: In 2008/09 the fund had an income of £22,000 and a total expenditure of £56,000.

Applications: On a form available from the correspondent or to download from the website. Applicants will need to prove their former residence in Zimbabwe and their right to remain in the UK. Applications can be submitted directly by the individual or through another charity or close relative. Trustees meet four times a year to consider applications, though urgent cases can be dealt with between meetings.

Correspondent: The Administrator, PO Box 213, Lingfield, Surrey RH7 6WW (email: ian@12buzz.com; website: zrwaf.com)

Zimbabwe Rhodesia Relief Fund

Eligibility: Zimbabwe Rhodesians living worldwide who are distressed or sick.

Types of grants: One-off and recurrent grants of £70 to £300.

Exclusions: Grants are not given for educational purposes or for travel.

Annual grant total: In 2008/09 the fund had assets of £46,000 and an income of £28,000. Grants were made to 120 individuals totalling £26,000.

Applications: In writing to the correspondent. Applications should be made through somebody known to the charity and include proof of past or present Zimbabwean citizenship.

Correspondent: W D Walker, Secretary, PO Box 5307, Bishop's Stonford, Hertfordshire CM23 3DY (01279 466121)

Holidays

The Family Holiday Association

Eligibility: Families who are referred by social workers, health visitors or other caring agencies as desperate for a holiday break. Applicants must not have had a holiday within the past four years, unless there are exceptional circumstances; and at least one child must be aged between 3 and 18.

Types of grants: Either the family has an idea about where they want to go and the association decides how much to give towards the total cost, or the association funds the entire holiday at a holiday centre and gives money towards the costs of food, spending money and so on. Grants are generally from £250 upwards.

Occasionally, the association also receives offers of holidays at short notice, e.g. a half board holiday in the UK or an activity holiday abroad. If a family can travel with only a few days' notice their chance of receiving a break may increase.

Annual grant total: In 2008/09 the trust had assets of £877,000 and an income of

£1.1 million. Grants were made to over 1,600 families totalling £610,000.

Applications: On a form available from the correspondent or to download from the website. Applications should be submitted in November each year. The association usually has enough applications to commit all its funds by December. Applications must be referred by a welfare agency, voluntary organisation and so on. Those made directly by the individual are not accepted.

Correspondent: Sophie Munro, Senior Grant and Project Officer, 16 Mortimer Street, London W1T 3JL (020 7436 3304; fax: 020 7323 7299; email: info@ familyholidayassociation.org.uk; website: www.fhaonline.org.uk)

The Lloyd Thomas Charity for Women & Girls

Eligibility: Women and girls on a low income in desperate need of a holiday.

Types of grants: Grants up to £130 for women and £65 for girls towards the cost of a holiday. Only in exceptional circumstances can a person be considered for a grant if they have had a holiday within the last four years.

Annual grant total: Grants usually total around £2,000 a year.

Applications: In writing through a social worker or other welfare agency requesting an application form. Applications are considered all year, though generally from November to May.

Correspondent: John McDonald, 2nd Floor Rear, Family Holiday Association, 16 Mortimer Street, London W1T 3JL (020 7436 3304; fax: 020 7323 7299; email: info@FamilyHolidayAssociation. org.uk; website: www.fhaonline.org.uk)

The Victoria Convalescent Trust

Eligibility: People in medical need of convalescence, recuperative and respite care in England and Wales. Preference is given to people living in Surrey and Croydon.

Types of grants: Grants ranging from £50 to £600 towards the cost of convalescence, respite care and recuperative holidays.

Exclusions: Grants are not made for holidays.

Annual grant total: In 2009 the trust made grants totalling £61,000, which consisted of sundry grants and grants made for convalescence and respite purposes.

Applications: On a form available from the correspondent. Applications must be submitted through a social worker, a health care worker or a welfare agency or another professional worker and will be considered every month. Medical and social reports supporting the need for a break must be provided.

Correspondent: The Grants Co-ordinator, 11 Cavendish Avenue, Woodford Green, Essex IG8 9DA (020 8502 9339)

Other information: Occasionally, support is given to women living in Greater London for vital equipment and services.

Homelessness

Housing the Homeless Central Fund

Eligibility: People who are either homeless or have serious accommodation problems. Priority may be given to expectant parents or those with children.

Types of grants: One-off grants of around £250 to £300 for household items and fuel bills.

Exclusions: No recurrent grants are given or grants for holidays, medical apparatus, funeral expenses, travel costs, removal costs, vehicles, educational expenses, structural improvements to property, computers or televisions.

Annual grant total: In 2008/09 the fund had assets of £290,000 and an income of £101,000. Grants were made totalling £79,000, of which approximately £54,000 was given to individuals and £25,000 to organisations.

Applications: Guidelines and applications should be requested by a social worker, who will receive the information, on headed paper and enclosing an sae. Decisions are usually made within a week, although no grants are made in March or December. No telephone calls can be accepted.

Correspondent: The Clerk to the Trustees, 2 Evershed House, 24 Old Castle Street, London E1 7NU

Other information: The trust has recently stated that while it still receives and processes individual applications, it now relies more and more upon organisations that it has known for some years, which accept a block grant of around £2,500 and distribute it to their clients on the trust's behalf.

Older people

Age Sentinel Trust

Eligibility: People over 60, who are living on a low income. Priority is given to people with dementia, particularly Alzheimer's disease, and those with other debilitating illnesses.

Types of grants: One-off and recurrent grants to help people through a financial crisis or to pay for services, such as emergency home repairs, access improvements, maintenance and gardening costs.

Annual grant total: This trust was registered with the Charity Commission in January 2010. It expects to have around £25,000 to £35,000 available for grantmaking in 2010/11 and aims to double this allowance for 2011/12.

Applications: On a form available from the correspondent.

Correspondent: Francesca Colverson, 2 Winchester Road, Bishops Waltham, Southampton SO32 1BE (020 8144 4774; email: agesentineltrust@googlemail.com; website: agesentinel.org.uk)

Aid for the Aged in Distress (AFTAID)

Eligibility: UK citizens of state pensionable age (60 years old for women and 65 for men) who reside in the UK and are living on a low income and have minimal savings.

Types of grants: Emergency grants for essential items to facilitate the beneficiary to maintain their independence in the familiar surroundings of their home, for example heating appliances, bedding, cookers, washing machines or other white goods, essential furniture and carpets. Grants are also made towards more expensive items such as a stair lift, walk-in shower, motorised scooter and so on. Applications can sometimes be considered towards costs for an elderly carer to enjoy a respite break.

Exclusions: Grants cannot be made for any on-going payments, arrears or debts of any kind.

Annual grant total: In 2009 the charity had an income of £101,000. Grants and services for elderly people totalled £100,000.

Applications: On a form available from the correspondent. Applications can be made directly by the individual or through a welfare organisation and should include written support from a social worker, doctor or similar professional of the official care services who are personally aware of the beneficiary's situation.

Correspondent: Lewis Greene, 18 Hand Court, High Holborn, London WC1V 6JF (0870 803 1950; fax: 0870 803 2128; email: info@aftaid.org.uk; website: www. aftaid.org.uk)

The Percy Bilton Charity

Eligibility: People who are on a low income and are either:

- over 65 years old
- have a physical or learning disability
- receiving hospital or other medical treatment for a long term illness (including mental illness).

Types of grants: One-off grants of up to £200 for specific essential items only. For example, laundry equipment, cooking and heating appliances, basic furniture, beds and bedding, floor coverings, clothing and footwear and other essential household items.

Exclusions: No payments are made towards items costing over £200; travel expenses, sponsorship, holidays or respite care; educational grants, computer equipment or software; house alterations and maintenance (including adaptations for disabled facilities); debts; dishwashers; reimbursement of cost for articles already purchased; garden fencing or clearance; motor vehicle purchase or expenses; nursing and residential home fees; funeral expenses; removal expenses; medical treatment of therapy; course fees including driving or IT lessons.

Annual grant total: In 2008/09 the charity had assets of £14 million and an income of £781,000. Grants were made totalling £112,000 and were distributed as follows:

Household goods and furniture	566	£68,000
Home appliances	268	£34,000
Clothing and footwear	135	£11,000

A further £40,000 was given in Christmas hampers and £467,000 was awarded to organisations.

Applications: On a form available from the correspondent: to be submitted by a social worker, community psychiatric nurse or occupational therapist, including a covering letter on headed paper. Full application guidelines are available on the website or on request. Applications can be made at any time.

Please note: the charity is unable to respond to applications made by anyone other than a social worker or occupation therapist or to requests which fall outside of the charity's funding criteria. Applicants should also ensure that they have applied to all statutory sources and any appropriate specialist charities (e.g. employment related funds and armed forces funds) before approaching the charity.

Correspondent: Tara Smith, Bilton House, 7 Culmington Road, Ealing, London W13 9NB (020 8579 2829; fax: 020 8579 3650; website: www. percybiltoncharity.org.uk)

Counsel & Care for the Elderly

Eligibility: People over 60 years old who are not eligible for statutory support and have savings of under £2,500 (£3,500 for couples).

Types of grants: One-off grants of £250 towards housing repairs, mobility aids, household items and holidays. Though, where appropriate, the trust prefers that individuals apply to more specific charities first.

Exclusions: Applications will only be considered if no statutory funding is available. If you are receiving Pension Guarantee Credit, a grant will not be considered unless you have first made an application to the Social Fund and a decision has been made (this does not apply if your item is in the excluded list for the Social Fund). Grants will not be considered to repay debt.

Annual grant total: In 2008/09 the charity had assets of £132,000 and an income of £868,000.

Information from the charity's accounts indicates that the charity is building up reserves. Therefore, it appears that no grants were made during the year.

Applications: On a form available from the correspondent. Applications can be submitted by the individual or a third party but must be countersigned by a social worker, advice worker or similar professional in order to be considered. Applications are processed on a quarterly basis, with decisions being made in April/July/October/January.

Correspondent: Mr S B Burke, Twyman House, 16 Bonny Street, London NW1 9PG (020 7241 8555; email: advice@ counselandcare.org.uk; website: www. counselandcare.org.uk)

Other information: The charity also provides an advice service (including fact sheets) for older people on matters such as help at home, accommodation and finance.

Monica Eyre Memorial Foundation

Eligibility: People in need, particularly older people and people with disabilities/special needs in the UK.

Types of grants: Grants are made to enable people with low-mobility in residential care to get a holiday with essential carer support.

Annual grant total: In 2008/09 the trust had an income of £6,000 and a total expenditure of £5,900.

Applications: In writing to the correspondent.

Correspondent: Michael Bidwell, 5 Clifton Road, Winchester, Hampshire SO22 5BN (email: michael.bidwell@talk21.com)

Other information: The trust also makes grants to organisations and to individuals for educational purposes.

Friends of the Elderly

Eligibility: Men and women who live in England and Wales aged 60 or over (over 50 for homeless people), with low income and with limited savings are eligible for support. The trust cannot help people living in residential care or those living in Scotland.

Types of grants: One-off grants are given for essential items such as mobility aids, clothing, basic furniture, household white goods and appliances, property repairs/adaptations and other expenses. A cheque will be made payable to the relevant organisation (or company providing the equipment or service).

The charity also distributes allowances, on a monthly or twice yearly basis, to support older people on low incomes in maintaining their independence.

Exclusions: Unfortunately, the charity cannot help those living in residential care or those living in Scotland. Grants are not available for care home fees, rent arrears, none-UK respite breaks or council tax payments.

Annual grant total: In 2008/09 grants were made to 954 older people totalling £365,000.

Applications: On a form available from the correspondent. Applications should be made through a third party organisation such as social services, Citizens Advice or Age UK.

Correspondent: Welfare and Grant Giving Manager, 40–42 Ebury Street, London SW1W 0LZ (020 7730 8263; fax: 020 7259 0154; email: wagg@fote.org. uk; website: www.fote.org.uk)

Home Warmth for the Aged

Eligibility: People of pensionable age, at risk from the cold in winter who have no resources other than their state pension/income support and have savings of less than £4,000.

Types of grants: Provision of heating appliances, bedding, clothing and solid fuel and to pay fuel debts where the supply has been disconnected. One-off grants only, ranging between £90 and £250.

Exclusions: No grants are made to people who have younger members of their family living with them.

Annual grant total: In 2008/09 the trust had an income of £29,000 and a total expenditure of £25,000. Grants totalled around £20,000.

Applications: On a form available from the correspondent and submitted through social workers, doctors, nurses etc. only, to whom grants are returned for disbursement. If there is an armed forces connection, applications should be made through SSAFA (see service section of this guide). Applications made directly by individuals are not considered. Applications are looked at monthly.

Correspondent: W J Berentemfel, 19 Towers Wood, South Darenth, Dartford, Kent DA4 9BQ (01322 863836; email: w.berentemfel@btinternet.com)

IndependentAge (RUKBA)

Eligibility: People over 70 years old who are lonely or isolated and find themselves in financial need. Preference is given to individuals who will benefit most from long-term support.

Types of grants: Annuities of £750, which are granted for life (unless there is an unexpected and considerable improvement in the recipient's circumstances), are the main form of help. One-off grants are also made towards, for example, unexpected, emergency household repairs and maintenance; mobility aids; convalescence and respite care; spectacles and dental treatment. The association also distributes parcels of clothing and bed linen.

Exclusions: One-off grants are only available to existing beneficiaries.

Annual grant total: In 2009 the association made regular payments totalling £4.7 million and one-off grants and loans totalling £532,000.

Applications: In the first instance the applicant should write to the care officer giving a brief description of their circumstances.

Correspondent: Care Services Department, 6 Avonmore Road, London W14 8RL (020 7605 4200; fax: 020 7605 4201; email: charity@ independentage.org.uk; website: www. independentage.org.uk)

Other information: The association provides information, advice and practical help through its network of staff and dedicated volunteers across the UK. It also manages three residential and nursing homes.

The Heinz, Anna and Carol Kroch Foundation

Eligibility: People who are older, have a chronic illness or have fled domestic situations and are in financial hardship.

Types of grants: One-off grants usually ranging from £100 to £500 towards hospital travel costs, household bills, furniture, other hospital expenses, clothing, food, medical and disability equipment, living costs, home adaptations, help in the home and so on.

Exclusions: No grants for education or holidays.

Annual grant total: In 2008/09 the foundation had assets of £2.9 million and an income of £171,000. Grants were made to 730 individuals totalling £98,000.

Applications: In writing to the correspondent. Most applications are submitted through other charities and local authorities. Applications should include full financial information including income and expenditure, what the grant will be used for and a why it is needed. Applicants should also state if they have approached any other charities for financial assistance and how successful

they have been to date. Applications are considered monthly.

Correspondent: Heather Astle, PO Box 5, Bentham, Lancaster LA2 7XA (01524 263001; fax: 01524 262721; email: hakf50@hotmail.com)

Morden College

Eligibility: People in need who are aged over 50, from a professional or managerial background, who have retired from paid employment either on medical grounds or because they have reached the statutory retirement age.

Types of grants: Quarterly allowances and one-off grants of between £200 and £1,000 towards household items, holidays and convalescence.

Exclusions: The trust does not give for nursing home top up fees or any services or products which should be funded by statutory authorities.

Annual grant total: In 2008/09 the trust had assets of £11 million and an income of £8.8 million. A total of £328,000 was paid out in donations and outpensions to 97 individuals during the year.

Applications: On a form available from the correspondent, for consideration throughout the year. Applications can be submitted either directly by the individual or through any third party.

Correspondent: Sir Iain Mackay-Dick, Clerk to the Trustees, 19 St German's Place, Blackheath, London SE3 0PW (020 8463 8330; fax: 020 8293 4887; email: amanda@mordencollege.org)

Other information: Morden College is the general title used for the administration of Sir John Morden's Charity and Dame Susan Morden's Charity. Sir John Morden's Charity provides grants and accommodation for the elderly. Dame Susan Morden's Charity is primarily concerned with the advancement of religion by assisting the Church of England with the upkeep of their churches and associated activities.

The National Benevolent Institution

Eligibility: Older people in need who live in their own homes (rented or owned) and have reached state retirement age or are over 50 and in receipt of the middle or higher rate of Disability Living Allowance (not fixed period). Net income, after certain expenses have been disregarded (e.g. rent and council tax), should be less than £6,600 per year for a single person and £10,200 for a couple. Savings should not exceed £10,000 for individual applicants or £18,000 for couples.

Please note that applications will not be considered unless the individual is claiming all the state benefits to which they are entitled.

Types of grants: Recurrent grants of up to £13 per week (£17.50 for couples) to allow people to live in their own homes in comfort and warmth. They are paid quarterly in March, June, September and December. One-off grants are also available for unexpected household costs and other items.

Exclusions: No grants are available for nursing home top up fees.

Annual grant total: In 2009 the institution had assets of £11 million, an income of £680,000 and a total expenditure of £674,000. Grants were made totalling £158,000.

Applications: On a form available from the correspondent including full income and expenditure details. Applications can be submitted either directly by the individual or through a third party such as a social worker. Help is available from the welfare officer should there be any problems in completing the form.

Correspondent: Rosie Jones, Welfare Officer, Peter Herve House, Eccles Court, Tetbury, Gloucestershire GL8 8EH (01666 505500; fax: 01666 503111; email: welfare@nbi.org.uk; website: www. nbi.org.uk)

Other information: The institution also operates two residential properties, providing accommodation for people over 50 who are in financial need.

The Nottingham Aged Persons' Trust see entry on page 234

The Roger Pilkington Young Trust

Eligibility: People over 60 years of age whose income has been reduced through no fault of their own, but prior to application was enough for them to live in a 'reasonable degree of comfort'.

Types of grants: Monthly pensions of about £45 for single people and £60 for married couples.

Annual grant total: In 2008/09 the trust had assets of £1.1 million and an income of £68,000. Grants were made to around 100 individuals totalling £62,000.

Applications: On a form available from the correspondent, after the pensions are advertised.

Correspondent: Ben Dixon, Everys Solicitors, Magnolia House, Church Street, Exmouth, Devon EX8 1HQ (01395 264384; email: ben.dixon@everys. co.uk)

The Florence Reiss Trust for Old People

Eligibility: Women over 55 and men over 60 who are in need. Priority is given to those who live in the parishes of Streatley in Berkshire and Goring-on-Thames in Oxfordshire.

Types of grants: One-off and recurrent grants according to need.

Annual grant total: In 2008/09 the trust had an income of £11,000 and a total expenditure of £10,000. Grants totalled around £9,000, most of which was given in grants to organisations.

Applications: In writing to the correspondent.

Correspondent: Dr Stephen Reiss, Trustee, 94 Tinwell Road, Stamford, Lincolnshire PE9 2SD (01780 762710)

The Skerritt Trust

Eligibility: Older people who live within ten miles of the market square in Nottingham.

Types of grants: Funding is given for house repairs and improvements to assist older people so that they can remain in their homes as long as possible.

Annual grant total: In 2008/09 the trust had assets of £1.6 million and an income of £82,000. Grants were made totalling £77,000, all of which was given to organisations.

Applications: In writing to the correspondent through a social worker, Age Concern, day centre or similar third party. Applications are considered all year round.

Correspondent: Nigel Cullen, Cumberland Court, 80 Mount Street, Nottingham NG1 6HH (0115 901 5558)

The Stanley Stein Charitable Trust

Eligibility: People with a disability and those over the age of 75 who are in need.

Types of grants: One-off and recurrent grants according to need.

Annual grant total: In 2008/09 the trust had an income of £19,000 and a total expenditure of £41,000.

Applications: On a form available from the correspondent.

Correspondent: Michael Lawson, Trustee, Burwood House, 14–16 Caxton Street, London SW1H 0GY (020 7873 1000)

The Straits Settlement & Malay States Benevolent Society

Eligibility: People in need who have lived in the Straits Settlements or Malay States for at least two years, and their dependants.

Types of grants: One-off and recurrent grants according to need. The society tends to support Europeans and dependants of Europeans, although this is not exclusively so.

Annual grant total: Grants average around £14,000 a year.

Applications: Applications should be sponsored by a subscriber.

Correspondent: Vince Cheshire, TMF Management (UK) Ltd, 400 Capability Green, Luton LU1 3AE (01582 439270; email: vince.cheshire@tmf-group.com)

Other information: In our last edition of this guide the society stated that its funds are fully committed and the society does not wish to incur further administration costs in replying to applications which cannot at present be considered.

Tancred's Charity for Pensioners

Eligibility: Men aged 50 or over who are UK citizens and clergy of the Church of England or Church in Wales, or officers in the armed forces.

Types of grants: Annual pensions of around £1,600 a year are paid quarterly to 13 to 15 beneficiaries.

Annual grant total: In 2009 the charity had an income of £21,000 and an expenditure of £24,000.

Applications: In writing to the correspondent. Individuals may apply at any time, but applications can only be considered when a vacancy occurs, which is approximately once a year.

Correspondent: Andrew Penny, Clerk, 31 Hill Street, London W1J 5LS (020 7863 8522; email: andrew.penny@forsters.co.uk)

The Universal Beneficent Society

Eligibility: People aged 65 and over and living at home (rented or owned). The society focuses on those who are severely isolated and who struggle to live on or below the UK poverty line. Individuals must have a weekly income of £140 or less (£200 for couples) and must have savings of less than £3,000 (£5,000 for couples).

Types of grants: The society provides a variety of support:

- Emergency grants: One-off grants of up to £100 in times of urgent need, for example, to help towards essential utility bills, mobility equipment and household goods or the installation of a telephone or security system.

- Regular allowances: An annual allowance of £258 (individuals) or £340 (couples) is given to supplement a low income. Please note, this service is currently closed to new applicants.

- Extras: Food hampers, bedding packs and thermal slippers are distributed in winter to help alleviate the risk of hypothermia. Small cash gifts are also made.

Annual grant total: In 2008 the society had assets of £1.4 million and an income of £543,000. Grants were made to over 1,000 individuals totalling £298,000.

Applications: On a form available from the correspondent. Applications can be made at anytime either directly by the individual or through a social worker or Citizens Advice.

Correspondent: Paramjit Sangha, Beneficiaries Caseworker, 6 Avonmore Road, London W14 8RL (020 7605 4228; fax: 020 7605 4201; email: paramjit. sangha@ubs.independentage.org.uk; website: www.u-b-s.org.uk)

Williamson Memorial Trust

Eligibility: People who are over 65 years of age.

Types of grants: One-off grants of between £20 and £100, given as gifts rather than maintenance. Grants are mainly given at Christmas.

Annual grant total: In 2008/09 the trust had an income of £8,800 and a total expenditure of £8,300. Grants are made for education and welfare purposes.

Applications: Due to a reduction of its funds and the instability of its income, the trust regrets that very few new applications will be considered to ensure it can meet its existing commitments. Support will generally only be given to cases known personally to the trustees and to those individuals the trust has existing commitments with.

Correspondent: Colin Williamson, 6 Windmill Close, Ashington, Pulborough, West Sussex RH20 3LG

Wireless for the Bedridden

Eligibility: People who are confined to their bed, largely housebound, elderly or disabled and in financial need.

Types of grants: Radios are provided and sent to the organisation supporting the application. Televisions are rented by the society on a full maintenance contract from a major rental company. The service is free to both recipient and sponsoring organisations. However, the sets remain the property of the society.

The society does not provide television licenses unless the applicant is in receipt of, or is applying for, equipment.

Exclusions: No grants to: individuals applying on their own behalf; organisations; grant-making bodies; statutory bodies; top up funding on under-priced contracts.

Annual grant total: In 2008/09 the society had an income of £282,000 and a total expenditure of £372,000. Grants were made totalling around £340,000.

Applications: On a form available directly from the correspondent or to download from the website. Applications must be submitted through a third party such as a social worker, Citizens Advice, religious organisation or other welfare agency. The society aims to respond to applications within ten working days.

Correspondent: Anny Mills, Applications Officer, 159a High Street, Hornchurch, Essex RM11 3YB (Freephone: 0800 018 2137; fax: 01708 620816; email: info@w4b.org.uk; website: www. w4b.org.uk)

Orders

Catenian Benevolent Association

Eligibility: Members of the association and their dependants who are in need.

Types of grants: One-off and recurrent grants according to need. Loans are also available.

Annual grant total: In 2008/09 the fund had assets of £6.4 million and an income of £312,000. Grants were made to 24 individuals totalling £87,000. Non-secured loans were also made amounting to £198,000.

Applications: In writing to the correspondent. Applications are considered four times a year.

Correspondent: Michael Tudor, 2nd Floor, 1 Copthall House, Station Square, Coventry CV1 2FY (02476 224533; email: catena@btconnect.com; website: www.thecatenians.com)

Grand Charitable Trust of the Order of Women Freemasons

Eligibility: Women freemasons who are in need.

Types of grants: One-off and recurrent grants to help towards medical, household and living expenses.

Annual grant total: In 2008/09 the trust had assets of £666,000, an income of £169,000 and made grants to individuals totalling £12,000.

Applications: In writing to the correspondent, usually through the local lodge. The trustees meet regularly throughout the year to consider applications.

Correspondent: Sylvia Joan Brown, Trustee, 27 Pembridge Gardens, London W2 4EF (020 7229 2368; website: www. owf.org.uk/)

The Grand Charity (of Freemasons under the United Grand Lodge of England)

Eligibility: Any freemason in need, whether they are currently a subscribing member or no longer belong to a Lodge, and their immediate dependants. Single

applicants should have savings of less than £13,000 (£18,000 for couples).

Types of grants: Grants of between £500 and £7,000, which can be renewed annually, to help with living expenses and unexpected needs.

Annual grant total: In 2008/09 the charity had assets of £61 million and an income of £16 million. Over 1,900 individuals received Masonic relief grants totalling £3.5 million. A further £2.9 million was distributed to organisations.

Applications: Applicants should first contact their Lodge Almoner or Provincial Grand Almoner who will provide support throughout the application process. Applications can be submitted at any time and a decision is usually reached within four to eight weeks of receipt.

For further information and questions on eligibility, applicants should contact Sandra Neary (020 7395 9391) or Mike Martin (020 7395 9293) at the charity's main office.

Correspondent: Ms Laura Chapman, Freemasons Hall, 60 Great Queen Street, London WC2B 5AZ (020 7395 9261; fax: 020 7395 9295; email: info@the-grand-charity.org; website: www.grandcharity. org)

Other information: The charity also manages the Relief Chest Scheme. Each 'relief chest' is used to accumulate funds collected by a Lodge, Chapter or Province for charitable purposes. These are then used by the individual Lodges to distribute grants to charities and individuals in need. Applications for these funds should be made through the relevant Lodge, Chapter or Province.

In 2002, the charity took over responsibility for the Transferred Beneficiaries Fund, which makes regular payments to former beneficiaries of the Royal Masonic Benevolent Institution Annuity Fund. This fund is not open to new applications for assistance.

Practical help and financial support for individuals in times personal distress and for local charities is also given independently of the Grand Charity by individual lodges and Provincial Grand Lodges. Addresses are available from the correspondent.

The separate entries for the Royal Masonic Benevolent Institution and the New Masonic Samaritan Fund in this *Guide* may be helpful. There is also the Masonic Trust for Girls and Boys, which helps children of any age (including adopted children and step-children) of Freemasons under the United Grand Lodge of England. (See entry in *The Guide to Educational Grants*, also published by DSC).

The Grand Lodge of Antient, Free & Accepted Masons of Scotland

Eligibility: Members and their dependants, and the widows and dependants of deceased members.

Types of grants: One-off and recurrent grants according to need.

Annual grant total: In 2008/09 the trust had an income of £1.9 million. About £155,000 is given in welfare grants each year and £25,000 in educational grants.

Applications: On a form available from the correspondent, or by direct approach to the local lodge. They are considered three times a year, although urgent requests can be dealt with between meetings.

Correspondent: D M Begg, Grand Secretary, Freemasons Hall, 96 George Street, Edinburgh EH2 3DH (0131 225 5304)

Other information: The trust also runs care homes for older people.

Adelaide Litten Charitable Trust

Eligibility: Women freemasons and their dependants who are in need.

Types of grants: One-off and recurrent grants according to need.

Annual grant total: In 2008/09 the trust had assets of £3.3 million and an income of £189,000. Grants to 'petitioners' totalled £3,900. A further £210 was paid in 'Christmas gratuities'.

Applications: In writing to the correspondent.

Correspondent: The Trustees, c/o Winckworth Sherwood, Minerva House, 5 Montague Close, London SE1 9BB (020 7593 5000; fax: 020 7593 5099)

The Masonic Province of Middlesex Charitable Trust

Eligibility: Freemasons or their families or dependants who are in need and live in the Middlesex area.

Types of grants: Grants are given according to need.

Annual grant total: In 2008/09 the trust had assets of £1.5 million and an income of £56,000. Grants totalled £36,000, all of which was given to organisations.

Applications: Requests should be made to the Provincial Grand Almoner and are considered on an ongoing basis.

Correspondent: Peter Gledhill, Secretary, 85 Fakenham Way, Sandhurst, Berkshire GU47 0YS (01344 777077)

The New Masonic Samaritan Fund

Eligibility: Freemasons, their families and dependants who are in both financial and medical need.

Types of grants: One-off grants ranging between £1,500 and £15,000 towards medical, respite and dental treatment.

Exclusions: No grants can be made towards treatment which has already been provided privately, or which can be made through the NHS without undue delay or hardship.

Annual grant total: In 2008/09 the trust had assets of £39 million and an income of £5.4 million. There were 471 grants made to individuals totalling £2.3 million.

Applications: On a form available from the correspondent or through the lodge almoner. The trustees meet each month (usually the last Thursday) to consider applications received in the previous 30 days.

Correspondent: The Secretary, 60 Great Queen Street, London WC2B 5AZ (020 7404 1550; email: mail@msfund.org. uk; website: www.msfund.org.uk)

The Royal Antediluvian Order of Buffaloes, Grand Lodge of England War Memorial Annuities

Eligibility: Members of the order who are elderly or who have disabilities, and their dependants.

Types of grants: Annuities, though the Grand Lodge may have other charitable funds available for one-off grants.

Annual grant total: In 2008/09 the trust had assets of £153,000 and an income of £48,000. Grants were made totalling £34,000.

Applications: Applications should be made through the member's lodge. All assistance originates at the local lodge level; if its resources are inadequate, the lodge may then seek assistance at provincial or ultimately national level. For dependants of deceased members, it is necessary to give the lodge to which the member belonged. If its name and number is known, the correspondent below will probably be able to identify a current local telephone number or address. If only the place is known, this may still be possible, but not in all cases, particularly when the lodge concerned does not belong to this Grand Lodge group.

Correspondent: The Secretary, Grove House, Skipton Road, Harrogate, North Yorkshire HG1 4LA (01423 502438; fax: 01423 533979; email: hq@raobgle.org. uk; website: www.raobgle.org.uk)

Other information: The Grand Lodge of England is the largest of 15 Separate and independent Buffalo groups in the country.

They appear to exist for mutual sociability and support as well as the support of their local communities. There are over 3,500 local lodges, all of which may be concerned to help members, dependants and perhaps others in time of need or distress. This fund was established as a tribute to members of the order who died during the First World War.

The Royal Masonic Benevolent Institution

Eligibility: Freemasons (usually over 60 years of age, unless unemployed due to incapacity) of the English Constitution (England, Wales and certain areas overseas) and their dependants.

Types of grants: Christmas gifts. In 2002, the responsibility for payment of annuities was transferred to The Grand Charity.

Annual grant total: In 2008/09 annuities and grants amounted to £100,000.

Applications: On a form available from the correspondent, usually submitted through the lodge of the relevant freemason. Applications are considered every month.

Correspondent: David R Innes, 60 Great Queen Street, London WC2B 5AZ (020 7596 2400; fax: 020 7404 0724; email: enquries@rmbi.org.uk; website: www.rmbi.org.uk)

Other information: The institution has a team of welfare visitors covering the whole of England and Wales and also runs 17 homes catering for around 1,000 older freemasons.

Francis Winham Foundation

Eligibility: People of retirement age who are in need and in live in England can apply for a grant.

Types of grants: The trust can assist with mobility equipment, home adaptations, fuel bills and home repairs.

Exclusions: No grants are given towards administration costs, debts, household extensions, respite care or funeral costs.

Annual grant total: In 2008/09 the trust had assets of £2.2 million and an income of £117,000. The majority of grants are made to organisations.

Applications: In writing to the correspondent. A third party must apply on behalf of an individual such as a welfare professional from Age Concern, social services, Citizens Advice for example. Applications are considered throughout the year.

Correspondent: Mrs J Winham, 41 Langton Street, London SW10 0JL (020 7795 1261; fax: 020 7795 1262; email: francinetrust@btopenworld.com)

Politics

Conservative and Unionist Agents' Benevolent Association

Eligibility: Individuals in need who are, or have been, Conservative and Unionist Agents, or Women Organisers, and their dependants. Support is also given to the dependants of deceased Conservative or Unionist Agents or Women Organisers.

Types of grants: Recurrent grants to help with living costs. One-off grants are given towards, for example, roof repairs, emergency plumbing, replacement kitchen equipment, stair-lifts, bathrooms suitable for those with disabilities, and new boilers. Support towards funeral costs, night nursing expenses and emergency medical care may also be given.

Annual grant total: In 2008/09 the association had assets of £1.9 million and an income of £101,000. Grants were made totalling £54,000.

Applications: Initial telephone calls are welcomed and application forms are available on request. Applications can be made either directly by the individual, or through a member of the management committee or local serving agent. All beneficiaries are allocated a 'visiting agent'.

Correspondent: Sally Smith, Conservative Campaign Headquarters, Millbank Tower, 30 Millbank, London SW1P 4DP (020 7984 8172; email: sally.smith@ conservatives.com)

Other information: The majority of the association's grants are made for relief-in-need purposes but some help is given to the children of deceased members for the costs of education.

Prisoners/ex-offenders

The Aldo Trust

Eligibility: People in need who are being held in detention pending their trial or after their conviction. The applicant must still be serving the sentence. Applicants must have less than £25 in private cash.

Types of grants: Grants up to a maximum of £10 a year towards any needs except toiletries and training shoes.

Annual grant total: In 2008 the trust had assets of £666,000 and an income of £30,000. There were 975 grants made to individuals totalling £9,500, which were administered by NACRO. The trust's accounts state that this form of grant giving will cease to exist in future as the administering costs are too high to maintain it.

Applications: On a form available from the correspondent. Applications must be made through prison service personnel (for example, probation, chaplaincy, education), and should include the name and number of the prisoner, age, length of sentence and expected date of release. No applications direct from prisoners will be considered.

Applicants may apply once only in each twelve-month period, and applications are considered monthly.

Correspondent: Grant Administrator, c/o NACRO, Coast Cottage, 90 Coast Road, West Mersea, Colchester CO5 8LS (01206 383809; fax: 01206 383809; email: owenwheatley@btinternet.com)

Other information: NACRO also offers a fund for people on probation; see separate entry in this guide.

The Michael and Shirley Hunt Charitable Trust

Eligibility: Prisoners and their relatives and dependants, such as their spouses and children.

Types of grants: One-off and recurrent grants for prisoners' families' welfare needs and for travel expenses for prisoners on care leave.

Annual grant total: In 2008/09 the trust had assets of £5.4 million, which generated an income of £349,000. Grants were made to 60 individuals totalling £6,000.

Applications: In writing to the correspondent. Applications can be made directly by the individual or through a third party such as Citizens Advice or a social worker.

Correspondent: Mrs D S Jenkins, Trustee, Ansty House, Henfield Road, Small Dole, West Sussex BN5 9XH (01903 817116)

Other information: Grants are also made to organisations (£59,000 in 2008/09).

The National Association for the Care & Resettlement of Offenders (NACRO)

Eligibility: Ex-offenders and their partners and families.

Types of grants: One-off grants only, usually of around £50. Only one grant can ever be made to an individual.

Annual grant total: Grants usually total around £50,000 per year.

Applications: Either directly by the individual or through the Probation Service, social service department, Citizens Advice or registered charity. Applications are considered every two months.

Correspondent: Finance Director, 169 Clapham Road, London SW9 0PU (020 7840 6464 or 0800 0181 259 (freephone for prisoners only); fax: 020 7840 6720; email: helpline@nacro.org.uk; website: www.nacro.org.uk)

SACRO Trust

Eligibility: People living in Scotland who are subject to a license/court order or who have been released from prison in the last two years.

Types of grants: Grants are usually to a maximum of £300, although applications for larger sums can be considered. Grants given include those for electrical goods, clothing, furniture, driving lessons and education and training.

Exclusions: No grants are made where financial help from other sources is available.

Annual grant total: Grants usually total around £10,000 per year.

Applications: On a form available from the correspondent. Applications can only be accepted if they are made through a local authority, voluntary sector worker, health visitor or so on. They are considered every two months. No payment can be made directly to an individual by the trust; payment will be made to the organisation making the application. Other sources of funding should be sought before applying to the trust.

Correspondent: Trust Fund Administrator, 29 Albany Street, Edinburgh EH1 3QN (0131 624 7270; fax: 0131 624 7269; email: info@national. sacro.org.uk; website: www.sacro.org.uk)

The Paul Stephenson Memorial Trust

Eligibility: People who have served at least two years of imprisonment and are near the end of their sentence or have been released recently.

Types of grants: One-off grants of up to £100. Grants can be in cash or in kind for a particular rehabilitative need of the applicant or their immediate family, e.g. home furnishings, clothing, tools for work or assistance with college expenses.

Exclusions: Grants are not given for recreational activities, setting up small businesses or becoming self employed, or for existing debts.

Annual grant total: Around £1,000.

Applications: On a form available from the correspondent, which must be submitted via a probation officer, prison education officer or voluntary associate. Applicants should mention other trusts or organisations that have been applied to and other grants promised or received, including any statutory grants. Trustees usually meet twice a year.

Correspondent: Pauline Austin, The New Bridge, 27A Medway Street, London SW3 2BD

The Sure Foundation

Eligibility: Christians seeking to share their faith in the UK or overseas and people needing a new start in employment, such as ex-offenders.

Types of grants: One-off grants in the range of £50 to £200.

Exclusions: Grants are not made to individuals with previous vocational or professional qualifications or for higher education.

Annual grant total: About £2,000.

Applications: In writing to the correspondent directly from the individual. References are considered helpful when assessing applications.

Correspondent: The Trustees, Hobbs Green Farm, Odell, Bedfordshire MK43 7AB

Quakers

The Westward Trust

Eligibility: Quakers in need who live in the UK.

Types of grants: One-off and recurrent grants according to need.

Annual grant total: In 2008/09 the trust had an income of £11,000 and a total expenditure of £15,000.

Applications: In writing to the correspondent.

Correspondent: Alison Ironside, 17 Green Meadow Road, Birmingham B29 4DD (0121 475 1179)

Other information: Grants are also made to organisations, particularly Quaker charities or projects in which members of the Religious Society of Friends are involved.

Vegetarian

The Vegetarian Charity

Eligibility: Children and young people under the age of 26 who are vegetarian or vegan and are sick or in need.

Types of grants: One-off and recurrent grants to relieve poverty and sickness, usually ranging from £250 to £1,000.

Annual grant total: In 2008/09 the charity had assets of £805,000 and an income of £60,000. There were 73 grants paid during the year to individuals and organisations totalling £46,000; a further breakdown was not available.

Applications: On a form available from the correspondent, including details of any other grants received, a CV, covering letter and three references. Applications are considered throughout the year.

Correspondent: Susan Lenihan, 56 Parliament Street, Chippenham, Wiltshire SN14 0DE

Other information: Grants are also made to organisations which promote vegetarianism among young people and to vegetarian children's homes.

Victims of crime or injustice

Caudwell Children (formerly The Caudwell Charitable Trust)

Eligibility: People under 18 who are sick or disabled.

Types of grants: One-off and recurrent donations for equipment, therapy and treatment.

Exclusions: No grants for: building works, fixtures and fittings; gardening and the making safe of gardens; respite care; dolphin therapy/faith healing; computers (unless specifically designed for people with special needs); motor vehicle purchase/adaptations; equipment repair or maintenance; or holidays (except those for terminally, ill children).

Annual grant total: In 2009 the trust had assets of £4.3 million and an income of £4.7 million. Grants made directly to children in the community totalled £1.9 million.

Applications: On a form available from the correspondent – requests can be made via telephone or email. Forms can also be downloaded from the charity's website.

Correspondent: Lisa Bates, Applications Manager, Minton Hollins, Shelton Old Road, Stoke-on-Trent, Staffordshire ST4 7RY (0845 300 1348; fax: 01782 600639; email: charity@caudwellchildren.com; website: www.caudwellchildren.com)

Other information: The trust also organises a holiday to Florida each year under the 'Destination Dreams' programme. There are approximately 25 fully-funded family places available. Applications for places should be made early in the year i.e. January to March. For further information please contact the trust directly.

The Heinz, Anna and Carol Kroch Foundation *see entry on page 34*

Women

Frederick Andrew Convalescent Trust

Eligibility: Professional women who are working or retired and are in need of convalescence.

Types of grants: One-off grants for convalescence of up to £700.

Annual grant total: In 2008 the trust made grants to individuals totalling £49,000.

Applications: On a form available from the correspondent, to be submitted directly by the individual or through a social worker, Citizens Advice, other welfare agency or other third party.

Correspondent: Mrs Karen Armitage, Clerk to the Trustees, Andrew & Co, St Swithin's Square, Lincoln LN2 1HB (01522 512123; fax: 01522 546713; email: andsol@enterprise.net; website: www.factonline.co.uk)

Barley Women's Institute

Eligibility: Women in need living in rural areas in the UK.

Types of grants: One-off and recurrent according to need.

Annual grant total: In 2008/09 the institute had both an income and expenditure of £1,200.

Applications: In writing to the correspondent.

Correspondent: Mrs M Ashworth, Higher Whitehough Farm, Barley, Lancashire BB12 9LF (01282 616063)

Bircham Dyson Bell Charitable Trust – The Crossley Fund

Eligibility: Single women, including widows, of at least 50 years of age, who are in need.

Types of grants: Grants of £4 per week towards rent.

Annual grant total: In 2008/09 the trust had assets of £94,000 and an income of £56,000. Grants to individuals were made totalling £4,200.

Applications: Applications are usually made with the assistance of welfare organisations or third parties such as vicars. A form is sent to likely applicants on request. The trustees meet in June and December.

Please note the following statement from the trust: 'The trustees have been affected by the current economic conditions and have decided reluctantly that as matters stand they must try to meet their existing commitments and have for the time being closed the fund to new applicants. They will review the position from time to time according to their resources and the number of beneficiaries.'

Correspondent: Helen Abbey, Bircham Dyson Bell, 50 Broadway, Westminster, London SW1H 0BL (020 7227 7000; fax: 020 7222 3480; email: helenabbey@bdb-law.co.uk)

Other information: The trust has previously stated: 'We receive lots of inappropriate applications; we can only help older people with rent.'

The Eaton Fund for Artists, Nurses & Gentlewomen

Eligibility: Artists, including painters, potters, sculptors and photographers but not performing artists; nurses, including SRN, SEN, medical carers and dental nurses who are in employment or retired; and women over 18, who are in need of financial assistance.

Types of grants: One-off grants for artist's materials and equipment; picture framing for an exhibition; wheelchairs; and the setting up of a new home after a family breakdown.

Exclusions: Grants are not given for educational fees, recurring expenses such as mortgage repayments, rent, fuel or phone bills, special diets, care home fees, private treatments or to clear debt.

Annual grant total: In 2008/09 the fund had assets of £8.3 million and an income of £276,000. Grants were made to 234 individuals totalling £74,000.

Applications: On a form available from the correspondent or to download from the website. Forms can be submitted directly by the individual but the trust strongly recommends that a supporting letter from an appropriate third party, such as a doctor or social worker, be included. Any relevant documents like invoices or quotations should also be sent in with the form. They are considered six times a year and applicants will be notified of the decision within a month of the application deadline. For more information on specific application deadlines see the 'calendar' section of the trust's website.

Correspondent: Lorna Stagg, 33 St Annes Crescent, Lewes, East Sussex BN7 1SB (01273 480606; email: admin@eatonfund.org.uk; website: www.eaton-fund.co.uk)

The Arthur Hurst Will Trust

Eligibility: Women and members of the clergy who are in need and who have been forced to give up their work because of ill health. The trust also supports widows and children of clergymen.

Types of grants: One-off grants according to need.

Annual grant total: In 2008/09 the trust had an income of £46,000 and gave approximately £30,000 in grants to individuals.

Applications: Applications can be submitted directly by the individual or through a social worker, Citizens Advice, a welfare agency or another third party. Applications can be considered at any time, although there is not always available funding to make payments.

Correspondent: Trustee, Office of the Official Solicitor, 81 Chancery Lane, London WC2A 1DD (020 7911 7127)

The Morris Beneficent Fund

Eligibility: 'Distressed gentlewomen' recommended by members of the fund. Grants generally go to older women.

Types of grants: Recurrent grants according to need.

Annual grant total: Grants and annuities usually total around £25,000 each year.

Applications: On an application form supplied by a member. No unsolicited applications will be considered.

Correspondent: Simon Jamison, No. 10 Evendons Centre, 171 Evendons Lane, Wokingham RG41 4EH (0118 979 8653)

Other information: The trustees decide each year how many annuitants can be supported, though this number rarely exceeds 20 as the trustees prefer to raise the level of grants rather than awarding a larger number of smaller annuities.

Mrs Alice Lilian Nash Will Trust

Eligibility: Women in need in the area comprising the Dioceses of London, Southwark and Chelmsford.

Types of grants: The provision of permanent accommodation, maintenance, holidays and so on.

Annual grant total: In 2008/09 the trust had an income of £19,000 and a total expenditure of £42,000. Charitable payments totalled £35,000, all of which were given to organisations.

Applications: In writing to the correspondent.

Correspondent: The Committee, Natwest Trust Services, 5th Floor, Trinity Quay 2, Avon Street, Bristol BN2 OPT (0117 940 3283)

Other information: The trust committee is formed of the Anglican Bishops of the Dioceses of London, Chelmsford and Southwark.

The Perry Fund

Eligibility: Older women who are not 'of the artisan class' and are in need of financial assistance for whatever reason.

Types of grants: One-off and recurrent grants generally ranging between £100 and £500.

Annual grant total: Grants usually total about £11,000 per year.

Applications: On a form available from the correspondent. Applications can be submitted directly by the individual or through a third party such as a social worker, nursing home manager or welfare organisation. The trustees usually meet twice a year to consider applications.

Correspondent: William Carter, Clerk to the Trustees, 7 Waterloo Road, Wolverhampton WV1 4DW

The Royal Society for the Relief of Indigent Gentlewomen of Scotland

Eligibility: Single women, widows or divorcees in need who are over 50 years of age, of Scottish birth or background, and have (or whose husband or father had) a professional or business background. Applicants need not live in Scotland.

Types of grants: Annuities, paid in quarterly instalments, of around £1,000 a year, or less if the beneficiary is under 60 years of age and receives help from DWP. Beneficiaries may also receive one-off grants for TV licences, telephone rental, holidays, nursing, property maintenance and so on.

Annual grant total: In 2009/10 the society had assets of £32 million and an income of £1.8 million. Grants were made totalling £1.1 million and were distributed as follows:

Annual annuities	£868,000
Supplementary grants	£57,000
Holidays	£78,000
TV licences	£15,000
Telephone costs	£55,000
Initial grants	£14,000
Other grants	£12,000

Applications: On a form available from the correspondent, to be submitted directly by the individual or through a social worker, Citizens Advice or other welfare agency or third party. Application deadlines are end of March and September for consideration in May and November. Details of applicant's age, current financial position, personal family background and a copy of the divorce document (if appropriate) are required.

Correspondent: The Secretary and Cashier, 14 Rutland Square, Edinburgh EH1 2BD (0131 229 2308; fax: 0131 229 0956; email: info@igf.org; website: www.igf.org)

Other information: The society also provides regular home visiting, counselling and assistance with application forms.

The Society for the Assistance of Ladies in Reduced Circumstances

Eligibility: Women who live completely alone, have savings less than £8,000, receive a means tested benefit, and are not eligible for help from any other charity.

Types of grants: Monthly payments towards day-to-day living expenses and one-off grants for TV licences, telephone rental charges and so on.

Exclusions: No grants for education, care or nursing home fees, holidays, repayment of debts or funeral expenses. The Trust is unable to assist women who work 16 hours or more a week.

Annual grant total: In 2009 the society had assets of £23 million and an income of £799,000. A total of £749,000 was given grants to individuals.

Applications: On a form available from the correspondent including information on employment history, financial situation and any other charities that have been approached. Applications can be submitted directly by the individual or through a third party such as Citizens Advice or a social worker.

Correspondent: John Sands, Lancaster House, 25 Hornyold Road, Malvern, Worcestershire WR14 1QQ (01684 574645 (Freephone: 0800 587 4696); email: info@salrc.org.uk; website: www.salrc.org.uk)

St Andrew's Society for Ladies in Need

Eligibility: Single women from a well-educated, professional or semi-professional background who are now living alone in reduced circumstances. Preference is given to elderly women who are over 80 years of age.

Types of grants: Recurrent grants, up to a maximum of £20 a week to help with daily living expenses, are paid each quarter. Priority is given to ladies who are trying to maintain their own homes but grants are also given to those struggling with nursing home fees. One-off special grants are also available for heating, the cost of moving house, domestic appliances, furniture, disability aids, holidays and convalescences.

Exclusions: No grants to younger women and non-retired ladies who are able to work. No assistance with the discharge of debts.

Annual grant total: In 2008 the society had assets of £968,000 and an income of £66,000. Grants were made to 69 individuals totalling £46,000. The vast majority of this (£45,000) was given in regular grants and the remaining £1,000 was awarded in one-off grants to meet particular short-term needs.

Applications: On a form available from the correspondent, to be submitted either directly by the individual or through a social worker, Citizens Advice, other welfare agency or somebody with power of attorney. They should include as much background detail as possible, such as education, occupation and so on. Applications are considered at quarterly committee meetings, though urgent cases can be dealt with between meetings.

Correspondent: Mrs M Pope, 20 Denmark Gardens, Ipswich Road, Holbrook, Ipswich, Suffolk IP9 2BG (01473 327408; email: mpope1@btinternet.com; website: www.standrewssociety.ik.com)

WRVS Benevolent Trust

Eligibility: Past or present members of the WRVS who have given at least five years of service and are in need.

Types of grants: One-off grants ranging from £50 to £6,000. Recent grants have been made for a washing machine, replacement windows, a new boiler, moving costs, a carbon monoxide alarm, car tax, nursing home top up fees and dry rot treatment.

Annual grant total: In 2008 grants were made to 21 people totalling £26,000.

Applications: In writing to the correspondent to be submitted directly by the individual or a WRVS contact. Applications are considered in March, July and November, however urgent cases can be considered on receipt.

Correspondent: Paulene Lambert, 14 Wykeham Road, Guildford, Surrey GU1 2SE (email: wrvsbenevolenttrust@ hotmail.co.uk)

ILLNESS & DISABILITY CHARITIES

There are many charities for people with illnesses or disabilities. The entries in this section are only for those which give financial help from their own resources. There are many others that do not have a large enough income to do this but may be the starting point for getting financial help. For this reason we have a list of organisations which provide advice and support on page 349.

This section starts with an index of illness or disability. The entries are arranged alphabetically within each category, with those trusts which support more than one illness or disability listed at the start of the chapter.

Local disability charities are not included in this section but are listed in the relevant local section of the book. Northern Irish, Scottish and Welsh disability charities are also listed in the relevant locality rather than in this section.

Index of illness and disability funds

A
AIDS/HIV 46
Alzheimer's disease 47
Arthritis and rheumatism 48
Ataxia 48

B
Blindness/partial sight 48
Brain tumours 49
Bowel conditions 49
Brittle bones 50

C
Cancer and Leukaemia 50
Cerebral palsy 51
Cystic fibrosis 51

D
Deafblind 51
Dystonia 51

H
Haematological disorders 51
Haemophilia 52
Huntingdon's disease 52

L
Liver 52

M
Meningitis 52
Mental illness 52
Motor neurone 53
Mucopolysaccharide diseases 53
Multiple sclerosis 53
Muscular dystrophy 54

N
Neurological disorders 54

P
Parkinson's disease 54
Polio 54

R
Renal 55

S
Spinal muscular 55
Sport injuries 55
Stroke 56

T
Tuberous sclerosis 56

Able Kidz Educational Trust

Eligibility: Disabled children and young adults under the age of 18 in the UK.

Types of grants: One-off and recurrent grants according to need.

Annual grant total: In 2008/09 the trust had assets of £32,000 and an income of £45,000. Donations paid amounted to £16,000.

Applications: In writing to the correspondent. Applications are not means tested. They should include the following:

- a summary of the child's circumstances
- what the child requires and how Able Kidz might be able to help
- an outline of the costs involved.

Correspondent: The Grants Officer, 6th Floor, 456–458 Strand, London, WC2R ODZ

Active Foundation *see entry on page 26*

ASPIRE (Association for Spinal Injury Research Rehabilitation and Reintegration) Human Needs Fund

Eligibility: People in need with a spinal cord injury. Priority is given to re-establishing independent mobility.

Types of grants: One-off grants to help towards the purchase of specialist equipment such as wheelchairs and computers.

Exclusions: Grants from the fund are solely for people with acquired non progressive spinal cord injury. The charity also states that it is unlikely to fund applications for holidays, standing wheelchairs, house adaptations, passive exercise equipment and vehicles.

Annual grant total: In 2008/09 the fund had assets of £1.8 million and an income £2.1 million. Human need grants totalled £63,000.

Applications: On a form available from the correspondent, for consideration on an ongoing basis. The assessment period is approximately four to six weeks and each application requires a supporting letter from an occupational therapist or medical consultant to explain why the specialist equipment is appropriate. A full list of application guidelines is available from the correspondent and on the website.

Correspondent: The Human Needs Manager, ASPIRE National Training Centre, Wood Lane, Stanmore, Middlesex HA7 4AP (020 8954 5759; fax: 020 8420 6352; email: info@aspire.org. uk; website: www.aspire.org.uk)

Other information: The fund also provides services for eligible individuals.

The Birchington Convalescent Benefit Fund

Eligibility: Children under the age of 18 who are chronically ill or recovering from surgery or long-term illness.

Types of grants: One-off grants of £200 towards part-payment of convalescent holidays for children.

Exclusions: Grants are rarely given for expensive or overseas holidays. Grants are not given for reasons other than holidays. This includes no grants to allow ill parents to have a break from their children.

Annual grant total: In 2009 the fund had assets of £2.1 million and an income of £119,000. Grants were made to eight individuals totalling £1,600.

Applications: On a form available from the correspondent or to download from the website. Applications should be made through a third party, for example, a doctor, social worker or hospital staff. Details of the sponsor of the application, type of illness or surgery, financial status and type and cost of the holiday needed should be included. Decisions on grant awards are made in February, April and June.

Correspondent: Rev David Phillips, Church Society, Dean Wace House, 16 Rosslyn Road, Watford WD18 0NY (01923 235111; fax: 01923 800362; email: admin@churchsociety.org; website: www.churchsociety.org)

Other information: Those awarded a grant also receive a complimentary children's bible.

Clevedon Forbes Fund

Eligibility: People of limited means who are recovering from surgery or who are in need of a break due to illness or trauma. Grants are also available to those caring for someone who is sick or disabled. The majority of grants are given to individuals living in the south west but those living further afield will be considered.

Types of grants: One-off grants to those in need.

Exclusions: Grants are not made for capital goods. Individuals cannot apply for another grant until a three year period has elapsed.

Annual grant total: In 2008/09 the fund had assets of £1.2 million and an income of £71,000. Grants to 107 individuals totalled £34,000.

Applications: Applications need to be made through a professional in the statutory or voluntary sector, such as a social worker or welfare officer. Application forms are available on the fund's website or directly from the correspondent.

Correspondent: Wendy Robinson, Director, 4 Kenn Road, Clevedon, BS21 6EL (01275 341777; fax: 01275 341777; email: wendy@ clevedonforbes.org; website: www. clevedonforbes.org)

Other information: A Christian gospel booklet is sent out to people receiving a grant unless there is a specific request to the contrary.

Equipment for Independent Living

Eligibility: People over 16 who are disabled in the UK and overseas.

Types of grants: One-off grants towards disability equipment enabling people to obtain mobility, independence and earning power. Awards are usually in the range of £100 to £1,000.

Exclusions: Normally grants are not made towards: medical equipment; course fees and materials; welfare expenditure of a non-capital nature, e.g. holiday or moving expenses; equipment which is supplied by the NHS or social services; equipment running costs; building adaptations and decorating; household equipment (unless specially adapted for the person's disability); or private treatment, home care fees or computers (unless they are used as a speech aid or to enable the individual to earn their living).

Funds are not normally granted to cases submitted by other charities which have much larger resources than the trust.

Annual grant total: In 2009 the trust had an income of £18,000 and a total expenditure £24,000.

Applications: Applicants must be referred in the first instance by a professional person involved with their welfare, for example, a social worker, occupational therapist or specialist nurse. The professional person should write to the Honorary Secretary – June Sutherland at 10 Pembroke Walk, London W8 6PQ – describing the applicant's circumstances and saying what equipment is needed and why. If appropriate, a full application form will then be sent out.

Applications can be submitted at any time and are considered in January, April, July and October.

Correspondent: Secretary, 10 Pembroke Walk, London, W8 6PQ

Monica Eyre Memorial Foundation see entry on page 33

Gardening for the Disabled Trust

Eligibility: Members of the trust who wish to participate in gardening regardless of age or disability.

Types of grants: One-off grants according to need to help towards tools, raised beds, paving and greenhouses.

Annual grant total: In 2008 the trust had assets of £194,000 and an income of £24,000. Grants were made totalling £27,000.

Applications: In writing to the correspondent detailing the work they would like done and an estimate of the cost of tools, materials and labour (if necessary). Applicants should also include a note from their GP, social worker or occupational therapist describing their disability. The committee meets every month to consider applications.

Correspondent: The Secretary, PO Box 285, Tunbridge Wells, Kent, TN2 9JD (01580 852372; website: www. gardeningfordisabledtrust.org.uk)

The Megan and Trevor Griffiths Trust

Eligibility: People with physical or mental disabilities. Preference is given to people living in the former administrative county of Carmarthen (Carmarthenshire and parts of Ceredigion and Pembrokeshire).

Types of grants: Grants are provided for goods or services that cannot be obtained through statutory agencies, and specifically to promote independence. This can include IT equipment, electrical goods, hospital expenses, respite care, holidays, special toys/instruments, fees for training courses and disabled and therapeutic equipment. Grants are one-off and are usually limited to £100.

Exclusions: Grants are very unlikely to be given for the payment of debt.

Annual grant total: In 2008/09 the trust had an income of £20,000 and a total expenditure of £18,000.

Applications: In writing to the correspondent from a third party such as a social worker or on a form available from the correspondent, which has to be supported by another person, preferably a professional, for verification. Application deadlines are in mid-October and at the end of May.

Correspondent: Janet Griffiths, Honorary Secretary, 46 Partridge Road, Roath, Cardiff CF24 3QX (029 2045 6680)

Other information: The trust also runs a rolling programme of leisure and respite care for adults with a learning disability.

The trust has rarely supported applications from outside of Carmarthenshire and states that 'we always have more than enough worthy applicants from Carmarthenshire and surrounding counties'.

The N & P Hartley Memorial Trust

Eligibility: People who are disabled, older or terminally ill. Priority is firstly given to those living in West Yorkshire, secondly to individuals living in the north of England and thirdly to those elsewhere in the UK and overseas.

Types of grants: One-off grants towards, for example, specialist equipment for people with disabilities.

Annual grant total: Grants to individuals total between £3,000 and £4,000 each year.

Applications: In writing to the correspondent, preferably through a social worker, Citizens Advice or other welfare agency, for consideration twice yearly. Re-applications from previous beneficiaries are welcomed.

Correspondent: Virginia Watson, Trustee, 24 Holywell Lane, Leeds, LS17 8HA

Other information: The trust also makes a number of grants to organisations and to individuals for educational purposes.

Independence at Home

Eligibility: People who are substantially disabled or severely ill and who live at home or who wish to do so.

Types of grants: Grants ranging between £100 and £500 towards specific additional costs associated with living at home with a disability, including equipment and adaptations. Grants can be made towards almost any expense which is not covered by statutory provision and which is related to a disabled person living at home.

Please note: the trust will not consider applications where more than £2,000 has still to be raised.

Exclusions: No grants are made to people living in residential care. Grants are not made towards medical treatment or therapies; funeral expenses; debts and arrears; leisure equipment such as televisions; motor vehicles (although we may be able to help towards the cost of adaptations); telephone rental or call charges; or TV licences. Only one grant can be held in any 12 month period.

Annual grant total: In 2008/09 the trust had assets of £2.6 million and an income of £445,000. Grants were made to 1312 individuals totalling £365,000.

Applications: On a form available from the correspondent or to download from the website. Applications should be submitted by post through a social worker, occupational therapist, specialist nurse or other welfare body. They are considered on an ongoing basis.

Correspondent: Mary Rose, Chief Executive, 4th Floor, Congress House, 14 Lyon Road, Harrow, HA1 2EN (020 8427 7929; fax: 020 8424 2937; email: iah@independenceathome.org.uk; website: www.independenceathome.org.uk)

The League of the Helping Hand

Eligibility: People who have a physical disability, learning difficulty or mental health problem and are in financial need. Those who care for somebody who is disabled, elderly or ill may also be eligible.

Types of grants: One-off grants ranging between £50 and £250 towards essential household items, specialist equipment and carer's breaks. Recurrent grants are also available to help with daily living costs.

Exclusions: No help is given for debts, mobility scooters, wheelchairs or for education-related items.

Annual grant total: In 2008/09 the trust had assets of £1.6 million and an income of £168,000. Grants were made to 604 individuals totalling £111,000.

Applications: On a form available from the correspondent or to download from trust's website. Applications must be submitted through a social worker, carers' support centre, Citizens Advice or other welfare body. An sae must be enclosed. Supportive letters accompanying completed forms are not required. The trustees meet every three weeks to consider applications, although emergency needs can be met more quickly. Telephone enquiries are welcome – for single grant enquiries Tel: 01444 236099 and for recurrent grants Tel: 01273 493551.

Correspondent: Moira Parrott, LHH, P O Box 342, Burgess Hill, RH15 5AQ (01444 236099; email: secretary@lhh.org.uk; website: www.lhh.org.uk)

Mobility Trust II

Eligibility: People with disabilities.

Types of grants: No grants are given. The trust provides powered wheelchairs or scooters for people who are unable to obtain such equipment through statutory sources or afford it themselves. If someone is unable to walk at all and requires a powered wheelchair they should apply to their local NHS Wheelchair Service before making an application to the trust.

Annual grant total: In 2008/09 the trust had assets of £277,000 and an income of £252,000. A total of £176,000 was spent on beneficiaries' equipment.

Applications: Applications must be submitted in the first instance by a letter directly by the individual or through a social worker, medical advisor or other welfare agency. If there is a possibility of helping the person they will be sent a form to complete. On confirmation of acceptance of the application the trust will arrange for an independent occupational therapist to assess the person in order that they receive the right equipment to suit their clinical need.

The trust insures the equipment for the first year but expects the beneficiary to take over the payments in the second year. Servicing and repairs will be their responsibility following the expiry of the warranty period.

Correspondent: Anne Munn, Chief Executive, 17b Reading Road, Pangbourne, Reading, Berkshire RG8 7LR (0118 984 2588; fax: 0118 984 2544; email: mobility@mobilitytrust.org.uk; website: www.mobilitytrust.org.uk)

The Florence Nightingale Aid-in-Sickness Trust

Eligibility: People who are in poor health, convalescent or who have disabilities. Preference will be given to people with professional, secretarial, or administrative qualifications or experience.

Types of grants: One-off grants are available for convalescence or respite care; medical equipment and other aids; sensory equipment; telephone installation (or mobile phones in rare cases); and hospital visiting expenses. Partial funding may be provided where a large grant is requested.

Exclusions: Grants are not available for: house alterations, adaptations, improvements or maintenance; car purchase or adaptations; electrical wheelchairs, scooters or buggies; holidays, carers' breaks, exchange visits or nursing home fees; debts or repayments; general clothing; computers and software; stairlifts; or general house furnishing. Under normal circumstances, grants can only be given to any one household at intervals of three years.

Annual grant total: In 2009 the trust had assets of £7.5 million and an income of £274,000. Grants were made to 262 individuals totalling £170,000.

Applications: On a form available from the correspondent or to download from the website. Applications should be submitted by a social worker, occupational therapist, doctor, health centre worker or a similar welfare professional. They should include a brief medical history of the applicant and proof of the need for assistance. Applications are considered monthly, although urgent requests can be dealt with between meetings.

Correspondent: Ann Griffiths, 6 Avonmore Road, London W14 8RL (020 7605 4244; email: fnaist@ independentage.org.uk; website: www.fnaist.org.uk)

React (Rapid Effective Assistance for Children with Potentially Terminal Illnesses)

Eligibility: Financially disadvantaged families caring for a child under 18 years living with a potentially terminal illness.

Types of grants: Grants in kind and one-off grants ranging from £50 to £5,000. They can be made for domestic or medical equipment which may contribute towards the child's quality of life. A broad variety of items may be considered including carpets, furniture, kitchen appliances, clothing, bedding, toys, car seats, travel expenses, specialist chairs and beds, sensory equipment, wheelchairs and hoists, as well as mobile home holidays at one of six sites around the UK. The charity can also contribute towards hospital expenses such as food and travel and funeral and memorial expenses.

Exclusions: No grants towards trips overseas, structural building works, private treatment or the purchase of vehicles.

Annual grant total: In 2008/09 the trust had assets of £370,000 and an income of £779,000. Grants to individuals totalled £364,000 and were broken down as follows:

Medical	87	£77,000
Domestic	360	£134,000
Respite holidays	16	£5,200
Mobile home holidays	237	£47,000
Funerals	53	£35,000
Travel and subsistence	169	£25,000
Equipment purchases	30	£13,000
Home adaptations	32	£23,000
Other	22	£5,400

Applications: On a form available from the correspondent or to download from the website. Forms must be completed and signed by a member of the family and endorsed by a medical or social care professional. Families are required to declare financial details and are asked to phone if in any doubt about eligibility. The charity aims to reply to every application within a few days, and the decision process in most cases takes less than a week.

Correspondent: Grants Administrator, St Luke's House, 270 Sandycombe Road, Richmond Upon Thames, Surrey TW9 3NP (020 8940 2575; fax: 020 8940 2050; email: react@reactcharity.org; website: www.reactcharity.org)

sfgroup Charitable Fund for Disabled People

Eligibility: Severely disabled people of all ages, primarily in the Midlands, North West and Yorkshire. This can include people with significant sensory, physical and intellectual impairments and those with complex and challenging behavioural needs.

Types of grants: Grants of up to £5,000 for specific items or services which will make a 'positive' difference to quality of life. Recent grants have been made towards manual/powered wheelchairs, household items, special mattresses and beds, computer equipment, small home improvements and holidays.

Exclusions: No grants for: education and course fees; debts; motor vehicle purchase or expenses; nursing and residential home fees; funeral expenses; removal expenses; driving lessons; items already purchased; therapies such as swimming with dolphins and hyperbaric therapy; alternative therapies such as reflexology, acupuncture and faith healing.

Annual grant total: In 2009 the fund had assets of £243,000 and an income of £104,000. Direct charitable expenditure totalled £99,000.

Applications: Applications are welcomed from individuals, professional workers and representatives of organisations and institutions. Where the request is from a private individual, a detailed letter of support from a professional (e.g. family doctor, hospital consultant, social worker, teacher or a worker from a community or disability organisation) is essential. If applying for specialist seating, manual or powered wheelchairs are requested, the letter must be from an occupational therapist or physiotherapist.

Applicants should first complete a short preliminary enquiry form. This can be done online at the sfgroup website, or by completing the form attached to the charity's information leaflet which can be requested by phone or email. The Fund Manager will make contact within two weeks of receiving the application to discuss the request in more detail.

Correspondent: Brenda Yong, Charitable Fund Manager, FREEPOST NAT13205, Nottingham, NG8 6ZZ (email: brenda.yong@sfcharity.co.uk; website: www.sfcharity.co.uk)

Other information: Grants are also made to organisations.

The Starfish Trust

Eligibility: People who are disabled or ill and living in the UK. Priority is given to those based within a 25-mile radius of central Bristol.

Types of grants: One-off grants to meet most welfare needs. Recent grants have included support for a house extension for a person with disabilities; a specially designed wheelchair; an electronic bed for a teenager with cerebral palsy; and sensory toys for a severely disabled child.

Annual grant total: In 2008/09 the trust had assets of £1.2 million and an income of £61,000. Grants to 11 individuals amounted to £25,000.

Applications: In writing to the correspondent. Applications can be submitted directly by the individual or family member, a social worker or Citizens Advice and should be supported by a member of the patient's medical team. Applications are considered at monthly trustee meetings.

The trust also suggests that it would be useful to enclose any information regarding whether the applicant has approached/will be approaching other funds and the results achieved so far.

Correspondent: Robert Woodward, Chief Executive, 3 Gloucester Road, Almondsbury, Bristol BS32 4BJ (01179 701756)

Other information: Grants are also made to organisations to support medical research (£71,000 in 2008/09).

Bruce Wake Charity

Eligibility: People who are disabled (predominantly wheelchair-users) in the UK.

Types of grants: One-off grants up to about £2,000 each for holidays and disabled equipment.

Annual grant total: In 2008/09 the charity had assets of £6.7 million, which generated an income of £246,000. Grants were made to 67 individuals totalling £49,000.

Applications: In writing through a charitable organisation or equivalent recognised body to: Mrs P Wake, BWCT, PO Box 9335, Oakham, Rutland LE15 0ET (Tel: 0844 879 3349). Applications should include all appropriate financial information. They are considered quarterly.

Correspondent: Peter Hems, Trustee, c/o Grant Thornton, Regent House, 80 Regent Road, Leicester, LE1 7NH (0116 247 1234; email: wake@webleicester.co.uk; website: www.brucewaketrust.co.uk)

Other information: Grants were made to 137 organisations totalling £461,000.

AIDS/HIV

The Crusaid Hardship Fund

Eligibility: People with HIV/AIDS, who face difficulty or extra expenditure because of their HIV status, and live in England, Northern Ireland or Wales.

Types of grants: One-off grants, usually of £40 but they can be up to £350, for items or services which cannot reasonably be afforded on current income, are not available from other sources and will improve the quality of life. Grants have been given towards, for example, a fridge to keep medication in; a washing machine for someone suffering from night sweats; help with higher gas bills for someone experiencing HIV-related pneumonia; and respite care for children whilst their carer is in hospital.

Exclusions: No grants for council tax, rent, holiday expenses, air fares or funeral costs.

Annual grant total: In 2008/09 the fund gave 2,485 grants to 2,106 individuals amounting to £381,000.

Applications: On a form available from the correspondent or from many HIV specialist centres around the country. Applications should be submitted by a social worker, welfare rights worker, health adviser or THT buddy. A diagnosis letter from a consultant or doctor should be enclosed.

Correspondent: Jordan Hay, Chief Executive, 1–5 Curtain Road, London, EC2A 3JX (020 7539 3881; fax: 020 7539 3890; email: office@crusaid.org.uk; website: www.crusaid.org.uk)

Other information: For applicants living in Scotland, even if they are English, Welsh or Northern Irish, please see entry for Waverly Care Scotland on page 143.

Eileen Trust

Eligibility: People who have become HIV positive because of NHS treatment, for example, following transfusions or a needlestick injury. It provides financial support in the form of small regular payments or one-off payments to affected individuals.

Types of grants: Financial help is given in three ways: regular monthly payments to contribute to meeting the additional costs of living with HIV, or assist those who have been bereaved; single payments in response to specific requests for help; and winter payments (supplements to regular payments made in recognition of the additional costs of keeping healthy during the winter months).

Annual grant total: In 2008/09 grants totalled £149,000. Grants consisted of regular monthly payments to individuals and families, winter payments and special winter payments.

Applications: Applications for assistance are received in the main via the trust's case worker and from time to time by direct approach.

Correspondent: The Secretary, Alliance House, 12 Caxton Street, London, SW1H 0QS (020 7808 1170)

JAT

Eligibility: Jewish people with HIV/AIDS.

Types of grants: One-off grants of up to £500 a year are available from the trust, which may share the cost of major items with other agencies. Recent grants have been given towards Passover food, travel expenses for respite care, washing machines, cookers, moving costs and so on.

Exclusions: No grants are given towards rent, mortgage arrears, luxury items or repayments of loans, debts or credit cards.

Annual grant total: In 2008/09 the trust had assets of £99,000 and an income of £94,000. Previously grants have totalled around £10,000.

Applications: On a form available from the correspondent. All referrals must be through a professional person such as a social worker, health visitor and so on. A referral must accompany every application and be on headed paper including client's name, date of birth, detailed breakdown of weekly income, details and nature of request, name, position and signature of referrer and details of whom the cheque should be made payable to. First applications require symptomatic proof of HIV diagnosis from the applicant's doctor.

Correspondent: Janine Clements, Director, Berkeley House, First Floor – Unit 4, 18–24 High Street, Edgware, Middlesex HA8 7RP (020 8952 5253; fax: 020 8952 8893; email: admin@jat-uk.org; website: www.jat-uk.org)

Other information: The trust was established to educate Jewish people about HIV and also provide support for those affected by it. The trust also carries out research into sex and relationships education in schools and manages sexual health information workshops in Jewish schools, clubs and in Jewish student unions in the UK.

The Macfarlane Trust

Eligibility: People with haemophilia who as a result of receiving contaminated blood products are living with AIDS or have been infected with HIV, and their dependants. No other people are eligible. The trust is in contact with those known to have haemophilia and to be HIV positive through infected blood products and therefore any further eligibility to register with the trust seems unlikely.

Types of grants: One-off and recurrent grants are available towards the additional costs associated in living with HIV. Grants can be given towards health-related needs such as convalescence, respite, travel, clothes, medical care, specialised equipment and so on.

Annual grant total: In 2008/09 the trust had assets of £4 million and an income of £4 million. Grants totalled £3.6 million and were distributed as follows:

One-off grants	961	£537,000
Summer payments	400	£437,000
Winter payments	390	£244,000
Additional winter payment	390	£55,000
Regular grants	509	£2,330,000

Applications: On an application form available from the correspondent, although requests by letter or telephone are also considered. A medical report and supporting letter from a doctor or similar

medical professional are required. Applicants must be registered with the trust in order to apply.

Correspondent: Linda Haigh, Finance Manager, Alliance House, 12 Caxton Street, London SW1H 0QS (020 7233 0057; fax: 020 7808 1169; email: linda@macfarlane.org.uk; website: www.macfarlane.org.uk)

Other information: The trust was established in 1988 to manage a £10 million fund given by the government to assist people with haemophilia who had contracted HIV through infected blood products administered by the NHS during their treatment.

Alzheimer's disease

Alzheimer's Society

Eligibility: People who live with Alzheimer's disease and related illnesses, and their carers, are welcome to receive emotional support from the society. Applicants must live in England, Northern Ireland or Wales.

The Helpline number is 020 7423 3500. The society is able to advise on insurance policies, gadgets, benefits, support for carers, practical help and support branches that are available.

Types of grants: One-off grants towards washing machines, clothing, telephone bills, respite breaks, aids, adaptations and replacement bedding, but not nursing home fees. Grants range up to £500.

Annual grant total: Grants made to individuals usually total between £200,000 and £300,000 each year.

Applications: On a form available from the correspondent, to be considered weekly. Applications can be submitted at any time either directly by the individual, or through a social worker, recognised welfare agency or other third party. It is essential that all applications are supported by references from a doctor and a social worker endorsing the stated need.

Correspondent: Mr N Hunt, Devon House, 58 St Katharine's Way, London E1W 1JX (020 7423 3500; fax: 020 7423 3501; email: info@alzheimers.org.uk; website: www.alzheimers.org.uk)

Other information: Grants are also made to organisations.

The Margaret and Alick Potter Charitable Trust *see entry on page 162*

Arthritis and rheumatism

The Arthritic Association

Eligibility: People who have arthritis or a related condition, and are in financial need. Grants are only available to: members of the Arthritic Association; those who are undertaking a dietary programme with the association; and, towards treatments associated with the programme.

Types of grants: One-off grants in kind for dietary supplements and remedial therapy.

Annual grant total: In 2007/08 the association had assets of £5.7 million and an income of £1.2 million. Grants totalled £53,000.

Applications: On a form available from the correspondent, for consideration in January, March, July and October. Applications can be submitted by the individual or through a social worker, Citizens Advice or other welfare agency.

Correspondent: Bruce Hester, Consultant; Ian Sketchley, Company Secretary, One Upperton Gardens, Eastbourne, East Sussex BN21 2AA (01323 416550; fax: 01323 639793; email: info@ arthriticassociation.org.uk; website: www. arthriticassociation.org.uk)

Other information: The association works to promote natural dietary treatments for arthritis and grants are also made for research in this area.

Strongbones Children's Charitable Trust

Eligibility: Children under 18 with scoliosis, brittle bone disease, rheumatoid arthritis or any other condition of the bone.

Types of grants: One-off grants, usually of around £250 for medical equipment, computers/software, toys, sensory equipment, short breaks away, days out and proven household bills.

Annual grant total: In 2008/09 the trust had assets of £19,000 and income of £298,000. Grants to individual children totalled about £36,000.

Applications: Forms are available directly from the correspondent or on the trust's website. Applications should include details of the child's condition and why a grant is needed. The trust also requires that forms be countersigned by a social worker or relevant medical consultant.

Correspondent: Grants Team, SCCT House, Kemp Road, Dagenham, Essex, RM8 1ST (020 8590 9283; fax: 020 8590 6262; email: grantsofficer@ strongbones.org.uk; website: www. strongbones.org.uk)

Ataxia

Ataxia UK (formerly Friedreich's Ataxia Group)

Eligibility: People who are in need and have Cerebellar Ataxia (Freidreich's Ataxia and spinocerebellar).

Types of grants: One-off grants for things such as respite care, holidays, computers, equipment, aids and adapted furniture.

Exclusions: People may apply only if they have not received a grant from the charity in the past two years: or, if applying for a respite break, in the previous 12 months.

Annual grant total: In 2008/09 the charity had assets of £1.5 million and an income of £1.6 million. There were 23 grants made to individuals totalling £13,700.

Applications: On a form available from the correspondent, to be submitted directly by the individual or a third party.

Correspondent: Ms Susan Millman, Chief Executive, Ground Floor, Lincoln House, 1–3 Brixton Road, London, SW9 6DE (020 7582 1444; email: enquiries@ataxia. org.uk; website: www.ataxia.org.uk)

Blindness/partial sight

Action for Blind People

Eligibility: Registered blind or partially sighted people who are in need and live within the boundaries of the charity's action areas. Applicants will need to show that they have exhausted other funding options.

Types of grants: Grant assistance is available for holiday breaks (excluding travel costs) and assistive software technology, e.g. Supernova, Zoomtext, Hal and Jaws.

Exclusions: If applying for a holiday grant, the applicant must not have had a holiday in the last five years.

Annual grant total: In 2008/09 the charity had assets of £24 million and a consolidated income of £18 million. Grants were made to 43 individuals totalling £15,000, of which £11,000 was given in grants for assistive technology software and £4,000 was given in holiday awards.

Applications: On a form available from the correspondent. Applications for assistance will only be accepted from people living within an action team area, supported by an action coordinator. A list of action areas can be found on the charity's website or by calling the national freephone helpline on 0800 915 4666.

Please note: Grants are usually paid directly to the service or product supplier.

Correspondent: Anita M South, 14–16 Verney Road, London SE16 3DZ (020 7635 4800; email: grants.team@ actionforblindpeople.org.uk; website: www.actionforblindpeople.org.uk)

Other information: Following a review of its services in 2007, the charity decided that it could no longer support an unrestricted national grants programme. The new grants service is limited to holiday and software grants and is only available to clients who live within the boundaries of the charity's 'action teams', which are all based in England (call 0303 123 9999 to check the boundaries). As a result it now gives far less in direct grants than it has done in previous years. However, the charity does provide help and advice on a wide range of issues including applying for benefits, housing, aids and adaptations, finding a job and accessing local services.

In 2009 the charity finalised an Association Agreement with the Royal National Institute for the Blind (RNIB), making it part of the RNIB Group. (*Please see the RNIB entry for further information on their activities*).

Gardner's Trust for the Blind

Eligibility: Registered blind or partially-sighted people who live in the UK.

Types of grants: One-off grants for domestic household tools and for educational purposes. The trust also gives grants in the form of pensions.

Exclusions: No grants for holidays, residential or nursing home fees or for loan repayments.

Annual grant total: In 2008/09 the trust had assets of £2.8 million and an income of £804,000. Grants to individuals totalled £67,000, through which £16,000 was given in general welfare grants and 51 pensioners were supported with grants totalling £34,000. A further £18,000 was given in education, trade and music grants.

Applications: In writing to the correspondent. Applications can be submitted either directly by the individual or by a third party, but they must also be supported by a third party who can confirm the disability and that the grant is needed. They are considered in March, June, September and December and should be submitted at least three weeks before the meeting.

Correspondent: Angela Stewart, 117 Charterhouse Street, London EC1M 6AA (020 7253 3757)

National Blind Children Society

Eligibility: People aged up to 25 years in full-time education who are (or are eligible to be) registered blind or partially sighted and live in the UK.

Types of grants: One-off grants towards IT equipment or sensory/recreational equipment for use in the home to aid with the individual's learning and development.

Annual grant total: In 2008 the society had assets of £1.2 million and an income of £1.9 million. There were 21 small grants made to individuals totalling £3,500 for holidays and recreational activities including riding lessons, music lessons and for medical and legal fees.

Applications: On a form available from the correspondent, for consideration at monthly meetings. Applications can be submitted either by the individual with a supporting letter, or via a social worker, welfare agency or qualified teacher of people who are visually impaired. They are considered on a monthly basis.

Correspondent: Hazel Russell, Bradbury House, Market Street, Highbridge, Somerset TA9 3BW (01278 764764; fax: 01278 764790; email: enquiries@nbcs.org.uk; website: www.nbcs.org.uk)

Other information: Grants are also made to organisations in support of groups of children with visual impairments.

The Royal Blind Society for the UK

Eligibility: People who are registered blind or partially sighted and on a low income.

Types of grants: One-off grants of up to £200 (one per household) and annual grants of £208 per annum (one per household). Grants can be made towards: household bills; specialist medical equipment such as thick-lens spectacles; daily living aids such as a washing machine with Braille controls; IT equipment, reading and literacy aids for young visually impaired people; holidays within the UK; and, other emergencies and unforeseen needs.

Annual grants run for a standard period of three years.

Annual grant total: In 2007/08 the trust had assets of £1.3 million and an income of £1.2 million. Grants totalled £112,000.

Applications: On a form available from the correspondent or to download from the website. Applications must be submitted through a professional welfare worker who knows the applicant well, for example, a social worker or similar welfare advisor. They are considered on a quarterly basis.

Correspondent: Grants Co-ordinator, RBS House, 59–61 Sea Lane, Rustington, West Sussex BN16 2RQ (01903 857023; fax: 01903 859166; email: grants@royalblindsociety.org; website: www.royalblindsociety.org.uk)

Other information: At the time of writing (autumn 2010), the trust's annual report and accounts for 2008/09 were overdue at the Charity Commission.

The Royal National Institute of Blind People

Eligibility: Registered blind and partially-sighted people who receive a means-tested benefit or are on a very low income and who have savings of £10,000 or less.

Types of grants: One-off and recurrent grants of up to £500, though the trust has strict guidelines on how much it will give for certain items.

● Essential household items: furniture (a maximum of £350); cookers, washing machines, carpets and curtains (£300); fridges and freezers (£200); and other domestic equipment (£100).

● Computer software or reading equipment: video magnifiers – CCTV (up to £350); and computer access software (£300).

● Miscellaneous: essential adaptations, repairs or redecoration (up to £300); holidays (up to £250 for the person with sight loss and £250 for an essential companion); clothing and debts for essential services (£150); and other items (£250).

There is a limit of £750 for each individual over three years and there should be a gap of one year between grants. Priority is given to items essential for day-to-day living.

Exclusions: Emergency grants are not available. No grants for recreational needs, nursing home fees, the costs of medical treatment, telephone installation, employment needs or repeatedly accruing debts. Holidays are only supported if the applicant has not had one for five years.

Annual grant total: Around £70,000.

Applications: Application forms are available from the correspondent or to download from the website. Applications must be supported by a social worker, rehabilitation officer or a voluntary organisation, such as Citizens Advice. They are considered throughout the year.

Correspondent: Grants Officer, Information Resource Team, RNIB, 105 Judd Street, London WC1H 9NE (Helpline: 0303 123 9999; email: helpline@rnib.org.uk; website: www.rnib.org.uk)

Other information: The RNIB provides a number of services for blind and partially sighted people. Financial and other assistance is also available from the wide range of local charities for blind people, almost all of which work in close partnership with the RNIB.

Bowel conditions

Crohn's and Colitis UK

Eligibility: People in need who have ulcerative colitis, Crohn's Disease or related inflammatory bowel diseases, and their carers.

Types of grants: One-off grants of up to £300 to meet special needs which have arisen as a direct result of illness. For example, funding has been given for washing machines, refrigerators, telephone installation, clothing, beds and bedding and recuperative holidays.

Exclusions: Ongoing grants for needs such as heating and food are not usually made.

Annual grant total: In 2009 the charity had assets of £2.4 million and an income of £2.1 million. Grants were made 206 individuals totalling £53,000.

Applications: On a form available from the correspondent or to download from the website. The form has two extra sections, one which should be completed by a doctor to confirm the individual's illness and one to be filled in by a social worker (or health visitor, district nurse or Citizens Advice advisor). Completed applications should be sent to the personal grants fund secretary at: PO Box 334, St Albans, Hertfordshire AL1 2WA.

Correspondent: Julia Devereux, NACC, 4 Beaumont House, Beaumont Works, Sutton Road, St. Albans AL1 5HH (01727 759654 or 01727 830038 (main switchboard); fax: 01727 759654; email: julia.devereux@nacc.org.uk; website: www.crohnsandcolitis.org.uk/)

Other information: The association also operates a Young Persons' Assistance Scheme which helps to meet special vocational and educational needs arising from inflammatory bowel disease (IBD). However, the association's main role is to provide information and advice to people living with IBD.

Brain tumours

The Denny Care and Relief Fund (Brain Tumour UK)

Eligibility: Brain tumour patients, their carers, family and friends.

Types of grants: One-off grants of up to £500 to help increase independence and quality of life.

Annual grant total: In 2009 the fund made grants totalling £38,000.

Applications: In the first instance, please contact the Brain Tumour UK support services (0845 4500 386).

Correspondent: Support Services, Tower House, Latimer Park, Chesham, Buckinghamshire HP5 1TU (0845 4500 386; website: www.braintumouruk.org.uk)

Brittle bones

The Brittle Bone Society

Eligibility: Children and others with osteogenesis imperfecta (brittle bones) or similar disorders.

Types of grants: Grants in the range of £200 to £5,000 towards wheelchairs and other specialist equipment. This could include home alternations, assistance with holiday costs and laptops for children who are unable to attend school for a prolonged period.

Annual grant total: In 2008/09 the society had assets of £336,000 and an income of £232,000. Charitable expenditure totalled £56,000 and included costs for wheelchair purchases, wheelchair repairs, welfare and equipment and holidays.

Applications: In writing to the correspondent at any time. Applications should include an occupational therapist's report showing a need for the item required.

Correspondent: Patricia Osborne, Chief Executive, 30 Guthrie Street, Dundee DD1 5BS (01382 204446; email: bbs@ brittlebone.org; website: www.brittlebone.org)

Cancer & Leukaemia

Brad's Cancer Foundation

Eligibility: Teenagers who have cancer and related illnesses throughout the East Midlands region.

Types of grants: The provision of financial assistance to teenagers and their families, including grants towards equipment.

Annual grant total: In 2008/09 the foundation had an income of £28,000 and a total expenditure of £14,000, around £4,000 was given in donations to families and children.

Applications: In writing to the correspondent.

Correspondent: Susan Bartlett, 14 Crosslands Meadow, Riverview Park, Colwick, Nottingham, NG4 2DJ (website: www.brads.org.uk)

Other information: Grants are also made to organisations.

CLIC Sargent (formerly Sargent Cancer Care for Children)

Eligibility: Children and young people under the age of 21 living in the UK who have cancer or have been under treatment in the past six months.

Types of grants: Grants of up to £170 to alleviate crises or help with the quality of life of the child and/or family during treatment. Exceptional grants of up to £400 may be issued where no other support is available.

Annual grant total: Previously the charity made nearly 5,000 care grants totalling £818,000. Grants are also made for educational purposes.

Applications: On a form, to be completed by the CLIC Sargent Care Professional working with the family.

Correspondent: Grants Department, 161 Hammersmith Road, London W6 8SG (020 8752 2800; website: www.clicsargent.org.uk)

Other information: The charity also provides respite holidays. Details of grants holidays and other services are available from the CLIC Sargent Care Professional.

The Leukaemia Care Society

Eligibility: People with leukaemia and allied blood disorders. Financial support is open to all patients and carers who are no more than four years post diagnosis or, if there has been bereavement, no more than two years after this.

Types of grants: The society gives limited financial assistance in the form one-off grants in kind and gift vouchers. The value of awards is usually in the range of £50 to £250. This can include help towards utility bills, holidays, supermarket vouchers which can be used for food, or petrol for travel to hospital or small necessary household items.

Annual grant total: In 2008/09 the society had assets of £1 million and an income of £975,000. Grants were made to 189 individuals totalling £33,000 towards general living costs and holidays.

Applications: Applicants should first call the CARE Line on 0800 169 6680 to discuss their case and request the necessary forms. Applications usually take 14–30 days to complete.

Correspondent: Tony Gavin, One Birch Court, Blackpole East, Worcester WR3 8SG (01905 755977; fax: 01905 755166; email: care@ leukaemiacare.org.uk; website: www.leukaemiacare.org.uk)

Other information: The society also provides a signposting service in respect of welfare rights and other charities and organisations that may be able to offer additional assistance.

Macmillan Cancer Relief – Patients Grants Scheme

Eligibility: People, of any age, who have cancer, or who are still affected by the illness, and are in financial need. 'To qualify, patients must not have capital savings of more than £8,000 per couple, or £6,000 for a single person. Individual household members must not have more than £100 each to spend each week, after allowing for basic costs.'

Types of grants: One-off grants towards daily expenses, including travel, heating, clothing, furnishings, care, telephones, convalescence, holidays and so on.

Annual grant total: In 2008 the charity had assets of £60 million and an income of £126 million. Grants to individuals totalled £9.6 million.

Applications: On a form available from the correspondent. No direct applications can be made; they must be made through a Macmillan or community nurse, health or social worker, hospital social worker or a health professional from another welfare charity. Welfare workers can receive more information about the scheme by calling Macmillan CancerLine on 0808 808 2020. Applications are usually processed on the day they are received and payments are sent out within three working days.

Correspondent: Grants Department, 87–90 Albert Embankment, London SE1 7UQ (020 7840 7833; fax: 020 7840 4832; website: www.macmillan.org.uk)

Other information: Grants to patients are only one feature of the fund's work. Others include funding Macmillan Nurses (who are skilled in providing advice and support on symptom control and pain relief), Macmillan buildings for in-patient and day care, and financing an education programme for professionals in palliative care. The fund also gives grants to three associated charities.

The Ada Oliver Will Trust

Eligibility: People who have cancer or rheumatism and are in financial need. Preference is given for people living in Surrey.

Types of grants: Monthly and one-off grants of up to £100 are given for a variety of needs. Recent grants have been given for settling rent arrears, nursing home fees and necessities.

Annual grant total: In 2008/09 the trust had an income of £2,900 and a total expenditure of £5,100. Grants are made to individuals and organisations.

Applications: In writing to the correspondent, including details of income and circumstances. Applications can be submitted throughout the year by a social worker, Citizens Advice or other welfare agency on behalf of the individual.

Correspondent: The Trustees, c/o Marshalls Solicitors, 102 High Street, Godalming, Surrey GU7 1DS (01483 416101)

The Shona Smile Foundation

Eligibility: Children and young people under the age of 18 who have one of the forms of rhabdomyosarcoma.

Types of grants: Cash donations towards, for example, everyday items, something that the child/young person wants or needs, or helping to fulfil a dream of his/her choosing.

Annual grant total: About £8,000.

Applications: In writing to the correspondent.

Correspondent: Pete Gill, 18 The Combers, Grange Farm, Kesgrave, Ipswich IP5 2EY (01473 614504; email: pete.gill@live.co.uk; website: www.shonassmile.org)

Cerebral palsy

The Nihal Armstrong Trust

Eligibility: Children living in the UK, up to and including the age of 18, with cerebral palsy.

Types of grants: Grants up to £1,000 towards equipment, communication aids or a particular service that will benefit children with cerebral palsy. Items/services must not be available from the local authority.

Annual grant total: In 2008/09 the trust had an income of £8,200 and a total expenditure of £10,000.

Applications: Applications can be made via the trust's website and must be supported by a doctor, school, social worker, health visitor, speech, occupational therapist or physiotherapist. Trustees meet three times a year.

The trustees prefer to receive applications via the website where possible. Individuals who are sending literature on equipment/services or suppliers' estimates, can forward any documents to the address provided in the 'contacts' section. A short list of supporting documents needed is given on the trust's website.

Correspondent: The Trustees, 111 Chatsworth Road, London, NW2 4BH (020 8459 6527; email: info@nihalarmstrongtrust.org.uk; website: www.nihalarmstrongtrust.org.uk)

Other information: The trust is managed by a small group of trustees who between them, have a wealth of experience in relating to families who care for someone with cerebral palsy. The Trust states it "is keen to make life easier for these families" and encourages individuals to apply.

Cystic fibrosis

Cystic Fibrosis Trust

Eligibility: People in need who have cystic fibrosis.

Types of grants: One off grants ranging from around £100 to £300 for household items directly beneficial to those with cystic fibrosis, assistance to new homeowners, holidays (mainly for adults with cystic fibrosis*), travelling costs during hospital admissions, and help to fund a first annual prescription prepayment certificate. Up to £750 is also available towards funeral costs.

* The trust tends to refer families who have children with cystic fibrosis to the Cystic Fibrosis Holiday Fund and other related charities (please contact the welfare officer for more information).

Exclusions: Unfortunately no grants are given for computers, cars, significant debts or to meet ongoing costs. Holiday grants are only awarded to people who have not had a holiday in the last two years (other than under exceptional circumstances).

Annual grant total: In 2008/09 the trust had assets of £1.1 million and an income of £9.3 million. Grants were made to individuals totalling £210,000.

Applications: Application forms are available from the correspondent or can be downloaded from the trust's website. Applications must be supported by a social worker or other professional and should state whether the applicant has applied to other charities and the outcome, the general financial circumstances and the reason for the application. The trust strongly advises that individuals or their health professionals contact the welfare grants officer before submitting an application.

Correspondent: Welfare Grants Officer, 11 London Road, Bromley, Kent BR1 1BY (0845 859 1020; fax: 020 8313 0472; email: enquiries@cftrust.org.uk; website: www.cftrust.org.uk)

Other information: The trust also provides confidential advice, support and information on all aspects of cystic fibrosis in the form of factsheets and dedicated helplines for general and welfare benefits advice.

Deafblind

Sense, the National Deaf-Blind & Rubella Association

Eligibility: People who are deaf-blind or multi-sensory impaired, and their families.

Types of grants: One-off emergency grants only, in exceptional circumstances. Grants are generally £50. Grants have been given towards clothing and travel fares to hospitals.

Annual grant total: In 2008/09 the trust had assets of £28 million and an income of £78 million. Grant totals vary from year to year.

Applications: In writing to the correspondent, to be considered as they arrive.

Correspondent: Yvonne Thomas, Sense, 101 Pentonville Road, London, N1 9LG (0845 127 0060, textphone: 0845 127 0062; fax: 0845 127 0061; email: info@sense.org.uk; website: www.sense.org.uk)

Other information: Sense provides a complete range of support and services for people with dual sensory impairments, or a sensory impairment and another disability (and their families) including holidays.

Dystonia

The Dystonia Society

Eligibility: People living with Dystonia in the UK.

Types of grants: One-off and recurrent grants according to need.

Exclusions: No grants for medical treatment or other therapies, or for items or services available from the NHS.

Annual grant total: In 2008/09 the society had assets of £539,000 and an income of £721,000. During the year six grants were made to individuals totalling £1,300.

Applications: On a form available from the correspondent. Application forms must be endorsed by a health or social care professional who has known the applicant for at least two years.

Grants do not usually exceed £300, except in special circumstances.

Correspondent: Val Wells, Service Development Manager, The Dystonia Society, 1st Floor, 89 Albert Embankment, London, SE1 7TP (0845 458 6211)

Haematological disorders

The Roald Dahl Foundation

Eligibility: Children and young adults aged 25 or under, who have a neurological or haematological condition and are from a low-income family. The only eligible cancer is benign brain tumour.

Families must be in receipt of Income Support, Working Tax Credit and/or Housing Benefit. Families who do not qualify for these benefits, but are on a low-income or whose income has been interrupted by the child's illness may also be considered.

Types of grants: One-off grants of up to £500. Grants can be given towards household appliances; clothing, beds and bedding; utility bills; respite care; medic alert bracelets; travel and subsistence payments whilst children are in hospital; and specialised equipment such as sensory toys, car seats, specialist tricycles, wheelchairs and motability vehicles.

Exclusions: No grants are given towards debts (except utility bills) or items that should be provided by statutory sources. Holidays are not funded as a rule, unless exceptional circumstances exist.

Annual grant total: In 2008/09 the foundation had assets of £1.5 million and an income of £751,000. Grants were made 295 families totalling £96,000.

Applications: On a form available from the correspondent or to download from the website. Applications must be completed and submitted by a social worker or healthcare professional who is willing to see the application through to completion, supplying and confirming the information contained. There are no deadlines and applications are considered as and when they arrive.

Assistance may be available to those who do not qualify for state benefits but have an income lower than £22,000. Applicants should provide full details of family income and expenditure for consideration.

Correspondent: Small Grants Manager, 81A High Street, Great Missenden, Buckinghamshire HP16 0AL (01494 892170; fax: 01494 890459; email: josmith@roalddahlfoundation.org; website: www.roalddahlfoundation.org)

Other information: The foundation also makes grants to charities and NHS hospitals working in the fields of neurology and haematology (£349,000 in 2008/09).

Haemophilia

The Haemophilia Society (The Tanner Fund)

Eligibility: People with haemophilia and related bleeding disorders, and their families.

Types of grants: One-off grants for items relating to applicants' medical problems, such as fridges to store treatment, floor coverings, washing machines and bedding.

Exclusions: No grants are given for debts, holidays, motor vehicles or ongoing bills such as gas or electricity.

Annual grant total: In 2009/10 the society had assets of £361,000 and an income of £697,000. Individual grants made through the Tanner Fund totalled £2,400.

Applications: On a form available from the correspondent. Applications must be completed in conjunction with a health care professional affiliated to their local haemophilia centre. They are considered as received. Please note each family may only make one application a year.

Correspondent: Rachel Goodkin, First Floor, Petersham House, 57A Hatton Garden, London EC1N 8JG (0800 018 6068 (freephone helpline) or 020 7831 1020; fax: 020 7405 4824; email: info@haemophilia.org.uk; website: www.haemophilia.org.uk)

Other information: The society has centres across the UK and provides a wide range of support and advice to people affected by bleeding disorders.

Huntingdon's disease

The Huntington's Disease Association

Eligibility: People with Huntington's disease, their immediate families and those at risk, who live in England or Wales.

Types of grants: One-off grants only, typically of up to £350, although each application is considered on merit. Recent grants have been for clothing, furniture, domestic equipment (e.g. washing machines and cookers) and flooring.

Exclusions: No grants towards equipment or services that should be provided by statutory services. Support will not be given for the payment of debts, loans, bills, funeral expenses, holidays or travel.

Annual grant total: Up to £30,000 a year.

Applications: On a form available from the correspondent. Applications should be submitted through a Regional Care Adviser or other professional. Requests are processed monthly. Full guidance notes are available on request.

Correspondent: Karen Crowder and Mark Ford, Neurosupport Centre, Norton Street, Liverpool, L3 8LR (0151 298 3298; fax: 0151 298 9440; email: info@hda.org.uk; website: www.hda.org.uk)

Liver

The Ben Hardwick Fund

Eligibility: Children with primary liver disease, and their families, who are in need.

Types of grants: One-off and recurrent grants, usually ranging between £150 and £500, to help with costs which are the direct result of the child's illness, such as hospital travel costs, in-hospital expenses, telephone bills and childminding for other children left at home.

Annual grant total: In 2008/09 the fund had an income of £6,900 and a total expenditure of £16,000.

Applications: In writing to the correspondent, usually through a hospital social worker or other welfare professional. Applications are considered at any time.

Correspondent: Anne Auber, 12 Nassau Road, Barnes, London SW13 9QE (020 8741 8499)

Other information: The fund also makes grants to organisations.

Meningitis

Meningitis Trust

Eligibility: People in need who have meningitis or who are disabled as a result of meningitis.

Types of grants: One-off and recurrent grants towards respite care, sign language lessons, specialist aids and equipment, travel and accommodation costs, therapeutic activities, re-education and special training, and funeral expenses and headstones.

Exclusions: Usually no grants will be given towards domestic bill arrears, clothing, bedding and furniture.

Annual grant total: In 2008/09 the trust had assets totalling £1.6 million and an income of £3.2 million. Grants for educational and welfare purposes were made to 144 families totalling £157,000.

Applications: On a form available from the correspondent. An initial telephone call to the grants coordinator Tracy Lewendon on 01453 769043 or the 24-hour helpline on 0800 028 18 28 to discuss the application process is welcomed. Applications should be submitted through a third party and are reviewed on a monthly basis.

Correspondent: Tracy Lewendon, Fern House, Bath Road, Stroud GL5 3TJ (01453 769043; fax: 01453 768001; email: TraceyL@meningitis-trust.org; website: www.meningitis-trust.org)

Other information: The trust runs a 'family day' for children who have meningitis and their families. The day includes arts, crafts and music for children and gives parents an opportunity to meet the trust's staff and other families. The trust also supports a range of professional counselling, home visits, therapy and information services.

Mental illness

The Matthew Trust

Eligibility: People aged 8 years and upwards, who have a mental health problem of any kind. The trust will accept applications from victims of aggression as well as those with a mental health problem, both in prisons and special hospitals and when they return to living in the community.

Types of grants: One-off grants of between £50 and £250 towards: counselling or medical bills; equipment and furniture to make a flat liveable; security equipment; clothing; second chance learning and skills training; taking up housing issues with local authorities; travel costs for prison visits; respite breaks; and debt support in special circumstances.

Annual grant total: In 2008/09 the trust had assets of £249,000 and an income of £86,000. Grants were made totalling £33,000.

Applications: In writing to the correspondent through a professional agency such as a social worker, probation officer, community care worker or GP. Applications should include the name, address and age of the applicant; the health and age of other close family members; a summary of the mental health problem; the type of support required, including costs where applicable; and, details of any other organisations which have been approached for support.

Please note: The Matthew Trust is a 'last-stop' agency and will only consider applications when all other avenues of statutory and voluntary funding have been exhausted and then only where a care programme has been established. The trust aims to provide a response within 14 days.

Correspondent: Annabel Thompson, Director, PO Box 604, London SW6 3AG (020 7736 5976; fax: 020 7731 6961; email: matthewtrust@ukonline.co.uk; website: www.matthewtrust.org)

Motor neurone

The Motor Neurone Disease Association

Eligibility: People with motor neurone disease, living in England, Wales and Northern Ireland.

Types of grants: i) Top-up of respite care (normally £500–£2,000).

ii) Equipment rental.

iii) Building adaptations.

Annual grant total: In 2008/09 the trust made grants totalling £721,000.

Applications: On a form available from the correspondent or a local regional care adviser. Applications must be submitted through a health or social care professional. In addition to stating what is requested, applications should include details of why the need is not met by statutory sources and where any payments should be made.

Correspondent: Malcolm Watkins, PO Box 246, Northampton NN1 2PR (01604 611814; email: enquiries@ mndassociation.org; website: www. mndassociation.org)

Other information: The trust has a network of association branches which can offer information about the grants available. Further information is available on the trust's website.

Mucopoly-saccharide diseases

Society for Mucopolysaccharide Diseases

Eligibility: Children and young adults with mucopolysaccharide and related disorders. Applicants must be members of the society.

Types of grants: One-off grants and loans ranging between £25 and £250, primarily to enable members to access activities and conferences organised by the society. Grants for equipment, holidays and bereavement costs are also considered.

Exclusions: No grants can be paid towards arrears or to non-members. Grants are not made retrospectively.

Annual grant total: In 2008/09 the society had assets of £1 million and an income of £1.1 million. A small annual budget of around £2,000 is available to help families in need of financial assistance.

Applications: On a form available from the correspondent, to be submitted directly by the individual or a family member. They are considered on a monthly basis.

Correspondent: Christine Lavery, Director, MPS Society, MPS House, Repton Place, White Lion Road, Amersham, Buckinghamshire, HP7 9LP (0845 389 9901; email: mps@mpssociety. co.uk; website: www.mpssociety.co.uk)

Other information: The society also funds research into mucopolysaccharide and related diseases.

Multiple sclerosis

The Multiple Sclerosis Society of Great Britain and Northern Ireland

Eligibility: People with multiple sclerosis and their families and carers, living in the

UK. People living in Scotland or Northern Ireland may be subject to other conditions, please contact MS Society Scotland (0131 335 4050) or MS Society Northern Ireland (028 9080 2803) for full details.

Types of grants: One-off grants towards: home adaptations or remedial work needed following adaptations; wheelchairs; mobility scooters; double profiling beds; riser-recliner chairs; car adaptations such as hoists or hand controls; motability advance payments (in certain circumstances); driving lessons; respite care; holidays for individuals or families who have not been away for three or more years; clinical and communication aids; bankruptcy and Debt Relief Order fees; removal costs; and furnishings, flooring and domestic appliances. Other needs may also be considered.

The society in England, Wales and Northern Ireland also has two specific funds for carers:

- Young Carers Fund – Grants of up to £300 are available for people aged 17 and under who help care for a parent or guardian with MS, or who have extra responsibilities at home due to there being someone with MS in the family.
- Carers Opportunities Fund – Grants of up to £400 for carers aged over 18 and those whose caring role has recently ended to develop an interest or undertake a course to get back into work.

In Scotland, carers can apply to the MS Society Scotland grants fund.

Exclusions: Applicants with more than £16,000 in savings are not eligible for financial assistance. Those with more than £8,000 in savings are expected to contribute towards the cost of the item.

Grants cannot be made for purchases already made; long-term financial commitments (such as top-up grants for residential care); loans, debt assistance or legal fees; and complimentary, alternative or conventional treatments and associated equipment (such as exercise equipment).

Annual grant total: In 2008 grants to individuals totalled £1.8 million.

Applications: On a form available from the correspondent or a local MS Society branch. Applications should include two quotes for the expenditure and a letter of support from a social worker, health professional or occupational therapist. Applicants in England, Wales or Northern Ireland should submit their form and supporting information to a local branch where the request will be considered confidentially by trained volunteers. If the branch is unable to award a grant for the full cost of the item, the form will be forwarded to the MS National Centre. Applicants in Scotland should submit their form to the Grants coordinator at the MS Society Scotland office.

Correspondent: The Grants Team, MS National Centre, 372 Edgware Road, Cricklewood, London NW2 6ND (020 8438 0700; fax: 020 8438 0701; email: grants@mssociety.org.uk; website: www.mssociety.org.uk)

Other information: The Society has a freephone helpline (0808 800 8000), dedicated respite centres, free information booklets on all aspects of living with MS for people with, and affected by, MS and a network of branches, manned by volunteers, across the UK offering local support to people with MS.

Muscular dystrophy

The Joseph Patrick Trust

Eligibility: People with muscular dystrophy or an allied neuromuscular condition.

Types of grants: On average about 200 one-off grants of between £200 and £1,250 are made each year to partially fund the purchase of wheelchairs (powered and manual), scooters, electric beds, trikes, computers, vehicle adaptations, riser chairs, mobile arm supports, portable aids, therapy equipment and so on. Discretionary payments can be made for funeral expenses and other emergencies.

Exclusions: Grants are not given for: holidays, household adaptations, building works or domestic appliances; equipment which has already been bought; recurring costs (e.g. wheelchair repairs); the purchase or lease of vehicles, vehicle deposits, maintenance or repair of vehicles. No grants outside of the UK.

Annual grant total: In 2008/09 the trust made grants totalling £156,000 to 220 individuals.

Applications: On a form available from the correspondent or to download from the website. Completed forms can be submitted directly by the individual or via a third party and should be supported by an assessment and quotation for the equipment requested, confirming the need and suitability of the equipment. Applications are considered six times a year. Grants are only be made payable to the supplier.

Correspondent: Robert Meadowcroft, c/o Muscular Dystrophy Campaign, 61 Southwark Street, London SE1 0HL (020 7803 4800; fax: 020 7401 3495; email: jptgrants@muscular-dystrophy.org; website: www.muscular-dystrophy.org/how_we_help_you/equipment_grants)

Neurological disorders

Cerebra for Brain Injured Children and Young People

Eligibility: Children and young people aged 16 or under who have disabilities because of a brain related condition or injury. The condition may be of a physical nature, a learning disability or both.

Types of grants: Equipment or resources that would improve quality of life not available from statutory agencies like the social services or the NHS. Examples of grants made include those towards touch screen computers, specialist car seats, power wheelchairs, therapies, trampolines, sensory toys, tricycles and quadricycles and digital drum kits.

For anything where there is a medical need the trust asks that potential applicants check with them as they may be able to help.

Exclusions: Grants are not given for: driving lessons; motorised vehicles such as quad bikes and motorbikes; anything that could be considered a home improvement e.g. paint for decorating, conservatories, carpet or other flooring; garden landscaping; household items e.g. vacuum cleaners, washing machines, wardrobes, standard beds (special beds may be considered); vehicle purchase or maintenance; assessments; general clothing; treatment centres outside of the UK; lycra suits; holidays; and educational items such as home tutors, standard teaching materials or the son-rise programme.

Annual grant total: Between £50,000 and £400,000 in recent years.

Applications: Application forms and guidance notes can be downloaded from the Cerebra website. Grants are all paid directly to the assistance provider.

Correspondent: Debbie Godsave, Grants Co-ordinator, Second Floor Offices, The Lyric Building, King Street, Carmarthen, SA31 1BD (01267 244216; email: debbieg@cerebra.org.uk; website: www.cerebra.org.uk)

Other information: The trust also provides other support services such as telephone counselling, speech and language therapy and a wills and trust voucher scheme.

Parkinson's disease

Parkinson's Disease Society

Eligibility: People with Parkinson's disease, with under £10,000 in individual savings or under £15,000 in joint savings.

Types of grants: One-off grants of up to £1,500 for equipment or home adaptations, up to £1,000 for respite breaks for people with Parkinson's disease and their carer, and up to £500 for other items such as domestic appliances or household goods.

Exclusions: No grants are given towards ongoing costs or regular payments such as care fees, bills, insurance, medical treatment, debts, retrospective funding or holidays.

Annual grant total: Grants to individuals usually total about £90,000 per year.

Applications: Application forms and guidance notes can be found on the Parkinson's Disease Society website. Applications are considered every two months.

Correspondent: Steve Ford, Chief Executive, 215 Vauxhall Bridge Road, London SW1V 1EJ (020 7931 8080; email: enquiries@parkinsons.org.uk; website: www.parkinsons.org.uk)

Polio

The British Polio Fellowship

Eligibility: People in need who have been disabled through poliomyelitis (polio) and live in the UK.

Types of grants: Welfare grants of up to £500 are given for scooters, electric or manual wheelchairs, riser/recliner chairs, specialist beds and mattresses; household aids and equipment to enable independence; and, home and car adaptations. Support may occasionally be given for essential home improvement and crisis prevention.

Grants of up to £100 are awarded each autumn to help with heating costs for those who are not eligible for state assistance. Help is also available towards the cost of holidays.

Exclusions: No grants are given for hospital expenses, household bills or home carers. Statutory sources e.g. Social Services, Social Fund must be approached before approaching the fellowship.

Annual grant total: In 2008 the fellowship had assets of £3.4 million and an income of £1.2 million. Charitable activities totalled

£923,000, of which £209,000 was given in grants to individuals.

Applications: Welfare and heating grant forms are available from the correspondent or a local branch welfare officer. Applications should be submitted by the individual or by an appropriate third party on their behalf and include a medical certificate or doctors note stating polio-disability. Welfare applications are considered throughout the year. Heating grants are awarded once a year in the autumn.

Holiday grant forms are available from the correspondent or by emailing holidays@britishpolio.org.uk. They are assessed every other month.

Correspondent: Support Services Team, Unit A, Eagle Office Centre, The Runway, South Ruislip, Middlesex HA4 6SE (0800 0180 586; fax: 020 8842 0555; email: info@britishpolio.org.uk; website: www.britishpolio.org.uk)

Other information: The fellowship has over 50 local branches and provides support and advice on a wide range of issues affecting people disabled through polio.

Renal

The British Kidney Patient Association

Eligibility: Renal patients of UK nationality, whether on dialysis or not.

Types of grants: One-off grants can be given for all kinds of need caused by the condition, including clothing costs, gas/electric/water bills, telephone installation, TV licenses, and domestic goods such as washing machines and carpets. Grants can also be made to cover the costs of hospital visits, such as travel expenses, car tax and insurance.

Help may also be offered towards holidays at specialist centres equipped with dialysis treatment facilities. Applicants interested in such grants should refer to the BKPA website for more information.

Exclusions: Grants are not made for: telephone bills; court fines; improvements to a patient's home e.g. showers, stair lifts, central heating; credit card and loan repayments; medical equipment such as wheel chairs; council tax payments; and reimbursement for loss of items due to theft.

Annual grant total: In 2009 the trust had an income of £2.8 million and a total expenditure £4.3 million. Patient Aid for children and adults totalled £393,000.

Applications: Via a kidney unit social worker or a member of the kidney care team on a form available from the correspondent, or to download from the BKPA website. Applications are considered on an ongoing basis.

Correspondent: Susan Lee, 3 The Windmills, St Mary's Close, Turk Street, Alton, GU34 1EF (01420 541424; fax: 01420 89438; email: info@britishkidney-pa.co.uk; website: www.britishkidney-pa.co.uk)

Other information: The trust also makes grants to hospitals and supports the Ronald McDonald Houses at the Alder Hey Children's Hospital, Liverpool, Bristol Royal Hospital for Children, Evelina Children's Hospital, London and the Royal Hospital for Sick Children, Yorkhill which provide support for the families of young renal patients attending the units at these hospitals.

Spinal muscular

The Jennifer Trust

Eligibility: People diagnosed as having the genetic condition spinal muscular atrophy. Please note that the trust cannot give grants to people with any other condition.

Types of grants: One-off grants for equipment to meet needs not provided by statutory services. Grants have been awarded for electric wheelchairs, beds, computers and chairs.

Exclusions: No grants towards vehicles or their adaptations.

Annual grant total: In 2008/09 the trust had assets of £175,000 and an income of £770,000. Welfare and equipment grants totalled £16,000.

Applications: On a form available from the correspondent.

Note: At the time of writing (autumn 2010) the trust was in the process of reviewing its grantmaking policy and was not accepting new applications. For the latest information, please go to the trust's website.

Correspondent: Heather Brown, General Manager, Elta House, Birmingham Road, Stratford-upon-Avon CV37 0AQ (01789 267520; fax: 01789 268371; email: heather.brown@jtsma.org.uk; website: www.jtsma.org.uk)

Other information: Individual financial grants are only one way in which the trust provides support. For more information, contact the trust and request an information pack or visit the website.

Sports injuries

RFU Injured Players Foundation

Eligibility: People who are seriously injured playing sport under the auspices of the Rugby Football Union.

Types of grants: Small grants of up to £2,000 per year and large grants of up to £20,000 for a variety of needs.

Annual grant total: In 2008/09 the foundation had assets of £1 million and an income of £769,000. A total of £260,000 was given in large grants to 37 individuals and a further £139,000 was given in 65 small grants.

Applications: Small grant application forms can be download from the website. Large grants have a more detailed application and assessment process and forms are only available by contacting Tim Bonnett.

Correspondent: Tim Bonnett, Client Support Executive, Rugby House, Twickenham Stadium, 200 Whitton Road, Middlesex, TW2 7BA (0800 783 1518; email: timbonnett@rfu.com; website: www.rfu.com)

Other information: The foundation is usually notified of players who receive injuries through the RFU's Injury Reporting process. When someone is catastrophically injured, the RFU Injured Player Welfare Officer will contact the family of the person involved and offer initial help with travel and other expenses to visit the player in hospital and support them through their recovery and rehabilitation.

The Rosslyn Park Injury Trust Fund

Eligibility: Young people who have a disability or are in poor health as a result of an injury suffered while playing sports (amateur sports). Help may also be available to their dependants.

Types of grants: One-off grants for computers, special care, medical equipment and disability aids.

Annual grant total: On average, about £3,000 is available each year to distribute in grants.

Applications: In writing to the correspondent. Applications can be submitted by either the individual or through social services and are considered as they are received.

Correspondent: Brian Carr, Trustee, 8 Burbage Road, London, SE24 9HJ (020 7733 9055; email: brian.carr@onetel.net)

Stroke

The Stroke Association

Eligibility: People who have had a stroke and are in need. Applicants must have less than £8,000 in savings.

Types of grants: One-off grants of up to £200 to help improve the individual's quality of life. Recent grants have been given for hospital travel costs, extra heating, holidays, household items, clothing, phone installation, house adaptations, computer equipment and so on.

Annual grant total: In 2008/09 the trust had assets of £9 million and an income of £22 million. Welfare grants were made totalling about £100,000.

Applications: On a form available from the correspondent to be completed by a social worker or health professional on the individual's behalf. Awards are means-tested, taking into account the total household income.

Correspondent: The Welfare Secretary, Stroke House, 240 City Road, London EC1V 2PR (020 7566 0300; fax: 020 7490 2686; email: info@stroke.org. uk; website: www.stroke.org.uk)

Tuberous sclerosis

Tuberous Sclerosis Association Benevolent Fund

Eligibility: People in need who have tuberous sclerosis complex and their carers.

Types of grants: One-off grants of up to £400 for hospital travel and accommodation costs, specialist equipment, furniture and so on. Up to £500 is also available for holidays.

Exclusions: There are no grants available for things which are the responsibility of a statutory service. No more than £800 can be given to one person in any five year period and only one application is allowed each year. No grants for car repairs or car purchase.

Annual grant total: In 2008/09 the fund had assets of £1.9 million and an income of £496,000. Grants were made totalling £21,000, of which £15,000 was given in family days and weekends and £5,500 in benevolent grants.

Applications: On a form available from the correspondent or to download from the website. Applications can be submitted either directly by the individual or through a parent or carer. If the application is for more than £100 a professional such as a social worker, therapist, doctor or TSA advisor should fill in a professional reference form supporting the request.

Applications for benevolent grants can be made at anytime and a decision is usually made within two to three weeks, though the fund can respond more quickly in urgent cases. Holiday applications should be submitted by 1 July and successful applicants will be notified in writing by 1 August.

Correspondent: Diane Sanson, Head of Administration, PO Box 12979, Barnt Green, Birmingham, B45 5AN (0121 445 6970; email: development-support@tuberous-sclerosis.org; website: www.tuberous-sclerosis.org)

Other information: The fund's main priority is to fund research into the causes and management of tuberous sclerosis (£165,000 in 2008/09). It also provides education and information about the condition.

OCCUPATIONAL CHARITIES

This section contains the following parts.

● An index of particular trades or professions. The categories of trades/professions are listed alphabetically.

● After the index, the charities themselves are arranged alphabetically within each trade/profession. Charities include both independent charities and benevolent funds associated with trade unions or professional bodies.

Trusts included are those which support both members of the occupation listed and their dependants. Individuals should also check for any trade unions listed which cover their area of work, as unions will sometimes have resources available for workers in their sector who are not members. When a possible occupation has been identified, go to the relevant page and read the entries carefully. Being a member of a profession is not necessarily enough; there may well be other criteria that make individuals ineligible.

We have grouped together certain occupations to make relevant trusts easier to identify. For instance, dance, magic, music, painting, theatre and writing have all been placed under 'Arts', as there are some trusts which support arts generally (and which would give to a number of these categories) and some that will give only to one specific branch. Being in paid employment is not always necessary for eligibility; for instance, there are trusts for certain amateur sportspeople.

We have placed all medical and health workers in the same category. The exceptions to this are the trusts that support carers, which have been included in the general section under the 'Carers and volunteers' category (see page 26). The category 'Food, drink and provision trade' (see page 76) contains many different individual roles within the industry. Trusts concerning clergy and missionaries have been listed in the 'Religious charities' chapter (see page 123). Please note that trusts which support a particular occupation but only give in a particular locality, such as Lancashire County Nursing Trust, are included in the relevant local section of this guide.

Index of occupational charity funds

A

Accountancy 58
Advertising and marketing 59
Agriculture & related rural issues 59
Airline pilots 60
Antiques 60
Architecture 60
Arts 60
    Dance 62
    Magic 62
    Music 62
    Painting 64
    Theatre 64
    Writing 65
Atomic energy 66

B

Banking, finance and insurance 66
Book retail 67
Building trade 67

C

Caravan 68
Ceramic 68
Chartered surveyors 68
Civil service 68
Clayworking 69
Clergy 70
Clothing and textiles 70
Coal industry 71
Commerce 71
Commercial travellers 72
Cooperative 72
Coopers 72
Corn exchange 72
Customs & excise 73

D

Driving Instructors 73

E

Electrical 73
Engineering 74
Environmental health 76
Estate workers 76

F

Farriers 76
Fire service 76
Food, drink and provision trades 76
Furnishing trade 79

G

Gardening 79
Gas engineering 79

H

Hairdressing 80
Horticulture 80
Hotel and catering 80

J

Jewellery 80

L

Laundry 81
Leather 81
Legal 81

M

Market research 82
Match manufacture 82
Media 82
Medicine and health 83
Metal trades 87
Mining 88
Motor industry 88

N

Naval architecture 88
Newsagents 88

P

Patent agents 89
Pawnbrokers 89
Petroleum 89
Police 89
Post office 90
Pottery and glass 91
Printing 91
Probation 91
Public relations 91
Public sector 91
Public transport 92

Q

Quarrying 92

R

Railways 92
Removal trade 93
Retail trade 93
Road haulage 93

S

School inspectors 94
Science 94
Seafaring and fishing 94
Secretaries 97
Self-employed and small businesses 97
Social workers 97
Solicitors 98

Sport 98
  Cricket 98
  Football 99
  Golf 99
  Horse racing 100
  Motor sport 100
  Snooker and billiards 101
Stationery 101
Stock Exchange 101

T

Tax inspectors 101
Teaching 102
Telecommunications 103
Tobacco 103
Travel agents 103

U

United Nations 104

V

Veterinary 104
Voluntary Sector 104

W

Watch and clock makers 105

Accountancy

AIA Educational and Benevolent Trust

Eligibility: Fellows and associates of the institute, and their close dependants, who are in need.

Types of grants: One-off grants according to need.

Annual grant total: About £7,000.

Applications: In writing to the correspondent.

Correspondent: Trust Administrator, Staithes 3, The Watermark, Metro Riverside, Tyne And Wear, NE11 9SN (0191 4930277; fax: 0191 4930278; website: www.aiaworldwide.com/)

Other information: Grants may also be given to those wishing to undergo education and training in accountancy.

The Chartered Accountants' Benevolent Association

Eligibility: Members, former members and employees of the Institute of Chartered Accountants in England and Wales and the Society of Incorporated Accountants, and their dependants. Also those without full membership, who are registered as studying for examinations, with the expectation of becoming a full member.

Types of grants: One-off and recurrent grants towards daily living costs, respite care, household essentials and so on. The association also provides interest-free loans.

Annual grant total: In 2009 the association gave £1.2 million in financial aid, including £100,000 in loans.

Applications: In writing to the correspondent.

Correspondent: Donna Cooper, Grants Coordinator, 8 Mitchell Court, Castle Mound Way, Rugby, CV23 0UY (01788 556366 /0800 107 6163 (24hr helpline); email: enquiries@caba.org.uk; website: www.caba.org.uk)

Other information: The association offers a wide range of support and advice on issues such as accessing state benefits, debt and financial problems and stress management.

The Chartered Certified Accountants' Benevolent Fund

Eligibility: Members, and former members, of the ACCA, and their dependants.

Types of grants: Grants range from £40 to £11,000. Recurrent grants are available to help with stairlifts, telephone bills, holidays, TV rental and so on; one-off grants in tragic circumstances to help beneficiaries get back on their feet; and low-interest or interest-free loans on property.

Exclusions: Grants are not available for the education of children.

Annual grant total: In 2008 the association had assets of £1.8 million and an income of £217,000. Grants were made to 15 individuals totalling £31,000.

Applications: On a form available from the correspondent or downloadable from the website (www.accaglobal.com/members/fund/apply). Applications can be submitted directly by the individual or through a social worker, Citizens Advice, welfare agency or other third party. They are considered at meetings held every two or three months.

Correspondent: Hugh McCash, Honorary Secretary, 2 Central Quay, 89 Hydepark Street, Glasgow G3 8BW (0141 534 4045; fax: 0141 534 4151; email: hugh.mccash@accaglobal.com; website: www.accaglobal.com)

The Chartered Institute of Management Accountants Benevolent Fund

Eligibility: Past and present CIMA members and their dependants anywhere in the world.

Types of grants: One-off grants for specific needs such as television licence/rental, telephone rental, motor insurance/tax, disability aids, some repairs and necessary household items such as fridges, cookers and so on. Regular grants are also made to help meet basic living costs. Loans may be provided in exceptional circumstances.

Exclusions: No grants to enhance property, for investment in business ventures, or for private medical care. Though, assistance may be given to members living outside the UK who do not have access to state-funded medical treatment or medical insurance and have large medical bills.

Annual grant total: In 2009 the fund had assets of £1.9 million and an income of £85,000. Grants were made totalling £109,000.

Applications: On a form available from the correspondent or to download from the website. Applications can be submitted directly by the individual or through a recognised referral agency (Citizens Advice, doctor, social worker and so on), or through a third party. They are considered monthly/as necessary.

Correspondent: Caroline Aldred, Secretary, CIMA, 26 Chapter Street, London SW1P 4NP (020 8849 2221; email: benevolent.fund@cimaglobal.com; website: www.cimaglobal.com)

Other information: Educational grants are also made for dependent children.

The Institute of Financial Accountants' & International Association of Book-Keepers' Benevolent Fund

Eligibility: Past and present members of the institute or the association, and their dependants.

Types of grants: One-off grants according to need. Grants are normally only given in real cases of financial need, and usually range between £100 and £2,000.

Annual grant total: In 2010 grants were made totalling about £10,000.

Applications: On a form available from the correspondent. Applications can be submitted directly by the individual or on their behalf by a family member. Details of income and expenditure should also be included. Every application is considered on its merits.

Correspondent: Carmel Fitzgerald, Burford House, 44 London Road, Sevenoaks, Kent TN13 1AS (01732 458080; fax: 01732 455848; email: carmelf@ifa.org.uk; website: www.ifa.org.uk)

Advertising and marketing

NABS

Eligibility: People who work or have worked in advertising, marketing, marketing services and related industries, and their dependants.

Types of grants: One-off and recurrent grants according to need. Welfare advice is available through a NABS helpline.

Annual grant total: In 2008 the trust had assets of £3.2 million and an income of £3.4 million. Grants were made to over 300 individuals totalling £405,000.

Applications: On a form available from the correspondent. Completed forms, which should include a career history, financial information and references, are considered monthly.

Correspondent: Ms Lucy T Owen, 47–50 Margaret Street, London, W1W 8SB (020 7462 3150; email: nabs@nabs.org.uk; website: www.nabs.org.uk)

Other information: The society also provides a wide range of services for members of the industry, including a telephone helpline, sheltered housing, residential care and nursing accommodation for older people, a flatshare scheme and a lonely-hearts service.

Agriculture & related rural issues

Confederation of Forest Industries

Eligibility: Members of the Forestry and Timber Association (or ConFor) and their dependants who are in need. Members must have been involved with the association for at least one year.

Types of grants: One-off grants usually in excess of £1,000 are made towards expenses for those experiencing hardship.

Annual grant total: This fund has an average income of around £4,500 per year and an average expenditure of £400.

Applications: Application forms are available from the correspondent.

Correspondent: Ms J Karthaus, Woodland Place, Belford, Northumberland NE70 7QA (01668 213937; fax: 01668 213555; email: jane@apfs.demon.co.uk; website: www.confor.org.uk)

Other information: Anyone can join ConFor who has an interest in trees, woodlands or timber.

The Gamekeepers Welfare Trust

Eligibility: Gamekeepers and those in similar occupations who are in need, and their dependants.

Types of grants: One-off and recurrent grants according to need.

Annual grant total: In 2009 the trust had assets of £154,000 and an income of £31,000. Welfare grants were made totalling £8,400.

Applications: On a form available from the correspondent or through the website. Applications can be made at any time.

Correspondent: Helen M J Benson, Keepers Cottage, Tanfield Lodge, West Tanfield, Ripon, North Yorkshire HG4 5LE (01677 470180; email: gamekeeperwtrust@btinternet.com; website: thegamekeeperswelfaretrust.com)

Other information: The trust also makes grants for educational purposes (£1,100 in 2009).

Kent Farmers Benevolent Fund

Eligibility: People who have been engaged in agriculture and their dependants who are in need. Beneficiaries must have a connection with Kent.

Types of grants: Grants given according to need.

Annual grant total: About £1,500.

Applications: In writing to the correspondent.

Correspondent: Simon Palmer, Trustee, Somerfield House, 59 London Road, Maidstone, Kent, ME16 8JH

The Royal Agricultural Benevolent Institution

Eligibility: Farmers and farm workers who are retired and over 60 years old and their families who are in need and have worked in the industry for at least 10 years. Although, age and years in the industry may be waived if the applicant has been forced to give up work due to illness or disability.

There is an emergency fund available for working farmers and farm workers who are experiencing financial hardship and exceptionally difficult circumstances.

Types of grants: One-off grants and regular financial assistance. Grants can be given towards white goods, disability equipment, TVs and licences, telephone rental, lifelines, help in the home, care home fees, replacement boilers and so on. Emergency relief is available for essential domestic expenses in times of financial difficulty. A significant number of emergency grants have been made recently to assist farmers who have struggled with flooding, foot and mouth and the subsequent movement restrictions imposed.

The institution can also pay for temporary help on the farm if the individual or an immediate dependant is seriously ill or has an accident.

Exclusions: No grants can be given towards business debts and expenses, medical expenses or private education costs.

Annual grant total: In 2008 the institution had assets of £37 million and an income of £5.2 million. Grants were made to over 1,600 individuals totalling £1.3 million.

Applications: Applications can be made by telephoning 01865 727888 or by letter or email to the correspondent either directly by the individual or through a social worker, Citizens Advice or other third party.

All new applicants for regular assistance will be visited by one of the institution's regional welfare offices. The grants committee meets every six weeks to consider applications, though emergency needs can be met immediately.

Correspondent: Welfare Team, Shaw House, 27 West Way, Oxford OX2 0QH (01865 724931; fax: 01865 202025; email: welfare@rabi.org.uk; website: www.rabi.org.uk)

Other information: The institution also operates two residential homes, one in Bury St Edmunds and one in Burnham on Sea and also associated sheltered flats for older members of the farming community.

The Timber Trades Benevolent Society

Eligibility: People engaged in the timber trade in the UK for at least 10 years, and their dependants, who are in need.

Types of grants: One-off grants towards car adaptations for disabled use, funeral costs, domestic appliances, house repairs, essential car maintenance and so on.

The trust also runs a television scheme, which makes payments to cover TV rental and licences, and a telephone rental scheme. A 'winter warmer' allowance has also been available in recent years to help with fuel bills.

Exclusions: No grants are made towards care or nursing home fees. The society will not support furniture manufacturers and carpenters servicing the building trade.

Annual grant total: In 2009 the society had assets of £2.1 million and an income of £178,000. Grants were made totalling £108,000 and were distributed as follows:

Allowances	£36,000
Spring gifts to beneficiaries and grantees	£5,200
Christmas gifts to beneficiaries and grantees	£16,000
Television rental and licences	£4,600
Telephone rental	£14,000
Holidays	£500
Winter warmer	£28,000
Individual grants	£4,400

Applications: On a form available from the correspondent. Applications can be submitted directly by the individual or through a social worker, Citizens Advice, welfare agency or other third party. They are considered on a regular basis.

Correspondent: Malcolm Job, General Manager, 31 Chelthorn Way, Solihull B91 3FW (08448 922205; email: info@ttbs.org.uk)

Airline pilots

The British Airline Pilots' Association Benevolent Fund (BALPA)

Eligibility: Serving and retired commercial pilots, flight engineers and navigators who are or have been members of BALPA, and their dependants.

Types of grants: One-off and recurrent grants and interest-free loans. The fund prefers to give grants for specific needs such as electricity bills, school books for children and so on.

Exclusions: Grants are not given for school fees.

Annual grant total: In 2009 the trust had an income of £515,000. The trust made grants of approximately £4,100 and gave about £27,000 in interest-free loans.

Applications: In writing to the correspondent requesting an application form. Applications are considered quarterly.

Correspondent: Sue Christie, BALPA House, 5 Heathrow Boulevard, 278 Bath Road, West Drayton, UB7 0DQ (020 8476 4000; fax: 020 8476 4077; email: balpa@balpa.org)

The Guild of Air Pilots Benevolent Fund

Eligibility: Members of the guild and those who have been engaged professionally as air pilots or air navigators in commercial aviation and their dependants.

Types of grants: One-off and recurrent grants ranging between £250 and £2,000. Loans can also be made to assist in the rehabilitation of people after accidents or to enable them to regain licences. The guild does not grant money for the repayment of debts or long-term expenses such as school fees or prolonged medical care.

Exclusions: Training and higher education are not usually supported.

Annual grant total: In 2008/09 the guild had assets of £603,000 and an income of £40,000. Scholarships totalling approximately £42,000 were made to seven individuals and a further £6,800 was given in 'regular and occasional' welfare grants.

Applications: On a form available from the website, including details of the individual's financial situation and proof of an aviation career. Applications are considered in January, April, July and October. The fund has helpers and visitors who can assist applicants fill in the form. The trust attaches great importance to the comments and recommendations of helpers.

Correspondent: Chris Ford, Almoner, Cobham House, 9 Warwick Court, Gray's Inn, London WC1R 5DJ (020 7404 4032; fax: 020 7404 4035; email: gapan@gapan.org; website: www.gapan.org)

Other information: The fund works closely with the other aviation trusts for individuals (both military and civilian). If an applicant has approached another such trust, they should say so in their application to this fund.

Antiques

The British Antique Dealers' Association Benevolent Fund

Eligibility: Members and former members of the association who are in need, and their dependants.

Types of grants: One-off or recurrent grants ranging from £100 to £2,000 for needs such as assistance with household bills.

Annual grant total: Grants usually total around £5,000 a year.

Applications: On a form available from the correspondent. Applicants should provide two references from members or former members of the association. Applications are considered on a regular basis.

Correspondent: Mark Dodgson, 20 Rutland Gate, London SW7 1BD (020 7589 4128; fax: 020 7581 9083)

Architecture

The Architects' Benevolent Society

Eligibility: People engaged or formerly engaged in the practice of architecture, and their dependants. This includes (but is not limited to) architects, assistants, technicians and technologists and landscape architects.

Types of grants: Recurrent grants, one-off grants and loans.

Exclusions: No educational grants.

Annual grant total: In 2008/09 the society had assets of £19 million and an income of £1 million. Grants and gifts were made to 301 individuals totalling £475,000

Applications: A short application form is available from the correspondent or to download from the website. Applications can be submitted directly by the individual or through a social worker, Citizens Advice or other welfare agency. Once received, the society will arrange a visit by one of their welfare officers. Applications are considered throughout the year.

Correspondent: Keith Robinson, Charity Secretary, 43 Portland Place, London W1B 1QH (020 7580 2823; fax: 020 7580 7075; email: help@absnet.org.uk; website: www.absnet.org.uk)

Other information: The society also provides sheltered accommodation.

Arts

The Artists' General Benevolent Institution

Eligibility: Professional artists, i.e. painters, sculptors, designers, who live in England, Wales and Northern Ireland whose work has been known to the public for some time. Artists widows/widowers and orphans are also supported.

Types of grants: One-off and recurrent grants to artists who through old age, illness or accident are unable to work and earn. Grants cover a wide range of items and uses, such as domestic and utility bills, repair of equipment or replacement of worn-out items, help to cover costs of car replacements, visits to family and friends and respite care.

Exclusions: The fund cannot help with career or legal difficulties, or (except in exceptional circumstances) student fees.

Annual grant total: In 2008/09 the fund had assets of £8.2 million and an income of £707,000. Grants were made to 135 individuals totalling £529,000.

Applications: Applications should initially be in writing, including a full CV listing all exhibitions in professional galleries and teaching experience (if any) at GCSE, A-level or higher education. They can be submitted directly by the individual, or through a recognised referral agency (Citizens Advice, doctor, social worker and so on). Appropriate applicants will then receive a form which they will need to complete. The trust visits most potential beneficiaries.

The council meets eight times a year to consider applications.

Correspondent: April Connett-Dance, Secretary, Burlington House, Piccadilly, London W1J 0BB (020 7734 1193; website: www.agbi.org.uk/)

Other information: The fund's website is currently very basic but is due to be expanded in the near future.

The Entertainment Artistes' Benevolent Fund

Eligibility: Entertainment artistes (that is professional performers in variety, pantomime, revue, circus, concert party, cabaret, clubs, television, radio, making of records and light entertainment in general), and their dependants.

Types of grants: Regular allowances and one-off grants for gas, electricity and fuel bills, medical and nursing needs, television licences and rentals, household repairs and telephone bills. Help may also be given with funeral costs.

Annual grant total: In 2008 the fund had assets of £2.1 million, an income of £2.7 million and a total expenditure of £2 million. Grants were made totalling £78,000.

Applications: On a form available from the correspondent. Applications can be made directly or through a social worker or welfare agency. They are considered on a regular basis.

Correspondent: Roger Kitter, Executive Administrator, Brinsworth House, 72 Staines Road, Twickenham TW2 5AL (020 8898 8164; fax: 020 8894 0093; email: peter@eabf.org.uk; website: www.eabf.org.uk)

Other information: The fund has its own home for older entertainment artistes in need of care.

Equity Trust Fund

Eligibility: Professional performers (under Equity or ITC contracts), stage managers and directors, and their dependants.

Types of grants: One-off grants for almost any welfare need.

Exclusions: No grants to amateur performers, musicians or drama students.

Annual grant total: In 2008/09 the fund had assets of £6.4 million and an income of £362,000. Grants were made to individuals and one organisation, with the majority of grants being made to individuals.

Applications: On a form available from the correspondent. Meetings are scheduled to take place every six weeks. For further details please contact the Welfare Case Worker, Miranda Connell (email: m.connell@equitytrustfund.org.uk).

Correspondent: Keith Carter, Secretary, Plouviez House, 19–20 Hatton Place, London, EC1N 8RU (020 7831 1926; email: keith@equitytrustfund.org.uk; website: www.equitytrustfund.org.uk)

Grand Order of Water Rats Charities Fund

Eligibility: People, and their dependants, who have been involved in a theatrical profession for at least seven years and are in need.

Types of grants: One-off and recurrent grants according to need.

Exclusions: No grants are given towards students' fees, education, taxes, overdrafts, credit card bills or bank loans.

Annual grant total: In 2008 the fund had assets of £1.4 million and an income of £245,000. Grants totalled £66,000 and were distributed as follows:

Donations	£19,000
Monthly allowances, grants and gifts	£45,000
Fruit and flowers	£2,400

Applications: In writing to the correspondent, including a CV of professional career. The trustees meet monthly to consider applications.

Correspondent: John Adrian, Secretary to the Trustees, 328 Gray's Inn Road, London WC1X 8BZ (020 7407 8007; fax: 020 7403 8610; email: charities@gowr.net; website: www.gowr.net)

Other information: From time to time the fund may also grant a general one-off payment to organisations or individuals who the trustees feel are in need of assistance.

The Evelyn Norris Trust

Eligibility: Members or ex-members of the concert or theatrical profession who are older, sick, disabled or in need.

Types of grants: One-off grants of up to £700 towards convalescence or recuperative holidays following illness, injury or surgery.

Exclusions: No grants for student/education course fees.

Annual grant total: In 2009 the trust had assets of £543,000 and an income of £29,000. Grants were made to 26 individuals totalling £18,000.

Applications: On a form available from the correspondent. Applications are considered monthly and can be submitted directly by the individual or through a social worker, Citizens Advice, welfare agency or any third party. Applications should include any relevant financial or personal information.

Correspondent: Keith Carter, Plouviez House, 19–20 Hatton Place, London, EC1N 8RU (020 7831 1926)

The Royal Opera House Benevolent Fund

Eligibility: People who work, or have worked, for the Royal Opera House or Birmingham Royal Ballet, and their widows, widowers, partners or children. Applicants must have savings of less than £10,000 if single and £15,000 if married. Please note: applicants do not have to have contributed to the fund in order to receive help.

Types of grants: Grants range from £50 per month to £3,000 as a one-off grant. Monthly allowances are towards food and clothing. One-off grants are towards essential home maintenance, domestic equipment, urgent medical costs, education, holidays and so on. Interest-free loans are also available.

Annual grant total: In 2008/09 the fund had assets of £5.4 million and an income of £208,000. There were 51 grants made to individuals totalling £103,000.

Applications: On a form available from the correspondent, providing details of income and expenditure. They should be submitted directly by the individual for consideration on receipt.

Correspondent: David Pilcher, Royal Opera House, Covent Garden, London WC2E 9DD (020 7212 9128; email: ben.fund@roh.org.uk)

The Scottish Artists' Benevolent Association

Eligibility: Scottish artists in need and their dependants.

Types of grants: Regular or one-off grants according to need and single payments can also be made to cover emergency situations. Grants are mainly given to people who are older or in poor health.

Annual grant total: In 2009/10 the association had an income of £29,000. Grants usually total about £30,000.

Applications: On a form available from the correspondent to be submitted directly by the individual.

Correspondent: G C McAllister, 2nd Floor, 5 Oswald Street, Glasgow G1 4QR (0141 248 7411)

Other information: The association also administrates the Gertroude Annie Leuder Trust which distributes grants to female artists. Those interested in further information should contact the correspondent.

The Show Business Benevolent Fund

Eligibility: Members of the Show Business Association who are in need, and their dependants, including widows/widowers. Emergency help may also be given to non-members through the W F Frame Fund.

Types of grants: One-off and recurrent grants towards clothing, fuel, living expenses, funeral costs, TV rental and licences and holidays to Blackpool.

Annual grant total: No recent financial information was available. In previous years grants have totalled about £50,000.

Applications: In writing to the correspondent.

Correspondent: T Davies Brock, Administrator, Royal Bank Buildings, 55 Main Street, Callander, Perthshire FK17 8DZ (01877 330033; fax: 01877 331248; email: info@ssbf.co.uk; website: www.ssbf.co.uk/)

Other information: The fund administers two smaller funds: the Mozart Allan Benevolent Fund (SC004768) and the W. F. Frame Benevolent Fund (SC008402).

The Mozart Allan Fund makes grants to members of the Show Business Fund and their dependants for convalescence and home comforts.

The W F Frame Fund grants emergency relief to people who have been connected with the entertainment profession. A maximum of £250 per year is available.

Arts – Dance

The Dance Teachers' Benevolent Fund

Eligibility: Dance teachers or ex-dance teachers who are experiencing short or long-term hardship.

Types of grants: Grants of £100 to £1,000 are usually awarded as 'disregard allowance', clothing grants or assistance with home improvements. Other possibilities could be considered. No grants are given towards training.

Annual grant total: In 2008/09 the fund had assets of £353,000 and an income of £31,000. Grants made to individuals totalled £7,000.

Applications: On a form available from the correspondent. Forms can be submitted by the individual or any third party, and are considered all year.

Correspondent: Miss Laura Jane Lavender, Rostron & Partners, Saint Peter's House, 23 Cattle Market Street, Norwich NR1 3DY (01603 619 166; email: dtbf@rostron.com)

The International Dance Teachers' Association Benevolent Fund

Eligibility: Members and former members of the association, other dancers, former dancers, teachers or former teachers of dance, employees or former employees of the association, and their dependants who are affected by hardship.

Types of grants: One-off grants ranging from £100 to £5,000. 'Grants are made of a benevolent nature for people in need during times of crisis or ill health. Grants are not for the purpose of developing career training or prospects.'

Annual grant total: In 2007 grants were made to 34 individuals totalling £28,000. Recent accounts have not been filed with the Charity Commission.

Applications: In writing to the correspondent.

Correspondent: Keith Holmes, Chief Executive, International House, 76 Bennett Road, Brighton BN2 5JL (01273 685652; fax: 01273 674388; email: info@idta.co.uk; website: www.idta.co.uk)

The Royal Ballet Benevolent Fund

Eligibility: Dancers and ex-dancers who have been members of UK repertory ballet and contemporary dance companies for at least seven years, unless illness or injury has forced early withdrawal. In special cases, the dependants of such people after their death.

Types of grants: One-off grants and regular payments are available to relieve any form of hardship. This includes financial assistance to older people on a low income, aids for people with a disability, help with the transition from dance to another career, or specialist surgery/therapy for injured dancers.

Exclusions: There are no grants available for students training to be dancers.

Annual grant total: In 2008/09 the fund had assets of £3.1 million and an income of £199,000. Grants were made to 56 individuals totalling £92,000.

Applications: On a form available from the correspondent or to download from the website. Applications should be submitted directly by the individual and include evidence of expenditure such as electricity and heating bills. The trustees meet to consider applications in March, June, September and December.

Correspondent: Clementine Cowl, Executive Secretary, Royal Opera House, Covent Garden, London WC2E 9DD (01273 626547; email: info@rbbf.org.uk; website: www.rbbf.org.uk)

Arts – Magic

The Magic Circle Benevolent Fund

Eligibility: Members/former members of the Magic Circle and their dependants.

Types of grants: One-off grants according to need.

Annual grant total: Grants average around £2,500 a year.

Applications: In writing to the correspondent either directly by the individual or by a third party. They can be considered at any time.

Correspondent: Fund Secretary, The Centre for the Magic Arts, 12 Stephenson Way, London NW1 2HD (020 7387 2222)

Arts – Music

The Concert Artistes' Association Benevolent Fund

Eligibility: Members of the association, and their dependants, who are in need. Applicants must have held their membership for at least two years (or five years if over 40 at the time of joining).

Types of grants: One-off and recurrent grants according to need. Recent grants have been given towards the payment of household bills, dentures, hearing aids, glasses, disability equipment and electrical goods. Monthly grants may also be made to pensioners.

Annual grant total: In 2008/09 the fund had both an income and a total expenditure of £19,000.

Applications: On a form available from the correspondent: to be submitted directly by the individual. Applications are considered on an ongoing basis.

Correspondent: Pamela Cundell, Trustee, 13 Holmdene Avenue, London, NW7 2LY (020 8959 3154)

The English National Opera Benevolent Fund

Eligibility: People who are or have been employed by the English National Opera and/or Sadlers Wells Companies.

Types of grants: Applicants for recurrent grants must be over 58 years old and grants 'would normally be to reimburse telephone, TV and insurance costs with small monthly cash payments or to reimburse such. One-off support is considered on a case by case basis'. Grants range between £150 and £3,000.

Medical/dental treatment is not normally supported, except where delay would affect a performing career. The fund will help with payments for treatment which is not generally available through the NHS.

Annual grant total: In 2008/09 the trust had assets of £278,000 and an income of £48,000. Grants were made to 16 individuals totalling £26,000.

Applications: Submitted directly by the individual on a form available from the correspondent, to be considered in March, June, September and December.

Correspondent: Humayun S Ahmed, ENO Benevolent Fund, London Coliseum, 38 St Martin's Lane, London WC2N 4ES (020 7845 9252; email: hahmed@eno.org)

The Incorporated Association of Organists' Benevolent Fund

Eligibility: Organists and/or choirmasters who are members/former members of any association or society affiliated to the Incorporated Association of Organists, and their dependants, who are in need.

Types of grants: Regular grants of around £20 per week and occasional one-off payments for specific items. Occasional help is given for music tuition, especially pipe organ tuition, for members' children.

Annual grant total: In 2009 the trust had assets of £225,000 and an income of £16,000. Grants were made to 14 individuals totalling £15,000.

Applications: On a form available from the correspondent. Applications can be made by the individual or through the secretary of the local organists' association. They should be submitted by 31 March for consideration at the trustees' annual meeting in May. In urgent cases the secretary may obtain approval at other times.

Correspondent: Michael Whitehall, 180 Lynn Road, Wisbech, Cambridgeshire PE13 3EB (01945 463826; email: michael@whitehalls.plus.com; website: www.iao.org.uk)

ISM Members' Fund (The Benevolent Fund of The Incorporated Society of Musicians)

Eligibility: Members and former members of the society and their dependants who are in need.

Types of grants: One-off and recurrent grants according to need.

Exclusions: No grants towards professional training.

Annual grant total: In 2008/09 the society had assets of £3 million and an income of £157,000. Grants were made to 61 individuals totalling £80,000.

Applications: On a form available from the correspondent, to be submitted directly by the individual at any time.

Correspondent: Deborah Annetts, 10 Stratford Place, London, W1C 1AA (020 7629 4413; email: membership@ism.org)

The Musicians Benevolent Fund

Eligibility: Professional musicians, and people who work, or have worked, in a closely related occupation who are in need as a result of old age, poor health, accident or other misfortune. Applicants must be UK citizens.

Types of grants: Grants range from small single payments for items such as telephones and TV licences to more substantial sums to help with medical costs, re-training, motoring and holiday costs. Regular grants are also available to support, for example, individuals in residential care. The fund will occasionally offer loans to assist with paying off debts or house adaptations.

Annual grant total: In 2008 the fund had assets of £37 million, an income of £4.8 million and a total expenditure of £5.5 million. Benevolence grants were made totalling £1.8 million. A further £449,000 was given in grants to organisations.

Applications: On a form available on request by calling the free helpline number: 0800 082 6700. Applications should be submitted directly by the individual and can be considered at any time. Potential beneficiaries are usually visited to discuss their circumstances and specific needs.

Correspondent: Sara Dixon, Director of Casework, 7–11 Britannia Street, London WC1X 9JS (020 7239 9100 or 0800 082 6700 (Helpline); fax: 020 7713 8942; email: helpline@helpmusicians.org.uk; website: www.helpmusicians.org.uk/)

Other information: The fund runs the Ivor Newton residential home in Bromley, Kent. It also provides educational grants for outstanding young musicians towards the cost of their musical development.

Musicians' Social & Benevolent Council

Eligibility: Musicians who are or were members of the London branches of the Musicians' Union who are facing sickness or distress. Members of other branches who have performed for a long run in London, such as the West End, are also eligible.

Types of grants: Monthly grants of £20 are given to older, retired members. One-off grants of up to £170 are available to any members in need.

Annual grant total: Grants average around £12,000 a year.

Applications: In writing to the correspondent, including the musicians' union branch and membership number. Applications should be submitted directly by the individual or by spouse or friend.

Correspondent: Geraldine Chalmers, 100a Weston Park, London N8 9PP (020 8348 9358)

The Organists' Benevolent League

Eligibility: Organists, and their dependants, who are in financial difficulties.

Types of grants: One-off grants ranging between £500 and £1,000.

Annual grant total: In 2009 the league had an income of £15,000 and a total expenditure of £11,000. Grants totalled around £10,000.

Applications: On a form available from the correspondent. Applications can be submitted directly by the individual or through a third party such as a social worker. They are considered at any time. Repeat applications are welcomed.

Correspondent: The Trustees, 10 Stratford Place, London W1C 1BA (0208 318 1471; email: secretary@organistscharitabletrust.org)

The Performing Right Society Members' Fund

Eligibility: Songwriters and composers of music who are or were members of the Performing Right Society, and their dependants.

Types of grants: The fund offers a variety of grants and loans:

- Special needs grants: one-off grants to elderly or disabled members towards, for example, essential property repairs or the replacement of domestic equipment.
- Regular grants: up to £20 per week to help members who are receiving benefits but still unable to maintain

basic standards of living. Help may also be given towards telephone and TV rental, TV licences and holidays.

- Holiday grants: provide help to elderly members who would otherwise be unable to afford a holiday.
- Short term loans: to help with an unexpected financial crisis.

Exclusions: No grants towards: the cost of buying a home; the promotion costs of any commercial venture; supporting composers who don't have any other employment; payments as an advance against future royalties.

Annual grant total: Usually grants to individuals total about £200,000.

Applications: On a form available from the correspondent or to download from the website. Applications can be submitted by the individual, through a social worker, Citizens Advice or other welfare agency, or by next of kin or associate. In cases of claims based on illness, a medical or GP's report is required.

Correspondent: John Logan, General Secretary, 29–33 Berners Street, London W1T 3AB (020 7306 4067; fax: 020 7306 4453; email: john.logan@ prsformusic.com; website: www. prsformusicfund.com)

The Royal Society of Musicians of Great Britain

Eligibility: Professional musicians and their families who are in need because of illness, accident or age. Membership of the society is not a requirement.

Types of grants: One-off grants from £50 to £5,000.

Exclusions: No grants are given to students or people whose only claim for relief arises from unemployment.

Annual grant total: In 2008/09 the society had assets of £13 million and an income of £689,000. Grants were made to individuals totalling £365,000.

Applications: On a form available from the correspondent. Enquiries from welfare organisations are welcomed as is the identification of need from any concerned individual. An application for financial assistance should have the support of a member, honorary member or officer of the society. A copy of the current membership list is supplied to applicants. Applications are considered monthly.

Correspondent: Maggie Gibb, Secretary, 10 Stratford Place, London W1C 1BA (020 7629 6137; fax: 020 7629 6137; website: royalsocietyofmusicians.co.uk/)

Other information: Specialist advice is also available from honorary officers, which include medical consultants.

Arts – Painting

The Eaton Fund for Artists, Nurses & Gentlewomen *see entry on page 39*

Arts – Theatre

The Actors' Benevolent Fund

Eligibility: Members of the theatrical profession, which includes actors and actresses, theatrical stage managers and people who have sung or spoken words professionally on the stage in English, including chorus singers whose efforts are devoted entirely to theatrical work, their spouses and dependants.

Types of grants: Recurrent grants of up to £30 per week (to be reviewed every 13 or 26 weeks). One-off grants are given for furniture, wheelchairs, convalescence, nursing home fees, household equipment and minor home adaptations. Help is also available for TV licence bills, insurance costs, phone bills and transport costs.

Exclusions: No grants are available to students. Grants are unlikely to be made for credit card debts, loans or private dental or medical treatment, which should be covered by the NHS, although the trust will consider such applications.

Annual grant total: In 2008 the fund had assets of £11 million and an income of £826,000. Grants were made to over 190 individuals totalling £385,000.

Applications: On a form available from the correspondent or on the fund's website. Applications should be submitted directly by the individual and include a photograph and detailed CV. If applying due to ill health or an accident, a recent doctor's letter giving details of the individual's condition should be included. It may also be helpful to include any Benefit Agency letters which confirm the level of benefits received. Applications are considered on the last Thursday of each month and forms should be submitted by the Friday before a meeting.

In cases of emergency, where potential beneficiaries need their application to be considered before the next scheduled meeting please contact the fund's office on 0207 836 6378 for advice.

Correspondent: Willie Bicket, 6 Adam Street, London WC2N 6AD (020 7836 6378; fax: 020 7836 8978; email: office@abf.org.uk; website: www. actorsbenevolentfund.co.uk)

The Actors' Charitable Trust (TACT)

Eligibility: Children (aged under 21) of professional actors who are in financial need. Please note: the trust cannot help those who have solely worked in variety, amateur dramatics or as an extra.

Types of grants: One off and recurrent grants of up to £1,200 for help with essential furnishings, utility bills (where this will benefit the children), holidays, childcare costs, clothing and special equipment. Additional grants at Christmas and crisis grants are also available.

Exclusions: Grants are not usually given for private school fees, however, the trust may consider making a grant if private education would be beneficial to the child i.e. due to special educational needs or family situation.

Annual grant total: In 2008/09 the trust had assets of £4.8 million and an income of £385,000. Grants to 111 families with 176 children between them totalled £233,000.

Applications: On a form available from the correspondent or to download from the website. Applications can be considered at any time and can be submitted either by the individual or a parent. Telephone and email enquiries are welcomed.

Correspondent: Robert Ashby, The Actors Charitable Trust, 58 Bloomsbury Street, London, WC1B 3QT (020 7636 7868; email: robert@tactactors.org; website: www.tactactors.org)

Other information: The Actors' Charitable Trust also offer nursing, residential, dementia and palliative care to those over 70 from the acting profession in Denville Hall, which they have run since 1965.

The Royal Theatrical Fund

Eligibility: People in need who have professionally practised or contributed to the theatrical arts (on stage, radio, film or television or any other medium) for a minimum of seven years, and the relief of families or dependants of such people.

Types of grants: One-off and recurrent grants of £250 to £3,000 are given towards domestic bills, monthly allowances, shortfall in nursing and residential fees, car tax, insurance, TV licences and so on.

Exclusions: No grants are made to students or towards courses or projects.

Annual grant total: In 2008/09 the fund had assets of £5.2 million and an income of £430,000. Welfare grants amounted to £272,000.

Applications: On a form available from the correspondent or to download from the website. Applications can be submitted at any time and should include a CV and a medical letter if appropriate. The welfare committee meets on the first Wednesday of each month except August to consider applications. Telephone enquiries are welcome.

Correspondent: Roslyn Margot Foster, Secretary, West Suite, 2nd Floor, 11 Garrick Street, London WC2E 9AR (020 7836 3322; fax: 020 7379 8273; email: admin@trtf.com; website: www.trtf.com)

The Theatrical Guild

Eligibility: People who work either backstage or front-of-house in a professional theatre and are pensioners or have retired due to accident or ill health. In special cases, support may be given to working members of the profession and to one-parent families who are prevented from accepting a job due to the cost of childcare.

Types of grants: Regular grants to retired members of the profession to enable them to maintain their independence; assistance with nursing fees and shortfalls in nursing/residential home fees; emergency child care grants to help one-parent families (limited to six weeks); and one-off payments to help with better heating, provide necessary appliances or to help out in any emergencies.

Exclusions: No grants are given for the repayment of credit card debt or to students.

Annual grant total: In 2009 the trust had assets of £1 million and an income of £108,000. Grants were made to 57 individuals totalling £54,000.

Applications: Application forms can be requested in writing or downloaded from the website. Applications can be submitted either directly by the individual, through a third party such as a social worker or through an organisation such as a Citizens Advice. They are considered monthly.

Correspondent: Karen Nichols, Chief Administrator, Ambassadors Theatre, West Street, London WC2H 9ND (020 7395 5460; email: admin@ttg.org.uk; website: www.ttg.org.uk)

Arts – Writing

The Authors' Contingency Fund

Eligibility: Professional authors in the UK and their dependants.

Types of grants: One-off grants of between £500 and £750 to relieve a temporary financial emergency.

Exclusions: The trust cannot help with the following:

- grants to cover publication costs
- grants to authors who are in financial difficulty through contributing towards publication costs

- tuition fees
- general support whilst writing a book.

Annual grant total: In 2008 the trust had an income of £18,000 and a total expenditure of £9,300.

Applications: On a form available from the correspondent or to download from the website, including information about the applicant's circumstances. Applications can be submitted directly by the individual and are considered on receipt. The assessment process usually takes around three weeks.

Correspondent: Sarah Baxter, The Society of Authors, 84 Drayton Gardens, London SW10 9SB (020 7373 6642; email: sbaxter@societyofauthors.org; website: www.societyofauthors.org)

Francis Head Award

Eligibility: Professional writers (writing in the English language) who were born in the UK and are over the age of 35. The focus of the trust is primarily on those who are temporarily unable to support themselves or their dependants due to illness or accident.

Types of grants: Emergency grants ranging from £1,000 to £2,000.

Exclusions: No grants are given to cover publication costs, tuition fees or general maintenance whilst writing a book. Support is also unavailable to authors who are in financial difficultly because they have invested money in publication costs.

Annual grant total: In 2008 charity had assets of £534,000 and an income of £26,000. Grants were made to ten authors totalling £13,000.

Applications: On a form available from the correspondent or to download from the trust's website. Applications can be submitted directly by the individual and should include a covering letter explaining the circumstances prompting the application. A decision is usually made within three weeks.

Correspondent: Sarah Baxter, 84 Drayton Gardens, London SW10 9SB (020 7373 6642; fax: 020 7373 5768; email: sbaxter@societyofauthors.org; website: www.societyofauthors.org)

Peggy Ramsay Foundation

Eligibility: Writers for the stage who have been produced publicly, are 'of promise' and are in need of time to write which they cannot afford, or are in need of other assistance. Applicants must live in the British Isles (including Republic of Ireland and the Channel Islands).

Types of grants: One-off grants. Individual awards rarely exceed £5,000 for writing time or £1,000 for word processors.

Exclusions: No grants towards production costs or to writers who have not been produced. Drama students or other artists

learning their trade are not supported, just experienced writers who could not otherwise follow their career. No grants are made for writing not intended for the theatre.

Annual grant total: In 2008 the foundation had assets of £4.1 million and an income of £270,000. There were 86 grants made to individuals totalling £190,000.

Applications: Apply by writing a short letter to the correspondent, submitted with a CV directly by the individual. Scripts and publicity material must not be included. Applications, which are always acknowledged, are considered four or five times a year.

Correspondent: G Laurence Harbottle, Trustee, Hanover House, 14 Hanover Square, London W1S 1HP (020 7667 5000; fax: 020 7667 5100; email: laurence.harbottle@harbottle.com; website: www.peggyramsayfoundation.org)

Other information: Grants were also made to organisations totalling £28,000.

The Royal Literary Fund

Eligibility: Authors of published work of literary merit and their dependants. The work must be written in English. Books stemming from a parallel career as an academic or practitioner are not eligible.

Types of grants: Awards range between £3,000 and £10,000. Most grants are an outright grant which means that there can be no reapplication within three years. Pensions run for five years and are then renewable according to circumstances. In special circumstances the trust gives interim grants which allow reapplication after one year.

Recent examples of beneficiaries include: (a) an older lady living on a low income who received a grant of £3,000 plus £20 per week for three years and (b) a writer living overseas recovering from a severe stroke who received a grant of £10,000.

Exclusions: No grants for projects or work in progress. The trust does not make loans.

Annual grant total: In 2008/09 grants and pensions amounted to £1.5 million.

Applications: On a form available from the correspondent, including details of all income and expenditure. Applicants are asked to supply copies of their published work which is then read by two members of the committee who decide on the question of literary merit. If this is approved, a grant/pension may be made based on an assessment of need. A home visit may also be arranged.

Correspondent: Eileen Gunn, Chief Executive, 3 Johnson's Court, off Fleet Street, London EC4A 3EA (020 7353 7159; email: egunnrlf@globalnet.co.uk; website: www.rlf.org.uk)

The Society of Authors Pension Fund

Eligibility: Authors over 65 who have been a member of the Society of Authors for at least 10 years.

Types of grants: Pensions of £1,500 a year are given.

Annual grant total: In 2009 the trust an income of £20,000 and a total expenditure of £24,000.

Applications: In writing to the correspondent when vacancies are announced in the society's journal.

Correspondent: The General Secretary, 84 Drayton Gardens, London SW10 9SB (020 7373 6642; fax: 020 7373 5768; email: info@societyofauthors.org; website: www.societyofauthors.org)

Atomic energy

UBA Benevolent Fund

Eligibility: Past and present members of the non-industrial staff of UKAEA, Amersham International plc and British Nuclear Fuels plc (or any successor organisation) and their dependants, who are in need. (Where single status has been adopted, all employees are eligible.) People who left the company as industrial employees are not eligible. Applicants do not need to have been a subscriber to the fund.

Types of grants: Allowances of between £5 and £20 per week. One-off grants are given for most purposes, except where this would affect state benefits. Interest-free loans against property and for serving officers are possible. Grants are given towards furniture, disability aids (stair lifts, wheelchairs, alarms and so on), holidays, nursing home fees, Christmas grants, television licences and sets, repairs, fuel bills (to prevent disconnection), telephone bills, removal costs, debts (in some cases), minor repairs and child minding.

Exclusions: Grants are not given for private health care (excluding convalescence and residential home fees) or private education.

Annual grant total: In 2008/09 the fund had assets of £2.5 million and an income of £102,000. Grants were made totalling £27,000, a decrease of £19,000 on the previous year.

Applications: On a form available from the correspondent. Applications may be channelled through the network of local representatives, located at or near the organisations' sites, direct to the fund's office, or through other charities or similar bodies. They are considered every two months from January onwards.

Correspondent: Marie Sims, Unit CU1, Warrington Business Park, Long Lane, Warrington, WA2 8TX (01925 633 005; fax: 01925 633 455; email: info@ubabenfund.com)

Banking, finance and insurance

The Bankers Benevolent Fund

Eligibility: People in need who are working or who have worked in a bank in the UK, and their families and dependants.

Types of grants: Regular grant payments for those on limited incomes; limited help with residential and nursing home fees; contributions towards the cost of wheelchairs, scooters, mobility aids and domestic appliances; carer's respite breaks and some family holidays; in special cases, assistance with telephone bills and TV licenses; grants towards house repairs and maintenance.

Exclusions: No grants for non-priority debts, private medical fees or home improvements, except when essential repairs are needed to ensure independent living, safety and security.

Annual grant total: In 2008/09 the trust had assets of £35 million and an income of £1.3 million. A total of £645,000 was given in welfare grants to individuals.

Applications: On a form available from the correspondent or to download from the website. Once the form has been received it will be reviewed by staff. Additional contact may be required to obtain further information or clarification. The trustees meet quarterly to consider new cases.

Correspondent: The Clerk, Pinners Hall, 105–108 Old Broad Street, London EC2N 1EX (020 7216 8981; email: info@bbfund.org.uk; website: www.bbfund.org.uk)

Other information: The trust also makes grants to children and students for educational purposes (£623,000 in 2008/09).

The Chartered Institute of Loss Adjusters Benevolent Fund

Eligibility: Members of the institute and their dependants who are 'distressed through sickness or other misfortune'.

Types of grants: One-off and recurrent grants according to need. Recent grants have been given to people diagnosed with terminal illnesses.

Annual grant total: In 2008/09 the trust had an income of £15,000 and a total expenditure of £2,400.

Applications: In writing to the correspondent. If a member passes away, the fund notifies his/her partner of the financial assistance available.

Correspondent: Executive Director, Warwick House, 65/66 Queen Street, London EC4R 1EB (020 7337 9960; fax: 020 7929 3082; email: info@cila.co.uk; website: www.cila.co.uk)

The Alfred Foster Settlement

Eligibility: Employees and former employees of banks and their dependants who are in need.

Types of grants: One-off grants according to need.

Annual grant total: In 2008/09 the trust had an income of £33,000 and a total expenditure of £26,000. Charitable expenditure came to £15,000.

Applications: By the employee's bank, to their local regional office or directly to the correspondent.

Correspondent: Robin Taylor, Barclays Bank Trust Co. Ltd, Executorship & Trustee Service, Osborne Court, Gadbrook Park, Rudheath, Northwich CW9 7UE, CW9 7UE (01606 313173)

Other information: The trust also makes grants to individuals for educational purposes.

The Insurance Charities – The Orphans' Fund

Eligibility: Children of people who have spent at least five years working in the insurance industry in UK or Eire. Adult children of insurance people can be considered where personal resources are insufficient to meet reasonable expenditure.

Types of grants: Ongoing grants and interest-free or low interest loans towards day-to-day expenses and one-off grants towards special needs such as domestic appliances, disability aids and property maintenance. Help is also given to students on first degree courses.

Annual grant total: In 2008/09 the charities had assets of £19 million and an income of £1.6 million. Grants were made totalling £807,000. A further £120,000 was given through the Paul Golmick Fund.

Applications: An initial form can be completed online or downloaded from the website.

Correspondent: Mrs A J Thornicroft, 20 Aldermanbury, London EC2V 7HY (020 7606 3763; fax: 020 7600 1170; email: info@theinsurancecharities.org.uk; website: www.theinsurancecharities.org.uk)

Other information: The charities also make grants to past and present employees of the insurance industry experiencing financial hardship.

The Paul Golmick Fund is administered by the charities and was set up to promote the maintenance and education of children and young people under the age of 24, but primarily under the age of 18, who reside in the UK or Republic of Ireland and who have at least one parent or guardian with service to the insurance industry.

The Insurance Charities

Eligibility: Past and present employees of the insurance industry and their dependants experiencing financial hardship as a result of misfortune, who live in the UK or Eire. Applicants or dependent relatives must usually have spent five years in the insurance industry with service taking place not more than 10 years before retirement or another event prompting the application.

Types of grants: Grants or interest-free or low-interest loans towards day-to-day expenses or special needs such as domestic appliances, disability aids, property maintenance, therapy and holidays.

Annual grant total: In 2008/09 the charities had assets of £19 million and an income of £1.6 million. Grants were made totalling £807,000.

Applications: An initial form can be completed online or downloaded from the website.

Correspondent: Mrs A J Thornicroft, Secretary, 20 Aldermanbury, London EC2V 7HY (020 7606 3763; fax: 020 7600 1170; email: info@ theinsurancecharities.org.uk; website: www.theinsurancecharities.org. uk)

Other information: The charities also assist the children of insurance employees through the Orphan Fund.

The Lloyd's Benevolent Fund

Eligibility: People who work or have worked in the Lloyd's insurance market and their dependants, anywhere in the world.

Types of grants: Recurrent grants can be given towards relieving general hardship but not medical costs or school fees.

Annual grant total: In 2008/09 the trust had assets of £7.7 million and an income of £531,000. There were 31 grants made totalling £200,000.

Applications: On a form available from the correspondent. Applications can be submitted by the individual or through a social worker, Citizens Advice, other welfare agency or other third party. They are considered throughout the year.

Correspondent: Raymond G Blaber, c/o Lloyd's, 1 Lime Street, London EC3M 7HA (020 7327 6453)

UNITE the Union Benevolent Fund

Eligibility: Members, former members, employees or ex-employees of the union and their dependants.

Types of grants: One-off grants of between £100 and £1,000 to people who have fallen on hard times through being absent from work through prolonged sickness, retirement through ill-health, family bereavements or a change in domestic circumstances. Grants have included payment towards a riser/recliner for person with back problems, help to somebody dismissed while on sick leave, heating grants for older people, Christmas bonuses for people who are elderly or have young children, and general assistance with bills.

Exclusions: Help with legal fees, educational grants and credit card bills is not usually available.

Annual grant total: In 2008 the trust had an income of £40,000 and a total expenditure of £23,000. Grants were made to 28 individuals totalling £21,000.

Applications: On a form available from the correspondent or to download from the website. Applications are considered quarterly.

Correspondent: Stephen Skinner, UNITE, Hayes Court, West Common Road, Hayes, Bromley, BR2 7AU (020 8462 7755; fax: 020 8315 8537; email: stephen. skinner@unitetheunion.org; website: www. unitetheunion.org)

Book retail

The Book Trade Charity

Eligibility: People in need who have worked in the book trade in the UK for at least one year (normally publishing/ distribution/book-selling), and their dependants. Priority will be given to people who are chronically sick, redundant, unemployed or over 50 years of age.

Types of grants: One-off grants of up to £1,500 and recurrent grants of around £1,300 a year. Grants are normally to supplement weekly/monthly income and for recuperative holidays. Other support is given in a variety of ways, for example, assistance with telephone and television rental, medical aid, aids for disabled people and house repairs/redecoration. Grants are also given to help retrain people from the book trade who have been made redundant.

Annual grant total: Grants for welfare and medical costs usually total around £100,000 a year.

Applications: On a form available from the correspondent. Applications can be submitted by the individual or through a recognised referral agency (social worker, Citizens Advice, doctor and so on). They are considered as they arrive.

Correspondent: David Hicks, Chief Executive, The Foyle Centre, The Retreat, Abbots Road, Kings Langley, Hertfordshire WD4 8LT (01329848731; email: david@ btbs.org; website: www.booktradecharity. org/)

Building trade

Builders' Benevolent Institution

Eligibility: Those who are or who have been master builders (employers in the building industry), and their dependants. Applicants with less than 10 years experience are not eligible, nor are those who have been employees.

Types of grants: Mostly pensions and Christmas vouchers. Occasionally, the trust distributes one-off grants towards the cost of necessary items such as home alterations and urgent house repairs.

Annual grant total: In 2009 the institution had assets of £861,000 and an income of £93,000. Grants were made totalling £57,000 and were distributed as follows:

Pensions	£52,000
Christmas gift vouchers	£4,100
Temporary relief	£400

Applications: On a form available from the correspondent, submitted directly by the individual, through a social worker, Citizens Advice, other welfare agency or third party. Applications are considered throughout the year.

Correspondent: The Secretary, 147 Trevor Drive, Maidstone, Kent, ME16 0QL (01622 681997; email: bbi@fmb.org.uk)

The Chartered Institute of Building Benevolent Fund

Eligibility: Members of the institute and their dependants who are in real need.

Types of grants: One-off and recurrent grants towards, for example, computer equipment for a housebound individual, help for a family in general financial hardship and continuing support for a member following redundancy and ill-health.

Please note: the fund cannot allocate grants for academic study but it may be able to help members who are in circumstances of hardship to obtain specialised, skill-based training.

Annual grant total: In 2009 the fund had assets of £734,000 and an income of £166,000. Grants were made totalling £62,000.

Applications: In writing to the correspondent. Applications are considered as they arrive.

Correspondent: Franklin MacDonald, Secretary, Englemere, Kings Ride, Ascot, Berkshire SL5 7TB (01344 630780; fax: 01344 630777; email: fmacdonald@ciob.org.uk; website: www.ciob.org.uk)

Other information: A significant part of the charitable expenditure is spent on providing practical advice, information and advocacy. The fund also provides a guide called 'Fresh Start' which offers information for members coping with unemployment or redundancy and is available to download from the website.

The Lighthouse Club Benevolent Fund

Eligibility: People, or dependants of people, who work or have recently worked in the construction industry, or in an industry associated with construction, in the UK or Republic of Ireland.

Types of grants: Recurrent grants to help towards living costs for those in need through accident, disability or ill-health and for those in need because a member of their family (who was in the construction industry) has died or has a fatal illness. One-off grants are also available towards essential items, such as a new bed, a replacement washing machine and school uniforms.

Exclusions: The maximum length of time for recurrent grants to be given is five years.

Annual grant total: In 2009 the fund had assets of £594,000 and an income of £658,000. Grants were made to 426 individuals totalling £666,000. Grants were also made for holidays for disabled individuals amounting to £12,000.

Applications: In the first instance contact the correspondent or a branch welfare officer (a list of local branches is available on the fund's website). A visit will then be arranged with a welfare officer to discuss the applicant's needs and complete an application form.

Correspondent: Peter Burns, Armstrong House, Swallow Street, Stockport, Cheshire SK1 3LG (0161 429 0022; email: peterb@cooksonhardware.com; website: www.lighthouseclub.org/)

Caravan

The National Caravan Council Benevolent Fund

Eligibility: People in need who are, or have been, employed in the caravan industry, and their dependants.

Types of grants: Normally one-off grants ranging from £200 to £2,500, although occasionally recurrent grants may be given. Recent grants have been made towards redecoration, medical expenses, food, education or special equipment such as computers for people who are housebound or disabled.

Annual grant total: In 2008/09 the fund had an income of £4,700 and a total expenditure of £7,200.

Applications: On a form available from the correspondent including details of employment within the caravan industry. Applications can be submitted directly by the individual or through an appropriate third party.

Correspondent: Mrs S J Amey, 176 Hermitage Woods Crescent, Woking, GU21 8UH (01252 318251; email: info@nationalcaravan.co.uk; website: www.nationalcaravan.co.uk/home/index.asp)

Ceramic

The Ceramic Industry Welfare Society

Eligibility: People in need who are or have been employed in the ceramics industry, or widows of former employees.

Types of grants: Recurrent grants are fixed at £45 per six week period depending on the circumstances of the applicant as confirmed by the visit of the society's representative. About 500 grants are given each year, about 60 people per six week period.

Exclusions: No grants are payable beyond 12 months of the date of retirement.

Annual grant total: In 2009 the society had an expenditure of £4,600.

Applications: In writing to the correspondent.

Correspondent: The Secretary, Unity Trades Union, Hillcrest House, Garth Street, Stoke-on-Trent, ST1 2AB (01782 272755; fax: 01782 284902)

Chartered surveyors

Lionheart (The Royal Institution of Chartered Surveyors Benevolent Fund)

Eligibility: Members and former members of the Royal Institution of Chartered Surveyors or organisations it has merged with and their dependants. Applications are welcome from people in the UK and those living overseas.

Types of grants: One-off and recurrent grants and loans are given towards: essential domestic appliances, furnishings, re-decorations and property repairs; living expenses; care in the community, residential and nursing care; respite care and holidays; and, medical aids, adaptations and equipment for children with disabilities and the elderly. Additional financial help is also available for those most in need at Christmas.

Annual grant total: In 2008 the trust had assets of £10 million and an income of £1.9 million. Grants of £702,000, together with £32,000 in loans, were made to 400 individuals. Of those individuals 362 were permanent UK residents and 38 lived overseas.

Applications: On a form available from the correspondent or to download from the website. Evidence of RICS membership or details of the member of whom the applicant is a dependant should be provided. Applications are considered quarterly, although urgent cases can be considered between meetings.

Correspondent: Brin Corotana, Welfare Administrator, Surveyor Court, Westwood Way, Coventry CV4 8BF (024 7646 6696; fax: 020 7647 4701; email: info@lionheart.org.uk; website: www.lionheart.org.uk)

Other information: The trust offers confidential advice, counselling, information and help in kind to members of the profession and their dependants on a range of social welfare, financial, employment and property-related matters. A helpline is operated on 0845 603 9057.

Civil service

Assist Fund (formerly known as the Century Benevolent Fund)

Eligibility: Employees and ex-employees of the Government Communications Bureau and its associated organisations, and their dependants.

Types of grants: One-off or recurrent grants and loans towards telephone bills, house repairs and so on.

Exclusions: There are no educational grants available.

Annual grant total: In 2008/09 the trust had assets of £633,000 and an income of £86,000. Regular grants to individuals totalled £39,000 and one-off grants amounted to £24,000.

Applications: In writing to the correspondent, although applications are often made by word of mouth. Applications are generally considered four times a year, but exceptions can be made in urgent cases.

Correspondent: The Administrator, PO Box 62849, London, SE1P 5AE

The Civil Service Benevolent Fund

Eligibility: Serving, former and retired staff of the Civil Service and associated organisations, and their dependants, who are in need.

Types of grants: Grants, loans and allowances according to need. Help has been given towards: daily living expenses and household bills; property repairs, adaptations, rent deposit and sheltered housing; respite care, nursing home top-ups and allowances; disabled vehicles and equipment; and, funeral costs.

Exclusions: Funding is not provided for house purchase, home improvements, strike action, legal costs, private medical treatment for infertility, private education, payment of fines or to those dismissed for gross misconduct.

Annual grant total: In 2009 the fund had assets of £35 million and an income of £10 million. Grants were made totalling £4.3 million and were distributed as follows:

Reduced or low incomes	£2,300,000
Debt	£929,000
Poor or inappropriate living arrangements	£715,000
Illness	£244,000
Immobility	£210,000
Bereavement	£255,000
Emergency situations	£28,000
Community projects	£1,000
Education	£65,000

A further 12 repayable grants were agreed during the year amounting to £17,000.

Applications: Application forms are available from the correspondent or to download from the website. The fund can assist with the completion of the form, by either giving advice over the telephone (call 0800 056 2424) or by sending one of its volunteer visiting officers to the applicant. The fund aims to consider completed application forms within five days of receipt, although they may occasionally take a little longer. In urgent cases payment can be made within 24 hours.

Correspondent: The Help and Advisory Team, Fund House, 5 Anne Boleyn's Walk, Cheam, Sutton, Surrey SM3 8DY (020 8240 2400 (Freephone: 0800 056 2424); fax: 020 8240 2401; email: help@csbf.org.uk; website: www.csbf.org.uk)

Other information: The fund also helps people by providing an information service on a range of community-based services and a confidential visiting service to aid and advise on funding opportunities.

Overseas Service Pensioners' Benevolent Society

Eligibility: Members of the Overseas Service Pensioners' Association or those with other relevant service in the Overseas Civil Service or in a former British dependent (colonial) territory, and their dependants, who are in need.

Types of grants: Grants of between £50 and £1,500 are usually paid quarterly to help with living expenses. Occasionally, single grants are given for special needs. All cases are reviewed annually.

Exclusions: No grants are made for residential care or nursing home fees.

Annual grant total: In 2008 the society provided financial assistance to beneficiaries totalling £94,000.

Applications: On a form available from the correspondent. Applications should normally be submitted directly by the individual or by a third party such as a close relative or a legal representative.

Correspondent: D F B Le Breton, Secretary, 138 High Street, Tonbridge, Kent TN9 1AX (01732 363836; fax: 01732 365070; email: mail@ospa.org.uk; website: www.ospa.org.uk)

Prospects Benevolent Fund (formerly The Institution of Professionals, Managers & Specialists Benevolent Fund and The Engineers' & Manager's Association (EMA) Benevolent Fund)

Eligibility: Members and retired members of the union (and the former Institution of Professional Civil Servants) and their dependants who are experiencing financial problems.

Types of grants: Generally one-off grants. Recurrent grants do not exceed £1,500. The trustees aim to relieve immediate problems and point applicants to other channels and agencies for long-term solutions. Grants are usually sent to the applicant, but for speed and/or reliability, some awards are sent direct to the utility/body owed money. Occasionally this is processed through an agency or second party (such as welfare officer, debt counsellor, branch officer or relative).

Exclusions: The trust does not make loans.

Annual grant total: In 2008 the trust made grants to 16 individuals totalling £18,000.

Applications: On a form available from the correspondent. Applications can be submitted directly by the individual or through employer's welfare officers or branch representatives. Applications are considered throughout the year and are processed quickly.

Correspondent: Finance Officer, New Prospect House, 8 Leake Street, London, SE1 7NN (020 7902 6600; fax: 020 7902 6667; website: www.prospect.org.uk)

The Public and Commercial Services Union Benevolent Fund

Eligibility: Members and associate members of the union who are suffering severe financial hardship, through sickness, family troubles or other problems. Applications will be rejected if the individual is not a fully paid-up member, or associate member, of the union.

Types of grants: One-off grants to a maximum of £500 in any 12 month period.

Exclusions: No grants are given for help with private legal or medical expenses. No grants are given for credit card debts, overdrafts or loans.

Annual grant total: About £140,000.

Applications: On a form available from the correspondent or to download from the website. Completed applications should be submitted either directly by the individual or a family member, or through a third party such as a union representative. They are reviewed every Monday.

Correspondent: Benevolent Fund Secretary, 160 Falcon Road, London SW11 2LN (020 7801 2601, option 3; fax: 020 7801 2675; email: membenefits@pcs.org.uk; website: www.pcs.org.uk)

Clayworking

The Institute of Clayworkers Benevolent Fund

Eligibility: People in need who had to retire early from the clayworking industry through accident or ill-health. Dependants of deceased clayworkers may also be eligible. The fund covers brick-making, roof tiles, clay drainage pipes and refractory industries, but not pottery workers.

Types of grants: One-off grants, usually of £250. In exceptional cases where applicants have been identified by other charitable bodies as being in extreme need, larger grants may be given.

Annual grant total: In 2009 the fund had an income of £3,100 and a total expenditure of £3,400.

Applications: In writing to the correspondent, including age, length of service, date of termination of employment (if applicable), brief description (two or three sentences) of circumstances leading to application, and brief testimonial (a sentence or two) from a supervisor/manager if appropriate. The fund only accepts applications made through a former employer and not usually those made directly by the individual. Applications may be made at any time.

Correspondent: Francis Morrall, Trustee, Federation House, Station Road, Stoke-on-Trent, Staffordshire ST4 2SA (01782 744631; email: francism@ceramfed.co.uk)

Clergy

Gibbons Charity

Eligibility: Widows and widowers and children of Shropshire Church of England clergy and clergy who have retired and face hardship.

Types of grants: One-off and recurrent grants according to need.

Annual grant total: On average this charity has a total annual expenditure of around £2,000.

Applications: In writing to the correspondent.

Correspondent: D G Woolford, The Swallows, Station Road, Admaston, Telford, Shropshire, TF5 0AW (01952 243846; email: don.woolford@btinternet.com)

The Rehoboth Trust

Eligibility: Christian ministers or retired ministers who are in need in England and Wales and Israel.

Types of grants: Grants given according to need.

Annual grant total: In 2009 the trust had an income of £35,000 and made grants totalling £26,000, including £7,900 to individuals.

Applications: In writing to the correspondent.

Correspondent: Shakti Sisodia, Trustee, 71 Rydal Gardens, Hounslow, TW3 2JJ

Other information: Grants are also made to organisations.

Clothing and textiles

The City of London Linen and Furnishings Trades Association

Eligibility: Members and former members of the association and their dependants.

Types of grants: One-off grants according to need. The trust can also contribute towards the cost of a holiday at one of the Textile Benevolent Association holiday homes.

Annual grant total: Grants usually total about £1,500 each year.

Applications: In writing to the correspondent.

Correspondent: Geoffrey Blake, Trustee, 69a Langley Hill, Kings Langley, Hertfordshire WD4 9HQ (01923 262857)

The Cotton Industry War Memorial Trust

Eligibility: People in need who have worked in the cotton textile industry in the north west of England. This includes weaving, spinning and dyeing. Cotton industry workers who were badly injured while fighting for HM Forces in wartime may also be eligible.

Types of grants: Convalescence grants are available to people who are in poor health or who have suffered injury due to their work in the cotton textiles industry. One-off grants are also awarded for specific needs.

Exclusions: People who have worked with clothing, footwear, hosiery and other man-made fabrics are not eligible.

Annual grant total: In 2009 the trust had assets of £5.4 million, an income of £287,000 and a total expenditure of £568,000. Grants were made to 267 individuals under the convalescence scheme totalling £158,000. A further £1,000 was paid in two individual grants and £105,000 was given to organisations.

Applications: On a form available from the correspondent. Please note that the correspondent cannot send forms directly to applicants, just to employers, trade unions, SSAFA or similar welfare agencies for them to pass on to potential beneficiaries. Applicants must show that they have worked in the textile industry and provide medical evidence if claiming assistance due to employment injury or disability. Applications are considered quarterly.

Correspondent: Hilda Ball, 42 Boot Lane, Heaton, Bolton BL1 5SS (01204 491810)

Other information: The trust gives substantial grants to educational bodies to assist eligible students in furthering their textile studies, to other bodies which encourage recruitment into or efficiency in the industry and to organisations furthering the interests of the industry by research and so on.

The Fashion and Textile Children's Trust

Eligibility: Children and young people under 18 whose parents work or have worked in the UK fashion and textile retailing and manufacturing industry.

Types of grants: The trust concentrates its grant giving on 'the essential costs of education'. However, it also makes some welfare grants to children from particularly poor backgrounds for items such as,

disability equipment, clothing, bedding and shoes.

Exclusions: No grants are given towards child care, study/travel abroad; overseas students studying in Britain; student exchange; or people starting work. No grants are available for those in higher education.

Annual grant total: In 2009/10 the trust had assets of £6.3 million and an income of £353,000. The majority of grants were made to individuals for educational purposes (£133,000), whilst the remainder was given in grants for general welfare purposes (£25,000).

Applications: On a form available from the correspondent or an initial enquiry form from the trust's website. Applications can be submitted at anytime either directly by the individual or through a third party such as a social worker, teacher or Citizens Advice.

Correspondent: Anna Pangbourne, Director, Winchester House, 259-269 Old Marylebone Road, London, NW1 5RA (020 7170 4117; email: anna@ftct.org.uk; website: www.ftct.org.uk)

The Feltmakers Charitable Foundation

Eligibility: Employees or former employees of the hat trade who are in need.

Types of grants: Annual pensions.

Annual grant total: In 2009/10 the foundation had assets of £400,000 and an income of £74,000. Grants were made totalling £8,700.

Applications: Applicants must be nominated in the first place by their employer or former employer, or in exceptional circumstances by a welfare organisation.

Correspondent: Maj. Jollyon Coombs, Post Cottage, The Street, Greywell, Hook, Hampshire RG29 1DA (01256 703174; email: jcpartnership@btopenworld.com; website: www.feltmakers.co.uk/)

Other information: The foundation also makes grants to organisations (£26,000 in 2009/10).

Footwear Benevolent Society (formerly The Boot Trade Benevolent Society)

Eligibility: People who are working or have worked in the boot trade and footwear industry, and their dependants.

Types of grants: One-off grants and quarterly allowances with a Christmas bonus to supplement low income or to purchase a specific item such as a new cooker. Holiday grants are also available.

Annual grant total: In 2008/09 the society had assets of £899,000 and an income of £199,000. Grants were made to 265 individuals totalling £102,000.

Applications: On a form available from the correspondent. Applications are considered every two months.

Correspondent: Gabi O'Sullivan, Secretary, 3 Queen Square, Bloomsbury, London WC1N 3AR (020 7843 9486; email: info@footwearfriends.org.uk; website: www.footwearfriends.org.uk)

Master Tailors' Benevolent Association

Eligibility: Master tailors who are in need, and their dependants. To qualify the individual must have worked as a master tailor for more than ten years. Master tailors who meet these criteria but live elsewhere are also considered if they were born in the UK or Eire.

Types of grants: Quarterly grants.

Annual grant total: In 2008/09 the association had assets of £496,000 and an income of £66,000. Grants were made to seven individuals totalling £23,000.

Applications: On a form available from the correspondent, to be submitted directly by the individual or another master tailor known to the trust.

Correspondent: Cyril Fox, Flat 5, Chestnut Court, Comerford Way, Winslow, Buckingham MK18 3FJ (01296 712173; email: foxcy101@hotmail.com)

Sydney Simmons Pension Fund

Eligibility: People in need who are or have been employed in the carpet trade.

Types of grants: One-off grants usually in the range of £300 to £500.

Annual grant total: Grants for individuals usually total about £2,000 a year.

Applications: On a form available from the correspondent.

Correspondent: David Matanle, Homefield, Fortyfoot Road, Leatherfield, Surrey KT22 8RP (01372 370073; email: luchar@btinternet.com)

Other information: The fund also makes grants to organisations.

The Tailors Benevolent Institute

Eligibility: Journeyman tailors, tailoresses and their near relatives who were employed in the bespoke (made to measure) tailoring trade. Preference is given to past and present members of the institute but help can be given to other eligible applicants.

Types of grants: Small one-off grants and regular allowances. Previously, allowances have been in the region of £20 a week.

Annual grant total: In 2009 the institute had assets of £1.8 million, an income of £35,000 and a total expenditure of £105,000. Grants were made to 114 individuals totalling £76,000.

Applications: On a form available from the correspondent. Applications should preferably be submitted through a social worker. However, those submitted directly by the individual or through another third party will be considered.

Correspondent: Susanne Smart, 68 Nightingale Road, Petts Wood, Orpington, Kent, BR5 1BQ (01689 824405)

The Textile Benevolent Association (1970)

Eligibility: People in need who are employees and former employees of: wholesalers and retailers engaged in the textile trade; and of manufacturers in the trade which distribute to retailers as well as manufacture. The wives, widows, husbands and widowers of such people can also benefit.

Types of grants: Grants are towards holidays, winter fuel bills, clothing, cookers, washing machines and so on.

Annual grant total: In 2009 the association had assets of £249,000 and an income of £307,000. Welfare grants were made to 108 individuals totalling £12,000.

Applications: On a form available from the correspondent, usually via employers, doctors or social services.

Correspondent: Mrs Sandra O'Hara, 72a Lee High Road, Lewisham, London SE13 5PT (020 8852 7239; fax: 020 8463 0303)

Coal industry

The Coal Industry Benevolent Trust

Eligibility: Widows and families of miners who have died as a result of industrial accident or disease (mainly pneumoconiosis). Help is also available to mineworkers and their dependants who are experiencing financial difficulties.

Types of grants:
- General hardship grants of up to £500 towards, for example, buying a motorised wheelchair, specialist equipment and home adaptations.
- Grants of up to £1,500 to the dependants of miners who have died as a result of their work (made soon after the death) and £500 for the following three years, if his widow remains single, and £250 to the children (£350 if the child has a disability).
- Grants of £50 every four weeks are available to miners who are in hospital as a result of their work, up to £200 a year.

- Grants of £5 per journey up to £200 for miners who have to travel to an outpatients centre as a result of an accident at work.

Annual grant total: In 2009 the trust had assets of £13 million and an income of £567,000. Grants were made to over 1,800 individuals totalling £864,000 and were distributed as follows:

Industrial accidents	£15,000
Industrial disease	£23,000
Pulmonary & cardio-pulmonary disease	£348,000
Employees' premises	£3,300
Hospital benefits	£50
Other grants	£475,000

Applications: In writing to the correspondent for consideration by the trustees. The trust usually sends one of its own social workers to visit the individual to assess their needs and assist with the application form.

Correspondent: Vernon Jones, Secretary, The Old Rectory, Rectory Drive, Whiston, Rotherham, South Yorkshire S60 4JG (01709 728115; fax: 01709 839164; email: cibt@ciswo.org.uk; website: www.ciswo.org.uk/cibt.htm)

The Coal Trade Benevolent Association

Eligibility: Non-manual workers of the coal industry in England and Wales who have worked in the production or distribution sectors and allied trades, and their dependants.

Types of grants: Weekly grants to supplement low income and one-off grants towards, for example, telephone costs, televisions, fuel payments, respite holidays and capital items.

Annual grant total: In 2009 the association had assets of £4.5 million and an income of £216,000. Grants were made to 338 individuals totalling £131,000.

Applications: On a form available from the correspondent for consideration throughout the year.

Correspondent: Nicholas Maxwell Ross, Unit 6 Bridge Wharf, 156 Caledonian Road, London N1 9UU (020 7278 3239; email: coalbenev@btconnect.com)

Commerce

The George Drexler Foundation

Eligibility: Former employees of the Ofrex Group and their dependants.

Types of grants: One-off and recurrent grants of £1,000 to £10,000.

Exclusions: We do not support funding for medical electives, volunteering or gap year projects.

Annual grant total: In 2009/10 grants awarded totalled £228,000, of which £64,000 was allocated for welfare purposes and £164,000 was given in educational grants.

Applications: On a form available from the correspondent, submitted directly by the individual, enclosing an sae. Applications should be submitted in May for consideration in June/July.

Correspondent: Jonathan Fountain, 35–43 Lincolns Inn Fields, London, WC2A 3PE (020 7869 6080; email: georgedrexler@rcseng.ac.uk)

Other information: The foundation also provides educational grants to people in need who have a direct link with commerce, that is, who have owned and run their own commercial business. Applicants whose parents or grandparents have this link can also be supported. This does not include professional people such as doctors, lawyers, dentists, architects or accountants. No exceptions can be made.

The Ruby & Will George Trust

Eligibility: People in need who have been or who are employed in commerce, and their dependants. Preference is given to people who live in the north east of England.

Types of grants: One-off or recurrent grants for items which are needed but cannot be afforded, usually related to sickness and disability, for example, wheelchairs, washing machines and clothes. Grants usually range from between £250 and £5,000.

Annual grant total: In 2008/09 the trust had assets of £2.6 million and an income of £90,000. Grants totalling £62,000 were made to 34 individuals, mainly for the advancement of education.

Applications: The trust has an online application process, though those without access to the internet can still submit a paper-based application. Applicants will need to prove their commerce connection and their income and expenditure. Two references are required.

The trust considers applications four times a year, usually in January, May, July and October. Applications should be submitted two weeks in advance. Note: upcoming deadline dates can be found on the trust's website.

Correspondent: David Simpson, Administrator, 18 Ghyll Edge, Lancaster Park, Morpeth, Northumberland NE61 3QZ (01670 516657; email: admin@rwgt.co.uk; website: www.rwgt.co.uk/)

Other information: The trust also makes grants to institutions.

Commercial travellers

The Commercial Travellers' Benevolent Institution

Eligibility: People in the UK who are in need and have worked as a sales representative/agent promoting or selling to the trade for at least five years. Applicants must have been employed for a minimum of six months in each of these years. Sales must be business to business and involve the representative leaving their office and visiting client sites.

Types of grants: Recurrent grants and gifts in kind. One-off grants are also given towards respite breaks, disability aids, home adaptations, TV licences and for critical one-off payments.

Exclusions: No help is given to those engaged in 'van sales' or who sell through retail outlets.

Annual grant total: In 2009 the trust had assets of £4.6 million and an income of £502,000. Grants were made totalling £469,000.

Applications: On a form available from the correspondent or to download from the website. Applications should include evidence of employment in commercial sales and be submitted either directly by the individual or through a third party. The trustees meet five times a year to consider applications, though emergency payments can be made quickly in cases of extreme hardship.

Correspondent: Mandi Leonard, 2 Fletcher Road, Ottershaw, Chertsey, Surrey KT16 0JY (01932 429636; email: sec.ctbi@ntlworld.com; website: www.ctbi.org)

UCTA Samaritan Benefit Fund Society

Eligibility: Commercial travellers and their dependants in the UK who are in need.

Types of grants: One-off and recurrent grants according to need.

Annual grant total: In 2009 the society had assets of £253,000, an income of £73,000 and made grants totalling £71,000.

Applications: On a form available from the correspondent.

Correspondent: Peter Brennan, The Cottage, Dairyhouse Lane, Dunham Massey, Altrincham, Cheshire WA14 5RD (0161 265 3462; email: pjb@pbrennan.freeserve.co.uk)

Cooperative

The National Association of Cooperative Officials' Benevolent Fund

Eligibility: Members and former members of the association and their families. Widows and children of deceased members are also eligible for assistance.

Types of grants: One-off grants up to a maximum of £1,000.

Annual grant total: In 2009 the association had an income of £18,000 and a total expenditure of £3,800.

Applications: On a form available from the correspondent to be submitted directly by the individual. Applications should include details of personal finance. They are usually considered quarterly.

Correspondent: Lynne Higginbottom, 6a Clarendon Place, Hyde, Cheshire SK14 2QZ (0161 351 7900; email: ich@nacoco-op.org)

Coopers

William Alexander Coopers Liverymen Fund

Eligibility: Members of the Coopers' Company, their widows and other dependants, who are in need.

Types of grants: Money can be given to supplement relief or assistance provided out of public funds, in the form of one-off grants and Christmas grants.

Exclusions: No funds are available for education.

Annual grant total: In 2008/09 the fund had an income of £5,600 and a total expenditure of £4,700.

Applications: In writing to the correspondent.

Correspondent: A D Carroll, The Clerk, Coopers' Hall, 13 Devonshire Square, London EC2M 4TH (email: clerk@coopers-hall.co.uk; website: www.coopers-hall.co.uk/coopers/)

Corn exchange

The Bristol Corn Trade Guild

Eligibility: People who work in the corn and feed trade, and their dependants, who are in need.

Types of grants: One-off grants ranging from £200 to £840. Recent grants have been given towards utility bills, medical equipment, repairs and as food vouchers.

Annual grant total: In 2009 the guild had an income of £7,400 and a total expenditure of £8,300.

Applications: In writing to the correspondent. Applications can be submitted directly by the individual or through a social worker, Citizens Advice or other welfare agency.

Correspondent: R Cooksley, Portbury House, Sheepway, Portbury, Bristol BS20 7TE (01275 373539; fax: 01275 374747; email: cooksleyandco@btconnect.com)

The Corn Exchange Benevolent Society

Eligibility: Members of the society and their dependants who are in need. Limited funds are also available for people who work or have been engaged in any aspect of grain trading in England and Wales (corn, grain, seed, animal feed stuffs, pulses, malt, flour or granary-keeping trades) and their dependants.

Types of grants: Quarterly grants are available to help towards day-to-day living costs. One-off grants are given for general household expenses, repairs, decorating materials, mobility aids, TV licenses, winter fuel, respite care and special therapy. Christmas gifts are also made to all beneficiaries.

Annual grant total: In 2009 the society had assets of £2.5 million and an income of £80,000. Grants were made to 36 individuals totalling £27,000.

Applications: On a form available from the correspondent. Applications can be submitted directly by the individual or through a social worker, Citizens Advice or other welfare agency.

Correspondent: Richard Butler, 20 St Dunstan's Hill, London EC3R 8HL (020 7283 6090; email: richard.butler@baltic-charities.co.uk)

Customs & excise

The North West Customs and Excise Benevolent Society

Eligibility: Serving or retired members of HM Revenue and Customs who are in need, and their dependants.

Types of grants: One-off grants according to need.

Annual grant total: Around £2,500 is usually available for grant making.

Applications: Potential applicants should contact the correspondent either in writing or by telephone.

Correspondent: Brian Roberts, Fifth Floor West, Commercial Directorate, Ralli Quays, Stanley Street, Manchester, M60 9LA (0161 827 0399; email: brian.roberts@hmrc.gsi.gov.uk)

Driving instructors

The Driving Instructors' Accident & Disability Fund

Eligibility: Driving instructors, former driving instructors and members of the Driving Instructors' Association who have been injured or disabled and their dependants.

Types of grants: One-off grants ranging from £150 to £250.

Annual grant total: Grants average around £650 a year, though the actual grant figure tends to fluctuate quite widely.

Applications: In writing to the correspondent.

Correspondent: Yusuf Dosani, 2 Alford Close, Guildford, Surrey, GU4 7YL (01483 574542)

Electrical

The Amalgamated Union Of Engineering Workers Fleet Street Branch Trust

Eligibility: Members and former members of the union and their dependants, who are in financial hardship caused by unemployment, ill health or age.

Types of grants: One-off grants and Christmas gifts.

Annual grant total: In 2009 the trust had an income of £1,200 and a total expenditure £9,000. Grants are given to both individuals and organisations.

Applications: In writing to the correspondent.

Correspondent: Arthur Beecham, 29 Birch Close, Longfield, Kent, DA3 7LH (01474 709237)

Electrical and Electronics Industries' Benevolent Association

Eligibility: Employees and former employees of the UK electrical and electronic industries and allied sciences, including mechanical engineering, and their dependants. There are no age limits.

Types of grants: Grants are: 'To provide practical help and support in any form most appropriate to each individual applicant including one-off grants, ongoing budget balancing grants, clothing, house repairs (specific criteria), aids for disabled people, holidays, wheelchairs (specific criteria), television and telephone rental and so on.'

Exclusions: Grants are not normally given to cover the costs of private medical care, educational fees or nursing/residential fees.

Annual grant total: In 2008 the association had assets of £3.8 million and an income of £2.1 million. Grants totalled £427,000.

Applications: On a form available from the head of welfare. They can be submitted directly by the individual or through a social worker, Citizens Advice, other welfare agency or a human resources department. They are considered throughout the year.

Correspondent: Timothy Lambert, 8 Station Parade, Balham High Road, London SW12 9AZ (0800 652 1618; website: www.eeiba.org)

Other information: The association also runs a sheltered housing scheme in Sellyoak, Birmingham.

The Institution of Engineering and Technology Benevolent Fund (IET Connect)

Eligibility: Members and former members who have held their membership for at least two years, and their dependants.

Types of grants: Grants given include those for living costs, care home fees, respite and home care, home adaptations, disability equipment, emergency grants, lifeline alarms and television and telephone costs.

Annual grant total: In 2008/09 the trust had assets of £14 million and an income of £2.3 million. Grants were made totalling £535,000.

Applications: On a form available from the correspondent. Applications are sent to a local welfare visitor who will visit the applicant to discuss the request and report the findings to the care committee. Applications are considered on receipt.

Correspondent: Christine Oxland, IET, 2 Savoy Place, London WC2R 0BL (020 7344 8474; email: ietconnect@theiet.org; website: www.ietconnect.org)

Other information: The fund also owns a residential home in New Malden, Surrey, for the benefit of its members and their dependants.

The RTRA Benevolent Fund

Eligibility: People in need who are directly connected with the electronic and electrical retailing industry.

Types of grants: One-off grants in the range of £250 to £1,000 to give short-term support to individuals in need.

Annual grant total: In 2008/09 the fund had an income of £12,000 and a total expenditure of £4,900.

Applications: In writing to the correspondent at any time. Applications should be submitted either directly by the individual or a family member, through an organisation such as a Citizens Advice or other welfare agency, or via a member of RTHA.

Correspondent: Jan Bray, Retra Ltd, 1 Ampthill Street, Bedford, MK42 9EY (01234 269110; email: retra@retra.co.uk)

Engineering

The Chartered Institution of Building Services Engineers' Benevolent Fund

Eligibility: Members and former members of the institution and their dependants (on death of member), who are in need.

Types of grants: Regular payments to supplement pensions and other income sources. One-off grants towards the cost of special equipment such as stair lifts or equipment which will enable the individual to work from home and major one-off bills such as essential repairs to the home. Help may also be given in the form of waived CIBSE subscriptions.

Exclusions: Private health care or education.

Annual grant total: Grants usually total around £200,000 a year. No further information was available.

Applications: Applications can be submitted at any time either directly by the individual or through a social worker, Citizens Advice or other welfare agency. An almoner will visit the applicant to obtain details. Applications are considered on receipt.

Correspondent: Stephen Matthews, CIBSE, 222 Balham High Road, London SW12 9BS (020 8675 5211; fax: 020 8675 5449; email: benfund@cibse.org; website: www.cibse.org)

The Benevolent Fund of the Engineering Employers' Federation (including the Dyer Memorial Funds)

Eligibility: 'The purpose of the fund is to enable federated employers to obtain financial assistance for their employees or their dependants. In order to be eligible the relevant employee should be or have been employed in a position of trust and this is

normally taken to mean under-foreman or equivalent status.'

Types of grants: Grants fall into the following categories:

(i) Income grants, where the applicant's income, after certain deductions, has fallen below the equivalent of a state pension (this can be increased when the applicant is elderly, infirm or has dependants). These grants range from £200 to £1,040.

(ii) Property grants, generally for modifications to the applicant's home due to their physical condition.

(iv) Bereavement grants, payable in respect of the death of an employee or their spouse, to assist with funeral costs.

(v) Mobility grants to help applicants in need of a wheelchair or to adapt other forms of transport.

Exclusions: The fund does not give loans.

Annual grant total: In 2008/09 the fund had an income of £15,000 and an expenditure of £133,000, most of which was given in grants to individuals.

Applications: The fund no longer issues grants to new applicants. It instead continues to fund its current grant recipients.

Correspondent: Simon Charlick, Broadway House, Tothill Street, London SW1H 9NQ (020 7654 1562)

The Worshipful Company of Engineers Charitable Trust Fund

Eligibility: Engineers who are in need. Applicants do not necessarily have to be members of the Worshipful Company.

Types of grants: Grants of up to £1,000 for welfare purposes.

Annual grant total: In 2008/09 the trust had assets of £498,000 and an income of £67,000. Grants totalled £8,000, with a further £14,000 having been spent on medals, prizes and associated costs.

Applications: In writing to the correspondent at any time providing as much detail about your circumstances as possible. Applications are considered throughout the year.

Correspondent: Air Vice-Marshal G Skinner, The Worshipful Company of Engineers, Wax Chandlers Hall, 6 Gresham Street, London EC2V 7AD (020 7726 4830; fax: 020 7726 4820; email: clerk@ engineerscompany.org.uk; website: www. engineerscompany.org.uk)

Other information: Grants are also made to organisations and individuals for educational purposes.

The Guild of Benevolence of The Institute of Marine Engineering Science and Technology

Eligibility: Qualified marine engineers, or their dependants, who are in need. Scientists and technologists are also eligible if past or present members of the Institute.

Types of grants: Regular grants are given to supplement a low income. One-off grants, to a maximum of £4,000, are also available for disability aids, debt relief, reasonable nursing home fees, funeral costs, home maintenance and respite care. All regular beneficiaries receive a Christmas gift of £120.

Exclusions: There are no grants for educational costs.

Annual grant total: In 2008/09 the trust had assets of £638,000, an income of £131,000 and a total expenditure of £381,000. Grants were made to 148 individuals totalling £209,000.

Applications: On a form available from the correspondent or to download from the website. Evidence of service or qualifications as a marine engineer must be produced if not already a member of the Institute of Marine Engineers, as well as full disclosure of financial situation. Applicants should expect a visit by a guild representative who will assess their needs and assist in completing the application form. Applications are considered every two months.

Correspondent: David Cusdin, Hon. Chairman, 80 Coleman Street, London EC2R 5BJ (020 7382 2600; fax: 020 7382 2670; email: guild@imarest. org; website: www.imarest.org)

Other information: This trust was launched as a response to the sinking of the Titanic in 1912, a disaster which no marine engineer aboard survived. Since 1989 the guild has administered the Marine Engineers' Benevolent Fund. The guild also gives a grant to the Royal Merchant Navy School Foundation, towards the education of eligible dependants.

The Benevolent Fund of the Institution of Civil Engineers Ltd

Eligibility: Past and present members of the institution, and their dependants. The dependants of former members of the Institution of Municipal Engineers.

Types of grants: One off grants towards: essential domestic appliances, furnishings, re-decorating and repairs to property; residential and nursing home care; aids, adaptations and equipment to promote independence; respite care and holidays; and Christmas and Easter gifts. Monthly payments may be made to those on very low incomes.

A small number of grants are also available to student members of the fund to help with living costs and course materials.

Annual grant total: In 2009 the fund had assets of £5.2 million and an income of £784,000. Grants were made to 194 individuals totalling £565,000.

Applications: On a form available from the correspondent. Applications can be submitted directly by the individual or through a social worker, Citizens Advice or other welfare agency, or through a close relative, solicitor or similar third party. They should include information about the individual's income, expenditure and capital and can be submitted at any time. Most applicants will be visited by one of the fund's volunteer visitors.

Correspondent: Kris Barnett, Chief Executive, 30 Mill Hill Close, Haywards Heath, West Sussex RH16 1NY (01444 417979; fax: 01444 453307; email: benfund@ice.org.uk; website: www.bfice.org.uk)

Other information: The fund owns properties in West Sussex and has nomination rights to the Hanover Housing Association which it uses to help (ex-)members and their families who are facing difficult circumstances and need somewhere to live.

It also runs a 24-hour helpline (0800 587 3428) which offers support and advice on a wide range of issues including, stress management, debt problems, childcare and substance abuse.

In 2008 the fund became incorporated and in January 2009 the assets of the unincorporated benevolent fund (Registered Charity No. 208229) were transferred to the new incorporated fund (Registered Charity No. 1126595).

The Benevolent Fund of the Institution of Mechanical Engineers

Eligibility: Past and present members of the Institution, and their dependants, who are in need. Former members must have paid subscription fees for at least five years. Priority is given to those on low incomes who qualify for means-tested state benefits.

Types of grants: One-off grants and loans are available towards a variety of needs, including house repairs and adaptations, medical equipment, domestic appliances, beds and bedding, furniture, respite care, holidays and carer's breaks. Recurrent grants are also available to help with living expenses.

Exclusions: No grants are given for school fees, business ventures, private medical treatment or the payment of debts.

Annual grant total: In 2009 the fund had assets of £14 million and an income of £810,000. Grants to 315 individuals totalled £480,000.

Applications: Applicants should first contact the fund, by phone, letter, email or fax, to confirm whether or not they are eligible for assistance. If so, they will be asked to complete an application form and meet with one of the fund's volunteer visitors. Applications are considered by the grants committee every two months.

Correspondent: Fiona Porter, Casework and Welfare Officer, 3 Birdcage Walk, London SW1H 9JJ (020 7304 6816; fax: 020 7973 1262; email: info@ supportnetwork.org.uk; website: www. bfime.org)

Other information: The fund also operates a free confidential helpline which offers advice on a range of issues from childcare to bereavement (call 0800 243 458 or minicom 020 8987 6574 and quote either: bfime or Support Network). It can also help those in search of a new job through its links with the HR firm, Chiumento and provides educational grants to mechanical engineering students.

The Institution of Plant Engineers Benevolent Fund

Eligibility: Members/former members of the institution, and their dependants living in England, Scotland and Wales.

Types of grants: One-off grants according to need. Most grants are given to people who are financially stressed through serious illness, unemployment or bereavement. For example, support for a young member no longer able to work due to multiple sclerosis.

Annual grant total: In 2009 the fund had an income of £15,000 and a total expenditure of £20,000.

Applications: In writing to the correspondent. Applications can be submitted directly by the individual or by a relative or close friend. They are considered in March, July and November.

Correspondent: Grants Administrator, 22 Greencoat Place, London SW1P 1DX (020 7630 1111)

The Institution of Structural Engineers' Benevolent Fund

Eligibility: Members of the institution and their dependants who are in financial difficulties due to circumstances such as: unemployment; illness, accident or disability; family problems; difficulties during retirement; bereavement.

Types of grants: One-off and recurrent grants and loans up to a maximum of £8,500 per year towards, for example, home repairs, household equipment, property adaptations, disability equipment, carers' breaks and daily living costs for those on very modest incomes.

Exclusions: No grants for private health care. If the fund settles debts for a

beneficiary, it will not usually pay any subsequent debts.

Annual grant total: In 2009 the fund had assets of £1.5 million and an income of £122,000. Grants were made to 28 individuals totalling £67,000.

Applications: On a form available from the correspondent which can be submitted by the individual or an appropriate third party. The trust likes to visit applicants before any grant is made.

NB. In cases of genuine emergency, the fund can pay up to £500, as a loan, normally within days.

Correspondent: Dr Susan Doran, 11 Upper Belgrave Street, London SW1X 8BH (020 7235 4535; fax: 020 7235 4294; email: benfund@ istructe.org; website: www.istructe.org)

The Matthew Hall Staff Trust Fund

Eligibility: Former employees of Matthew Hall (1992) plc may apply for grants if they are in financial hardship and only when they have reached the age of 65.

Types of grants: One-off and recurrent grants according to need.

Annual grant total: In 2008/09 the fund had assets of £2.1 million and an income of £79,000. Grants were made to 184 former employees totalling £168,000.

Applications: In writing to the correspondent.

Correspondent: Mrs P R Pritchard, AMEC, Booths Hall, Chelford Road, Knutsford, WA16 8QZ (01565 683281)

Royal Engineers' Association

Eligibility: Past or present members of the corps, and their dependants, who are in need.

Types of grants: One-off and recurrent grants. Grants are given for a wide range of purposes including mobility aids and walk-in showers. Regular weekly allowances are made to around 140 people and Christmas cards and monetary gifts are sent out in November to around 900 people who are resident in elderly people's homes, hospitals and homes for the mentally infirm and to those in receipt of weekly pensions. Annuities for top-up fees for nursing homes are given in exceptional circumstances.

Exclusions: No grants for private education, private medical fees, court or legal fees or debts.

Annual grant total: In 2008 the association had assets of £7.5 million and an income of £1.3 million. Grants were made to nearly 1,000 individuals totalling £551,000 and were distributed as follows:

Grants	£432,000
Christmas Grants	£32,000
Weekly Allowances	£87,000

Applications: On a form available from the correspondent, to be submitted through SSAFA or the Royal British Legion. Applications for less than £500 will be considered at any time, while cases requiring over £500 are considered at monthly committee meetings.

Correspondent: Lt Col John McLennan, Brompton Barracks, Dock Road, Chatham, Kent ME4 4UG (01634 822982; fax: 01634 822394; email: benevolence@reahq.org.uk; website: www2.army.mod.uk/royalengineers/rea/)

Environmental health

Environmental Health Officers Welfare Fund

Eligibility: Past and present members of Chartered Institute of Environmental Health Officers, Association of Public Health Inspectors or the Guild of Public Health Inspection and their dependants, who are in need.

Types of grants: One-off and recurrent grants according to need.

Annual grant total: Grants usually total around £3,000.

Applications: In writing to the correspondent, usually via centre or branch networks.

Correspondent: Graham Jukes, Chadwick Court, 15 Hatfields, London SE1 8DJ (020 7928 6006; fax: 020 7827 5866; email: membership@cieh.org; website: www.cieh.org)

Estate workers

Midhurst Pensions Trust

Eligibility: People in need who have been employed by the Third Viscount Cowdray, Lady Anne Cowdray, any family company or on the Cowdray Estate, and their dependants.

Types of grants: One-off grants usually in the range of £25 to £2,000.

Annual grant total: In 2008/09 the trust had an income of £138,000 and a total expenditure of £144,000. Grants were made totalling about £50,000.

Applications: In writing to the correspondent.

Correspondent: Laura Gosling, Millbank Financial Services Ltd, 10 Cork Street, London W1S 3LW (020 7439 9061; email: charity@mfs.co.uk)

Farriers

The Worshipful Company of Farriers Charitable Trust

Eligibility: Registered farriers, their widows and dependants who are in need.

Types of grants: One-off and recurrent grants according to need. Grants are usually given to people who are unable to work through injury or sickness.

Annual grant total: In 2008/09 the trust had assets of £1.1 million and an income of £58,000. Grants were made to individuals totalling £3,400.

Applications: In writing to the correspondent. Applications are considered eight times a year.

Correspondent: The Clerk, 19 Queen Street, Chipperfield, Kings Langley, Hertfordshire WD4 9BT (01923 260747; fax: 01923 261677; email: theclerk@wcf.org.uk; website: www.wcf.org.uk)

Fire service

The British Fire Services Association Member's Fund

Eligibility: Fire-fighters and ex-fire-fighters who have held BFSA membership, and their dependants.

Types of grants: One-off grants according to need. It assists with one-off hardship grants, mobility aids, furniture, domestic appliances, emergency property repairs, convalescence and travel costs.

Annual grant total: In 2008 the fund had assets of £499,000 and an income of £89,000. Grants to 32 individuals totalled £12,000.

Applications: In writing to the correspondent, including details of income and expenditure and a record of fire service employment. Applicants are usually visited at home by a representative of the fund to assess their needs.

Correspondent: David Stevens, Secretary & Treasurer, 9 Brooksfield, South Kirkby, Pontefract, West Yorkshire, WF9 3DL (01977 650245; email: welfare.bfsa@btinternet.com)

The Fire Fighters Charity

Eligibility: Serving and retired fire service fire-fighters (having served five years or been medically discharged), non uniformed fire service personnel, retained and works fire-fighters and their dependants (including widows and widowers). The charity has defined eligibility criteria for each of these categories.

Types of grants: The charity looks to assist its beneficiaries by providing practical solutions to meet beneficiary need. The majority of these solutions are one off and the type of solution can vary depending on the need, in some cases this may be a monetary solution in the form of a grant or the charity may assist practically by purchasing the solution (for example equipment or home adaptations that are required due to disability/ill health). Assessments are made under either a health or general category and the cost of the solution can vary according to the needs of the beneficiary.

Exclusions: The charity cannot finance private medical care, pay off debts or cover funeral or repatriation costs. The charity does not provide loans to beneficiaries, pay university/educational fees or residential care/nursing fees. Statutory provision must be exhausted in the first instance.

Annual grant total: In 2008/09 the charity made grants to 420 individuals totalling £211,000.

Applications: Initial contact should be through the helpline but requests for assistance can be made by email or in writing. Initial assessment is made on the helpline and if the beneficiary cannot be helped through advice then a referral is made to the regional team who will arrange a home visit. An application form will be completed at the home visit and an assessment of need (including financial assessment) is carried out

Correspondent: Grants and Services, Beneficiary Support Department, Level 6, Belvedere, Basing View, Basingstoke, Hampshire RG21 4HG (0800 389 8820; fax: 01256 366599; email: helpline@firefighterscharity.org.uk; website: www.firefighterscharity.org.uk)

Other information: The charity also provides recuperation and rehabilitation services to all eligible beneficiaries.

Food, drink and provision trades

The Bakers' Benevolent Society

Eligibility: People in need who have worked in the baking industry and its allied trades and are now retired, and their dependants.

Types of grants: Recurrent grants to top-up a low income. One-off grants are also available towards essential items such as, mobility aids, lifelines and telephone rental.

Annual grant total: In 2008/09 the society had assets of £1.5 million, an income of £394,000 and a total expenditure of £306,000. Pensions and grants to individuals totalled £12,000.

Applications: On a form available from the correspondent to be submitted either directly by the individual or a family member or through an appropriate welfare agency. Applications should include details of occupational history, age and financial circumstances. Applications are considered upon receipt.

Correspondent: Suzanne Pitts, Clerk to the Society, The Mill House, 23 Bakers Lane, Epping, Essex CM16 5DQ (01992 575951; fax: 01992 561163; email: bbs@bakersbenevolent.co.uk; website: www.bakersbenevolent.co.uk)

Other information: The society also manages almshouses and sheltered housing in Congleton and Epping.

Barham Benevolent Foundation

Eligibility: People who have been employed in the milk business, and possibly their dependants, who are in need.

Types of grants: One-off grants according to need. In some circumstances the foundation will provide holiday accommodation in Southsea for employees, their close relations and former employees of the milk business.

Annual grant total: In 2008/09 the foundation had an income of £169,000 and a total expenditure of £188,000. Grants to individuals usually total around £15,000.

Applications: In writing to the correspondent.

Correspondent: Michael Cook, Hobson & Arditti, 5 Staple Inn, London WC1V 7QH (020 7242 5031; fax: 0207 831 4909)

Other information: Bursaries are also made available for the benefit of eligible students who study dairy related subjects.

The Butchers' & Drovers' Charitable Institution

Eligibility: People in the UK, who have worked in any aspect of the meat industry whether wholesale, retail or otherwise, and their close family members.

Types of grants: Pensions, one-off grants and loans. One-off grants range from £100 to £1,000 and are made towards heating bills, mobility aids, house repairs and clothing. Grants of up to £50 a week are made to top up nursing home fees.

Annual grant total: In 2008 the trust had assets of £7.8 million and an income of £460,000. Grants were made to individuals totalling £191,000, which included pensions, one-off grants and assistance towards the cost of nursing fees.

Applications: On a form available from the correspondent or to download from the website. Applications can be submitted directly by the individual or through a social worker, Citizens Advice, other welfare agency or third party and are considered on a regular basis.

Preference is given to applications which provide details of meat trade connections, verified in writing by existing meat traders or by production of other documentation.

Correspondent: The Clerk to the Trustees, Butchers' and Drovers' Charitable Institution, 105 St Peter's Street, St Albans, Hertfordshire, AL1 3EJ (01727 896094; fax: 01727 896026; email: info@bdci.uk. com; website: www.bdci.uk.com)

Caravan (the trading name of The National Grocers' Benevolent Fund)

Eligibility: To qualify for assistance applicants must:

- have worked for a minimum of 10 years in the UK grocery industry (including food manufacturing, wholesaling and retailing in all its aspects and the retail off-licence trade)
- have no more than £12,000 in savings/capital (excluding property)
- be able to demonstrate a degree of financial hardship.

Full-time and part-time workers are eligible and the grant can transfer to spouses or long term partners in the event of the beneficiary's death.

Types of grants: Annual grants of £780, paid quarterly (roughly £15 per week). Emergency grants for specific financial problems such as house repairs, disability aids and household equipment are also available.

Annual grant total: In 2008/09 the fund had assets of £7 million and a consolidated income of £3.5 million. Grants were made totalling £1.3 million.

Applications: On a form available from the correspondent or to download from the website. Applications can be submitted directly by the individual, through a social worker, Citizens Advice, other welfare agency, or via a third party such as a relative. Applications are considered throughout the year.

Correspondent: Gillian Barker, Director General, Unit 2, Lakeside Business Park, Swan Lane, Sandhurst, Berkshire, GU47 9DN (01252 875925; fax: 01252 890562; email: info@caravan-charity org.uk; website: www.caravan-charity.org.uk)

The Fishmongers' & Poulterers' Institution

Eligibility: People in need who are, or have been, involved in the processing, wholesale and retail fish and poultry trades for at least ten years, and their dependants.

Types of grants: Pensions and one-off grants. Grants average about £250 and have been given for mobility aids, respite holidays, property repairs and heating systems.

Annual grant total: In 2009 the institution had assets of £477,000 and an income of £30,000. Grants were made totalling £26,000, of which £22,000 was given in pensions and the remaining £3,900 was distributed in one-off grants.

Applications: On a form available from the correspondent. Applications can be submitted directly by the individual or through a third party. They are considered three times a year.

Correspondent: Ali Mackey, Secretary, Butchers' Hall, 87 Bartholomew Close, London EC1A 7EB (020 7600 4106; fax: 020 7606 4108; email: fpi@ butchershall.com; website: www. butchershall.com)

Sir Percival Griffiths' Tea Planters Trust

Eligibility: People who live in the UK who are or have been involved in tea planting in India and their dependants.

Types of grants: One-off and recurrent grants up to £3,000 to help with general living expenses. One-off grants include those for assistance with medical equipment, electrical goods and so on.

Annual grant total: In 2009 the charity had an income of £7,000 and a total expenditure of £11,000.

Applications: On a form available from the correspondent including details of career in India (dates, tea garden and so on). Applications can be submitted directly by the individual, through a social worker, Citizens Advice, welfare agency, or third party and are considered at any time.

Correspondent: Stephen Buckland, Trustee, Wrotham Place, High Street, Wrotham, Sevenoaks, Kent TN15 7AE (020 7201 3065)

Licensed Trade Charity (Licensed Trade Support and Care)

Eligibility: People in need who are working, or have worked, in the licensed drinks industry, including their spouses/partners and dependent children. To qualify for assistance applicants should have worked in the trade for a minimum of three years.

Types of grants: Recurrent grants are given to those on a very low income to help with utility bills, food costs and hospital travel expenses. One-off grants are also made towards: urgently needed equipment, such as household appliances and mobility aids; household improvements like door widening, stair-lifts and ramps; convalescent care and nursing costs for those recovering from illness; and funeral expenses.

Exclusions: No grants for: education related costs such as fees for educational courses, student maintenance, and student loan repayments; top up fees for residential care; or private medical treatments.

Annual grant total: In 2009 the charity had assets of £48 million and an income of £15 million. Welfare grants to individuals totalled £535,000 and were given under the following categories:

- Quarterly grants to help with living costs
- Winter payments to assist with additional costs associated with colder weather
- Grants to help with one-off assistance

Applications: On a form available from the correspondent, including proof of membership, personal details, personal history and full financial circumstances. Applications can be submitted either directly by the individual or through a social worker, Citizens Advice or other welfare agency.

Correspondent: Head of Welfare, Heatherley, London Road, Ascot, Berkshire SL5 8DR (01344 884440; fax: 01344 884703; email: support&care@ ltcharity.org.uk; website: www. licensedtradecharity.org.uk)

Other information: The charity also operates two schools in Brighton and Ascot and offers bursaries to students whose parents have worked in the licensed drinks industry amounting to around £650,000 in 2009.

The Benevolent Society of the Licensed Trade of Scotland

Eligibility: Members of the society and people who have been employed full time in the licensed trade in Scotland for at least three years.

Types of grants: Annual pensions of up to £640. Each pensioner also receives a substantial Christmas and holiday gift. One-off grants are also available for temporary emergencies.

Annual grant total: In 2009/10 the society had an income of £454,000. The society provides pensions and one-off grants to over 200 individuals totalling about £175,000 each year.

Applications: On a form available from the correspondent at any time. Applications can be made directly by the individual or through a social worker, Citizens Advice or other welfare agency.

Correspondent: Chris Gardner, Chief Executive, 79 West Regent Street, Glasgow G2 2AW (0141 353 3596; fax: 0141 353 3597; email: chris@bensoc. org.uk; website: www.bensoc.org.uk)

The National Association of Master Bakers, Confectioners and Caterers Benevolent Fund

Eligibility: Former master bakers and their families who are in need.

Types of grants: Quarterly grants to help towards living costs such as gas, electricity and telephone bills. One-off grants are also available for specific items such as wheelchairs and household adaptations.

Exclusions: No grants are given for business debt or towards nursing home fees.

Annual grant total: In 2008 the fund had assets of £586,000 and an income of £32,000. Grants were made totalling £10,000.

Applications: On a form available from the correspondent, to be submitted by the individual or through a recognised referral agency such as a social worker, Citizens Advice or doctor. Applications are usually considered on a monthly basis.

Correspondent: The Secretary, 21 Baldock Street, Ware, Hertfordshire SG12 9DH (01920 468061)

National Dairymen's Benevolent Institution

Eligibility: People who have worked in the dairy trade in the UK for a continuous period of seven years and have since retired through age or ill health.

Types of grants: One-off grants are available towards outstanding bills, house repairs and medical equipment/aids. Regular payments of £210 to £250 per quarter are only made to existing beneficiaries.

Annual grant total: In 2008/09 the institution had assets of £215,000 and an income of £115,000. Grants were made totalling £34,000 of which £26,000 was given in pensions and £7,900 in one-off grants.

Applications: On a form available from the correspondent, submitted either directly by the individual, through a third party such as a social worker or through an organisation such as a Citizens Advice or other welfare agency. Applications are considered bi-monthly in January, March, May, July, September and November.

Correspondent: Tina Scott, Secretary, First Floor, Front Office, 8 High Street, Worthing, West Sussex BN11 1NU (01903 213065; email: tinascott@ndbi. freeserve.co.uk)

The National Federation of Fish Friers Benevolent Fund

Eligibility: Members or former members of the federation and their dependants (whether subscribers to the fund or not).

Types of grants: One-off grants in the range of £150 to £300 for necessities and convalescent holidays in the UK.

Exclusions: No grants are available for debts due to poor business practice or to organisations.

Annual grant total: Grants average about £3,000 a year, though the actual grant figure tends to fluctuate quite widely.

Applications: On a form available from the correspondent. Applications can be submitted by the individual, through a recognised referral agency (such as a social worker, Citizens Advice or AFF Associations/branches) or by the individual's family, and are considered throughout the year.

Correspondent: The General Secretary, New Federation House, 4 Greenwood Mount, Meanwood, Leeds LS6 4LQ (0113 230 7044; fax: 0113 230 7010; email: mail@federationoffishfriers.co.uk; website: www.federationoffishfriers.co.uk)

Other information: The fund maintains several convalescent homes.

The Provision Trade Charity

Eligibility: People in need in the provision and allied trade, and their dependants. Applicants are normally retired and must have been employed in the trade for at least 10 years.

Types of grants: Grants are issued quarterly. Summer and winter gifts and one-off grants can also be awarded where appropriate.

Exclusions: The charity does not provide loans.

Annual grant total: In 2008 the charity had assets of £36,000 and an income of £65,000. Grants totalled £47,000.

Applications: On a form available from the correspondent. Applications are usually considered in February, May, August and November. They can be submitted directly by the individual or through a social worker, Citizens Advice, other welfare agency or through a relation or friend. Prospective beneficiaries are visited by the trust's welfare visitor.

Correspondent: Mette Barwick, Secretary, 17 Clerkenwell Green, London EC1R 0DP (020 7253 2114; fax: 020 7608 1645; email: secretary@ptbi.org.uk; website: www.ptbi.org.uk)

Other information: This trust was founded as the Cheesemonger's Benevolent Institution in 1835 'for pensionary relief of indigent or incapacitated members of the Provision Trade and their widows'.

The trust is also referred to as 'PTBI'.

Sweet Charity

Eligibility: People in need who have worked in the confectionery or related industries for more than five years and are living on a low income, with less than £6,000 in savings (or less than £12,000 for people who have worked in the industry for more than ten years).

Types of grants: Quarterly grants of up to £260 are given to those in need who have worked in the industry for more than ten years. One-off grants of up to £600 are available to people with at least five years service for disability aids, heating repairs and household items and adaptations. Grants are also given for convalescence, holidays and respite breaks.

Annual grant total: In 2008/09 the charity had assets of £2.3 million, an income of £1.3 million and a total expenditure of £1.4 million. Grants were made totalling £390,000 and were distributed as follows:

Quarterly grants	£233,000
One-off grants	£62,000
Birthday vouchers and TV licenses	£34,000
Christmas hampers	£39,000
Holidays and beneficiary outings	£16,000

Applications: On a form available from the correspondent or to download from the website. Applications can be submitted directly by the individual or through a social worker, Citizens Advice or other welfare agency. Applicants will then be contacted by one of the charity's welfare officers who will arrange a home visit.

Correspondent: Welfare Manager, 19–20 Hatton Place, London, EC1N 8RU (020 7404 5222; fax: 020 7404 5221; email: info@sweetcharity.net; website: www.sweetcharity.net)

Other information: Sweet Charity is the working name of the Confectioners Benevolent Fund.

The charity has bases across the UK, each with a welfare officer and team of volunteers who offer support and advice to people in their area.

The Wine & Spirits Trades' Benevolent Society

Eligibility: People living in England, Northern Ireland or Wales who have worked for more than five years, directly or indirectly, in the buying, selling, producing or distributing of wines and spirits, and their dependants.

Types of grants: Regular beneficial grants towards general living expenses of up to £65 paid monthly and one-off grants of up to £250 for a variety of items, including cookers, fridges, other household furniture, structural repairs, respite breaks, electric scooters and stairlifts. The society also makes Christmas gift donations and gives grants towards TV licence fees.

Exclusions: No grants are given towards business equipment.

Annual grant total: In 2008 the society had assets of £4.1 million and an income of £1.2 million. Grants to individuals totalled £336,000 and were broken down as follows:

Beneficial grants	427	£276,000
Discretionary grants	149	£52,000
TV License scheme	57	£7,600

Applications: On a form available from the correspondent or to download from the website. Applications can be submitted directly by the individual, or through a

social worker or welfare agency. They are considered throughout the year and should include history of employment within the drinks industry. All new beneficiaries are visited by the society's welfare officer before a regular donation is made.

Correspondent: Mrs Cheng Loo, Chief Executive, 39–45 Bermondsey Street, London SE1 3XF (020 7089 3888; fax: 020 7089 3889; email: chengloo@ thebenevolent.org.uk; website: www.the benevolent.org.uk)

Other information: The society also has two residential estates and a care home and offers personal welfare support and advice.

The Wine Trade Foundation

Eligibility: People in need who are or were employed in the wine and spirit and ancillary trades in the UK and Republic of Ireland, and their dependants.

Types of grants: One-off grants for the general relief of poverty.

Annual grant total: In 2008 the trust had an income of £13,000 and a total expenditure of £10,000.

Applications: In writing to the correspondent, preferably submitted directly by the individual. Applications are considered throughout the year.

Correspondent: Michael Hasslacher, Trustee, Broomwood, Kettlewell Hill, Woking, Surrey GU21 4JJ

Furnishing trade

Furnishing Trades Benevolent Association

Eligibility: People (and their dependants) who are, or have been, employed in the furnishing industry, for a minimum of two years, and are now in financial need.

Types of grants: One-off grants averaging about £250 to help towards the purchase of scooters, recliner chairs, TV licences, the installation of walk-in showers, central heating and telephone lines. Help is also given towards the payment of rent arrears, interior decorating costs and holidays. Weekly grants of £9 per person are given to those struggling to live on state pension benefits.

Annual grant total: In 2008 the association had assets of £4.8 million and an income of £379,000. Grants were made to £119,000, with £95,000 paid in weekly grants, £20,000 paid in one-off grants and £3,300 paid towards the Edenfield Holiday Scheme.

Applications: To request an application pack write, email or telephone the association giving a brief summary of your employment history and the reasons why you are applying for financial or medical

assistance. Applications should be submitted through a third party such as a social worker, teacher, Citizens Advice or school.

Correspondent: Welfare Officer, Furniture Maker's Hall, 12 Austin Friars, London, EC2N 2HE (020 7256 5954; fax: 020 7256 6035; email: welfare@ftba.co. uk; website: www.ftba.co.uk)

Other information: The trust states that grants are mainly for the relief of need; education grants are of secondary importance.

Gardening

The Royal Fund for Gardeners' Children

Eligibility: Children in need, particularly orphans, whose parents are or have been employed full-time in horticulture. Assistance is also given to children of horticulturists who are mentally or physically disabled. Applicants should be under 25.

Types of grants: Quarterly allowances to orphaned children who are still in full-time education. One-off grants for items such as clothing, beds, bedding, holidays and so on, to other children. Grants usually range from £50 to £500.

Annual grant total: In 2008/09 the fund had assets of £808,000 and an income of £96,000. Grants and allowances made to orphaned children amounted to £57,000.

Applications: On a form available from the correspondent, with details of parents' and/or applicant's income and expenditure. Applications can be submitted either directly by the individual, or through a social worker, Citizens Advice or other welfare agency. Ideally, this should be at least two weeks before one of the committee meetings which take place in March, September and November each year.

Correspondent: Sally Hanson, Hon Secretary, 115–117 Kingston Road, Leatherhead, Surrey, KT22 7SU (email: Online contact form; website: www.rfgc.org.uk)

Gas engineering

The Institution of Gas Engineers Benevolent Fund

Eligibility: Members and ex-members of the Institution of Gas Engineers, and their dependants. Please note that other people in the gas industry who have no such connection with the institution are not eligible.

Types of grants: One-off and recurrent grants according to need.

Annual grant total: In 2009 the trust had an income of £7,000 and a total expenditure of £11,000.

Applications: In writing to the correspondent.

Correspondent: Lesley Ecob, IGEM Secretariat, IGEM House, High Street, Kegworth, Derbyshire, DE74 2DA (01509 678167; email: lesley@igem.org.uk; website: www.igem.org.uk)

Hairdressing

The Barbers' Amalgamated Charity

Eligibility: Poor, generally older, members of the medical, barber or hairdressing professions.

Types of grants: Annual pensions to those in need.

Annual grant total: In 2008/09 the charity had an income of £16,000 and a total expenditure of £14,000.

Applications: In writing to the correspondent directly by the individual or via a family member, or through an organisation such as a Citizens Advice or other welfare agency. Applications are considered throughout the year.

Correspondent: Colonel P J Durrant, The Worshipful Company of Barbers, Barber-Surgeons' Hall, 1A Monkwell Square, Wood Street, London EC2Y 5BL (020 7606 0741; fax: 020 7606 3857; email: clerk@barberscompany.org; website: www.barberscompany.org)

Horticulture

The Horticultural Trades Association Benevolent Fund

Eligibility: Nurserymen and seedsmen and their dependants who are in need.

Types of grants: Usually one-off grants.

Annual grant total: Grants average around £2,000 a year, though the actual grant figure tends to fluctuate quite widely.

Applications: In writing to the correspondent.

Correspondent: David Gwyther, 19 High Street, Theale, Reading, Berkshire RG7 5AH (0118 930 3132)

Perennial

Eligibility: People who are, or have been, employed in the horticultural industry and their spouses/partners. This includes qualified and unqualified gardeners, nursery workers, garden centre employees, arboriculturists and many more.

Types of grants: One-off grants ranging from £20 to £2,000 towards a variety of needs, including support for mobility aids, property adaptations, property maintenance, domestic appliances, furniture and fittings, personal items, funeral expenses, travel and other costs linked to training, holidays, and support for micro-businesses. In certain circumstances grants may also be available for debt clearance. Quarterly payments and support for care fees of up to £50 a week are also given.

Exclusions: No grants are given for items not allowable under DWP regulations, with special reference to people receiving Income Support. No help is available for maintaining council or other rented property.

Annual grant total: In 2009 grants totalled in excess of £640,000.

Applications: Perennial has a regionally based caseworker team. Initial contact should be via the correspondent or direct to the relevant caseworker team (telephone numbers are on the website) and can be made directly by the individual or through any welfare organisation or other third party. All applicants are visited by a caseworker, usually within 14 days, who will make and initial assessment and fill in an application form with the prospective client.

Correspondent: Sheila Thomson, Director of Services, 115–117 Kingston Road, Leatherhead, Surrey KT22 7SU (0845 230 1839; fax: 01372 384055; email: info@perennial.org.uk; website: www.perennial.org.uk)

Other information: The trust provides advice, advocacy and support on welfare rights, entitlement to benefit, and accommodation issues. It also has a specialist debt advisor and a dedicated debt helpline (Tel: 0800 2944 244). Further details can be found on the website or by contacting the trust.

Hotel and catering

Hospitality Action (formerly Hotel And Catering Benevolent Association)

Eligibility: Former and current workers in the hospitality industry in the UK. The individuals or the company they work for would need to have been involved in the direct provision of food, drink and accommodation away from home.

Types of grants: One-off grants for essential needs, including short-term crisis grants to the maximum amount of £5,000.

Exclusions: The trust does not give to organisations. Funding is not available towards the following: private school fees, fees for educational courses, student maintenance, student loan repayment, private medical treatment, legal costs, residential care fee shortages.

Annual grant total: Income and expenditure for the charity was significantly higher in 2004 and 2005. However in recent years, income and expenditure for the charity has been around £3,000.

Grants made to individuals are roughly between £250 and £500 each, but this can vary depending on each individual's particular circumstances and length of service in the industry.

Applications: On a form available from the correspondent. If writing please include the individual's work history, savings available and specific need. Applications should be supported by an independent third party such as a social worker, Citizens Advice or other welfare agency. They are considered weekly.

Correspondent: Grants and Advisory Team, 62 Britton Street, London, EC1M 5UY (020 3004 5500; fax: 020 7253 2094; email: help@ hospitalityaction.org.uk; website: www. hospitalityaction.org.uk)

Other information: Hospitality Action runs The Ark Foundation Programme which offers seminars on drugs and alcohol misuse. The organisation has a membership scheme for retirees of the hospitality industry.

It also has a contact scheme for retirees of the hospitality industry which includes a bi-monthly newsletter and birthday card.

Jewellery

The British Jewellery, Giftware & Finishing Federation Benevolent Society

Eligibility: People in need who have worked in the industries covered by the federation, and their dependants. Eligible trades are jewellery manufacture and distribution, giftware, leather goods, brass and copperware manufacture and the processing or out-work finishing of metal.

Types of grants: One-off grants and loans are given towards the provision of essential items such as cookers, washing machines, fridges, freezers, bedding, telephone rental, television licence fees and household repairs. Recurrent grants are also paid to those on a low income.

Annual grant total: In 2009 the society had assets of £518,000 and an income of £157,000. Grants were made to 88 individuals totalling £54,000.

Applications: On a form available from the correspondent. Applications can be submitted either directly by the individual or through a social worker, Citizens Advice, welfare agency or other third party. Applications are considered quarterly.

Correspondent: Lynn Snead, Secretary, Federation House, 10 Vyse Street, Hockley, Birmingham B18 6LT (0121 236 2657; fax: 0121 236 3921; email: lynn@teg.co.uk; website: www.bjgf.org.uk)

The Silversmiths and Jewellers Charity

Eligibility: People in need who are, or have been, employed in any sector of the gold and silver smithing trade or the jewellery trade, and their dependants.

Types of grants: Quarterly payments of £105, a summer gift of £50 and a Christmas gift of £150 are given to regular grantees. One-off grants are also made for special needs such as domestic goods, furniture, bedding and hospital travel costs.

Of the 35 applications for assistance that were made in 2008, three were accepted as regular grantees. The remaining 34 were awarded one-off grants, referred to other organisations or rejected as ineligible.

Annual grant total: In 2008 the society had assets of £1.3 million and an income of £147,000. Grants were made totalling £59,000.

Applications: On a form available from the correspondent. Applications can be submitted directly by the individual or through a social worker, Citizens Advice or other welfare agency.

Correspondent: Julie Griffin, PO Box 2319, Leagrave, Luton LU3 3WG (01582 599800; fax: 01582 599810; email: info@thesjcharity.com)

Other information: This charity was previously known as the Goldsmiths', Silversmiths' & Jewellers' Benevolent Society.

Laundry

The Worshipful Company of Launderers Benevolent Trust

Eligibility: Existing and retired members of the laundry industry and their dependants.

Types of grants: Grants can be paid annually (towards fuel bills); biannually (fuel bills and a summer grant), or monthly (towards general living expenses).

Annual grant total: In 2009/10 the trust had assets of £465,000 and an income of £39,000. Grants made to individuals totalled £7,600.

Applications: In writing to the correspondent.

Correspondent: Mrs Jacqueline Polek, Launderers' Hall, 9 Montague Close, London SE1 9DD (020 7378 1430; fax: 020 7378 9364; email: clerk.launderers@btconnect.com; website: www.launderers.co.uk)

Leather

The Leather & Hides Trades' Benevolent Institution

Eligibility: People who work or have worked in the leather trade (i.e. in the production of leather or in the handling of hide and skin) for 10 years or more, and their dependants. Applicants are usually over 60, though people under 60 may also be considered.

Types of grants: Annuities of between £340 and £1,000 a year (paid quarterly) plus bonuses at Christmas and in the summer. Also, one-off grants to annuitants and others for special needs, and help towards shortfalls in nursing home fees.

Exclusions: No grants for funeral expenses.

Annual grant total: In 2008 the charity had assets of £718,000 and an income of £59,000. Annuities and grants were made totalling £83,000.

Applications: On a form available from the correspondent or through the charity's website. Applications can be submitted directly by the individual or through a social worker, Citizens Advice or other welfare agency. Applications can be considered at any time.

Note: Recurrent grants are subject to annual review.

Correspondent: Karen Harriman, Secretary, 107 Barkby Road, Leicester, LE4 9LG (0116 274 1500; fax: 0116 274 1500; email: karenharriman@btconnect.com; website: www.lhtbi.org.uk)

Legal

The Barristers' Benevolent Association

Eligibility: Past or present practising members of the Bar in England and Wales, and their spouses, former spouses and dependants. No grants to those who when qualified went straight into commerce.

Types of grants: One-off grants, maintenance allowances and loans. The correspondent states that some form of grant is given in most cases.

Annual grant total: In 2008 grants were made to individuals totalling £336,000.

Applications: On a form available from the correspondent. Applications can be submitted by the individual or through a social worker or other welfare agency. They are considered at monthly meetings of the management committee.

Correspondent: Janet South, Director, 14 Gray's Inn Square, London WC1R 5JP (020 7242 4764 /0207 242 4761; email: enquiries@the-baa.com; website: www.the-bba.com)

Other information: Grants are also made for educational purposes.

The Institute of Legal Executives' Benevolent Fund

Eligibility: Members and former members of the institute (including associates, fellows and student members), and their dependants.

Types of grants: One-off grants ranging between £100 and £1,000 for specific purposes such as telephone/fuel bills, nursing/residential care, medical equipment and so on. Grants can also be made to members who are unable to pay their membership subscriptions through redundancy or illness and so on.

Annual grant total: In 2009 the fund had an income of £7,600 and a total expenditure of £3,800.

Applications: On a form available from the correspondent. Applications should be submitted directly by the individual or a dependant and can be considered at any time.

Correspondent: Valerie Robertson, The Institute Of Legal Executives, Kempston Manor, Kempston, Bedford MK42 7AB (01234 845763; email: vrobertson@ilex.org.uk; website: www.ilex.org.uk)

The United Law Clerks Society

Eligibility: People employed or who were employed by any person of the legal profession in England, Scotland and Wales, and their dependants.

Types of grants: One-off and recurrent grants according to need, mainly to pensioners and people who are sick. Recurrent grants are usually for £5 to £10 a week, but can be for up to £720 a year. One-off grants can be for up to £500 or £600 a year, for example, towards cookers, roof repairs, special chairs/beds and so on.

Exclusions: No grants for students.

Annual grant total: In 2008/09 the trust had an income of £4,400 and a total expenditure of £22,000.

Applications: On a form available from the correspondent at any time. Applications can be submitted either directly by the individual, through a third party such as a social worker, or through an organisation such as a Citizens Advice or other welfare agency.

Correspondent: John Dungay, Innellan House, 109 Nutfield Road, Merstham, Surrey RH1 3HD (01737 643261; email: john_a_dungay@hotmail.com)

Market research

The Market Research Benevolent Association

Eligibility: People who are or have been engaged in market research, and their dependants.

Types of grants: Generally one-off grants for people in need. Interest free loans are also made on occasions.

Annual grant total: In 2008/09 the association had assets of £460,000 and an income of £38,000. Grants to individuals totalled £34,000.

Applications: On a form available from the correspondent. Applications can be submitted either directly by the individual or by a third party and are considered throughout the year.

Correspondent: Danielle Scott, Secretary and Treasurer, 11 Tremayne Walk, Camberley, Surrey GU15 1AH (0845 652 0303; fax: 0845 652 0303; email: info@mrba.org.uk; website: www.mrba.org.uk)

Match manufacture

The Joint Industrial Council & the Match Manufacturing Industry Charitable Fund

Eligibility: People who are or have been involved in the manufacture of matches, and their dependants.

Types of grants: One-off grants towards, for instance, medical expenses, dental and optical expenses, home security, removal costs (to sheltered accommodation) and winter fuel costs. Christmas grants are also available.

Annual grant total: In 2008 the fund had an income of £1,100 and a total expenditure of £20. No further information was available.

Applications: In writing to the correspondent, directly by the individual.

Applications are considered throughout the year.

Correspondent: Rachel Perks, Republic Technologies Ltd, Sword House, Totteridge Road, High Wycombe, Buckinghamshire HP13 6DG (01494 533300)

Media

The Chartered Institute of Journalists Orphan Fund

Eligibility: Orphaned children of institute members who are in need, aged between 5 and 22 and in full-time education.

Types of grants: Monthly grants (plus birthday/Christmas/summer holiday payments).

Annual grant total: Grants to individuals usually total around £30,000 a year.

Applications: In writing to the correspondent.

Correspondent: Norman Barlett, The Honorary Treasurer, 2 Dock Offices, Surrey Quays Road, London SE16 2XU (020 7252 1187; fax: 020 7232 2302; email: memberservices@cioj.co.uk; website: www.cioj.co.uk)

Other information: This fund also gives grants for educational purposes.

The Cinema & Television Benevolent Fund

Eligibility: People who have worked behind the scenes in the cinema, film and commercial television industries in the UK for two years in any capacity, i.e. production, exhibition, distribution, administration or transmission of film or commercial television. Help is also available to dependants.

Types of grants: One-off and recurrent grants towards the payment of television licences, medical equipment, bankruptcy fees, household essentials and so on.

Annual grant total: In 2008/09 the fund had assets of £26 million and a consolidated income of £4.2 million. Grants to individuals totalled £871,000.

Applications: On a form available from the welfare department. Applications are considered on an ongoing basis and should be submitted either directly by the individual or through a third party such as a social worker. Most applicants will be assessed by a visitor from the fund.

Correspondent: Diana Mead, 22 Golden Square, London W1F 9AD (020 7437 6567; email: charity@ctbf.co.uk; website: www.ctbf.co.uk)

Other information: The fund owns and manages a home for the elderly at Glebelands, which gives priority to those

who have worked in the world of film, cinema and television. For more information please contact the fund or go to the Glebelands website (www.glebelands.org).

The Grace Wyndham Goldie (BBC) Trust Fund

Eligibility: Employees and ex-employees worldwide engaged in broadcasting or an associated activity, and their dependants.

Types of grants: One-off grants to help relieve continuing hardship not covered by aid from other sources.

Exclusions: Grants are not given for medical, nursing or care home fees, or funeral expenses. Recurrent grants are not made.

Annual grant total: In 2009 the trust had assets of £1.1 million and an income of £39,000. Grants were made to individuals to alleviate hardship amounting to £5,000.

Applications: On a form available from the correspondent. The deadline for applications is 31 July; they are considered in September. As the income of the fund is limited, and to ensure help can be given where it is most needed, applicants must be prepared to give full information about their circumstances.

Correspondent: Christine Geen, Secretary, BBC Pension and Benefits Centre, Broadcasting House, Cardiff CF5 2YQ (029 2032 3772; fax: 029 2032 2408; website: www.bbc.co.uk/charityappeals/grant/gwg.shtml)

The Journalists' Charity

Eligibility: British journalists and dependants who are in need.

Types of grants: One-off grants, typically in the range of £250 and £500.

Annual grant total: In 2009 the charity had an income of £1.4 million and a total expenditure of £2.1 million. Grants were made totalling £305,000.

Applications: On a form available from the correspondent, including details of the career in journalism. Applications are considered monthly.

Correspondent: David Ilott, Director and Secretary, Dickens House, 35 Wathen Road, Dorking, Surrey RH4 1JY (01306 887511; fax: 01306 888212; email: enquiries@journalistscharity.org.uk; website: www.journalistscharity.org.uk)

Other information: The fund also runs residential homes in Dorking.

The Guild of Motoring Writers Benevolent Fund

Eligibility: Motoring writers, photographers and historians who are in need and are, or have been, members of the guild. Their dependants may also be supported.

Types of grants: One-off and recurrent grants according to need. For example, to help with short-term financial difficulties following redundancy or injury. Grants are also available to retired members for stair lifts, orthopaedic beds, interim nursing costs and so on.

Annual grant total: In 2008 the fund had assets of £475,000 and an income of £44,000. Grants were made totalling £7,300.

Applications: In writing to the correspondent at any time. Applications can be made either directly by the individual through a third party.

Correspondent: Elizabeth Aves, 23 Stockwell Park Crescent, London, SW9 0DQ (020 7737 2377; email: benfundamin@gomw.co.uk; website: www.gomw.co.uk/)

The National Union of Journalists Provident Fund

Eligibility: Members and former members of the National Union of Journalists and the dependants of deceased members. Applicants must have paid at least one year's full subscription to the NUJ. Please note: current members are only eligible for short-term assistance.

Types of grants: One-off grants are given for urgent bills (mainly rent and utilities), wheelchairs, beds, domestic goods, medical equipment and minor home adaptations. Bills or rent payments will generally be made directly to the supplier or landlord. Recurrent grants of up to £175 a week are also available to top up the income of those living on a state pension and/or other benefits.

Exclusions: No grants for: legal expenses, private medical treatment or private education. Members who left owing the union contributions are not eligible for help.

Annual grant total: In 2009 the fund had assets of £2.1 million and an income of £98,000. Grants were made totalling £94,000.

Applications: On a form available from the correspondent or to download from the website. Applications can be submitted by the individual or through an NUJ welfare officer or other third party. They are considered throughout the year.

Correspondent: Lena Calvert, Headland House, 308–312 Gray's Inn Road, London WC1X 8DP (020 7278 7916; email: lenac@nuj.org.uk; website: www.nujextra.org.uk/)

Other information: NUJ Extra is an amalgamation of charities previously known as National Union of Journalists Members in Need Fund and National Union of Journalists Provident Fund.

Medicine and health

The 1930 Fund for District Nurses

Eligibility: Qualified nurses who have worked in the community as a district nurse, community nurse, school nurse, health visitor, community midwife or community psychiatric nurse.

Types of grants: One-off grants usually ranging from £100 to £300 for a variety of needs, including bathroom and kitchen equipment, household essentials, mobility aids, spectacles, dentures and specialist equipment. The fund also provides recurrent grants to help with living expenses.

Exclusions: No grants are given for care home fees, educational fees, private healthcare, payment of debt, payment of rent/council tax.

Annual grant total: In 2008/09 the fund had assets of £1.4 million and an income of £59,000. Grants were made totalling £35,000.

Applications: On a form available from the correspondent or to download from the website. Applications can be submitted directly by the individual, through a social worker, a Citizens Advice, other welfare agency or third party. They are considered throughout the year and should include details of nursing experience and an invoice or quote for any work or item being applied for. A third party applying on the individual's behalf should also include a letter of endorsement.

Correspondent: Mia Duddridge, The Trust Partnership, 6 Trull Farm Buildings, Tetbury, Gloucestershire GL8 8SQ (01285 841904; fax: 01285 841576; email: 1930fund@thetrustpartnership.com; website: www.1930fundfornurses.org/)

Ambulance Service Workers' Hardship Fund

Eligibility: Employees and ex-employees in the ambulance service and their dependants.

Types of grants: One-off and recurrent grants according to need.

Annual grant total: Grants usually total around £6,000 per year.

Applications: On a form available from the ambulance service trade union.

Correspondent: Simon Oestreicher, UNISON, 1 Mabledon Place, London WC1H 9AJ (020 7551 1356; email: welfare@unison.co.uk)

Ambulance Services Benevolent Fund

Eligibility: Present and former ambulancemen/women, who have been employed by the NHS ambulance services, and their dependants. If retired, it must be for age or medical reason. People who only served for a couple of years before seeking other employment for the rest of their working life are not considered.

Types of grants: One-off grants of £100 to £1,000 are awarded to relieve genuine hardship, poverty or distress, or to assist medically.

Annual grant total: In 2008/09 the fund had assets of £161,000 and an income of £37,000. Grants were made to 35 individuals totalling £20,000 and distributed as follows:

Long term sickness	£5,600
Convalescence/respite care	£5,300
Disability aid	£4,300
Financial hardship	£2,000
Bereavement	£1,400
Problems caused by theft	£1,000

Applications: Applications are considered throughout the year and should be made in writing to the correspondent. The application should include: age, length of service with dates, name of the service, specific details of hardship, number of dependants, support received from other agencies and any other relevant information to support the claim. Applications are generally expected to come through a recognised referral agency (social worker, Citizens Advice, doctor or ambulance officer/manager) but they can be accepted directly from the individual if the matter is of a very personal or confidential nature.

Correspondent: Simon Fermor, Secretary, Cherith, 150 Willingdon Road, Eastbourne, East Sussex BN21 1TS (01323 721150; email: enquiries@asbf.co.uk; website: www.asbf.co.uk)

BMA Charities Trust Fund

Eligibility: Medical doctors and their dependants who are in financial need due to illness or unemployment, whether or not they are BMA members.

Types of grants: One-off grants of up to £6,000 for specific items in times of crisis and the payment of debts. Support is also available for terminal and palliative care, including night sitter services, respite breaks for carers, personal care, domestic help or a holiday break for the patient and their family.

Exclusions: The trust does not help with legal fees, private medical treatment or career enhancement projects. There are no general grants for 'living costs'.

Annual grant total: In 2009 the trust made grants totalling £181,000.

Applications: On a form available from the correspondent, to be submitted at any time. Two personal references are required, one of which must be from a doctor.

Correspondent: Marian Flint, BMA House, Tavistock Square, London, WC1H 9JP (020 7383 6142; email: info. bmacharities@bma.org.uk; website: www. bma.org.uk/about_bma/charities)

Other information: The BMA Charities Trust Fund incorporates the Hastings Benevolent Fund and the BMA Educational Fund.

The British Dental Association Benevolent Fund

Eligibility: Dentists who are or have been on the UK dental register and their dependants.

Types of grants: One-off grants to help meet specific needs such as washing machines, TV licences, fridges, fuels costs, household repairs, holidays and respite care. Regular grants to supplement income are also available as are interest-free loans to relieve difficulties with a limited time span.

Exclusions: Help is not usually given with private medical fees or private school fees. The trust does not generally help people with a considerable amount of capital.

Annual grant total: In 2009 the fund had assets of £4.9 million and an income of £273,000. Grants were made totalling £220,000.

Applications: On a form available from the correspondent. Applications are considered as they are received. Enquiries can be made directly by the individual or through a social worker, Citizens Advice, welfare agency or other third party.

Correspondent: Mrs Sally Atkinson, 63–64 Wimpole Street, London W1G 8YS (020 7486 4994; email: dentistshelp@ btconnect.com; website: bdabenevolentfund.org.uk)

The Cameron Fund

Eligibility: General practitioners and their dependants who are in need.

Types of grants: One-off and recurrent grants towards general expenses, holidays, house repairs, replacement of household equipment, children's needs, nursing home fees and so on. Each application is considered on its own merits. Occasionally support may be offered in the form of an interest-free loan.

Exclusions: No grants can be made towards items which should be provided through statutory sources. Educational grants are only given to families previously supported by the trust.

Annual grant total: In 2008 the trust had assets of £3.8 million and an income of £258,000. Grants were made totalling £157,000.

Although submitted on time, 2009 accounts were not available to view at the Charity Commission.

Applications: On a form available from the correspondent or to download from the website. Applications can be submitted at any time, either directly by the individual or through a social worker, Citizens Advice, solicitor or other welfare agency. Applications are considered on a quarterly basis, though decisions can be made sooner in urgent cases. A trustee will usually visit the applicant before agreeing a grant.

Correspondent: Jane Cope, Services Manager, Tavistock House North, Tavistock Square, London WC1H 9HR (020 7388 0796; email: info@cameronfund. org.uk; website: www.cameronfund. uk)

The Chartered Society of Physiotherapy Members' Benevolent Fund

Eligibility: Members, past members, assistant members and student members of the society.

Types of grants: One-off grants for emergency needs such as respite care or house repairs. Recurrent grants to help with living expenses, household repairs, heating bills and road tax (where car use is essential). The fund also supplements low income. Grants can range from £80 a month to £220 a month.

Exclusions: No grants towards payment of debts or when statutory help is available.

Annual grant total: In 2008 the society had assets of £1.2 million and an income of £151,000. Grants were made to 40 beneficiaries totalling £44,000.

Applications: On a form available from the correspondent. Applications should be submitted directly by the individual or by a third party such as a carer or partner. Applications are considered in January, April, July and October.

Correspondent: Christine Cox, 14 Bedford Row, London WC1R 4ED (020 7306 6642; fax: 020 7306 6643; email: coxc@csp.org. uk; website: www.csp.org.uk)

Other information: Grants are made for educational purposes.

The Benevolent Fund of the College of Optometrists and the Association of Optometrists

Eligibility: Current and retired members of the optical profession and their dependants.

Types of grants: Regular monthly payments to elderly or ill members towards bills and other living expenses. One-off grants are occasionally given towards costly items of expenditure such as house repairs,

wheelchairs and holidays. Christmas grants are also given. For younger practitioners unable to work, the fund may assist with professional fees. Grants usually range from £20 to £200.

Exclusions: No grants to students.

Annual grant total: In 2008/09 the fund had assets of £906,000 and an income of £101,000. Grants were made to individuals totalling £53,000.

Applications: Application forms are available from the correspondent and a financial form must be completed. Applications are considered all year round and applicants are usually visited by a member of the profession.

Correspondent: David Lacey, Administrative Secretary, PO Box 10, Swanley, Kent BR8 8ZF (01322 660388; email: davidflacey@aol.com)

The Eaton Fund for Artists, Nurses & Gentlewomen *see entry on page 39*

Ethel Mary Fund For Nurses

Eligibility: Registered, or retired, state nurses over 40 years of age who are sick and disabled and who live in the UK.

Types of grants: Pensions are given.

Annual grant total: Grants total around £3,000 per year.

Applications: On a form available from the correspondent. Applications are considered quarterly.

Correspondent: Miss H M Campbell, Vice President, The Princess Royal House, The TA Centre, London Road, Stonecot Hill, Sutton, Surrey, SM3 9HG (020 8335 3691; email: enquiries@rbna.org.uk; website: www.rbna.org.uk/)

The Institute of Healthcare Management Benevolent Fund

Eligibility: Members and former members of the institute and their dependants.

Types of grants: Emergency one-off grants (usually around £200); monthly grants (variable according to circumstances, presently £40 to £100 a month); special Christmas and summer holiday grants usually paid to people receiving regular grants (variable but with emphasis on dependent children); and top-up nursing/ residential home fees and similar.

Exclusions: Generally no grants given to students but some educational grants may be given to members of the institute, not their children.

Annual grant total: In 2009 the fund had an income of £13,000 and a total expenditure of £11,000.

Applications: Should be submitted through a regional representative on the national council of the institute. Applications are considered on receipt.

Correspondent: Grants Administrator, c/o Institute of Healthcare Management Ltd, 18–21 Morley Street, London, SE1 7Q2 (020 7620 1030; fax: 020 7620 1040; email: enquiries@ihm.org.uk; website: www.ihm.org.uk)

The Junius S Morgan Benevolent Fund

Eligibility: Registered nurses and auxiliaries who have practised in the UK for a minimum of five years.

Types of grants: One-off grants of up to £1,500 for a variety of purposes including electricity and fuel bills, telephone charges, household renewal costs (decorating, furniture, furnishings) and television rental and licence fees.

Exclusions: Grants are not given towards educational fees, funeral costs, bankruptcy fees, residential/nursing home fees, holidays or respite care.

Annual grant total: In 2008 the fund had assets of £1.4 million and an income of £198,000. Grants were made to 127 individuals totalling £148,000.

Applications: On a form available from the correspondent or to download from the website. Applications must be submitted through a third party (i.e. a social worker, care worker or Citizens Advice) who has reviewed the application and provided a letter of support. Applications should include: three months of recent bank statements and gas/electricity bills; a current mortgage statement or rental agreement; and a written quotation if a purchase or repair is required. They are considered on a weekly basis.

Correspondent: Shirley Baines, SG Hambros Trust Company Ltd, Norfolk House, 31 St James's Square, London SW1Y 4JR (020 7597 3166; email: grantadmin@juniusmorgan.org.uk; website: www.juniusmorgan.org.uk)

The NHS Pensioners' Trust

Eligibility: i) Any person who has retired from service in any capacity in the NHS in England, Wales or Scotland; ii) Any person who has retired from service in England, Wales or Scotland for any of the related health service organisations or caring professions prior to the creation of the NHS; and iii) Any person who is the wife, husband, widow, widower or other dependant of those specified above.

Types of grants: Grants of up to £350, for general upkeep to ease financial difficulty in cases of hardship, including the cost of disabled living, aids and equipment, repairs to the home and fuel bills. Larger grants can be considered in particular circumstances. Grants are one-off, but

individuals can reapply in the following year.

Annual grant total: In 2008/09 the fund had assets of £840,000 and an income of £55,000. Grants totalled £70,000 and were distributed in 314 individual grants.

Applications: On a form available from the correspondent following receipt of an sae. Applications containing supporting information and/or the backing of social work agencies will be processed more quickly. A trust representative may follow up applications to verify information.

Correspondent: Frank Jackson, Director, PO Box 456, Esher, KT10 1DP (020 7307 2506; fax: 020 7307 2800; email: frankjackson1945@yahoo.com; website: www.nhspt.org.uk)

NurseAid – The Edith Cavell Fund for Nurses

Eligibility: Nurses of limited means who are already claiming all appropriate state benefits. To qualify for assistance, registered/enrolled nurses must have more than three years post qualification experience. Auxiliary nurses should have at least five years experience of working in a hospital or under the guidance of a registered nurse (e.g. Marie Curie community nursing). In exceptional circumstances, help may also be given to student nurses.

Types of grants: One-off and recurrent grants towards, for example, household repairs and equipment, current utility and telephone bills, specialist aids, spectacles, dental work, convalescence and respite breaks. One-off grants usually range from £100 to £500, but are occasionally up to £1,000. Regular grants range from £5 to £30 per week.

Exclusions: No grants for debt repayment, holidays, bankruptcy fees, funeral expenses, educational costs or nursing home fees.

Annual grant total: The fund gives around £500,000 in grants each year.

Applications: On a form available from the correspondent or to download from the website. Applications should include a letter of support from someone who is aware of the applicant's situation, for example, a senior nurse, GP, social worker, Citizens Advice worker or minister of religion. They can be submitted at anytime.

Correspondent: Peter Farrall, Chief Executive Officer, Grosvenor House, Prospect Hill, Redditch, Worcestershire B97 4DL (01527 595999; email: admin@nurseaid.org.uk; website: www.nurseaid.org.uk/)

Other information: This fund incorporates 'The Groves Trust for Nurses'.

Pharmacist Support (formerly Royal Pharmaceutical Society's Benevolent Fund)

Eligibility: Pharmacists and their families, pre registration trainees and those retired from the profession. Support is also available to pharmacists no longer on the register of the RPSGB or General Pharmaceutical Council e.g. those taking a break from pharmacy, on maternity leave or those who have been removed from the register (for whatever reason).

Types of grants: Health and wellbeing grants, one off and regular grants. Typical funding examples include grants to support mental or physical quality of life (for counselling, convalescence after an illness or accident or for purchasing a particular disability aid); to support those who cannot meet a specific cost and require temporary assistance (perhaps due to an unforeseen loss of work); to support those on a very low income who are finding it difficult to make ends meet without getting into debt. Grants may also be made to support students facing particular hardship due to unforeseen circumstances such as family issues, ill-health or bereavement.

Exclusions: There are no grants available for pharmacy technicians or pharmacy assistants. Support is not available in Northern Ireland.

Annual grant total: In 2009 the charity's assets stood at £11 million and it had an income of £358,000. Grants were made to 164 individuals totalling £253,000.

Applications: On a form available to download from the charity's website, or by contacting the correspondent. Applications will be considered year round and can be submitted either directly by the individual or through a social worker, Citizens Advice, other welfare agency, or other third party on behalf of an individual. An initial phone call is welcomed.

Correspondent: Grant Administrator, 3rd Floor, The Pinnacle, 73–79 King Street, Manchester M2 4NG (0808 168 2233; Fax: 0161 441 0319; email: info@pharmacistsupport.org; Website: www.pharmacistsupport.org)

Other information: The charity also provides debt, benefits and employment advice, a Listening Friends stress helpline (run by trained volunteer pharmacists), addiction support and information and signposting services.

The Queen's Nursing Institute

Eligibility: Qualified district, community and Queen's nurses, usually who are unable to work due to age, illness or disability. Help may also be given to those who need some financial assistance at crucial times to help them remain in the profession.

Types of grants: One-off and recurrent grants ranging between £300 and £3,500 to help with household essentials, building repairs and adaptations, bills, specialist aids and equipment, respite care and holidays.

Exclusions: No grants for residential or nursing home fees, debt, cost of medical treatment or funeral expenses.

Annual grant total: In 2008 the institute had assets of £6.5 million and an income of £694,000. Grants were made totalling £92,000 in providing welfare support.

Applications: On a form available from the correspondent or to download from the website. Applications can be submitted by the individual, or through a recognised referral agency (social worker, Citizens Advice or doctor) or other third party and are considered in February, May, August and November.

Correspondent: Joanne Moorby, 3 Albemarle Way, Clerkenwell, London EC1V 4RQ (0207 549 1405; fax: 020 7490 1269; email: joanne. moorby@qni.org.uk; website: www.qni. org.uk)

The Royal College of Midwives Trust

Eligibility: Midwives, former midwives and student midwives who are in need.

Types of grants: Usually one-off grants for emergency or other unexpected needs (typically £50 to £200); very occasionally regular allowances where needed. Grants are given, for instance, towards the cost of a wheelchair, removal expenses, furniture, disability chairs, personal items and household equipment.

Exclusions: Dependants of those eligible are unable to receive grants.

Annual grant total: In 2008/09 the trust had assets of £5.1 million and an income of £3.3 million. Support to members amounted to £37,000.

Applications: On a form available from the correspondent. Applications should be submitted either directly by the individual or through a third party such as a nursing organisation. They are considered every six to eight weeks.

Correspondent: Clifford Crisp, The Royal College of Midwives, 15 Mansfield Street, London W1G 9NH (020 7312 3535; fax: 020 7312 3536; email: info@rcm.org. uk; website: www.rcm.org.uk)

Royal College of Nursing Benevolent Fund

Eligibility: Registered or retired nurses and members of the RCN, who are sick or in need.

Types of grants: One-off grants ranging from £50 to £1,000. Grants can be given towards: aids for daily living; mobility and communication; household repairs or

equipment, if health, safety or well-being are at risk; payment of gas, electricity, phone and water bills; and respite care and convalescence.

Exclusions: No grants towards student nurses (except student members who are in ill health), care home fees, regular grants, costs of study or further education or private medical treatment and care.

Annual grant total: In 2008/09 grants were made totalling £170,000.

Applications: On a form available from the correspondent, providing details of income, savings and outgoings, nursing career history, confirmation of need for a grant and information to assist in advising on other sources of grant aid and welfare. Applications can be submitted directly by the individual or a family member and are considered throughout the year.

Correspondent: Jane Clarke, Welfare Service, 20 Cavendish Square, London W1G 0RN (020 7647 3599; email: jane. clarke@rcn.org.uk; website: www.rcn.org. uk)

The Royal Medical Benevolent Fund

Eligibility: Registered medical practitioners whose names are on the UK General Medical Council (GMC) register, their wives, husbands, widows, widowers and dependent children who are in need and are resident in Great Britain.

Types of grants: One-off gifts/loans and regular grants are only provided for the relief of poverty and are made entirely at the discretion of the fund's case committee.

Exclusions: No grants for second degrees, private health care and medical insurance, private education, legal fees, Inland Revenue payments, the repayment of loans from family and friends, improvements and repairs to rented property. Medical students can only receive support if their parents are beneficiaries in their own right.

Annual grant total: In 2008/09 the fund had assets of £20 million and an income of £2.1 million. Grants were made to individuals totalling £785,000.

Applications: On a form available from the correspondent, which can be submitted either directly by the individual or through a social worker, Citizens Advice, other welfare agency, medical colleague or other medical and general charities.

Two references are required (at least one of which should be from a medical practitioner). All applicants are visited before a report is submitted to the case committee. Income/capital and expenditure are fully investigated, with similar rules applying as for those receiving Income Support. Applications are considered bi-monthly.

Correspondent: The Senior Case Manager, 24 King's Road, Wimbledon, London

SW19 8QN (020 8540 9194; email: enquiries@rmbf.org; website: www. rmbf.org)

Other information: Voluntary visitors liaise between beneficiaries and the office.

The Royal Medical Foundation

Eligibility: Medical practitioners and their dependants who are in need.

Types of grants: One-off grants, monthly pensions and maintenance grants of £500 to £15,000. Previous applications have included support for doctors with debt problems, fall-out from divorce or suspension, re-training expenses, practical financial support during/after rehabilitation, help with essential domestic bills, respite breaks, home alterations for the elderly or people with disabilities and nursing home fees.

Annual grant total: In 2008/09 the foundation gave grants to individuals totalling £200,000, which were broken down as follows:

Regular payments to medical practitioners and their widows/widowers	11	£25,000
Short-term or one-off grants for urgent assistance	19	£38,000
Financial assistance with educational expenses	16	£109,000
Financial assistance with educational expenses at Epsom College	1	£26,000
Other grants	2	£650

Applications: On a form available from the correspondent, for consideration throughout the year. Applications can be submitted either by the individual or a family member, through a third party such as a social worker or teacher, or through an organisation such as Citizens Advice or a school. The trust advises applicants to be honest about their needs. All applicants are means tested.

Correspondent: Fiona Anderson and Helen Jones, RMF Office, Epsom College, College Road, Epsom, Surrey KT17 4JQ (01372 821010/11; email: caseworker@ royalmedicalfoundation.org; website: www.epsomcollege.org.uk/royal-medical-foundation)

The Society for Relief of Widows & Orphans of Medical Men

Eligibility: Widows, widowers or orphans of any doctor who was at the time of his/ her death, and for the preceding two years, a member of the society. In certain circumstances members and their dependants may also be eligible. Any surplus income may be used to help medical practitioners and their dependants who are in need but are not members of the society.

Types of grants: One-off and recurrent grants of between £500 and £3,000

towards: helping family hardship at times of illness or loss of 'bread-winner'; debt repayments; home alterations to accommodate wheelchairs; household repairs; retraining; and for medical students who are the children of doctors where the family is in need.

Exclusions: Grants are not normally made towards nursing home fees, loans, long-term assistance or second degrees.

Annual grant total: In 2009 a total of 104 grants were made to widows and orphans totalling £64,000.

Applications: On a form available from the correspondent or to download from the website. Applications should be submitted directly by the individual and are considered in February, May, August and November.

Correspondent: The Secretary, Medical Society of London, Lettsom House, 11 Chandos Street, Cavendish Square, London W1G 9EB (01234 217522; email: info@widowsandorphans.org.uk; website: www.widowsandorphans.org.uk)

Benevolent Fund of the Society of Chiropodists

Eligibility: Members/former members of the society or one of its constituent bodies and their dependants.

Types of grants: One-off grants according to need, ranging from £50 to £1,000.

Annual grant total: In 2009 the fund had an income of £19,000 and a total expenditure of £28,000.

Applications: On a form available from the correspondent, to be submitted directly by the individual or through a third party. Applications are considered monthly.

Correspondent: Honorary Secretary, 1 Fellmongers Path, Tower Bridge Road, London SE1 3LY (020 7234 8623; email: dg@scpod.org)

The Society of Radiographers Benevolent Fund

Eligibility: Past and present members of the society and their dependants, with a possible preference for people who are in ill health, elderly or incapacitated.

Types of grants: One-off grants towards, for example, stairlifts, re-training, orthopaedic beds, house adaptations, car repairs, healthcare travel costs, long term residential care, computer equipment and washing machines.

Exclusions: There are no grants available for further education.

Annual grant total: In 2008/09 the fund had an income of £11,000 and a total expenditure of £8,900.

Applications: Applicants must complete an application form and a financial circumstances form, both of which are available on request from the correspondent or to download directly from the fund's website. Applications can be submitted by the individual or through a third party such as a colleague or relative.

Correspondent: Grants Officer, 207 Providence Square, Mill Street, London SE1 2EW (020 7740 7200; email: info@sor.org; website: www.sor.org)

The Trained Nurses Annuity Fund

Eligibility: Nurses aged 40 or over who are disabled and have at least seven years service.

Types of grants: Annuities and occasionally one-off grants. Each year beneficiaries of recurrent grants send a short report explaining whether financial circumstances have changed and whether they are still in need of assistance.

Exclusions: No grants for education or house improvements.

Annual grant total: Grants usually total around £24,000 a year.

Applications: On a form available from the correspondent. These should normally be submitted by doctors or social workers along with a doctor's certificate or by the individual. Applications are considered at executive meetings and payments are made in July and December.

Correspondent: Miss H M Campbell, The Princess Royal House T.A.C, Stonecot Hill, Sutton, Surrey, SM3 9HG (020 8335 3691; email: enquires@rbna.org)

Metal trades

The Institution of Materials, Minerals & Mining

Eligibility: Members of the institution and former members and their dependants.

Types of grants: One-off and recurrent grants in the range of £250 and £3,500. One-off grants in kind are also made.

Annual grant total: In 2008/09 the institution had assets of £8.4 million and an income of £6.5 million. Total outgoing resources amounted to £4.2 million, but it was not clear how much of this was given directly in support of individuals.

Applications: On a form available from the correspondent for consideration at any time.

Correspondent: R Milbank, Finance Director, c/o The Institution of Materials, Minerals & Mining, 1 Carlton House Terrace, London, SW1Y 5DB (website: www.iom3.org)

London Metal Exchange Benevolent Fund

Eligibility: People in need who are members of, or have been connected with, the London Metal Exchange, and their dependants.

Types of grants: One-off and recurrent grants according to need.

Annual grant total: In 2008/09 the fund had an income of £8,500 and a total expenditure of £22,000, the majority of which was distributed in individual grants.

Applications: On a form available from the correspondent.

Correspondent: Philip Needham, The London Metal Exchange Ltd, 56 Leadenhall Street, London EC3A 2DX (020 7264 5555)

Rainy Day Trust (formerly Royal Metal Trades Benevolent Society)

Eligibility: People who are in need and have worked in any of the DIY, hardware, housewares, ironmongery, builders merchants and brushware industries – normally for at least ten years. The trust tends to focus on people who are over 60 years old but younger individuals may also be eligible for assistance.

Types of grants: One-off grants towards, for example, mobility equipment and installations, travel expenses to see distant relatives, nursing home or residential fees, holidays, TV licences, funeral expenses, food hampers at Christmas, utility bills, household equipment and so on. Pensions are also given.

Exclusions: No grants are given to children, or to people working in the steel and motor industries.

Annual grant total: In 2008 the trust had assets of £1.3 million and an income of £142,000. Grants were made to 112 individuals totalling £123,000, and were distributed as follows:

Quarterly pensions	£104,000
Christmas hampers/grants	£6,200
Holiday grants	£1,500
TV licence grants	£550
Funeral grants	£600
Telephone	£5,200
Other grants	£4,900

Applications: On a form available from the correspondent or the trust website. Applications can be submitted directly by the individual or through a social worker, Citizens Advice or other welfare agency. Applications are considered at any time.

Correspondent: Martina Farragher, Administration Manager, Federation House, 10 Vyse Street, Birmingham, B18 6LT (0121 237 1130; fax: 0121 237 1133; email: rainyday@ brookehouse.co.uk; website: www. rainydaytrust.org.uk)

Mining

Mining Institute of Scotland Trust

Eligibility: Members or former members of the Mining Institute of Scotland and their dependants.

Types of grants: One-off and recurrent hardship grants of up to £1,000 a year. Widows of members can receive Christmas and summer holiday grants.

Annual grant total: The trust has about £25,000 available to give in grants each year, for both education and hardship purposes. It has difficulty in finding enough eligible applicants to support.

Applications: In writing to the correspondent, in the first instance, to request an application form.

Correspondent: The Secretary, 2 Ashfield Gardens, Kelty, Fife, KY4 0JY

Other information: Schools are also supported.

Motor industry

Ben – Motor & Allied Trades' Benevolent Fund

Eligibility: People from the UK or Republic of Ireland employed or formerly employed in the motor, motorcycle, commercial vehicle, or agricultural engineering industries plus all associated trades, organisations and industries. Dependants of employees can also apply.

Types of grants: One-off grants are usually under £500, although larger grants up to and over £1,750 are not uncommon. Recurrent grants and loans are also made. In the past grants have been given towards travel costs, specialist medical equipment, home adaptations, respite breaks and help with household bills.

Exclusions: The trust cannot assist with property repairs, education costs, or private medical costs.

Annual grant total: In 2008/09 the fund had assets of £13 million and an income of £12 million. There were 2,227 grants made to individuals totalling £616,000.

Applications: On a form available from the correspondent. Applications can be submitted directly by the individual or through a social worker, Citizens Advice or other welfare agency. An initial phone call is welcomed.

Correspondent: Brian Cottrell, Lynwood, Sunninghill, Ascot, Berkshire SL5 0AJ (01344 620191; fax: 01344 622042; email: careservices@ben.org.uk; website: www.ben.org.uk)

Other information: The fund also manages an extensive range of residential and nursing accommodation for people who are older or living with a disability, including sheltered accommodation.

H T Pickles Memorial Benevolent Fund

Eligibility: Present and former members, and employees of members, of the Vehicle Builders and Repairers Association who are in need, and their dependants. Applicants must have been a member or employee for at least five years.

Types of grants: One-off and recurrent grants according to need.

Annual grant total: In 2009 the fund had an income of £1,000 and a total expenditure of £3,400.

Applications: On a form available from the correspondent.

Correspondent: David C Hudson, c/o Vehicle Builders' & Repairers' Association Ltd, Belmont House, Gildersome, Leeds LS27 7TW (0113 253 8333; fax: 0113 238 0496; email: vbra@vbra.co.uk; website: www.vbra.co.uk)

Other information: The fund is also known as the VBRA Benevolent Fund.

The Society of Motor Manufacturers & Traders Charitable Trust Fund

Eligibility: People in need who held 'responsible positions' in the motor industry, and their dependants.

Types of grants: One-off and recurrent grants and loans according to need.

Annual grant total: In 2009 the society had assets of £735,000 and an income of £27,000. Grants were made totalling £12,000.

Applications: In writing to the correspondent.

Correspondent: Sefton Samuels, SMMT, Forbes House, Halkin Street, London SW1X 7DS (0207 344 9267; email: charitabletrust@smmt.co.uk)

Naval architecture

Royal Institution of Naval Architects

Eligibility: Members and their dependants who are in need.

Types of grants: One-off grants for a variety of needs.

Annual grant total: In 2008/09 the trust had assets of £2.6 million and an income of £2.3 million. Grants were made totalling £25,000.

Applications: In writing to the correspondent, to be considered as they arrive.

Correspondent: Trevor Blakeley, Chief Executive, 10 Upper Belgrave Street, London SW1X 8BQ (020 7235 4122; fax: 020 7259 5912; email: hq@rina.org.uk; website: www.rina.org.uk)

Other information: This trust also provides scholarships and training programmes.

Newsagents

The National Federation of Retail Newsagents Convalescence Fund

Eligibility: Members of the federation and their spouses. Other people in the retail newsagency trade who are not members of the federation are not eligible.

Types of grants: One-off grants for convalescent holidays.

Annual grant total: In 2007 the fund had an income of £20,000 and a total expenditure of £13,000.

Applications: In writing to the correspondent. Applications can be submitted directly by the individual, through a third party such as a social worker or through a district office of the federation. They are considered at any time.

Correspondent: Michael Jenkins, Yeoman House, Sekforde Street, Clerkenwell Green, London EC1R 0HF (020 7017 8855; email: info@nfrn.org.uk; website: www.nfrnonline.com)

Other information: Recent accounts were overdue at the Charity Commission.

NewstrAid Benevolent Society

Eligibility: Retired people and their dependants, and those who cannot work through ill health, who have been engaged in the distribution and sale of newspapers and magazines in the UK, normally for at least five years, and are not currently trading or working. The trust has stated that all applications are considered on their own merit and that the applicant must have a proven trade connection and be in need.

Types of grants: Annual payments and one-off grants for various items including household appliances, special chairs, mobility aids, small repairs and disability equipment. The charity offers interest free loans to home owners in respect of costly repairs, repayable on the sale of their property.

Exclusions: No grants for private medicine or school or college fees.

Annual grant total: In 2009 the charity had assets of £5.5 million and an income of £1.8 million. Approximately £532,000 was given in grants to individuals for welfare purposes.

Applications: On a form available from the correspondent or to download from the website. Applications should be referred through an almoner, NewstrAid volunteer, social worker, welfare agency or any third party who can confirm the individual's background. They are considered every two months.

Correspondent: Welfare Manager, Barnetson Court, Braintree Road, Great Dunmow, Essex CM6 1HS (01371 874198; fax: 01371 873816; email: sinead@ newstraid.org.uk; website: www.newstraid. org.uk)

Other information: The charity also manages a care home in Great Dunmow, Essex.

Patent agents

The Incorporated Benevolent Association of the Chartered Institute of Patent Attorneys

Eligibility: British members and former members of the institute, and their dependants.

Types of grants: One-off and recurrent grants or loans according to need.

Annual grant total: In 2008/09 the association had assets of £579,000 and an income of £54,000. Welfare grants totalled £14,000.

Applications: In writing to the correspondent, marked 'Private and Confidential'. Applications can be submitted at any time. Where possible, grants are provided via a third party.

Correspondent: Derek Chandler, 95 Chancery Lane, London WC2A 1DT

Other information: The association also makes grants for educational purposes.

Pawnbrokers

The Pawnbrokers' Charitable Institution

Eligibility: Pawnbrokers in need who have been in the business for at least five years, and their dependants. Help is primarily given to people over 60 but assistance may also be available to younger people if there is sufficient need.

Types of grants: Regular payments for those on a low income and one-off grants to meet emergency needs. Recent grants have been given towards new furniture, a cooker and a reclining chair. Christmas and summer grants of about £250 each are also available to beneficiaries.

Annual grant total: In 2008/09 the institution had assets of £2.6 million and an income of £88,000. Grants were made to 39 individuals totalling £98,000.

Applications: On a form available from the correspondent. The trustees meet on the first Tuesday of every month to consider applications.

Correspondent: Mrs K Way, Secretary, 184 Crofton Lane, Orpington, Kent BR6 0BW (01689 811978)

Petroleum

BP Benevolent Fund

Eligibility: Former employees of BP plc or subsidiary or associated companies and the dependants of such persons.

Types of grants: One-off and recurrent according to need and vouchers.

Annual grant total: In 2008/09 the fund had assets of £1.1 million and an income of £33,000. Grants were made to individuals totalling £19,000, which consisted of 13 occasional hardship grants totalling £7,000 and £12,000 given in other grants to nine individuals.

Applications: In writing to the correspondent.

Correspondent: Peter Darnell, BP Benevolent Fund Trustees Ltd, 4 Woodside Close, Shermanbury, Horsham RH13 8HH (01403 710437; email: peter.darnell@uk. bp.com)

Police

Indian Police Benevolent Fund

Eligibility: Former members of the Indian police, and their widows and children, worldwide.

Types of grants: One-off and recurrent grants in the range of £1,000 to £2,000.

Annual grant total: Grants usually total around £20,000 per year.

Applications: On a form available from the correspondent, for consideration throughout the year. Completed forms should be submitted directly by the individual. Widows and children should include details of their connection with the former member of the Indian police.

Correspondent: Paul Dean, Executive Trustee, 97 Verulam Road, St Albans, Hertfordshire AL3 4DL (01727 845229)

The Metropolitan Police Benevolent Fund

Eligibility: Metropolitan Police officers and ex-officers who are in need, and their widows/widowers and orphans.

Types of grants: Generally one-off grants according to need.

Annual grant total: In the period covering July 2008 to December 2009 the fund had assets of £3.7 million and an income of £4.8 million. Charitable activities totalled £1.2 million.

Applications: In writing to the correspondent directly by the individual. Applications are considered throughout the year.

Correspondent: Janice Berry, Exchequer Services (Charities), Metropolitan Police Services, Empress State Building, Empress Approach, London SW6 1TR (020 7161 1909; email: janice.berry@met. police.uk)

Other information: In 2008 the Metropolitan Police Combined Benevolent Fund and its constituent charities amalgamated into one major fund that would encompass all the objectives of the current charities (Metropolitan Police Convalescent Home Fund, Metropolitan and City Police Orphans Fund, Metropolitan Police Relief Fund and Metropolitan Police Widows and Widowers Fund). This new fund is known as the Metropolitan Police Benevolent Fund.

Metropolitan Police Civil Staff Welfare Fund

Eligibility: Members and past members of the Metropolitan Police Staff and the Metropolitan Police Authority and their families and dependants who, through poverty, hardship or distress, are in need.

Types of grants: One-off grants and loans, generally ranging between £100 and £1,000 according to need.

Exclusions: Grants are unlikely to be made towards private healthcare, private education fees, legal costs, business debts or bills that have already been paid.

Annual grant total: In 2008/09 the fund had assets of £272,000 and an income of £39,000. Grants were made to 39 individuals totalling £28,000.

Applications: On a form available from the correspondent. Applications should be submitted directly by the individual or through a social worker, Citizens Advice or other welfare agency.

Correspondent: Welfare Funds Manager, Metropolitan Police Service, 2nd Floor, Empress State Building, Empress Approach, London SW6 1TR

(020 7161 1909; email: welfarefunds@met. police.uk)

Police Dependants' Trust

Eligibility: (i) Dependants of current police officers or former police officers who have died from injuries received in the execution of duty.

(ii) Police officers or former police officers incapacitated as a result of injury received in the execution of duty, or their dependants.

Types of grants: One-off grants in the range of £120 to £100,000, averaging about £1,400 each. Grants are available for specialist equipment, disability aids, clothing, holidays (including support for accompanying professional carers) and funeral expenses. Residential care grants may also be considered to assist with incidental expenses. Annual maintenance grants are given to help incapacitated officers and police dependants enjoy a reasonable standard of living.

Annual grant total: In 2008/09 the trust had assets of £20.1 million and an income of £1,9 million. Grants totalled £1.8 million and were distributed as follows:

Maintenance Grants	339
Children's grants	272
Special Purpose Grants	180
Holiday Grants	729
Funeral Grants	4

Applications: On a form available from the correspondent, to be submitted through one of the force's welfare officers. Applications are generally considered every two months although urgent decisions can be made between meetings.

Correspondent: David French, Chief Executive, 3 Mount Mews, High Street, Hampton, Middlesex TW12 2SH (020 8941 6907; fax: 020 8979 4323; email: office@policedependantstrust.org. uk; website: www.policedependantstrust. org.uk)

St George's Police Trust (formerly the Northern Police Orphans' Trust)

Eligibility: Children in full time education with at least one parent who was a member of a police force covered by the trust (see 'Other Information'), and who is now deceased or incapacitated due to their work. Young people not in full time education who have lost a police officer parent, but who are unable to earn their own living as a result of having special needs, may also be eligible.

Please note: to be eligible the police officer parent must have donated to the trust whilst serving.

Types of grants: One-off and recurrent grants towards living costs, holidays,

clothing, birthday and Christmas gifts and so on.

Annual grant total: In 2009 the trust had assets of £8.5 million and an income of £793,000. Grants to individuals totalled £364,000.

Applications: Applications should be submitted via the police force in which the parent served. This is usually done through the police federation office, the occupational health and welfare department or occasionally the force benevolent fund. Applications are considered as they arrive.

Correspondent: Michael Baxter, St Andrews, Harlow Moor Road, Harrogate, North Yorkshire HG2 0AD (01423 504448; email: enquiries@ thepolicetreatmentcentres.org; website: www.thepolicetreatmentcentres. org)

Other information: The trust covers the following police forces: Central Scotland; Cheshire; Cleveland; Cumbria; Derbyshire; Dumfries & Galloway; Durham; Fife; Grampian; Greater Manchester Police; Humberside; Lancashire; Lincolnshire; Lothian & Borders; Merseyside; Northern; Northumbria; North Wales; North Yorkshire; Nottinghamshire; South Yorkshire; Staffordshire; Strathclyde; Tayside; West Mercia; West Yorkshire.

Post office

The Rowland Hill Memorial And Benevolent Fund

Eligibility: People in need who have been employed by the Royal Mail, Post Office, Parcelforce Worldwide or General Logistics for at least six months (full or part-time, not casual); retired employees in receipt of an occupational pension; and people who have a deferred pension. The direct dependants of such people may also be eligible for assistance.

Types of grants: One-off grants of up to £5,000 but usually less than £1,000 for disability aids, house adaptations, hospital travel costs, funeral expenses, medical equipment, essential household items and so on. Recurrent cost of living grants and help with nursing home fees are also available to older people.

Annual grant total: In 2008/09 the fund had assets of £2.4 million and an income of £419,000. Grants were made totalling £246,000.

Applications: Employees of the Royal mail group or people in receipt of an occupational pension or deferred pension should call the free 24 hour helpline operated by Royal Mail (0800 6888777). A trained advisor will conduct a short telephone assessment and, with permission, forward a report of the case to

the fund for consideration. Some medical and/or financial evidence of need may also be required.

People applying through a third party such as a social worker or Citizens Advice should apply in writing to the correspondent, including as much background information and supporting documentation as possible.

Correspondent: Mary Jeffery, Room 412, POB, Royal Mail Mount Pleasant, Farringdon Road, London EC1A 1BB (020 7239 2271; fax: 020 7239 2265; email: rowland_hill_fund@royalmail.com; website: www.rowlandhillfund.org)

The National Federation of Sub-Postmasters Benevolent Fund

Eligibility: People in need who fall into one of the following categories:

(i) Serving or retired sub-postmasters and sub-postmistresses;

(ii) Serving or retired full-time employees of the NFSP; and

(iii) The widows, widowers and children of the above in the event of a breakdown in health; the death of a husband, father, wife or mother; or domestic distress.

Types of grants: One-off and recurrent grants according to need. Recent examples include: fencing; a second hand scooter; a downstairs shower for a person who is disabled; house and roof repairs; an adjustable bed; a reconditioned stair-lift; and a holiday for somebody with disabilities.

Recurrent grants are also available.

Annual grant total: In 2008 the fund had assets of £1.4 million, an income of £105,000 and a total expenditure of £124,000. Grants were made to 56 individuals totalling £88,000.

Applications: On a form available from the correspondent, submitted directly by the individual or a welfare charity. Applications are usually considered quarterly, but emergency cases can be dealt with as they arise.

Correspondent: George Thomson, Evelyn House, 22 Windlesham Gardens, Shoreham-by-Sea, West Sussex BN43 5AZ (01273 452324; fax: 01273 465403; email: admin@nfsp.org.uk; website: www. nfsp.org.uk/)

Other information: The fund also provides access to a one on one counselling service with qualified counsellors who offer counselling and emotional support on all issues to sub-postmasters, their immediate family members and sub-post office staff.

Pottery and glass

The Pottery & Glass Trade Benevolent Fund (formerly the Pottery and Glass Trade Benevolent Institution)

Eligibility: People who are or were employed in manufacturing, wholesale or retail aspects of china or glass.

Types of grants: One-off grants and pensions. Recent grants have been made towards priority debts, house adaptations, central heating repairs, mobility scooters, essential household items and car repairs.

Annual grant total: In 2008/09 the fund had an income of £20,000 and a total expenditure of £29,000. Grants were made totalling about £25,000.

Applications: On a form available from the correspondent. Applications can be submitted directly by the individual or through a social worker, Citizens Advice or other welfare agency. They are considered quarterly in March, June, September and December and should be submitted by 1 March, June, September and December.

Correspondent: Audrey Smith, Flat 57, Witley Court, Coram Street, London WC1N 1HD (020 7837 2231; fax: 020 7837 2231)

Printing

The Printing Charity (formerly the Printers' Charitable Corporation)

Eligibility: Ex-printers, or people who have worked in the printing, paper, publishing and graphics industries, and their dependants.

Types of grants: One-off and recurrent grants ranging from £100 to £1,000 for help with mobility needs, household items, house repairs, convalescence, bankruptcy fees, 'top up' fees for nursing homes and emergency relief for people affected by flooding. Biannual financial assistance grants are also available to help with everyday living costs.

Annual grant total: In 2008 regular financial assistance totalled £43,000.

Applications: On a form available from the correspondent or from the website. Assistance is 'means tested' so applicants should be prepared to make a full declaration of their finances, including state benefits and funding from other charitable sources. Application forms can be submitted either directly by the individual or through a social worker, Citizens Advice or other third party.

The trust strongly advises potential applicants to contact them before submitting an application.

Correspondent: Henry Smith, Grants Officer, Suite B Underwood House, 235 Three Bridges Road, Crawley, West Sussex RH10 1LS (01293 542820; fax: 01293 542826; email: info@ theprintingcharity.org.uk; website: www. theprintingcharity.org.uk)

Other information: The trust provides sheltered homes for older people at Basildon and Bletchley plus a nursing home at Bletchley. It also advises pensioners on their statutory entitlements.

Probation

The Edridge Fund

Eligibility: Members, and ex-members, of the probation service and CAFCASS who are (or were) eligible to be members of NAPO and their bereaved partners, spouses and dependants.

Types of grants: Financial and welfare support, generally in a one-off grant, to alleviate cases of distress and hardship such as debt, relationship breakdown, accident or ill health.

Annual grant total: In 2008 the fund had assets of £173,000 and an income of £59,000. Grants to 123 individuals totalled £44,000 and were distributed as follows:

Bereavement	£1,200
Special	£43,000
Christmas	£140

Applications: On a form available from the correspondent, a local representative or on the fund's website. Applications can be submitted either directly by the individual or through the local representative of the fund. A decision is usually made within three weeks, though emergency cases can be dealt with more quickly.

NB. If applicants do not wish their local representative to be aware of their application it should be stated clearly on their form.

Correspondent: Richard Martin, Secretary, The Limes, Lynn Road, Gayton, King's Lynn, Norfolk PE32 1QJ (01553 636570; email: edridge@btinternet.com; website: www.edridgefund.org)

Public relations

Iprovision (formerly The Institute of Public Relations Benevolent Fund)

Eligibility: Members of the institute and dependants of members or deceased members.

Types of grants: One-off and recurrent grants according to need as well as interest free loans.

Annual grant total: In 2009 grants were made to 10 individuals totalling over £16,000.

Applications: In writing to the correspondent. Applications are considered every two months, although urgent applications can be considered at any time.

Correspondent: Jane Wharam, Administrator, 9 Eyston Drive, Weybridge, KT13 0XD (020 8144 5536; email: administrator@iprovision.org.uk; website: www.cipr.co.uk/iprovision)

Public sector

Corporation of London Benevolent Association

Eligibility: People in need who are, or have been, members of the Court of Common Council, and their dependants.

Types of grants: One-off grants according to need.

Annual grant total: In 2008/09 the charity had an income of £13,000 and a total expenditure of £3,900. Grants totalled around £3,800.

Applications: In writing to the correspondent.

Correspondent: David Milnes, Town Clerk's Office, City of London, PO Box 270, London EC2P 2EJ (020 7332 1410 (9.15–5pm); website: www.cityoflondon. gov.uk)

Other information: In recent years, the charity's investment income has exceeded its expenditure and the trustees are keen to ensure that all members, and particularly their families, are aware of the opportunity for financial assistance.

UNISON Welfare

Eligibility: Members of UNISON and past members of NALGO, and their dependants, who are in need.

Types of grants: One-off grants for individuals experiencing unforeseen difficulties such as redundancy, illness, bereavement or relationship breakdown.

Recent awards have been given to help with household bills, travel costs, childcare, furniture, domestic appliances, funeral expenses, disability aids and so on. Emergency grants of up to £150 are available when there is a crisis and money is needed quickly. For example, if an individual has been forced to leave their home and is in need of food and temporary shelter. Weekly grants may be considered if the applicant is in a temporary period of reduced income, especially if they have considerable debt.

Funding is also available for holidays, convalescence and respite breaks under the trust's 'Wellbeing Breaks' scheme.

Annual grant total: In 2009 the trust had assets of £5.6 million, an income of £1.1 million and a total expenditure of £1.3 million. Grants were made to over 2,100 individuals totalling £709,000.

Applications: Individuals should first contact their branch welfare officer or secretary who will help them to fill in an application form. Applications are usually processed within two weeks, though urgent requests can be dealt with more quickly, sometimes within 48 hours. People who are having difficulty contacting their local branch should speak to the national office.

Please note that there are separate application forms for welfare grants and wellbeing breaks.

Correspondent: Julie Grant, Head of UNISON Welfare, 1 Mabledon Place, London WC1H 9AJ (020 7551 1620; email: welfare@unison.co.uk; website: www.unison.org.uk/welfare)

Other information: The trust provides support and advice on a variety of issues including personal debt and state benefits.

Public transport

The Worshipful Company of Carmen Benevolent Trust

Eligibility: People based in the UK and have worked in the transport industry (for example, HGV drivers or bus drivers).

Types of grants: One-off grants usually in the region of £50 to £500, where the grant will make an exceptional difference to the individual. A recent grant was given, for example, to a disabled person who needed computer equipment.

Exclusions: The trust cannot help with holidays or bankruptcy fees.

Annual grant total: In 2008/09 the trust had assets of £841,000 and an income of £124,000. Grants totalled £73,000, however nearly all of this went to organisations during the year.

Applications: In writing to the correspondent. Please note, this trust only occasionally makes grants to individuals. The trustees meet four times a year.

Correspondent: Robin East, Hon. Secretary, 5 Kings House, Queen St Place, London, EC4R 1QS (020 7489 8289; fax: 020 7236 3133; email: enquiries@ thecarmen.co.uk; website: www. thecarmen.co.uk)

The Transport Benevolent Fund

Eligibility: Employees and former employees of the public transport industry who are in need (often due to being sick, disabled or convalescent), their partners and dependants. Only members of the benevolent fund are supported.

Types of grants: Grants are to meet unexpected one-off situations, where help is not available from other sources. They can be given towards medical equipment, complementary medical treatments and other needs.

Exclusions: There is no funding towards dental or optical treatment and funerals, except in special circumstances.

Annual grant total: In 2008/09 grants were made to individuals totalling £313,000, which were broken down as follows:

Hardship grants from trustees (i) Transport Benevolent Fund (TBF)	1166	£173,000
Hardship grants from trustees (ii) Staff Welfare Fund (SWF)	6	£1,000
Hardship grants for beneficiaries by Local Committees	830	£125,000
Medical and equipment aids (i) TBF	40	£9,000
Medical and equipment aids (ii) SWF	1	£1,000
Convalescence and recuperation expenses	70	£4,000

Applications: On a form available from the correspondent to be submitted either directly by the individual, through a third party such as a social worker, or through an organisation such as a Citizens Advice or other welfare agency. They are considered monthly or when required.

Correspondent: Chris Godbold, Director, 87a Leonard Street, London EC2A 4QS (08450 100 500; email: help@tbf.org.uk; website: www.tbf.org.uk)

Other information: In 2006 the charity acquired the assets of the Transport for London Staff Welfare Fund, which had been established in 1948 to provide help for staff of the London Transport Executive. The assets are held separately and used only for the relief of persons specified by Transport for London in the Deed of Grant.

Quarrying

The Institute of Quarrying Educational Development and Benevolent Fund

Eligibility: Members or former members of the Institute of Quarrying, and/or their dependants. People who are involved in the quarrying industry but are not members of the institute cannot be considered.

Types of grants: One-off grants ranging from £100 to £2,500. No recurrent grants are made, although most beneficiaries successfully reapply each year.

Annual grant total: In 2009/10 the trust had assets of £858,000 and an income of £37,000. Welfare grants were made to six individuals totalling £15,000.

Applications: On a form available from the correspondent. Applications may be submitted at any time.

Correspondent: Mrs Lyn Bryden, 7 Regent Street, Nottingham NG1 5BS (0115 9453882; fax: 0115 9484035; email: mail@quarrying.org; website: www. quarrying.org)

Other information: Projects which advance the education and research of quarrying are also supported.

Railways

Associated Society of Locomotive Engineers & Firemen (ASLEF) Hardship Fund

Eligibility: Members of ASLEF, and their dependants, who are in need.

Types of grants: One-off grants according to need.

Annual grant total: Grants to individuals probably total around £500 each year.

Applications: In writing to the correspondent.

Correspondent: The General Secretary, ASLEF, 9 Arkwright Road, Hampstead, London NW3 6AB (020 7317 8600; fax: 020 7794 6406; email: info@aslef.org. uk; website: www.aslef.org.uk)

Railway Benevolent Institution

Eligibility: Active and retired members of the British Railway Board, its subsidiaries and related organisations, and their spouses and children.

Types of grants: One-off and recurrent grants of £100 to £1,500.

- Single benevolent grants include help for mobility aids, minor house repairs, funeral expenses, household equipment, clothing, debt relief, convalescence and household bills.

- Annuities are paid quarterly and are available to people on a low income. They are reviewed periodically.
- Residential care grants are paid monthly to 'top up' care home fees.
- Grants from the Webb Fund are paid quarterly to parents to assist underprivileged children.
- Child care grants are given towards clothing, footwear and educational necessities like books and equipment.

Annual grant total: In 2009 the institution had assets of £3.2 million and an income of £348,000. Grants were made to over 600 individuals totalling £385,000 and distributed in the following areas:

Annuities	197	£98,000
Single Benevolent Grants	375	£264,000
Residential Care Grants	3	£7,800
Webb Fund Grants	30	£12,000
Child Care Grants	9	£2,800
Other	0	0

Applications: On a form available from the correspondent. Applications can be submitted either directly by the individual or a family member or through a third party such as a social worker, teacher or Citizens Advice. Applicants must be able to provide verification of railway service.

Correspondent: Margaret Skerratt, Electra Way, Crewe, Cheshire CW1 6HS (01270 251316; email: director@ railwaybenefitfund.org.uk; website: www. railwaybenefitfund.org.uk)

The Railway Housing Association & Benefit Fund

Eligibility: People who are working or who have worked in the railway industry, and their dependants, in England, Scotland and Wales.

Types of grants: One-off grants towards house repairs, care attendants, respite care, essential household items, aids and adaptations and general financial assistance.

Annual grant total: In 2008/09 grants to beneficiaries amounted to £37,000.

Applications: The association has transferred the administration of its grants to the Railway Benefit Fund and potential applicants should contact them directly at: Electra Way, Crewe Business Park, Crewe, Cheshire CW1 6HS – 01270 251316. However, the association is happy to help and advise any individual who wishes to discuss their case prior to making an application.

Correspondent: Anne Rowlands, Railway Housing Association and Benefit Fund, Bank Top House, Garbutt Square, Darlington, County Durham DL1 4DR (01325 482125; fax: 01325 384641; email: info@railwayha.co.uk)

Other information: The association's primary concern is the management of affordable accommodation for the benefit of older people in need.

RMT (National Union of Rail, Maritime & Transport Workers) Orphan Fund

Eligibility: The children (aged under 22) of deceased members of the union.

Types of grants: Grants are made of £12 per week per child up to 16 years of age and £12.75 per week per child continuing to receive full-time education from 16 up to 22 years of age, payable on member's death. Grants are paid quarterly in March, June, September and December.

Annual grant total: About £150,000.

Applications: Application forms are available from the branch secretary or to download from the union's website. Applications should be made through the local union branch and endorsed by the branch secretary.

Correspondent: The Benefits Section, Unity House, 39 Chalton Street, London NW1 1JD (020 7387 4771; fax: 020 7387 4123; email: info@rmt.org. uk; website: www.rmt.org.uk)

Other information: The union also provides accident, retirement, death and demotion benefits and grants for widows or widowers of members of the union.

Removal trade

The Removers Benevolent Association

Eligibility: People in need who are, or have been, employed for a minimum of one year by a member or former member of the British Association of Removers Ltd, and their dependants.

Types of grants: One-off grants, usually in the range of £250 to £750, to help those experiencing a temporary period of financial difficulty. Occasionally, recurrent grants may be given.

Annual grant total: In 2009 the association had an income of £9,400 and a total expenditure of £4,600.

Applications: In writing to the correspondent, to be submitted by the member company the employee has worked for. Applications are considered as they arrive.

Correspondent: Grants Officer, British Association of Removers, Tangent House, 62 Exchange Road, Watford, Hertfordshire WD18 0TG (01923 699480; fax: 01923 699481; email: info@bar.co.uk; website: www.bar.co.uk)

Retail trade

Retail Trust (formerly Cottage Homes)

Eligibility: People in need (and their dependants) who have worked in the retail, wholesale, manufacturing and distribution trades for at least:

- two years if still in the trade
- two years if returning to work in retail after recovering from an illness/accident
- two years (within the last five) if returning to work after bringing up a family or experiencing circumstances such as domestic violence, homelessness or caring responsibilities
- five years if retired
- ten years for former retail employees who have moved on to other trades.

Types of grants: One-off and recurrent grants ranging from £300 to £1,000 towards medical equipment, essential household items and so on.

Exclusions: No grants are given to students or for items purchased prior to the application.

Annual grant total: In 2008/09 grants for financial assistance amounted to £818,000.

Applications: On a form available from the correspondent or to download from the website. Applications should be submitted either directly by the individual or through a social worker, Citizens Advice or other welfare agency. They are usually considered in February, April, June, October and December.

Correspondent: Grants Manager, Marshall Estate, Hammers Lane, London NW7 4DQ (080 8801 0808; email: grants@retailtrust. org.uk; website: www.retailtrust.org.uk)

Other information: This trust also runs a help and support line for its beneficiaries (080 8801 0808), offers respite care and runs sheltered, residential and nursing homes and a day centre.

Road haulage

The Road Haulage Association Benevolent Fund

Eligibility: Current and former members and employees/ex-employees of members, of the association, and their dependants.

Types of grants: One-off grants according to need.

Exclusions: Grants are not usually awarded towards holidays (unless there are exceptional circumstances).

Annual grant total: In 2009 the fund had assets of £750,000 and an income of £48,000. Grants were made totalling

£11,000. In the past the fund has given a total of £30,000.

Applications: On a form available from the correspondent, to be submitted directly by the individual or through a social worker, Citizens Advice or other third party. Applications are considered throughout the year.

Correspondent: Alistair Morrow, Road Haulage Association, Roadway House, The Rural Centre, Newbridge EH28 8NZ (0131 333 4900; website: www.rha.uk.net)

School inspectors

HM Inspectors of Schools' Benevolent Fund

Eligibility: Present and retired HM Inspectors of schools in England and Wales and their dependants who are in need or distress.

Types of grants: One-off grants of £500 to £5,000 and loans of up to £10,000.

Annual grant total: In 2009 the trust had an income of £20,000 and a total expenditure of £25,000. Grants totalled around £4,000.

Applications: In writing to the correspondent, either directly by the individual or through a third party such as a friend or colleague. Applications are considered as they arise, and should include the applicant's financial situation, and for example, arrangements for repaying loans.

Correspondent: Clive Rowe, Hassocks House, 58 Main Street, Newtown Linford, Leicester LE6 0AD (01530 243989)

Other information: The trust also provides information and support services.

Science

The Institute of Physics Benevolent Fund

Eligibility: Physicists and members of their family in need, whether members of the institute or not.

Types of grants: One-off and recurrent grants according to need.

Annual grant total: No recent financial information was available. In previous years grants have totalled about £50,000.

Applications: In writing to the correspondent, marked 'Private and Confidential'.

Correspondent: Susan McGoldrick, Secretary, Crosswinds, Ferry Road, Iwade,

Sittingbourne, Kent ME9 8RE (01795 424348)

The John Murdoch Trust

Eligibility: People in need who are over 50 and have pursued science, in any of its branches, either as amateurs or professionals.

Types of grants: Yearly allowances and one-off grants, on average of about £200 to £1,000. Grants are given for relief-in-need rather than scientific needs.

Annual grant total: In 2008/09 the trust had an income of £42,000. The grant total varies, but is usually in the range of about £4,000 a year.

Applications: On a form available from the correspondent. Applications are normally considered twice a year.

Correspondent: Grant Administrator, c/o The Royal Bank of Scotland plc, Trust and Estate Services, Eden Lakeside, Chester Business Park, Wrexham Road, Chester CH4 9QT (01244 688292)

Royal Society of Chemistry Benevolent Fund

Eligibility: People who have been members of the society for the last three years, or ex-members who were in the society for at least 10 years, and their dependants, who are in need.

Types of grants: Regular allowances, one-off grants and loans. Recent grants have been towards essential home maintenance, help with transport costs, household equipment and furniture, school uniforms, Christmas bonuses and funeral costs.

Exclusions: Anything which should be provided by the government or local authority is ineligible.

Annual grant total: In 2009 bursaries and travel grants were made to over 250 individuals totalling £130,000.

Applications: In writing or by telephone in the first instance, to the correspondent. Applicants will be requested to provide a financial statement (forms supplied by the secretary) and include a covering letter describing their application as fully as possible. Applications can be made either directly by the individual, or through a third party such as a social worker or Citizens Advice. They are considered every other month, although urgent appeals can be considered at any time.

Correspondent: Jennifer Tunbridge, 290–292 Science Park, Milton Road, Cambridge, CB4 0WF (01223 432237; website: www.rsc.org)

Other information: The fund acts as an advisory service, as well as a grant provider.

The Scientific Relief Fund of the Royal Society

Eligibility: Scientists professionally involved in the natural sciences, or their families, in need of assistance, and retired scientists who need help to continue their research. Whilst there is no nationality requirement, the scientist concerned must have some connection with British or Irish science.

Types of grants: One-off grants of between £1,000 and £10,000. Recent grants have been made for travel to and from hospital, residential care costs, a sighted assistant to aid scientific research, computer equipment for scientific reasons, medical and surgical treatment and therapeutic drugs.

Exclusions: No grants are given towards scientist's salaries.

Annual grant total: In 2009/10 the fund had an income of £71 million and a total expenditure of £66 million. Around £25,000 is usually available for relief in need.

Applications: Applications can be submitted directly by the individual or through a third party such as a social worker or an officer of any nationally recognised scientific society within the British Commonwealth or the Republic of Ireland. Applicants should contact the correspondent for instructions about what they should put in their application. They can be considered at any time.

Correspondent: The Executive Director, The Royal Society, 6–9 Carlton House Terrace, London SW1Y 5AG (020 7451 2500; email: info@royalsociety. org; website: royalsociety.org)

Seafaring and fishing

The Baltic Exchange Charitable Society

Eligibility: Members of the society and their dependants. Help is usually given to retired or elderly people and occasionally to younger people who find themselves in a difficult situation.

Types of grants: One-off grants usually in the range of £50 to £10,000. Recent grants have been made for household items, repairs to property, mobility aids, debt relief, therapy and respite care. Recurrent grants are also paid to help with living expenses.

Annual grant total: In 2009 the society had assets of £4.2 million and an income of £165,000. Grants were made to 40 individuals totalling £118,000. Of this,

£107,000 was given in quarterly payments and £11,000 in one-off grants.

Applications: On a form available from the correspondent. Applications can be submitted at any time.

Correspondent: Richard Butler, Nordic House, 20 St Dunstan's Hill, London EC3R 8HL (020 7283 6090; fax: 020 7283 6133; email: richard.butler@baltic-charities.co.uk)

Other information: Help can also be given in the form of loans.

Fawcett Johnston Charity

Eligibility: Grants for poor and destitute sailors and ship carpenters and their dependants who live in Maryport, Cumbria.

Types of grants: One-off and recurrent according to need.

Annual grant total: In 2008/09 the trust had an income of £2,600 and a total expenditure of £1,800.

Applications: In writing to the correspondent.

Correspondent: Mrs Lisa Douglas, The Town Hall, Senhouse Street, Maryport, CA15 6BH

Grimsby Sailors and Fishing Charity

Eligibility: Primarily the children of Grimsby fishermen lost at sea or dying ashore while still fishermen. However, help may also be available to other beneficiaries living in Grimsby and the surrounding area, at the trustees' discretion.

Types of grants: Weekly and quarterly grants to support children of deceased fishermen while they are still in full-time education. Weekly grants are usually around £13 and quarterly grants range from £100 to £250.

Annual grant total: In 2009 the charity had an income of £609,000 and a total expenditure of £492,000. The majority of the charity's expenditure is spent on providing and maintaining almshouses. Grants to individuals usually total around £35,000 each year.

Applications: On a form available from the correspondent or from the Port Missioner. Applications should be submitted directly by the individual or through an appropriate welfare agency. They are considered when received.

Correspondent: Duncan Watt, Charities Administrator, 1st Floor, 23 Bargate, Grimsby, South Humberside DN34 4SS (01472 347914; fax: 01472 347914; email: duncan.watt@btinternet.com)

Other information: The Grimsby Fishermen's Dependants Fund has recently transferred its funds to this charity and is now a subsidiary.

The Honourable Company of Master Mariners

Eligibility: British Master Mariners, navigating officers of the merchant navy, and their wives, widows and dependants who are in need.

Types of grants: One-off and quarterly grants according to need.

Annual grant total: About £30,000 per year.

Applications: In writing to the correspondent. Applications can be submitted directly by the individual, through a social worker, Citizens Advice, or other welfare agency, or by a friend or relative. They are considered quarterly.

Correspondent: The Clerk, HQS Wellington, Temple Stairs, Victoria Embankment, London, WC2R 2PN (020 7836 8179; email: info@hcmm.org.uk; website: www.hcmm.org.uk)

Other information: This trust is an amalgamation of four separate funds: the Education Fund, the Benevolent Fund, the London Maritime Institution and the Howard Leopold Davis Fund.

The London Shipowners' & Shipbrokers' Benevolent Society

Eligibility: Shipowners and shipbrokers and their dependants.

Types of grants: Annual cost of living grants, paid quarterly and special one-off grants.

Annual grant total: In 2009 the society had assets of £1 million and an income of £46,000. Grants were made to 12 individuals totalling £29,000, of which £19,000 was given in quarterly grants and £9,300 was given in special grants.

Applications: On a form available from the correspondent. Applications can be submitted at any time either directly by the individual or a family member, through a third party such as a social worker, or through an organisation such as a Citizens Advice or other welfare agency.

Correspondent: Richard Butler, Secretary, 20 St Dunstan's Hill, London EC3R 8HL (020 7283 6090; email: richard.butler@baltic-charities.co.uk)

The Marine Society and Sea Cadets

Eligibility: Professional seafarers, active and retired, who are in need.

Types of grants: Bursaries, scholarships, one-off grants and loans. Interest-free loans rather than grants are given where the need is short-term and the applicant expects to be earning again.

Exclusions: Recurrent grants are not made.

Annual grant total: In 2008/09 the trust had assets of £13 million and an income of £12 million. Grants to individuals totalled £1.4 million, although the trust states that 'individual grants given are small and not material within the overall total'.

Applications: In writing to the correspondent in the first instance, requesting an application form.

Correspondent: Claire E Barnett, 202 Lambeth Road, London SE1 7JW (020 7654 7011; fax: 020 7928 8914; email: info@ms-sc.org; website: www.ms-sc.org)

Other information: Grants are also made to sea cadet units.

The Nautilus Welfare Fund (previously The NUMAST Welfare Fund)

Eligibility: Seafarers, former seafarers and their dependants. Applicants should normally be over 50 but exceptions are made, for example in cases of ill-health.

Types of grants: Regular payments of up to £12 a week and one-off grants towards household items, medical expenses, home adaptations to aid independent living and electrically powered vehicles.

Annual grant total: In 2009 the fund had assets of £18 million and an income of £2.2 million. Grants were made to 345 individuals totalling £217,000, of which £177,000 was given in regular awards and the remaining £40,000 was distributed in one-off grants.

Applications: On a form available from the correspondent: to be submitted directly by the individual or through a third party such as SSAFA. Proof of sea-service, medical and birth certificates and details of income and expenditure, bills and so on are required to support the application. Applications are usually processed within two weeks.

Correspondent: Peter McEwen, Secretary, Nautilus House, Mariners' Park, Wallasey, CH45 7PH (0151 639 8454; fax: 0151 346 8801; email: welfare@nautilusuk.org; website: www.nautilusuk.org)

Other information: The fund also manages the Mariners Park welfare complex in Wallasey, which accommodates independent older seafarers and their dependants in bungalows and flats, and older seafarers and their dependants assessed for residential or nursing care in the NUMAST Mariners Park Care Home. The management and maintenance of this site takes up a large proportion of the fund's income.

Royal Liverpool Seamen's Orphan Institution

Eligibility: Children of deceased British merchant seafarers, who are of pre-school age or in full-time education (including further education). Help can also be given to seafarers who are at home caring for their family alone.

Types of grants: Monthly maintenance and annual clothing grants. Grants usually range from £80 to £300 a month for each child. They are reviewed annually. Help may also be given for school fees.

Annual grant total: In 2009 the institution had assets of £3.1 million and an income of £496,000. Grants were made to 122 individuals totalling £427,000, of which £325,000 was given in maintenance grants and £12,000 was awarded in Christmas grants.

Applications: On a form available from the correspondent, to be considered at any time. Applications can be submitted either directly by the individual, or by the parent or guardian. They need to include confirmation of the seafarer's death and the child's birth certificate.

Correspondent: Linda Gidman, Secretary, C/O Mrs Linda Gidman Room 19, 2nd Floor, Tower Building, 22 Water Street, Liverpool L3 1BA (0151 227 3417; fax: 0151 227 3417; email: enquiries@rlsoi-uk.org; website: www.rlsoi-uk.org)

Other information: It was not possible to obtain a grant total for direct education purposes. However, all grants are given to children and young people who are in attendance at school and further or higher education institutions.

Royal National Mission to Deep Sea Fishermen

Eligibility: Commercial fishermen, including retired fishermen, and their wives and widows who are experiencing unforeseen tragedy or hardship.

Types of grants: Immediate one-off payments to widows of fishermen lost at sea. There are also other individual grants to alleviate cases of hardship (e.g. provision of basic furniture for impoverished older fishermen). Grants are almost always one-off.

Annual grant total: In 2009 the mission had an income of £2.5 million and a total expenditure of £2.8 million. Welfare payments were made totalling around £40,000.

Applications: In writing to the correspondent or the local superintendent, either directly by the individual or through a social worker, Citizens Advice or other welfare agency. Record of sea service and names of fishing vessels and/or owners is required.

Correspondent: Dan Conley, Chief Executive, Fishermen's Mission Head Office, Mather House, 4400 Parkway, Solent Business Park, Hampshire PO15 7FJ (01489 566910; email: enquiries@rnmdsf. org.uk; website: www.fishermensmission. org.uk/)

Sailors' Society

Eligibility: Merchant seafarers and their dependants who are in need.

Types of grants: Emergency grants to ease financial hardship.

Annual grant total: In 2009 the society had assets of £13 million and an income of £3 million. Grants were made totalling £23,000, of which £13,000 was given in welfare grants and £10,000 in educational awards.

Applications: In the first instance a short application should be sent by email to welfare@sailors-society.org.

Correspondent: Welfare Fund Manager, 350 Shirley Road, Southampton, SO15 3HY (023 8051 5950; fax: 023 8051 5951; email: welfare@sailors-society.org)

Other information: The society maintains a network of Chaplains at the various key ports around the world who carry out ship visiting routines and minister to seafarers. It also provides centres and clubs for seafarers and associated maritime workers at strategic seaports.

The society administers the Leith Aged Mariners' Fund and the Dundee Seaman's Friend Society.

The Sailors' Families' Society

Eligibility: Seafarers from the UK or who sail on UK ships, or their dependants, who are in one-parent families with children aged below 16 years. Grants can also be given if the seafarer is in a two-parent family but is permanently disabled. Usually, the only source of income for the family is Income Support or Incapacity Benefit.

Types of grants: (i) Monthly grants of £48 per family are available, to help pay for the basic necessities of family life. (ii) A discretionary clothing grant payable per child twice a year – £75 in August and £40 in January – to help children start off the new school year and to buy a new winter coat. (iii) Discretionary Christmas grants of £25 per child to help to buy a special Christmas present. (iv) Educational holiday grants of up to £250 per child for holidays 'with a difference' (Outward Bound Courses, Sail Training Association trips), where the experience can be character building. (v) Special equipment grants of up to £250 to help with non-academic abilities such as musical instruments and sports equipment, or for training in special skills which may benefit them in securing employment. (vi) Household replacement grants of up to £250 to help with debt relief or replace essential items such as washing machines, cookers, children's bedding or redecoration of children's rooms. (vii) Caravan holidays. The society provides a week's free holiday to families in one of the seven caravans it owns around the coast.

Annual grant total: In 2008/09 the society had assets of £3.1 million and an income of £483,000. The sum of £306,000 went to seafarers families.

Applications: On a form available from the correspondent, with details about children, income and expenditure, including copies of relevant certificates, for example, birth certificates and proof of seafaring service. Applications can be submitted directly by the individual or through a social worker, Citizens Advice, other welfare agency, or through seafaring organisations. Applications are considered every other month, beginning in February.

Correspondent: Ian Scott, Welfare Manager, Newland, Cottingham Road, Hull HU6 7RJ (01482 342331; fax: 01482 447868; email: info@sailors-families.org.uk; website: www.sailors-families.org.uk)

Other information: This trust is essentially set up to give relief-in-need to seafarers, but some of their grants are of an educational nature.

The Seamen's Hospital Society

Eligibility: Seamen and seawomen who are in need, and their dependants. Applicants must be seafarers with a long service except where accident or illness has interrupted intended long-term service. They may have worked anywhere in the UK and be of any nationality.

Types of grants: One-off grants can be given towards medical treatment and items such as wheelchairs, riser recliner chairs, stair lifts and installation of disabled access; household items such as cookers, beds and decorating costs; holidays, convalescence and respite breaks; clothing; priority bills; and funeral expenses.

Exclusions: No grants are given towards study costs or re-training costs. Members and former members of the Royal Navy are not eligible.

Annual grant total: In 2009 the society had assets of £7.7 million, an income of £496,000 and a total expenditure of £718,000. Grants were made to 286 individuals totalling £128,000. A further £259,000 was given to organisations.

Applications: On a form available from the correspondent, including full details of sea service and need. Applications can be submitted directly by the individual or through a social worker, Citizens Advice or other welfare agency.

Correspondent: Peter Coulson, General Secretary, 29 King William Walk, Greenwich, London SE10 9HX (020 8858 3696; fax: 020 8293 9630; email: admin@seahospital.org.uk; website: www.seahospital.org.uk)

Other information: The society supports Dreadnought patients at Guys and St Thomas' Hospital in London. It also helps to fund the Seafarers' Benefits Advice Line

(0845 741 3318), which provides advice and information on a wide range of issues.

The Shipwrecked Fishermen & Mariners' Royal Benevolent Society

Eligibility: Fishermen, mariners and their widows and dependants, who are on a low income, especially those who are over 60 or in poor health. Priority is given to widows with young children. There is a minimum sea service of five years for one-off grants (10 for recurrent grants), although this is reviewed periodically to reflect employment patterns. Grants are available in the UK and Republic of Ireland only. Applicants must be receiving all the state benefits they are entitled to.

Types of grants: Mainly regular grants of £624 a year (usually to people aged over 60). One-off grants ranging from about £250 to £2,000 are available for those who do not qualify for regular support for help towards electrical appliances, household repairs, beds and bedding, rent deposits, debt relief, stair-lifts, scooters and so on. Immediate grants are given to widows and children left in need following the death of a serving fisherman or mariner. Death benefit grants are also given to the widows of life members of the society.

Annual grant total: In 2008/09 the society had assets of £19 million and an income of £1.7 million. Grants were made to over 2,900 individuals totalling £1.7 million, of which £1.5 million was given in regular donations and the remaining £189,000 in one-off grants.

Applications: On a form available from the correspondent or to download from the website. Applications can be submitted by the individual or through a third party and are considered on a weekly basis.

Correspondent: Malcolm Williams, Chief Executive, 1 North Pallant, Chichester, West Sussex PO19 1TL (01243 787761; fax: 01243 530853; email: grants@ shipwreckedmariners.org.uk; website: www.shipwreckedmariners.org. uk)

Other information: The Royal Seamen's Pension Fund and the Hull Fishermen's Trust Fund have been integrated into this society.

Trinity House Maritime Charity

Eligibility: Former mariners over 60 who have normally served at least 15 years in UK or Commonwealth vessels, their wives and dependent children.

Types of grants: One-off grants of between £200 and £700 and annuities not exceeding £624 a year. Christmas grants are also available to annuitants.

Annual grant total: In 2008/09 the charity had assets of £122 million and an income of £5.9 million. Grants were made to 45 individuals totalling £31,000.

Applications: On a form available from the correspondent. Applications are considered six times a year and can be submitted directly by the individual, through a recognised referral agency (Citizens Advice, doctor, social worker etc.), or via another charity. In all cases proof of sea service and rank must be provided.

Correspondent: Graham Hockley, Corporation of Trinity House, Trinity House, Tower Hill, London EC3N 4DH (020 7481 6900; email: graham.hockley@ thls.org; website: www.trinityhouse.co.uk)

Other information: The primary objects are to provide almshouse accommodation for mariners and their dependants who are in need and to provide financial assistance to individuals in need.

The secondary objects are to advance the education and training of mariners and cadets in all matters pertaining to navigation and seamanship; research for the safety and welfare of mariners; cooperation with other charities and similar causes and the promotion of any matter for the advancement of education in navigation, shipping and seamanship.

Secretaries

The Institute of Chartered Secretaries & Administrators' Benevolent Fund

Eligibility: Members and former members of the institute and their dependants who are in need, living in UK, Eire and associated territories.

Types of grants: Weekly allowances and regular support according to need, for example towards telephone line rental, rental for emergency alarm systems and TV rental and licences. One-off grants are given for specific items and services, often paid directly to the supplier, including those for clothing, clearance of debts, decorating, property repairs. Loans are also considered.

Annual grant total: In 2008/09 the fund had assets of £4.6 million and an income of £41,000. Welfare grants and allowances were made totalling £69,000.

Applications: On a form available from the correspondent or to download from the website, indicating full current income and expenditure details. Institute members (volunteers) visit beneficiaries where necessary. Applications can be made throughout the year. Contact the correspondent if assistance in making the application is required.

Correspondent: Elizabeth Howarth, Charities Officer, 16 Park Crescent, London W1B 1AH (020 7580 4741;

fax: 020 7323 1132; email: icsacharities@ icsa.co.uk; website: www.icsa.org.uk)

Self-employed and small businesses

The Prime Charitable Trust

Eligibility: Members or former members of the National Federation of Self-Employed and Small Businesses Ltd and their family and dependants, who due to illness or incapacity are unable to maintain themselves.

Types of grants: One-off and recurrent grants according to need.

Annual grant total: In 2008/09 the trust had an income of £6,900 and a total expenditure of £12,000.

Applications: In writing to the correspondent.

Correspondent: Louise Withers, Federation of Small Businesses, Sir Frank Whittle Way, Blackpool FY4 2FE (01253 336000; fax: 01253 348046; email: head.operations@fsb.org.uk)

Social workers

The Social Workers' Benevolent Trust

Eligibility: Social workers who hold a professional social work qualification and are experiencing financial difficulties, and their dependants. Unqualified social workers may also be considered depending upon the nature and length of their employment.

Types of grants: One-off grants up to £500 are given for specific debts and other needs.

Exclusions: No grants for: daily living costs; social work training; private health care; private education; or private social care.

Annual grant total: In 2008/09 the trust had an income of £23,000 and a total expenditure of £25,000. On average approximately 65 applications are considered and grants totalling £20,000 are distributed each year.

Applications: On a form available from the correspondent or to download from the website. Applications should be submitted directly by the individual and are considered bi-monthly.

Correspondent: Gail Tucker, 16 Kent Street, Birmingham B5 6RD

(01543 878311; email: swbt@basw.co.uk; website: www.basw.co.uk)

Solicitors

The Solicitors' Benevolent Association Ltd

Eligibility: Solicitors on the Roll for England and Wales, and their dependants, who are in need.

Types of grants: One-off and recurrent grants and interest-free loans (if sufficient equity is available). They can be made towards living expenses, nursing home fees, TV licences, telephone rental, essential travel, emergency repairs or replacement of household appliances, holidays and medical or special equipment not provided for by the state.

Exclusions: Solicitors who have been considered to have brought the profession into disrepute are not eligible.

Annual grant total: In 2009 the association had assets of £15 million and an income of £1.5 million. Grants totalled £759,000 and were distributed as follows:

Cost of living allowances	£399,000
Supplementary, leisure, special and miscellaneous grants	£209,000
Nursing home fees	£6,500
Educational support	£144,000

Applications: On a form available on request from the correspondent.

Correspondent: John Platt, 1 Jaggard Way, Wandsworth Common, London SW12 8SG (020 8675 6440; email: sec@sba.org.uk; website: www.sba.org.uk)

Sport

The Mark Davies Injured Riders' Fund

Eligibility: People injured in horse-related accidents (excluding professional and amateur jockeys and those injured in the horse racing industry) and their carers.

Types of grants: One-off cash grants and grants in kind according to need; loans are also made. Recent grants have been given towards wheelchairs, special beds, house adaptations, stair lifts, physiotherapy, stable help and other living costs.

Annual grant total: Grants usually total around £35,000 a year.

Applications: In writing to the correspondent at any time. All applicants are visited by a local fund volunteer to discuss their medical and financial needs. A report is then made to the trustees, who will consider whether or not to award a grant.

Correspondent: Rosemary Lang, Lancrow Farmhouse, Penpillick Hill, Penpillick, Cornwall, PL24 2SA (01726 813156; email: rosemary@mdirf.co.uk; website: www.mdirf.co.uk)

Other information: The fund also provides practical advice on rider safety issues and produces a number of help sheets on the subject. These are available to download from the website.

The Francis Drake Fellowship

Eligibility: Widows, dependants and orphans of members of the fellowship who have died.

Types of grants: One-off and recurrent grants according to need. There is a sliding scale of grants depending on surplus income. If after general household/living expenses (excluding food, clothing etc.) the applicant has a surplus of under £70 per week, grants are £550; if the surplus income is between £70 and £90, grants are £450; between £90 and £110, grants are £350; between £110 and £130, grants are £200; and for incomes over £130, grants are £50.

Annual grant total: Previously the fellowship made grants totalling £14,000.

Applications: In writing to the correspondent, requesting an application form. Applications should be submitted through the bowling club's Francis Drake Fellowship delegate. Applications are accepted two years after the date of the member's death.

Correspondent: Joan Jupp, 24 Haldane Close, London N10 2PB (020 8883 8725)

The Rugby Football League Benevolent Fund

Eligibility: People who play or assist, or who have played or assisted, in the game of Rugby League in the UK or for a team affiliated to an association primarily based in the UK and their dependants. Beneficiaries should be in hardship or distress, in particular, as a result of injury through playing or training, or when travelling to or from a game or training session.

Types of grants: Hardship grants, also donations towards special vehicles and repairs, home improvements, furniture, wheelchairs, gym equipment, computers, hotel accommodation, travel, physiotherapy, home appliances, educational courses and Christmas presents.

Annual grant total: In 2008 the fund had assets of £299,000, an income of £228,000 and a total expenditure of £175,000. Grants were made totalling about £84,000.

Applications: In the case of serious injury applicants should notify the RFL Operations Department (Tel. 0844 477713 Ext. 6), who will then contact Dave Phillips, the RFL Benevolent Fund Welfare Officer.

Correspondent: Steve Ball, Rugby Football League, Red Hall, Red Hall Lane, Leeds, West Yorkshire LS17 8NB (0844 477 7113; email: steve.ball@rflbenevolentfund.co.uk; website: www.rflbenevolentfund.co.uk/)

Sport – Cricket

The Cricketers Association Charity

Eligibility: Members and former members of the association and any person who has played cricket on at least one occasion for any county which at the relevant time was recognised by the English Cricket Board (formerly the Test and County Cricket Board), and their dependants.

Types of grants: One-off or recurrent grants according to need.

Annual grant total: In 2008/09 the association had an income of £13,000 and a total expenditure of £26,000.

Applications: In writing to the correspondent, to be considered as they arrive.

Correspondent: David Graveney, 6 Southover Close, Westbury On Trym, Bristol, BS9 3NG

The Hornsby Professional Cricketers Fund Charity

Eligibility: Former professional cricketers and their dependants who are in need.

Types of grants: Recurrent grants and special payments at Christmas or in mid-summer. Help is also given towards winter fuel bills, medical costs and special equipment such as electric wheelchairs and stairlifts.

Annual grant total: In 2008/09 grants totalled £41,000 and were distributed in the following categories:

Monthly allowances	£16,000
Summer allowances	£5,400
Heating allowances	£3,700
Winter allowances	£6,500
Walter Hammond allowances	£600
Special allowances	£8,600

Applications: In writing to the correspondent. Applications can be submitted either directly by the individual or by the county cricket club.

Correspondent: The Revd Michael Vockins, Birchwood Lodge, Birchwood, Storridge, Malvern, Worcestershire WR13 5EZ (01886 884366)

Sport – Football

The Football Association Benevolent Fund

Eligibility: People who have been involved in Association Football in any capacity, such as players and referees, and their dependants, who are in need. The fund interprets people involved in football as broadly as possible, although it tends not to support professional footballers, passing their details on to the occupational benevolent funds which they can apply to.

Types of grants: One-off and recurrent grants ranging from £250 to £2,000 are given to meet any need.

Annual grant total: In 2008 the fund had assets of £3.2 million and an income of £159,000. Grants were made to 63 individuals totalling £41,000.

Applications: On a form available from the correspondent. Applications should be made through the County Football Associations. They are considered on a regular basis.

Correspondent: Mike Appleby, Wembley Stadium, Wembley, London HA9 0WS (0844 980 8200; email: mike.appleby@thefa.com)

The Institute of Football Management & Administration Charity Trust

Eligibility: Members or former members of the institute (formerly the Football League Executive Staffs Association) who have worked for a Football League or Premier League Club and who are in need, and their widows/widowers.

Types of grants: One-off grants in particular cases of need, and Christmas vouchers.

Annual grant total: In 2008/09 the trust had an income of £3,100 and a total expenditure of £5,800.

Applications: In writing to the correspondent. Applications can be submitted directly by the individual or through a family member, friend or colleague.

Correspondent: Graham Mackrell, The Camkin Suite, 1 Pegasus House, Tachbrook Park, Warwick, CV34 6LW (01926 831556; fax: 01926 429781; email: ifma@lmasecure.com)

The League Managers Benevolent Trust

Eligibility: Members of the League Managers Association who are in need and their wives, widows and children.

Types of grants: One-off and recurrent grants according to need.

Annual grant total: Grants usually total around £5,000 a year.

Applications: In writing to the correspondent. Applications are considered throughout the year.

Correspondent: The Trustees, League Managers Association, Unit 1 Pegasus House, Pegasus Court, Tachbrook Park, Warwick CV34 6LW (01926 411884; email: ifma@lmasecure.com; website: www.leaguemanagers.com)

Professional Footballers' Association Accident Insurance Fund

Eligibility: Members or former members of the association in England and Wales who require medical treatment as a result of a specific injury or illness which results in their permanent total disability to play professional football.

Types of grants: Grants are to provide private medical treatment for all members and for members unable to claim under the terms of the PFA accident insurance policy due to the nature/circumstances of the injury. Grants are also given to meet operation costs which may not be covered by the insurance and free places are available at Lilleshall Rehabilitation Centre. Grants are also available to former members for treatment on injuries received as a result of their playing career.

Annual grant total: Grants usually total around £2 million each year.

Applications: On a form available from the correspondent. Completed applications should be returned directly by the individual or by a family member/social worker on their behalf. There are no deadlines and applications are considered as they are received.

Correspondent: Darren Wilson, Director of Finance, 20 Oxford Court, Bishopsgate, Manchester M2 3WQ (0161 236 0575; fax: 0161 228 7229; email: info@thepfa.co.uk; website: www.givemefootball.com/)

Other information: Contributions are made to FAPL and FH Club to ensure all PFA members are covered by private medical insurance.

Professional Footballers' Association Benevolent Insurance Fund

Eligibility: Current and former members of the association in England and Wales who are experiencing financial hardship and are on a low income.

Types of grants: One-off grants in the range of £50 to £2,000 to help relieve financial difficulties such as the threat of losing a home due to mortgage/rent arrears or threat of bailiffs in respect of debts. Where appropriate, general advice regarding financial management and options concerning further education may be offered as required. There is also funding available in the event of the death of any member whilst under contract, up to a maximum of £1 million.

Exclusions: No grants are made for cars, holidays or to set up businesses. Loans are not available to former members and there are no recurrent grants.

Annual grant total: In 2008/09 the fund had assets of £18 million and an income of £1.6 million. There were 526 grants made to members totalling £460,000.

Applications: On a form available from the correspondent. Completed applications should be returned directly by the individual or by a family member/social worker on their behalf. There are no deadlines and applications are considered as they are received.

Correspondent: Darren Wilson, Financial Controller, 20 Oxford Court, Bishopsgate, Manchester M2 3WQ (0161 236 0575; fax: 0161 228 7229; email: info@thepfa.co.uk; website: www.givemefootball.com/)

The Referees' Association Members' Benevolent Fund

Eligibility: Members and former members of the association in England, and their dependants, who are in need.

Types of grants: One-off and recurrent grants to relieve an immediate financial need such as hospital expenses, convalescence, clothing, living costs, household bills, medical equipment and help in the home.

Annual grant total: In 2009/10 the fund had an income of £18,000 and a total expenditure of £8,000.

Applications: On a form available from the correspondent. Applications should be submitted directly by the individual for consideration at any time.

Correspondent: The General Secretary, Unit 12, Ensign Business Centre, Westwood Way, Westwood Business Park, Coventry CV4 8JA (02476 420360; fax: 02476 677234; email: ra@footballreferee.org; website: www.footballreferee.org)

Sport – Golf

The PGA European Tour Benevolent Trust

Eligibility: Members and former members of the PGA European Tour and other people whose main livelihood is, or has been, earned by providing services to professional golf, and their dependants.

Types of grants: One-off or recurrent grants according to need.

Annual grant total: In 2008 the trust had assets of £704,000 and an income of £48,000. There were 19 grants made to individuals totalling £188,000.

Applications: In writing to the correspondent at any time. Applications can be submitted directly by the individual or through a social worker, Citizens Advice, other welfare agency or another third party.

Correspondent: The Secretary, Wentworth Drive, Virginia Water, Surrey GU25 4LX (01344 840400; email: cduffain@europeantour.com; website: www.europeantour.com)

Other information: The trust does not give to organisations.

Sport – Horse racing

The Injured Jockeys Fund

Eligibility: Jockeys who have suffered through injury, and their families. Applicants must hold (or have held) a licence to ride under the Rules of Racing.

Types of grants: One-off and recurrent grants to assist with medical care and to help alleviate financial problems and stress. Recent grants have included help with medical treatment and equipment, contributions to private medical insurance, wheelchairs, holidays, televisions and emergency cash. Assistance may also be given to help with the cost of education where children have special needs.

Annual grant total: In 2008/09 the fund had assets of £26 million, an income of £3.4 million and a total expenditure of £2.1 million. Grants were made to 357 individuals totalling £989,000. A further £8,800 was distributed in grants to organisations.

Applications: On a form available from the correspondent. The fund has nine almoners who cover the whole of the UK and visit potential beneficiaries to assess their needs.

Correspondent: Jeremy Richardson, Chief Executive, 1 Victoria Way, Newmarket, Suffolk CB8 7SH (01638 662246; fax: 01638 668988; email: jr@ijf.org.uk; website: www.injuredjockeys.co.uk)

Other information: The fund also provides accommodation for families and individuals in need. A range of permanent family homes, single apartments and disabled accommodation is available.

Racing Welfare

Eligibility: People in need who are, or have been, employed in the thoroughbred horse-racing and breeding industry, and their dependants.

Types of grants: One-off and recurrent grants and loans according to need. The majority of funding is given in the form of quarterly benefits of about £1,000 to retired staff. The rest is given in one-off grants to help towards disability aids and equipment, house adaptations, clothing, food, medical expenses, car adaptations, drugs rehabilitation and bedding.

Annual grant total: In 2008 the charity had assets of £12 million and an income of £1.6 million. Grants were made to 369 individuals totalling £235,000.

Applications: On a form available from the welfare officer at most racing centres or from the correspondent. Applicants are visited by a welfare officer before the application is considered by the trustees.

Correspondent: Brig. Cedric Burton, Robin McAlpine House, 20b Park Lane, Newmarket, Suffolk CB8 8QD (01638 560763; email: info@racingwelfare.co.uk; website: www.racingwelfare.co.uk)

Other information: The trust has welfare officers based all over the country who offer support and advice on financial issues, diet and nutrition and housing. It also runs a holiday scheme for its elderly and disabled beneficiaries.

Sport – Motor sport

The Auto Cycle Union Benevolent Fund

Eligibility: Past and present members of the Auto Cycle Union, and their dependants, who are in need through accident, illness or hardship in England, Scotland or Wales.

Types of grants: One-off and recurrent grants to supplement low income.

Annual grant total: In 2009 the fund had assets of £1.6 million and an income of £118,000. Grants were made to 85 individuals totalling £56,000.

Applications: On a form available from the local ACU officer. Applications should be made directly by the individual and include details on current income and expenses. They are considered monthly. In very special circumstances the committee has the power to make emergency payments pending full information.

Correspondent: Emma Connop, Secretary, ACU House, Wood Street, Rugby, Warwickshire, CV21 2YX (01788 566413; fax: 01788 573585; email: emma@acu.org.uk; website: www.acu.org.uk)

Other information: For details of the nearest ACU officer, please contact the correspondent.

British Motor Cycle Racing Club Benevolent Fund

Eligibility: Members of the club and their dependants, who are in need.

Types of grants: One-off grants towards subsistence, travel and medical care costs.

Annual grant total: In 2009 the trust had an income of £10,000 and a total expenditure of £8,000. Grants totalled around £8,000.

Applications: In writing to: David Stewart, c/o British Motor Cycle Racing Club Ltd, Lydden Motor Racing Circuit, Wootton, Canterbury, Kent CT4 6RX. Applications can be submitted at any time, either directly by the individual, or through a third party such as a spouse or next of kin.

Correspondent: John Wilson, 13 Watchet Lane, Holmer Green, High Wycombe HP15 6UA (01494 711210)

British Racing Drivers Club (BRDC) Benevolent Fund

Eligibility: Members of the BRDC and their families and dependants or persons involved with motor racing generally and their families and dependants.

Types of grants: One-off and recurrent grants according to need.

Annual grant total: In 2008/09 the fund had assets of £403,000 and an unusually large income of £237,000 (£41,000 in 2007/08). This was due to several large individual donations made during the year. Grants were made to four individuals totalling £9,000.

Applications: On a form available from the correspondent including details of income and expenditure, assets and liabilities. Applications can be submitted directly by the individual, by an organisation such as Citizens Advice or through a third party such as a social worker. There are no deadlines and applications are considered at trustee meetings.

Correspondent: The Trustees, c/o Rawlinson and Hunter, Eighth Floor, 6 New Street Square, London, EC4A 3AQ (0207 8422000; website: www.brdc.co.uk/)

Other information: During 2008/09 the British Racing Drivers Club (BRDC) Benevolent Fund merged with the British Motoring Sport Relief Fund and the assets of the latter have been transferred under the control of the trustees of the BRDC Benevolent Fund.

The Grand Prix Mechanics Charitable Trust

Eligibility: Past and present Grand Prix mechanics and their dependants who are in need.

Types of grants: One-off and recurrent grants towards medical costs, bills and living expenses and so on.

Annual grant total: In 2008/09 the trust had assets of £1.4 million and an income of £133,000. Grants were made to four individuals totalling £13,000.

Applications: In writing to the correspondent at: PO Box 38540, London SW1Y 6YF.

Correspondent: Ann Wood, Administrator, Eighth Floor, 6 New Street Square, London, EC4A 3AQ (01896 820263; fax: 01896 820264; email: enquiries@gpmechanicstrust.com; website: www.gpmechanicstrust.com)

Sport – Snooker and billiards

The Professional Billiards & Snooker Players Benevolent Fund

Eligibility: Members of the World Professional Billiards and Snooker Association and their dependants, who are in need.

Types of grants: One-off and recurrent grants and loans according to need.

Annual grant total: In 2008/09 the trust had an income of £5,400 and a total expenditure of £7,200, almost all of which was given in grants.

Applications: In writing to the correspondent, to be considered within one month.

Correspondent: Elaine Eyers, World Snooker Ltd, Suite 2.1, Albert House, 111–117 Victoria Street, Bristol BS1 6AX (0117 317 8216)

Stationery

The British Office Supplies and Services Federation Benevolent Fund

Eligibility: Applications are welcome from those who work or have worked in the stationery, office products and office machines sector, and their dependants.

Types of grants: One-off grants according to need are given towards, for example, wheelchairs or property repair. Regular quarterly payments are also made.

Annual grant total: Grants usually total around £50,000 each year.

Applications: On a form available from the correspondent. Applications can be submitted directly by the individual or through a relevant welfare agency or third party. Applicants will usually be visited by one of the fund's volunteers who will assess their needs and offer support.

Correspondent: Benevolent Fund Secretary, Farringdon Point, 29–35 Farringdon Road, London EC1M 3JF (020 7915 8326; fax: 020 7405 7784; email: info@bossfederation.co.uk; website: www.bossfederation.co.uk)

Other information: This fund was previously known as the British Office Systems & Stationery Federation Benevolent Fund.

Stock Exchange

The Stock Exchange Benevolent Fund

Eligibility: Former members of the Stock Exchange and their dependants. In exceptional circumstances, existing members and children of education age (i.e. last year of schooling, not further/higher education) of ex-members.

Types of grants: Annuities and one-off grants according to need. Recent grants have been made for medical equipment, motor repairs and household essentials.

Annual grant total: In 2009 the fund had assets of £17 million, an income of £669,000 and a total expenditure of £907,000. Grants were made totalling £600,000, of which £433,000 was given in pensions to 83 individuals and £167,000 in one-off grants to 20 beneficiaries.

Applications: On a form available from the correspondent or to download from the website. Applications are considered quarterly, on the first Tuesday of March, June, September and December, though emergency grants can be made between meetings. Forms should be submitted two months before the next meeting.

Correspondent: James Cox, Secretary, 1–5 Earl Street, London EC2A 2AL (020 7797 1092/3120; fax: 020 7374 4963; email: stockxbf@yahoo.co.uk; website: www.sebf.co.uk/)

Other information: The fund tries to keep in regular contact with its beneficiaries and is there to offer advice and support if needed.

The Stock Exchange Clerks Fund

Eligibility: Former members of the fund and former employees of the London Stock Exchange or member firms of the London Stock Exchange, who are in need, and their dependants.

Types of grants: Monthly payments to help with living costs. One-off grants are available for medical equipment, domestic appliances, mobility vehicles, driving lessons for specialised vehicles, moving costs and so on. Most beneficiaries also receive a Christmas food parcel.

Exclusions: No grants are given towards items provided for by Income Support.

Annual grant total: In 2009 the trust had assets of £902,000, an income of £40,000 and a total expenditure of £110,000. Grants were made to 44 individuals totalling £67,000.

Applications: On a form available from the correspondent. Applications can be submitted at anytime by the individual or through a third party. New applicants are visited by the Fund's Liaison Officer who will then make a report to the trustees.

Any information concerning individuals who were previously employed in the industry and who may be in need of assistance can be given in complete confidence to either the correspondent or any of the trustees.

Correspondent: Alfred Barnard, 1–5 Earl Street, London EC2A 2AL (020 7797 4373 or 01245 322985; email: alf.barnard@btconnect.com)

Tax inspectors

The Benevolent Fund of the Association of Her Majesty's Inspectors of Taxes

Eligibility: Current and former tax inspectors and other senior officers in the Inland Revenue who are members of the association, and their dependants, who are ill or in other necessitous circumstances.

Types of grants: One-off and recurrent grants of up to £500 for people on sick leave to help towards the cost of medical equipment, hospital travel and medicines.

Exclusions: Clerical grade inspectors are not normally eligible.

Annual grant total: Grants average around £2,500 a year, though the actual grant figure tends to fluctuate quite widely.

Applications: In writing to the correspondent at any time. Applications can be submitted directly by the individual.

Correspondent: Jim Ferguson, Room 1/72, HM Revenue and Customs, 100 Parliament Street, London, SW1A 2BQ (020 7147 2807)

Teaching

Association of Principals of Colleges Benevolent Fund

Eligibility: Members and ex-members of the association, and their dependants, who are in need.

Types of grants: One-off and recurrent grants according to need. Grants have been given to widows and dependants of members who have died.

Annual grant total: Grants usually total around £1,000 per year.

Applications: In writing to the correspondent.

Correspondent: Ms D Stych, Association of Colleges, 5th Floor, Centre Point, 103 New Oxford Street, London WC1A 1RG (0207 827 4600; fax: 0207 827 4645)

Church School Masters and School Mistresses Benevolent Institution

Eligibility: Retired teachers and their dependants throughout the UK who are in need.

Types of grants: One-off grants according to need.

Annual grant total: Total annual grants are generally in the region of £200. Though this is expected to increase following the sale of the Glen Arun care home.

Applications: On a form available from the correspondent to be submitted directly by the individual or a family member. Applications are considered upon receipt.

Correspondent: The Trustees, 3 Kings Court, Harwood Road, Horsham, RH13 5UR (01403 250798; email: info@cssbi.org.uk; website: www.cssbi.org.uk/)

Other information: The institution has traditionally maintained a care home, Glen Arun, for the benefit of retired teachers and their dependants. However, in early 2009 the institution decided to sell the home, freeing up much of its income for other purposes.

The Headmasters' Association Benevolent Fund

Eligibility: The widows and dependants of deceased secondary school headmasters who were members of the association. Help is also given to headmasters and ex-headmasters who are, or were members of the association and are in urgent need of assistance.

Types of grants: One-off and recurrent grants according to need.

Annual grant total: Grants usually total about £10,000 a year.

Applications: In writing to the correspondent. Applications are considered as they arrive.

Correspondent: Andrew Smetham, Trustee, The Water Barn, Water Meadow Lane, Wool, Wareham BH20 6HL (01929 463727)

The Incorporated Association of Preparatory Schools' Benevolent Fund

Eligibility: Past and present members of the association, or their staff, and their dependants, who are in need.

Types of grants: One-off and recurrent grants according to need.

Annual grant total: In 2009/10 the fund had an income of £14,000 and a total expenditure of £15,000.

Applications: In writing to the correspondent.

Correspondent: Richard Flower, Trustee, 11 Waterloo Place, Leamington Spa, Warwickshire CV32 5LA (01926 887833)

The National Association of Schoolmasters Union of Women Teachers (NASUWT) Benevolent Fund

Eligibility: Members and former members of the association who are in need, and their dependants. Applicants should have less than £5,000 in savings and investments (though this limit may be waived in extenuating circumstances).

Types of grants: One-off and recurrent grants and interest-free loans according to need. Recent grants have been given to people with terminal illnesses to visit relatives; to pay for the services of an occupational therapist to assess disability home conversion needs; to buy a converted vehicle for a member who is paralysed; and a monthly grant to a member's widow with no occupational pension.

Exclusions: No grants/loans available for private health care, dental treatment, private school fees, student loans or legal fees. Assistance is not given if it would affect the applicant's entitlement to means-tested state benefits.

Annual grant total: About £250,000.

Applications: Potential applicants should either contact their local association secretary or the correspondent to arrange a meeting with a benevolence visitor. The visitor will complete an application form with the individual and submit a recommendation to the benevolence committee. The committee meets monthly (except August) to consider new applications. However, emergency cases can be processed more quickly.

Correspondent: Legal and Casework Team, NASUWT, Hillscourt Education Centre, Rose Hill, Rednal, Birmingham B45 8RS (0121 453 6150; fax: 0121 457 6210; email: legalandcasework@mail.nasuwt.org.uk; website: www.nasuwt.org.uk/)

The Ogilvie Charities

Eligibility: People who are, or have been, teachers or governesses in England and Wales, and, children resident in any London borough who are in need, hardship or distress by assisting with the cost of holidays or days out in the country; accompanied by or unaccompanied by other family members.

Types of grants: One-off grants of £100 to £250.

Annual grant total: In 2009 the charities had assets of £1.5 million and an income of £59,000. Grants totalling £1,000 were made to four families for holidays.

Applications: In writing to the correspondent, to be submitted through a social worker, Citizens Advice or other welfare agency. The referring agency may telephone the trust if there are doubts about their client's eligibility. Applications can be considered at any time.

Correspondent: Gillian Galvan, General Manager, The Gate House, 9 Burkitt Road, Woodbridge, Suffolk IP12 4JJ (01394 388746; fax: 01394 388746; email: ogilviecharities@btconnect.com; website: theogilvietrust.org.uk)

Other information: The charities also make grants to organisations.

Schoolmistresses' & Governesses' Benevolent Institution

Eligibility: Women who work, or have worked, as a schoolmistress, matron, bursar, secretary or librarian in the private sector of education. Self-employed teachers may also be assisted.

Types of grants: All types of help including annuities and one-off grants towards telephone bills, TV licences, household items, clothing, medical needs, holidays and mobility equipment. Grants usually range from £50 to £500.

Annual grant total: In 2008/09 the institution had assets of £3.2 million and an income of £986,000. Grants were made to 166 individuals totalling £116,000.

Applications: On a form available from the correspondent, to be submitted at any time directly by the individual or family member. Applications are considered monthly.

Correspondent: Case Secretary, SGBI Office, Queen Mary House, Manor Park Road, Chislehurst, Kent BR7 5PY (020 8468 7997; email: sgbi@fsmail.net)

Other information: The institution arranges annual visits to beneficiaries.

The Society of Schoolmasters and Schoolmistresses

Eligibility: Schoolmasters or schoolmistresses (employed/retired) of any independent or maintained school who have 10 years of continuous service, and their dependants.

Types of grants: One-off and recurrent grants up to a maximum of £600 per year. Grants are normally made to retired schoolmasters or schoolmistresses who have no adequate pension, but exceptions can sometimes be made for younger teachers.

Annual grant total: In 2009 the trust had an income of £5,800 and a total expenditure of £4,800.

Applications: On a form available from the correspondent. Applications can be submitted directly by the individual. They are considered quarterly.

Correspondent: Laurence Baggott, Queen Mary House, Manor Park Road, Chislehurst, Kent BR7 5PY (020 8468 7997; email: sgbi@fsmail.net; website: www. sossandsgbi.org.uk)

Mrs Rona P Strattons Bequest

Eligibility: Female teachers in Scotland and members of the Educational Institute of Scotland who are in need due to ill health.

Types of grants: One-off payments of up to £500.

Annual grant total: Grants usually total around £700 each year.

Applications: In writing to the correspondent. Applications can be submitted directly by the individual or family member and are considered every two months.

Correspondent: The General Secretary, The Educational Institute of Scotland, 46 Moray Place, Edinburgh EH3 6BH (0131 225 6244; fax: 0131 220 3151)

Teacher Support Network (formerly The Teachers Benevolent Fund – TBF)

Eligibility: Serving, former and retired teachers (regardless of teacher union affiliation) and their dependants. Applicants must have less than £4,000 in savings.

Types of grants: One-off grants between £300 and £3,000 towards a range of needs, including low income, illness and injury. Grants can be for special needs equipment, living expenses, clothing, funeral expenses, removal costs and household repairs.

Exclusions: No grants for private school fees, educational course fees, school trips, unsecured debts, house purchases or private medical treatment. Student loans are not made.

Annual grant total: In 2008 the trust had assets of £3.9 million, an income of £2.8 million and a total expenditure of £3.1 million. Grants were made totalling £232,000.

Note: Although submitted on time, 2009 accounts were not available to view at the Charity Commission at the time of writing (summer 2010).

Applications: On a form available from the correspondent. Applications are usually considered on a monthly basis and can be submitted directly by the individual. Applications are means-tested so financial information is needed, alongside other supporting information such as proof of need.

Correspondent: Grants Manager, 40a Drayton Park, London, N5 1EW (020 7697 2750; email: enquiries@ teachersupport.info; website: www. teachersupport.info)

Other information: Grant-making is just one aspect of the work of this trust, hence the change of name. In 1999, it established Teacher Support Line (formerly Teacherline), 'providing day-to-day support for teachers in both their personal and professional lives'. There is also a financial and welfare benefits advice service and a dedicated service for retired teachers.

Telecommunications

The BT Benevolent Fund

Eligibility: People who work, or have worked, for British Telecom or its predecessors (GPO/Post Office Telephones), and their dependants.

Types of grants: One-off grants of up to £2,000 are given towards: household appliances, disability aids, home adaptations, convalescence, carer's breaks and debt arrears, especially when there is a risk of eviction and small children are involved. Weekly grants of up to £20 a week are also available to older former employees, and their dependants, who are living on a low income.

Annual grant total: In 2009 the fund had assets of £2.6 million and an income of £803,000. Grants totalled £609,000, of which £444,000 was given in single grants and £165,000 in weekly grants.

Applications: On a form available from the correspondent. Applications are considered when received and can be submitted either directly by the individual or through a third party such as a welfare agency.

Correspondent: Phil Jennings/Steve Melhuish, Room 323, Reading Central Telephone Exchange, 41 Minister Street, Reading RG1 2JB (0845 602 9714; fax: 0118 959 0668; email: benevolent@bt. com; website: www.benevolent.bt.com)

Other information: The fund also operates a 'contact scheme' to provide advice and support for BT pensioners who are over 75 years old.

Tobacco

Tobacco Trade Benevolent Association

Eligibility: People who have been engaged in the manufacture, wholesale or retail sections of the tobacco industry and their dependants, who are in need. Both full-time and part-time workers are eligible for assistance. Applicants should have no more than £12,000 in savings/capital (excluding property).

Types of grants: Monthly allowances and one-off grants for household items and house repairs.

Annual grant total: In 2008/09 the association had assets of £2.1 million and an income of £259,000. Grants were made totalling £230,000 and were broken down as follows:

Pensions and general relief	£99,000
Maintenance grant	£49,000
One off grants	£37,000
Welfare assistance	£18,000
Christmas gifts	£18,000
TV rentals and licences	£9,300

Applications: Application forms are available from the correspondent or to download from the website. They can be submitted directly by the individual or through a social worker, Citizens Advice, welfare agency or other third party. Applicants are asked to provide details of the length of their service in the tobacco trade, financial position and whether they own their own home. Applications are considered every two months.

Correspondent: Dianne Jennings, Company Secretary, Forum Court, 83 Copers Cope Road, Beckenham, Kent BR3 1NR (020 8663 3050; fax: 020 8663 0949; email: ttba@ tobaccocharity.org.uk; website: www. tobaccocharity.org.uk)

Travel agents

ABTA Lifeline

Eligibility: People who are or have been employed by ABTA members (or ABTA itself) and their dependants.

Types of grants: One-off and recurrent grants and loans unrestricted in size. Recent grants have been given for holidays, disability aids, bills, redecorating costs and so on.

Exclusions: The fund generally does not have any restrictions in relation to their grant criteria, except it cannot help with costs arising from the failure of a company.

Annual grant total: In 2009 the fund had assets of £540,000 and an income of £74,000. Grants were made to 26 individuals totalling £16,000.

Applications: On a form available from the correspondent or to download from the website. Applications should be submitted either directly by the individual, through a third party such as a social worker, or through an organisation such as a Citizens Advice. They are considered every two months.

Correspondent: Grants Administrator, 3rd Floor, 30 Park Street, London SE1 9EQ (020 3117 0547; fax: 020 3117 0581; email: lifeline@abtalifeline.org.uk; website: www.abtalifeline.org.uk)

Thomas Cook Pensioners' Benevolent Fund

Eligibility: Retired former employees of Thomas Cook and their dependants and the dependants of deceased former employees who are in need.

Types of grants: One-off grants to alleviate hardship, for example, the replacement of worn out electrical equipment or modifications to property to accommodate disability or immobility.

Annual grant total: Grants average around £1,100 a year.

Applications: In writing to the correspondent. If eligible the individual will be required to complete a claim form.

Correspondent: Stewart Grant, Thomas Cook Pensions Department, Unit 15/18, Thomas Cook Business Park, Coningsby Road, Peterborough PE3 8SB (01733 416434; fax: 01733 416780; email: lin.creed@thomascook.com)

Other information: If eligibility is established for an individual, the fund would consider an application in conjunction with another charity or organisation.

The Guild of Registered Tourist Guides Benevolent Fund

Eligibility: Institute registered (blue badge) guides who are in need and have been qualified for at least one year and former and retired guides who have been qualified for five years or more. The dependants of guides qualified for at least five years may also be eligible for support.

Types of grants: One-off grants to relieve need and enable a guide to work. Grants can be up to £700, but are normally between £300 and £400.

Exclusions: Grants are not given for debts or private hospital care.

Annual grant total: In 2009 the fund had an income of £10,000 and a total expenditure of £6,700.

Applications: In writing to the correspondent, including the tourist board with which the applicant was registered, whether any statutory bodies have been approached and details of the specific need. Applications can be made directly by the individual or through a third party. They can be considered at any time. Each trustee has a portfolio of clients and is responsible for checking how the beneficiaries are getting on, sometimes through home visits.

Correspondent: Elizabeth Keatinge, c/o GRTG, The Guild House, 52D Borough High Street, London SE1 1XN (01908 623463; fax: 01908 625597)

United Nations

British Association of Former United Nations Civil Servants Benevolent Fund

Eligibility: Former employees of the United Nations organisation or its specialised agencies and their dependants who are in need. Applicants must be resident in the UK, but do not have to be UK nationals.

Types of grants: One-off grants, grants in kind and loans of between £100 and £500. Grants can be made towards a wide range of needs, including health and convalescence needs, help in the home, living costs, electrical goods, furniture, aids for older people or those who are disabled and assistance towards hospital visits. Loans include those to people who are recently widowed, prior to establishing their pension rights.

Annual grant total: Grants usually total around £3,000 per year.

Applications: In writing in the first instance, to the correspondent. Applications are normally referred to appropriate BAFUNCS registered welfare officer for immediate follow-up. Applications are considered throughout the year.

Correspondent: Nanda Wijayatilake, Trustee, 41 Riverine, Grosvenor Drive, Maidenhead, Berkshire SL6 8PF (01628 636000)

Veterinary

Veterinary Benevolent Fund

Eligibility: Veterinary surgeons and retired veterinary surgeons that are in need, and their dependants.

Types of grants: Regular monthly payments for people living on a low income. One-off grants up to a maximum of £1,000 are also made towards TV licences, telephone line rental, additional heating costs, car tax and insurance, holidays, medical equipment and disability aids. Short-term loans may also be made to tide beneficiaries over in times of crisis.

Exclusions: No grants towards: business or partnership debt; mandatory training courses; indemnity insurance; private education; private medical care; repaying loans to family and friends; improvements and repairs to rented property. Grants are not available to veterinary students. Financial support is not given simply because someone is unemployed.

Annual grant total: In 2009 the fund had assets of £5.3 million, an income of £393,000 and a total expenditure of £336,000. Grants were made totalling £177,000, of which £149,000 was given in regular payments and £28,000 was awarded in special gifts.

Applications: Applicants should first fill in a preliminary application form, which is available from the correspondent or to download from the website. An initial assessment will be made and those in need of urgent assistance may be awarded payment immediately. Others deemed eligible but not in urgent need will be asked to complete a more detailed application form and may be visited by one of the fund's trustees. A decision will usually be made within two weeks of receipt of the completed form.

Correspondent: Vanessa Kearns, Administration Manager, 7 Mansfield Street, London W1G 9NQ (020 7908 6385; fax: 020 7980 4890; email: info@vetlife.org.uk; website: www.vetlife.org.uk/)

Other information: The fund owns four properties in Burton near Christchurch, Dorset which are available for veterinary surgeons and their families in need of support.

Voluntary Sector

Charity Employees Benevolent Fund

Eligibility: People in need who have been in paid employment with a UK charity (or any other charitable body: either an exempt charity or recognised as a charity by the Inland Revenue). Help may also be extended to partners and dependants.

Types of grants: One-off grants according to need.

Annual grant total: In 2008/09 the fund had assets of £52,000 and an income of £54,000. Grants were made totalling £150.

Applications: On a form which can be obtained from the correspondent or via the website.

Please note: the fund has stated that its resources are currently quite limited.

Correspondent: David Prescott, The Finsbury Business Centre, 40 Bowling Green Lane, Clerkenwell, London EC1R 0NE (020 7415 7004; email: info@ cebf.org.uk; website: www.cebf.org.uk/ index.html)

Other information: The CEBF was established in 2003 to help charity employees and their families. So far, the fund has only been able to offer welfare advice and financial support on a small scale. However, as it grows it aims to extend its services to include:

● welfare support and advice on benefits

● a friendship network and a caring community

● longer term allowances to help individuals get back on their feet after a sudden setback such as bereavement, serious illness or redundancy.

Watch and clock makers

The National Benevolent Society of Watch and Clock Makers

Eligibility: Members of the UK watch and clock trade and their widows/widowers and dependants that are in need.

Types of grants: Help is usually offered in the form of quarterly grants and occasional gifts.

Annual grant total: In 2008/09 the charity had assets of £2.5 million and an income of £99,000. Grants totalled £131,000 and were broken down as follows:

Grants in aid	£82,000
Heating and seasonal gifts	£33,000
Television licence fees	£2,400

Applications: Applications for grants should be made by contacting the secretary who will send out an application form. All applications are treated in strict confidence. Completed application forms should be submitted by individuals or, if they require assistance, through a family member, social worker, welfare agency or Citizens Advice.

Correspondent: Anne Baker, Secretary, 18a Westbury Road, New Malden, Surrey, KT3 5BE (020 8288 9559; email: sec@ nbswcm.org; website: www.nbswcm.org/)

SERVICE AND EX-SERVICE CHARITIES

Service and ex-service charities have been given their own section in this guide owing to the number of trusts available and because they can support a large number of people. This branch of the sector is committed to helping anyone who has at least one day's paid service in any of the armed forces, including reserves and those who did National Service and their husbands, wives, children, widows, widowers and other dependants.

These charities are exceptionally well organised. Much of this is due to the work of SSAFA Forces Help, which has an extensive network of trained caseworkers around the country who act on behalf of SSAFA Forces Help and other service charities. Many of the trusts in this section use the same application forms and procedures as SSAFA and assist a specified group of people within the service and ex-service community, while others (such as the Royal British Legion) have their own procedures and support the services as a whole.

There is a standard application form which is used by many service and ex-service charities. This form should not be filled in by the applicant, but rather by a trained caseworker at the applicant's home. The completed form is sent to the appropriate service, regimental or corps benevolent fund (and, where appropriate, copies may be sent to other relevant funds, both service and non-service).

Although many service benevolent funds rely on trained SSAFA volunteer caseworkers to prepare application forms, some do have their own volunteers who can complete the form. However, these may not be spread so comprehensively around the country. Alternatively, some funds ask applicants to write to a central correspondent. In such cases, applicants may like to follow the guidelines in the article 'How to make an application' (see page 13). Most entries in this section state whether the applicant should apply directly to the trust or through a caseworker. If in doubt, the applicant should contact the trust concerned or the local SSAFA Forces Help office.

Some people may prefer to approach their (or their former spouse's) regimental or corps association. Each corps has its own entry in this guide and the regimental associations are listed at the end of this section (see 'Service and regimental funds' on page 116). Many of them have their own charitable funds and volunteers, especially in their own recruiting areas. In other cases they will work through SSAFA Forces Help or another benevolent fund with which they have links. Again, if in doubt or difficulty, the applicant should ring up the regimental/corps association or the local SSAFA Forces Help office.

SSAFA Forces Help is much more than just a provider of financial assistance; it also provides advice, support and training. It can assist members of the service and ex-service communities on many issues, ranging from how to replace lost medals to advice on adoption. Its website (www.ssafa.org.uk) is an excellent resource for the members of the community, giving a wide range of useful information and links. Local SSAFA Forces Help offices generally can be found in the local telephone directories (usually under Soldiers', Sailors' & Airmen's Families Association – Forces Help) or advertised in such places as Citizens Advice, doctors' waiting rooms or libraries. Alternatively, the central office is based at 19 Queen Elizabeth Street, London, SE1 2LP (tel: 0845 1300 975; email: info@ssafa.org.uk; www.ssafa.org.uk).

ABF The Soldiers' Charity (also known as The Army Benevolent Fund)

Eligibility: Members and ex-members of the British Regular Army and the Reserve Army (TA) and their dependants who are in need. Serving TA soldiers must have completed at least one year's satisfactory service, and former TA soldiers should have completed at least three years' satisfactory service.

Types of grants: Grants are made in the following areas: debt relief; mobility assistance and home modifications; annuities and care home fees; war widow and family financial support; and holidays.

Annual grant total: In 2008/09 the fund had assets of £31 million, an income of £9.7 million and a total expenditure of £9.2 million. Grants to individuals totalled £2.5 million.

Applications: The fund does not deal directly with individual cases. Soldiers who are still serving should contact their regimental or corps association, who will then approach the fund on their behalf. Former soldiers should first contact SSAFA Forces Help or the Royal British Legion. Applications are considered at anytime, but all are reviewed annually in July.

Enquiries may be made directly to the fund to determine the appropriate corps or regimental association. See also, in particular, the entries for SSAFA Forces Help and the Royal British Legion.

Correspondent: The Director of Grants and Welfare, Mountbarrow House, 6–20 Elizabeth Street, London, SW1W 9RB (0845 241 4820; fax: 0845 241 4821; email: info@soldierscharity.org; website: www.soldierscharity.org)

Other information: The trust also gives grants to individuals for educational purposes and to organisations.

The Airborne Forces' Security Fund

Eligibility: Serving and former members of the Parachute Regiment, the Glider Regiment and other units of airborne forces, and their dependants.

Types of grants: One-off grants according to need.

Annual grant total: In 2009 the fund had assets of £4.5 million and an income of £407,000. Grants were made to 254 individuals totalling £187,000.

Applications: In writing to the correspondent, usually through ABF The Soldiers' Charity, SSAFA or the Royal British Legion.

Correspondent: The Controller, Regimental Headquarters, The Parachute Regiment, Merville Barracks, Colchester, Essex, CO2 7UT (01206 817079; email: parafunds@btconnect.com)

The Aircrew Association Charitable Fund

Eligibility: Serving or ex-serving aircrew of the allied forces and their dependants. Most, but not all, of the trust's beneficiaries are Second World War veterans or the dependants of such persons.

Types of grants: One-off grants of up to £1,500 for electrical goods, convalescence, household bills, holidays, travel expenses, medical equipment and disability equipment. Recent grants have included those for a CCTV magnifier for a claimant who could not otherwise read (£1,400); a respite holiday for an older couple (£880); clothing for a couple who both suffer from Alzheimer's disease (£500); and debt relief for one claimant (£300).

Annual grant total: In 2008/09 the trust had an income of £11,000 and a total expenditure of £14,000.

Applications: On a form available from the correspondent. Applications can be submitted either directly by the individual or through a third party such as SSAFA, RAFA, RBL and so on. Applications are considered on receipt, and are assessed according to need; financial and other information may be requested.

Correspondent: Graham Watson, Honorary Secretary, 14 Holmdale, Eastergate, Chichester, West Sussex, PO20 3AA (01243 543355; email: graham0885@yahoo.co.uk)

AJEX Charitable Foundation (formerly known as The Association of Jewish Ex-Servicemen & Women)

Eligibility: Jewish ex-servicemen and women, and their dependants, who are in need.

Types of grants: One-off and recurrent grants according to need. Special grants are also made to cover emergencies and exceptional circumstances.

Annual grant total: In 2008 the foundation had an income of £328,000 and

assets that stood at £2.4 million. Grants were made totalling £37,000.

Applications: On a form available from the correspondent, to be returned directly by the individual or through a third party. Evidence of service in the British army and of Jewish religious status is required.

Correspondent: Ronald Shelley, Shield House, Harmony Way, Hendon, London NW4 2BZ (020 8202 2323; fax: 020 8202 9900; email: headoffice@ajex.org.uk; website: www.ajex.org.uk)

Other information: Although submitted on time, 2009 accounts were not available to view at the Charity Commission.

ATS & WRAC Benevolent Fund

Eligibility: Former members of the Auxiliary Territorial Service during the Second World War and the Women's Royal Army Corps between 1949–1992 who are in financial hardship or who are disabled or have mobility problems.

Types of grants: One-off grants to those in need. The fund can also help with making up the shortfall for nursing home fees and supports some annuitants who receive regular payments throughout the year.

Annual grant total: In 2008/09 the trust had assets of £5.2 million and an income of £315,000. Grants were made to 538 individuals totalling £146,000.

Applications: All applications for financial assistance should go through the Soldiers, Sailors, Airman and Families Association (SSAFA) or the Royal British Legion caseworkers who will visit the applicants and submit whatever forms are necessary.

Correspondent: J Freebairn, AGC Centre, Worthy Down, Winchester SO21 2RG (01962 887570; fax: 01962 887478; email: benfund@wracassociation.co.uk; website: www.wracassociation.co.uk)

Other information: If you feel that you might qualify for financial assistance, please apply to your local Royal British Legion or SSAFA office in the first instance.

The Black Watch Association

Eligibility: Serving and retired soldiers of the regiment, their wives, widows and families.

Types of grants: One-off grants towards rent arrears, clothing, household equipment, funeral expenses and mobility aids. Support is also given towards holidays for widows and dependent children and former members of the regiment in necessitous circumstances.

Exclusions: No grants towards council tax arrears, loans or large debts.

Annual grant total: In 2009 the trust had an income of £247,000.

Applications: On an application form to be completed by a caseworker from SSAFA Forces Help (19 Queen Elizabeth Street,

London SE1 2LP; Tel: 0845 1300 975; website: www.ssafa.org.uk). Applications are considered throughout the year.

Correspondent: Maj. A R McKinnell, Balhousie Castle, Hay Street, Perth PH1 5HR (01738 623214; fax: 01738 643245; email: bwassociation@btconnect.com)

British Limbless Ex-Service Men's Association (BLESMA)

Eligibility: Serving and ex-serving members of HM or auxiliary forces who have lost a limb or eye or have a permanent loss of speech, hearing or sight, and their widows/widowers. Despite the association's name, it serves members of both sexes.

Types of grants: One-off and recurrent grants towards, for example, wheelchairs and Electric Propelled Vehicles, stair lifts, car adaptations and gardening costs.

Annual grant total: In 2009 the association had assets of £18 million and an income of £4.1 million. Welfare grants were made totalling £362,000.

Applications: On a form available from the correspondent. Applications can be submitted at any time, either directly by the individual or through their local BLESMA representative, SSAFA Forces Help, Citizens Advice or similar welfare agency.

Correspondent: Jerome W Church, General Secretary, Frankland Moore House, 185–187 High Road, Chadwell Heath, Romford, Essex RM6 6NA (020 8590 1124; fax: 020 8599 2932; email: headquarters@blesma.org; website: www.blesma.org)

Other information: The association provides permanent residential and respite accommodation through its two nursing and residential care homes at Blackpool and Crieff in Perthshire.

The Burma Star Association

Eligibility: People who were awarded the Burma Star Campaign Medal (or the Pacific Star with Burma clasp) during the Second World War, and their immediate dependants, who live in the UK, Republic of Ireland or other Commonwealth country.

Types of grants: One-off grants usually in the range of £200 to £1,000 towards: top-up fees for nursing, care and residential homes; respite care and holidays; domestic goods; debts; disability aids; funeral expenses; repairs and adaptations; travel costs; mobility aids and so on.

Exclusions: No grants are available towards private medical treatment, headstones or plaques. The association does not give loans.

Annual grant total: In 2009 the association had an income of £132,000 and a total expenditure of £349,000. Grants totalled around £200,000.

Applications: In writing to the correspondent. Applications can be made by the individual or through a third party. They should either be sent directly to the correspondent or submitted via branches of the association or other ex-service organisations. Grants are made through the local branches, SSAFA, the Royal British Legion or other ex-service organisations after investigation and completion of an application form giving full particulars of circumstances and eligibility (including service particulars verifying the award of the Burma Star). Applications are considered throughout the year.

Correspondent: Glynis Longhurst, 34 Grosvenor Gardens, London, SW1W 0DH (020 7823 4273; email: burmastar@btconnect.com; website: www.burmastar.org.uk)

Other information: The association has over 100 branches across the UK and overseas, which offer support and advice to their local members and make small grants where possible. The contact details for local branch officers can be obtained from the correspondent.

The Commandos' Benevolent Fund

Eligibility: People who served with the Army Commandos during the Second World War, and their dependants. Unfortunately service with any other commando group does not make people eligible for help from this fund.

Types of grants: One-off grants towards, hospital transport, household bills, stair-lifts, flooding costs, holidays, respite breaks, removal expenses, home adaptations, medical costs, funeral expenses and so on. The fund states that it will consider all applications on a case by case basis.

Annual grant total: In 2009 the fund had an income of £97,000 and a total expenditure of £78,000. Grants were made totalling £67,000.

Applications: In writing, with service details, to the Assistant Secretary, PO Box 104, Selby, Yorkshire, YO8 5YY: or on a form available from the website. Applications can be submitted directly by the individual or through a social worker, Citizens Advice or other welfare agency such as SSAFA Forces Help. Applications are considered as soon as possible after receipt.

Correspondent: Michael Copland, Old Pinkneys, Lee Lane, Maidenhead, Berkshire SL6 6PE (01628 630375; email: mandlcopland@yahoo.co.uk; website: commandosbenevolentfund.org.uk/)

W J & Mrs C G Dunnachie's Charitable Trust

Eligibility: People who are in poor health or who have a disability as a result of their service during the Second World War.

Types of grants: One-off and recurrent grants according to need.

Annual grant total: Grants average about £80,000 a year.

Applications: In writing to the correspondent at any time. Most applications are submitted via SSAFA Forces Help or through a regimental association.

Correspondent: Trust Administrator, c/o Low Beaton Richmond, Sterling House, 20 Renfield Street, Glasgow G2 5AP (0141 221 8931; fax: 0141 248 4411; email: murdoch@lbr-city.demon.co.uk)

The Hampshire & Isle of Wight Military Aid Fund (1903)

Eligibility: Members, or former members, of the British Army (whether regular, territorial, militia, yeomanry or volunteer), and their dependants, who are in need, and who are, or were:

a) Members or former members of any Regiment or Corps raised in Hampshire.

b) Members or former members of The Princess of Wales's Royal Regiment (Queen's and Royal Hampshire's) who were resident in Hampshire at the time of their enlistment.

Types of grants: One-off grants for stair-lifts, recliner chairs, walk-in showers, electrically powered vehicles and so on. Grants usually range from £250 to £350.

Annual grant total: In 2009 the fund had assets of £397,000 and an income £39,000. Individual grants were made totalling £19,000.

Applications: Normally through the local branch of SSAFA or the Royal British Legion. Applications are considered as they are received.

Correspondent: Lt Col Keith Bryan, Serle's House, Southgate Street, Winchester, Hampshire SO23 9EG (01962 852933; email: hantsandiowmaf@dsl.pipex.com)

Other information: The fund also distributes grants and monthly allowances on behalf of ABF The Soldiers' Charity for nursing home top up fees and support for individuals on a low income trying to stay in their own homes (£17,000 in 2009).

The Household Division Queen's Jubilee Trust

Eligibility: Children who are physically and/or mentally disabled whose parents are officers, warrant officers, non commissioned officers and soldiers of the Household Division, and other such children. Applicants must have been born while their fathers were serving in the Household Division unless they died whilst serving in it.

Types of grants: One-off and recurrent grants 'to assist in the care, upbringing, maintenance and education' of such children.

Annual grant total: Grants total around £3,000 each year.

Applications: In the first instance ring 020 7930 4466 and ask for the assistant regimental adjutant of the regiment concerned who will tell you how to contact the relevant headquarters. In some cases SSAFA Forces Help will be asked to investigate and make recommendations on grants.

Correspondent: Major William Style, Household Division Funds, Horse Guards, Whitehall, London SW1A 2AX (email: william.style901@mod.uk)

Lloyd's Patriotic Fund

Eligibility: Ex-servicemen and women who are in need, and their dependants.

Types of grants: One-off grants averaging about £300 are provided for essential domestic items, electric wheelchairs, home adaptations and exceptional expenses. In deserving cases grants may also be given for debt relief and help with utility bills. Annuity payments are also made.

Annual grant total: In 2008/09 the fund had assets of £1.4 million and an income of £95,000. Grants for welfare purposes were made to 150 individuals totalling £45,000. A further £15,000 was distributed in 14 educational grants and £17,000 was given in 36 annuity payments.

Applications: Applications should be made through SSAFA, using their application form.

Correspondent: The Secretary, Lloyd's, One Lime Street, London EC3M 7HA (020 7327 6075; email: communityaffairs@lloyds.com; website: www.lloyds.com)

Other information: The fund makes an annual grant to The Gurkha Welfare Trust.

The Nash Charity

Eligibility: Ex-service personnel who have been wounded or disabled during wartime.

Types of grants: Grants are usually paid through social services, Citizens Advice or other welfare agencies to purchase specific items.

Annual grant total: In 2008/09 the charity had an income of £16,000 and a total expenditure of £22,000.

Applications: In writing to the correspondent at any time. Applications can be submitted directly by the individual or through an appropriate third party.

Correspondent: P A Williamson, Peachey & Co, 95 Aldwych, London WC2B 4JF (020 7316 5200; fax: 020 7316 5222)

The 'Not Forgotten' Association

Eligibility: Service and ex-service men and women who are disabled or suffering from some form of ill health. Applicants must have served in the Armed Forces of the Crown (or Merchant Navy during hostilities). The association cannot help wives, widows or families (unless they are themselves ex-members of the forces or they are acting as carers).

Types of grants: The association does not give financial grants direct to applicants; rather it gives help in kind of between £150 and £250 in the following areas: televisions and licences for those with restricted mobility or who are otherwise largely housebound; holidays (accompanied by carers if required) and day outings to events and places of interest; entertainment at ex-service care homes.

The association does not give cash grants, but in certain cases cheques may be sent to individual applicants for holidays or to office holders of bona fide ex-service organisations. The association does not have the resources to undertake case work.

Annual grant total: In 2008/09 the association had assets of £596,000 and an income of just over £850,000. Grants were made totalling £546,000.

Applications: Applications should be submitted through SSAFA Forces Help, Royal British Legion, Combat Stress or the Welfare Service of the Service Personnel and Veterans' Agency. These agencies will complete the common application form on behalf of the applicant and then make the appropriate recommendation to the association, with the applicant's income and expenditure details and degree of disability. Applications are considered throughout the year. Successful applicants can reapply after a three-year gap.

Correspondent: Col. S D Rowland-Jones, 4th Floor, 2 Grosvenor Gardens, London SW1W 0DH (020 7730 2400/3660; fax: 020 7730 0020; email: director@ nfassociation.org; website: www. nfassociation.org)

Other information: The association holds a summer garden party and Christmas party for war pensioners or for those in receipt of compensation from the Armed Force Compensation Scheme in London each year.

The Officers' Association Scotland

Eligibility: Ex-officers of the armed forces of Great Britain, or of the merchant navy or Polish forces during World War Two, (including the women's and nursing services) and their widows/widowers and dependants who are in distress, and ex-officers of all ages seeking employment.

Types of grants: One-off and recurrent grants according to need. Previously, annual grants have been made in four quarterly payments of up to £380. One-off grants are investigated and dealt with as they arise.

Annual grant total: In 2009/10 the association had an income of £310,000. Last year the association gave grants to 121 individuals totalling £169,000.

Applications: Potential beneficiaries should first contact the benevolence secretary on 0131 550 1593.

Correspondent: Gary Grey, Benevolence Secretary, New Haig House, Logie Green Road, Edinburgh EH7 4HR (0131 550 1593; fax: 0131 557 5819; email: g.gray@poppyscotland.org.uk; website: www.oascotland.org.uk/)

Other information: The association runs a 'friendship visits programme' to provide company for retired officers and their dependants who are feeling isolated. It also provides support and advice to officers making the transition from service to civilian employment.

The Officers' Association

Eligibility: Officers who have held a commission in HM Forces, their widows and dependants. Officers on the active list will normally be helped only with resettlement and employment.

Types of grants: One-off and recurrent grants according to need. Cash grants are made for specific items such as disability equipment, property repairs, convalescence, holidays or to help set up a new home following a family crisis. Regular allowances are given mainly to older people who are living on a low income. Help is also given towards residential care and nursing home fees.

Limited assistance may be given for education or training needs in exceptional circumstances.

Annual grant total: In 2008/09 the association had assets of £12 million and an income of £3.2 million. Grants were made to 912 individuals totalling £1.4 million and were given mainly for relief-in-need purposes.

Applications: On a form available from the Benevolence Secretary. Applications can be submitted either directly by the individual or via a third party. The association has a network of honorary representatives throughout the UK who will normally visit the applicant to discuss their problems and offer advice.

Correspondent: Benevolence Department, 1st Floor, Mountbarrow House, 6–20 Elizabeth Street, London SW1W 9RB (020 7808 4175 /0845 873 7150; email: k. wallis@officersassociation.org.uk; website: www.officersassociation.org.uk)

Other information: The association has a residential home at Bishopsteignton, South Devon, for ex-officers (male and female) over the age of 65 who do not need special care. There is also a small estate of 12 bungalows in Leavesden specially designed for disabled officers and their families.

The association provides a series of advice leaflets on finding accommodation in residential care or nursing homes, how to get financial assistance and how to find short-term convalescence accommodation and sheltered accommodation for older people who are disabled. It also has an employment department to help ex-officers up to the age of 60 find suitable employment. This service is open to officers just leaving the services and to those who have lost their civilian jobs.

For applicants in Scotland: See entry for the Officers' Association Scotland.

The REME Benevolent Fund

Eligibility: Members and former members of the REME who are in need, and their immediate dependants.

Types of grants: One-off grants of up to £1,000 for any need. For example, a recent grant was made to a REME staff sergeant who lost a leg in a traffic accident to help towards the cost of an automatic car. Annuities and help with nursing home fees are also available.

Exclusions: No grants for medical expenses, funeral expenses, litigation costs or debts.

Annual grant total: In 2009 the fund had assets of £657,000 and an income of £680,000. Grants were made to individuals totalling about £432,000 and were distributed as follows:

Grants in aid – Individuals	£368,000
Grants to Royal Star & Garter Homes	£1,500
Erskine & Queen Alexandra' Hospitals	£4,700
Nursing Home Fees	£20,000
Annuity allowances	£38,000

Applications: On a form available from the correspondent or a local branch of SSAFA or the Royal British Legion. Grants are only made through a third party (e.g. SSAFA/RBL), and applications made direct will be referred to a welfare agency for investigation. Applications are screened immediately on receipt and are either rejected on sight, referred back for more information or to a committee which meets every three weeks. Grants of under £500 can be paid immediately on receipt of a suitable application.

Correspondent: Corps Secretariat, RHQ REME, HQ DEME (A), Isaac Newton Road, Arborfield, Reading RG2 9NJ (0118 976 3220; email: deme-corpssecro1@ mod.uk)

Other information: The fund also makes grants to other service organisations.

Royal Air Force Benevolent Fund

Eligibility: Past and present members of the Royal Air Force or associated forces and their immediate dependants.

Types of grants: Almost all types of assistance can be considered in the form of grants or loans. Common types of awards cover house repairs or modifications, mobility aids, maintenance and immediate need grants, specialist equipment and, in some cases, education and housing.

Exclusions: No grants for private medical costs or for legal fees.

Annual grant total: In 2009 the fund had assets of £141 million and an income of £17.7 million. Grants totalled £18 million, the majority of which were given in welfare grants.

Applications: On a form available directly from the correspondent or on their website via an online application form. Applications can be submitted by the individual or through an ex-service welfare agency such as RAFA or SSAFA. The fund runs a free helpline which potential applicants are welcome to call for advice and support on the application process. Applications are considered on a continual basis.

Correspondent: The Welfare Director, RAF Benevolent Fund, 12 Park Crescent, London, W1B 1PH (0800 169 2942; email: info@rafbf.org.uk; website: www.raf-benfund.org.uk)

Other information: The fund maintains a short-term care home in Sussex and a further three homes in Northumberland, Avon and Lancashire which are operated jointly with the RAFA.

The fund also gives grants to organisations (£2.7 million in 2009).

The Royal Air Forces Association

Eligibility: Serving and former members of the Royal Air Force (including National Service), and their dependants. The widows and widowers and dependants of those that have died in service, or subsequently, are also eligible for assistance.

Types of grants: Small, one-off grants when all other sources of funding have been exhausted. Recent grants have been awarded for gas and electricity bills, clothing, bedding, electrical goods, furniture and hospital travel costs. The trust may also assist with nursing, convalescent and respite care costs.

Exclusions: Credit card debts are not eligible, nor are medical fees.

Annual grant total: In 2009 the association had assets of £17 million, an income of £9.4 million and a total expenditure of £7.7 million. Welfare grants were made totalling £19,000.

Applications: On a form available from the relevant area welfare officer. They are contactable on the numbers below. Confirmation of RAF service is required. Applications may be submitted directly by the individual, or through SSAFA Forces Help, Royal British Legion or other welfare agency.

North West	Michael Grell	01772 426930
North East	Alan Robson	01904 870691
Eastern Area	Chris Fear	0116 268 8781
South West	Glenford Bishop	01392 462088
South East	Sue Smith	020 8286 6667
Midlands	Tracey Khan	0121 449 9356
Scotland and Overseas	Mike McCourt	0131 225 5221
Wales Area	Barbara Howells	01495 249 522
Northern Ireland	Sarah Waugh	02890 325718

Correspondent: Welfare Director, 117.5 Loughborough Road, Leicester LE4 5ND (0208 286 6667; email: welfare@rafa.org.uk; website: www.rafa.org.uk)

Other information: The association provides support and advice on state benefits, including war pensions. It also manages two sheltered housing complexes, a residential home and three respite care homes.

The Royal Army Service Corps & Royal Corps of Transport Benevolent Fund

Eligibility: People in need who have at any time served in or with the former RASC or the former RCT, including people who served and are now serving in the Royal Logistics Corp. Members of the women's services and the dependants of any of the above are also eligible.

Types of grants: One-off grants averaging about £420 towards wheelchairs and other mobility aids, house repairs, utility bills, bathroom conversions, house adaptations and so on.

Exclusions: No grants for repayment of general debts or loans.

Annual grant total: In 2008 the fund had assets of £9 million, an income of £592,000 and a total expenditure of £497,000. Grants were made to 809 individuals totalling £342,000.

Applications: Applications should be made through SSAFA Forces Help, the Royal British Legion, PoppyScotland or similar welfare organisation. Grants are made to the sponsoring organisation rather than directly to the individual. Applications can be made at any time, though requests for larger amounts need to be considered by the executive committee, making them longer to process.

Correspondent: Lt Col M J B Graham, RASC/RCT Association, Dettingen House, The Princess Royal Barracks, Deepcut, Camberley, Surrey GU16 6RW (01252 833391; email: controller@rascrct.org.uk; website: www.rascrctassociation.co.uk/)

Royal Artillery Charitable Fund

Eligibility: Serving and ex-serving members of the Royal Regiment of Artillery and their dependants.

Types of grants: One-off and recurrent grants of £250 to £700 for essential needs such as household bills, kitchen and domestic equipment, rent, water rates, nursing home fees, disability equipment, clothing, council tax and utility or power bills.

Exclusions: No grants towards income tax, loans, credit card debts, telephone bills, legal fees or private medical treatment.

Annual grant total: In 2009 the fund had assets of £13 million and an income of £1.3 million. Welfare grants were made to over 2,000 individuals amounting to £901,000.

Applications: In writing to SSAFA Forces Help (details of local branches can be found in telephone directories or from Citizens Advice). Applications can also be made to the Royal British Legion or to Poppy Scotland (Earl Haig Fund Scotland) – see Scotland section of this guide. Applications can be considered at any time.

Correspondent: The Welfare Secretary, Artillery House, Royal Artillery Barracks, Larkill, Salisbury, SP4 8QT (01980 845698; website: www.forums.theraa.co.uk)

The Royal British Legion

Eligibility: Serving and ex-serving members of the armed forces and their wives, widows, children and other dependants in England, Wales and Northern Ireland (for Scotland see the entry for Poppy Scotland (Earl Haig Fund Scotland) in the Scotland section of the guide).

Types of grants: Following a standard assessment of the beneficiary's financial situation, the Legion makes grants to individuals, either financial or by the provision of goods or services. Grants can be given for any purpose within the scope of the Royal Charter, which governs the Legion, and includes an Immediate Needs Scheme, help for homelessness, and a Property Repair Loan Scheme.

Annual grant total: In 2009 the Legion had assets of £224 million, an income of £125 million and a total expenditure of £112 million. Welfare grants to just under 27,000 individuals totalled £23 million.

Applications: Individual applications to any local branch or the county field officers. A local telephone number for an initial enquiry can usually be found in any telephone directory. Extensive information and contact details can also be found on the website.

Note: Most charities for ex-servicemen and women co-operate together in their work and the British Legion may also be approached through other service organisations and vice versa.

Correspondent: Welfare Services, 199 Borough High Street, London, SE1 1AA (Telephone Legionline on 08457 725 725 Tel: 020 3207 2100; email: info@britishlegion.org.uk; website: www.britishlegion.org.uk)

Other information: The Royal British Legion is one of the largest providers of charitable help for individuals in the country and is financed mainly by gifts from individuals, especially through its annual Poppy Day collection.

The Legion provides a comprehensive service for advising and helping ex-servicemen and women and their dependants (though for ex-service women, wives, widows and dependants, see also the entry for Royal British Legion Women's Section). Direct financial assistance is but one aspect of this work. There are over 3,000 branches of the Legion, all of which can act as centres for organising whatever help the circumstances may require. The support of the Legion is available to all who served in the forces, whether in war or peace-time, as regulars or those who have done national service.

The Legion has seven care homes which are exclusively for ex-service people and their dependants. They also have four Welfare Break centres designed to give a break to those who have been ill or bereaved or to relieve carers for two to three weeks of caring for ex-service people with severe disabilities.

There is a 'Poppy Calls' service, offering help with awkward jobs such as minor repairs or fitting essential devices such as smoke detectors and care phones, allowing ex-service members and their dependants to stay independent in their own homes.

The Legion also works with SSAFA Forces Help on a Prison In-Reach programme, which gives advice and practical support to ex-service people who are serving a prison sentence and their immediate dependants.

Royal British Legion Women's Section

Eligibility: Ex-servicewomen, the wives and widows of servicemen and the dependant children of ex-servicemen and women who are in need.

Types of grants: Women's Section Allowance: a small means-tested allowance, paid quarterly, intended to help pay for daily living expenses. To be eligible applicants must be over 60 and have served in the armed forces. Spouses, widows, widowers, surviving civil partners, partners and divorced spouses (who have never remarried or entered another long-term cohabiting relationship) are also eligible. Applicants must live alone, be in real financial need and in receipt of all appropriate benefits.

Children's Welfare Scheme: grants are available to children for clothing, beds and bedding. To qualify the children must be dependants of ex-service personnel and, if over the age of 16, be in full-time education. Parents and guardians of eligible children must be in financial need i.e. being a subsistence wage earner and/or in receipt of Income Support, Housing Benefit or Council Tax Benefit.

Family Welfare Breaks: respite breaks at various holiday parks such as Pontin's, Butlin's or Haven for ex-Service families and particularly for child carers. Additional funds may also be given for travel, children's pocket money and holiday clothing. The following groups are eligible to apply: families where a member is disabled and in receipt of a disability benefit; young carers looking after dependants, parents or siblings who are in need of a family break; and families with other special circumstances.

Welfare Breaks Scheme: grants for one to two week holidays on a half-board basis at hotels and guesthouses around the country. Welfare breaks are available to ex-service personnel and their spouses, particularly those who are pre or post hospitalization or have recently suffered a bereavement of a close relative.

Annual grant total: In 2009 the trust's total charitable expenditure amounted to £1.4 million. No further information was available.

Applications: Initial enquiries by telephone or in writing requesting a visit by a welfare visitor who will submit an application form, which includes a financial statement. Applications are considered on a regular basis.

Correspondent: Welfare Advisor, 199 Borough High Street, London, SE1 1AA (020 3207 2182; email: WSWelfare@britishlegion.org.uk; website: www.womensbritishlegion.org.uk)

Other information: Grants are made through the Women's Section, which is an autonomous organisation within the Royal British Legion concentrating on the needs of widows and ex-servicewomen and dependant children of ex-service personnel. It works in close association with the Legion but has its own funds and its own local welfare visitors.

Royal Commonwealth Ex-Services League

Eligibility: Ex-servicemen and women of the crown, their widows or dependants, who are living outside the UK. There are 56 member organisations in 48 countries.

Types of grants: All types of help can be considered. Grants are one-off, usually ranging from £100 to £500 and renewable on application. Grants are generally for medically related costs such as hearing aids, wheelchairs, artificial limbs, food or

repairs to homes wrecked by floods or hurricanes and so on.

Annual grant total: In 2009 the fund had an income of £1.3 million and a total expenditure of £1.7 million. Approximately £1.6 million was given for welfare and benevolence to individuals and projects.

Applications: Considered daily on receipt of applications from member organisations or British Embassies/High Commissions, but not directly from individuals. Applications should include proof of military service to the crown.

Correspondent: Secretary General, Haig House, 199 Borough High Street, London SE1 1AA (020 3207 2413; email: mgordon-roe@commonwealthveterans.org.uk; website: www.commonwealthveterans.org.uk)

Other information: The league has members or representatives in most parts of the world through whom former servicemen or their dependants living abroad can seek help. The local British Embassy or High Commission can normally supply the relevant local contact. In a Commonwealth country the local ex-service association will probably be affiliated to the league.

Royal Military Police Central Benevolent Fund

Eligibility: People who are serving or have served in the Royal Military Police corps, or any of its predecessors, and their dependants.

Types of grants: One-off cash grants of £100 to £1,000 towards heating, funeral expenses, household furniture, debts, clothing and bedding, mobility aids, holidays, medical needs, special chairs, removals and other needs. Christmas grants of £85 are distributed to people who have received an individual benefit grant and are over 80 years of age.

Annual grant total: In 2008/09 the fund had assets of £2.2 million and an income of £253,000. Grants were made totalling £104,000 and were distributed as follows:

Individual grants	£77,000
Christmas grants	£16,000
Nursing home fees	£4,200
Annuities	£6,800

Applications: In writing to the correspondent. All applications are passed to the Royal British Legion or SSAFA Forces Help, who will visit applicants to verify eligibility and financial need.

Correspondent: Col John H Baber, Defence Police College & Guarding, Postal Point 38, Southwick Park, Nr Fareham, Hampshire PO17 6EJ (01243 534237; email: rhqrmp@btconnect.com)

The Royal Naval Benevolent Society for Officers

Eligibility: Officers, both active service and retired, of the Royal Navy, Royal Marines, QARNNS and WRNS and their respective reserves, of the equivalent rank of Sub-Lieutenant RN and above, and their spouses, former spouses, families and dependants. There are no age limits.

Types of grants: One-off and recurrent grants to augment inadequate incomes or to meet specific, unforeseen expenses. Grants have been given to help with: house repairs; car maintenance; removal costs; mobility aids; retraining and nursing home fees. Education grants may be given to complete a particular stage of a child's education (not school fees).

Exclusions: The society does not make grants for school fees or medical care.

Annual grant total: In 2008 the society had assets of £8.8 million and an income of £4.5 million. Grants were made to individuals (17 members and 227 non-members) totalling £264,000.

Although submitted on time, at the time of writing (winter 2010), 2009 accounts were not available to view at the Charity Commission.

Applications: On a form available from the correspondent. Applications can be submitted either directly by the individual, or through a third party such as a social worker or Citizens Advice. They are considered monthly.

Correspondent: Cmdr W K Ridley, Secretary, 70 Porchester Terrace, Bayswater, London W2 3TP (020 7402 5231; email: rnoc@arno.org.uk)

Other information: The society was founded on 16 May 1739 by a group of naval officers suffering from unreasonable treatment by the Admiralty. The benevolent function of the society emerged later and became its sole purpose in 1791. In 2008, the Association of Royal Navy Officers Charitable Trust transferred its assets to the society.

Royal Naval Benevolent Trust

Eligibility: Serving and ex-serving men and women of the Royal Navy and Royal Marines (not officers) and their dependants.

Types of grants: Recurrent grants of £100 a quarter to older people and one-off grants towards a variety of needs, including rent and mortgage payments, food, clothing, fuel, childcare, medical treatment, disability aids, respite and recuperative holidays, household goods and repairs, removal expenses, debts and training for a second career.

Annual grant total: In 2009 the trust had assets of £31 million and an income of £4 million. Grants amounted to £1.3 million, with an additional £790,000 given in annuity payments.

Applications: On a form available from the correspondent, to be submitted through a social worker, welfare agency, SSAFA Forces Help, Royal British Legion or any Royal Naval Association branch. Applications are considered twice a week.

Correspondent: The Grants Administrator, Castaway House, 311 Twyford Avenue, Portsmouth PO2 8NR (023 9269 0112; fax: 023 9266 0852; email: rnbt@rnbt.org.uk; website: www.rnbt.org.uk)

Other information: The trust pays 1,300 annuities of up to £12 a week to older beneficiaries. These are called Jellicoe (Greenwich Hospital) Annuities. They cost about £811,000 a year.

The trust also runs a residential and nursing home for older ex-naval men (not women) namely, Pembroke House, Oxford Road, Gillingham, Kent.

The Royal Naval Reserve (V) Benevolent Fund

Eligibility: Members or former members of the Royal Naval Volunteer Reserve, Women's Royal Naval Volunteer Reserve, Royal Naval Reserve and the Women's Royal Naval Reserve, who are serving or have served as non-commissioned rates. The fund also caters for wives, widows and young children of the above.

Types of grants: One-off grants only, ranging from £50 to £350. Grants have been given for gas, electricity, removal expenses (i.e. to be near children/following divorce); clothing; travel to visit sick relatives or for treatment; essential furniture and domestic equipment; help on bereavement. Schoolchildren from poor families may very occasionally receive help for clothes, books or necessary educational visits, and help can also go to eligible children with aptitudes or disabilities which need special provision.

Annual grant total: About £3,000.

Applications: In writing to the correspondent directly by the individual or through the local reserve division, Royal British Legion, SSAFA Forces Help or Royal Naval Benevolent Trust, which investigates applications.

Correspondent: Commander J M D Curteis, Hon. Secretary and Treasurer, The Cottage, St Hilary, Cowbridge, Vale of Glamorgan CF71 7DP (01446 771108)

The Royal Navy & Royal Marines Children's Fund

Eligibility: Young people under 25 who are in need and are the dependant of somebody who has served, or is serving, in the Royal Navy, Royal Marines, the Queen Alexandra's Royal Naval Nursing Service or the former Women's Royal Naval Service.

Types of grants: One-off and recurrent grants ranging between £20 and £20,000 for general welfare needs including, help in the home, hospital travel expenses, respite care, specialist equipment, house adaptations and childcare. Assistance is also available to children who had been traumatised by death or family break-up.

Annual grant total: In 2008/09 the fund had assets of £6.8 million and an income of £1.2 million. The sum of £359,000 was distributed in children's miscellaneous grants and a further £767,000 was given in special needs education grants.

Applications: On a form available from the correspondent or to download from the website. Applications can be submitted directly by the individual or through the individual's school/college, SSAFA, Naval Personal, social services or other third party. They can be submitted at any time and are considered on a monthly basis, though urgent cases can be dealt with between meetings.

Correspondent: Monique Bateman, Director, 311 Twyford Avenue, Stamshaw, Portsmouth PO2 8RN (023 9263 9534; fax: 023 9267 7574; email: rnchildren@btconnect.com; website: www.rnrmchildrensfund.org)

The Royal Observer Corps Benevolent Fund

Eligibility: All former members of the Royal Observer Corps who are in need, hardship or distress. Length of service is not a consideration, except that the person on whom the application has been made must have served long enough to have received their Royal Observer Corps official number.

Types of grants: Almost all types of grants can be considered. Typically the fund can provide financial help for mobility aids, debt relief, essential home repairs or modification and respite care.

Exclusions: Grants are not given towards debts or arrears owed to government bodies.

Annual grant total: In 2009 the trust had assets of £846,000 and an income of £28,000. Grants were made totalling £34,000.

Applications: By direct contact with the fund or through SSAFA, the Royal British Legion or the Royal Air Forces Association. Applications are considered on receipt and normally a decision is given within days.

Correspondent: The Secretary, 120 Perry Hall Road, Orpington, Kent BR6 0EF (email: info@rocbf.org.uk; website: www.rocbf.org.uk)

The Royal Signals Benevolent Fund

Eligibility: Members and former members of the Royal Signals, regular or territorial volunteer reserve, and their widows and other dependants.

Types of grants: One-off and recurrent grants according to need. Grants are given towards fuel and lighting costs, funeral expenses, domestic and medical appliances, convalescence, nursing home top-up fees, supplementary and Christmas allowances.

Exclusions: The fund does not distribute loans.

Annual grant total: In 2009 the fund had an income of £1.5 million and a total expenditure of £1.4 million. Benevolence grants were made totalling around £360,000.

Applications: Applications should be made through SSAFA Forces Help or another charitable organisation and are considered as required.

Correspondent: The Regimental Secretary, RHQ Royal Signals, Blandford Camp, Blandford Forum, Dorset DT11 8RH (01258 482081; email: SOINC-RHQ-RegtSec@mod.uk)

Other information: The fund also gives funding to other service charities.

The Sister Agnes Benevolent Fund

Eligibility: People who have served in the armed forces, regardless of rank or length of service, who are uninsured and are either inpatients or outpatients at King Edward VII's Hospital Sister Agnes, and their spouses, ex-spouses, widows and widowers.

Types of grants: Means tested grants for up to 100% of hospital fees. In some cases, consultant fees may also be covered.

Annual grant total: In 2008/09 the fund had assets of £511,000 and an income of £64,000. Grants were made to 18 individuals totalling £96,000.

Applications: On a form available from the correspondent or to download from the website, including evidence of service and financial details.

Please note: Uninsured service personnel, their spouses, ex-spouses, widows and widowers are all eligible for a 20% subsidy on their hospital bill (this is not means-tested). To claim, eligible individuals need to notify the hospital when booking their procedure.

Correspondent: PA to the Chief Executive, Beaumont Street, London, W1G 6AA (020 7486 4411; email: info@kingedwardvii.co.uk; website: www.kingedwardvii.co.uk)

Other information: The Sister Agnes Benevolent Fund is a restricted fund of King Edward VII's Hospital Sister Agnes. The hospital also administers the Charity of Alexander Michael Levy, which can provide grants to people who have lived in London and have at least one parent who was born in the UK.

SSAFA Forces Help

Eligibility: Service and ex-service men and women and their immediate dependants who are in need.

Types of grants: One-off grants are available for a variety of needs, for example, electrically powered vehicles, white goods, household items, holidays and carers' breaks.

Exclusions: The trust does not assist with legal issues, private medical care costs, educational grants and anything the state has a statutory duty to provide.

Annual grant total: In 2009 the trust had assets of £7 million and an income of £47 million. Grants for welfare purposes totalled £14 million, of which £489,000 was paid from charity funds and £13 million was given on behalf of service funds and other charities.

Applications: Contact should normally be made by letter direct to the honorary secretary of the local branch. The appropriate address can usually be obtained from the SSAFA website, a Citizens Advice, the local telephone directory (under SSAFA Forces Help) and most main post offices. In case of difficulty, the local address can be obtained from the correspondent.

Correspondent: Director of Welfare and Housing, 19 Queen Elizabeth Street, London SE1 2LP (0845 1300 975; fax: 020 7403 8815; email: info@ssafa.org.uk; website: www.ssafa.org.uk)

Other information: SSAFA Forces Help operates throughout the UK and in garrisons and stations overseas. It is concerned with the welfare of service and ex-service men and women and their families and provides a wide range of advice and support services.

All SSAFA branches are empowered to give immediate help without reference to higher committees. Also, because of their extensive coverage of the UK, they act as agents for service and other associated funds. Indeed, SSAFA is much more of a case-working organisation than a benevolent fund.

A residential home is maintained on the Isle of Wight for older ex-service personnel and their dependants. Eligible men and women can be accepted from any part of the UK. SSAFA also manages cottage homes for ex-service men and women and their spouses, some purpose-built for people with disabilities, for which residents pay no rent but make a modest maintenance payment.

Two SSAFA Norton Homes provide short term accommodation so that families can stay nearby whilst visiting a loved one at Selly Oak Hospital in Birmingham or the Defence Medical Rehabilitation Centre at Headley Court, Surrey. The houses are designed as 'home from home' and are both located in secure and peaceful environments.

Stepping Stone homes are provided for women, with or without children, who are serving, ex-service or dependants of service or ex-service personnel, who are facing homelessness and need somewhere to live.

Support services for serving and ex-service prisoners, with the aim of reducing re-offending and helping prisoners resettle into society, are also available.

SSAFA provides a confidential telephone support line for serving personnel which is staffed all year round and is outside the chain of command (call 0800 731 4880 or +44 (0)1980 630854 from overseas). It is also developing its health and social care services for serving personnel around the world and provides family support groups and adoption services.

For further information on all of the services listed here, and more, go to the trust's website or visit a local branch.

St Andrew's Scottish Soldiers Club Fund

Eligibility: Serving and former Scottish soldiers, and their dependants, who are in need.

Types of grants: One-off grants according to need.

Annual grant total: In 2008/09 the fund had an income of £4,900 and a total expenditure of £1,600.

Applications: In writing to the correspondent usually through an ex-service body such as SSAFA Forces Help or the Royal British Legion.

Correspondent: The Grants Officer, 37 King Street, Covent Garden, London WC2E 8JS (020 7240 3718; fax: 020 7497 0184; email: info@scotscare.com; website: www.scotscare.com)

St Dunstan's

Eligibility: There are two conditions that must be fulfilled to be eligible for St Dunstan's:

1 All applicants must have served at any time in the Regular or Reserve UK Armed Forces, or in the Merchant Navy during World War Two, or in the Polish Forces under British Command.

2 The Ophthalmic criteria is presenting at best a current visual acuity in both eyes of roughly halfway between being able to count fingers at arm's length and read the largest line on an eye chart.

Types of grants: Grants are given to allow applicants to develop their independence by a combination of training, rehabilitation, holiday and respite care. An annual support grant is given to all beneficiaries and further assistance is available for specific needs such as, help in the garden, a domestic help allowance, healthcare needs, nursing home fees and assistance with mobility and employment. Grants are provided according to need once an applicant has become a beneficiary of St Dunstan's.

Annual grant total: In 2008/09 the trust had assets of £128 million and an income of £15 million. Grants totalled about £17 million and were distributed as follows:

Independent Living Assistance (grants for a variety of welfare purposes)	£3,400,000
Housing Provision (purchase of accommodation and grants for household essentials and IT equipment)	£3,000,000
Nursing and Residential Care (permanent residents, respite care, holidays and rehabilitation)	£11,000,000

Applications: On a form available from the admissions department, with details of the applicant's service (including service number and dates of service) and details of their ophthalmic consultant. On receipt the trust will contact the respective service office and ophthalmic consultant for reports. The process should take about 10 weeks.

Correspondent: Admissions & Pensions Manager, 12–14 Harcourt Street, London W1H 4HD (020 7723 5021; fax: 020 7262 6199; email: admissions@st-dunstans.org.uk; website: www.st-dunstans.org.uk)

Other information: St Dunstan's provides lifelong support and advice to its beneficiaries and dependants. Its National Centre at Ovingdean (Brighton) provides rehabilitation and training to individuals learning to cope with blindness and also serves as a nursing, residential and respite care centre.

St Dunstan's administers the Diana Gubbay Trust which exists for the benefit of men and women in the Emergency Services (Police, Fire and Ambulance) who suffer severe loss of sight whilst on duty. The ophthalmic criteria is the same as for St Dunstan's

The WRNS Benevolent Trust

Eligibility: Ex-Wrens and female serving members of the Royal Navy (officers and ratings) who joined the service between 3 September 1939 and 1 November 1993 who are in need. People who deserted from the service are not eligible.

Types of grants: Recurrent grants of £221 a quarter for people of pensionable age who are living on a low income. These grants may also be awarded to younger people in exceptional circumstances. Amenity grants totalling up to £480 per annum are made in June and December and Christmas bonuses dependent on need, with an extra £45 per child being added to the Christmas bonus for parents of children of school age or below. There is also provision for recurrent grants to assist with telephone helplines and TV licences.

One-off grants are also available towards needs such as debts and arrears, household goods, medical aids, household repairs, funeral expenses, convalescent care, medical expenses, travel fares, education, removal costs, clothing and food.

Annual grant total: In 2009 the trust had assets of £3.1 million and an income of £500,000. Grants, mainly for welfare purposes, totalled £376,000. Grants for educational purposes totalled £160.

Applications: Applications can be made direct to the correspondent, or through SSAFA.

Correspondent: Sarah Ayton, General Secretary, Castaway House, 311 Twyford Avenue, Portsmouth, Hampshire PO2 8RN (023 9265 5301; fax: 023 9267 9040 (mark 'for the attention of WRNS BT'); email: generalsecretary@wrnsbt.org.uk; website: www.wrnsbt.org.uk/)

SERVICE AND REGIMENTAL FUNDS

Royal Navy and Royal Marines

Royal Marines Benevolent Fund
RM Corps Secretary, Building 32, HMS Excellent, Whale Island, Portsmouth, PO2 8ER (tel: 02392 651304; fax: 02392 547207).

Royal Naval Association
General Secretary, Room 209, Semaphore Tower (PP70), HM Naval Base, Portsmouth, Hampshire PO1 3LT (tel: 02392 722983; fax: 02392 723371).

Women's Royal Naval Service Benevolent Trust
General Secretary, Castaway House, 311 Twyford Avenue, Portsmouth, Hampshire, P02 8RN (tel: 02392 655301; fax: 02392 679040).

Merchant Navy

Merchant Navy Welfare Board
Welfare Officer, 30 Palmerston Road, Southampton SO14 1LL (tel: 023 8033 7799; fax: 023 8063 4444).

Royal Alfred Seafarers Society
Western Acres, Woodmansterne Lane, Banstead SM7 3HA (tel: 01737 353763; fax: 01737 362678).

Royal Air Force

Princess Mary's Royal Air Force Nursing Services Trust
Secretary, PMA21(RAF), PMA, RAF Innsworth, Gloucester, GL3 1EZ (tel: 01452 712612 ext. 7020).

Royal Air Force Disabled Holiday Trust
Administrator, 67 Portland Place, London, W1B 1AR (tel: 020 7307 3303; fax: 020 7307 3363).

Royal Air Forces Ex-POW Association Charitable Fund
Welfare Officer, Mill House, Great Bedwyn, Marlborough, Wiltshire, SN8 3LY (tel: 01672 870529).

Royal Observer Corps Benevolent Fund
Secretary, 120 Perry Hall Lane, Orpington, BR6 0EF (tel & fax: 01689 839031).

Army

The Adjutant General's Corps Regiment Association
Gould House, Worthy Down, Winchester, SO21 2RG (tel: 01962 887254; fax: 01962 887690).

Afghan Trust, the Parachute Regiment
RHQ PARA, PO4, Merville Barracks, Colchester, CO2 7UT (tel: 01235 847614).

Argyll and Sutherland Highlanders' Regimental Association
Secretary, The Castle, Stirling FK8 1EH (tel: 01786 475165; fax: 01786 446038).

Army Air Corps Fund (post Sept 1957)
Headquarters Army Air Corps, Middle Wallop, Stockbridge, Hampshire, SO20 8DY (tel: 01264 784565; fax: 01264 784163).

Army Physical Training Corps Association
Regimental Secretary, Fox Lines, Queen's Avenue, Aldershot, GU11 2LB (tel: 01252 349197; fax: 01252 340785).

Ayrshire Yeomanry
(See Yeomanry Benevolent Fund)

Bedfordshire and Hertfordshire Regiment
(See Royal Anglian Regiment Benevolent Charity)

Berkshire Yeomanry
(See Yeomanry Benevolent Fund)

Berkshire and Westminster Dragoons
(See Yeomanry Benevolent Fund)

Blues and Royals Association
Honorary Secretary, Home HQ, Household Cavalry, Combermere Barracks, St Leonards Road, Windsor, SL4 3DN (tel: 01753 755132; fax: 01753 755161).

Border Regiment
(See Duke of Lancaster's Regiment)

Buckinghamshire, Berkshire & Oxfordshire Yeomanry
(See Yeomanry Benevolent Fund)

Cambridgeshire Regiment
(See Royal Anglian Regiment Benevolent Charity)

Cameronians (Scottish Rifles)
(See King's Own Scottish Borders Association)

Cheshire Regiment
(See Mercian Regiment Benevolent Fund)

Cheshire Yeomanry
(See Yeomanry Benevolent Fund)

Coldstream Guards Association
Assistant Regimental Adjutant, Wellington Barracks, Birdcage Walk, London, SW1E 6HQ (tel: 020 7414 3263; fax: 020 7414 3444).

Connaught Rangers Association
Applications should be forwarded directly to ABF The Soldiers' Charity: see page 107.

Corps of Army Music
Corps Secretary, Kneller Hall, Kneller Road, Twickenham TW2 7DU (tel: 020 8744 8652).

County of London Yeomanry (3rd)
(See Yeomanry Benevolent Fund)

Derbyshire Yeomanry
(See Yeomanry Benevolent Fund)

Devonshire and Dorset Regiment
(See the Rifles – Exeter)

Devonshire Regiment
(See the Rifles – Exeter)

Dorset Regiment
(See the Rifles – Exeter)

Dragoons:
1st King's Dragoon Guards
(See Queen's Dragoon Guards Benevolent Fund)

2nd (Queen's Bays)
(See Queen's Dragoon Guards Benevolent Fund)

3rd Carabiniers (Prince of Wales's Dragoon Guards)
(See Royal Scots Dragoon Guards Association)

4th/7th Royal Dragoon Guards
(See Royal Dragoon Guards Benevolent Fund)

5th Royal Inniskilling Dragoon Guards
(See Royal Dragoon Guards Benevolent Fund)

2nd Royal Scots Greys
(See Royal Scots Dragoon Guards Association)

3rd Dragoon Guards
(See Royal Scots Dragoon Guards Association)

6th Dragoon Guards
(See Royal Scots Dragoon Guards Association)

25th Dragoon Guards
(See Royal Scots Dragoon Guards Association)

Westminster Dragoons
(See Yeomanry Benevolent Fund).

Duke of Albany's Seaforth Highlanders
(See Queens Own Highlanders (Seaforth and Camerons) Regimental Association)

Duke of Cornwall's Light Infantry
(See the Rifles – Bodmin)

Duke of Edinburgh's Royal Regiment
(See the Rifles – Salisbury).

Duke of Lancaster's Regiment
The Castle, Carlisle CA3 8UR (tel & fax: 01228 521275)

Duke of Wellington's Regiment
(See Yorkshire Regiment)

Durham Light Infantry
(See the Rifles – Durham)

East Anglian Regiment
(See Royal Anglian Regiment Benevolent Charity)

East Lancashire Regiment
(See Duke of Lancaster's Regiment)

East Yorkshire Regiment
(See Yorkshire Regiment)

Essex Regiment
(See Royal Anglian Regiment Benevolent Charity)

Fife and Forfar Yeomanry
(See Yeomanry Benevolent Fund)

Fusiliers Aid Society
c/o RHQ The Royal Regiment of Fusiliers, HM Tower of London, London, EC3N 4AB (tel: 020 3166 6906; fax: 020 3166 6920).

Glasgow Highlanders
(See Royal Highland Fusiliers Benevolent Association)

Glider Pilot Regimental Association Benevolent Fund
26 North Quay, Abingdon Marina, Abingdon, Oxon, OX14 5RY (tel: 01235 200353).

Gloucestershire Regimental
(See the Rifles – Gloucester)

The Gordon Highlanders' Association
Home HQ The Highlanders, St Luke's, Viewfield Road, Aberdeen, AB15 7XH (tel: 01224 318174; fax: 01224 208652).

Green Howards
(See Yorkshire Regiment)

Grenadier Guards Association
General Secretary, Wellington Barracks, Birdcage Walk, London, SW1E 6HQ (tel: 020 7414 3285; fax: 020 7222 4309).

Gurkha Brigade Association Trust
Brigade Secretary, c/o HQ Brigade of Gurkhas, Airfield Camp, Netheravon, Salisbury, SP4 9SF (tel: 01980 628569; fax: 01980 628564).

The Gurkha Welfare Trust
PO Box 2170, 22 Queen Street, Salisbury, Wiltshire, SP2 2EX (tel: 01722 323955; fax: 01722 343119)

Hampshire and Isle of Wight Military Aid Fund
Secretary, Serles House, Southgate Street, Winchester, SP10 3EP (tel: 01962 852933; fax: 01962 863658).

Herefordshire Light Infantry Regiment
(See the Rifles – Shrewsbury)

Highland Light Infantry
(See Royal Highland Fusiliers Benevolent Association)

Highlanders (Seaforth, Gordons & Camerons) Regiment
(See Highlanders Regimental Association)

The Highlanders Association
Regimental Secretary, HHQ The Highlanders, Cameron Barracks, Inverness, IV2 3XE (tel: 01463 224380; fax: 01313 108172).

Honourable Artillery Company Benevolent Fund
Armoury House, City Road, London, EC1Y 2BQ (tel: 020 7382 1543; fax: 020 7382 1538).

Hussars:
 3rd The King's Own
 (See Queen's Royal Hussars)
 7th Queen's Own
 (See Queen's Royal Hussars)
 8th King's Royal Irish
 (See Queen's Royal Hussars)

10th Royal Hussars
(See King's Royal Hussars Welfare Fund)

11th Hussars
(See King's Royal Hussars Welfare Fund)

14th King's Hussars
(See King's Royal Hussars Welfare Fund)

14th/20th King's Hussars
(See King's Royal Hussars Welfare Fund)

20th Hussars
(See King's Royal Hussars Welfare Fund)

23rd Hussars
(See King's Royal Hussars Welfare Fund)

26th Hussars
(See King's Royal Hussars Welfare Fund)

13th/18th Royal (Queen Mary's Own)
(See Light Dragoons Charitable Trust)

15th/19th King's Royal Hussars Regiment
(See Light Dragoons Charitable Trust)

The Queen's Own Hussars
(See Queen's Royal Hussars)

Queen's Royal Irish Hussars
(See Queen's Royal Hussars)

Imperial Yeomanry
(See Yeomanry Benevolent Fund).

Indian Army Association
c/o British Commonwealth Ex-Services League, Haig House, 199 Borough High Street, London, SE1 1AA (tel: 020 3207 2413).

Inns of Court and City Yeomanry
(See Yeomanry Benevolent Fund).

Intelligence Corps Association
Corps Adjutant, Building 200, Chicksands, Shefford, Bedfordshire, SG17 5PR (tel: 01462 752341; fax: 01462 752374).

Irish Guards Association
RHQ Irish Guards, Wellington Barracks, Birdcage Walk, London, SW1E 6HQ (tel: 020 7414 3295; fax: 020 7414 3446).

King's Royal Hussars Welfare Fund
Secretary, Fulwood Barracks, Preston, PR2 8AA (tel: 01772 260310).

King's Regiment Liverpool/Manchester
(See Duke of Lancaster's Regiment)

King's Own Royal Border Regimental Association
(See Duke of Lancaster's Regiment)

King's Own Royal Regiment
(See Duke of Lancaster's Regiment)

King's Own Scottish Borderers Association
The Parade, The Barracks, Berwick-upon-Tweed, Northumberland, TD15 1DG (tel: 01289 307426; fax: 01289 331928).

King's Own Yorkshire Light Infantry Regiment
(See the Rifles – Pontefract)

King's Royal Rifle Corps
(See the Rifles – Winchester)

King's Shropshire Light Infantry
(See the Rifles – Shrewsbury)

Labour Corps
Applications should be forwarded directly to ABF The Soldiers' Charity: see page 107.

Lancashire Fusiliers
(See Fusiliers Aid Society)

Lancashire Regiment (Prince of Wales's Royal Volunteers) Regiment
(See Duke of Lancaster's Regiment)

Lancers:
 9th/12th/27th Royal Lancers
 (See 9th/12th Royal Lancers (Prince of Wales) Charitable Association)
 16th, 5th, 17th & 21st Lancers
 (See Queen's Royal Lancers)
 9th Queen's Royal Lancers
 (See 9th/12th Royal Lancers (Prince of Wales) Charitable Association)

Leinster Regiment (for those resident in UK)
Applications should be forwarded directly to ABF The Soldiers' Charity: see page 107.

The Life Guards Association
Honorary Secretary, Home HQ Household Cavalry, Combermere Barracks, St Leonards Road, Windsor, SL4 3DN (tel: 01753 755229; fax: 01753 755161).

Light Dragoons Regimental Association Charitable Trust
Fenham Barracks, Newcastle upon Tyne, NE2 4NP (tel: 0191 2393 138; fax: 0191 239 3139).

Light Infantry
(See the Rifles – appropriate local office)

London Irish Rifles Benevolent Fund
Connaught House, 4 Flodden Road, Camberwell, London, SE5 9LL (tel: 020 7390 4466 ext. 2406).

London Regiment
Applications should be forwarded directly to ABF The Soldiers' Charity: see page 107.

London Scottish Regiment Benevolent Fund
16 Highfields Mead, East Hanningfield, Chelmsford, Essex, CM3 8XA (tel: 020 7630 1639).

Lothian & Border Horse
(See Yeomanry Benevolent Fund)

Lovat Scouts
(See Yeomanry Benevolent Fund)

Loyal Regiment (North Lancashire)
(See Duke of Lancaster's Regiment).

Machine Gun Corps
Applications should be forwarded directly to ABF The Soldiers' Charity: see page 107. (For Heavy Branch Machine Gun Corps see **Royal Tank Regiment Association and Benevolent Fund**).

Manchester Regiment Aid Society and Benevolent Fund
(See Duke of Lancaster's Regiment)

Mercian Benevolent Fund
Heath Avenue, Whittington Barracks, Lichfield, Staffordshire, WS14 9TJ (tel: 01543 434351; fax: 01543 434359).

Middlesex Regiment (Duke of Cambridge's Own)
(See Princess of Wales's Royal Regiment)

Military Provost Staff Corps Association
Regimental Secretary, Berechurch Hall Camp, Berechurch Hall Road, Colchester, Essex, CO2 9NU (tel: 01206 816795).

North Staffordshire Regiment
(See Mercian Benevolent Fund)

Northamptonshire Regiment
(See Royal Anglian Regiment Benevolent Charity)

Northamptonshire Yeomanry Association (1st and 2nd Regiments)
(See Yeomanry Benevolent Fund)

Nottinghamshire and Derbyshire Regiment
(See Mercian Benevolent Fund)

'Old Contemptibles'
Applications should be forwarded directly to ABF The Soldiers' Charity: see page 107.

Oxfordshire and Buckinghamshire Light Infantry
(See the Rifles – Winchester)

Oxfordshire Yeomanry
(See Yeomanry Benevolent Fund).

Parachute Regiment
(See Airborne Forces Security Fund)

Post Office Rifles
Applications should be forwarded directly to ABF The Soldiers' Charity: see page 107.

Prince of Wales Leinster Regiment
c/o Royal British Legion Ireland, 26 South Frederick Street, Dublin 2. (tel: 00 353 1671 3044).

Prince of Wales's Own (West & East Yorkshire) Regiment
(See Yorkshire Regiment)

Princess of Wales's Royal Regiment
Benevolence Secretary, Howe Barracks, Canterbury, Kent, CT1 1JY (tel: 01227 818053; fax: 01227 818057).

Queen Alexandra's Royal Army Nursing Corps Association
Secretary, AMS Headquarters, Slim Road, Camberley, Surrey, GU15 4NP (tel: 01159 573252).

Queen's Dragoon Guards
Regimental Secretary, Maindy Barracks, Whitchurch Road, Cardiff, CF14 3YE (tel: 029 2078 1227; fax: 029 2078 1384).

Queen's Lancashire Regiment
(See Duke of Lancaster's Regiment)

Queen's Own Buffs, The Royal Kent Regiment
(See Princess of Wales's Royal Regiment)

Queen's Own Cameron Highlanders' Regiment
(See Queen's Own Highlanders (Seaforth and Camerons) Regimental Association)

Queen's Own Highlanders (Seaforth and Camerons) Regimental Association
RHQ HLDRS, Cameron Barracks, Inverness, IV2 3XD (tel: 01463 224380).

Queen's Own Yorkshire Dragoons
(See Yeomanry Benevolent Fund)

Queen's Regiment
(See Princess of Wales's Royal Regiment)

Queen's Royal Hussars
Regimental Secretary, Regent Park Barracks, Albany Street, London, NW1 4AL (tel: 020 7756 2273; fax: 020 7756 2276).

Queen's Royal Lancers
Regimental Secretary, HHQ, QRL Lancer House, Prince William of Gloucester Barracks, Grantham, Lincolnshire, NG31 7TJ (tel: 0115 957 3252).

Queen's Royal Surrey Regiment
(See Princess of Wales's Royal Regiment)

Reconnaissance Corps
(See Royal Armoured Corps War Memorial Benevolent Fund)

Rifle Brigade
(See the Rifles – Winchester)

The Rifles
Main Office: Benevolence Secretary, Peninsula Barracks, Romsey Road, Winchester, Hampshire, SO23 8TS (tel: 01962 828530; fax: 01962 828534).

Regional Offices:

Bodmin – The Keep, Victoria Barracks, Bodmin, Cornwall, PL31 1EG (tel: 01208 72810; email: bodmin@the-rifles.co.uk)

Durham – Elvet Waterside, Durham City, Durham, DH1 3BW (tel: 01913 865496: email: durham@the-rifles.co.uk)

Exeter – Block 11, Wyvern Barracks, Exeter, Devon, EX2 6AR (tel: 01392 492435: email: exeter2@the-rifles.co.uk)

Gloucester – Custom House, 31 Commercial Road, Gloucester, Gloucestershire, GL1 2HE (tel: 01452 522682; email: gloucester@the-rifles.co.uk)

London – 52–56 Davies Street, London W1K 5HR (tel: 020 7491 4936; email: london@the-rifles.co.uk)

Salisbury – The Wardrobe, 58 The Close, Salisbury, Wiltshire, SP1 2EX (tel: 01722 414536; email: salisbury@the-rifles.co.uk)

Shrewsbury – Copthorne Barracks, Shrewsbury, Shropshire, SY3 8LZ (tel: 01743 262425; email: shrewsbury@the-rifles.co.uk)

Taunton – 14 Mount Street, Taunton, Somerset, TA1 3QB (tel: 01823 333434; email: taunton@the-rifles.co.uk)

Yorkshire – Minden House, Wakefield Road, Pontefract, West Yorkshire, WF8 4ES (tel: 01977 703181; email: yorkshire@the-rifles.co.uk)

Ross-Shire Buffs, Duke of Albany's Seaforth Highlanders
(See Queen's Own Highlanders (Seaforth and Camerons) Regimental Association)

Royal Anglian Regiment Benevolent Charity
Blenheim House, Eagle Way, Warley, Brentwood, Essex, CM13 3BN (tel & fax: 01277 213051).

Royal Armoured Corps War Memorial Benevolent Fund
c/o RHQ Royal Tank Regiment, Stanley Barracks, Bovington Camp, Wareham, Dorset, BH20 6JB (tel: 01929 403331; fax: 01929 403488).

Royal Army Chaplains' Department Association
Ramillies, Marlborough Lines, Monxton Road, Andover, SP11 8HJ (email: jackie.footitt255@mod.uk).

Royal Army Dental Corps Association
RHQ RADC, HQ AMD, The Former Staff College, Slim Road, Camberley, Surrey, GU15 4NP (tel: 01276 412753; fax: 01276 412793).

Royal Army Medical Corps Association
Secretary, RHQ RAMC, Slim Road, Camberley, Surrey, GU15 4NP (tel: 01276 412791; fax: 01276 412793).

Royal Army Ordnance Corps Charitable Trust
(See Royal Logistics Corps Association Trust)

Royal Army Pay Corps
Secretary, RHQ AGC Centre, Winchester, Hampshire, SO21 2RG (tel: 01962 887436; fax: 01962 887074).

Royal Army Veterinary Corps Benevolent Fund
Secretary, RHQ RAVC, HQ AMD, The Former Army Staff College, Slim Road, Camberley, Surrey, GU15 4NP (tel: 01276 412749; fax: 01276 412793).

Royal Berkshire Regiment
(See the Rifles – Salisbury)

Royal Dragoon Guards Benevolent Fund
3 Tower Street, York, YO1 9SB (tel & fax: 01904 642036).

Royal Dublin Fusiliers
Applications should be forwarded directly to ABF The Soldiers' Charity: see page 107.

Royal Electrical and Mechanical Engineers Association & Benevolent Fund
RHQ REME, Headquarters DEME (A), Isaac Newton Road, Arbofield, Reading, RG2 9NJ (tel: 0118 976 3219).

Royal Engineers Association
Ravelin Building, Brompton Barracks, Chatham, Kent, ME4 4UG (tel: 01634 847005; fax: 01634 822394).

Royal Fusiliers Aid Society
City of London Headquarters, HM Tower of London, London EC3N 4AB (email: royalfusiliers@fsmail.net).

Royal Gloucestershire Hussars
(See Yeomanry Benevolent Fund)

Royal Gloucestershire, Berkshire & Wiltshire Regiment
(See the Rifles – Gloucester)

Royal Green Jackets
(See the Rifles – Winchester)

Royal Hampshire Regiment
(See Princess of Wales's Royal Regiment)

Royal Highland Fusiliers Benevolent Association
518 Sauchiehall Street, Glasgow, G2 3LW (tel: 0141 332 0961; fax: 0141 353 1493).

Royal Inniskilling Fusiliers
(See Royal Irish Regiment Benevolent Fund)

Royal Irish Fusiliers
(See Royal Irish Regiment Benevolent Fund)

Royal Irish Rangers
(See Royal Irish Regiment Benevolent Fund)

Royal Irish Regiment Benevolent Fund
RHQ The Royal Irish Regiment, Palace Barracks, Londonderry, BFPO 807, Northern Ireland (tel: 02891 420632).

Royal Irish Rifles
(See Royal Irish Regiment Benevolent Fund)

9th/12th Royal Lancers (Prince of Wales) Charitable Association
Regimental Secretary, TA Centre, Saffron Road, South Wigston, Leicestershire, LE18 4UX (tel: 0116 278 5425).

Royal Lincolnshire Regiment
(See Royal Anglian Regiment Benevolent Charity)

Royal Logistic Corps Association Trust
RHQ The RLC, Dettingen House, Deepcut, Camberley, Surrey, GU16 6RW (tel: 01252 833363; fax: 01252 833390).

Royal Military Academy Sandhurst Band
Applications should be forwarded directly to ABF The Soldiers' Charity: see page 107.

Royal Munster Fusiliers Charitable Fund
Applications should be forwarded to ABF The Soldiers' Charity: see page 107.

Royal Norfolk Regimental Association
(See Royal Anglian Regiment Benevolent Charity)

Royal Northumberland Fusiliers
(See Fusiliers Aid Society)

Royal Regiment of Fusiliers (post 1968)
(See Fusiliers Aid Society)

Royal Regiment of Scotland
Regimental Secretary, Edinburgh Castle, Edinburgh, EH1 2YT (tel: 0131 310 5090; fax: 0131 310 5075).

Royal Scots Benevolent Society
c/o HHQ RS, The Castle, Castle Hill, Edinburgh, EH1 2YT (tel: 0131 310 5016; fax: 0131 310 5019).

Royal Scots Dragoon Guards Association
The Castle, Edinburgh, EH1 2YT (tel: 0131 310 5100; fax: 0131 310 5101).

Royal Scots Fusiliers
(See Royal Highland Fusiliers Benevolent Association).

Royal Sussex Regiment
(See Princess of Wales's Royal Regiment).

Royal Tank Regiment Association and Benevolent Fund
RHQ Royal Tank Regiment, Stanley Barracks, Bovington Camp, Dorset, BH20 6JA (tel: 01929 403331).

Royal Ulster Rifles Benevolent Fund
(See Royal Irish Regiment Benevolent Fund)

Royal Warwickshire Regimental Association
Area Headquarters, St John's House, Warwick, CV34 4NF (tel: 01926 491653; fax: 01869 497707).

Royal Welch Fusilier Comrades' Association
RHQ The Royal Welsh, Hightown Barracks, Wrexham, Clwyd, LL13 8RD (tel: 01978 316176; fax: 01978 316121).

Royal Welsh Benevolent Fund
RHQ, Maindy Barracks, Cardiff, CF14 3YE (tel: 029 2078 1215; fax: 029 2078 1357).

Scots Guards Association
Scots Guards Office, The Castle, Edinburgh, EH1 2YT (tel: 0131 310 5042; fax: 0131 310 5026).

Seaforth Highlanders' Regiment
(See Queens Own Highlanders (Seaforth and Camerons) Regimental Association)

Sharpshooters Yeomanry
(See Yeomanry Benevolent Fund)

Sherwood Foresters
(See Mercian Regiment Benevolent Fund)

Sherwood Rangers Yeomanry
(See Yeomanry Benevolent Fund)

Small Arms School Corps Comrades' Association
HQ SASC, Land Warfare Centre, Imber Road, Warminster, Wiltshire, BA12 0DJ (tel: 01985 222487; fax: 01985 222972).

Somerset Light Infantry
(See the Rifles – Taunton)

South Lancashire Regiment (Prince of Wales's Volunteers)
(See Duke of Lancaster's Regiment).

South Staffordshire Regiment
(See Mercian Regiment Benevolent Fund)

Special Air Service Association
PO Box 35051, London, NW1 4WF (tel: 020 7756 2408; Fax; 020 7756 2409).

Staffordshire Regiment
(See Mercian Regiment Benevolent Fund)

Staffordshire Yeomanry
(See Yeomanry Benevolent Fund)

Suffolk Regiment
(See Royal Anglian Regiment Benevolent Charity)

Sussex Regiment
(See Princess of Wales's Royal Regiment)

Ulster Defence Regiment Benevolent Fund
Regimental Secretary, RHQ The Royal Irish Regiment, Palace Barracks, Londonderry, BFPO 807, Northern Ireland (tel: 02891 420632).

Welsh Guards Benevolent Fund
Assistant Regimental Adjutant, Maindy Barracks, Whitchurch Road, Cardiff, CF14 3YE (tel: 029 2078 1219).

West Riding Regiment
(See Yorkshire Regiment)

West Yorkshire Regimental Association
(See Yorkshire Regiment)

Wiltshire Regiment
(See the Rifles – Salisbury)

Women's Royal Army Corps Benevolent Fund
Gould House, Worthy Down, Winchester, SO21 2RG (tel: 01962 887612; fax: 01962 887478).

Worcestershire Regiment
(See the Mercian Regimental Benevolent Fund)

Worcestershire & Sherwood Foresters Regiment
(See the Mercian Regimental Benevolent Fund)

Yeoman of the Guard – Queen's Bodyguard
(See Yeomanry Benevolent Fund)

Yeoman Warders
(See Yeomanry Benevolent Fund)

Yeomanry Benevolent Fund
Honorary Secretary, 10 Stone Buildings, Lincolns Inn, London, WC2A 3TG (tel: 01962 779227). This fund covers all Yeomanry Regiments.

York and Lancaster Regiment
(See Yorkshire Regiment)

Yorkshire Hussars
(See Yeomanry Benevolent Fund)

Yorkshire Regiment
RHQ, 3 Tower Street, York, YO1 9SB (tel: 01904 461019; fax: 011904 461021).

All services funds

Funds marked with a (*) also have an entry in the main 'Service and ex-service charities' section which starts on page 107.

*Association of Jewish Ex-servicemen and Women

Shield House, Harmony Way, London, NW4 2BZ (tel: 020 8208 2323; fax: 020 8202 9900).

Fund dedicated to the welfare of Jewish veterans and their dependants.

*Barnsley Prisoner of War Fund

Applications to Town Clerk, Town Hall, Church Street, Barnsley, S70 2TA (tel: 01226 773027).

Makes grants to needy ex-Servicemen and women (not necessarily ex-prisoners-of-war) living in the Barnsley Metropolitan area.

British Korean Veterans (1981) Relief Fund

c/o Royal British Legion, 199 Borough High Street, London, SE1 1AA (tel: 020 3207 2133).

Fund for the relief of distress amongst men and women who served with the British Forces during the Korean Campaign between June 1950 and July 1954, who are holders of, or entitled to, the British Korean Medal or United Nations Medal, their widows and dependants. Applicants need not be members of the British Korean Veterans Association to qualify for assistance.

*British Limbless Ex-Service Men's Association (BLESMA)

General Secretary, Frankland Moore House, 185–187 High Road, Chadwell Heath, Romford RM6 6NA (tel: 020 8590 1124; fax: 020 8599 2932).

To promote the welfare of all those of either sex who have lost a limb or limbs, or one, or both eyes, whilst in service or as a result of service in any branch of her Majesty's Forces or auxiliary Forces and to assist needy dependants of such limbless ex-Servicemen and women. It will also help those ex-Servicemen and women who suffer amputation of a limb or limbs after service.

*Burma Star Association

Benevolence Secretary, 34 Grosvenor Gardens, London, SW1W 0DH (tel: 020 7823 4273).

Grants for men and women who served with his Majesty's or Allied Forces or in the Nursing Services during the Burma campaign and are Burma Star medal holders.

Cambridgeshire County Remembrance Fund

Mariah Hugh, Hon. Secretary (tel: 01480 890942), Brig P Williams, Managing Trustee, Croxton Old Rectory, Croxton, St Neots, PE19 6SU (tel: 01480 890942)

Grants to alleviate hardship among members of the Armed Forces and Merchant Navy who served in World War I and II in the Cambridgeshire Regiment or were at the time of enlistment living in the old county of Cambridgeshire or the Isle of Ely, and their dependants. Application forms are available from Mrs Hugh.

Canadian Veterans' Affairs

Welfare Officer, Department of Veterans' Affairs, Canadian High Commission, MacDonald House, 1 Grosvenor Square, London, W1K 4AB (tel: 020 7258 6339; fax: 020 7258 6645).

Support for Canadian veterans, and their widows and dependants, living in the UK.

Chindits Old Comrades Association

Capt B K Wilson, Secretary & Welfare Officer, c/o The TA Centre, Wolsley House, Park Lane, Fallings Park, Wolverhampton, WV10 9QR (tel: 01902 731841; fax: FAO Capt B K Wilson – 01902 303830).

The aim of the association is to provide and aid (including, in appropriate cases, financial aid) to people who served in Burma with the Chindit Forces in 1943 and 1944, and their widows.

Ex-Services Mental Welfare Society (Combat Stress)

Tyrwhitt House, Oaklawn Road, Leatherhead, KT22 0BX (tel: 01372 841600; fax: 01372 841601; website: www.combatstress.org.uk).

The society is the only organisation specialising in helping those of all ranks of the armed services and merchant navy suffering from combat related psychological injury caused by the traumatic events they have experienced in service. Remedial treatment is offered at three centres in Surrey, Shropshire and Ayrshire. The society also has a network of 12 welfare officers who visit at home or hospital, and can help with war pensions and appeals. Information packs on request.

The Far East Prisoners of War (FEPOW) Trust Funds

c/o Royal British Legion, 199 Borough High Street, London, SE1 1AA (tel: 020 3207 2133).

Support for people who were FEPOW and their spouses, widows/widowers and dependants from the Far East Prisoner of War Fund and the FEPOW Central Welfare Fund.

Forces Pensions Society

68 South Lambeth Road, London, SW8 1RL (tel: 020 7820 9988; email: memsec@forpen.co.uk; website: www.forcespensionsociety.org).

This society provides advice on all aspects of Armed Forces Pensions Schemes. No financial assistance is given.

Irish Ex-Service Trust

c/o Royal British Legion, 199 Borough High Street, London, SE1 1AA (tel: 020 3207 2133).

This is a government fund for those ex-service persons of the British Armed Forces who are resident in Northern Ireland or the Republic of Ireland, and their dependants. The trust makes one-off and recurrent grants for a variety of needs, particularly in those cases that might not normally be considered by other trusts/welfare organisations.

JAFFE Relief Fund

c/o Welfare Department, SSAFA Forces Help, 19 Queen Elizabeth Street, London, SE1 2LP (tel: 020 7463 9224).

This is a general fund providing relief for poverty and homelessness. Grants of up to £250 are available for essential items, immediate needs and daily living costs.

Joint Committee of the Order of St John and British Red Cross

c/o Royal British Legion, 199 Borough High Street, London, SE1 1AA (tel: 020 3207 2133).

Help is available mainly by grants administered through other voluntary organisations, for War Pensioners and their widows/widowers, primarily those disabled in the first and Second World wars and the subsequent recognised conflicts, but not including Falklands War, the Gulf War 1990/91 or service in Northern Ireland.

*Lloyd's Patriotic Fund

c/o Welfare Department, SSAFA Forces Help, 19 Queen Elizabeth Street, London, SE1 2LP (tel: 020 7463 9224; fax: 020 7403 8815).

The fund aims to help former members of the armed forces and their dependants who are in need. Grants will be given to a limited number of cases for one-off single grants for those with chronic illness or living in poverty, or in need of respite holidays.

National Ex-Prisoners of War Association

99 Parlaunt Road, Langley, Slough, SL3 8BE (tel & fax: 01753 818308)

To relieve poverty and sickness among members of all ranks of the forces or nursing services and who during such service were prisoners of war in any theatre of war, and their widows and dependants.

Normandy Veterans Association Benevolent/Welfare Fund

Tilden Cottage, Grove Road, Hindhead, Surrey, GU26 6QR (tel: 01428 605672).

The purpose of the fund is to give practical help to members, and to dependants of veterans, whose circumstances require it.

*"Not Forgotten" Association

4th Floor, 2 Grosvenor Gardens, London, SW1W 0DH (tel: 020 7730 2400; fax: 020 7730 0020; website: www.nfassociation.org).

Provides recreational facilities for wounded service and disabled ex-service men and women as follows: TV sets (applicants whose mobility is severely restricted), TV licences, holidays, day outings and, for those confined to care homes, in-house entertainments.

Please note: the association is unable to make cash grants, undertake welfare casework or assist widows.

*Officers' Association

First Floor, Mountbarrow House, 6–20 Elizabeth Street, London, SW1W 9RB (tel: 0845 873 7150; fax: 0845 873 7154; website: www.officersassociation.org.uk).

The association awards regular and one-off financial help and advice to those in distress at home. Help is also provided towards care home third party shortfalls. Advice papers are also available on Care in the Community Legislation, Pension Credit and associated benefits, and accommodation e.g. Care Homes and sheltered accommodation.

*Officers' Association Scotland

New Haig House, Logie Green Road, Edinburgh, EH7 4HR (tel: 0131 557 2782; fax: 0131 557 5819)

Benevolence Secretary: Gary Gray (tel: 0131 550 1593); Benevolence Administrator: Mrs Lillias Reid (tel: 0131 550 1558); Employment Manager: Mrs Stephanie Sharpe (tel: 0131 550 1581).

The association aims to relieve distress among all those who have at any time held a Sovereign's Commission with embodied service in HM Naval, Military, or Air Forces, and among their wives, widows, husbands, widowers, children and dependants. This includes ex-officers who were commissioned into the Reserve, Auxiliary, or Territorial Forces. Applicants must be resident in Scotland at the time of their initial application or have been

members of a Scottish Regiment. Financial assistance is available through the Benevolence Service and help to ex-officers looking for employment is given through the Employment Service.

*Poppyscotland (Earl Haig Fund Scotland)

New Haig House, Logie Green Road, Edinburgh, EH7 4HR (tel: 0131 557 2782; fax: 0131 557 5819)

Head of Charitable Services: Gary Gray; Benevolence Secretary: Capt. Jim Macfarlane.

To relieve financially all ex-servicemen and women in need residing in Scotland, and their dependants. Poppyscotland also assists Merchant Seamen who have served in a war environment and Polish ex-Servicemen provided, in both cases, they are resident in Scotland. Grants may be given either following an annual review or as an individual one-off payment.

Prisoners Families Fund

c/o Welfare Department, SSAFA Forces Help, 19 Queen Elizabeth Street, London, SE1 2LP (tel: 020 7463 9224).

This fund makes grants of up to £500 where a prisoner's family is struggling as a result of imprisonment.

Royal Patriotic Fund Corporation

4 North John Street, Wilton, Salisbury, SP2 0HE (tel & fax: 01722 744030).

The corporation provides financial help to widows, children and other dependants of officers and men of the Armed Forces who

are in need, in the form of continuing allowances and grants, including education grants or bursaries.

Special Forces Benevolent Fund

c/o Brig Roger Dillon, D Group, 23 Grafton Street, London, W1S 4EY (tel: 020 7318 9200)

Grants and pastoral support to 1939–1945 members of Special Operations Executive and their dependants.

Veterans Aid

40 Buckingham Palace Road, London SW1W 0RE (tel: 020 7828 2468; fax: 020 7630 6784; website: www.veterans-aid.net).

This organisation provides advice and assistance to homeless or 'pending' homeless ex-service personnel and their families in the UK and overseas. Help can be given in the form of food, clothing and shelter. Assistance is also given with drug, alcohol and gambling addictions and issues around mental health.

War Widows Association of Great Britain

c/o Royal British Legion, 199 Borough High Street, London, SE1 1AA (tel: 020 3207 2133; website: www.warwidowsassociation.org.uk).

The association, formed in 1971 to improve conditions for all service widows and their dependants, works with government departments and service and ex-service organisations to help with all matters of its members' welfare. The association does not make grants.

121

Christian

The Alexis Trust

Eligibility: Members of the Christian faith.

Types of grants: Grants of between £50 and £100 are available, mostly for Christian-based activities.

Annual grant total: In 2008/09 the trust had assets of £363,000 and an income of £42,000. Grants were made totalling £37,000, of which £5,800 was given in grants to individuals. A further £31,000 was given in grants to institutions.

Applications: In writing to the correspondent.

Correspondent: Prof. Duncan Wright Vere, 14 Broadfield Way, Buckhurst Hill, Essex IG9 5AG

Other information: The grants given to individuals are usually from the surplus funds from the grants to organisations and are given for welfare and educational purposes.

Frances Ashton's Charity

Eligibility: Serving and retired Church of England clergy, or their widows/widowers, who are in need.

Types of grants: One-off grants of between £150 and £880.

Exclusions: Grants are not given towards property purchase, school fees, parochial expenses or office furniture/equipment.

Annual grant total: In 2008 the charity had assets of £1.2 million and an income of £71,000.

Grants totalled £53,000 and were distributed as follows: grants to serving clergy (27) £31,000; grants to retired clergy (14) £14,000; grants to widows/widowers (5) £4,000; and emergency grants (3) £1,400.

Applications: On a form available from the correspondent, to be submitted directly by the individual by 1 June each year. They are considered in September.

Correspondent: The Receiver, CAF, Kings Hill, West Malling, Kent ME19 4TA

(01732 520334; fax: 01732 520159; email: grants@cafonline.org)

Other information: There was one grant made to an institution during the year totalling £95.

The Auxiliary Fund of the Methodist Church

Eligibility: Retired ministers and deacons of the Methodist church and their dependants. Grants can also be made to enable ministers and deacons to continue to work where otherwise they would have to retire.

Types of grants: One-off grants to meet all kinds of need including, unexpected household expenditure (e.g. replacement of boiler/cooker/washing machine), gardening, property maintenance and repairs, bills, recarpeting, redecorating and medical needs (e.g. stair lifts, mobility scooters, opticians and dental costs). Grants of up to £3,000 are also available for residential care fees.

Annual grant total: Grants usually total around £200,000 each year.

Applications: In writing to the correspondent at any time.

Correspondent: Philip Bedford-Smith, 25 Marylebone Road, London NW1 5JR (020 7467 5266; email: smithb@ methodistchurch.org.uk; website: www. methodist.org.uk/)

Other information: The fund is also known as the Fund for the Support of Presbyters and Deacons.

Archdeaconry of Bath Clerical Families Fund

Eligibility: Widows and children of clergymen who have died and who last served in the deaneries of Bath, Chew Magna and Portishead.

Types of grants: One-off and recurrent grants according to need.

Annual grant total: Grants are generally in the region of £900.

Applications: In writing to the correspondent.

Buckingham Trust

Eligibility: People in need who are missionaries or Christian workers, or people with some Christian connection. Applicants must be known to the trustees.

Types of grants: One-off and recurrent grants according to need.

Annual grant total: In 2008/09 the trust had assets of £702,000 and an income of £298,000. Grants were made totalling £327,000, of which £275,000 was given to charities, £47,000 to churches and the remaining £4,200 to individuals.

Applications: In writing to the correspondent. However, the trust has previously stated that its funds are fully committed each year and not given to new applicants.

Correspondent: Richard Foot, Trustee, 17 Church Road, Tunbridge Wells, Kent, TN1 1LG (01892 774774)

The Chasah Trust

Eligibility: Missionaries who are known to the trustees, or are a contact of the trustees.

Types of grants: One-off and recurrent grants to support Christian work.

Annual grant total: In 2008/09 the trust had assets of £23,000 and an income of £38,000. Grants were made to individuals totalling £15,000. Organisations received a further £31,000.

Applications: In writing to the correspondent.

Correspondent: Richard Collier-Keywood, Trustee, Glydwish Hall, Fontridge Lane, Etchingham, East Sussex TN19 7DG (01435 882768)

Children of the Clergy Trust

Eligibility: Children of deceased ministers of the Church of Scotland.

Types of grants: One-off or recurrent grants according to need. Previously grants have ranged from £500 to £1,000 to relieve poverty, hardship or distress.

Annual grant total: About £2,000.

Applications: In writing to the correspondent. Applications should be submitted directly by the individual and should include information about the applicant's ministerial parent, general family circumstances and other relevant information.

Correspondent: Revd Iain U Thomson, The Manse, Manse Road, Kirkton of Skene, Westhill, Aberdeenshire AB32 6LX (01224 743277)

Christadelphian Benevolent Fund

Eligibility: Members of the Christadelphian body who are experiencing difficult times.

Types of grants: One-off and recurrent grants according to need.

Annual grant total: In 2009 the trust had assets of £2.1 million and an income of £106,000. Grants to individuals totalled £66,000 and were broken down as follows:

Annual holiday scheme	£12,000
Fuel aid	£8,300
Water aid	£4,500
Regular grants	£24,000
Compassionate grants	£15,000
Christmas bounty	£2,400

Applications: In writing to the correspondent. Compassionate grants are given to individuals on the basis of representations made by the ecclesia of which those individuals are members.

Correspondent: Kenneth Smith, Westhaven House, Arleston Way, Shirley, Solihull, West Midlands B90 4LH (0121 713 7100)

The Church of England Pensions Board

Eligibility: Retired clergy and licensed layworkers of the Church of England, their widows, widowers and dependants.

Types of grants: Allowances for those participating in the retirement housing scheme and to clergy widow(er)s to supplement their low income. Assistance is also available for help with fees in residential or nursing homes.

Annual grant total: In 2008 the trust had assets of £87 million, an income of £21 million and a total expenditure of £20 million. Grants were made totalling £334,000.

Applications: On a form available from the correspondent.

Correspondent: Peter Lowings, 29 Great Smith Street, London SW1P 3PS (0207 898 1602; email: enquiries@cepb.c-of-e.org.uk; website: www.cofe.anglican.org/about/cepb)

Other information: The trust's main concern is the administration of the pension scheme and the provision of supported housing and nursing care. It operates seven such complexes across the country. The trust also runs a retirement housing scheme which offers mortgages and loans to assist those vacating 'tied' housing.

The Clergy Rest Fund

Eligibility: Church of England clergy who are in need.

Types of grants: One-off grants ranging from £500 to £1,500 for a variety of needs.

Annual grant total: In 2009 the fund had assets of £869,000 and an income of £43,000. Grants were made to 38 individuals totalling £45,000.

Applications: In writing to the correspondent.

Correspondent: Hugh MacDougald, Wickworth & Sherwood Solicitors, Minerva House, 5 Montague Close, London SE1 9BB (020 7593 5000; fax: 020 7593 5099; email: info@wslaw.co.uk; website: www.wslaw.co.uk/)

Other information: The fund also makes grants to institutions connected with the Church of England.

The Collier Charitable Trust

Eligibility: Retired Christian missionaries and teachers in the UK and overseas.

Types of grants: One-off and recurrent grants of around £300 each.

Annual grant total: Grants usually total about £6,000 a year.

Applications: In writing to the correspondent.

Correspondent: M A Blagden, Secretary, Cherry Tree Cottage, Old Kiln Lane, Churt, Farnham, Surrey GU10 2HX

Other information: Current financial information was not available.

The Corporation of the Sons of the Clergy

Eligibility: Anglican clergy of the dioceses of the UK and Ireland and the diocese in Europe, their widows/widowers and dependants under 25, separated or divorced spouses of such clergy and mature unmarried daughters of such clergy.

Types of grants: The corporation provides a guide as to what it will give grants for, however this is by no means exhaustive. The secretary and staff are happy to discuss individual cases for other areas of funding and will try and help with any problem.

Bereavement expenses

- Grants may be considered for clergy and their widows/widowers towards the costs of their spouse's funeral.

Cars for individuals with disabilities

- Help cannot be provided towards the cost of acquiring a car, but grants can sometimes be considered towards the cost of converting a standard car to enable its use by a person with disabilities who needs the car for the purposes of mobility.

Child maintenance

- Grants can be considered for widows/widowers and divorced and separated clergy/spouses in respect of their children who are under the age of 25 and who are still in full-time education or are below school age.

Clothing

- Grants can be given towards adult clothing (including clerical clothing) as well as towards necessities for infants.

Counselling

- Grants can be considered towards the cost of professional counselling, including marriage guidance counselling. A supporting letter from the counsellor will usually be required.

Debts

- Help towards debts can sometimes be considered. It should be noted that debt relief is a formal procedure involving both the charity's and the applicant's diocese, and permission for consultation by the charities with the diocese will be required. Anyone seeking help towards debts is advised to discuss the matter with the Registrar/Secretary at an early stage.

Heating expenses

- Normally for retired clergy, widows/widowers and unmarried daughters over pensionable age who find these expenses particularly difficult to meet. Help is sometimes given to serving clergy where family illness necessitates extra heating.

Holidays

Applications can be considered from:

- serving clergy, particularly those in parochial work
- retired clergy
- widows/widowers
- separated or divorced spouses if still dependent on their clergy spouses.

In addition, applicants who live in an area that is considered 'unsafe' may, with their archdeacon's support, apply for a grant to help with the cost of employing someone to look after their home while they are away.

House repairs and decoration

- For retired clergy, widows/widowers, unmarried daughters and separated or divorced spouses. Help can be considered for essential work only. No assistance can be given in respect of repairs or decorations to property that is not owned by the applicant, nor to property for which a third party is responsible for the work in question.

Medical expenses

- Grants towards the costs of medical treatment and medical aids can be considered where the treatment/aids cannot be provided on the NHS. A supporting letter from the applicant's doctor or other specialist will be required. The possibility of using St Luke's Hospital for the Clergy at 14 Fitzroy Square, London W1T 6AH (telephone number 020 7388 4954) should be explored in appropriate cases.

Nursing home fees

- Help can be considered towards the costs of nursing home care where the shortfall in fees cannot be met by the State, church pension authority, local authority or family.

Ordinands

- Book grants can be considered for those training for the ordained ministry. Applications will need to be supported by the principal of the applicant's training establishment. A maximum of two grants can be considered during the period of training.

Removals and resettlement

Grants can be considered for:

- serving clergy on taking up a new appointment, where costs are not covered by diocesan and other grants
- clergy moving to the UK or Ireland from an overseas appointment (but only from the point of entry into the UK/Ireland)
- clergy at the time of retirement, although any lump sum payable on retirement will be taken into account
- retired clergy, widows/widowers, elderly unmarried daughters and separated or divorced spouses.

Sabbaticals

- Grants towards sabbatical costs can be considered provided that the sabbatical is supported financially by the Diocese

Financial management courses

- Grants can be considered towards the costs of financial management courses for clergy where the relevant course is approved by the applicant's bishop or archdeacon.

Exclusions: Grants for any one purpose will not normally be awarded more frequently than annually. Holiday grants, however, will not normally be awarded more frequently than once every two years.

Grants are not normally made:

- to augment stipends or pensions
- in connection with the purchase of a house or flat
- in connection with the purchase or maintenance of motor vehicles (save in limited circumstances for applicants with disabilities)
- for the cost of fares or freight in connection with removals to or from the United Kingdom
- to reimburse litigation costs or other legal costs.

Help for separated or divorced spouses can only be considered if the ordained spouse is still in Holy Orders.

The corporation does not make loans.

Annual grant total: In 2008 the corporation had assets of £27 million and an income of £2.5 million. Grants to individuals totalled £1.2 million and were distributed as follows:

General welfare	£381,000
School fees	£283,000
University maintenance	£103,000
Other educational expenses	£183,000
Resettlement and house expenses	£139,000
Bereavement	£7,000
Debt	£36,000
Ordinand book grants	£33,000

Applications: Application forms can be requested from the corporation via email, through which applicants must provide details of their request for a grant. All applications are means-tested.

Applications from non-stipendiary clergy or their dependants must be supported by the applicant's bishop or archdeacon, with details of the role performed by the relevant clergy person in his or her parish or diocese.

Correspondent: Robert Welsford, Registrar, 1 Dean Trench Street, Westminster, London SW1P 3HB (020 7799 3696; fax: 020 7222 3468; email: enquiries@clergycharities.org.uk; website: www.clergycharities.org.uk)

Other information: The Sons of the Clergy and the Friends of the Clergy (*see separate entry*) have traditionally worked in conjunction with each other in their grant work. Since January 2005 the two charities have been working even more closely together in their grant administration following the establishment of a single body of trustees common to both organisations and a combined staff. As a result, it no longer matters whether an applicant applies to the Sons or to the Friends as there is a common application form for both charities and all applications are automatically considered by both organisations.

The Deakin and Withers Fund

Eligibility: Single women in the UK, whether divorced, unmarried or widowed, who are in reduced circumstances and who are members of the Church of England or of a church having full membership of the Council of Churches for Britain and Ireland. Grants are not given to ladies under 40 years of age and beneficiaries are usually over 55 years.

Types of grants: Annuities of around £700 paid in December.

Exclusions: No one-off grants are made.

Annual grant total: In 2008/09 the fund had assets of £1.2 million and an income £177,000. Grants were made to 81 individuals totalling £60,000.

Applications: On a form available from the correspondent submitted directly by the individual, through a third party such as a social worker, or through an organisation such as a Citizens Advice or other welfare agency.

Correspondent: Sandra Mullins, c/o South Yorkshire Community Foundation, Unit 3 – G1 Building, 6 Leeds Road, Sheffield, S9 3TY (0114 2424857; email: peggy.murton@sycf.org.uk)

Other information: In 2008 the Deakin Institute and the Withers Pension amalgamated and became the Deakin and Withers Fund.

The Four Winds Trust

Eligibility: Evangelists, missionaries and ministers, including those who have retired, and their widows, widowers and other dependants who are in need.

Types of grants: One-off and recurrent grants according to need.

Annual grant total: In 2008/09 the trust had assets of £860,000 and an income of £37,000. Grants were made totalling £28,000, of which £5,700 was given in individual grants and the remaining £22,000 was distributed to organisations.

Applications: In writing to the correspondent, although the trust states that it does not consider unsolicited applications. Applications without a sae will not receive a response.

Correspondent: P A Charters, Trustee, Four Winds, Church Lane, Ashbury, Swindon, Wiltshire SN6 8LZ (01793 710431)

The Friends of the Clergy Corporation

Eligibility: Ordained Anglican ministers, their widows/widowers, children or other dependants, including separated or divorced spouses and their children. Clergy missionaries who are working abroad may also be eligible for assistance if they are sponsored financially by a UK based missionary society.

Types of grants: One-off and recurrent grants usually ranging between £200 and £2,000 for convalescence, travel expenses, furniture, clothing, holidays, overseas medical expenses, retirement living costs and hospital expenses. This is not an exhaustive list and the trust is happy to discuss individual cases for other areas of funding and will try and help with any problem.

Annual grant total: In 2008 the trust had assets of £28 million and an income of £2.4 million. Grants totalled £690,000 and were distributed as follows:

Holidays	£230,000
University maintenance	£103,000
General welfare	£161,000
School clothing	£19,000
Removals	£58,000
Debts	£30,000
Bereavement	£9,000
Christmas	£17,000
Repairs to property	£16,000
Overseas medical	£48,000

Applications: Applicants should first write to the correspondent (post or email) providing a brief summary of their circumstances and requesting an application form. Forms should be completed as fully as possible and returned with all necessary supporting information.

Applications from non-stipendiary clergy or their dependants must be supported by the applicant's bishop or archdeacon, with details of the role performed by the relevant clergy person in his or her parish or diocese.

Correspondent: Robert Welsford, Registrar, 1 Dean Trench Street, Westminster, London SW1P 3HB (020 7799 3696; fax: 020 7222 3468; email: enquiries@clergycharities.org.uk; website: www.clergycharities.org.uk)

Other information: This trust works very closely with The Corporation of the Sons of the Clergy and the two organisations now share a common application form. As a result, applicants can apply to either the Sons or the Friends as any application is automatically considered by both.

For a more detailed description of the trust's grant giving policy please see *The Corporation of the Sons of the Clergy* entry in this section.

The I W Griffiths Trust

Eligibility: People who are, or have been, engaged in Christian mission and are in need.

Types of grants: One-off and recurrent grants according to need.

Annual grant total: In 2008 the trust had assets of £196,000 and an income of £19,000. Grants were made totalling £45,000.

Applications: In writing to the correspondent.

Correspondent: Lord Brian Griffiths of Fforestfach, 19 Chester Square, London, SW1W 9HS (020 7774 4015)

The Lady Hewley Trust

Eligibility: Present or retired ministers of the United Reformed, Congregational and Baptist churches and their widows who are in need. This is a national trust, although preference is given to applicants whose ministry is in the northern counties of England.

Types of grants: Welfare grants to a maximum of about £1,000 (unless outside the scope of social security payments).

Exclusions: No grants will be given when local authority funds are available.

Annual grant total: In 2008/09 the trust had assets of £11 million and an income of £365,000. Grants to individuals totalled £90,000, of which £28,000 was given in student grants.

Applications: On a form available from the correspondent. Applications should be submitted by 15 March for the June meeting of the trustees and by 15 July for the October meeting.

Correspondent: Neil Blake, Clerk, Pursglove & Brown, Military House, 24 Castle Street, Chester, CH1 2DS (01244 400315)

The Hounsfield Pension

Eligibility: Unmarried women, widows and widowers who are over 50 years old, live in England or Wales, are members of the Church of England and have never received parochial relief or public assistance.

Types of grants: Grants are fixed annually and paid in two instalments.

Annual grant total: In 2008/09 the charity had an income of £5,100 and a total expenditure of £11,000. Grants totalled around £10,000.

Applications: In writing to the correspondent. Only a limited number of pensions are available, and places become available at irregular intervals.

Correspondent: Godfrey Smallman, c/o Wrigleys Solicitors, 3rd Floor, Fountain Precinct, Balm Green, Sheffield S1 2JA (0114 267 5594; fax: 0114 276 3176)

The H E Knight Charitable Trust

Eligibility: Individuals involved in missionary Christian work and spiritual teaching in the UK.

Types of grants: Ongoing support for Christian workers. Grants of up to £500 are awarded.

Annual grant total: Grants average around £6,000 a year.

Applications: In writing to the correspondent. Please note, the trust has stated that the majority of its funds go to missionaries known to the trustees and as such, other applicants are unlikely to be successful. The trust does not accept unsolicited applications.

Correspondent: Aubrey Curry, 14 Bramley Gardens, Whimple, Exeter, EX5 2SJ (01404 822295)

The Leaders of Worship and Preachers Trust

Eligibility: Preachers and leaders of worship who are in need, and their dependants.

Types of grants: One-off and recurrent grants towards the cost of care, mobility equipment and other aids.

Annual grant total: In 2008/09 the trust had assets of £516,000 and an income of £2.4 million. Grants were made totalling £25,000.

Applications: On a form available from the correspondent or to download from the website.

Correspondent: Adrian J Needham, Unit 35 First Floor Offices, Orbital 25 Business Park, Dwight Road, Watford, Hertfordshire WD18 9DA (01923 231811; email: lwptoffice@lwpt.org.uk; website: www.lwpt.org.uk)

The Lind Trust

Eligibility: Individuals in full-time Christian ministry.

Types of grants: One-off and recurrent grants according to need.

Annual grant total: In 2008/09 the trust had assets of £20 million and an income of £3.7 million. Grants and donations were made totalling £178,000 to various organisations, churches and individuals.

Applications: In writing to the correspondent at any time. The trust commits most of its money early, giving the remaining funds to eligible applicants.

Correspondent: Gavin Wilcock, Tithe Barn, Attlebridge, Norwich NR9 5AA (01603 262626)

Other information: This trust was previously called Cross House Trust.

The Lyall Bequest

Eligibility: Church of Scotland ministers who are in need.

Types of grants: One-off grants generally in the range of £100 to £200 are given towards convalescence and holidays.

Annual grant total: Grants usually total about £1,000 each year.

Applications: In writing to the correspondent to be submitted directly by the individual.

Correspondent: Miss E L Calderwood, c/o Pagan Osborne, 106 South Street, St Andrews, Fife KY16 9QD (01334 475001; email: elcalderwood@pagan.co.uk)

Ministers' Relief Society

Eligibility: Protestant ministers, their widows and dependants who are in need. Children of deceased ministers must be under 21 and of 'genuine evangelical and protestant convictions' to be eligible.

Types of grants: One-off and recurrent grants according to need. Recent grants have been given to: ministers who are retired or disabled, and their widows, with inadequate income or savings; specific emergencies, such as serious illness, removal costs, enforced resignation or dismissal by congregation; and candidates and students seeking vocational training in the ministry.

Annual grant total: In 2008 the society had an income of £24,000 and a total expenditure of £17,000.

Applications: On a form available from the correspondent, to be submitted directly by the individual.

Correspondent: A Lathey, 8 Marston Avenue, Chessington, Surrey KT9 2HF (020 8397 2483)

The Mylne Trust

Eligibility: Members of the Protestant faith who have been engaged in evangelistic work, including missionaries and retired missionaries, and Christian workers whose finances are inadequate. Married ordinands with children are also supported when all other sources of funding have failed to cover their needs.

Types of grants: Annual and one-off grants for living costs and training expenses.

Annual grant total: In 2008/09 grants were made to over 180 people totalling £65,000.

Applications: On a form available from the correspondent or to download from the trust's website. The trustees meet quarterly to consider applications.

Correspondent: Paul Jenkins, PO Box 530, Farnham, GU9 1BP (email: admin@mylnetrust.org.uk; website: www.mylnetrust.org.uk)

Other information: Grants are also made for educational purposes.

Nazareth Trust Fund

Eligibility: The trust gives support to individuals known to the trustees who promote the Christian faith and/or are Christian missionaries.

Types of grants: One-off grants ranging between £100 and £750.

Exclusions: No support for individuals not known to the trustees.

Annual grant total: Grants are made to individuals totalling between £2,000 and £3,000 per year.

Applications: In writing to the correspondent, although the trust tends to only support individuals and organisations personally known to the trustees.

Correspondent: Mrs E M Hunt, Barrowpoint, 18 Millennium Close, Salisbury, Wiltshire SP2 8TB (01722 349322)

The Paton Trust

Eligibility: Ministers of the Established Church of Scotland who are elderly or in poor health.

Types of grants: One-off grants up to £100. Grants are given to ministers who are in need of a convalescence break and to ministers who are retiring to provide them with a holiday at the time of retirement.

Annual grant total: Grants usually total about £1,600 each year.

Applications: On a form available from the correspondent. Applications are considered throughout the year and should be submitted directly by the individual.

Correspondent: Trust Administrator, c/o Alexander Sloan, Chartered Accountants, 38 Cadogan Street, Glasgow G2 7HF (0141 204 8989)

Lady Peel Legacy Trust

Eligibility: Priests in the Anglo-Catholic tradition who, due to ill health or age, have had to resign their work or livings.

Types of grants: One-off or recurrent grants according to need.

Annual grant total: About £5,000 a year towards both educational and welfare purposes.

Applications: In writing to the correspondent. The closing dates for applications are 1 April and 1 November each year. Telephone contact is not invited.

Correspondent: Revd Preb James Trevelyan, Bridge End, Barbon, Carnforth, Lancashire LA6 2LT

The Podde Trust

Eligibility: Individuals involved in Christian work in the UK and overseas.

Types of grants: One-off and recurrent grants.

Annual grant total: In 2008/09 the trust had assets of £3,100 and an income of £37,000. There were 29 grants to individuals for education and relief-in-need purposes totalling £8,700.

Applications: In writing to the correspondent: please note, the trust states that it has very limited resources, and those it does have are mostly already committed. Requests from new applicants therefore have very little chance of success.

Correspondent: Peter Godfrey, 68 Green Lane, Hucclecote, Gloucester GL3 3QX (01452 613563; email: podde@supanet.com)

Other information: Organisations involved in Christian work are also supported (£28,000 in 2008/09).

The Pyncombe Charity

Eligibility: Serving Anglican clergy under 70 years of age and their immediate families who are resident with them, who are in financial need resulting from a serious illness or accident or special circumstance.

Types of grants: Small one-off grants.

Exclusions: No grants towards educational expenses.

Annual grant total: In 2009/10 the charity had an income of £15,000 and a total expenditure of £20,000.

Applications: Applications must be made through the diocesan bishop on a form available from the correspondent. Applications are considered in April. No direct applications can be considered.

Correspondent: Rita Butterworth, Wingletye, Lawford, Crowcombe,

Taunton, TA4 4AL (01984 618388; email: joeandrita@waitrose.com)

The Retired Ministers' and Widows' Fund

Eligibility: Retired ministers, and ministers' widows of Presbyterian, Independent (including Unitarian, Free Christian, Congregational and the United Reformed) and Baptist churches, who live in England and Wales and are on a low income. This is defined as those with an income (not including state benefits) of less than £4,600 (£6,900 for married couples) and savings not exceeding £37,000. The savings limit for one-off grants is £9,000.

Types of grants: Biannual payments totalling £500 a year for widows and single ministers and £700 a year for married ministers. One-off grants may also be given to help in an emergency.

Annual grant total: In 2008/09 the fund had assets of £452,000 and an income of £41,000. Grants were made to 50 individuals totalling £31,000.

Applications: On a form available from the correspondent. Applications can be submitted by the individual but should be signed by a local minister.

Correspondent: Bill Allen, 7 Wendover Lodge, Church Street, Welwyn AL6 9LR (01438 489171; email: willallen@tinyonline.co.uk)

Retired Missionary Aid Fund

Eligibility: Retired missionaries from the Christian Brethren Assemblies who are in need. Help may also be given to their dependants.

Types of grants: Quarterly grants, birthday gifts and Christmas hampers are given.

Annual grant total: In 2008/09 the fund had an income of £418,000 and a total expenditure of £647,000. Grants were made totalling about £630,000.

Applications: The fund only gives support to its members, who should make their circumstances known to the correspondent.

Correspondent: Roger Herbert, Secretary, 5 Beaconhill Drive, Worcester WR2 6DL (01905 422779; email: enquiries@rmaf.co.uk; website: www.rmaf.co.uk)

The Rev Dr George Richards' Charity

Eligibility: Church of England clergy who are in need and their widows and dependants. Preference is given to older people and those in poor health.

Types of grants: One-off and recurrent grants for heating expenses, household costs, travel, education, clothing, Christmas gifts and medical care. Pensions are available for those who have been forced to retire early from active ministry and are on a low income.

Exclusions: No grants for repaying debt.

Annual grant total: In 2009 the charity had an income of £20,000 and a total expenditure of £22,000.

Applications: On a form available from the correspondent, including details of all sources of income. Applications should be submitted directly by the individual. They are usually considered twice a year.

Correspondent: Dr Paul Simmons, Flat 98, Thomas More House, Barbican, London EC2Y 8BU (020 7588 5583)

The Silverwood Trust

Eligibility: Christian missionaries in need through illness or retirement.

Types of grants: One-off or small recurrent grants according to need. (Normally restricted to people known to the trustees.)

Exclusions: No grants for computers or school fees.

Annual grant total: Around £1,000 is allocated each year in grants to individuals in need.

Applications: In writing to the correspondent, directly by the individual.

Correspondent: J N Shergold, Trustee, 35 Orchard Grove, New Milton, Hampshire BH25 6NZ

The Henry Smith Charity (UK)

Eligibility: Clergy grants are only made to ordained clergy of the Church of England. Preference is given to those who work in 'tough and demanding' parishes.

Kindred grants are open to direct legitimate descendants of one of the kindred previously registered, or the spouse, widow or widower of a kindred member. The onus is on the individual to prove their descent.

Types of grants: The charity manages two funds for the benefit of individuals:

Poor clergy fund: one-off grants to help clergy families take a break and fund emergency or exceptional costs which cannot be afforded from family incomes.

Kindred grants: one-off and recurrent grants, for example, to help those on low incomes, provide training for young people and cover funeral costs.

Annual grant total: In 2008 the charity had assets of £582 million and an income of £21 million. Grants were made to individuals totalling £991,000, of which £524,000 was given in grants to clergy and £467,000 was given in grants to 'poor kindred'.

Applications: On a form available from the correspondent. Clergy must be recommended to the charity by their Bishop.

Applications for kindred grants should be made in writing to the Kindred Administrator.

Correspondent: Genevieve Ford-Saville, Grants Officer, Sixth Floor, 65–68 Leadenhall Street, London, EC3A 2AD (020 7264 4970; fax: 020 7488 9097; website: www. henrysmithcharity.org.uk)

Other information: The charity also makes a large number of grants to organisations (£26 million in 2008).

The Society for the Relief of Poor Clergymen

Eligibility: Evangelical ordained ministers and accredited lay workers and their dependants or widows/widowers in the Church of England and the Church in Wales.

Types of grants: One-off grants for illness or financial support when it can be shown that it has caused distress and hardship to the individual or family.

Exclusions: Grants are not given towards educational costs or travel expenses.

Annual grant total: In 2009 the trust had an income of £22,000 and a total expenditure of £18,000.

Applications: On a form available from the correspondent. The committee meets twice yearly (normally in March and September). Applications can be submitted directly by the individual or through a third party without the knowledge of the individual and in confidence if the individual is not inclined to apply.

Correspondent: Secretary, c/o CPAS, Athena Drive, Tachbrook Park, Warwickshire CV34 6NG (01926 458458)

The Foundation of Edward Storey

Eligibility: 'Financially unsupported' (i.e. single, separated, divorced or widowed) women who fall into either of two qualifying categories:

a) Women over 40 living within the county of Cambridgeshire

b) Widows or ex-wives of Church of England clergy, retired clergywomen, missionaries, or other women with a close professional connection with the Church of England.

Types of grants: Recurrent grants and pensions (which are annually reviewable and renewable). Pensions are usually only available to those over 60.

Annual grant total: In 2008/09 the foundation had assets of £12 million and an income of £2.3 million. Grants and pensions were made totalling £171,000.

Applications: On an application form available from the correspondent. Applications can be submitted directly by the individual or a family member (if sponsored by a suitable third party), through a third party such as a social worker, Diocesan Widows' Officers, Diocesan Visitors, clergy and so on, or through an organisation such as a Citizens Advice or other welfare agency. Applicants may be interviewed by the foundation's case officer. Applications are considered on a regular basis.

Correspondent: Timothy Burgess, Clerk to the Trustees, Storey's House, Mount Pleasant, Cambridge CB3 0BZ (01223 364405; email: info@edwardstorey. org.uk; website: www.edwardstorey.org. uk)

The Thornton Fund

Eligibility: Ministers and ministerial students of the Unitarian church and their families who are in need.

Types of grants: One-off grants ranging from £250 to £1,500. Recent grants have been given towards convalescence, counselling, replacement of equipment not covered by insurance and taxis for somebody unable to drive for medical reasons.

Annual grant total: Grants usually total around £15,000 per year.

Applications: In writing to the correspondent through a third party such as a minister. They are considered on an ongoing basis.

Correspondent: Dr Jane Williams, 93 Fitzjohn Avenue, Barnet, Hertfordshire EN5 2HR (020 8440 2211)

Other information: The fund occasionally makes grants to the general assembly of Unitarian and Free Christian Churches for special projects.

Torchbearer Trust Fund

Eligibility: People engaged in full-time Christian missionary work. Preference is given to students and former students of Torchbearer Bible schools.

Types of grants: One-off and recurrent grants according to need.

Annual grant total: In 2008/09 the fund had assets of £140,000 and an income of £34,000. Grants totalled £48,000.

Applications: In writing to the correspondent.

Correspondent: The Secretary, Capernwray Hall, Carnforth, Lancashire LA6 1AG (01524 733908; fax: 01524 736681; email: info@ capernwray.org.uk; website: www. capernwray.org.uk)

Other information: Grants are also available for missionary work.

Arthur Townrow Pensions Fund

Eligibility: Women in need who are unmarried or widows and are over 40 years of age. The fund specifies that the applicant should be 'of good character' and be a member of the Church of England or a Protestant dissenting church that acknowledges the doctrine of the Holy Trinity.

Types of grants: Recurrent grants of £50 a month are made to women who have an income below £8,000. One half of the pensions granted must be paid to unmarried women and widows living in Chesterfield, Bolsover and north east Derbyshire. The remaining grants may be paid anywhere in England but only to eligible unmarried women over the age of 40.

Annual grant total: In 2008/09 the fund had assets of £2.4 million which generated an income of £147,000. Grants were made to 179 individuals totalling £130,000.

Applications: On a form available from the correspondent. Applications should be submitted either directly by the individual or through a third party.

Correspondent: P I King, Secretary, PO Box 48, Chesterfield, Derbyshire S40 1XT (01246 560560; website: www. townrowfund.org.uk)

The Widows Fund

Eligibility: Protestant ministers over 60 and their widows, widowers and children who are in need. Ministers who have been prevented from continuing in their ministries due to poor health or disability may also qualify for assistance.

Types of grants: Recurrent grants to supplement a low income and one-off emergency grants for specific purposes.

Annual grant total: In 2008/09 the fund had assets of £625,000 and an income of £37,000. Grants were made totalling £43,000, of which £41,000 was given in annuities and £1,900 in benevolent grants.

Applications: In writing to the correspondent.

Correspondent: John Cook, Kingsmead, Upton Road, Prenton, Merseyside, CH43 7QQ (0151 652 4943)

Christian Science

The Morval Foundation

Eligibility: Older Christian Scientists living in the UK who are members of The Mother Church, The First Church of Christ, Scientist in Boston, USA.

Types of grants: Monthly grants of between £75 and £120 to allow older Christian Scientists to continue living independently in their own homes.

Annual grant total: In 2008/09 the foundation had assets of £1.3 million and an income of £36,000. Grants to individuals were made totalling £24,000.

The foundation also administers two subsidiary charities, the New Chickering Fund and the Ruston Bequest. In 2008/09 the two charities gave a total of £14,000 in grants to Christian Scientists.

Applications: On a form available from the correspondent, to be submitted directly by the individual for consideration at any time.

Correspondent: Shirley Tarboton, 52 Milbourne Lane, Esher, KT10 9EA (01372 210106)

Jewish

The AJR Charitable Trust

Eligibility: Jewish refugees from Nazi oppression, their dependants and descendants, who are settled in the UK. Potential applicants must be members of the Association of Jewish Refugees (AJR) or be eligible to become members and be willing to join the association.

Types of grants: The association administers emergency social, welfare and care funds on behalf of the Conference on Jewish Material Claims Against Germany, which can be used to pay for a number of services and essential items including dental treatment and specialist clothing as well as urgent house repairs, recuperative convalescence, respite breaks and homecare packages.

Annual grant total: In 2009 the association had assets of £15 million and an income of £2.7 million. Social work and welfare activities amounted to £1.3 million, of which £991,000 was given in direct payments to beneficiaries.

Applications: In writing to the correspondent directly by the individual. Applications can be made at any time.

Correspondent: Social Services Department, Jubilee House, Merrion Avenue, Stanmore, Middlesex HA7 4RL (020 8385 3070; fax: 020 8385 3080; email: enquiries@ajr.org.uk; website: www. ajr.org.uk)

Other information: The association provides support and advice on welfare benefits, foreign pension entitlements and reparations. It also has a day centre in Hampstead which runs entertainment programmes and a Meals-on-Wheels service for the surrounding area.

Carlee Ltd

Eligibility: Jewish people in need.

Types of grants: One-off and recurrent grants according to need.

Annual grant total: Grants to individuals usually total about £10,000 per year.

Applications: In writing to the correspondent.

Correspondent: Secretary, 32 Pagent Road, London N16 5NQ

Other information: Grants are also made to organisations.

Chasdei Tovim Me'oros

Eligibility: People of the Jewish faith who are in need.

Types of grants: Grants given according to need.

Annual grant total: In 2008/09 the trust had an income of £43,000 and made grants totalling £38,000 of which £32,000 went to organisations and £5,700 to individuals.

Applications: In writing to the correspondent.

Correspondent: Yoel Bleier, Trustee, 17 Durlston Road, London, E5 8RP (020 8806 2406)

Closehelm Ltd

Eligibility: People of the Jewish faith who are in need.

Types of grants: Grants and loans are given to needy families for wedding costs and other needs.

Annual grant total: In 2008/09 the trust had assets of £3.5 million and an income of £274,000. Grants were made totalling around £430,000.

Applications: In writing to the correspondent.

Correspondent: A Van Praagh, Trustee, 30 Armitage Road, London NW11 8RD (0208 201 8688)

Other information: This trust also gives to organisations.

The Engler Family Charitable Trust

Eligibility: Members of the Jewish faith living in England and Wales.

Types of grants: Grants given according to need.

Annual grant total: About £5,000 a year.

Applications: In writing to the correspondent.

Correspondent: J Engler, Trustee, Motley Bank, South Downs Road, Bowdon, Altrincham WA14 3HB (email: jengleruk@ yahoo.co.uk)

Other information: The trust also makes grants to Jewish organisations.

Finnart House School Trust

Eligibility: Young people of the Jewish faith who are in need through sickness or disadvantage. Priority is given to people over 16, although all applicants are considered.

Types of grants: Grants of between £100 and £1,000 to provide care or education.

Exclusions: Only members of the Jewish faith can be supported.

Annual grant total: Funding is given to secondary schools to provide bursaries to students from low income families. Funding was given to four secondary schools in the UK totalling £29,000.

Applications: On a form available from the correspondent. Applications must be submitted through a social worker or social welfare organisation and are considered three or four times a year.

Correspondent: Peter Shaw, Clerk to the Trustees, PO Box 603, Edgware, Middlesex, HA8 4EQ (020 3209 6006; email: info@finnart.org; website: www.finnart.org)

Other information: This trust also gives grants for educational purposes and to organisations which work with children and young people of the Jewish faith who are in need.

Gur Trust

Eligibility: People connected to the Jewish faith in the UK.

Types of grants: One-off and recurrent grants according to need.

Annual grant total: In 2008/09 the trust had an income of £78,000 and a total expenditure of £92,000. At the time of writing, further information was not available.

Applications: 'Funds are raised by the trustees. All calls for help are carefully considered and help is given according to circumstances and funds then available.'

Correspondent: The Trustees, 5 Windus Road, London, N16 6UT (020 8880 8910)

Other information: The trust also makes grants to organisations and to individuals for educational purposes.

The Nathan and Adolphe Haendler Charity

Eligibility: Jewish people who, as a consequence of religious persecution or other misfortune, have taken (or need to take) refuge in the UK, and are in need.

Types of grants: One-off or recurrent grants according to need.

Annual grant total: In 2008/09 the charity had an income of £1,700 and a total expenditure of £63,000. Grants were made totalling about £58,000.

Applications: In writing to the correspondent at any time.

Correspondent: Company Secretary, World Jewish Relief, Oscar Joseph House, 54 Crewys Road, London NW2 2AD (020 8736 1250; email: info@wjr.org.uk; website: www.wjr.org.uk)

The Jewish Aged Needy Pension Society

Eligibility: Members of the Jewish community aged 60 or over, who have known better circumstances and have lived in the UK for at least 10 years or are of British nationality.

Types of grants: Up to 60 pensions of up to £10 per week for all kinds of need.

Annual grant total: In 2008 the society had an income of £21,000 and a total expenditure of £28,000. Pensions and grants were given totalling £21,000.

Applications: In writing to the correspondent. Applications are considered quarterly.

Correspondent: Sheila Taylor, Secretary, 34 Dalkeith Grove, Stanmore, Middlesex HA7 4SG (020 8958 5390)

Kupath Gemach Chaim Bechesed Viznitz Trust

Eligibility: Members of the Jewish faith who are in need.

Types of grants: One-off and recurrent grants according to need.

Annual grant total: In 2008/09 the trust had assets of £181,000 and an income of £237,000, mainly from donations. Grants were made totalling £115,000, of which £56,000 was given to organisations and £58,000 to 'poor and needy' individuals.

Applications: In writing to the correspondent.

Correspondent: Saul Weiss, Trustee, 171 Kyverdale Road, London, N16 6PS (0208 442 9604)

Mercaz Torah Vechesed Ltd

Eligibility: Members of the orthodox Jewish community who are in need.

Types of grants: One off and recurrent grants according to need.

Annual grant total: In 2008/09 the charity had an income of £1.4 million from donations, nearly all of which was distributed in grants. Assets stood at £59,000. The majority of grants are made to organisations but funding for individuals is also available.

Applications: In writing to the correspondent.

Correspondent: Joseph Ostreicher, Trustee, 28 Braydon Road, London, N16 6QB (020 8880 5366)

The Chevras Ezras Nitzrochim

Eligibility: Jewish people who are in need, with a focus on those living in the Greater London area. Though help can also be given to individuals living further away.

Types of grants: One-off and recurrent grants according to need.

Annual grant total: In 2008 the trust had assets of £1,000, an income of £249,000 and a total expenditure of £251,000. Grants were made to 710 individuals and families totalling £195,000.

Applications: In writing to the correspondent. Applications can be made at any time.

Correspondent: H Kahan, Trustee, 53 Heathland Road, London N16 5PQ

Other information: Grants are also made to organisations (£50,000 in 2008).

NJD Charitable Trust

Eligibility: Members of the Jewish faith who are in need.

Types of grants: One off and recurrent grants according to need.

Annual grant total: In 2008/09 the trust had assets of £108,000 and an income of £101,000. Grants were made totalling £94,000. Grants are made to organisations and individuals.

Applications: In writing to the correspondent.

Correspondent: J C Dwek, Trustee, 35 Frognal, Hampstead, London, NW3 6YD (email: info@igpinvest.com)

Norwood (formerly Norwood Ravenswood)

Eligibility: Mostly Jewish children and their families, although one-quarter of their clients are of mixed faith. This is a national trust but concentrates on London and the south east of England.

Types of grants: According to need, but no regular allowances. Grants towards the celebration of Jewish religious festivals, social need and occasional holidays.

Annual grant total: In 2008/09 the trust had assets of £14 million and an income of £34 million. Grants total about £55,000 each year.

Applications: Grants are recommended by Norwood staff.

Correspondent: The Chief Executive, Broadway House, 80–82 The Broadway, Stanmore, Middlesex HA7 4HB (020 8954 4555; email: info@norwood.org.uk; website: www.norwood.org.uk/)

Other information: Grants are made in conjunction with a comprehensive welfare service. Norwood provides a range of social services for Jewish children and families, including social work, day facilities, residential and foster care.

Taldus Ltd

Eligibility: People of the Orthodox Jewish faith who are in need.

Types of grants: One-off and recurrent grants according to need.

Annual grant total: In 2008/09 the trust had an income of £259,000 and a total expenditure of £137,000, most of which was spent on governance costs. At the end of year the trust had a deficit of over £1 million in its reserves. No grants were made.

Applications: In writing to the correspondent.

Correspondent: Jacob Grosskopf, 6 Spring Hill, London, E5 9BE (020 8806 5010)

Toras Chesed (London) Trust

Eligibility: Members of the Jewish faith who are in need.

Types of grants: One-off and recurrent grants according to need.

Annual grant total: In 2008/09 the trust had an income of £216,000 and made grants totalling £206,000.

Applications: In writing to the correspondent. 'Applications for grants are considered by the trustees and reviewed in depth for final approval.'

Correspondent: A Langberg, Trustee, 14 Lampard Grove, London, N16 6UZ (020 8806 9589; email: ari@toraschesed.co. uk)

Other information: Grants are also made to organisations.

The ZSV Trust

Eligibility: Jewish people in need, particularly older people, refugees, orphans and families in distress.

Types of grants: One-off and recurrent grants according to need. Most of the trust's funds are spent on providing food parcels. Other recent grants have been given towards medical assistance, clothing, shoes and weddings.

Annual grant total: In 2008 the trust had assets of £35,000 and an income of £783,000. Grants totalled £744,000 and were broken down as follows:

Food parcels	£478,000
Relief of poverty	£130,000
Endowments to poor brides	£49,000
Families undergoing stress	£51,000
House repairs and utilities	£21,000
Assistance with healthcare	£5,700
Clothing and shoes	£4,900
Youth activities	£4,400
General donations	£1,200

Applications: In writing to the correspondent. Individuals need to apply through social services.

Correspondent: Z V I Friedman, 12 Grange Court Road, London N16 5EG

LOCAL CHARITIES

This section lists local charities that give grants to individuals for welfare purposes. The information in the entries applies only to welfare grants and concentrates on what the charity actually does rather than on what its trust deed allows it to do.

All the charities listed have a grant-making potential of £500 a year for individuals, but most give considerably more than this.

Regional classification

We have divided the UK into nine geographical areas, as numbered on the map on page 134. Scotland, Wales and England have been separated into areas or counties in a similar way to previous editions of this guide. On page 135, we have included the 'Geographical areas' list which shows the unitary and local authorities within each such area or county. (Please note: not all of these unitary or local authorities have a trust included in this guide.)

The Northern Ireland section has not been subdivided into smaller areas. Within the other sections, the trusts are ordered as follows.

Scotland:

- Firstly, the charities which apply to the whole of Scotland, or at least two areas in Scotland.
- Secondly, Scotland is sub-divided into five areas. The entries which apply to the whole area, or to at least two unitary authorities within, appear first.
- The rest of the charities in the area are listed in alphabetical order of unitary authority.

Wales:

- Firstly, the charities which apply to the whole of Wales, or at least two areas in Wales.
- Secondly, Wales is sub-divided into three areas. The entries which apply to the whole area, or to at least two unitary authorities within, appear first.
- The rest of the charities in the area are listed in alphabetical order of unitary authority.

England:

- Firstly, the charities which apply to the whole area, or at least two counties in the area.
- Secondly, each area is sub-divided into counties. The entries which apply to the whole county, or to at least two towns within it, appear first.
- The rest of the charities in the county are listed in alphabetical order of parish, town or city.

London:

- Firstly, the charities which apply to the whole of Greater London, or to at least two boroughs.
- Secondly, London is sub-divided into the boroughs. The entries are listed in alphabetical order within each borough.

In summary, within each county or area section, the trusts in Scotland and Wales are arranged alphabetically by the unitary or local authority which they benefit, while in England they are listed by the city, town or parish and in London by borough.

To be sure of identifying every relevant local charity, look first at the entries under the heading for your:

- unitary authority for people in Scotland and Wales
- city, town or parish under the relevant regional chapter heading for people living in England
- borough for people living in London.

People in London should then go straight to the start of the London chapter, where trusts which give to individuals in more than one borough in London are listed.

Other individuals should look at the sections for trusts which give to more than one unitary authority or town before finally considering those trusts at the start of the chapter that make grants across different areas or counties in your country or region.

For example, if you live in Liverpool, first establish which region Merseyside is in by looking at the map on page 134. Then having established that Merseyside is in region 5, look at the 'Geographical areas' list on page 135 and see on which page the entries for Merseyside start. Then look under the heading for Liverpool to see if there are any relevant charities. Next check the charities which apply to Merseyside generally. Finally, check under the heading for the North West generally.

Having found the trusts covering your area, please read any other eligibility requirements carefully. While some trusts can and do give for any need for people in their area of benefit, most have other criteria which potential applicants must meet.

Geographical areas

1. Northern Ireland *137*

2. Scotland *139*

Aberdeen & Perthshire *146*
Aberdeen & Aberdeenshire; Angus; Dundee; Laurencekirk; Moray; Perth and Kinross

Central *151*
Clackmannanshire; Falkirk; Fife; Stirling

Edinburgh, the Lothians & Scottish Borders *152*
Edinburgh; Scottish Borders; West Lothian

Glasgow & West of Scotland *155*
Argyll & Bute; Dumfries & Galloway; East Ayrshire; East Renfrewshire; Glasgow; Inverclyde; South Ayrshire; West Dunbartonshire

Highlands & Islands *159*
Highland; Shetland Islands; Western Isles

3. Wales *161*

Mid-Wales *162*
Ceredigion; Powys

North Wales *162*
Anglesey; Conwy; Denbighshire; Flintshire; Gwynedd; Wrexham

South Wales *164*
Cardiff; Carmarthenshire; Merthyr Tydfil; Monmouthshire; Pembrokeshire; Swansea; Torfaen; Vale of Glamorgan

4. North East *169*

County Durham *172*
East Yorkshire *173*
Aldbrough; Barmby on the Marsh; Bridlington; Kingston-upon-Hull; Newton on Derwent; Ottringham; Walkington

North Yorkshire *175*
Carperby-cum-Thoresby; Craven; Danby; Knaresborough; Lothersdale; Northallerton; Scarborough; St Margaret; West Witton; York

Northumberland *178*
Berwick-upon-Tweed

South Yorkshire *178*
Armthorpe; Barnsley; Beighton; Bramley; Doncaster; Epworth; Finningly; Rotherham; Sheffield

Teesside *181*
Hartlepool; Middlesbrough; Middleton

Tyne & Wear *181*
Gateshead; Horton; Newcastle upon Tyne; Sunderland; Tynemouth; Wallsend

West Yorkshire *183*
Baildon; Bingley; Bradford; Calderdale; Dewsbury; Halifax; Horbury; Horton; Huddersfield; Keighley; Leeds; Sandal Magna; Todmorden; Wakefield

5. North West *191*

Cheshire *192*
Chester; Congleton; Frodsham; Macclesfield; Mottram St Andrew; Warrington; Widnes; Wilmslow; Wybunbury

Cumbria *194*
Ambleside; Carlisle; Cockermouth; Crosby Ravensworth; Kirkby Lonsdale; Workington

Greater Manchester *196*
Bolton; Bury; Denton; Golborne; Manchester; New Mills; Oldham; Rochdale; Salford; Stockport; Tameside

Isle of Man *200*

Lancashire *200*
Blackpool; Caton-with-Littledale; Darwen; Lancaster; Littleborough; Lowton; Lytham St Anne's; Nelson

Merseyside *203*
Billinge; Birkenhead; Higher Bebington; Huyton with Roby; Liverpool; Lydiate; Sefton; Wirral

6. Midlands *209*

Derbyshire *213*
Buxton; Chesterfield; Clay Cross; Derby; Glossop; Ilkeston; Spondon

Herefordshire *215*
Hereford; Middleton-on-the-Hill; Norton Canon

Leicestershire & Rutland *216*
Cossington; Great Glen; Groby; Illston; Keyham; Leicester; Market Harborough; Market Overton; Markfield; Mountsorrel; Oadby; Queniborough; Quorn; Rutland; Smisby; Syston; Wymeswold

Lincolnshire *221*
Barrow-upon-Humber; Barton-upon-Humber; Deeping; Dorrington; Frampton; Friskney; Grimsby; Hacconby & Stainfield; Kesteven; Lincoln; Moulton; Navenby; South Holland; Spilsby; Stamford; Stickford; Surfleet; Sutterton; Sutton St James; Swineshead

Northamptonshire *225*
Blakesley; Brackley; Braunston; Brington; Byfield; Chipping Warden; Daventry; Desborough; East Farndon; Harpole; Kettering; Litchborough; Northampton; Pattishall; Ringstead; Roade; Scaldwell; Towcester; Wappenham; Welton

Nottinghamshire *229*
Balderton; Bingham; Carlton in Lindrick; Coddington; Farndon; Gotham; Hucknall; Long Bennington and Foston; Mansfield; Newark; Nottingham; Warsop

Shropshire *234*
Alveley; Bridgnorth; Clun; Hodnet; Hopesay; Lilleshall; Shrewsbury

Staffordshire *237*
Church Eaton; Enville; Leek; Lichfield; Newcastle-under-Lyme; Stoke-on-Trent; Tamworth; Trentham; Tutbury

Warwickshire *240*
Atherstone; Barford; Bedworth; Bilton & New Bilton; Coleshill; Grandborough; Kenilworth; Leamington Spa; Napton-on-the-Hill; Rugby; Stratford-upon-Avon; Sutton Cheney; Thurlaston; Warwick

West Midlands *244*
Bilston; Birmingham; Bushbury; Castle Bromwich; Coventry; Dudley; King's Norton; Meriden; Sandwell; Stourbridge; Sutton Coldfield; Tettenhall; Walsall; West Bromwich; Wolverhampton

Worcestershire *251*
Cropthorpe; Kidderminster; Worcester

7. South West *255*

Avon *256*
Almondsbury; Bath; Bath & North East Somerset; Bristol; Midsomer Norton; North Somerset; Portishead; South Gloucestershire; Stanton Prior; Thornbury

Cornwall *260*
Gunwalloe; Gwennap; Helston; Penzance

Devon *261*
Barnstaple; Bratton Fleming; Brixham; Brixton; Broadhempston; Budleigh Salterton; Colyton; Cornwood; Crediton; Culmstock; Dartmouth; Exeter; Exminster; Exmouth; Gittisham; Great Torrington; Highweek; Holsworthy; Honiton; Litton Cheney; Ottery St Mary; Paignton; Plymouth; Sandford; Sheepwash; Sidmouth; Silverton; South Brent; Sowton; Teignbridge; Topsham; Torbay

Dorset *269*
  Charmouth; Christchurch; Corfe Castle; Dorchester; Poole; Shaftesbury; Wimborne Minster

Gloucestershire *271*
  Bisley; Charlton Kings; Cirencester; Gloucester; Minchinhampton; Tewkesbury; Wotton-under-Edge

Somerset *272*
  Axbridge; Bridgewater; Cannington; Draycott; Ilchester; Newton St Loe; Pitminster; Porlock; Rimpton; Street; Taunton

Wiltshire *275*
  Aldbourne; Ashton Keynes; Chippenham; East Knoyle; Salisbury; Trowbridge; Westbury

8. South East *277*

Bedfordshire *279*
  Bedford; Clophill; Dunstable; Flitwick; Husborne Crawley; Kempston; Luton; Potton; Ravensden; Shefford

Berkshire *281*
  Binfield; Burnham; Datchet; Hedgerley; Newbury; Reading; Sunninghill

Buckinghamshire *283*
  Aylesbury; Bletchley; Calverton; Cheddington; Denham; Emberton; Great Linford; High Wycombe; Hitcham; Radnage; Stoke Poges; Stony Stratford; Water Eaton; Wolverton

Cambridgeshire *286*
  Cambridge; Chatteris; Downham; Elsworth; Ely; Grantchester; Hilton; Ickleton; Landbeach; Little Wilbraham; Pampisford; Peterborough; Sawston; Soham; Stetchworth; Swaffham Bulbeck; Swavesey; Walsoken; Whittlesey; Whittlesford

East Sussex *289*
  Battle; Brighton & Hove; Eastbourne; Hastings; Mayfield; Newick; St Leonards-on-Sea; Warbleton

Essex *291*
  Braintree; Broomfield; Chigwell & Chigwell Row; Dovercourt; East Bergholt; East Tilbury; Halstead; Harlow; Hutton; Saffron Walden; Springfield; Thaxed; Waltham Forest

Hampshire *294*
  Brockenhurst; Fareham; Gosport; Hawley; Hordle; Isle of Wight; Lyndhurst; New Forest; Portsmouth; Ryde; Southampton

Hertfordshire *299*
  Buntingford; Dacorum; Harpenden; Hatfield; Letchworth Garden City; Watford; Wormley

Kent *301*
  Borden; Canterbury; Chatham; Dover; Folkstone; Fordwich; Gillingham; Godmersham; Gravesham; Hayes; Herne Bay; Hildenborough; Hothfield; Hythe; Leigh; Maidstone; Margate; Rochester; Sevenoaks; Tunbridge Wells; Wilmington

Norfolk *306*
  Banham; Barton Bendish; Burnham Market; Buxton with Lammas; Diss; Downham Market and Downham West; East Dereham; East Tuddenham; Feltwell; Foulden; Garboldisham; Gayton; Gaywood; Harling; Hilgay; Horstead with Stanninghall; Little Dunham; Lyng; Marham Village; Northwold; Norwich; Old Buckenham; Pentney; Saham Toney; Saxlingham; Shipdham; South Creake; Swaffham; Swanton Morley; Walpole; Watton; Welney; West Walton; Wiveton; Woodton; Wretton

Oxfordshire *312*
  Bletchington; Eynsham; Great Rollright; Henley-on-Thames; Over Norton; Oxford; Sibford Gower; Souldern; Steventon; Wallingford

Suffolk *315*
  Aldeburgh; Brockley; Bungay; Carlton and Calton Colville; Chediston; Chelsworth; Corton; Dennington; Dunwich; Earl Stonham; Framlingham; Gisleham; Gislingham; Halesworth; Ipswich; Kirkley; Lakenheath; Lowestoft; Melton; Mendlesham; Mildenhall; Pakenham; Reydon; Risby; Rushbrooke; Stanton; Stowmarket; Stutton; Sudbury; Walberswick

Surrey *320*
  Abinger; Ashford; Betchworth; Bisley; Bletchingley; Bramley; Byfleet; Capel; Charlwood; Cheam; Chertsey; Chessington; Chobham; Crowhurst; East Horsley; Effingham; Egham; Epsom; Esher; Gatton; Guildford; Headley; Horley and Salfords; Horne; Kingston-upon-Thames; Leatherhead; Leigh; Nutfield; Ockley; Oxted; Pirbright; Shottermill; Staines; Stoke D'Abernon; Thorpe; Thursley; Walton-on-the-Hill; West Clandon; West Horsley; Weybridge; Woking; Worplesdon; Wotton

West Sussex *328*
  Horsham; Midhurst; Wisborough Green

9. London *331*

Barking & Dagenham *334*
Barnet *335*
Bexley *335*
Brent *336*
Bromley *336*
Camden *336*
City of London *337*
Ealing *338*
Enfield *338*
Greenwich *338*
Hackney *339*
Hammersmith & Fulham *339*
Haringey *340*
Harrow *340*
Hillingdon *340*
Hounslow *341*
Islington *341*
Kensington & Chelsea *341*
Kingston-upon-Thames *342*
Lambeth *342*
Lewisham *343*
Merton *343*
Newham *343*
Redbridge *343*
Richmond-upon-Thames *344*
Southwark *345*
Sutton *346*
Tower Hamlets *346*
Wandsworth *347*
Westminster *347*

1. NORTHERN IRELAND

The Belfast Association for the Blind

Eligibility: People who are registered blind in Northern Ireland. Consideration may also be given to those registered as partially sighted.

Types of grants: One-off grants of towards holidays, house repairs, visual aids and so on. Grants are also given for educational purposes.

Annual grant total: Previously around £16,000 was given in grants to individuals.

Applications: In writing to the correspondent through a social worker. Applications are considered throughout the year.

Correspondent: R Gillespie, Hon. Secretary, 30 Glenwell Crescent, Newtownabbey, County Antrim, BT36 7TF (028 9083 6407)

Other information: Grants are also made to organisations.

The Belfast Sick Poor Fund

Eligibility: Families in Northern Ireland with children aged under 18 who are in poor health or who have a disability and are in receipt of benefits or on a low income and who are in need.

Types of grants: One-off grants ranging from £50 to £200 for necessities and comforts.

Annual grant total: Grants usually total about £4,000 each year.

Applications: In writing to the correspondent by a social worker. Applications should include: background information on the applicant with a breakdown of needs; why the request is being made; how a grant will benefit the applicant; details of income and expenditure on a weekly or monthly basis; and details of other sources of financial assistance and outcomes of any applications.

Correspondent: Grants Officer, c/o Bryson House, 28 Bedford Street, Belfast BT2 7FE (028 9032 5835; fax: 028 9043 9156)

The Londonderry Methodist City Mission

Eligibility: People in need who live in Londonderry and the surrounding area.

Types of grants: One-off grants according to need up to £500 per application.

Annual grant total: Grants usually total around £1,500.

Applications: In writing to the correspondent. Applications can be submitted directly by the individual or family member, through an organisation such as Citizens Advice or through a third party such as a social worker. References are required to support applications made directly by individuals.

Correspondent: Fund Administrator, Mission Office, Clooney Hall Centre, 36 Clooney Terrace, Londonderry BT47 6AR (028 7134 8531; fax: 028 7134 8531; email: office@clooneyhall.org.uk; website: www.methodistcitymission.com)

Other information: The trust has a specific interest in the homeless and runs a hostel for homeless men.

The Newtownabbey Methodist Mission

Eligibility: Socially disadvantaged children, adults, families and older people who live in Rathcoole and the surrounding area and Newtownabbey.

Types of grants: One-off grants for food, clothing and fuel bills throughout the year, and food/toy parcels at Christmas.

Annual grant total: Grants usually total around £10,000 per year.

Applications: By personal application or through a referral by a minister of religion, social worker or Citizens Advice at any time.

Correspondent: The Administrator, 35a Rathcoole Drive, Newtownabbey, County Antrim BT37 9AQ (028 9085 2546; fax: 028 9085 9956; email: office@newtownabbeymethodist.org.uk; website: www.nireland.com/nmm)

Other information: The mission also has a playgroup, a charity shop and provides hot meals for older people.

The Presbyterian Old Age Fund, Women's Fund & Indigent Ladies Fund

Eligibility: Needy, elderly or infirm members of the Presbyterian Church who live at home in any part of Ireland.

Types of grants: Recurrent grants of up to £280 paid quarterly, plus a Christmas gift; one-off grants are occasionally considered in emergencies.

Annual grant total: In 2009 the fund made grants to 92 individuals totalling £110,000.

Applications: In writing through a minister to the correspondent. Applications are considered in January, April, June and October.

Correspondent: The Secretary, Glengall Exchange, 3 Glengall Street, Belfast, BT12 5AB

Other information: The Women's Fund and Indigent Ladies Fund are administered with the Old Age Fund.

The Presbyterian Orphan and Children's Society

Eligibility: Children aged 23 or under who are in full or part-time education, living in Northern Ireland and Republic of Ireland, usually in single parent families. One parent must be a Presbyterian.

Types of grants: Regular grants paid each quarter. Depending on financial resources, a summer grant and Christmas grant is paid to each family. Exceptional grants of up to £300 (very occasionally up to £500) are also available.

Annual grant total: Around £500,000 per year.

Applications: Applications are made by Presbyterian clergy; forms are available from the correspondent or to download from the website. They are considered in April and October. As recurrent grants are means tested, applications should be submitted with details of the applicant's income and expenditure. Any application for an exceptional grant must be made on the 'Exceptional Grant' application form.

Correspondent: Dr Paul Gray, Glengall Exchange, 3 Glengall Street, Belfast, BT12 5AB (028 9032 3737;

fax: 028 9043 4352; email: paul-gray@
presbyterianorphanandchildrenssociety.
org; website: www.presbyterianorphanand
childrenssociety.org)

The Protestant Orphan Society for the Counties of Antrim & Down (Inc)

Eligibility: Orphaned children who live in the counties of Antrim or Down and who are members of the Church of Ireland.

Types of grants: Annual grants of up to £500 and one-off bereavement grants of £1,000 to a family on the death of a parent.

Exclusions: No grants to applicants living outside the beneficial area.

Annual grant total: About £70,000 is available each year.

Applications: Applications can be made at any time through the clergy of the parish in which the individual lives.

Correspondent: Jane Butler, Secretary, Church of Ireland House, 61–67 Donegall Street, Belfast BT1 2QH (028 9032 2268)

The Retired Ministers' House Fund

Eligibility: Retired full-time members and servants of the Presbyterian Church in Ireland, and those contemplating retirement.

Types of grants: Provision of rented accommodation, equity sharing arrangements and loans.

Exclusions: The fund does not distribute one-off grants.

Annual grant total: About £150,000, although this varies each year.

Applications: In writing to the correspondent. Applications are considered as they arrive.

Correspondent: Ian McElhinly, Secretary, Church House, Fisherwick Place, Belfast BT1 6DW (028 9041 7220)

The Royal Ulster Constabulary Benevolent Fund

Eligibility: Members and ex-members of the Royal Ulster Constabulary and their dependants who are in need. The main objectives being to look after widows and their dependants, parents of deceased officers, injured officers, police officers who are disabled, pensioners, serving police officers and ex-police officers.

Types of grants: One-off and recurrent grants and loans according to need. The fund offers a wide range of assistance including adventure holidays for children, short breaks for widows, convalescence for injured officers and financial help when required.

Exclusions: No grants for NHS treatment.

Annual grant total: Around £800,000.

Applications: In writing to the correspondent at any time. Applications must be submitted via a regional representative. Grants below £500 are considered throughout the year, while larger donations up to £10,000 are assessed monthly.

Correspondent: The Secretary, Police Federation for Northern Ireland, 77–79 Garnerville Road, Belfast BT4 2NX (028 9076 4215; email: info@rucbenevolentfund.org; website: www.rucbenevolentfund.org)

The Society for the Orphans and Children of Ministers & Missionaries of the Presbyterian Church in Ireland

Eligibility: Children and young people aged under 26 who are orphaned and whose parents were ministers, missionaries or deaconesses of the Presbyterian Church in Ireland.

Types of grants: One-off grants of £300 to £2,000 for general welfare purposes.

Annual grant total: Grants to individuals for educational and welfare purposes total about £30,000.

Applications: On a form available from the correspondent. Applications should be submitted directly by the individual in March for consideration in April.

Correspondent: Paul Gray, Glengall Exchange, 3 Glengall Street, Belfast, BT12 5AB (028 9032 3737)

Other information: The trust also gives educational grants to the children of living ministers and missionaries.

The Sunshine Society Fund

Eligibility: Families in Northern Ireland with children aged under 18 who are ill, disabled or facing financial hardship.

Types of grants: One-off grants for necessities and comforts. Only 12 grants can be made each year.

Annual grant total: Around £3,000 is available each year for grants.

Applications: In writing to the correspondent by a social worker. Applications should include: background information on the applicant with a breakdown of needs; why the request is being made; how a grant will benefit the applicant; details of income and expenditure on a weekly or monthly basis; and details of other sources of financial assistance and outcomes of any applications.

Correspondent: Grants Administrator, c/o Bryson House, 28 Bedford Street, Belfast BT2 7FE (028 9032 5835; fax: 028 9043 9156)

The Victoria Homes Trust

Eligibility: Young people under 21 who live in Northern Ireland. The trust prefers to fund groups or organisations for a specific project involving young people under 21 years old, rather than funding individual young people.

Types of grants: One-off grants of £200 to £2,500 to help with problems associated with homelessness, alcohol and drug abuse and towards the cost of counselling for young people. Grants are occasionally made for educational purposes.

Exclusions: No grants for: projects whose beneficiaries are outside Northern Ireland; projects which do not target the needs of children and young people; and, projects for which expenditure has already been incurred.

Annual grant total: About £5,000.

Applications: Forms can be downloaded from the trust's website. Applications should be submitted through a social worker, Citizens Advice or other welfare agency. They are considered twice a year and should be received on or before the 30 April or 30 November.

Correspondent: Derek H Catney, Secretary, 2 Tudor Court, Rochester Road, Belfast BT6 9LB (028 9079 4306; email: derek.catney@victoriahomestrust.org.uk; website: www.victoriahomestrust.org.uk)

2. SCOTLAND

The Adamson Trust

Eligibility: Children aged 17 or under who have a physical or mental disability.

Types of grants: Grants range from £150 to £5,000 and are given to help with the cost of a holiday or respite break. Grant recipients must take the trip before their 18th birthday.

Exclusions: No grants can be given towards the costs of accompanying adults.

Annual grant total: In 2008/09 the trust had an income of £83,000. Grants to individuals have previously totalled around £20,000 annually, with a further £50,000 distributed to organisations and schools. However, the trust states that the relatively low amount given in individual grants was due to a lack of suitable applications rather than a desire to set aside funding for organisations and schools. Consequently, it is possible that in future years the whole sum could be awarded to individuals should there be enough worthy applications.

Applications: On a form available from the correspondent, to be returned with: details of the planned holiday; booking confirmations (if possible); and information about the child beneficiary. All applications are considered by the trustees four times a year in February, May, August and November with closing dates of December 31, March 31, June and September 30 respectively.

Correspondent: Edward Elworthy, Orchil Den, Braco, Dunblane, Perthshire, FK15 9LF (07770 842502; fax: 01764 682359; email: edward@ elworthy.net)

The Aged Christian Friend Society of Scotland

Eligibility: Christians in need living in Scotland who are over 60 years of age.

Types of grants: Pensions of about £200 a year.

Annual grant total: In 2008 the society had an income of £221,000. Previously pensions have totalled around £3,000.

Applications: The trust is not inviting new applications for pensions at present. The number of awards is gradually declining.

Correspondent: Hugh Stevens, Brodies, 15 Atholl Crescent, Edinburgh, EH3 8HA (0131 228 3777; website: www.acfsos.org. uk)

Other information: The society is now a company limited by guarantee. Its principal activity is the provision of sheltered housing for older people in Scotland.

The Airth Benefaction Trust

Eligibility: People in need, 'who are incapable of gaining a livelihood'.

Types of grants: Recurrent grants and pensions are available up to £120.

Annual grant total: Grants usually total around £6,000 a year.

Applications: On a form available from the correspondent to be submitted either directly by the individual or through a third party such as a social worker. These should be returned not later than 30 September for consideration in December. Beneficiaries are invited to reapply each year.

Correspondent: Douglas Hunter, HBJ Gateley Wareing, Exchange Tower, 19 Canning Street, Edinburgh EH3 8EH (0131 228 2400; fax: 0131 222 9800; email: info@hbj-gw.com)

The Avenel Trust

Eligibility: Children in need under 18 and students of nursery nursing living in Scotland.

Types of grants: One-off grants of £10 to £500 are given for safety items such as fireguards and safety gates, shoes, clothing, bedding, cots and pushchairs, money for bus passes, recreational activities for young carers and washing machines.

Exclusions: Grants are not given for holidays or household furnishings.

Annual grant total: In 2009 the trust had an income of £16,000.

Applications: Applications are considered every two months and should be submitted through a tutor or third party such as a social worker, health visitor or teacher. Applicants are encouraged to provide as much information about their family or individual circumstances and needs as possible in their applications. Applications can only be accepted from people currently residing in Scotland.

Correspondent: Administrator, Vale Cottage, 52 Forth Street, North Berwick, EH39 4JJ

The John Boyd Baxter Charitable Trust

Eligibility: Women over 55, who live in and around Dundee, or in and around Newport or Fife and have done so for at least 10 years.

Types of grants: About 10 individuals receive about £100 a year. Beneficiaries must be 'deserving respectable females to whom a little help may bring comparative comfort'.

Annual grant total: Grants usually total around £1,000 a year.

Applications: In writing to the correspondent. Applications can be submitted either directly by the individual or through a social worker, Citizens Advice or other welfare agency or other third party on behalf of an individual.

Correspondent: The Trustees, Whitehall House, 33 Yeaman Shore, Dundee DD1 4BJ (01382 229111)

The Benevolent Fund for Nurses in Scotland

Eligibility: Nurses who have worked or were trained in Scotland and are experiencing financial difficulties.

Types of grants: One-off and quarterly grants to applicants with limited income owing to illness or disability, or in the case of retired nurses, those with little or no superannuation pension. The fund can also help by buying furnishings or equipment.

Annual grant total: In 2008/09 the association had an income of £220,000. Grants usually total about £150,000 a year.

Applications: Application forms, available from the correspondent, can be submitted by the individual or through a recognised referral agency (social worker, Citizens Advice, doctor and so on) and are considered as they are received. The trust may decide to visit potential beneficiaries.

Correspondent: Margaret Sturgeon, 15 Camp Road, Motherwell, ML1 2RQ (01698 252034; email: m.sturgeon@bfns. org.uk; website: www.bfns.org.uk)

The Elizabeth Bibby Bequest

Eligibility: Seafarers or ex-seafarers in financial or other need who are either former employees of north of Scotland, Shetland and Orkney Shipping Company, native or one time residents of the counties of Aberdeen, Orkney or Shetland or residents of the Seamen's Institute, Leith.

Types of grants: One-off grants in the range of £100 and £500.

Annual grant total: Generally, the charity gives around £1,000 a year, all of which is distributed in grants.

Applications: On a form available from the correspondent.

Correspondent: The General Secretary, Sailors' Society, 350 Shirley Road, Southampton, Hampshire SO14 3AT (02380 515 950; fax: 02380 515 951; email: chaplains@sailors-society.org; website: www.biss.org.uk)

Other information: The Elizabeth Bibby Fund (237778–12) is a subsidiary of the Sailors Society.

The Biggart Trust

Eligibility: People in need, with preference for people related to the founders and their descendants.

Types of grants: One-off and recurrent grants (half-yearly), ranging from £600 to £1,100.

Annual grant total: In 2008/09 the trust had an income of £13,000.

Applications: In writing to the correspondent, directly by the individual.

Correspondent: Andrew S Biggart, McClay Murray & Spens, 151 St Vincent Street, Glasgow G2 5NJ (0141 248 5011; fax: 0141 271 5319)

The Blyth Benevolent Trust

Eligibility: Women aged over 60 and in need. Preference is given to people who are blind or partially-sighted with the surname Bell or Blyth, and who live in or are connected with Newport-on-Tay, Fife or Dundee.

Types of grants: Annuities paid twice a year of £65. A Christmas bonus may be paid, if funds permit.

Annual grant total: In 2009/10 the trust had an income of £5,800.

Applications: In writing to the correspondent to be submitted either directly by the individual, through a third party such as a social worker, or through an organisation such as a Citizens Advice or other welfare agency.

Correspondent: Trust Administrator, Bowman Solicitors, 27 Bank Street, Dundee DD1 1RP (01382 322267)

The Boath & Milne Trust

Eligibility: People in need who were born in or who have been resident in Kirriemuir for at least 10 years and are aged 70 and over. Preference is given to those who were bakers by profession.

Types of grants: Grants of around £90 each.

Annual grant total: In 2008/09 the trust had an income of £21,000.

Applications: There is a local press advertisement each year and further information can be gained from the correspondent.

Correspondent: The Trustees, Wilkie & Dundas Solicitors, 28 Marywell Brae, Kirriemuir, Angus DD8 4BP (01575 572608; email: admin@wdws.co. uk)

The Buchanan Society

Eligibility: Only people with the following surnames: Buchanan, McAuslan (any spelling), McWattie or Risk.

Types of grants: Pensions for older people in need. One-off grants can also be given.

Annual grant total: In 2009 the society had an income of £46,000. Around 70 people are supported each year. Grants are also made for educational purposes.

Applications: On a form available from the correspondent, to be submitted either directly by the individual or a family member, or through a third party such as a social worker or teacher. Applications are considered throughout the year.

Correspondent: The Secretary, 2 Broadcroft, Kirkintilloch, G66 1HP

Other information: The Buchanan Society is the oldest Clan Society in Scotland having been founded in 1725. Grantmaking is its sole function.

Challenger Children's Fund

Eligibility: The trust aims to help any child in Scotland under the age of 18 years living with a disability through a physical impairment of the musclo-skeletal, neurological or cardio-respiratory system of the body

The following conditions on their own however, are not accepted: psychiatric disorders, learning disabilities, behavioural disorders, development delay, Down's Syndrome, autism, visual or hearing impairment, cancer, diabetes, epilepsy, HIV, back pain and chronic fatigue syndrome.

Types of grants: One-off grants averaging £250 but consideration is given to grants as large as £500. More may be granted in some circumstances. Grants can be given

towards anything which is not provided by statutory sources and have previously included holidays, specialised equipment, a washing machine, clothing, fridges, beds and so on. In case of a holiday grant, if it is essential that a child must be accompanied, consideration will be given to the cost.

Exclusions: Grants cannot be made retrospectively.

Annual grant total: In 2008/09 the trust had an income of £24,000. Grants to individuals totalled around £22,000.

Applications: On a form which can be obtained from the correspondent or via the website. Applications should be submitted by a social worker, GP, health visitor, district nurse or therapist. Trainee workers and community care assistants may also apply, but a qualified person must countersign the application. Grants are given to the agency sponsoring the application, or company the purchase(s) are being made from. They cannot be given direct to the child or child's family. Applications can be submitted once a year.

Correspondent: John Ritchie, Barstow Miller, Midlothian Innovation Centre, Pentlandfield, Roslin, Midlothian, EH25 9RE (0131 312 8508; email: info@ ccfscotland.org; website: www.ccfscotland. org)

The Craigcrook Mortification

Eligibility: People in need who are over 60 and were born in Scotland or have lived there for more than 10 years.

Types of grants: Pensions of between £600 and £850 per annum payable in half-yearly instalments. One-off payments are not available.

Exclusions: Assistance is not normally given to those living with relations or in nursing homes.

Annual grant total: About £20,000 is available for distribution each year.

Applications: On a form available from the correspondent or to download from the website. Applications should be supported by a minister of religion, doctor, bank manager, lawyer or similar professional.

Correspondent: Fiona Watson or Janice Couper, Scott-Moncrieff, Exchange Place, 3 Semple Street, Edinburgh EH3 8BL (0131 473 3500; fax: 0131 473 3535; website: www.scott-moncrieff.com)

Other information: The trust has limited capacity to take on new applicants.

The Alastair Crerar Trust for Single Poor

Eligibility: Single people aged 16 or over who are on low incomes. Applicants or the person applying on their behalf must have an active Christian faith. Grants are preferably given to people in Scotland.

Types of grants: One-off grants of up to £300.

Exclusions: No grants for students except in very exceptional circumstances.

Annual grant total: Set up in 1985, this trust is a small charitable trust with limited funds. The object of the trust is to provide financial assistance for eligible people in order to improve their quality of life. Grants are normally limited to a maximum of £300 each.

Applications: On a form available from the correspondent to be submitted either directly by the individual or through a social worker, Citizens Advice or other welfare agency or other third party. Applications are considered every three to four weeks.

Correspondent: James D Crerar, the Secretary, Alastair Crerar Trust for Single Poor, 1 Beechwood Mains, Edinburgh, EH12 6XN (0131 337 3831; email: jandvcrerar@yahoo.com)

Other information: Grants can also be made to organisations.

The Educational Institute of Scotland Benevolent Fund

Eligibility: Members of the institute suffering from financial hardship due to unexpected illness, long term health problems or a sudden change in financial circumstances and their widows/widowers and dependants. Applicants must have held a membership for at least one year prior to application.

Types of grants: One-off and recurrent grants towards, for example, daily living costs, television licences, telephone rental, hairdressing and holidays. Emergency grants may also be available to members who have had an arrestment on their salary, who face eviction, or who have had their gas or electricity cut off.

Annual grant total: Previously, grants have totalled around £60,000. No further information was available.

Applications: On a form available from the correspondent or a local EIS association. Meetings are normally held in January, March, May, June, September and November. Applications should be received two weeks prior to a meeting.

Correspondent: The General Secretary, Educational Institute of Scotland, 46 Moray Place, Edinburgh EH3 6BH (0131 225 6244; fax: 0131 220 3151; email: enquiries@eis.org.uk; website: www.eis.org.uk)

The Faculty of Advocates 1985 Charitable Trust

Eligibility: 1. Widows, widowers, children or former dependants of deceased members of the Faculty of Advocates.

2. Members of the faculty who are unable to practise by reason of permanent ill health.

Types of grants: Single grants, annuities or loans appropriate to the circumstances. Grants range from £500 to £17,000.

Annual grant total: Grants to individuals usually total around £125,000.

Applications: In writing to the correspondent.

Correspondent: J W Macpherson, Bursar, Advocate's Library, Parliament House, Edinburgh EH1 1RF (0131 332 1750)

The Hugh Fraser Foundation (Emily Fraser Trust)

Eligibility: People in need who work or worked in the drapery, printing, publishing, bookselling, stationery and newspaper and allied trades and their dependants. The trustees consider applications particularly from individuals who are or were in the employment of House of Fraser Ltd, Scottish Universal Investments Ltd and Paisleys.

Types of grants: One-off grants of £100 to £4,000.

Annual grant total: Grants to individuals usually total about £30,000 each year.

Applications: In writing to the correspondent. The trustees meet on a quarterly basis, normally in January, April, July and October. Applications should be received one month before the meeting.

Please note: the foundation's focus is on making grants to charitable organisations and only in exceptional circumstances will the trustees consider applications from individuals and their dependants.

Correspondent: Heather Thompson, Turcan Connell, Princes Exchange, 1 Earl Grey Street, Edinburgh EH3 9EE (0131 228 8111; fax: 0131 228 8118; email: ht@turcanconnell.com)

Other information: The Emily Fraser Trust has recently merged with the Hugh Fraser Foundation and been removed from the Scottish Charity Register.

The Glasgow Society of the Sons and Daughters of Ministers of the Church of Scotland

Eligibility: Children of ministers of the Church of Scotland who are in need, particularly students and the children of deceased ministers.

Types of grants: One-off and recurrent grants according to need.

Annual grant total: About £55,000 a year is given in educational and welfare grants to individuals.

Applications: On a form available from the correspondent. Applications from children of deceased ministers are considered in February.

Correspondent: The Secretary, Exchange Place, 3 Semple Street, Edinburgh EH3 8BL

The Douglas Hay Trust

Eligibility: Children aged under 18 who are physically disabled and live in Scotland.

Types of grants: One-off grants ranging from £40 to £500 towards shoes, clothes, bedding, home improvements, holidays, computers, equipment and education.

Annual grant total: In 2008/09 the trust had an income of £46,000. Grants are usually made totalling about £20,000 each year.

Applications: On a form available from the correspondent: to be submitted through a social worker, medical practitioner or other welfare agency. Applications are considered monthly.

Correspondent: John D Ritchie, Barstow & Millar, Midlothian Innovation Centre, Pentlandfield, Roslin, Midlothian, EH25 9RE (0131 440 9030; fax: 0131 440 9872; email: enquiries@barstowmillar.com; website: www.douglashay.org.uk/)

The Anne Herd Memorial Trust

Eligibility: People who are blind or partially sighted who live in Broughty Ferry (applicants from the city of Dundee, region of Tayside or those who have connections with these areas and reside in Scotland will also be considered).

Types of grants: Grants are usually given for educational equipment such as computers and books. Grants are usually at least £50.

Annual grant total: In 2008/09 the trust had an income of £38,000. The trust gives approximately £25,000 a year in grants.

Applications: In writing to the correspondent, to be submitted directly by the individual in March/April for consideration in June.

Correspondent: The Trustees, Bowman Solicitors, 27 Bank Street, Dundee, DD1 1RP (01382 322267; fax: 01382 225000)

William Hunter Old Men's Fund

Eligibility: Older men in need who were born in Scotland and are of Scottish parentage and who are/were merchants, manufacturers or master tradesmen.

Types of grants: Recurrent grants paid twice a year of £370 for people under 80, and £385 for those over 80.

Annual grant total: In 2008/09 the fund had an income of £12,000. Grants were made totalling around £10,000.

Applications: In writing to the correspondent.

Correspondent: The Trustees, Ground Floor, Capital House, 2 Festival Square, Edinburgh EH3 9SU

The George Jamieson Fund

Eligibility: Widows and single women who are in need and live in the city of Aberdeen or the counties of Aberdeen and Kincardine.

Types of grants: Annual grants of about £220, payable half yearly.

Annual grant total: In 2008/09 the fund had an income of £14,000. Grants usually total around £3,000.

Applications: In writing to the correspondent. Applications can be submitted directly by the individual or through a social worker, Citizens Advice or other welfare agency. Applications should include details of circumstances and are considered on a regular basis.

Correspondent: The Trustees, Wilsone & Duffus, 7 Golden Square, Aberdeen AB10 1EP (01224 651700; email: info@key-moves.co.uk; website: www.key-moves.co.uk)

Jewish Care Scotland

Eligibility: Jewish people in need living in Scotland.

Types of grants: One-off grants of £50 to £750 towards clothing, food, household goods, rent, holidays, equipment, travel and education.

Exclusions: No grants are given to postgraduates.

Annual grant total: Welfare grants total around £1,000 each year.

Applications: The charity has previously stated that it will not be accepting applications for the foreseeable future.

Correspondent: Ethne Woldman, The Walton Community Care Centre, May Terrace, Giffnock, Glasgow, G46 6LD (0141 620 1800; email: admin@jcarescot.org.uk; website: www.jcarescot.org.uk)

Other information: The board also helps with friendship clubs, housing requirements, clothing, meals-on-wheels, counselling and so on.

Key Trust

Eligibility: People living in Scotland who are in need due to age, ill health or disability.

Types of grants: One off grants according to need. Recent grants have been given to help people setting up home, for example, towards furnishings such as carpets and to enable people to gain independence and 'experience more out of life'.

Annual grant total: Grants usually total around £4,000 per year.

Applications: On a form available from the correspondent, submitted either directly by the individual or through a social worker, Citizens Advice or other welfare agency.

Correspondent: The Trustees, c/o Key Housing, Savoy Tower, 77 Renfrew Street, Glasgow G2 3BZ

The Law Society of Scotland Benevolent Fund

Eligibility: People who have practised as a solicitor in Scotland or their dependants who are experiencing hardship.

Types of grants: One-off and recurrent grants according to need.

Annual grant total: Grants usually total around £10,000 per year.

Applications: In writing to the correspondent. Applications are considered in May and November and should be submitted by April and October respectively, including a reference from a solicitor.

Correspondent: M Sheridan, The Scottish Law Agents Society, 166 Buchanan Street, Glasgow G1 2LW (0141 332 3536; email: secretary@slas.co.uk; website: www.slas.co.uk)

John A Longmore's Trust

Eligibility: People who live in Scotland and have an incurable disease.

Types of grants: Annuities of £330 in two instalments. One-off grants of up to £1,000 to improve the quality of life on a day-to-day basis. Equipment sought can be either fixed or moveable such as a wheelchair.

Exclusions: No grants are given towards holidays or house decoration.

Annual grant total: Grants usually total around £18,000 per year.

Applications: On a form available from the correspondent, to be returned with a covering letter detailing income and expenses of the household and a breakdown of how the grant will be used. Applications are considered in the third week of every month and should be submitted by the 16th of the month.

Correspondent: Robin D Fulton, Trustee, Turcan Connell, Princes Exchange, 1 Earl Grey Street, Edinburgh EH3 9EE (0131 228 8111; fax: 0131 228 8118; email: rdf@turcanconnell.com)

Other information: The trust will not be issuing any grants for the foreseeable future. It intends to concentrate on its current beneficiaries instead.

The Agnes Macleod Memorial Fund

Eligibility: Women in need who are over 60, living in Scotland and were born with the name Macleod or whose mothers were born Macleod.

Types of grants: To provide monetary grants or donations of gift vouchers when benefits from the state are either not sufficient or not appropriate. Grants range from £100 to £250 and are one-off.

Annual grant total: In 2008/09 the fund had an income of £4,900.

Applications: In writing to the correspondent. Advertisements are also put in newspapers. Applications are considered in May and November. Doctors, social workers, Citizens Advice, other welfare agencies, health visitors, ministers and priests may also submit applications on behalf of an individual.

Correspondent: Linda Orr, Secretary, Nurses Cottage, Hallin, Waternish, Isle of Skye, IV55 8GJ (email: linda@m-orr.freeserve.co.uk; website: www.clan-macleod-scotland.org.uk)

The Catherine McCallum Memorial Fund

Eligibility: Women who are in poor health and have been teachers or governesses. (It is not necessary to have been members of the institute.)

Types of grants: One-off grants of up to £500.

Annual grant total: Grants usually to total about £4,000 each year.

Applications: On a form available from the correspondent to be submitted directly by the individual or a family member. Applications are considered on a regular basis. Applicants will be advised of deadlines.

Correspondent: The General Secretary, Educational Institute of Scotland, 46 Moray Place, Edinburgh EH3 6BH (0131 225 6244; fax: 0131 220 3151; email: enquiries@eis.org.uk; website: www.eis.org.uk)

The McLaren Fund for Indigent Ladies

Eligibility: To benefit widows and unmarried women over 40. Priority is given to women who are:

i) widows and daughters of officers in the Highland Regiment;

ii) widows and daughters of Scotsmen.

Types of grants: Regular allowances made according to need.

Annual grant total: Grants usually total about £1,000 each year.

Applications: On a form available from the correspondent. Applications to be made throughout the year for consideration when the trustees meet in March, July and December. Beneficiaries' payments are reviewed annually at the discretion of the trustees.

Correspondent: Rosina M Dolan, BMK Wilson, Second Floor, 90 St Vincent Street, Glasgow G2 5UB (0141 221 8004; fax: 0141 221 8088; email: bmkw@bmkwilson.co.uk)

The Annie Ramsay McLean Trust for the Elderly

Eligibility: People aged 60 or over who live in Fife and Tayside.

Types of grants: One-off and recurrent grants of £100 to £1,000 towards needs such as convalescence, travel expenses, furniture, clothing, medical and disability equipment, electrical goods, holidays, nursing home fees, help in the home, household items, electrically operated chairs, motorised scooters and so on.

Exclusions: No grants are given towards debts.

Annual grant total: In 2009 the trust had an income of £48,000. Previously grants to individuals have totalled around £3,000.

Applications: On a form available from the correspondent. Applications can be submitted directly by the individual or thorough any third party. They are considered monthly.

Correspondent: The Trustees, Blackadders Solicitors, 30–34 Reform Street, Dundee DD1 1RJ (01382 229222; fax: 01382 342220; email: beth.anderson@ blackadders.co.uk)

The George McLean Trust

Eligibility: People in need who are living with a mental or physical disability and reside in Fife and Tayside. Older people may also qualify for assistance.

Types of grants: Grants are made towards convalescence, hospital expenses, electrical goods, clothing, holidays, travel expenses, medical equipment, nursing fees, furniture, disability aids and help in the home.

Exclusions: No grants are made towards debts.

Annual grant total: In 2009/10 the trust had an income of £29,000. Grants are made annually totalling about £25,000.

Applications: On a form available from the correspondent. Applications can be submitted directly by the individual or through any third party. They are considered monthly.

Correspondent: Grants Administrator, Blackadders Solicitors, 30–34 Reform Street, Dundee DD1 1RJ (01382 229222; fax: 01382 342220; email: enquiries@ blackadders.co.uk)

Other information: The trust also makes grants to organisations.

The Alexander Naysmyth Fund

Eligibility: Scottish artists of established reputation in painting, sculpture, architecture or engraving who are in need.

Types of grants: One-off payments of up to £1,000.

Annual grant total: In 2009 the trust had an income of £12,000. Grants usually total £2,000 each year.

Applications: In writing to the correspondent directly by the individual for consideration in mid-June.

Correspondent: Bruce Laidlaw, Administrative Secretary, Royal Scottish Academy, The Mound, Edinburgh, EH2 2EL (0131 225 6671; fax: 0131 220 6016)

North of Scotland Quaker Trust

Eligibility: People who are associated with the Religious Society of Friends in the North of Scotland Monthly Meeting area, namely Aberdeen City, Aberdeenshire, Moray, Highland, Orkney, Shetland, Western Isles and that part of Argyll and Bute from Oban northwards.

Types of grants: One-off and recurrent grants according to need.

Exclusions: No grants are given to people studying above first degree level.

Annual grant total: About £10,000 is given in grants annually, for educational and welfare purposes.

Applications: Children of people who are associated with the Religious Society of Friends in the North of Scotland Monthly Meeting area.

Correspondent: The Clerk, Quaker Meeting House, 98 Crown Street, Aberdeen, AB11 6HJ

Other information: This trust was previously known as The Aberdeen Two Months' Meeting Trust.

The Nurses' Memorial to King Edward VII Edinburgh Committee

Eligibility: Nurses with a strong connection to Scotland (including nurses who have worked in Scotland, or Scottish nurses working outside Scotland) who are retired, ill or otherwise in need. Retired nurses are given priority.

Types of grants: One-off and monthly grants towards accommodation charges, domestic bills and to supplement inadequate income.

Annual grant total: In 2009 the trust had an income of £193,000. Between 50 and 60 nurses are usually supported each year, with grants totalling around £60,000.

Applications: Details of present financial and other circumstances are required on a form available from the correspondent. The information given should be confirmed by a social worker, health visitor, doctor or similar professional.

Correspondent: Mr Byers, Byers & Company, 2b Roseburn Terrace, Edinburgh EH12 6AW (0131 313 5555)

The Mrs Jeane Panton and Miss Anne Stirling Trust

Eligibility: Ministers or pastors (not bishops) of the Scottish Episcopal Church who were born in Scotland and have small incomes.

Types of grants: One-off grants are given to supplement the individual's regular income.

Annual grant total: Grants usually total around £3,000 per year.

Applications: In writing via bishops of the dioceses, who are the trustees and recommend ministers in need. Ministers cannot apply directly.

Correspondent: John Stuart, General Synod, 21 Grosvenor Crescent, Edinburgh EH12 5EE (0131 225 6357)

Waverly Care Scotland – Crusaid Hardship Fund In Scotland

Eligibility: People with HIV positive diagnosis who are currently living in Scotland, including people currently resident in Scottish prisons or detention centres. There are no citizenship or permanent residency requirements.

Types of grants: Generally, one-off grants of up to £150 towards items such as white goods, start-up costs for a new home and needs directly related to the individual's condition. The level of support available is means-tested.

Exclusions: No grants for: travel or accommodation of any kind outside of the UK; funeral costs; or luxury items. Applicants eligible to apply for statutory funds should seek this funding before approaching the fund.

Annual grant total: Grants were made totalling around £70,000.

Applications: On a form available from the correspondent or to download from the website. Applications should be completed by a recognised referring agent such as a social worker or HIV nurse, who must send the application on behalf of the applicant.

Correspondent: Grants Administrator, 3 Mansfield Place, Edinburgh EH3 6NB (0131 558 1425; fax: 0131 466 9883; email: crusaid@waverleycare.org; website: www.waverleycare.org)

Other information: People with HIV/AIDS living in other parts of the UK, even if of Scottish origin, should apply to The Crusaid Hardship Fund (see separate entry).

Poppyscotland (The Earl Haig Fund Scotland)

Eligibility: People in Scotland who have served in the UK Armed Forces (regular or reserve) and their widows/widowers and dependants.

Types of grants: Annual and one-off grants towards household items, medicine, respite breaks, mobility aids, travel expenses, clothing, living costs, home repairs and so on.

Exclusions: Grants are not normally given towards non-priority debt, headstones or the replacement of medals. Loans are not available.

Annual grant total: In 2009 the fund had an income of £3.3 million. Grants were made to over 1,400 individuals totalling £777,000, mostly for welfare purposes.

Applications: In the first instance applicants should contact the correspondent or complete a 'request for assistance' form (available to download from the website). A representative from SSAFA Forces Help will then visit the individual to assess the level of need and complete any further forms. Applications can be made at anytime.

Correspondent: Gail Beaton, Charitable Services Department, New Haig House, Logie Green Road, Edinburgh EH7 4HR (0131 550 1557; email: g.beaton@ poppyscotland.org.uk; website: www. poppyscotland.org.uk/)

Other information: Poppyscotland is in many respects the Scottish equivalent of the benevolence department of the Royal British Legion in the rest of Britain. Like the legion, it runs the Poppy Appeal, which is a major source of income to help those in need. There is, however, a Royal British Legion Scotland, which has a separate entry in this guide. The two organisations share the same premises and work together.

In 2006 the Earl Haig Fund Scotland launched a new identity – 'Poppyscotland' – and is now generally known by this name.

Radio Forth Cash for Kids Appeal

Eligibility: Children under the age of 18 who have a disability or are disadvantaged and live in Edinburgh, the Lothians and Fife.

Types of grants: Grants are given towards clothing, hospital expenses and medical and disability equipment.

Annual grant total: Grants have previously totalled around £200,000.

Applications: Application forms are available on request from the correspondent or by filling in a short request form on the website. A letter of support is required from a GP, health visitor, social worker, occupational therapist or other professional involved with the child who can support the claim.

Correspondent: Lesley Fraser-Taylor, Charity Coordinator, Forth House, Forth Street, Edinburgh EH1 3LE (0131 556 9255; email: lesley@forthone. com; website: www.forthonline.co.uk)

Radio Tay – Cash for Kids

Eligibility: Children and young people aged under 18 who are in need and live within Radio Tay's transmission area (Dundee, Angus, Perth and North East Fife).

Types of grants: One-off grants of £50 to £5,000 towards needs such as clothing, beds, bedding, holidays, disability equipment and so on.

Exclusions: Grants are not made to pay salaries or rent.

Annual grant total: About £200,000 is given to individuals and organisations each year.

Applications: On a form available from the correspondent or to download from the website. Applications must be submitted with a letter of reference from a social worker, doctor, minister or health visitor. They are accepted from 1 November to 31 January.

Correspondent: Lynda Curran, Cash for Kids, 6 North Isla Street, Dundee DD3 7JQ (01382 200800; email: lynda.curran@ radiotay.co.uk; website: www.tayfm.co.uk)

The Royal Scottish Corporation (also known as The Scottish Hospital of the Foundation of King Charles II)

Eligibility: Scottish people, and their children and widows, who are in need, hardship or distress and live within a 35-mile radius of Charing Cross. Beneficiaries are usually in receipt of state benefits.

Types of grants: The trust gives weekly allowances to older people, one-off grants to people unable to improve their circumstances, help with respite holidays, outings and social events, sheltered housing and help to come off benefits.

Exclusions: No grants are made for debts or for items that have already been purchased.

Annual grant total: In 2008/09 the trust had assets of £31 million and an income of £2 million. Welfare grants amounted to around £400,000.

Applications: On a form available from the correspondent or to download from the website. After receiving the completed form, which should include copies of the birth/wedding certificates, the corporation decides whether to submit the application for consideration at the trustees' monthly meeting. They may also decide to visit or ask the applicant to visit the corporation's office to discuss their case.

Correspondent: Willie Docherty, Chief Executive, 37 King Street, Covent Garden, London WC2E 8JS (020 7240 3718 (UK helpline 0800 652 2989); fax: 020 7497 0184; email: info@scotscare. com; website: www.scotscare.com)

The Royal Society for Home Relief to Incurables, Edinburgh (General Fund)

Eligibility: Adult people throughout Scotland under retirement age, who have earned a livelihood (or been a housewife) and are no longer able to do so because of an incurable illness.

Types of grants: An annuity is given quarterly (totalling £540 per year) to help provide extra comforts.

Exclusions: The fund is not in a position to consider isolated requests to meet single emergencies.

Annual grant total: About £90,000 a year.

Applications: On a form available from the correspondent.

Correspondent: R Graeme Thom, Scott-Moncrieff, 17 Melville Street, Edinburgh EH3 7PH (0131 473 3500; email: graeme. thom@scott-moncrieff.com)

Sailors' Orphan Society of Scotland

Eligibility: Orphaned or fatherless children of seafaring men throughout Scotland who are in need.

Types of grants: Grants are given to help towards the cost of clothes, food, education and other necessities.

Annual grant total: In 2008/09 the trust had an income of £61,000. Grants usually total about £50,000.

Applications: In writing to the correspondent. There is a small management committee who decide all cases. The local representatives look after and report on the children in their area.

Correspondent: John Dow, 18 Woodside Crescent, Glasgow G3 7UL (0141 353 2090; fax: 0141 353 2196)

The Scottish Artists' Benevolent Association see entry on page 61

The Scottish Association of Master Bakers' Benevolent Fund

Eligibility: Members or ex-members of the Scottish Association of Master Bakers and their families who are in need. Other members of the Scottish baking industry may also be supported.

Types of grants: One-off grants of up to £700 towards electrical goods, household repairs, repayment of small debts and so on.

Annual grant total: In 2009 the association had an income of £7,800.

Applications: On a form available from the correspondent.

Correspondent: Grants Administrator, Atholl House, 4 Torphichen Street, Edinburgh EH3 8JQ

The Scottish Chartered Accountants' Benevolent Association

Eligibility: Members of the Institute of Chartered Accountants of Scotland who are in need, and their dependants.

Types of grants: One-off and recurrent grants for a variety of needs. Recent grants have been given for hospital travel costs, house repairs, general living expenses, mobility aids, retraining and home help.

Annual grant total: Grants usually total about £120,000 each year.

Applications: An initial letter or telephone call should be made to the correspondent. A member of the fund will then make contact and arrange a visit if appropriate. Following this, an application, report and recommendation will be made to the fund's council for approval.

Correspondent: Robert Linton, Secretary, Robert Linton & Co, 53 Bothwell Street, Glasgow, G2 6TS (0141 572 8465; fax: 0141 248 7456; email: mail@robertlinton.co.uk)

Other information: Grants are also given for educational purposes.

The Scottish Cinematograph Trade Benevolent Fund

Eligibility: People in need who are, or have been, working in the cinema industry in Scotland for at least two years.

Types of grants: One-off and recurrent grants for living costs, household essentials, 'Aid Call' systems and convalescence.

Annual grant total: In 2009 the fund had an income of £21,000. Grants were made totalling about £18,000.

Applications: In writing to the correspondent. Applications can be submitted either directly by the individual, or through a social worker, Citizens Advice or other welfare agency or third party.

Correspondent: The Secretary, c/o Grant Thornton, Scottish Legal Life Building, 95 Bothwell Street, Glasgow G2 7JZ (0141 223 0000; email: info@sctbf.co.uk; website: www.sctbf.co.uk)

Other information: The fund also offers advice on state benefits and pensions and employs a welfare visitor.

Scottish Grocers' Federation Benevolent Fund

Eligibility: Past members or employees of the grocery trade in Scotland who are in need.

Types of grants: One-off grants or recurrent grants distributed quarterly totalling £900 a year.

Annual grant total: In 2008 the fund had an income of £25,000. Grants have previously totalled about £14,000.

Applications: On a form available from the correspondent. Applicants are then visited to assess the most appropriate form of help.

Correspondent: Scott Landsburgh, Secretary, Federation House, 222–224 Queensferry Road, Edinburgh, EH4 2BN (0131 343 3300; fax: 0131 343 6147; email: info@scottishshop.org.uk)

The Scottish Hide & Leather Trades' Provident & Benevolent Society

Eligibility: People of retirement age who have worked in the Scottish hide and leather trades.

Types of grants: The society exists principally to provide pensions to its members. It also pays pensions to the widows and widowers of members who have survived their pensionable spouse. Donations equivalent to the annual pensions are also paid to people who have been employed in the trades but who are not members. Very occasionally one-off payments of about £100 to £200 are made for specific purposes, usually for the replacement of household equipment, such as a washing machine, fridge and so on.

Annual grant total: Grants usually total about £10,000 each year.

Applications: Most applicants have been recommended by other members of the society or local organisations.

Correspondent: David Ballantine, c/o Mitchells Roberton Solicitors, George House, 36 North Hanover Street, Glasgow G1 2AD (0141 552 3422; fax: 0141 552 2935; email: info@mitchells-roberton.co.uk)

Scottish Hydro Electric Community Trust

Eligibility: People living in the Scottish Hydro Electric supply area. Grants can be given for domestic properties and properties used for not-for-profit community projects. Domestic properties must be the sole residence of the applicant.

Types of grants: Grants are given towards the costs of domestic electricity connections. Grants are awarded at the trustees' discretion and range from a few hundred pounds to a few thousand, however the usual level is 30% of the connection cost.

Exclusions: Applications for holiday homes or second homes will not be considered.

Annual grant total: In 2008/09 the trust had an income of £82,000. No further information was available concerning grants total.

Applications: On a form available from the correspondent. Applications should be submitted directly by the individual and are considered about three times a year.

Correspondent: Alisa Gray, Secretary, 200 Dunkeld Road, Perth, PH1 3AQ (01738 455154; fax: 01738 455281; website: www.scottish-southern.co.uk/)

Other information: Grants are also given to community ventures for electricity connections.

The Scottish National Institution for the War-Blinded

Eligibility: Visually impaired ex-service personnel who live in Scotland.

Types of grants: Mainly regular monthly grants for aftercare and workshop allowances. Occasional hardship grants are also given.

Annual grant total: In 2009/10 the trust had assets of £49 million and an income of £2.5 million. Approximately £1.5 million was given in veterans' grants.

Applications: Through the Workshops and After-Care Department (Tel: 0131 333 1369). Applications are considered as required.

Correspondent: Richard Hellewell, Chief Executive and Secretary, PO Box 500, Gillespie Crescent, Edinburgh EH10 4HZ (0131 229 1456; website: www.royalblind.org/warblinded)

The Scottish Nautical Welfare Society

Eligibility: Active, retired and disabled seafarers with ten years in service who are in need and their widows.

Types of grants: Recurrent quarterly grants of £156.

Annual grant total: In 2008/09 the trust had an income of £116,000. Grants have previously totalled £56,000.

Applications: In writing to the correspondent.

Correspondent: Mrs Gail Haldane, Administrator, 937 Dumbarton Road, Glasgow, G14 9UF (0141 337 2632; fax: 0141 337 2632; email: gvsa@hotmail.com)

Other information: This society was established in April 2002 as an amalgamation of Glasgow Aged Seaman Relief Fund, Glasgow Seaman's Friend Society and Glasgow Veteran Seafarers' Association.

Scottish Prison Service Benevolent Fund

Eligibility: Scottish prison officers, both serving and retired, and their families who are in need.

Types of grants: One-off and recurrent grants according to need.

Annual grant total: In 2008/09 the trust had an income of £23,000. About £15,000 is distributed in grants annually.

Applications: In writing to the correspondent.

Correspondent: The Governor, H M Prison, South Road, Peterhead, AB42 2YY

The Scottish Solicitors' Benevolent Fund (incorporating The Scottish Law Agents' Society Benevolent Fund)

Eligibility: People in need who were members of the solicitor profession in Scotland and their dependants. Grants are generally awarded to minor dependent children, widows and widowers of solicitors who practised in Scotland and have died. Occasional help is given to practising solicitors who are in need.

Types of grants: One-off and recurrent grants according to need.

Annual grant total: In 2008/09 the fund had an income of £24,000. Grants were made totalling about £22,000.

Applications: On a form available from the correspondent, including financial details and two referees.

Correspondent: The Secretary, c/o Sheridans Solicitors, 166 Buchanan Street, Glasgow G1 2LW (0141 332 3536; fax: 0141 353 3819; email: secretary@slas. co.uk; website: www.slas.co.uk)

Dr J R Sibbald's Trust

Eligibility: Adults living in Scotland who have an incurable disease and who are in financial need.

Types of grants: Usually £140 a year payable in two instalments in May and November. Occasional one-off grants are given in exceptional circumstances.

Annual grant total: Grants to individuals usually total about £4,000 per year.

Applications: On a form available from the correspondent. Applications should be accompanied by a certificate from a surgeon or physician giving full details of the disease and certify that in their opinion it is incurable. As much background information about the applicant as possible is also required which can be in the form of a letter from a social worker or friend describing the family circumstances and giving other personal information. Applications should be submitted by 15 November for consideration in late November/early December.

Correspondent: H J Stevens, Brodies, 15 Atholl Crescent, Edinburgh EH3 8HA (0131 228 3777; fax: 0131 228 3878)

The Miss M O Taylor's Trust

Eligibility: Impoverished artists in Scotland of sufficient standing to deserve the title. The applicant must have had some measure of success in the profession that they have adopted and must have earned money in it.

Types of grants: One-off payments according to need.

Annual grant total: The fund has approximately £800 a year from which to make awards.

Applications: In writing to the correspondent directly by the individual for consideration in mid-June. Applications should be received by 30 April and include an example of the artist's work.

Correspondent: Trust Administrator, Royal Scottish Academy, The Mound, Edinburgh EH2 2EL (0131 225 6671; fax: 0131 220 6016; email: info@ royalscottishacademy.org; website: www. royalscottishacademy.org)

The Royal Society for the Relief of Indigent Gentlewomen of Scotland see entry on page 40

Mrs S H Troughton Charitable Trust

Eligibility: People in need who receive a pension and live on the estates of Ardchatten in Argyll, and Blair Atholl.

Types of grants: One-off and recurrent grants ranging from £400 to £600.

Exclusions: Grants are not given to people whose income is £1,000 above their personal allowance for income tax.

Annual grant total: In 2008/09 the trust had an income of £20,000 and a total expenditure of £12,000.

Applications: In writing to the correspondent at any time by the individual or via a third party such as a social worker or through an organisation such as a Citizens Advice or other welfare agency. Unsuccessful applications will not be acknowledged.

Correspondent: Laura Gosling, Pollen House, 10–12 Cork Street, London W1S 3LW (020 7439 9061; email: charity@ mfs.co.uk)

Other information: The trust also makes grants to organisations.

The Eliza Haldane Wylie Fund

Eligibility: People in need who are related to or associated with Eliza Haldane Wylie or her family and 'gentlefolk of the middle class' in need.

Types of grants: Small one-off payments.

Annual grant total: In 2008/09 the fund had an income of £54,000.

Applications: In writing to the correspondent

Correspondent: Trust Administrator, 9–11 Hill Street, Edinburgh EH2 3JT (0131 225 8371; fax: 0131 225 2048)

Aberdeen & Perthshire

The Cyril and Margaret Gates Charitable Trust

Eligibility: Journalists under 30, born or working in Aberdeen, the north east and north of Scotland (the area north of Stonehaven), and their dependants, who are in need.

Types of grants: Usually one-off payments according to need. Maximum grant is normally in the region of £1,000.

Annual grant total: Approximately £1,000 is distributed annually, mostly for welfare purposes.

Applications: In writing to the correspondent.

Correspondent: Alan J Innes, 100 Union Street, Aberdeen AB10 1QR (01224 428000)

The Neil Gow Charitable Trust

Eligibility: People in need who live in the district of Perth and Kinross or the immediate neighbourhood.

Types of grants: Annuities of around £90 each, paid quarterly.

Annual grant total: In 2009/10 the trust had an income of £12,000.

Applications: In writing to the correspondent.

Correspondent: A G Dorward, Messrs Miller Hendry, 10 Blackfriars Street, Perth PH1 5NS (01738 637311; fax: 01738 638685)

Grampian Police Diced Cap Charitable Fund

Eligibility: People in need who live in the Grampian police force area.

Types of grants: One-off and recurrent grants to improve the health and well being of any deserving persons.

Annual grant total: In 2008/09 the fund had an income of £112,000. Grants usually total about £50,000, although most of this is given to organisations.

Applications: In writing to the correspondent.

Correspondent: The Secretary, Grampian Police, Queen Street, Aberdeen AB10 1ZX (email: dicedcap@grampian.pnn.police.uk)

The Gertrude Muriel Pattullo Trust for Handicapped Boys

Eligibility: Boys aged 18 or under who are living with a physical disability and have resided in the city of Dundee or the county of Angus.

Types of grants: Gifts in kind and one-off cash grants. Recent grants have been given for electrical goods, clothing, hospital expenses, holidays, medical and disability equipment, travel expenses, furniture, nursing fees, help in the home and so on.

Exclusions: No grants are given towards repayment of debts.

Annual grant total: Grants usually total about £4,000 each year.

Applications: On a form available from the correspondent at any time. Applications can be submitted directly by the individual or through a social worker, Citizens Advice or other welfare agency.

Correspondent: Toni McNicoll, Blackadders Solicitors, 30–34 Reform Street, Dundee DD1 1RJ (01382 229222; fax: 01382 342220; email: toni.mcnicoll@ blackadders.co.uk)

Other information: Grants are also made to organisations.

The Gertrude Muriel Pattullo Trust for Handicapped Girls

Eligibility: Girls aged 18 years or under who have physical disabilities and live in the city of Dundee or the county of Angus.

Types of grants: One-off grants ranging from £100 to £500 for electrical goods, clothing, hospital expenses, holidays, medical and disabled equipment, travel expenses, furniture, nursing fees, help in the home and so on.

Exclusions: No grants are given for the repayment of debts.

Annual grant total: In 2008/09 the trust had an income of £5,500. No further information was available.

Applications: On a form available from the correspondent at any time. Applications can be submitted directly by the individual or through a social worker, Citizens Advice, or other welfare agency. Applications are considered monthly.

Correspondent: Toni McNicoll, Blackadders Solicitors, 30–34 Reform Street, Dundee DD1 1RJ (01382 229222; fax: 01382 342220; email: toni.mcnicoll@ blackadders.co.uk)

Other information: Grants are also made to organisations.

The Gertrude Muriel Pattullo Trust for the Elderly

Eligibility: Older people (i.e. generally those of state pensionable age), especially those living with a disability, resident in the city of Dundee and county of Angus.

Types of grants: One-off grants for general welfare purposes. Recent grants have included help towards house adaptation and a grant to purchase a portable cylinder.

Exclusions: No grants are given for debt repayment.

Annual grant total: Grants usually total about £4,000 each year.

Applications: On a form available from the correspondent at any time. Applications can be submitted either directly by the individual or through a third party such as a social worker.

Correspondent: Toni McNicoll, Blackadders Solicitors, 30–34 Reform Street, Dundee DD1 1RJ (01382 229222; fax: 01382 342220; email: toni.mcnicoll@ blackadders.co.uk)

Other information: Grants are also given to organisations.

Miss Jessie Ann Thomson's Trust

Eligibility: Women, either single or widowed, in financial need who live in the city of Aberdeen. There is a preference for those whose maiden name is Thomson or Middleton.

Types of grants: Recurrent grants of £330 per year, paid in May and November.

Annual grant total: About £7,000.

Applications: On a form available from the correspondent, to be submitted either directly by the individual or through a social worker, Citizens Advice or another welfare agency. Applications are considered at any time.

Correspondent: Douglas M Watson, Adam Cochran Solicitors, 6 Bon-Accord Square, Aberdeen AB11 6XU (01224 588913; fax: 01224 581149; email: dmwatson@adamcochran.co.uk)

Aberdeen & Aberdeenshire

Aberdeen Indigent Mental Patients' Fund

Eligibility: People who live in Aberdeen and are, or have been, mentally ill on their discharge from hospital.

Types of grants: One-off and recurrent grants according to need.

Annual grant total: In 2009 the fund had an income of £2,900.

Applications: In writing to the correspondent.

Correspondent: Alan Innes, Peterkins Solicitors, 100 Union Street, Aberdeen AB10 1QR (01224 428000)

The Aberdeen Widows' & Spinsters' Benevolent Fund

Eligibility: Widows and unmarried women over 60 years of age who live in the city or county of Aberdeen; in cases of special need and where surplus income is available, those between 40 and 60 are considered.

Types of grants: Generally yearly allowances of up to £360 paid in two instalments in June and December.

Annual grant total: In 2008/09 the fund had an income of £48,000. Grants usually total around £40,000.

Applications: On a form available from the correspondent.

Correspondent: Trust Administrator, 12–16 Albyn Place, Aberdeen, AB10 1PS (01224 332400)

The James Allan of Midbeltie Trust

Eligibility: Widows who live in Aberdeen and are in need.

Types of grants: Recurrent yearly allowances of £250 a year payable in two instalments in May and November.

Annual grant total: About £13,000.

Applications: On a form available from the correspondent. Applications can be submitted either directly by the individual, through a third party such as a social worker or through an organisation such as Citizens Advice or another welfare agency. Applications are usually considered in April and October.

Correspondent: Michael D McMillan, Burnett & Reid, 15 Golden Square, Aberdeen AB10 1WF (01224 644333; fax: 01224 632173; email: MDMcMillan@ burnett-reid.co.uk)

Dr John Calder's Fund

Eligibility: People in need who live in the parish of Machar, or within the city of Aberdeen.

Types of grants: This trust deals primarily with educational grants, although relief-in-need grants can be considered.

Annual grant total: Around £2,000 is available for individuals. A further £8,000 is given in grants towards educational projects or organisations.

Applications: The trust stated in January 2006 that funds were fully committed and that this situation was likely to remain so for the medium to long term.

Correspondent: Clive Phillips, Paull & Williamsons, New Investment House, 214 Union Row, Aberdeen AB10 1QY

The George, James & Alexander Chalmers Trust

Eligibility: Women living in Aberdeen who have fallen on hard times as a result of misfortune and not through any fault of their own.

Types of grants: Recurrent grants of about £450 a year, payable in half-yearly instalments.

Annual grant total: In 2008/09 the trust had an income of £104,000. Grants usually total about £50,000.

Applications: On a form available from the correspondent.

Correspondent: Grant Administrator, 2 Bon Accord Crescent, Aberdeen AB11 6DH (01224 587261)

The Gordon Cheyne Trust Fund

Eligibility: Widows and daughters of deceased merchants, shopkeepers and other businessmen who are elderly natives of Aberdeen or who have lived there for at least 25 years.

Types of grants: Annual allowances of about £400, paid twice yearly.

Annual grant total: In 2008/09 the trust had an income of £25,000.

Applications: On a form available from the correspondent via a social worker, Citizens Advice or other welfare agency.

Correspondent: Grant Administrator, 12–16 Albyn Place, Aberdeen, AB10 1PS (01224 332400; fax: 01224 332401)

The Crisis Fund of Voluntary Service Aberdeen

Eligibility: People in Aberdeen who are facing extreme hardship.

Types of grants: Immediate grants ranging from about £50 to £150 for emergency needs such as food, beds and bedding, clothing and essential household items.

Annual grant total: Grants usually total about £40,000 each year.

Applications: On a form available from Voluntary Service Aberdeen: to be submitted through a third party such as a social worker, Citizens Advice or similar welfare agency. Applications are considered as received.

Correspondent: Crisis Fund Administrator, Voluntary Service Aberdeen, 38 Castle Street, Aberdeen AB11 5YU (01224 212021; fax: 01224 580 722; email: info@vsa.org.uk; website: www.vsa.org.uk/)

The Donald Trust

Eligibility: People in need who 'belong to' the city of Aberdeen and former county of Aberdeen. 'Advanced age, lack of health, inability to work, high character and former industry are strong recommendations.'

Types of grants: An annuity of £400 a year, paid in two instalments.

Exclusions: Generally, people under the age of 60 are not eligible.

Annual grant total: In 2009 the trust had an income of £26,000. Grants usually total about £10,000 each year.

Applications: On a form available from the correspondent. Applications should be submitted through a third party such as a social worker. They are considered twice a year.

Correspondent: Anne Henderson, 12–16 Albyn Place, Aberdeen, AB10 1PS (01224 332400; fax: 01224 332401; email: anne.henderson@raeburns.co.uk)

Garden Nicol Benevolent Fund

Eligibility: Women in need who live in Aberdeen.

Types of grants: One-off and recurrent grants according to need.

Annual grant total: Grants usually total about £6,000 a year.

Applications: In writing to the correspondent.

Correspondent: Alan J Innes, 100 Union Street, Aberdeen, AB10 1QR (01224 428000)

John Harrow's Mortification

Eligibility: People in need who live in the parishes of Old Machar and Denburn, Aberdeen and attend the church in Denburn or St Machar Cathedral.

Types of grants: About £800 is given to the ministers of each parish at Christmas for distribution to older people.

Annual grant total: Grants total around £1,600 each year.

Applications: Applications are made via the ministers of the parishes of Old Machar and Denburn, not directly to the trust.

Correspondent: Alan J Innes, Peterkins Solicitors, 100 Union Street, Aberdeen AB10 1QR (01224 428250)

The Mary Morrison Cox Fund

Eligibility: People in need who live in the parish of Dyce, Aberdeen. Preference is given to older people and people living with disabilities.

Types of grants: One-off grants ranging from £100 to £400 to help with general living expenses.

Annual grant total: Grants usually total around £10,000 a year.

Applications: The trust has a list of potential beneficiaries to whom it sends application forms each year, usually in November. Applicants can contact the trust at any time to ask to be added to the list.

Correspondent: The Trustees, 18 Bon-Accord Crescent, Aberdeen AB11 6XY (01224 573321)

The Matilda Murray Trust

Eligibility: People in need who have lived in Old Aberdeen for at least five years immediately before the date of application.

Types of grants: Annual grants generally in the range of £50 to £60.

Annual grant total: In 2008/09 the trust had an income of £11,000.

Applications: On a form available from the correspondent. Applications must be submitted by mid-October for consideration in November and grants are distributed in December.

Correspondent: Trust Administrator, Stronachs, 34 Albyn Place, Aberdeen, AB10 1FW (01224 845845; fax: 01224 845800; email: info@stronachs.com)

Simpson Trust

Eligibility: Older people in need who are in poor health and live in the burgh of Macduff.

Types of grants: Annual payments of around £75 to £200, usually made in two instalments.

Annual grant total: Grants average around £10,000 a year.

Applications: On a form available from the correspondent. When there are vacancies on the list of annuitants, applications are invited through the local press.

Correspondent: Trustees of the Simpson Trust, c/o Alexander George and Co. Solicitors, 25 High Street, Banff, AB45 1AN

Miss Caroline Jane Spence's Fund

Eligibility: Widows or unmarried females living within the city or county of Aberdeen who are in need.

Types of grants: Recurrent grants are made.

Exclusions: No grants are made where statutory funding is available.

Annual grant total: Grants usually total about £30,000 each year.

Applications: On a form available from the correspondent. Applications can be submitted either directly by the individual, or through a social worker, Citizens Advice or other welfare agency or other third party. Applications are considered in November, January and April.

Correspondent: Charles Scott, c/o Mackinnons, 14 Carden Place, Aberdeen AB10 1UR (01224 632464)

The Fuel Fund of Voluntary Service Aberdeen

Eligibility: People living in Aberdeen who need help in maintaining a warm home, particularly older people, people with a disability and families with young children.

Types of grants: One-off grants of about £30.

Annual grant total: Grants usually total about £8,000 each year.

Applications: By interview with a member of the Voluntary Service Aberdeen's social work team, or on an application form available from the correspondent, to be submitted through a social worker or other professional welfare agency.

Correspondent: Fuel Fund Administrator, 38 Castle Street, Aberdeen AB11 5YU (01224 212021; fax: 01224 580722; email: info@vsa.org.uk; website: www.vsa.org.uk)

Angus

Charities Administered by Angus Council

Eligibility: Residents of Arbroath, Brechin, Carnoustie, Forfar, Kirnemuir, Montrose, Kettins, Carmyllie and Arbirlot (particularly older people and people who are in need).

Types of grants: One-off grants generally of £30 or more.

Annual grant total: The combined grant totals of these charities is about £2,500 per year.

Applications: On a form available from the correspondent.

Correspondent: Sarah Forsyth, Angus Council, Angus House, Orchardbank Business Park, Forfar DD8 2AL (01307 476269)

Other information: Over 100 charitable trusts are administered by Angus Council including: Brechin Charitable Funds, Arbroath Charitable Funds, Forfar Charitable Funds, Forfar Landward Charities, Carnoustie Charitable Funds and Kirriemuir Charitable Funds.

The Colvill Charity

Eligibility: People who are in need and live in the town of Arbroath and the parish of St Vigeans and the surrounding area.

Types of grants: Annual grants of up to about £100 are given to older people. Special one-off grants of up to about £250 are also available for specific medical or household needs.

Annual grant total: In 2008/09 the charity had an income of £20,000. Grants usually total about £8,000 each year.

Applications: On a form available from the correspondent to be submitted directly by the individual or through a social worker, Citizens Advice or other welfare agency. Applications can be made at any time, though requests for regular grants are usually assessed once a year.

Correspondent: Grants Administrator, Thorntons WS, Brothockbank House, Arbroath, Angus DD11 1NJ (01241 872683; fax: 01241 871541; email: arbroath@thorntons-law.co.uk)

The Mrs Marie Dargie Trust

Eligibility: People of pensionable age living within the city boundaries of Brechin.

Types of grants: One-off grants of around £20 are given for a range of purposes, including television licenses.

Annual grant total: Grants usually total around £8,000 a year.

Applications: In writing to the correspondent including documentation proving the age of the applicant. Applications can be submitted either directly by the individual or a family member or through an organisation such as a Citizens Advice or other welfare agency. Applications can be considered at any time.

Correspondent: David H Will, Trustee, Ferguson & Will, 28 Clerk Street, Brechin, Angus DD9 6AY (01356 622289)

The St Cyrus Benevolent Fund

Eligibility: People who are sick, infirm and in need and live in the parish of St Cyrus, Montrose only.

Types of grants: One-off grants of £25 to £100 are given as well as gift vouchers and grants in kind. Grants given include those towards clothing, food, travel expenses, medical equipment and disability equipment. Parcels are distributed at Christmas time.

Annual grant total: Grants usually total around £1,000 a year.

Applications: In writing to the correspondent. Recommendation by social worker, minister, doctor, nurse or similar is essential. The trust stated: 'An individual may make a direct application in the first instance but it will be thoroughly checked through the usual type of referee.' Applications are considered at any time.

Correspondent: The Secretary, Scotston of Kirkside, St Cyrus, Montrose, Angus DD10 0DA

Other information: The trust also makes grants to organisations for medical equipment and welfare.

The Angus Walker Benevolent Fund

Eligibility: People in need who live in Montrose.

Types of grants: One-off grants.

Annual grant total: In 2008/09 the trust had an income of £5,900. About £6,000 is given each year in grants.

Applications: By formal application through a trustee, local district councillors, the minister of Montrose Old Church or the rector of St Mary's & St Peter's Episcopal Church, Montrose.

Correspondent: Messrs T Duncan & Co., Solicitors, 192 High Street, Montrose, DD10 8NA (01674 672533)

Dundee

The Broughty Ferry Benevolent Fund

Eligibility: People in need living in Broughty Ferry, Dundee, who are not in residential care.

Types of grants: One-off grants according to need.

Annual grant total: In 2008/09 the trust had an income of £10,000.

Applications: On a form available from the correspondent. Applications can be submitted either directly by the individual or through a social worker, Citizens Advice or other welfare agency.

Correspondent: The Trustees, 12 Tircarra Gardens, Broughty Ferry, Dundee DD5 2QF

The Dundee Indigent Sick Society

Eligibility: People in need, who are in poor health or who have a disability and live in Dundee.

Types of grants: One-off grants of up to £100, although more can be given in exceptional circumstances.

Annual grant total: Grants usually total about £2,000 each year.

Applications: In writing to the correspondent either directly by the individual or a family member, or through a third party such as a social worker. Potential applicants are normally visited by the trust.

Correspondent: Donald Gordon, Blackadders, 30–34 Reform Street, Dundee DD1 1RJ (01382 229222; fax: 01382 342220; email: donald.gordon@blackadders.co.uk)

Johnston Charity

Eligibility: Older people who are infirm and in need who live in the old City of Dundee boundary.

Types of grants: Yearly pensions of £50.

Annual grant total: Grants usually total around £600 per year.

Applications: Individuals should first contact their councillor who will submit an application form on the individual's behalf to the Director of Finance of Dundee City Council.

Correspondent: Director of Finance, Dundee City Council, Floor 4, Tayside House, 28 Crichton Street, Dundee, DD1 3RF

John Normansell Kyd's Trust for Walton & Rashiewell Employees

Eligibility: Ex-employees of the former Walton Works and Rashiewell Works in Dundee (which closed over 20 years ago) and their dependants who are in need.

Types of grants: Currently beneficiaries receive £250 a year (£100 summer grant and £150 winter grant.)

Annual grant total: About £750.

Applications: No new applications will be eligible as there are only three remaining ex-employees who receive grants.

Correspondent: The Trustees, 5 Bank Street, Dundee, DD1 1RL

The Mair Robertson Benevolent Fund

Eligibility: Older women living in Dundee and Blairgowrie who are suffering from financial difficulties or are on a low income.

Types of grants: One-off grants of up to about £300.

Annual grant total: Grants usually total about £4,000 each year.

Applications: On a form available from the correspondent. Applications can be submitted directly by the individual or through a social worker, Citizens Advice, other welfare agency or other third party.

Correspondent: The Trustees, 17 Crichton Street, Dundee DD1 3AR

Mrs Margaret T Petrie's Mortification

Eligibility: Aged, infirm and indigent individuals over 55 years of age belonging to, or settled in, Dundee.

Types of grants: One-off and recurrent according to need.

Annual grant total: Grants to individuals usually total about £2,000 per year.

Applications: In writing to the correspondent. Applications can be submitted either directly by the individual, or through a social worker, Citizens Advice or other welfare agency, or another third party.

Correspondent: Administrator, Thorntons Solicitors, Whitehall House, 33 Yeaman Shore, Dundee, DD1 4BJ (01382 229111; fax: 01382 202288; email: dundee@ thorntons-law.co.uk)

The Hannah & Margaret Thomson Trust

Eligibility: Firstly, people in need who live in Dundee and were wounded during the Second World War, and their spouses. Secondly, ex-employees of Thomson Shepherd & Co. who are in need.

Types of grants: One-off and recurrent grants according to need.

Annual grant total: In 2009/10 the trust had an income of £64,000. Grants were previously made totalling about £8,000, however this amount may have risen in line with the trust's sharp increase in income during recent years.

Applications: In writing to the correspondent. Applications can be submitted either directly by the individual or through a social worker, Citizens Advice or other welfare agency.

Correspondent: Administrator, Thorntons Solicitors, Whitehall House, 33 Yeaman Shore, Dundee, DD1 4BJ (01382 229111; fax: 01382 202288; email: dundee@ thorntons-law.co.uk)

Laurencekirk

The Cameron Fund

Eligibility: People of pensionable age who live in the burgh of Laurencekirk and are in need.

Types of grants: One off and recurrent grants according to need.

Annual grant total: Grants average around £3,500 a year.

Applications: In writing to the correspondent, directly by the individual.

Correspondent: Trust Administrator, Banski & Co, 19a High St, Laurencekirk, Aberdeenshire AB30 1AF (01561 377245)

Moray

The Auchray Trust

Eligibility: Older people or people who are infirm and were in business in the burgh of Elgin and who are now in financial need.

Types of grants: Help with council house rent.

Annual grant total: This trust's annual income is around £4,500. In previous years grants have totalled around £2,200.

Applications: On an application form available from the correspondent to be submitted by the individual or family member. There are no deadlines for applications.

Correspondent: Grants Administrator, Finance and Information Technology Services, Moray Council, District Headquarters, High Street, Elgin, IV30 1BX (01343 563124)

Other information: The council also administers various small charities (under £500 grant total) for residents of the following areas: Kirkmichael, Inveravon, Mortlach, Keith and Aberlour (Keith/Dufftown Poor Funds & Keith Nursing Fund); Dufftown (Watt Bequest); Lossiemouth; the parishes of Boharm, Deskford, Dibble, Knockando, Rothes and Speymouth; and the burgh of Cullen. Further details are available from the correspondent.

Perth and Kinross

The Anderson Trust

Eligibility: Women in need who live in the parish of Kinnoull or Perth and who belong to the established Church of Scotland.

Types of grants: Grants are limited to a maximum of £500 per person each year.

Annual grant total: In 2008/09 the trust had an income of £6,400. About £5,500 is available each year for grant distribution.

Applications: On a form available from the correspondent at any time.

Correspondent: A G Dorward, Messrs Miler Hendry, 10 Blackfriars Street, Perth, PH1 5NS (01738 637311)

Mrs Agnes W Carmichael's Trust (incorporating Ferguson and West Charitable Trust)

Eligibility: The relief of poverty, sickness and distress of people who are older, disabled and needy resident in Coupar Angus.

Types of grants: Grants of £50 to £250.

Annual grant total: In 2008/09 the trust had an income of £20,000.

Applications: On a form available from the correspondent. Applications should give details of the individual's financial circumstances. Deadlines are in November and applications are considered in December.

Correspondent: Alison Hodge, Watson Lyall Bowie, Union Bank Building, Coupar Angus, Blairgowrie PH13 9AJ (01828 628395)

Other information: The trust also supports older people's organisations.

The Guildry Incorporation of Perth

Eligibility: People in need who live in Perth.

Types of grants: One-off and recurrent grants usually ranging between £100 and £500.

Annual grant total: In 2009/10 the guild had an income of £204,000. In previous years around £80,000 was given in grants to individuals, of which approximately £31,000 was given for welfare purposes, namely weekly pensions (£18,000); quarterly pensions (£8,500); and coal allowances (£4,800).

Applications: Application forms can be requested from the correspondent. They are considered at the trustees' meetings on the last Tuesday of every month.

Correspondent: Lorna Peacock, Secretary, 42 George Street, Perth PH1 5JL (01738 623195)

Scones Lethendy Mortifications

Eligibility: People in need who live in the burgh of Perth and are poor descendents of Alexander Jackson, or with the surname Jackson and other people who are in need (Jackson Mortifications)

Types of grants: Grants of about £65 a quarter.

Annual grant total: Grants usually total about £7,000 per year.

Applications: On a form available from correspondent. Both trusts have a waiting list to which applications would be added, although successful applicants are judged on need rather than when they applied.

Correspondent: Graham MacKenzie, Treasurer, King James VI Hospital, Hospital Street, Perth, PH2 8HP (01738 624660)

Other information: A third trust is the Cairnie Mortification: Recurrent grants lasting for 10 years can be given to two young men, starting when they are near the age of 14. Priority is given to those who are direct descendants of Charles Cairnie or any of his five brothers, otherwise grants can be given to people with the surname Cairnie.

Central

Clackmannanshire

The Clackmannan District Charitable Trust

Eligibility: People in need who have lived in Clackmannanshire for 12 consecutive months preceding the application being considered or who have lived in Clackmannanshire for three years at some time in the past and continuously for the six consecutive months preceding the application being considered.

Types of grants: Assistance is mainly given for essential household goods such as, electric cookers, washing machines, beds and bedding.

Annual grant total: Grants usually total about £1,000 each year.

Applications: On a form available either directly from the correspondent, at community access points or to download from the website. Applications can be submitted at any time but are only considered in March and September.

Correspondent: Trusts Administrator, Trusts Administrator, Legal & Administration, Clackmannanshire Council, Greenfield House, Alloa, FK10 2AD (01259 452108; email: adminservices@clacks.gov.uk; website: www.clacksweb.org.uk/)

The Spittal Trust

Eligibility: People in need who have lived in Alloa for at least 10 years immediately before applying to the trust.

Types of grants: Assistance is mainly given for essential household goods, for example, electric cookers, washing machines, beds and bedding.

Annual grant total: Grants usually total around £2,000 a year.

Applications: On a form available from the correspondent. The trust also requires proof of income. Applications deadlines are at the end of February, May, August and November for consideration in March, June, September and December.

Correspondent: Ann Lomax, Administration Officer, Administrative Services, Clackmannanshire Council, Greenfield, Alloa FK10 2AD (01259 452108)

Falkirk

The Anderson Bequest

Eligibility: People in need who live in Boaness.

Types of grants: Annual grants of about £150 per year.

Annual grant total: In 2008/09 the fund had an income of £20,000. About £7,500 is given a year in grants to individuals.

Applications: In writing to the correspondent.

Correspondent: J W Johnston, 11 Register Street, Boaness, West Lothian, EH51 9AE (01506 822112)

Falkirk Temperance Trust

Eligibility: Individuals who have alcohol, drug or other substance abuse problems and live in the former burgh of Falkirk.

Types of grants: One-off grants according to need ranging from £1,000 to £2,000.

Annual grant total: Grants total around £4,000 per year.

Applications: In writing to the correspondent at any time giving details of the specific funding required and what it is for. Applications can be made directly by the individual or family member or by a third party such as Citizens Advice or a social worker.

Correspondent: Hazel Jones Director of Finance Dept, Falkirk Council, Municipal Buildings, Falkirk FK1 5RS (01324 506070; fax: 01324 506363)

The Shanks Bequest

Eligibility: People in need who live in Denny.

Types of grants: There is a list of beneficiaries, which is updated each year, who receive a share of the income (about £40) as a Christmas gift.

Annual grant total: Grants usually total around £1,000 per year.

Applications: In writing to the correspondent.

Correspondent: Hillary McArthur, Finance Services, Falkirk Council, Municipal Buildings, West Bridge Street, Falkirk FK1 5RS (01324 506354)

Other information: Falkirk Council also administers other small trusts for individuals in need who live in the Falkirk area. Further details from the correspondent above.

Fife

Charities Administered by Fife Council (West Fife Area)

Eligibility: The beneficial area differs from charity to charity, the largest of which are the McGregor Bequest and the Wildridge Memorial Fund. The majority refer only to Dunfermline, but smaller ones exist for Aberdour, Culross, Lochgelly, Limekilns, Kincardine, Ballingry and Tulliallan.

Types of grants: Generally one-off grants, usually to poor and/or older people, including help in the form of annual pensions, coal and groceries.

Annual grant total: Grants usually total around £4,000 per year.

Applications: Applications should be made to one of the eight local panels in the communities. A list of local service centres can be found on the council website (www.fifedirect.org.uk).

Correspondent: Linda Purdie, Team Leader, Fife Council, Fife House, North

Street, Glenrothes, Fife, KY7 5LT
(018451 555555 ext. 442175)

The Fleming Bequest

Eligibility: People living in the parish of St Andrews and St Leonards in the town of St Andrews who are older, in poor health or in financial difficulty.

Types of grants: One-off grants, of up to around £300 each, for a specific household need such as clothing, carpets, fridge/freezers, special chairs and so on.

Annual grant total: In 2009/10 the bequest had an income of £13,000. Grants were made totalling about £12,000.

Applications: In writing to the correspondent preferably through a social worker, Citizens Advice or similar welfare agency. Applications are considered at any time and should include details of the applicant's postal address, date of birth and reason for request.

Correspondent: Elizabeth Calderwood, Pagan Osborne, 106 South Street, St Andrews, Fife KY16 9QD (01334 475001; fax: 01334 476322)

The Kirkcaldy Charitable Trust

Eligibility: People in need who live in Kirkcaldy.

Types of grants: One-off grants to those in urgent need. Recent grants have ranged from £10 to £250 for heating, fuel, clothing, aids, appliances and food.

Annual grant total: In 2009 the trust had an income of £4,200.

Applications: In writing to the correspondent either directly by the individual or through a social worker, Citizens Advice or other welfare agency. The trust requires evidence of Social Fund refusal before considering giving a grant.

Correspondent: Trust Administrator, Fife Council, Finance and Procurement, Fife House, Glenrothes, Fife KY7 5LT

Macdonald Bequest

Eligibility: Young people in need who live in the city of St Andrews or in the parish of St Andrews and St Leonards.

Types of grants: One-off and recurrent grants according to need. Recent grants have been given towards living costs, holidays and disability equipment.

Annual grant total: Grants usually total about £600 each year.

Applications: In writing to the correspondent to be submitted either through a third party such as a social worker, or through an organisation such as a Citizens Advice or other welfare agency. Applications are considered throughout the year and should include details of the individual's financial position (which will be treated in confidence).

Correspondent: Elizabeth Calderwood, c/o Pagan Osborne, 106 South Street, St Andrews, Fife KY16 9QD (01334 475001; email: elcalderwood@pagan.co.uk)

Other information: The trust also gives grants to organisations in the area of benefit.

The St Andrews Welfare Trust

Eligibility: Young and older or infirm people in need who live within a four mile radius of St Andrews.

Types of grants: One-off grants of up to £400 are given towards carpeting, cookers, clothing, fireguards and so on.

Exclusions: No grants for educational purposes, such as gap year projects.

Annual grant total: About £10,000 is given to individuals and about £4,000 to organisations each year.

Applications: In writing to the correspondent through a social worker, Citizens Advice or other welfare agency. Applications should include applicant's date of birth, postal address and reason for request and are considered throughout the year.

Correspondent: Elizabeth Calderwood, Pagan Osborne, 106 South Street, St Andrews, Fife KY16 9QD (01334 475001; fax: 01334 476332)

Other information: Grants are also given to playgroups and senior citizen Christmas teas.

Stirling

The George Hogg Trust

Eligibility: People who live in Killin and are in need.

Types of grants: One-off and recurrent grants according to need. For example, a recent grant of £200 was given towards an electric wheelchair.

Annual grant total: Grants usually total about £15,000 each year.

Applications: In writing to the correspondent via a third party such as a local doctor or minister. There are no deadlines and applications are normally considered at the Annual General Meeting.

Correspondent: Secretary, Tayview, Main Street, Killin, Perthshire FK21 8UT

Edinburgh, the Lothians & Scottish Borders

The Blackstock Trust

Eligibility: People who are elderly or sick and live in the counties of Roxburgh, Berwick and Selkirk.

Types of grants: Financial assistance (usually up to £500) for accommodation, maintenance or welfare, short holiday breaks, respite care and the provision of amenities.

Annual grant total: About £25,000 to over 100 individuals.

Applications: In writing to the correspondent. Applicants must provide details of financial position (income and capital).

Correspondent: William Windram, Secretary, Messrs Pike & Chapman, 36 Bank Street, Galashiels TD1 1ER (01896 752379)

The Capital Charitable Trust

Eligibility: People in need who live in the Edinburgh and Lothians area.

Types of grants: Small one-off grants of about £10 to £20 for clothes, decorating, household goods and so on.

Annual grant total: In 2008/09 the trust had an income £24,000. Grants were made totalling around £20,000.

Applications: Application forms are available from the Lothian Regional Council Social Work Departments and other responsible bodies who will forward them to the correspondent. Applications are not accepted directly from the individual.

Correspondent: Yvonne Rafferty, 7 Abercromby Place, Edinburgh EH3 6LA (0131 556 6644)

The Robert Christie Bequest Fund

Eligibility: People over 60 who are in need, live in Edinburgh or Midlothian and have an acutely painful disease.

Types of grants: Annual allowances are given according to need.

Annual grant total: In 2009 the fund had an income of £31,000. Grants were made totalling about £29,000.

Applications: On a form available from the correspondent. Applications can be submitted directly by the individual or through a social worker, Citizens Advice or other welfare agency. Applications are usually considered twice a year.

Correspondent: Trust Administrator, Gibson McKerrell Brown, 14 Rutland Square, Edinburgh EH1 2BD (0131 228 8319)

The ECAS (Access/Holiday Fund)

Eligibility: People who are long-term and significantly disabled through impairment of the musculoskeletal, neurological or cardiorespiratory systems of the body.

Unfortunately, people with the following conditions do not fall within the fund's eligibility criteria: psychiatric disorders, learning difficulties, behavioural disorders, developmental delay, Down's syndrome, autism, visual or hearing impairment, cancer, diabetes, epilepsy, HIV, back pain and chronic fatigue syndrome.

Types of grants: One-off grants of up to £500 for special equipment, white goods, special furniture, household equipment and so on. The fund also awards grants towards holidays and may contribute towards the cost of an accompanying carer or partner.

Exclusions: There are no grants available for: bills, debts, wheelchairs or scooters. Funding is not given to pay for items which have already been bought.

Annual grant total: In 2009/10 the trust had an income of £200,000. Around £25,000 is available for grantmaking each year.

Applications: On a form available from the correspondent or to download from the website. Applications must be supported by a social worker or health care professional. A short GP report is also required unless the applicant can provide a recent DLA (Care or Mobility) or Attendance Allowance award letter, or a taxi card. Applications can be made at any time but individuals should allow around four weeks (12 weeks for holiday applications) for the administration of any grant.

Correspondent: Grants Administrator, ECAS, Norton Park, 57 Albion Road, Edinburgh EH7 5QY (0131 475 2344; fax: 0131 475 2341; website: www.ecas-edinburgh.org)

The Edinburgh Merchant Company Endowment Trust

Eligibility: 'Decent, indigent men and women' who are over the age of 55 and have lived or worked in the city of Edinburgh or in Midlothian. Help may also be given to younger individuals who are certified on medical grounds as unable to earn their living.

Types of grants: The majority of funding is given in biannual pensions of about £500 per person. However, one-off cash grants and gifts in kind for household goods are also available.

Annual grant total: In 2008/09 the trust had an income of £2 million. Grants were made totalling around £100,000.

Applications: On a form available from the correspondent. Applications can be submitted at any time either directly by the individual, through a third party such as a social worker, or through an organisation such as Citizens Advice. The trust employs an almoner who assesses need and reports to the trust prior to any grant being made.

Correspondent: The Secretary, The Merchants Hall, 22 Hanover Street, Edinburgh EH2 2EP (0131 225 7202; fax: 0131 220 4842; email: info@mcoe.org.uk; website: www.mcoe.org.uk/)

Other information: The trust also administers various other trust funds.

The Edinburgh Voluntary Organisations' Trusts

Eligibility: Individuals in need who live in the city of Edinburgh and the Lothians. Priority is given where there is a serious illness of the individual or in the family.

Types of grants: One-off grants of up to £200 where they will be of real benefit to the family or individual. For example, grants are given for a specific need such as clothing and household essentials.

Exclusions: No grants for electrical equipment, white goods, holidays (except in special circumstances), students' fees/equipment or the repayment of debt.

Annual grant total: In 2008/09 the trust had an income of £174,000. Grants were made totalling £54,000, of which £35,000 was given to individuals and the remaining £19,000 to organisations.

Applications: On a form available from the correspondent. Applications should be submitted through a local authority or hospital social worker or an approved voluntary body. They are considered monthly.

Correspondent: Janette Scappaticcio, Trust Fund Administrator, 14 Ashley Place, Edinburgh EH6 5PX (0131 555 9100; fax: 0131 555 9101; email: janette.scappaticcio@evoc.org.uk; website: www.evoc.org.uk)

Other information: The Edinburgh Voluntary Organisations' Council (EVOC) previously administered a number of small trust funds which have now been amalgamated into a new fund, EVOT. EVOC separately administers the BBC Children in Need grants for the Edinburgh and Lothian region.

John Watt's Trust

Eligibility:
- People over 55 who have the name Watt and who live in the parish of South Leith or those who have done so for at least 10 years prior to their application.

- People in need who have lived or are living in the City of Edinburgh or any part of Midlothian may apply.

Types of grants: Grants are given in quarterly instalments.

Annual grant total: Grants usually total around £400 each year.

Applications: Prospective applicants must respond to an advertisement in the local press or through the local Leith churches, but more information can be gained from the correspondent. Applications are generally requested in November for consideration in January.

Correspondent: Mrs Elspeth Williamson, Mowat Hall Dick, 45 Queen Charlotte Street, Leith, Edinburgh EH6 7HT (0131 555 0616; email: elspeth.williamson@mhdlaw.co.uk)

Other information: The trust has a visitor who is a member of South Leith Parish Church. He visits the pensioners throughout the year and reports to the trustees on their state of health and needs.

Edinburgh

Alexander Darling Silk Mercer's Fund

Eligibility: Unmarried or widowed women, over 55, who live in Edinburgh or have worked in Edinburgh in the manufacture or sale of textile garments for ladies and children. Preference is given to women bearing the surname Darling, Millar, Small or Scott and to women born in the town of Lanark. Unfortunately, women who have only been involved in the manufacture and sale of textiles for men do not qualify for these grants.

Types of grants: Recurrent grants of £250 every six months to support living costs. The fund also helps with the cost of 'white goods' to qualifying people over the age of 55.

Annual grant total: In 2008/09 the fund had an income of £34,000 and made grants totalling £36,000.

Applications: Applications should be made in writing to the secretary of the Merchant Company, either directly by the individual or through a third party such as a social worker or Citizens Advice. Every written application is followed up by a visit by the almoner, during which a declaration regarding the applicant's financial circumstances is required.

The Edinburgh Royal Infirmary Samaritan Society

Eligibility: Patients of NHS hospitals in Edinburgh who are in need.

Types of grants: Specific sums of money for clothing, bills, travel expenses or other help for patients while in these hospitals or on leaving (such as grants for travel expenses for members of families visiting or accompanying patients). Grants range from £5 to £150.

Annual grant total: In 2008/09 the fund had an income of £20,000. Grants were made totalling around £18,000.

Applications: Through a medical social worker (at Edinburgh Royal Infirmary Social Work Department) on an application form. Applications are considered fortnightly.

Correspondent: The Honorary Secretary, 6a Randolph Crescent, Edinburgh EH3 7TH

EMMS International

Eligibility: People of good character, who live in Edinburgh city, are recovering from an illness and are in need of a convalescent holiday, which they are unable to pay for themselves.

Types of grants: Grants are awarded to help with the travel costs and accommodation for a convalescent holiday and are considered at up to £300 per adult and £150 per child (aged 16 or under). The maximum grant per family is £900. Grants will only be awarded once to each individual, or family, within a five-year period, unless there are very exceptional circumstances.

Exclusions: The trust cannot give grants towards spending money.

Annual grant total: In 2009 the trust had an income of £850,000. The trust gives around £13,000 annually to individuals in need.

Applications: On a form available from the correspondent. Applications must be sponsored by a social worker, health visitor or minister and be supported by a medical reference from a GP. Applications are considered throughout the year and usually take up to six to eight weeks to process.

Applicants can refer to the trust's website for details on how to apply and application guidelines.

Correspondent: James Wells, Chief Executive, 7 Washington Lane, Edinburgh EH11 2HA (0131 313 3828; fax: 0131 313 4662; email: info@emms.org; website: www.emms.org)

Other information: Grants are not paid to individuals but to sponsoring agencies or accredited guesthouses or travel agents. Only one successful application per individual is allowed.

Miss Jane Campbell Fraser's Trust

Eligibility: People in need who are over 60 and live in Leith.

Types of grants: One-off and recurrent grants of about £250 normally paid at Christmas.

Annual grant total: In 2008/09 the trust had an income of £5,300.

Applications: In writing to the correspondent. Applications can be submitted either directly by the individual or though a social worker or other welfare agency. They are considered throughout the year.

Correspondent: The Trustees, Wallace & Menzies, 21 Westgate, North Berwick EH39 4AE (01620 892307)

Leith Benevolent Association Ltd

Eligibility: People in financial need who live in Leith.

Types of grants: One-off grants, usually of £10 to £15 per person.

Annual grant total: About £500 a year.

Applications: In writing to the correspondent with supporting evidence from a social worker.

Correspondent: C Thomson, Catchpell House, Carpet Lane, Bernard Street, Leith, Edinburgh EH6 6SP (0131 467 7453; fax: 0131 467 0099; email: applications@leithbenevolentassociation.co.uk; website: www.leithbenevolentassociation.co.uk)

The William Brown Nimmo Charitable Trust

Eligibility: Older women living on a low income who were born, and permanently live, in Leith or Edinburgh.

Types of grants: Annual grants of about £80.

Annual grant total: Grants total about £20,000 each year. The trust usually accepts several new beneficiaries a year, but this is dependent on available income and existing beneficiaries failing to re-qualify for a grant.

Applications: On a form only available from 1 June from the correspondent. They should be returned by 31 July for consideration in September/October. Applicants are visited.

Correspondent: Grants Administrator, Shepherd & Wedderburn, 1 Exchange Crescent, Conference Square, Edinburgh EH3 8UL (0131 228 9900; fax: 0131 228 1222; email: info@shepwedd.co.uk)

The Police Aided Clothing Scheme of Edinburgh

Eligibility: Children in need who live in the area administered by City of Edinburgh Council.

Types of grants: In kind gifts of socks, shoes and a coat or jacket are given to children.

Exclusions: No cash grants are made, or help towards school uniforms.

Annual grant total: About 300 children are supported each year and grants total about £1,000.

Applications: Applications can be submitted at any time, by the individual or any third party. All applicants are visited in their homes by a police officer in uniform.

Correspondent: Administrator, Lothian & Borders Police Headquarters, Fettes Avenue, Edinburgh EH4 1RB (0131 311 3131; fax: 0131 440 6889)

The Surplus Fire Fund

Eligibility: Injured fire-fighters and widows and orphans of any who lost, or may lose, their lives through fires in Edinburgh.

Types of grants: One-off payments.

Annual grant total: In 2009/10 the fund had an income of £34,000. Grants previously totalled about £29,000.

Applications: In writing to the correspondent.

Correspondent: Grants Officer, Waverley Court, 4 East Market Street, Edinburgh, EH8 8BG

Other information: Grants are also made to organisations.

Scottish Borders

Black's Bequest

Eligibility: People in need who live in Coldstream and Coldstream Newton.

Types of grants: One-off grants according to need.

Annual grant total: About £300 a year.

Applications: In writing to the correspondent.

Correspondent: Anne Isles, Legal and Licensing Services Manager, Scottish Borders Council, Council Headquarters, Newtown St Boswells TD6 0SA (01835 825002; email: aisles@scotborders.gov.uk)

Christie Fund

Eligibility: People in need in Duns Parish.

Types of grants: One-off grants to a usual maximum of £200. Funds are available to help with specific items where the applicant does not have access to other means of funding.

Annual grant total: The trust usually has an income of less than £1,000.

Applications: In writing to the correspondent at any time, through a social worker, Citizens Advice or other welfare agency. Applications should include full details of the assistance needed, stating why funding is unavailable from other sources.

Correspondent: John Grant, Trustee, Iain Smith & Partners, 11 - 13 Murray Street,

Duns TD11 3DF (01361 882733; fax: 01361 883517)

The R S Hayward Trust

Eligibility: People in need who have been employed in Galashiels for at least 10 years, and have retired or become incapacitated, either permanently or temporarily, from work, and their wives or widows.

Types of grants: Recurrent grants of around £8 per week.

Annual grant total: Approximately £20,000 a year.

Applications: In writing to the correspondent.

Correspondent: Trust Administrator, c/o Pike & Chapman Solicitors, 36 Bank Street, Galashiels, Selkirkshire TD1 1ER (01896 752379)

The Elizabeth Hume Trust

Eligibility: People in need who live in the parish of Chirnside.

Types of grants: 'Grants are made at the sole discretion of the minister.'

Annual grant total: This trust generally has an income of around £19,000. No further information was available.

Applications: Applications can be made either directly by an individual or family member, through a third party such as a social worker or teacher, through an organisation such as a Citizens Advice or school or through a church elder.

Correspondent: The Minister, The Manse, The Glebe, Chirnside, Duns, Berwickshire TD11 3XL

Roxburghshire Landward Benevolent Trust

Eligibility: People in need who live in the Landward area of the former Roxburgh County Council.

Types of grants: One-off grants up to £500. Grants are normally given to assist people with health and social problems where government assistance is not available. Financial help can be towards travel to hospital, respite care, equipment such as wheelchairs, and the purchase of domestic equipment.

Exclusions: No grants to settle debts or to duplicate state aid.

Annual grant total: Grants to individuals generally total around £500. The trust also makes grants to organisations.

Applications: In writing to the correspondent. Applications can be submitted directly by the individual, through a social worker, Citizens Advice or other welfare agency, or through other third party on behalf of an individual. They are considered in April and October. Applicants will be visited by a trustee before any decision to make a payment is made.

West Lothian

The James Wood Bequest and the James Wood & Christina Shaw Bequests

Eligibility: There are three separate James Wood Bequests: the first is for poorer people who live in Armadale; the second for poorer people who live in Blackridge and Torphichen; and the third for people who live in Blackridge and Torphichen who are sick or in need. The Christina Shaw Bequest is also for people who are sick and in need who live in Armadale and Blackridge/Torphichen. For all trusts, applicants must have an income of less than £130 per week.

Types of grants: One-off grants at Christmas. The Christina Shaw Bequest gives grants for comforts and home help, whilst the others are given for general relief in need.

Few grants have been made in recent years due to lack of applicants.

Exclusions: Individuals in employment are not eligible for funding.

Annual grant total: In 2008/09 the trusts had a collective income of around £2,000.

Applications: Advertisements for applicants are placed in the local papers in November each year. Further information can be obtained from the correspondent.

Correspondent: Finance Manager, Finance Management Unit, West Lothian Council, West Lothian Civic Centre, Howden South Road, Livingston EH54 6FF (01506 775000)

Glasgow & West of Scotland

The Association for the Relief of Incurables in Glasgow & the West of Scotland

Eligibility: People over 18 years of age in financial need with long-term illnesses and are living at home. Applicants must be living in Glasgow or the West of Scotland.

Types of grants: Pensions of £388 a year paid quarterly. One-off grants of up to £350 per person, for specific needs such as telephone installation, washing machines and cookers.

Exclusions: No grants given to clear debts or towards holidays.

Annual grant total: In 2009 the charity had an income of £142,000. Previously grants have been made to approximately 350 people totalling £130,000.

Applications: Applications must be made through a social worker, Citizens Advice or another welfare agency on a form available from the correspondent. GP must confirm medical condition. Applications are considered quarterly with deadlines 14 days prior to each meeting.

Correspondent: BMK Wilson, Solicitors, BMK Wilson Solicitors, 90 St. Vincent Street, Glasgow, G2 5UB (0141 221 8004; fax: 0141 221 8088)

The Robert Hart Trust

Eligibility: Working men over 50 who live in Glasgow or the surrounding area and are in need.

Types of grants: One-off and recurrent grants according to need.

Annual grant total: Grants usually total about £1,000 each year.

Applications: In writing to the: Glasgow Society of Social Services, 30 George Square, Glasgow G2 1EG.

Correspondent: Trust Administrator, James Patrick and Muir, 44 New Street, Dalry, Ayrshire KA24 5AE (01294 832442)

Other information: The trust also gives small grants to institutions in Glasgow.

Merchants House of Glasgow

Eligibility: Pensioners who are in need and live in Glasgow and the West of Scotland.

Types of grants: Recurrent pensions are paid to help elderly people who are facing hardship.

Annual grant total: In 2009 the trust had an income of £931,000. Pensions usually total around £150,000 a year.

Applications: In writing to the correspondent at any time.

Correspondent: The Collector, 7 West George Street, Glasgow G2 1BA (0141 221 8272; fax: 0141 226 2275; email: theoffice@merchantshouse.org.uk; website: www.merchantshouse.org.uk)

Other information: The Merchants House administers several funds in trust, including the Inverclyde Bequest Fund for Seamen, RNVR Club (Scotland) Memorial Trust and the Commercial Travellers of Scotland Benevolent Fund for Widows and Orphans.

James Paterson's Trust

Eligibility: Women who have worked in factories or mills in the Glasgow area, consisting of the district of the City of Glasgow and the contiguous districts of Dumbarton, Clydebank, Bearsden and Milngavie, Bishopbriggs and Kirkintilloch, East Kilbride, Eastwood and Renfrew.

Types of grants: Grants are given to pay primarily for short term convalescent accommodation and occasionally for medical expenses and private accommodation in any private hospital.

Grants are usually one-off payments of around £250.

Annual grant total: In 2009 the trust had an income of £30,000. Grants to individuals usually total about £25,000.

Applications: In writing to the correspondent. Applications can be submitted directly by the individual or through a social worker, Citizens Advice or other welfare agency. They are considered throughout the year.

Correspondent: Alastair Campbell, Mitchells Roberton Solicitors, George House, 36 North Hanover Street, Glasgow G1 2AD (0141 552 3422; fax: 0141 552 2935)

Radio Clyde – Cash for Kids at Christmas

Eligibility: Families with children under 16 who live in west central Scotland, including Dumfries and Galloway, and are sick or underprivileged.

Types of grants: Christmas grants usually ranging from £15 to £25.

Annual grant total: In 2008/09 the charity had an unusually low income of £370,000. Grants to individuals usually total about £50,000.

Applications: On a form available from the correspondent, to be submitted by a head teacher, priest or minister who is aware of the family circumstances and will take responsibility for cashing the cheque. The deadline for applications is usually around the end of October.

Correspondent: Grants Manager, Radio Clyde Cash for Kids, 3 South Avenue, Clydebank Business Park, Glasgow, G81 2RX (0141 204 1025; email: cashforkids@radioclyde.com; website: www.cashforkids.org.uk)

Other information: Details of the scheme are broadcast on radio Clyde in the run up to Christmas. Grants are also awarded to organisations.

Mairi Semple Fund for Cancer Relief & Research

Eligibility: People with cancer who live in Kintyre or the Island of Gigha.

Types of grants: Provision of equipment and/or nursing help in the home and help with hospital travel costs for patients or relatives.

Exclusions: No grants are given to students for research.

Annual grant total: Grants usually total about £10,000 each year.

Applications: In writing through the doctor, nurse or church minister of the patient, at the relevant address:

(i) Minister, Killean & Kilchenzie Church, Manse, Muasdale, Tarbert, Argyll.

(ii) Doctor, The Surgery, Muasdale, Tarbert, Argyll.

(iii) Nurse, The Surgery (same address as (ii)).

Correspondent: Mrs Margaret S Semple, Secretary, Rhonadale, Muasdale, Tarbert, Argyll, PA29 6XD (01583 421234)

Strathclyde Police Benevolent Fund

Eligibility: Members and former members of the Strathclyde Police Force and former members of the constituent forces, their families and dependants.

Types of grants: One-off and recurrent grants according to need.

Annual grant total: In 2009 the fund had an income of £159,000. Grants usually total over £100,000 each year.

Applications: In writing to the correspondent. Applications are considered on a monthly basis.

Correspondent: Grants Manager, Strathclyde Police Federation, 151 Merrylee Road, Glasgow, G44 3DL (0141 633 2020; fax: 0141 633 0276; website: www.strathclydepolicefederation. org.uk)

Argyll & Bute

The Glasgow Bute Benevolent Society

Eligibility: People in need, particularly older people, who live in Bute. The length of time a person has lived in Bute and how long they have been connected with the area is taken into consideration.

Types of grants: The society does not award grants as such; suitable applicants are admitted to the Society's Roll of Pensioners and receive a pension payable half-yearly and a Christmas bonus payment. The half-yearly pension is about £50; the value and availability of the bonus depends on income available.

Annual grant total: In 2009 the society had an income of £19,000. Grants were made totalling around £15,000.

Applications: On a form available from the correspondent, with a supporting recommendation by a minister of religion, doctor, solicitor or other responsible person.

Correspondent: The Secretary, 29 St Vincent Place, Glasgow G1 2DT (0141 248 4134; fax: 0141 226 3118)

Dumfries & Galloway

Elizabeth Armstrong Charitable Trust

Eligibility: People in need living in Canonbie in Dumfriesshire.

Types of grants: One-off and recurrent grants according to need.

Annual grant total: This trust's income fluctuates between £400 and £1,000 each year.

Applications: In writing to the correspondent.

Correspondent: Kenneth Hill, Senior Partner, 38 High Street, Langholm, Dumfries & Galloway, DG13 0JH (01387 380428; fax: 01387 381144)

Samuel Elliot Bequest

Eligibility: Older people who are in need and live in the burgh of Lockerbie and the parishes of Dryfesdale and Johnstone.

Types of grants: Recurrent grants according to need.

Annual grant total: Grants total around £500 each year.

Applications: In writing to the correspondent. Dates for submission are advertised in the local newspaper.

Correspondent: Alex Haswell, Corporate Finance, Carruthers House, English Street, Dumfries DG1 2HP (01387 260031; fax: 01776 704819)

The Holywood Trust

Eligibility: Young people aged 15 to 25 living in the Dumfries and Galloway region, with a preference for people who are mentally, physically or socially disadvantaged.

Types of grants: One-off and recurrent grants of £50 to £500. The trust supports a wide range of causes, however applications which contribute to their personal development are more likely to receive support. This could include financial or material assistance to participate in education or training, access to employment, establish a home or involvement in a project or activity which will help the individual or their community.

Exclusions: No grants are given towards carpets or accommodation deposits.

Annual grant total: Grants to individuals total around £150,000 annually.

Applications: Forms are available from the correspondent, or can be downloaded from the trust's website. Applications are considered at least four times a year. The trust encourages applicants to provide additional information about any disadvantage which affects them where their application form has not given them an opportunity to do so. It also welcomes any supporting information from third party workers.

Correspondent: Richard Lye, Trust Administrator, Mount St Michael, Craigs Road, Dumfries DG1 4UT (01387 269176; fax: 01387 269175; email: funds@ holywood-trust.org.uk; website: www. holywood-trust.org.uk)

Other information: The trust also gives educational grants to individuals and supports groups and project applications which benefit young people.

Lockerbie & District Sick Benevolent Association

Eligibility: People in Lockerbie and the surrounding parishes who are in need, with a preference for older people.

Types of grants: Grants are given towards food, appliances, clothing, convalescence and so on.

Annual grant total: In 2009/10 the association had an income of £3,000.

Applications: In writing to the correspondent.

Correspondent: Mrs Rosemary V Scott, Henderland, Greenhill, Lockerbie, Dumfriesshire DG11 1JB

The Lockerbie Trust

Eligibility: People in need who live in Lockerbie.

Types of grants: One-off grants according to need. Occasionally annual payments will be considered but only in exceptional circumstances.

Exclusions: Education grants are not awarded where Scottish Office grants are available.

Annual grant total: In 2008/09 the trust had an income of £19,000. Grants totalled around £15,000 and were made to both individuals and organisations.

Applications: On a form available from the correspondent, to be submitted directly by the individual. Applicants should note that the availability of grants from other sources will be taken into account in assessing applications.

Correspondent: Alex Haswell, Service Director, Chief Executive Services, Dumfries & Galloway Council, Council Offices, English Street, Dumfries DG1 2DD (01387 260006; fax: 01387 260034)

The James McKune Mortification

Eligibility: People in need who are natives of the parish of Kirkbean and have lived there for 20 years.

Types of grants: Annual pensions of £30 a year.

Annual grant total: In 2009 the trust had an income of £7,200. Grants usually total around £500 a year.

Applications: On a form available from the correspondent. Applications should be submitted directly by the individual before 31 January for consideration in March.

Correspondent: The Trustees, Blawearie, Kirkbean, Dumfries DG2 8DW

Nithsdale District Charities

Eligibility: People in need who live in the former Nithsdale district.

Types of grants: The council administers a number of very small trusts. The largest has a grant total of £400.

Annual grant total: Previous research indicates that grants total about £8,000 each year.

Applications: In writing to the correspondent.

Correspondent: Alex Haswell, Deputy Secretary, Dumfries & Galloway District Council, Council Offices, English Street, Dumfries, DG1 2DD (01387 260000)

The Nivison Trust

Eligibility: People in need who live in Sanquhar.

Types of grants: Quarterly payments of £20.

Annual grant total: About £1,000.

Applications: In writing to the correspondent.

Correspondent: Alex Haswell, Service Director, Dumfries & Galloway District Council, Carruthers House, English Street, Dumfries DG1 2HP

John Primrose Trust

Eligibility: People in need with a connection to Dumfries and Maxwelltown by parentage or by living there.

Types of grants: Grants of £100 to £150 are given twice a year to 10 to 20 older people.

Annual grant total: About £14,000, half of which is given to individuals for relief-in-need and educational purposes.

Applications: On an application form available from the correspondent, to be considered in June and December.

Correspondent: The Trustees, 92 Irish Street, Dumfries DG1 2PF

East Ayrshire

The Shearer Bequest

Eligibility: Unmarried women and widows in need, who are native to Kilmarnock.

Types of grants: Grants are given for general relief-in-need purposes.

Annual grant total: Over the last six years the trust's annual income has ranged from £11 to £9,500.

Applications: In writing to the correspondent.

Correspondent: Grants Administrator, 13 Central Avenue, Kilmarnock, Ayrshire KA1 4PT

Miss Annie Smith Mair Bequest

Eligibility: People in need who live, or were born in, Newmilns.

Types of grants: One-off grants usually in the range of £50 to £1,000, towards household essentials, minor house or garden maintenance work/adaptations, short breaks, mobility and personal aids, clothing, and small donations for living expenses.

Annual grant total: Grants average about £4,000 per year.

Applications: On a form available from the correspondent or from the East Ayrshire Council website (www.east-ayrshire.gov.uk/corpres/admin/trusts/trusts.asp). Applications can be made directly by the individual or through a GP, social worker, Citizens Advice or other welfare agency.

Please note: if an application is being made on health grounds alone, a GP's certification of need will also be required.

Correspondent: Gillian Hamilton, Administrative Officer, Democratic Services, East Ayrshire Council, Council Headquarters, London Road, Kilmarnock KA3 7BU (01563 576093; email: gillian.hamilton@east-ayrshire.gov.uk; website: www.east-ayrshire.gov.uk)

The Archibald Taylor Fund

Eligibility: Unmarried women in need, who are aged 45 or over and originate from, or live in, Kilmarnock.

Types of grants: Grants are given for the provision of special nursing or convalescent treatment and convalescent holidays of up to three weeks. Previously, awards have ranged from £250 to £1,000.

Annual grant total: In 2008/09 the fund had an income of £13,000.

Applications: On a form available from the correspondent, for consideration throughout the year. Applications can be made either directly by the individual, or through a social worker, Citizens Advice or other third party such as a GP. The following should be submitted with the application: details of the proposed holiday and cost, household income, employer's certificate of earnings and a declaration by a medical attendant.

Correspondent: Administration Manager, East Ayrshire Council, Council Headquarters, London Road, Kilmarnock KA3 7BU (01563 576093; fax: 01563 576245; email: gillian.hamilton@east-ayrshire.gov.uk)

East Renfrewshire

The Janet Hamilton Memorial Fund

Eligibility: People who are chronically sick or infirm, who live in the former burgh of Barrhead and are of pensionable age.

Types of grants: Postal orders of £15, distributed at Christmas.

Annual grant total: Grants usually total around £2,000 a year.

Applications: Directly by the individual on a form available from the correspondent. A signature from a doctor confirming the person's state of health is necessary, as well as a signed copy of his/her life certificate. Grants are distributed in early December.

Correspondent: Finance Department, East Renfrewshire Council, Council Headquarters, Eastwood Park, Rouken Glen Road, Giffnock, Glasgow G46 6UG (0141 577 3000)

Glasgow

Glasgow Dunbartonshire Benevolent Association

Eligibility: People born in the county of Dumbarton, or their children living in and around Glasgow, who are in need.

Types of grants: One-off and recurrent grants to relieve low incomes, illness or a sudden emergency.

Annual grant total: Grants usually total about £2,000 each year.

Applications: In writing to the correspondent. Applications are considered throughout the year.

Correspondent: General Secretary, City of Glasgow Society of Social Service, Fifth Floor, 30 George Square, Glasgow G2 1EG (0141 248 3535)

Incorporation of Bakers of Glasgow

Eligibility: People who are members of the incorporation and their dependants.

Types of grants: One-off and recurrent grants according to need.

Annual grant total: Grants to individuals total about £500 each year.

Applications: In writing to the correspondent.

Correspondent: R Graham Davidson, 3 Newton Place, Glasgow G3 7PU (0141 332 3265; fax: 0141 332 2613; email: gdavidson@hillbrown.co.uk)

Other information: The exact date on which the Incorporation of Bakers was founded is uncertain but it is known that the Incorporation existed long prior to its first official mention in 1556.

Today the incorporation is engaged in works of charity and benevolence. Christmas and holiday gifts are paid to numerous needy pensioners and the incorporation provides prizes for students of baking and allied subjects at Glasgow College of Food Technology.

Lethbridge – Abell Charitable Bequest

Eligibility: People in Glasgow who are in need.

Types of grants: One-off grants, usually up to £300.

Annual grant total: Grants usually total around £1,000 per year.

Applications: In writing to the correspondent.

Correspondent: The Private Secretary to the Lord Provost, 266 George Street, Glasgow, G1 1QX

Francis Lipton Memorial Fund

Eligibility: Single mothers experiencing financial hardship and their children under 16 or between 16 and 21 years who have a physical or mental disability and are substantially dependent on their mother. Applicants must live within the city of Glasgow.

Types of grants: One-off and recurrent grants according to need.

Exclusions: 'Motherless' children are not eligible.

Annual grant total: In 2008/09 the trust had an income of £6,800 and a total expenditure of £8,400.

Applications: In writing to the correspondent or through a third party such as a social worker.

Correspondent: Mary McLean, Secretary, c/o City of Glasgow Society of Social Service, Fifth Floor, 30 George Square, Glasgow G2 1EG (0141 248 3535)

The Andrew & Mary Elizabeth Little Charitable Trust

Eligibility: People in need whose sole source of income is income support, disability benefit or pension, and who live in the city of Glasgow.

Types of grants: One-off and recurrent grants according to need.

Annual grant total: In 2008/09 the trust had an income of £46,000. Grants total about £56,000 a year, of which 80% is given to individuals and 20% to organisations.

Applications: In writing to the correspondent, to be submitted through social services. Applications should include financial details and are considered monthly.

Correspondent: R Munton, Low Beaton Richmond Solicitors, 20 Renfield Street, Glasgow, G2 5AP

The Lord Provost Charities Fund, the D M Stevenson Fund & the Lethbridge Abell Fund

Eligibility: People in need who live in Glasgow.

Types of grants: One-off and recurrent grants of up to £300.

Annual grant total: Grants usually total about £500 each year.

Applications: In writing to the correspondent. Applications should be submitted by a third party such as a recognised charity, Citizens Advice or social worker.

Correspondent: Fund Administrator, Glasgow City Council, 266 George Street, Glasgow G1 1QX (0141 287 2000)

Mrs Esther Ross Bequest

Eligibility: People in need who live in Glasgow. Preference is given to people who are elderly or disabled.

Types of grants: One-off grants of £50 for shoes, clothes, bedding or other essentials.

Exclusions: No grants are made towards holidays or respite care.

Annual grant total: Grants usually total around £1,500 per year.

Applications: In writing to the correspondent by a social worker or another individual of authority, who should supervise how the grant is spent. Applications are considered as received and should contain details of weekly or monthly income and expenditure.

Correspondent: Grant Administrator, Glasgow City Council, City Chambers, 266 George Street, Glasgow G1 1QX

The Trades House of Glasgow

Eligibility: People in need who live in Glasgow, especially those receiving only a pension.

Types of grants: One-off grants of between £5 and £5,000.

Annual grant total: About £100,000 in relief-in-need grants to individuals.

Applications: In writing to the correspondent.

Correspondent: The Clerk, Administration Centre, North Gallery – Trades Hall, 85 Glassford Street, Glasgow, G1 1UH (0141 553 1605; website: www.tradeshouse.org.uk/)

Other information: Grants are also made to organisations.

The Ure Elder Fund for Widows

Eligibility: Widows in need who live in Glasgow, particularly Govan.

Types of grants: Annual grants paid twice a year plus a bonus at Christmas.

Annual grant total: In 2008/09 the trust had an income £11,000.

Applications: On a form available from the correspondent. Applications can be submitted directly by the individual or through a third party. They are considered in April and October.

Correspondent: Eleanor Kerr, Maclay Murray and Spens Solicitors, 151 St Vincent Street, Glasgow G2 5NJ (0141 248 5011)

Inverclyde

The Gourock Coal & Benevolent Fund

Eligibility: People in need who live in the former burgh of Gourock. There is a preference for older people, especially people who live on their own.

Types of grants: Gas and electricity vouchers are available and coal deliveries can also be made.

Annual grant total: Grants usually total about £3,000 each year.

Applications: In writing to any minister or parish priest in the town, or the local branch of the WRVS (not to the correspondent). Applications are normally considered in December and can be submitted either directly by the individual or through a social worker, Citizens Advice or other welfare agency.

Correspondent: The Trustees, 4D Cragburn Gate, Albert Road, Gourock, Renfrewshire, PA19 1NZ

Seamans' Friend Charitable Society

Eligibility: Seafarers in need in Greenock and Port Glasgow.

Types of grants: One-off grants usually of about £150, distributed once a year at Christmas.

Annual grant total: About £800.

Applications: In writing to the correspondent.

Correspondent: William G Mitchell, Patten & Prentice Solicitors, 2 Ardgowan Square, Greenock PA16 8PP (01475 720306; fax: 01475 888127)

The Lady Alice Shaw-Stewart Memorial Fund

Eligibility: Female ex-prisoners recommended by the probation officer in the Inverclyde Council area.

Types of grants: On average one-off grants total about £200 each and are given for general welfare purposes, such as electrical goods, holidays and driving lessons.

Annual grant total: Grants usually total about £1,000 each year

Applications: In writing to the correspondent. Applications should be submitted by a probation officer on behalf of the individual.

Correspondent: Director of Finance, Inverclyde Council, Municipal Buildings, Greenock, Inverclyde PA15 1JA (01475 717171)

Other information: The council administers about 20 other small trusts for people living in Greenock, Gourock, Inverkip and Kilmalcolm.

Mrs Mary Sinclair's Trust

Eligibility: Older seafarers who were born or sailed out of Greenock, their widows and children, who are in need.

Types of grants: A twice yearly pension to each beneficiary of £12.

Annual grant total: Grants generally total around £500 a year.

Applications: Application forms can be obtained from the correspondent.

Correspondent: D I Banner, Neill Clerk & Murray Solicitors, 3 Ardgowan Square, Greenock PA16 8NW (01475 724522)

South Ayrshire

The James and Jane Knox Fund

Eligibility: Older men in need, preferably bachelors, in the parish of Monkton and Prestwick.

Types of grants: One-off and recurrent grants for the provision of comforts.

Annual grant total: About £1,000.

Applications: In writing to the correspondent directly by the individual with as much information as possible. Applications are considered as and when required.

Correspondent: Head of Legal and Administration Services, South Ayrshire Council, County Buildings, Wellington Square, Ayr, KA7 1DR (0300 123 0900)

Other information: South Ayrshire Council administers 93 smaller trusts, details of which can be obtained from the correspondent.

The Loudoun Bequest

Eligibility: People in need who live in Monkton and Prestwick.

Types of grants: Gifts of coal to individuals who meet the criteria.

Annual grant total: Grants usually total about £500 each year.

Applications: In writing to the correspondent directly by the individual, providing detailed information.

Correspondent: Valerie Andrews, Head of Legal and Administration, South Ayrshire

Council, County Buildings, Wellington Square, Ayr KA7 1DR (01292 612000)

West Dunbartonshire

Dumbarton Children's Trust

Eligibility: Children in Dumbarton and district up to the age of 18 who have physical, mental or sensory difficulties or are suffering the effects of deprivation.

Types of grants: On average 150 one-off grants are made a year of up to £100 per child according to need. Medical and disability equipment is only available where it is not provided by statutory services. Toys and educational aids/ equipment are available.

Exclusions: No grants are given for household equipment (unless specifically for children), debts or items which should be provided by statutory services.

Annual grant total: Grants usually total around £15,000 per year.

Applications: On a form available from the correspondent. Applications should be submitted by a social worker, health visitor or other third party and are considered every six weeks to two months. Deadlines for applications are a week before each meeting.

Correspondent: Liz Cochrane, Secretary, c/o Citizens Advice, 6–14 Bridge Street, Dumbarton G82 1NP (01389 841333)

Lennox Children's Trust

Eligibility: Children who are in need and live in the Dunbartonshire area.

Types of grants: One-off and recurrent grants according to need. Recent grants have been given for medical equipment, disability aids, toys and educational equipment.

Annual grant total: Grants usually total around £1,000 per year.

Applications: On a form available from the correspondent, to be submitted by a third party with a connection to the child.

Correspondent: Administrator, c/o Citizens Advice Bureau, 6–14 Bridge Street, Dumbarton G82 1NP (01389 765345)

Highlands & Islands

Lady McCorquodale's Charity Trust

Eligibility: People who are in need, with a preference for older people.

Types of grants: One-off and recurrent grants are given for day-to-day needs, such as clothing and food.

Annual grant total: In 2008/09 the trust had an income of £20,000 and a total expenditure of £18,000.

Applications: In writing to the correspondent. Applications can be submitted either directly by the individual or via a social worker, Citizens Advice or other third party.

Correspondent: Laura Gosling, Millbank Financial Services Ltd, 10–12 Cork Street, London W1S 3LW (020 7439 9061; email: charity@mfs.co.uk)

Other information: This trust also makes grants to organisations.

Dr Sutherland's Fund

Eligibility: People in need who live in the parishes of Olrig – Caithness and Kirkwall and St Ola in the Orkney Isles.

Types of grants: Grants of around £50 each typically.

Annual grant total: Grants usually total around £1,500 per year.

Applications: No grants given on application. The fund's administrators write to the relevant social work departments and ask for a list of eligible beneficiaries, who the administrators then contact.

Correspondent: Secretary, Stewarts & Murdochs, Tontine House, 8 Gordon Street, Glasgow, G1 3PL

Highland

Dr Forbes Inverness Trust

Eligibility: People with a medical or similar need who live in the former burgh of Inverness or immediately surrounding areas to the south of the Beauly/Inverness Firth.

Types of grants: Generally one-off grants to help with the cost of medical treatment and equipment, convalescence, food, clothing and travel expenses to visit sick relatives. Help has also been given with holidays for people who, from a medical point of view, would benefit from it.

Annual grant total: Grants usually total about £9,000 each year.

Applications: On a form available from the correspondent, can be submitted by the individual or through a recognised referral agency (e.g. social worker, Citizens Advice or doctor) or other third party. Forms are considered throughout the year and must be signed by the applicant's doctor. Supporting letters can also help the application.

Correspondent: D J Hewitson, Secretary & Treasurer, Munro & Noble Solicitors, 26 Church Street, Inverness IV1 1HX

(01463 221727; fax: 01463 225165; email: legal@munronoble.com)

The Highland Children's Trust

Eligibility: Children and young people in need who are under 25 and live in the Highlands.

Types of grants: One-off grants of £50 to £500 are available for the following purposes:

- Student hardship funding
- School or educational trips
- Family holidays
- Educational items for children with special educational needs

Exclusions: Grants are not given for postgraduate study, to pay off debts, nor to purchase clothing, footwear, food, furniture or cars and so on.

Annual grant total: Around £20,000.

Applications: On a form available from the correspondent. They can be submitted at any time either directly by the individual or through a social worker, Citizens Advice or other welfare agency. Applications must include details of income and savings.

Correspondent: Mrs Alison Harbinson, 105 Castle Street, Inverness IV2 3EA (01463 243872; fax: 01463 243872; email: info@hctrust.co.uk; website: www.hctrust.co.uk)

The Morar Trust

Eligibility: People who live in the community of Morar and environs.

Types of grants: Funds are used to support educational, social and charitable occasions in the local community. The trust has in the past assisted with payments for educational equipment, trips and festivities along with supporting the hospital, ambulance and welfare purposes. Grants are given in one-off payments.

Annual grant total: £1,000 for educational and welfare purposes.

Applications: In writing to the council via the correspondent or through a social or medical worker.

Correspondent: The Secretary, Mallaig and Morar Community Centre, West Bay, Mallaig, PH41 4PX

Miss M C Stuart's Legacy

Eligibility: Older people in need who live in Grantown and district.

Types of grants: In practice Christmas donations are made to Senior Citizens Welfare Association and individuals.

Annual grant total: Grants usually total around £3,000.

Applications: In writing to the correspondent at any time.

Correspondent: Director of Finance, Finance Department, The Highland

Council, Glenurquhart Road, Inverness, IV3 5NX

Shetland Islands

Shetland Charitable Trust

Eligibility: People who have disabilities or are of pensionable age and have been resident in Shetland for more than a year.

Types of grants: An annual payment is made at Christmas.

Annual grant total: In 2008/09 the trust had an income of £19 million. Previously, grants to individuals totalled £1.6 million, which were distributed through the Independence at Home scheme (£394,000), the Social Assistance scheme (£55,000), special equipment grants (£261,000), Christmas bonuses (£882,000) and replacing community alarms (£70,000).

Applications: Applications directly from the general public are not considered. The trustees meet every six to eight weeks.

Correspondent: Mary Anderson, 22–24 North Road, Lerwick, Shetland, ZE1 0NQ (01595 744992; fax: 01595 690206)

Other information: Grants are also given to organisations.

Western Isles

The William MacKenzie Trust

Eligibility: People who are older or in poor health and live in Stornoway.

Types of grants: One-off grants to enable individuals to continue living in their own homes. Recent grants have been given for house adaptations, reclining chairs and domestic equipment such as washing machines.

Annual grant total: In 2008/09 the trust had an income of £43,000. Grants were made totalling about £30,000.

Applications: In writing to the correspondent. Applications can be submitted directly by the individual, or through a social worker, Citizens Advice or other welfare agency.

Correspondent: Jack Kernahan, 26 Lewis Street, Stornoway, Isle of Lewis HS1 2JF (01851 702335; fax: 01851 706132; email: jack@mannjudd.co.uk)

Other information: The trust also makes grants to organisations.

3. WALES

Children's Leukaemia Society

Eligibility: Children under 16 who are in need and have leukaemia. Grants are made to those living in south Wales and the West Country.

Types of grants: One-off gifts to those in need. Previously, a gift of the child's choice was made to them while they were in hospital for example, a TV, video, or a games console.

Annual grant total: In 2009/10 the society had assets of £107,000 and an income of £53,000. Holidays and gifts made to children amounted to £19,000.

Applications: In writing to the correspondent.

Correspondent: Peter Robinson, 140 Broadway, Cardiff, CF24 1NL

Other information: The society also makes caravans available for the children when they are well enough and their families, to have a free holiday.

LATCH (Llandough Aim to Treat Children with Cancer and Leukaemia with Hope)

Eligibility: Children who have cancer or leukaemia (including tumours) and have been referred to the Paediatric Oncology Unit at The Children's Hospital for Wales.

Types of grants: One-off and recurrent grants for children and the families of children who are in need of financial assistance. Recent grants have been given for travel expenses, living costs, car repairs, washing machines, holidays and outings.

Annual grant total: In 2009 the charity had assets of £2.8 million and an income of £630,000. Grants were made totalling £151,000.

Applications: Through one of the LATCH social workers, who submit applications for consideration by the trust.

Correspondent: Grants Manager, LATCH Office, Children's Hospital for Wales, Heath Park, Cardiff CF14 4XW (029 2074 8858/9; fax: 029 2074 8868; email: info@latchwales.org; website: www. latchwales.org)

Other information: The charity also supports the development of the specialist medical care the Unit provides for the children and their families.

The North Wales Society for the Blind

Eligibility: People in need who are registered blind or partially sighted and live in the county authorities of Gwynedd, Anglesey, Conwy, Denbigh, Wrexham and Powys.

Types of grants: One-off grants are given according to need. Recent grants have been given for assistive equipment, holidays, hospital travel expenses and computer equipment/software to aid communication.

Exclusions: Grants are not given if there is a statutory obligation to provide such items.

Annual grant total: In 2008/09 the society had assets of £347,000, an income of £216,000. Grants were made totalling £9,000 to a single beneficiary, Bangor Resource Centre.

Applications: On a form available from the correspondent. Applications should be submitted through a social worker or rehabilitation officer and are considered monthly. All other potential sources of funding should be explored before making an application to the society.

Correspondent: G J Bowen, Director, 325 High Street, Bangor, Gwynedd, LL57 1YB (01248 353604; email: admin. nwsb@btconnect.com; website: www.nwsb. org.uk)

Other information: The society also provides information and counselling services and promotes the interests of blind and partially sighted people living in the area.

The Welsh Rugby Charitable Trust

Eligibility: People who have been severely injured whilst playing rugby football in Wales, and their dependants.

Types of grants: One-off grants to help injured players regain their independence. Grants can be made towards cars, wheelchairs, hoists, domestic aids, holidays and Christmas gifts.

Annual grant total: In 2008/09 the trust had an income of £154,000 and a total expenditure of £118,000. Grants totalled around £70,000.

Applications: In writing to the correspondent, including the circumstances of the injury and the effect it has on the applicant's career. Information on the financial position before and after the accident should also be included. Applications are considered every two months (or sooner in emergency cases) and can be submitted either directly by the individual or by a club representative. Players who have been seriously injured but not permanently disabled are usually visited by the trust to assess the degree of need before any grant is made.

Correspondent: Edward Jones, Hon. Secretary, 55 West Road, Bridgend, Mid Glamorgan, CF31 4HQ (01656 653042; email: ehjones100@googlemail.com; website: www.wrct.org.uk)

The Widows, Orphans & Dependants Society of the Church in Wales

Eligibility: Widows, orphans and dependants of deceased clergy of the Church in Wales only, who are living on a low income.

Types of grants: One-off grants in the form of birthday, Christmas and Easter bonuses.

Annual grant total: In 2009 the society had assets of £521,000 and an income of £92,000, nearly all of which was given in grants.

Applications: In writing to the correspondent, including details of the individual's income and their relationship to the relevant member of the clergy and the last parish they served in. Applications can be considered at any time. Grants should be made through one of the six diocesan committees of the Church in Wales.

Correspondent: Louise Davies, 39 Cathedral Road, Cardiff CF11 9XF (02920 348228; email: louisedavies@ churchinwales.org.uk; website: www. churchinwales.org.uk)

Mid-Wales

Ceredigion

The Margaret and Alick Potter Charitable Trust

Eligibility: People with all types of dementia (including Alzheimer's disease) and their families who live in North Ceredigion.

Types of grants: Grants given according to need.

Annual grant total: In 2008/09 the trust had an income of £5,200 and a total expenditure of £10,000.

Applications: In writing to the correspondent.

Correspondent: Joan Miller, Y Nyth, Capel Bangor, Aberystwyth, SY23 3LR (01970 880637)

Other information: The trust also makes grants to local organisations.

Powys

The Brecknock Association for the Welfare of the Blind

Eligibility: Blind and partially-sighted people living in Brecknock.

Types of grants: One-off grants at Christmas and for special equipment/ special needs, for example, cookers and talking books.

Annual grant total: Grants average around £1,700 a year, though the actual grant figure tends to fluctuate quite widely.

Applications: In writing to the correspondent, to be considered when received.

Correspondent: E J Vince, Ken Dy Gwair, Aber, Talybont-on-Usk, Brecon, LD3 7YS (01874 676202)

The Brecknock Welfare Trust

Eligibility: People in need who live in the town of Brecon.

Types of grants: One-off grants in kind according to need, such as electrical goods, clothing, medical and disabled equipment and furniture.

Exclusions: Grants are in kind and no cash awards are made.

Annual grant total: Over the last five years the trust's annual expenditure has ranged from £0 to £6,200. Grants are primarily made to organisations.

Applications: In writing to the correspondent. Applications should be submitted through a recognised referral agency (such as a social worker, Citizens Advice or doctor and so on).

Correspondent: Gail Rofe, Brecon Town Council, The Guildhall, High Street, Brecon, Powys LD3 7AL (01874 622884; email: brecon.guildhall@btinternet.com)

The Llanidloes Relief-in-Need Charity

Eligibility: People in need who live in the communities of Llanidloes and Llanidloes Without only.

Types of grants: One-off grants for fuel, equipment for people who are disabled and to families and students in need.

Annual grant total: About £1,000.

Applications: In writing to the correspondent. Applications should be made through social service, doctors, Citizens Advice or churches.

Correspondent: Mrs S J Jarman, Clerk, Llwynderw, Old Hall, Llanidloes, Powys SY18 6PW (01686 412636)

The Montgomery Welfare Fund

Eligibility: People in need who live permanently in the ecclesiastical parish of Montgomery (not the county).

Types of grants: One-off grants ranging from £25 to £100. Reapplications can be made. Grants cover a wide range of needs.

Exclusions: No grants to pay rates, tax or other public funds.

Annual grant total: Grants usually total around £2,500 per year.

Applications: In writing to the correspondent. Applications can be submitted directly by the individual or family member. Applications can be received all year round.

Correspondent: J Sexton, Maviri, Withy Avenue Forden, Welshpool, Powys SY21 8NJ (01938 580494)

Other information: Grants can also be given to individuals for education, 'development in life' and so on.

North Wales

The Corwen College Pension Charity

Eligibility: Needy widows or widowers of clergy of the Church in Wales who have held office in the district of Merionydd in Gwynedd or the communities of Betws Gwerfil Goch, Corwen Gwyddelern, Llandrillo, Llangar and Llansantffraid Glyndyfrdwy (all in Clwyd).

Types of grants: Recurrent grants according to need.

Annual grant total: Grants generally total around £1,000 a year.

Applications: In writing to the correspondent, for consideration in February.

Correspondent: Diane McCarthy, The Diocese of St Asaph, Diocesan Office, High Street, St Asaph, Denbighshire LL17 0RD (01745 582245; fax: 01745 530078; email: dianemccarthy@churchinwales.org. uk)

The North Wales Association for Spina Bifida & Hydrocephalus

Eligibility: People with spina bifida and/or hydrocephalus who live in North Wales, i.e. the counties of Conwy, Denbighshire, Gwynedd, Flintshire, Isle of Anglesey and Wrexham.

Types of grants: One-off grants ranging from £50 to £400 to help with maximising 'opportunities for independence' for people with spina bifida or hydrocephalus in order to 'extend their choices and so help their integration into society'.

Grants are given to support mobility needs, funeral expenses, household items and travel expenses incurred when visiting members in hospital out of the area.

Exclusions: Grants are not given for housing adaptations and improvements, house purchase or pilgrimages. No grants for things that are within the remit of the Local Authority. No loans.

Annual grant total: In 2009/10 the association had an income of £13,000 and a total expenditure of £15,000.

Applications: Applications must be submitted by the association's area advisers and are considered monthly. Applications for assistance must be related to the person's disability and the statutory authorities' responsibility should be determined. Only one welfare grant can be given in 12 months, except in exceptional circumstances.

Correspondent: Mike Mason, 14 Holland Drive, Abergele, LL22 9AF (01745 825738; email: northwalesasbah@hotmail.co.uk; website: www.asbah.org)

The North Wales Police Benevolent Fund

Eligibility: Members of the North Wales Police Force and former members of this and previous forces amalgamated within constituent forces, and their families and immediate dependants who are in need.

Types of grants: One-off and recurrent grants according to need. Grants are also made at Christmas.

Annual grant total: In 2009/10 the fund had an income of £10,000 and an unusually low expenditure of £500 (£5,100 in 2008/09).

Applications: In writing to the correspondent. Applications are considered quarterly, although urgent applicants can be considered as they arrive.

Correspondent: Mel Jones, North Wales Police Federation, 311 Abergele Road, Old Colwyn, Colwyn Bay LL29 9YF (01492 805404)

The North Wales Psychiatric Fund

Eligibility: People in North Wales who are mentally ill and are under the care of a social worker or health professional.

Types of grants: One-off grants for clothes, furniture, holidays and learning courses.

Exclusions: There are no grants available for the payment of debts.

Annual grant total: Grants average around £5,000 a year.

Applications: In writing to the correspondent through a social worker or health professional, including details of income and other possible grant sources. Applications are considered throughout the year.

Correspondent: Mr A Banks, Finance Department, Stanley Hospital, Upper Denbigh Road, St Asaph LL17 0RS (01745 589646)

The Evan & Catherine Roberts Home

Eligibility: People who live within a 40-mile radius of the Bethesda Welsh Methodist Church in Old Colwyn.

Types of grants: One-off grants ranging from £50 to £150.

Annual grant total: In 2009 the trust had an income of £2,900 and a total expenditure of £5,100.

Applications: On a form available from the correspondent.

Correspondent: Ken Owen, Ael Y Garth, 81 Bryn Avenue, Yn Conwy LL29 8AH (01492 515209)

Elizabeth Williams Charities

Eligibility: People in need who live in the communities of St Asaph, Bodelwyddan, Cefn and Waen in Denbighshire.

Types of grants: One-off grants, generally between £50 and £100, are given as Christmas bonuses for people who are older, to families with parents suffering serious illnesses and for particular needs.

Exclusions: Grants are not given for aid that can be met specifically by public funds, for private education or if the grant would affect a claimant's benefit from the DWP.

Annual grant total: Grants usually total around £7,000 per year.

Applications: In writing to the correspondent, to be submitted either directly by the individual or through a social worker, Citizens Advice or other welfare agency. Applications can also be submitted via a trustee. They are generally considered in November, although specific cases can be considered at any time.

Correspondent: Mrs Alison R Alexander, Arfon Cottage, 19 Roe Parc, St Asaph, Denbighshire LL17 0LD (01745 583798; email: alison.alexander@btinternet.com)

Anglesey

Anglesey Society for the Welfare of Handicapped People

Eligibility: People living in Anglesey who have tuberculosis or any other disease, illness or disability.

Types of grants: One-off or recurrent grants according to need.

Annual grant total: Around £2,000 each year is given in grants to individuals.

Applications: In writing to the correspondent.

Correspondent: Hugh Neville Pritchard, 5 Cwm Tecaf, Rhosybol, Amlwch, Gwynedd LL68 9PU (01407 831496)

Other information: The trust also makes grants to organisations.

John Theodore Wood Charity

Eligibility: Pensioners in need, especially married couples, who live in Anglesey. Women must be over 60 and men over 65.

Types of grants: One-off grants towards warm clothing, bed linen, coal and towards heating bills and telephone installation in isolated houses. Grants range from £100 to £200.

Exclusions: Help cannot be given where statutory provision is available.

Annual grant total: Grants average around £2,000 a year.

Applications: On a form available from the correspondent. Applications can be submitted directly by the individual or through a social worker, Citizens Advice, other welfare agency or other third party. Applications are considered in April.

Correspondent: Mrs Brenda Randall, Trust Secretary, Trefnant, Chapel Street, Menai Bridge, Anglesey LL59 5HW (01248 712478)

Conwy

Conwy Welsh Church Acts Fund

Eligibility: People in need living in the County Borough of Conwy.

Types of grants: One-off grants ranging from £50 to £2,000, for relief of poverty and sickness, financial aid for older people, medical treatment, help for people on probation, assistance for the blind or visually impaired and to relieve emergencies and disasters.

Exclusions: Grants are not made to individuals for sport or tuition fees.

Annual grant total: The fund generates approximately £10,000 per annum for distribution.

Applications: On a form available from the correspondent, to be submitted directly by the individual or through a third party. The closing date for applications is the first week in October, for consideration in November/December.

Correspondent: Mrs Catherine Dowber, Conwy County Borough Council, Bodlondeb, Conwy LL32 8DU (01492 576201 - For Welsh Language Officer call 01492 576130; email: cath. dowber@conwy.gov.uk)

Other information: The fund also supports organisations.

Denbighshire

The Freeman Evans St David's Day Denbigh Charity

Eligibility: People in need who are older, in poor health or who have a disability and live in Denbigh and Henllan.

Types of grants: One-off grants towards disability aids, furniture, travel costs, home adaptations, Christmas gifts and so on.

Annual grant total: In 2008/09 the charity made five grants to individuals totalling just under £5,000. The rest were made to organisations which amounted to £25,000.

Applications: In writing to the correspondent. Applications can be made either directly by the individual or through a third party such as a social worker, Citizens Advice or other welfare agency. The trustees meet regularly throughout the year to consider applications.

Correspondent: Medwyn Jones, Denbigh Town Council, Town Hall, Crown Square, Denbigh, Clwyd LL16 3TB (01745 815 984; email: townclerk@denbightowncouncil. gov.uk)

Other information: Grants are also given for educational purposes.

Flintshire

Flintshire Welsh Church Acts Fund

Eligibility: People who are sick or who have disabilities and are living in Flintshire.

Types of grants: One-off and recurrent grants, ranging between £100 and £500.

Annual grant total: In 2008/09 grants to four individuals totalled £800.

Applications: On a form available from the correspondent. Applications are considered quarterly.

Correspondent: Philip Latham, Funds and Treasury, Flintshire County Council, County Hall, Mold, CH7 6NA (01352 702264; fax: 01352 702279; email: philip.latham@flintshire.gov.uk)

Other information: This trust was previously listed as County Council of Clwyd Welsh Church Acts Fund.

It also makes grants to organisations.

The Owen Jones Charity

Eligibility: People in need who live in Northop.

Types of grants: One-off and recurrent grants according to need.

Annual grant total: In 2008/09 the charity made grants to individuals totalling £700, which included several university students and three local primary schools in educational projects.

The charity states that it has struggled to identify people eligible for support and hopes that in future years more of its expenditure can go to individuals in need.

Applications: In writing to the correspondent. An application form for students to use is currently being drafted and should be used when available.

Correspondent: Jack Wolstenholme, Secretary, 18 St Peter's Park, Northop, Mold, Clwyd CH7 6DP (01352 840739)

Other information: The charity also makes grants to local schools.

Gwynedd

The Freeman Evans St David's Day Ffestiniog Charity

Eligibility: People who are older, in poor health, or who have disabilities and live in the districts of Blaenau Ffestiniog and Llan Ffestiniog as they were prior to the 1974 reorganisation.

Types of grants: One-off and recurrent grants for home adaptations, specialist chairs, stair-lifts, electric wheelchairs and phone lifelines.

Annual grant total: In 2009/10 the charity had assets of £1.2 million and an income of £59,000. Grants were made totalling £37,000.

Applications: Applications can be submitted in writing directly by the individual or through a recognised referral agency such as a social worker, minister of religion, councillor, Citizens Advice or doctor. Applications are considered by the trustees twice a year, though urgent cases can be dealt with between meetings.

Correspondent: Maldwyn Evans, Natwest Bank plc, Merionnydd Business Centre, Bridge Street, Dolgellau, Gwynedd LL40 1AU (01341 421242)

Wrexham

William and John Jones Trust

Eligibility: People who are sick, convalescing, disabled or infirm in the county of Wrexham.

Types of grants: Grants for respite care in residential and nursing homes and convalescence. Grants for appliances and surgical aids not readily available through the health service are also considered.

Annual grant total: In 2009 the trust had both an income and a total expenditure of £31,000.

Applications: In writing to the correspondent.

Correspondent: Mrs Melissa Thomas, College House, 1 Temple Row, Wrexham LL13 8LY (01978 261684)

The Ruabon & District Relief-in-Need Charity

Eligibility: All People who are considered to be in need who live in the county borough of Wrexham, which covers the community council districts of Cefn Mawr, Penycae, Rhosllanerchrugog (including Johnstown) and Ruabon.

Types of grants: One-off and occasionally recurrent grants of up to £200. Grants can be towards installation of a telephone, heating costs, children's clothing, cookers, furniture, musical instruments, electric wheelchairs, clothing for adults in hospital, travel costs for hospital visits and books and travel for university students. One-off grants in kind are also given. On average, 15 grants are given by the charity each year.

Exclusions: Grants are not given for instigating bankruptcy proceedings. Loans are not given.

Annual grant total: About £1,400 in educational and relief-in-need grants.

Applications: In writing to the correspondent either directly by the individual or a family member, through a third party such as a social worker or teacher, or through an organisation such as Citizens Advice or a school. Applications are considered on an ongoing basis.

Correspondent: J R Fenner, Secretary, Cyncoed, 65 Albert Grove, Ruabon, Wrexham LL14 6AF (01978 820102; email: jamesrfenner@tiscali.co.uk)

The Wrexham & District Relief in Need Charity

Eligibility: People in need who live in the former borough of Wrexham or the communities of Abenbury, Bersham, Bieston, Broughton, Brymbo, Esclusham Above, Esclusham Below, Gresford, Gwersyllt and Minera in Wrexham.

Types of grants: One-off or recurrent grants according to need ranging from £40 to £500. For example, grants have been given towards the cost of maternity necessities, household equipment, wheelchairs, clothing and a stairlift.

Annual grant total: In 2009 the charity had an income of £15,000 and a total expenditure of £14,000.

Applications: In writing to the correspondent. Applications should be submitted directly by the individual, or by a third party, and should include full details of the applicant's weekly income and expenditure together with the cost of the item required where applicable. Applications are considered throughout the year.

Correspondent: P J Blore, Clerk, 49 Norfolk Road, Borras Park, Wrexham LL12 7RT (01978 356901; email: panda@chezblore.wanadoo.co.uk)

South Wales

Gwalia Housing Trust

Eligibility: People in need who live in areas where Grwp Gwalia Cyf owns properties (south Wales, including Newport, Haverfordwest, Newtown, Machynlleth, Carmarthenshire, Swansea and Neath Port Talbot).

Types of grants: One-off grants for housing related needs.

Annual grant total: In 2008/09 the trust had assets of £1.5 million and an income of £117,000. Grants to individuals totalled £18,000.

Applications: On a form available from the correspondent or to download from the website. Applications can be submitted directly by the individual or through an appropriate third party and should include a supporting letter. They are considered on a quarterly basis.

Correspondent: Sarah Rowland, Trust Administrator, Grwp Gwalia Cyf, Ty Gwalia, 7–13 The Kingsway, Swansea, SA1 5JN (01792 460609; fax: 01792 466198; email: ght@gwalia.com; website: www.gwalia.com/main.cfm)

Other information: The trust provides housing for people in necessitous circumstances, particularly older people, students and those living with disabilities. The trust also makes grants to organisations.

The Harley Charity (formerly The Honourable Miss Frances Harley Charity)

Eligibility: (i) Church of England clergy and their widows/widowers who are in need and live primarily, but not exclusively, in the diocese of Hereford.

(ii) People who are blind, in need and are members of the Church of England. Usually grants are given to those people living within the area defined above.

Types of grants: One-off grants, but individuals who receive a grant can reapply each year.

Annual grant total: Grants usually total around £1,000 each year.

Applications: In writing to the correspondent.

Correspondent: Thomas Davies, Trustee, Elgar House, Holmer Road, Hereford HR4 9SF (01432 352222)

Other information: When funds allow, the charity also supports Hereford Cathedral and other local churches and charities.

James Edward Harris Trust

Eligibility: People in need who live in South Wales. There is a preference for older people 'of good character' (described as 'gentlefolk'), who are in distressed circumstances and in need of regular assistance through no fault of their own.

Types of grants: Regular grants of between £100 and £1,400 a year, given in quarterly payments. One-off grants are very rarely given.

Exclusions: No grants for students.

Annual grant total: In 2008/09 the trust had an income of £15,000 and a total expenditure of £11,000.

Applications: In writing either directly by the individual or through a recognised referral agency (e.g. social worker, Citizens Advice or doctor) or other third party. Grants are made in January, April, July and October.

Correspondent: Richard H Read, Holmlea, Bradford Place, Penarth, CF64 1AF (029 2070 8258; email: richard. read@culver-holdings.com)

Local Aid for Children & Community Special Needs

Eligibility: People with special needs/learning difficulties, between the ages of 3 and 30, who live in Swansea or Neath Port Talbot.

Types of grants: One-off grants or grants in kind ranging from £50 to £150 for specialist equipment such as a specialist bed, chair or bike, or towards the costs of travel.

Exclusions: No grants are given for items which should be funded by statutory sources.

Annual grant total: In 2008/09 the charity had assets of £62,000 and an income of £109,000.

Applications: In writing to the correspondent, including confirmation that the amount requested is not available from statutory sources. Applications should be submitted through a social worker, Citizens Advice or other welfare agency or professional. They are considered quarterly.

Correspondent: Sandra Anne Mylan, Secretary, 89 Clase Road, Morriston, Swansea, SA6 8DY (01792 405041; email: terrance.richardson@ntlworld.com; website: www.localaid.co.uk)

Other information: Grants are occasionally made to individuals in need, however the majority of expenditure is allocated to funding the charity's own projects working with children with disabilities.

The South Wales Police Benevolent Fund

Eligibility: Serving or retired members of the South Wales Police or constituent force pre-1968 and their dependants, who are in need.

Types of grants: One-off and recurrent grants to meet relief in cases of financial need for those who are sick, convalescent, disabled, infirm, poor or aged. Recent grants have been made to assist with travel expenses to and from a police convalescent home; to assist in buying orthopaedic beds for older people with disabilities and specialist equipment for children with disabilities in hospitals; to assist in travel expenses for specialist treatment in hospitals; and to help with financial hardship 'not brought about by folly'.

Exclusions: Grants are not made for private medical treatment or for holidays of convalescence other than at a police home. Loans are not given.

Annual grant total: In 2007/08 the trust made welfare payments totalling £400, death benefits to 30 individuals totalling £15,000 and benevolence assistance to 15 individuals totalling £27,000.

Applications: On a form available from the correspondent. Applications should be submitted either by the individual or by any committee member or member of the Force's Welfare Staff on behalf of the individual. Applications are considered quarterly, but emergency payments can be made more quickly.

Correspondent: Head of Performance Management, Communications Division, Cowbridge Road, Bridgend, Mid Glamorgan CF31 3SU (01656 869342; website: www.south-wales.police.uk)

Other information: At the time of writing (winter 2010) the charity's accounts for 2008/09 were overdue at the Charity Commission.

Vision Impaired West Glamorgan

Eligibility: People who are registered blind or partially sighted and live in the areas of the city and county of Swansea and Neath Port Talbot.

Types of grants: One-off grants for special items for blind people (for example RNIB aids) and towards computer/technical equipment. Items costing less than £25 cannot be considered, with the exception of big button telephones. In addition to these grants the association loans out equipment. Grants usually range from £25 to £300.

Exclusions: No grants for domestic/household equipment.

Annual grant total: In 2008/09 the trust had an unusually low income and expenditure of £1,000 and £3,200 respectively, compared with an income of £11,000 and expenditure of £19,000 in 2007/08. Grants were made totalling about £3,000.

Applications: Applications should be made on a form via a specialist social worker for visual impairment based at the Sensory Impairment Teams in Swansea and Neath Port Talbot. If the grant is made as part of the total cost of items required, the association needs details of other sources/charities that will be making up the balance. Applications are considered continually, subject to funds available.

Correspondent: Pini Patel, City & County Of Swansea Council, Civic Centre, Oystermouth Road, Swansea, SA1 3SN (01792 637731; email: karen.cobb@ swansea.gov.uk)

Other information: The trust was formally known as the West Glamorgan County Blind Welfare Association.

Cardiff

The Cardiff Caledonian Society

Eligibility: People of Scottish nationality and their families, who live in Cardiff or the surrounding district and are in need.

Types of grants: One-off grants are given for clothing, food, household bills, travel expenses and furniture. Support may be given to people who are homeless, disabled or affected by hardship.

Annual grant total: Grants usually total around £7,000 each year, although most of this is given in grants to organisations.

Applications: In writing to the correspondent. Applications can be submitted directly by the individual or through a social worker, Citizens Advice or other welfare agency at any time. Applications are considered on a regular basis.

Correspondent: Mrs Cathy Rogers, 2 Llandinam Crescent, Cardiff, CF14 2RB (02920 623 680)

Other information: Grants are also made for educational purposes.

Cardiff Citizens Charity

Eligibility: People in need who live in the city of Cardiff.

Types of grants: One-off grants in the range of £100 to £400 for funeral expenses, clothes, specialist computer software, household appliances and so on.

Exclusions: No grants are made for educational purposes.

Annual grant total: On average the charity has an annual total expenditure of around £500.

Applications: On a form available from the correspondent, to be submitted through a recognised referral agency (such as a social worker, Citizens Advice or doctor) or other third party. Evidence of weekly/monthly expenditure must be submitted. Trustees meet twice yearly to consider applications.

Correspondent: Paul Leverett, County Events Coordinator, Cardiff County Council, City Hall, Cardiff CF10 3ND (02920 871769)

Other information: This charity was formally known as the Cardiff Charity for Special Relief.

The Duffryn Trust

Eligibility: People in need with a preference for those who live in Cardiff.

Types of grants: One-off and recurrent grants according to need.

Annual grant total: In 2008/09 the trust had an income of £7,000 and a total expenditure of £6,000. Grants have averaged around £7,500 over the last five years.

Applications: In writing to the correspondent.

Correspondent: D C Williams, 89 Cyncoed Road, Cardiff, CF23 5SD

The Poor's Charity of Margaret Evans

Eligibility: People in need who live in the parish of Roath, Cardiff.

Types of grants: One-off grants, Christmas gifts and heating allowances.

Annual grant total: In 2009 the trust had an income of £4,200 and a total expenditure of £3,000.

Applications: In writing to the correspondent.

Correspondent: Sue Oxenham, 5 Melrose Avenue, Penylan, Cardiff CF23 9AR (029 2045 5272)

Carmarthenshire

The Abergwili Relief-in-Need Charity

Eligibility: People in need who live in the parish of Abergwili.

Types of grants: One-off cash grants.

Annual grant total: This trust has an income of almost £1,000 but no expenditure has been made for the last five years.

Applications: In writing to the correspondent by the individual or the parent/guardian. Applications are considered at any time.

Correspondent: Mrs J M Kemp-Smith, Maenllwyd, Llanybri, Carmarthen, Dyfed, SA33 5JA (01267 211342)

Merthyr Tydfil

Merthyr Mendicants

Eligibility: People in need who live in the borough of Merthyr Tydfil.

Types of grants: One-off grants according to need. Recent grants have been given towards medical equipment not available from the National Health Service (providing it is recommended by a medical authority); Christmas parcels; holidays for children; telephone helplines for incapacitated people; and help with domestic equipment such as cookers, refrigerators, washing machines, bedding and beds.

Annual grant total: Grants average around £10,000 a year.

Applications: In writing to the correspondent, including information on any other sources of income. Applications can be submitted directly by the individual or through a social worker, Citizens Advice or other welfare agency.

Correspondent: A G Lane, 4 Georgetown Villas, Georgetown, Merthyr Tydfil, Mid Glamorgan CF48 1BD (01685 373308)

Monmouthshire

Llandenny Charities

Eligibility: People over 65 and in need who are in receipt of a state pension, live in the parish of Llandenny and have lived there for more than one year.

Types of grants: Pensions to people receiving a state pension.

Annual grant total: About £1,000 for educational and welfare purposes.

Applications: In writing to the correspondent, to be submitted directly by the individual. Applications should be submitted by 15 January for consideration in February.

Correspondent: Dr Graham Russell, Forge Cottage, Llandenny, Usk, Monmouthshire NP15 1DL (01633 432536; email: gsrussell@btinternet.com)

Monmouth Charity

Eligibility: People in need who live within an eight-mile radius of Monmouth and neighbourhood.

Types of grants: One-off grants usually up to a maximum of £500.

Annual grant total: In 2009/10 the charity had both an income and expenditure of £10,400. Grants are made for both educational and welfare purposes.

Applications: The trust advertises in the local press each September/October and applications should be made in response to this advertisement for consideration in November. Emergency grants can be considered at any time. There is no application form. Applications can be submitted directly by the individual or through a social worker, Citizens Advice or other welfare agency.

Correspondent: A R Pirie, Pen-y-Bryn, Oakfield Road, Monmouth NP25 3JJ

Monmouth Relief-in-Need Charity

Eligibility: People in need who live in Monmouth town.

Types of grants: One-off grants of up to £60 including those towards winter heating costs.

Annual grant total: Total expenditure for this charity averages around £800.

Applications: In writing to the correspondent by 1 January for consideration in the same month. Applications can be submitted directly by the individual, through a social worker, Citizens Advice, other welfare agency or a member of the clergy.

Correspondent: Derek H Jones, New Ways, 19 The Gardens, Monmouth, Monmouthshire NP25 3HF (01600 712221; email: mojonesnewways@aol.com)

The Monmouthshire Welsh Church Acts Fund

Eligibility: People living in the boundaries of Monmouthshire County Council who are in need.

Types of grants: Grants of money or payment for items, services or facilities. Accommodation can be provided to older people who need it because of infirmities or disabilities. People who are blind may also be given access to charitable homes and holiday homes. Grants range from £50 to £500.

Annual grant total: In 2008/09 the fund had assets of £5 million and an income of £280,000. Grants to organisations and individuals totalled £136,000.

Applications: On a form available from the correspondent which can be submitted at any time, and must be signed by a County Councillor. Applications can be made either directly by the individual, or through a third party such as a social worker or Citizens Advice and are usually considered in June, September, December and March.

Correspondent: S K F Greenslade, Treasurer's Department, Monmouthshire County Council, County Hall, Cwmbran, Monmouthshire NP44 2XH (01633 644644)

Other information: Following the reorganisation of local councils the funds from the Gwent Welsh Church Fund were divided and are now administered by five new councils. The above council is the only one which makes grants directly to individuals.

Pembrokeshire

The Gild of Freemen of Haverfordwest

Eligibility: Hereditary freemen of Haverfordwest aged 18 years and over.

Types of grants: One-off grants according to need.

Annual grant total: In 2008/09 the trust had an income of £24,000 and a total expenditure of £23,000.

Applications: Freemen must be enrolled by the chairman of the local authority. The honour is hereditary being passed down through the male or female line.

Correspondent: P K Lucas, R K Lucas & Son, The Tithe Exchange, 9 Victoria Place, Haverfordwest, Pembrokeshire SA61 2JX (01437 762538)

Other information: Grants are also made to organisations.

The William Sanders Charity

Eligibility: Widows and unmarried women in need who live within a five mile radius of the parish of St John's, Pembroke Dock.

Types of grants: Christmas grants ranging from £25 to £40.

Annual grant total: In 2008/09 the charity had an income of £8,500 and a total expenditure of £4,400.

Applications: In writing to the correspondent directly by the individual or family member.

Correspondent: Henry Johnston, St Johns Parish Office, St Johns Community Hall, Church Street, Pembroke Dock SA72 6AR (01646 680024)

The Tenby Relief-in-Need & Pensions Charity

Eligibility: Older people in need who live in the community of Tenby.

Types of grants: Pensions of £17 a month to help relieve financial difficulties. Most beneficiaries will also receive a small Christmas bonus of £18. Usually, once a grant has been agreed it will be paid indefinitely.

Annual grant total: In 2009 the charity had assets of £651,000 and an income of £35,000. Grants were made to 130 individuals totalling £27,000.

Applications: On a form available from the correspondent: to be submitted directly by the individual or a family member.

Correspondent: Clive Mathias, Clerk to the Trustees, Lewis Lewis & Co, County Chambers, Pentre Road, St Clears, Carmarthen, SA33 4AA (01994 231044)

William Vawer's Charity

Eligibility: People in need who live in the town of Haverfordwest.

Types of grants: Pensions to existing pensioners. Other grants to those in need, hardship or distress.

Annual grant total: Grants usually total around £1,500 per year.

Applications: In writing to the correspondent.

Correspondent: R K Lucas, The Tithe Exchange, 9 Victoria Place, Haverfordwest, Pembrokeshire SA61 2JX (01437 762538; fax: 01437 765404; email: mail@ pembrokeshirecoastproperties.co.uk)

Swansea

The Swansea & District Friends of the Blind

Eligibility: People who are registered blind and live in Swansea.

Types of grants: One-off grants towards talking watches, kitchen equipment, computers and so on. Gifts are also given out at Christmas and Easter.

Annual grant total: In 2007/08 the trust had assets of £213,000 and an income of £49,000. Grants were made totalling around £2,000. At the time of writing, recent accounts had not been filed with the Charity Commission.

Applications: In writing to the correspondent. Applications are considered on a regular basis.

Correspondent: John Allan, Secretary, 3 De La Beche Street, Swansea SA1 3EY (01792 655424; email: allan.john@ btconnect.com)

Other information: The majority of the trust's funds go towards organising events such as summer outings and Christmas dinners and generally providing advice and information for visually impaired people in the area.

Torfaen

The Cwmbran Trust

Eligibility: People in need living in the town of Cwmbran, Gwent.

Types of grants: One-off and recurrent grants are awarded for a wide variety of educational and welfare purposes, such as stair-lifts, home-study courses, computer equipment, wheelchairs, holidays, debt clearance, removal costs, building renovation, funeral costs and respite care. Grants usually range between £125 to £2,500.

Annual grant total: In 2009 the trust had assets of £1.8 million and an income of £69,000. Grants were made to 21 individuals totalling £22,000.

Applications: In writing to the correspondent. Applications can be submitted directly by the individual or through a social worker, Citizens Advice, welfare agency or other third party. Applications are usually considered in March, May, July, October and December.

Correspondent: K L Maddox, Arvinheritor HVBS (UK) Ltd, Grange Road, Cwmbran, Gwent NP44 3XU (01633 834040; fax: 01633 834051; email: cwmbrantrust@ arvinmeritor.com)

Other information: Grants are also made to individuals for educational purposes.

Vale of Glamorgan

The Cowbridge with Llanblethian United Charities

Eligibility: People in need who live in the town of Cowbridge with Llanblethian.

Types of grants: The provision of items, services or facilities that will reduce the person's need.

Annual grant total: In 2008/09, Christmas and summer grants totalled £23,000, with a further £300 given in general grants locally.

Applications: In writing to the correspondent. Applications can be submitted directly by the individual or through a welfare agency.

Correspondent: H G Phillips, 66 Broadway, Llanblethian, Cowbridge, Vale of Glamorgan CF71 7EW (01446 773287; email: unitedcharities@aol. com)

Other information: Grants are also made for educational purposes.

The Dinas Powis Relief-in-Sickness Fund

Eligibility: People in need who live in Dinas Powis with a preference for those who are sick or who have disabilities.

Types of grants: One-off grants according to need.

Annual grant total: In both 2006 and 2007 the trust had an unusually high income of £19,000, however, there has been no expenditure by the trust for the past five years.

Applications: In writing to the correspondent. Applications can be submitted directly by the individual or family member, by an organisation such as Citizens Advice, or through a third party such as a social worker. There is no deadline and applications can be considered at any time.

Correspondent: Rev David H Rhydderch, The Rectory, Lettons Way, Dinas Powys, Vale of Glamorgan CF64 4BY (029 20512555)

Other information: Grants are also made to organisations.

The Neale Trust Fund for Poor Children

Eligibility: Schoolchildren in need who live in the district of Barry and are aged 16 or under.

Types of grants: One-off grants of up to £500 each for: clothes; shoes; educational, medical or disability equipment; and travel expenses.

Exclusions: No grants are given for video/computer equipment.

Annual grant total: On average, about £1,000 is available each year to distribute in grants.

Applications: In writing to the correspondent, who will then send out a form to be completed. The need for support has to be shown by the applicant. Applications are considered in January and September according to availability of funds or in special cases by home visit of the secretary. Applications can be made through the social services, Citizens Advice or local childcare officer, or directly by the individual. The trust does not accept unsolicited applications.

Correspondent: David Ward Jenkins, Trustee, Lanby, 16 White House, Barry, CF62 6FB (01446 730204)

4. NORTH EAST

The Christina Aitchison Trust

Eligibility: People who are blind or have any ophthalmic disease or disability, and people who have a terminal illness, who are in need, and live in north east or south west England.

Types of grants: One-off and recurrent grants for up to £200 to relieve blindness, ophthalmic disease or disability, and terminal illness.

Annual grant total: In 2008/09 the trust had an income of £1,900 and a total expenditure of £2,300.

Applications: On a form available from the correspondent, to be submitted in March or September for consideration in April or November.

Correspondent: R Massingberd-Mundy, c/o The Old Post Office, The Street, West Raynham, Fakenham, Norfolk NR21 7AD

Other information: Grants are also given to individuals and organisations concerned with education, equitation, sailing and music.

Mrs El Blakeley-Marillier Charitable Fund

Eligibility: Ladies over 55 who are in need and are not of the Roman Catholic faith or members of the Salvation Army. Preference is given to women from the counties of Yorkshire and Devon and in particular the towns of Scarborough and Torquay.

Types of grants: Annuities of about £520 a year paid twice a year. Grants will not be given if the effect is to reduce income support or other benefits or to reduce debt.

Annual grant total: In 2008/09 the fund had an income of £10,000 and a total expenditure of £12,000.

Applications: On a form available from the correspondent to be submitted directly by the individual including a general financial overview. Applications are usually considered in November and May.

Correspondent: Karen Tristram, Messrs Hooper & Wollen, Carlton House, 30 The Terrace, Torquay, Devon TQ1 1BS (01803 213251; fax: 01803 296871; email: karen.tristram@hooperwollen.co.uk; website: www.hooperwollen.co.uk/)

The Charity of Miss Ann Farrar Brideoake

Eligibility: Communicant members of the Church of England living within the dioceses of York, Liverpool and Manchester, who are in need. This includes clergy and retired clergy.

Types of grants: Recurrent grants of £500 to £1,500 are given to help in 'making ends meet'. Support is given towards household outgoings, domestic equipment, holidays, children's entertainment and so on as well as special medical needs. One-off payments are made in special circumstances and debt relief can be supported in exceptional circumstances.

Annual grant total: In 2008/09 the charity had assets of £1.5 million and an income of £84,000. Grants totalled around £60,000.

Applications: On a form available from the correspondent, to be countersigned by the local vicar as confirmation of communicant status. Applications should be submitted in April or May for consideration in July/August.

Correspondent: Alan Ware, Cowling Swift & Kitchin, 8 Blake Street, York YO1 8XJ (01904 625678; fax: 01904 620214)

Lord Crewe's Charity

Eligibility: Necessitous clergy, their widows and dependants who live in the dioceses of Durham and Newcastle. Grants may also be given more generally to people in need who live in the area.

Types of grants: One-off and recurrent grants according to need.

Annual grant total: In 2009 relief in need grants made to clergy amounted to £9,000.

Applications: On a form available from the correspondent.

Correspondent: Peter Church, Durham Cathedral, The Chapter Office, The College, Durham DH1 3EH (0191 375 1226; email: peter.church@ durhamcathedral.co.uk)

The Olive & Norman Field Charity

Eligibility: People who are in poor health, convalescent or who have disabilities and live in the former North Riding of Yorkshire (the counties of Durham and North Yorkshire and the unitary authorities of Darlington, Hartlepool, Middlesbrough, Redcar & Cleveland, Stockton-on-Tees and York).

Types of grants: One-off grants, usually in the range of £100 to £350, are given towards electric goods, convalescence, medical equipment, furniture and disability equipment.

Annual grant total: In 2009 the charity had an income of £25,000 and a total expenditure of £38,000. Grants are made to both individuals and organisations.

Applications: On a form available from the correspondent or social services. Applications should be submitted either through a social worker, Citizens Advice or other welfare agency. Applications are considered in February, April, June, September and December.

Correspondent: John Pelter, British Red Cross Society, Red Cross House, Zetland Street, Northallerton, North Yorkshire DL6 1NB (01609 771554)

The Greggs Foundation

Eligibility: Individuals and families in extreme financial hardship in the north east of England. Priority is given to dependent children within family units.

Types of grants: Grants range from £50 to £150 and are given for essential items such as, washing machines, fridges, cookers, furniture, baby equipment, flooring, clothing and school uniforms.

Exclusions: No grants for unspecified costs, repayment of loans, bankruptcy petition fees, holidays, funeral expenses, medical equipment and computer equipment. Most household items can be considered but the foundation states that, 'realistically, non-priority items are hard to fund'.

Annual grant total: In 2009 the foundation had assets of £9.7 million and an income of £1.4 million. Grants totalled

£1.7 million, of which £194,000 was given to individuals in hardship grants.

Applications: On a form available to download from the website. The form is designed to be completed and submitted electronically (to greggs.foundation@greggs.co.uk). Applications should be made through a welfare agency, such as social services, probation service, Citizens Advice, victim support, health, disability and housing projects or other similar organisations. Applications submitted directly by the individual will not be considered.

Applications received by Friday at 5pm will be processed in the following week. The foundation asks that applicants do not send any additional information as this will not be considered.

Note: following the economic recession the foundation has experienced a significant rise in applications. Consequently, the success rate for applications has fallen from 60% in 2008 to 40% in 2009.

Correspondent: Foundation Manager, Fernwood House, Clayton Road, Jesmond, Newcastle-upon-Tyne NE2 1TL (0191 212 7626; fax: 0191 281 9536; email: greggsfoundation@greggs.co.uk; website: www.greggsfoundation.org.uk)

Other information: Through the Hardship Fund, Greggs Foundation administers funds on behalf of a number of other local charitable trusts, including the Brough Benevolent Fund, Hadrian Trust, the 1989 Willan Charitable Trust, Sir James Knott Trust, Joicey Trust and the Rothley Trust. Only one form from each applicant should be submitted to the joint trusts, as the payment will be made from joint funds.

Lady Elizabeth Hastings' Non-Educational Charity

Eligibility: Clergy working in the parish of Burton Salmon, in the county of north Yorkshire, the ecclesiastical parishes of Thorp Arch, Collingham with Harewood, Bardsey with East Keswick and Shadwell, in the county of west Yorkshire and the ecclesiastical parish of Ledsham with Fairburn in the counties of north and west Yorkshire, and their dependants.

Types of grants: One-off grants averaging about £700 per person are given for welfare purposes.

Annual grant total: In 2008/09 the non-educational branch of the charity gave 120 individual grants totalling £86,000.

Applications: In writing to the correspondent.

Correspondent: E F V Waterson, Carter Jonas, 82 Micklegate, York YO1 6LF (01904 558201)

Other information: The trust is managed by and derives its income from the Lady Elizabeth Hastings Estate Charity.

The John Routledge Hunter Memorial Fund

Eligibility: People who live in Northumberland and Tyne and Wear (north of River Tyne) who have (or recently have had) chest, lung or catarrhal complaints.

Types of grants: Grants of £200 to £500 towards a two or three week recuperative holiday in a hotel in Lytham St Annes or Southport (including rail travel expenses, bed, breakfast, evening meal and £25 in cash). Holidays are taken between Easter and September.

Annual grant total: Grants to individuals usually total around £13,000 each year.

Applications: On a form available from the correspondent, supported by a certificate signed by a doctor. Applications should be submitted directly by the individual and are considered from January to April.

Correspondent: Mary Waugh, Dickinson Dees (Solicitors), One Trinity, Newcastle-Upon-Tyne, NE1 2HF (0844 984 1500; fax: 0844 984 1501)

Hylton House Fund

Eligibility: People in the North East (County Durham, Darlington, Gateshead, South Shields, Sunderland and Cleveland) with cerebral palsy and related disabilities, and their families and carers. Applicants (or their family members, if the applicant is aged under 18) must be on income support or a low income or have a degree of disability in the family, which creates a heavy financial demand.

Types of grants: Grants of up to £350 towards: holidays and respite support for carers of up to two weeks in the UK or abroad; education, training and therapy; training and support for carers and self-help groups (if there is no statutory support available); domestic equipment (maximum award £200); aids and equipment, particularly specialist clothing, communication and mobility aids; travel costs to allow applicants and their carers to attend a specific activity, specialist centre or hospital if no alternative transport is available; respite support to pay for an employed carer in the home or for visiting a specialist centre where care is provided; costs of setting up home (unless this is a SCOPE or Local Authority led move); debts, if it can be proved that they were incurred by the disability.

Exclusions: No grants for: legal costs; ongoing education; medical treatment; decorating and/or refurbishment costs (unless the work is due to the nature of the applicant's disability); motor vehicle adaptations; motor insurance, deposits or running costs; televisions or DVD players; assessments, such as the costs involved in the Scope Living Options Schemes; or retrospective funding. Only one grant can be held in each financial year starting in April.

Annual grant total: In 2008/09 grants were made totalling £8,500. Grants are given for both educational and welfare purposes.

Applications: On a form available from the correspondent or to download from the website. All applications must include a reference from a social worker or professional adviser in a related field, with a telephone number and the individual's permission for them to be contacted about an application. A full breakdown of costs should also be included. For specialist equipment and therapy, confirmation from an occupational therapist/doctor/physiotherapist or other professional advisor that the equipment is suitable, is also required.

Appeals are considered in January, April, July and October and should be received before the start of the month. They can be considered between these dates within a month of application if the need is urgent, but the applicant will need to request this and provide a reason why an exception to the usual policy needs to be made.

Correspondent: Brenda Dye, Jordan House, Forster Business Centre, Finchale Road, Durham DH1 5HL (0191 383 0055; fax: 0191 383 2969; email: info@cdcf.org.uk; website: www.countydurhamfoundation.co.uk)

The Rose Joicey Fund

Eligibility: Families or individuals in need who live in the counties of Durham, Northumberland or Tyne & Wear.

Priority for grants is given to groups which organise holidays for people in need. Requests from individuals will only be considered if made through a proper social work agency. Preference will be given to people in poor health or who have a disability.

Types of grants: One-off grants usually ranging from £100 to £200 for holidays and short breaks.

Exclusions: Grants are not given for furniture, clothing, building restoration or medical care and equipment.

Annual grant total: In 2008/09 the fund had assets of £86,000 and an income of £4,700. Grants were made totalling about £5,000.

Applications: In writing to the correspondent by a social worker. Details of costs, the amount requested and information on any other sources of funding that have been approached should be included.

Correspondent: Graeme Lyall, Finance Officer, c/o Newcastle Council for Voluntary Service, Mea House, Ellison Place, Newcastle upon Tyne NE1 8XS (0191 232 7445; fax: 0191 230 5640; email: ncvs@cvsnewcastle.org.uk; website: www.cvsnewcastle.org.uk)

The Kelly Charitable Trust

Eligibility: People in need in England and Wales, primarily in the north east of England.

Types of grants: One-off and recurrent grants according to need, mainly for relief-in-need purposes.

Annual grant total: In 2008/09 the trust had an income of £4,700 and a total expenditure of £9,000.

Applications: In writing to the correspondent.

Correspondent: Sir David Kelly, Stanton Fence, Stanton, Morpeth, Northumberland NE65 8PP (email: stantonfence@hotmail.com)

The Leeds Jewish Welfare Board

Eligibility: Jewish people who live in Leeds or North and West Yorkshire.

Types of grants: Grants may be given as part of a 'support package'. They are rarely given as a one-off without a full assessment of the situation. Loans may also be given and depending on individual circumstances may be part-grant/part-loan. A flexible approach together with budgeting advice is offered. The majority of grants are given to families with children. These may be for clothes, bedding requirements and so on. Grants are also given at Jewish festivals such as Passover. Counselling and meals-on-wheels services along with a comprehensive range of services and resources are also offered to Jewish children, families and older people.

Annual grant total: In 2008/09 the board had assets of £4 million and an income of £879,000. It appears that no grants were made to individuals during the year.

Applications: Applications for help can be made at any time by individuals, welfare agencies, friends or relatives. The board can respond quickly in urgent cases. The applicant will be seen by a social worker who will assess the application and gather the relevant information.

Correspondent: Rebecca Weinberg, 311 Stonegate Road, Leeds LS17 6AZ (0113 268 4211; email: enquiries@ljwb.co.uk)

The North East Area Miners Social Welfare Trust Fund

Eligibility: People in need living in Durham, Northumberland and Tyne and Wear who are employed by the coal industry, or who have not been employed since retirement or redundancy from the coal industry.

Types of grants: One-off grants according to need.

Annual grant total: In 2008/09 the trust had assets of £4.2 million and an unusually high income of £2.7 million, due to the transfer of assets from the North East Area Mineworkers' Convalescent Fund (£2 million) and the Sam Watson Rest Home (£582,000) in June 2009. Grants to individuals totalled £1,400.

Applications: In writing to the correspondent. Applications can be submitted directly by the individual or through a social worker, Citizens Advice or other welfare agency. They are usually considered four times a year.

Correspondent: Vincent B Clements, Coal Industry Social Welfare Organisation, 6 Bewick Road, Gateshead, Tyne & Wear NE8 4DP (0191 477 7242; email: vincent.clements@ciswo.org.uk)

Other information: The trust also makes a number of grants to organisations (£70,000 in 2008/09).

The Northern Ladies Annuity Society

Eligibility: Governesses and single and unmarried ladies in need who live or were born in the northern counties of England. At present only those over 60 years of age are considered. The applicant should have an annual income of less than £7,000.

Types of grants: Annuities of £1,300 paid quarterly. One-off grants are also available for those in receipt of an annuity for expenses such as, holidays, domestic appliances, household items and other unexpected costs. Christmas hampers are also distributed to most annuitants.

Please note individuals not already in receipt of an annuity are ineligible for any other form of help from the society.

Exclusions: The trust does not give one-off grants to non-annuitants, nor support students, and will ignore any such requests for assistance.

Annual grant total: In 2008/09 the society had assets of £6.2 million and an income of £329,000. Grants were made totalling £163,000, of which £139,000 was given in annuities and £25,000 in special grants.

Applications: Applications to become an annuitant should be made on a form available from the correspondent. Completed forms can be submitted directly by the individual or through a third party such as Citizens Advice or a social worker. Applications are considered monthly.

Correspondent: Jean Ferry, Secretary, MEA House, Ellison Place, Newcastle-upon-Tyne NE1 8XS (0191 232 1518)

Other information: The society also owns a number of properties, which are available on a low rent to annuitants in need.

The Sir John Priestman Charity Trust

Eligibility: Clergy and their families in need who live in the historic counties of Durham and York (especially the county borough of Sunderland).

Types of grants: One-off and recurrent grants ranging from £50 to £1,000.

Annual grant total: In 2008 the trust had assets of £7.5 million and an income of £369,000. Grants to clergy and their families totalled around £20,000.

Applications: In writing to the correspondent. Applications are considered quarterly.

Correspondent: P W Taylor, McKenzie Bell, 19 John Street, Sunderland, Tyne & Wear SR1 1JG (0191 567 4857)

Other information: The trust also assists charities serving County Durham (especially the Sunderland area) and helps maintain Church of England churches and buildings in the area.

The Rycroft Children's Fund

Eligibility: Children in need who live in Cheshire, Derbyshire, Greater Manchester, Lancashire, Staffordshire, South and West Yorkshire. There is a preference for children living in the cities of Manchester and Salford and the borough of Trafford. Applicants should be aged 18 or under.

Types of grants: One-off grants according to need.

Exclusions: Grants are not given to individuals for education, holidays or computers.

Annual grant total: In 2008/09 the fund had an income and expenditure of around £50,000. Grants totalled £44,000.

Applications: On a form available from the correspondent either directly by the individual or through a social worker, Citizens Advice or other welfare agency. Details of the applicant's available income and contributions from other sources must also be included. Applications can be made at any time.

Correspondent: J N Smith, 10 Heybridge Drive, Northernden, Manchester M22 4HB (0161 998 3127)

sfgroup Charitable Fund for Disabled People *see entry on page 46*

Sherburn House Charity

Eligibility: People in 'extreme social need' who live in the North East of England between the rivers Tweed and Tees.

Types of grants: One-off grants according to need.

Exclusions: No grants for central heating; driving licences; telephones and/or telephone arrears; specialist medical equipment; funeral expenses and holidays (unless there are exceptional circumstances). Applicants should wait two years before reapplying.

Annual grant total: In 2008/09 the charity had assets of £22 million and an income of £748,000. Grants to individuals totalled £767,000.

Applications: The charity prefers applicants to apply online via the website, though there is an option to download a hardcopy of the form to complete by hand. Applications must be made through a welfare agency such as, social services, probation service, Citizens Advice and so on. They are normally assessed on a monthly basis.

Correspondent: Stephen Black, Administration Manager, Ramsey House, Sherburn Hospital, Durham, DH1 2SE (0191 372 2551; fax: 0191 372 0035; email: admin@sherburnhouse.org; website: www.sherburnhouse.org)

Wright Funk Fund

Eligibility: Families in need in Darlington and County Durham.

Types of grants: Hardship grants of up to £500 per applicant to help keep families together or to support families in crisis. Recent grants have been made for domestic equipment e.g. fridges, washing machines and cookers; carpets and bedding; support for carers; and, in exceptional circumstances, household bills.

Exclusions: The fund does not assist with bankruptcy fees.

Annual grant total: Grants are for a maximum of £500 each.

Applications: In writing to the correspondent, explaining what is needed and why it cannot be afforded without a grant. Application forms and guidance notes can be downloaded from the County Durham Foundation's website. Alternatively, a paper copy can be requested from the correspondent.

Correspondent: Brenda Dye, Grants Officer, Victoria House, Whitfield Court, St John's Road, Meadowfield Industrial Estate, Durham, DH7 8XL (0191 378 6340; fax: 0191 383 2969; email: brenda@cdcf.org.uk; website: www.countydurhamfoundation.co.uk)

Yorkshire County Bowling Association Benevolent Fund

Eligibility: Bowlers and their dependants from Yorkshire County EBA Clubs who are in need.

Types of grants: Christmas grants of £100.

Annual grant total: About £800.

Applications: On a form available from the correspondent submitted via club secretaries. Applications are usually considered in November.

Correspondent: David Oliver, 31 Redland Drive, Kirk Ella, Hull, HU10 7UX (01482 656411)

Yorkshire Water Community Trust

Eligibility: People who are in arrears with Yorkshire Water and have at least one other priority debt.

Types of grants: No cash grants are given. One-off payments are made to Yorkshire Water and credited to the applicant's account.

Annual grant total: In 2008/09 the trust had an income of £650,000 and made grants to 1,891 individuals totalling £585,000.

Applications: On a form available from the correspondent. Although applications can be submitted directly by the individual or a friend or relative, the trust prefers them to be submitted by a social worker, Citizens Advice or other welfare agency. Successful applicants may not reapply within two years.

Correspondent: Mark Lee, Trust Officer, Freepost BD3074, Bradford BD3 7BR (0845 124 2426; fax: 01274 262265; email: info@ywct.org.uk; website: www.ywct.co.uk)

Other information: Small grants may also be available to advice agencies dealing with debt.

County Durham

County Durham Community Foundation

Eligibility: People in need who live in County Durham and Darlington.

Types of grants: Usually one-off grants of between £50 to £2,000. Please visit the foundation's website for further details. Individuals can only hold one grant per each financial year starting in April.

Exclusions: No grants are made towards medical treatment, nursing care or anything which is the responsibility of social services or the NHS. Grants are not made retrospectively.

Annual grant total: In 2008/09 the foundation had assets of £5.5 million and an income of £2 million. Grants were made totalling £113,000. The foundation administers eight funds that give for both educational and welfare purposes.

Applications: Applicants can either: use a form available from the correspondent or the website; or write to the correspondent including their name, address, how they fit the criteria, what is needed and why, costs, when the grant is needed, details of income and savings, details of why the need can't be met, where any other money will be coming from (if not requesting the full amount), names of other organisations approached and details of how a cheque should be made payable to (unless directly

to the provider, such as a residential home, rather than to the applicant).

In all cases, applications must include a reference from a professional third party, such as a GP, community nurse or social worker. The foundation will give a decision within one month, although this can be sooner if the request is particularly urgent.

Correspondent: Mrs Barbara Gubbins, Chief Executive, Jordan House, Forster Business Centre, Finchale Road, Durham, DH1 5HL (0191 383 0055; email: info@countydurhamfoundation.co.uk; website: www.countydurhamfoundation.co.uk)

Other information: Grants are also made to organisations.

The Ferryhill Station, Mainsforth & Bishop Middleham Aid-in-Sickness Charity

Eligibility: People in need who are in poor health, convalescent or who have disabilities and live in the parishes of Ferryhill Station, Mainsforth and Bishop Middleham.

Types of grants: One-off grants ranging from £250 to £1,000 towards medical care and equipment, holidays for people with disabilities (and their carers) and for special needs arising from disability or illness.

Annual grant total: About £2,000 a year. Grants are given to both individuals and organisations.

Applications: In writing to the correspondent, either directly by the individual or via a third party such as a district nurse, social worker, Citizens Advice or other welfare agency. Applications are considered on a regular basis.

Correspondent: Zoe Whent, Dunelm, Mainsforth Village, Ferryhill, County Durham DL17 9AA (01740 652434)

The Ropner Centenary Trust

Eligibility: Present and former maritime employees who are in need, and their dependants. Preference is generally given to people living in the North East of England and particularly those who have worked for Ropner Shipping Company Ltd.

Types of grants: One-off and recurrent grants according to need.

Annual grant total: In 2008/09 the trust had assets of £782,000 and an income of £39,000. Grants were made totalling £26,000, of which £19,000 was given in grants to 41 individuals and the remaining £7,000 was awarded to organisations.

Applications: In writing to the correspondent. Applications are considered annually, although urgent requests can be dealt with between meetings.

Correspondent: Alan Theakston, 15 The Green, High Coniscliffe, Darlington, County Durham, DL2 2LJ (01325 374249)

The Sedgefield District Relief-in-Need Charity

Eligibility: People in need who live in the parishes of Bishop Middleham, Bradbury, Cornforth, Fishburn, Mordon, Sedgefield and Trimdon in County Durham.

Types of grants: One-off grants, including those for furnishings, bedding, medical requisites, mobility aids, hospital travel costs, living expenses and respite care.

Annual grant total: About £5,000 to individuals for welfare and educational purposes.

Applications: In writing to the correspondent. Applications can be submitted directly by the individual or through a social worker, Citizens Advice, welfare agency or other third party such as a carer or relative. They are considered as they arise.

Correspondent: John Hannon, Clerk, East House, Mordon, Sedgefield, County Durham, TS21 2EY (01740 622512; email: east.house@btinternet.com)

Other information: The trust has previously given annual payments to individuals at Christmas and is phasing these out. Whilst current beneficiaries will continue to receive payments, no new names will be added to the list. The trust also makes grants to local organisations.

East Yorkshire

The Joseph & Annie Cattle Trust

Eligibility: Primarily people who live in the Hull or East Riding of Yorkshire area and are in need. Preference is given to people who are older, disabled or disadvantaged, particularly children who are dyslexic.

Types of grants: One-off grants of £200 to £500 for needs such as travel expenses, furniture, medical and disability equipment, electric goods and help in the home.

Annual grant total: In 2008/09 the trust had assets of £5.4 million and an income of £463,000. Grants for educational and welfare purposes were made to 36 individuals totalling £25,000.

Applications: In writing to the correspondent, only via a welfare organisation, for consideration on the third Monday of every month. Please note, if applicants approach the trust directly

they will be referred to an organisation, such as Disability Rights Advisory Service, or social services.

Correspondent: Roger Waudby, Administrator, Morpeth House, 114 Spring Bank, Hull HU3 1QJ (01482 211198; fax: 01482 211198)

Other information: Grants are also made to organisations (£284,000, 2008/09).

The Hesslewood Children's Trust (Hull Seamen's & General Orphanage)

Eligibility: People under 25 in need who are native to, or have family connections with, the former county of Humberside and North Lincolnshire. Students who have come to the area to study are not eligible.

Types of grants: One-off and recurrent grants according to need. Grants have been given for specified short periods of time at special schools, holiday funding for individuals and youth organisations in the UK and overseas, and for musical instruments and special equipment for children who are disabled.

Exclusions: Loans are not made.

Annual grant total: In 2008/09 the trust had assets of £1.8 million and an income of £108,000. Grants made to or on behalf of individuals totalled £22,000.

Applications: On a form available from the correspondent. Applications can be made either directly by the individual or through the individual's school/college/welfare agency or another third party on their behalf. Applicants must give their own or their parental financial details, the grant required, and why parents cannot provide the money. If possible, a contact telephone number should be provided. Applications must be accompanied by a letter from the tutor or an educational welfare officer (or from medical and social services for a disability grant). The deadlines are 16 February, 16 June and 16 September.

Correspondent: Michael Mitchell, Graham & Rosen (Solicitors), 8 Parliament St, Hull, HU1 2BB (01482 323123; fax: 01482 223542; email: law@graham-rosen.co.uk)

Other information: Grants are also made to organisations (£53,000 in 2008/09)

The Hull Aid in Sickness Trust

Eligibility: People in need, on a low income, who live in the city and county of Kingston-upon-Hull and are sick, disabled, infirm or convalescent.

Types of grants: One-off and recurrent grants, to a usual maximum of £500, to aid and improve quality of life. This can include grants for electrical goods, medical and disability equipment, food and living costs and so on.

Exclusions: No grants are given towards debts or where money is available from public funds.

Annual grant total: In 2008/09 the trust had assets of £954,000 and an income of £69,000. Grants were made totalling £31,000, of which around £15,000 was given in grants to individuals.

Applications: On a form available from the correspondent, to be submitted directly by the individual or through a social worker, Citizens Advice, other welfare agency or other third party. Applications must be supported by a doctor's certificate or similar.

Correspondent: Dawn Singleton, 34 Thurstan Road, Beverley, Hull HU17 8LP (01482 860133; email: haist@thesingletons.karoo.co.uk)

Other information: Grants of £1,000 or more were made to five organisations: Kids, Marie Curie Cancer Care, Parkinson's Disease Society (Hull & East Yorkshire Branch), CRUSE Bereavement Care and Dove House Hospice.

Humberside Police Welfare and Benevolent Fund

Eligibility: Serving and retired officers of the Humberside Police and retired officers from other forces who live in Humberside, and their partners and dependants; and civilian employees of Humberside Police Authority, retired civilian employees and their partners and dependants.

Types of grants: One-off and recurrent grants of up to £500.

Annual grant total: In 2009 the fund had an income of £21,000 and a total expenditure of £11,000.

Applications: In writing to the correspondent at any time, either through the branch/divisional representative or the headquarters.

Correspondent: Mrs J Jeffrey, Priory Police Station, Priory Road, Hull, HU5 5SF (0845 6060 222; email: webmail@humberside.pnn.police.uk; website: www.humberside.police.uk)

The Nafferton Feoffee Charity Trust

Eligibility: People in need who live in the parish of All Saints Nafferton with St Mary's Wansford.

Types of grants: One-off grants in the range of £100 to £250. Recent grants have been given for hospital travel costs, heating expenses and food vouchers. Bursaries are also available to local students.

Exclusions: The trust stated that the parish only consists of 3,000 people and every household receives a copy of a leaflet outlining the trust's work. People from outside this area are not eligible to apply.

Annual grant total: In 2009 the trust had assets of £1.5 million and an income of

£56,000. Welfare grants to individuals totalled around £500.

Applications: In writing to the correspondent at any time, directly by the individual.

Correspondent: Margaret Buckton, South Cattleholmes, Wansford, Driffield, East Yorkshire YO25 8NW (01377 254293)

Other information: Grants are also made to organisations.

Ethel Maude Townend Charity

Eligibility: People in need who live in Hull and the East Riding of Yorkshire. Applicants should have been in the medical, nursing or legal professions or have been ministers of religion, accountants or architects, or members of other professions generally. Their widows can also be supported.

Types of grants: Usually weekly payments plus a Christmas bonus. Also one-off grants towards, for example, nursing registration fees; outstanding telephone bills; washing machines; roof and window repairs; medical equipment; and Tens machines.

Exclusions: There are no grants available for educational purposes.

Annual grant total: In 2008/09 the fund had an income of £5,300 and a total expenditure of £4,400.

Applications: On a form available from the correspondent following an advertisement. Applications can be submitted directly by the individual or through a social worker, Citizens Advice, doctor or other welfare agency. Applications can be made at any time of the year.

Correspondent: Stephen Walker, Gosschalks, 61 Queens Gardens, Hull HU1 3DZ (01482 324252; email: sw@gosschalks.co.uk)

Robert Towries Charity

Eligibility: People in need who live in Aldbrough and Burton Constable.

Types of grants: One-off and recurrent grants for food and fuel.

Annual grant total: In 2008/09 the charity had an income of £9,000 and a total expenditure of £7,000. Approximately £3,500 was given in grants for welfare purposes.

Applications: In writing to the correspondent directly by the individual.

Correspondent: Mrs P M Auty, 6 Willow Grove, Headlands Park, Aldbrough, Hull HU11 4SH (01964 527553)

Other information: Grants are also given for educational needs.

Aldbrough

Aldbrough Poor Fields

Eligibility: People aged over 65 and widows who are in need and live in Aldbrough village.

Types of grants: Grants are given towards food and fuel. Gifts in kind are also made.

Annual grant total: The total annual expenditure for this charity is on average around £490.

Applications: In writing to the correspondent for consideration in November.

Correspondent: Janet North, 4 Sandpits Lane, Aldbrough, Hull, HU11 4RL (01964 527608; email: janetnorth@homecall.co.uk)

Barmby on the Marsh

Garlthorpes Charity

Eligibility: People in need who live in the parish of Barmby on the Marsh.

Types of grants: One-off grants according to need.

Annual grant total: In 2008/09 the charity had an income of £7,000 and a total expenditure of £4,000.

Applications: In writing to the correspondent.

Correspondent: John Burman, c/o Hepstonstalls Solicitors, 7–15 Gladstone Terrace, Goole, North Humberside, DN14 5AH (01405 765661)

Bridlington

The Bridlington Charities

Eligibility: People in need who live in the parish of Bridlington and Bridlington Quay.

Types of grants: Grants of between £50 and £150 for the purchase of fuel (gas, coal, electricity). Payment is made direct to the suppliers. One-off grants towards school clothing can also be made.

Exclusions: No loans or grants for meals or paid help.

Annual grant total: In 2008 the charities had assets of £41,000 and an income of £58,000. The charity paid £30,000 to fuel suppliers on behalf of 207 beneficiaries.

Applications: In writing to the correspondent, usually for consideration in February, May, August and November. Applications can be submitted through a social worker, Citizens Advice or other welfare agency. The charities' field officers visit the applicants and report to the trustees in writing.

Correspondent: Andrew Mead, 118 St. James Road, Bridlington, North Humberside, YO15 3NJ

Kingston-upon-Hull

The Charity of Miss Eliza Clubley Middleton

Eligibility: Poor women of the Catholic faith who have lived in the Hull area for over 10 years.

Types of grants: Grants are distributed twice a year, at Christmas and in the summer. The typical average value of any individual grant is less than £75.

Annual grant total: In 2008/09 the charity had assets of £206,000 and an income of £13,000. Grants were made totalling £8,800.

Applications: A list of current beneficiaries is circulated to all local priests each year. They then recommend any additions or note changes in circumstances.

Correspondent: Trust Administrator, Rollits, Rowntree Wharf, Navigation Road, York YO1 9WE (01904 625790; fax: 01904 625807)

The 'Mother Humber' Memorial Fund

Eligibility: People in need who live in the city of Kingston-upon-Hull.

Types of grants: One-off grants ranging from £50 to £500 for individuals

Exclusions: No grants are made for: educational appeals and sponsorship e.g. of Duke of Edinburgh Award students; the payment of debts; and the payment of wages or administration expenses.

Annual grant total: In 2008/09 the fund had an income of £36,000. Grants to individuals totalled approximately £20,000.

Applications: On a form available from the correspondent, submitted through a social worker, Citizens Advice or other welfare agency.

Correspondent: Malcom Welford, Secretary, 14 Kendale View, Driffield, East Yorkshire, YO25 5YY (01482 679888)

The Joseph Rank Benevolent Fund

Eligibility: Men aged 65 or over and women aged 60 or over who are retired and have lived in Hull for at least 10 of the last 15 years. If the applicant is married, their partner must also meet these age limits.

Types of grants: Recurrent grants of £30 per quarter to single people and £60 per quarter to married couples.

Annual grant total: In 2009 the fund had assets of £2.7 million which generated an income of £111,000. Grants were made to individuals totalling £77,000.

Applications: On a form available from the correspondent. Applications are considered throughout the year.

Correspondent: Mrs M Burman, Clerk to the Trustees, Artlink Centre, 87 Princes Avenue, Hull HU5 3QP (01482 225542)

Other information: The fund also makes grants to local charities (£3,000 in 2009).

The Wilmington Trust

Eligibility: People in need who live in Kingston-upon-Hull (east of the river Hull).

Types of grants: One-off grants ranging from £50 to £100 towards, for instance, clothing, holidays, emergencies, furniture, white goods and other household items.

Annual grant total: In 2009 the trust had an income of £9,600 and a total expenditure of £7,800.

Applications: On a form available from the correspondent. Applications must be made through Citizens Advice, social workers or members of the clergy. The trustees meet twice a year to consider grants, although decisions can be made between meetings.

Correspondent: Rev Heather Nesbitt, 25 Church Street, Sutton-On-Hull, Hull HU7 4TL (01482 782154)

Other information: The trust also makes grants to local organisations.

Newton on Derwent

Newton on Derwent Charity

Eligibility: People who are sick, older or in need who live in the parish of Newton on Derwent.

Types of grants: One-off grants according to need.

Annual grant total: Welfare grants usually total around £3,000 per annum.

Applications: In writing to the correspondent.

Correspondent: The Clerk to the Charity, FAO, Grays Solicitors, Duncombe Place, York YO1 7DY

Ottringham

The Ottringham Church Lands Charity

Eligibility: People in hardship and/or distress who live in the parish of Ottringham.

Types of grants: Normally one-off grants, but recurrent grants may be considered.

Exclusions: No grants are given which would affect the applicant's state benefits.

Annual grant total: About £6,000.

Applications: In writing to the correspondent at any time. Applications can be submitted either directly by the individual, through a third party such as a social worker or teacher, or through an organisation such as Citizens Advice or a school.

Correspondent: J R Hinchliffe, 'Hallgarth', Station Road, Ottringham, East Yorkshire HU12 0BJ (01964 622230)

Walkington

Sherwood and Waudby Charity

Eligibility: People of any age who are in need, due for example to hardship, disability or sickness and living in the parish of Walkington only.

Types of grants: One-off grants ranging between £200 and £500 towards items, services or facilities calculated to alleviate need.

Annual grant total: Grants usually total around £5,000 per year; however the majority of grants are made to organisations.

Applications: In writing to the correspondent for consideration in November. Applications from outside the parish of Walkington are not considered.

Correspondent: Mrs Sue Sugars, 11 Waudby Close, Walkington, Beverley HU17 8SA (01482 861056; email: sugars@waudby-close.karoo.co.uk)

North Yorkshire

Bauer Radio's Cash for Kids Charities

Eligibility: People who are 19 or under and either live or go to school in the East Yorkshire and Northern Lincolnshire area. This area extends to Mablethorpe in the South, York and Carlton in the West and Flamborough in the North.

Types of grants: Grants are made towards children who are sick, disabled or have learning disabilities.

Annual grant total: In 2009 the charities made grants to organisations amounting to £34,000. No grants were made to individuals during the year.

Applications: On a form available from the correspondent. They are considered quarterly. Cheques are paid to a charity on the individual's behalf to ensure it is spent for the intended purpose.

Correspondent: Rebecca Poppleton, Trust Manager (01482 593193; email: rebecca.poppleton@vikingfm.co.uk; Website: www.vikingfm.co.uk)

Bedale Welfare Charity

Eligibility: Older people who are infirm and/or in need who live in Bedale and the immediate surrounding area.

Types of grants: One-off grants usually ranging from £40 to £500.

Annual grant total: In 2008/09 the charity had an income of £15,000 and a total expenditure of £5,000, most of which is distributed in relief-in-need grants and to organisations to a larger extent.

Applications: On a form available from the correspondent, to be submitted at any time either directly by the individual or through a third party such as a social worker or teacher.

Correspondent: John Winkle, 25 Burrill Road, Bedale, North Yorkshire, DL8 1ET (01677 424306; email: johnwinkle@awinkle.freeserve.co.uk)

Broughton, Kirkby & District Good Samaritan Fund

Eligibility: People who are over 65 years of age or infirm and resident in the parishes of Kirkby and Ingleby Greenhow.

Types of grants: A simple Christmas present and visit.

Annual grant total: Grants average around £1,000 a year, though the actual grant figure tends to fluctuate quite widely.

Applications: In writing to the correspondent.

Correspondent: R Cooper, Hon. Secretary, Roseworth House, Great Broughton, Middlesbrough, Cleveland TS9 7EN (01642 370073)

The Gargrave Poor's Land Charity

Eligibility: People in need who live in Gargrave, Banknewton, Coniston Cold, Flasby, Eshton or Winterburn.

Types of grants: One-off and recurrent grants for debt relief, travel to hospital, household equipment, furniture, respite care, electrical goods and essential repairs. Christmas gifts are also made each year to permanent residents who are poor, older, disadvantaged or disabled.

Annual grant total: In 2008/09 the charity had assets of £344,000 and an income of £45,000. Grants were made totalling £18,000, nearly £16,000 of which was given for welfare purposes and distributed as follows:

Christmas distribution	£10,000
Debt repayments	£2,500
Purchase of appliances	£1,400
Sundry assistance to the poor	£1,600

Applications: On a form available from the correspondent. Applications can be submitted at any time.

Correspondent: The Trustees, Kirk Syke, High Street, Gargrave, Skipton, North Yorkshire, BD23 3RA

Other information: Grants are also given for educational purposes.

The Goldsborough Poor's Charity

Eligibility: Older people who live in Goldsborough, Flaxby or Coneythorpe (or near Knaresborough). Most recipients tend to be widows or widowers.

Types of grants: Recurrent grants are given to supplement pensions or low incomes.

Annual grant total: Grants usually total around £1,500 a year.

Applications: In writing to the correspondent. Applications can be submitted either directly by the individual, through a third party or via a social worker, Citizens Advice or other welfare agency.

Correspondent: J L Clarkson, 25 Princess Mead, Goldsborough, Knaresborough, North Yorkshire HG5 8NP (01423 865102)

Reverend Matthew Hutchinson Trust (Gilling and Richmond)

Eligibility: People who are in need and live in the parishes of Gilling and Richmond in North Yorkshire.

Types of grants: One-off grants according to need. Recent grants have been given towards medical care, telephone rental, a violin, running shoes and children's nursery fees.

Annual grant total: This charity has branches in both Gilling and Richmond, which are administered jointly, but have separate funding. In 2009 the combined income of the charities was £21,000 and their combined expenditure was £16,000. The combined grant total is usually about £10,000 a year.

Applications: In writing to the correspondent by March or November. Applications can be submitted directly by the individual or through a trustee, social worker, Citizens Advice or other welfare agency.

Correspondent: Mrs C Wiper, 3 Smithson Close, Moulton, Richmond, North Yorkshire, DL10 6QP (01325 377328)

Other information: Grants are also made to local schools and hospitals.

The Purey Cust Fund

Eligibility: People with medical needs who live in York and the surrounding area.

Types of grants: One-off grants ranging between £100 and £1,500, for healthcare equipment, specialist medical equipment and medical education.

Annual grant total: About £2,500.

Applications: Applications must show evidence of the medical need and can be submitted directly by the individual or through a social worker, Citizens Advice, other welfare agency or third party. Applications are considered throughout the year.

Correspondent: Nicholas Turner, Trustee, Stockton Hermitage, Malton Road, York, YO32 9TL (01904 400 070)

The Rowlandson & Eggleston Relief-in-Need Charity

Eligibility: People in the parishes of Barton and Newton Morrell who are in need.

Types of grants: One-off grants usually in the range of £100 to £500. Recent grants have been given towards funeral expenses, medical equipment, disability aids and lifeline telephone systems for older people.

Annual grant total: In 2008/09 the charity had an income of £4,000 and a total expenditure of £7,600.

Applications: In writing to the correspondent including details of circumstances and specific need(s). Applications may be submitted directly by the individual or through a social worker, Citizens Advice or other third party.

Correspondent: Peter Vaux, Chair, Brettanby Manor, Barton, Richmond, North Yorkshire DL10 6HD (01325 377233; fax: 01325 377647)

Other information: This charity also provides other facilities and make grants to individuals for educational purposes.

The York Dispensary Charitable Trust

Eligibility: People living in York and the surrounding districts who are experiencing poverty and ill health.

Types of grants: One-off grants for specific needs such as clothing, domestic equipment or holidays.

Annual grant total: Grants usually total around £1,500 per year.

Applications: In writing to the correspondent, preferably through social services or a similar welfare agency, although direct application is possible. Applications are considered regularly.

Correspondent: The Secretary, 1 St Saviourgate, York YO1 8ZQ (01904 558600)

Carperby-cum-Thoresby

The Carperby Poor's Land Charity

Eligibility: People in need who live in the parish of Carperby-cum-Thoresby.

Types of grants: One-off and recurrent grants are given according to need.

Annual grant total: Grants average around £1,700 a year.

Applications: In writing to the correspondent, with details of the financial need. Applications can be submitted directly by the individual or through a social worker, Citizens Advice or other welfare agency. They are usually considered quarterly.

Correspondent: David Brampton, The Bastlehouse, Carperby, Leyburn, North Yorkshire DL8 4DD (email: brampton@ bastlehouse.freeserve.co.uk)

Craven

The Gertrude Beasley Charitable Trust

Eligibility: Children and young people who are disabled and live in Craven.

Types of grants: Grants given according to need.

Annual grant total: About £1,000.

Applications: In writing to the correspondent.

Correspondent: J C Mewies, J P Mewies and Co. Solicitors, Clifford House, Keighley Road, Skipton, North Yorkshire BD23 2NB (01756 799000)

Other information: Grants are also made to organisations.

Danby

The Joseph Ford's Trust

Eligibility: People who live within the original parish of Danby and are blind, aged or in poverty or misfortune.

Types of grants: One-off or recurrent grants according to need.

Annual grant total: About £1,200.

Applications: In writing to the correspondent or any other trustee, at any time.

Correspondent: Liz Sheard, Trustee, 28 West Lane, Danby, Whitby, YO21 2LY (01642 711289)

Knaresborough

The Knaresborough Relief-in-Need Charity

Eligibility: People in need who live in the parish of Knaresborough, with a preference for people who have lived there for at least five years.

Types of grants: Pensions of £25 a year and occasional one-off grants of up to £1,000.

Annual grant total: Pensions were made to over 200 individuals totalling £5,000.

Applications: In writing to the correspondent.

Correspondent: Mike Dixon, Administrator, 9 Netheredge Drive, Knaresborough, North Yorkshire HG5 9DA (01423 863378; email: thedixongang@btinternet.com)

Lothersdale

Raygill Trust

Eligibility: Older people who live in the ecclesiastical parish of Lothersdale.

Types of grants: One-off grants are available to assist with the cost of living.

Annual grant total: In 2008/09 the trust had an income of £11,000 and a total expenditure of £8,000.

Applications: In writing to the correspondent. Applications can be submitted directly by the individual or through a third party or welfare agency.

Correspondent: Roger Armstrong, Armstrong Wood & Bridgman, 12–16 North Street, Keighley, West Yorkshire BD21 3SE (01535 613660)

Northallerton

The Grace Gardner Trust

Eligibility: Older people, people with disabilities or those who are disadvantaged who live within the boundary of Northallerton parish.

Types of grants: One-off grants of up to £200 according to need including those for electric goods, home improvements, travel expenses, furniture and disability equipment.

Annual grant total: In 2008/09 the trust had an income of £5,700 and a total expenditure of £3,700.

Applications: In writing to the correspondent including details of age and place of residence. Applications can be submitted directly by the individual or through a recognised referral agency (such as social worker, Citizens Advice or doctor) at any time.

Correspondent: The Secretary, c/o Town Hall, High Street, Northallerton, North Yorkshire DL7 8QR (01609 776718; email: northallertontc@btconnect.com)

Other information: The trust also makes grants to local organisations for day trips.

Scarborough

The Scarborough Municipal Charities

Eligibility: People in need who are of retirement age and live in Scarborough.

Types of grants: Grants are one-off and range between £250 and £1,500. Support is given towards livings costs and travel expenses.

Annual grant total: In 2009 grants were made for both educational and welfare purposes totalling £13,000.

Applications: In writing to the correspondent. Applications are considered quarterly.

Correspondent: Mrs E Greening, 42 Green Lane, Scarborough, YO12 6HT (01723 371063)

St Margaret

Robert Winterscale's Charity

Eligibility: People over 60 years of age who have lived in the ancient parishes of St Margaret's and St Denys for more than five years and are in need.

Types of grants: Biannual pensions totalling about £25 a year.

Annual grant total: Grants average around £1,600 each year.

Applications: On a form available from the correspondent. Applications can be submitted directly by the individual, through an organisation such as Citizens Advice or through a third party such as a social worker. Applications are considered on a regular basis.

Correspondent: Richard Watson, Crombie Wilkinson, 17–19 Clifford Street, York YO1 9RJ (01904 624185; email: r.watson@crombiewilkinson.co.uk)

West Witton

The Smorthwaite Charity

Eligibility: Older people in need who live in West Witton.

Types of grants: Annual grants of ranging from £100 to £150.

Annual grant total: In 2008/09 the charity had an income of £15,000 and a total expenditure of £39,000. Grants usually total about £5,000 each year.

Applications: The charity usually advertises in the local post office. Most applications tend to be submitted by word of mouth and through conversations with the trustees rather than through a formal application process.

Correspondent: Geoff Clarke, Pen Cottage, Main Street, West Witton, Leyburn, North Yorkshire DL8 4LX (01969 624393)

Other information: The charity also maintains five rental properties in the area.

York

The Micklegate Strays Charity

Eligibility: Freemen of the city of York and their dependants living in the Micklegate Strays ward. (This area is now defined as the whole of that part of the city of York to the west of the River Ouse.)

Types of grants: Pensions and medical grants of £30 a year.

Annual grant total: About £600 a year for educational and welfare purposes.

Applications: On a form available from the correspondent. Applications should include the date of the freeman's oath and are considered in November.

Correspondent: Roger Lee, 29 Albemarle Road, York, YO23 1EW (01904 653698)

Other information: The trust was created by the 1907 Micklegate Strays Act. The city of York agreed to pay the freemen £1,000 a year in perpetuity for extinguishing their rights over Micklegate Stray. This sum has been reduced due to the forced divestment of the trust government stock, following the Charities Act of 1992.

The Charity of Jane Wright

Eligibility: People in need who live in the city of York.

Types of grants: One-off grants and vouchers according to need.

Annual grant total: In 2008/09 the charity made grants totalling £24,000, distributed as follows:

School uniforms	£16,000
Residence fees	£2,500
Miscellaneous purposes	£5,400

Applications: Applications must be made directly or via recognised welfare agencies. They are considered at or between trustees' meetings.

Correspondent: Diane Grayson, Clerk, 18 St Saviourgate, York YO1 8NS (01904 655555; email: post@harlandsolicitors.co.uk)

York City Charities

Eligibility: People in need who live within the pre-1996 York city boundaries (the area within the city walls).

Types of grants: One-off grants of between £50 and £200. Recent grants have been given towards furniture and to people on probation to set up a new home.

Annual grant total: In 2008 the charities had assets of just over £1 million and an income of £205,000. Grants made to individuals totalled £1,500.

Applications: In writing to the correspondent, to be submitted by a doctor, occupational nurse, head teacher, social worker, Citizens Advice or other third party or welfare agency. Applications are considered throughout the year.

Correspondent: M Richard Watson, Clerk, 19 Clifford Street, YORK, YO1 9RJ (01904 624185; email: r.watson@ crombiewilkinson.co.uk)

The York Fund for Women & Girls

Eligibility: Women and girls under the age of 50, who live in York and who are in need.

Types of grants: Generally one-off grants, between £50 and £150, to help with essential household items, fuel bills, furnishings, baby equipment and children's clothes.

Exclusions: No grants for education or travel costs.

Annual grant total: Grants usually total around £2,000 per year.

Applications: On a form available from the correspondent. Applications should be made through a recognised agency and include details of the individual's income. They are considered on an ongoing basis.

Correspondent: Rosemary Suttill, Administrator to the Trustees, c/o York & District CAB, 3 Blossom Street, York YO24 1AU (01904 623648; email: rosemary.suttill@yorkcab.org.uk)

Northumberland

The Henry Bell Trust

Eligibility: People in need who live in the parish of Hexham or the Hexhamshire area.

Types of grants: One-off and recurrent grants ranging from £50 to £400.

Annual grant total: In 2008/09 the trust had an income of £13,000 and a total expenditure of £6,500. Grants are available both to individuals and organisations.

Applications: In writing to the correspondent directly by the individual or family member. Applications are considered in March and September.

Correspondent: A Sharp, Secretary, Land Factor, Market Place, Haltwhistle, Northumberland, NE49 0BP (01434 320363)

The Eleemosynary Charity of Giles Heron

Eligibility: People in need who live in the ancient parish of Simonburn.

Types of grants: One-off grants ranging from £100 to £500.

Annual grant total: In 2008/09 the charity had both an income and a total expenditure of £14,000. Grants were made totalling around £8,000, of which about £4,000 was given in individual awards, with the rest being donated to local organisations.

Applications: In writing to the correspondent directly by the individual.

Correspondent: George Benson, Trustee, Brunton House, Wall, Hexham, Northumberland NE46 4EJ (01434 681203)

Other information: Individual grants are also made for educational purposes.

The Morpeth Dispensary

Eligibility: People who are sick and poor and live in or around Morpeth.

Types of grants: Grants are one-off and range from £40 to £300 including those for new washing machines, household bills, cookers, decorating costs, clothing, furniture and so on.

Annual grant total: Grants average around £2,000 per year.

Applications: In writing to the correspondent at any time through a third party such as a social worker, GP, Citizens Advice or other welfare agency. Applications must include detail of the applicant's age, whether a single parent, whether on benefit, their address and any details regarding health matters. Grants are made directly to the third party, not the applicant.

Correspondent: Michael Gaunt, Trustee, 15 Bridge Street, Morpeth, Northumberland NE61 1NX (01670 512336)

Other information: Grants are also made to organisations to provide additional help at Christmas, for instance a trip to the theatre at Christmas for those individuals meeting the eligibility criteria.

Berwick-upon-Tweed

The Berwick-upon-Tweed Nursing Amenities Fund

Eligibility: People who are sick, poor or in need and live in the borough of Berwick-upon-Tweed.

Types of grants: One-off grants up to £200.

Annual grant total: About £650.

Applications: In writing to the correspondent through a social worker, Citizens Advice or other welfare agency at any time.

Correspondent: Alan J Patterson, Greaves West & Ayre, 1–3 Sandgate, Berwick-upon-Tweed TD15 1EW (01289 306688; fax: 01289 307189; email: ap@gwayre.co.uk)

South Yorkshire

The Aston-cum-Aughton Charity Estate

Eligibility: People in need who live in Aston, Aughton or Swallowness.

Types of grants: One-off and recurrent grants according to need. Recent grants have been made towards the cost of holidays for a single parent family and an unemployed couple and their three children. Help has also been given towards installing a telephone for an older couple. The trust does not normally give cash grants instead it pays the supplier of the services.

Exclusions: The charity does not make loans or give to profit-making concerns.

Annual grant total: In 2009 the charity had an income of £24,000 and a total expenditure of £21,000.

Applications: In writing to the correspondent or any trustee, directly by the individual or through a social worker, Citizens Advice or other welfare agency. Applications are considered quarterly.

Correspondent: Jim Nuttall, Clerk, 3 Rosegarth Avenue, Aston, Sheffield S26 2DB (0114 287 6047)

Other information: Grants are also made to organisations catering for the elderly.

The Brampton Bierlow Welfare Trust

Eligibility: People in need who live in Brampton Bierlow and West Melton, and those parts of Wentworth and Elscar within the ancient parish of Brampton Bierlow.

Types of grants: One-off grants from £100 to £250 for necessities and comforts, and Christmas grocery vouchers of £6.

Annual grant total: In 2009 the trust had an income of £9,700 and a total expenditure of £5,300.

Applications: Applications in writing to the correspondent can be submitted by the individual and are considered at any time.

Correspondent: Jill Leece, Newman & Bond, 35 Church Street, Barnsley S70 2AP (01226 213434)

Other information: The trust also makes grants to local organisations.

The Cantley Poor's Land Trust

Eligibility: People in need who live in the ancient parish of Cantley with Branton.

Types of grants: One-off grants ranging from £50 to £500 including those towards electric goods, clothing, medical equipment, furniture and disabled equipment.

Exclusions: Restrictions apply to the relief of rates, taxes and repeat grants.

Annual grant total: In 2008/09 the trust had assets of £726,000 and an income of £34,000. Grants were made to 110 individuals totalling £15,000.

Applications: On a form available from the correspondent, to be submitted directly by the individual or through a welfare agency. Applications are considered on a monthly basis.

Correspondent: Margaret Jackson, Clerk to the Trustees, 30 Selhurst Crescent, Bessacarr, Doncaster, South Yorkshire DN4 6EF (01302 530566)

William Fisher

Eligibility: Unitarian and Roman Catholic widows and unmarried women in need who are over 45 and live in and around Sheffield.

Types of grants: Annual allowances of £100 to £150 to help supplement low incomes.

Annual grant total: Grants usually total about £1,000 each year.

Applications: On a form available from the correspondent, to be submitted via the applicant's minister. Applications are normally considered in April.

Correspondent: Jennifer Laister, 77 Woodburn Drive, Chapeltown, Sheffield, S35 1YT (0114 246 2293)

Other information: This trust is also known as the Fisher Trust.

The George & Clara Ann Hall Charity

Eligibility: Widows and unmarried women over 45 who have lived in the city of Sheffield or the township and chapelry of Bradfield for the past five years and are in receipt of benefits.

Types of grants: Annual grants of £600 are paid half yearly to a small number of beneficiaries.

Annual grant total: In 2008/09 the charity had an income of £5,000 and a total expenditure of £5,600.

Applications: In writing to the correspondent. However, the charity has only a limited amount of funds and wants to ensure that the annual grants it awards are a meaningful amount. As a result, new applicants are only considered when an existing beneficiary has died.

Correspondent: Nick Warren, Chief Executive, c/o Voluntary Action Sheffield, The Circle, 33 Rockingham Lane, Sheffield S1 4FW (0114 2536605; fax: 0114 2536601; email: n.warren@vas.org.uk)

Rebecca Guest Robinson Charity

Eligibility: People who live in the villages of Birdwell and Worsbrough, near Barnsley, and are in need. Preference is given to children, young people and older people.

Types of grants: One-off grants, usually ranging between £50 and £250, towards clothing, household equipment, disability equipment, holidays and childcare.

Annual grant total: This trust generally has an income of around £1,500 and a total expenditure of £1,000 to £2,000.

Applications: On a form available from the correspondent. Applications should be submitted directly by the individual or a family member.

Correspondent: John Armitage, 10 St Mary's Gardens, Worsbrough, Barnsley, South Yorkshire S70 5LU (01226 290179)

Other information: Local organisations are also supported.

The Sheffield West Riding Charitable Society Trust

Eligibility: Clergymen of the Church of England in the diocese of Sheffield who are in need. Also their widows, orphans or distressed families, and people keeping house, or who have kept house, for clergymen of the Church of England in the diocese or their families.

Types of grants: One-off and recurrent grants of £100 to £1,000.

Annual grant total: In 2009 the trust had an income of £11,000 and a total expenditure of £14,000. Around 20 grants are made each year.

Applications: On a form available from the correspondent.

Correspondent: Malcolm Fair, Diocesan Secretary, Diocesan Church House, 95–99 Effingham Street, Rotherham S65 1BL (01709 309100; email: malcolm.fair@sheffield.anglican.org; website: www.sheffield.anglican.org)

Other information: Welfare grants are also made to the clergy, house-keepers and disadvantaged families in the diocese.

Armthorpe

Armthorpe Poors Estate Charity

Eligibility: People who are in need and live in Armthorpe.

Types of grants: One-off and recurrent grants of £50 to £500 towards items such as mobility aids, aids for people with visual difficulties, hospital visiting and care of older people.

Annual grant total: In 2008/09 the charity had an income of £10,000 and a total expenditure of £8,000.

Applications: Contact the clerk by telephone who will advise if a letter of application is needed. Applicants outside of Armthorpe will be declined.

Correspondent: Frank Pratt, 32 Gurth Avenue, Edenthorpe, Doncaster DN3 2LW (01302 882806)

Other information: The trust gives to both individuals and organisations

Barnsley

The Barnsley Tradesmen's Benevolent Institution

Eligibility: Merchants and traders, their widows and unmarried daughters, who are in need and have lived in the old borough of Barnsley for at least seven years.

Types of grants: Recurrent grants are given towards general daily living expenses such as food, medical care and equipment and travel to and from hospital.

Annual grant total: Generally this trust gives grants totalling around £1,800 a year.

Applications: In writing to the correspondent, either directly by the individual or through a third party such as a Citizens Advice or other welfare agency. Applications are considered monthly.

Correspondent: David Bishop Richards, 9 Kensington Road, Barnsley, South Yorkshire S75 2TX

The Fountain Nursing Trust

Eligibility: People in need who are in poor health, convalescent or who have a disability and live in the urban district of Darton, Barnsley.

Types of grants: One-off and recurrent grants according to need. Recent grants have been given for medical equipment and expenses, nursing fees and help in the home.

Annual grant total: Grants average about £2,000 a year, though the actual grant figure tends to fluctuate quite widely.

Applications: In writing to the correspondent.

Correspondent: The Trustees, Newman & Bond, 35 Church Street, Barnsley, South Yorkshire S70 2AP (01226 213434; fax: 01226 213435)

Beighton

Beighton Relief-in-Need Charity

Eligibility: People in need who live in the former parish of Beighton.

Types of grants: One off grants according to need. Recent grants have been given towards bath lifts and child care seats for people who are disabled. Winter fuel grants of £15 per household were also given to older people.

Annual grant total: Grants usually total around £9,000 per year.

Applications: In writing to the correspondent. Applications can be submitted directly by the individual or through a social worker, Citizens Advice, other welfare agency or a third party such as a relative, neighbour or trustee.

Correspondent: Michael Lowe, Elms Bungalow, Queens Road, Beighton, Sheffield S20 1AW (0114 2692875)

Other information: Grants are also made for educational purposes.

Bramley

The Bramley Poor's Allotment Trust

Eligibility: People in need who live in the ancient township of Bramley, especially people who are elderly, poor and sick.

Annual grant total: In 2008/09 the trust had an income of £6,000 and a total expenditure of £4,800.

Applications: In writing to the correspondent. The trust likes applications to be submitted through a recognised referral agency (social worker, Citizens Advice, doctor, headmaster or minister). They are considered monthly.

Correspondent: Len Barnett, Mrs Marian Houseman, 9 Horton Rise, Rodley, Leeds, LS13 1PH (0113 2360115)

Doncaster

The John William Chapman Charitable Trust

Eligibility: People in need who live in the metropolitan borough of Doncaster.

Types of grants: One-off grants in kind, not cash, up to the value of £500 towards fridges, cookers, washing machines, beds, cots, carpets and clothing.

Exclusions: No grants are given towards wardrobes, cupboards, drawers, living room suites, TV, hi-fi, video players, educational course fees, funeral expenses, external work to a property, payment of debts including rent bonds, decorating materials, toys, removal expenses, baby high chairs or gates.

Annual grant total: In 2008/09 the trust had assets of £3.4 million and an income of £172,000. Grants to individuals totalled £23,000.

Applications: On a form available from the correspondent or to download from the website. Applications must be accompanied by a letter from a social worker, GP or welfare agency and are considered monthly. The trust visits all applicants.

Correspondent: Rosemary Sharp, Jordans, 4 Priory Place, Doncaster DN1 1BP (01302 365374; email: info@chapmantrust.org)

Other information: Grants to organisations amounted to £26,000.

Epworth

Epworth Charities

Eligibility: People in need who live in Epworth.

Types of grants: One-off and recurrent grants in the range of £50 and £250.

Annual grant total: Grants usually total between £400 and £1,000 per year.

Applications: In writing to the correspondent to be submitted directly by the individual. Applications are considered on an ongoing basis.

Correspondent: Mrs Margaret Draper, 16 Fern Croft, Epworth, Doncaster, South Yorkshire DN9 1GE (01427 873234; email: margaret.draper@btinternet.com)

Other information: Grants are also made for educational purposes.

Finningly

The Sir Stuart & Lady Florence Goodwin Charity

Eligibility: People over 60 who are need and live in the former rural district of East Retford. Consideration may be given to younger applicants.

Types of grants: One-off grants to improve quality of life. Recent grants have been given for medical equipment such as nebulisers, access ramps, walk-in baths and mobility scooters.

Annual grant total: In 2008/09 the charity had an income of £9,900 and a total expenditure of £9,400.

Applications: In writing to the correspondent. Applications can be submitted directly by the individual or through a third party such as Age Concern or social services. Grants will only be made to the person raising the invoice, not the individual.

Correspondent: Grants Administrator, Bassetlaw District Council, Finance Department, Queen's Buildings, Potter Street, Worksop, Nottinghamshire S80 2AH (01909 533296; email: memberssupport@bassetlaw.gov.uk)

Rotherham

The Common Lands of Rotherham Charity

Eligibility: People in need who live in Rotherham. Preference is usually given to older people.

Types of grants: One-off and recurrent grants according to need.

Annual grant total: Grants usually total about £5,000 a year.

Applications: In writing to the correspondent following advertisement in September.

Correspondent: W B Copley, Barn Cottage, 5 Crossland Gardens, Tickhill, Doncaster, South Yorkshire DN11 9QS (01302 743947)

The Stoddart Samaritan Fund

Eligibility: People in need who have medical problems and would benefit from financial assistance to help their recovery. Applicants must live in Rotherham and the surrounding area.

Types of grants: One-off grants to assist recovery.

Annual grant total: Grants usually total around £15,000 a year.

Applications: On a form available from the correspondent, to be submitted by the applicant's doctor. Applications are considered on a regular basis.

Correspondent: Peter Wright, 7 Melrose Grove, Rotherham, South Yorkshire S60 3NA (01709 376448)

Sheffield

John Walsh Fund

Eligibility: Those working in or retired from the retail, fashion and department store trade who are in conditions of need, hardship or distress and live in Sheffield.

Types of grants: One-off grants ranging between £200 and £1,000 towards equipment or services.

Annual grant total: Generally the fund has a total expenditure of around £2,000 but no grants have been made for the past five years. The trust has stated that grants will be made again in the future but the capital used to generate income is small (approximately £40,000) and so income will be limited.

Applications: Applications should be made through the website or by calling 0808 801 0808.

Correspondent: Rob Mansell, Marshall Hall, Marshall Estate, Hammers Lane, London, NW7 4DQ (020 8358 7225; email: rmansell@retailtrust.org.uk; website: www.retailtrust.org.uk)

Teesside

The Teesside Emergency Relief Fund

Eligibility: People in need who live in the county borough of Teesside.

Types of grants: One-off grants of between £100 and £1,000 to meet a specific need.

Annual grant total: In 2008/09 the fund had an income of £28,000 and a total expenditure of £57,000. Grants were made totalling about £50,000.

Applications: On a form available from the correspondent. Applications should be supported by a letter from a social worker, health visitor, welfare officer, GP, probation officer, local tenancy office or other welfare agency representative. They are considered on a regular basis.

Correspondent: D E Bond, Stockton-on-Tees Borough Council, Municipal Buildings, Church Road, Stockton-on-Tees TS18 1LD (01642 393939)

Hartlepool

The Furness Seamen's Pension Fund

Eligibility: Seamen in need who are 50 or over and live in the borough of Hartlepool or the former county borough of West Hartlepool, or who had their permanent residence there during their sea service. All applicants must have served as seamen for at least 15 years and with some part of the sea service in vessels registered in Hartlepool, West Hartlepool or the Port of Hartlepool, or vessels trading to/from any of these ports.

Types of grants: Quarterly pensions.

Annual grant total: In 2008/09 the fund had an income of £9,900 and total expenditure of £8,800.

Applications: On a form available from the correspondent. Advertisements are placed in the Hartlepool Mail when vacancies are available.

Correspondent: Heather O'Driscoll, Trust Administrator, c/o Horwath Clark Whitehill, Oakland House, 38–42 Victoria Road, Hartlepool, Cleveland TS26 8DD (01429 234414; fax: 01429 231263; email: heather.o'driscoll@horwath.co.uk)

Middlesbrough

The Lady Crosthwaite Bequest

Eligibility: Pensioners in need who live in the former county borough of Middlesbrough.

Types of grants: Small grants at Christmas, and occasional day trips, via the social services and community councils, together with one-off lump sums to organisations.

Annual grant total: In 2008/09 the bequest had an income of £17,000 and a total expenditure of £20,000.

Applications: In writing to the correspondent, through social services.

Correspondent: Mark Taylor, Middlesbrough Council, PO Box 340, Middlesbrough, Cleveland TS1 2XP (01642 727337)

Middleton

Ralph Gowland Trust

Eligibility: People in need aged 60 or over who live in the parish of Middleton in Teesdale.

Types of grants: One-off and recurrent grants according to need.

Annual grant total: About £1,000.

Applications: In writing to the correspondent.

Correspondent: Joan Staley, 38 Hill Terrace, Middleton-in-Teesdale, Barnard Castle, County Durham DL12 0SL (01833 640542)

Tyne & Wear

Community Foundation Serving Tyne & Wear and Northumberland

Eligibility: People in need who live in Northumberland or Tyne and Wear.

Types of grants: The Community Foundation is essentially a local umbrella organisation of grant making trusts, which pools together money from various sources to maximise the interest levels on the investments. There are over 100 smaller funds administered by the foundation and only a handful support individuals. Information on funds is available from the foundation, or on its website.

Annual grant total: In 2008/09 the there were over 300 grants made to individuals for educational and welfare needs totalling £180,000.

Applications: On a form available from the correspondent. The foundation is responsible for managing many different funds and will forward any application to the one most suitable, though it is important to note that several funds do have a separate application form and it is worth contacting the foundation prior to completing any submission. Applications can be made at any time and the foundation will generally reply within three months of receipt.

Correspondent: George Hepburn, Cale Cross, 156 Pilgrim Street, Newcastle upon Tyne, NE1 6SU (0191 222 0945; fax: 0191 230 0689; email: general@ communityfoundation.org.uk; website: www.communityfoundation.org. uk)

Other information: More detailed information on this foundation can be found in DSC's *The Guide to the Major Trusts Volume 1*. Also see the foundation's website for more information on the application process and the different grant-making funds.

Charity of John McKie Elliott Deceased

Eligibility: People who are blind in Gateshead or Newcastle upon Tyne.

Types of grants: One-off and recurrent grants according to need.

Annual grant total: Annual income usually ranges between £500 and £2,500.

Applications: In writing to the correspondent.

Correspondent: Roger Eager, 9 Beaumont Court, Whitley Bay, Tyne & Wear, NE25 9TZ (0191 2537079; email: eager6@ msn.com)

Other information: The trust gives educational grants and grants to individuals in need

The Sunderland Guild of Help

Eligibility: People in need who live in Sunderland.

Types of grants: Support is given for the advancement of health and the relief of poverty.

Exclusions: No grants for new goods or goods made to order.

Annual grant total: In 2008/09 the guild had assets of £133,000 and an income of £17,000. Grants to individuals usually total around £4,000.

Applications: Applications can only be considered if they are submitted through a social worker. They should include an income and expenditure statement and are considered throughout the year.

Correspondent: Norman Taylor, Chair, 4 Toward Road, Sunderland, Tyne & Wear SR1 2QG (0191 567 2895; email: info@ guildofhelp.co.uk; website: www. guildofhelp.co.uk)

Other information: The guild administers the Sunderland Queen Victoria Memorial

Fund 1901, the Sunderland Convalescent Fund and the Chest and Heart Fund. It also manages the trust funds connected with the tuberculosis care committee of the guild.

In addition, the guild acts as an enabling charity through its premises on Toward Road, Sunderland where other small charities are provided accommodation at rents that reflect their charitable status.

The Sunderland Orphanage & Educational Foundation

Eligibility: Young people under 25 who are resident in or around Sunderland who have a parent who is disabled or has died, or whose parents are divorced or legally separated.

Types of grants: Grants are given to children for clothing and living expenses. Grants are also made to students.

Annual grant total: In 2008/09 the trust had an income of £22,000 and a total expenditure of £25,000.

Applications: Applications should be made in writing to the correspondent. They are considered every other month.

Correspondent: Peter Taylor, McKenzie Bell, 19 John Street, Sunderland SR1 1JG (0191 567 4857)

The Thomas Thompson Poors Rate Gift

Eligibility: People in need who live in Byker.

Types of grants: One-off grants for items such as washing machines, furniture and cookers. Grants have also been given to replace Christmas presents and children's bikes which have been stolen.

Annual grant total: Grants average around £3,000 a year.

Applications: In writing to the correspondent, for consideration throughout the year. Grants to replace stolen property are usually submitted through Victim Support.

Correspondent: Anthony Francis, Newcastle City Council, 5th Floor, Civic Centre, Barras Bridge, Newcastle NE99 1RD (0191 2116919; email: anthony.francis@newcastle.gov.uk)

The Tyne Mariners' Benevolent Institution

Eligibility: Former merchant seamen who live in Tyneside (about five miles either side of the River Tyne) and their widows. Applicants must be: (a) at least 55 years old and have served at least 15 years at sea; (b) under the age of 55, but unable to work owing to ill-health; or (c) the widows of such people.

Types of grants: Recurrent grants of about £40 per calendar month and two bonuses of varying value.

Annual grant total: In 2009 the trust had assets of £1 million and an income of £212,000. Grants were made to over 200 individuals totalling £124,000

Applications: On a form available from the correspondent, to be submitted either directly by the individual or through a social worker, Citizens Advice or other welfare agency. Applications can be considered at any time.

Correspondent: Janet Littlefield, Hadaway & Hadaway, 58 Howard Street, North Shields, Tyne & Wear NE30 1AL (0191 2570 382; email: janetl@hadaway.co.uk)

Other information: The institution also administers The Master Mariners Homes in Tynemouth which provides 30 flats for its beneficiaries.

Gateshead

The Gateshead Blind Trust Fund

Eligibility: People who are registered blind or partially sighted and live in the borough of Gateshead.

Types of grants: One-off grants up to £500 towards household items such as cookers, fridges, washing machines, as well as furniture, computer equipment, educational expenses and any aids that will benefit people who are blind or partially sighted in their daily living.

Exclusions: Grants are not given for debts of any kind, television or car licences, cars, holidays, funeral expenses or nursing or residential home fees.

Annual grant total: There has been no expenditure by this fund since 2007, although it still has an income of around £900. Previously total expenditure was between £200 and £1,100.

Applications: All applications must be submitted via the Technical Officers for the Blind, employed in the social services department, on the form available. Applications are considered throughout the year. Re-application for grants is not allowed for two years once a grant has been awarded.

Correspondent: Mike Barker, Gateshead Council, Legal & Corporate Services, Civic Centre, Regent Street, Gateshead NE8 1HH (0191 433 3000)

The Gateshead Relief-in-Sickness Fund

Eligibility: People who are in poor health, convalescent or who have disabilities and live in the borough of Gateshead.

Types of grants: One-off grants towards providing or paying for items, services or facilities, which will alleviate need or assist with recovery, and are not readily available from other sources. Recent grants have

been given to adapt a bathroom for a boy with learning and physical disabilities and for computers and talking typewriters for people who are registered blind.

Annual grant total: About £1,700 a year. Grants are given to both individuals and organisations.

Applications: In writing to the correspondent. Applications can be submitted directly by the individual or through a social worker, Citizens Advice or other welfare agency.

Correspondent: Victoria Spark, Thomas Magnay & Co, 8 St Mary's Green, Whickham, Newcastle on Tyne, NE16 4DN (0191 4887459)

Horton

Houghton-Le-Spring Relief in Need Charity

Eligibility: People in need living in the Ancient Parish Of Houghton-Le-Spring.

Types of grants: One-off and recurrent according to need.

Annual grant total: In 2008/09 the charity had an income of £6,500 and a total expenditure of £5,000.

Applications: In writing to the correspondent.

Correspondent: Mrs Angela Fitzroy Morris JP, 24 Sancroft Drive, Houghton Le Spring, DH5 8NE (01915672312; email: rectorstmichaels@btinternet.com)

Newcastle upon Tyne

The Non-Ecclesiastical Charity of William Moulton

Eligibility: People in need who have lived within the boundaries of the city of Newcastle upon Tyne for at least the past 12 months.

Types of grants: Grants range between £50 and £200 towards general household/personal needs such as washing machines, cookers, furniture, clothing and so on.

Exclusions: No grants are given for education, training or rent arrears.

Annual grant total: In 2009 the charity had assets of £1.1 million and an income of £48,000. Grants made to individuals totalled £32,000.

Applications: On a form available from the correspondent. Applications should be submitted through a social worker, Citizens Advice or other welfare agency and are considered monthly.

Correspondent: George Jackson, Clerk to the Trustees, 10 Sunlea Avenue, Cullercoats, Tyne & Wear NE30 3DS (0191 251 0971; email: jgeorgelvis@blueyonder.co.uk)

The Town Moor Money Charity

Eligibility: Freemen of Newcastle upon Tyne and their widows and children who are in need.

Types of grants: One-off and recurrent grants according to need. Grants are means-tested and paid in June and December.

Annual grant total: In 2008/09 the charity had assets of £354,000 and an income of £35,000. Grants were made to 385 beneficiaries totalling £107,000.

Applications: Application forms are available in April and October from the senior steward of the appropriate company. They are usually considered in May and November.

Correspondent: Richard Grey, Moor Bank Lodge, Claremont Road, Newcastle upon Tyne NE2 4NL (0191 261 5970; email: admin@freemenofnewcastle.org; website: www.freemenofnewcastle.org)

Sunderland

The Mayor's Fund for Necessitous Children

Eligibility: Children in need (under 16, occasionally under 19) who are in full-time education, live in the city of Sunderland and whose family are on a low income.

Types of grants: Grants of about £25 for the provision of clothing and footwear, paid every six months.

Exclusions: No grants are made to asylum seekers.

Annual grant total: About £500.

Applications: Applicants must visit the civic centre and fill in a form with a member of staff. The decision is then posted at a later date. Proof of low income is necessary.

Correspondent: Children's Services Financial Manager, Sunderland City Council, Civic Centre, Sunderland SR2 7DN (0191 5531826)

Tynemouth

The Charlton Bequest & Dispensary Trust

Eligibility: People who are sick, poor, have disabilities or who are convalescent and live in the former county borough of Tynemouth, now part of North Tyneside County Borough. Preference is given to people resident at one of the trust's almshouses.

Types of grants: Grants to pay for items, services or facilities which are calculated to alleviate the suffering or assist the recovery of eligible people who do not have funds

readily available to them from other sources.

Annual grant total: In 2008/09 the trust had assets of £1.5 million and an income of £63,000. Grants were made totalling £310.

Applications: In writing to the correspondent.

Correspondent: Roy King, Trustee, 50 The Broadway, North Shields, NE30 2LQ (0191 257 5297)

Other information: This trust was formed from the North Shields & Tynemouth Dispensary and the County Borough of Tynemouth Nursing Association. It is primarily concerned with the provision of apartments for older people in poor health.

Wallsend

The Victor Mann Trust (also known as The Wallsend Charitable Trust)

Eligibility: People over 60 who are on or just above state benefit income levels and live in the former borough of Wallsend.

Types of grants: One-off grants ranging between £10 to £500 to help meet extra requirements, for example, washing machines, fridge-freezers, carpets, home decoration, safety and security measures and medical equipment.

Exclusions: The trust will not help with continuing costs such as residential care or telephone rentals and will not help a person whose income is significantly above state benefit levels. Applicants must have exhausted all statutory avenues such as DWP, Social Fund, social services department and so on.

Annual grant total: In 2009 the trust had an income of £99,000 and a total expenditure of £110,000. The majority of grants are usually given to organisations.

Applications: In writing to the correspondent either directly by the individual or through a social worker, Citizens Advice or other welfare agency or third party, such as a friend or relative. Applications are considered quarterly in April, July, September and December. They must include details of the purpose of the grant and an estimate of the cost.

Correspondent: The Secretary, North Tyneside Council, Cobalt 16, The Silverlink North, Newcastle Upon Tyne, NE27 0BY (0191 643 7006)

Other information: Grants can be given to organisations provided that the majority of members meet the same criteria as apply to individuals.

West Yorkshire

Bradford & District Wool Association Benevolent Fund

Eligibility: Former workers in the wool trade in Bradford and district or their spouses, who are in need. Preference is given to those who are elderly or disabled.

Types of grants: Normally recurrent grants up to a maximum of £200 towards heating, electricity and telephone costs. Special cases (such as the need for an invalid chair) are considered.

Annual grant total: Grants total around £4,000 per year.

Applications: In writing to the correspondent either directly by the individual or through a relative or friend. Applications are considered at any time.

Correspondent: Sir James F Hill, Chair, Unit 2, Baildon Mills, Northgate, Baildon, Shipley, West Yorkshire, BD17 6JX (01274 532200)

The Bradford Jewish Benevolent Fund

Eligibility: Older people in need who are Jewish and live in the city of Bradford and district.

Types of grants: One-off and recurrent grants according to need. Grants are to relieve poverty and sickness.

Annual grant total: Grants average around £1,800 a year.

Applications: In writing to the correspondent, directly by the individual or through a third party such as a social worker.

Correspondent: Walter Behrend, 1 Fern Chase, Leeds, LS14 3JL (0113 2893274)

Mary Farrar's Benevolent Trust Fund

Eligibility: Women of limited means who are over 55 years of age and have lived in the parish of Halifax for more than five years.

Types of grants: Annual pensions are paid quarterly.

Exclusions: No more than six grants are given to married women and widows.

Annual grant total: In 2008/09 the fund had an income of £8,000 and a total expenditure of £10,000. Grants usually total around £10,000.

Applications: On a form available from the correspondent. Applications can be submitted by the individual, through a recognised referral agency (such as a social worker, Citizens Advice, or doctor) or another third party such as a relative, friend, minister of religion or trustee.

Correspondent: Peter Haley, P Haley & Co, Poverty Hall, Lower Ellistones, Saddleworth Road Greetland, Halifax HX4 8NG (01422 376690)

The Harrison & Potter Trust (incorporating Josias Jenkinson Relief-in-Need Charity)

Eligibility: People in need who live in Leeds.

Types of grants: One-off grants range from £100 to £200 with a monthly budget limit of £2,500. Grants are made primarily for household equipment, furniture, bedding and electrical goods, although help may also be given for gas and electricity bills.

Annual grant total: In 2009 the trust had assets of £4.6 million and an income of £330,000. Grants totalled £32,000, of which £29,000 was given in small individual grants and £3,000 was given in vouchers to almshouse residents. A further £15,000 was given to external bodies.

Applications: On a form available from the correspondent and supported by a detailed breakdown of income and expenditure. Applicants should also indicate any other charities approached. Forms should be submitted through a Citizens Advice, social worker or other welfare agency and are considered at the end of each month.

Correspondent: Ann Duchart, Clerk, Wrigleys Solicitors, 17–21 Cookridge Street, Leeds LS2 3AG (0113 244 6100)

Other information: The trust owns and operates two housing schemes for older people in Leeds. Eligible applicants must be in financial hardship and under the terms of the scheme preference must be given to women. Suitable applicants are eligible for grants to meet removal costs, furnishings and so on.

The trust also makes grants to institutions or groups which provide services or facilities to those in need.

Huddersfield and District Army Veterans' Association Benevolent Fund

Eligibility: Veterans of the army, navy and air force who are in need, aged over 60 years, and who were discharged from the forces 'with good character' and live in Huddersfield and part of Brighouse.

Types of grants: One-off and recurrent grants according to need.

Annual grant total: In 2009 the fund had an income of £24,000 and a total expenditure of £29,000. Grants to individuals usually total around £10,000.

Applications: In writing to the correspondent, or on a form published in the fund's applications leaflet. The leaflet is available from doctor's surgeries, local libraries and so on.

Correspondent: Mrs Sarah Lamont, 10 Belton Grove, Huddersfield, HD3 3RF (01484 310193)

The Lucy Lund Holiday Grants

Eligibility: Present and former teachers who need a recuperative holiday. Preference is given to female teachers and particularly those from the former west riding of Yorkshire. No grants are given to dependants or students.

Types of grants: One-off grants for recuperative holidays.

Annual grant total: Grants average around £500 a year.

Applications: On a form available from the correspondent to be submitted by the individual.

Correspondent: Tina Cogan, Teachers Assurance, Tringham House, Deansleigh Road, Bournemouth BH7 7DT

Sir Titus Salt's Charity

Eligibility: People in need who are over the age of 75 and live in Shipley, Baildon, Saltaire, Nab Wood and Wrose of Bradford.

Types of grants: Food vouchers paid once a year, available from Shipley Information Centre. On average 300 grants of £5 each are made every year.

Annual grant total: Grants usually total about £1,500 each year.

Applications: Applications should be made through the Shipley Information Centre to be considered in November/December each year.

Correspondent: Dr Norman Roper, 6 Carlton Road, Shipley, West Yorkshire BD18 4NE (01274 599540)

West Yorkshire Police (Employees) Benevolent Fund

Eligibility: Employees and ex-employees of the West Yorkshire Police Force or the West Yorkshire Metropolitan County Council under the direct control of the chief constable who are in need, and their widows, orphans and other dependants.

Types of grants: One-off and recurrent grants according to need.

Annual grant total: In 2008/09 the fund had an income of £2,800 and a total expenditure of £3,600.

Applications: In writing to the correspondent. Trustee meetings are held every three months, although urgent cases can be considered at any time.

Correspondent: Pat Maknia, West Yorkshire Police Finance Department, PO Box 9, Wakefield WF1 3QP (01924 292841)

Baildon

The Butterfield Trust

Eligibility: People in need who live in the parish of Baildon.

Types of grants: One-off grants for emergencies.

Annual grant total: Grants usually total around £2,500 a year.

Applications: In writing to the correspondent. Decisions can be made immediately.

Correspondent: Revd John Nowell, The Vicarage, Browgate, Baildon, West Yorkshire BD17 6NE (01274 594941)

Bingley

The Bingley Diamond Jubilee Relief-in-Sickness Charity

Eligibility: People who live in the parish of Bingley (as constituted on 14 February 1898) who are sick, convalescent, have disabilities or are infirm.

Types of grants: Emergency payments or annual grants.

Annual grant total: Grants average around £1,000 a year.

Applications: In writing to the correspondent through a social worker, Citizens Advice, other welfare agency or a third party. For specific items, estimates of costs are required. The trustees meet in February and November. A sub-committee of trustees can deal promptly with emergency payments.

Correspondent: John Daykin, Clerk, Weatherhead & Butcher, Solicitors, 120 Main Street, Bingley BD16 2JJ (01274 562322; email: info@wandb.uk.com)

Other information: The charity also makes grants to local organisations.

The Samuel Sunderland Relief-in-Need Charity

Eligibility: People who live in the former parish of Bingley (as constituted on 14 February 1898) and are in need, hardship or distress.

Types of grants: Emergency payments and annual grants averaging £500 each.

Annual grant total: In 2009 the charity had an income of £6,600 and a total expenditure of £4,400.

Applications: In writing to the correspondent through a social worker, Citizens Advice, other welfare agency or any other third party on behalf of the individual. When specific items are required estimates of the cost must be provided. Applications are considered in February and November.

Correspondent: John Daykin, Clerk, Weatherhead & Butcher Solicitors, 120 Main Street, Bingley BD16 2JJ (01274 562322; email: info@wandb.uk.com)

Other information: Grants are also given to local organisations which serve a similar purpose.

Bradford

The Bradford & District Children's Charity Circle

Eligibility: Children in need under 16 who live in Bradford.

Types of grants: One-off grants usually of £100 towards disability equipment, holidays, bedding and clothing.

Exclusions: No grants are given towards domestic bills or electrical goods.

Annual grant total: Grants to individuals generally total around £500 a year. Grants are also made to organisations.

Applications: In writing to the correspondent through a social worker, Citizens Advice or other welfare agency. They are considered monthly. Individuals should not apply directly.

Correspondent: Julie Cadman, 14 Oakwood Drive, Bingley, West Yorkshire, BD16 4AH (01274 561204)

The Bradford Tradesmen's Homes

Eligibility: Unmarried women over the age of 60 who have lived in Bradford metropolitan district for at least seven years who are not in employment and are in need.

Types of grants: Pensions of £65 per quarter, plus a Christmas grant of £80.

Annual grant total: In 2010 the trust made grants to individuals totalling £6,600. Annuities made to 'spinsters' amounted to £1,600 and Christmas gifts totalled £5,000.

Applications: On a form available from the correspondent. Applications can be submitted directly by the individual or through a social worker, Citizens Advice, other welfare agency, doctor, clergy or other third party. Applicants will be visited before an award is made and they must provide the names of two referees. Applications are considered throughout the year.

Correspondent: Colin Askew, Trust Administrator, 44 Lily Croft, Heaton Road, Bradford BD8 8QY (01274 543022; email: admin.bth@btconnect.com)

Other information: The trust also runs almshouses.

The Emmandjay Charitable Trust

Eligibility: People in need, for example, those in financial difficulties and people living with disabilities or a terminal illness.

Types of grants: Generally one-off grants, though payments can be spread over three years.

Exclusions: No grants are given towards rent, debts, utility/telephone bills or to students.

Annual grant total: Grants are made primarily to organisations but in previous years around £5,000 has been available to individuals.

Applications: Applications must be submitted by a social services worker. Direct applications by the individual will not be considered or acknowledged.

Correspondent: Mrs A E Bancroft, PO Box 60, Skipton, North Yorkshire BD23 9DP

The Moser Benevolent Trust Fund

Eligibility: People in need who are 60 or over and have lived or worked in the former county borough of Bradford for at least three years.

Types of grants: On average around 10 recipients receive pensions of £400 a year.

Annual grant total: In 2008/09 the trust had an income of £5,900 and a total expenditure of £3,500.

Applications: In writing at any time to: M Chappell, 56 Carr Lane, Shipley, West Yorkshire BD18 2LB. Applicants should include details of income and assets.

Correspondent: D C Stokes, 33 Mossy Bank Close, Queensbury, Bradford, West Yorkshire BD13 1PX (01274 817414)

Joseph Nutter's Foundation

Eligibility: People aged 18 or under who live in the metropolitan district of Bradford and have suffered the loss of a parent.

Types of grants: One-off grants of around £100 to £200 are given towards clothing, bedding, beds and household equipment which specifically benefit the child, such as cookers, fires and washing machines. Other needs may occasionally be considered on an individual basis.

Annual grant total: In 2008/09 the foundation had an income of £21,000 and a total expenditure of £23,000.

Applications: In writing to the correspondent at any time. Applications can be submitted directly by the individual or family member.

Correspondent: Mrs J M Barraclough, Administrator, The Ballroom, Hawkswick, Skipton BD23 5QA (01756 770361; email: comedancing@hawkswick.net)

Paul and Nancy Speak's Charity

Eligibility: Women in need who are over the age of 50 and live in Bradford.

Types of grants: Regular allowances of £500 a year, paid quarterly.

Annual grant total: In 2008 the charity had both an income and expenditure of £14,000.

Applications: In writing to the correspondent.

Correspondent: Michael Chapel, Secretary, 56 Carr Lane, Windhill, Shipley, North Yorkshire BD18 2LD (01274 585301)

Calderdale

The Community Foundation for Calderdale

Eligibility: People in need who live in Calderdale.

Types of grants: One-off grants of up to £100 and occasionally small loans to meet urgent needs, such as household equipment, clothing and food which cannot be readily funded from other sources.

Annual grant total: In 2008/09 the foundation had assets of £5.7 million and an income of £1.3 million. Grants were made totalling £778,000, of which £22,000 went to individuals, mostly for relief-in-need purposes.

Applications: Individuals must apply through a referring agency, such as Citizens Advice, on an application form available from the correspondent. Grants will only be awarded to individuals in the form of a cheque; cash is not given.

Correspondent: Grants Department, Community Foundation for Calderdale, Community Foundation House, 162A King Cross Road, Halifax, West Yorkshire, HX1 3LN (01422 438738; fax: 01422 350017; email: enquiries@cffc.co.uk; website: www.cffc.co.uk)

Other information: The foundation also gives to organisations and to individuals for educational purposes.

The Halifax Society for the Blind

Eligibility: People in need who are registered blind or partially sighted and live in Calderdale.

Types of grants: One-off grants of cash or equipment according to need. Recent grants have been given towards beds, school equipment, televisions and decorating costs.

Annual grant total: In 2009 the society had an income of £151,000 and a total expenditure £96,000. Grants were made totalling £8,000.

Applications: On a form available from the correspondent, to be submitted through one of the visiting staff of the society. Applications are considered on a regular basis.

Correspondent: Eileen Holmes, 34 Clare Road, Halifax, West Yorkshire HX1 2HX (01422 352383)

Other information: The society visits each of its 433 members three to four times a year and also provides four social centres, a drop in centre, resource centre, subsidised holidays and a mini bus service.

The Halifax Tradesmen's Benevolent Institution

Eligibility: People in need aged 60 or over who have been self-employed or a manager of a business for at least seven years and live in the parish of Halifax and the surrounding area. Applicants should have no other income than a pension and have only modest savings.

Types of grants: Pensions of about £550 a year.

Annual grant total: In 2008/09 the institution had an income of £27,000 and a total expenditure of £23,000.

Applications: In writing to the correspondent for consideration quarterly.

Correspondent: Anthony Wannan, West House, Kings Cross Road, Halifax, HX1 1EB (01422 352517)

Dewsbury

Dewsbury & District Sick Poor Fund

Eligibility: People who are sick and in need who live in the county borough of Dewsbury and the ecclesiastical parish of Hanging Heaton.

Types of grants: One-off grants according to need.

Annual grant total: Grants average around £6,000 each year.

Applications: In writing to the correspondent including details of illness and residential qualifications. Applications can be submitted either directly by the individual, through a third party such as a social worker or through an organisation such as a Citizens Advice.

Correspondent: John Alan Winder, 130 Boothroyd Lane, Dewsbury, West Yorkshire WF13 2LW (01924 463308)

Halifax

The Goodall Trust

Eligibility: Widows and unmarried women who are in need and live in the present Calderdale ward of Skircoat or the parts of the parishes of St Jude and All Saints (Halifax) which are within the ancient township of Skircoat.

Types of grants: Recurrent grants are given according to need.

Annual grant total: Grants usually total about £2,000 each year.

Applications: On a form available from the correspondent. Applications should be submitted by mid September either directly by the individual; by a relative, friend or neighbour; or through a welfare agency. They are considered in October.

Correspondent: Andrew Buck, 122 Skircoat Road, Halifax HX1 2RE (email: atbuck@tiscali.co.uk)

Charity of Ann Holt

Eligibility: Single women who are over the age of 50 and in need and have lived in Halifax for at least five years.

Types of grants: Pensions of around £200 a year, paid in quarterly instalments until the recipient dies, moves out of the area or moves into a residential home. About 75 grants are given each year.

Annual grant total: Grants to individuals usually total around £10,000 per year.

Applications: In writing to the correspondent, directly by the individual. Applicants will need to be prepared to provide two referees who are not relations, such as a vicar, ex-employer or someone else they have known for a number of years.

Correspondent: G D Jacobs, Oak House, 9 Cross Street, Oakenshaw, Bradford, West Yorkshire BD12 7EA (01274 679835; email: oakey9uk@yahoo.co.uk)

Horbury

St Leonards Hospital Charity

Eligibility: People in need, hardship or distress who live in the former urban district of Horbury.

Types of grants: One-off grants usually ranging from £20 to £200. Recent grants have been given towards adaptations, convalescence, nursing, renovation and repairs to homes for disabled access and helping people who are homeless or experiencing marital problems.

Exclusions: No grants are made towards maintenance of equipment already paid for. No loans are made although recurrent grants are considered if necessary.

Annual grant total: Grants usually total about £2,000 a year.

Applications: In writing to the following address: The Priest, 2 Elm Grove, Horbury, Wakefield WF4 5EP. Applications can be submitted directly by the individual, through a social worker, Citizens Advice or other welfare agency or through a church member. They are considered at any time and the trustees can act quickly in urgent cases.

Correspondent: Ian Whittell, 31 New Road, Horbury, Wakefield, West Yorkshire WF4 5LS (01924 272762)

Horton

The John Ashton Charity (including the Gift of Ellis Smethurst).

Eligibility: People in need who are over 65 and live alone in the Great Horton area of Bradford.

Types of grants: Small grants, according to need.

Annual grant total: Grants usually total about £2,000 per year.

Applications: On a form available from the correspondent to be submitted directly by the individual or through a family member for consideration in June and December.

Correspondent: Gordon Doble, Trustee, Upper Beck House, 22 Hammerton Drive, Hellifield, Skipton, BD23 4LZ (01729 851329)

Huddersfield

The Beaumont & Jessop Relief-in-Need Charity

Eligibility: People in need who are over 65 and live in the ancient township of Honley (near Huddersfield).

Types of grants: One-off grants ranging from £60 to £500 towards, for instance, Winged Fellowship holidays, heating grants (nominated by doctors), medical equipment, spectacles, transport to luncheon clubs and so on.

Annual grant total: Grants usually total around £1,000 a year.

Applications: In writing to the correspondent, indicating the purpose of the grant. Applications can be submitted directly by the individual or through a social worker, Citizens Advice, other welfare agency or other third party (nurses or doctors). Applications are considered throughout the year.

Correspondent: Leslie Chadwick, 35 Westcroft, Honley, Holmfirth, HD9 6JP (01484 662880)

The Charles Brook Convalescent Fund

Eligibility: People in need who live within the old Huddersfield Health Authority catchment area.

Types of grants: One-off grants for medical comforts, items essential to live independently and convalescent holidays.

Exclusions: No loans.

Annual grant total: In 2008/09 the fund had had an income of £12,000 and a total expenditure of £15,000.

Applications: On a form available from the social work department at Royal Infirmary, Huddersfield and St Luke's Hospital, Huddersfield. Applications must be submitted through a social worker and include details of weekly income/ expenditure and family situation. Applications sent directly to the correspondent cannot be considered.

Correspondent: Carol Thompson, Mistal Barn, Lower Castle Hill, Almondsbury, Huddersfield, HD4 6TA (01484 532183)

The Henry Percy Dugdale Charity

Eligibility: People in need who live in the county borough of Huddersfield (comprising the urban districts of Colne Valley, Kirkburton, Meltham and Holmfirth). People who have previously lived in the area for a period of 10 consecutive years are also eligible for assistance.

Types of grants: One-off and recurrent grants according to need.

Annual grant total: In 2008/09 the trust had assets of £1.3 million and an income of £64,000. Grants were made totalling £53,000, and were distributed as follows:

Regular payments	47	£40,000
One-off payments	19	£5,000
Christmas gifts	39	£7,800

Applications: Application forms are given to local organisations such as social services and churches. They are then submitted by or on behalf of the individual. The trustees meet twice a year to consider applications.

Correspondent: T J Green, Clerk, Bank Chambers, Market Street, Huddersfield HD1 2EW (01484 648482)

The Huddersfield Education Trust

Eligibility: Children under 16 who live in the former county borough of Huddersfield.

Types of grants: The trustees do not normally like to be the sole funders of the proposal. The trust stated that it is currently fully subscribed and any new beneficiaries would result in all beneficiaries receiving slightly less, although this is not something which would necessarily mean applications would be declined.

Annual grant total: In 2008/09 the trust had an income of £3,600 and a total expenditure of £5,600. Grants to both individuals and organisations total around £2,500 each year.

Applications: In writing to the correspondent, preferably through a school, educational welfare agency or a social worker. Applications are considered in April/May.

Correspondent: Carole Hardern, Kirklees Metropolitan Council, Room 806, Oldgate House, 2 Oldgate, Huddersfield HD1 6QW (01484 225226)

Keighley

Bowcocks Trust Fund for Keighley

Eligibility: People in need who live in the municipal borough of Keighley as constituted on 31 March 1974.

Types of grants: One-off grants according to need.

Annual grant total: In 2008/09 the trust had an income of £10,000 and a total expenditure of £9,700. Grants for education and welfare purposes totalled around £8,500. In previous years a majority of the grant total has gone towards educational grants.

Applications: Initial telephone calls are welcomed. Applications should be made in writing to the correspondent by a third party.

Correspondent: Mr P Vaux, Clerk, Old Mill House, 6 Dockroyd, Oakworth, Keighley, West Yorkshire BD22 7RH (01535 643029)

The William & Sarah Midgley Charity

Eligibility: People who are in need and live in Barcroft, Lees and Cross Roads in the former borough of Keighley, West Yorkshire.

Types of grants: Christmas hampers are normally given to older people in the area. Occasional one-off cash grants and grants in kind have also been made for electrical goods, clothing, food, travel expenses, medical and disability equipment and furniture.

Annual grant total: In 2008/09 the charity had an income of £6,400 and a total expenditure of £1,900.

Applications: In writing to the correspondent.

Correspondent: Eileen Proctor, 7 Lachman Road, Trawden, Colne, Lancashire BB8 8TA (01282 862757)

Leeds

The Bramhope Trust

Eligibility: People in need within the parish of Bramhope.

Types of grants: Gifts of varying amounts are given to organisations and individuals.

Annual grant total: In 2008/09 the trust had assets of £397,000 and both an income and grant expenditure of £28,000. Eighteen grants were given including one to an individual of £2,000.

Applications: In writing to the correspondent directly by the individual or through a doctor. Applications are considered throughout the year.

Correspondent: Anne Schofield, Wharfe Croft, 51 Breary Lane East, Bramhope, Leeds LS16 9EU (0113 2678813)

The Chapel Allerton & Potternewton Relief-in-Need Charity (Leeds)

Eligibility: People who live in the parish boundaries of Chapel Allerton, Chapeltown and Potternewton, Leeds.

Types of grants: One-off grants of £5 to £150 mainly for white electrical goods. Grants can also be to assist with arrears of fuel bills, rent (where housing benefit is not available); telephone (where required by people who are sick or housebound); to replace cookers beyond repair; and to provide food in emergencies when social security is not available.

Exclusions: No grants for furniture as there are two local furniture stores organised by churches.

Annual grant total: Grants average around £1,000 per year.

Applications: Applications must be made through the Leeds or Chapeltown Citizens Advice, a social services department, probation officer, health visitor and so on. Trustees meet in March but applications can be dealt with at any time according to need.

Correspondent: D Milner, 6 Grosvenor Park, Leeds, LS7 3QD (0113 268 0600)

The Community Shop Holiday Fund

Eligibility: Families with a child of over three years old living in the Leeds boundaries for whom a holiday would be beneficial.

Types of grants: One-off grants to allow families to take a break away where circumstances show a need. Though children aged three or under are not specifically eligible for a grant on their own, they may receive funding if they have an older sibling who the trust is supporting.

Annual grant total: In 2008 the trust had assets of £5,200 and an income of £64,000. Grants were made to 507 individuals totalling £64,000 and were distributed as follows:

Emergency grants	280	£46,000
Christmas grants	178	£8,600
Holidays	35	£6,700
'Kosy Kids'	10	£1,800
'Keen Kids'	4	£1,300

Applications: In writing to the correspondent through a social worker, Citizens Advice or other welfare agency. Potential applicants are then sent an application form to complete. For this reason the initial letter must give full details of the personal circumstances. Applications are considered as received between April and September.

Correspondent: Lynn Higo, Unit 4, Clayton Wood Bank, West Park Ring Road, Leeds LS16 6QZ (0113 274 5551; fax: 0113 278 3184; email: info@ leedscommunitytrust.org; website: www. leedscommunity.trust.org)

Other information: The charity runs a shop and distributes the profits to local charities, groups and individuals in need, particularly people in vulnerable situations. Grants are also given for general welfare and educational purposes: please see the separate entry for *The Community Shop Trust* for details.

The Community Shop Trust

Eligibility: People in need who live in the Leeds area.

Types of grants: One-off grants are given under a number of different schemes.

Emergency Grants
Usually for household items such as, white goods, carpets or removal costs which people are desperately in need of but have no means to pay for. Families with children are given priority.

Christmas grants
Grants for food, presents, and possibly cookers. A grocery voucher will be issued about one to two weeks before Christmas.

Kosy Kids
Grants towards beds, bedding, paint, curtains, carpet, heaters and furniture for children's bedrooms.

The Holiday Fund
Grants are also made to families in real need of a holiday. Please see the separate *Community Shop Holiday Fund* entry in this section for more information.

Annual grant total: In 2008 the trust had assets of £5,200 and an income of £64,000. Grants were made to 507 individuals totalling £64,000 and were distributed as follows:

Emergency grants	280	£46,000
Christmas grants	178	£8,600
Holidays	35	£6,700
'Kosy Kids'	10	£1,800
'Keen Kids'	4	£1,300

Applications: In writing to the correspondent through a social worker, Citizens Advice or other welfare agency. Potential applicants are then sent an application form to complete. For this reason the initial letter must give details of the personal circumstances. Decisions on emergency grant applications are usually made within two days.

Correspondent: Lynn Higo, Unit 4, Clayton Wood Bank, West Park Ring Road, Leeds LS16 6QZ (0113 274 5551; fax: 0113 278 3184; email: info@ leedscommunitytrust.org; website: www. leedscommunity.trust.org)

Other information: The trust is also known as the Leeds Community Trust. It runs a shop and distributes the profits to local charities, groups and individuals in need, particularly people in vulnerable situations.

Kirke Charity

Eligibility: People in need who live in the ancient parishes of Adel, Arthington or Cookridge.

Types of grants: One-off grants, generally of around £100.

Annual grant total: In 2008/09 the charity had an income of £9,000 and a total expenditure of £7,000. Grants usually total around £6,000.

Applications: Applications can be submitted directly by the individual or through a social worker, Citizens Advice or other welfare agency.

Correspondent: J A B Buchan, 8 St Helens Croft, Leeds LS16 8JY (01924 465860)

The Leeds Benevolent Society for Single Ladies

Eligibility: Single ladies in need who are over 60 and have lived in the Leeds metropolitan area for seven years.

Types of grants: Mainly regular allowance of £10 a week paid quarterly. The society also pays telephone rental and television licence fees and helps with holiday payments.

Annual grant total: In 2009 the trust had assets of £3.3 million, an income of £92,000 and a total expenditure of £100,000. Grants were made totalling £65,000.

Applications: On a form available by telephoning the correspondent or writing to: Applications Secretary, 36 Holland Road, Kippax, Leeds LS25 7PP.

Applications can be submitted directly by the individual or through a social worker, Citizens Advice, other welfare agency or other third party. Applicants are visited to assess their needs.

Correspondent: Elisabeth A Stephens, Chair, 5 Scarcroft Grange, Wetherby Road, Scarcroft, Leeds LS14 3HJ (0113 289 2482)

The Leeds District Aid-in-Sickness Fund

Eligibility: People who live in the city of Leeds and are in need through unexpected illness or accident ('city of Leeds' refers to the Leeds boundaries as they were prior to the re-organisation of 1974 and the establishment of the metropolitan district of Leeds).

Types of grants: One-off cash grants of £50 to £250 towards domestic appliances, furnishings, food, medical aid, travel, holidays, adapted computers and so on.

Exclusions: No recurrent grants or loans are given and there is no support for debts, rates or taxes.

Annual grant total: About £2,000 a year. Grants are given to both individuals and organisations.

Applications: On a form available from the correspondent, sent on behalf of the applicant by a social worker, welfare agency, doctor, teacher, clergyman or similar third party (personal applications will not be accepted). Application deadlines are March, June, September and December with decisions made quarterly.

Correspondent: Valerie Kaye, Nidd View Cottage, 39 Kirkgate, Knaresborough, North Yorkshire, HG5 8BZ (01423 797842; email: vjk@kaye-estates.co.uk)

The Leeds Tradesmen's Trust

Eligibility: People over 50 who have carried on business, practised a profession or been a tradesperson for at least five years (either consecutively or in total) and who, during that time, lived in Leeds or whose business premises (rented or owned) were in the city of Leeds. Grants are also given to self-employed business/professional people who 'have fallen upon misfortune in business'; normally older people. Widows and unmarried daughters of the former are also eligible.

Types of grants: Quarterly pensions of £10 to £500 a year, plus Christmas grants and spring fuel grants only to those already receiving a pension.

Annual grant total: In 2009 the trust had assets of £816,000 and an income of £39,000. Grants were made totalling £46,000, which consisted of £21,000 given in pensions and £25,000 given in special grants to 51 individuals.

Applications: In writing to the correspondent, including details of the business or professional addresses, length of time spent there and financial position. All applicants are visited by the assistant secretary.

Correspondent: John C Suttenstall, Secretary, 17 Wayside Crescent, Scarcroft, Leeds LS14 3BD (0113 289 3346)

The Metcalfe Smith Trust

Eligibility: Adults and children who live in Leeds and have 'a physical disability, long term illness or a mental health difficulty'.

Types of grants: One-off grants ranging from £250 to £1,000 towards items or services that will significantly improve quality of life. For example, disability equipment, computers, respite breaks, heating costs, small items of furniture and course fees.

Exclusions: No support for individuals outside the area of benefit, general appeals or recurrent grants.

Annual grant total: In 2008/09 the trust had an income of £24,000. There were 19 grants made to individuals totalling £9,000.

Applications: Application forms are available on request by filling in the 'application request form' on the trust's website. Individual applications must be supported by a social worker or local welfare organisation. They are considered twice a year in May and November and should be submitted in April and October respectively. Emergency grants of up to £100 can be made at any time.

Correspondent: Geoff Hill, Secretary, c/o Voluntary Action Leeds, Stringer House, 34 Lupton Street, Hunslet, Leeds LS10 2QW (email: secretary@ metcalfesmithtrust.org; website: www. metcalfesmithtrust.org.uk)

Other information: The trust also makes grants to organisations (£15,000 in 2008/09).

Sandal Magna

The Henry & Ada Chalker Trust

Eligibility: People in need who live in Sandal Magna, with a preference for elderly residents.

Types of grants: Recurrent grants of around £10 a year are distributed in the first week of December.

Annual grant total: Grants to individuals total around £1,000 each year. Approximately 90 grants are awarded.

Applications: On a form available from the correspondent. As this is a recurrent grant new applications are stockpiled until there is a vacancy on the current list.

Correspondent: The Trustees, Beaumont Legal, Beaumont House, 1 Paragon Avenue, Wakefield, West Yorkshire, WF1 2UF (0845 122 8100)

The Sandal Magna Relief-in-Need Charity

Eligibility: People in need who live in the old parish of Sandal Magna (this includes Sandal, Walton, Crigglestone, Painthorpe and West Bretton).

Types of grants: One-off grants of about £50 to £300 are made each year to 6 to 10 individuals. Recent grants have been used for the purchase of a second-hand washing machine, decorating materials, bedding for a child and a safety gate for the stairs.

Annual grant total: Grants usually total around £1,000 per year.

Applications: In writing to the correspondent. Applications can be sent directly by the individual or through a social worker, Citizens Advice or other welfare agency.

Correspondent: Martin J Perry, 50 Dukewood Road, Clayton West, Huddersfield HD8 9HF (01484 860594; email: marpam@fsmail.net)

Todmorden

Todmorden War Memorial Fund

Eligibility: Veterans of the First and Second World Wars who are sick or in need and live in the former borough of Todmorden, and their dependants.

Types of grants: Grants are mostly one-off; recurrent grants are very occasionally given. TV licences are given to First and Second World War families. Food vouchers, medicine, medical comforts, bedding, fuel, domestic help and convalescence expenses are also given.

Annual grant total: Grants to individuals usually total about £800 a year.

Applications: In writing to: Mrs M Gunton, Case Secretary, Stile House, Stilerd, Todmorden OL14 8NU. Applications must be through a welfare agency or similar organisation and they are considered monthly.

Correspondent: Paul Butterworth, Cinder Hill Farm, Cinderhill Road, Todmorden, West Yorkshire OL14 8AA

Other information: The fund also makes grants to organisations.

Wakefield

The Brotherton Charity Fund

Eligibility: People in need who are over 60 years old and live in Wakefield.

Types of grants: Annual pensions.

Annual grant total: Grants usually total about £2,000 each year.

Applications: On a form available from the correspondent. When vacancies arise an advert is placed in the Wakefield Express and a waiting list is then drawn up. Applications can be made directly by the individual or family member.

Correspondent: C Brotherton-Ratcliffe, PO Box 374, Harrogate HG1 4YW

The Charity of Miss Ann Farrar Brideoake see entry on page 169

Cockshot Foundation

Eligibility: People in need, hardship or distress resident in the counties of Cumbria, Lancashire and Greater Manchester.

Types of grants: On-off and recurrent grants according to need.

Annual grant total: In 2008/09 the foundation had assets of £407,000 and an income of £202,000. It appears that no grants were made during the year either to organisations or individuals.

Applications: In writing to the correspondent.

Correspondent: The Trustees, Belle Isle, Windermere, Cumbria, LA23 1BG (01539 447087; email: cockshotfoundation@belleisle.net)

The Cotton Districts Convalescent Fund and the Barnes Samaritan Charity

Eligibility: People in need who have a severe/long term illness, are convalescent or who have a disability and live in Lancashire and Greater Manchester.

Types of grants: The fund makes grants to enable a subsidised convalescent holiday of one week to be taken at hotels in Blackpool and St Annes. Applicants are expected to pay approximately £80 towards the cost of a week's half board holiday with the fund paying the difference. Consideration will be given to making a grant towards the costs of a special needs holiday proposed by the applicant (for example where nursing or other care is required).

Monthly grants of £40 are also available towards living costs for those who are in poor health, convalescent or who have a disability.

Annual grant total: In 2008 the trust had assets of £788,000 and an income of £48,000. Grants from the convalescence fund were made to 75 individuals totalling £23,000. A further £22,000 was awarded in recurrent grants to 36 individuals.

Applications: In writing to the secretary. Applications may be submitted directly by the individual or through a social worker, Citizens Advice or other welfare agency. Please note: the trust has stated that due to a lack of income, future grant-making will be limited.

Correspondent: Nicholas Stockton, c/o Cassons Chartered Accountants, Rational House, 64 Bridge Street, Manchester M3 3BN (0845 337 9409; fax: 0845 337 9408; email: manchester@cassons.co.uk; website: www.cotton-districts.co.uk/)

Other information: This trust was previously known as The Cotton Districts Convalescent Fund.

George House Trust

Eligibility: People with HIV who live in the north west of England.

Types of grants: One off grants ranging from £20 to £150 to help with essential items. Small emergency grants can be made to help with immediate hardship, for example, food.

Exclusions: No grants are made to people without original proof of HIV diagnosis. Normally no more than one payment per person can be made each year.

Annual grant total: In 2008/09 the trust had assets of £1 million and an income of £888,000. Welfare grants were made to 699 individuals totalling £37,000.

Applications: Applications should be made in writing through the trust's website or on a form available from their office (those living outside of Manchester can have one sent to their home). Evidence that the individual has been diagnosed HIV positive, such as a letter from the consultant at a HIV testing clinic, should be enclosed with the form. The committee considers the applications on the last working day of the month. If funding is a matter of emergency (i.e. people with no money for food or gas) then it is worth contacting the trust as they may be able to make a small grant straight away.

Correspondent: The Honorary Secretary, 77 Ardwick Green North, Manchester M12 6FX (0161 274 4499; email: ght@ght.org.uk; website: www.ght.org.uk)

Other information: The trust also provides advice and information for people with HIV.

The Grant, Bagshaw, Rogers & Tidswell Fund

Eligibility: Older people in need who live, or were born in, Liverpool, the Wirral, Ellesmere Port or Chester.

Types of grants: Pensions, currently around £425 per annum, are paid half yearly. Occasional one-off grants may also be given.

Annual grant total: In 2008/09 the fund had an income of £13,000 and a total expenditure £16,000.

Applications: On a form available from the correspondent. Applications should be returned by 31 March and 30 October for consideration in April and November respectively. Applications should be submitted through a social worker, Citizens Advice or other welfare agency, although direct applications will also be considered.

Correspondent: Lawrence Downey, Mace & Jones, Drury House, 19 Water Street, Liverpool L2 0RP (0151 236 8989; fax: 0151 227 5010; email: lawrence.downey@maceandjones.co.uk)

The Gregson Memorial Annuities

Eligibility: Female domestic servants who have been in service for at least 10 years in Liverpool, Southport, Malpas and the surrounding area and who cannot work now for health reasons.

Governesses and other 'gentlewomen', widows and unmarried daughters or sisters of professional men and merchants, who are over 50 years old and members of the Church of England, may also be eligible for assistance.

Types of grants: Annuities of about £300 a year, payable in two six-monthly instalments.

Annual grant total: Grants usually total about £2,000 each year.

Applications: Applications in writing to the correspondent are considered throughout the year.

Correspondent: Robin Miller, Trustee, Brabners Chaffe Street Solicitors, Horton House, Exchange Flags, Liverpool L2 3YL (0151 600 3000; fax: 0151 227 3185; email: lisa.sutton@brabnerscs.com)

The Lancashire Infirm Secular Clergy Fund

Eligibility: Catholic secular clergy of the dioceses of Liverpool, Salford and Lancaster who are unable, through age or infirmity, to attend to their duties of office and are in need.

Types of grants: Annual grants mostly of £1,300 each although smaller grants of around £600 are also available.

Annual grant total: In 2008/09 the fund had assets of £2.7 million and an income of £175,000. Grants to infirm clergy totalled £102,000.

Applications: On a form available from the correspondent, to be submitted directly by the individual.

Correspondent: Rev Peter Stanley, St Josephs Presbytery, Harpers Lane, Chorley, PR6 0HR (01257 262713)

North West Police Benevolent Fund

Eligibility: Serving officers and pensioners of Cheshire County Constabulary, Greater Manchester and Merseyside Police Forces and amalgamated forces of those areas. Also their dependants.

Types of grants: Recurrent grants and loans for convalescence and medical equipment (but not for private health care), financial help for cases of need arising from unforeseen circumstances. Orphaned children of police officers can receive a weekly allowance. Christmas gifts and holiday grants are made through the subsidiary St George's Fund.

Exclusions: No grants available for private health, education or legal fees.

Annual grant total: In 2008 the fund had assets of just over £4 million and an income of £1.7 million. Grants were made totalling £157,000.

Applications: On a form available from the correspondent. Applications are usually made through a force welfare officer or a member of the management committee. They are considered each month and should be submitted by the second Wednesday in January or by the first Wednesday in any other month.

Correspondent: Constable Jackie Smithies, Progress House, Broadstone Hall Road South, Reddish, Stockport SK5 7DE (0161 355 4420; fax: 0161 355 4410; email: jsmithies@gmpf.polfed.org; website: www.nwpbf.org)

Other information: The fund does not give grants to organisations.

sfgroup Charitable Fund for Disabled People *see entry on page 46*

United Utilities Trust Fund

Eligibility: People in need who live in the area supplied by United Utilities Water (predominantly the north west of England).

Types of grants: Payments for water and/or sewerage charges due to United Utilities Water. The trust can also help with water or sewerage charges which are collected by other companies or organisations on behalf of United Utilities Water. In certain cases, the trust can also consider giving some help to meet other essential bills, household needs or priority debts.

Exclusions: No grants for court fines, catalogue debts, credit cards, personal loans or other forms of borrowing; social fund loans/benefit overpayments/tax credit overpayments now being reclaimed; retrospective payments.

Annual grant total: In 2008/09 the trust had an income of £3 million. The sum of £2.5 million was given on behalf of individuals.

Applications: Application forms and full guidelines are available on the website. They are also available on request from the correspondent.

Correspondent: The Secretary (Auriga Services Ltd), FREEPOST RLYY-JHEJ-XCXS, Sutton Coldfield, B72 1TJ (0845 179 1791; email: contact@uutf.org.uk; website: www.uutf.org.uk)

Other information: Grants were also made to 13 debt counselling organisations in 2008/09 totalling £223,000.

Cheshire

The Charity of Letitia Beaumont

Eligibility: People in need who were born or who have lived for some time in the borough of Warrington or the parish of Moore.

Types of grants: Annual pensions of approximately £160 per person, paid quarterly.

Annual grant total: About £2,500.

Applications: In writing to the correspondent.

Correspondent: Norman Banner, Forshaws Davies Ridgway LLP, 21 Palmyra Square, Warrington, WA1 1BW (01925 230000)

The Cheshire Provincial Fund of Benevolence

Eligibility: Freemasons of Cheshire, and their dependants, who are in need.

Types of grants: One-off and recurrent grants according to need.

Annual grant total: In 2008/09 the fund had assets of £2.9 million and an income of £337,000. Grants were made to individuals and charities totalling £161,000.

Applications: In writing to the correspondent.

Correspondent: Peter Carroll, Ashcroft House, 36 Clay Lane, Timperley, Altrincham WA15 7AB (0161 980 6090; email: enquiries@cheshiremasons.co.uk)

Other information: Grants are also available for masons connected to the lodge through the grand charity fund.

John Holford Charity

Eligibility: People in need who live in the parishes of Astbury, Clutton and Middlewich, and the borough of Congleton.

Types of grants: One-off and recurrent grants for a variety of needs, ranging from £100 to £2,500.

Exclusions: No grants for education, or for medical treatment.

Annual grant total: In 2009 grants totalled £19,000, the majority of which was given to individuals.

Applications: On a form available from the correspondent. Applications should be submitted by a social worker, carer, Citizens Advice, other welfare agency or other third party such as a relative. They are considered at any time.

Correspondent: Kerris Owen, Friars, 20 White Friars, Chester CH1 1XS (01244 356789; email: kerris.owen@cullimoredutton.co.uk; website: www.bclaw.co.uk)

The Ursula Keyes Trust

Eligibility: People in need, especially those with a medical condition, who live in the area administered by Chester District Council and in particular those within the boundaries of the former City of Chester and the adjoining parishes of Great Boughton and Upton.

Types of grants: One-off grants towards, for example, washing machines for families in need or computers for children with disabilities.

Exclusions: No grants to repay debts or loans or to reimburse expenditure already incurred.

Annual grant total: In 2009 the trust had assets of £5.2 million and an income of £295,000. Grants were made to 36 individuals totalling £18,000.

Applications: In writing to the correspondent, with details of applicant's income and expenditure. Applications must be supported by a social worker, a doctor (if relevant) or another professional or welfare agency. A summary form, which is available to download from the website, should also be included with the application.

Applications are considered at the end of January, April, July and October and should be received at least four weeks in advance to be certain of consideration at any particular meeting.

Correspondent: Dot Lawless, Baker Tilly, Steam Mill, Chester, CH3 5AN (01244 505100; fax: 01244 505101; website: www.ursula-keyes-trust.org.uk)

The Wilmslow Aid Trust

Eligibility: People in need who live in Wilmslow and the surrounding neighbourhood.

Types of grants: One-off grants according to need for items such as replacement beds and bedding after a house fire, fridge/ freezers for single parents, removal costs due to bankruptcy, heating system repairs, furniture, clothing and decorating materials.

Annual grant total: Grants usually total about £1,000 each year.

Applications: In writing to the correspondent: to be submitted through a welfare agency, church, social worker or Citizens Advice. Applications should include the individual's address, income and a summary of what is needed and why.

Correspondent: W T Hall, 38 Broad Walk, Wilmslow, Cheshire SK9 5PL (01625 524974)

Other information: The trust also gives grants to organisations.

The Wrenbury Consolidated Charities

Eligibility: People in need who live in the parishes of Chorley, Sound, Broomhall, Newhall, Wrenbury and Dodcott-cum-Wilkesley.

Types of grants: Payments on St Marks' (25 April) and St Thomas' (21 December) days to pensioners and students. Grants are also given for one-off necessities. Grants range from £120 to £130.

Annual grant total: About £7,000.

Applications: In writing to the correspondent either directly by the individual or through another third party on behalf of the individual. The Vicar of Wrenbury and the parish council can give details of the six nominated trustees who can help with applications. Applications are considered in December and March.

Correspondent: Helen Smith, Eagle Hall Cottage, Smeatonwood, Wrenbury, North Nantwich CW5 8HD

Other information: Grants are also given to churches, the village hall and for educational purposes.

Chester

The Chester Parochial Relief-in-Need Charity

Eligibility: People in need who live in the city of Chester, with preference given to the area of the ecclesiastical parish called the Chester Team Parish in the county of Chester.

Types of grants: One-off grants, usually ranging from £50 to £1,000, are given for furniture, washing machines, cookers, electrical items, clothing, carpets, and so on. A supermarket vouchers scheme is also available to help low-income families, mainly over the Christmas period.

Annual grant total: In 2008/09 the charity had an income of £26,000 and a total expenditure of £27,000. Grants were made totalling £19,000.

Applications: On a form available from the correspondent. Applications can be made directly by the individual, through a recognised referral agency or through a third party such as a family member. All applicants will be visited by a trustee who will then report back to the sub-committee for a final decision. Applications are considered at any time.

Correspondent: Kerris Owen, Birch Cullimore, Friars, 20 White Friars, Chester CH1 1XS (01244 356789; fax: 01244 312582; email: info@bclaw.co.uk; website: www.bclaw.co.uk)

Other information: Grants are also made to organisations.

Congleton

The Congleton Town Trust

Eligibility: People in need who live in the town of Congleton (this does not include the other two towns which have constituted the borough of Congleton since 1975).

Types of grants: Grants in the range of £200 and £3,000 are given to individuals in need or to organisations who provide relief, services or facilities to those in need.

Annual grant total: In 2008 the trust had an income of £24,000 and a total expenditure of £20,000.

Applications: On a form available from the correspondent, to be submitted directly by the individual or a family member. Applications are considered quarterly, on the second Monday in March, June, September and December.

Correspondent: Ms J Money, Clerk, c/o Congleton Town Hall, High Street, Congleton CW12 1BN (01260 291156)

Other information: The trust also administers several smaller trusts.

Frodsham

Frodsham Nursing Fund

Eligibility: People in need who are sick, convalescent or living with disabilities and are resident in the town of Frodsham.

Types of grants: One off grants according to need. Recently grants have been given for items such as bedding, clothing, medical aids, heating and other domestic appliances. Temporary relief may also be provided to those caring for somebody who is sick or disabled.

Annual grant total: In 2008/09 the fund had an income of £3,000 and a total expenditure of £2,000.

Applications: In writing to the correspondent, either directly by the individual or on their behalf by a doctor, nurse or social worker. Applicants should briefly state their circumstances and what help is being sought.

Correspondent: Miss J Pollen, 22 Fluin Lane, Frodsham, WA6 7QH (01928 731043)

Macclesfield

The Macclesfield Relief-in-Sickness Fund

Eligibility: People in need who live in Macclesfield town and who have a chronic illness or a learning disability.

Types of grants: One-off grants only for necessary items such as washing machines, telephone installation, removals or specialist wheelchairs and especially for health-related items that would improve the quality of the applicant's situation.

Annual grant total: About £1,500.

Applications: Applications must be made through a local social services office, doctor's surgery or other welfare agencies and they should verify the need of the applicant.

Correspondent: Lynette Cookson, c/o Community and Voluntary Services Cheshire East, 81 Park Lane, Macclesfield, Cheshire SK11 6TX (01625 428301)

Mottram St Andrew

The Mottram St Andrew United Charities

Eligibility: People in need who live in the parish of Mottram St Andrew.

Types of grants: On average 35 one-off grants ranging from £35 to £250 reviewed annually; recurrent grants according to need. Recent grants have been given in cases of illness and death, for travel to and from hospital and Christmas bonuses to pensioners.

Annual grant total: Grants usually total around £3,000 a year.

Applications: In writing to the correspondent or to individual trustees. Applications can be submitted directly by the individual or through a social worker, Citizens Advice, other welfare agency or other third party. They are considered in November and should be received by early November.

Correspondent: J D Carr, Thornlea, Oak Road, Mottram St Andrew, Macclesfield, Cheshire SK10 4RA (01625 829634)

Warrington

The Police-Aided Children's Relief-in-Need Fund

Eligibility: Children of pre-school or primary school age living in the borough of Warrington and whose families are in financial or physical need. Applications from students of secondary school age and over will be considered in exceptional circumstances.

Types of grants: Vouchers to help with the cost of clothing and footwear. Vouchers are only redeemable at selected retailers in the borough.

Annual grant total: In 2008/09 the fund had an income of £5,000 and made 190 awards totalling £11,400, facilitated through an unusually high income of £30,000 gained in the previous financial year.

Applications: On a form available from the correspondent.

Correspondent: The Administrator, Warrington Council For Voluntary Services, The Gateway, 89 Sankey St, Warrington, WA1 1SR

The Warrington Sick & Disabled Trust

Eligibility: People in need, especially those who are disabled or infirm, who live in a six-mile radius of the Nurses' Home at 21 Arpley Street, Warrington.

Types of grants: One-off grants for holidays, Christmas parcels and other needs.

Annual grant total: Grants usually total around £2,000 per year.

Applications: In writing to the correspondent.

Correspondent: Norman L Banner, Ridgway Greenall Solicitors, 17–21 Palmyra Square, Warrington WA1 1BW (01925 654221)

Widnes

The Knight's House Charity

Eligibility: People in need who live in Widnes.

Types of grants: One-off grants for kitchen appliances, clothing, carpets, and decorating materials. Second-hand furniture and beds may also be provided through an informal partnership with a separate organisation, Justice and Peace.

Annual grant total: In 2008/09 the charity had an income of £13,000 and a total expenditure of £19,000.

Applications: On a form available from the correspondent.

Correspondent: Wendy Jefferies, Halton Borough Council, Municipal Building, Kingsway, Widnes, Cheshire WA8 7QF (0151 424 2061; email: wendy.jefferies@halton-borough.gov.uk)

Wilmslow

The Lindow Workhouse Trust

Eligibility: People in need who live in the ancient parish of Wilmslow.

Types of grants: One-off grants to help with, for example, fuel bills, equipment repairs, property repairs. Any cases of real need are considered.

Exclusions: No grants are made towards relief of rates, taxes or other public funds.

Annual grant total: About £5,000 for welfare and educational purposes.

Applications: In writing to the correspondent at any time. Applications can be submitted either directly by the individual or a family member, through a third party such as a social worker or teacher, or through an organisation such as Citizens Advice or a school.

Correspondent: Jacquie Bilsborough, 15 Westward Road, Wilmslow, SK9 5JY

Wybunbury

The Wybunbury United Charities

Eligibility: People in need who live in the 18 townships of the ancient parish of Wybunbury as it was in the 1600s and 1700s. The townships are Basford, Batherton, Blakenhall, Bridgemere, Chorlton, Checkley-cum-Wrinehill, Doddington, Hatherton, Hough, Hunsterson, Lea, Rope, Shavington-cum-Gresty, Stapeley, Walgherton, Weston, Willaston and Wybunbury.

Types of grants: The three administering trustees for each township are responsible for distribution of grants. Some make annual payments to individuals in need

but funds are also kept in most townships to cover emergency payments for accidents, bereavement or sudden distress.

Annual grant total: Grants usually total around £5,000 a year.

Applications: By direct application to one of three administering trustees.

Correspondent: Barnabas Pettman, 12 Lyndhurst Grove, Stone, Staffordshire ST15 8TP (01785 819677; fax: 01785 819677)

Cumbria

Barrow Thornborrow Charity

Eligibility: People who are disabled or sick and live, or were born in, the former county of Westmorland, the former county borough of Barrow, the former rural districts of Sedbergh and North Lonsdale, or the former urban districts of Dalton-in-Furness, Grange and Ulverston.

Types of grants: One-off grants towards items, services or facilities which are calculated to alleviate suffering and assist recovery and which are not available from other sources. In previous years grants have been given for household equipment, assistance with travelling expenses in case of hospitalisation, clothing, computer aids and assistance with essential property repairs.

Annual grant total: Grants normally total around £5,000 per year.

Applications: In writing to the correspondent including details of the applicant's circumstances. Applications can be submitted through a social worker, Citizens Advice or other welfare agency.

Correspondent: R J Morgan, 103 Sedbergh Road, Kendal, Cumbria LA9 6BE (01539 725871)

The Cumbria Constabulary Benevolent Fund

Eligibility: Members and former members of the Cumbria Constabulary in need, and their widows and dependants.

Types of grants: One-off cash grants ranging from £250 to £750, usually for the purchase of medical equipment.

Annual grant total: Grants to individuals and organisations average around £14,000 a year.

Applications: In writing to the correspondent directly by the individual or family member. Applications are considered within 14 days.

Correspondent: Federation Representative, Federation Office, 1 The Green, Carleton Hall, Penrith, Cumbria, CA10 2BW (01768 217426; fax: 01708 217425)

The Cumbria Miners' Welfare Trust Fund

Eligibility: Miners and their families who are in need and live or work in Cumbria.

Types of grants: Grants are given mainly to miners' welfare schemes in the Cumbria area, but individuals may also apply.

Exclusions: Mineworkers who have taken up other employment since leaving the industry are excluded from applying. No recurrent grants are made.

Annual grant total: About £12,000 a year.

Applications: In writing to the correspondent either directly by the individual, through the union or via a CISWO social worker.

Correspondent: Vincent Clements, c/o CISWO, 6 Bewick Road, Gateshead, Tyne & Wear NE8 4DP (0191 477 7242; fax: 0191 477 1021; email: vincent. clements@ciswo.org.uk)

Edmond Castle Educational Trust

Eligibility: Children and young people who are or have been in the care of, or provided with accommodation, by Cumbria County Council and, also children and young people who are in need who have experienced mental health problems.

Types of grants: Grants given according to need.

Annual grant total: In 2008/09 the trust has an income of £1,300 and a total expenditure of £5,700.

Applications: In writing to the correspondent.

Correspondent: The Administrator, Cumbria Community Foundation, Dovenby Hall, Dovenby, Cockermouth, CA13 0PN

Other information: Grants are also made to organisations.

The Jane Fisher Trust

Eligibility: People in need over 50, and people who are disabled, who have lived in the townships of Ulverston and Osmotherly or the parish of Pennington for at least 20 years.

Types of grants: Small monthly payments. No lump sum grants have been made for many years.

Annual grant total: Grants usually total around £5,000 a year.

Applications: On a form available from the correspondent. Applications are considered when they are received. They must include details of income, capital, age, disabilities, marital status and how long the applicant has lived in the area.

Correspondent: Steven Marsden, Secretary, Livingstons Solicitors, 9 Benson Street, Ulverston, Cumbria LA12 7AU (01229 585555; fax: 01229 584950)

The Joseph Hutchinson Poors Charity

Eligibility: People in need who are over 65 year old or are widows, and have lived in the villages of Hunsonby or Winskill for over one year.

Types of grants: One-off grants of around £60 according to need.

Annual grant total: Grants to individuals usually total around £3,000.

Applications: In writing to the correspondent.

Correspondent: Stephen Holliday, Trustee, South View Farm, Hunsonby, Penrith CA10 1PN (01768 881364)

Lakeland Disability Support

Eligibility: People with physical disabilities who live in South Lakeland, Cumbria.

Types of grants: Grants for respite care, day care, equipment and services that will enhance the life of people with disabilities and which the applicant or social services are unable to provide.

Exclusions: No grants for long-term care provision.

Annual grant total: In 2008 the trust had assets of £1 million, an income of £143,000 and a total expenditure of £1,900. No grants were made during the year (see 'other information' for full details).

Applications: On a form available from the correspondent. Trustees meet quarterly in January, April, July and October. Applications must be received on or before the 15th of the preceding month.

Correspondent: Brenda Robinson, Trust Secretary, 46 Victoria Road North, Windermere, Cumbria LA23 2DS (01539 442800)

Other information: This trust was established in 2004 following an announcement in October 2003 that Leonard Cheshire would vacate Holehird (a home for people with disabilities in South Lakeland) in two to three years' time. The trust aimed to raise sufficient funds to allow it to keep the home open for the benefit of present and future residents. However, in 2008 Leonard Cheshire surprisingly reversed its decision and announced its intention to remain at Holehird for the foreseeable future.

By this time the trust had raised a significant amount of money and so, after consulting with donors and the Charity Commission, decided to retain the donations and use them to support people with a physical disabilities in other ways. Grantmaking is expected to start in 2010.

Ambleside

The Ambleside Welfare Charity

Eligibility: People in need who live in the parish of Ambleside, especially those who are ill.

Types of grants: One-off and recurrent grants according to need. Help is also given to local relatives for hospital visits.

Annual grant total: In 2008 the charity had assets of £942,000 and an income of £45,000. Welfare grants came to £6,500.

Applications: In writing to the correspondent.

Correspondent: Marjorie Blackburn, The Coach House, Rydal Road, Ambleside, LA22 9PL (01539 434087)

Agnes Backhouse Annuity Fund

Eligibility: Unmarried women (widows and spinsters) aged over 50 who live in the parish of Ambleside.

Types of grants: Recurrent grants of £50.

Annual grant total: In 2008 the fund had an income of £21,000 and a total expenditure of £15,000.

Applications: In writing to the correspondent.

Correspondent: James Hamilton, Temple Heelis Solicitors, Bridge Mills, Stramongate, Kendal LA9 4UB (01539 723757)

Other information: The trust states that people who currently fit the above criteria should be receiving a grant, whether rich or poor.

Carlisle

The Carlisle Sick Poor Fund

Eligibility: People living in Carlisle who are in financial hardship due to ill health.

Types of grants: One-off grants of up to £200 towards bedding, food, fuel, medical aids and equipment, convalescence, holidays and home help.

Annual grant total: In 2009 the fund had an income of £8,000 and a total expenditure of £4,200.

Applications: On a form available from the correspondent.

Correspondent: Brenda Newbegin, Atkinson Ritson Solicitors, 15 Fisher Street, Carlisle, Cumbria CA3 8RW (01228 674507)

Cockermouth

The Cockermouth Relief-in-Need Charity

Eligibility: Older people in need who live in Cockermouth.

Types of grants: One-off grants in the range of £25 to £35.

Annual grant total: Grants average around £800 a year and are divided between individuals and local organisations.

Applications: In writing to the correspondent. Applications can be made directly by the individual or family member.

Correspondent: Revd Wendy Sanders, Parish Administration, Christ Church Rooms, South Street, Cockermouth, Cumbria CA13 9RU (01900 829926)

Crosby Ravensworth

The Crosby Ravensworth Relief-in-Need Charities

Eligibility: People in need who have lived in the ancient parish of Crosby Ravensworth for at least 12 months. Preference is given to older people.

Types of grants: One-off and recurrent grants. Grants include £30 coal vouchers to senior citizens and a basket of fruit (or other gift) to people who have been in hospital. Grants can also be given to local students entering university if they have been educated in the parish.

Annual grant total: In 2009 the trust had an income of £12,000 and a total expenditure of £6,000.

Applications: In writing to the correspondent submitted directly by the individual including details of the applicant's financial situation. Applications are considered in February, May and October.

Correspondent: G Bowness, Ravenseat, Crosby Ravensworth, Penrith, Cumbria CA10 3JB (01931 715382; email: gordonbowness@aol.com)

Kirkby Lonsdale

The Kirkby Lonsdale Relief-in-Need Charity

Eligibility: People in need who live in the parish of Kirkby Lonsdale.

Types of grants: One-off grants of £30, usually given just before Christmas.

Annual grant total: Grants usually total around £900.

Applications: In writing to the correspondent directly by the individual, or by a third party on his or her behalf.

Applications are considered in early December.

Correspondent: Mary Quinn, 19 Fairgarth Drive, Kirkby Lonsdale, Carnforth, Lancashire LA6 2DT (0152 427 1258)

Workington

The Bowness Trust

Eligibility: People in need who live in Workington and live at home (not in institutions).

Types of grants: One-off grants only.

Annual grant total: Generally grants total around £1,500 a year.

Applications: In writing to the correspondent.

Correspondent: Richard Atkinson, Milburns Solicitors, Oxford House, 19 Oxford Street, Workington, Cumbria CA14 2AW (01900 67363; fax: 01900 65552)

Greater Manchester

J T Blair's Charity

Eligibility: People over 65 who live in Manchester and Salford and who are in need.

Types of grants: Weekly pensions of up to £10, paid at four-weekly intervals.

Annual grant total: In 2008/09 the charity had an income of £18,000 and a total expenditure of £16,000.

Applications: On a form available from the correspondent, to be submitted by a social worker or other professional person. The trustees meet three or four times a year. Applicants should contact the charity for specific deadlines. Those in receipt of a pension are visited at least once a year.

Correspondent: Anne Hosker, Gaddum Centre, Gaddum House, 6 Great Jackson Street, Manchester M15 4AX (0161 834 6069; fax: 0161 839 8573; website: www.gaddumcentre.co.uk)

The Lawrence Brownlow Charity

Eligibility: People (usually children and older people) in need who live in the ancient townships of Tonge, Haulgh and Darcy Lever in Bolton.

Types of grants: One-off grants given for a variety of purposes including household bills, living costs and help in the home.

Annual grant total: Grants usually total around £1,400 a year.

Applications: In writing to the correspondent. Applications can be submitted either directly by the individual, through a social worker, a Citizens Advice or another welfare agency. Applications are considered in November.

Correspondent: R Hill, 24 Exford Drive, Bolton BL2 6TB (01204 524823; email: brownlow.trust@ntlworld.com)

The Manchester District Nursing Institution Fund

Eligibility: People with health related needs in the cities of Manchester and Salford and the borough of Trafford.

Types of grants: One-off grants. It is important that the request is directly related to the health issue of the applicant and is not related to a general condition of poverty.

Annual grant total: In 2009 the fund had assets of £650,000, which generated an income of £26,000. Grants were made to 107 individuals totalling £20,000.

Applications: On a form available from the correspondent which must be completed by a sponsor from a recognised social and/or health agency. Trustees meet monthly and the deadline for any meeting is the first Wednesday of the month.

Correspondent: Anne Hosker, Gaddum Centre, Gaddum House, 6 Great Jackson Street, Manchester M15 4AX (0161 834 6069; fax: 0161 839 8573; website: www.gaddumcentre.co.uk)

Other information: Grants were also made to organisations totalling £5,000 (2009).

The Manchester Jewish Federation

Eligibility: Jewish people in need who live in Greater Manchester.

Types of grants: Small grants of up to £100 to people on low income or one-off help with utility bills, childcare support, respite care, essential household items and the additional food costs of Passover and other religious festivals. The federation also provides help for children's holidays and play schemes and help to re-establish within the community i.e. removal.

Annual grant total: In 2008/09 the trust had assets of £1.4 million and an income of £940,000. Grants were made to 120 families totalling £10,000.

Applications: On a form available from the correspondent, submitted directly by the individual or, with the applicant's permission, through a social worker, Citizens Advice, other welfare agency or other third party. Applications are considered throughout the year. A referral and advice officer is available each day from 9.30 to 12.30 to discuss requests for financial assistance (call 0161 795 0024 for North Manchester or 0161 941 4442 for South Manchester).

Correspondent: Francine Heilig, 12 Holland Road, Crumpsall, Manchester M8 4NP (0161 795 0024; fax: 0161 795 3688; email: enquiries@ thefed.org.uk; website: www.thefed.org.uk)

Other information: Other services are also provided, including a full social work service, a centre for people with mental health needs, respite support for parents of children with special needs, a carer's helpline, a luncheon club, a toy library and other help for people who are isolated or housebound.

The Manchester Jewish Soup Kitchen

Eligibility: Poor, older and housebound Jewish people who live in the Greater Manchester area, who are in poor health and are unable to care for themselves.

Types of grants: Meals twice a week, and extra food for the Jewish holidays; additionally, a day trip to St Anne's is arranged each year.

Annual grant total: In 2008/09 the trust had assets of £154,000 and an income of £28,000. The trust spent £25,000 towards the provision of food for individuals.

Applications: In writing to the correspondent direct or through a hospital, social worker, member of the clergy, doctor or other welfare agency.

Correspondent: Mrs Nina Mocton, Joint Hon. Treasurer, 27 Old Hall Road, Salford, M7 4JJ (0161 740 1068)

The Mellor Fund

Eligibility: People who are sick or in need and live in Radcliffe, Whitefield and Unsworth.

Types of grants: One-off grants towards fuel, food and clothing, domestic necessities, medical needs, recuperative breaks and so on. Recurrent grants are generally not given.

Annual grant total: Grants usually total around £1,000 per year.

Applications: In writing to the correspondent. Applications can be submitted directly by the individual or through a social worker, Citizens Advice, other welfare agency or a relative, and should include brief details of need, resources, income and commitments. Applications are considered when received.

Correspondent: Peter James-Robinson, 95 Salisbury Road, Radcliffe, Manchester M26 4NQ (0161 723 5835)

The Pratt Charity

Eligibility: Women over 60 who live in or near Manchester and have done so for a period of not less than five years.

Types of grants: Grants are given towards education, health and relief of poverty, distress and sickness.

Annual grant total: About £1,000 per year.

Applications: In writing to the correspondent via a social worker.

Correspondent: Anne Hosker, Gaddum Centre, Gaddum House, 6 Great Jackson Street, Manchester M15 4AX (0161 834 6069; email: amh@ gaddumcentre.co.uk)

Bolton

The Bolton & District Nursing Association

Eligibility: People who are sick, convalescing, have disabilities or who are infirm and live in the area of Bolton Metropolitan Borough Council.

Types of grants: One-off grants for items and services, such as the provision of medical equipment, disability equipment and convalescence.

Annual grant total: This trust's income is around £3,000 a year but its total expenditure has been steadily decreasing and in 2009 was £35.

Applications: On a form available from the correspondent. Applications can be submitted directly by the individual or through a third party such as a social worker, health visitor or welfare agency. Initial telephone enquiries are encouraged to establish eligibility.

Correspondent: David Wrennall, Trustee, Bolton Guild of Help (Inc), Scott House, 27 Silverwell Street, Bolton BL1 1PP (01204 524858)

The Bolton Poor Protection Society

Eligibility: People in need who live in the former county borough of Bolton.

Types of grants: One-off grants for emergencies and all kinds of need, ranging from £25 to £50.

Annual grant total: The total annual expenditure for this charity averages around £870.

Applications: Initial telephone enquiries are encouraged to establish eligibility. Application forms are sent out thereafter.

Correspondent: The Trustees, Bolton Guild of Help, Scott House, 27 Silverwell Street, Bolton BL1 1PP (01204 524858)

The Louisa Alice Kay Fund

Eligibility: People in need who live in Bolton.

Types of grants: One-off grants for emergencies and relief-in-need, mostly for replacing household equipment and furniture.

Annual grant total: In 2009 grants were made to 131 individuals totalling £22,000 and were distributed in the following areas:

Cookers	£7,000
Washing machines	£9,000
Beds and furniture	£1,700
Fridges/freezers	£3,800

Applications: On a form available from the correspondent. Applications can be submitted either directly by the individual or a family member, through a third party such as a social worker, or through an organisation such as a Citizens Advice or other welfare agency. Applicants will sometimes be interviewed before a grant is awarded.

Correspondent: Diana Brierley, Bolton Guild of Help (Inc), Scott House, 27 Silverwell Street, Bolton BL1 1PP (01204 524858)

Other information: The fund is the main subsidiary of the Bolton Guild of Help Incorporated.

Bury

The Bury Relief-in-Sickness Fund

Eligibility: People living in the metropolitan borough of Bury who are in poor health, convalescent or who have disabilities.

Types of grants: One-off grants towards convalescence, medical equipment and necessities in the home which are not available from other sources.

Annual grant total: Grants usually total about £3,000 each year.

Applications: In writing to the correspondent.

Correspondent: Gill Warburton, The Royal Bank of Scotland plc, PO Box 26, 40 The Rock, Bury, Lancashire BL9 0NX (0161 797 8040)

Denton

The Denton Relief in Sickness Charity

Eligibility: People in need who are sick, convalescent, disabled or infirm who live in the parish of Denton.

Types of grants: One-off grants ranging from £250 to £500. Grants are given to provide a medical need not available from the NHS.

Annual grant total: Grants usually total around £2,800 a year.

Applications: In writing to the correspondent. Applications can be submitted directly by the individual, by an organisation such as Citizens Advice or through a third party such as a social worker.

Correspondent: Mary Goodliffe, Apartment 44, Enfield Court, Garside Street, Hyde SK14 5GU (0161 366 0586)

Other information: Grants are given to individuals and organisations.

Golborne

The Golborne Charities

Eligibility: People in need who live in the parish of Golborne as it was in 1892.

Types of grants: One-off grants between £50 and £80 but occasionally up to £250. Grants are usually cash payments, but are occasionally in kind, for example for food, bedding, fireguards, clothing and shoes. Also help with hospital travel and necessary holidays.

Exclusions: Loans or grants for the payments of rates are not made. Grants are not repeated in less than two years.

Annual grant total: The charities have an average expenditure of £5,000 per year.

Applications: In writing to the correspondent through a third party such as a social worker or a teacher, or via a trustee. Applications are considered at three-monthly intervals. Grant recipients tend to be known by at least one trustee.

Correspondent: Paul Gleave, 56 Nook Lane, Golborne, Warrington WA3 3JQ

Other information: Grants are also given to charitable organisations in the area of benefit, and for educational purposes

Manchester

The Crosland Fund

Eligibility: People affected by hardship who live in central Manchester.

Types of grants: One-off grants, usually of £40 to £50, for basic necessities such as clothing, food, bedding, furniture, repairs and household materials. Children's Christmas presents may also be given.

Annual grant total: In 2008/09 the fund had an income of £6,400 and a total expenditure of £3,500.

Applications: In writing to the correspondent, through a social worker, Citizens Advice or other welfare agency. Applications are considered in February, May, August and November.

Correspondent: John Atherden, Accountant, Manchester Cathedral, Victoria Street, Manchester M3 1SX (0161 833 2220)

The Dr Garrett Memorial Trust

Eligibility: Families or groups in need who live in Manchester.

Types of grants: Grants are given towards the cost of convalescence or holidays for individual families and groups.

Exclusions: Applicants should not have had a funded holiday during the past three years.

Annual grant total: In 2009/10 the trust had an income of £13,000 and a total expenditure of £11,000.

Applications: On a form available from the correspondent which should be completed by a sponsor from a recognised social or health agency. Applications must be submitted by the end of April each year.

Correspondent: Anne Hosker, Gaddum Centre, Gaddum House, 6 Great Jackson Street, Manchester M15 4AX (0161 834 6069; fax: 0161 839 8573; email: amh@gaddumcentre.co.uk; website: www.gaddumcentre.co.uk)

Other information: The trust also provides information and advice on a range of social and health care issues.

The Manchester Relief-in-Need Charity and Manchester Children's Relief-in-Need Charity

Eligibility: People in need who live in the city of Manchester and are over 25 (Relief-in-Need) or under 25 (Children's Relief-in-Need).

Types of grants: One-off grants for domestic appliances, furniture, clothing, heating and fuel bills and other general necessities. Cheques are made out to the supplier of the goods or services.

Exclusions: Debts are very rarely paid and council tax and rent debts are never met.

Annual grant total: In 2008/09 both charities had a combined income of £78,000. Grants were made totalling about £42,000.

Applications: On a form available from the correspondent which should be completed by a sponsor from a recognised social or health related agency. The trustees meet during the last week of every month. Applications must be received by the 15th of the month.

Correspondent: Anne Hosker, Gaddum Centre, Gaddum House, 6 Great Jackson Street, Manchester M15 4AX (0161 834 6069; fax: 0161 839 8573; email: amh@gaddumcentre.co.uk; website: www.gaddumcentre.co.uk)

Other information: Both charities also make grants to organisations (about £22,000 in 2008/09).

New Mills

John Mackie Memorial Ladies' Home

Eligibility: Widows or 'spinsters' who are members of the Church of England, are over 50 and are in need.

Types of grants: Christmas gifts to about 80 individuals of £65 each. Applicants will not receive help if they re-marry.

Annual grant total: In 2009 the trust had an income of £2,000 and a total expenditure of £4,000.

Applications: In writing to the correspondent, with (i) evidence of the birth, marriage and death of the applicant's husband, (ii) references from three house-owners, confirming her character, respectability and needy circumstances, (iii) proof that she has a small income and (iv) evidence that she is a member of the Church of England. Applications can be submitted either directly by the individual, through a third party such as a social worker, or through an organisation such as Citizens Advice or other welfare agency. Applications are considered throughout the year.

Correspondent: Mrs Margaret Wood, 27 Low Leighton Road, New Mills, High Peak SK22 4PG (01663 743243)

Oldham

The Sarah Lees Relief Trust

Eligibility: People living in Oldham who are sick, convalescent, disabled or infirm.

Types of grants: One-off grants and gifts in kind. Approximately 12 grants are made each year of up to £500 each.

Exclusions: No grants for items, services or facilities that are readily available from other sources.

Annual grant total: Grants average around £4,000 a year.

Applications: In writing to the correspondent through a social worker, Citizens Advice or other recognised welfare agency. Trustees meet three times a year, but urgent requests will be considered in between meetings.

Correspondent: Catherine Sykes, 10 Chew Brook Drive, Greenfield, Oldham, OL3 7PD (01457 876606)

The Oldham United Charities

Eligibility: People in need who live in the borough of Oldham.

Types of grants: One-off grants according to need. Recent grants have been mainly for medical needs, for example, wheelchairs and washing machines for people who are incontinent. Some grants are given to students towards educational expenses.

Annual grant total: About £3,000 is available each year for relief-in-need purposes.

Applications: In writing to the correspondent. Grants are usually considered quarterly.

Correspondent: Brian McKown, c/o Mills McKown, 85 Union Street, Oldham OL1 1PF (0161 624 9977)

Rochdale

Heywood Relief-in-Need Trust Fund

Eligibility: People in need who live in the former municipal borough of Heywood.

Types of grants: One-off grants usually ranging from £50 to £400. Recent grants have been given to help with fuel arrears, clothing and furniture.

Annual grant total: In 2008/09 the fund had an income of £7,500 and a total expenditure of £8,400.

Applications: On a form available from the correspondent. Applications should preferably be supported by a social worker, health visitor or similar professional.

Correspondent: Jim Murphy, Head of Finance Services, Central Finance – Finance Services, Rochdale MBC, PO BOX 530, Level 7 Telegraph House, Baillie Street, Rochdale OL16 9DJ (01706 925651; fax: 01706 924185; email: jim.murphy@rochdale.gov.uk)

The Middleton Relief-in-Need Charity

Eligibility: People in need who live in the former borough of Middleton.

Types of grants: One-off grants (typically £200) for emergencies, for example, travel expenses to visit people in hospital or similar institutions, fuel bills, television licence fees, arrears, holidays for disadvantaged families and general household necessities.

Annual grant total: About £1,600.

Applications: Made by individual application and through social workers, health visitors, victim support schemes and Citizens Advice.

Correspondent: Jim Murphy, Rochdale Metropolitan Borough Council, Head Of Finance Services, PO Box 530, Floor 7, Telegraph House, Baillie Street, Rochdale OL16 9DJ (01706 925651; email: jim. murphy@rochdale.gov.uk)

The Nurses' Benefit Fund

Eligibility: Nurses or any other person formerly in the employment of Rochdale District Nursing Association and any retired or district nurse living in the borough of Rochdale.

Types of grants: Recurrent grants paid either once or twice a year.

Annual grant total: About £1,100 a year. Grants are given to both individuals and organisations.

Applications: In writing to the correspondent.

Correspondent: Susan M Stoney, Clerk, The Old Parsonage, 2 St Mary's Gate, Rochdale OL16 1AP (01706 644187; email: law@jbhs.co.uk)

The Rochdale Fund for Relief-in-Sickness

Eligibility: People living in Rochdale who are in poor health, convalescent or who have disabilities. Help may also be given to those whose physical or mental health is likely to be impaired by poverty, deprivation or other adversity.

Types of grants: One-off grants according to need. The trustees will consider any requests for items which will make life more comfortable or productive for the individual. For example, recent grants have been given towards wheelchairs, hoists, IT equipment, house adaptations, special leisure equipment, medical aids, washing machines, cookers, clothing, beds, bedding and respite breaks.

Exclusions: Grants are not given for the payment of debts, including utility bills, council tax and Inland Revenue payments or to help with hardship not directly related to, or caused as a result of, sickness.

Annual grant total: In 2008/09 the fund had assets of £937,000 and an income of £48,000. Grants were made totalling £37,000, of which £24,000 was awarded to organisations and £13,000 was given to specific families.

Applications: On a form available from the correspondent or to download from the website. Applications can be made either directly by the individual (if no other route is available) or through a social worker, Citizens Advice, other welfare agency or other third party such as a doctor.

Correspondent: Susan Stoney, The Old Parsonage, 2 St Mary's Gate, Rochdale OL16 1AP (01706 644187; email: law@jbhs.co.uk; website: www.rochdalefund.org.uk)

Rochdale United Charity

Eligibility: People in need who live in the ancient parish of Rochdale (the former county borough of Rochdale, Castleton, Wardle, Whitworth, Littleborough, Todmorden and Saddleworth).

Types of grants: One-off grants ranging from £50 to £250. Grants have been given to help with washing machines, cookers, fridges/freezers, bedding, clothing, recuperative holidays for people long deprived of such, special food, medical or other aids, and telephones, televisions or radios for people who live alone.

Annual grant total: In 2009/10 the charity had an income of £14,000 and a total expenditure of £22,000.

Applications: On a form available from the correspondent, to be submitted through a social worker, GP, health visitor, Citizens Advice or other welfare agency. Though, applications can be made directly by the individual if they include a supporting letter from any of those listed above. Applications are usually considered quarterly.

Correspondent: Julie Baker, Rochdale Metropolitan Borough Council, Finance Services, Po Box 530, Floor 7, Telegraph House, Baillie Street, Rochdale, Lancashire OL16 9DJ

Salford

The Booth Charities

Eligibility: People who are retired, over 60, on a basic pension, live in the city of Salford and are in need.

Types of grants: Annual pensions of up to £105 and one-off grants towards TV licences and other needs.

Annual grant total: In 2008/09 the trust had assets of £24,000 and an income of £1.1 million. Grants were made to individuals totalling £3,600. A further £1.9 million was given in grants to organisations.

Applications: On a form available from the correspondent. Applications for one-off grants must be made by social services, ministers of religion, doctors and so on. Distribution meetings are held regularly throughout the year.

Correspondent: Jonathan Shelmerdine, Butcher & Barlow, 31 Middlewich Road, Sandbach, CW11 1HW (01270 762521; fax: 01270 764795)

The City of Salford Relief-in-Distress Fund

Eligibility: People in need who live in the city of Salford.

Types of grants: One-off grants to families and individuals of up to £250 (although grants over this amount may be considered). Applications will be considered for clothing, convalescence/holidays, furniture, special equipment for those with special needs, bedding and so on. Recent grants have included funds for a memorial to a young person's father, a grant to enable a family to partially equip their home after a fire, and a holiday for a family where the mother had terminal cancer.

Exclusions: Grants cannot be considered for local authority rent or council tax arrears.

Annual grant total: About £1,000 each year.

Applications: On a form submitted by a city of Salford social worker, who must be prepared to attend a meeting with the trustees to present the case.

Correspondent: Keith Darragh, c/o Salford City Council: Social Services, Crompton House, 100 Chorley Road, Swinton, Manchester M27 6BP (0161 727 8875)

Stockport

Sir Ralph Pendlebury's Charity for Orphans

Eligibility: People who have been orphaned and live, or whose parents lived, in the borough of Stockport for at least two years.

Types of grants: Grants can be for £5 or £6 a week and orphans can also receive a clothing allowance twice a year.

Annual grant total: Previously about £16,000 a year for welfare purposes.

Applications: In writing to the correspondent.

Correspondent: S M Tattersall, Carlyle House, 107–109 Wellington Road South, Stockport, SK1 3TL

Other information: Grants are also made for educational purposes.

The Stockport Sick Poor Nursing Association

Eligibility: People in need who are sick, poor or infirm and who live in the old county borough of Stockport.

Types of grants: One-off grants up to £400 for household goods and appliances, carpets and other flooring, bedding, medical equipment and so on.

Exclusions: Recurrent grants are not given.

Annual grant total: Grants usually total around £2,000 a year.

Applications: In writing to the correspondent through social services or a welfare agency. Direct applications from individuals are not accepted. The trustees meet on the third Wednesday of every other month to discuss applications. If grants are approved, cheques are sent out straight away. Cheques are made payable to the agency that supports the application who will then buy the items for the applicant.

Correspondent: Janet Heap, Trustee, 20 Charlestown Road West, Stockport, SK3 8TW (0161 483 8816)

Tameside

The Mayor of Tameside's Distress Fund

Eligibility: People in need who live in Tameside. Preference is generally given to older people and those who are, or have been, homeless.

Types of grants: One-off cash grants of up to about £200.

Annual grant total: Grants average about £1,500 each year.

Applications: On a form available from the correspondent: to be submitted through a social worker or similar third party. Applications should include details of personal income and expenditure, the amount requested, why it is needed and any other organisations approached.

Correspondent: Scott Littlewood, Tameside M B C, Room 2.23, Wellington Road Offices, Ashton-under-Lyne, Tameside OL6 6DL (0161 342 2878)

Isle of Man

The Manx Marine Society

Eligibility: Seafarers, retired or disabled seafarers and their widows, children and dependants, who live on the Isle of Man. Young Manx people under 18 who wish to attend sea school or become a cadet are also eligible.

Types of grants: One-off and recurrent grants of up to £400 according to need.

Annual grant total: About £5,000.

Applications: On a form available from the correspondent. Applications are considered at any time and can be submitted either by the individual, or through a social worker, Citizens Advice or other welfare agency.

Correspondent: Capt. R K Cringle, 10 Carrick Bay View, Ballagawne Road, Colby, Isle of Man IM9 4DD (01624 838233)

Lancashire

The Accrington & District Helping Hands Fund

Eligibility: People living in the former borough of Accrington, Clayton-Le-Moors and Altham, who are in poor health and are either supported by benefits or are on a low income.

Types of grants: One-off grants usually ranging from £100 to £300 towards the cost of: (i) special foods and medicines, medical comforts, extra bedding, fuel and medical and surgical appliances; (ii) provision of domestic help; (iii) convalescence; (iv) provision of mobile physiotherapy service. Grants are usually made directly to the supplier.

Annual grant total: In 2009 the fund had an income of £11,000 and a total expenditure of £6,000. Grants usually total about £5,000 a year.

Applications: On a form available from the correspondent submitted either directly by the individual or through a social worker, Citizens Advice or other welfare agency. Applications should include evidence of income and state of health, as well as estimates of what is required.

Correspondent: Mrs Mary-Ann Renton, The Coach House, Clitheroe Road, Waddington, Lancashire BB7 3HQ (01200 422062)

The Baines Charity

Eligibility: People in need who live in the ancient townships of Carleton, Hardhorn-cum-Newton, Marton, Poulton and Thornton.

Types of grants: One-off grants ranging from £100 to £250. 'Each case is discussed in its merits.'

Annual grant total: In 2009 the charity had an income of £17,000 and a total expenditure of £15,000. Grants are made for both welfare and educational purposes.

Applications: On a form available from the correspondent, either directly by the individual, or through a social worker, Citizens Advice or other welfare agency. Applications are considered upon receipt.

Correspondent: Duncan Waddilove, 2 The Chase, Normoss Road, Blackpool, Lancashire FY3 0BF (01253 893459)

The Blackpool, Fylde & Wyre Society for the Blind

Eligibility: People who are blind, or who suffer substantially from a visual impairment whether or not registered as blind or partially sighted, living in Blackpool, Fylde and Wyre districts of Lancashire.

Types of grants: One-off grants of between £10 and £250 to relieve difficulties arising from visual impairment.

Annual grant total: In 2008/09 the society had assets of £3.4 million and an income of £1.2 million. Charitable expenditure totalled £938,000, but only about £2,500 is available in grants each year.

Applications: On a form available from the correspondent to be submitted through a society welfare officer. Applications are considered throughout the year.

Correspondent: John Booth, Company Secretary, Princess Alexandra Home for the Blind, Bosworth Place, Blackpool, FY4 1SH (01253 362688; email: kevin@bfwsb.co.uk; website: www.bfwsb.co.uk)

Other information: The society provides a range of services including a resource and rehabilitation centre, a talking newspaper service and a library with over 1,000 audio book titles.

James Bond/Henry Welch Trust

Eligibility: People in need who live in the area covered by Lancaster City Council and have diseases of the chest/lung and early forms of phthisis. Children with disabilities and other special needs are also eligible.

Types of grants: One-off and recurrent grants ranging from £100 to £500 towards, for example, computer equipment, household essentials and holidays.

Annual grant total: In 2008/09 the trust had assets of £262,000 and an income of £11,000. Grants were made to 13 individuals totalling £4,700.

Applications: The trust's home visitor will visit the individual and complete the form. Applications can be submitted at anytime.

Correspondent: Jane Glenton, The Clerk to the Trustees, c/o Democratic Services, Lancaster City Council, Town Hall, Dalton Square, Lancaster LA1 1PJ (01524 582068)

Other information: This trust also gives to organisations.

Brentwood Charity

Eligibility: Individuals in need who live in Lancashire (boundaries pre-1974).

Types of grants: One-off grants ranging from £50 to £150, towards such items as necessary household appliances, furnishings and special equipment.

Exclusions: No grants to pay for debts or rent bonds.

Annual grant total: About £2,500 is available each year for grants to individuals.

Applications: On a form available directly from the correspondent or to download from the website. Applications should be submitted through a social worker, Citizens Advice or other welfare agency. No response is made without an sae. Applications are considered quarterly, in January, April, July and October.

Correspondent: Marion Bolton, Community Futures, 15 Victoria Road, Fulwood, Preston, Lancashire PR2 8PS (01772 717461; fax: 01772 900250; email: ccl@communityfutures.org.uk; website: www.communityfutures.org.uk)

The Chronicle Cinderella Fund

Eligibility: Children who are disadvantaged, aged under 18 and live in the pre-1974 boundaries of Lancashire.

Types of grants: Grants of up to £250 to help with the cost of holidays in the UK. Grants are given to individual children to allow them to go on group holidays and to children and mothers for family holidays on referral from agencies.

Annual grant total: In 2008/09 the fund had an income of £5,900 and a total expenditure of £4,900.

Applications: On a form available from the correspondent or to download from the website. Applications must be made through, and completed by, a referral agent such as a social worker or similar professional. Applications are considered quarterly in January, April, July and October. No response is made without an sae.

Correspondent: Lorraine Wilson, Clerk to the Trustees, Community Futures, 15 Victoria Road, Fulwood, Preston PR2 8PS (01772 717461; fax: 01772 900250; email: ccl@communityfutures.org.uk; website: www.communityfutures.org.uk)

Other information: The fund also makes grants to organisations running holidays for children who are disadvantaged.

Daniel's and Houghton's Charity

Eligibility: People in need who live in Lancashire with preference given to those living in Preston, Grimsargh, Broughton, Woodplumpton, Eaves, Catforth, Bartle, Alston and Elston.

Types of grants: One-off and recurrent grants according to need.

Exclusions: No grants are given for items or services where statutory funds are available.

Annual grant total: In 2008/09 grants were made totalling £33,000.

Applications: In writing to the correspondent.

Correspondent: Miss H A Ryan, Brabners Chaffe Street LLP, 7–8 Chapel Street, Preston PR1 8AN (01772 823921)

Other information: Grants are also made to organisations.

The Foxton Dispensary

Eligibility: People in need who are in poor health, convalescent or who have a disability and live in the urban district of Poulton-le-Fylde and the county borough of Blackpool.

Types of grants: One-off grants towards food and other necessities such as household equipment.

Annual grant total: In 2009 the dispensary had assets of £607,000 and an income of £58,000. Grants were made totalling £17,000.

Applications: On a form available from the correspondent or through the website. Applications should be made via a doctor, healthcare professional or social services department. They are considered on an ongoing basis. All applicants are visited by one of the trustees before a grant is made.

Correspondent: Robert Dunn, PO Box 227, Lytham St. Annes, FY8 9BJ (01253 722277; email: clerk@foxtoncharity.co.uk; website: www.foxtoncharity.co.uk)

The Harris Charity

Eligibility: People in need under 25 who live in Lancashire, with a preference for the Preston district.

Types of grants: One-off grants of £100 to £5,000 for electrical goods, travel expenses and disability equipment.

Exclusions: No grants for course fees or to supplement living expenses.

Annual grant total: In 2008/09 the charity had assets of £2.5 million, an income of £136,000 and a total expenditure of £90,000, of which £13,000 was given in grants to individuals and a further £11,000 given in five loans.

Applications: In writing to the correspondent with information about financial income and outgoings. Applications are considered during the three months after 31 March and 30 September and must be submitted before these dates either directly by the individual or a third party on behalf of the individual (social worker, Citizens Advice and so on).

Correspondent: P R Metcalf, Richard House, 9 Winckley Square, Preston PR1 3HP (01772 821021; fax: 01772 259441; email: harrischarity@mooreandsmalley.co.uk; website: theharrischarity.co.uk/)

Other information: The charity also supports charitable institutions that benefit individuals, recreation and leisure and the training and education of individuals.

Lancashire County Nursing Trust

Eligibility: Retired nurses who are in need and have been employed in Lancashire, south Cumbria or Greater Manchester. Grants are also given to people who are in need in the area but it is important to note that most of the trust's income is for the benefit nurses and only a relatively small amount is available for others.

Types of grants: One-off grants usually ranging from £100 to £300. Support for retired nurses can be for any purpose but funding for people who are sick and in need is generally focused on medical care, holidays and equipment.

Annual grant total: In 2009 the trust had an income of £11,000 and a total expenditure of £5,900.

Applications: In writing to the correspondent. Applications can be submitted directly by the individual or through a social worker, Citizens Advice, nursing authority or other welfare agency.

Correspondent: Hadyn Gigg, 16 Richmond Avenue, Wrea Green, Preston, PR4 2NJ (01772 683946; email: hadyngigg@yahoo.co.uk)

The Lancashire Football Association Benevolent Fund

Eligibility: People in need who are members of clubs associated with Lancashire Football Association and players or officials injured during, or travelling to or from, matches organised by the association.

Types of grants: One-off grants ranging from £100 to £300 towards, for example, hospital expenses, living costs and household bills.

Annual grant total: Grants average around £600 a year.

Applications: On a form available from the correspondent. Applications can be submitted directly by the individual or through a personal representative or a friend.

Correspondent: David Burgess, The County Ground, Thurston Road, Leyland, Preston, Lancashire PR25 2LF (01772 624000; fax: 01772 624700)

Peter Lathom's Charity

Eligibility: People in need living in West Lancashire.

Types of grants: One-off grants in November/December.

Annual grant total: In 2008 the charity had assets of £1.1 million and an income of £33,000. Grants made for welfare purposes totalled £1,100.

Applications: On a form available from the correspondent.

Correspondent: Mark Abbott, c/o The Kennedy Partnership, 15 Railway Road, Ormskirk, Lancashire L39 2DW (01695 575271)

The Shaw Charities

Eligibility: People over 60 who are on low incomes and live in Rivington, Anglezarke, Heath Charnock and Anderton, Lancashire.

Types of grants: Recurrent grants at Easter and Christmas. Grants range from £15 to £20.

Annual grant total: In 2008/09 the charities had an income of £3,600 and a total expenditure of £2,600.

Applications: On a form available from the correspondent to be submitted by the individual for consideration in March and November.

Correspondent: Mrs E Woodrow, 99 Rawlinson Lane, Heath Charnock, Chorley, Lancashire, PR7 4DE (01257 480515; email: woodrows@ tinyworld.co.uk)

Other information: Grants for the purchase of books by undergraduates are also given through the Shaw's Educational Endowment.

The Skelton Swindells Trust

Eligibility: Women in need, usually those not supported by a partner, who live in Lancashire (pre-1974 boundaries).

Types of grants: One-off grants of up to £150 for heating, furnishings, special equipment, household appliances, provision of services and so on.

Annual grant total: Grants usually total about £1,500 each year.

Applications: On a form available from the correspondent or to download from the website. Applications should be completed and submitted by a social worker or similar professional or by a voluntary agency such as Citizens Advice. They are considered three times a year in March, June and November. A sae must be included.

Correspondent: Marion Bolton, Community Futures, 15 Victoria Road, Fulwood, Preston PR2 8PS (01772 717461; fax: 01772 900250; email: ccl@ communityfutures.org.uk; website: www. communityfutures.org.uk)

Blackpool

The Blackpool Ladies' Sick Poor Association

Eligibility: People in need who live in Blackpool.

Types of grants: Mainly food vouchers of £12 to £20 a month per family. Special relief grants can be made for immediate needs such as rent, second-hand cookers and washers, clothing, heaters, fireguards, stair gates and so on.

Annual grant total: In 2008/09 the association had assets of £306,000 and an income of £36,000. Grants were made totalling £35,000.

Applications: Applications must include proof of extreme hardship and must be in writing via health visitors, social workers, Citizens Advice or other welfare agencies such as Age Concern, MIND and so on. Health visitors and social workers can write to the association's treasurer directly, otherwise letters should be sent to the correspondent. Applications are considered all year round, excluding August.

Correspondent: Ronald A Shaw, 156 Highcross Road, Poulton-Le-Fylde, Lancashire, FY6 8DA (01253 893188)

Other information: The association occasionally makes grants to organisations.

The Swallowdale Children's Trust

Eligibility: People who live in the Blackpool area who are under the age of 25. Orphans are given preference.

Types of grants: One-off grants are given for a wide variety of needs, including hospital expenses, clothing, food, travel expenses, medical equipment, nursing fees, furniture, disabled equipment and help in the home.

Annual grant total: In 2008/09 the trust had assets of £698,000 and an income of £43,000. There were 262 relief-in-need grants made during the year totalling £25,000. No grants were made for educational purposes.

Applications: On a form available from the correspondent, with the financial details of the individual or family. Applications must be made through a social worker or teacher. They are considered every two months.

Correspondent: The Secretary, 145 Mayfield Road, St Annes on Sea, FY8 2DS

Caton-with-Littledale

The Cottam Charities

Eligibility: People in need who are over 50 and have lived in the parish of Caton-with-Littledale for at least five years.

Types of grants: One-off grants ranging from about £100 to £140.

Annual grant total: Grants usually total around £25,000 each year.

Applications: In writing to the correspondent directly by the individual or family member by mid-November for consideration in November/December each year. Applicants must reapply each year.

Correspondent: Amanda Owen, Blackhurst Swainson Goodier Solicitors, 3 & 4 Aalborg Square, Lancaster LA1 1GG (01524 32471; email: ajo@bsglaw.co.uk)

Darwen

The W M & B W Lloyd Trust

Eligibility: People in need who live in the old borough of Darwen in Lancashire. Preference is given to single parents.

Types of grants: One-off and recurrent grants according to need. Educational grants are given priority over social or medical grants.

Annual grant total: In 2008/09 the trust had an income of £72,000 and made grants totalling £96,000 to organisations and individuals.

Applications: On a form available from the correspondent, only through a social worker, Citizens Advice, other welfare agency, doctor or health visitor. Applications are considered quarterly in March, June, September and December.

Correspondent: John Jacklin, Trustee, Gorse Barn, Rock Lane, Tockholes, Darwen, Lancashire BB3 0LX (01254 771367)

Lancaster

The Gibson, Simpson & Brockbank Annuities Trust

Eligibility: Unmarried women or widows in need (with an income of less than £1,000 from sources other than their state pension), who are over 50 years old and have lived in Lancaster for the last three years.

Types of grants: Quarterly grants.

Annual grant total: In 2009 the trust had an income of £6,700 and a total expenditure of £5,800.

Applications: On a form available from the correspondent to be submitted directly by the individual. Applications are usually considered every three months.

Correspondent: Amanda Owen, Blackhurst Swainson Goodier Solicitors, 3 & 4 Allborg Square, Lancaster LA1 1GG (01524 32471; fax: 01524 386515; email: ajo@bsglaw.co.uk)

The Lancaster Charity

Eligibility: People over 60 who are in need and have lived in the old city of Lancaster for at least three years. People under 60 may be considered if they are unable to work to maintain themselves due to age, accident or infirmity.

Types of grants: Individual grants according to need.

Annual grant total: In 2009 the charity had assets of £1.8 million and an income of £131,000. During the year, payments totalling £1,900 were made to pensioners. The majority of income is spent on maintaining the charity's almshouses.

Applications: On a form available from the correspondent. Applications are considered when vacancies occur.

Correspondent: Philip Oglethorpe, 16 Castle Park, Lancaster LA1 1YG (01524 846846)

Littleborough

The Littleborough Nursing Association Fund

Eligibility: People in need who are sick, convalescent, disabled or infirm and live in the former urban district of Littleborough.

Types of grants: Recurrent grants according to need.

Exclusions: Grants are not given for costs which are normally covered by the DWP or NHS.

Annual grant total: Grants to individuals usually total around £500 each year.

Applications: In writing to the correspondent for consideration in October. Applications can be submitted directly by the individual or through a social worker, Citizens Advice, other welfare agency or other third party.

Correspondent: Marilyn Aldred, 26 Hodder Avenue, Shore, Littleborough OL15 8EU (01706 370738)

Lowton

The Lowton United Charity

Eligibility: People in need who live in the parishes of St Luke's and St Mary's in Lowton.

Types of grants: One-off grants at Christmas and emergency one-off grants at any time.

Annual grant total: Grants total about £4,000 a year. About half of grants are given at Christmas for relief-in-need purposes and the rest throughout the year.

Applications: Usually through the rectors of the parishes or other trustees.

Correspondent: J Naughton, Secretary, 51 Kenilworth Road, Lowton, Warrington, WA3 2AZ

Lytham St Anne's

The Lytham St Anne's Relief-in-Sickness Charity

Eligibility: People with a physical or mental disability or long term illness who are in need and live in the borough of Fylde, mainly St Annes.

Types of grants: One-off grants of up to £500, for example, fuel bills, washing machines, special beds/chairs, respite holidays and travel for medical treatment or to visit sick relatives.

Exclusions: No grants for court fees or funeral costs.

Annual grant total: About £8,000 a year.

Applications: In writing to the correspondent with financial details and information about the illness or the reason for need. Applications can be submitted directly by the individual or through a social worker, Citizens Advice, other welfare agency or other third party.

Correspondent: The Trustees, c/o Blackpool CVS, 95 Abingdon Street, Blackpool FY1 1PP (01253 624505 (Ext. 214))

Nelson

The Nelson District Nursing Association Fund

Eligibility: Sick, poor people who live in Nelson, Lancashire.

Types of grants: One-off grants according to need, ranging from £50 to £500.

Annual grant total: In 2009/10 the fund had an income of £4,700 and a total expenditure of £2,100.

Applications: In writing to the correspondent. Applications can be submitted directly by the individual or through a social worker, Citizens Advice or other welfare agency. All applicants will be visited by the association's welfare officer before a decision is taken.

Correspondent: Joanne Eccles, Democratic & Legal Services, Pendle Borough Council, Nelson Town Hall, Market Street, Nelson, Lancashire BB9 7LG (01282 661654)

Merseyside

Channel – Supporting Family Social Work in Liverpool

Eligibility: Children living in Merseyside who are in need, where the need cannot be met by statutory grants from the social services.

Types of grants: One-off grants up to £100 for clothing, food, furniture, kitchen equipment and childcare.

Annual grant total: In 2008/09 the trust had an income of £18,000 and a total expenditure of £11,000.

Applications: Applications can only be made through a social worker, health worker or voluntary agency, who should contact the correspondent for advice on funding, an application form and guidelines. Applications are considered on an ongoing basis.

Correspondent: Janet Corke, 294 Aigburth Road, Liverpool, L17 9PW (0151 726 0443; fax: 0151 726 0443)

The Girls' Welfare Fund

Eligibility: Girls and young women (usually aged 15 to 25) who are in need and were born, educated and live in Merseyside. Applications from other areas will not be acknowledged.

Types of grants: One-off and recurrent grants according to need. Grants range from £50 to £750.

Exclusions: Grants are not made to charities that request funds to pass on and give to individuals.

Annual grant total: In 2009 the fund had an income of £8,000 and a total expenditure of £100.

Applications: By letter to the correspondent or via email (including full details of what is needed and for what purpose). Applications can be submitted directly by the individual or through a social worker, Citizens Advice or another welfare agency. Applications are considered quarterly in March, June, September and December.

Correspondent: Mrs S M O'Leary, West Hey, Dawstone Road, Heswall, Wirral CH60 4RP (email: gwf_charity@hotmail.com)

Other information: The trust also gives grants to organisations benefiting girls and young women on Merseyside, and to eligible individuals for leisure, creative activities, sports, arts and education.

The Liverpool Caledonian Association

Eligibility: People of Scottish descent, or their immediate family, who are in need and who live within a 15-mile radius of Liverpool Town Hall. The association states: 'Generally speaking we do not welcome applications from people who have fewer than one grandparent who was Scots born.'

Types of grants: Regular monthly payment of annuities, heating grants and a limited number of Christmas food parcels. The usual maximum grant is £50.

Exclusions: Holidays are generally excluded.

Annual grant total: In 2009 the association had an income of £9,700 and a total expenditure of £19,000.

Applications: In writing to the correspondent either directly by the individual, through a social worker, Citizens Advice, or other welfare agency or through any other third party. Applications are considered at any time and applicants will be visited.

Correspondent: I A Fisher, Secretary, 72 Cambridge Road, Crosby, Liverpool L23 7TZ (0151 924 3909)

The Liverpool Ladies' Institution

Eligibility: Single women in need who were either born in the city of Liverpool or live in Merseyside. Preference is given to such women who are members of the Church of England, and to older women.

Types of grants: Recurrent grants.

Annual grant total: In 2009 the trust had an income of £4,800 and a total expenditure of £6,100.

Applications: On a form available from the correspondent. Applications should be submitted, at any time, through a social worker, Citizens Advice or other welfare agency. The trust has stated that it receives a lot of inappropriate applications.

Correspondent: David Anderton, 15 Childwall Park Avenue, Childwall, Liverpool L16 0JE (0151 722 9823; email: d.anderton68@btinternet.com)

The Liverpool Merchants' Guild

Eligibility: Retired, professional, clerical or self-employed people and their dependants who live on Merseyside (or who have lived there for a continuous period of at least 15 years), are aged over 50, and are in need or distress.

Types of grants: Annual pensions of £200 upwards. One-off grants of up to £5,000 for items of exceptional expenditure e.g. equipment or adaptations to support independent living.

Annual grant total: In 2008 the guild had assets of £22 million and an income of £1.3 million. Grants were made totalling £782,000. This included £658,000 given in pensions and £124,000 given in grants.

Applications: On a form available from the correspondent or to download from the website. Applications must be countersigned by two unrelated referees and include all relevant supporting documentation. They can be submitted at any time and are considered every three months.

Note: Applicants wishing to apply for a one-off grant will need to fill in the standard application form and a supplementary grants form (also available on the website).

Correspondent: Brian McGain, Moore Stephens, 110–114 Duke Street, Liverpool L1 5AG (0151 703 1080; fax: 0151 703 1085; email: info@liverpoolmerchantsguild.org.uk; website: www.liverpoolmerchantsguild.org.uk)

The Liverpool Provision Trade Guild

Eligibility: Members of the guild and their dependants who are in need. If funds permit, benefits can be extended to other members of the provision trade on Merseyside who are in need and their dependants.

Types of grants: Recurrent grants of £400 to £900 paid monthly, half-yearly or annually.

Annual grant total: In 2008/09 the trust had an income of £5,000 and a total expenditure of £6,800.

Applications: In writing to the correspondent, directly by the individual. Meetings are held in May and December to discuss applications.

Correspondent: The Secretary, KBH Accountants Ltd, 255 Poulton Road, Wallasey, Wirral CH44 4BT (0151 638 8550)

The Liverpool Queen Victoria District Nursing Association (LCSS)

Eligibility: People who are sick or disabled, live in Merseyside and are in need. No help

is given where this should be provided by the 'public purse'.

Types of grants: One-off grants of between £10 and £200 to provide financial help towards food, appliances or other items to help alleviate suffering or assist the recovery of eligible people.

Exclusions: No grants for debts, holidays, pilgrimages or medical treatment.

Annual grant total: Grants have previously totalled £28,000.

Applications: On a form only available from the Community Nursing Services of Merseyside Health Districts (not from the correspondent) via district nurses, health visitors or through a social worker. An initial telephone call to the correspondent to discuss eligibility and needs is welcomed. Applications are considered all year round.

Correspondent: Company Secretaries, Liverpool Charity and Voluntary Services, 151 Dale Street, Liverpool L2 2AH (0151 227 5177; fax: 0151 237 3998; email: email@merseytrusts.org.uk; website: www.merseytrusts.org.uk/)

The Liverpool Queen Victoria Nursing Association (PSS)

Eligibility: People in need who are in poor health, convalescent or who have a disability and live in Merseyside.

Types of grants: One-off grants up to £150 for essential items which will alleviate suffering or assist recovery, such as bedding, clothing and household equipment.

Annual grant total: Grants usually total about £4,000 each year.

Applications: On a form available from the correspondent. Applications must be made through a social worker, health visitor or occupational therapist.

Correspondent: Louise Nightingale, Liverpool Charity and Voluntary Services, 151 Dale Street, Liverpool L2 2AH (0151 227 5177; fax: 0151 237 3998; email: email@merseytrusts.org.uk; website: www.merseytrusts.org.uk/)

Other information: The association is administered by Liverpool Charity and Voluntary Services.

The Mersey Mission To Seafarers

Eligibility: Active, retired or disabled seafarers and fishermen, their children, widows and dependants.

Types of grants: One-off and recurrent grants according to need.

Annual grant total: It appears that no grants were made during 2009, although in previous years a small proportion of income, around £2,000, was given in grants to individuals and assistance given to other funding sources.

Applications: In writing to the correspondent.

Correspondent: Capt David Nutman, Colonsay House, 20 Crosby Road South, Waterloo, Liverpool, Merseyside L22 1 RQ (0151 920 3253; fax: 0151 928 0244; email: dnbnutman@talktalk.net)

Merseyside Jewish Community Care

Eligibility: People of Jewish faith who live in Merseyside and are in need due to poverty, illness, old age, social disadvantage, disability or mental health problems.

Types of grants: Small one-off grants and loans to help towards medical equipment, respite breaks and basic essentials such as food and clothing. Grants are only paid on the provision of receipts for the goods/services purchased or are simply made directly to the supplier.

Annual grant total: In 2008/09 the trust had assets of £1.6 million and an income of £2.2 million. 'Relief grants' were made totalling £18,000.

Applications: By letter or telephone to the correspondent, directly by the individual.

Correspondent: Lisa Dolan, Chief Executive, Shifrin House, 433 Smithdown Road, Liverpool L15 3JL (0151 733 2292; email: info@mjccshifrin.co.uk)

The Merseyside Police Orphans' Fund

Eligibility: Children/adopted children of deceased police officers or police officers who are incapacitated and will never work again. The police officers must have been members of the Merseyside Police Force.

Types of grants: Allowances of £200 a quarter and a parting gift of £150. Allowances are paid until the child is 16 (unless he/she remains in full-time secondary education). Christmas and summer gifts are also available.

Exclusions: No grants for students being educated at university level.

Annual grant total: In 2008/09 the trust had assets of £47,000, an income of £21,000 and made grants to children totalling £16,000.

Applications: In writing to the correspondent.

Correspondent: C Pierce, 178 Higher Bebington Road, Wirral, Merseyside CH63 2PT (0151 233 4708)

Billinge

John Eddleston's Charity

Eligibility: People in need who live in the ecclesiastical parish of Billinge.

Types of grants: One-off and recurrent grants according to need.

Annual grant total: Grants to individuals usually total around £1,000 for education and welfare purposes.

Applications: In writing to the correspondent by the end of March. The annual meeting of the trustees takes place after the end of March.

Correspondent: Graham Bartlett, Parkinson Commercial Property Consultants, 10 Bridgeman Terrace, Wigan, Lancashire, WN1 1SX (01942 7401800)

Birkenhead

The Birkenhead Relief in Sickness Fund

Eligibility: People in need through ill health who are on a low income and live in the old county borough of Birkenhead. Applicants should have tried to obtain a social fund loan before approaching the trust.

Types of grants: One-off grants to a usual maximum of £250. Grants are given for essential items such as clothing, electrical appliances, furniture (e.g. beds), travel costs and household items (e.g. bedding, towels).

Annual grant total: In 2008/09 the fund had an income of £2,300 and a total expenditure of £1,800.

Applications: Applications can be submitted through a recognised referral agency (e.g. social worker, Citizens Advice or doctor) or other third party, and are considered throughout the year. A doctor's note will be needed to back up the claim if the applicant is not in receipt of Disability Living Allowance. An appointment will be made with the claimant, or a member of the family if they are unable to attend, to discuss the claim.

Correspondent: Viv Kenwright, Wirral CVS, 46 Hamilton Square, Birkenhead CH41 5AR (0151 647 5432; email: viv@wirralcvs.org.uk)

The Christ Church Fund for Children

Eligibility: Children in need up to the age of 17 whose parents are members of the Church of England and who live in the county borough of Birkenhead. Preference is given to children living in the ecclesiastical parish of Christ Church, Birkenhead.

Types of grants: Grants for any kind of need, but typically for bedding, furniture, clothing and trips.

Annual grant total: About £1,500.

Applications: In writing through a recognised referral agency (for example, a social worker or Citizens Advice) or other third party. Applications are usually considered quarterly (around January, April, September and December), but emergency applications can be considered at any time.

Correspondent: Robert Perry, 28 Beresford Road, Prenton, CH43 1XG

Higher Bebington

The Thomas Robinson Charity

Eligibility: People in need who live in Higher Bebington.

Types of grants: One-off grants of £50 to £500. Grants can be made for educational purposes.

Annual grant total: About £1,000.

Applications: In writing to: The Vicar, Christ Church Vicarage, King's Road, Higher Bebington, Wirral CH43 8LX. Applications can be submitted directly by the individual or a family member, through a social worker, or a relevant third party such as Citizens Advice or a school. They are considered at any time.

Correspondent: Charles F Van Ingen, 1 Blakeley Brow, Wirral, Merseyside CH63 0PS

Huyton with Roby

The Huyton with Roby Distress Fund

Eligibility: People in need who live in the former urban district of Huyton with Roby (in Knowsley).

Types of grants: One-off grants ranging from £100 to £350 towards the cost of items such as washing machines, carpets and beds.

Exclusions: No grants for debts or fuel costs or to buy non-essential items.

Annual grant total: Grants average around £900 per year.

Applications: In writing to the correspondent through a social worker, Citizens Advice or other welfare agency. A social worker would usually assess the need and should inform the trust about the applicant's full circumstances and give details about the item required (e.g. the cost). Applications are considered on receipt.

Correspondent: The Trustees, Knowsley MBC, KMBC Finance, Po Box 23, Nutgrove Villa, Westmorland Road, Huyton, Liverpool L36 6GA (0151 443 3757; fax: 0151 443 3452)

Liverpool

The Charles Dixon Pension Fund

Eligibility: Merchants who are married men, widowers or bachelors of good character, who are practising members of the Church of England, and widows of pensioners who are in reduced circumstances. Applicants must live in Bristol, Liverpool or London and must be over 60 years.

Types of grants: Pensions of between £520 and £2,000 a year.

Annual grant total: In 2009/10 the fund had an income of £7,200 and a total expenditure of £7,100.

Applications: On a form available from the correspondent. Applications can be submitted directly by the individual or through a social worker, Citizens Advice, other welfare agency or a third party such as a clergyman. They are dealt with as received.

Correspondent: Richard J Morris, Treasurer, The Society of Merchant Venturers, Merchants' Hall, The Promenade, Clifton Down, Bristol BS8 3NH (0117 973 8058; fax: 0117 973 5884; email: enquiries@ merchantventurers.com)

The Liverpool Corn Trade Guild

Eligibility: Members of the guild and their dependants who are in need. If funds permit benefits can be extended to former members and their dependants. Membership is open to anyone employed by any firm engaged in the Liverpool Corn and Feed Trade.

Types of grants: One-off and recurrent grants according to need.

Annual grant total: Grants average around £11,000 a year.

Applications: In writing to the correspondent. Applications should be made directly by the individual.

Correspondent: S N Gooderham, c/o Criddle & Co. Ltd, 3rd Floor Cunard Building, Liverpool L3 1EL (0151 243 9111; fax: 0151 243 9012)

The Liverpool Wholesale Fresh Produce Benevolent Fund

Eligibility: People in need, who are or have been associated with the Liverpool fruit trade either as importers or wholesalers, and their families.

Types of grants: One-off and recurrent grants usually ranging from £50 to £80.

Annual grant total: In 2009/10 the trust had an income of £6,100 and a total expenditure of £12,000.

Applications: In writing to the correspondent.

Correspondent: Thomas J C Dobbin, Secretary, 207 Childwall Road, Liverpool L15 6UT (0151 722 0621)

The Ann Molyneux Charity

Eligibility: Seamen living in the city of Liverpool. Preference for men who sailed from the city for most of the last five years that they were at sea. Applicants must receive Income Support, rent or council tax rebate.

Types of grants: Pensions of £200 a year (paid quarterly).

Annual grant total: In 2008/09 the charity had assets of £384,000 and an income of £26,000. Grants were made totalling £23,000.

Applications: On a form available from Liverpool Parish Church and Our Lady & St Nicholas. Applications should be accompanied by seamen's books, details of income and a testimonial from a person of good standing in the community.

Correspondent: The Trustees, Macfarlane & Co, 2nd Floor, Cunard Building, Water Street, Liverpool L3 1DS (0151 236 6161)

The Pritt Fund

Eligibility: Solicitors who are in need and have practised in the city of Liverpool or within the area of Liverpool Law Society, and their dependants.

Types of grants: One-off and recurrent grants according to need.

Annual grant total: Previously grants have totalled about £14,000.

Applications: On a form available from the correspondent.

Correspondent: D J Tournafond, Liverpool Law Society, The Cotton Exchange Building, Second Floor, Old Hall Street, Liverpool L3 9LQ (0151 236 5998)

Lydiate

John Goore's Charity

Eligibility: People in need living in the parish of Lydiate only.

Types of grants: Grants of up to £500 to alleviate some of the difficulties faced by people with a physical or mental disability, for example, small home improvements, travel to community activities/facilities and specialist equipment. Grants of up to £250 are also available to local carers for respite breaks, travel expenses and additional costs of living incurred as a direct result of being a carer.

Exclusions: No grants for payment of debts.

Annual grant total: In 2008/09 the charity had an income of £22,000 and a total expenditure of £16,000.

Applications: Applications should be made through the Community Foundation for Merseyside. Forms are available on request either by post, telephone or email, or to download directly from the foundation's website (see contact information below).

Address: c/o Alliance & Leicester, Bridle Road, Bootle GIR 0AA

Tel: 0151 966 3504 – email: grants@cfmerseyside.org.uk – Web: www.cfmerseyside.org.uk

Applications should include written proof of residence in Lydiate and a letter of support from the person being cared for (if appropriate).

Correspondent: E R Bostock, 124 Liverpool Road, Lydiate, Merseyside L31 2NB (0151 526 4919)

Other information: The charity also makes grants to organisations and to individuals for educational purposes.

Sefton

Southport & Birkdale Provident Society

Eligibility: People in need who live in the metropolitan borough of Sefton.

Types of grants: One-off grants in kind only after social services have confirmed that all other benefits have been fully explored. Recent grants have been given towards clothing, bedding, cookers, washing machines and other basic household needs.

Exclusions: No cash payments. Grants are not given for education, training experience, rental deposits, personal debt relief or hire purchase. Medical services are not supported.

Annual grant total: In 2009 the society had assets of £540,000 and an income of £25,000. Grants were made to 90 individuals totalling £11,000.

Applications: In writing to the correspondent with as much background information of family and reasons for request as possible. Applications should be submitted through social services. They are considered at any time.

Correspondent: Ian P Jones, 12 Ascot Close, Southport, Merseyside PR8 2DD (01704 560 095)

Other information: Local groups supporting people in need in the beneficial area will also be considered.

Wirral

The Emily Clover Trust

Eligibility: Individuals and families who are in need and live within a 10-mile radius of Bidston Parish Church, Birkenhead.

Types of grants: One-off grants of between £70 and £200 for needs such as beds and bedding, lycra support suits, a disability toilet, holidays for disadvantaged children and household grants.

Exclusions: No grants towards further or adult education, adventure holidays or to relieve debts.

Annual grant total: Grants to individuals generally total around £900.

Applications: In writing to the correspondent. Support from a social worker or other welfare agency is useful. Applications are considered as they are received.

Correspondent: Anthony Endean, Trustee, Park Lodge, 126 Eleanor Road, Prenton, CH43 7QS (0151 652 7328)

Other information: The trust also gives grants to organisations.

The Conroy Trust

Eligibility: People in need who live in the parish of Bebington.

Types of grants: Bi-monthly payments to regular beneficiaries and one-off grants for special needs. Grants usually range from £50 to £300.

Exclusions: No grants are made for educational purposes.

Annual grant total: About £3,500 a year. Grants are given to both individuals and local organisations.

Applications: In writing to the correspondent directly by the individual.

Correspondent: Tom Bates, 22 Waterford Road, Prenton, Wirral CH43 6UU (0151 652 2128)

The John Lloyd Corkhill Trust

Eligibility: People with lung conditions who live in the metropolitan borough of Wirral.

Types of grants: Mostly for equipment (e.g. nebulisers). Help is also given towards services and amenities, for example holidays and occasionally to buy domestic appliances such as fires, washing machines and so on.

Annual grant total: On average, about £3,000 is available each year to distribute in grants.

Applications: Clients are generally referred by their social worker or doctor and have a low income. Supporting medical evidence must be supplied. Applications are considered in June and December.

Correspondent: Michelle Jafrate, 5 Broadway, Greasby, Wirral, Merseyside CH49 2NG (0151 678 4428; email: jlct. wirral@tiscali.co.uk)

The Maud Beattie Murchie Charitable Trust

Eligibility: People in need who live on the Wirral.

Types of grants: One-off and recurrent grants according to need. Grants to organisations are mostly recurrent.

Exclusions: No grants for educational purposes.

Annual grant total: In 2008/09 the trust had assets of £589,000 and an income of £37,000. Grants were made totalling £27,000 of which £13,000 was given to individuals and the remaining £14,000 to institutions.

Applications: Applications should be made through Wirral Social Services. They are usually considered in June and December.

Correspondent: W M Pattison, Duncan Sheard Glass, Castle Chambers, 43 Castle Street, Liverpool L2 9TL (0151 243 1200)

The West Kirby Charity

Eligibility: People in need who have lived in the old urban district of Hoylake (Caldy, Frankby, Greasby, Hoylake, Meols and West Kirby) for at least three years. Preference is given to older people and people who have a disability.

Types of grants: Pensions of about £20 a month. Christmas gifts and one-off grants are also made.

Annual grant total: In 2009 the trust had an income of £15,000 and a total expenditure of £12,000.

Applications: On a form available from the correspondent. Applications are usually considered quarterly.

Correspondent: Jane Boulton, 14 Surrey Drive, Wirral, CH48 2HP (0151 625 4794)

6. MIDLANDS

The Beacon Centre for the Blind

Eligibility: People who are registered blind or partially sighted and live in the metropolitan boroughs of Dudley (except Halesowen and Stourbridge), Sandwell and Wolverhampton, and part of the South Staffordshire District Council area.

Types of grants: One-off grants up to £250 towards socials and outings; holidays; and talking books and newspapers. Grants for specific items of equipment can be given to those who are visually impaired.

Annual grant total: In 2009/10 the charity had assets of £8.7 million, an income of £2.5 million and a total expenditure of £2.3 million. In previous years a small number of grants have been made to individuals.

Applications: In writing to the correspondent stating the degree of vision and age of the applicant, and their monthly income and expenditure. Applications can be submitted through a social worker or a school, and are considered throughout the year.

Correspondent: Chief Executive, Beacon Centre for the Blind, Wolverhampton Road East, Wolverhampton WV4 6AZ (01902 880111; fax: 01902 886795; email: enquiries@beacon4blind.co.uk; website: www.beacon4blind.co.uk)

The Birmingham & Three Counties Trust for Nurses

Eligibility: Nurses on any statutory register, who have practiced or practice in the city of Birmingham and the counties of Staffordshire, Warwickshire and Worcestershire.

Types of grants: One-off or recurrent grants according to need. Grants are given to meet the costs of heating, telephone bills, cordless phones for the infirm, household equipment, household repairs, car repairs, electric scooters, wheelchairs, medical equipment and personal expenses such as spectacles and clothing. Grants are also made for convalescent care, recuperative holidays and to clear debt.

Annual grant total: In 2008/09 the trust had an income of £19,000 and a total expenditure of £25,000.

Applications: On a form available from the correspondent. Applications can be submitted either directly by the individual or through a friend, relative or a social worker, Citizens Advice or other welfare agency. Details of financial status including income and expenditure, reasons for application, and health status where relevant should be included. Applications are considered throughout the year.

Applicants are visited by a trustee (where distance allows) for assessment. Supportive visiting continues where considered necessary.

Correspondent: Mrs Ruth Adams, Hon. Secretary, 26 Whitnash Road, Leamington Spa, Warwickshire CV31 2HL (01926 743660; email: ruthmadams_45@msn.com)

The Charities of Susanna Cole & Others

Eligibility: Quakers in need who live in parts of Worcestershire and most of Warwickshire and are 'a member or attendee of one of the constituent meetings of the Warwickshire Monthly Meeting of the Society of Friends'. Preference is given to younger children, and retired people on an inadequate pension.

Types of grants: One-off and recurrent grants according to need. Help may be given with domestic running costs, rent or accommodation fees, convalescence, recreation and home help, and to those seeking education or re-training.

Annual grant total: In 2008 the charity had an income of £12,000 and a total expenditure of £8,000. Grants are made for welfare and educational purposes.

Applications: In writing to the correspondent via the overseer of the applicant's Quaker meeting. Applications should be received by early March and October for consideration later in the same months.

Correspondent: Peter Gallimore, Trustee, 19 Oak Tree House, 153 Oak Tree Lane, Bournville, Birmingham, B30 1TU (0121 471 4064)

Thomas Corbett's Charity

Eligibility: People in need who live in Worcestershire, Staffordshire and Birmingham.

Types of grants: One-off grants according to need.

Annual grant total: In 2009 the charity had assets of £625,000 and an income of £40,000. Grants were made totalling £200.

Applications: In writing to the clerk directly by the individual.

Correspondent: Andrew G Duncan, Clerk, 16 The Tything, Worcester WR1 1HD (01905 731731)

Other information: The charity has stated that most of its income is used for the upkeep of the Wychbold almshouses and that, therefore, very few grants are made to individuals.

Baron Davenport's Charity

Eligibility: Widows, unmarried women and divorcees aged over 60 and in need; women abandoned by their partners and their children; and people under 25 whose fathers are dead. Exceptions may be made for younger widows with limited income and school-age children living at home who are in financial need. Applicants must live in the West Midlands, Shropshire, Staffordshire, Warwickshire or Worcestershire and have a net income of less than £160 per week and savings that do not exceed £5,000.

Types of grants: Recurrent grants, typically of £170 to £200, paid twice annually. In very special circumstances one-off grants of up to £250 are given for varying cases of need.

Exclusions: Applications will not be accepted from those in receipt of Low/High Rate Attendance Allowance; Middle/High rates of Disability Living Allowance or Mobility Allowance (or car allowance).

Annual grant total: In 2008 the charity had assets of £25 million and an income of £1.2 million. Grants were made to 1,946 individuals totalling £385,000.

Applications: Except for emergency cases, applications should be made through local authority social services departments or recognised welfare agencies, although direct applications from individuals may also be considered.

Application forms are available from the secretary and should be submitted by 15 March or 15 September. Grants awarded are paid in June and November. Applications where prompt relief is needed should be addressed to the local Council of Voluntary Service, as listed under their separate entries.

Correspondent: Marlene Keenan, Charity Administrator, Portman House, 5–7 Temple Row West, Birmingham B2 5NY (0121 236 8004; fax: 0121 233 2500; email: enquiries@ barondavenportscharity.org; website: www.barondavenportscharity.org)

Other information: The trust and CVS regard as fatherless those whose fathers are dead, and in some cases children abandoned by their fathers.

For emergency needs, see the separate entries in: Staffordshire, Warwickshire, Worcestershire, and West Midlands.

The W E Dunn Trust

Eligibility: People who are in need and live in the West Midlands, particularly Wolverhampton, Wednesbury, north Staffordshire and the surrounding area. Preference is given to people who are very old or very young, who the trust recognises as possibly being the least able to fund for themselves.

Types of grants: One-off grants ranging from £50 to £200.

Exclusions: Grants are not made to settle or reduce debts already incurred.

Annual grant total: In 2008/09 the trust had assets of £3.1 million and an income of £207,000. Grants totalling £47,000 were distributed in the following areas:

Clothing and furniture	164	£20,000
Convalescence and holidays	4	£700
Domestic equipment	87	£14,000
Education	36	£6,000
Radio, TV and licences	4	£640
Social and welfare	31	£5,500

Applications: Applications should be made in writing via a social worker, Citizens Advice or other welfare agency. The trustees meet on a regular basis to consider applications.

Correspondent: Alan H Smith, Secretary, The Trust Office, 30 Bentley Heath Cottages, Tilehouse Green Lane, Knowle, Solihull B93 9EL (01564 773407)

Other information: Grants are also made to organisations (£99,000 in 2008/09).

Friends Hall Farm Street Trust

Eligibility: Individuals with membership of or links with the Religious Society of Friends (Quakers) who live within 35 miles of the centre of Birmingham.

Types of grants: One-off grants ranging from between £100 and £250 are given for academic courses, travel costs and learning experiences.

Annual grant total: In 2008/09 the trust had an income of £17,000 and a total expenditure of £123,000.

Applications: In writing to the correspondent, directly by the individual. Applications should be submitted between March and October for consideration in October/November. Ineligible applications will not receive a reply.

Correspondent: Eric Adams, 36 Grove Avenue, Birmingham B13 9RY

The Frimley Fuel Allotments Charity

Eligibility: People in need who live in the parish of Frimley. Priority is given to people who are older or who have a disability, and those who care for them.

Types of grants: One-off grants ranging from about £100 to £1,500 for a variety of needs.

Annual grant total: In 2009 the trust had assets of £1.6 million, an income of £127,000 and a total expenditure of £111,000. Grants totalled £103,000 of which £58,000 was awarded to individuals, £18,000 was given in heating grants and the remaining £27,000 was donated to organisations.

Applications: On a form available from a local Citizens Advice or social services centre. Applications for the Christmas heating grants should be returned to the respective social service centre by mid November and can be made directly by the individual. Applications for other grants can be made at any time and are considered on a regular basis. The charity has limited resources so accurate and complete data on the form is essential.

Correspondent: Kim Murray, Hon. Secretary, 2a Hampshire Road, Camberley, Surrey GU15 4DW (01276 23958)

Other information: A book 200 Years of Frimley's History – The Story of Frimley Fuel Allotments Charity and Pine Ridge Golf Course has been published by Gordon Wellard, Camberley's historian. The book is available in local book shops and libraries.

Francis Butcher Gill's Charity

Eligibility: Unmarried or widowed women aged over 50 in need, who are regular attendees of Christian worship, or prevented from being by bodily infirmity. Applicants must also be of good standing and live in Nottinghamshire primarily, but those living in Derbyshire or Lincolnshire may also be considered.

Types of grants: Pensions of £250 per quarter are given to a fixed number of pensioners. One-off grants may also

occasionally be available for items such as gas fires.

Annual grant total: In 2008/09 the charity had an income £15,000 and a total expenditure of £18,000.

Applications: On a form available from the correspondent. Applications should be submitted either through a doctor or member of the clergy or directly by the individual supported by a reference from the one of the aforementioned. Applications can be submitted at any time for consideration in March and October, or at other times in emergency situations.

For pensions, applications will only be considered as a vacancy arises.

Correspondent: Charles N Cullen, Clerk, Cumberland Court, 80 Mount Street, Nottingham NG1 6HH (0115 936 9369; fax: 0115 901 5500)

The Edmund Godson Charity

Eligibility: People in need who wish to emigrate and who currently live in and around Woolwich, Shinfield and Spencers Wood near Reading, north east Herefordshire and Tenbury Wells in Worcestershire.

Types of grants: One-off grants according to need.

Annual grant total: In 2008/09 the charity had an income of £9,800 and an unusually low total expenditure of £580 (£5,300 in 2007/08).

Applications: Directly by the individual on a form available from the correspondent. Details of the proposed destination, occupation, emigration eligibility and financial circumstances should be given.

Correspondent: Freya Villis, 30 Hemingford Road, Cambridge, CB1 3BZ (email: fv221@cam.ac.uk)

Other information: The charity mainly makes grants to organisations.

Jordison and Hossell Animal Welfare Charity

Eligibility: People in the Midlands who are on low incomes and are in need of financial assistance in meeting vets' bills for their pets.

Types of grants: One-off grants of up to £500 towards vets' bills.

Exclusions: No grants for vets' bills for larger animals such as horses and farm animals.

Annual grant total: In 2008/09 the charity had an income of £2,600 and a total expenditure of £3,900.

Applications: In writing to the correspondent. Applications must be made by the vet in question or a third party such as Citizens Advice, rather than from the client. The charity does not deal with the client directly. Evidence that the beneficiary is on benefits is required.

Correspondent: Sally Reid, 173 Tanworth Lane, Shirley, Solihull, West Midlands B90 4BZ (0121 745 4274)

Melton Mowbray Building Society Charitable Foundation

Eligibility: Individuals in need who live within a 30 mile radius of Melton Mowbray.

Types of grants: One-off grants in the range of £100 and £250, for example to provide security and protection for older people.

Exclusions: No grants are made for circular appeals or for projects of a high capital nature.

Annual grant total: About £3,000.

Applications: In writing to the correspondent to be submitted either directly by the individual or a family member, through a third party such as a social worker or teacher, or through an organisation such as Citizens Advice or a school. Applications should include details of the cash value sought, the nature of the expense, the reason for application and the location of the applicant. Applications are considered at meetings held on a quarterly basis.

Correspondent: Miss M D Swainston, Leicester Road, Melton Mowbray, LE13 0D3 (01664 414141; fax: 01664 414040; email: m.swainston@mmbs.co.uk)

Other information: Grants may also be given to local organisations and community projects.

Thomas Monke's Charity

Eligibility: Young individuals between the ages of 17 and 21 who live in Austrey in Warwickshire and Measham, Shenton and Whitwick in Leicestershire.

Types of grants: One-off and recurrent grants of £100 to £250 according to need.

Exclusions: Expeditions and scholarships are not funded.

Annual grant total: About £1,500 a year for educational and welfare purposes.

Applications: Application forms are available from the correspondent and should be submitted directly by the individual before the end of March, in time for the trustees' yearly meeting held in April.

Correspondent: C P Kitto, Steward, 20 St John Street, Lichfield, Staffordshire WS13 6PD (01543 262491; fax: 01543 254986)

The Newfield Charitable Trust

Eligibility: Girls and women (under 30) who are in need of care and assistance and live in Coventry or Leamington Spa.

Types of grants: 'The relief of the physical, mental and moral needs of, and the promotion of the physical, social and educational training of' eligible people. Most grants are under £500 towards things such as clothing, electrical goods, holidays, travel expenses and furniture.

Exclusions: No grants for arrears or utility bills.

Annual grant total: In 2008/09 the trust had assets of £1.5 million and an income of £60,000. During the year, the trustees received a total of 166 applications, from which 163 applicants were awarded. Grants totalled just over £37,500.

Applications: Write to the correspondent for an application form. Applications are accepted from individuals or third parties e.g. social services, Citizens Advice, school/college etc. A letter of support/reference from someone not a friend or relative of the applicant (i.e. school, social services etc.) is always required. Details of income/expenditure and personal circumstances should also be given.

Applications are considered eight times a year.

Correspondent: D J Dumbleton, Clerk, Rotherham & Co. Solicitors, 8–9 The Quadrant, Coventry CV1 2EG (024 7622 7331; fax: 024 7622 1293; email: d.dumbleton@rotherham-solicitors.co.uk)

The Norton Foundation

Eligibility: Young people under 25 who live in Birmingham, Coventry or Warwickshire and are in need of care, rehabilitation or aid of any kind, 'particularly as a result of delinquency, maltreatment or neglect or who are in danger of lapsing or relapsing into delinquency'.

Types of grants: One-off grants of up to £500 are given towards clothing, household items and holidays.

Annual grant total: In 2008/09 the trust had assets of £3 million and an income of £145,000. Grants were made totalling £107,000, of which £14,000 was given in individual grants, £33,000 was awarded in discretionary grants and the remaining £59,000 was given to institutions. Grants to individuals were distributed as follows:

Clothing	34	£3,500
Education and training	27	£3,100
Household	55	£7,400
Holidays	2	£300

Applications: By a letter which should contain all the information required as detailed in the guidance notes for applicants. Guidance notes are available from the correspondent or the website. Applications must be submitted through a social worker, Citizens Advice, probation service, school or other welfare agency. They are considered quarterly.

Correspondent: The Correspondent, PO Box 10282, Redditch, Worcestershire B97 9ZA (01527 544446; email: correspondent@nortonfoundation.org; website: www.nortonfoundation.org)

The Pargeter & Wand Trust

Eligibility: Women who have never been married, are aged over 55 and live in their own homes. There is a preference for those living in the West Midlands area, but other areas of the country are considered.

Types of grants: Annuities of around £300 are paid quarterly and reviewed annually. One-off grants, usually in the range of £50 to £150, are also available.

Annual grant total: In 2009 the trust had an income of £12,000 and a total expenditure of £10,000.

Applications: Applications should be made via Age Concern.

Correspondent: Peter Hewis, 1 Little Blenheim, Yarton, Kidlington, Oxfordshire OX5 1LX (01865 372265; email: peter.hewis@hmc.ox.ac.uk)

The Pedmore Sporting Club Trust Fund

Eligibility: People in need who live in the West Midlands.

Types of grants: One-off grants have included those for medical care equipment, travel to and from hospital, wheelchairs and IT equipment. Christmas and Easter parcels are also given.

Annual grant total: In 2009 the trust had assets of £272,000 and an income of £38,000. Grants were made totalling £6,700.

Applications: Applicants for the Easter food parcels should be recommended by a member of the sporting club. Other applications should be made in writing to the correspondent. The trustees meet four or five times a year.

Correspondent: The Secretary, Nicklin LLP, Church Court, Stourbridge Road, Halesowen, West Midlands B63 3TT (email: psclub@pedmorehouse.co.uk)

Other information: Grants are also made to organisations (£32,000 in 2009).

The Persehouse Pensions Fund

Eligibility: Elderly or distressed people belonging to the upper or middle classes of society who were born in the counties of Staffordshire or Worcestershire, or people who have lived in either county for 10 years or more.

Types of grants: Mainly pensions, but occasional one-off grants.

Annual grant total: In 2008/09 the trust had an income of £12,000 and a total expenditure of £4,500.

Applications: On a form available from the correspondent to be submitted directly by the individual.

Correspondent: C S Wheatley, 12a Oakleigh Road, Stourbridge, West Midlands DY8 2JX

The Roddam Charity

Eligibility: People in need who live in the TF10 postcode area, including the parishes of Newport, Chetwynd, Church Aston, Chetwynd Aston, Woodcote, Moreton, Sambrook, Tibberton, Edgmond and Lilleshall in Shropshire and Forton in Staffordshire.

Types of grants: One-off grants in the range of about £50 to £200. Grants are made to help with items, services or facilities that are not readily available from other sources and which will relieve the suffering or assist the recovery of individuals in poor health and people living with disabilities.

Annual grant total: Grants usually total about £3,000 each year.

Applications: On a form available from the correspondent to be submitted directly by the individual. Applications are usually considered quarterly.

Correspondent: Stuart Barber, Merewood, Springfields, Newport TF10 7EZ (01952 814628; email: bougheyroddamha@btinternet.com)

sfgroup Charitable Fund for Disabled People *see entry on page 46*

Richard Smedley's Charity

Eligibility: People in need who live in the parishes of Breaston, Dale Abbey, Draycott with Church Wilne, Heanor, Hopwell, Ilkerton, Ockbrook and Risley (all in Derbyshire) and of Awsworth, Bilborough, Brinsley, Greasley and Strelley (all in Nottinghamshire).

Types of grants: One-off grants generally in the range of £50 to £350 are given towards items such as furniture, washing machines, mobility aids, clothing and carpets.

Annual grant total: Grants usually total about £5,000 a year.

Applications: On an application form available from the correspondent to be submitted either directly by the individual or through a social worker, Citizens Advice or other welfare agency. Applications can be submitted at any time and are usually considered quarterly.

Correspondent: M T E Ward Esq., Robinsons Solicitors Co, 21–22 Burns Street, Ilkeston, Derbyshire DE7 8AA (0115 932 4101; email: maurice.ward@robinsons-solicitors.co.uk)

Other information: Grants are also made to organisations.

The Snowball Trust

Eligibility: Children and young people under 21 who are in poor health or who have a disability and live in Coventry and Warwickshire.

Types of grants: One-off grants mainly for medical equipment and disability aids. The charity's policy is, 'to grant sums of money for the provision of moveable equipment and other resources for qualifying individuals or organisations'.

Annual grant total: In 2008/09 the trust had assets of £121,000 and an income of £54,000. Grants to individuals totalled £15,000.

Applications: On a form available from the correspondent: to be submitted either by the individual or through a third party such as a special school, social worker or other welfare agency. Applications should include a firm quote for the equipment to be supplied, a letter of support from the individual's school and/or a medical professional, and confirmation of the parents'/guardians' financial need.

Correspondent: Shaun Flaherty, 80 Howes Lane, Coventry, CV3 6PJ (02476 415 733)

Other information: The trust also makes grants to organisations (£42,000 in 2008/09).

The Eric W Vincent Trust Fund

Eligibility: People in need living within a 20 mile radius of Halesowen.

Types of grants: Grants range from £50 to £250 and can be for clothing, furniture, hospital travel expenses, equipment and holidays.

Exclusions: The trust does not make loans or give grants for gap year projects, any educational purposes or to pay off debts.

Annual grant total: In 2008/09 the trust had assets of £928,000 and an income of £51,000. Grants were made to 51 individuals totalling £4,400.

Applications: Trustees normally meet bimonthly. Applications should be in writing through a health professional, social worker, Citizens Advice or other welfare agency. Details of financial circumstances must be included.

Correspondent: Mrs Janet Stephen, Clerk, 4–5 Summer Hill, Halesowen, West Midlands B63 3BU

The Anthony & Gwendoline Wylde Memorial Charity

Eligibility: People in need with a preference for residents of Stourbridge (West Midlands) and Kinver (Staffordshire).

Types of grants: One-off grants in the range of £50 and £500.

Exclusions: No grants are made towards bills or debts.

Annual grant total: In 2008/09 the charity had assets of £843,000 and an income of £46,000. Grants were made totalling £36,000, of which £6,800 was given to individuals for educational and relief-in-need purposes. The remaining £29,000 was given to organisations.

Applications: In writing to the correspondent. Applications can be submitted directly by the individual or a family member and are considered on an ongoing basis.

Correspondent: D J Nightingale, Clerk, Blythe House, 134 High Street, Brierley Hill, West Midlands DY5 3BG (01384 342100)

The Jonathan Young Memorial Trust

Eligibility: People who are living with a disability and would benefit from access to computer technology. The trust operates primarily within the East Midlands (Nottinghamshire, Derbyshire, Leicestershire, Lincolnshire and South Yorkshire) but will occasionally consider applications from further afield.

Types of grants: Grants of £200 to £500 towards the cost of computer equipment.

Exclusions: The trust does not make grants for general living expenses, course or college fees, disability aids such as wheelchairs or any non-electronic items.

Annual grant total: In 2009 the trust had an income of £11,000 and a total expenditure of £17,000.

Applications: In writing to the correspondent, either directly by the individual, carer or parent or through a welfare organisation such as social services or a Citizens Advice. Applications should include:

- name, address, telephone number and age
- background information
- the nature and extent of the disability
- financial information – income/expenditure and how much can be contributed towards the equipment
- why a computer would be beneficial
- the specific equipment needed, including any software and a quotation if possible.

For individuals applying directly, a supporting letter from a GP, social worker, teacher or similar should be included. Applications are considered in April and October.

Correspondent: John Young, Trustee, 10 Huntingdon Drive, The Park,

Nottingham NG7 1BW (0115 947 0493; email: info@jonathan-young-trust.co.uk; website: www.joanthan-young-trust.co.uk)

Derbyshire

The Alfreton Welfare Trust

Eligibility: People in need who live in the former urban district of Alfreton (i.e. the parishes of Alfreton, Ironville, Leabrooks, Somercotes and Swanwick).

Types of grants: Grants have included travel expenses to hospital; provision of necessary household items and installation costs; recuperative holidays; relief of sudden distress (such as theft of pension or purse, funeral costs, marital difficulties); telephone installation; and outstanding bills. Support is also given to people who are disabled (including helping to buy wheelchairs and so on).

Exclusions: Grants are not given to organisations or for educational purposes.

Annual grant total: About £1,500.

Applications: In writing to the correspondent directly by the individual. Applications are considered throughout the year.

Correspondent: Celia Johnson, Clerk, 30 South Street, Swanwick, Alfreton, Derbyshire DE55 1BZ (01773 609782)

The Dronfield Relief-in-Need Charity

Eligibility: People in need who live in the ecclesiastical parishes of Dronfield, Holmesfield, Unstone and West Handley.

Types of grants: One-off grants, up to a value of £100, towards household needs (such as washing machines), food, clothing, medical appliances (such as a nebulizer) and visitors' fares to and from hospital.

Exclusions: No support for rates, taxes and so on.

Annual grant total: This charity gives around £1,000 a year in grants for welfare purposes.

Applications: In writing to the correspondent though a social worker, doctor, member of the clergy of any denomination, a local councillor, Citizens Advice or other welfare agency. The applicants should ensure they are receiving all practical/financial assistance they are entitled to from statutory sources.

Correspondent: Dr A N Bethell, Ramshaw Lodge, Crow Lane, Unstone, Dronfield, Derbyshire S18 4AL (01246 413276)

Other information: Grants are also given to local organisations.

The Margaret Harrison Trust

Eligibility: 'Gentlewomen of good character' aged 50 or over who have lived within a 15-mile radius of St Giles Parish Church, Matlock for at least five years.

Types of grants: Small quarterly pensions.

Annual grant total: Grants usually total around £3,000 per year.

Applications: On a form available from the correspondent, although the trust is already spending all its income and will not be looking for applicants until interest rates rise.

Correspondent: Alexandra Mastin, 5 The Avenue, Darley Dale, Matlock, Derbyshire, DE4 2HT

The Sawley Charities

Eligibility: People over 60 years of age in need who have lived in the parishes of Sawley and Wilsthorpe in Derbyshire for at least six years. Normally only state pensioners are considered.

Types of grants: One-off cash grants, usually of around £15 each, towards heating costs.

Annual grant total: Grants usually total around £2,300 per year.

Applications: On an application form available from the correspondent. Applications can be submitted directly by the individual or family member and should be received by September for consideration in October/November.

Correspondent: Monica Boursnell, 35 Weston Crescent, Long Eaton, Nottingham NG10 3BS

Other information: Grants are also made to welfare organisations.

The Stanton Charitable Trust

Eligibility: People of any age or occupation who are in need, due for example to hardship, disability or sickness, and who live near Staveley Works in Chesterfield, Derbyshire, namely Staveley, Brimington, Barrowhill, Hollingwold and Inkersall.

Types of grants: One-off cash grants towards items, services or facilities.

Annual grant total: This trust has an annual income of around £2,000.

Applications: In writing either directly by the individual or a family member, or through an organisation such as Citizens Advice or a school. Applications should state the specific amount for a specific item.

Correspondent: Clive Turner, Saint-Gobain Pipelines plc, Lows Lane, Stanton-by-Dale, Ilkeston, DE7 4QU

Other information: Grants are also made to schools, churches, scouts, guides and local fundraising events.

The Wirksworth and District Trust Fund

Eligibility: People in need who live in the parishes of Alderwasley, Ashleyhay, Callow, Cromford, Hopton, Ible, Idridgehay & Alton, Middleton-by-Wirksworth and Wirksworth.

Types of grants: One-off cash grants of between £25 and £200.

Annual grant total: About £2,000 a year. Grants are given to both individuals and organisations.

Applications: In writing to the correspondent for consideration in March and November, although urgent needs can be considered at any time. Applications can be submitted either directly by the individual or through a social worker, Citizens Advice or other welfare agency.

Correspondent: Dorothy Jill Hughes, Clerk, 8 Lady Flatts Road, Wirksworth, Matlock, Derbyshire DE4 4BQ (01629 822706)

Other information: The Wirksworth Charities are made up of 21 smaller charities, the funds from which are distributed as one sum.

The Woodthorpe Relief-in-Need Charity

Eligibility: People in need who live in the ancient parishes of Barlborough, Staveley and Unstone.

Types of grants: One-off grants, up to £750 for general purposes such as fuel, beds, washing machines, furnishings, mobility chairs and so on.

Annual grant total: The charity usually has an income of approximately £5,000 and gives £1,500 in grants to individuals annually.

Applications: In writing to the correspondent.

Correspondent: M Scott, Clerk, 8 Wigley Road, Inkersall, Chesterfield, Derbyshire S43 3ER (01246 474457)

Buxton

The Bingham Trust

Eligibility: People in need, primarily those who live in Buxton. Most applicants from outside Buxton are rejected unless there is a Buxton connection.

Types of grants: One-off grants ranging from £200 to £1,500. Grants are made for a wide variety of needs, for example, to relieve poverty, to further education and for religious and community causes.

Exclusions: No grants are made for debts or higher education study.

Annual grant total: In 2008/09 the trust had assets of £1.8 million and an income of

£108,000. Around £15,000 was given in grants to individuals.

Applications: On a form available from the correspondent or to download from the website. Applications should include a supporting letter from a third party such as a social worker, Citizens Advice, doctor or minister. They are considered during the first two weeks of January, April, July and October and should be received before the end of the previous month.

Correspondent: Roger Horne, Trustee, Blinder House, Flagg, Buxton, Derbyshire SK17 9QG (01298 83328; email: binghamtrust@aol.com; website: www.binghamtrust.org.uk/)

Other information: The trust also makes grants to organisations (£79,000 in 2008/09).

Chesterfield

The Chesterfield General Charitable Fund

Eligibility: People in need in the parliamentary constituency of Chesterfield.

Types of grants: One-off and recurrent grants ranging from £200 to £800.

Annual grant total: In 2008/09 the trust had an income of £7,300 and a total expenditure of £5,100.

Applications: In writing to the correspondent, directly by the individual. Applications are considered quarterly.

Correspondent: Keith Pollard, 266 Old Road, Chesterfield, Derbyshire, S40 3QN (01246 221872)

The Chesterfield Municipal Charities

Eligibility: There are two charities, one for older and poor people who were born or live in Hasland; the other for respectable widows and older spinsters who were born or live in Chesterfield.

Types of grants: One-off grants and regular payments of about £100 made twice a year.

Annual grant total: In 2009 the charities had an income of £9,000 and a total expenditure of £13,000.

Applications: In writing to the correspondent.

Correspondent: David Dolman, Shipton Halliwell & Co, 23 West Bars, Chesterfield, Derbyshire S40 1AB (01246 232140)

Other information: The existing beneficiaries have remained the same for a number of years, although the charity welcomes new applicants.

Clay Cross

The Eliza Ann Cresswell Memorial

Eligibility: People in any kind of need who live in the former urban district of Clay Cross (now the civil parish of Clay Cross), particularly needy families with young children.

Types of grants: Usually one-off grants in whole or part payment of a particular need for example heating costs, housing, debts, replacement of bedding and damaged furniture, removal costs, and holidays.

Exclusions: The trust does not give cash directly to applicants nor does it usually pay the full amount of a debt unless any repayment is beyond the individual's means.

Annual grant total: Grants average around £950 a year.

Applications: In writing to the correspondent. A description of the person's financial position, the gaps in statutory provision, what contribution the applicant can make towards the need and what help can be given to prevent the need for future applications should be included. Applications are considered throughout the year. Grants are given on the recommendation of social workers, health visitors, probation officers, home nurses, doctors, clergy and welfare organisations (for example Citizens Advice), and are paid through these bodies.

Correspondent: Dr Christine Fowler, Correspondent Trustee, Blue Dykes Surgery, Eldon Street, Clay Cross, Chesterfield, Derbyshire S45 9NR (0844 4127 333; fax: 01246 861058)

Derby

The Derby City Charity

Eligibility: People under 25 who live in the city of Derby and are in need.

Types of grants: One-off grants only according to need.

Exclusions: No grants are given for the relief of taxes or other public funds.

Annual grant total: In 2008/09 the charity had an income of £4,000 and a total expenditure of £2,300. About £2,000 is given in grants each year. At least 5% of the trust's grant total must be used for educational purposes; the rest is used for welfare grants.

Applications: On a form available from the correspondent on written request. Applications can be submitted either through a relevant third party such as a social worker, Citizens Advice or other welfare agency; or directly by the individual. The trustees meet at least twice a year to consider applications.

Correspondent: Ms Laura Braithwaite, Derby City Council, Room 129, The Council House, Corporation Street, Derby DE1 2YL (01332 293111)

The Liversage Trust

Eligibility: Older people in need who live in the city of Derby.

Types of grants: Cash grants for the relief of poverty, usually limited to a maximum of £150 although most grants are of between £30/£40 and £150. Grants can be made towards clothing, food or consumer durables.

Annual grant total: In 2008/09 the trust had assets of £14 million and an income of £1.7 million. Grants usually total around £20,000.

Applications: On a form available from the correspondent. Applications should be submitted through a recognised referral agency such as a social worker, Citizens Advice or doctor. They are considered throughout the year.

Correspondent: R Pike, Clerk, The Boardroom, 6b Liversage Almshouses, London Road, Derby DE1 2QW (01332 348155; fax: 01332 349674; email: kim.mannion@liversagetrust.org)

Other information: The trust's main concern is the management of almshouses and the care home, Liversage Court.

Glossop

The Mary Ellen Allen Charity

Eligibility: People over 60 who are in need and live in the former borough of Glossop (as it was in 1947). There is a preference for those who have lived in the area for at least five years in total.

Types of grants: About 15 one-off grants a year in the range of £50 to £500.

Annual grant total: In 2008/09 the charity had both an income and a total expenditure of £6,800.

Applications: In writing to the correspondent either through a social worker, Citizens Advice or other welfare agency, or directly by the individual. Applications can be submitted at any time for consideration in January, April, July and October.

Correspondent: Philip Sills, 1 Bowden Road, Glossop, Derbyshire SK13 7BD (01457 865685)

Ilkeston

The Old Park Ward Old Age Pensioners Fund

Eligibility: People over 65 who are in need and live in the Old Park ward of the former borough of Ilkeston.

Types of grants: One-off cash grants, usually at Christmas time.

Annual grant total: In 2008/09 the fund had an income of £16,000 and a total expenditure of £15,000. Grants were made totalling about £1,200.

Applications: In writing to the correspondent.

Correspondent: J Dack, 3 Knole Road, Nottingham, NG8 2DB (0115 913 2118)

Other information: The majority of the fund's income is spent on providing recreational facilities and events such as dancing, bingo, a monthly Sunday lunch club and other outings.

Spondon

The Spondon Relief-in-Need Charity

Eligibility: People in need who live in the ancient township of Spondon.

Types of grants: One-off grants in kind up to the value of £500, including those towards electric goods, clothing, furniture, disabled equipment, carpets and so on. Christmas goodwill gifts are also made.

Exclusions: The charity does not contribute towards domestic debts and so on.

Annual grant total: In 2009 the trust had an income of £25,000 and a total expenditure of £26,000. Grants are made for educational and welfare purposes.

Applications: On a form available from the correspondent. Each form must be accompanied by a letter of support from a sponsor such as a doctor, health authority official, social worker, city councillor, clergyman, head teacher, school liaison officer, youth leader or probation officer. The sponsor must justify the applicant's need. The latter is particularly important. The applicant should provide as much information on the form as possible. It is better to ask for a visit by a trustee if possible.

The trustees meet four times a year and applications must be received by the end of January, April, July and October; grants are given one month later.

Correspondent: Richard J Pooles, Secretary and Treasurer, PO Box 5073, Spondon, Derby, DE21 7ZJ (01332 669879; email: info@spondonreliefinneedcharity.org; website: www.spondonreliefinneedcharity.org/)

Herefordshire

The Hereford Corn Exchange Fund

Eligibility: People in Herefordshire who have been employed at one farm for over 30 years.

Types of grants: Grants of between £100 and £500 for the advancement of agriculture in the county of Herefordshire.

Annual grant total: In 2009/10 the fund had an income of £3,700 and a total expenditure of £2,700. The fund gives about £1,000 to individuals and £1,000 to agricultural organisations each year.

Applications: In writing to the correspondent in March/April for consideration in May.

Correspondent: E P Edwards, Secretary, 7 Yew Tree Gardens, Kings Acre, Hereford HR4 0TH (01432 263040)

The Hereford Society for Aiding the Industrious

Eligibility: People in need who live in Herefordshire (particularly Hereford City) and are trying to better themselves by their own efforts.

The early history of the society involved aid to the 'industrious poor' and those who would not make an effort to help themselves were excluded. This is reflected today by priority being given to individuals who are trying to obtain training to get back to work, often as mature students.

Grants will be considered when a person is required to fund a gap between formal education and training for a career. The society also considers applications from girl guides and boy scouts for assistance with the cost of camp, but need must be proved in all cases.

Types of grants: Grants or interest free loans, of £50 to £1,000, according to need.

Annual grant total: In 2008/09 the trust had assets of £721,000 and an income of £93,000. Grants to individuals totalled £9,200, of which approximately £1,000 was spent on Christmas gifts for elderly residents and £8,200 on educational grants ranging from £170 to £1,000.

Applications: On a form available from the correspondent. Applicants are then interviewed by the secretary. Trustees usually meet on the third Monday of every month.

Correspondent: Sally Robertson, Secretary, 18 Venns Close, Bath Street, Hereford HR1 2HH (01432 274014 – Thursdays only; email: hsaialms@talktalkbusiness.net)

Other information: Grants are also made to organisations.

The Herefordshire Community Foundation

Eligibility: People in need who live in Herefordshire.

Types of grants: One-off and recurrent grants according to need.

Annual grant total: In 2008/09 the foundation had assets of £935,000 and an income of £1 million. Approximately £5,000 is given each year to individuals.

Applications: In writing to the correspondent including standard information such as contact details, what the grant is to be used for and why it is needed.

Correspondent: The Secretary, The Fred Bulmer Centre, Wall Street, Hereford, Herefordshire HR4 9HP (01432 272550; email: info@herefordshirecommunityfoundation.org)

Other information: Grants are also made to organisations (£204,000 in 2008/09).

Open House Darts League

Eligibility: People who are in poor health or who have a disability and live in Herefordshire.

Types of grants: Recurrent grants in the form of purchased goods only (not cash).

Exclusions: The charity does not sponsor students.

Annual grant total: About £1,000.

Applications: Applications can be submitted either directly by the individual or by a relevant third party. They are usually considered monthly between April and September.

Other information: Grants are also given to schools, hospitals and hospices.

The Rathbone Moral Aid Charity

Eligibility: People who live in Herefordshire who are under 25 and in need of rehabilitation, 'particularly as a result of crime, delinquency, prostitution, addiction to drugs or drink, maltreatment or neglect'.

Types of grants: One-off and recurrent grants according to need.

Exclusions: No grants are given for nursery fees.

Annual grant total: In 2009 the trust had an income of £8,500 and a total expenditure of £7,600.

Applications: In writing to the correspondent. Individual applications are considered throughout the year. All individual applications must be supported by a welfare agency or doctor, social worker, teacher or other professional.

Correspondent: Carol Thompson, Clerk, Herefordshire Community Council, PO Box 181, Hereford HR2 9YN (01981 250899)

Other information: Grants are also made to organisations.

Hereford

All Saints Relief-in-Need Charity

Eligibility: Individuals in need who live in the city of Hereford, with a preference for those resident in the ancient parish of All Saints.

Types of grants: In previous years the charity has preferred to provide items rather than giving cash grants. However, one-off grants are available to those in need.

Annual grant total: In 2008/09 the charity had an income of £8,600 and a total expenditure of £4,300.

Applications: On a form available from the correspondent.

Correspondent: Douglas Harding, Trustee, 6 St Ethelbert Street, Hereford HR1 2NR (01432 267821)

The Hereford Municipal Charities

Eligibility: People in need who live in the city of Hereford.

Types of grants: One-off grants of amounts up to £200. Grants are given to help with household equipment, clothes, educational equipment, emergencies and so on.

Exclusions: No grants towards debts or nursery fees.

Annual grant total: In 2009 the charities had assets of £3.5 million and an income of £382,000. Grants to individuals totalled approximately £32,000.

Applications: On a form available from the correspondent to be submitted directly by the individual or through a relevant third party. Applications are considered monthly.

Correspondent: The Trustees, 147 St Owen Street, Hereford HR1 2JR (01432 354 002; email: herefordmunicipal@btconnect.com)

Other information: Most of the charity's expenditure is allocated to the running costs of its almshouses.

Middleton-on-the-Hill

The Middleton-on-the-Hill Parish Charity

Eligibility: People living in the parish of Middleton-on-the-Hill.

Types of grants: One-off and recurrent grants for both welfare and educational purposes.

Annual grant total: About £1,000 a year is given in grants.

Applications: In writing to the correspondent.

Correspondent: Clare Halls, Secretary, Highlands, Leysters, Leominster, Herefordshire HR6 0HP

Norton Canon

The Norton Canon Parochial Charities

Eligibility: People in need who live in the parish of Norton Canon.

Types of grants: One-off and recurrent grants according to need.

Annual grant total: Grants total around £10,000 a year and are given for educational and welfare purposes.

Applications: In writing to the correspondent at any time.

Correspondent: Mary Gittins, Ivy Cottage, Norton Canon, Hereford HR4 7BQ (01544 318984)

Leicestershire & Rutland

The Ashby-de-la-Zouch Relief-in-Sickness Fund

Eligibility: People in need who live in Ashby-de-la-Zouch and Blackfordby.

Types of grants: One-off grants in the range of £50 to £60 for things such as hospital expenses, electrical goods, convalescence, clothing, holidays, travel expenses, medical equipment, furniture, disabled equipment and help in the home.

Annual grant total: Grants total around £650 each year.

Applications: In writing to the correspondent at any time directly from the individual, or through a social worker, Citizens Advice or other welfare agency. Anybody who thinks they know someone who needs help is welcome to submit an application. It is useful to know whether any other source of help has been approached. Applications are considered at all times.

Correspondent: Jeanette Cowan McCarthy, Crane & Walton, 30 South Street, Ashby-de-la-Zouch, Leicestershire LE65 1BT (01530 414111; fax: 01530 417022; email: jeanettemccarthy@craneandwalton.co.uk)

William Clayton Barnes Trust

Eligibility: People in need who are sick and infirm and live in Melton Mowbray, Eye Kettleby or Great Dalby and have lived there for three years.

Types of grants: One-off grants for a range of needs, including wheelchairs, stairlifts (purchase and rental), household equipment for special needs, food and travel to hospital.

Annual grant total: In 2008/09 the trust had an income of £2,500 and a total expenditure of £3,800. Grants totalled about £3,500.

Applications: The trust welcomes an initial telephone call. Applications should be in writing to the correspondent either directly by the individual or through a doctor, church leader, social worker, Citizens Advice or other welfare agency. They are considered all year round.

Correspondent: John Thornton, The Old Rectory, Main Road, Wyfordby, Melton Mowbray, Leicestershire LE14 4RY (01664 564437)

The John Heggs Bates' Charity for Convalescents

Eligibility: 'Necessitous convalescents' and their carers who reside in Leicester, Leicestershire and Rutland.

Types of grants: One-off grants of £100 to £600 for convalescence breaks.

Annual grant total: Around £10,000 a year.

Applications: On a form available from: Leicester Charity Link, 20a Millstone Lane, Leicester LE1 5JN. Applications should be submitted through a social worker, Citizens Advice, doctor or church and are considered throughout the year.

Correspondent: Barbara Amos, Charnwood Court, 58 New Walk, Leicester, LE1 6TE (0116 204 6620; email: barbara.amos@stwcharity.co.uk)

The Brooke Charity

Eligibility: People in need who live in the parishes of Brooke, Oakham, Braunston, Ridlington and Morcott.

Types of grants: One-off grants to relieve financial difficulty, usually in the range of £50 to £250.

Annual grant total: In 2008/09 the charity had an income of £5,400 and a total expenditure of £5,800.

Applications: In writing to the correspondent. Applications can be submitted directly by the individual or through a social worker, Citizens Advice or other welfare agency. They are considered at any time.

Correspondent: Barbara J Clemence, Old Rectory Farm, Main Street, Brooke, Oakham, Leicestershire LE15 8DE (01572 770558)

Other information: The charity also provides support to organisations.

The Elizabeth Clarke Relief-in-Need Fund & The Wigston Relief-in-Need Fund

Eligibility: People in need who live in the urban district of Wigston.

Types of grants: One-off grants towards general relief-in-need, including clothing, safety alarms, special chairs, wheelchairs, orthopaedic footwear, travel costs for medical treatment, bedding, spectacles and so on.

Annual grant total: In 2009 the two funds gave approximately £2,300 in grants to individuals and organisations.

Applications: In writing to the correspondent, accompanied by a supporting letter from a social worker or other welfare agency if possible.

Correspondent: Debbie Watson, Oadby & Wigston Borough Council, Council Offices, Station Road, Wigston, Leicestershire, LE18 2DR (0116 2572680)

Other information: These two trusts work closely together, and often large grants are paid from both funds. However, grants from the Elizabeth Clarke Relief-in-Need Fund can only be given to those who live in the All Saints, Central, Westfield and Wolstan's wards of the urban district of Wigston.

Coalville and District Relief in Sickness Fund

Eligibility: People in need of medical equipment not provided by the NHS who live in Coalville and district.

Types of grants: One-off grants in the range of £100 to £1,000 towards, for example, medical needs, special mattresses, gas fires, washing machines, reconditioned computers and home alterations.

Annual grant total: In 2008/09 the trust had an income of £2,000 and a total expenditure of £3,500.

Applications: In writing to the correspondent to be submitted directly by the individual. Applications are considered at quarterly intervals.

Correspondent: Sue Clarke, 6 Meadow Lane, Coalville, Leicestershire, LE67 4DL (01530 834992)

Other information: The trust gives grants to both individuals and organisations.

Leicester ARC (also known as Leicester and County Convalescent Homes Society)

Eligibility: Existing contributors (see below) and people in need who are ill, disabled or receiving medical care and live in Leicester, Leicestershire and Rutland.

Types of grants: Generally small grants to assist with medical needs with the aim of achieving a better quality of life, whether it be the purchase or hire of a piece of equipment, or a period of 'quality' time away. Consideration will be given to both short and long-term medically-related needs.

Annual grant total: Grants usually total around £1,000 each year.

Applications: On a form available form the correspondent. Applications must be returned with supporting evidence from a doctor/occupational therapist. In the case of powered/manual wheelchairs or other medical equipment – no application is considered without an assessment from an occupational therapist or physiotherapist as to the best type of chair, make, model, price and adaptations (if any).

Correspondent: J A S Pooley, 22 St George's Way, Leicester LE1 1SH (0116 262 0617; fax: 0116 262 1323; email: enquiries@leicesterarc.org)

Other information: The organisation operates a scheme in which people contribute towards, via pay roll or annual subscription, the costs of any future convalescent needs that may be required.

The Leicester Charity Link (formerly Leicester Charity Organisation Society)

Eligibility: People in need who live in the city of Leicester and the vicinity, which includes the whole of Leicestershire and Rutland.

Types of grants: One-off grants and occasionally recurrent grants or pensions. The society makes payments from its own funds, administers funds on behalf of other charities and puts potential beneficiaries into contact with funds and charities which may be able to help. A very wide range of grants is considered from small immediate payments, for example, for food, to larger payments of, for example, £6,500 for a special computer for a man with disabilities.

Annual grant total: In 2008/09 the trust had an income of £1,300 and a total expenditure of £2,600.

Applications: Generally through a social worker, health visitor, doctor or welfare agency on an application form.

Correspondent: James Munton, Director of Operations, 20a Millstone Lane, Leicester, Leicestershire LE1 5JN (0116 222 2200; fax: 0116 222 2201; email: info@charity-link.org)

The Leicester Freemen's Estate

Eligibility: Needy freemen of Leicester and their widows who are elderly or infirm.

Types of grants: One-off cash grants, recurrent grants/pensions and loans are available.

Annual grant total: In 2009 the trust had assets of £4.6 million and an income of £209,000. Grants were made to nine freemen and 20 widows through monthly payments and a Christmas bonus which totalled £21,000.

Applications: On a form available from the correspondent and including proof of status as a freeman/widow of a freeman. Applications can be submitted directly by the individual and are considered monthly throughout the year.

Correspondent: Mrs Lynda Bramley, Estate Office, 32 Freemen's Holt, Old Church Street, Aylestone, Leicester LE2 8NH (0116 283 4017; fax: 0116 283 4017; email: leicester. freemen@talktalkbusiness.net; website: www.leicester-freemen.com)

Other information: The trust also provides accommodation for needy freemen and their widows. Applications should be made to the above address.

The Leicestershire Coal Industry Welfare Trust Fund

Eligibility: Miners and their dependants working in the British coal mining industry aged over 16, who have not taken up other full-time work.

Types of grants: Grants have been given towards special needs assistance, house repairs, house conversions and televisions.

Annual grant total: In 2008 the trust had an income of £12,000 and a total expenditure of £15,000. Grants are made to individuals and organisations.

Applications: In writing to the correspondent, including details of the individual's mining connection, proof of their residence in Leicestershire and dependence on the mineworker (in the case of children).

Correspondent: Peter Smith, Trustee, NUM, Springboard Centre, 18 Mantle Lane, Coalville, Leicestershire LE67 3DW (01530 832085; email: leicesternum@ ukinbox.com)

The Leicestershire County Nursing Association

Eligibility: Retired district nurses and people who are sick and in need, who live in Leicestershire or Rutland (excluding the city of Leicester). Priority is given to retired district nurses.

Types of grants: One-off grants up to £3,000 for any need. Recent grants have been given towards hospital costs, bedding and convalescence.

Annual grant total: In 2008/09 the trust had assets of £952,000 and an income of £54,000. Grants were made to retired nurses totalling £6,000.

Applications: In writing to the correspondent, directly by the individual in the case of retired district nurses or through Leicester Charity Organisation Society (see separate entry) in other cases. Applications are considered in January and October.

Correspondent: Edward Cufflin, Brewin Dolphin, Permanent House, 31 Horsefair Street, Leicester, LE1 5BU (0116 242 0700)

Other information: The trust also makes grants to organisations (£46,000 in 2008/09).

The Loughborough Welfare Trusts

Eligibility: People in need who live in Loughborough and Hathern.

Types of grants: One-off and recurrent grants are given generally to families on low income for decoration costs, second-hand fridges, cookers and so on. Grants are also made towards clothing for primary schoolchildren aged under 11.

Annual grant total: In 2009 the trust had assets of £556,000 and an income of £25,000. Grants were made totalling £8,300, which included £6,200 relief in need grants and £2,100 in relief in sickness grants.

Applications: In writing to the correspondent for consideration in January, March, May, July, September or November.

Correspondent: Mrs Lesley Cutler, Bird Wilford & Sale Solicitors, 20 Churchgate, Loughborough LE11 1UD (01509 232611; email: loughweltrsts@fsmail.net)

Other information: This trust administers Edgar Corah Charity, John Storer Education Foundation, The Reg Burton Fund, Loughborough Adult Schools, Herrick Charities, and The Loughborough Community Chest.

The Nicholson Memorial Fund

Eligibility: Young people and children 'who are delinquent, deprived, neglected or in need of care' in Leicestershire.

Types of grants: One-off grants according to need.

Annual grant total: In 2008/09 the trust had assets of £176,000 and an income of £13,000. Grants were made totalling £21,000, of which £14,000 was given to individuals and the remaining £7,000 to organisations.

Applications: On a form available from the correspondent.

Correspondent: Jim Munton, c/o Leicester Charity Link, 20a Millstone Lane, Leicester LE1 5JN (0116 222 2200; email: info@ charity-link.org; website: www.charity-link.org)

Other information: Leicester Charity Link, the administrator of this fund, provides a wide range of support and advice to people in need, for example through directing them to suitable funding bodies.

The Thomas Stanley Shipman Charitable Trust

Eligibility: People in need who live in the city and county of Leicester.

Types of grants: One-off and recurrent grants ranging from between £500 to £5,000 for living expenses, garden alterations and gifts at Christmas.

Annual grant total: In 2008/09 the charity had assets of £887,000 and an income of just under £50,000. Grants were made totalling £49,000, of which £38,000 was given to individuals and £11,000 to organisations.

Applications: In writing to the correspondent either directly by the individual or via a relevant third party such as a social worker, Citizens Advice or other welfare agency, or through Leicester Charity Link. Applications should be submitted in mid-October and mid-April for consideration in November and June.

Correspondent: Andrew York, 6 Magnolia Close, Leicester, LE2 8PS (0116 283 5345)

Other information: The trust does not usually provide educational grants due to lack of resources, and in light of its other objectives.

Cossington

Babington's Charity

Eligibility: People in need in the parish of Cossington.

Types of grants: One-off and recurrent grants according to need.

Annual grant total: In 2008 the trust had assets of £439,000, an income of £31,000 and a total expenditure of £28,000. Grants totalled £5,300, of which £2,800 was given in welfare grants.

Applications: In writing to the correspondent.

Correspondent: The Trustees, Fintry, 58 Main Street, Cossington, Leicester, Leicestershire, LE7 4UU (01509 812340)

Great Glen

Great Glen Relief in Need Charity

Eligibility: People in need (especially older people) who live in the parish of Great Glen and have been living there for a number of years.

Types of grants: One-off grants according to need. Older people receive grants in the form of vouchers at Christmas, at a rate of £15 per individual and £30 per couple.

Annual grant total: In 2009 the charity had an income of £2,200 and a total expenditure of £3,600.

Applications: In writing to the correspondent. Applications are considered twice a year, usually in November and April.

Correspondent: Major Gerald Hincks, Trustee, 19 Naseby Way, Great Glen, Leicester LE8 9GS (0116 259 3155)

Other information: In recent years the charity has also made grants to a local church project and to young people in the parish undertaking voluntary work abroad.

Groby

Thomas Herbert Smith's Trust Fund

Eligibility: People who live in the parish of Groby in Leicestershire.

Types of grants: One-off and recurrent grants ranging from £100 to £500.

Annual grant total: In 2008/09 the fund had an income of £19,000 and a total expenditure of £12,000. Grants are made to organisations and individuals.

Applications: On a form available from the correspondent, for consideration throughout the year. Applications can be submitted either directly by the individual, or through a social worker, Citizens Advice or other third party.

Correspondent: A R York, 6 Magnolia Close, Leicester, LE2 8PS

Illston

Illston Town Land Charity

Eligibility: People in need who live in the town of Illston in Leicestershire.

Types of grants: Grants towards the costs of Council Tax charges.

Annual grant total: In 2008/09 the charity had an income of £6,900 and a total expenditure of £6,600.

Applications: In writing to the correspondent.

Correspondent: J F Tillotson, Warwick House, 5 Barnards Way, Kibworth Harcourt, Leicester, LE8 0RS (0116 2792524)

Keyham

Keyham Relief in Need Charity

Eligibility: People who live in the parish of Keyham (Leicestershire) and are in need. Though, applications from people who do not live in the area but have strong connections to residents in Keyham have previously been considered.

Types of grants: One-off grants according to need.

Annual grant total: In 2009 the charity had an income of £18,000 and a total expenditure of £10,000. Grants usually total around £10,000 each year.

Applications: In writing to the correspondent, to be submitted directly by the individual. If the applicant does not live in Keyham, information about their connection with residents should be provided with the application.

Correspondent: D B Witcomb, Tanglewood, Snows Lane, Leicester, Leicestershire LE7 9JS (0116 2595663)

Leicester

The Leicester Aid-in-Sickness Fund

Eligibility: People who are in poor health and financial need and live in the city of Leicester.

Types of grants: One-off grants, generally ranging from £20 to £125.

Annual grant total: Grants usually total around £12,000 each year.

Applications: In writing to the correspondent. Applications are usually considered quarterly.

Correspondent: M K Dunkley, Clerk, 20 New Walk, Leicester LE1 6TX (0116 254 5454; email: mark.dunkley@ harveyingram.com)

The Leicester Indigent Old Age Society

Eligibility: People aged 65 or over who are in need and live in the city of Leicester.

Types of grants: Pensions of £80 a year paid in quarterly instalments.

Annual grant total: In 2008/09 the trust had an income of £5,800 and a total expenditure of £6,800. Grants totalled around £6,500.

Please note the following statement from the trust's website: 'Due to pressure on funds help is only given once every two years unless there are exceptional circumstances.'

Applications: Applications should be made though Leicester Charity Link using their application form which can be found on the trust's website. Telephone calls should be made between 9am and 12 noon and 2pm to 4.30pm daily, Monday through to Friday.

Correspondent: Jim Munton, 20a Millstone Lane, Leicester LE1 5JN (0116 222 2200; fax: 0116 222 2201; email: info@charity-link.org; website: www.charity-link.org/leicester-indigent-old-age)

Other information: The trust also makes grants for coach trips and outings for older people living in Leicester.

The Parish Piece Charity

Eligibility: People in need who live in the parish of St Margaret in Leicester. Priority is usually given to older people and people with disabilities.

Types of grants: One-off grants and small pensions. Recent grants have been given for heating and electrical appliances.

Annual grant total: Grants usually total around £6,000 a year.

Applications: In writing to the correspondent or via Leicester Charity Link.

Correspondent: John E Adams, 19 Rowley Fields Avenue, Leicester LE3 2ER (0116 289 7432)

Other information: The charity also gives grants to organisations.

St Margaret's Charity

Eligibility: People in need who live in the city of Leicester.

Types of grants: One-off grants, usually ranging from £25 to £100.

Annual grant total: In 2009/10 the charity had an income of £4,200 and a total expenditure of £3,000.

Applications: In writing to the correspondent or via the Leicester Charity Organisation Society.

Correspondent: Stephen Franklin, 58 Park View, Sharnford, Hinckley, LE10 3PT (01455 272160; email: stephen.franklin@ lineone.net)

Other information: The charity also makes grants to local organisations.

Sir Edward Wood's Bequest Fund For Gentlewomen

Eligibility: Women who are 55 years old or over, are either unmarried or widows, who have lived in the area administered by Leicester City Council for at least 10 years, and who are members of a Protestant Non-conformist church.

Types of grants: Pensions only of £400 a year, paid quarterly.

Annual grant total: In 2009 the fund had an income of £4,300 and a total expenditure of £900.

Applications: On a form available from the correspondent either directly by the individual or through a third party. A reference from a church minister is also needed. There are only a limited number of pensions available and applications can only be considered when a vacancy arises.

Correspondent: J A Norris, 63 Carisbrooke Road, Leicester LE2 3PF (0116 270 4223)

Market Harborough

The Market Harborough & the Bowdens Charity

Eligibility: People in need who live in the former urban council district area of Market Harborough. 'The charity prefers prevention to palliatives. It wishes to foster self-help and the participation of those intended to benefit; enable less advantaged people to be independent, gain useful skills and overcome handicaps; and encourage volunteer involvement.'

Types of grants: Grants are one-off and are wide-ranging, providing they meet with the charity's scheme and geographical area.

Annual grant total: In 2009 the charity had assets of £14 million and an income of £540,000. Grants were made to 91 individuals totalling £51,000. A further £13,000 was given in Christmas donations to 260 children.

Applications: On a form available from the correspondent or to download from the website. Applications can be submitted either directly by the individual or via a relevant third party such as a social worker, Citizens Advice or other welfare agency. Potential applicants are welcome to contact the correspondent directly for further guidance.

Correspondent: James G Jacobs, Steward, 149 St Mary's Road, Market Harborough, Leicester LE16 7DZ (01858 462467; fax: 01858 431898; email: steward@ mhbcharity.co.uk; website: www. mhbcharity.co.uk)

Market Overton

Market Overton Charity

Eligibility: People in need who live in the parish of Market Overton.

Types of grants: One-off grants of up to £250 for those in need, typically for help towards replacement domestic appliances, but also help towards education needs e.g. school educational visits.

Annual grant total: In 2009 the charity had assets of around £2,500 and an income of about £400.

Applications: In writing to the correspondent. Applications can be submitted directly by the individual or through a social worker, Citizens Advice, Church or other welfare agency. They are considered at any time.

Correspondent: M Crowther, Trustee, 6 The Limes, Market Overton, Oakham, LE15 7PX (01572 767779)

Markfield

Jane Avery Charity – Markfield

Eligibility: People in need who live in the ancient parish of Markfield.

Types of grants: Normally one-off grants of £25 to £300. Grants have included those towards holiday costs, nursery school fees, a wheelchair and house repairs.

Exclusions: There are no grants available for educational purposes.

Annual grant total: The trust gives on average around £500 a year.

Applications: In writing to the correspondent. Applications can be submitted directly by the individual or through a social worker, Citizens Advice, other welfare agency, or through a third party such as a doctor, minister, neighbour or relative. They can be considered at any time.

Correspondent: Revd Simon Nicholls, The Rectory, 3a The Nook, Markfield, Leicestershire, LE67 9WE (01530 242844)

Mountsorrel

The Mountsorrel Relief-in-Need Charity

Eligibility: People in need who live in the parish of Mountsorrel.

Types of grants: One-off grants towards electrical household goods, garden maintenance, decorating costs, carpets/flooring, Charnwood Piper Lifelines, mobility equipment, child care expenses, hospital travel expenses and so on.

Annual grant total: In 2009 the charity made grants to 140 individuals totalling £87,000.

Applications: To apply, contact Anni Reid, Benefit Secretary at 3 Heron Close, Mountsorrel, Loughborough LE12 7FH (Tel: 0116 237 5132 or 0753 460 4337), who will visit the applicant in their home and help them to complete the application form.

Correspondent: Paul Blakemore, KDB Accountants and Consultants Ltd, 21 Hollytree Close, Hoton, Loughborough LE12 5SE (01509 889369; website: mountsorrelunitedcharities.co.uk)

Other information: This charity is closely linked to the Mountsorrel United Charities.

Oadby

The Oadby Educational Foundation

Eligibility: People in need in the parish of Oadby only.

Types of grants: One-off and recurrent grants in the range of £50 and £200.

Annual grant total: About £12,000 to individuals, mostly for educational purposes.

Applications: In writing to the correspondent, to be submitted either through a social worker, Citizens Advice or other welfare agency, or directly by the individual. They are considered in March, June and October.

Correspondent: Rodney Waterfield, 2 Silverton Road, Oadby, Leicester, LE2 4NN

Other information: Grants are also made to organisations.

Queniborough

Alex Neale Charity

Eligibility: Older people in need who live in the parish of Queniborough.

Types of grants: Grants towards gas and electricity bills.

Annual grant total: Grants usually total around £2,000 each year.

Applications: The trustees publicise the grants, usually every two years, in The Queniborough Gazette. An application form is then available from the correspondent. The trust may ask for copies of fuel bills for the two years prior to application, and then a grant would be made towards the costs of these bills.

Correspondent: Maurice Kirk, 6 Ervin Way, Queniborough, Leicester LE7 3TT (0116 260 6851)

Quorn

The Quorn Town Lands Charity

Eligibility: People in need who live in the parish of Quorn.

Types of grants: One-off and recurrent grants in the range of £50 to £250. Grants given include those for hospital expenses, convalescence, living costs, household bills, food, travel expenses and help in the home.

Annual grant total: In 2008/09 the trust had an income of £5,900 and a total expenditure of £3,800.

Applications: In writing to the correspondent. Applications should be submitted directly by the individual or through a relevant third party. They are considered quarterly.

Correspondent: Geoffrey Gibson, Clerk, 2 Wallis Close, Thurcaston, Leicester LE7 7JS (0116 235 0946; fax: 0116 235 0946)

Other information: This charity consists of three different funds: Quorn Town Lands Charity, Quorn Aid in Sickness Fund and Quorn Education Fund.

Rutland

The Rutland Dispensary

Eligibility: People who are poor, old or sick and live in Rutland.

Types of grants: One-off and recurrent grants ranging from £100 to £250.

Annual grant total: About £3,000.

Applications: In writing to the correspondent including details of any medical conditions and the general circumstances.

Correspondent: Fred Bellingall, 8 Holyrood Close, Oakham, Leicestershire LE15 6SF (01572 723480; email: fredbellingall@aol.com)

The Rutland Trust

Eligibility: People who are disabled and live in Rutland and are in need.

Types of grants: One-off and recurrent grants ranging between £50 and £400, to buy equipment.

Annual grant total: In 2009 the trust had an income of £14,000 and a total expenditure of £11,000. Grants are also made for educational purposes and to organisations.

Applications: An initial telephone call is recommended.

Correspondent: Richard Adams, Clerk, 35 Trent Road, Oakham, Rutland, LE15 6HE (01572 756706; email: adams@ apair.wanadoo.co.uk)

Smisby

The Smisby Parochial Charity

Eligibility: People in need who live in Smisby.

Types of grants: Christmas hampers to older people.

Annual grant total: About £1,500, mostly for welfare purposes.

Applications: In writing to the correspondent. Applications can be submitted either directly by the individual or a relevant third party, or through a social worker, Citizens Advice or other welfare agency. They can be considered at any time.

Correspondent: Mrs S Heap, Clerk, Cedar Lawns, Forties Lane, Smisby, Ashby-De-La-Zouch, Leicestershire LE65 2SN (01530 414179)

Syston

The H A Taylor Fund

Eligibility: People in need who have been in resident in the parish of Syston for at least one year.

Types of grants: One-off grants ranging from £50 to £1,000 towards, for example, travel costs, furniture, clothing, fuel, household repairs, medical treatment, books and course fees, mobility aids and telephone and television expenses.

Exclusions: Repeat applications can only be made every two years unless there are exceptional circumstances.

Annual grant total: In 2008/09 the fund had assets of £478,000 and an income of £26,000. Grants were made to 21 individuals totalling £6,800. A further £4,900 was given to Age Concern (Syston).

Applications: Application forms are available from Syston & District Volunteer Centre, Syston Health Centre and Syston Library or can be downloaded from the website. They can be submitted at any time either through a third party or directly by the individual and are considered every two months.

Correspondent: James Munton, LCOS, 20a Millstone Lane, Leicester LE1 5JN (0116 222 2200; fax: 0116 222 2201; email: info@charity-link.org; website: www.charity-link.org/)

Wymeswold

The Wymeswold Parochial Charities

Eligibility: People in need who have lived in Wymeswold for the last two years.

Types of grants: Winter gifts to senior citizens, widows and widowers. One-off grants are also given to people who are ill.

Annual grant total: Grants total about £4,000 a year.

Applications: In writing to the correspondent at any time.

Correspondent: The Trustees, 26 Church Street, Wymeswold, Loughborough LE12 6TX (01509 881146)

Lincolnshire

The Addlethorpe Parochial Charity

Eligibility: People in need who live in the parish of Addlethorpe, or who previously lived in Addlethorpe and now live in an adjoining parish. Applicants must be either living on a low income, with limited savings or investments of less than £10,000, or have a disability or illness that renders them unable to work.

Types of grants: Most grants are in the form of solid fuel or electricity/gas cheques. One-off grants are given towards funeral expenses, household repairs and other necessities. Grants have also been given for hospital or doctor's visits. Grants of £60 are available, and may be given up to three times during the year.

Annual grant total: The trust usually has both and income and a total expenditure of around £4,000, all of which is given in grants to individuals.

Applications: In writing to the correspondent to be submitted either directly by the individual or a family member, through a third party such as a social worker, or through an organisation such as Citizens Advice or other welfare agency. Applications must state that they are living on a reduced income and that savings/investments are below £10,000. Applications are considered on an ongoing basis.

Correspondent: Sara Marshall, Beck Cottage, Welton-Le-Marsh, Spilsby, Lincolnshire, PE23 5TA (01754 890377; email: mrsh225@aol.com)

Bauer Radio's Cash for Kids Charities *see entry on page 175*

The Bishop of Lincoln's Discretionary Fund

Eligibility: Ministers of the Church of England who live and work in the Diocese of Lincoln.

Types of grants: One-off grants of £25 to £450 according to need. Grants are usually to assist sick clergy and their families and for holiday grants.

Annual grant total: About £12,000 a year.

Applications: In writing by the individual or one of the other local bishops to the Bishop of Lincoln. Applications are considered throughout the year.

Correspondent: Revd Michael Silley, Bishop's House, Eastgate, Lincoln LN2 1QQ (01522 534701)

The Charity of John Dawber

Eligibility: People in need who live in the city of Lincoln and the parish of Bracebridge.

Types of grants: Christmas grocery vouchers and quarterly payments.

Annual grant total: In 2008/09 the charity had assets of £991,000, which generated an income of £51,000. During the year, charitable expenditure totalled £16,000, which went to 17 annuities and 977 recipients of Christmas vouchers.

Applications: In writing to the correspondent. There are no deadlines for applications.

Correspondent: Messrs Andrew & Co., St Swithins Square, 1 Flavian Road, Lincoln LN2 1HB (01522 512123; email: helen. newson@andre-solicitors.co.uk)

Other information: The trust also makes grants to organisations that benefit people living in the beneficial area.

The Farmers' Benevolent Institution

Eligibility: People living within a 15-mile radius of Grantham who have 'been owners or occupiers of land, but who from losses or other untoward circumstances have become destitute'. Applicants must be over 60 if they have been a subscriber of the fund for ten years or more. Otherwise they should be over 65.

Types of grants: Annual payments of around £150 and a supplementary payment at Christmas.

Annual grant total: Grants usually total about £3,000 each year.

Applications: In writing to the correspondent.

Correspondent: J D Andrew, c/o Duncan & Toplis, 3 Castlegate, Grantham, Lincolnshire NG31 6SF (01476 591200; fax: 01476 591222; email: info@grantham. duntop.co.uk)

Hunstone's Charity

Eligibility: Gentlemen in need who live in Lincolnshire with preference for 'decayed gentlemen of the family of Edward Hunstone or of the several families of the Gedneys or of Robert Smith or of the Woodliffes and decayed gentlemen living in the county of Lincoln'. Particular mention is also made of retired clergymen, members of HM Forces, farmers, farm labourers or anyone connected with land, and people with disabilities.

Types of grants: Recipients receive £250 per year, paid in two instalments of £125 in April and October. The assistance will be given as long as the trustees consider necessary or until the death of the recipient.

Exclusions: Grants are not given to women.

Annual grant total: In 2009 the charity had an income of £22,000 and a total expenditure of £17,000. Grants were made totalling around £15,000.

Applications: On a form available from the correspondent. Applications should be submitted either through a social worker, Citizens Advice or other welfare agency, or directly by the individual. They are considered in May each year and should be received by 30 April; urgent applications can be considered at other times. Two references are required with each application.

Correspondent: Tony Bradley, 58 Eastwood Road, Boston, Lincolnshire PE21 0PH (01205 364175)

The Kitchings General Charity

Eligibility: People in need who live in the parish of Bardney (covers Stainfield, Apley, Tupholme and Bucknall).

Types of grants: One-off grants to relieve hardship or distress e.g. holidays/respite care for disabled people (mostly at a special home at Sandringham), specialised nursing equipment and funeral expenses. Grants are in the range of £200 and £500.

Annual grant total: Grants usually total around £10,000 per year, which includes welfare and educational grants and widows pensions.

Applications: In writing to the correspondent directly by the individual, only basic details are required. Applications are considered in May, October and January.

Correspondent: Mrs J Smith, Secretary, 42 Abbey Road, Bardney, Lincoln LN3 5XA (01526 398505)

The Lincoln General Dispensary Fund

Eligibility: People who are in poor health, convalescent or who have disabilities and live within the 10 mile radius of the Stonebow (Lincoln).

Types of grants: One-off grants up to about £250 to alleviate suffering or aid recovery. Recent grants have been given for orthopaedic beds, alarm systems and recuperative holidays.

Exclusions: No grants are given for building adaptations, debts already incurred or anything that could be provided by public funds.

Annual grant total: In 2009 grants were made totalling about £12,000.

Applications: On a form available from the correspondent: to be submitted through a recognised social or medical agency. Applications are considered throughout the year.

Correspondent: M Bonass, Durrus, Scothern Lane, Dunholme, Lincoln LN2 3QP (01673 860660; fax: 01673 861701)

Other information: Grants are also given to local organisations.

Lincolnshire Police Charitable Fund

Eligibility: People in need who are present or former employees of Lincolnshire Police Authority, and their dependants. Former employees of other Police Authorities who have retired and now live in Lincolnshire may also qualify for assistance.

Types of grants: One-off grants according to need.

Annual grant total: In 2008/09 the trust had assets of £140,000 and an income of £38,000. Grants were made totalling just

over £38,000 and were distributed as follows:

General cases	£17,000
Medical, travel and expenses	£11,000
Death grants	£7,200
Christmas gifts	£1,200
Fruit, flowers and donations	£1,200
Comforts fund	£125

Applications: On a form available from the Welfare Officer. Applications can be submitted directly by the individual or through a social worker, Citizens Advice or other welfare agency.

Correspondent: Mrs Cilla Smith, Lincolnshire Police Welfare Department, 19 Sixfield Close, Lincoln LN6 0EJ (01522 805757)

The Tyler Charity for the Poor

Eligibility: People in need who live in the parishes of Morton and Thornock.

Types of grants: One-off and recurrent grants according to need.

Annual grant total: About £900.

Applications: In writing to the correspondent.

Correspondent: Mrs E M Bradley, 22 Market Place, Gainsborough, Lincolnshire, DN21 2BZ

The Willingham & District Relief-in-Sickness Charity

Eligibility: People in need who live in the parishes of Corringham, Heapham, Kexby, Springthorpe, Upton and Willingham.

Types of grants: One-off and recurrent grants according to need, such as for one-off items or respite care. Priority is usually given to help with bills.

Annual grant total: Grants usually total around £4,000 a year.

Applications: In writing to the correspondent by 1 April or 1 October for meetings at the end of those months.

Correspondent: Mrs J C Spencer, Secretary, 4 Church Road, Upton, Gainsborough, Lincolnshire DN21 5NS (01427 838385)

Barrow-upon-Humber

The Beeton, Barrick & Beck Relief-in-Need Charity

Eligibility: People in need who are over 60 and live in the parish of Barrow-upon-Humber.

Types of grants: Christmas vouchers and one-off grants for a variety of purposes, for example, travel costs to hospital.

Annual grant total: In 2008/09 the trust had both an income and a total expenditure of £3,600.

Applications: On a form available from the correspondent.

Correspondent: Mrs A Lawe, Barrow Wold Farm, Deepdale, Barton-upon-Humber, North Lincolnshire DN18 6ED (01469 531928)

Barton-upon-Humber

The Barton-upon-Humber Relief-in-Sickness Fund

Eligibility: People in the parish of Barton-upon-Humber who are suffering from ill-health and their relatives/carers (in appropriate cases).

Types of grants: Discretionary grants are given for all kinds of need, but usually for medical aids and equipment.

Annual grant total: Grants usually total around £2,000 each year.

Applications: In writing to the correspondent. The trustees discuss cases which are known personally to them, although written applications are equally welcome and are considered when received.

Correspondent: H K Ready, Market Place, Barton-upon-Humber, North Lincolnshire DN18 5DD (01652 632215)

The Charity of John Tripp (Blue Coat)

Eligibility: People in need who live in Barton-upon-Humber.

Types of grants: One-off grants, usually of around £25 to £30, towards footwear, clothing, bedding and other essential items.

Annual grant total: In 2008/09 the charity had an income of £8,400 and a total expenditure of £6,600.

Applications: In writing to the correspondent. Unless urgent, applications are considered each November.

Correspondent: Keith Ready, Market Place, Barton-upon-Humber, North Lincolnshire DN18 5DD (01652 632215)

Deeping

The Deeping St James United Charities

Eligibility: People in need living in the parish of St James, Deeping. Grants are also paid to widows over 60 who have lived in the parish for three years or more.

Types of grants: One-off and recurrent grants according to need are given for a variety of purposes. Previous causes have included the assistance for a young person to attend a residential training course, contributions towards food bills for an older person, living expenses whilst a benefits claim was pending and the funding towards the cost of a replacement cooker for a family, assistance with hospital visiting costs and special equipment for the family of a seriously ill child.

Annual grant total: In 2008 the charities had assets of £2.3 million and an income of £109,000. Relief in need and relief of sickness grants totalled £18,000.

Applications: In writing to the correspondent for consideration at the start of March, June, September and December. The trust welcomes telephone calls to discuss suggestions for grants with potential applicants.

Correspondent: Julie Banks, Clerk, The Institute, 38 Church Street, Deeping St James, Lincolnshire, PE6 8HD (01778 344707 (Tues/Thurs 9am-12pm); email: clerk@dsjunitedcharities.org.uk; website: www.dsjunitedcharities.org.uk)

Other information: This trust also gives grants to college and university students and local organisations.

Dorrington

Dorrington Welfare Charity

Eligibility: People over the age of 18 who are in need and have lived in the village of Dorrington for at least the last year.

Types of grants: In the past one-off grants of up to £200 have been made along with Christmas payments to children of primary school age and to persons over 65.

Annual grant total: Grants usually total around £1,000 per year.

Applications: In writing to the correspondent, or a trustee, directly by the individual. Applications are considered at any time. Applications should include a general explanation of assistance required, an estimate of the expenses involved, details of any other assistance received or confirmation that no assistance has been or can be received from public funds.

Correspondent: Mrs Susan Tong, Penneshaw Farm, Sleaford Road, Dorrington, Lincoln LN4 3PU (01526 833395; email: susantong@ btinternet.com)

Frampton

The Frampton Town Land & United Charities

Eligibility: People in need who have lived in the ancient parish of Frampton for at least five years. Preference is usually given to older people (over 65) and recently bereaved widows.

Types of grants: One-off grants towards electricity bills, Christmas gifts for older people and so on.

Annual grant total: In 2008/09 the charities had both an income and expenditure of £8,800.

Applications: In writing to the correspondent. Applications are normally considered in October.

Correspondent: Mark Hildred, Moore Thompson, Bank House, Broad Street, Spalding, Lincolnshire PE11 1TB (01775 711333; fax: 01775 711307)

Friskney

The Friskney United Charities

Eligibility: Older people in need who live in Friskney, particularly those who have a connection with agricultural work.

Types of grants: Annual grants of 3cwt of coal and/or £10 each, classed as Christmas gifts.

Annual grant total: This trust's main purpose is the provision of housing for older people. Coal and charitable gifts given usually total around £400.

Applications: In writing to the correspondent. Applications are considered in November. A list of applicants is produced by the trustees based upon their local knowledge.

Correspondent: Jacquie Scott, Sigtoft Farm, Low Road South, Friskney, Boston, PE22 8QH (01754 820554)

Grimsby

Sir Alec Black's Charity

Eligibility: Fishermen and dockworkers who are sick and poor, who live in the borough of Grimsby. Grants are also available to people employed by Sir Alec Black during his lifetime.

Types of grants: One-off and recurrent grants according to need.

Annual grant total: In 2008/09 the charity had an income of £473,000. Grants to fishermen and dockworkers totalled £3,500, former employees received £16,000 and grants to organisations totalled £136,000.

Applications: In writing to the correspondent. The trustees meet twice a year, in May and November, to consider applications.

Correspondent: Stewart Wilson, Trustee, Messrs Wilson Sharpe & Co, 27 Osborne Street, Grimsby, North East Lincolnshire DN31 1NU (01472 348315; email: sc@ wilsonsharpe.co.uk)

Hacconby & Stainfield

Hacconby Poor's Money & Others

Eligibility: People in need who live in the parish of Hacconby and Stainfield.

Types of grants: One-off and recurrent grants according to need. Recent grants have included Christmas grants to people aged over 60, help with home alterations for disabled people and grants towards funeral expenses and hospital travel costs.

Annual grant total: In 2008/09 the trust had an income of £3,500 and a total expenditure of £3,000.

Applications: In writing to the correspondent. Applications can be submitted directly by the individual or through a third party such as a social worker, Citizens Advice, welfare agency or neighbour.

Correspondent: Gillian Stoneman, 8 Church Street, Hacconby, Bourne, Lincolnshire PE10 0UJ (01778 570607; email: beamsend@tiscali.co.uk)

Kesteven

The Kesteven Children in Need

Eligibility: Children/young people up to the age of 16 who live in Kesteven.

Types of grants: One-off and recurrent grants of up to £500. Examples of grants include clothing, educational holidays, days out, prams/pushchairs, beds/sheets, fireguards, second-hand washing machines, educational toys and playschool fees.

Annual grant total: In 2008 the charity had assets of £12,000 and a total income of £25,000. The majority of grants were made for welfare purposes totalling £19,000, with an additional £500 made for educational purposes.

Applications: Generally through local social workers, health visitors, teachers and education officers. Information should include the family situation, the age of the child and his/her special needs. Applications are considered throughout the year.

Correspondent: Mrs Jane Howard, Nocton Rise, Sleaford Road, Nocton, Lincoln LN4 2AF (01522 791217; email: enquiries@kcin.org)

A L Padley Charity Fund

Eligibility: People living in Kesteven who are: couples wishing to get married where the man is 24 years or older and the woman is 21 years or older; pensioners; or people who have been experiencing prolonged illness.

Types of grants: One-off and recurrent grants according to need.

Annual grant total: In 2008/09 the trust had both an income and total expenditure of £3,900.

Applications: The trust asks applicants to write a short initial letter to see if their interests match those of the trustees. Please mark all correspondence with ref. WECC.

Correspondent: William Cursham, Fraser Brown Solicitors, 84 Friar Lane, Nottingham NG1 6ED (0115 947 2541)

Other information: Grants are also made to organisations.

Lincoln

The Lincoln Municipal Relief-in-Need Charities

Eligibility: People in need who live in the city of Lincoln.

Types of grants: One-off grants up to £500 each, for all kinds of need except relief with rates, taxes or public funds; improvement to properties; or debts already incurred.

Annual grant total: In 2009/10 the trust had assets of £737,000 and an income of £39,000. Grants were made to individuals totalling £33,000, of which £4,600 was given in quarterly payments.

Applications: On a form available from the correspondent, to be submitted through a social worker, Citizens Advice or other welfare agency. Applications are considered at any time.

Correspondent: M G Bonass, Clerk, Durrus, Scothern Lane, Dunholme, Lincoln LN2 3QP (01673 860660)

Other information: Grants are occasionally made to organisations.

The Herbert William Sollitt Memorial Trust

Eligibility: Older people in need who are widows or widowers and live in the city of Lincoln.

Types of grants: One-off grants towards, for example, household items, life line alarms, decoration, convalescent holidays and telephone installation.

Exclusions: Grants are not given to married people or people who live outside the area of benefit.

Annual grant total: About £1,500 a year. Grants are given to both individuals and organisations.

Applications: On a form available from the correspondent to be submitted through a social worker, Citizens Advice or other welfare agency. Applications are considered on a regular basis.

Correspondent: Jacqueline Smith, Secretary, 24 Sunfield Crescent, Birchwood, Lincoln LN6 0LL

(01522 885006; email: jacq.smith@ntlworld.com)

Moulton

The Moulton Poors' Lands Charity

Eligibility: People in need, generally older people, who live in the civil parish of Moulton.

Types of grants: Grants can be paid in cash or in kind. Relief-in-need grants are generally paid following a severe accident, unexpected loss or misfortune.

Annual grant total: Previously grants to individuals and organisations have totalled around £15,000.

Applications: In writing to the correspondent, usually through a trustee. Applications are considered in April and December.

Correspondent: R W Lewis, Clerk for the Charity, Maples & Son Solicitors, 23 New Road, Spalding, Lincolnshire PE11 1DH

Navenby

The Navenby Towns Farm Trust

Eligibility: People in need who live in the village of Navenby.

Types of grants: One-off grants according to need.

Exclusions: No grants can be given outside the village.

Annual grant total: About £11,000 to individuals and organisations.

Applications: On a form available from the correspondent, the village post office, or Smith and Willows the newsagents. Applications are considered in September. Urgent applications may occasionally be considered at other times. Unsolicited applications are not responded to.

Correspondent: The Secretary, 17 North Lane, Navenby, Lincoln LN5 0EH

South Holland

The Spalding Relief-in-Need Charity

Eligibility: People in need who live in the area covered by South Holland District Council with priority to residents of the parishes of Spalding, Cowbit, Deeping St Nicholas, Pinchbeck and Weston.

Types of grants: One-off grants in the range of £100 to £400 towards furniture and domestic appliances, rent arrears and other debts and children's clothing.

Annual grant total: In 2009 the charity had both an income and an expenditure of approximately £40,000. Grants to individuals totalled £31,000.

Applications: On a form available from the charity. Applications can be submitted directly by the individual or assisted if appropriate by a social worker, Citizens Advice, other welfare agency or third party. Grants are considered on a weekly basis.

Correspondent: R A Knipe, Clerk and Solicitor, Dembleby House, 12 Broad Street, Spalding, Lincolnshire PE11 1ES (01775 768774)

Other information: Grants can also be made to organisations. Normally payments are made directly to suppliers.

Spilsby

The Spilsby Feoffees (Poorlands) Charities

Eligibility: People of retirement age in need who have lived in Spilsby for at least five years.

Types of grants: Grants of up to £25 are made twice a year in June and December.

Annual grant total: About £2,000.

Applications: On a form available from the correspondent. Applications must be submitted directly by the individual and are considered in June and December. Applicants must state how long they have lived in Spilsby.

Correspondent: Mrs J Tong, Clerk, Rosedale Lodge, Ashby Road, Spilsby, Lincolnshire PE23 5DW (01790 752885)

Stamford

Winifrede Browne's Charity

Eligibility: People in need who are sick or elderly and live in Stamford.

Types of grants: Grants given include those for clothing, medical and disabled equipment, household bills, help in the home, travel to hospital and assistance with funeral expenses.

Exclusions: Grants are not given for 'relief of rates, taxes or other public funds'.

Annual grant total: About £3,500 a year.

Applications: In writing to the correspondent, to be submitted either through a social worker, Citizens Advice or other welfare agency, or directly by the individual. They are considered quarterly unless urgent.

Correspondent: N P Fluck, Messrs Stapleton & Son, 1 Broad Street, Stamford, Lincolnshire PE9 1PD (01780 751226; fax: 01780 766407)

Stickford

The Stickford Relief-in-Need Charity

Eligibility: People in need who live in the parish of Stickford.

Types of grants: One-off and recurrent grants for relief-in-need purposes, towards school uniforms, and a Christmas bonus. Further grants are given towards a bus service for older people, youth club outings and so on.

Annual grant total: About £15,000.

Applications: In writing to the correspondent. Applications should be submitted directly by the individual and are considered all year.

Correspondent: Katherine Bunting, Clerk, The Old Vicarage, Church Road, Stickford, Boston, Lincolnshire PE22 8EP (01205 480455)

Surfleet

The Surfleet United Charities

Eligibility: Retired people in need who have lived in the parish of Surfleet for over 10 years (exceptions will be made on the age restriction in cases of extreme need).

Types of grants: Normally grants before Christmas each year of £15 (individuals) and £25 (couples). Other one-off grants according to need.

Annual grant total: In 2008 the charities had an income of £26,000 and a total expenditure of £27,000. Grants were made totalling £2,800.

Applications: In writing to the correspondent. Applications can be submitted directly by the individual and are considered in November.

Correspondent: Leanne Barlow, Beck Cottage, Beck Bank, Quadring Fen, Spalding, Lincolnshire PE11 4RA (01775 750183)

Sutterton

The Sutterton Parochial Charity Trust

Eligibility: People in need who live in the parishes of Sutterton and Amber Hill.

Types of grants: One-off grants of about £50 are given at Christmas time.

Annual grant total: In 2008/09 the trust had an income of £16,000 and a total expenditure of £17,000.

Applications: On a form available from the correspondent which can be submitted directly by the individual or a family member. Applications should be received

by the trust by the end of November for consideration in early December.

Correspondent: Mrs D P McCumiskey, 6 Hillside Gardens, Wittering, Peterborough, PE8 6DX (01780 782668)

Other information: Grants are also made to organisations.

Sutton St James

The Sutton St James United Charities

Eligibility: People in need who live in the parish of Sutton St James.

Types of grants: One-off and recurrent grants according to need. Recent grants have been given for funeral expenses and to help people who have been evicted.

Annual grant total: In 2008/09 the charities had an income of £17,000 and a total expenditure of £27,000. Grants are made for educational and welfare purposes.

Applications: On a form available from the correspondent. Applications are only considered when all other available avenues have been explored.

Correspondent: Keith Savage, Clerk, Lenton Lodge, 94 Wignals Gate, Holbeach, Spalding, Lincolnshire PE12 7HR (01406 490157; email: keithsavage@btinternet.com)

Swineshead

The Swineshead Poor Charities

Eligibility: People in need who live in the parish of Swineshead.

Types of grants: One-off and recurrent grants and loans according to need.

Annual grant total: In 2009/10 the charities had an income of £14,000 and a total expenditure of £19,000.

Applications: In writing to the correspondent.

Correspondent: Lynne Richardson, Hawthorn Farm, Station Road, Swineshead, Boston, Lincolnshire PE20 3NZ (01205 821628)

Other information: The charities also make grants to organisations.

Northampton-shire

Edmund Arnold's Charity (Poors Branch)

Eligibility: People in need who live in the parish of Nether Heyford, Northamptonshire, the ancient parish of St Giles in Northampton and the parish of Stony Stratford, Buckinghamshire.

Types of grants: One-off cash grants of between £50 and £400 for 'extra comforts'.

Annual grant total: In 2008 grants to individuals totalled £3,300.

Applications: On a form available on written request from the correspondent. Applications can be submitted either directly by the individual or through a third party such as a social worker, Citizens Advice or another welfare agency. They are considered in March/April and September/October.

Correspondent: Jane Forsyth, Clerk, 4 Grange Park Court, Roman Way, Grange Park, Northampton NN4 5EA (01604 876697)

The Valentine Goodman Estate Charity

Eligibility: People in need who live in the parishes of Blaston, Bringhurst, Drayton, East Magna, Hallaton and Medbourne.

Types of grants: One-off or recurrent grants according to need.

Annual grant total: In 2009 the charity had an income of £12,000 and a total expenditure of £11,000.

Applications: In writing to the correspondent. Grants are distributed in February each year.

Correspondent: John Stones, Administrator, Blaston Lodge, Blaston Road, Blaston, Market Harborough, LE16 8DB (01858 555688)

The Henry & Elizabeth Lineham Charity

Eligibility: Women in need, generally widows or unmarried daughters of professional men who have died, or school teachers and governesses. Applicants must be at least 55 and live in the borough of Northampton.

Types of grants: Annuities are paid half yearly.

Annual grant total: In 2009 the trust had assets of £1 million, and an income of £48,000. Grants were made 67 individuals totalling £26,000.

Applications: In writing to the correspondent. Beneficiaries are usually nominated by one of the trustees, mostly councillors or ex-councillors.

Correspondent: Angela Moon, Hewitson's LLP, 7 Spencer Parade, Northampton NN1 5AB (01604 233233; email: mail@ hewitsons.com)

The Page Fund

Eligibility: People in need who live in the borough of Northampton or within five miles of the Guild Hall and have done so for more than five years. Preference is given to older people, and to those with a sudden and unforeseen drop in income, for example widows following the death of a husband.

Types of grants: Pensions of up to £800 per year for people who have experienced a reduction in income due to widowhood or old age.

Annual grant total: In 2008/09 the fund had assets of £535,000 and an income of £38,000. Grants were made totalling £35,000, of which £4,200 was given to four individuals and the remaining £31,000 to ten organisations.

Applications: On a form available from the correspondent. Applications can be submitted directly by the individual or through a social worker, Citizens Advice or other welfare agency. They are accepted at any time and are considered in May and November.

Correspondent: Jane Forsyth, Wilson Browne Solicitors, 4 Grange Park Court, Roman Way, Northampton NN4 5EA (01604 876697; fax: 01604 768606; email: jforsyth@wilsonbrowne.co.uk)

Saint Giles Charity Estate

Eligibility: People in need who live in Northamptonshire.

Types of grants: Grants of £50 to £400 to individuals and families towards, for example, helping to fund individual household requirements such as carpets/ washing machines and so on. Grants are always made for a specific purpose, not as a financial 'top up'.

Exclusions: The charity does not normally make grants towards paying off debts, tuition fees or for building projects.

Annual grant total: In 2008 the charity had assets of £2.8 million and an income of £561,000. Grants were made totalling £40,000 and were given to both individuals and institutions.

Applications: On a form available from the correspondent. The charity prefers applications to be supported by a third party such as a social worker, or to come through an organisation such as Citizens Advice or another welfare agency. Applications should be submitted by the end of January, April, July and October for consideration in the next month.

All enquiries must be made by post.

Correspondent: Grants Administrator, 7 Spinney Close, Boughton, Northampton, NN2 8SD

Other information: The charity's main activity is the provision of almshouses and the support of Nicholas Rothwell House, a specially designed and purpose built complex dedicated to providing both short and long term residential care.

Sir Thomas White's Loan Fund

Eligibility: People aged between 21 and 34 years of age who live in the extended borough of Northampton.

Types of grants: One-off grants towards buying a house, home improvements (e.g. central heating/double glazing installation, bathroom improvements), wedding expenses, car expenses, etc.

The fund was originally set up for the provision of tools for people setting up in a trade or profession and it also gives educational grants and interest-free loans for education and new businesses.

Annual grant total: In 2009 the fund had assets of £3.2 million and an income of £253,000, with grants totalling £94,000.

Applications: Apply in writing for a form in November, following a public notice advertising the grants.

Correspondent: Clerk to the Trustees, Hewitsons, 7 Spencer Parade, Northampton NN1 5AB (01604 233233; email: angelamoon@hewitsons.com)

Other information: Grants are also made to individuals for educational purposes.

The Yelvertoft & District Relief-in-Sickness Fund

Eligibility: People in need who live in the parishes of Yelvertoft, West Haddon, Crick, Winwick, Clay Coton and Elkington, who are sick, convalescent, disabled or infirm.

Types of grants: On average 70 one-off grants ranging between £25 and £150.

Annual grant total: No recent financial information was available. In previous years grants totalled around £8,000.

Applications: In writing to the correspondent. Applications should be submitted directly by the individual, a relative or district nurse, and can be considered at any time.

Correspondent: Anne Drewett, Secretary and Trustee, 6 Monks Way, Crick, Northampton NN6 7XB (01788 823499)

Blakesley

The Blakesley Parochial Charities

Eligibility: People in need who live in Blakesley.

Types of grants: One-off and recurrent grants according to need. Grants are given towards the fuel bills of older people and as pensions to widows.

Annual grant total: In 2009 the charities had an income of £5,500 and a total expenditure of £5,200.

Applications: In writing to the correspondent. Applications are considered in December.

Correspondent: Derek Lucas, Bradworthy, Main Street, Woodend, Towcester, NN12 8RX (01327 860517; email: derekjlucas@tiscali.co.uk)

Other information: The charities also make grants for educational purposes.

Brackley

The Brackley United Feoffee Charity

Eligibility: People in need who live in Brackley.

Types of grants: The trust gives funding to a wide range of causes, including the distribution of Christmas donations to around 60 elderly residents of Brackley. Previous grants have included: help towards the cost of aids for people with disabilities, temporary accommodation for a couple following a serious house fire, the purchase of a new washing machine for the young mother of a child with disabilities, help with childcare for parents deemed vulnerable and a contribution towards the repair of the headstone of a young child.

Annual grant total: In 2008/09 the charity had an income of £38,000. Grants to individuals totalled £9,000, with £6,500 going to welfare causes.

Applications: In writing to the correspondent preferably by the individual or through a social worker, Citizens Advice or other welfare agency. Trustees meet every three to four months.

Correspondent: Mrs R Hedges, 7 Easthill Close, Brackley, Northamptonshire NN13 7BS (01280 702420; email: caryl. billingham@tesco.net)

Braunston

The Braunston Town Lands Charity

Eligibility: People who live in Braunston and have to spend four nights or more in a hospital. Grants are given to patients and to their relatives. The size of grant depends on the distance that has to be travelled to the hospital and the amount of time spent at hospital.

Types of grants: One-off grants in the form of cash donations for those over 90 years of age and Christmas gifts for people who are hospitalised or housebound. Grants generally range from £15 to £25.

Exclusions: No grants to individuals living outside the beneficial area.

Annual grant total: Grant giving to individuals generally totals around £800 a year.

Applications: In writing to the correspondent, directly by the individual.

Correspondent: Sheila Rowley, 5 Danecourt, Church Road, Braunston, Daventry, Northamptonshire NN11 7HG (01788 890559)

Other information: Grants are also made to organisations.

Brington

The Chauntry Estate

Eligibility: Elderly people and other people in need who live in the parish of Brington. Applicants must have lived in the parish for at least five years.

Types of grants: One-off grants to relieve sudden distress or infirmity are made, for example, towards travel expenses for visits to hospital, food, fuel and heating appliances, and comforts or aids not provided by health authorities.

Annual grant total: In 2008/09 the trust had an income of £10,000 and a total expenditure of £8,000. Grants are made for welfare and educational purposes.

Applications: In writing to the correspondent.

Correspondent: Rita Tank, Walnut Tree Cottage, Main Street, Great Brington, Northampton NN7 4JA (01604 770809)

Byfield

The Byfield Poors Allotment

Eligibility: People in need who live in the parish of Byfield.

Types of grants: One-off grants of £10 and £100, towards household bills, travel expenses, dental costs, spectacles and other 'minor medical items'. Grants, usually to older people, are also given for Christmas expenses.

Annual grant total: In 2008/09 the allotment had both an income and total expenditure of £800.

Applications: On a form available from the correspondent. Applications can be made directly by the individual or a relevant third party. They can be submitted at any time for consideration in March, June, September and December.

Correspondent: Ms Delith Jones, 15 Banbury Lane, Byfield, Daventry, Northamptonshire, NN11 6UX (01327 261405)

Chipping Warden

Relief in Need Charity of Reverend William Smart

Eligibility: People in need who live in the parish of Chipping Warden, Northamptonshire. Preference is given to elderly people and young people in education.

Types of grants: One-off grants according to need.

Annual grant total: About £3,000 each year.

Applications: In writing to the correspondent either directly by the individual or by another third party such as a social worker. Applications are considered at any time.

Correspondent: N J Galletly, 3 Allens Orchard, Chipping Warden, Banbury, Oxfordshire OX17 1LX (01295 660365)

Daventry

The Daventry Consolidated Charity

Eligibility: People in need who live in the borough of Daventry.

Types of grants: One-off grants for a specific need such as a special chair for a child with cerebral palsy, travel to hospital 45 miles from home and help with the costs of adaptations to a motability vehicle.

Exclusions: There are no grants available towards debts or ongoing expenses.

Annual grant total: Grants average around £22,000 a year, though the actual grant figure tends to fluctuate quite widely.

Applications: In writing to the correspondent. Trustees meet three times a year in March, July and November. Applications must include financial circumstances and the specific purpose for the grant. Relevant information not included will be requested if required.

Correspondent: Maggie Dowie, 15 Astbury Close, Daventry, Northamptonshire NN11 4RL

Other information: The charity also makes grants to organisations.

Desborough

The Desborough Town Welfare Committee

Eligibility: People who are older, sick or in need and living in Desborough.

Types of grants: One-off and recurrent grants, paid mainly at Christmas.

Annual grant total: Grants usually total around £6,000 a year.

Applications: In writing to the correspondent, for consideration within two to three months.

Correspondent: Ann King, 190 Dunkirk Avenue, Desborough, Kettering, Northamptonshire NN14 2PP (01536 763390)

East Farndon

The United Charities of East Farndon

Eligibility: Families in need who live in East Farndon.

Types of grants: One-off cash grants of up to £50 are provided for travel expenses to hospital, fuel grants towards electricity, disabled equipment, living costs and household bills.

Annual grant total: In 2009 the charities had an income of £2,500 and a total expenditure of just under £2,000.

Applications: In writing to the correspondent directly by the individual or a family member for consideration as they are received.

Correspondent: C L Fraser, Linden Lea, Main Street, Market Harborough, Northamptonshire LE16 9SJ (01858 464218; email: fraser-cameron@ hotmail.com)

Other information: Grants are also made for educational purposes.

Harpole

The Harpole Parochial Charities

Eligibility: People in need who have lived in Harpole for more than seven years, with a preference for those over 65.

Types of grants: Recurrent grants ranging from £25 to £30.

Annual grant total: Grants usually total around £1,200 a year.

Applications: On a form available from the correspondent including details of financial status; benefits and income. Applications can be submitted either directly by the individual or through a relative. They are considered in December and should be submitted in November.

Correspondent: Jeremy Calderwood, 39 Upper High Street, Harpole, Northampton NN7 4DJ (01604 830099)

Kettering

The Broadway Cottages Trust

Eligibility: People in need who live or have lived in or near Kettering.

Types of grants: One-off and recurrent grants according to need.

227

Annual grant total: Generally around £600 a year is given to individuals.

Applications: In writing to the correspondent.

Correspondent: Peter Wilson, Chair, 35 Westhill Drive, Kettering, Northamptonshire, NN15 7LG (01536 482017)

Other information: The trust also provides housing with affordable rent and makes grants to organisations.

The Kettering Charities (Fuel Grants)

Eligibility: Widows, widowers and single people over the age of 60 who live alone in Kettering or Baron Seagrave and who are in receipt of retirement pension.

Types of grants: Grants of £25 towards winter fuel bills.

Annual grant total: In 2008/09 the charities had an income of £14,000 and a total expenditure of £16,000.

Applications: On a form available from the correspondent which can be obtained after advertisements have been placed in local newspapers in November each year. Applications are considered in November. Applicants must include details of income, status, age and address.

Correspondent: Anne Ireson, Kettering Borough Council, Council Offices, Bowling Green Road, Kettering NN15 7QX (01536 534398; email: anneireson@kettering.gov.uk)

Other information: The charities also make grants towards education expenses to people over 16 (please see our sister publication, *The Guide to Educational Grants* for further details).

The Stockburn Memorial Trust Fund

Eligibility: People in need who live in the town of Kettering.

Types of grants: One-off grants according to need.

Annual grant total: In 2009 the fund had an income of £7,900 and a total expenditure of £5,900.

Applications: In writing to the correspondent through a social worker, Citizens Advice or other welfare agency. Applicants should include details of age, address, telephone number, financial situation and health circumstances.

Correspondent: Mrs P M Reynolds, 70 Windermere Road, Kettering, Northamptonshire NN16 8UF (01536 524662)

Litchborough

The Litchborough Parochial Charities

Eligibility: People in need who live in Litchborough.

Types of grants: One-off grants and pensions.

Annual grant total: In 2009/10 the charities had both an income and expenditure of £5,200.

Applications: In writing to the correspondent.

Correspondent: Maureen Pickford, 18 Banbury Road, Litchborough, Towcester, Northamptonshire NN12 8JF (01327 830110)

Northampton

The Northampton Municipal Church Charities

Eligibility: People in need who live in the borough of Northampton.

Types of grants: People aged over 55 are eligible for payments of £85 a quarter and a Christmas voucher of £45. People of any age can receive one-off grants of up to a maximum of £500.

Exclusions: The charity is unable to assist with debt.

Annual grant total: In 2007/08 the charities had assets of £4.4 million and an income of £233,000. Grants were made totalling £65,000, and were distributed as follows:

Individual grants	£24,000
Pension payments	£35,000
Christmas vouchers	£5,600

A further £60,000 was given to organisations.

Note: Although submitted on time, 2008/09 accounts were not available to view at the Charity Commission.

Applications: On a form available from the correspondent, including details of age, residence, income, assets and expenditure. Applications can be submitted either directly by the individual or through a third party such as a social worker, Citizens Advice or other welfare agency. They are considered on a regular basis.

Correspondent: Jane Forsyth, Wilson Browne Solicitors, 4 Grange Park Court, Roman Way, Grange Park, Northampton NN4 5EA (01604 876697; fax: 01604 768606; email: jforsyth@wilsonbrowne.co.uk)

Other information: The charity runs a sheltered housing scheme at St Thomas House in St Giles Street, Northampton. It is warden controlled and has 17 small flats for people over 55. The charities' income must firstly be used for maintaining St

Thomas House, secondly for the benefit of residents, and thirdly for the relief-in-need of people who live in Northampton.

Pattishall

The Pattishall Parochial Charities

Eligibility: People in need who have lived in the parish of Pattishall for at least three years. Preference is given to people who are over 65.

Types of grants: One-off grants of between £15 and £500 for a variety of needs, for example provision of a downstairs toilet and a contribution towards a child's playgroup fees. 15 widows and widowers receive monthly pensions of £15, and around 40 older people receive grants for fuel at Christmas (£40 to single people and £55 to couples).

Annual grant total: Grants usually total around £6,000 a year.

Applications: In writing to the correspondent. Applications are usually considered in November for fuel grants, July for pensions, and throughout the year for other grants. Applications can be submitted either directly by the individual or by anybody who hears of a need such as one of the trustees or the rector of the parish. Receipts (copies will do) should be included for the cost of travel for hospital visits and estimates for the purchases of large equipment, for example wheelchairs.

Correspondent: Wendy Watts, 59 Leys Road, Pattishall, Towcester, Northamptonshire, NN12 8JY (01327 830583)

Ringstead

The Ringstead Gift

Eligibility: People in need who live in the parish of Ringstead.

Types of grants: One-off grants in kind. 'The trustees would consider all applications'.

Exclusions: No grants to cover the cost of rent or rates.

Annual grant total: About £1,000 a year for educational and welfare purposes.

Applications: In writing to the correspondent, to be submitted either directly by the individual or a family member, through a third party such as a social worker or teacher or through an organisation such as Citizens Advice or a school. Applications are considered in June and November and should be submitted at least two weeks prior to this.

Correspondent: Mrs D Pentelow, 20 Carlow Street, Ringstead, Kettering, Northamptonshire NN14 4DN

Roade

The Roade Feoffee and Chivall Charity

Eligibility: People in need who live in the ancient parish of Roade.

Types of grants: One-off grants usually ranging from £15 to £100. Recent grants have been given at Christmas time and for such things as travel expenses to visit relatives in hospital.

Annual grant total: In 2009 the charity had an income of £18,000 and a total expenditure of £9,500.

Applications: In writing to the correspondent, specifying the reason for the application.

Correspondent: Michael Dowden, 67 High Street, Roade, Northampton NN7 2NW

Scaldwell

The Scaldwell Relief-in-Need Charity

Eligibility: People in need who live in the parish of Scaldwell only.

Types of grants: One-off grants ranging from £50 to £250.

Annual grant total: Grants average around £1,200 a year.

Applications: In writing to the correspondent. Applications can be submitted directly by the individual or family member and are considered in November and February.

Correspondent: Mrs S K Dodds-Smith, The Old Barn, High Street, Scaldwell, Northampton, NN6 9JS (01604 881950; email: d.doddssmith@btinternet.com)

Towcester

The Sponne & Bickerstaffe Charity

Eligibility: People in need who live in the civil parish of Towcester.

Types of grants: One-off grants of £50 to £250 towards household essentials, such as furniture, clothing and electrical goods.

Annual grant total: About £1,700 for welfare and educational purposes.

Applications: In writing to the correspondent, through a social worker, Citizens Advice or other welfare agency. Applications are considered monthly.

Correspondent: Mrs T Richardson, Moorfield, Buckingham Way, Towcester, Northamptonshire NN12 6PE (01327 351206; email: sponneandbickerstaffe@btconnect. com)

Wappenham

The Wappenham Poors Land Charity

Eligibility: People in need who live in the ecclesiastical parish of Wappenham.

Types of grants: The trust gives a small standard grant to pensioners in need. Grants are also given to widows, widowers and people who are sick or disabled and are in need of specific items e.g. wheelchairs, orthopaedic beds, home improvements, shower installation, redecoration and so on.

Annual grant total: Grants average around £3,000 a year.

Applications: In writing to the correspondent.

Correspondent: Mrs J E McNeil, Flat 1, Green Norton Park, Greens Norton, Towcester NN12 8DP (01327 350873)

Welton

Welton Village Hall (formerly The Welton Town Lands Trust)

Eligibility: People in need, irrespective of age, who have lived in the village of Welton for at least two years.

Types of grants: One-off grants of around £50 per family. The amount varies according to the total number of applicants as it is divided in equal shares.

Annual grant total: In 2009/10 the charity had an income of £11,000 and a total expenditure of £9,000. Previously, grants were made to individuals totalling £2,000, of which £700 was given in educational grants and £1,400 was distributed in welfare awards.

Applications: On a form available from the correspondent. Applications are considered in November for distribution in December. The details of the trust are usually well publicised within the village.

Correspondent: Mr Peter O'Mahoney, Orchard House, Halford Way, Welton, Daventry, NN11 2XZ

Other information: The trust also makes grants to local schools and churches.

Nottinghamshire

The John and Nellie Brown Farnsfield Trust

Eligibility: People in need who live in the Farnsfield, Edingley Halam and Southwell areas of Nottinghamshire.

Types of grants: Grants given according to need.

Annual grant total: In 2008/09 the trust had an income of £7,000 and a total expenditure of £23,000, a marked increase on the previous years spending (£6,600).

Applications: In writing to the correspondent.

Correspondent: J A Brown, Trustee, Blue Haze, Tippings Lane, Farnsfield, Newark, NG22 8EP

Other information: Grants are also made to organisations and for educational purposes.

The Lucy Derbyshire Annuity Fund

Eligibility: People of good character who are in reduced circumstances or of limited means and have lived in Nottinghamshire for at least five years preceding their application. The fund has a preference for older people.

Types of grants: Recurrent grants are given according to need.

Annual grant total: In 2007/08 the fund had assets of £500,000 and an income of £246,000. 'Due to financial constraints no grants were made during the year'. Recent accounts have not been filed with the Charity Commission.

Applications: In writing to the correspondent. Applications can be submitted directly by the individual or through a social worker, Citizens Advice or other welfare agency.

Correspondent: Richard Minshall, Minshalls, 370–374 Nottingham Road, Newthorpe, Nottingham NG16 2ED (01773 538930; email: mco@minshall.co. uk)

Other information: The fund also runs a small care home in Wollaton, Nottingham.

The Mary Dickinson Charity

Eligibility: Older people in need who live in the city or county of Nottingham. Preference is given to Christians.

Types of grants: Pensions are given to a fixed number of older people. One-off grants may also be available for emergency items such as replacing gas fires and safety alarm and telephone systems.

Annual grant total: In 2009 the charity had assets of £1.1 million and an income of £31,000. Pensions and grants amounted to £18,000.

Applications: On a form available from the correspondent. Applications should be submitted through a doctor/member of the clergy or directly by the individual, supported by a reference from one of the aforementioned. Applications can be submitted all year round and are considered in March, June, September and December, although emergency cases can be considered at any time.

Correspondent: Neil Cullen, Freeth Cartwright LLP, Cumberland Court,

80 Mount Street, Nottingham NG1 6HH
(0115 936 9369; fax: 0115 859 9600)

Other information: This charity is also known as the Dickinson Massey Underwood Charity.

Dickinson Massey Underwood Charity

Eligibility: The object of the charity is the relief of persons resident, or who have at some time resided, in the City of Nottingham or the County of Nottinghamshire who are in need, hardship or distress.

In exceptional cases the trustees may decide to assist someone (who is otherwise qualified) who is resident outside the area of the City of Nottingham or the County of Nottinghamshire or only temporarily resident in the City of Nottingham or the County of Nottinghamshire.

Types of grants: One-off grants ranging from £50 to £200.

The trustees may relieve persons in need by making grants of money to them; or providing or paying for goods, services, or facilities for them; or making grants of money to persons or bodies who provide goods, services or facilities to those in need.

Annual grant total: In 2009 the charity had assets of £1.1 million and an income of £31,000. Pensions and grants to 34 individuals amounted to £18,000.

Applications: In writing to the correspondent.

Correspondent: Anna Chandler, Freeth Cartwright LLP, 80 Mount Street, Nottingham NG1 6HH (01159 015562; fax: 01158599652; email: anna.chandler@freethcartwright.co.uk)

The Fifty Fund

Eligibility: People in need who live in and around Nottingham.

Types of grants: Payments of about £130 a quarter and one-off grants and loans to help with debts, disability equipment and white goods.

Exclusions: No grants are given for education or sponsorship.

Annual grant total: In 2008 the fund had assets of £5.8 million and an income of £332,000. Grants were made to 104 individuals totalling £65,000 and were distributed as follows:

Payments to beneficiaries	£53,000
Summer gifts	£6,300
Christmas gifts	£5,500

Applications: Applications, in writing to the correspondent, can be submitted either by the individual or through a recognised referral agency (such as a social worker, Citizens Advice or doctor) or other third party. The trustees meet twice a year to consider applications.

Correspondent: Stephen Moore, Nelsons Solicitors, Pennine House, 8 Stanford Street, Nottingham, NG1 7BQ (0115 989 5251)

Other information: Grants are also made to organisations (£209,000 in 2008).

The Charles Wright Gowthorpe Fund & Clergy Augmentation Fund

Eligibility: (i) The Gowthorpe Fund supports widows and other women in need who live within a 12-mile radius of the Market Square, Nottingham.

(ii) The Clergy Augmentation Fund generally supports clergymen within a 10-mile radius of St Peter's Church, Nottingham.

Types of grants: Grants usually of £100, paid once a year in December.

Annual grant total: In 2008/09 the Gowthorpe Fund had an income of £7,100 and a total expenditure of £8,700. In the same year, the Clergy Augmentation Fund had an income of £3,600 and a total expenditure of £7,400.

Applications: On a form available from local Church of England vicars, to be returned by the end of October. Do not write to the correspondent initially; only send the application form once it has been completed.

Correspondent: Geoff Gleeson, Lloyds TSB Private Banking Ltd, UK Trust Centre, 22–26 Ock Street, Abingdon, Oxfordshire OX14 5SW (01235 232761)

The John William Lamb Charity

Eligibility: People in need who have been living for at least one year within the city of Nottingham, or within 20 miles of the Nottingham Exchange.

Types of grants: Annuities of around £130 a quarter.

Annual grant total: In 2008/09 the trust had assets of £694,000, which generated an income of £37,000. Annuities were made totalling £17,000.

Applications: In writing to the correspondent. Applicants will be visited by a member of the trust.

Correspondent: The Trustees, Cooper Parry, 14 Park Row, Nottingham NG1 6GR (0115 958 0212; fax: 0115 958 8800)

Manor House Charitable Trust (incorporating The Charity of Lily Taylor)

Eligibility: People in need, principally those who live in Nottinghamshire. For The Charity of Lily Taylor, applicants must live within 15 miles of the Market Place, Nottingham.

Types of grants: One-off grants in the range of £50 to £250.

Annual grant total: In 2008/09 the trust had assets of £539,000 and an income of £29,000. Grants were made to 87 individuals totalling £10,000.

Applications: In writing to the correspondent, to be submitted by a social worker, Citizens Advice or other welfare agency. Applications must be supported by a sponsoring organisation or they will not be considered.

Correspondent: W F Whysall, Berrymen Shacklock, Park House, Friar Lane, Nottingham, NG1 6DN (0115 945 3700)

Other information: The trust also makes grants to organisations (£12,000 in 2008/09).

The New Appeals Organisation for the City & County of Nottingham

Eligibility: People in need who live in the city and county of Nottingham.

Types of grants: One-off grants ranging from £50 to £2,000 to meet needs which cannot be met from any other source. For example, wheelchairs, white goods, flooring, beds and bedding, rise/recliner chairs, adapted vehicles, holidays, computers and other electrical goods. Much of the money is raised for specific projects or people.

Exclusions: The trust does not usually help with debt arrears, building works, wages or educational costs.

Annual grant total: In 2008/09 the organisation had assets of £65,000 and an income of £58,000. There were 89 grants made to individuals totalling £25,000.

Applications: On a form available from the correspondent. Applications should ideally be made through a social worker, Citizens Advice, medical establishment or other welfare agency, although those submitted directly by the individual are considered. Applications are considered on the first Monday of each month.

Correspondent: Phil Everett, Joint Chairman, 4 Rise Court, Hamilton Road, Nottingham NG5 1EU (0115 960 9644 (answering service); email: enquiries@newappeals.org.uk; website: www.newappeals.org)

Other information: The trust has a 'library of equipment' for adults and children including electric scooters, sports wheelchairs and computers.

The Nottingham Annuity Charity

Eligibility: People in need who live in Nottinghamshire. Preference is given to widows and unmarried women.

Types of grants: Regular yearly allowances of about £200 (paid in quarterly grants).

Annual grant total: In 2008/09 the charity had an income of £13,000 and a total expenditure of £11,000. Grants were made totalling about £10,000.

Applications: On a form available from the correspondent to be submitted either directly by the individual or via an appropriate third party such as a social worker, Citizens Advice or other welfare agency. Applications are usually considered quarterly.

Correspondent: Tim Ward, c/o Nottingham Community Housing Association, Property Management Services, 12–14 Pelham Road, Sherwood Rise, Nottingham NG5 1AP (0115 8443420)

The Nottingham Children's Welfare Fund

Eligibility: Children under 18, with priority given to young children, who live in Nottinghamshire especially in Nottingham and especially those who have lost either or both of their parents.

Types of grants: One-off grants of around £50 to £75. Recent awards have been made for domestic appliances, furniture, furnishings, clothing, toys and contributions to school trips and family holidays.

Annual grant total: About £1,800.

Applications: On a form available from the correspondent: to be submitted by social services, the probation service or another welfare agency or third party such as a teacher. Applications are usually considered four times a year.

Correspondent: Gwen Derry, 37 Main Road, Wilford, Nottingham NG11 7AP (0115 981 1830)

The Nottingham General Dispensary

Eligibility: People who are in poor health, convalescent or who have disabilities and live in the county of Nottinghamshire.

Types of grants: One-off grants ranging from £20 to £1,000 are given for a variety of needs including, home adaptations, mobility equipment, medical aids, hospital travel costs, computer equipment, holidays and respite breaks.

Exclusions: No grants are given where funds are available from statutory sources. No recurrent grants are made.

Annual grant total: In 2008/09 the trust had assets of £970,000 and an income of £55,000. Grants were made to over 60 individuals totalling £20,000.

Applications: In writing to the correspondent through a social worker, Citizens Advice, other welfare agency or a professional, for example a doctor or teacher. Individuals can apply directly, but they must include supportive medical evidence with their application. Applications are considered all year round.

Correspondent: Nigel Cullen, Cumberland Court, 80 Mount Street, Nottingham NG1 6HH (0115 901 5558)

Nottingham Gordon Memorial Trust for Boys & Girls

Eligibility: Children and young people aged up to 25 who are in need and who live in Nottingham and the area immediately around the city.

Types of grants: One-off grants are made for needs such as clothing, bedding, electrical goods, basic equipment for people who are disabled, family holidays and educational courses.

Annual grant total: About £40,000 a year, mostly for relief-in-need purposes. Around £3,000 per year is given in educational grants.

Applications: On a form available from the correspondent to be submitted through the individual's school, college, educational welfare agency, health visitor, social worker or probation officer. Individuals, supported by a reference from their school/college, can also apply directly. Applications are considered all year round.

Correspondent: Mrs Colleen Douglas, Cumberland Court, 80 Mount Street, Nottingham NG1 6HH

Other information: The trust also supports organisations in the Nottingham area.

Nottinghamshire County Council Fund for Disabled People

Eligibility: People who are disabled, live in Nottinghamshire and are in need. This does not include residents of the city of Nottingham.

The fund also gives to voluntary groups working with people with disabilities.

Types of grants: Grants are available at set amounts per piece of equipment, as follows:

- Electric scooter £500
- Electric wheelchair £500
- Riser-recliner chair £600
- High-backed chair £350
- Electric profiling bed £400
- Orthopaedic bed £350
- Computer equipment £350
- Dropped kerbs £250 (please note, these can only be funded after all other sources of funding have been pursued)

Exclusions: The fund does not make grants for: driving lessons, car purchase or mobility deposits; stair lifts; decorating, house repairs and general maintenance costs; showers; items available elsewhere, for example from social security or NHS or leisure service departments; or medical equipment.

Successful applicants cannot reapply for the next three years.

No retrospective grants are made.

Annual grant total: Grants usually total around £45,000 each year.

Applications: On a form available from the correspondent. Applications can be submitted either through a social worker, Citizens Advice, other welfare agency or a relative or friend; or directly by the individual. Letters of support are required from professionals, for example a doctor, social worker or occupational therapist. People applying for electric scooters/ electric wheelchairs or riser-recliner chairs (over 65s only) are required to have an assessment carried out at the Disabilities Living Centre (Middleton Court, Glaisdale Parkway, Glaisdale Drive West, Bilborough, Nottingham NG8 4GP). Meetings are held on a six-weekly basis.

Correspondent: Miss Janet Lowe, Accounting Services, Policy and Resources Department, County Hall, West Bridgford, Nottingham NG2 7QP (0115 977 3662; email: customerservice.centre@nottscc.gov. uk; website: www.nottinghamshire.gov.uk)

Other information: 'The Disability Discrimination Act 1995 defines a disabled person as someone who has a disability i.e. "a physical or mental impairment which has a substantial and long-term adverse effect on his/her ability to carry out normal day-to-day activities". This includes people with sensory impairments and learning disabilities, as well as people with physical impairments. It does not include any impairment resulting from or consisting of a mental illness, unless that illness is clinically well-recognised.'

The Nottinghamshire Miners' Welfare Trust Fund

Eligibility: Members of the mining community in Nottinghamshire who are in need, and their dependants.

Types of grants: One-off and recurrent grants are given to improve health and living conditions. Recent grants have been given for bathroom alterations, mortgage repayments, stair lifts, wheelchairs, scooters, beds and bedding, furniture and replacement boilers. Holiday grants of £100 to £250 are also available.

Annual grant total: In 2009 the fund had assets of £2.4 million and an income of £74,000. Grants were made totalling £84,000 and were distributed as follows:

Personal welfare and hardship grants	£58,000
Holiday grants	£9,000
Grants to organisations	£17,000

Applications: On a form available from the correspondent, to be submitted directly by the individual or through a third party such as the Coal Industry Social Welfare Organisation (CISWO), a Citizens Advice, social worker or similar welfare organisation. Applications are considered regularly throughout the year.

Correspondent: D A Brookes, Welfare Offices, Berry Hill Lane, Mansfield, Nottinghamshire NG18 4JR (01623 625767)

The Perry Trust Gift Fund

Eligibility: In order of preference: (a) people in need who have lived in the city of Nottingham for at least five years; (b) people in need who have lived in Nottinghamshire for at least five years. Grants are mainly given to older people with low incomes but some help is also available to younger people in need.

Types of grants: One-off grants up to £200 towards, for example, electric bills, clothing, living costs, household bills, food, furniture, disabled equipment and help in the home.

Annual grant total: In 2008/09 the fund had an income of £17,000 and a total expenditure of £14,000.

Applications: On a form available from the correspondent. Applications can be made through a third party such as a social worker, Citizens Advice or other welfare agency. They are considered in May and November.

Correspondent: Anna Chandler, c/o Freeth Cartwright LLP, Cumberland Court, 80 Mount Street, Nottingham NG1 6HH (0115 901 5562)

The Puri Foundation

Eligibility: Individuals in need living in Nottinghamshire who are from India (particularly the towns of Mullan Pur near Chandigarh and Ambala). Employees/past employees of the Melton Medes Group Ltd, Blugilt Holdings or Melham Inc and their dependants, who are in need, are also eligible

The trust wants to support people who have exhausted state support and other avenues, in other words to be a 'last resort'.

Types of grants: One-off and recurrent grants according to need, for items such as furniture or clothes. The maximum donation is usually between £150 and £200.

Annual grant total: In 2008/09 the foundation had assets of £2.8 million and an income of £979,000. Grants mostly to organisations totalled approximately £730,000.

Applications: In writing to the correspondent, either directly by the individual or through a social worker.

Correspondent: Nathu Ram Puri, Environment House, 6 Union Road, Nottingham NG3 1FH (0115 901 3000)

The Skerritt Trust *see entry on page 35*

The West Gate Benevolent Trust

Eligibility: People in need who live in Nottinghamshire.

Types of grants: One-off grants ranging from £50 to £5,000 for household essentials, such as washing machines; holidays; and travel to visit relations in hospital.

Annual grant total: In 2008/09 the trust had assets of £116 and an income of £70,000, almost all of which was given in grants.

Applications: Through a third party such as a social worker or Citizens Advice. Applications directly by the individual cannot be considered.

Correspondent: Stephen Carey, Secretary, 17 Storcroft Road, Retford, Nottinghamshire DN22 7EG (01777 707677)

Balderton

The Balderton Parochial Charity

Eligibility: People in need who live in the parish of Balderton.

Types of grants: One-off grants according to need. Recent grants have been given for cookers, electric wheelchairs, cycle trailers and garden alterations.

Exclusions: No donations for the relief of rates, taxes, fines or other public funds.

Annual grant total: In 2009/10 the charity had an income of £3,000 and a total expenditure of £7,800. Grants are given to both individuals and organisations.

Applications: In writing to the correspondent either directly by the individual or through a social worker, Citizens Advice or other welfare agency. Applications are considered at any time.

Correspondent: P C Holland, 8 Meadow Road, New Balderton, Newark, Nottinghamshire NG24 3BP (01636 682083; email: p.c.holland@ ntlworld.com)

Bingham

The Bingham Trust Scheme

Eligibility: People under the age of 21 living in Bingham.

Types of grants: Grants in the range of £50 and £150 to help with expenses incurred in the course of education, religious and physical welfare and so on. They are made in January and early July each year.

Annual grant total: In 2008/09 the scheme had an income of £1,700 and a total expenditure of £2,000.

Applications: Application forms are available from: Mrs R Pingula, 74

Nottingham Road, Bingham, Nottinghamshire NG13 8AW. They can be submitted directly by the individual or a family member by 30 April and 31 October each year.

Correspondent: Gillian M Bailey, 20 Tithby Road, Bingham, Nottingham NG13 8GN (01949 838673)

Bingham United Charities

Eligibility: People in need who live in the parish of Bingham.

Types of grants: One-off grants in the range of £50 to £600. Grants given have included those towards: Christmas gifts for a struggling family; carpets for a recently rehabilitated man; respite care; and visiting expenses for local clergy members.

Exclusions: Grants are not given to the same person twice.

Annual grant total: In 2008/09 the trust had an income of £8,700 and a total expenditure of £6,500.

Applications: In writing to the correspondent, preferably directly by the individual; alternatively, they can be submitted through a social worker, Citizens Advice or other welfare agency. Applications are considered on the second Tuesday in alternate months, commencing in May. Details of the purpose of the grant and other grants being sought should be included.

Correspondent: Claire Pegg, c/o Bingham Town Council, The Old Court House, Church Street, Bingham, Nottinghamshire NG13 8AL (01949 831445)

Other information: Grants are also given to organisations and individuals for educational purposes.

Carlton in Lindrick

The Christopher Johnson & the Green Charity

Eligibility: People in need who live in the village of Carlton in Lindrick.

Types of grants: One-off grants according to need.

Annual grant total: Grants usually total about £2,000 each year and are given for educational and welfare purposes.

Applications: In writing to the correspondent either directly by the individual, via a third party such as a social worker, doctor or district nurse or through a Citizens Advice or other welfare agency. Applications are considered throughout the year.

Correspondent: C E R Towle, Hon. Secretary and Treasurer, 135 Windsor Road, Carlton in Lindrick, Worksop, Nottinghamshire S81 9DH (01909 731069; email: 1cert@tiscali.co.uk)

Coddington

The Coddington United Charities

Eligibility: People in need who live in the parish of Coddington.

Types of grants: One-off grants for individuals resident in the charity's almshouses and general relief in need.

Annual grant total: In 2009 the charities had an income of £22,000 and a total expenditure of £26,000.

Applications: In writing to the correspondent. Applications can be submitted at any time, either through a third party such as a social worker or Citizens Advice or directly by the individual.

Correspondent: A Morrison, Clerk to the Trustees, Alasdair Morrison and Partners, 26 Kirkgate, Newark, Nottinghamshire NG24 1AB (01636 700888; fax: 01636 700885)

Farndon

The Farndon Relief-in-Need Charity

Eligibility: People in need who live in the parish of Farndon.

Types of grants: One-off grants, Christmas hampers and clothing vouchers.

Annual grant total: About £1,200 a year. Grants are given to both individuals and organisations.

Applications: In writing to the correspondent directly by the individual or through a third party such as Citizens Advice or a social worker. The trustees meet twice a year, usually in May and October. Emergency applications can be considered at other times.

Correspondent: L G Aslin, Trustee, 1 Village Close, Farndon, Newark, Nottinghamshire, NG24 4SY (01636 705798)

Gotham

Doctor M A Gerrard's Gotham Old People's Benevolent Fund

Eligibility: Older people in need who live, or have lived, in the parish of Gotham.

Types of grants: One-off grants according to need. Gifts in kind are also available.

Annual grant total: Grants usually total around £500 per year.

Applications: In writing to the correspondent, submitted directly by the individual or via a third party such as a social worker.

Correspondent: Ms J Raven, The Old Rectory, 33 Leake Road, Gotham, Nottingham NG11 0HW (0115 983 0863)

Other information: The fund also makes grants to organisations.

Hucknall

The Hucknall Relief-in-Need Charity

Eligibility: People in need who live in Hucknall, with a preference for 'poor householders'.

Types of grants: One-off and recurrent grants according to need.

Exclusions: No grants for the relief of rates, taxes or other public funds.

Annual grant total: About £1,000.

Applications: In writing to the correspondent at any time. Individuals should apply through a social worker, minister of religion or similar third party.

Correspondent: Kenneth Creed, 67 Glendon Drive, Hucknall, Nottingham, NG15 6DF (0115 963 5929)

Long Bennington and Foston

Long Bennington Charities

Eligibility: People in need who live in the parish of Long Bennington.

Types of grants: One-off grants according to need. Recent grants have been given for garden maintenance and disability aids like wheelchairs and ramps.

Annual grant total: In 2009 the charity had an income of £6,200 and a total expenditure of £4,200.

Applications: In writing to the correspondent directly by the individual or through a third party.

Correspondent: Mrs G Baggaley, Trustee, 6 Lilley Street, Long Bennington, Newark, Nottinghamshire NG23 5EJ (01400 281364)

Mansfield

The Brunts Charity

Eligibility: Older people over 60 who are in need and have lived in the former borough of Mansfield (as constituted in 1958) for at least five years.

Types of grants: Regular allowances in the form of small pensions. Christmas gifts are also available.

Annual grant total: In 2008/09 the charity had assets of £11 million and an income of £608,000. During the year £740 was given in pensions and £2,700 in welfare grants.

Applications: On a form available from the correspondent to be submitted directly by the individual. Applications are considered regularly.

Correspondent: K F Williams, Brunts Chambers, 2 Toothill Lane, Mansfield, Notts NG18 1NJ (01623 623055)

Other information: The charity's main concern is the provision of almshouses for elderly residents in financial difficulty. It also makes grants to local organisations.

Newark

The Mary Elizabeth Siebel Charity

Eligibility: People over 60 years of age who are in poor health and live within a 12 mile radius of Newark Town Hall.

Types of grants: One-off grants ranging from £50 to £2,500. The trust aims to enable individual applicants to live in their own homes e.g. help with the cost of stairlifts, essential home repairs, aids for disabled people, care at home, relief for carers and so on.

Annual grant total: In 2008/09 the trust had assets of £2.3 million, an income of £137,000 and a total expenditure of £121,000. Grants were made to 67 individuals totalling £63,000. A further £18,000 was given in two organisational grants.

Applications: On a form available from the correspondent. Applications can be submitted at anytime but must be endorsed by a recognised third party such as a doctor or social worker. Individuals are usually visited by the charity's assessor who will then make a recommendation to the trustees. The trustees meet every two months to consider applications.

Correspondent: Frances Kelly, Tallents Solicitors, 3 Middlegate, Newark, Nottinghamshire NG24 1AQ (01636 671881; fax: 01636 700148; email: frances.kelly@tallents.co.uk)

Nottingham

Bilby's and Cooper's Relief in Need Charity

Eligibility: People in need who live in the city of Nottingham.

Types of grants: One-off grants ranging from £50 to £200.

Annual grant total: About £500.

Applications: In writing to the correspondent either through a social worker, Citizens Advice or other welfare agency, or directly by the individual. Applications are considered at any time.

Correspondent: The Trustees, Smith Cooper, Haydn House, 309–329 Haydn

Road, Sherwood, Nottingham NG5 1HG (0115 960 7111; fax: 0115 969 1313)

The Frank Hodson Foundation Ltd

Eligibility: People who live in one of the trust's properties and are in need.

Types of grants: Small grants and other benefits to residents.

Exclusions: The foundation does not provide grants for lifts nor for any nursing or warden-aided assistance.

Annual grant total: In 2008/09 the trust had assets of £6.2 million and an income of £272,000. 'Gifts to residents' totalled £1,600.

Applications: On a form available from the correspondent, submitted directly by the individual. Applications should be sent to Mrs E Ellis, 9 Old Hall Drive, Mapperly Park, Nottingham NG3 5EZ.

Correspondent: Sidney J Christophers, Trustee, 12 Killerton Park Drive, West Bridgford, Nottingham NG2 7SB (0115 984 5377)

Other information: The trust provides rent free accommodation for people over 60 years old.

The Nottingham Aged Persons' Trust

Eligibility: People in need, over 60 years of age, who live in the city of Nottingham and are in receipt of, or eligible for, the state retirement pension.

Types of grants: One-off grants ranging from £15 to £200 towards, for example, travel expenses to visit sick or older relatives; help for victims of crime; medical items; household costs.

Exclusions: Only one award per year will be made to any individual who makes a successful application.

Annual grant total: There has been no expenditure by this fund since 2007, although it still has an income of around £1,500. Previously total expenditure was around £200.

Applications: On a form available from the correspondent. Applications can be submitted directly by the individual or family member. There are no deadlines.

Correspondent: Vicky Richards, Nottingham City Council, Single Gateway Unit, Communities Courtyard, Wollaton Annex, Wollaton Road, Nottingham NG8 2AD (0115 8762179)

The Thorpe Trust

Eligibility: Widows and spinsters in need who live within a mile radius of Nottingham city centre. The recipients must be the widows or fatherless daughters of clergymen, gentlemen or professional people or of people engaged (otherwise than in a menial capacity) in trade or agriculture.

Types of grants: Recurrent grants according to need.

Annual grant total: In 2008/09 the trust had an income of £21,000 and a total expenditure of £19,000.

Applications: On a form available from the correspondent. Applications can be submitted directly by the individual or through a social worker, Citizens Advice or other welfare agency. They are considered once during the summer and at Christmas.

Correspondent: Mrs Mandy Kelly, Actons Solicitors, 20 Regent Street, Nottingham, NG1 5BQ (email: mandy.kelly@actons.co.uk)

Warsop

The Warsop United Charities

Eligibility: People in need who live in the urban district of Warsop (Warsop, Church Warsop, Warsop Vale, Meden Vale, Spion Kop and Skoonholme).

Types of grants: One-off grants for necessities and quarterly grants to about 60 individuals.

Annual grant total: Previously about £5,000.

Applications: In writing to the correspondent. Trustees meet three or four times a year.

Correspondent: Mrs J R Simmons, Newquay, Clumber Street, Warsop, Mansfield, Nottinghamshire, NG20 0LX

Other information: Grants are also made for educational purposes.

Shropshire

The Atherton Trust

Eligibility: People who are widowed, orphaned, sick, have disabilities or are otherwise in need and live in the parishes of Pontesbury and Hanwood and the villages of Annscroft and Hook-a-Gate in the county of Shropshire.

Types of grants: One-off and recurrent grants according to need.

Annual grant total: In 2008/09 the trust had an income of £20,000 and a total expenditure of £6,000. Generally the trust gives around £900 annually to individuals for welfare purposes.

Applications: On a form available from the correspondent, to be submitted directly by the individual. Applications are considered in February, May, August and November.

Correspondent: Richard Thornhill Tudor, Whittingham Riddell LLP, Belmont House, Shrewsbury Business Park, Shrewsbury SY2 6LG (01743 273273; email: rtt@whittinghamriddell.co.uk)

Other information: The trust also supports institutions that give support and services to people who need aid due to loss of sight, limb or health by accident or inevitable causes.

The Ellen Barnes Charitable Trust

Eligibility: People in need who live in Weston Rhyn and adjoining parishes.

Types of grants: Although the trust's income is mainly used to run six almshouses, one-off grants are considered.

Annual grant total: In 2009 the trust had both an income and a total expenditure of £20,000. Grants were made totalling about £5,000.

Applications: In writing to the correspondent either directly by the individual or through a social worker, Citizens Advice, doctor or other welfare agency. Applications are considered throughout the year.

Correspondent: Mark Haddon Woodward, Crampton Pym & Lewis, 47 Willow Street, Oswestry, Shropshire SY11 1PR (01691 653301; fax: 01691 658699; email: info@crampton-pym-lewis.co.uk; website: www.crampton-pym-lewis.co.uk/)

The Lady Forester Trust

Eligibility: Firstly, people who live in the ancient Borough of Wenlock and then to the inhabitants of the county of Shropshire who are sick, disabled, convalescent or infirm.

Types of grants: One-off grants for medical equipment, nursing care, travel to and from hospitals and other medical needs not otherwise available on the NHS.

Exclusions: No retrospective grants are made, nor are grants given for building repairs/alterations, home/garden improvements or household bills.

Annual grant total: In 2008 the trust had assets of £3.4 million and an income of £161,000. Grants to 54 individuals totalled £23,000.

Applications: On a form available from the correspondent. Applications should be made through a doctor (or social services in exceptional circumstances) and are considered on a quarterly basis.

Correspondent: The Administrator, Willey Park, Broseley, Shropshire TF12 5JJ (01952 882146; fax: 01952 883680; email: ladyforesttrust@willeyestates.co.uk)

Other information: The trust also gives to local charities whenever possible.

Dr Gardner's Charity for Sick Nurses

Eligibility: Nurses in need who live in Shropshire.

Types of grants: One-off grants, usually of up to about £300, to help sick nurses to convalesce or to have further help to enable them to return to work. Grants are made to individuals and organisations.

Annual grant total: Grants average around £1,000 per year.

Applications: On a form available from the correspondent. Applications can be submitted at any time either through a social worker, Citizens Advice or other welfare agency, or directly by the individual or a relevant third party.

Correspondent: Dr L F Hill, Radbrook Stables, Radbrook Road, Shrewsbury, SY3 9BQ

Gibbons Charity see entry on page 70

The Basil Houghton Memorial Trust

Eligibility: People with learning disabilities who are in need and live in Shropshire.

Types of grants: One-off grants usually of no more than £250. Grants should be additional to any services provided by statutory bodies.

Annual grant total: In 2008/09 the trust had an income of £13,000 and a total expenditure of £12,000.

Applications: On a form available from the correspondent.

Correspondent: Julia Baron, c/o Community Council Building, The Creative Quarter, Shrewsbury Business Park, Shrewsbury, SY2 6LG (01743 360641; email: houghton.trust@shropshire-rcc.org.uk)

Other information: Grants are also made to organisations.

The Oswestry Dispensary Fund

Eligibility: People who are in poor health and financial difficulties and live in the borough of Oswestry and its surrounding district.

Types of grants: One-off grants, normally up to £300, for items such as medical equipment and care and second-hand television sets.

Annual grant total: Grants usually total about £400 each year.

Applications: In writing to the correspondent either directly by the individual or via a relevant third party such as a social worker, Citizens Advice or other welfare agency.

Correspondent: Emyr Richard Lloyd, Brown and Lloyd, The Albany, 37–39 Willow Street, Oswestry, Shropshire SY11 1AQ (01691 659194)

The Shrewsbury Municipal Charity

Eligibility: People in need who live in the borough of Shrewsbury and Atcham. 60% of the disposable income is for education/training of people under 25 years of age; the balance is for general relief of need.

Types of grants: One-off grants of £50 to £250.

Annual grant total: About £500.

Applications: In writing to the correspondent, either directly by the individual or through a social worker, Citizens Advice, welfare agency or other third party. Applications are considered in January, May, and September, but emergencies can be considered at any time. Please include details of any other charities that have been contacted for assistance.

Correspondent: John Goldsworthy, 21 Eastwood Road, Shrewsbury SY3 8ES

Shrewsbury Staff Welfare Society

Eligibility: Royal Mail employees who work at the Shrewsbury sorting office.

Types of grants: Loans and one-off grants according to need. Recurrent grants may be available for people who are long-term sick.

Annual grant total: About £2,000.

Applications: In writing to the correspondent.

Correspondent: Treasurer, Royal Mail, Shrewsbury Mail Centre, Castle Foregate, Shrewsbury SY1 1AA (01743 277307)

Other information: Recent accounts have not been filed with the Charity Commission.

The Shropshire Football Association Benevolent Fund

Eligibility: People in need who live in Shropshire, who are: (i) amateur and professional footballers; (ii) apprentices; (iii) coaches; (iv) managers; (v) any other official or employee of any football team; (vi) referees and referees' assistants and widows and orphans of other persons dependant wholly or partially on any of the above people who may die or be disadvantaged.

Types of grants: One-off and recurrent grants according to need.

Annual grant total: About £1,000.

Applications: Applications can be submitted at any time and should include details of present income, occupation and any dependants along with any other information which may be helpful.

Correspondent: David Rowe, Chief Executive, New Stadium, Oteley Road, Shrewsbury, Shropshire SY2 6ST (01743 362769; fax: 01743 270494; email: secretary@shropsfa.com)

The Shropshire Welfare Trust

Eligibility: Patients and members of staff in specified hospitals in Shropshire who are in need. People living in Shropshire with medically-related and disability-related expenses may also be eligible for assistance.

Types of grants: One-off grants ranging from £50 to £300 towards: travel from hospitals for poor patients to their homes or elsewhere; linen or other clothing for hospital patients or those who have been discharged; and, medical aids for patients.

Annual grant total: Grants usually total about £1,500 each year.

Applications: On a form available from the correspondent; advice is also available. Applications can be submitted directly by the individual or through a social worker, Citizens Advice or similar third party.

Correspondent: Dr Len Hill, Hon. Secretary, Radbrook Stables, Radbrook Road, Shrewsbury SY3 9BQ (01743 236863; email: dr.lenhill@tiscali.co.uk)

Other information: Occasional grants are given to organisations with similar objects.

The St Chad's and St Alkmund's Charity

Eligibility: People in need who have lived in the ecclesiastical districts of St Chad and St George, Shrewsbury, Astley, Kinnerley, Guildsfield, Great Ness, Annscroft, Oxon and Bicton for not less than five years immediately before their application.

Types of grants: One-off grants of up to £50 to help with the cost of clothes, linen, bedding, tools, medical or other aid in sickness, food or other articles in kind.

Annual grant total: About £1,000.

Applications: On a form available from the correspondent. Applications should be submitted directly by the individual and they are considered at any time.

Correspondent: L E Smith, Little Garth, 3 Roman Road, Shrewsbury SY3 9AZ (01743 353869; email: lawson-smith@tiscali.co.uk)

Other information: The charity also gives support to religious work of the Church of England and to promote education for people under 25.

The Thompson Pritchard Trust

Eligibility: Individuals who live in Shropshire and have medically-related and disability-related expenses and problems. Preference is given to those who have recently been discharged from hospital.

Types of grants: One-off grants up to £300 are given towards: medical equipment (and repairs); convalescent treatment; domestic equipment which affects health such as washing machine or fridge repairs; expenses incurred during illness, including treatment; and travel and occasional accommodation for relatives during major operations.

Exclusions: No recurrent grants or grants towards purchasing, repairing or maintaining buildings or to pay off debts.

Annual grant total: In 2009 the trust had an income of £18,000 and a total expenditure of £19,000.

Applications: On a form available from the correspondent. Applications for small grants can be submitted at any time either directly by the individual or through a relevant third party such as a social worker, Citizens Advice or other welfare agency. Advice is available from the trust.

Correspondent: Dr Len Hill, Radbrook Stables, Radbrook Road, Shrewsbury, SY3 9BQ (01743 236863)

Alveley

The Alveley Charity

Eligibility: People in need who live in the parishes of Alveley and Romsley.

Types of grants: One-off grants according to need.

Annual grant total: In 2008/09 the charity had an income of £19,000 and a total expenditure of £12,000.

Applications: In writing to the correspondent either directly by the individual, or through a social worker, Citizens Advice or other welfare agency.

Correspondent: The Trustees, MFG Solicitors, Carlton House, Worcester Street, Kidderminster DY10 1BA (01562 820181)

Bridgnorth

The Bridgnorth Parish Charity

Eligibility: People living in Bridgnorth parish, including Oldbury and Eardington, who are in need.

Types of grants: One-off grants according to need, including those towards playgroup fees, school visits, funeral expenses and heating costs.

Annual grant total: In 2009 the trust had an income of £7,000 and a total expenditure of £5,000

Applications: In writing to the correspondent either directly by the individual or through a doctor, nurse, member of the local clergy, social worker, Citizens Advice or other welfare agency.

Correspondent: Elizabeth Smallman, Clerk, 37 Stourbridge Road, Bridgnorth, WV15 5AZ (email: eeesmallman@aol.com)

Other information: Grants are also made to organisations.

Clun

The Earl of Northampton's Charity

Eligibility: Preference is given to older people in need who live in Castle Rising and Shotesham in Norfolk, Clun in Shropshire and Greenwich and Tower Hamlets in London.

Types of grants: Pensions of £20 a week.

Annual grant total: In 2008/09 the charity had assets of £19 million and an income of £1.6 million. Grants totalling £9,300 were made to organisations for the purposes of relieving poverty. It appears that no grants were made to individuals during the year.

Applications: On a form available from the correspondent. However, the charity has stated: 'Funds for individual grants are currently fully committed. Therefore, no further applications will be considered for the time being.'

Correspondent: Head of Charity Services, Mercers' Company, Mercers' Hall, Ironmonger Lane, London EC2V 8HE (020 7726 4991; fax: 020 7600 1158; email: mail@mercers.co.uk; website: www.mercers.co.uk)

Other information: The charity's principal object is the administration of almshouses in Greenwich and Shotesham. These properties are currently being redeveloped and significant grantmaking activity is unlikely to take place until the refurbishment has been completed.

Hodnet

The Hodnet Consolidated Eleemosynary Charities

Eligibility: People in need who live in Hodnet parish.

Types of grants: Grants include Christmas parcels for people of pensionable age.

Annual grant total: In 2008/09 the charities had an income of £3,800 and a total expenditure of £3,300. Grants usually total around £2,000.

Applications: In writing to the correspondent for consideration throughout the year. Applications can be submitted directly by the individual or through a social worker, Citizens Advice or other welfare agency.

Correspondent: Mrs S W France, 26 The Meadows, Hodnet, Market Drayton, Shropshire TF9 3QF

Other information: This is essentially a relief-in-need charity that also gives money to students for books.

Hopesay

Hopesay Parish Trust

Eligibility: People in need living in the parish of Hopesay. Priority is given to those under 25 years old.

Types of grants: One-off grants between £25 and £650 according to need.

Exclusions: Grants are not made where the funding is the responsibility of central or local government, whether or not the individual has taken up such provision.

Annual grant total: Grants usually total around £1,000 per year.

Applications: Preferably on an application form, available from the correspondent. The application form covers the essential information required, and the trustees will ask for further details if necessary. Applications can be made at any time, either directly by the individual, or by a third party on their behalf, such as parent/guardian, teacher or social worker, or through an organisation such as Citizens Advice or a school. They can be submitted at any time.

Correspondent: David Evans, Park Farm, The Fish, Hopesay, Craven Arms, Shropshire SY7 8HG (01588 660545)

Other information: The trust gives priority to educational grants. At the trustees' discretion, any surplus income may be applied for any other charitable purposes but only within the parish.

Lilleshall

The Charity of Edith Emily Todd

Eligibility: Pensioners in need who live in the ecclesiastical parish of Lilleshall.

Types of grants: Pensions of £15 a month with a bonus payment of around £30 at Christmas.

Annual grant total: In 2008/09 the charity had an income of £7,000 and a total expenditure of £7,700.

Applications: In writing directly by the individual to the correspondent. Applications are considered on receipt.

Correspondent: Mary Heather Ayres, Kenilworth, 4 Willmoor Lane, Lilleshall, Newport, Shropshire TF10 9EE (01952 606053)

Shrewsbury

The Gorsuch, Langley & Prynce Charity

Eligibility: People in need who live in the parishes of Holy Cross (the Abbey) and St Giles in Shrewsbury.

Types of grants: One-off and recurrent grants ranging from £50 to £500. Recent grants have been given towards furniture, carpets, washing machines, cookers, fridges, baby clothes and cots.

Annual grant total: In 2009 the charity had assets of £827,000 and an income of £37,000. Grants were made to 155 individuals totalling £34,000.

Applications: In writing to the correspondent through a social worker, healthcare professional, Citizens Advice or other welfare agency such as Homestart. Applications should include details of the full the amount required and why it is needed. They are considered on a regular basis.

Correspondent: Pamela Moseley, 116 Underdale Road, Shrewsbury SY2 5EF

Staffordshire

Albrighton Relief in Need Charity

Eligibility: People in need who live in the parishes of Albrighton and Boningale.

Types of grants: One-off grants according to need. Recent grants have been made for clothing, electrical goods, food, holidays, travel expenses, specialised computers, furniture and medical and disability equipment. Christmas hampers are also distributed.

Annual grant total: Grants average around £1,500 a year, though the actual grant figure tends to fluctuate quite widely.

Applications: In writing to the correspondent either directly by the individual or through a third party such as a social worker, Citizens Advice, GP, district nurse or health visitor.

Correspondent: David Beechey, 34 Station Road, Albrighton, Wolverhampton WV7 3QG (01902 372779; email: dabeechey@blueyonder.co.uk)

The Burton on Trent Nursing Endowment Fund

Eligibility: People in need who live in the former county borough of Burton-on-Trent.

Types of grants: One-off grants towards, for example, chiropody treatment, bedding, removal costs, electric scooter batteries, fridges, freezers and childcare provision.

Annual grant total: Grants to individuals average around £3,000 per year.

Applications: On a form available from the correspondent. Applications can come directly via the individual or through a recognised referral agency (social worker, Citizens Advice, local GP and so on).

Correspondent: Marilyn Arnold, Community Action & Support – East, Voluntary Services Centre, Union Street, Burton-On-Trent, DE14 1AA (01283 543414)

Other information: The fund also makes grants to organisations.

Consolidated Charity of Burton-upon-Trent

Eligibility: People in need who live in the former county of Burton upon Trent or the parishes of Branston, Stretton or Outwoods.

Types of grants: One-off grants of up to £1,000 (£250 for applicants who have been living in the area for less than two years) for essential items such as cookers, fridge-freezers, washing machines, carpets, furniture, bedding, mobility aids and children's clothing.

Exclusions: Grants are not awarded for the relief of debt. Only one item per applicant.

Annual grant total: In 2009 the trust had assets of £10 million and an income of £437,000. The trust gave £48,000 in 156 grants to individuals for relief-in-need purposes

Applications: On a form available from the correspondent, supported by evidence of income and outgoings, quotes from recommended suppliers and a letter of support from an appropriate welfare agency. Applications can be made at any time.

Correspondent: Thomas J Bramall, Clerk, Talbot & Co, 148 High Street, Burton upon Trent, Staffordshire DE14 1JY (01283 564716; email: consolidatedcharity@talbotandco. freeserve.co.uk)

Other information: The trust also makes grants to local organisations and to individuals for educational purposes.

The Baron Davenport Emergency Grant (North Staffordshire)

Eligibility: Women (widows, singles and divorcees) who have lived in North Staffordshire for at least 10 years and are over the age of 60. Applicants must live alone and have a household income of less than £164 and no more than £5,000 in savings.

Types of grants: One-off grants for emergencies only.

Annual grant total: Grants usually total about £5,000 a year.

Applications: On a form available from the correspondent. Applications are considered upon receipt.

Correspondent: Information and Advice Service, c/o Age UK, 83–85 Trinity Street, Hanley, Stoke-on-Trent ST1 5NA (01782 204995)

Other information: For information on Baron Davenport's Charity Trust, see entry in the Midlands general section.

The Baron Davenport's Charity Trust Emergency Fund

Eligibility: Women over 60 who are widowed, unmarried or divorced and have lived in the midlands for at least 10 years. Exceptions may be made for younger widows who are in financial need. Applicants must live alone (except for school age children), have an income of less than £148 a week and savings of less than £3,500. Applicants must not be in receipt of attendance allowance, higher rate disability living allowance or mobility allowance (including car allowance).

Types of grants: One-off grants up to about £200 for emergencies only.

Annual grant total: Grants usually total about £1,000 each year.

Applications: On a form available from the correspondent. Applications can be submitted directly by the individual or through a social worker, Citizens Advice or other welfare agency. The applicant must have a bank, building society or post office account into which to pay a cheque.

Correspondent: Marilyn Arnold, Voluntary Services Centre, Union Street, Burton upon Trent, Staffordshire DE14 1AA (01283 543414; fax: 01283 536168; email: marilyn@cases-vol.org.uk)

Other information: For information on Baron Davenport's Charity Trust, see entry in the Midlands general section.

The Heath Memorial Trust Fund

Eligibility: Primarily older people who live in North Staffordshire.

Types of grants: One-off grants are available for recuperative holidays/convalescence only. Christmas vouchers, for which applications should not be submitted, are also distributed by trustees to eligible people.

Annual grant total: Grants usually total about £2,000 each year.

Applications: On a form available from the correspondent and countersigned by a trustee, local councillor, health visitor, social worker or doctor. Applications are considered throughout the year.

Correspondent: Mrs Lynn Thorley, Business Management Unit, Corporate Resources Department, PO Box 632, Swann House, Boothen Road, Stoke-on-Trent ST4 4UJ (01782 232 655)

The Fred Linford Charitable Trust

Eligibility: People who live in the south Staffordshire area and are in need.

Types of grants: One-off and recurrent grants according to need.

Annual grant total: There has been no expenditure by this trust in 2008/09. Previously grants have totalled around £7,000.

Applications: In writing to the correspondent.

Correspondent: David Linford, Trustee, The Kennels, Stockings Lane, Upper Longdon, Rugeley, Staffordshire WS15 1QF (01543 491230)

The Edward Malam Convalescent Fund

Eligibility: Adults in need, who live in Stoke-on-Trent, are in receipt of benefits and need a holiday as part of their convalescence.

Types of grants: One-off grants to contribute towards the cost of recuperative holidays.

Annual grant total: Grants usually total about £1,000 each year.

Applications: On a form available from the correspondent. Applications are considered throughout the year, however, due to limited finance it is best to apply early in the year.

Correspondent: Lynn Thorley, Business Management Unit, Corporate Resources Department, PO Box 632, Swann House, Stoke-on-Trent ST4 4UJ (01782 232655)

The North Staffordshire Coalfield Miners Relief Fund

Eligibility: Mineworkers or retired mineworkers who worked in the North Staffordshire coalfield (including Cheadle), and their widows or dependants. The mineworker must have suffered an industrial accident or disease or died as a result of their duties.

Types of grants: One-off grants according to need.

Annual grant total: In 2008/09 the trust had an income of £3,500 and a total expenditure of £21,000. Grants were made totalling around £20,000.

Applications: In writing to the correspondent or by telephone either directly by the individual or via a third party such as a social worker, Citizens Advice or other welfare agency. Grants are given after a home visit. Applications are considered throughout the year.

Correspondent: Susan Jackson, c/o Coal Industry Social Welfare Organisation, 142 Queens Road, Penkhull, Stoke-on-Trent, Staffordshire ST4 7LH (01782 744996; fax: 01782 749117)

Other information: Grants are also made to organisations.

The Strasser Foundation

Eligibility: Individuals in need in the local area, with a preference for North Staffordshire.

Types of grants: Usually one-off grants for a specific cause or need, to help with the relief of poverty.

Annual grant total: In 2008/09 the trust had an income of £25,000. Grants were made totalling £24,000, of which about £2,000 was given to individuals for educational and welfare purposes. The remaining £22,000 was awarded to organisations.

Applications: In writing to the correspondent. The trustees meet quarterly. Applications are only acknowledged if an sae is sent.

Correspondent: The Trustees, c/o Knight & Sons, The Brampton, Newcastle-Under-Lyme, Staffordshire ST5 0QW (01782 619225)

Church Eaton

The Church Eaton Relief-in-Need Charity

Eligibility: People in need who live in the parish of Church Eaton.

Types of grants: Payment for, or provision of, items, services or facilities that would reduce the individual's need. Recent grants have been given for TV licences, winter fuel payments and lifeline telephones.

Annual grant total: In 2009 the charity had an income of £9,000 and a total expenditure of £13,000.

Applications: In writing to the correspondent. Applications are considered when received.

Correspondent: Stephen Rutherford, 5 Ashley Court, Church Eaton, Stafford ST20 0BJ (01785 823958)

Enville

The Enville Village Trust

Eligibility: People in need who live in the parish of Enville, with a preference for older people.

Types of grants: One-off grants ranging from £50 to £150. Grants may not always be given directly to individuals; sometimes they may be to provide a service to individuals, which they cannot themselves afford. Grants have been given for telephone installation/connection (including an emergency contact line), emergency medical help, optician bills for partially-sighted people, special dental treatment, travel to hospital, food parcels, clothing and fuel in winter.

Annual grant total: On average this trust has an income of around £2,000 and a total expenditure of between £1,500 and £2,500.

Applications: In writing to the correspondent. Applications can be submitted either directly by the individual or through a social worker, the vicar of the parish church or the village welfare group. They are considered at any time.

Correspondent: J A Gloss, Walls Cottage, Kinver Road, Enville, Stourbridge DY7 5HE (01384 873691)

Leek

The Carr Trust

Eligibility: People in need who live in Leek.

Types of grants: Primarily recurrent grants, usually of around £20 a month towards items, services and facilities that will help to reduce need or hardship. One-off grants are also available and most beneficiaries receive a Christmas bonus.

Annual grant total: In 2008 the trust had assets of £490,000 and an income of £32,000. Grants and pensions were given to 54 individuals totalling £15,000.

Applications: In writing to the correspondent. An advert about the grants appears in a local paper in March each year. The trustees require details of the applicant's age, marital status, income, savings and details of any property owned.

Correspondent: Andrew Burrows, Tinsdills Solicitors, 10 Derby Street, Leek, Staffordshire ST13 5AW (01538 399332; fax: 01538 399180; email: andrew.burrows@tinsdills.co.uk)

Lichfield

The Lichfield Municipal Charities

Eligibility: Individuals in need who live in the city of Lichfield (as it was pre-1974).

Types of grants: One-off grants according to need.

Annual grant total: In 2009 the charity had assets £1.9 million and an income of £65,000. Grants were made to 39 individuals totalling £15,000.

Applications: On a form available from the correspondent. Trustees meet four times a year in March, June, September and December.

Correspondent: Simon R James, Clerk, Ansons Solicitors, St Mary's Chambers, 5 Breadmarket Street, Lichfield, Staffordshire WS13 6LQ (01543 263456; fax: 01543 250942; email: sjames@ansonsllp.com)

Other information: Grants are also made to organisations (£13,000 in 2009).

Michael Lowe's & Associated Charities

Eligibility: People in need who live in the city of Lichfield, particularly older people and those requiring help in an emergency.

Types of grants: One-off grants ranging from £50 to £800 for domestic items, special chairs, school uniforms, wheelchairs and so on. People who are over 70 and living on a low income can also apply for fuel grants.

Annual grant total: In 2008/09 the trust had assets of £1.5 million and an income of £100,000. Grants were made to 233 individuals totalling £49,000 and were distributed as follows:

Individual grants	102	£39,000
Fuel grants	131	£9,800

A further £44,000 was made in grants to organisations.

Applications: On a form available from the correspondent. Applications are considered on their own merits and individuals are usually interviewed before any grant is awarded. The trustees meet on average five times a year to consider grant applications, though special meetings may be called to deal with urgent requests.

Correspondent: C P Kitto, Hinckley Birch & Brown, 20 St John Street, Lichfield, Staffordshire WS13 6PD (01543 262491)

Other information: The trust also operates a 'furniture transfer scheme' whereby families are recommended by local welfare agencies and, depending on their circumstances, invited to choose suitable items from the furniture warehouse.

Newcastle-under-Lyme

The Newcastle-under-Lyme United Charities

Eligibility: People in need who live in the borough of Newcastle-under-Lyme (as it was before 1974).

Types of grants: Christmas grants.

Exclusions: No grants are given to older people living in sheltered housing.

Annual grant total: In 2008/09 the trust had an income of £3,900 and a total expenditure of £3,100.

Applications: In writing to the correspondent. Applications should be submitted either directly by the individual or via a friend or family member. They are considered in October each year. The circumstances of beneficiaries are assessed on an annual basis by trustees.

Correspondent: Caroline Horne, Civic Offices, Merrial Street, Newcastle-Under-Lyme, Staffordshire, ST5 2AG (01782 742232; email: caroline.horne@newcastle-staffs.gov.uk)

Stoke-on-Trent

The Stoke-on-Trent Children's Holiday Trust Fund

Eligibility: Children who live in Stoke-on-Trent and whose parents could not otherwise afford to pay for a recuperative holiday.

Types of grants: One-off grants between £95 and £165 for children only, towards a holiday or day trip.

Exclusions: It is very rare that the trustees will give retrospective grants.

Annual grant total: Grants average about £2,000 per annum.

Applications: On a form available from the correspondent. Applications should be submitted at least six weeks prior to the date of the holiday either by the individual or through a third party.

Correspondent: The Grants Officer, The Staffordshire Community Foundation, The Dudson Centre, Hope Street, Hanley, Stoke-On-Trent ST1 5DD (01782 683 000; email: jean@staffsfoundation.org.uk; website: www.staffsfoundation.org.uk)

Tamworth

Beardsley's Relief-in-Need Charity

Eligibility: People in need who live in the borough of Tamworth.

Types of grants: One-off grants for health and welfare purposes.

Annual grant total: In 2008/09 the charity had an income of £11,000 and a total expenditure of £8,000.

Applications: In writing to the correspondent, either directly by the individual or through a social worker, Citizens Advice or other welfare agency.

Correspondent: Derek Tomkinson, 'Torview', 95 Main Road, Wigginton, Tamworth, Staffordshire B79 9DU (01543 255612)

The Rawlet Trust

Eligibility: People in need who live in the borough of Tamworth.

Types of grants: One-off and recurrent grants towards disability aids, bathroom adaptations, holidays, bibles for children and Home Link telephone expenses.

Annual grant total: In 2008/09 the trust had both an income and a total expenditure of £22,000. Grants were made totalling £20,000, of which £4,600 was given in educational grants and £15,000 in non-educational grants.

Applications: On a form available from the correspondent, to be submitted either directly by the individual or through a

third party such as a social worker or Citizens Advice. The clerk or one of the trustees will follow up applications if any further information is needed. The trustees meet in January, April, July and October to consider applications.

Correspondent: Christine Gilbert, 47 Hedging Lane, Wilnecote, Tamworth B77 5EX (01827 704815; email: christine.gilbert@mail.com)

Other information: Grants are also made to organisations.

The Tamworth Municipal Charity

Eligibility: People in need who live in the borough of Tamworth.

Types of grants: One-off grants towards, for example, equipment, household items and hospital travel costs.

Annual grant total: About £3,000.

Applications: In writing to the correspondent: to be submitted either directly by the individual or through a social worker, Citizens Advice or other welfare agency. Applications should include details of the individual's financial circumstances.

Correspondent: D J Weatherley, Tamworth Borough Council, Marmion House, Lichfield Street, Tamworth, Staffordshire B79 7BZ (01827 709709)

Trentham

The Lady Katherine and Sir Richard Leveson Charity

Eligibility: People in need who live in the ancient parish of Trentham.

Types of grants: One-off and recurrent grants according to need.

Annual grant total: In 2009 the charity had an income of £2,200 and a total expenditure of £3,600.

Applications: In writing to the correspondent either directly by the individual or a relevant third party, or through a social worker, Citizens Advice or other welfare agency. Applications are usually considered in spring and autumn.

Correspondent: Adam Bainbridge, 67 Jonathan Road, Stoke-on-Trent, ST4 8LP

Other information: The charity also makes grants to organisations and to individuals for educational purposes.

The Charity of Edith Emily Todd Deceased

Eligibility: People in need who live in the ecclesiastical parish of St Mary and All Saints, Trentham.

Types of grants: Older people can receive a recurrent grant, which are reviewed twice a year. The trust can also make one-off grants.

Annual grant total: Grants total around £1,500 each year.

Applications: In writing to the correspondent at any time. Applications can be submitted either through a third party such as a social worker, Citizens Advice or other welfare agency, or directly by the individual.

Correspondent: Adam Bainbridge, Clerk to the Trustees, 67 Jonathan Road, Trentham, Stoke-on-Trent ST4 8LP

Tutbury

The Tutbury General Charities

Eligibility: Only people in need who live in the parish of Tutbury.

Types of grants: One-off and recurrent grants according to need. All residents in the parish who are over 70 receive a birthday card and £2 to be spent at a local shop. Vouchers for fuel or goods at a local store (from £5 to £12.50) are also given to about 200 people in need who live within the parish regardless of their age at Christmas.

Special cases are considered on their merits by the trustees but applicants must live in the parish of Tutbury.

Annual grant total: In 2008/09 the charities had an income of £8,300 and a total expenditure of £10,500. Grants are made for welfare and educational purposes.

Applications: The charities have application forms, available from the correspondent, which should be submitted for consideration in November for Christmas vouchers. Inclusion in the birthday voucher scheme can be done at any time (all that is needed is the name, address and date of birth of the person).

Correspondent: Mrs J M Minchin, 66 Redhill Lane, Tutbury, Burton-on-Trent, Staffordshire DE13 9JW (01283 813310)

Other information: The clerk of the trust states that details of the trust are well publicised within the village.

Warwickshire

Sir Edward Boughton Long Lawford Charity

Eligibility: People in need who live in the parish of Long Lawford or Rugby. Applicants for pensions must have lived in the parish for the last five years.

Types of grants: Pensions of £10 a month and Christmas bonuses of £40. One-off

grants are awarded for various welfare purposes, including disability aids, TV licences and stairlifts. Small awards have also been made for swimming classes.

Annual grant total: In 2009 the charity had assets of £1.5 million and an income of £120,000. Grants were made totalling £29,000, of which £18,000 was given in pensions to 113 individuals and £11,000 in 8 one-off grants.

Applications: On a form available from the correspondent, to be considered by the trustees every three months, usually February, May, August and November.

Correspondent: Jean Taylor, 12 Millfields Avenue, Rugby, Warwickshire, CV21 4HJ (01788 571140)

Other information: Grants are also made to local schools and organisations (£62,000 in 2009).

The Baron Davenport Emergency Grant (Leamington Spa, Kenilworth or Warwick)

Eligibility: Widows, single women over 60, and occasionally, young single women who are in need. The children (aged under 25) of these individuals may also qualify for assistance. All beneficiaries must live alone apart from school aged children and have resided in the Midlands for at least five years. The applicant's household income should not be more than £165 a week and savings should amount to no more than £5,000. Applicants must not be in receipt of low/high Rate Attendance Allowance; middle/high rates of Disability Living Allowance; Mobility Allowance (or car allowance).

Types of grants: One-off grants of about £100 can be given for cookers, bath lifts, baby equipment, carpets, telephone extensions, showers, pushchairs and so on.

Annual grant total: About £2,000 each year is available for distribution.

Applications: Applications should be made by letter, including details of status, circumstances, financial situation and a supporting statement from a GP, social worker or similar professional. Grants will only be paid to individuals via the person supporting the applications. Applications from those in the Warwick district should be sent to the correspondent address. Individuals in Birmingham should forward their forms to:

Baron Davenport's Charity
Portman House
5/7 Temple Row West
Birmingham
B2 5NY

Tel: 0121 236 8004

Correspondent: Grants Administrator, c/o WCAVA – Warwick District, 4–6 Clemens, Leamington Spa, Warwickshire CV31 2DL (01926 477512; fax: 01926 315112; email: warwickinfo@wcava.org.uk; website: www.wcava.org.uk)

Other information: For information on Baron Davenport's Charity Trust, see entry in the Midlands general section.

The Baron Davenport Emergency Grant (North Warwickshire)

Eligibility: (i) Widows, unmarried women and divorcees over 50 years old, and women abandoned by their partners; and (ii) children under the age of 25 whose mothers are in the first category, in the borough of North Warwickshire. Applicants must have been resident in the West Midlands for 10–15 years, be living alone (except where school age children are living with their mother) and have a bank, building society or Post Office account.

The total income of the household should be no more than about £141 a week; this figure changes in line with state benefits.

Types of grants: One-off grants of between £150 and £200 for house repairs, furniture, school clothes, bedding, emergencies and so on. Pensions are also given of either £110 or £90 at each half-yearly distribution.

Annual grant total: Grants average around £1,000 a year.

Applications: On an form available from the correspondent. Applications should be submitted through a social worker or welfare agency. They are considered throughout the year.

Correspondent: The Manager, c/o North Warwickshire Citizens Advice Bureau, The Parish Rooms, Welcome Street, Atherstone, Warwickshire CV9 1DU (0844 855 2322; fax: 01827 721944; email: nwcab.advice@cabnet.org.uk)

Other information: For information on Baron Davenport's Charity Trust, see entry in the Midlands general section.

The Baron Davenport Emergency Grant (Nuneaton and Bedworth)

Eligibility: Widows, unmarried women and divorcees aged over 50 and young women abandoned by their partners who are in need and live in Nuneaton and Bedworth.

Types of grants: Small one-off grants for electrical goods, clothing, household bills and furniture.

Annual grant total: Grants usually total about £200 each year.

Applications: On a form available from the correspondent: to be submitted via a social worker, Citizens Advice or similar welfare agency.

Correspondent: Grants Administrator, Warwickshire Community and Voluntary Action – Nuneaton and Bedworth Office, 72 High Street, Nuneaton, Warwickshire CV11 5DA (024 7638 5765;

fax: 024 7637 4891; email: nunbedinfo@ wcava.org.uk)

Other information: For information on Baron Davenport's Charity, see entry in the Midlands general section.

The Baron Davenport Emergency Grant (Warwickshire)

Eligibility: Widows, unmarried women (over 18) and children whose fathers are dead (under 21) who are in need. Applicants should not have savings over £1,000. Applicants must have lived within the old county boundaries of Warwickshire for at least 10 years (this includes Coventry).

Types of grants: One-off grants for emergencies only, particularly unexpected domestic expenses, heavy funeral expenses or similar instances where state benefit is not available or undue delay would cause hardship. Grants are normally between £100 and £200.

Annual grant total: Grants total about £1,000 each year.

Applications: In writing to the correspondent. Applications can be submitted through a social worker, Citizens Advice or other welfare agency; or directly by the individual. They are considered at any time.

Correspondent: Pauline Dye, Coventry Carers Centre, 3 City Arcade, Coventry CV1 3HX (024 7663 2972; email: contactus@coventrycarers.org.uk; website: www.coventrycarers.org.uk)

Other information: For information on Baron Davenport's Charity Trust, see entry in the Midlands general section.

The Hatton Consolidated Charities

Eligibility: People in need who live in the parishes of Hatton, Beausale and Shrewley. Applications from outside these areas will not be considered.

Types of grants: One-off grants usually in the range of £50 to £500.

Exclusions: Grants are not given to schoolchildren.

Annual grant total: In 2008/09 the charities had an income of £10,000 and expenditure of £8,700. Grants are made for both educational and welfare purposes.

Applications: In writing to the trustees or the correspondent.

Correspondent: Mrs M H Sparks, Clerk, Weare Giffard, 32 Shrewley Common, Shrewley, Warwick CV35 7AP (01926 842533)

Other information: Grants are also given to help students and young people starting work to help buy books and tools.

The South Warwickshire Welfare Trust

Eligibility: People who are sick and in need and live in Warwick district and the former rural district of Southam.

Types of grants: One-off grants of £25 to £400 for items, services or facilities to alleviate suffering or assist recovery for people who are sick, convalescent, disabled or infirm. Recent grants have been given towards household goods such as washing machines, carpets, beds and fridges; school uniforms; and towards larger items such as central heating, conditional upon the full amount being raised elsewhere.

Exclusions: Grants are not repeated and are not given for relief of taxes or other public funds.

Annual grant total: In 2009 the trust had an income £9,000 and a total expenditure of £7,500.

Applications: On an application form available from the correspondent to be submitted through a social worker, Citizens Advice or other welfare agency, or through a doctor, church official or similar third party. Applications are considered in January, April, July and October and should be submitted in the preceding months. Details of income/expenditure must be disclosed on the application form.

Correspondent: Mrs V Grimmer, Clerk, 62 Foxes Way, Warwick CV34 6AY (01926 492226)

Warwick Relief in Need Charity

Eligibility: People in need who live in the town of Warwick.

Types of grants: One-off grants of up to £1,000 for washing machines, beds, mattresses, vacuum cleaners, carpets, holidays and so on.

Annual grant total: In 2008 the charity had assets of £2.6 million, an income of £142,000 and a total expenditure of £86,000. Grants were made to 10 individuals totalling £9,900.

Applications: On a form available from the correspondent with a covering letter explaining the nature of the need. Applications are normally submitted through social services or a similar welfare organisation.

Correspondent: Christopher Houghton, c/o Moore & Tibbits Solicitors, 34 High Street, Warwick CV34 4BE (01926 491181; fax: 01926 402692; email: choughton@ moore-tibbits.co.uk)

Other information: Grants are also made to organisations (£54,000 in 2008).

Warwickshire Constabulary Benevolent Fund

Eligibility: Police officers of the Warwickshire Constabulary who regularly subscribe to the fund, retired members

who take on honorary membership, and their immediate dependants.

Types of grants: One-off and recurrent grants and loans of up to £5,000 for individuals in financial difficulty. Help is also given to members attending a police convalescence home to assist with their travel costs and other expenditure.

Annual grant total: About £6,000.

Applications: On a form available from the correspondent to be submitted either directly by the individual or through a work colleague, occupational health department or local NARPO secretary. Applications are considered on a regular basis.

Correspondent: Grants Officer, PO Box 4, Leek Wootton, Warwick, CV35 7QB (01926 415000)

The Warwickshire Miners' Welfare Fund

Eligibility: Mineworkers and former mineworkers who have worked within the coal industry in Warwickshire and their dependants.

Types of grants: One-off grants from £50 to £1,500 towards convalescent holidays, hospital visits to spouse (or applicant), electrical appliances such as cookers and vacuum cleaners, carpets, beds and other furniture, wheelchairs, stairlifts, scooters, and medical reports for industrial diseases.

Exclusions: No death grants or grants to people who have received redundancy pay in the last 10 years. Grants will not be given for any purpose for which the DWP will pay.

Annual grant total: About £15,000 a year.

Applications: In writing to the correspondent. Applications can be submitted directly by the individual or through a social worker, Citizens Advice or other welfare agency or other third party. Applications should include weekly income and medical proof from a doctor (if applicable). They are considered at any time.

Correspondent: David Thomas, CISWO, 142 Queens Road, Stoke-on-Trent ST4 7LH (01782 744996; email: david. thomas@ciswo.org.uk)

Atherstone

The Charity of Priscilla Gent & Others

Eligibility: People in need who live in Atherstone, Warwickshire.

Types of grants: One-off grants ranging from £50 to £250. Grants have included those to clear rent arrears and towards the cost of furniture and bedding, clothes, shoes (particularly for children), heaters and washing machines, travel expenses to hospital and short breaks for poor children and families.

Annual grant total: In 2009 the charity had an income of £5,100 and a total expenditure of £12,000. Grants are given to both individuals and organisations.

Applications: Applications can be submitted in writing by the individual or through a recognised referral agency (e.g. social worker, Citizens Advice or doctor). They are considered in May and November. Emergency applications can be considered at other times.

Correspondent: M L R Harris, Clerk, 42 King Street, Seagrave, Loughborough, Leicestershire LE12 7LY (01509 812366)

Barford

The Barford Relief-in-Need Charity

Eligibility: People in need who live in the parish of Barford.

Types of grants: One-off cash grants and gifts in kind are given towards 'any reasonable need', including hospital expenses, electric goods, convalescence, living costs, household bills, holidays, travel expenses, medical equipment, nursing fees, furniture, disabled equipment and help in the home.

Exclusions: No loans are given.

Annual grant total: Around £8,000.

Applications: In writing to the correspondent, directly by the individual or a family member. Applications are considered upon receipt. One of the trustees will visit to elicit all necessary information. Applications are usually considered in May and October.

Correspondent: Mr and Mrs T Offiler, 14 Dugard, Barford, Warwick, CV35 8DX (01926 624153)

Bedworth

The Henry Smith Charity (Bedworth)

Eligibility: Older people in need who live in Bedworth.

Types of grants: Small Christmas food vouchers to be used at a local shop.

Annual grant total: Grants usually total about £1,000 each year.

Applications: In writing to the correspondent before September, for consideration in December.

Correspondent: Pam Matthews, Democratic Support Services, Nuneaton & Bedworth Borough Council, Town Hall, Coton Road, Nuneaton, Warwickshire CV11 5AA (024 7637 6204)

Other information: This charity is also known as the 'Consolidated Charity of Hammersley, Smith and Orton'.

Bilton & New Bilton

The Bilton Poors' Land & Other Charities

Eligibility: People in need who live in the ancient parish of Bilton (now part of Rugby). Preference is given to older people and those referred by social services.

Types of grants: One-off grants, generally of between £15 and £250.

Annual grant total: In 2008/09 the charity had assets of £399,000 and an income of £34,000. Grants to individuals and organisations totalled £11,000.

Applications: In writing to the correspondent, by the individual or through a third party such as a minister, although often applications are forwarded by social services. They are considered three times a year.

Correspondent: Robin Walls, Trustee, 6 Scotts Close, Rugby, CV22 7QY (01788 810930)

Coleshill

Relief in Need Charity of Simon Lord Digby and Others

Eligibility: People in extreme hardship who live in the parish of Coleshill.

Types of grants: One-off grants according to need. Recent grants have been given to an individual with multiple sclerosis towards the cost of electric reclining/rising chair and to a family of an eight year old with leukaemia for help with extra expenses.

Annual grant total: About £1,000.

Applications: In writing to the correspondent. Applications are usually decided in March and November although decisions can be made more quickly in an emergency. They should be submitted directly by the individual or through a social worker, Citizens Advice or other welfare agency and should give as much detail as possible including information about applications to other organisations/trusts.

Correspondent: Ann Latimer, The Vicarage Office, High Street, Coleshill, Birmingham B46 3BP (01675 462188)

Grandborough

The Grandborough & Sutton Charities

Eligibility: People in need who live in the parish of Grandborough.

Types of grants: Small one-off grants to help with optician's fees, hospital travel expenses and other general needs. Support is also available for older people at Christmas time.

Exclusions: Grants are not given when the need is covered by the state.

Annual grant total: About £700.

Applications: In writing to the correspondent directly by the individual or family member. Applications are considered on an ongoing basis. Evidence of expenditure is required.

Correspondent: Mrs Joy Coling, Manor Farm, Grandborough Fields Road, Grandborough, Rugby, Warwickshire, CV23 8DT (01788 813 825)

Other information: Grants may be given towards educational books for students.

Kenilworth

The Kenilworth Carnival Comforts Fund

Eligibility: People in need who live in Kenilworth.

Types of grants: Mainly one-off grants of £15 per person or £20 per couple, usually in the form of a grocery voucher redeemable at various shops in Kenilworth, hampers of food or bouquets of flowers. About 60 grants are given at Christmas, the rest are given throughout the year. Grants are not made to charities.

Annual grant total: About £1,000.

Applications: In writing to the correspondent. Applications can be submitted directly by the individual or through a social worker, Citizens Advice, other welfare agency or a third party, for example, a friend or relative. They are considered bi-monthly from February.

Correspondent: James A Evans, Treasurer, 7 Queens Road, Kenilworth, Warwickshire CV8 1JQ (01926 859161)

The Kenilworth United Charities

Eligibility: People in need who live in the ancient parish of Kenilworth.

Types of grants: Generally grocery vouchers given to one-parent families. One-off grants have also been made towards white goods.

Annual grant total: Grants have previously totalled around £5,000 a year.

Applications: On a form available from the correspondent. Applications are considered quarterly, although urgent cases will receive special consideration.

Correspondent: The Trustees, Damian J Plant & Co, 29b Warwick Road, Kenilworth, Warwickshire CV8 1HN (01926 857741)

Other information: Recent accounts have not been filed with the Charity Commission.

Leamington Spa

The Leamington Relief-in-Sickness Fund

Eligibility: People suffering from ill-health who live in the former borough of Leamington Spa and the neighbourhood and are in need. People with disabilities or mental health problems are especially welcomed.

Types of grants: One-off grants only from around £25, including help with fuel debts, television licences, baby necessities, food for special diets, fares for visiting hospitals or sick relatives, replacing locks after a burglary, children's clothing, and repairs to washing machines and so on.

Exclusions: Applicants can only receive one grant each year.

Annual grant total: About £2,000.

Applications: In writing through a social worker, Citizens Advice, health visitor, doctor, probation service, Mind or other welfare agency. Applications submitted by individuals will not be acknowledged or considered. Applications are considered throughout the year.

Correspondent: Peter Byrd, Trustee, 2 Oakley Wood Cottages, Banbury Road, Bishops Tachbrook, Leamington Spa, CV33 9QJ (01926 651789; email: peterandsuebyrd@hotmail.com)

Napton-on-the-Hill

The Napton Charities

Eligibility: People in need who live in the parish of Napton-on-the-Hill only.

Types of grants: One-off grants ranging from £30 to £35 mainly towards heating for older people (e.g. gas, electricity, solid fuel) although other applications are considered, including clothing and living costs.

Annual grant total: Grants usually total about £1,000 each year.

Applications: On a form available from the correspondent. Applications can be submitted either directly by the individual or by a relative or friend with the consent of the individual. Proof of having lived in Napton for over a year is required.

Correspondent: Trevor Griffin, 1 Howcombe Lane, Napton-on-the-Hill, Southam, Warwickshire, CV47 8NX

Rugby

The Baron Davenport Emergency Grant (Rugby)

Eligibility: Single women over 60 years old who live alone, have a weekly income of £165 or less and savings of no more than £5,000. Exceptions may be made for younger widows on limited income with school-age children living at home. Applicants must have lived in the Midlands area for at least five years and not be in receipt of Attendance Allowance, Disability Living Allowance or Mobility Allowance (or car allowance).

Types of grants: Recurrent grants of £200 to £230 paid twice a year.

Annual grant total: About £2,000 is usually available for distribution.

Applications: On a form available from the correspondent, preferably submitted through a referring body, such as Age Concern, social services or a Neighbourhood Office.

Recipients receive two grants each year: one at the end of May/beginning of June and another at the end of November/beginning of December. Applications for the spring distribution should be received by 15 March and for the autumn distribution, by 15 September.

Correspondent: Pam Luck, c/o Warwickshire Community and Voluntary Action – Rugby Office, 19–20 North Street, Rugby CV21 2AG (01788 574258; fax: 01788 550786; email: pam@wcava.org.uk; website: www.wcava.org.uk/baron-davenport-trust-rugby-borough)

Other information: For information on Baron Davenport's Charity Trust, see the entry in the Midlands general section.

Rugby Relief in Need Charity

Eligibility: People in need who live in the ancient parish of Rugby, which includes the parishes of St Andrew's and St Matthew's.

Types of grants: One-off grants, usually for people of pensionable age although general relief-in-need grants are also given. Grants are usually paid at Christmas.

Annual grant total: In 2008/09 the charities had an income of £4,000 and a total expenditure of £3,300.

Applications: In writing to the correspondent. Applications are generally considered three or four times a year, although urgent cases can be considered at any time.

Correspondent: Mrs Mary Poxon, Clerk, Parish Office, St Andrew's Church, Rugby, Warwickshire CV21 3PT (01788 565609)

Stratford-upon-Avon

The Stratford-upon-Avon Municipal Charities – Relief in Need

Eligibility: People in need, generally older people, living in the town of Stratford-upon-Avon.

Types of grants: One-off and recurrent grants in the range of £100 and £500 towards essential items of furniture and household equipment (e.g. bed, support chair, cooker, microwave, fridge, freezer, washing machine), mobility aids and unexpected household bills. Educational grants are occasionally given.

Exclusions: No grants for: the repayment of debts; rent and council tax arrears; or, rental deposits.

Annual grant total: About £25,000 a year is given to individuals for educational and welfare purposes.

Applications: On a form available from the correspondent, including details of the financial circumstances of the applicant and parent(s) if appropriate. When applying for financial assistance in connection with a specific health condition, applicants are asked to include a letter from a GP, occupational therapist, social worker or similar professional.

Correspondent: Mrs Ros Dobson, Clerk to the Trustees, 6 Guild Cottages, Church Street, Stratford-upon-Avon, Warwickshire CV37 6HD (01789 293749; email: municharities@btinternet.com; website: www.municipal-charities-stratforduponavon.org.uk/)

Mayor's Fund Society of Stratford-upon-Avon

Eligibility: Older people in need who live in the former borough of Stratford-upon-Avon.

Types of grants: One-off and recurrent grants are usually given in the form of grocery vouchers.

Annual grant total: Grants usually total about £3,000 a year.

Applications: In writing to the correspondent. Applications can be submitted directly by the individual or through a social worker, Citizens Advice, other welfare agency or other third party such as a member of the clergy. They should include a general summary of income, other relief received (for example housing benefits) and financial commitments.

Correspondent: Mrs R Dobson, 155 Evesham Road, Stratford upon Avon, Warwickshire, CV37 9BP (01789 293749; email: themayorsfund@yahoo.com)

Sutton Cheney

Sir William Roberts Relief in Need Charity

Eligibility: People who live in the village of Sutton Cheney and are in need.

Types of grants: One-off grants, usually in the range of £150 to £200, for basic necessities only.

Annual grant total: Grants to individuals generally total around £1,000 a year.

Applications: In writing to the correspondent, or any of the trustees. Applications may be submitted directly by the individual at any time.

Correspondent: Miss D A Read, Secretary, Chatsmoth Cottage, Main Street, Sutton Cheney, Nuneaton, Warwickshire CV13 0AG (01455 291037)

Other information: Grants are also made to organisations based in Sutton Cheney.

Thurlaston

The King Henry VIII Endowed Trust – Warwick

Eligibility: People who live in the old borough of Warwick (CV34 postal district).

Types of grants: One-off grants according to need. Grants to individuals in need are usually made only if a previous application to the Warwick Relief in Need Charity has been unsuccessful.

Annual grant total: In 2008 the trust had assets of £25 million and an income of £1.8 million. Grants were made to 16 individuals totalling £12,000.

Applications: On an application form available from the correspondent or from the trust's website. Though deadline dates are listed in the guidelines found on the trust website, applications can be submitted at any time. These can be submitted directly by the individual, a relevant third party or through a social worker, Citizens Advice or educational welfare agency.

Correspondent: Mr Jonathan Wassall, Clerk & Receiver, 12 High Street, Warwick CV34 4AP (01926 495533; email: jwassall@kinghenryviii.org.uk; website: www.kinghenryviii.org.uk/)

Other information: Grants are also made to organisations.

Thurlaston Poor's Plot Charity

Eligibility: People of pensionable age who are in need and live in Thurlaston.

Types of grants: The charity gives help with the payment of bills.

Annual grant total: About £2,000 a year.

Applications: In writing to the correspondent directly by the individual.

Applications are considered in January, September and November.

Correspondent: Mrs K Owen, Clerk, Congreaves, Main Street, Thurlaston, Rugby CV23 9JS (01788 817466)

Other information: Educational grants are also made to students.

Warwick

The Austin Edwards Charity

Eligibility: People living in the old borough of Warwick.

Types of grants: Grants ranging from £250 to £500 for relief-in-need purposes.

Annual grant total: In 2008/09 the trust had an income of £12,000 and a total expenditure of £8,000.

Applications: In writing to the correspondent. Applications are considered throughout the year.

Correspondent: Mrs Jackie Newton, 26 Mountford Close, Wellesbourne, Warwick CV35 9QQ (01789 840135; website: www.warwickcharities.org.uk/)

The Warwick Provident Dispensary

Eligibility: People in need who are in poor health, convalescent or who have a disability and live in the borough of Warwick.

Types of grants: One-off and recurrent grants according to need.

Annual grant total: In 2009 the trust had both an income and a total expenditure of £21,000. Around £1,500 a year is given in grants to individuals.

Applications: In writing to the correspondent, directly by the individual or through a third party.

Correspondent: Christopher Houghton, Messrs Moore & Tibbits, 34 High Street, Warwick CV34 4BE (01926 491181; email: choughton@moore-tibbits.co.uk)

Other information: The trust also makes grants to organisations.

West Midlands

The Avon Trust

Eligibility: Retired Methodist ministers and their dependants with some preference for those living in the West Midlands, and people in residential homes who live in the West Midlands.

Types of grants: One-off and recurrent grants according to need.

Annual grant total: In 2009/10 the trust had an income of £10,000 and a total expenditure of £4,600.

Applications: In writing to the correspondent. The trustees meet once a year in July but can consider applications at other times.

Correspondent: Andrew Cashmore, Trehue, 8 Trenwith Place, St Ives TR26 1QD (01736 793369)

The Badley Memorial Trust

Eligibility: People in need who are in poor health, convalescent or who have disabilities and live in the former county borough of Dudley (as constituted in 1953). In certain cases the present metropolitan boroughs of Dudley and Sandwell may be included.

Types of grants: One-off grants have been made towards medical aids, clothing, beds/bedding, heating appliances, domestic appliances, televisions, radios, fuel, respite holidays, and adaptations for people with disabilities. Recurrent grants are only given in exceptional cases.

Exclusions: Grants are not given to pay off debts or for educational fees.

Annual grant total: In 2009/10 the trust had assets of £1.2 million and an income of £48,000. Grants were made to 61 individuals totalling £31,000.

Applications: On a form available from the correspondent to be submitted directly by the individual, or through a social worker, Citizens Advice, other welfare agency; or a third party, for example a relative, doctor or member of the clergy. Applications are considered quarterly.

Correspondent: Christopher Williams, 16 Manderville Gardens, Kingswinford, DY6 9QW (01384 294019)

Other information: The trust also gives grants to organisations.

The Birmingham and District Butchers and Pork Butchers Association Benevolent Fund

Eligibility: Past and present members of the association and their dependants and any other person connected with the meat trade in Birmingham and district.

Types of grants: One-off and recurrent grants ranging from £120 to £175 according to need.

Annual grant total: Grants average around £2,700 a year.

Applications: In writing to the correspondent. Applications can be submitted directly by the individual or through a social worker, Citizens Advice or other welfare agency. They are considered in June and November.

Correspondent: Glenda Richards, 97 Cherry Orchard Road, Birmingham, B20 2LA (0121 622 4900)

Birmingham Jewish Community Care

Eligibility: Jewish people in need living in the West Midlands.

Types of grants: Mainly one-off grants ranging from £10 to £250. Grants have been given to a small number of clients at Jewish festivals and for school clothing, music lessons for a gifted child, holidays for disadvantaged children and travel expenses for visiting distant cemeteries and occasionally to pay household or car bills. There is also a kosher meals-on-wheels service.

Regular payments are no longer made. Applicants must be prepared to update their circumstances before a second grant is made (other than in the case of regular telephone rental payment in some cases).

Exclusions: Grants are not made for setting up businesses.

Annual grant total: In 2008/09 the trust had assets of £4.6 million and an income of £2 million. Grants were made totalling £1,400.

Applications: In writing to the correspondent, including information on length of residence in the area, other applications made and whether or not the applicant is in receipt of income support or support from other charities. Applications are considered monthly and may be submitted directly by the individual or through a social worker, Citizens Advice or other welfare agency or third party such as a rabbi. No grant is ever made without personal contact with someone from the trust's social work department.

Correspondent: Grants Administrator, Bill Steiner Suite, 1 River Brook Drive, Birmingham, B30 2SH (0121 459 3819; email: admin@bhamjcc.co.uk)

Other information: The trust also runs a residential and nursing home, Andrew Cohen House, at Stirchley in Birmingham.

Blakemore Foundation

Eligibility: People in need in the UK wide, with a preference for the West Midlands.

Types of grants: Grants are given according to need.

Annual grant total: In 2009/10 the foundation made grants totalling £217,000 to organisations and individuals.

Applications: Unsolicited applications are not accepted.

Correspondent: P F Blakemore, A F Blakemore and Sons Ltd, Longacre, Willenhall, West Midlands, WV13 2JP (01902 366066)

The Thomas Bromwich Charity

Eligibility: People in need living in Handsworth (that is, the ecclesiastical parishes of St Mary, St Andrew, St James, St Michael, St Peter and the Holy Trinity,

Birdfield and St Paul, and Hanstead); Great Barr (that is, the ecclesiastical parish of St Margaret), and Perry Barr (that is, the ecclesiastical parishes of St John the Evangelist, Perry Barr, St Luke, Kingstanding, and St Matthews and Perry Beeches).

Types of grants: One-off grants towards electric goods, clothing, household bills, food and help in the home.

Annual grant total: In 2009/10 the charity had an income of £19,000 and a total expenditure of £18,000. Around £5,000 is distributed in grants each year.

Applications: In writing to the correspondent either directly by the individual or through a social worker, Citizens Advice or other welfare agency. Applications are considered at any time.

Correspondent: Rev Dr Crispin Pailing, Vicarage, Church Road, Perry Barr, Birmingham, B42 2LB (0121 356 7998; email: vicar@st-johns-perry-barr.org.uk)

The Chance Trust

Eligibility: People in need in the rural deaneries of Warley and West Bromwich.

Types of grants: One-off grants ranging from £50 to £400.

Annual grant total: The trust makes grants of between £2,500 and £3,000 a year to individuals for both educational and relief-in-need purposes.

Applications: In writing to the correspondent, outlining the need and the amount required. Applications are considered in January and July.

Correspondent: Revd Anthony Perry, Trustee, St Mary's Vicarage, 27 Poplar Avenue, Edgbaston, Birmingham B17 8EG (0121 4292165)

The Coventry Freemen's Charity

Eligibility: Freemen and their dependants who are in need and live within seven miles of St Mary's Hall, Coventry.

Types of grants: Recurrent grants of £40 to £60 are paid quarterly to individuals who are 67 or over. Lump sum grants are given to other applicants.

Annual grant total: In 2009 the charity had assets of £12 million and an income of £680,000. Grants totalled £497,000 and were distributed as follows:

Freeman and women	£389,000
Freemens' widows	£103,000
Special cases	£3,400
Payments for relief and need	£1,800

Applications: On a form available from the correspondent directly by the individual, for consideration bi-monthly.

Correspondent: David J Evans, Clerk, Abbey House, Manor Road, Coventry CV1 2FW (024 7625 7317;

fax: 024 7655 2845; email: john@foxevans.co.uk; website: www.foxevans.co.uk)

Friends of the Animals

Eligibility: People who live in the West Midlands, Dorset and Hampshire.

Types of grants: Subsidised veterinary treatment, such as spaying, neutering, inoculations and treatment of accidents.

Annual grant total: In 2008/09 the charity had assets of £308,000 and an income of £376,000. Charitable activities totalled £310,000, including administration costs amounting to £120,000.

Applications: In writing to the correspondent.

Correspondent: Martin J Gomez, 408 Bearwood Road, Bearwood, Warley, West Midlands B66 4EX (0121 420 4201; email: friendsoftheanimals@btinternet.com; website: www.friendsoftheanimals.co.uk)

Grantham Yorke Trust

Eligibility: People under 25 who were born in the old West Midlands metropolitan county area (basically: Birmingham, Coventry, Dudley, Redditch, Sandwell, Solihull, Tamworth, Walsall or Wolverhampton).

Types of grants: One-off grants according to need.

Annual grant total: In 2008/09 the trust had assets of £4.4 million and an income of £263,000. Grants were made to 15 individuals totalling £8,300.

Applications: On a form available from the correspondent. Applications should be submitted directly by the individual or via a relevant third party such as a social worker, Citizens Advice or other welfare agency, in February, May, August and November for consideration in the following month.

Correspondent: Christine Norgrove, Martineau, 1 Colmore Square, Birmingham B4 6AA (0800 763 1000; email: christine.norgrove@martineau-uk.com)

Other information: The trust also makes grants to organisations and to individuals for educational purposes.

The Harborne Parish Lands Charity

Eligibility: People in need who live in the ancient parish of Harborne, which includes parts of Harborne, Smethwick, Bearwood and Quinton. A map of the old parish is available to view on the website and individuals are advised to check that they reside in the area of benefit before making an application.

Types of grants: One-off grants ranging from £50 to £700. Grants cover a wide range of needs, including furniture, aids and adaptations, clothing, and assistance with transport.

Exclusions: Grants are not made for help with statutory bills, such as taxes.

Annual grant total: In 2008/09 the charity had assets of £13 million, an income of £943,000 and a total expenditure of £978,000. Grants were made to individuals totalling £50,000. A further £156,000 was given in general grants to organisations and £548,000 was spent on the charity's almshouses.

Applications: A short application form is available from the correspondent. Applications can be made at any time and should be submitted through a local agency or organisation, such as social services or a Citizens Advice. All applicants are visited.

Correspondent: Lynda Bending, 109 Court Oak Road, Birmingham, B17 9AA (0121 426 1600; fax: 0121 428 2267; email: theclerk@hplc. fednet.org.uk; website: www. harborneparishlandscharity.org.uk)

The CB & AB Holinsworth Fund of Help

Eligibility: People in need who live in or near to the city of Birmingham and are sick or convalescing.

Types of grants: One-off grants ranging from £50 to £300. Grants are given towards the cost of respite holidays, travelling expenses to and from hospital, clothing, beds and carpets.

Exclusions: Generally grants are not given for bills or debt.

Annual grant total: About £1,500.

Applications: On a form available from the correspondent. Applications are considered throughout the year and should be submitted through a social worker, Citizens Advice or other welfare agency. Confirmation of illness is needed, for example a letter from a doctor, consultant or nurse.

Correspondent: Phil Wright, Room B19, Birmingham City Council, The Council House, Victoria Square, Birmingham B1 1BB (0121 303 2023)

The Lant Trust

Eligibility: People in need, especially those who are older, living in the ecclesiastical parishes of Berkswell (St John the Baptist), Balsall Common (St Peter) and Temple Balsall (St Mary). The trust also augments three clergy stipends, gives grants to residents of Berkswell, Burton Green and Temple Balsall, and helps maintain some playing fields.

Types of grants: One-off and recurrent grants according to need.

Annual grant total: No recent financial information was available. In previous years grants have totalled about £8,000.

Applications: In writing to the correspondent.

Correspondent: Professor A F Lant, 61 Wimpole Street, London W1G 8AH (020 7486 1800)

The James Frederick & Ethel Anne Measures Charity

Eligibility: The following criteria apply:

1 applicants must usually originate in the West Midlands

2 applicants must show evidence of self-help in their application

3 trustees have a preference for disadvantaged people

4 trustees have a dislike for applications from students who have a full local authority grant and want finance for a different course or study

5 trustees favour grants towards the cost of equipment

6 applications by individuals in cases of hardship will not usually be considered unless sponsored by a local authority, health professional or other welfare agency.

Types of grants: One-off or recurrent grants, usually between £50 and £500.

Annual grant total: In 2008/09 the charity had assets of £900,000, which generated an income of £46,000. Grants were made totalling £43,000, although previous research indicates that most of this is awarded to organisations.

Applications: In writing to the correspondent. No reply is given to unsuccessful applicants unless an sae is enclosed.

Correspondent: The Clerk to the Trustees, Harris Allday, 2nd Floor, 33 Great Charles Street, Birmingham B3 3JN

Other information: Grants were made to 51 organisations during the year.

The Newman Trust Homes

Eligibility: People who are in need, hardship or distress who live, or have formerly lived, in the City of Birmingham. Grants are primarily paid to benefit people who are older, people with housing difficulties and people living within the area of Handsworth and its immediate vicinity.

Types of grants: One-off and recurrent grants according to need.

Exclusions: No funding for: salaries or office equipment/furniture; play schemes/summer schemes; community sports/play area facilities; pre-schools or play groups (excluding special needs groups); medical or academic research; the arts; schools, colleges and universities (excluding special schools); animals; funerals.

Annual grant total: In 2008/09 the trust gave grants to 26 individuals totalling £9,700.

Applications: Application forms are available from the charity. Applicants are encouraged to detail any additional information they believe may assist the trustees in their decision.

Correspondent: Judy Dyke, Tydallwoods Solicitors, 29 Woodbourne Road, Harborne, Birmingham B17 8BY (0121 693 2222; email: jdyke@ tyndallwoods.co.uk)

The Samuel Smith Charity, Coventry

Eligibility: People in need who live in Coventry and the ancient parish of Bedworth.

Types of grants: Pensions and one-off grants.

Annual grant total: In 2009 the charity had assets of £826,000 and an income of £31,000. Grants were distributed as follows:

Pensions	£16,000
Payments in lieu of coal	£2,200
Christmas gifts to pensioners	£1,800
May gifts	£1,300
Bibles	£300

Applications: Applications can be made in writing to the correspondent, but most beneficiaries are referred by the charity's almoner.

Correspondent: J C B Leech, Fourwinds, 9 Highland Road, Kenilworth, Warwickshire CV8 2EU (01926 852846)

The Joanne Webb Memorial Fund

Eligibility: People in need who live in the north Shropshire area.

Types of grants: One-off and recurrent grants according to need.

Annual grant total: About £500.

Applications: In writing to the correspondent.

Correspondent: Barry Hale, Trustee, 40 Queensway, Whitchurch, Shropshire, SY13 1HD

Bilston

The Bilston Relief-in-Need Charity

Eligibility: People in need living in the ecclesiastical parish of Bilston and the area of the former borough of Bilston.

Types of grants: Generally one-off grants in the range of £10 to £300 including, for example, those for electric goods, clothing, living costs, household bills, food, holidays, travel expenses and furniture.

Annual grant total: Grants to individuals generally total around £600 a year.

Applications: Applications, in writing to the correspondent, can be submitted by the individual or through a recognised referral agency for example a social worker, Citizens Advice, doctor or medical worker. They are considered at any time.

Correspondent: Desmond Smith, 36 Springfield Road, Bilston, West Midlands WV14 6LN (01902 493928)

Other information: Grants are given both to individuals and organisations.

Birmingham

The Freda & Howard Ballance Trust

Eligibility: People in need who live in Birmingham.

Types of grants: One-off grants usually ranging from £50 to £200. Recent grants have been given for clothing, furniture and disability aids. A small amount is also available for educational items.

Annual grant total: Grants usually total between £1,000 and £2,000 each year.

Applications: On a form available from the correspondent. A letter giving brief details of the application is required before an application form is sent out. Applications can be made either directly by the individual or via a third party such as a charity, social worker or Citizens Advice. They are usually considered quarterly.

Correspondent: Michael Stocks, Appeals Secretary and Trustee, Blackhams, Lancaster House, 67 Newhall Street, Birmingham B3 1NR (0121 233 0062; fax: 0121 233 9880; email: stocks87@blackhams.com)

The Richard & Samuel Banner Trust

Eligibility: Men and widows who are in need and live in the city of Birmingham.

Types of grants: Clothing grants up to £100.

Annual grant total: In 2008/09 the trust had an income of £9,000 and a total expenditure of £7,900.

Applications: Applicants must be nominated by a trustee, doctor or the Council for Old People. Applications are considered on 1 November and grants are distributed immediately after this date.

Correspondent: Anne Holmes, c/o Cobbetts Solicitors, 1 Colmore Square, Birmingham, B4 6AJ (0845 404 2505)

Other information: The trust can also give apprenticing grants to male students under 21, but this is done through certain colleges; applicants should not apply directly.

Friends of Home Nursing in Birmingham

Eligibility: Sick and older people who live in Birmingham city and who are patients nursed at home by the district nurse.

Types of grants: The trust provides goods, equipment and occasional monetary grants which are not available from other sources. In the past this has included digital thermometers, a dressing trolley, cameras and films for ulcer recordings, and part of the cost of holidays. Grants are usually one-off and range from £50 to £500.

No grants are made for double glazing or electrical work.

Annual grant total: Financial information has not been available the last set of accounts were submitted for the year 2006.

Applications: In writing, via a district nurse, to the correspondent. Applications can be submitted at any time, for consideration in the spring and autumn, 'but if a real case of need occurs we deal with it as soon as possible'.

Correspondent: Mrs J Burns, Hon. Treasurer, 46 Underwood Road, Handsworth Wood, Birmingham B20 1JS (0121 686 5565)

The Charity of Jane Kate Gilbert

Eligibility: People in need who are over 60 years of age and have lived in Birmingham for at least two years.

Types of grants: Small quarterly pensions with a possible Christmas bonus. One-off hardship payments up to a maximum of £100 will also be considered.

Annual grant total: Grants average around £1,900 a year.

Applications: On a form available from the correspondent to be submitted through a social worker, Citizens Advice or other welfare agency. Applications are usually considered in March and November.

Correspondent: Phil Wright, Committee Services, Room B43, Council House, Victoria Square, Birmingham, B1 1BB (0121 303 2023)

The Handsworth Charity

Eligibility: People in need who live in the parish of Handsworth (now in Birmingham).

Types of grants: One-off grants of up to £500 according to need.

Annual grant total: In 2009 the charity had an income of £17,000 and a total expenditure of £9,600. Grants were made totalling around £8,000.

Applications: In writing to the correspondent: to be submitted directly by the individual or through a referral organisation.

Correspondent: Dipali Chandra, 109 Court Oak Road, Birmingham B17 9AA

Harriet Louisa Loxton Trust Fund

Eligibility: People in need who live in Birmingham, with a preference for older people.

Types of grants: One-off grants ranging from £100 to £2,000, though the average is generally around £400. Examples of grants given include £500 to an older person with disabilities for a washing machine and drier, £100 for a vacuum cleaner for an older woman who was ill, £1,700 for central heating for a woman who was blind and £500 towards an electric scooter for a man who was totally immobile.

Exclusions: There are no grants available to pay off debts, relieve public funds or towards the community charge and no grants to organisations.

Annual grant total: In 2008/09 the fund had assets of £1.2 million and an income of £56,000. Grants were made to 25 individuals totalling £11,000.

Applications: On a form available from the correspondent. The trustees meet four times a year to consider applications. Applications may take some considerable time to process. Immediate decisions on applications cannot be given.

Correspondent: Gloria Zachariou, Adults and Communities Finance Section, 67 Sutton New Road, Birmingham, B23 6QT (0121 464 5325)

Other information: The fund was established from proceeds of the sale of Icknield, a property donated to the city by Harriet Louisa Loxton for use as a home for older people.

Sands Cox Relief in Sickness Charity

Eligibility: People in need who live in Birmingham.

Types of grants: One off grants of up to £500.

Annual grant total: About £2,500.

Applications: In writing to the correspondent, either directly by the individual or through a responsible person, e.g. a trustee, doctor or social service professional.

Correspondent: Ann Andrew, Secretary, 12 Hayfield Gardens, Moseley, Birmingham, B13 9LE

Other information: The charity also makes grants to local organisations.

The Yardley Great Trust

Eligibility: People living in the ancient parish of Yardley in the city of Birmingham. This includes the wards of Yardley, Acocks Green, Fox Hollies,

Billesley, Hall Green and part of the wards of Hodge Hill, Shard End, Sheldon, Small Heath, Sparkhill, Moseley, Sparkbrook and Brandwood. (A map is produced by the trust outlining the beneficial area.)

Types of grants: One-off grants towards washing machines, fridges, cookers, clothing, beds and bedding and household furniture.

Exclusions: No grants are given for educational needs or for items that should be met by local authorities, health authorities or social services.

Annual grant total: In 2009 the trust had assets of £5.8 million and an income of £1.7 million. Grants were made to individuals totalling £37,000.

Applications: Application forms are available in hardcopy from the correspondent or can be completed online via the website. Applications should be made through a Council Neighbourhood Office, Citizens Advice or other welfare agency. They are considered monthly.

Correspondent: Mrs K L Grice, Clerk to the Trustees, 31 Old Brookside, Yardley Fields Road, Stechford, Birmingham B33 8QL (0121 784 7889; fax: 0121 785 1386; email: enquiries@ygtrust.org.uk; website: www.yardley-great-trust.org.uk)

Other information: The trust also makes grants to organisations (£27,000 in 2009).

Bushbury

The Bushbury United Charities

Eligibility: People in need living in the ancient parish of Bushbury.

Types of grants: Annual grants paid at Christmas.

Annual grant total: In 2009 the charity had an income of £7,200 and a total expenditure of £9,500.

Applications: In writing to the correspondent.

Correspondent: Administrator, Dallow & Dallow, 23 Waterloo Road, Wolverhampton, West Midlands WV1 4TJ (01902 420208)

Castle Bromwich

The Mary Dame Bridgeman Charity Trust

Eligibility: People in need living in the ecclesiastical parishes of St Mary and St Margaret, and St Clement, Castle Bromwich.

Types of grants: One-off grants have in the past been used to meet the cost of heating bills or respite care.

Exclusions: Grants are not given if they will affect any statutory benefits.

Annual grant total: About £1,000.

Applications: In writing to the correspondent, directly by the individual or through a social worker, welfare agency or other third party such as a parent, partner or relative. Applications should include the applicant's income and expenditure. The trustees meet twice a year in May and November.

Correspondent: Revd Michael Sears, 67 Chester Road, Castle Bromwich, Solihull, West Midlands B36 0AL

Other information: This entry is an amalgamation of three separate charity funds which are administered as one.

Coventry

The Children's Boot Fund

Eligibility: Schoolchildren in the city of Coventry, aged 4 to 16.

Types of grants: Grants for school footwear for children in need. No other type of help is given. Grants are made direct to footwear suppliers in the form of vouchers.

Annual grant total: In 2008/09 the fund had an income of £11,000 and a total expenditure of £15,000.

Applications: Application forms are available from schools in the area and should be completed, verified and signed by the head teacher of the child's school. Applications are considered four times a year.

Correspondent: Mrs Janet McConkey, 123A Birmingham Road, Coventry CV5 9GR (024 7640 2837)

The Coventry Nursing Trust

Eligibility: People in need living in, and who have been patients in, the city of Coventry.

Types of grants: Grants for the relief of sickness are mainly given to help with night sitting costs, although day sitting is also provided for. A large proportion of the grant total is also given towards convalescence recommended by a doctor or social worker and may occasionally include the cost of the patient's travel to and from the convalescent home.

Exclusions: Help with day-to-day expenses is not given.

Annual grant total: In 2008 the trust had an income of £6,700 and a total expenditure of £13,000.

Applications: In writing to the correspondent. Please note: convalescent care applications can only be made by a social worker on a form available from the trust and payments are made directly to convalescent homes.

Correspondent: Mrs E A Martin, Clerk, 44 Madeira Croft, Chapelfields, Coventry CV5 8NY (024 7671 1082)

The General Charities of the City of Coventry

Eligibility: People in need living in the city of Coventry.

Types of grants: One-off grants in kind and recurrent grants, but not cash grants. Recurrent grants of £45 a quarter can be given to a maximum of 650 pensioners.

Exclusions: Cash grants are not given.

Annual grant total: In 2009 welfare grants totalled £77,000.

Applications: Applications should be made through social workers, probation officers, Citizens Advice or other welfare agencies.

Correspondent: Mrs V A Tosh, General Charities Office, Old Bablake, Hill Street, Coventry CV1 4AN (024 7622 2769; email: cov.genchar@virgin.net)

Other information: The charities receive income from Sir Thomas White's Charity including the allocation for the Sir Thomas White's Loan Fund in Coventry.

John Moore's Bequest

Eligibility: People in need, generally older people, living in the city of Coventry.

Types of grants: Grants of up to £20 given in December.

Annual grant total: In 2008/09 the bequest had an income of £4,100 and an unusually low total expenditure of £950 (£3,500 in 2007/08).

Applications: The charity's trustees each select around 25 recipients either directly or through local churches.

Correspondent: Ian Cox, Sarginsons, 10 The Quadrant, Coventry CV1 2EL (024 7655 3181)

The Dr William MacDonald of Johannesburg Trust

Eligibility: People in need who live in the city of Coventry.

Types of grants: One-off welfare grants, typically about £50, usual maximum £200.

Exclusions: No grants for the relief of debt.

Annual grant total: Grants usually total around £2,000 each year.

Applications: In writing to the correspondent. Applications can be submitted directly by the individual or through a third party such as a social worker.

Correspondent: Jane Barlow, Lord Mayor's Office, Council House, Earl Street, Coventry, CV1 5RR (024 7683 3047)

Spencer's Charity

Eligibility: Women in need who are over 65, still living in their own homes and able to prove that they have lived in the city of Coventry for at least seven years. The charity stipulates that they must not be in receipt of 'too many' other benefits.

Types of grants: Pensions amounting to £200 per year are paid every six months.

Annual grant total: In 2009 the charity had assets of £579,000 and an income of £23,000. Pensions were paid to 97 individuals totalling £19,000.

Applications: Application forms are available from the clerk to the trustees, Mr G Foottit, at the above address.

Correspondent: G T W Foottit, Mander Hadley & Co. Solicitors, 1 The Quadrant, Coventry CV1 2DZ (02476 631212)

The Tansley Charity Trust

Eligibility: Women over 50 years old who are in poor health and live in the city of Coventry.

Types of grants: One-off grants up to £200. Recent grants have been given towards the purchase of clothing, household items and the payment of bills.

Exclusions: No grants for council tax or Inland Revenue payments.

Annual grant total: In 2009/10 the trust had both an income of £6,200 and a total expenditure of £880.

Applications: On a form available from the correspondent. Applications can be submitted by the individual or through a recognised referral agency (e.g. a social worker, Citizens Advice or doctor). Grants are considered twice a year.

Correspondent: Lara M Knight, Governance Services, Room 60, Council House, Earl Street, Coventry CV1 5RR (02476 833 237)

The Tile Hill & Westwood Charities for the Needy Sick

Eligibility: People who are both sick and in need and live in the parish of Westwood and parts of the parish of Berkswell, Kenilworth and Stoneleigh and elsewhere within a three and a half mile radius of 93 Cromwell Lane, Coventry.

Types of grants: One-off grants according to need. The trust is often able to provide assistance where a potential beneficiary 'falls between the cracks' of other providers.

Annual grant total: In 2009 the trust had an income of £20,000 and a total expenditure of £4,800.

Applications: In writing to the correspondent.

Correspondent: John Ruddick, Clerk, 4 Poundgate Lane, Coventry CV4 8HJ (024 7646 6917; email: john.ruddick@bttj. com)

The Harry Weston Memorial Fund

Eligibility: Pensioners, aged 65–75, who are in financial difficulty (usually those on pension credit) and live in the city of Coventry.

Types of grants: One-off grants up to about £50, mainly towards the cost of television licences. The fund has also helped with the provision of reconditioned television sets.

Annual grant total: Grants usually total about £2,000 each year.

Applications: In writing to the correspondent either directly by the individual or through a third party such as a social worker, Citizens Advice, other welfare agency or a relative or neighbour. Applications must include information on the applicant's age, circumstances and date of TV licence renewal if relevant.

Correspondent: The Secretary, 8 Eaton Road, Coventry CV1 2FF (0247 671 3942)

Dudley

The Dudley Charity

Eligibility: People in need who live in the town of Dudley (as constituted prior to 1 April 1966) and its immediate surroundings, including Netherton.

Types of grants: One-off grants in the range of £100 to £250.

Annual grant total: In 2008/09 the charity had an income of £6,100 and a total expenditure of £6,200. Grants were made totalling about £6,000.

Applications: On a form available from the correspondent. Applications can be submitted directly by the individual or through a third party such as a social worker. They are normally considered monthly.

Correspondent: Dennis Jones, Secretary to the Trustees, St Barnabas Vicarage, Middlepark Road, Dudley DY1 2LD (01384 392704)

Other information: The charity also makes grants to organisations.

The Reginald Unwin Dudley Charity

Eligibility: People in need who live in Dudley.

Types of grants: One-off grants of up to about £200.

Annual grant total: In 2009/10 the charity had an income of £3,000 and a total expenditure of £5,700.

Applications: On a form available from the correspondent.

Correspondent: David Hughes, 53 The Broadway, Dudley, West Midlands,

DY1 4AP (01384 259277; email: rududley@ hotmail.com)

King's Norton

The King's Norton United Charities

Eligibility: People who live in the ancient parish of King's Norton in Birmingham and the West Midlands.

Types of grants: One-off and recurrent grants according to need.

Annual grant total: Grants usually total around £5,000.

Applications: Grants are made to named individuals only.

Correspondent: Revd M Blood, Chair, The Rectory, 273 Pershore Road, Kings Norton, Birmingham, B30 8EX (0121 459 0560)

Meriden

Meriden United Charities

Eligibility: People in need who have lived in the parish of Meriden for at least two years.

Types of grants: One-off grants towards people such as older people, children or those experiencing a sudden illness.

Annual grant total: The charity has an income of about £1,500 a year. Grants are made for education and welfare purposes.

Applications: Applications can be submitted either directly by the individual or a family member or through a third party such as a social worker or teacher. The existence of the charities is made known by a notice in the Meriden magazine and by a notice in the library.

Correspondent: Alan Barker, 163 Avon Street, Coventry CV2 3GQ (024 7645 3342)

Sandwell

The Fordath Foundation

Eligibility: People who are in need and live in the Metropolitan Borough of Sandwell. Preference is given to older people and those in poor health.

Types of grants: One-off grants to meet a specific expense.

Annual grant total: Grants usually total about £5,000 each year.

Applications: Applications are usually made through Sandwell Social Services, Citizens Advice, Carers' Centre or a similar organisation and should include brief details of the individual's circumstances. They are considered throughout the year, funds permitting.

Correspondent: John Sutcliffe, 33 Thornyfields Lane, Stafford ST17 9YS (01785 247035; email: fordath-foundation@ntlworld.com)

The Mayor's General Fund (Sandwell)

Eligibility: People in need who live in the area covered by Sandwell Metropolitan Borough Council.

Types of grants: Generally small grants (usually about £25, but up to £100) to help with one-off expenses such as clothing and fuel bills.

Annual grant total: Grants usually total about £1,000 each year.

Applications: In writing to the correspondent through a social worker, Citizens Advice or other welfare agency. Applications are considered at any time.

Correspondent: The Mayor, The Big House, PO Box 2374, Freeth Street, Oldbury, West Midlands B69 3DE (0121 569 3041; email: pauline_white@sandwell.gov.uk)

The George & Thomas Henry Salter Trust

Eligibility: People in need who live in the borough of Sandwell.

Types of grants: One-off grants usually in the range of £50 to £1,000 towards clothing, household equipment and so on.

Annual grant total: In 2009 the trust had assets of £1.3 million and an income of £43,000. The education fund gave £600 in education grants to local schools and £45,000 to local trainees at colleges and universities. The relief in need fund made grants totalling £25,000 to 'poor persons in need'.

Applications: On a form available from the correspondent. Applications are considered on a regular basis.

Correspondent: Mrs J S Styler, Clerk, Lombard House, Cronehills Linkway, West Bromwich, West Midlands B70 7PL (0121 553 3286)

Stourbridge

The Palmer & Seabright Charity

Eligibility: Elderly people in need living in the parish of Stourbridge.

Types of grants: One-off and recurrent grants according to need.

Annual grant total: In 2008 the trust had assets of £205,000 and an income of £51,000. Grants given for welfare and education totalled £9,400.

Applications: On a form available from the correspondent. Applications can be submitted either directly by the individual or a family member, through a third party

such as a social worker or teacher, or through an organisation such as Citizens Advice or a school.

Correspondent: Susannah Griffiths, c/o Wall, James & Chappell, 15–23 Hagley Road, Stourbridge, West Midlands DY8 1QW (01384 371622; fax: 01384 374057)

Chris Westwood Charity

Eligibility: Children and young people in Stourbridge, and the surrounding areas, with physical disabilities.

Types of grants: Typical examples of support have included: special exercise equipment to assist in regaining and maintaining mobility; wheelchairs, special mobility chairs and lifting equipment; and contributions towards the cost of home modifications, to improve access, or provide specialised facilities that may be required.

Annual grant total: In 2009 the charity had an income of £20,000 and a total expenditure of £19,000.

Applications: In writing to the correspondent.

Correspondent: Martyn Morgan, Talbots Solicitors, 63 Market Street, Stourbridge DY8 1AQ (01384 445850; email: martynmorgan@talbotssolicitors.co.uk; website: www.talbotssolicitors.co.uk/charity)

Sutton Coldfield

Sutton Coldfield Municipal Charities

Eligibility: People in need living in the Four Oaks, New Hall and Vesey wards of Sutton Coldfield.

Types of grants: One-off grants are given to individuals in the range of £100 and £1,500. Grants are given for special needs, for example, stair lifts, adapted bathrooms and mobility vehicles for people who are elderly or disabled, school clothing, building repairs and essential household equipment e.g. carpets, washing machine, cookers.

Exclusions: Grants are not given to people in receipt of benefits from other sources, for example social services, family, DWP and so on.

Annual grant total: In 2008/09 the charities had assets of £41 million and an income of £1.8 million. Grants to four individuals for educational and personal needs totalled £2,700. A further 280 school clothing grants were made to individuals totalling £27,000. Relief-in-need grants to 32 individuals totalled £35,000. Grants to 69 organisations totalled £908,000.

Applications: On a form available from the correspondent. Applications should be made directly by the individual or through

a parent or carer. They are considered every month, except April, August and December. Telephone enquiries are welcomed.

Correspondent: Grants Officer, Lingard House, Fox Hollies Road, Sutton Coldfield, West Midlands B76 2RJ (0121 351 2262; fax: 0121 313 0651; website: www.suttoncoldfieldmunicipalcharities.com/)

Other information: The principal objective of the charities is the provision of almshouses, the distribution of funds and other measures for the alleviation of poverty and other needs for inhabitants and other organisations within the boundaries of the former borough of Sutton Coldfield.

Tettenhall

The Tettenhall Relief-in-Need & Educational Charity

Eligibility: People in need who live in the parish of Tettenhall, as constituted on 22 June 1888.

Types of grants: Grants are given mainly for clothing and food and range from £25 to £50.

Annual grant total: About £1,000 is available each year for relief-in-need purposes.

Applications: In writing to the correspondent. Applications should be made through a social worker, Citizens Advice or other welfare agency, doctor or senior citizen's organisation. They should be submitted in October for consideration in November.

Correspondent: Andrew Graham, Clerk to the Trustees, 4 Mayswood Drive, Wolverhampton WV6 8EF (01902 762021)

Walsall

The Blanch Woolaston Walsall Charity

Eligibility: People in need living in the borough of Walsall. Educational grants will only be given to those under 21 years of age. There is no age limit for relief-in-need grants.

Types of grants: Around 20 one-off grants are made each year ranging from £50 to £300 for school uniforms and small household items. The trustees cannot undertake to repeat/renew any grants.

Exclusions: No grants are made for the payment of rates, taxes or other public funds (including gas, electricity and so on).

Annual grant total: Grants average around £1,200 a year, though the actual grant figure tends to fluctuate quite widely.

Applications: On a form available from the correspondent. Applications are considered four times a year.

Correspondent: Stephen Brooke, Constitutional Services, Walsall Metropolitan Borough Council, Civic Centre, Darwall Street, Walsall WS1 1EU (01922 652014; email: brookes@walsall.gov.uk)

West Bromwich

The Charity of Jane Patricia Eccles

Eligibility: Older women in need who live in Sandwell.

Types of grants: One-off grants in kind to meet specific needs, for example phone installation, showers and Braille reader machines for the blind.

Annual grant total: Grants average around £500 a year, though the actual grant figure tends to fluctuate quite widely.

Applications: In writing to the correspondent for consideration at any time. Applications can be submitted either directly by the individual or a family member, through a third party such as a social worker, or through an organisation such as Citizens Advice or other welfare agency. Applications must be made through, and include, a letter of support from a doctor, church minister or welfare agency.

Correspondent: David Coles, 9 Highcroft Drive, Sutton Coldfield, West Midlands, B74 4SX (01283 513065)

Wolverhampton

The Greenway Benefaction Trust

Eligibility: Children in need living in the Bradley area of the city of Wolverhampton.

Types of grants: One-off grants towards the cost of holidays, convalescence, toys, entertainment and so on.

Annual grant total: This trust generally has an income of around £1,000. There has been no expenditure by the trust for the last five years.

Applications: In writing to the correspondent. They can be submitted either by the individual or a relevant third party for example a parent, social worker, Citizens Advice or other welfare agency. They are considered as received.

Correspondent: Mr G Entwistle, Customer and Shared Services, Wolverhampton City Council, Civic Centre, St Peter's Square, Wolverhampton WV1 1RL (01902 554432)

The Power Pleas Trust

Eligibility: Mainly young people, under 18 years, with muscular dystrophy and similar diseases living in the Wolverhampton area.

Types of grants: Grants are given primarily towards the purchase and provision of outdoor electric powered wheelchairs and other aids.

Annual grant total: In 2008/09 the trust had an income of £3,900 and a total expenditure of £6,400.

Applications: In writing to the correspondent directly by the individual or family member.

Correspondent: Keith Berry, 80 York Avenue, Wolverhampton WV3 9BU (01902 655962; email: keithoberry@hotmail.com)

Worcestershire

The Astley and Areley Kings Sick Fund

Eligibility: People who have disabilities and who live in the parishes of St Peter Astley, St Bartholomew Areley Kings, St Michael & All Angels Stourport-on-Severn and All Saints Wilden.

Types of grants: One-off grants are made towards specialist equipment for home-care, disabled facilities and additional home support.

Annual grant total: Grants to individuals average around £1,000 a year.

Applications: In writing to the correspondent. Applications can be submitted either directly by the individual, or through a social worker, Citizens Advice or another third party. Trustees meet regularly throughout the year.

Correspondent: Mary Wood, Muldoon, Areley Common, Stourport-on-Severn, Worcestershire, DY13 0NG (01299 823619)

The Baron Davenport Emergency Fund (Worcestershire)

Eligibility: Divorcees over 55, young single women/women abandoned by their partners, fatherless children under 25 and widows. Applicants must have been resident in the West Midlands for at least 10 years, have an income of less than £141 per week and savings of less than £3,500.

Types of grants: One-off grants ranging from £100 to £150 for emergencies only. Grants have been given towards telephone debt, removal expenses and electrical goods.

Annual grant total: Grants are generally around £800 a year.

Applications: On a form available from the correspondent. A personal income and expenditure breakdown must accompany all applications. Applications can be made through a social worker, Citizens Advice or other welfare agency, or directly by the individual or family member. They are considered on receipt.

Correspondent: The Administrator, Community Action Malvern District, 28–30 Belle Vue Terrace, Worcestershire WR14 4PZ (01684 892381; fax: 01684 575155; email: info@communityaction.org.uk)

John Martin's Charity

Eligibility: People resident in Evesham, Worcestershire. Applicants or a parent/guardian must have lived in the town for at least 12 months at the date of application.

Please note: Applications may also be considered from residents in a number of designated villages close to Evesham if they are suffering from chronic ill health conditions.

Types of grants: 'Grants are available for the benefit of children, single parent families, the disabled and people who have fallen on hard times for a variety of circumstances beyond their control. Applications are subject to income assessment and will be considered for a variety of reasons including help with clothing, essential household items, medical and mobility equipment.'

Annual Heating Allowance – an annual award is currently made to assist those aged 60 and over in meeting their energy bills.

Exclusions: Support is not normally approved for the repayment of debts, rent or council tax arrears, nor are rental deposits provided. Grants are not considered unless all statutory benefits are being claimed.

Annual grant total: In 2008/09 the charity had assets of £15 million and an income of £751,000. Welfare grants were made to individuals totalling £200,000 and were broken down as follows:

Relief in need	£173,000
Health	£15,000
Religious support	£11,000

Applications: On a form available from the correspondent. Applications can be submitted directly by the individual or through a social worker, Citizens Advice or other welfare agency. They are considered twice monthly.

Correspondent: The Clerk, 16 Queen's Road, Evesham, Worcester WR11 4JN (01386 765440; fax: 01386 765340; email: enquires@johnmartins.org.uk; website: www.johnmartins.org.uk)

Other information: Grants are also made to organisations and to individuals for educational purposes.

Pershore United Charity

Eligibility: People in need who live in private or rented accommodation (not residential or nursing homes) in the parishes of Pershore and Pensham. Priority is given to older people and people in need who have lived in the town for several years.

Types of grants: Recurrent and occasional one-off grants to help with heating costs at Christmas.

Annual grant total: The charity usually has both an income and a total expenditure of approximately £4,000, all of which is distributed in grants to individuals.

Applications: In writing to the correspondent. Applications are considered in October.

Correspondent: Ken Myers, 3 Old School Close, Pershore, Worcestershire, WR10 1RG (01386 561308; fax: 01386 561996)

The Ancient Parish of Ripple Trust

Eligibility: People in need living in the parishes of Ripple, Holdfast, Queenhill and Bushley.

Types of grants: Small one-off cash grants are made. Ongoing Christmas grants can also be made to older people.

Annual grant total: In 2008/09 the trust had an income of £14,000 and a total expenditure £13,000.

Applications: In writing to the correspondent. Grants are considered at any time of year.

Correspondent: John Willis, Secretary, 7 Court Lea, Holly Green, Upton-upon-Severn, Worcestershire WR8 0PE (01684 594570; email: willis.courtlea@ btopenworld.com)

Other information: Grants are also made to registered charities that serve local people.

The Henry & James Willis Trust

Eligibility: People who are convalescing and live in the city of Worcester.

Types of grants: One-off grants to allow convalescents to spend six weeks at the seaside or other health resort. Travel costs and accommodation are included and in special cases the cost of a carer. Patients are usually asked for a small weekly contribution.

Annual grant total: In 2008/09 the trust had an income of £5,600 and a total expenditure of £5,300.

Applications: On a form available from the clerk. Applications can be submitted directly by the individual, or through a social worker, Citizens Advice or other welfare agency.

Correspondent: John Wagstaff, Clerk, The Laurels, 4 Norton Close, Worcester WR5 3EY (01905 355659)

The Worcestershire Cancer Aid Committee

Eligibility: People with cancer who live in the old county of Worcestershire.

Types of grants: One-off and recurrent grants and loans, including grants in kind to assist cancer patients in financial distress with home nursing, transport to hospital, specialist equipment and so on.

Annual grant total: In 2008/09 the committee had an income of £17,000 and a total expenditure of £20,000.

Applications: On a form to be submitted through a third party such as a social worker, doctor or nurse. Applications are considered within one week.

Correspondent: Anthony T Atkinson, c/o Kennel Ground, Gilberts End, Hanley Castle, Worcestershire WR8 0AS (01684 310408)

Other information: The committee also makes grants to organisations.

Cropthorpe

Randolph Meakins Patty's Farm & the Widows Lyes Charity

Eligibility: People in need who live in the village of Cropthorne (Worcestershire).

Types of grants: As well as general welfare grants, Christmas parcels are also given.

Annual grant total: Grants are given for educational and welfare purposes and usually total about £3,000 per year.

Applications: In writing to the correspondent.

Correspondent: Mrs J Ayliffe, Orchard House, Main Street, Cropthorne, Pershore, Worcestershire WR10 3LT (01386 860011)

Kidderminster

The Kidderminster Aid In Sickness Fund

Eligibility: People who are in poor health and financial need, and live in the borough of Kidderminster.

Types of grants: One-off grants towards, for example, fuel expenses, equipment, furniture, beds and bedding.

Annual grant total: Grants average around £8,000 per year.

Applications: In writing to the correspondent. Applications can be considered at any time.

Correspondent: Peter Hill, M F G Solicitors, Carlton House, Marlborough Street, Kidderminster, DY10 1BA (01562 820181)

Other information: Grants are also made to organisations.

Worcester

Armchair

Eligibility: People in need, who have no savings, who live within a five-mile radius of Worcester City.

Types of grants: The charity provides good quality second hand furniture to families and individuals, for example, beds, wardrobes, tables/chairs and so on.

Annual grant total: In 2008/09 it had assets of £74,000 and an income of £27,000. There were no grants made during the year.

Applications: Applications should be submitted through a social worker, Citizens Advice or other welfare agency. They are considered all year round.

Correspondent: Margaret Jones, 66 Riverview Close, Worcester, WR2 6DA (01905 29377; fax: 01905 729133)

The Mary Hill Trust

Eligibility: People in need who live within the boundaries of the city of Worcester.

Types of grants: One-off grants ranging from £50 to £500.

Annual grant total: Grants usually total around £6,000 per year.

Applications: In writing to the correspondent either through a third party such as a social worker, Citizens Advice or other welfare agency, or directly by the individual. Applications from individuals are considered upon receipt. Applicants should include as many financial details as possible, for example income and weekly outgoings.

Correspondent: Andrew G Duncan, Clerk, 16 The Tything, Worcester WR1 1HD (01905 731731)

The United Charities of Saint Martin

Eligibility: People in need who live in the parish of St Martin, Worcester.

Types of grants: One-off grants and pensions, according to need.

Annual grant total: In 2009 the charities had an income of £6,000 and a total expenditure of £7,000.

Applications: In application to the correspondent.

Correspondent: Michael Bunclark, 4 St Catherine's Hill, London Road, Worcester, WR5 2EA

The Worcester Consolidated Municipal Charity

Eligibility: People in need who live in the city of Worcester.

Types of grants: One-off grants of £20 to £1,000, principally towards electrical goods, carpets, household items, clothing and so on.

Annual grant total: In 2008 grants made were made to individuals totalling £80,000, the vast majority were made for less than £1,000.

Applications: Applications are usually through a social worker, Citizens Advice or other welfare agency. Statutory sources must have first been exhausted. Applications are submitted on a form available from the correspondent and are considered every month.

Correspondent: The Clerk to the Trustees, Hallmark Solicitors, 4 & 5 Sansome Place, Worcester WR1 1UQ (01905 726600; email: icp@hallmarkslaw.co.uk)

7. SOUTH WEST

Viscount Amory's Charitable Trust

Eligibility: People in need in the south west of England, with a preference for Devon (due to limited funds).

Types of grants: One-off and recurrent grants according to need.

Annual grant total: In 2008/09 the trust had assets of £10 million and an income of £470,000. The trust made 17 grants to individuals totalling £8,700, mostly for educational purposes. A further £396,000 was given to organisations.

Applications: In writing to the correspondent, for consideration every month.

Correspondent: The Trust Secretary, The Island, Lowman Green, Tiverton, Devon EX16 4LA (01884 254899)

Avon & Somerset Constabulary Benevolent Fund

Eligibility: Mainly serving and retired members of the Avon & Somerset Constabulary who are in need. Their dependants may also be supported.

Types of grants: One-off grants, ranging from £500 to £2,000, for equipment and house repairs, travel costs for hospital visits and holidays in extreme cases; interest free loans to cover debts or other urgent needs.

Exclusions: No grants for private medical treatment, legal representation or private education.

Annual grant total: In 2008 the fund had assets of £783,000 and an income of £72,000. Grants to organisations and individuals totalled £50,000.

Applications: Applications must be submitted with a report and recommendation by a force welfare officer. They can be considered at any time.

Correspondent: Mr D J Hayler, Company Secretary, Police Headquarters, PO Box 37, Portishead, Bristol, BS20 8QJ (01275 816507; email: dave.hayler@avonandsomerset.police.uk)

Avon Local Medical Committee Benevolent Fund

Eligibility: Medical practitioners who are practicing or have practiced in the former county of Avon, and his or her dependants who are in need.

Types of grants: One-off and recurrent grants according to need.

Annual grant total: Each year the fund has a consistent income and total expenditure of around £10,000. Grants to individuals usually total around £5,000.

Applications: In writing to the correspondent.

Correspondent: Dr J C D Rawlins, Acacia House, Chew Magna, Bristol BS40 8PW (01275 332344; fax: 01275 332344)

Other information: Grants are also made to organisations.

The Beckly Trust

Eligibility: Children under 18 who live in the city of Plymouth or district of Caradon, Cornwall and who are sick or disabled and in need.

Types of grants: One-off grants of £200 to £500.

Annual grant total: Grants usually total around £5,000 per year.

Applications: In writing to the correspondent giving brief details of income and outgoings of the applicant's parent/guardian and a description of the child's need. Applications should be made preferably through a social worker, Citizens Advice or other welfare agency but can also be made directly by the individual or through another third party. They are considered on an ongoing basis.

Correspondent: Stephen Trahair, 10 South Hill, Stoke, Plymouth, PL1 5RR (01752 675071)

Other information: The fund occasionally gives to charities/organisations that support such children.

Gloucestershire Football Association Benevolent Fund

Eligibility: The fund website states that it will assist: 'players of clubs affiliated to the Gloucestershire Football Association and in membership of the Fund, and players of Representative League and County Teams, who may be injured whilst playing football in a recognised match.' The fund also helps affiliated referees who are injured whilst officiating at sanctioned matches. Applicants must be unable to work normally for at least two weeks before they will be considered eligible for a grant.

Types of grants: One-off and recurrent grants according to the nature of the accident and the applicant's personal circumstances.

Annual grant total: Grants usually total around £10,000 per year.

Applications: Forms are available from the correspondent or can be downloaded from the website. Applications must be made within 28 days of the injury unless there are exceptional circumstances. All forms must also include a report by a member of council and a doctor's certificate.

Correspondent: Tony Stone, Gloucestershire Football Association Ltd, Oaklands Park Stadium, Gloucester Road, Almondsbury, Bristol, BS32 4AG (01454 615888; email: secretary@gloucestershirefa.com; website: www.gloucestershirefa.com)

The Douglas Martin Trust

Eligibility: People in need who live in southern England but only in cases personally known to the trustees. Unsolicited applications cannot be responded to.

Types of grants: On average 400 one-off grants are made a year of up to £300 for items such as bedding, furniture, children's holidays, debt relief and educational grants. Grants are never made to organisations.

Exclusions: The trust can only support cases known to the trustees.

Annual grant total: In 2008/09 the trust had assets of £798,000 and an income of £51,000. Grants were made totalling £52,000.

Applications: Applications will not be accepted unless applicants are known by the trustees or referred by an organisation known by the trustees.

Correspondent: David Evans, 45 Burnards Field Road, Colyton, Devon EX24 6PE (01297 553007; email: d.d.evans@btinternet.com)

The Pirate Trust

Eligibility: People in need living within the Pirate FM 102 broadcast area (Cornwall, Plymouth and west Devon). Preference is given to people with disabilities.

Types of grants: One-off and recurrent grants mainly towards disability equipment.

Annual grant total: In 2008/09 the trust had an income of £21,000 and a total expenditure of £20,000. Grants are given to both individuals and organisations.

Applications: In writing to the correspondent at any time.

Correspondent: Nicholas Lake, Pirate FM Ltd, Carn Brea Studios, Barncoose Industrial Estate, Redruth, Cornwall TR15 3XX (01209 314400)

The Plymouth & Cornwall Cancer Fund

Eligibility: People in need who have cancer, or who have a dependant or relative with cancer, and live in the county of Cornwall and within a radius of 40 miles of Plymouth Civic Centre in Devon. Also in-patients or out-patients of any hospital controlled by Plymouth Hospital NHS Trust.

Types of grants: One-off grants to relieve hardship which is caused by cancer, for example, towards the cost of travel to hospital for patients and visitors, additional clothing, bed linen, stairlifts and telephone installations and bills. In 2009 grants ranged between £16 and £500.

Annual grant total: In 2008/09 the fund had assets of £183,000 and an income of £47,000. Hardship grants to individuals were made totalling £8,600.

Applications: In writing to the correspondent at any time. Applicants should have exhausted all other potential sources of help before approaching the fund.

Correspondent: P W Harker, Whiteford Crocker, 28 Outland Road, Plymouth PL2 3DE (01752 550711; email: annepccf@blueyonder.co.uk)

St Monica Trust Community Fund

Eligibility: People who have a physical or sensory impairment or a long term physical health problem and live in Bristol or the surrounding area (Gloucestershire, Somerset, Bath and Wiltshire). Applicants must have a low income, limited savings and be over 16 years old.

Types of grants:

Gifts

One-off grants ranging from £50 to £500 to help towards mobility aids, home/car adaptations, domestic appliances, furniture and flooring, bedding, clothing, health costs, driving lessons, communication aids, bills and debts.

Help will not be given for holidays; gardening; bankruptcy fees; funeral expenses; decorating labour costs; respite care and care home fees.

Short-Term Grants

A period of monthly payments designed to help a person through a time of crisis. For example, help can be given for: debt relief; adjusting to a sudden loss of income; unexpected costs; and, the extra costs involved when undergoing chemotherapy, interferon or similar treatments. Usually up to £25 each week is paid for anywhere between a couple of months up to a maximum of three years. It is important to note that help will only be given if the fund believes that the grants it can offer will make a substantial difference in the long-term.

Exclusions: No help is given to people with mental health problems or people with a learning disability unless they also have a physical disability or long-term physical health problem. Help is available to people who are in recovery from substance misuse or alcoholism, provided they have been drug or alcohol free for at least six months and also have a physical disability or long-term physical health problem. Help is not generally given to people who have more than £3,000 in savings.

Annual grant total: In 2008 the fund had assets of £182 million, an income of £16 million and a total expenditure of £15 million. Grants were made to over 1,000 individuals totalling £500,000. Of this, £286,000 was given in gifts, £190,000 in short term grants and £23,000 in annuities.

Applications: On a form available from the correspondent or to download from the fund's website. If possible, applications should be submitted via a social worker, advice worker or a similar professional, although individuals can apply themselves. Depending on the request, a letter may be needed from an occupational therapist confirming the need for a particular item and why it is not available from statutory funds. Individuals should contact the trust if they are having any difficulties in filling out the form, and if needed a home visit can be arranged to help complete their application. Applicants are usually contacted within two weeks of receipt.

Correspondent: Community Fund Manager, Cote Lane, Westbury-on-Trym, Bristol, BS9 3UN (0117 949 4003; email: communityfund@stmonicatrust.org.uk; website: www.communityfund.stmonicatrust.org.uk)

Other information: Grants are also made to organisations (£136,000 in 2008).

Avon

The Anchor Society

Eligibility: Women over 60 and men over 65 who are in need and live in the Bristol postcode area (BS).

Types of grants: Annuities and Christmas gifts, usually up to £500.

Annual grant total: In 2008/09 the charity had assets of £2.4 million and an income of £171,000. Grants were made totalling £87,000, of which around £17,000 was given to individuals.

Applications: In writing to the correspondent.

Correspondent: Siobhan Barker, Administrator, 29 Alma Vale Road, Clifton, Bristol, BS8 2HL (0117 973 4161; email: info@anchorsociety.co.uk; website: www.anchorsociety.co.uk/)

Other information: The society has also invested in the provision of sheltered living and day care accommodation for elderly people and has close links with other welfare charities in the area.

Backwell Foundation

Eligibility: People in need who live in the civil parishes of Backwell and Brockley.

Types of grants: One-off and recurrent grants according to need.

Annual grant total: Grants usually average around £650 per year.

Applications: In writing to the correspondent. The trust does not respond to applications made outside its area of interest.

Correspondent: David James Pike, Sedalia, Brockley Hall, Brockley Lane, Brockley, Bristol, BS48 3AZ (01275 463261)

Bath Dispensary Charity

Eligibility: People who are sick and in need and live in, or very near, Bath.

Types of grants: Grants generally not for more than £750, usually towards medical equipment, but other requests are considered.

Annual grant total: In 2008 the charity had assets of £1.1 million and an income of £63,000 generated from investments. Grants were made to 33 individuals totalling £9,000.

Applications: On a form available from the correspondent. Applications should be made either by the individual or through a third party.

Correspondent: J Money-Kyrle, St John's Hospital, 4–5 Chapel Court, Westgate

Buildings, Bath BA1 1SQ (01225 486410; email: james.money-kyrle@stjohnsbath.org.uk)

The Federation of Master Builders (Bristol Branch) Benevolent Fund

Eligibility: Members of the building trade who live in, or have worked in, Bristol, and their dependants who are in need, usually through illness or infirmity. New entrants training in the construction industry in the Bristol area are also eligible.

Types of grants: One-off grants ranging from £200 to £300 for help with living costs, household bills and disabled equipment.

'The fund is not rich. It provides short-term help to cover difficult or crisis periods. It also gives grants to assist in funding larger items where there are other agencies involved.'

Annual grant total: The total annual expenditure of this charity varies from £300 to £3,300.

Applications: In writing to the correspondent. Applications can be submitted either directly by the individual, through a third party such as a social worker, or through a member of the federation and should include details of the applicant's social circumstances. Applications are considered three times a year.

Correspondent: Geoff White, 15 Ransford, Clevedon, BS21 7YW (01275 870744)

The Grateful Society

Eligibility: Ladies over 50 who have lived in Bristol and the surrounding area for at least 10 years and would benefit from financial assistance in order to pursue an independent life in their own home.

Types of grants: Regular allowances of £100 to £200 a year. One-off grants can be paid towards, for example, electrical goods, clothing, household bills, food, holidays, travel expenses, heating repairs, medical equipment, furniture and disability equipment.

Annual grant total: In 2009 the society had an income of £87,000 and a total expenditure of £79,000. Annuities and gifts were made totalling around £50,000.

Applications: In writing to the correspondent: to be submitted directly by the individual or through a third party.

Correspondent: June Moody, Administrator, 17 St Augustines Parade, Bristol, BS1 4UL (0117 929 1929; fax: 0117 925 3824; email: g-s.moody@btconnect.com; website: gratefulsociety.org)

The Peter Herve Benevolent Institution

Eligibility: People aged 60 and over who live within a 25-mile radius of Bristol city centre, own their own homes and have fallen on hard times.

Types of grants: Recurrent grants, averaging £200 a quarter and one-off emergency grants of up to £300, for example, towards a new boiler.

Annual grant total: In 2008 the trust had assets of £2.4 million and an income of £130,000. Annuities and regular gifts totalled £44,000 and emergency grants totalled £21,000.

Applications: In writing to the correspondent, for consideration throughout the year.

Correspondent: June Moody, 17 St Augustine Parade, Bristol BS1 4UL (0117 929 1929; fax: 0117 925 3824; email: g-s.moody@btconnect.com)

Almondsbury

Almondsbury Charity

Eligibility: People in need in the old parish of Almondsbury.

Types of grants: One-off grants according to need, for instance for household appliances.

Exclusions: Grants are not given towards fuel bills.

Annual grant total: In 2008/09 the trust had assets of £1.8 million and an income from investments totalling £54,000. Grants were made to 16 individuals totalling £5,000. Grants are also made to individuals for educational purposes.

Applications: On a form available from the correspondent. Cash grants are never made directly to the individual; the grant is either paid via a third party such as social services, or the trust pays for the item directly and donates the item to the individual.

Correspondent: A B Gaydon, Chair, Highbank, 7a The Scop, Almondsbury, Bristol BS32 4DU (01454 613424; email: highbankabg@tiscali.co.uk)

Other information: Grants were also made to schools and organisations totalling £25,000 (2008/09).

Bath

The Mayor of Bath's Relief Fund

Eligibility: People in need who live in Bath.

Types of grants: One-off grants ranging from £50 to £350 for carpets, second-hand furniture and appliances, school uniforms and bills. The trust states that its key aim is to ensure that children have 'clean clothes, hot food and a warm house.'

Exclusions: No grants are given for tuition fees or rent arrears.

Annual grant total: In 2008/09 the trust had an income of £7,200 and a total expenditure of £10,000.

Applications: On a form available from local health visitors, social services or Citizens Advice. Applications should be submitted through one of these organisations or a similar third party and are considered throughout the year. Please note grants are only made as a last resort for those who have already exhausted all other funding channels such as Social Security, social services and other local charities.

Correspondent: James Money-Kyrle, c/o St John's Hospital, 4–5 Chapel Court, Bath BA1 1SQ (01225 486400; email: james.money-kyrle@stjohnsbath.org.uk)

The Monmouth Street Society, Bath

Eligibility: The 'deserving poor' who live in Bath and have done so for at least two years.

Types of grants: One-off grants up to £150 towards essential household equipment.

Annual grant total: In 2009 the society had an income of £6,500 and a total expenditure of £5,400.

Applications: Preference for personal applications, but will accept any received through social workers and such like. All cases are investigated by a member of the society, and are considered throughout the year.

Correspondent: James Money-Kyrle, St John's Hospital & Bath, Municipal Charities, 4–5 Chapel Court, Bath BA1 1SQ (01225 486400; email: james.money-kyrle@stjohnsbath.org.uk)

The St John's Hospital, Bath

Eligibility: People in need living in Bath. There are no age restrictions.

Types of grants: Grants, which may be made up of several payments, but generally not for more than a total of £1,500. Help is given towards: food; clothing; TV licenses; furniture; white goods; carpets (if there is a child in the family, there are medical reasons or there are any other exceptional circumstances); bankruptcy fees; rent arrears; utility bills; and counselling. Other requests may be considered.

Exclusions: No grants for: DWP loans; funeral expenses; magistrates court fines; deposits or rent in advance for accommodation; washing machines (unless there is a child in the family or there are medical grounds, in which case medical confirmation must be supplied).

Only one grant per individual/family unit is considered in any twelve-month period. No family or individual shall receive more than three grants within five years or up to a limit set by the trustees.

Annual grant total: In 2009 relief-in-need grants to individuals totalled £176,000.

Applications: On a form available from most local welfare agencies, such as Citizens Advice, Housing Advice Centre and social services. This will be forwarded with a recommendation to the correspondent.

Correspondent: James Money-Kyrle, Director of Support Services, St John's Hospital, 4–5 Chapel Court, Bath BA1 1SQ (01225 486400; email: info@stjohnsbath. org.uk; website: www.stjohnsbath.org.uk)

Bath & North East Somerset

Combe Down Holiday Trust

Eligibility: People who are disabled, their families and carers, who live in the Bath and North East Somerset area.

Types of grants: One-off grants averaging around £130 towards the cost of a holiday, short break or respite care.

Annual grant total: In 2009 the trust had assets of £815,000 and an income of £52,000. There were 235 welfare grants made totalling £31,000.

Applications: On a form available from the correspondent, to be submitted directly by the individual or through a social worker, Citizens Advice or other welfare agency.

Correspondent: John Carter, c/o Combe Down Surgery, The Avenue, Combe Down, Bath BA2 5EG (01225 837181; email: ro@cdht.org.uk; website: beehive. thisisbath.com/cdht)

Other information: Please note, specialised accommodation is usually booked months in advance, so applicants are advised to apply as early as possible to avoid disappointment.

Bristol

Thomas Beames' Charity

Eligibility: People in need who live in the ancient parish of St George with St Augustine, Bristol or the parishes of Christchurch with St George, St Stephen with St James or St John the Baptist with St Michael, Bristol. In exceptional cases, the charity may help people who live outside this area and who produce sufficient good reason why they should be treated as being resident within the parish.

Types of grants: Grants are made at the discretion of the trustees, towards, for

example, bedding, food and electrical cookers.

Annual grant total: In 2009/10 the charity had an income of £5,600 and a total expenditure of £5,000.

Applications: In writing to the correspondent including details of why help is needed. Applications are usually considered quarterly.

Correspondent: David Cross, 1 All Saints Court, Bristol, BS1 1JN (01179 665739)

The Bristol Benevolent Institution

Eligibility: Older people living in their own homes with small fixed incomes and little or no capital. Applicants must be over 60 and have lived in Bristol for 15 years or more.

Types of grants: Mostly small recurrent grants paid quarterly in advance within the level disregarded by the DWP when calculating benefits. Also, for people aged 70 or over who own their own house, free of mortgage, interest free loans of £1,500 a year can be given against the security of their deeds. Loans to be repaid on death or the sale of property. There is no charge for redemption at any time.

Annual grant total: In 2009 the trust had assets of £11 million and an income of £421,000. Grants to individuals totalled £336,000.

Applications: On a form available from the correspondent. Applications can be submitted directly by the individual or by a third party such as a social worker or Citizens Advice. Applicants are asked to provide details of income and expenditure. All applicants are visited. The trustees meet quarterly in March, June, September and December to discuss applications.

Correspondent: Maureen Nicholls, Secretary, 45 High Street, Nailsea, Bristol, BS48 1AW (01275 810 365; email: maureen.nicholls1@btinternet.com)

Bristol Charities

Eligibility: People in need who have lived in Bristol for more than two consecutive years.

Types of grants: Grants will normally be considered for bedding/beds, carpets, clothing for school age children, white goods, furniture, medical equipment, decorating materials and respite care.

The following items, purchased through the 'retained ownership scheme' will be considered: wheelchairs, electric wheelchairs, electric powered chairs/ electric scooters, standard stair lifts, stair lifts with a manual platform and stair lifts with a powered platform.

Exclusions: No grants for debts or rent arrears. Only one grant is given per applicant per year and there is a limit of three grants per person.

Annual grant total: In 2008/09 grants to over 1400 individuals totalled £140,000.

Applications: On a form available from social workers, health visitors, Citizens Advice, housing associations, and so on, who make the application on behalf of the individual. Applications are considered daily.

Correspondent: D W Jones, Chief Executive, 17 Augustines Parade, Bristol BS1 4UL (0117 930 0303; fax: 0117 925 3824; email: info@ bristolcharities.org.uk; website: www. bristolcharities.org.uk)

The Lord Mayor of Bristol's Christmas Appeal for Children

Eligibility: Children under 16 who are in need and who live in the city of Bristol.

Types of grants: One-off grants of around £20 in the form of vouchers for food, clothes and toys at Christmas.

Annual grant total: In 2008/09 the trust had assets of £110,000 and an income of £42,000. Grants were made totalling £43,000.

Applications: Through a social worker, Citizens Advice, welfare agency or other third party such as a parent or a person who can confirm the individual's needs.

Correspondent: B N Simmonds, Hon. Treasurer, 3 Park Crescent, Frenchay, Bristol, BS16 1PD

The Dolphin Society

Eligibility: People in need and/or at risk through poor health, disability or financial difficulty and who live in Bristol. Preference is given to older people who need help in maintaining their independence and security in their own homes.

Types of grants: Help with telephone installations, smoke alarms, pendant alarms, minor repairs and security items such as door and window locks. One-off cash grants are given occasionally and can range from £10 to £1,000.

Exclusions: No grants to applicants living outside the area of benefit.

Annual grant total: In 2008/09 the society had an income of £76,000 and a total expenditure of £142,000. Grants were made totalling about £130,000.

Applications: On a form available from the correspondent. Applications can be submitted directly by the individual or family member or by an appropriate third party. There are no deadlines and applications are considered throughout the year.

Correspondent: June Moody, Administrator, 17 Augustines Parade, Bristol, BS1 4UL (0117 929 9649; email: dolphinsociety@btconnect.com; website: dolphin-society.org.uk)

Other information: The society also makes grants to local self-help groups, community centres and day care centres.

The Redcliffe Parish Charity

Eligibility: People in need who live in the city of Bristol.

Types of grants: One-off grants usually of £25 to £50. 'The trustees generally limit grants to families or individuals who can usually manage, but who are overwhelmed by circumstances and are in particular financial stress rather than continuing need.' Grants are typically given for electric goods, clothing, living costs, food, holidays, furniture and disabled equipment.

Exclusions: No grants for bankruptcy fees, debts in respect of Council Tax, rent arrears or credit debts.

Annual grant total: In 2008/09 the charity had an income of £10,000 and a total expenditure of £7,000.

Applications: In writing to the correspondent. Applications should be submitted on the individual's behalf by a social worker, doctor, health visitor, Citizens Advice or appropriate third party, and will be considered early in each month. Ages of family members should be supplied in addition to financial circumstances and the reason for the request.

Correspondent: Margaret Jardine, Jowayne, Hobbs Wall, Farmborough, Bath BA2 0BJ (01761 471713)

Other information: Grants to schoolchildren occur as part of the trust's wider welfare work.

The Unity Fund for the Elderly

Eligibility: People over 60 in need, hardship or distress in the Bristol area.

Types of grants: One-off grants towards repairs, clothing, electric goods, household bills, medical equipment, furniture, disability equipment and so on.

Annual grant total: In 2009 the fund had an income of £14,000 and a total expenditure of £19,000.

Applications: In writing to the correspondent. Applications should be submitted through a social worker, Citizens Advice or other welfare agency. They are considered at any time.

Correspondent: D H T Rowcliffe, Secretary, 5 Bishop Road, Emersons Green, Bristol BS16 7ET (0117 956 1289)

Other information: Grants are also made to organisations.

Wraxall Parochial Charities

Eligibility: People living in the parish of Wraxall and Failand, Bristol who are in need due to hardship or disability.

Types of grants: One-off grants.

Annual grant total: In 2008 the charity had an income of £16,000 and a total expenditure of £17,000.

Applications: In writing to the correspondent, directly by the individual. Applications are considered in February, June, September and November.

Correspondent: Mrs A Sissons, Clerk to the Trustees, 2 Short Way, Failand, Bristol BS8 3UF (01275 392691)

Other information: Grants are also made for educational purposes.

Midsomer Norton

Ralph and Irma Sperring Charity

Eligibility: People in need who live within a five-mile radius of the Church of St John the Baptist in Midsomer Norton, Bath.

Types of grants: One-off and recurrent grants according to need.

Annual grant total: In 2009/10 the foundation had assets of £5.8 million, which generated an income of £201,000. Awards to local causes amounted to £117,000. Further details were not available, however the trust makes grants to both individuals and organisations.

Applications: In writing to the correspondent, to be considered quarterly.

Correspondent: The Secretary, Thatcher & Hallam Solicitors, Island House, Midsomer Norton, Bath BA3 2HJ (01761 414646)

North Somerset

Nailsea Community Trust Ltd

Eligibility: People of any age or occupation who are in need due, for example, to hardship, disability or sickness, and who live in the town of Nailsea and the immediate area in North Somerset.

Types of grants: One-off grants, usually up to £500, towards items, services or facilities.

Annual grant total: About £5,000 for educational and welfare purposes.

Applications: On a form available from the correspondent. Applications can be submitted either directly by the individual or via a relevant third party such as a school, social worker or Citizens Advice. Applications are considered at meetings held every three months.

Correspondent: Phil Williams, 11 Walnut Close, Nailsea, Bristol, BS48 4YT

Charles Graham Stone's Relief-in-Need Charity

Eligibility: People in need who live in the parishes of Churchill and Langford, North Somerset.

Types of grants: One-off grants of £50 to £150 towards travel expenses of visiting relatives in hospitals or nursing homes, help in the home, household bills or medical/disability equipment.

Exclusions: No grants for payment of national or local taxes or rates.

Annual grant total: In 2009 the charity had an income of £4,200 and an expenditure of £4,000. Grants are made to individuals for educational purposes.

Applications: In writing to the correspondent with a full explanation of the personal circumstances. Applications should be submitted by the end of February or August for consideration in the following month. Initial telephone calls are not welcomed.

Correspondent: John Gravell, Easton Grey, Webbington Road, Cross, Axbridge, BS26 2EL

Other information: Grants are also made to vocational students in the parishes.

Portishead

The Portishead Nautical Trust

Eligibility: People in need, usually under 25, who live in Portishead. Preference is given to people who are: homeless; unemployed; experiencing problems related to drug or solvent abuse; being ill-treated; being neglected, in the areas of physical, moral and educational well-being; or 'people who have committed criminal acts, or are in danger of doing so'.

Types of grants: Small grants and bursaries, 'where such a grant will enable a young person to realise their full potential'.

Annual grant total: In 2008/09 the trust had an income of £97,000. Grants totalled £50,000, of which £2,500 was donated to individuals.

Applications: On a form available from the correspondent. Applications must be supported by a sponsor, such as a welfare officer or health visitor. Trustees meet four times a year to consider applications

Correspondent: P C Dingley-Brown, Secretary, 108 High Street, Portishead, Bristol, BS20 6AJ (01275 847463; fax: 01275 818871)

South Gloucestershire

The Chipping Sodbury Town Lands

Eligibility: People in need who live in Chipping Sodbury or Old Sodbury.

Types of grants: One-off and recurrent grants according to need.

Annual grant total: In 2009 grants made towards winter heating bills totalled £9,000.

Applications: In writing to the correspondent.

Correspondent: Mrs Nicola Gideon, Clerk, Town Hall, 57–59 Broad Street, Chipping Sodbury, South Gloucestershire BS37 6AD (01454 852223; email: nicola.gideon@ chippingsodburytownhall.co.uk)

Stanton Prior

The Henry Smith Charity (Longnet Estate)

Eligibility: People in need who have lived in Stanton Prior for more than three years. Preference is usually given to those living in rented accommodation.

Types of grants: One-off cash grants and gift vouchers.

Annual grant total: Grants usually total around £1,000 each year.

Applications: In writing to the correspondent, directly by the individual, for consideration by the trustees in November and December.

Correspondent: Alistair Hardwick, Church Farm, Stanton Prior, Bath BA2 9HT (01761 479625)

Thornbury

Thornbury Consolidated Charities (administered by Thornbury Town Trust)

Eligibility: People in need who live in the parish of Thornbury. Beneficiaries are often of pensionable age or disabled but anyone in the parish can apply.

Types of grants: One-off grants usually ranging from £80 to £120 to help with the extra expense of Christmas but they are also given at other times.

Exclusions: No grants for educational purposes. Grants are not given where the need is covered by statutory authorities.

Annual grant total: In 2009 the charities had assets of £814,000 and an income of £36,000. Grants were made totalling £27,000.

Applications: By letter to the correspondent. Applications can be submitted directly by the individual or through a social worker, Citizens Advice or other welfare agency and should include details of income. They are considered in November for Christmas but applications for special needs can be made at any time.

Correspondent: Margaret Powell, 9 Elmdale Crescent, Thornbury, Bristol, BS35 2JH (01454 281777; email: margaret. towntrust@googlemail.com)

Other information: Grants are also given to organisations.

Cornwall

The Blanchminster Trust

Eligibility: People who live in the parishes of Bude, Stratton and Poughill (the former urban district of Bude-Stratton).

Types of grants: Generally one-off grants up to a maximum of £25,000 for the relief of need, hardship or distress, for example for clothing, food, electrical goods, furniture, medical care and equipment, and travel to and from hospital.

Exclusions: Grants are not given to foreign students studying in Britain.

Annual grant total: The majority of grants to individuals are given for educational purposes and total around £180,000 each year. In addition, a smaller number of grants are given for relief in need purposes which total around £20,000.

Applications: On a form available from the correspondent. Applications are considered monthly and should be submitted directly by the individual. Where possible the application should include a request for a specific amount and be supported with quotes for the costs needed and/or written support from a social worker or other welfare agency. Applications must include evidence of financial need.

Correspondent: Owen A May, Clerk, Blanchminster Building, 38 Lansdown Road, Bude, Cornwall EX23 8EE (01288 352851; fax: 01288 352851; email: office@blanchminster.plus.com)

Other information: Grants are also made to community projects.

The Lizzie Brooke Charity

Eligibility: Older people, people who are sick and those in need who live in West Cornwall.

Types of grants: One-off grants ranging from £100 to £200 for the necessities of everyday living. Grants can be given towards electric goods, clothing, holidays, travel expenses, furniture and hospital expenses.

Exclusions: Grants are not made to people living in other parts of Cornwall or for students for fees.

Annual grant total: In 2009 the charity had an income of £30 and a total expenditure of £8,500. Grants were made totalling around £8,000.

Applications: On a form available from the correspondent and completed by a sponsor. Applications should be submitted through a social worker, Citizens Advice or other welfare agency. They are considered at any time.

Correspondent: Mrs Sheila Bates, 13 Church Close, Lelant, St Ives TR26 3JX

(01736 752383; email: mail@anthony-williams.co.uk)

Cornwall Community Foundation

Eligibility: People in need living in Cornwall.

Types of grants: Usually one-off.

Annual grant total: In 2009 the foundation had assets of £1.6 million and an income of £1.1 million. Grants were made to individuals through three funds totalling £26,000.

Applications: Initial enquiries should be directed to the grants team to check what funds are available.

Please visit the foundation's website for further information.

Correspondent: The Grants Team, Suite 1, Sheers Barton, Lawhitton, Launceston, Cornwall PL15 9NJ (01566 779333; email: grants@cornwallfoundation.com; website: www.cornwallfoundation.com/)

The Cornwall Retired Clergy, Widows of the Clergy and their Dependants Fund

Eligibility: Widows, widowers and dependants of deceased members of the clergy who live in, or have worked in, the diocese of Truro. Retired Anglican clergy who are in need and have links with Truro are also eligible for support.

Types of grants: Grants are one-off and occasionally recurrent according to need. Recent grants have ranged from £50 to £500 and included funding for dentist's fees, spectacles, travel to hospital and assistance with equipment for people with disabilities.

Exclusions: No grants for assistance with school fees or university fees.

Annual grant total: In 2009 the fund had an income of £14,000 and a total expenditure of £13,000.

Applications: In writing to the correspondent. Applications can be submitted directly by the individual or through a relative or a carer. They are usually considered monthly.

Correspondent: C M Kent, Truro Diocesan Board Of Finance, Diocesan House, Truro, Cornwall, TR1 1JQ (01872 274351; email: accountant@truro. anglican.org)

The Duke of Cornwall's Benevolent Fund

Eligibility: People who are in need, though in practice funds are steered towards the West Country and areas related to Duchy lands, which are principally in Cornwall.

Types of grants: One-off and recurrent grants according to need.

Annual grant total: In 2008/09 the fund had assets of £2.5 million and an income of £113,000. Grants totalled £109,000, of which £2,000 was awarded to one individual.

Applications: In writing to the correspondent.

Correspondent: Robert G Mitchell, 10 Buckingham Gate, London SW1E 6LA (020 7834 7346)

Other information: The fund's main focus is on awarding grants to charitable organisations.

The United Charities of Liskeard

Eligibility: For the relief-in-need fund, people in need who live in the town of Liskeard (formerly the borough of Liskeard). For the relief-in-sickness fund, people in need who live in Liskeard, the parish of Dobwalls with Trewidland (formerly the parish of Liskeard) and the parishes of Menheniot and St Cleer.

Types of grants: One-off and recurrent grants according to need.

Annual grant total: Grants usually total around £1,000 each year.

Applications: In writing to the correspondent.

Correspondent: A J Ball, Tremellick, Pengover Road, Liskeard, Cornwall PL14 3EW (01579 343577)

Gunwalloe

The Charity of Thomas Henwood

Eligibility: People who are unemployed, sick and retired and live in the parish of Gunwalloe.

Types of grants: One-off or recurrent grants according to need, and grants for the provision of nurses and to assist people recovering from illness. All by periodic distribution. Grants range from £60 to £100. Income is also used to care for graves in the churchyard if no relatives are still alive.

Annual grant total: In 2008 the charity had an income of £9,100 and a total expenditure of £7,600.

Applications: In writing to the trustees. Applications are considered in March and December.

Correspondent: Beryl Pollard, Trustee, 31 Cunnack Close, Helston, Cornwall TR13 8XQ (01326 564535)

Gwennap

Charity of John Davey

Eligibility: Ex-miners over 70 years of age, or their widows, who live in the ancient parish of Gwennap, near Redruth in Cornwall and are in need.

Types of grants: Quarterly grants of £10 to £40 for general living expenses.

Annual grant total: In 2008/09 the charity had an income of £13,000 and a total expenditure of £11,000. Grants usually total around £10,000.

Applications: Initial telephone calls to the correspondent are welcome and application forms are available on request. Applications can be submitted directly by the individual or family member.

Correspondent: E T Pascoe, Tregenna Lodge, Crane, Camborne TR14 7QX (01209 718853)

Helston

The Helston Welfare Trust

Eligibility: People in need who live in the area administered by Helston Town Council.

Types of grants: One-off grants in kind. The trust will purchase essential electrical goods like cookers, refrigerators or furniture on behalf of the individual.

Annual grant total: This trust's income is generally in the region of £2,500 a year. Total expenditure averages around £880.

Applications: In writing to the correspondent. Applications can be submitted directly by the individual or through a third party such as a social worker or an organisation such as Citizens Advice. Details of need and the financial circumstances of the applicant should be included. Applications are considered as they are received.

Correspondent: Chris Dawson, Guildhall, Helston, Cornwall TR13 8ST (01326 572063; email: townclerk@ helstontc.com)

Penzance

Mayor's Welfare Fund

Eligibility: People who live in Penzance and who are suffering from hardship.

Types of grants: One-off and recurrent grants according to need.

Annual grant total: This trust generally has a yearly income and total expenditure of around £2,000.

Applications: In writing to the correspondent by the end of October, directly by the individual or through a

third party on their behalf. Applications are considered in November.

Correspondent: Town Clerk, Town Clerk's Office, Alverton Street, Penzance, Cornwall TR18 2QP (01736 363405; fax: 01736 330221; email: townclerk@pz-towncouncil.fsnet.co.uk)

Devon

The Barnstaple & North Devon Dispensary Fund

Eligibility: People in need who live in the North Devon parishes.

Types of grants: One-off grants towards coal and heating bills, convalescence, medical equipment and other costs, bedding, clothing, travel expenses and food.

Annual grant total: In 2009 the fund had an income of £13,000 and a total expenditure of £12,000.

Applications: In writing to the correspondent, preferably through a doctor, health visitor, social worker or other third party.

Correspondent: Christina Ford, 17 Sloe Lane, Landkey, Barnstaple, Devon, EX32 0UF (01271 831551; email: bandnddf@gmail.com)

Bideford Bridge Trust

Eligibility: People in need who live in Bideford and the immediate neighbourhood.

Types of grants: One-off grants ranging from £150 to £500.

Exclusions: Grants are not given for computers for personal use.

Annual grant total: In 2009 welfare grants totalled £24,000.

Applications: On a form available from the correspondent, to be submitted at any time during the year by the individual, although a sponsor is usually required.

Correspondent: P R Sims, Steward, 24 Bridgeland Street, Bideford, Devon EX39 2QB (01237 473122)

Edward Blagdon's Charity

Eligibility: People in need who live in Tiverton and Washfield in Devon.

Types of grants: One-off grants only ranging from £10 to £500.

Annual grant total: In 2008/09 the trust had an income of £15,000 and a total expenditure of £5,100.

Applications: In writing to the correspondent directly by the individual or through a social worker, Citizens Advice or other welfare agency.

Correspondent: Joan McCahon, Clerk to the Trustees, Gunshot Cottage, Lower Washfield, Tiverton, Devon, EX16 9PD (01884 253468)

The Brownsdon & Tremayne Estate Charity (also known as the Nicholas Watts' Gift)

Eligibility: For the Brownsdon Fund, men in need who live in Devon, with a preference for Tavistock applicants, preferably owner/occupiers. For the Tremayne Estate Charity, people in need who live in Tavistock.

Types of grants: One-off grants averaging around £300 each. In addition to general relief-in-need, the trustees help towards the maintenance of homes owned by beneficiaries, for example, providing new carpets, grants towards the costs of roof repairs and occasionally supplying computers to people with disabilities.

Exclusions: The trust does not assist with mortgage repayments.

Annual grant total: In 2008/09 the charity had an income of £18,000 and a total expenditure £9,800. Grants were made to 22 individuals totalling £7,100.

Applications: On a form available from the correspondent. The trustees advertise for applications in July, to be considered in September, but at other times for emergencies. Applications can be submitted directly by the individual.

Correspondent: Joan Stewart, 17 Chapel Street, Tavistock, Devon, PL19 8DX

Cranbrook Charity

Eligibility: People in need who live in the parishes of Dunsford, Doddiscombeleigh and 'that part of the parish of Holcombe Burnel as in 1982 constituted part of the parish of Dunsford'.

Types of grants: One off and recurrent grants to those in need. Recently, grants of £80 have been given every six months for relief-in-need and educational purposes.

Annual grant total: In 2008/09 the charity had both an income and total expenditure of £10,000.

Applications: In writing to the correspondent.

Correspondent: Stephen Purser, Venn Farm, Bridford, Exeter EX6 7LF (01647 252328; email: purseratvenn@ hotmail.com)

Other information: Grants are also made for educational purposes.

The Devon County Association for the Blind

Eligibility: People who are blind or partially sighted who live in Devon (excluding the city of Exeter and Plymouth).

Types of grants: Grants of up to £250 to cover specific needs including holidays, travel expenses, medical equipment, furniture and disabled equipment.

Annual grant total: In 2008/09 the charity had assets of £923,000 and an income of £240,000. Grants were made to 17 individuals totalling £4,500.

Applications: On a form available from the correspondent. Applications are considered quarterly and should be submitted either directly by the individual or through a third party such as a social worker.

Correspondent: Mrs Sue Auton, Director, Station House, Holman Way, Topsham, Exeter EX3 0EN (01392 876666; fax: 01392 874442; email: devon-blind@ btconnect.com; website: www.devonblind. org.uk)

Other information: Grants are also made to organisations and to individuals for education.

The Dodbrooke Parish Charity

Eligibility: People in need who live in the parishes of Dodbrooke and Kingsbridge.

Types of grants: One-off grants and pensions to older people.

Annual grant total: In 2009 the trust had an income of £25,000 and a total expenditure of £30,000.

Applications: In writing to the correspondent. Applications are considered in January, March, June and September.

Correspondent: David Tucker, 6 Alvington Terrace, Westville, Kingsbridge, Devon TQ7 1HD

The Exeter Relief-in-Need Charity

Eligibility: People in need who live in the city of Exeter.

Types of grants: One-off grants of between £50 and £150; individuals can reapply in subsequent years. Grants are made towards household furniture and equipment, floor coverings, school uniforms, essential travelling expenses, heating costs and so on.

Exclusions: No grants for debt repayment, interest on loans, rent, mortgage, or council tax arrears.

Annual grant total: In 2009 the charity had an income of £13,000 and a total expenditure of £23,000.

Applications: On a form available from the correspondent, submitted directly by the individual, or through a social worker, Citizens Advice or other welfare agency. Applications should include details of the income, including benefits and outgoings of the applicant. Three references must normally be supplied. Awards are made following interviews of the applicants by

trustees in February, May, August and November.

Correspondent: Martin R King, Clerk, Exeter Municipal Charities, Chichester Mews, 22A Southernhay East, Exeter EX1 1QU (01392 201550; email: admin@ exetermunicipalcharities.org.uk; website: www.exetermunicipalcharities.org. uk/)

Other information: This charity is part of Exeter Municipal Charities.

The Heathcoat Trust

Eligibility: People who are older, in poor health or financial need and live in Tiverton and the mid-Devon area. Applicants need to have a personal connection with either the John Heathcoat or the Lowman Companies.

Types of grants: One-off and recurrent grants according to need.

Annual grant total: In 2008/09 the trust had assets of £16 million and an income of £798,000. There were 4,446 grants made to individuals totalling £479,000, distributed as follows:

In cases of hardship	4,000
Chiropody	17,000
Consolidated grant	214,000
General	20,000
Educational bodies	131,000
In cases of hardship	6,000
Hospital visiting	24,000
Death grants	21,000
Communication grant	10,000
Opticians' charges	21,000
Dentists' charges	13,000
Death grants	20,000

Applications: In writing to the correspondent.

Correspondent: Mrs C J Twose, Secretary, The Factory, Tiverton, Devon EX16 5LL

Other information: Grants were also made to charitable organisations (£114,000 in 2008/09).

The Christopher Hill Charity

Eligibility: People in need who live in the former parish of Netherexe or in the surrounding parishes in Devon.

Types of grants: One-off grants according to need.

Annual grant total: Grants to individuals are in the region of £600 a year.

Applications: In writing to the correspondent. Applications can be submitted directly by the individual or through a third party such as Citizens Advice or a social worker. Applications are considered in December or anytime in urgent cases.

Correspondent: Colin Bond, Trustee, Fortescue Crossing, Thorverton, Exeter EX5 5JN (01392 841512)

Other information: Grants are also given to organisations.

The Maudlyn Lands Charity

Eligibility: People who live in the Plympton St Mary and Sparkwell areas and are in financial need.

Types of grants: One-off or recurrent grants, usually ranging between £250 and £500.

Annual grant total: Grants total around £7,000 each year.

Applications: In writing to the correspondent. Applications are considered in November.

Correspondent: Anthony Peter Golding, Clerk to the Trustees, Blue Haze, Down Road, Tavistock, Devon PL19 9AG (01822 612983)

Other information: The charity also makes grants to local organisations.

Northcott Devon Foundation

Eligibility: People living in Devon who are in need as the result of illness, injury, bereavement or exceptional disadvantages.

Types of grants: One-off and recurrent grants of up to £200 can be given towards, for example, computers for children with physical disabilities, adaptations, repairs, holidays, clothing, furniture and wheelchairs.

Exclusions: No grants towards long-term educational needs, funeral expenses or to relieve debts.

Annual grant total: In 2008/09 the foundation had assets of £4.5 million and an income of £214,000. Grants were made to 995 individuals totalling £187,000.

Applications: On a form available from the correspondent. Applications can be submitted through a social worker, Citizens Advice, welfare agency or a third party such as a doctor, health visitor or SSAFA. Applications should include the individual's name and address, and details of income and expenditure, type of household, age and children. They are considered every month.

Correspondent: G Folland, 1b Victoria Road, Exmouth, Devon EX8 1DL (01395 269204; fax: 01395 269204)

Other information: Grants are also made to organisations (£12,000 in 2008/09).

South West Peninsula Football League Benevolent Fund

Eligibility: People in need who live in the county of Devon who are or were involved with a club in the Devon County Football League, and referees in the league. Grants are given to people who have disabilities, have a serious illness, or who have experienced personal misfortune.

Types of grants: One-off and recurrent grants ranging from £50 to £250. A recent grant was made to a player with a depressed cheekbone fracture.

Exclusions: There are no grants available to people with short term injuries, or anyone not considered to be 'in need'.

Annual grant total: Grants to individuals are generally around £800 a year.

Applications: In writing to the correspondent either directly by the individual, or through a social worker, Citizens Advice, or other third party such as the club secretary. The trustees meet to consider applications on the first Thursdays in January, March, May, September and November. Applications should include the individual's marital and employment status, number of children and length of incapacity.

Correspondent: Mark Hayman, SCONICCA, 17 Nelson Place, Newton Abbot, Devon TQ12 2JH (01626 363376; website: www.swpleague.co.uk)

Other information: Grants are also given to organisations.

The Tavistock, Whitchurch & District Nursing Association Trust Fund

Eligibility: People in poor health who are in need and live in Tavistock, Whitchurch, Brentor, Mary Tavy and Peter Tavy, Lamerton, Tavistock Hamlets and part of the parish of Lydford.

Types of grants: One-off grants of up to about £100 to help with heating and water bills, travel to medical appointments, stair lifts and alarm systems to help people stay in their own homes and to assist carers in caring for spouses. Grants can occasionally be recurrent.

Annual grant total: Grants usually total about £1,500 each year.

Applications: In writing to the correspondent: to be submitted either directly by the individual or through a social worker, Citizens Advice or similar third party.

Correspondent: Brenda Mary Moyse, Beechwood Lodge, 7 Wheal Josiah Cottages, Tavistock PL19 8NZ (01822 834358)

Other information: The fund also gives to organisations.

The Christine Woodmancy Charitable Foundation

Eligibility: Children and young people under the age of 21 who live in the Plymouth area and are in need.

Types of grants: One-off grants to help maintain and educate young people in need.

Annual grant total: In 2008/09 the foundation had an income of £23,000 and a total expenditure of £15,000. However, in previous years grants have tended to be given mostly to organisations rather than individuals.

Applications: In writing to the correspondent, directly by the individual or via a social worker, Citizens Advice or other welfare agency. Applications should include background information and provide evidence of financial need.

Correspondent: Jill Hill, Thompson and Jackson, 4–5 Lawrence Road, Plymouth, PL4 6HR (01752 665037; email: jill@ thompsonandjackson.co.uk)

Barnstaple

The Barnstaple Municipal Charities (The Poors Charity Section)

Eligibility: People in need who live in the parish of Barnstaple.

Types of grants: One-off grants available to people in need.

Annual grant total: In 2008/09 the Poors Charity section had an income of £760. No grants were made during the year.

Applications: In writing to the correspondent. Applications are considered quarterly.

Correspondent: M Steele, 29 Carrington Terrace, Yeo Vale, Barnstaple, Devon EX32 7AF (01271 346354; email: barnstaplemunicipalcharities@msn. com)

Bridge Trust

Eligibility: People who live in the borough of Barnstaple, Devon, with a preference for people who have disabilities, older and young people.

Types of grants: Emergency grants of up to £100.

Exclusions: Educational grants are not given.

Annual grant total: About £3,000 a year is available for individuals.

Applications: In writing to the correspondent. Applications must be made via a social worker, Citizens Advice or other welfare agency or third party.

Correspondent: C J Bartlett, Clerk to the Trustees, 7 Bridge Chambers, Barnstaple, Devon EX31 1HB (01271 343995)

Other information: The trust's main priority is the maintenance of 24 properties in Barnstaple and making grants to local organisations.

Bratton Fleming

The Bratton Fleming Relief-in-Need Charity

Eligibility: People in any kind of need living within the parish of Bratton Fleming.

Types of grants: One-off and recurrent grants towards, for example, extra expenses caused by children going to new schools, heating during the winter or medical expenses.

Annual grant total: Grants usually average around £2,100 a year.

Applications: In writing to the correspondent or by word of mouth by the individual or a third party on their behalf, to be considered in early June and early December.

Correspondent: Terrence Squire, Haxlea, 2 Threeways, Bratton Fleming, Barnstaple, Devon EX31 4TG (01598 710526)

Brixham

John Mitchelmore's Charity

Eligibility: People who live in Brixham who are in need, for example due to hardship, disability or sickness.

Types of grants: One-off or recurrent grants according to need.

Annual grant total: Grants average around £1,800 a year, though the actual grant figure tends to fluctuate quite widely.

Applications: In writing to the correspondent.

Correspondent: Russell Denny Postlethwaite, The Tern, 38 Station Hill, Brixham, Devon, TQ5 8BN (01803 851036; email: russelldenny@onetel.com)

Brixton

The Brixton Feoffee Trust

Eligibility: People in need who live in the parish of Brixton, near Plymouth.

Types of grants: One-off and recurrent grants according to need. Recent grants have been given for disability aids, driving lessons, pre-school costs and an orthopaedic chair.

Exclusions: The charity cannot give grants where the funds can be obtained from state sources.

Annual grant total: In 2008/09 the trust had assets of £1 million and an income of £63,000. Grants were made totalling £18,000 of which £1,600 was given to individuals, £7,900 to St Mary's Church and £8,300 to local organisations and initiatives.

Applications: In writing to the correspondent including as much detail as possible. Applications can be submitted directly by the individual or through a social worker, Citizens Advice or other welfare agency or third party. They are considered throughout the year.

Correspondent: Sally Axell, 15 Cherry Tree Drive, Brixton, Plymouth PL8 2DD (01752 880262)

Other information: The trust's scheme states that its net income should be shared equally between people in need in the parish of Brixton and a local church, St Mary's in Brixton, for its upkeep and maintenance. If any of the allotted money is unspent at the end of the financial year it is transferred to a third fund which is distributed to charitable schemes that benefit Brixton parish as a whole.

Broadhempston

The Broadhempston Relief-in-Need Charity

Eligibility: People in need who live in the parish of Broadhempston.

Types of grants: One-off or recurrent grants ranging from £40 to £100. Recent grants have included assistance with food and fuel for older people, residential school trips for special needs families and aids for older people and people with disabilities. Grants are also made towards children's educational trips and aids for educational purposes.

Annual grant total: Grants for both welfare and educational purposes generally total around £1,000 a year.

Applications: In writing to the correspondent directly by the individual to be considered in June and December.

Correspondent: Mrs R H E Brown, Meadows, Broadhempston, Totnes, Devon TQ9 6BW (01803 813130)

Other information: The charity also gives grants for educational purposes.

Budleigh Salterton

The Budleigh Salterton Nursing Association

Eligibility: People living in the parish of Budleigh Salterton who are in poor health, convalescent or who have disabilities.

Types of grants: One-off grants according to need. Recent grants have been given for wheelchairs, raised beds, reclining chairs, stair lifts, telephone extensions and travel allowances.

Annual grant total: Grants usually total about £1,500 each year.

Applications: In writing to the correspondent. Applications can be submitted directly by the individual or through a social worker, Citizens Advice or other appropriate third party.

Correspondent: Mrs B Tilbury, Hayes End, 1 Boucher Way, Budleigh Salterton, Devon EX9 6HQ (01395 442304)

Fryer Welfare and Recreational Trusts

Eligibility: People in need living in the local authority boundary of Budleigh Salterton.

Types of grants: One-off grants of £200 to £500 for recreational and welfare purposes.

Annual grant total: In 2008/09 the trusts had an income of £1,800 and a total expenditure of £900.

Applications: In writing to the correspondent at any time. Applications can be submitted directly by the individual or through a social worker, Citizens Advice or other welfare agency.

Correspondent: W K H Coxe, Council Chambers, Station Road, Budleigh Salterton, Devon EX9 6RL (01395 442223)

Colyton

The Colyton Parish Lands Charity

Eligibility: People in need in the ancient parish of Colyton.

Types of grants: One-off and recurrent grants towards electrical goods, convalescence, clothing, household bills, holidays, travel expenses, medical equipment, furniture and disability equipment.

Annual grant total: In 2008/09 the charity had an income of £56,000. Grants totalled £900 which included grants made to the local primary school, local individuals and organisations.

Applications: In writing to the correspondent to be submitted either directly by the individual or a family member, through a third party such as a social worker or teacher, or through a welfare agency such as a Citizens Advice. Applications are considered monthly.

Correspondent: A Kekwick, Colyton Chamber of Feoffees, Town Hall, Market Place, Colyton, Devon EX24 6JR (01297 552129)

Other information: Grants are made to both individuals and organisations.

Cornwood

Reverend Duke Yonge Charity

Eligibility: People in need who live in the parish of Cornwood.

Types of grants: One-off and recurrent grants according to need. Recent grants have included help with playgroup attendance fees, a sit-in shower facility, a support chair and winter heating costs.

Annual grant total: In 2009 the charity had both an income and total expenditure of around £14,000. Grants for welfare purposes usually total about £5,000 a year.

Applications: In writing to the correspondent via the trustees, who are expected to make themselves aware of any need. Applications are considered at trustees' meetings.

Correspondent: Mrs J M Milligan, 8 Chipple Park, Lutton, Nr Cornwood, Ivybridge, Devon PL21 9TA

Other information: Grants are also made for education purposes and to organisations.

Crediton

The Crediton Relief-in-Need Charity

Eligibility: People in need who have been resident in Crediton town and the parish of Crediton Hamlets for at least 12 months.

Types of grants: One-off grants of up to £300 towards, for example, nursery school costs, travel expenses, furniture, medical equipment, food, hospital expenses, electric goods, household bills and disability equipment. 'General benefit tickets' of £5 each to buy food in local shops are also available from local health visitors.

As much as possible the charity tries to provide goods or services for the applicant – money is not usually given directly.

Exclusions: Grants are not given towards house improvements or to repay existing debts.

Annual grant total: In 2008/09 the charity gave grants to 15 individuals totalling £4,800.

Applications: On a form available from the correspondent. Applications can be submitted directly by the individual, or through a third party such as a social worker. Applications are considered early every month (except August) and should be submitted before the end of the month. 'A supplementary letter is always useful.'

Correspondent: Mike Armstrong, 5 Parr House, Lennard Road, Crediton, EX17 2AP (01363 776529)

Culmstock

Culmstock Fuel Allotment Charity

Eligibility: People in need who live in the ancient parish of Culmstock.

Types of grants: Recurrent grants according to need. Recently, grants have ranged from £20 to £70 for electricity and solid fuel bills and gifts for the eight oldest applicants.

Annual grant total: Grants usually total around £1,500.

Applications: In writing to the correspondent, directly by the individual.

Correspondent: Mrs Elaine Artus, Clerk, Pendle, Culmstock, Cullompton, Devon EX15 3JQ (01884 840577)

Other information: Grants are also made for educational purposes.

Dartmouth

The Saint Petrox Trust Lands

Eligibility: People in need who live in the parish of Dartmouth and particularly within the ancient parish of St Petrox.

Types of grants: One-off grants of £100 to £500, to people affected by hardship through illness, homelessness, hospitalisation and so on for items including electrical goods, hospital expenses, household bills, travel expenses, medical equipment and furniture.

Exclusions: Recurring grants are not made.

Annual grant total: In 2008/09 the trust had assets of £384,000 and an income of £62,000. Grants totalled £3,300.

Applications: In writing to the correspondent either directly by the individual or through a social worker, Citizens Advice, other welfare agency, or other third party on behalf of the individual. Applications should include details on the purpose of grant, proof of need and estimates of costs. They are considered in January, April, July and October.

Correspondent: Hilary Bastone, Clerk, 30 Rosemary Gardens, Paignton, Devon TQ3 3NP (01803 666322; fax: 01803 666322; email: hilarybastone@hotmail.co.uk)

Other information: The trustees recently stated that they would like to support more individuals in need. They have therefore widened the trust's beneficial area to cover the whole of the Parish of Dartmouth.

Grants are also given towards the upkeep of ancient buildings within the ancient parish of St Petrox.

Exeter

The Central Exeter Relief-in-Need Fund

Eligibility: People in need who live in the parish of Central Exeter.

Types of grants: One-off grants usually of £50 to £150 for basic needs such as furniture, assistance with heating bills, children's clothing and mobility aids.

Exclusions: Grants are not made for educational and training needs.

Annual grant total: About £2,500.

Applications: In writing to the correspondent with the support of a social worker, health visitor or other welfare agency. Applications are considered in June and December.

Correspondent: M J Richards, 32 Oakley Close, Exeter, EX1 3SB (01392 468531)

Exeter Dispensary & Aid-in-Sickness Fund

Eligibility: Sick or disabled poor people who live in the city of Exeter.

Types of grants: One-off grants for day-to-day needs including convalescence breaks, help with fuel or telephone bills, cooking or heating appliances, clothing, food, medical care, bedding, travel to and from hospitals and so on. The average such grant is £100. Larger grants are made towards medical appliances and aids.

Exclusions: Grants are not given for items which are available from public funds or for structural alterations to property.

Annual grant total: In 2008 the fund had assets of £490,000 and an income of £51,000. There were 115 grants made to individuals totalling £19,000.

Applications: Applications should be made through Citizens Advice, other welfare agency, a social worker or other third party such as a doctor. They should include brief details of the medical condition, the financial circumstances and the specific need. Applications are considered throughout the year for day-to-day needs and in March and November for medical appliances and so on.

Applications should be sent to: A R Gladstone, 'Blanchland', 18 Streatham Drive, Exeter EX4 4PD for day-to-day needs; otherwise, in writing to the correspondent.

Correspondent: David W Fanson, Hon. Secretary, 85 Beacon Lane, Whipton, Exeter EX4 8LL (01392 256381)

Other information: Grants are also given to other organisations with similar objectives.

Exminster

Exminster Feoffees

Eligibility: People in need living in the parish of Exminster.

Types of grants: One-off grants and loans usually of up to £200 each. Grants have previously included cash grants and goods in kind. About four to five grants are made each year.

Annual grant total: Over five years, expenditure for this charity has averaged £800.

Applications: In writing to the correspondent. Applications can be submitted either directly by the individual, through a third party such as a social worker, or through an organisation such as a Citizens Advice or another welfare agency. They are dealt with within three weeks of receipt.

Correspondent: R H Adams, 26 Exe View, Exminster, Exeter, EX6 8AL (01392 833024)

Other information: The trust gives to both individuals and organisations

Exmouth

Exmouth Welfare Trust

Eligibility: People living in the former urban district of Exmouth, comprising the parishes of Withycombe Raleigh and Littleham-cum-Exmouth who are convalescent, disabled, infirm or in need. A fund is available for modest awards for those setting up home on a minimal budget.

Types of grants: One-off grants and gift vouchers, for example, towards dietary needs, childcare, respite costs, safety equipment, hospital expenses, electrical goods, convalescence, clothing, travel expenses, medical equipment, furniture, disability equipment and help in the home. Cheques will be payable to charities, suppliers, service providers and official departments. Payments will not be made personally to individuals.

Exclusions: No grants for rents, rates, debts and outstanding liabilities.

Annual grant total: In 2008 the charity had an income of £22,000 and a total expenditure of £34,000. Grants totalled around £28,000.

Applications: On a form available from the correspondent, submitted through an independent third party (not a relative) such as a social worker, Citizens Advice, other welfare agency, or another professional or well experienced person with detailed knowledge. Applications are considered throughout the year.

Correspondent: The Secretary, PO Box 16, Exmouth, EX8 3YT

Gittisham

Elizabeth Beaumont Charity

Eligibility: People in need who live in the parish of Gittisham.

Types of grants: Quarterly pensions and Christmas bonus paid to qualifying local pensioners.

Annual grant total: Grants usually total around £4,000 per year.

Applications: In writing to the correspondent at any time throughout the year. Applications can be submitted directly by the individual or through a third party such as a social worker and should include details of income and any savings.

Correspondent: Mrs Paula S Land, The Laurels, 46 New Street, Honiton, Devon, EX14 1BY (01404 43431; email: paula. land@everys.co.uk)

Great Torrington

The Great Torrington Town Lands Poors Charities

Eligibility: People in need who live in the former borough of Great Torrington.

Types of grants: Usually one-off grants according to need.

Annual grant total: In 2008/09 the charity had assets of £5.8 million and an income of £252,000. Welfare grants were made to individuals totalling £7,000, a slight increase from the year before.

Applications: In writing to the correspondent, with all relevant personal information.

Correspondent: Chris J Styles, The Town Hall Office, High Street, Torrington, Devon EX38 8HN (01805 623517; email: gtc@greattorringtoncharities. fsbusiness.co.uk)

Other information: Grants are also made to organisations and to individuals for educational purposes.

Highweek

Highweek Charities

Eligibility: People in need over the age of 65 who live in the ancient parish of Highweek.

Types of grants: One-off Christmas grants and other grants of around £50 to £60.

Annual grant total: In 2009 the charity had an income of £36,000 and a total expenditure of £34,000. Grants usually total around £2,000.

Applications: In writing to the correspondent, directly by the individual. Applications should be submitted in October, for consideration in November.

Correspondent: Trevor Keen, Clerk and Collector, Lark Rise, 13 Gaze Hill, Newton Abbot, Devon, TQ12 1QL (01626 353831; email: highweekcharities@hotmail.co.uk)

Other information: The charity's main priority is the management of almshouses in Highweek.

Holsworthy

The Peter Speccott Charity

Eligibility: People in need who live in Holsworthy and Holsworthy Hamlet.

Types of grants: Grants and loans are given to provide temporary relief for people facing unexpected loss or sudden destitution.

Annual grant total: About £800.

Applications: In writing to the correspondent. The trust also advertises in local colleges, careers offices, social services and so on.

Correspondent: Denzil C Blackman, 8 Fore Street, Holsworthy, Devon EX22 6ED (01409 253262; email: denzilblackman@ppwhol.co.uk)

Honiton

Honiton United Charities

Eligibility: People in need who live in the borough of Honiton.

Types of grants: One-off and recurrent grants ranging from £50 to £100. Pensions are paid quarterly.

Exclusions: No grants to people living outside the beneficial area or for funding a gap year.

Annual grant total: In 2009 the trust had an income of £10,000 and a total expenditure of £9,700.

Applications: In writing to the correspondent including details of income and savings. Applications can be submitted directly by the individual or through a social worker, Citizens Advice or other welfare agency, and are considered throughout the year.

Correspondent: Paula Land, The Laurels, 46 New Street, Honiton, Devon, EX14 1BY (01404 43431; email: paula.land@everys.co. uk)

Other information: Grants are also made to organisations.

Litton Cheney

The Litton Cheney Relief-in-Need Trust

Eligibility: People in need who live in the parish of Litton Cheney.

Types of grants: Grants ranging from £100 to £220 are distributed once a year at the beginning of December. One-off emergency grants can be made at any time, for example, where there is a serious illness in the family.

Annual grant total: About £2,000.

Applications: Applications, on a form available from the correspondent, should be submitted directly by the individual, and are considered throughout the year.

Correspondent: B P Prentice, Steddings, Chalk Pit Lane, Litton Cheney, Dorchester, Dorset DT2 9AN (01308 482535)

Ottery St Mary

The Non-Ecclesiastical Charity of Thomas Axe

Eligibility: Older people living in Ottery St Mary (the old Ottery St Mary Urban District Council area).

Types of grants: One-off grants ranging from £25 to £200 in 'marriage portions', and aids for elderly and disabled people.

Exclusions: Recurrent support cannot be given.

Annual grant total: Grants average about £1,900 a year.

Applications: In writing to the correspondent directly by the individual. Applications are considered quarterly.

Correspondent: David Roberts, Eminence, Otter Close, Tipton St John, Sidmouth, Devon EX10 0JU (01404 813961; email: david@coral683844.freeserve.co.uk)

The Ottery Feoffee Charity

Eligibility: People in need who live in the ancient parish of Ottery St Mary. Priority is usually given to older people and people with disabilities.

Types of grants: One-off grants according to need.

Annual grant total: Grants to individuals usually total about £500 per year.

The vast majority of this charity's funds are spent on the provision of 22 flats for people in need. So while the charity has the ability to apply up to one half of its income in grants, in reality, the costs associated with property upkeep mean that only a small amount is usually available for welfare grants.

Applications: In writing to the correspondent.

Correspondent: John Akers, 7 Broad Street, Ottery St Mary, Devon EX11 1BS (01404 812 228; email: osmlaw@gilbertstephens.co.uk)

Other information: The charity also runs a small day centre.

Paignton

Paignton Parish Charity

Eligibility: Poor people who are long-term residents of Paignton.

Types of grants: Cash payments of £50 to £60 are given twice a year for use as the recipient wishes.

Exclusions: Payments are not made for living expenses.

Annual grant total: In 2008/09 the charity had an income of £10,000 and a total expenditure of £8,000.

Applications: On a form available from the correspondent. Applications are considered in May and November and should be submitted by the end of April and October respectively. They should include the applicant's age and length of residency in Paignton.

Correspondent: c/o Mrs A Palmer, 12 Monastery Road, Paignton, Devon TQ3 3BU (01803 556680)

Other information: The trust also makes annual donations to surgery support groups.

Plymouth

The Joseph Jory's Charity

Eligibility: Widows over 50 who are in need and have lived in the city of Plymouth for the last seven years.

Types of grants: Small pensions, paid quarterly. Amounts vary according to available income.

Annual grant total: In 2009 the trust had both an income and expenditure of £11,000.

Applications: The trust advertises locally when funds are available; because ongoing grants are made funds only become available to new applicants when someone leaves the fund's list of beneficiaries. New applications made are, however, kept on file.

Correspondent: Jennifer Rogers, c/o Wolferstans, 60–66 North Hill, Plymouth PL4 8EP (01752 292 347)

The Ladies' Aid Society and the Eyre Charity

Eligibility: Widows and unmarried women in need who live, or have lived, in Plymouth. Unfortunately, women who are divorced are not eligible for grants.

Types of grants: Annuities of around £100 are given quarterly to each recipient.

Annual grant total: In 2009 the trust had an income of £11,000 and a total expenditure of £8,500.

Applications: On a form available from the correspondent: to be submitted through a social worker, Citizens Advice, clergy, doctor, solicitor or similar third party. Before applying to the trust, the applicant should have obtained any statutory help they are entitled to.

Correspondent: Mrs J M Stephens, 14 Court Park, Thurlestone, Kingsbridge, Devon TQ7 3LX (01548 560891; email: r_john_venngrove@hotmail.com)

Plymouth Charity Trust

Eligibility: People in need who live in the city of Plymouth.

Types of grants: Grants are one-off and can be towards the cost of clothes for children of families with very limited income and to relieve sudden distress, sickness or infirmity. Grants range between £50 and £100. The trust usually makes the donation in the form of vouchers or credit at a relevant shop. They prefer not to give payment directly to the applicant.

Exclusions: No grants are given to other charities, to clear debts or for any need that can be met by social services.

Annual grant total: The trust makes a total of around £1,000 to individuals in need.

Applications: On a form available from the correspondent, to be submitted directly by the individual or through a social worker, Citizens Advice or other third party. Applications are considered on the first Monday of every month.

Correspondent: Susan Dale, Trust Manager, Charity Trust Office, 41 Heles Terrace, Prince Rock, Plymouth PL4 9LH (01752 663107)

Other information: The trust also gives around £1,000 a year in educational grants.

Sandford

The Sandford Relief-in-Need Charity

Eligibility: Pensioners in need who live in Sandford parish.

Types of grants: One-off grants usually of £10 to £50 towards such things as repair of household utility items, bereavement expenses or recurrent grants of £12 a month (to about 30 households). Christmas vouchers of £25 are given to existing pensioners and other parishioners towards fuel bills to be exchanged at local suppliers.

Annual grant total: Grants usually total around £6,000 per year.

Applications: On a form available from the correspondent. Applications can be submitted either directly by the individual or through a social worker, Citizens Advice, or other welfare agency. They are usually considered in March, September and November, but they can also be considered outside of these times.

Correspondent: Mrs H D Edworthy, 7 Snows Estate, Sandford, Crediton, Devon EX17 4NJ (01363 772550)

Sheepwash

The Bridgeland Charity

Eligibility: Older people in need who live in the parish of Sheepwash.

Types of grants: One-off grants ranging from £50 to £500.

Annual grant total: In 2008/09 the trust had an income of £3,400 and a total expenditure of £3,000.

Applications: In writing to the correspondent through a third party such as a social worker for consideration throughout the year.

Correspondent: Mrs D Tubby, Bramble Cottage, East Street, Sheepwash, Beaworthy, North Devon EX21 5NW (01409 231694)

Other information: The trust also supports local schools and community projects.

Sidmouth

Sidmouth Consolidated Charities

Eligibility: People in need who live in Sidmouth.

Types of grants: One-off grants of up to £1,000, towards, for example, new cookers, washing machines and stairlifts, and to help with travel expenses to visit someone in hospital.

Annual grant total: In 2009 grants totalled just under £5,000 and were made for both educational and welfare purposes.

Applications: In writing to the correspondent, either directly by the individual, or through a social worker, Citizens Advice or welfare agency. Applications are considered at monthly meetings.

Correspondent: Mrs Ruth Rose, 22 Alexandria Road, Sidmouth, Devon EX10 9HB (01395 513079; email: ruth.rose@eclipse.co.uk)

Silverton

Silverton Parochial Charity

Eligibility: People in need in the parish of Silverton.

Types of grants: One-off grants, with no minimum or maximum limit. Grants are towards anything that will help relieve hardship or need, such as alarms for people who are infirm, stairlifts, hospital travel costs, heating costs, medical equipment, children's clothing and wheelchairs.

Exclusions: No grants are made towards state or local authority taxes.

Annual grant total: In 2008/09 the charity had an income of £25,800 and an expenditure of £26,900.

Applications: Application forms can be obtained from the Silverton Post Office or the Community Hall, or prospective beneficiaries can write or speak to the correspondent. Completed forms can be submitted to the correspondent by the individual or by a carer or welfare department, and so on. The trustees will need details of the applicant's financial situation. Applications are considered monthly.

Correspondent: A Williams, Henbury, Old Butterleigh Road, Silverton, Devon EX5 4JE (01392 860408)

Other information: Grants are also made to organisations providing assistance to people in need who live in the parish and for educational purposes.

South Brent

The South Brent Parish Lands Charity

Eligibility: People in need who live in the parish of South Brent.

Types of grants: One-off or recurrent grants and Christmas gifts. Grants can be £50 to £300 and can be for a variety of needs including hospital transport/travel costs and special treatment to adults and/ or children where the family is desperately in need of help.

Annual grant total: Grants usually total around £10,000 for welfare purposes.

Applications: On a form available from the correspondent which can be submitted at any time either directly by the individual or a family member, through a third party such as a social worker or teacher, or through an organisation such as Citizens Advice or a school.

Correspondent: J I G Blackler, Luscombe Maye, 6 Fore Street, South Brent, Devon TQ10 9BQ (01364 646173; email: luscombe@ukonline.co.uk)

Sowton

Sowton In Need Charity

Eligibility: People in need who live in the parish of Sowton.

Types of grants: One-off grants for any specific educational or personal need. Grants have been given towards funeral expenses in the past.

Annual grant total: Grants total around £1,000 a year for individuals in need.

Applications: In writing to the correspondent, to be submitted either directly by the individual or through a social worker, Citizens Advice, other welfare agency or any third party.

Correspondent: N Waine, Meadowsweet, Sowton, Exeter, EX5 2AE (01392 368289; email: noelwaine@aol.com)

Other information: Grants are also given to organisations and to individuals for educational purposes.

Teignbridge

The Special People Fund

Eligibility: 'Children who live in Teignbridge who have learning difficulties, or a disability, or are suffering emotional trauma arising from the breakdown of marriage or family life, or bereavement or social circumstances.'

Types of grants: Grants are given according to need.

Annual grant total: In 2009/10 the fund had an income of £5,500 and a total expenditure of £5,600. Grants are made to organisations and individuals.

Applications: In writing to the correspondent.

Correspondent: M Nosworthy, 5 Higher Drive, Dawlish EX7 0AS

Topsham

The Charity of John Shere & Others

Eligibility: People in need who have lived in the parish of Topsham (as its boundaries were in 1966) for at least three years.

Types of grants: One-off and recurrent grants in the range of £350 to £400 are given where assistance cannot be obtained from any other means.

Annual grant total: In 2008/09 the charity had an income of £5,200 and a total expenditure of £5,000.

Applications: On a form available from the correspondent. Applications can be submitted at any time either directly by the individual or through a third party such as a social worker.

Correspondent: David John Tucker, 5 Elm Grove Gardens, Topsham, Exeter, EX3 0EL (01392 873168; email: tucker-david@ talktalk.net)

Torbay

The Leonora Carlow Trust Fund

Eligibility: Children up to 18 who have a physical or mental disability and live in Torbay.

Types of grants: One-off grants ranging up to £300 for computer equipment, holidays, furniture or disability equipment. Usually three or four grants are made each year.

Annual grant total: Grants average around £500 a year.

Applications: On a form available from the correspondent, to be submitted directly by the individual or family member, or through a social worker, Citizens Advice or other welfare agency. Applications are considered throughout the year and should include details of help sought from any other source and the outcome and details of any previous assistance from the fund.

Correspondent: Michael Deeley, Administrative Officer, Torbay Council, Children's Services, Oldway Mansion, Torquay Road, Paignton, Devon TQ3 2TE (01803 208227; email: michael.deeley@ torbay.gov.uk)

Dorset

Cole Anderson Charitable Foundation

Eligibility: People in need who live in Bournemouth and Poole.

Types of grants: Grants for providing or paying for services or facilities.

Annual grant total: About £10,000 for welfare and educational purposes.

Applications: In writing to the correspondent.

Correspondent: Martin Davies, Rawlins Davy, Rowlands House, Hinton Road, Bournemouth, BH1 2EG (01202 558 844; email: martin.davies@rawlinsdavy.com)

The Beaminster Charities

Eligibility: People in need who live in Beaminster, Netherbury and Stoke Abbott.

Types of grants: One-off grants in the range of £50 and £1,000. The trustees will consider any application. About 50 grants are made each year.

Annual grant total: In 2009 the charities had an income of £10,000 and a total expenditure of £17,000.

Applications: Applications can be submitted in writing to the correspondent by the individual or through a recognised referral agency such as social worker, Citizens Advice or doctor. The trustees meet throughout the year.

Correspondent: J Groves, 24 Church Street, Beaminster, Dorset DT8 3BA (01308 862313 or 01308 862192)

The Boveridge Charity

Eligibility: Poor people who are in need and have lived in the ancient parish of Cranborne (which includes the present parishes of Cranborne-cum-Boveridge, Wimborne St Giles, Alderholt, Verwood, Ferndown, West Parley and Edmondsham) for at least two years.

People in need who live outside the beneficial area may also be supported in exceptional circumstances.

Types of grants: Pensions of £500 per annum. One-off grants ranging from £100 to £500.

Annual grant total: In 2009/10 the charity had an income of £4,800 and an expenditure of £6,400.

Applications: In writing to the correspondent, submitted directly by the individual, through a third party such as a social worker or through an organisation such as a Citizens Advice or other welfare agency. Applications are considered throughout the year and should contain details of the individual's annual income and capital, detail of need, age and occupation.

Correspondent: Mrs R D Hunt, Brinscombe House, Lower Blandford Road, Shaftesbury, Dorset, SP7 0BG (01747 852511)

The MacDougall Trust

Eligibility: People in need who live in Dorset. Preference is given to those who live in Bournemouth and Poole.

Types of grants: One-off grants of up to £250 for all kinds of personal need. Only in exceptional circumstances will more than £250 be awarded.

Exclusions: No grants are given to organisations or for educational purposes, sponsorship, debt or childcare.

Annual grant total: In 2009/10 the trust had an income of £22,000 and a total expenditure of £18,000.

Applications: On a form available from the correspondent or to download from the trust's website. Applications should be supported by a recognised agency such as, Citizens Advice, local GP, social services or similar organisation. Forms should be returned to the administrative secretary at; 96 Scarf Road, Poole, Dorset, BH17 8QL. Applications are considered quarterly, though urgent requests may be considered between meetings.

Please note: if the application is being made on behalf of a minor, then details of the whole family will need to be included.

Correspondent: P D Malpas, 7 Church Road, Parkstone, Poole, Dorset BH14 8UF (01202 730002; email: adminsecretary@ macdougalltrust.com; website: www. macdougalltrust.com/)

The Pitt-Rivers Charitable Trust

Eligibility: People who live in rural Dorset and North Dorset in particular who are in need, for example due to hardship, disability or sickness.

Types of grants: One-off grants, ranging from £100 and £1,000.

Annual grant total: In 2008/09 the trust had assets of £149,000 and an income of £50,000. No grants were made to individuals during the year. Grants to organisations totalled £47,000.

Applications: In writing to the correspondent. Applications can be submitted directly by the individual or

family member and are considered at any time.

Correspondent: George Pitt-Rivers, Hinton St Mary Estate Office, Sturminster Newton, Dorset DT10 1NA (01258 472623)

Other information: The trust stated that because of the geographical limitations of this trust, grants are only occasionally given to individuals.

St Martin's Trust

Eligibility: People who are in need, people who are disabled and older people who live in Dorset.

Types of grants: One-off and recurrent grants according to need.

Annual grant total: In 2008/09 the trust had an income of £7,300 and a total expenditure of £6,500.

Applications: In writing to the correspondent.

Correspondent: The Revd David J Ayton, 201 Kinson Road, Bournemouth, BH10 5HB (01202 547054; website: www. stmartinsbooks.co.uk/)

Other information: Grants are also made to organisations.

The William Williams Charity

Eligibility: People in need who live in the ancient parishes of Blandford, Shaftesbury or Sturminster Newton.

Types of grants: One-off grants of £500 to £1,000 according to need.

Annual grant total: In 2009 the charity's assets stood at £5.6 million, which generated an income of £299,000. Grants for relief-in-need purposes totalled £42,000.

Applications: Applicants should apply directly to one of the trustees; in the first instance contact the correspondent to find which of the trustees is most relevant, and what their address is. The trustees meet quarterly to discuss applications.

Correspondent: Ian Winsor, Steward, Stafford House, 10 Prince of Wales Road, Dorchester, Dorset DT1 1PW (01305 264573; email: wwc@kennedylegg. co.uk)

Charmouth

The Almshouse Charity

Eligibility: People in need who, or whose immediate family, live in the parish of Charmouth.

Types of grants: One-off and recurrent grants, generally of £25 to £250. Grants have been given for hospital expenses, nursing fees, funeral expenses, special needs, health, sports and general living expenses. Grants can also be towards the total or part payment of the costs of equipment, such as electric chairs and cars, arthritic supports, shopping trolleys, washing machines and nebulisers. Annual grocery vouchers are given to selected people ranging from £40 to £60. The trust also makes interest-free loans.

Annual grant total: In 2008/09 the trust had an income of £3,100 and a total expenditure of £2,300.

Applications: In writing to the correspondent or other trustees. Applications can be submitted directly by the individual or through a third party such as a rector, doctor or trustee. They are usually considered at quarterly periods; emergencies can be considered at other times. Applications should include details of the purpose of the grant, the total costs involved, and an official letter or programme/itinerary.

Correspondent: Mrs M Comley, Secretary, Pebbles, Five Acres, Charmouth, Birdport, Dorset, DT6 6BE (01297 560812)

Other information: Grants are also given to individuals for further and higher education and overseas voluntary work, and to youth clubs for specific purposes.

Christchurch

Legate's Charity

Eligibility: People in need who live in the borough of Christchurch and the immediate surrounding area.

Types of grants: One-off grants for domestic items and clothes and small weekly allowances to help towards household bills.

Annual grant total: Grants average around £8,000 per year.

Applications: On a form available from the correspondent submitted either directly by the individual or through a friend, relative, social worker, Citizens Advice or other welfare agency.

Correspondent: Mrs M Parsa, Christchurch Borough Council, Civic Offices, Bridge Street, Christchurch, Dorset BH23 1AZ (01202 495050)

Mayor's Goodwill Fund

Eligibility: People in need who live in the borough of Christchurch.

Types of grants: One-off grants for grocery parcels, potted plants, sweets and chocolates.

Annual grant total: About £1,000.

Applications: On a form available from the correspondent, to be submitted through a social worker, Citizens Advice, other welfare agency, friend, neighbour or clergy. Applications should include the applicant's name and address and details of their circumstances.

Correspondent: The Mayor's Secretary, Civic Offices, Bridge Street, Christchurch,

Dorset BH23 1AZ (01202 495134; email: m.parsa@christchurch.gov.uk)

Other information: The fund also gives grants to organisations.

Corfe Castle

Corfe Castle Charities

Eligibility: People in need who live in the parish of Corfe Castle.

Types of grants: One-off grants or interest free loans according to need. In recent years grants have been given to relieve sickness, infirmity or distress, such as rental of emergency lifelines, help with recuperative hospital costs and payment of travel expenses for patients and visiting relatives in hospital.

Annual grant total: In 2008/09 the charity had assets of £4 million and an income of £457,000. There were six relief-in-need grants made to individuals totalling £3,600.

Applications: On a form available from the correspondent, to be submitted directly by the individual. The trustees meet monthly, but emergency requests are dealt with as they arise.

Correspondent: Mrs J Wilson, The Spinney, Springbrook Close, Corfe Castle, Wareham, Dorset BH20 5HS (01929 480 873)

Other information: Grants are also made to organisations.

Dorchester

Dorchester Relief-in-Need Charity

Eligibility: People in need who live in the ecclesiastical parish of Dorchester.

Types of grants: One-off grants according to need.

Annual grant total: Grants for welfare purposes usually total around £1,000 per year.

Applications: Application forms are available from the correspondent and can be submitted through a social worker, health visitor, Citizens Advice or social services.

Correspondent: R R E Potter, 8 Mithras Close, Dorchester, Dorset, DT1 2RF (01305 262041)

Other information: This charity also gives educational grants.

Poole

The Poole Children's Fund

Eligibility: Children up to 18 who are disadvantaged, disabled or otherwise in need and live in the borough of Poole.

Preference is given to children with behavioural and social difficulties who have limited opportunities for leisure and recreational activities of a positive nature, for schoolchildren with serious family difficulties so the child has to be educated away from home and people with special educational needs.

Types of grants: One-off grants of £10 to £50 towards the cost of holidays, educational or recreational opportunities.

Annual grant total: About £1,000 for welfare and educational purposes.

Applications: On a form available from the correspondent completed by a third party such as a social worker, health visitor, minister or teacher. Applications are considered throughout the year. They should include details of family structure including: ages; reason for application; family income and any other sources of funding which have been tried; what agencies (if any) are involved in helping the family; and any statutory orders (for example, care orders) relating to the child or their family members.

Correspondent: Julia Palmer, 52 Hennings Park Road, Poole, BH15 3QX (01202 633623)

Shaftesbury

John Foyle's Charity

Eligibility: People in need who live in the town of Shaftesbury.

Types of grants: One-off and recurrent grants and loans, including those for educational toys for people who are disabled, moving expenses, fuel, equipment, carpets and decoration. Around 15 grants a year are made ranging from £30 to £500.

Exclusions: No grants for items/services that are the responsibility of the state.

Annual grant total: Grants usually total around £3,000 per year.

Applications: In writing to the correspondent at any time. Applications can be submitted directly by the individual or through an appropriate third party; and should show evidence of need, for example, benefit record, and proof of address. They can be submitted at any time, for consideration at the discretion of the trustees.

Correspondent: Simon Rutter, Cann Field House, Cann Common, Shaftesbury, Dorset SP7 8DQ (01747 851881)

Wimborne Minster

Brown Habgood Hall and Higden Charity

Eligibility: Usually retired people on low income living in the ancient parish of Wimborne Minster, in Dorset.

Types of grants: One off grants, but mainly quarterly payments. Grants are not usually for more than £200, and are mainly for smaller amounts. About 26 regular grants are given plus one-off grants.

Annual grant total: In 2009 the charity had an income of £14,000 and a total expenditure of £16,000. Grants usually total around £10,000 per year.

Applications: In writing to the correspondent either directly by the individual, through a social worker, Citizens Advice, other welfare agency or through another third party such as a doctor, health visitor or clergy. The applicant's full name, address, age and employment should be included.

Correspondent: Mrs Hilary S Motson, Whiteoaks, Colehill Lane, Colehill, Wimborne, Dorset, BH21 7AN (01202 886303; email: bhhh.charity@ btinternet.com)

Gloucestershire

The Barnwood House Trust

Eligibility: People in need who have a serious and non-remedial physical or mental disability and have lived in the county of Gloucestershire for at least 12 months.

Types of grants: One-off grants ranging from £50 to £750 are given for household items, disability equipment, respite care breaks, holidays, clothes, selected bills and so on.

Exclusions: No grants for: funeral costs; medical equipment; private healthcare (e.g. assessment, treatment or medication); counselling or psychotherapy; top-up nursing home fees; private education or university tuition fees; council tax; court fines; house purchase, rent deposits, or rent in advance; regular payments to supplement income; the needs of non-disabled dependants or carers. No retrospective grants are given.

Annual grant total: In 2009 the trust had assets of £65 million and an income of £2.1 million. Grants were made to nearly 800 individuals totalling £254,000.

Applications: On a form available from the correspondent or to download from the website. All applications should be made through, or endorsed by, a social or healthcare professional, such as an

occupational therapist, social worker, health visitor, district nurse or community psychiatric nurse. The trust aims to respond to requests for grants under £600 within 15 working days. Wherever possible, the trust will visit applicants at home to discuss their needs in greater detail.

Correspondent: Gail Rodway, Grants Manager, The Manor House, 162 Barnwood Road, Gloucester GL4 3JX (01452 611292; fax: 01452 634018; email: gail.rodway@barnwoodtrust.org; website: www.barnwoodtrust.org)

Other information: Grants are also given to organisations and for medical research in Gloucestershire (£602,000 in 2009).

Cheltenham Aid-in-Sickness & Nurses Welfare Fund and the Cheltenham Family Welfare Association – Gooding Fund

Eligibility: People in need who are engaged in domiciliary nursing in the Cheltenham area, or to retired nurses who were so engaged.

Types of grants: One-off and recurrent grants to those in need.

Annual grant total: In 2008/09 the fund had an income of £15,000 and a total expenditure of £8,000. Grants totalled about £7,000.

Applications: On a form available from the correspondent. Applications should be submitted through a third party, such as a health visitor, social worker or Citizens Advice.

Correspondent: Mrs P Newman, Cheltenham Family Welfare Association, 21 Rodney Road, Cheltenham, Gloucestershire GL50 1HX (01242 522180; email: info@cheltenhamfamilywelfare.co. uk; website: www. cheltenhamfamilywelfare.co.uk)

The Fluck Convalescent Fund

Eligibility: Women of all ages and children under 16 who live in the city of Gloucester and its surrounding area, and are in poor health or convalescing after illness or operative treatment.

Types of grants: One-off grants between £50 and £350 for recuperative holidays, clothing, bedding, furniture, fuel, food, household equipment, domestic help, respite care and medical or other aids.

Exclusions: No grants are made for the repayment of debts or for recurrent payments such as rent and rates.

Annual grant total: In 2008/09 the fund had assets of £705,000 and an income of £40,000. Grants were made to 113 individuals totalling £40,000.

Applications: In writing to the correspondent through a 'responsible person' such as a social worker, medical professional or welfare organisation.

Applications are considered throughout the year.

Correspondent: Peter Francis Sanigar, c/o Whitemans Solicitors, Second Floor, 65 London Road, Gloucester GL1 3HF (01452 411601; fax: 01452 300922; email: info@whitemans.com)

Gloucestershire Bowling Association Benevolent Fund

Eligibility: Bowlers, ex-bowlers and their immediate dependants, who are in need and are present or past members of the association.

Types of grants: One-off and recurrent grants towards, for example, hospital visits.

Annual grant total: About £1,000.

Applications: In writing to the correspondent.

Correspondent: Derek Severs, 1 Wolfridge Ride, Alveston, Bristol, BS35 3RA (01454 414179)

Sylvanus Lyson's Charity

Eligibility: Clergy of the Church of England and their widows and dependants who are in need and are serving in or retired from the diocese of Gloucester.

Types of grants: One-off grants according to need.

Annual grant total: In 2008/09 the trust had assets of £8.4 million and an income of £315,000. Grants were made to 69 individuals totalling £21,000.

Applications: In writing to the correspondent, directly by the individual, for consideration in March, July, September and November.

Correspondent: A Holloway, Morroway House, Station Road, Gloucester GL1 1DW (01452 301903)

The Prestbury Charity (also known as The Prestbury United Charities)

Eligibility: People in need who live in the ecclesiastical parish of Prestbury and the adjoining parishes of Southam and Swindon village.

Types of grants: One-off grants according to need. Recent support has been given towards: heating costs for a person with disabilities; security lights for an elderly person; repairs and decorating costs; and, assistance for single parent families.

Annual grant total: In 2009 the charity had an income of £13,000 and a total expenditure of £11,000.

Applications: In writing to the correspondent, either directly by the individual, or via a social worker, Citizens Advice or other welfare agency or third party. Applications should include the individual's home address, so that the trust can see that they live in the area of benefit.

Correspondent: Brian Wood, Clerk, 2 Honeysuckle Close, Prestbury, Cheltenham, Gloucestershire, GL52 5LN (01242 515941; email: puc.clerk@ prestbury.net; website: www.prestbury.net/ puc)

Other information: Local organisations are also supported.

Bisley

The Ancient Charity of the Parish of Bisley

Eligibility: People in need who live in the ancient parish of Bisley.

Types of grants: One-off or recurrent grants according to need.

Annual grant total: In 2008/09 the charity had an income of £10,000 and a total expenditure of £7,400.

Applications: In writing to the correspondent.

Correspondent: Jane Bentley, The Old Post Office, High Street, Bisley, Stroud GL6 7AA (01452 770756)

Charlton Kings

Charlton Kings Relief in Need Charity

Eligibility: People in need who live in the parish of Charlton Kings or have a connection with the parish.

Types of grants: One-off grants of £50 to £1,000, according to need. In the past grants have been given towards travel expenses and medical equipment and can be used to help people to make a fresh start.

Annual grant total: About £2,500 a year. Grants are given to both individuals and organisations.

Applications: In writing to the correspondent.

Correspondent: Martin Fry, 7 Branch Hill Rise, Charlton Kings, Cheltenham, GL53 9HN

Cirencester

The Smith's Cirencester Poor Charity

Eligibility: People in need who have lived in the parish of Cirencester for the last three years.

Types of grants: One-off and recurrent grants towards disability aids, domestic appliances, furniture, heating bills and living expenses.

Annual grant total: Grants average around £3,500 each year.

Applications: On a form available from the correspondent. Applications are usually considered quarterly.

Correspondent: Mrs Maria Ann Bell, 7 Dollar Street, Cirencester, Gloucestershire GL7 2AS (01285 650000)

Other information: Grants are also made to local organisations.

Gloucester

The United Charity of Palling Burgess

Eligibility: People in need who live in the Gloucester city council administrative area, including people with disabilities, single parent families and people on a low income.

Types of grants: One-off cash grants and grants in kind up to a maximum value of £250.

Annual grant total: In 2008/09 the charity had an income of £1,800 and a total expenditure of £3,600.

Applications: In writing to the correspondent. Applications should be submitted through a social worker, nurse, health visitor, minister of religion or similar third party and are considered twice a year in March and October. Applications should be submitted by the end of February and September respectively.

Correspondent: Margaret Churchill, 30 Gambier Parry Gardens, Gloucester GL2 9RD (01452 421304)

Minchinhampton

Albert Edward Pash Charitable Trust Fund

Eligibility: People who live in the civil parish of Minchinhampton, of any age or occupation, who are in need due, for example, to hardship, disability or sickness.

Types of grants: One-off grants according to need.

Annual grant total: A minimum of 25% of the income must be given towards hospital research each year, with the rest donated to individuals. Generally there is a total annual expenditure of between £900 and £1,500.

Applications: In writing to the correspondent, directly by the individual or family member. Applications should be received by 31 March for consideration in April.

Correspondent: Diana Wall, Clerk, The Parish Office, The Trap House, West End, Minchinhampton, Gloucestershire, GL6 9JA (01453 731186; fax: 01453 731186; email: minchparish@ btconnect.com)

Tewkesbury

Gyles Geest Charity

Eligibility: People in need who live in the borough of Tewkesbury.

Types of grants: Grants usually average about £30 per household and are given as vouchers for use in local shops.

Annual grant total: In 2008/09 the charity had an income of £7,700 and a total expenditure of £7,300.

Applications: On a form available from the correspondent, to be submitted directly by the individual or through a third party.

Correspondent: Mrs M Simmonds, 10 Troughton Place, Tewkesbury, GL20 8EA (01684 850697)

Wotton-under-Edge

Edith Strain Nursing Charity

Eligibility: People who live in the town of Wotton-under-Edge and who are in need due to sickness or infirmity.

Types of grants: One-off and recurrent grants normally ranging between £50 and £100. Grants are not made where statutory money is available.

Annual grant total: Generally this charity has both an income and expenditure of around £2,000 with approximately £600 paid to individuals who are in need due to sickness or infirmity.

Applications: In writing to the correspondent, either directly by the individual, or via a social worker, Citizens Advice or other welfare agency. An sae is required. Applications are usually considered in May and November.

Correspondent: Mrs Jean Deveney, 85 Shepherds Leaze, Wotton-under-Edge, Gloucestershire GL12 7LJ (01453 844370)

Other information: Grants are also made to local organisations which care for people who are sick.

Somerset

J A F Luttrell Memorial Charity

Eligibility: People in need who live in Edington, Catcott, Chilton Polden and Burtle.

Types of grants: On average 30 one-off grants are made a year ranging from £25 to £500.

Annual grant total: In 2008/09 the charity had an income of £5,100 and a total expenditure of £6,500.

Applications: In writing to the correspondent, directly by the individual or a family member. Applications are considered in March and October and should be received by February and September respectively.

Correspondent: Agnes Auld, West Close, Church Road, Edington, Bridgwater, Somerset TA7 9JT (01278 722529)

Other information: Grants are also given to organisations supporting older people, environmental needs and cardiac rehabilitation.

The Nuttall Trust

Eligibility: People in need who live in the parishes of Brent Knoll, East Brent, Mark and Lympsham in Somerset.

Types of grants: One-off grants according to need.

Annual grant total: Grants generally average about £10,000, though this amount tends to fluctuate quite widely from year to year.

Applications: In writing to the correspondent. Applications can be submitted directly by the individual or via a third party.

Correspondent: Nicholas Redding, 60 High Street, Burnham-on-Sea, Somerset TA8 1AG (01278 782371)

Other information: The trust also makes grants to local organisations.

The Somerset Local Medical Benevolent Fund

Eligibility: General medical practitioners who are practising or have practised in Somerset and their dependants, who are in need.

Types of grants: One-off or recurrent grants according to need. Recently a quarterly grant was given to the widow of a Somerset GP and another grant was given to cover expenses incurred by a doctor who was involved in a serious accident.

Annual grant total: In 2008/09 the trust had an income of £24,000 and a total expenditure of £20,000.

Applications: In writing to the correspondent. Applications can be submitted directly by the individual or by any person on their behalf.

Correspondent: Dr J H Yoxall, Secretary to the Trustees, The Crown Medical Centre, Crown Industrial Estate, Venture Way, Taunton, TA2 8QY (01823 331428; email: lmcoffice@somerset.nhs.uk)

Axbridge

Axbridge Parochial Charities

Eligibility: People in need who live in the town of Axbridge.

Types of grants: One-off grants according to need. Previously, the majority of funding has been given for Christmas gifts of about £25 to older people.

Annual grant total: In 2008/09 the charities had an income of £16,000 and a total expenditure of £18,000. Grants were made totalling about £15,000.

Applications: In writing to the correspondent.

Correspondent: Julia Hill, Moonacre, Hillside, Axbridge, Somerset, BS26 2AN (01934 732915)

Other information: The charities also give grants to local organisations.

Bridgewater

The Tamlin Charity

Eligibility: Older people, generally those over 65, who are in need and live in Bridgwater.

Types of grants: Small quarterly pensions.

Annual grant total: Grants average around £900 a year.

Applications: On a form available from a trustee or from the correspondent. Applications can be submitted directly by the individual or through a third party such as a social worker, Citizens Advice or other welfare agency.

Correspondent: Richard Young, Clerk, 5 Channel Court, Burnham-on-Sea, Somerset TA8 1NE (01278 789859)

Cannington

The Cannington Combined Charity

Eligibility: People in need who live in the parish of Cannington. There is some preference for older people and those with disabilities.

Types of grants: Grants to meet regular or one-off bills where applicants cannot receive additional assistance from any other source. Other grants have been given towards a shower for a woman following major surgery, help with household expenses and travel expenses to a special school.

Annual grant total: Grants usually total around £2,000 per year.

Applications: On a form available from the correspondent. Applications can be submitted directly by the individual or through a social worker, family member, doctor or similar third party. Trustees

meet quarterly in January, April, August and November.

Correspondent: Betty Edney, Clerk to the Trustees, Down Stream, 1 Mill Close, Cannington, Bridgwater, Somerset TA5 2JA (01278 653026)

Draycott

Charity of John & Joseph Card (also known as Draycott Charity)

Eligibility: People in need who live in the hamlet of Draycott, near Cheddar, with a preference for those who receive a pension from the charity.

Types of grants: Pensions usually range from £100 to £500 a year and are made to people of pensionable age on low incomes (i.e. basic pensions). One-off hardship payments range from £50 to £250 and can be made to people of all ages. One-off grants have recently been made for clothing and travel to and from hospital.

Exclusions: No grants to pay normal household bills.

Annual grant total: In 2008/09 the charity had an income of £5,400 and a total expenditure of £4,600.

Applications: For pensions apply on a form available from the correspondent and for hardship grants apply in writing. Applications for pensions are considered in November and hardship grants are considered at any time. Applications can be submitted directly by the individual or by a family member.

Correspondent: Helen Dance, Leighurst, The Street, Draycott, Cheddar, Somerset BS27 3TH (01934 742811)

Other information: Grants are also made to organisations such as playgroups, churches and so on.

Ilchester

Ilchester Relief-in-Need and Educational Charity

Eligibility: People in need who live in the parish of Ilchester only.

Types of grants: One-off grants according to need.

Exclusions: Support will not be given to individuals who live outside the parish of Ilchester.

Annual grant total: In 2009 the charity had assets of £18,000 and an income of £34,000. Relief in need payments amounted to £2,600.

Applications: On a form available from the correspondent. Applications can be submitted directly by the individual or through a social worker, Citizens Advice or other welfare agency or third party.

Unsolicited applications are not responded to.

Correspondent: Mrs Wendy Scrivener, Milton House, Podimore, Yeovil, Somerset BA22 8JF (01935 840070)

Newton St Loe

The Henry Smith Charity (Newton St Loe)

Eligibility: People in need who live in Newton St Loe, and have done so for at least five years.

Types of grants: Annual grants of food vouchers and clothing tickets.

Annual grant total: Grants usually total around £1,500 per year.

Applications: In writing to the correspondent. Applications should be submitted directly by the individual by 25 September, for payment in November/ December each year.

Correspondent: Mrs J Ringham, 51 Claysend Cottages, Newton St Loe, Bath BA2 9DE

Pitminster

The Pitminster Charity

Eligibility: People who live or have recently lived in the parish of Pitminster and are in need.

Types of grants: One-off grants of at least £250 for items, services or facilities to reduce need.

Annual grant total: In 2008/09 the charity had an income of £5,700 and a total expenditure of £6,200.

Applications: In writing to the correspondent. Applications can be submitted at any time directly by the individual or family member. Please enclose an sae.

Correspondent: Bryan Thomas, Greencrest, Sellicks Green, Taunton, Somerset TA3 7SD

Other information: The trust also supports the upkeep of a recreation ground in the parish.

Porlock

The Henry Rogers Charity (Porlock Branch)

Eligibility: Older people who live in Porlock.

Types of grants: One-off grants and small monthly payments.

Annual grant total: Grants usually total about £1,600 each year.

Applications: On a form available from the correspondent, to be submitted directly by the individual.

Correspondent: Mrs C M Corner, Tyrol, Villes Lane, Porlock, Minehead, Somerset TA24 8NQ (01643 862645)

Rimpton

The Rimpton Relief-in-Need Charities

Eligibility: People in need who live in the parish of Rimpton only. Preference is generally given to older people.

Types of grants: One-off or recurrent grants according to need.

Annual grant total: Grants usually total about £1,500 each year.

Applications: On a form available from the correspondent, to be submitted either by the individual, a family member or through a third party.

Correspondent: J N Spencer, Secretary, Field End House, Home Farm Lane, Rimpton, Yeovil, Somerset, BA22 8AS (01935 850530)

Street

The George Cox Charity

Eligibility: People in need who live in the parish of Street.

Types of grants: One-off grants generally ranging from £50 to £100. Recent grants have been given for holidays; repair of domestic appliances such as washing machines and cookers; equipment for older people such as visual aids and Helping Hands; second hand furniture and carpets; and hospital travel costs. Grants are usually paid through the social services.

Annual grant total: In 2009 the charity had an income of £3,000 and a total expenditure of £4,200.

Applications: In writing to the correspondent. Applications are usually submitted through a social worker, Citizens Advice or other welfare agency, or through one of the trustees or someone known to the trustees.

Correspondent: Andrew Wride, 79 West End, Street, Somerset BA16 0LQ (01458 443990)

Other information: Grants are made to both organisations and individuals.

Taunton

The Taunton Aid in Sickness Fund

Eligibility: People in poor health who are in need and live within a four mile radius of St Mary's Church, Taunton. Priority is given to those living in the former borough of Taunton and the parish of Trull.

Types of grants: One-off grants generally up to £200. Recent grants have been given towards holidays, travel costs, outings and entertainments, laundering, furniture, food for special diets, help with child care costs, and many other benefits for those in poor health.

Exclusions: Grants cannot be used in place of public/statutory funds, but can be used as a supplement to support those where need is proven. Grants cannot be made on a recurring basis.

Annual grant total: In 2008/09 the fund had an income of £30,000 and a total expenditure of £20,000. Grants were made to 47 individuals totalling £13,000.

Applications: On a form available from the correspondent. Applications should be completed and signed by a recognised referral agency such as social services or a local NHS trust. They should include details of any benefits received by the applicant and a summary of all applications made to other charities or other sources of help. Specific items of basic need should be costed and the actual amount required should be given. Applications can be made at any time.

Correspondent: Lynne Durman, Clerk, Stafford House, Blackbrook Park Avenue, Taunton, Somerset TA1 2PX (01823 624450)

Taunton Town Charity

Eligibility: People in need who live in the borough of Taunton Deane.

Types of grants: One-off grants for specific items such as, furniture, white goods, equipment for babies/children, household repairs/decoration, flooring, holidays, clothing and disability aids.

Exclusions: Support is not given towards clearing debts.

Annual grant total: In 2009 grants were made to over 200 individuals for welfare purposes totalling £65,000.

Applications: On a form available from the correspondent, for consideration throughout the year. Applications should be submitted through a third party, such as a social worker, Citizens Advice or other welfare agency. The third party should verify that the applicant is in receipt of all statutory benefits to which they are entitled.

Correspondent: Mrs D Stodgell, Clerk, The Committee Room, Huish Homes,

Magdalene Street, Taunton, Somerset
TA1 1SG (01823 335348)

Other information: The prime role of the charity is to provide sheltered accommodation for older people. Grants are also made for educational purposes.

Wiltshire

Malmesbury Community Trust

Eligibility: People in need who live in Malmesbury and the surrounding area, with priority given to older residents.

Types of grants: One-off grants according to need.

Annual grant total: In 2008/09 the trust had an income of £5,400 and a total expenditure of £4,300.

Applications: On an application form available from the correspondent.

Correspondent: A C Neve, 3 Common Road, Malmesbury, Wiltshire SN16 0HN (01666 823864; email: mrtonyneve@googlemail.com)

Other information: The trust also makes grants to local organisations.

Salisbury City Almshouse & Welfare Charities

Eligibility: People in need who live in Salisbury and district.

Types of grants: One-off grants of between £100 and £300, to meet all kinds of emergency or other needs that cannot be met from public funds. Grants can be towards, for example, essential items such as reconditioned cookers, washing machines, refrigerators, school clothing, shoes, moving costs, beds/bedding, holidays and wheelchairs.

Exclusions: No grants for debts.

Annual grant total: In 2008 the charities had assets of £11.2 million and an income of £1.3 million. Welfare grants made to individuals totalled £16,500; it appears that no grants were made for educational purposes.

Applications: Applications are considered in the second week of each month. Application forms should be submitted at least 15 days before and should be sponsored by a recognised professional who is fully aware of statutory entitlements and is capable of giving advice/supervision in budgeting and so on. Application forms, together with guidance notes, are available from the clerk.

Correspondent: Clerk to the Trustees, Trinity Hospital, Trinity Street, Salisbury SP1 2BD (01722 325640; fax: 01722 325640; email: clerk@almshouses.demon.co.uk)

Wiltshire Ambulance Service Benevolent Fund

Eligibility: Serving and retired members of the Wiltshire Ambulance Service and their dependants.

Types of grants: One-off and recurrent grants according to need.

Annual grant total: In 2008/09 the trust had an income of £18,000 and a total expenditure of £27,000. Grants totalled around £2,500.

Applications: Applicants should contact their station benevolent fund representative, who will then contact the chair on their behalf.

Correspondent: A C Newman, Treasurer, 82 Dunch Lane, Melksham, Wiltshire SN12 8DX

Other information: The fund also owns and supports three properties that provide convalescence.

Aldbourne

Aldbourne Poors' Gorse Charity

Eligibility: People in need who live in the parish of Aldbourne, with a preference for those over 65.

Types of grants: One-off grants towards fuel costs.

Annual grant total: Grants usually total around £1,900 each year.

Applications: In writing to the correspondent, directly by the individual, usually on the charity's invitation.

Correspondent: Terence Gilligan, Poors Allotment, 9 Cook Road, Aldbourne, Marlborough, Wiltshire SN8 2EG (01672 540205)

Ashton Keynes

The Ashton Keynes Charity

Eligibility: Older people in need who live in Ashton Keynes.

Types of grants: Grants to pensioners. In previous years around 180 individuals have benefited.

Annual grant total: In 2009 the trust had an income of £6,600 and a total expenditure of £5,600.

Applications: In writing to the correspondent.

Correspondent: Richard Smith, Trustee, Amberley, 4 Gosditch, Ashton Keynes, Swindon, Wiltshire SN6 6NZ (01285 861461)

Other information: Grants are also given to organisations.

Chippenham

Chippenham Borough Lands Charity

Eligibility: People in need who are living within the parish of Chippenham at the date of application, and have been for a minimum of two years immediately prior to applying.

Types of grants: One-off, and occasionally recurrent, grants and loans are made according to need. Recent grants have included help with living costs, mobility aids, domestic appliances, debt relief, travel passes, food vouchers, furniture and childcare.

Exclusions: Grants are not given in any circumstances where the charity considers the award to be a substitute for statutory provision. The charity will not consider an application if a grant has been received within the past two years (or one year for mobility aids) unless the circumstances are exceptional.

Annual grant total: In 2008/09 the charity had assets of £9 million and an income of £364,000. There were 54 grants made for relief-in-need purposes totalling £22,000.

Applications: On a form available from the correspondent. Once received the application will be looked at in detail by a welfare officer. It is possible that the charity will visit, or ask applicants to call in at this stage. Applications are considered every month and can be submitted directly by the individual or through a third party such as a Citizens Advice, social worker or GP.

Correspondent: Catherine Flynn, Jubilee Building, 32 Market Place, Chippenham, Wiltshire SN15 3HP (01249 658180; fax: 01249 446048; email: admin@cblc.org.uk; website: www.cblc.org.uk)

Other information: People applying for mobility equipment will be asked to attend the Independent Living Centre in order for them to assess which equipment would be most appropriate.

East Knoyle

The East Knoyle Welfare Trust

Eligibility: People in need who live in the parish of East Knoyle.

Types of grants: One-off grants only, usually for heating bills.

Annual grant total: Grants usually total around £800.

Applications: Applications to the correspondent or any other trustee by the end of May to receive fuel payments for the next winter.

Correspondent: Miss Sabrina Sully, Old Byre House, Millbrook Lane, East Knoyle, Salisbury SP3 6AW

Other information: Grants are also made for educational purposes.

Salisbury

Charity of William Botley

Eligibility: Women in need who live in the city of Salisbury.

Types of grants: One-off grants ranging from about £100 to £200, to meet all kinds of emergency and other needs which cannot be met from public funds. Recent grants have been made for second hand white goods, clothing for mothers and children, carpets and floor coverings and holiday costs.

Exclusions: No grants for the payment of debts.

Annual grant total: In 2009 the charity had an income of £9,100 and a total expenditure of £5,700. Grants were made to 21 individuals totalling £4,000.

Applications: Application forms, together with guidance notes, are available from the clerk. Applications are considered during the second week of every month and should be received at least two weeks prior to this. They should be submitted through a recognised professional such as a social worker.

Correspondent: Clerk to the Trustees, Trinity Hospital, Trinity Street, Salisbury, Wiltshire SP1 2BD (01722 325640; email: clerk@almshouses.demon.co.uk)

Trowbridge

Dr C S Kingston Fund

Eligibility: People in need who live in the urban district of Trowbridge.

Types of grants: One-off grants according to need. Recent grants have been given towards electrical goods (cookers, washing machines), school uniforms and school trips for families not otherwise able to afford them. Occasionally, financial grants (but *not* payable to individuals), help towards childcare and help towards holidays has been given.

Annual grant total: In 2008/09 grants totalled around £2,300.

Applications: On a form available from the correspondent. Applications can be submitted directly by the individual, but are generally made through a social worker, doctor, Citizens Advice or other welfare agency.

Correspondent: Matthew Ridley, Castle House, Castle Street, Trowbridge, Wiltshire, BA14 8AX (01225 755621)

Westbury

The Henry Smith Charity (Westbury)

Eligibility: People in need who live in Westbury and are aged over 40 years.

Types of grants: Grants of around £40 are given towards, for example, fuel, food and clothing.

Annual grant total: Grants usually total around £1,000 a year.

Applications: In writing to the correspondent.

Correspondent: W H White, Pinniger Finch & Co, Solicitors, 35–37 Church Street, Westbury, Wiltshire BA13 3BZ (01373 823791; email: info@pinngerfinch. co.uk)

8. SOUTH EAST

Anglia Care Trust

Eligibility: People in need who live in East Anglia and are experiencing or have experienced a legal restriction on their liberty, and their families. Namely offenders, ex-offenders or people who are at risk of offending.

Types of grants: One-off grants towards rehabilitation and education. Grants usually range from £10 to £70. Sums of money are not usually paid direct, but itemised bills will be met directly. If items can be reclaimed from either housing benefit or returnable deposit, this must be considered.

Applicants will usually already be supported by, or are known to, ACT and should have exhausted all possible sources of statutory funds.

The areas that will be supported are:

- education and/or training
- basic equipment/tools
- furniture
- moving into new accommodation
- clothing to enable people to seek employment/return to work
- others on merit.

Exclusions: Grants are not given towards payment of debts, fines, legal costs or hire purchases.

Annual grant total: Grants usually total around £900.

Applications: In writing to the correspondent. All applications must be supported by a probation officer or other professional person and are considered quarterly.

Correspondent: Jane Sharpe, 65 St Matthew's Street, Ipswich, Suffolk IP1 3EW (01473 213140; email: admin@angliacaretrust.org.uk; website: www.angliacaretrust.org.uk)

Other information: For this entry, the information relates to the money available from ACT. For more information on what is available throughout East Anglia, contact the correspondent.

The Argus Appeal

Eligibility: People in need, particularly older people and underprivileged children, who live in the Sussex area.

Types of grants: One-off and recurrent grants according to need and food parcels for older people.

Annual grant total: In 2008 the charity had assets of £50,000 and an income of £223,000. Grants were made to individuals totalling £46,000.

Applications: In writing to the correspondent including details on who you are, what you do, how much is needed, how it will be spent and what has been done so far to raise the necessary funds.

Correspondent: Elsa Gillio, Argus House, Crowhurst Road, Hollingbury, Brighton BN1 8AR (01273 544320; email: elsa.gillio@theargus.co.uk; website: www.theargus.co.uk/argusappeal)

The Berkshire Nurses & Relief-in-Sickness Trust

Eligibility: 1. People in need through sickness or disability who live in the county of Berkshire and those areas of Oxfordshire formerly in Berkshire.

2. Nurses and midwives employed as district nurses in the county of Berkshire and those areas of Oxfordshire formerly in Berkshire and people employed before August 1980 as administrative and clerical staff by Berkshire County Nursing Association.

Types of grants: One-off grants only towards household accounts (excluding those below), holidays, some medical aids, special diets, clothing, wheelchairs, electronic aids for people with disabilities, hospital travel costs, prescription season tickets and so on.

Exclusions: No grants for rent or mortgage payments, community charge, water rates, funeral bills, on-going payments such as nursing home fees or any items thought to be the responsibility of statutory authorities.

Annual grant total: In 2009/10 the trust had assets of £1.2 million, which generated an income of £62,000. Grants were made to 189 individuals totalling £50,000.

Applications: On a form available from the correspondent. Applications should be made through a social worker, Citizens Advice or other welfare agency and supported by a member of the statutory authorities. They are considered as received. Applications are not accepted directly from members of the public.

Correspondent: Mrs R Pottinger, Honorary Secretary, 26 Montrose Walk, Fords Farm, Calcot, Reading RG31 7YH (0118 942 4556; email: rosandken@aol.com)

Other information: Grants are also made to local caring organisations, when funds allow.

The Chownes Foundation

Eligibility: Individuals and small charities primarily in Sussex, particularly Mid-Sussex, being the former home of the founder.

Types of grants: One-off and recurrent grants according to need.

Annual grant total: In 2008/09 the foundation had assets of £1.6 million, which generated an income of £103,000. Grants were made to individuals for 'social problems' and relief of poverty totalling £35,000.

Applications: The trustees prefer a one page document and will request further information if they require it.

Correspondent: Sylvia J Spencer, Secretary, The Courtyard, Beeding Court, Steyning, West Sussex, BN44 3TN (01903 816699)

Other information: The majority of the charity's funds are committed to long term support for poor and vulnerable beneficiaries, so only very few applications are successful.

The Derek & Eileen Dodgson Foundation

Eligibility: People in need over 55, who live in East and West Sussex, with a strong preference for connections with Brighton and Hove.

Types of grants: On average 500 one-off grants or loans of up to £1,000 are made, mainly to older people. Most of the funds are given to local non-governmental organisations to pass on to individuals.

Annual grant total: In 2008/09 the foundation had assets of £1.7 million and an income of £148,000. Grants were made totalling £98,000.

Applications: On a form available from the correspondent. Applications can be submitted either directly by the individual or through a social worker, Citizens Advice or other third party.

Correspondent: Ian W Dodd, 8 Locks Hill, Portslade, Brighton and Hove BN41 2LB (01273 419802; email: lanw.dodd@ ntlworld.com)

East Sussex Farmers' Union Benevolent Fund

Eligibility: People in need who are farmers, farm workers or their dependants, with priority for those who live in the county of East Sussex. When funds are available eligible people living in Kent, Surrey and West Sussex may also be supported.

Types of grants: One-off and recurrent grants according to need.

Annual grant total: In 2008/09 the fund had assets of nearly £1 million and an income of £31,000. Grants and donations to individuals totalled £16,000, with costs for hampers amounting to £2,000.

Applications: In writing or by telephone to the correspondent.

Correspondent: c/o Gordon J Fowlie, Farthings, North Road, Ringmer, Lewes, West Sussex, BN8 5JP (01273 812406)

The Eos Foundation

Eligibility: Customers of, or people living in a household supplied by, a company who donates to the foundation. These companies are Bournemouth and West Hampshire Water, Cambridge Water, Portsmouth Water, South East Water, Veolia Water East (formerly known as Tendring Hundred Water) and Veolia Water Southeast (formerly Folkestone and Dover Water).

Types of grants: The foundation can help with arrears of domestic water charges and other essential domestic bills and costs.

Exclusions: No grants for: educational or training needs; medical equipment, aids and adaptations; fines for criminal offences; overpayments of benefits; business debts; debts to central government departments, e.g. tax and national insurance; catalogues, credit cards, personal loans and other forms of non-secured lending; deposits to secure accommodation; or holidays. The foundation does not give loans or help with bills that have already been paid or items already purchased.

Annual grant total: In 2008/09 the foundation had assets of £49,000 and an

income of £218,000. Grants made to individuals totalled £186,000.

Applications: Application forms can be downloaded from the foundation's website or requested in writing or by telephone (01733 421060). A local money advice centre such as a Citizens Advice may be able to provide help in completing the form.

Those in receipt of an award from the foundation cannot reapply for two years. Applicants who do not receive an award can apply again after six months.

Correspondent: Grants Administrator, PO Box 42, Peterborough, PE3 8XH (01733 421021; fax: 01733 421020; email: eos@charisgrants.com; website: www.eosfoundation.org.uk)

Other information: The Eos Foundation is administered by Charis Grants alongside a number of other utility trust funds, namely the British Gas Energy Trust, the EDF Energy Trust, the Three Valleys Water Trust and the Anglian Water Assistance Fund. All the trusts operate within a shared scheme and have a common application form and assessment process so it may be possible for customers of these companies to arrange for water, sewerage and/or energy debts to be cleared at the same time. For further information please contact the foundation.

Grizzles Foundation

Eligibility: Babies and children up to the age 16 who are terminally or seriously ill with ongoing symptoms and who live within the Kent and Sussex boundaries.

Types of grants: Grants of up to £150 can be applied for towards the costs of equipment, specialist clothing, toys, holidays, outings and other special events for the benefit of children.

Annual grant total: Grants average around £2,000 a year, though the actual grant figure tends to fluctuate quite widely.

Applications: Application forms are available from the correspondent or to download from the foundation's website.

Correspondent: Sheila Woodcock, 13 Celtic Way, Rhoose, Vale of Glamorgan, CF62 3FT (email: grizzlefund@aol.com; website: www.grizzlesfoundation.org)

The Hunstanton Convalescent Trust

Eligibility: People who are on a low income, physically or mentally unwell and in need of a convalescent or recuperative holiday, with a preference for those living in Norfolk, Cambridgeshire and Suffolk.

Types of grants: Grants ranging from £100 to £350 are given to provide or assist towards the expenses of recuperative holidays, including for carers. The trust can sometimes provide other items, services or facilities which will help the individual's recovery.

Annual grant total: In 2008/09 the trust had an income of £12,000 and a total expenditure of £10,000.

Applications: On a form available from the correspondent, through a social worker, doctor or other welfare workers. Applications should be submitted at least one month before the proposed holiday. The full board of trustees meet in January, June and September.

Correspondent: Mrs F Wilby, 66 Collingwood Road, Hunstanton, Norfolk, PE36 5DY (01485 533788)

Jewish Care

Eligibility: Members of the Jewish faith who are older, mentally ill, visually impaired or physically disabled, and their families, who live in London and the south east of England.

Types of grants: Jewish Care (includes the former Jewish Welfare Board, Jewish Blind Society and the Jewish Home and Hospital at Tottenham) is the largest Jewish social work agency, providing a range of services, both domiciliary and residential. Financial assistance is not a normal part of the trust's work, though some such expenditure is inevitably associated with its social work service.

Exclusions: No help with burial expenses or education fees.

Annual grant total: In 2008/09 the trust had assets of £61 million, an income of £58 million and a total expenditure of £46 million, the majority of which went on the provision and administration of Jewish social services. Some direct financial help was, however, provided in the form of grants.

Applications: In writing to the correspondent either direct by the individual or through a social worker.

Correspondent: Grants Officer, Jewish Care, Merit House, 508 Edgware Road, London, NW9 5AB (020 8922 2000; email: info@jewishcare.org; website: www.jewishcare.org)

The Elaine & Angus Lloyd Charitable Trust

Eligibility: People 'whose circumstances are such they come within the legal conception of poverty'.

Types of grants: One-off and recurrent grants according to need.

Annual grant total: In 2009/10 the trust had assets of £2.3 million and an income of £86,000. Grants to individuals totalled £5,100 and grants to organisations amounted to £73,000.

Applications: In writing to the correspondent. The trustees meet regularly to consider grants.

Correspondent: Ross Badger, 3rd Floor, North Side, Dukes Court, 32 Duke Street,

St James's, London SW1Y 6DF
(020 7930 7797)

The B V MacAndrew Trust

Eligibility: People in need who live in East and West Sussex.

Types of grants: One-off grants ranging from £50 to £200 for a variety of needs including emergencies and household appliances.

Annual grant total: In 2008/09 the trust had an income of £21,000 and a total expenditure of £25,000. Grants were made to 152 individuals totalling £22,000.

Applications: In writing to the correspondent at any time including the amount required and the name of the person the cheque is to be made out to. Applications can be made either through a third party such as a social worker or through an organisation such as Citizens Advice or other welfare agency. Applications are usually considered a month following receipt.

Correspondent: Roger Clow, 9 Albert Mews, Third Avenue, Hove, East Sussex, BN3 2PP (01273 736272)

The Sussex Police Charitable Trust

Eligibility: Members and retired members of the Sussex Police Welfare Fund who are in need, and their dependants.

Types of grants: One-off grants averaging about £330 for convalescence, clothing, household bills, food, holidays, travel expenses, medical equipment, nursing fees, furniture, disability equipment, help in the home and short-term childcare. Grants are also given to facilitate mediation and initial legal advice.

Discretionary loans may be given to serving officers subscribing to the fund who are facing financial difficulties. Loans are repayable from salary at source per pay period.

Annual grant total: In 2009 the trust had assets of £981,000, an income of £114,000 and a total expenditure of £177,000. Grants were made to 118 individuals totalling £36,000.

Applications: In writing to the correspondent. Applications can be submitted directly by the individual or through a third party such as a social worker or Citizens Advice. They are considered monthly, though a decision can be made between meetings in urgent cases.

Correspondent: Barbara Castle, Sussex Police, Malling House, Church Lane, Lewes, East Sussex, BN7 2DZ (0845 6070999 (ext. 44137); email: spct@ sussex.pnn.police.uk)

Other information: The trust employs two welfare liaison officers who offer advice, information and practical support particularly to older members of the fund

and those struggling with debt problems. The trust also owns a bungalow in Highcliffe, Christchurch, which is available to members in need of a recuperative break.

NB The trust is also known as the Sussex Police Welfare Fund.

The Kathryn Turner Trust

Eligibility: Children, young people, the elderly and people with disabilities/special needs in the area of the old county of Middlesex.

Types of grants: Grants towards the costs of equipment.

Annual grant total: In 2009 the trust had an income of £104,000 and a total expenditure of £107,000. Grants are made to organisations and individuals.

Applications: In writing to the correspondent.

Correspondent: Kathryn Turner, 58 Addlestone Moor, Addlestone, KT15 2QL

Other information: The trust is also known as 'Whitton's Wishes'.

The Vokins Charitable Trust

Eligibility: People in need and live in Kent and Surrey.

Types of grants: One-off and recurrent grants according to need.

Annual grant total: In 2009 the trust had an income of £2,800 and a total expenditure of £4,100.

Applications: In writing to the correspondent.

Correspondent: T W D Vokins, 56 Hove Park Road, Hove, East Sussex, BN3 6LN

Other information: Grants are also made to organisations.

The Wantage District Coronation Memorial & Nursing Amenities Fund

Eligibility: People who are in poor health, convalescent or who have disabilities and live in the parishes of Wantage, East Challow, Grove, Letcombe Regis, Letcombe Bassett, West Challow, Childrey, Denchworth, Goosey, East Hanney, West Hanney and Lockridge in the county of Oxfordshire and the parishes of Farnborough and Fawley in the county of Berkshire.

Types of grants: One-off and recurrent grants ranging from about £20 to £100.

Exclusions: The income of the charity is not to be applied directly for the relief of taxes, rates or other public funds, but may be applied in supplementing relief or assistance provided out of public funds.

Annual grant total: Grants usually total about £3,000 each year.

Applications: In writing to the correspondent.

Correspondent: Carol Clubb, 133 Stockham Park, Wantage, Oxfordshire OX12 9HJ (01235 767355)

Other information: Grants are also made to organisations.

Bedfordshire

The Norah Mavis Campbell Trust

Eligibility: People who are elderly and in need who reside in the area of Bedford Borough Council area.

Types of grants: Grants are given according to need.

Annual grant total: In 2008/09 the trust had an income of £12,000 and a total expenditure of £5,000.

Applications: In writing to the correspondent.

Correspondent: David Baker, Committee Services Officer, Bedfordshire County Council, Borough Hall, Cauldwell Street, Bedford, MK42 9AP (email: david.baker@ bedford.gov.uk)

Other information: The trust also provides additional benefits for residents at the Puttenhoe Home in Bedford.

Mary Lockingtons' Charity

Eligibility: Individuals living in the parishes of Dunstable, Leighton Buzzard and Hockliffe who are in need, for example due to hardship, disability or sickness.

Types of grants: One-off grants towards items, services or facilities.

Annual grant total: In 2008/09 the charity had an income of £11,000 and a total expenditure of £5,300.

Applications: In writing to the correspondent.

Correspondent: Yvonne E Beaumont, Grove House, 76 High Street North, Dunstable, Bedfordshire LU6 1NF (01582 890 619)

The Sandy Charities

Eligibility: People who live in Sandy and Beeston and are in need.

Types of grants: One-off grants only ranging from £100 to £1,000, towards, for instance, motorised wheelchairs, decorating costs and children's' clothing.

Annual grant total: In 2008/09 the charities had an income of £8,800 and a total expenditure of £9,100.

Applications: In writing to the correspondent who will supply a personal details form for completion. Applications can be considered in any month, depending on the urgency for the grant; they should be submitted either directly by the individual or via a social worker, Citizens Advice or other welfare agency.

Correspondent: P J Mount, Clerk, Woodfines Solicitors, 6 Bedford Road, Sandy, Bedfordshire SG19 1EN (01767 680251; email: pmount@ woodfines.co.uk)

Other information: Grants are also made to organisations and to individuals for educational purposes.

Bedford

Municipal Charities

Eligibility: People in need who live in the borough of Bedford.

Types of grants: Pensions; grants towards fuel bills and other necessities; occasional one-off grants for special purposes in the range of £25 to £700 and Christmas bonuses.

Annual grant total: In 2008/09 the trust had assets of £790,000 and an income of £27,000. Grants totalled £26,000 and were distributed as follows:

Almoners allowance	£2,900
Pensions	£4,200
Christmas distribution	£1,600
Fuel grants	£4,900
Emergency fund	£11,000
Church distribution	£500
Other grants	£1,400

Applications: In writing to the correspondent. Applications can be submitted directly by the individual or through an appropriate third party. Individual applicants may be visited to assess the degree of need.

Correspondent: David Baker, Bedford Borough Council, Borough Hall, Cauldwell Street, Bedford MK42 9AP (01234 228788; email: dbaker@bedford.gov.uk)

Clophill

Clophill United Charities

Eligibility: People who live in the parish of Clophill and are in need.

Types of grants: One-off and recurrent grants according to need.

Exclusions: No grants where statutory funds are available.

Annual grant total: Grants usually total around £3,000 per year.

Applications: On a form available from the correspondent.

Correspondent: Richard Pearson, 8 Little Lane, Clophill, Bedford, MK45 4BG (01525 861110)

Dunstable

The Dunstable Poor's Land Charity

Eligibility: People, usually pensioners, who live in the parish of Dunstable.

Types of grants: Grants of around £20 each are made annually on Maundy Thursday mostly to older people on Income Support or other benefits.

Annual grant total: Grants usually total about £3,000 each year.

Applications: By personal application to the trustees. Applicants must provide evidence of their income.

Correspondent: Yvonne E Beaumont, Grove House, 76 High Street North, Dunstable, Bedfordshire LU6 1NF (01582 890619)

The Dunstable Welfare Trust

Eligibility: People in need who live in the borough of Dunstable or in exceptional cases 'immediately' outside Dunstable. Preference is given to people who attend Church of England services.

Types of grants: One-off grants ranging from £50 to £100 for those in need.

Exclusions: Grants are not given for relief of rates, taxes or other public funds. The trust may also give donations to organisations that provide services.

Annual grant total: Grants average about £400 a year.

Applications: In writing to the correspondent through a social worker, Citizens Advice or other welfare agency or clergy. Applications are considered regularly.

Correspondent: Revd Richard Andrews, The Rectory, 8 Furness Avenue, Dunstable, LU6 3BN (01582 703271)

Flitwick

The Flitwick Town Lands Charity

Eligibility: People in need who live in the parish of Flitwick.

Types of grants: Usually one-off grants.

Annual grant total: In 2008/09 the charity had an income of £8,800 and a total expenditure of £6,400. Grants are given for education and welfare purposes.

Applications: On a form available from the correspondent.

Correspondent: David Empson, Trustee, 28 Orchard Way, Flitwick, Bedford MK45 1LF (01525 718145; email: Deflitwick8145@aol.com)

Husborne Crawley

The Husborne Crawley Charities of the Poor

Eligibility: People in need who live in the ancient parish of Husborne Crawley.

Types of grants: Grants to all pensioners for fuel and death grants to relatives.

Annual grant total: About £5,000 a year.

Applications: In writing to the correspondent either directly by the individual or via a third party. Applications are considered throughout the year.

Correspondent: Charles Lousada, Estate Office, Crawley Park, Husborne Crawley, Bedford MK43 0UU (01908 282860)

Kempston

The Kempston Charities

Eligibility: People in need who live in Kempston (including Kempston rural).

Types of grants: One-off grants according to need.

Exclusions: No recurrent grants are made.

Annual grant total: Grants average around £5,000 a year.

Applications: In writing to the correspondent. Applications should be made either directly by the individual or through a social worker, Citizens Advice or other welfare agency. They are considered in March, July and November.

Correspondent: Mrs L Smith, 14 Riverview Way, Kempston, Bedford MK42 7BB

Other information: Grants are also given to local schools and other local institutions.

Luton

The Emily Ada Sibthorpe Trust

Eligibility: Women over 60 and men over 65 who are in need and live in Luton.

Types of grants: One-off grants which have been given towards household items, electric scooters and specialist items. Sometimes a contribution is made towards the cost of an item, rather than to cover the full amount.

Annual grant total: About £1,000.

Applications: In writing to the correspondent through the social services department.

Correspondent: Ruth Francis-Foster, Luton Borough Council, Apex House, 30–34 Upper George Street, Luton, LU1 2RD (01582 546030; email: ruth. francis-foster@luton.gov.uk)

Potton

The Potton Consolidated Charities

Eligibility: People in need who live in the parish of Potton.

Types of grants: Grants given according to need.

Annual grant total: In 2008/09 grants to individuals for welfare purposes totalled £2,000.

Applications: Directly by the individual on a form available from the correspondent. Applications are considered in November and should be received by 31 October.

Correspondent: Christine Hall, 1a Potton Road, Everton, Sandy, Bedfordshire SG19 2LD (01767 680663; email: pot. concha@tiscali.co.uk)

Ravensden

The Ravensden Town & Poor Estate

Eligibility: Older people who are in need and live in the parish of Ravensden.

Types of grants: One-off and recurrent grants according to need.

Annual grant total: Grants usually total about £3,000 each year.

Applications: In writing to the correspondent. Applications can be submitted directly by the individual. They are usually considered in November, although urgent cases can be responded to at any time.

Correspondent: Ronald Watson, The Plantation, Church Hill, Ravensden, Bedford MK44 2RL (01234 772434; email: rowmanser@kbnet.co.uk)

Other information: This charity also gives grants to a local school.

Shefford

The Charity of Robert Lucas for the Poor & for Public Purposes

Eligibility: People in need who live in the ancient township of Shefford.

Types of grants: One-off or recurrent grants for needs which cannot be met by statutory sources.

Annual grant total: About £1,000 to individuals.

Applications: In writing to the correspondent. Applications should be submitted directly by the individual and are considered every two months.

Correspondent: Keith Bland, 47 Lucas Way, Shefford, Bedfordshire, SG17 5DX (01462 812870)

Other information: The charity primarily makes grants to organisations.

Berkshire

The Earley Charity

Eligibility: People in need who have lived in Earley and the surrounding neighbourhood for at least six months. Applicants must be living in permanent accommodation and have UK citizenship or have been granted indefinite leave to remain in the UK.

Types of grants: One-off grants according to need. Recent grants have been given for stairlifts, gardening tools; specialist computer software, laptop computer, counselling sessions, washing machines, cookers, fridges/freezers and beds/mattresses.

Exclusions: No grants can be made to those who are planning to move out of the area of benefit, have been awarded a grant within the last two years or have received three grants in the past.

Annual grant total: In 2009 the trust had assets of £12 million, an income of £1 million and a total expenditure of £1.5 million. Grants were made totalling £604,000, of which £7,200 was given in grants to 57 individuals. Grants to organisations totalled £596,000.

Applications: On a form available from the correspondent to be submitted either directly by the individual or through a social worker, Citizens Advice or other welfare agency. Applications are considered every six weeks, though requests for grants of less than £500 may be dealt with more quickly.

Correspondent: Jane Wittig, The Liberty of Earley House, Strand Way, Earley, Reading RG6 4EA (0118 975 5663; fax: 0118 975 2263; email: enquiries@ earleycharity.org.uk; website: www. earleycharity.org.uk)

The Finchampstead & Barkham Relief-in-Sickness Fund

Eligibility: People in need who are sick, convalescent, who have mental or physical disabilities, or who are infirm and who live in the parish of Finchampstead and Barkham.

Types of grants: One-off grants ranging from £100 to £1,000 towards the cost of, for example, electric goods, convalescence, clothing, living costs, household bills, food, holidays, travel expenses, medical equipment, nursing fees, furniture, equipment, help in the home and respite care.

Exclusions: No grants for relief of rates or taxes. Grants cannot be repeated or renewed.

Annual grant total: Grants average around £2,000 a year.

Applications: In writing to the correspondent including confirmation of eligibility. Applications can be made directly by the individual, through a social worker, Citizens Advice or other welfare agency or through a third party on behalf of the individual. Applications can be submitted throughout the year.

Correspondent: Dr John Dewhurst, Fourwinds, The Ridges, Finchampstead, Wokingham, Berkshire RG40 3SY

The Polehampton Charity

Eligibility: People in need who live in Twyford and Ruscombe.

Types of grants: One-off grants of £100 to £250 for items such as clothing, domestic appliances, holidays, medical equipment, furniture and equipment for people who are disabled.

Annual grant total: In 2008 the charity had assets of £1.2 million and an income of £64,000. Grants made for other purposes and Christmas grants amounted to £1,500.

Applications: Applications should be submitted either directly by the individual or a family member, through a third party such as a social worker or teacher, or through and organisation such as Citizens Advice or a school. Applications can be made at any time and are considered at trustee meetings.

Correspondent: Mrs Caroline J White, 65 The Hawthorns, Charvil, Reading, RG10 9TS (0118 934 0852)

Other information: In 2008 grants were also made to schools totalling £21,000 and other organisations totalling £3,600.

Reading Dispensary Trust

Eligibility: People in need who are in poor health, convalescent or who have a physical or mental disability and live in Reading and the surrounding area (roughly within a seven-mile radius of the centre of Reading).

Types of grants: One-off grants for a wide range of needs including, clothing and footwear, beds and bedding, holidays and travel, house adaptations and repairs, food bills, utility arrears, respite care, medical equipment, domestic appliances, wheelchair equipment, scooters, telephones and so on.

Annual grant total: In 2009 the trust had assets of £1 million and an income of £45,000. Grants were made to individuals for educational and welfare purposes totalling £22,000.

Applications: On a form available from the correspondent. Applications should be submitted directly by the individual or through a social worker, Citizens Advice or other third party. They are considered on a monthly basis.

Correspondent: W E Gilbert, Clerk, 16 Wokingham Road, Reading RG6 1JQ (0118 926 5698)

Other information: Grants are also made to organisations (£3,000, 2009).

The Slough and District Community Fund

Eligibility: People who are in need and live in Slough, New Windsor and Eton.

Types of grants: One-off grants according to need. Recent grants have been given towards household items, clothing, food and fuel costs, child and baby expenses and so on.

Annual grant total: In 2009 the fund had an income of £4,500 and a total expenditure of £6,000.

Applications: On a form available from the correspondent.

Correspondent: John Brooks, 14 Shaggy Calf Lane, Slough, SL2 5HJ (01753 530 101)

Other information: This trust was formed by the amalgamation of 'All Good Causes' and 'The Slough Nursing Fund'.

The Wokingham United Charities

Eligibility: People in need who live in the civil parishes of Wokingham, Wokingham Without, St Nicholas, Hurst, Ruscombe and that part of Finchampstead known as Finchampstead North.

Types of grants: One-off grants between £25 and £150. Grants have been given towards household items, utility arrears and clothing.

Annual grant total: Grants usually total around £10,000 a year.

Applications: On a form available from the correspondent. Applications are considered each month (except August) and can be submitted directly by the individual, or through a social worker, school liaison officer or similar third party.

Correspondent: P Robinson, Clerk, 66 Upper Broadmoor Road, Crowthorne, Berkshire RG45 7DF (01344 762637; email: peter.westende@btinternet.com)

Binfield

The Fritillary Trust

Eligibility: Older people who are in need.

Types of grants: One-off and recurrent grants ranging from £300 to £1,500.

Annual grant total: In 2008/09 the trust had an income of £10,000 and a total expenditure of £11,000. Grants are made to both organisations and individuals.

Applications: In writing to the correspondent.

Correspondent: The Trustees, SG Hambros Trust Company Ltd, SG House, 41 Tower Hill, London EC3N 4SG (020 7597 3060)

Other information: The trust is also known by its working name, 'The Muir Family Charitable Trust'.

Burnham

The Cornelius O'Sullivan Fund

Eligibility: People in need who are in poor health, convalescent, or who have a disability and live in or near the parish of Burnham.

Types of grants: One-off grants of up to about £500 towards specialist medical equipment.

Annual grant total: Grants average around £1,000, though this figure tends to fluctuate quite widely from year to year. In 2007/08 no grants were made at all.

Applications: Applications can be submitted by the individual, through a recognised referral agency (e.g. social worker, Citizens Advice or doctor) or by a similar third party.

Correspondent: Barbara Julie O'Brien, Our Lady of Peace Junior School, Derwent Drive, Slough, SL1 6HW (01628 666715; email: post@ourlady-jun.slough.sch.uk)

Datchet

The Datchet United Charities

Eligibility: People in need who live in the ancient parish of Datchet.

Types of grants: Grants of £15 to £1,500 are given for clothing, fuel bills, living costs, food, holidays, travel expenses and household bills. Christmas vouchers are also distributed.

Annual grant total: In 2008/09 the charities had assets of £608,000 and an income of £27,000. Grants were made to individuals totalling £4,300. A further £7,100 was given to organisations.

Applications: In writing to the correspondent either directly by the individual or through a social worker, Citizens Advice or other welfare agency. All applicants will be visited by the charities' social worker.

Correspondent: Gwenna Mary Howard, 59 London Road, Datchet, Slough SL3 9JY (01753 541883; email: gwennahoward@ btinternet.com)

Other information: The trust also owns a day centre which local groups are able to use for free, loans medical equipment from its emergency centre and supports a 'people to places' car scheme.

Hedgerley

The Tracy Trust

Eligibility: People of a pensionable age who are in need and live in the parish of Hedgerley.

Types of grants: One-off grants towards medical and welfare needs such as, spectacles, chiropody, hospital travel costs, aid alarms, TV licenses, stairlifts and so on.

Annual grant total: In 2008/09 the trust made grants to individuals totalling £26,000.

Applications: In writing to the correspondent.

Correspondent: Jim Cannon, Two Pins, Andrew Hill Lane, Hedgerley, Slough, SL2 3UL

Newbury

Newbury & Thatcham Welfare Trust

Eligibility: People in need who are sick, disabled, convalescent or infirm and live in the former borough of Newbury as constituted on 31 March 1974 and the parishes of Greenham, Enborne, Hampstead, Marshall, Shaw-cum-Donnington, Speen and Thatcham.

Types of grants: One-off grants up to £250. Grants given include those for medical aids, food, holidays, respite care, travel, special equipment, TV licences, furniture and appliances.

Exclusions: Grants are not given towards housing or rent costs and debts.

Annual grant total: In 2009 the trust had an income of £3,000 and a total expenditure of £2,000.

Applications: By application form submitted either through a social worker, Citizens Advice or other welfare agency or through a third party on behalf of an individual such as a doctor, health visitor or other health professional. They can be considered at any time.

Correspondent: Mrs Heather Codling, Volunteer Centre West Berkshire, 1 Bolton Place, Northbrook Street, Newbury, Berkshire, RG14 1AJ (01635 49004; email: ntwt@hotmail.com)

Reading

St Laurence Relief in Need Trust

Eligibility: People in need who live in the ancient parish of St Laurence in Reading. Surplus money can be given to people living in the county borough of Reading.

Types of grants: One-off and annual grants are awarded according to need. The minimum grant is £100.

Exclusions: Grants are not made to students for training research grants or to people not resident in the area of benefit.

Annual grant total: Grants to individuals generally total around £1,000 a year.

Applications: In writing to the correspondent including details of requirements and place of residence. Applications can be made directly by the individual or by a third party such as a social worker or Citizens Advice. They are generally considered in April and November.

Correspondent: John Michael James, c/o Vale & West, Victoria House, 26 Queen Victoria Street, Reading RG1 1TG (0118 957 3238)

Other information: The trust also gives to other charities provided they benefit individuals in St Laurence.

Sunninghill

Sunninghill Fuel Allotment Trust

Eligibility: People in need who live in the parish of Sunninghill.

Types of grants: One-off grants ranging from about £100 to £1,000. Recent awards have been made to relieve sudden distress, to purchase essential equipment or household appliances and to cover utility bills.

Annual grant total: In 2008/09 the trust had assets of £1.8 million and an income of £90,000. Grants were made totalling £56,000, of which £3,300 was given to seven individuals for educational and relief-in-need purposes. The remaining £53,000 was awarded to organisations.

Applications: In writing to the correspondent either directly by the individual or through a third party such as a social worker, Citizens Advice or similar welfare agency. The trustees meet four times a year to consider applications, though urgent cases may be dealt with between meetings. Applicants should be prepared to provide documentary evidence of their difficulties and circumstances.

Correspondent: Richard J Dugdale, 101 Victoria Road, Ascot, Berkshire SL5 9DS (01344 620614; email: r723@ btinternet.com)

Buckinghamshire

1067 Trust Fund

Eligibility: People in need who live in the parishes of Wooburn Green, Little Marlow, Flackwell Heath, Hedsor, Bourne End, Well End and Loudwater (south of the A40).

Types of grants: One-off grants, usually ranging from £30 to £500, are given towards utility bills, rent, hampers, medicine and equipment. Gifts in kind and loans of 'useful articles' are also available.

Annual grant total: Grants average around £1,400 each year.

Applications: In writing to the correspondent. Applications should be made either through a social worker, Citizens Advice or other welfare agency or directly by the individual or a third party on behalf on an individual. Applications can be submitted at any time for consideration in March, June, September or December. Emergency applications can be considered at any time.

Correspondent: David Tracey, Uplands, New Road, Bourne End, Buckinghamshire SL8 5BY (01628 528699; email: tracey@ brantridge.net)

The Amersham United Charities

Eligibility: Persons under the age of 21 who are in need of financial assistance and are resident in the parishes of Amersham and Coleshill, Buckinghamshire.

Types of grants: One-off grants to relieve persons who are in need, hardship or distress.

Annual grant total: Grants usually total around £500 per year.

Applications: In writing to the correspondent.

Correspondent: Mrs S Pounce, 86 High Street, Amersham, Buckinghamshire HP7 0DS (01494 727674)

Other information: The main work of the charity is the administration and management of 13 almshouses.

The Iver Heath Sick Poor Fund

Eligibility: People who are sick, convalescing, physically or mentally disabled or infirm and who live in the Iver Heath ward of the parish of Iver and part of the parish of Wexham.

Types of grants: Usually one-off grants for clothing, medical needs, home help, fuel, lighting, chiropody and other necessities, although recurrent grants will be considered.

Annual grant total: Grants to individuals total around £2,000 each year.

Applications: In writing to the correspondent. Applications are considered twice a year in spring and autumn, although in emergencies they can be considered at other times.

Correspondent: John Shepherd, Loch Luichart, Bangors Road North, Iver, SL0 0BN (01753 651398)

Iver United Charities

Eligibility: People in need who live in the parishes of Iver, Iver Heath and Richings Park.

Types of grants: One-off grants and hampers.

Annual grant total: In 2008/09 the charities had an income of £4,200 and a total expenditure of £2,500.

Applications: In writing to the correspondent by a social worker, health visitor, vicar, district nurse or other appropriate third party on behalf of the individual. Applications must include details of the applicant's weekly income, housing and sick benefit, council tax benefit and any other income.

Correspondent: Robert Penn, 26 Chequers Orchard, Iver, Buckinghamshire SL0 9NH (01753 655839)

The Salford Town Lands

Eligibility: People in need who live in the parish of Hulcote and Salford.

Types of grants: Grants are made for social purposes and to individuals for the relief of need, hardship and distress. Donations are usually one-off ranging from £60 to £200, including those for older people at Christmas and children's Christmas tokens.

Annual grant total: Previously about £5,000.

Applications: In writing to the correspondent. Applications can be submitted directly by the individual or through any other parishioner.

Correspondent: Julian Barrett, South Cottage, 18 Broughton Road, Salford, Milton Keynes MK17 8BH

Other information: Grants are also made to organisations supporting the community.

The Stoke Mandeville & Other Parishes Charity

Eligibility: People in need who live in the parishes of Stoke Mandeville, Great and Little Hampden and Great Missenden.

Types of grants: Annual Christmas grants to people over 70 and one-off grants to people who are disabled for specific needs such as wheelchairs or stairlifts.

Annual grant total: About £8,800 a year towards aids for people who are disabled and £6,000 in Christmas grants to pensioners.

Applications: On a form available from the correspondent, considered in January, April, July and October.

Correspondent: G Crombie, Secretary, Blackwells, Great Hampden, Great Missenden, Buckinghamshire HP16 9RJ

Other information: The charity also gives grants to organisations.

Tyringham Pension Fund for the Blind

Eligibility: People in need who are blind or partially sighted and live in Newport Pagnell and Wolverton.

Types of grants: Pensions of around £100 per year.

Annual grant total: Grants usually total about £1,000 each year.

Applications: Applications should not be made directly to the trust. Individuals should contact Buckinghamshire Association for the Blind (Tel. 01296 487 556), who will approach the trust on their behalf.

Correspondent: Vanessa Jones, Trustee, St Faiths Close, Newton Longville, Milton Keynes, MK17 0BA (01908 643 816)

Wooburn, Bourne End & District Relief-in-Sickness Charity

Eligibility: People who live in the parishes of Wooburn, Bourne End, Hedsor or parts of Little Marlow who are sick, convalescent, physically or mentally disabled or infirm.

Types of grants: One-off grants and gift vouchers in the range of £50 to £400 for telephone installation, help with nursing costs, convalescence, holidays, home help and other necessities. All items for which a grant is requested must have a direct connection with the applicant's illness.

Exclusions: No recurrent grants are given.

Annual grant total: Grants average around £10,000 a year.

Applications: In writing to the correspondent through a doctor, health visitor, priest or other third party. Applications are considered throughout the year and should contain details of the nature of illness or disability.

Correspondent: Dorothea Heyes, 11 Telston Close, Bourne End, Buckingham SL8 5TY (01628 523498)

Other information: Grants are also made to organisations.

Aylesbury

Elizabeth Eman Trust

Eligibility: Women in need in the following order of priority: 1) widows born in the former borough of Aylesbury as constituted immediately before 1 April 1974; 2) widows living in the present district of Aylesbury Vale; 3) women living in the present district of Aylesbury Vale.

Types of grants: Allowances of £65 per quarter. Grants are for life.

Annual grant total: In 2008 the charity had assets of £602,000 and an income of

£61,000. Annuities to pensioners totalled £45,000.

Applications: On a form available from the correspondent after a public advertisement. Applications can be submitted directly by the individual or through a social worker or other welfare agency, or by a member of the individual's immediate family. Original birth, marriage and husband's death certificates should be included as appropriate. Applications are normally considered in May and November each year, although they can be considered at other times.

Correspondent: Neil Freeman, Horwood & James, 7 Temple Square, Aylesbury, Buckinghamshire HP20 2QB (01296 487361; fax: 01296 427155)

William Harding's Charity

Eligibility: People in need who live in the town of Aylesbury.

Types of grants: One-off grants and grants in kind are given, including those for living costs, furniture, disabled equipment and help in the home.

Annual grant total: In 2008 the charity had assets of £18 million and an income of £687,000. Grants were made for welfare purposes to organisations totalling £76,000, although it appears that there were no welfare grants made to individuals during the year.

Applications: On a form available from the correspondent to be submitted directly by the individual or a family member, through a third party such as a social worker or teacher or through an organisation such as Citizens Advice. Trustees meet 10 times each year to consider applications. Applications should include details of family income.

Correspondent: John Leggett, Clerk to the Trustees, Messrs Parrott & Coales, Solicitors, 14 Bourbon Street, Aylesbury HP20 2RS (01296 318500; website: www. whardingcharity.org.uk)

Other information: Grants are also made for educational purposes.

Thomas Hickman's Charity

Eligibility: People in need who live in Aylesbury town.

Types of grants: One-off grants according to need.

Annual grant total: In 2008/09 the charity had assets of £16 million and an income of £565,000. Grants were made to 91 individuals totalling £40,000.

Applications: On a form available from the correspondent. Applications should be submitted either directly by the individual or a family member, through a third party such as social worker or school, or through an organisation such as Citizens Advice or a school. Trustees meet on a regular basis and applications are considered as they arise.

Correspondent: J Leggett, Parrott & Coales, 14–16 Bourbon Street, Aylesbury, Buckinghamshire HP20 2RS (01296 318500)

Other information: The charity also provides almshouses.

Bletchley

The Poor's Allotments Charity

Eligibility: People in need who live in the MK3 area of Bletchley. Beneficiaries tend mainly to be older people.

Types of grants: Christmas grants of around £30 per family.

Annual grant total: Grants usually total about £1,000 each year.

Applications: In writing to the correspondent to be submitted either directly by the individual or through a third party such as a social worker. Applications are normally considered in November and should be received by the end of October.

Correspondent: Mrs E A Cumberland, 9 Katrine Place, Bletchley, Milton Keynes, MK2 3DW (01908 642713)

Calverton

Calverton Apprenticing Charity

Eligibility: People in need who have lived in the parish of All Saints, Calverton for at least five years. Preference is given to widows and those over 65.

Types of grants: Grants in the range of £100 to £150 are awarded for items such as clothing, medical equipment, nursing fees, furniture, heating and so on.

Annual grant total: Grants for welfare purposes usually total around £1,000 each year.

Applications: On a form available from the correspondent, to be submitted either directly by the individual or a family member.

Correspondent: Karen Phillips, 78 London Road, Stony Stratford, Milton Keynes MK11 1JH (01908 563350; email: karen. phillips20@yahoo.co.uk)

Other information: The charity also makes grants to organisations and to individuals for educational purposes.

Cheddington

Cheddington Town Lands Charity

Eligibility: People in need who live in Cheddington.

Types of grants: One-off and recurrent grants according to need.

Annual grant total: Grants usually total around £4,000.

Applications: In writing to the correspondent, directly by the individual or a family member.

Correspondent: Stuart Minall, 10 Hillside, Cheddington, Leighton Buzzard, LU7 0SP (01296 661987)

Denham

The Denham Nursing Fund

Eligibility: People in need who are sick and infirm and who live in the parish of Denham.

Types of grants: One-off grants given at Christmas only, except in emergencies.

Annual grant total: Generally grants total around £600 a year.

Applications: In writing to the correspondent.

Correspondent: Anne Leigh, Woodland Cottage, Wapseys Lane, Hedgerley, Slough, SL2 3XG (01753 888839)

Emberton

Emberton United Charity

Eligibility: Older people in need who live in the parish of Emberton.

Types of grants: One-off and recurrent grants, usually of up to £350.

Annual grant total: In 2008 charitable expenditure amounted to £3,400, this included £1,600 given in grants and £1,800 given in gifts.

Applications: In writing to the correspondent, directly by the individual.

Correspondent: George Davies, Secretary to the Trustees, 59 Olney Road, Emberton, Olney, Buckinghamshire MK46 5BU (fax: 0870 164 0662; email: george@ taipooshan.demon.co.uk)

Other information: Grants are also given for educational purposes.

Great Linford

Great Linford Relief in Need Charity

Eligibility: People in need who live in the parish of Great Linford.

Types of grants: One-off grants of up to £200. Grants have been given towards educational activities and to assist with the cost of sheltered housing.

Annual grant total: Grants usually total about £500 each year.

Applications: On a form available from the charity. Applications can be submitted either directly by the individual or through

a social worker, Citizens Advice, other welfare agency or a third party such as a relative, teacher or carer. Applications are usually considered in January, June and September.

Correspondent: Michael Williamson, 2 Lodge Gate, Great Linford, Milton Keynes MK14 5EW (01908 605664; email: greatlinfordfc@btopenworld.com)

High Wycombe

The High Wycombe Central Aid Society

Eligibility: People in need, usually older people and those in receipt of benefits, who live in the old borough of High Wycombe. The society will also help ex-service personnel and their dependants.

Types of grants: Mainly one-off grants in kind and gift vouchers to a maximum of £100. Recent grants have been given for food, clothing and furniture.

Exclusions: No grants towards council tax.

Annual grant total: In 2009/10 the society had assets of £422,000 and an income of £91,000. Grants were made totalling £8,900.

Applications: In writing to the correspondent including details of income, savings, family situation and a quote for the goods needed along with any relevant supporting documents. Applications can be submitted through a social worker, Citizens Advice or other welfare agency and are considered on a monthly basis.

Correspondent: Clyde Perkins, Secretary, West Richardson Street, High Wycombe, Buckinghamshire HP11 2SB (01494 535890; fax: 01494 538256; email: office@central-aid.org.uk; website: www.central-aid.org.uk)

Other information: The society also runs a Pensioners Pop-In for people over 50 twice a week and facilitates a division of SSAFA Forces help.

The society also has a second-hand furniture warehouse and clothes and soft furnishings store (Tel: 01494 443459).

Hitcham

Hitcham Poor Lands Charity

Eligibility: People in need who live in the parishes of Hitcham, Burnham and Cippenham.

Types of grants: Grants in kind including furniture, white goods and so on. Around 300 Christmas parcels are also distributed each year.

Annual grant total: In 2008/09 the trust had both an income and expenditure of £11,000.

Applications: In writing to the correspondent. Applications can be submitted directly by the individual or through a third party such as Citizens Advice or a social worker. There are no deadlines for applications and they are considered frequently.

Correspondent: Donald Cecil Lindskog, Little Orchard, Poyle Lane, Burnham, Slough SL1 8JZ (01628 605652)

Other information: The charity also makes grants to organisations that support people in Burnham in other ways.

Radnage

Radnage Poor's Land Estate (Poor's Branch)

Eligibility: People in need who live in the parish of Radnage.

Types of grants: One-off and recurrent grants of around £50 to £200. Recent grants have been given towards hospital visits and food.

Annual grant total: In 2009 the trust had both an income and expenditure of £10,000. Grants usually total about £5,000 per year.

Applications: In writing to the correspondent either directly by the individual or through a social worker, Citizens Advice or other third party.

Correspondent: I K Blaylock, Clerk to the Trustees, Hilltop, Green End Road, Radnage, High Wycombe, Buckinghamshire HP14 4BY (01494 483346)

Stoke Poges

Stoke Poges United Charities

Eligibility: People in need who live in the parish of Stoke Poges, including parts of the parish of Slough Borough – Stoke wards. Preference is given to widows and people who are sick.

Types of grants: Grants can be given for clothing, food, household necessities, medical care and equipment.

Annual grant total: Grants usually total around £500.

Applications: In writing to the correspondent, to be submitted either directly by the individual or through a social worker, Citizens Advice, other welfare agency or any third party.

Correspondent: Anthony Levings, Clerk, The Cedars, Stratford Drive, Wooburn Green, High Wycombe, HP10 0QH (01628 524 342)

Other information: This charity consists of five separate funds which provide grants for relief-in-need or educational purposes.

Stony Stratford

The Ancell Trust

Eligibility: People in need in the town of Stony Stratford.

Types of grants: Grants are given to students for books and are occasionally made to individuals for welfare purposes and to organisations.

Annual grant total: In 2008/09 the trust had an income of £9,100 and a total expenditure of £20,000.

Applications: In writing to the correspondent at any time.

Correspondent: Karen Phillips, Secretary, 78 London Road, Stony Stratford, Milton Keynes, MK11 1JH (01908 563350; email: karen.phillips20@yahoo.co.uk)

Water Eaton

Fuel Allotment

Eligibility: People of pensionable age who live in Water Eaton.

Types of grants: Pensions of between £10 and £12.

Annual grant total: Grants usually total around £1,000 per year.

Applications: In writing to the correspondent for consideration in November.

Correspondent: Mrs E A Cumberland, 9 Katrine Place, Betchley, Milton Keynes MK2 3DW

Wolverton

The Catherine Featherstone Charity

Eligibility: People in need who live in the ancient parish of Wolverton.

Types of grants: One-off and recurrent grants ranging from £150 to £500. Recent grants have been given for household bills, food, medical and disability equipment, electrical goods, living costs and home help.

Annual grant total: In 2009 the charity had an income of £8,100 and a total expenditure of £5,200. Grants usually total about £5,000 each year.

Applications: On a form available from the correspondent, to be submitted either directly by the individual or through a social worker, Citizens Advice or other welfare agency. Applications are considered in March, July and October.

Correspondent: Miss K Phillips, Secretary, 78 London Road, Stony Stratford, Milton Keynes, Buckinghamshire MK11 1JH (01908 563350; email: karen.phillips20@ yahoo.co.uk)

Cambridgeshire

Cambridgeshire County Bowling Association – Benevolent Fund

Eligibility: Bowlers who are or have been affiliated members of Cambridgeshire County Bowling Association and their dependants. Applicants must be in need.

Types of grants: One-off and recurrent grants in the range of £40 to £50.

Annual grant total: Grants usually total around £150 each year.

Applications: In writing to the correspondent by October, for consideration in December.

Correspondent: Barry Grimwood, 108 Northfield Park, Soham, Ely, Cambridgeshire CB7 5XA (01353 722781; email: barrygrimwood@aol.com)

The Farthing Trust

Eligibility: People in need, with a priority given to those either personally known to the trustees or recommended by those personally known to the trustees.

Types of grants: One-off and recurrent grants are given to meet 'charitable causes' in the UK and overseas.

Annual grant total: In 2009/10 the trust had assets of £3.1 million and an income of £85,000. Grants were made totalling £194,000, of which £16,000 was given to individuals and the remaining £177,000 was awarded to organisations.

Applications: In writing to the correspondent. Applications can be submitted directly by the individual or through a social worker, Citizens Advice or other welfare agency. They are considered quarterly. Please note applicants will only be notified of a refusal if a sae is enclosed.

Correspondent: Heber Martin, PO Box 277, Cambridge, CB7 9DE

Other information: The trusts states that it receives around 10 letters a week and is able to help about one in a 100. Therefore success is unlikely unless a personal contact with a trustee is established.

The Leverington Town Lands Charity

Eligibility: People in need who live in the parishes of Leverington, Gorefield and Newton.

Types of grants: One-off grants towards, for example, glasses, new teeth or household appliances.

Annual grant total: Grants were made totalling £10,000.

Applications: On a form available from the correspondent. Applications are considered in May and November.

Correspondent: Mrs R J Gagen, 78 High Road, Gorefield, Wisbech, Cambridgeshire, PE13 4NB (01945 870454; email: levfeoffees@aol.com)

The Upwell (Cambridgeshire) Consolidated Charities

Eligibility: People in need who are over 65 (unless widowed) and live in the parish of Upwell (on the Isle of Ely) and have done so for at least five years.

Types of grants: Christmas grants in the range of £10 to £40.

Annual grant total: In 2009 the trust had an income of £4,500 and a total expenditure of £3,500.

Applications: In writing to the correspondent. Applications should be submitted directly by the individual and are considered in November.

Correspondent: Ronald Stannard, Riverside Farm, Birchfield Road, Nordelph, Downham Market, Norfolk PE38 0BP (01366 324217; email: ronstannard@waitrose.com)

Cambridge

The Cambridge Community Nursing Trust

Eligibility: People in need who live in the boundaries of the city of Cambridge.

Types of grants: Grants of up to around £300 are given to provide extra care, comforts and special aids which are not available from any other source.

Annual grant total: In 2009 the trust had an income of £6,000 and a total expenditure of £3,500.

Applications: In writing to the correspondent. Applications are considered as received. The correspondent is happy to speak to potential applicants over the telephone before an application is submitted.

Correspondent: Mrs M Hoskins, 11 Rutherford Road, Cambridge CB2 8HH (01223 840259)

Chatteris

The Chatteris Feoffee Charity

Eligibility: People who are 'poor and needy' and have lived in Chatteris for at least 10 years.

Types of grants: Grants of around £25 given annually in January.

Annual grant total: In 2008/09 the charity had an income of £3,800 and a total expenditure of £3,600.

Applications: In writing to the correspondent, or upon recommendation of a trustee.

Correspondent: Brian Hawden, Brian Hawden & Co. Solicitors, Beechwood Court, Beechwood Gardens, London Road, Chatteris, Cambridgeshire PE16 6PX (01354 692133; email: hawden.co@ talktalkbusiness.net)

Downham

The Downham Feoffee Charity

Eligibility: People in need who live in the ancient parish of Downham.

Types of grants: One-off and recurrent grants according to need.

Annual grant total: In 2008/09 the charity had assets of £3.3 million and an income of £74,000. Grants to individuals totalled around £1,800.

Applications: In writing to the correspondent.

Correspondent: Win Hughes, 12 St Andrews Way, Ely, Cambridgeshire, CB6 3DZ (01353 610890; email: downham. feoffees@ntlworld.com)

Other information: The charity's main focus is the provision of housing and allotments. It also gives grants to local schools.

Elsworth

The Samuel Franklin Fund

Eligibility: Children, young people, older people and families, who are in need and who live in the parish of Elsworth. Preference is given to older people, those who are facing financial difficulties and people affected by hardship who are disabled.

Types of grants: One-off or recurrent grants of £10 to £1,000 according to need towards hospital expenses, convalescence, household bills, medical equipment, nursing fees, disability equipment and home help.

Annual grant total: In 2009 the trust had an income of £40,000 and a total expenditure of £18,000. Grants were made to 32 individuals totalling £6,000, mainly for welfare purposes.

Applications: In writing to the correspondent including brief details of requirements.

Correspondent: Helen Oborne, Low Farm, 45 Brook Street, Elsworth, Cambridge, CB23 4HX (01954 267197; email: helenobornesft@googlemail.com)

Ely

Thomas Parson's Charity

Eligibility: People in need who live in the city of Ely.

Types of grants: One-off and occasionally recurrent grants and loans, ranging from £1,000 to £4,000.

Annual grant total: In 2008/09 the charity had assets of £5.7 million and an income of £236,000. Grants were made totalling £4,900.

Applications: In writing to the correspondent, for consideration on the first Friday in each month. Applications can be submitted either directly by the individual, or through a social worker, Citizens Advice or other welfare agency.

Correspondent: Secretary, Hall Ennion & Young, 8 High Street, Ely, Cambridgeshire CB7 4JY (01353 662918; fax: 01353 662747; email: john@heysolicitors.co.uk)

Other information: The charity is primarily concerned with the management and maintenance of its almshouses.

Grantchester

The Grantchester Relief in Need Charity

Eligibility: People in need who live in the ancient parish of Grantchester.

Types of grants: One-off grants according to need.

Annual grant total: Over the last five years the charity's annual expenditure has ranged from £0 to £7,000.

Applications: In writing to the correspondent.

Correspondent: Allen Wheelwright, 67 Coton Road, Grantchester, Cambridge, CB3 9NT

Other information: The charity also makes grants to local organisations.

Hilton

Hilton Town Charity

Eligibility: People who live in the village of Hilton, Cambridgeshire, of any age or occupation, who may have unforeseen needs, due to for example hardship, disability or sickness.

Types of grants: One-off grants according to need.

Annual grant total: In 2008/09 the charity had an income of £4,900 and a total expenditure of £1,900. On average about £2,000 is available in grants.

Applications: In writing to the correspondent.

Correspondent: Ms S Sheppard, Treasurer, 20 Chequers Croft, Hilton, Huntingdon PE28 9PD

Other information: Grants in the main are directed towards organisations that serve the direct needs of the village.

Ickleton

The Ickleton United Charities (Relief-in-Need Branch)

Eligibility: People in need who live in the parish of Ickleton, Cambridgeshire.

Types of grants: One-off grants of around £40 towards fuel costs and necessities, and gift vouchers at Christmas.

Annual grant total: In 2009 the trust had an income of £9,000 and a total expenditure of £5,800.

Applications: In writing to the correspondent to be submitted directly by the individual.

Correspondent: John Statham, 35 Abbey Street, Ickleton, Saffron Walden, Essex CB10 1SS (01799 530258)

Landbeach

Rev Robert Masters Charity for Widows

Eligibility: People in need who live in the parish of Landbeach, with a preference for widows.

Types of grants: One-off and recurrent grants according to need.

Annual grant total: Grants total around £500 each year.

Applications: In writing to the correspondent.

Correspondent: Brian Marshall, Trustee, Flat 2 Cootes Court, Cootes Lane, Fen Drayton, Cambridge, CB24 4YP

Little Wilbraham

The Johnson Bede & Lane Charitable Trust

Eligibility: People in need who live in the civil parish of Little Wilbraham.

Types of grants: One-off grants usually between £50 and £150 for a wide range of welfare needs.

Annual grant total: In 2009/10 the trust had an income of £4,200 and a total expenditure of £4,500. Grants to individuals usually total around £3,000.

Applications: In writing to the correspondent directly by the individual or by a third party such as a social worker, Citizens Advice or neighbour. Applications are considered on an ongoing basis.

Correspondent: Mrs J Collins, The Gate House, Church Road, Little Wilbraham, Cambridge, CB21 5LE (01223 811465)

Other information: Grants are also made to organisations.

Pampisford

Pampisford Relief-in-Need Charity

Eligibility: People in need who live in the parish of Pampisford.

Types of grants: People who are older or disabled may receive Christmas gifts or individual grants of up to £250. Contributions are also made for the improvement of village amenities, which can then be enjoyed by people who are older or disabled.

Annual grant total: Grants are mostly made to organisations, but about £3,000 is available each year for individuals.

Applications: In writing to the correspondent directly by the individual. Applications can be considered at any time.

Correspondent: A J S Rogers, Clerk, 7 Hammond Close, Pampisford, Cambridgeshire CB2 4EP (01223 835954)

Other information: Half of the charity's income goes to the Pampisford Ecclesiastical Charity.

Peterborough

The Florence Saunders Relief-in-Sickness Charity

Eligibility: People in need who are in poor health, convalescent, or who have disabilities and live in the former city of Peterborough.

Types of grants: One-off grants between £100 and £500 for hospital expenses, convalescence, holidays, travel expenses, electrical goods, medical equipment, furniture, disability equipment and help in the home.

Exclusions: No grants are given for the repayment of debts.

Annual grant total: In 2008/09 the charity had both an income and expenditure of £8,300.

Applications: In writing to the correspondent to be submitted either directly by the individual or through a third party such as a family member, social worker or other welfare agency. Applications are considered at trustees' meetings, usually held three times per year.

Correspondent: Paula Lawson, Stephenson House, 15 Church Walk, Peterborough PE1 2TP (01733 343 275; email: paula.lawson@stephensonsmart.com)

Other information: Grants are also made to organisations.

Sawston

John Huntingdon's Charity

Eligibility: People in need who live in the parish of Sawston in Cambridgeshire.

Types of grants: One-off grants, usually ranging from £25 to £250. Grants can be given for essential household items such as cookers, beds or fridges, TV licences, holidays, household bills, food, clothing, travel expenses, medical equipment, debts, transport costs, and nursery/playgroup fees.

Annual grant total: In 2009 the charity had assets of £7.3 million and an income of £332,000. Grants were made to individuals for welfare purposes totalling £23,000.

Applications: On an application form available from Sawston Support Services at the address above or by telephone. Office opening hours are 9am to 2pm Monday to Friday.

Correspondent: Revd Mary Irish, Charity Manager, John Huntingdon House, Tannery Road, Sawston, Cambridge CB2 4UW (01223 830599 (Sawston Support Service Tel: 01223 836289); fax: 01223 830599; email: office@johnhuntingdon.org.uk)

Soham

Soham United Charities

Eligibility: People in need of all ages who live in the parish of Soham.

Types of grants: One-off grants can be made for items and services such as furniture, bedding, clothing, food, tools, books, holidays, house decorating, insulation and repairs, laundering, meals on wheels, child-minding and so on.

Exclusions: No grants towards education.

Annual grant total: Grants to individuals total around £5,000 each year.

Applications: In writing to the correspondent directly by the individual. Applicants should include a financial statement giving details of assets and liabilities, and reasons in support of the application. They are usually considered in November and February. There is also an emergency committee which can meet during the rest of the year. The trustees will discuss and investigate in detail the circumstances arising for the grant to be requested before making any award.

Correspondent: Elizabeth Stevenson, Ivy House, 33 Pratt Street, Soham, Ely, Cambridgeshire CB7 5BH (01353 722884)

Other information: Grants are also made to organisations.

Stetchworth

The Stetchworth Relief-in-Need Charity

Eligibility: People in need who live in the parish of Stetchworth and have done so for at least two years.

Types of grants: One-off grants according to need. Grants have been given towards, for example, electricity bills, fuel, groceries (through an account at the local community shop), transport to hospital and educational needs.

Annual grant total: In 2009/10 the charity had an income of £2,400 and a total expenditure of £2,200.

Applications: On a form available from the correspondent or the Ellesmere Centre, Stetchworth which should include details of income, expenditure and any other applications for help, rebates or discounts. Applications are considered at any time. The charity says: 'We welcome information from anyone who knows someone in need.'

Correspondent: Judith Mahoney, 26 High Street, Stetchworth, Newmarket, Suffolk CB8 9TJ (01638 508336)

Other information: Grants are available at any time of the year, although many of the elderly applicants tend to apply for a Christmas bonus in December. Whilst it is not the policy of the charity to give Christmas bonuses, it is happy to be used in this way.

Swaffham Bulbeck

The Swaffham Bulbeck Relief-in-Need Charity

Eligibility: People in need who are over 65 and live in the parish of Swaffham Bulbeck.

Types of grants: One-off and annual grants (in kind or in cash). Grants do not usually amount to more than £20 each.

Annual grant total: In 2009 the charity had an income of £7,500 and a total expenditure of £5,800. Grants are given to individuals and to local clubs, schools and churches.

Applications: In writing to the correspondent.

Correspondent: Cheryl Ling, 43 High Street, Swaffham Bulbeck, Cambridge CB25 0HP (01223 811733)

Swavesey

Thomas Galon's Charity

Eligibility: People in need who live in the parish of Swavesey. Preference is given to those who are over 70, single or widowed; married couples when one partner reaches

70; and, widows and widowers with dependent children up to 18 years old.

Types of grants: An annual gift, to be agreed in November, for people in need. One-off grants for hospital travel expenses, fuel costs and other needs. Grants of at least £35 are generally made.

Exclusions: No grants for capital projects such as buildings.

Annual grant total: About £6,000 a year. Grants are given to both individuals and organisations.

Applications: In writing to the correspondent for consideration in November. Grants will be delivered in December.

Correspondent: Linda Miller, Clerk, 21 Thistle Green, Swavesey, Cambridge CB24 4RJ (01954 202982; email: thomasgaloncharity@swavesey.org. uk; website: www.swavesey.org.uk/ thomas_galon_charity)

Walsoken

The Walsoken United Charities

Eligibility: Older people in need who have lived in the parish of Walsoken for at least two years.

Types of grants: Small one-off grants and gifts in kind.

Annual grant total: Grants usually total about £1,500 each year.

Applications: In writing to the correspondent, directly by the individual.

Correspondent: Derek Mews, Clerk, 7 Pickards Way, Wisbech, Cambridgeshire, PE13 1SD (01945 587982)

Whittlesey

The Whittlesey Charity

Eligibility: People in need who live in the ancient parishes of Whittlesey Urban and Whittlesey Rural only.

Types of grants: Small annual cash grants, plus the occasional one-off grant.

Annual grant total: In 2009 the charity had assets of £1.7 million and an income of £54,000. Grants were made totalling £35,000, of which £1,200 was given in one grant to an individual.

Applications: In writing to the correspondent. Applications are considered in February, May and September, but urgent applications can be dealt with at fairly short notice. Please note, the trust will not respond to ineligible applicants.

Correspondent: P S Gray, 33 Bellamy Road, Oundle, Peterborough PE8 4NE (01832 273085)

Other information: The charity makes grants to organisations and individuals, for relief in need, educational purposes, public purposes and it also makes grants to churches.

Whittlesford

The Charities of Nicholas Swallow & Others

Eligibility: People in need who live in the parish of Whittlesford (near Cambridge) and adjacent area.

Types of grants: One-off cash grants at Christmas; help can also be given towards hospital travel and educational costs.

Annual grant total: In 2008/09 the charities had assets of £570,000 and an income of £237,000. Welfare grants totalled around £1,700.

Applications: In writing to the correspondent directly by the individual.

Correspondent: Nicholas Tufton, Clerk, 11 High Street, Barkway, Royston, Hertfordshire SG8 8EA (01763 848888)

Other information: The principal activity of this charity is as a housing association managing 11 bungalows and 9 garages.

East Sussex

The Catharine House Trust

Eligibility: Older individuals and people in poor health who live in the borough of Hastings.

Types of grants: One-off grants ranging between £100 and £400. Funding is available for medical equipment and treatment; household goods when they are essential for maintaining health (but not general furniture); respite breaks for the client or carer; and relevant courses for instruction.

Exclusions: Usually only one application is accepted per person.

Annual grant total: In 2008/09 the trust had an income of £36,000 and a total expenditure of £32,000. Grants were made totalling £31,000.

Applications: In writing to the correspondent, supported by a written statement from a medical professional or social worker. Most applications are made through NHS trusts, local authority social services departments and other charities.

Correspondent: Jenny Ridd, Trustee, 23 The Meadway, Shoreham-By-Sea, BN43 5RN

Hart Charitable Trust

Eligibility: People in need who live in East Sussex.

Types of grants: One off grants, usually of around £75, are given towards clothing, bedding, travel and most other needs. Small amounts are also given to meet immediate needs.

Annual grant total: In 2008/09 the trust had assets of £556,000 and an income of £29,000. Grants were made to 254 individuals totalling £19,000.

Applications: On a form available from the correspondent, to be submitted through a third party such as a social worker, Citizens Advice or other welfare agency.

Correspondent: M R Bugden, Gaby Hardwicke, 2 Eversley Road, Bexhill-on-Sea, East Sussex TN40 1EY (01424 730945)

Other information: The trust also makes grants to institutions (£2,100 in 2008/09).

The Relief – Hastings Area Community Trust

Eligibility: People in need who are under 60 and live in Hastings and St Leonards-on-Sea who are on a very low income and have children, or who have medical reasons for not working.

Types of grants: One-off grants of £80 to £100 mainly in the form of payments to suppliers for essential furniture and household items, including cookers, washing machines, beds and baby items.

Exclusions: No grants for carpets, curtains or televisions.

Annual grant total: In 2008/09 the trust had assets of £469,000 and an income of £380,000. Grants were made totalling £11,000.

Applications: On a form available from the correspondent. Applications can only be accepted from a recognised referral agency (e.g. social worker, Citizens Advice or recognised advice agency) and are considered throughout the year. The trust encourages applicants who wish to telephone to leave a message on the answer phone if there is no reply as messages are listened to daily.

Correspondent: Anthony Bonds, Bolton Tomson House, 49 Cambridge Gardens, Hastings, East Sussex TN34 1EN (01424 718880)

The Mrs A Lacy Tate Trust

Eligibility: People in need who live in East Sussex.

Types of grants: One-off and recurrent grants according to need.

Annual grant total: In 2008/09 the trust made 164 grants to individuals for both welfare and educational purposes totalling £16,000.

Applications: In writing to the correspondent.

Correspondent: The Trustees, Heringtons Solicitors, 39 Gildredge Road, Eastbourne, East Sussex BN21 4RY (01323 411020)

Other information: Grants are also made to individuals for educational purposes and to organisations.

Battle

The Battle Charities

Eligibility: People in need who live in Battle and Netherfield, East Sussex.

Types of grants: Grants are usually made towards fuel and children's' clothing, and range from £50 to £200.

Annual grant total: Grants usually total about £2,000 each year.

Applications: In writing to the correspondent. Applications can be sent directly by the individual or family member, through an organisation such as a Citizens Advice or through a third party such as a social worker. Full details of the applicant's circumstances are required.

Correspondent: Timothy P Roberts, 1 Upper Lake, Battle, East Sussex TN33 0AN (01424 772401; email: troberts@heringtons.net)

Brighton & Hove

The Brighton District Nursing Association Trust

Eligibility: People in need who are in poor health, convalescent or who have a disability and live in the county borough of Brighton and Hove.

Types of grants: One-off grants of up to £250 for items in respect of medical treatment and for convalescence; some limited allowances for nurses may also be available.

Annual grant total: In 2008 the trust had assets of £1.6 million and an income of £73,000. Grants to individuals totalled £4,000. A further £49,000 was given in grants to organisations.

Applications: In writing to the correspondent: preferably supported by a doctor or health visitor. Applications are considered quarterly, though emergency grants may be awarded between meetings in urgent cases.

Correspondent: Anthony Druce, Hon. Secretary, Fitzhugh Gates, 3 Pavilion Parade, Brighton BN2 1RY (01273 686811; fax: 01273 676837; email: anthonyd@fitzhugh.co.uk)

The Brighton Fund

Eligibility: Usually people over 60 who are in need who live in Brighton and Hove administrative boundary.

Types of grants: One-off cash grants according to need including those for household items, medical equipment and subsistence.

Christmas gifts of £20 in the form of gift vouchers.

Annual grant total: In 2008/09 the fund had assets of £836,000 and an income of £62,000. Grants totalled just over £25,000 and were distributed between: individuals in need over 60 (£16,000); individuals in need under 60 (£6,000); and exception awards (£3,600).

Applications: On a form available from the correspondent to be submitted either through an organisation such as Citizens Advice or a school or through a third party such as a social worker or teacher. Applications are considered upon receipt.

Correspondent: The Secretary, c/o Welfare Rights Team, 3rd Floor, Bartholomew House, Bartholomew Square, Brighton, BN1 1JP (01273 291 118; email: welfarerights@brighton-hove.gov.uk; website: www.brighton-hove.gov.uk)

The Mayor of Brighton and Hove's Welfare Charity

Eligibility: Individuals in need living in the old borough of Hove and Portslade.

Types of grants: One-off grants up to a maximum of £250. The committee will only consider one grant for each applicant and successful applicants should not reapply.

Exclusions: No retrospective grants are made.

Annual grant total: Grants usually total around £6,000 a year.

Applications: On a form available from the correspondent along with full guidelines. Applications should be submitted directly by the individual or a relevant third party, for example, a friend, carer or professional (social worker, health visitor). Grants are considered bi-monthly, in January, March, May, July, September and November. No money is given directly to the applicant, but rather directly to settle invoices.

Correspondent: Michael Hill, Selborne Centre, 5 Selborne Place, Hove, East Sussex BH3 3ET (01273 779432; email: hill.michael4@sky.com)

Eastbourne

The Mayor's Poor Fund, Eastbourne

Eligibility: People living in the borough of Eastbourne who are in need of temporary financial assistance.

Types of grants: One-off grants, generally ranging between £25 and £100.

Annual grant total: Grants average around £600 a year.

Applications: In writing to the correspondent, including all relevant information. Applications are usually

submitted through a social worker or health visitor but individuals can apply directly if they wish.

Correspondent: The Mayor's Secretary, The Town Hall, Grove Road, Eastbourne, East Sussex BN21 4UG (01323 415002)

The Doctor Merry Memorial Fund

Eligibility: People who are ill and who live in the Eastbourne Health Authority area.

Types of grants: One-off grants for nursing home care, help with Lifeline rentals and medical equipment.

Annual grant total: In 2008/09 the fund had an income of £8,900 and a total expenditure of £5,600.

Applications: Individuals should apply via their doctor on a form available from the correspondent. Applications are considered throughout the year.

Correspondent: Ronald Pringle, Friston Corner, 3 Mill Close, East Dean, Eastbourne, East Sussex BN20 0EG (01323 423319; email: ronpringle@hotmail.com)

Other information: This charity was founded in 1922 as a memorial to Dr Merry who died of exhaustion after caring for the people of Eastbourne in the 'flu epidemic of that time'.

Hastings

Isabel Blackman Foundation

Eligibility: People in need who live in Hastings and the surrounding district.

Types of grants: One-off grants.

Annual grant total: In 2008/09 the trust had assets of £4 million and an income of £283,000. Approximately £23,000 was given in grants to individuals, of which £18,000 was given to 29 individuals for educational purposes. The remaining £5,000 was given to 12 individuals for health and social welfare purposes.

Applications: In writing to the correspondent through a third party such as a social worker, Citizens Advice or other welfare agency.

Correspondent: D J Jukes, Trustee and Secretary, Stonehenge, 13 Laton Road, Hastings, East Sussex TN34 2ES (01424 431756)

Other information: The foundation mainly supports organisations.

William Shadwell Charity

Eligibility: People in need who are sick and live in the borough of Hastings.

Types of grants: One-off and recurrent grants.

Exclusions: No grants are given for the payment of debt, taxes and so on.

Annual grant total: Grants usually total around £2,500 each year.

Applications: In writing to the correspondent to be submitted in March and September for consideration in April and October, but urgent cases can be considered at any time. Applications can be submitted directly by the individual or through a third party.

Correspondent: C R Morris, 4 Barley Lane, Hastings, East Sussex TN35 5NX (01424 433586)

Mayfield

The Mayfield Charity

Eligibility: People in need who live in the ancient parish of Mayfield.

Types of grants: One-off grants of £50 to £500 according to need. Grants have been given towards hospital travel, clothing, equipment for people who are disabled, purchase of aids and Christmas gifts for older people.

Exclusions: Grants are not made for religious or political causes.

Annual grant total: Grants are made for relief-in-need and educational purposes and total about £2,000 each year

Applications: In writing to the correspondent at any time either directly by the individual or a family member, through a third party such as a social worker or teacher, or through an organisation such as Citizens Advice or a school. Proof of need should be included where possible.

Correspondent: Brenda Hopkin, Appletrees, Alexandra Road, Mayfield, East Sussex, TN20 6DU

Newick

The Newick Distress Trust

Eligibility: People in need who live in the village of Newick. Preference is given to those who have experienced a drastically reduced income due to bereavement, ill-health, unemployment and broken marriages.

Types of grants: One-off or recurrent grants towards, for example, heating bills in very cold weather, school uniforms required due to a change of school and other basic living costs.

Annual grant total: Grants usually total about £1,000 a year, but it depends on the number of requests.

Applications: In writing to the correspondent or one of the trustees.

Correspondent: Geoffrey Clinton, Dolphin Cottage, 3 High Hurst Close, Newick, East Sussex BN8 4NJ (01825 722512)

St Leonards-on-Sea

The Sarah Brisco Charity

Eligibility: People in need who live in the parish of St Peter and St Paul, St Leonards-on-Sea.

Types of grants: One-off cash grants between £25 and £100 and gifts in kind (such as £100 at Christmas, £25 vouchers and so on).

Annual grant total: In 2008 the charity had an income of £8,300 and a total expenditure of £5,100.

Applications: In writing to the correspondent. Applications should be submitted directly by the individual and are considered at any time.

Correspondent: Steven Sleight, Chichester Diocesan Fund and Board Church House, 211 New Church Road, Hove BN3 4ED

Other information: The trust donates to other local charities when funds allow.

Warbleton

Warbleton Charity

Eligibility: People in need who live in the parish of Warbleton. Preference is usually given to older people.

Types of grants: One-off grants according to need. Recent awards have been made for fuel and Christmas hampers.

Annual grant total: Grants usually total about £1,000 each year.

Applications: In writing to the correspondent either directly by the individual or through a third party. Applications are considered on a regular basis.

Correspondent: John Leeves, 4 Berners Court Yard, Berners Hill, Flimwell, Wadhurst, East Sussex TN5 7NH (01580 879744; email: warbletonpc@ freeuk.com)

Other information: Grants are also made for educational purposes.

Essex

The Colchester Catalyst Charity

Eligibility: People in north east Essex who are living with a disability or sickness.

Types of grants: One-off and recurrent grants for special equipment. Items can include wheelchairs, mobility scooters and other mobility aids, special beds, pressure relieving mattresses and cushions, computers for specific needs and communication aids. Funding may also be given for respite care and specialist therapy.

Exclusions: Funding will not be given for items already purchased or where there is an obligation for provision by a statutory authority. The charity states that it does not take responsibility for the insurance, maintenance and repairs of any items funded.

Annual grant total: In 2008/09 the charity had assets of £8 million and an income of £352,000. Grant to individuals totalled £266,000 and were distributed as follows:

Special individual needs	£78,000
Respite care	£152,000
Equipment pools	£36,000

Applications: On a form available directly from the correspondent or on the charity's website. Applications should include supporting statements, professional assessments by an appropriate professional practitioner (GP, occupational therapist, district nurse) and any quotes or estimates.

Correspondent: Stephanie Grant, Administrator, Catalyst House, Newcomen Way, Colchester, Essex CO4 9YR (01206 752545; fax: 01206 842259; email: info@colchestercatalyst.co.uk; website: www.colchestercatalyst.co.uk)

Other information: The charity also gives grants to organisations (£133,000 in 2008/09) and will consider making loans to individuals when a grant is not suitable.

The Colchester Society for the Blind

Eligibility: People who are blind or sight impaired and live in the borough of Colchester and district.

Types of grants: One-off or recurrent grants according to need.

Annual grant total: In 2008/09 the society had an income of £8,900 and a total expenditure of £3,100.

Applications: In writing to the correspondent.

Correspondent: Marilyn Theresa Peck, Kestrels, Harwich Road, Beaumont, Clacton-on-Sea, Essex CO16 0AU (01255 862062)

Essex Police Support Staff Benevolent Fund

Eligibility: People in need who work or worked full-time or part-time for Essex Police Authority, and their dependants.

Types of grants: One-off grants or loans for essential needs such as travel expenses for hospital visits and unforeseen bills such as car repairs.

Exclusions: No grants towards medical treatment.

Annual grant total: In 2008/09 the fund had assets of £93,000 and an income of £34,000. Grants were made totalling £11,000.

Applications: Individuals should apply via the benevolent fund representative of their division or subdivision of Essex Police Authority. Applications are considered quarterly, although this can be sooner in emergencies.

Correspondent: B G Faber, Essex Police Headquarters, PO Box 2, Chelmsford, Essex CM2 6DA (01245 452597)

Help-in-Need Association (HINA)

Eligibility: People in need who live in the Tower Hamlets health district.

Types of grants: One-off and recurrent grants, usually up to £300 each.

Annual grant total: About £1,000.

Applications: On a form available from the correspondent.

Correspondent: Grant Administrator, Students Union Building, St Bartholomews and Royal London, School of Medicine and Dentistry, Stepney Way, Whitechapel, London E1 2AD (email: blhina@hotmail.co.uk)

The Kay Jenkins Trust

Eligibility: People in need, especially older or disabled people, who live in Great and Little Leighs.

Types of grants: One-off, mainly small, grants to help with household expenditure, medical aids and equipment. Occasionally up to £1,000 is given for a large item. No loans are made.

Annual grant total: About £2,000.

Applications: In writing to the correspondent directly by the individual or through a relative. Grants are considered throughout the year.

Correspondent: Diana Tritton, Hole Farmhouse, Great Leighs, Chelmsford, Essex CM3 1QR (01245 361204; email: dstritton@yahoo.com)

Braintree

The Braintree United Charities

Eligibility: People in need who live in the parishes of St Michael's and St Paul's, Braintree; usually those in receipt of an old age pension.

Types of grants: One-off and recurrent grants ranging from £50 to £100. Annual grants are given at Christmas to people in need who are registered with the charity.

Exclusions: Loans are not made.

Annual grant total: In 2008/09 the charities had an income of £3,700 and a total expenditure of £3,500. Grants are given to both individuals and organisations.

Applications: On a form available from the correspondent. Applications should be submitted through a social worker, Citizens Advice, other welfare agency or

other third party, or directly by the individual. They are considered in May and October and should be received in April and September respectively.

Correspondent: Sue Carlile, Smith Law Partnership, Gordon House, 22 Rayne Road, Braintree CM7 2QW (01376 321311; fax: 01376 559239; email: suecarlile@slpsolicitors.co.uk)

Broomfield

Broomfield United Charities

Eligibility: People in need who live in the civil parish of Broomfield.

Types of grants: One-off grants according to need and vouchers at Christmas.

Annual grant total: In 2008/09 the charities had both an income and expenditure of £8,400.

Applications: In writing to the correspondent directly by the individual for consideration at any time.

Correspondent: Brian H Worboys, 5 Butlers Close, Chelmsford, CM1 7BE (01245 440540; email: brian.worboys@virgin.net)

Chigwell & Chigwell Row

The George and Alfred Lewis (of Chigwell) Memorial Fund

Eligibility: People in need who served in HM Forces or the Merchant Service during the Second World War and were living in the parishes of Chigwell and Chigwell Row at the time of their enlistment.

Types of grants: One-off grants to help people who are in need due to family illness, old age, domestic emergencies and so on.

Annual grant total: Grants average around £4,200 a year.

Applications: In writing to the correspondent. Applications can be made either directly by the individual or through a third party on behalf of the individual, such as a spouse or child, and should include as much detail of personal circumstances as is deemed appropriate. Applications are considered at any time.

Correspondent: Miss Enid Smart, 16 Forest Terrace, High Road, Chigwell, Essex IG7 5BW (0208 504 9408)

Dovercourt

The Henry Smith Charity (Dovercourt)

Eligibility: People in need who live in the ancient parish of All Saints, Dovercourt.

Types of grants: The trust prefers to contribute towards the total cost of items and services rather than cash grants i.e. the purchase of a buggy for a disabled person, TV licence costs, food, and washing machine purchase and fitting. One-off cash donations up to a maximum of £100.

Annual grant total: This trust has an annual income of around £1,000. Total annual expenditure varies between £600 and £2,500.

Applications: In writing to the correspondent for consideration at any time. Applications should be submitted through Citizens Advice or other welfare agency or through a third party such as a priest who can recommend the applicant. After receiving a letter, the trustees usually visit the applicant. Applications should contain family details and are considered throughout the year.

Correspondent: Anthony Peake, 2 Kings Court, Kings Road, Dovercourt, Harwich, Essex CO12 4DT (01255 502209)

East Bergholt

The East Bergholt United Charities

Eligibility: People in need who live in East Bergholt.

Types of grants: One-off grants according to need. If no cases of hardship are brought to the attention of the trustees, they usually give £20 each at Christmas to 10 to 20 older people who are known to have small incomes. These are not given to the same person two years running, although additional help can be given if needed.

Annual grant total: The main purpose of this charity is the provision and maintenance of almshouses. Grants to individuals are usually under £500.

Applications: In writing to the correspondent, although most cases are brought to the attention of the trustees. Applications can be submitted directly by the individual or by a relative at any time. Proof of the financial situation of the applicant is required.

Correspondent: Greta Abbs, 31 Fiddlers Lane, East Bergholt, Colchester CO7 6SJ (01206 299 822)

East Tilbury

East Tilbury Relief-in-Need Charity

Eligibility: People in need who live in the parish of East Tilbury.

Types of grants: One-off and recurrent grants have been given towards hospital visits and children in need.

Annual grant total: Grants usually total about £6,000 per year.

Applications: In writing to the correspondent, to be considered in November.

Correspondent: Reginald F Fowler, Treasurer, 27 Ward Avenue, Grays, Essex RM17 5RE (01375 372304)

Halstead

Helena Sant's Residuary Trust Fund

Eligibility: People in need who live in the parish of St Andrew with Holy Trinity, Halstead who have at any time been a member of the Church of England.

Types of grants: One-off cash grants according to need.

Exclusions: Grants are not given to pay rates, taxes or public funds.

Annual grant total: In 2009 the trust had an income of £7,000 and a total expenditure of £8,000.

Applications: In writing to the correspondent directly by the individual, through an organisation such as Citizens Advice or through a third party such as a social worker. Applications are considered at any time.

Correspondent: M R R Willis, Trustee, Greenway, Church Street, Gestingthorpe, Halstead, Essex CO9 3AX (01787 469920)

Harlow

The Harlow Community Chest

Eligibility: Individuals and families in financial need, particularly where a small financial contribution will help to arrest the spiral of debt. Applicants must live in Harlow.

Types of grants: One-off grants up to £250. Recent grants have been made for: payment of outstanding utility bills for people in special need; clothing (for example for unemployed young people going for a job interview); household items; funeral expenses; removal costs; lodging deposits; and, nursery fees. Small emergency grants are also available.

Exclusions: No grants for housing rents or rates. Only one main grant to an individual/family can be made in any one year.

Annual grant total: In 2009/10 the trust had both an income and expenditure of £12,000.

Applications: On a form available from the correspondent: to be submitted through a recognised referral agency (for example a social worker, welfare organisation or doctor). Applications are considered on a monthly basis. Emergency payments can be made between meetings.

Correspondent: Connie Freeman, 245 Long Banks, Harlow, CM18 7PB (01279 410601; email: conniefre@hotmail.com)

Hutton

Ecclesiastical Charity of George White

Eligibility: People in need who live in the parish of All Saints with St Peter, Hutton. Particular favour is given to children, young adults and older people. The usual length of residency is seven years.

Types of grants: Pensions and one-off grants usually in the range of £100 and £400 towards necessary living expenses.

Annual grant total: Grants usually total around £9,000 per year.

Applications: In writing to the correspondent at any time. Applications can be submitted either directly by the individual, through a third party such as a social worker, or through an organisation such as Citizens Advice or other welfare agency. They are considered at any time.

Correspondent: The Reverend, c/o St Peter's Parish Office, Claughton Way, Hutton, Brentwood, Essex CM13 1JS (01277 362864)

Saffron Walden

The Saffron Walden United Charities

Eligibility: People in need who live in Saffron Walden including the hamlets of Little Walden and Sewards End.

Types of grants: One-off grants in kind and gift vouchers. A range of help is considered including, for example, electrical goods, convalescence, clothing, household bills, food, holidays, travel expenses, furniture, disability equipment and nursery fees.

Exclusions: No grants for credit card debt.

Annual grant total: In 2009 the charities had assets of £913,000 and an income of £37,000. Grants were made totalling £30,000.

Applications: In writing to the correspondent either directly by the individual, through a third party such as a social worker, or through an organisation such as a Citizens Advice or other welfare agency. Applications are considered as they arrive.

Correspondent: Jim Ketteridge, c/o Community Hospital, Radwinter Road, Saffron Walden, Essex CB11 3HY (01799 526122)

Springfield

The Springfield United Charities

Eligibility: Individuals in need living in the parish of Springfield.

Types of grants: One-off grants according to need.

Annual grant total: In 2008/09 the charities had an income of £11,000 and a total expenditure of £13,000.

Applications: In writing to the correspondent.

Correspondent: Nick Eveleigh, Civic Centre, Duke Street, Chelmsford, Essex CM1 2YJ (01245 606606)

Thaxed

Lord Maynard's Charity

Eligibility: People who live in the parish of Thaxted.

Types of grants: One-off and recurrent grants for general relief-in-need.

Annual grant total: About £2,000.

Applications: In writing to the correspondent. Applicants traditionally queue in the local church on 1 August for the money to be handed out, but postal applications prior to this are accepted.

Correspondent: Michael Chapman, Messrs Wade & Davies Solicitors, 28 High Street, Great Dunmow, Essex CM6 1AH (01371 872816)

The Thaxted Relief-in-Need Charities

Eligibility: People in need who live in the parish of Thaxted.

Types of grants: One-off and recurrent grants according to need.

Annual grant total: In 2009 the charities had an income of £23,000 and a total expenditure of £14,000. Around £2,000 a year is given in grants to individuals.

Applications: In writing to the correspondent.

Correspondent: M B Hughes, Secretary, Yardley Farm, Walden Road, Thaxted, Essex CM6 2RQ (01371 830642)

Other information: The main priority for the charities is to maintain its almshouses.

A small number of grants are also made to local organisations.

Waltham Forest

The E D Speed Trust

Eligibility: People in need who live in Waltham Forest.

Types of grants: One-off and recurrent grants according to need.

Annual grant total: The trust has an average income of around £800 but has only made grants in one of the last five years.

Applications: In writing to the correspondent. However, the trust has recently stated that it is unlikely that new applications will be supported.

Correspondent: Eric Darby, Trustee, 76 Grenville Gardens, Woodford Green, Essex IG8 7AQ (020 8504 8696)

Hampshire

The Alverstoke Trust

Eligibility: People in need who live in Alverstoke or nearby.

Types of grants: One-off grants, usually of amounts up to £200.

Exclusions: The trust does not make loans, grants to other charities or recurring awards.

Annual grant total: In 2008/09 the trust had an income of £1,100 and a total expenditure of £300.

Applications: In writing to the correspondent, either directly or through a third party such as a Citizens Advice, social worker, welfare agency or other third party. Applications are considered at any time.

Correspondent: Mrs Jane Hodgman, 5 Constable Close, Gosport, Hampshire PO12 2UF (023 9258 9822)

The Bordon and Liphook Charity

Eligibility: People in need who live in Bordon and Liphook and the surrounding villages.

Types of grants: One-off grants of between £50 and £3,000 can be awarded. The trustees consider a wide range of applications including heating and rent arrears.

Annual grant total: In 2009 grants were made to individuals and organisations totalling £61,000.

Applications: On a form available from the correspondent or to download from the website. Applications can be made either directly by the individual or through a social worker, Citizens Advice, other welfare agency, health visitor or district nurse. Applications are considered monthly and the trust reserves the right to commission a case worker's report.

Correspondent: Carl Tantum, Room 32, The Forest Centre, Pinehill Road, Bordon, Hampshire GU35 0TN (01420 477787; fax: 01420 477787; email: bordoncharity@aol.com; website: www.bordonandliphookcharity.co.uk/)

Dibden Allotments Charity

Eligibility: People in need who live in the parishes of Hythe, Dibden, Marshwood and Fawley.

Types of grants: One-off grants according to need, for the relief of hardship or distress. Recent grants were made towards items and services such as the provision of household goods to families, hospital travel costs, assistance with gardening for older people, and childcare costs for full-time students.

Annual grant total: In 2008/09 the charity had assets of £6.2 million and an income of £400,000. There were 398 grants made for general purposes totalling £157,000 and a further £12,000 spent towards a shoe project.

Applications: On a form available from the correspondent.

Correspondent: Barrie Smallcalder, 7 Drummond Court, Hythe, Southampton S045 6HD (023 8084 1305; email: dibdenallotments@btconnect.com)

Other information: Grants are also made to charitable and voluntary organisations.

The Farnborough (Hampshire) Welfare Trust

Eligibility: People in need who live in the urban district of Farnborough, Hampshire.

Types of grants: One-off and recurrent grants mainly to older people at Christmas. Grants are generally between £20 and £50.

Annual grant total: Grants usually total about £3,000 each year.

Applications: In writing to the correspondent: to be submitted either directly by the individual or by a third party. Applications are usually considered in early December.

Correspondent: M R Evans, Bowmarsh, 45 Church Avenue, Farnborough, Hampshire GU14 7AP (01252 542726)

Hampshire Ambulance Service Benevolent Fund

Eligibility: Serving and retired members of Hampshire Ambulance Service and their dependants.

Types of grants: One-off grants according to need.

Annual grant total: In 2008/09 the trust had an income of £16,000 and a total expenditure of £4,300.

Applications: In writing to the correspondent.

Correspondent: Terence Forgham, Trustee, 8 Ashley Gardens, Chandler's Ford, Eastleigh, Hampshire SO53 2JH (02380 269600)

Hampshire Association for the Care of the Blind (HACB)

Eligibility: People who are visually impaired, in need and live in Hampshire, excluding the cities of Portsmouth and Southampton.

Types of grants: One-off grants of up to £500 each to aid independent living for eligible people, e.g. towards special equipment, aids to daily living, holiday costs and costs incurred when moving into independent living.

Exclusions: No grants are given for educational purposes or to groups.

Annual grant total: In 2008/09 the trust had assets of £972,000 and an income of £558,000. Grants to individuals totalled £2,100.

Applications: On a form available from the correspondent. Applications can be made directly by the individual or through a third party (as long as it is signed by the individual). The trust encourages a supporting statement from the individual. Applications are usually processed within five weeks.

Correspondent: Grants Officer, Open Sight, 25 Church Road, Eastleigh, Hampshire SO50 6BL (023 8064 1244; email: info@opensight.org.uk; website: www.opensight.org.uk)

Other information: The trust also administers the Scale Trust (see separate entry for further information).

The Hampshire Constabulary Welfare Fund

Eligibility: Members, pensioners and civilian employees of the Hampshire Constabulary and their dependants. Assistance may also be available to special constables injured during police duty.

Types of grants: One-off and recurrent grants or loans to help support people experiencing family crisis or recovering from injury or illness. Recent grants have been given towards stair-lifts, bath-lifts, wheelchairs and general living costs.

Annual grant total: In 2008/09 the trust had assets of £497,000 and an income of £282,000. Grants totalled £99,000 and were distributed as follows:

Assistance and grants for individuals	£62,000
Widows and children's Christmas gifts	£28,000

Gifts to sick members, wreaths and donations to late members   £8,900

Applications: Applications should be made through a local police welfare officer. They are considered on a regular basis.

Correspondent: Ian Trueman, Hampshire Constabulary, West Hill, Romsey Road, Winchester, SO22 5DB (01962 871588; email: info@hantspolfed.com)

Hampshire Football Association Benevolent Fund

Eligibility: People in need who have been injured whilst playing football, and others who have 'done service' to the game of football. Applicants must be playing for a team affiliated with Hampshire Football Association.

Types of grants: One-off and recurrent grants, usually ranging from £50 to £1,000 according to need.

Annual grant total: Grants usually total around £5,000 per year.

Applications: In writing to the correspondent.

Correspondent: Robin Osborne, Winklebury Football Complex, Winklebury Way, Basingstoke, Hampshire, RG23 8BF (01256 853000; email: robin. osborne@hampshirefa.com)

Hampshire Golfers' Benevolent Fund

Eligibility: Priority is given to people who are members of Hampshire Professional Golfers' Association and their dependants. When funds are available the trust may also fund other people who have been employed as professional golfers and their dependants.

Types of grants: One-off and recurrent grants according to need.

Annual grant total: About £2,000.

Applications: In writing to the correspondent.

Correspondent: M J Dyer, Verisona, 64 West Street, Havant, Hampshire, PO9 1PA (02392 380112; email: hampshirepga@yahoo.co.uk)

The Kingsclere Welfare Charities

Eligibility: People in need who live in the parishes of Ashford Hill, Headley and Kingsclere.

Types of grants: The provision or payment for items, services or facilities such as medical equipment, expenses for travel to hospital and grants to relieve hardship. Grants are mostly one-off, but recurrent grants can be considered. They range from around £100 to £2,500.

Annual grant total: In 2009 the trust had an income of £4,800 and a total expenditure of £800.

Applications: In writing to the correspondent. Applications are considered in February, April, June, September and November.

Correspondent: Roy Forth, PO Box 7721, Kingsclere, RG20 5WQ (0118 981 1602; email: kclerecharities@aol.co.uk)

The Penton Trust

Eligibility: People in need who are over 65, have a limited income and live in Basingstoke. Applicants should either live in their own homes or be in sheltered accommodation.

Types of grants: Regular allowances to enable people to live in a comfortable residential hotel, boarding house or care home. Grants are also available for those living in their own home to pay for domestic help.

Annual grant total: In 2009/10 the trust had an income of £12,000 and a total expenditure of £9,200.

Applications: In writing to the correspondent.

Correspondent: Wilson Clark, Trustee, 12 Dever Way, Oakley, Basingstoke, Hampshire RG23 7AQ (01256 780872)

The Portsmouth Victoria Nursing Association

Eligibility: People in need who are sick and live in the areas covered by the Portsmouth City Primary Care Trust, the Fareham and Gosport Primary Care Trust and the East Hampshire Primary Care Trust.

Types of grants: One-off grants of up to £750 towards medical equipment, household essentials, special clothing and respite care.

Exclusions: Items that should be provided by the NHS.

Annual grant total: In 2009 grants were made to individuals amounting to £13,000, for patients welfare (£12,000) and to assist nurses in need (£740).

Applications: All applications must be made through the community nursing staff and help is confined to those on whom the nurses are in attendance. Referrals are made by the district nurses on a form which is considered by the committee at monthly meetings.

Correspondent: Susan Resouly, Secretary, Southlands, Prinsted Lane, Prinsted, Emsworth, Hampshire PO10 8HS (01243 373900; email: portsmouth.victoria. nursing@gmail.com)

Other information: Assistance is also given to the community nurses of the area to improve the care they give to their patients.

The Scale Charitable Trust Fund

Eligibility: People over 30 who are blind and in need. Applicants must have been born or have lived in Hampshire for at least five years.

Types of grants: Grants to aid independent living for eligible people, for example, towards equipment, course fees or transport costs.

Annual grant total: In 2008/09 the fund had an income of £4,500 and a total expenditure of £5,000.

Applications: Portsmouth City Council still administer the trust, however, people living in Hampshire, excluding those living in Portsmouth, should apply in writing directly to: Elaine Bellamy, Hampshire Association for the Blind (Open Sight), 25 Church Road, Bishopstoke, Eastleigh, Hampshire SO50 6BL (02380 641244). People living in Portsmouth should apply in writing directly to: Jim Tolley, Portsmouth Association for the Blind, 48 Stubbington Avenue, Portsmouth PO2 0HY (023 9266 1717).

Correspondent: Local Democracy Manager, Portsmouth City Council, Civic Offices, Guildhall Square, Portsmouth PO1 2AL (02392 834057; email: joanne. wildsmith@portsmouthcc.gov.uk)

The Earl of Southampton Trust

Eligibility: People in need who live in the ancient parish of Titchfield (now subdivided into the parishes of Titchfield, Sarisbury, Locks Heath, Warsash, Stubbington and Lee-on-the-Solent). Groups catering for people in need are sometimes considered.

Types of grants: One-off grants in the range of £25 and £1,000 towards motorised wheelchairs, stairlifts, specialist furniture for people who are disabled, respite care, household equipment, redecoration, home help, childminding, holiday activities, legal fees, respite holidays and so on.

Exclusions: The trust will not supply items or services which should be provided for by the state.

Annual grant total: In 2009/10 the trust had assets of £1.5 million and an income of £85,000. There were 58 grants made totalling £17,000 for welfare and educational purposes.

Applications: In writing to the correspondent through a social worker, Citizens Advice, other welfare agency or third party (for example, doctor, district nurse, clergy or councillor). Applications must include details of medical/financial status. Applications are considered on the last Tuesday of every month, although in the event of extreme urgency requests can be fast tracked between meetings.

Correspondent: Mrs S C Boden, Clerk to the Trustees, 24 The Square, Titchfield, Hampshire PO14 4RU (01329 513294; email: earlstrust@yahoo.co.uk)

Other information: The trust runs almshouses and a day centre for old people.

The Sway Welfare Aid Group

Eligibility: People who are older, in poor health or who have disabilities and live in the parish of Sway and its immediate neighbourhood.

Types of grants: One-off grants towards: household equipment; rent (to avoid eviction); bereavement costs; hospital travel costs; heating bills; essential decorating costs and home repairs; insulation; reasonable recreational equipment; and, disability aids. Help may also be given towards training courses and school trips.

Annual grant total: In 2008/09 the group had an income of £13,000 and a total expenditure of £15,000. Grants are made to both individuals and organisations.

Applications: In writing to the correspondent or by personal introduction.

Correspondent: J R Stevens, Driftway, Mead End Road, Sway, Lymington, Hampshire SO41 6EH (01590 682843; email: info@swaghants.org.uk; website: www.swaghants.org.uk/)

Other information: The group runs a lunch club for people living on their own. It also has a team of volunteer drivers that can help local residents who have difficulty in getting to, for example, hospital appointments.

The Three Parishes Fund

Eligibility: People in need who live in the parishes of Headley, Grayshott and Lindford and the town of Whitehill/ Bordon.

Types of grants: One-off grants.

Annual grant total: In 2009 the trust had an income of £5,700 and a total expenditure of £5,800.

Applications: In writing or by application form available from the correspondent. Applications are considered at any time and can be submitted directly by the individual, or by a social worker, doctor, clergy or similar third party.

Correspondent: George Wilson, Fremont, 23 Taylor's Lane, Lindford, Bordon, Hampshire GU35 0SW (01420 472899; email: ttpf@gofast.co.uk)

The Trant Goodwill Trust

Eligibility: People in need with a preference for Hampshire and the south of England.

Types of grants: One-off and recurrent grants according to need.

Annual grant total: In 2009 the trust had an income of £12,000 and a total expenditure of £13,000.

Applications: In writing to the correspondent.

Correspondent: Robin Horgan, Rushington House, Rushington, Southampton, Hampshire, SO40 9LT (023 8066 5544)

Other information: Grants are also made to organisations.

Twyford and District Nursing Association

Eligibility: People who are in need and live in the parishes of Twyford, Compton and Shawford, Colden Common and Owslebury, in the county of Hampshire.

Types of grants: One-off grants according to need. Recent awards have been given for electric goods, convalescence, clothing, travel expenses, medical equipment, nursing fees, furniture, disability equipment and help in the home.

Exclusions: The association cannot offer long term care.

Annual grant total: Grants average around £5,000 a year.

Applications: On a form available from the correspondent. Applications are usually made through the medical practices in the area (mainly the Twyford Practice) and people can also apply through the social services, a doctor or community nurse, or if they do not have a direct medical contact, directly to the correspondent or through a relevant third party.

Correspondent: Veronica Sowton, Bourne Cottage, Bourne Lane, Twyford, Winchester SO21 1NX (01962 713354)

The Winchester Rural District Welfare Trust

Eligibility: People in need who live in the former Winchester Rural District. This includes the parishes of Bighton, Bramdean, Compton, Headbourne Worthy and Abbot's Barton, Hursley, Itchen Valley, King's Worthy, Micheldever, Old Alresford, Owslebury, Sparsholt, Twyford, Wonston, Beauworth, Bishop's Sutton, Cheriton, Chilcomb, Crawley, Itchen Stoke and Ovington, Kilmeston, Littleton, New Alresford, Northington, Oliver's Battery and Tichborne. It does not include the city of Winchester.

Types of grants: One-off grants towards, for example, bedding, clothing, special food, fuel and heating appliances, telephone, nursing requirements, house repairs, hospital travel costs and convalescent care. Support may also be given to students seeking employment and other educational needs.

Annual grant total: Grants usually total about £1,000 each year.

Applications: In writing to the correspondent, to be submitted through a social worker, Citizens Advice or other welfare agency.

Correspondent: Sue Lane, Witts Cottage, Oxford Road, Sutton Scotney, Winchester, Hampshire SO21 3JG (01962 760858)

Other information: This trust was formed by merging the endowments of 26 charities in 25 parishes in the Winchester Rural District.

The Winchester Welfare Charities

Eligibility: People who are in need or distress, or who are sick, convalescing, disabled or infirm and live in Winchester and its immediate surroundings.

Types of grants: The trust gives winter fuel payments in December and emergency grants throughout the year. These one-off grants (typically £25 to £50) have been towards repairs to an electric wheelchair, special shoes for people with disabilities, repairs to a washing machine and so on. Help can also be given for furniture, bedding, clothing, food, fuel and nursing requirements.

Annual grant total: Grants usually total around £1,700 each year.

Applications: Recipients of Christmas vouchers are nominated by the trustees and local agencies. Applications for emergency payments should be made through a social worker, Citizens Advice or similar third party.

Correspondent: D Shaw, Hon. Clerk, Winchester Council, City Offices, Colebrook Street, Winchester, Hampshire SO23 9LJ (01962 848221; email: dshaw@ winchester.gov.uk)

Other information: A leaflet is available from the correspondent.

Brockenhurst

The Groome Trust

Eligibility: People in need who live in the parish of Brockenhurst.

Types of grants: One-off grants towards talking books for the blind, lifelines for people living alone, Christmas gifts to nursing home residents and food vouchers for older people at Christmas.

Annual grant total: In 2009 the trust had an income of £6,500 and a total expenditure of £7,300.

Applications: In writing to the correspondent, although often the applicant is known to the trustees. Applications are considered as received.

Correspondent: Patricia Dunkinson, Belmont, Burford Lane, Brockenhurst SO42 7TN (01590 622303)

Other information: The trust mainly makes grants to local organisations.

Fareham

The Fareham Welfare Trust

Eligibility: People in need who live in the ecclesiastical parishes of St Peter & Paul, St John and Holy Trinity, all in Fareham. Preference is given to widows in need.

Types of grants: One-off and recurrent grants up to a maximum of about £250 a year. Recent grants have been given for clothing, furniture, food, cookers, washing machines and other essential electrical items.

Annual grant total: In 2008/09 the trust had an income of £12,000 and a total expenditure of £11,000.

Applications: Applications should be submitted through a recognised referral agency (e.g. social worker, health visitor, Citizens Advice or doctor) or trustee. They are considered throughout the year. Details of the individual's income and circumstances must be included.

Correspondent: Anne Butcher, Clerk, 44 Old Turnpike, Fareham, Hampshire PO16 7HA (01329 235186)

Gosport

Thorngate Relief-in-Need and General Charity

Eligibility: People in need who live in Gosport.

Types of grants: One-off grants mostly between £100 and £500.

Exclusions: No grants are made towards legal expenses.

Annual grant total: In 2008/09 the charity's income was £11,000 and it had a total expenditure of £20,000. Grants are made for welfare and educational purposes.

Applications: On a form available from the correspondent. Applications can be made either directly by the individual or through a social worker, Citizens Advice, Probation Service or other welfare agency.

Correspondent: Kay Brent, 16 Peakfield, Waterlooville, PO7 6YP (023 9226 4400; email: kay@brentco.co.uk)

Hawley

The Hawley Almshouse & Relief-in-Need Charity

Eligibility: People in need who live in the area covered by Hart District Council and Rushmoor Borough Council. Beneficiaries are generally women aged 60 or over and men aged 65 or over.

Types of grants: Generally one-off grants for needs that cannot be met from any other source. Recent grants have been given for very high heating bills during cold weather and the installation of equipment such as chairlifts.

Annual grant total: In 2008/09 the charity had assets of £1.5 million and an income of £99,000. Grants were made totalling £1,300.

Applications: Applications can be submitted directly by the individual or by an appropriate third party such as a social worker or close family member. They are normally considered quarterly, but small emergency grants can be made between meetings.

Correspondent: The Secretary, Trustees' Office, Ratcliffe House, Hawley Road, Blackwater, Camberley, Surrey GU17 9DD (01276 33515)

Other information: The trust also provides warden-operated individual accommodation for elderly people in the area.

Hordle

The Hordle District Nursing Association

Eligibility: People in need who live in the parish of Hordle (New Forest).

Types of grants: Grants are given to help with the costs incurred by illness. They are usually one-off.

Annual grant total: About £1,000.

Applications: In writing to the correspondent. Applications can be made either directly by the individual or by anyone with knowledge of the applicant's need. They are considered at any time throughout the year.

Correspondent: Mrs A Hill, 7 Firmount Close, Everton, Lymington, Hampshire SO41 0JN (01590 642272)

Isle of Wight

The Broadlands Home Trust

Eligibility: Widows of pensionable age who are in need and live on the Isle of Wight.

Types of grants: Pensions of around £450 a year and Christmas boxes of between £50 and £100. General relief-in-need grants may occasionally be given.

Exclusions: No grants for married women or graduates.

Annual grant total: In 2008/09 the trust had assets of £243,000 and an income of £14,000. Grants were made totalling £12,000 and were distributed as follows:

Pensions	£7,800
Advancement of life grants	£2,100
Christmas boxes to pensioners	£800

Applications: On a form available from the correspondent, to be submitted either directly by the individual or a family member. Applications are considered quarterly in January, April, July and October.

Correspondent: Mrs M Groves, 2 Winchester Close, Newport, Isle of Wight PO30 1DR (01983 525630)

Other information: Please note: the trust stated in its latest accounts that, 'over the last few years it has not been possible to utilise all of the moneys in the pension branch and the trustees are at present actively seeking new pensioners'.

The Mary Pittis Charity for Widows

Eligibility: Widows who are aged 60 and over, who live on the Isle of Wight and express Christian (Protestant only) beliefs. Applicants must be known to the minister and have some connection with the church detailed on the application form.

Types of grants: One-off grants ranging from £50 to £200 towards essential kitchen equipment, semi-medical items such as easy-lift armchairs, alarm systems and so on.

Annual grant total: Grants average around £4,500 a year.

Applications: On a form available from the correspondent, giving details of the church attended and the minister. Applications can be made directly, through a welfare agency or a minister of religion. They are considered at any time.

Correspondent: Anthony Holmes, 62–66 Lugley Street, Newport, Isle of Wight PO30 5EU (01983 524431)

Lyndhurst

The Lyndhurst Welfare Charity

Eligibility: People in need who live in the parish of Lyndhurst.

Types of grants: Grants are normally one-off and are made towards items, services or facilities, e.g. household items, respite care and counselling. Grants usually range between £50 and £500.

Annual grant total: In 2008/09 the trust had an income of £4,600 and a total expenditure of £6,700. Grants to individuals usually total around £1,000 per year.

Applications: Applicants should telephone or write to the correspondent, either directly themselves, or through a social worker, Citizens Advice or other welfare agency. Applications are usually considered in April and October, but emergency applications can be considered in between those times.

Correspondent: A G Herbert, Trustee, 59 The Meadows, Lyndhurst, Hampshire SO43 7EJ (023 8028 3895)

Other information: Grants are also made to organisations.

New Forest

The New Forest Keepers Widows Fund

Eligibility: Retired keepers or widows and children of deceased keepers who are in need and live in the New Forest.

Types of grants: One-off and recurrent grants ranging from £50 to £2,500.

Annual grant total: In 2008/09 the fund had an income of £14,000 and a total expenditure of £5,300.

Applications: In writing to the correspondent directly by the individual or family member. Applications can be submitted at any time.

Correspondent: Richard Mihalop, 17 Ferndale Road, Marchwood, Southampton, SO40 4XR (023 8086 1136)

Portsmouth

The Isaac & Annie Fogelman Relief Trust

Eligibility: People of the Jewish faith aged 40 and over who live in Portsmouth and worship at the Portsmouth Jewish Synagogue.

Types of grants: One-off and recurrent grants according to need.

Annual grant total: In 2008/09 the trust had an income of £10,000 and a total expenditure of £4,900.

Applications: In writing to: The Secretary, Portsmouth & Southsea Hebrew Congregation, The Thicket, Elm Grove, Southsea PO5 2AA. Applications are considered quarterly.

Correspondent: S J Forman, Torrington House, 47 Holywell Hill, St Albans, Hertfordshire, AL1 1HD (01727 885560)

Thomas King Trust

Eligibility: People in need who have lived in Portsmouth for 10 years.

Types of grants: Mainly one-off grants according to need ranging from £20 to £50.

Annual grant total: In 2008/09 the trust had an income of £3,600 and a total expenditure of £3,100.

Applications: Application forms are available from the correspondent in October for decisions in December. They can be submitted either directly by the individual, or through a social worker, Citizens Advice or other third party.

Correspondent: Mrs Joanne Wildsmith, Local Democracy Manager, Portsmouth City Council, Civic Offices, Guildhall Square, Portsmouth PO1 2AL (023 9283 4092; email: joanne.wildsmith@portsmouthcc.gov.uk)

Other information: The John Wallace Peck Trust and three other local charities were amalgamated with this trust in 1999.

The Montagu Neville Durnford & Saint Leo Cawthan Memorial Trust

Eligibility: People over 60 who are in need and who live in the city of Portsmouth. Preference is given to ex-naval personnel and their dependants/widows.

Types of grants: Annual grants of £50 given by the Royal Naval Benevolent Trust (RNBT) and to those recommended by Age Concern.

Annual grant total: In 2008/09 the trust had an income of £17,000 and made grants totalling £20,000.

Applications: In writing to The Royal Naval Benevolent Trust (RNBT). Grants are made to the RNBT and Age Concern in November, for redistribution.

Correspondent: Local Democracy Manager, Portsmouth City Council, Civic Offices, Guildhall Square, Portsmouth PO1 2QR (023 9283 4057)

The Lord Mayor of Portsmouth's Charity

Eligibility: Individuals in need who live in the City of Portsmouth, or former residents who now live in Havant, Waterlooville, Fareham or Droxford.

Types of grants: One-off grants ranging between £100 and £500.

Exclusions: Educational fees, scholarships, travel costs or arrears/debts are not funded.

Annual grant total: In 2008/09 the trust had an income of £18,000 and a total expenditure of £14,000. Grants were made totalling around £12,000.

Applications: In writing to the correspondent. Unsuccessful applicants will be informed.

Correspondent: Hilary Thorpe, Local Democracy Manager, Portsmouth City Council, Civic Offices, Guildhall Square, Portsmouth, Hampshire PO1 2QR (023 9283 4057; email: hilary.thorpe@portsmouthcc.gov.uk)

The E C Roberts Charitable Trust

Eligibility: Children in need who live in the city of Portsmouth, with a preference for those living with blindness or disability.

Types of grants: One-off or recurrent grants according to need.

Annual grant total: Grants usually total around £1,000 a year.

Applications: In writing to the correspondent. Applications can be submitted either directly by the individual, through a third party such as a social worker, or through an organisation such as a Citizens Advice or other welfare agency. Applications are considered upon receipt.

Correspondent: Rev Wendy Kennedy, First Floor, Peninsular House, Wharf Road, Portsmouth, PO2 8HB (023 9289 9668; email: wendy.kennedy@portsmouth.anglican.org)

Ryde

The Ryde Sick Poor Fund (also known as Greater Ryde Benevolent Trust)

Eligibility: Sick people in need who live in the former borough of Ryde.

Types of grants: Small, one-off grants only. The trust is unable to give recurrent grants.

Annual grant total: In 2009 the trust had an income of £6,800 and a total expenditure of £5,200.

Applications: In writing to the correspondent.

Correspondent: Rachel Mckernan, Secretary, 29 John Street, Ryde, PO33 2PZ (01983 812552; email: rachel.mckernan@btinternet.com)

Southampton

The Southampton (City Centre) Relief-in-Need Charity

Eligibility: People in need who live in the ecclesiastical parish of Southampton (in practice, the city centre).

Types of grants: One-off grants ranging from £50 to £100 for a wide range of needs such as travel to hospital, convalescence, heating, medical equipment, holidays, special food or equipment, book recordings and chiropody.

Exclusions: No grants towards rent, debts or council tax.

Annual grant total: In 2009 the charity had an income of £11,000 and a total expenditure of £13,000.

Applications: In writing to the correspondent submitted through a social worker, Citizens Advice, health visitor or other welfare agency. Applications are considered quarterly in March, June, September and December; those made directly by the individual will not be considered.

Correspondent: Valerie Warren, 4 Morley Close, Burton Christchurch, BH23 7LA (01202 481984)

Southampton and District Sick Poor Fund and Humane Society

Eligibility: People who are sick and poor and live in Southampton and the immediate surrounding area.

Types of grants: One-off grants usually ranging from £50 to £250 for bedding, food, fuel and specialist equipment to alleviate an existing condition or to assist with day-to-day living.

Annual grant total: In 2009 the society had an income of £12,000 and a total expenditure of £10,000.

Applications: In writing to the correspondent. Applications should preferably be submitted through a social worker, Citizens Advice or other welfare agency. The trustees usually meet twice a year, but applications can be dealt with outside these meetings. Applicants must clearly demonstrate that they are both sick and poor (such as evidence of Income Support or other state benefits).

Correspondent: Paul Bricknell, Arcadia House, Maritime Walk, Southampton SO14 3TL (023 8088 1700)

Other information: Grants and certificates are also awarded to people for saving or attempting to save someone from drowning or other dangers.

Hertfordshire

The Bowley Charity for Deprived Children

Eligibility: Disadvantaged children up to 16 years (or 18 if in full-time education) who live in South West Hertfordshire.

Types of grants: Small one-off grants of between £50 and £500 (the upper limit is for larger families), for items such as cookers, beds, bedding, prams, cots and other essential household items. Grants are also given for essential items of clothing for children.

Exclusions: No grants for school uniforms

Annual grant total: In 2009/10 the charity had an income of £8,500 and a total expenditure of £16,000.

Applications: On a form available from the correspondent. Applications should be made through a social worker, Citizens Advice or other welfare agency. Trustees meet quarterly to consider grants.

Correspondent: Kay Rees, 175 Cassiobury Drive, Watford WD17 3AL (01923 226710; email: kayrees@hotmail.com)

The Hertfordshire Charity for Deprived Children

Eligibility: Disadvantaged children up to the age of 17 living in Hertfordshire (excluding the Watford area).

Types of grants: One-off grants generally for holidays (not overseas), clothing (such as school or cub uniforms or general clothing), and household items (such as cookers or washing machines, where this would improve the quality of life for the child). Grants usually range between £30 and £300.

Annual grant total: In 2008/09 the charity had an income of £7,800 and a total expenditure £9,400.

Applications: On a form available from the correspondent. Applications should be made through a health visitor, social worker, probation officer or similar third party. Trustees normally meet in May and November, but applications can be considered between meetings and can be approved on the agreement of two trustees.

Correspondent: Ralph Paddock, 86 Ware Road, Hertford, SG13 7HN (01992 551 128; email: ralphiegerry@btopenworld.com)

Hertfordshire Community Foundation

Eligibility: People up to 18 years of age who live in Hertfordshire and are disabled, disadvantaged or who have been in care.

Types of grants: One-off grants of up to £300. Recent grants include the purchase of beds and bedding for two families living in one house with four children between them; a tumble drier and an ironing board for a mother and her two young children fleeing domestic violence; a cooker for a young woman living with her 12 year old sibling whose mother has recently died; a wardrobe and changing unit for a single parent with a new baby who has special needs.

Exclusions: Grants are not given for holidays, school trips, debt payment, rent arrears or one-off events.

Annual grant total: Grants to individuals usually total around £20,000 per year.

Applications: On a form available from the correspondent. Applications can be made at any time through a recognised professional such as a social worker or health visitor. Evidence of income and expenditure should be provided. Please note: grants are only payable to third parties, such as a shop, in order to purchase a much needed item.

Correspondent: Grants Administrator, Foundation House, 2–4 Forum Place, Fiddlebridge Lane, Hatfield, Hertfordshire AL10 0RN (01707 251351; email: grants@hertscf.org.uk; website: www.hertscf.org.uk)

Other information: The foundation mainly supports organisations.

The Hertfordshire Convalescent Trust

Eligibility: People in need who are chronically sick, terminally ill or children with special needs and their carers. Families suffering from domestic violence or relationship breakdown may also be eligible for assistance. Applicants must live in Hertfordshire.

Types of grants: One-off grants in the range of £300 to £450 for traditional convalescence in a nursing home or for respite breaks and recuperative holidays in hotels and caravans.

Exclusions: There are no grants available for equipment or transport costs.

Annual grant total: In 2009 the trust had an income of £24,000 and a total expenditure of £39,000.

Applications: On a form available from the correspondent. Applications should be sponsored by a health professional, social worker or member of the clergy. They are considered throughout the year.

Correspondent: Janet Bird, Administrator, 140 North Road, Hertford SG14 2BZ (01992 587544; fax: 01992 582595; email: janet_l_bird@hotmail.com)

The Ware Charities

Eligibility: People in need who live in the area of Ware Town Council, the Parish of Wareside and the parish of Thundridge.

Types of grants: Grants are made towards items or services not readily available from any other source.

Annual grant total: In 2009/10 the charities had assets of £1.1 million and an income of £56,000. There were 37 grants made to individuals totalling £25,000.

Applications: In writing to the correspondent at any time, to be submitted directly by the individual or a family member. Applications must include brief details of the applicant's income and savings and be supported and signed by a head teacher, doctor, nurse or social worker.

Correspondent: D C Wardrop, 38 Scotts Road, Ware, Hertfordshire, SG12 9JQ

Other information: Grants are also made to local organisations.

Buntingford

The Buntingford Relief in Need Charity

Eligibility: Older people on state registered pensions who live in Buntingford and have lived there for 10 years.

Types of grants: £20 per household given in early December towards fuel.

Annual grant total: In 2009 the charity had an income of £50,000 and a total expenditure of £20,000. Grants were made totalling around £15,000.

Applications: In writing to the correspondent.

Correspondent: Valerie R Hume, 38 Monks Walk, Buntingford, Hertfordshire SG9 9EE (01763 272480)

Dacorum

The Dacorum Community Trust

Eligibility: People in need who live in the borough of Dacorum.

Types of grants: Generally one-off grants up to £500 towards domestic equipment; disability equipment; clothes and shoes; funeral expenses; respite breaks and holidays for families; debt relief; and the costs involved in making homes habitable and safe for young and old.

Exclusions: Grants are not normally given for the costs of further or mainstream education and only in exceptional circumstances for gap-year travel.

Annual grant total: In 2008/09 the trust had assets of £300,000 and received an income of £228,000, of which £93,000 was spent on grants. Around £20,000 is given annually to individuals for welfare and educational purposes.

Applications: On a form available from the correspondent or to download from the website. Applications can be submitted by the individual, through a recognised referral agency (such as social services or Citizens Advice) or through an MP, doctor or school. Applications are considered in March, June, September and December. The trust asks for details of family finances. A preliminary telephone call is always welcome.

Correspondent: The Trust Manager, Cementaprise Centre, Paradise, Hemel Hempstead, HP2 4TF (01442 231396; email: admin@dctrust.org.uk; website: www.dctrust.org.uk)

Other information: The trust manages the DCT Mayor's Recovery Fund for Hemel Hempstead which was set up following the Buncefield Oil Depot fire to help and support those affected.

Harpenden

The Harpenden Trust

Eligibility: People in need who live in the 'AL5' postal district of Harpenden, with a preference for younger and older people.

Types of grants: One-off grants for up to £200 are made, for example, for large unexpected bills, essential household items and children's food and clothing. Grants towards the cost of utility bills are available

to pensioners on a low income. Educational grants may also be made.

Exclusions: Grants are not given to individuals living outside of Harpenden.

Annual grant total: In 2008/09 the trust had assets of £2.9 million and an income of £177,000. Grants were made to 665 individuals totalling £50,000 and were distributed as follows:

Grants	344	£26,000
Utilities grants	83	£12,000
Christmas parcels	148	£1,300
Youth grants	90	£11,000

A further £67,000 was given to local organisations.

Applications: In writing to the correspondent, either directly by the individual or through a third party such as a social worker or Citizens Advice.

Correspondent: Dennis Andrews, The Trust Centre, 90 Southdown Road, Harpenden, AL5 1PS (01582 460457; email: admin@theharpendentrust.org.uk)

Other information: The trust runs its own centres in Southdown Road and at the High Street Methodist Church. There is a weekly coffee morning and summer coach trips are often organised. The trust also delivers a Christmas dinner to housebound residents on Christmas day.

Hatfield

Hatfield Broad Oak Non-Ecclesiastical Charities

Eligibility: People in need who live in Hatfield Broad Oak.

Types of grants: One-off and recurrent grants ranging from £20 to £25.

Annual grant total: In 2009 the trust had an income of £5,900 and a total expenditure of £2,600.

Applications: In writing to the correspondent directly by the individual or family member.

Correspondent: Martin Gandy, Carters Barn, Cage End, Hatfield Broad Oak, Bishop's Stortford, Hertfordshire, CM22 7HL (01279 718316)

Wellfield Trust

Eligibility: People in need who are on a low income and who have lived in the parish of Hatfield for six months.

Types of grants: One-off grants of £100 to £500 towards a range of welfare needs. The trust also loans motorised scooters.

Exclusions: Grants are not made for council tax arrears, rent or funeral costs.

Annual grant total: In 2008/09 grants to individuals totalled £13,000, with a further £1,800 given towards projects.

The majority of grants are given for welfare purposes.

Applications: On a form available from the correspondent only via a third party such as social services or Citizens Advice. Most of the local appropriate third parties also have the application form. Applications are considered monthly and should be received by the first Monday of every month.

Correspondent: Mrs Jeanette Bayford, Birchwood Leisure Centre, Longmead, Hatfield, Hertfordshire AL10 0AS (01707 251018; email: wellfieldtrust@aol.com; website: www.wellfieldtrust.co.uk)

Letchworth Garden City

The Letchworth Civic Trust

Eligibility: People who are in need, sick or require accommodation and live in Letchworth Garden City, and have lived there for two years or more.

Types of grants: One-off grants and occasionally loans in the range of £50 to £500. Grants aim to make a 'significant difference', for example the balance needed to purchase a wheelchair, tools for an ex-prisoner or 'key money' for a homeless person finding accommodation.

Annual grant total: In 2008/09 the trust had assets of £494,000 and an income of £62,000. Educational grants totalled £43,000. This comprised of grants made to:

- 144 university students who received average grants for educational learning materials of £227 (£33,000)
- 51 school students with disadvantaged home backgrounds received average grants of £54 (£3,000)
- 22 other individuals received average grants for educational or medical support of £325 (£7,000).

Applications: By letter or on an application form available from the correspondent. Applications can be made at any time, either directly by the individual or through a third party such as a probation officer or social worker.

The trust does not respond to applications made outside of its area of interest.

Correspondent: Peter Jackson, Secretary, 32 South View, Letchworth Garden City, Hertfordshire, SG6 3JJ (01462 484413; email: peterjackson99@btinternet.com; website: letchworthct.org.uk/)

Other information: Grants are also made to schoolchildren and students, and to groups and societies, but not religious or political groups.

Watford

The Watford Health Trust

Eligibility: People in need who are in poor health, convalescent or who have a disability and live in the borough of Watford and the surrounding neighbourhood.

Types of grants: One-off and recurrent grants to assist recovery or improve quality of life.

Annual grant total: In 2008/09 the trust had an income of £25,000 and a total expenditure of £23,000.

Applications: In writing to the correspondent. Grants are generally made through official bodies or practices familiar with the applicant's needs.

Correspondent: D I Scleater, Allways, 23 Shepherds Road, Watford, WD18 7HU (01923 222745; email: ian@scleater.co.uk)

Other information: Grants are also made to local organisations.

Wormley

The Wormley Parochial Charity

Eligibility: People in need who live in the parish of Wormley as it was defined before 31 March 1935, particularly those who are elderly, sick or newly bereaved.

Types of grants: Grants towards (i) transport to or from hospital, either as a patient or visitor; (ii) Christmas vouchers to spent locally for food and other necessities for people who are in need, sick, frail, elderly, bereaved and so on; (iii) one-off grants for people with special needs.

Exclusions: The trust does not give loans.

Annual grant total: About £3,000.

Applications: In writing to the charity, either directly by the individual, or through a social worker, Citizens Advice, welfare agency or a third party such as a friend who is aware of the situation. Applications are considered in April and October.

Correspondent: Mrs C Proctor, 5 Lammasmead, Broxbourne, Hertfordshire, EN10 6PF

Kent

The Appleton Trust (Canterbury)

Eligibility: People in need connected with the Church of England in the diocese of Canterbury.

Types of grants: One-off grants ranging between £100 and £500. Recent grants

include those made to youth workers and wives of the clergy. The trust also makes loans to member of the clergy, local parishes and widows of clergymen for items such as cars, computer equipment and equity loans.

Exclusions: Grants are not given for further education.

Annual grant total: In 2009 the trust had assets of £677,000 and an income of £33,000. Grants were made to six individuals totalling £28,000.

Applications: In writing to the correspondent. Applications should be submitted directly by the individual or a church organisation and are considered every two months.

Correspondent: J Hills, Diocesan House, Lady Wootton's Green, Canterbury, Kent CT1 1NQ (01227 459401; email: rtrice@ diocant.org)

Other information: Organisations connected to the Church of England in Canterbury Diocese are also supported.

The Christmas Gift Fund for the Old City of Canterbury

Eligibility: People in need who live in Canterbury and the surrounding area comprised in the former district of Bridge Blean. Preference is generally given to older residents.

Types of grants: Food parcels and toy vouchers are distributed at Christmas time.

Annual grant total: In 2008/09 the fund had assets of £44,000 and an income of £18,000. Grants were made totalling £18,000.

Applications: A list is compiled over the year from local doctors, clergy, Age Concern, direct applications and other sources. Direct applications should be made in writing to the correspondent.

Correspondent: Jennifer Sherwood, Larkings Chartered Accountants, 31 St George's Place, Canterbury, Kent, CT1 1XD (01227 464991)

Other information: The fund was previously known as the Christmas Gift Fund for the Old City of Canterbury.

R V Coleman Trust

Eligibility: People who live in Dover and the immediate neighbourhood and are sick, convalescing, or living with a mental or physical disability.

Types of grants: One-off grants according to need. Recent grants have been given for periods in residential care and nursing homes, disability aids, telephone facilities and convalescent holiday breaks.

Exclusions: No grants for furniture, home repairs or debts.

Annual grant total: In 2008 there were 999 cases supported which amounted to £58,000.

Applications: Applications should be made through a social worker, Citizens Advice, welfare agency, doctor or consultant and sent to Mrs Barbara Godfrey, Welfare Officer, 41 The Ridgeway, River, Dover, Kent, CT16 1RT.

Correspondent: Peter Sherred, Clerk, Bradleys, 19 Castle Street, Dover, Kent CT16 1PU (01304 204080; email: sherred@ invictawiz.co.uk)

Cornwallis Memorial Fund

Eligibility: People in need who live in Kent. Only those who were born in, or have lived in Kent for some time will be considered.

Types of grants: One-off grants of £50 to £300.

Annual grant total: In 2008/09 the fund had an income of £7,400 and a total expenditure of £17,000.

Applications: On a form available from the correspondent, on receipt of an sae. Applications can be made either directly by the individual, or through a social worker, Citizens Advice or other third party. Applicants should provide as much detail as possible, including extra information sheets with the application as relevant.

Correspondent: Richard Bushrod, Honorary Secretary, Beech Cottage, Lidwells Lane, Goudhurst, Kent, TN17 1EP (01580 211875; email: cornwallis.sec@ btinternet.com)

Headley-Pitt Charitable Trust

Eligibility: Individuals in need who live in Kent with a preference for Ashford. There is also a preference for older people.

Types of grants: One-off grants, usually in the range of £100 to £300.

Annual grant total: In 2008/09 the trust had assets of £2.3 million and an income of £69,000. Grants made to individuals totalled £29,000.

Applications: In writing to the correspondent, either directly by the individual or through a third party.

Correspondent: Thelma Pitt, Old Mill Cottage, Ulley Road, Kennington, Ashford, Kent, TN24 9HX (01233 626189; email: thelma.pitt@headley.co.uk)

Other information: Grants are also made to organisations and to individuals for educational purposes.

The Kent County Football Association Benevolent Fund

Eligibility: Players and others directly connected with affiliated bodies or within the jurisdiction of the association who may be injured whilst playing football or who may be incapacitated through illness definitely attributable to participation in the game.

Types of grants: One-off grants according to need.

Annual grant total: Grants average around £1,600 a year.

Applications: On a form available from the correspondent.

Correspondent: Keith Masters, Chief Executive, Invicta House, Cobdown Park, London Road, Ditton, Aylesford, Kent ME20 6DQ (01622 792140)

The Kent Fund for Children

Eligibility: Children and young people up to the age of 21, who are in need and live in Kent County Council area.

The trust is keen to support children and young people who have not had the opportunities that most children and young people enjoy, either because they have physical or learning disabilities, a sensory impairment, or difficult social circumstances.

Types of grants: Usually one-off grants up to £1,000. Grants must be of direct benefit to the child or young person. The trust is particularly keen to enable children and young people to pursue activities, hobbies and interests which cannot be financed through usual sources, i.e. local authorities, schools and community groups and where applicants show self-help through fundraising. Grants may be for equipment for personal development, or to allow the opportunity to learn new skills, or being involved in an expedition or outing.

Annual grant total: Grants usually total around £10,000 per year.

Applications: Applications must be made on behalf of individuals by a charity, an organised group, society or professional. This includes schools, youth, and community groups and so on.

Correspondent: Mike Ballard, Kent County Council, Room 1.60, Sessions House, County Hall, Maidstone, Kent ME14 1XQ (01622 694845; fax: 01622 694911; website: www. kenttrustweb.org.uk)

Other information: Formerly known as The Kent Children's Trust

Kent Nursing Institution

Eligibility: People in need who are sick, convalescent, disabled or infirm and live in west Kent.

Types of grants: One-off grants ranging between £200 and £500. Recent grants have been given in cases of known hardship caused by family illness (to help cover the costs of hospital visits etc.) and to assist in buying specialist equipment to relieve discomfort (special beds, ultrasound matching etc.).

Exclusions: The trust does not assist with debt or bankruptcy fees.

Annual grant total: In 2009 the trust had an income of £6,700 and a total expenditure of £3,900.

Applications: In writing to the correspondent either directly by the individual or through a social worker, doctor, priest, Citizens Advice or other welfare agency. Applications are usually considered in March and October.

Correspondent: Canon R B Stevenson, The Vicarage, 138 High Street, West Malling, Kent ME19 6NE (01732 842245; email: woolystevenson@yahoo.co.uk)

Other information: The trust also makes grants to organisations.

Littledown Trust

Eligibility: People in need with a preference for those who live in Kent.

Types of grants: One-off and recurrent grants according to need.

Annual grant total: In 2008/09 the trust had both an income and a total expenditure of £9,900.

Applications: In writing to the correspondent.

Correspondent: P G Brown, Littledown Farmhouse, Lamberhurst Down, Lamberhurst, Tunbridge Wells, TN3 8HD

The Dorothy Parrott Trust Fund

Eligibility: People in need who live in the area administered by Sevenoaks Town Council and adjoining parishes. Young children and older people are given preference.

Types of grants: Usually one-off grants ranging from £25 to £100 according to need. Recent grants have been given towards a fridge, a school outing for the child of a single parent, house decoration, boots, ballet shoes, a mattress for twins and project trips such as Operation Raleigh.

Annual grant total: Grants usually total about £2,000 per year.

Applications: Either direct to the correspondent or through a social worker, Citizens Advice or similar third party, including a general history of the family. Applications are considered on the last Monday of January, April, July and October.

Correspondent: Gina Short, 10 The Landway, Kemsing, Sevenoaks, TN15 6TG (01732 760263)

Sir Thomas Smythe's Charity

Eligibility: People of pensionable age who are in need and live within the 26 parishes of Tonbridge and Tunbridge Wells.

Types of grants: Pensions of £560 are distributed in quarterly payments of £140. Grants are typically made for items not covered by benefits, for example, unexpected household repairs or the replacement of domestic appliances.

Exclusions: Grants are not made to people in residential care and cannot be given to cover funeral costs or debt repayments.

Annual grant total: In 2008/09 the charity had assets of £949,000 and an income of £37,000. Pension payments totalled £27,000 and three grants were made for household items totalling £530.

Applications: Applications are only recommended via local trustees.

Correspondent: Charities Administrator, The Skinners' Company, Skinners' Hall, 8 Dowgate Hill, London EC4R 2SP (020 7213 0562; fax: 020 7236 6590; email: charitiesadmin@skinners.org.uk)

Borden

The William Barrow's Charity

Eligibility: People in need who live in the ancient ecclesiastical parish of Borden or have lived in the parish and now live nearby. There is a preference for people of 60 years or over and disabled people.

Types of grants: One-off grants and twice-yearly allowances may be given for pensions, disability and medical equipment, travel expenses, convalescence and living costs. Grants typically range from £350 to £500.

Annual grant total: In 2008 the foundation had assets of £5.3 million and an income of £175,000. Grants made to pensioners totalled £10,000.

Applications: On a form available from the correspondent. Applications are considered in January, April, July and October.

Correspondent: S J Mair, Clerk, c/o George Webb Finn, 43 Park Road, Sittingbourne, Kent ME10 1DY (email: stuart@georgewebbfinn.com)

Canterbury

The Canterbury United Municipal Charities

Eligibility: People in need who have lived within the boundaries of what was the old city of Canterbury for at least two years.

Types of grants: One-off and recurrent grants and pensions. Annual pensions of £100 are given to about 20 needy older people. Also at Christmas, vouchers/tokens of £25 are given for: clothing for children aged 6 to 16 (30 children); and people who are elderly and in need (120 adults).

Annual grant total: In 2008/09 the charities had an income of £8,000 and an expenditure of £7,000. Approximately £3,500 was given towards welfare needs.

Applications: In writing to the correspondent through the individual's school/college/educational welfare agency or directly by the individual. Applications are considered on an ongoing basis and should include a brief statement of circumstances and proof of residence in the area.

Correspondent: Aaron Spencer, Furley Page, 39–40 St Margaret's Street, Canterbury, Kent CT1 2TX (01227 863140; email: aas@furleypage.co.uk)

Other information: Grants are also given for educational purposes and to organisations with similar objects.

Streynsham's Charity

Eligibility: People who live in the ancient parish of St Dunstan's.

Types of grants: One-off grants, up to a maximum of about £300.

Annual grant total: Relief in need grants are usually made in three categories: 'lifeline grant', 'individual regular grants', and 'individual specific grants'. Combined relief in need grants usually total around £14,000 per year.

Applications: In writing to the correspondent. Applications should be made directly by the individual. They are usually considered in March and October but can be made at any time and should include an sae and telephone number if applicable.

Correspondent: The Clerk to the Trustees, PO Box 970, Canterbury, Kent CT1 9DJ (0845 0944769)

Chatham

Chatham District Masonic Trust

Eligibility: Freemasons and their widows and children, living in Chatham.

Types of grants: One-off and recurrent grants according to need.

Annual grant total: In 2008/09 the trust had assets of £17,000 and an income of £30,000. No charitable donations were made during the year. Previously, grants have totalled around £250.

Applications: In writing to the correspondent.

Correspondent: Jeremy Tivers, 59 Street End Road, Chatham, Kent, ME5 0BG (01634 301289; email: jell@blueyonder.co.uk)

Other information: The principal activity of the trust is the running of the Masonic Centre at Manor Road, Chatham.

Dover

The Casselden Trust

Eligibility: People in need who live in the Dover Town Council area.

Types of grants: One-off and recurrent grants, up to a maximum of £250.

Annual grant total: Grants usually total around £2,000 each year.

Applications: In writing to the correspondent.

Correspondent: Leslie Alton, 26 The Shrubbery, Walmer, Deal, Kent CT14 7PZ (01304 375499)

Folkstone

The Folkestone Municipal Charities

Eligibility: People in need who live in the borough of Folkestone and have done so for at least five years. Preference is usually given to older people and single parent families.

Types of grants: One-off and recurrent grants ranging from about £200 to £400 for a variety of needs. Recent grants have been given for telephone installation, help after a burglary, loss of a purse/wallet, shoes for disadvantaged children, gas/electricity bills, beds/bedding, prams, clothing and household repairs.

Annual grant total: In 2008/09 the trust had assets of £1.9 million and an income of £101,000. Grants were made totalling £77,000, of which £53,000 was given in pensions and £18,000 in one-off grants. Donations to organisations totalled £7,000.

Applications: On a form available from the correspondent. Applications should be submitted through a third party such as a social worker, Citizens Advice or similar welfare agency. They are considered on a monthly basis, though urgent requests can be dealt with between meetings.

Correspondent: Michael A Cox, Romney House, Cliff Road, Hythe CT21 5XA (01303 260144; email: gillyjc@btinternet.com)

Fordwich

The Fordwich United Charities

Eligibility: People in need or with disabilities living in Fordwich.

Types of grants: One-off grants mostly given towards household bills.

Annual grant total: In 2008 the charity had an income of £22,000 and a total expenditure of £35,000.

Applications: In writing to: M R Clayton, Ladywell House, Fordwich, Canterbury CT2 0DL. The deadline for applications is 1 September and a decision will be made within a month.

Correspondent: A Spencer, Furley Page Solicitors, 39 St Margaret's Street, Canterbury CT1 2TX (01227 863140; fax: 01227 863220)

Gillingham

Dobson Trust

Eligibility: People in receipt of a state pension or over the age of 60 who are in financial need and live in the former borough of Gillingham.

Types of grants: One-off grants according to need. Recent grants ranged from £70 for audio books to £2500 for a replacement boiler. Grants are generally given to help cover exceptional outgoings or unexpected bills, such as to repair or replace an essential domestic appliance or piece of furniture; specialist equipment associated with disability or impairment; or the costs associated with the death of a partner (excluding funeral costs).

Annual grant total: In 2008/09 the trust had an income of £1,800 and a total expenditure of £2,400. Grants totalled around £2,000.

Applications: On a form available from Mrs Ellen Wright at the above address. Applications can be submitted at any time and the trustees meet about four times a year to consider them.

Correspondent: Mrs Margaret Taylor, Resources, Medway Council, Gun Wharf, Dock Road, Chatham, Kent ME4 4TR (01634 332144; email: margaret.taylor@medway.gov.uk)

Other information: Local organisations are also supported.

Godmersham

Godmersham Relief in Need Charity

Eligibility: People in need who live in the ancient parish of Godmersham.

Types of grants: One-off grants according to need, towards items, services or facilities.

Annual grant total: In 2009 the charity had an income of £7,000 and a total expenditure of £6,000. Grants were given for both educational and relief-in-need purposes.

Applications: In writing to the correspondent, either directly by the individual or through a third party.

Correspondent: David T Swan, Feleberge, Canterbury Road, Bilting, Ashford, Kent TN25 4HE (01233 812125)

Gravesham

William Frank Pinn Charitable Trust

Eligibility: People of pensionable age who live in the borough of Gravesham. Priority is given to those on lower incomes.

Types of grants: One-off grants averaging £95 are made for specific purposes only, such as clothing, furniture, holidays and fuel.

Exclusions: No more than two grants may be made to any household per calendar year.

Annual grant total: In 2008/09 the trust had assets of £5.7 million and an income of £252,000. There were 2,063 grants made totalling £185,000.

Applications: On a form available from the correspondent. Applications should be submitted directly by the individual and are considered monthly.

Correspondent: Trust Officer, HSBC Trust Company (UK) Ltd, 10th Floor Norwich House, Nelson Gate, Commercial Road, Southampton, Hampshire SO15 1GX, SO15 1GX (023 8072 2226)

Hayes

Hayes (Kent) Trust

Eligibility: People in need who live in the parish of Hayes.

Types of grants: One-off grants in the region of £75 to £1,500 are given according to need.

Annual grant total: In 2008/09 the trust had assets of £738,000 and an income of £27,000. There were 11 welfare grants made totalling £4,200.

Applications: In writing to the correspondent. Applications should include the full name of the applicant, postal address in Hayes (Kent), telephone number and date of birth. Applications can be made either directly by the individual, or through a third party such as a social worker, Citizens Advice or other welfare agency.

Correspondent: Richard Marlin, 43 Eastry Avenue, Hayes, Bromley, Kent BR2 7PE (020 8462 1363)

Other information: The trust also makes grants to organisations and to individuals for educational purposes.

Herne Bay

The Herne Bay Parochial Charity

Eligibility: People in need who live in Herne Bay. Applicants preferably should be on income support or in receipt of similar financial assistance.

Types of grants: Both one-off and regular grants during the year and at Christmas. The usual grant to individuals consists of:

(i) a monthly voucher for £6 which can be exchanged at certain shops or the local council office

(ii) a cash grant of £20 at Christmas

(iii) a cash grant of £10 in February towards fuel

(iv) a cash grant of £10 in November towards fuel.

The charities make a £10 Christmas grant to several other individuals. Examples of other grants are to purchase a particular necessary item such as providing a telephone or to clear a debt, for example, an electricity bill.

Annual grant total: Grants average about £1,500 a year.

Applications: In writing to the correspondent through a social worker, Citizens Advice or other welfare agency or directly by the individual or some relevant third party. Applications are normally considered in April and October and ideally should be received in the preceding month. The charities have to be satisfied that the applicant is financially in need, such as by providing supporting evidence of Income Support, housing benefit and so on. Particulars of what the grant is required for should be included.

Correspondent: Susan Emily Record, 39 William Street, Herne Bay, Kent, CT6 5NR (01227 367355)

Other information: Grants are also made to organisations helping people in need.

Hildenborough

Helen Georgie Hills Charity

Eligibility: People who are sick and in need and live in the village of Hildenborough.

Types of grants: One-off grants according to need including those for convalescence, medical equipment, nursing fees and disability equipment.

Exclusions: Grants are not given to replace statutory responsibilities.

Annual grant total: Grants average around £900 a year.

Applications: In writing to the correspondent. Applications can be submitted directly by the individual, or through a social worker, Citizens Advice or other welfare agency or another third party. They are considered at any time.

Correspondent: David E Williams, 19 Elm Grove, Hildenborough, Tonbridge, Kent TN11 9HF (01732 833540)

Other information: The trust also supports local organisations.

Hothfield

The Thanet Charities

Eligibility: People in need who live in the parish of Hothfield.

Types of grants: One-off grants according to need.

Annual grant total: Grants average around £2,500 a year.

Applications: In writing to the correspondent.

Correspondent: Mrs Pat Guy, The Garden House, Bethesden Road, Hothfield, Ashford, Kent TN26 1EP (01233 612449)

Hythe

Anne Peirson Charitable Trust

Eligibility: People who live the parish of Hythe and are in need, due for example to hardship, disability or sickness. Support is primarily given for educational needs but grants for emergency needs will be made if financial hardship is demonstrated.

Types of grants: One-off grants ranging from £100 to £600. Recent grants were made towards nursery school fees, special needs for people with children who have disabilities, household goods and so on.

Exclusions: No grants are made where statutory support is available.

Annual grant total: In 2008 the trust had an income of £14,000 and a total expenditure of £16,000. Further information was not available.

Applications: In writing to the correspondent via either Citizens Advice, a social worker, health visitor, school head teacher or other third party. Grants are considered on an ongoing basis.

Correspondent: Mrs Ina Tomkinson, Trustee/Secretary, Tyrol House, Cannongate Road, Hythe, Kent, CT21 5PX (01303 260779)

Other information: Grants are also made to organisations.

Leigh

The Leigh United Charities

Eligibility: People in need who live in the ancient parish of Leigh.

Annual grant total: In 2008/09 the charities made grants totalling £38,000, which included monthly payments to 80 beneficiaries, annual Christmas grants to 99 individuals and grants to seven individuals under special circumstances.

Applications: In writing to the correspondent directly by the individual. Applications are considered throughout the year.

Correspondent: Sally Bresnahan, 3 Oak Cottages, High Street, Leigh, Tonbridge, Kent TN11 8RW (01732 838544; email: sally@bresnahan.co.uk)

Maidstone

The Edmett & Fisher Charity

Eligibility: People in need who are aged over 60 and live in the former borough of Maidstone (as it was before April 1974).

Types of grants: One-off and recurrent grants according to need. Christmas gifts have also been given in previous years.

Annual grant total: In 2008/09 the charity had an income of £6,400 and a total expenditure of £8,700.

Applications: On a form available from the correspondent to be submitted directly by the individual. Applications are usually considered twice a year.

Correspondent: R P Rogers, 72 King Street, Maidstone, Kent ME14 1BL (01622 698000)

The Hollands-Warren Charitable Trust

Eligibility: People in need of temporary medical and nursing services in their own homes and/or domestic help, who live in the old borough of Maidstone.

Types of grants: Grants towards the cost of such services and/or domestic help.

Annual grant total: In 2008/09 the trust had assets of £1.6 million and an income of £58,000. Grants were made totalling £96,000, all of which were paid to organisations.

Applications: In writing to the correspondent. Applications should be submitted directly by the individual.

Correspondent: Kim Harrington, c/o Brachers Solicitors, Somerfield House, 59 London Road, Maidstone, Kent ME16 8JH (01622 690691; fax: 01622 681430; email: kimharrington@ brachers.co.uk)

Other information: The trust states: 'The trustees do not have funds to monitor individual applications. Accordingly funds are allocated in bulk and individual applications are only considered via personal recommendation by a trustee.'

The Maidstone Relief-in-Need Charities

Eligibility: People in need, hardship or distress who live in the former borough of Maidstone.

Types of grants: One-off grants of up to around £300. Grants given include those for hospital expenses, electrical goods, convalescence, clothing, household bills, food, travel expenses, medical equipment, nursing fees, furniture, disability equipment and help in the home.

Annual grant total: In 2008/09 the trust had an income of £4,500 and a total expenditure of £3,200. Grants are given to both individuals and organisations.

Applications: Applications must be made through a social worker, health visitor, doctor or similar third party on a form available from the correspondent.

Correspondent: Debbie Snook, Maidstone Borough Council, Maidstone House, King Street, Maidstone, ME15 6JQ (01622 602030)

Margate

Margate and Dr Peete's Charity

Eligibility: People in need who live in the former borough of Margate (as constituted before 1974).

Types of grants: One-off and recurrent grants generally in the range of £50 to £250.

Annual grant total: In 2008/09 the charity had an income of £8,000 and a total expenditure of £5,200.

Applications: On a form available from the correspondent, to be submitted either directly by the individual or through a social worker, Citizens Advice or other welfare agency.

Correspondent: Hugh Mockett, 39 Hawley Square, Margate, Kent CT9 1NZ (01843 220567)

Rochester

Cliffe at Hoo Parochial Charity

Eligibility: People in need who live in the ancient parish of Cliffe-at-Hoo.

Types of grants: One-off grants according to need. For example, grants towards household bills and nursing fees.

Annual grant total: In 2008/09 the charity had an income of £6,000 and a total expenditure of £13,000. Around £6,500 worth of grants were given for welfare purposes.

Applications: In writing to the correspondent, to be submitted directly by the individual or a family member, or through a third party such as a social worker or Citizens Advice.

Correspondent: P Kingman, Clerk, 52 Reed Street, Cliffe, Rochester, Kent ME3 7UL (01634 220422; email: paul. kingman@btopenworld.com)

The William Mantle Trust

Eligibility: People in need who are over 60 and were either born in that part of Rochester which lies to the south and east of the River Medway, or have at any time lived in that part of the city for a continuous period of at least 15 years.

Types of grants: Recurrent grants of about £65 per person, per month.

Annual grant total: In 2009/10 the trust had an income of £9,200 and a total expenditure of £11,000.

Applications: On a form available from the correspondent. Applications should be submitted directly by the individual or through a third party on their behalf. They are considered on a regular basis.

Correspondent: Barbara Emery, Clerk, Administrative Offices, Watt's Almshouses, Maidstone Road, Rochester, Kent ME1 1SE (01634 842194; email: wattscharity@ btconnect.com)

Richard Watts and The City of Rochester Almshouse Charities

Eligibility: People in need who live in the city of Rochester.

Types of grants: Pensions for retired people and one-off grants towards a wide variety of needs, including clothing, electrical goods, travel expenses, medical equipment, furniture, disabled equipment and help in the home. In kind grants are also made. Grants are usually in excess of £50.

Annual grant total: In 2008 the charity had assets of £17 million and an income of £965,000. Grants were made totalling £43,000, which was distributed as follows:

Type	No. of Grants	£
Almhouse	17	2,700
Outpensions	10	9,000
Home help	37	29,000
Grants payable	5	2,500

Applications: In writing to the correspondent, directly by the individual or a family member. Applications can be submitted at any time and are considered on a monthly basis.

Correspondent: Mrs B A Emery, Watts Almhouses, Maidstone Road, Rochester, Kent ME1 1SE (01634 842194; email: wattscharity@btconnect.com)

Other information: Grants are also given to organisations which benefit the local community (£17,000 in 2008). The charity also runs an almshouse.

Sevenoaks

The Kate Drummond Trust

Eligibility: People in need who live in Sevenoaks, preference is given to young people.

Types of grants: The majority of grants are one-off.

Annual grant total: Grants tend to total around £2,000 each year.

Applications: In writing to the correspondent, with an sae if a reply is required.

Correspondent: The Rector, St Nicholas' Rectory, Rectory Lane, Sevenoaks, Kent TN13 1JA (01732 740340)

Tunbridge Wells

Miss Ethel Mary Fletcher's Charitable Bequest

Eligibility: Older people in need who live in the Tunbridge Wells area.

Types of grants: One-off and recurrent grants according to need.

Annual grant total: In 2008/09 the charity had an income of £12,000 and a total expenditure of £19,000.

Applications: In writing to the correspondent, through a social worker, Citizens Advice or other welfare agency. The charity has recently stated: 'funds are fully committed, although consideration will be given to extreme applications'.

Correspondent: Mrs S Currie, Thomson, Snell & Passmore, 3 Lonsdale Gardens, Tunbridge Wells, Kent TN1 1NX (01892 510000)

Other information: Occasional grants are made to organisations with similar objectives.

Wilmington

The Wilmington Parochial Charity

Eligibility: People in need, living in the parish of Wilmington, who are receiving a statutory means-tested benefit, such as Income Support, Housing Benefit or help towards their council tax.

Types of grants: Recurrent grants are available as follows: grocery vouchers of £30, cash grants of £10 at Christmas and heating grants of £60 at Easter.

Annual grant total: Welfare grants to individuals total about £8,500 a year. Educational grants total about £1,500 a year.

Applications: Applications should be submitted by the individual, or through a social worker, Citizens Advice or other welfare agency. The trustees meet in February and November. Urgent applications can be considered between meetings in exceptional circumstances.

Correspondent: Derek Maidment, 23 The Close, Dartford, DA2 7ES

Other information: Grants are also given to local schools at Christmas.

Norfolk

The Blakeney Twelve

Eligibility: Individuals who are older, infirm or disabled and who live in the parish of Blakeney, Morston and surrounding district.

Types of grants: One-off and recurrent grants, donations of coal and the payment of insurance.

Annual grant total: In 2008/09 the trust had an income of £8,900 and a total expenditure of £12,000. Grants usually total around £10,000.

Applications: In writing to the correspondent.

Correspondent: Christopher Scargill, 24 Kingsway, Blakeney, Holt, Norfolk, NR25 7PL (01263 741020)

The Calibut's Estate & the Hillington Charities

Eligibility: People in need, usually over 65, who live in Hillington and East Walton.

Types of grants: One-off and recurrent grants, generally ranging from £25 to £100.

Exclusions: Owner occupiers are not eligible for support.

Annual grant total: Between £600 and £800 a year is distributed in grants.

Applications: In writing to the correspondent to be submitted directly by the individual. Applications are considered in November.

Correspondent: William J Tawn, Trustee/Chair, 2 Wheatfields, Hillington, King's Lynn, Norfolk PE31 6BH (01485 600641)

The Anne French Memorial Trust

Eligibility: Members of the Anglican clergy in the diocese of Norwich.

Types of grants: Holiday and other relief-in-need grants.

Annual grant total: In 2008/09 the trust had assets of £4.2 million and an income of £253,000. Grants to individuals totalled around £59,000 and were broken down as follows:

Gifts to clergy	£45,000
Youth and training	£11,000
Training of the clergy	£2,500

Applications: In writing to the correspondent.

Correspondent: Christopher H Dicker, c/o Lovewell Blake, 66 North Quay, Great Yarmouth, Norfolk NR30 1HE (01493 335100; email: chd@lovewell-blake. co.uk)

Other information: The charity has a close association with the Bishop of Norwich Fabric Fund Trust and the Norwich Diocesan Board of Finance Ltd.

The King's Lynn & West Norfolk Borough Charity

Eligibility: People in need who live in the borough of King's Lynn and West Norfolk.

Types of grants: One-off grants up to £300 towards furniture (such as beds), washing machines, carpets, bedding, cookers, electric scooters and so on.

Exclusions: Grants are not given to relieve public funds.

Annual grant total: Grants usually total around £8,000 a year.

Applications: On a form available from the correspondent. Applications should be submitted through a social worker, Citizens Advice or other welfare agency. They are usually considered in March, June, September and December and should be received in the preceding month.

Correspondent: Veronica Stiles, Secretary to the Trustees, 54 Park Road, Hunstanton, Norfolk PE36 5DL (01485 533352)

The Lavender Trust

Eligibility: Christians, particularly young Christians, living in London, the south east counties and Norfolk.

Types of grants: One-off and recurrent grants according to need.

Annual grant total: In 2008/09 the trust had an income of £5,200 and a total expenditure of £5,000. Grants to individuals usually total around £2,500.

Applications: In writing to the correspondent at any time.

Correspondent: C D Leck, Trustee, Le Chalenet, Le Vier Mont, Grouville, Jersey JE3 9GF (01534 859662)

The Saham Toney Fuel Allotment & Perkins Charity

Eligibility: People in need who have lived in Saham Toney, Saham Hills or Saham Waite for at least two years.

Types of grants: Recurrent grants of between £40 and £120, to help with the cost of fuel.

Annual grant total: In 2009 the charity had both an income and expenditure of £5,000.

Applications: On a form available from the correspondent, submitted directly by the individual, giving details of dependants and income. Applications should be submitted in May for consideration in June.

Correspondent: Jill Glenn, Orchard House, 1 Cressingham Road, Ashill, Thetford, Norfolk IP25 7DG (01760 441738; email: jill@glenn8530. freeserve.co.uk)

The Shelroy Trust

Eligibility: Residents of East Norfolk and Norwich, with a preference for Christians, older people and people with disabilities.

Types of grants: One-off grants, ranging from £200 to £500 to cover a specific need.

Exclusions: The trust does not assist with bankruptcy costs.

Annual grant total: In 2008/09 the trust had an income of £33,000 and a total expenditure of £25,000. Grants to individuals for relief-in-need totalled around £4,600.

Applications: In writing to the correspondent at any time. Individuals applying for grants must provide full information and two referees are required. Applications can be made directly by the individual or through a social worker, Citizens Advice or other third party. They are considered at the trustees' quarterly meetings in March, June, September and December. The trust is not able to reply to unsuccessful applicants unless an sae is provided.

Correspondent: Roger Wiltshire, 4 Brandon Court, Brundall, Norwich NR13 5NW (01603 715605)

The Southery, Feltwell & Methwold Relief in Need Charity

Eligibility: People in need who live in the parishes of Southery, Feltwell and Methwold.

Types of grants: One-off grants in the range of £25 to £100. Grants are often given towards the costs of travel to and from hospital.

Annual grant total: About £1,000.

Applications: In writing to the correspondent. Applications are to be submitted by a third party such as a parishioner or committee member, and must be received by the application deadline of 31 March.

Correspondent: Mrs J K Hodson, 36a Lynn Road, Southery, Downham Market, Norfolk PE38 0HU (01366 377303)

Witton Charity

Eligibility: Pensioners and other people in need who live in Witton and Ridlington.

Types of grants: Grants of coal twice a year and food parcels at Christmas.

Annual grant total: Grants usually total about £1,000 each year.

Applications: In writing to the correspondent.

Correspondent: Beryl Lodge, Trustee, The Old Chapel, Chapel Road, Witton, North Walsham, NR28 9UA (01692 650546)

Banham

The Banham Parochial Charities

Eligibility: People in need who live in the parish of Banham.

Types of grants: One-off grants according to need. Grants have been given towards such things as heating bills, fuel, clothing and funeral expenses.

Annual grant total: Grants usually total about £7,000 a year.

Applications: In writing to the correspondent. Applications can be considered at any time.

Correspondent: Martin Baglin, Norfolk House, The Green, Banham, Norwich NR16 2AA (01953 887216)

Barton Bendish

The Barton Bendish Poor's Charity

Eligibility: Widows and people in need who live in Barton Bendish, including Eastmoor.

Types of grants: One-off grants of about £40 to help with fuel expenses during the winter and towards travel to hospitals and funeral expenses.

Annual grant total: Grants usually total around £1,000 a year.

Applications: In writing to the correspondent at any time throughout the year.

Correspondent: Freda Rumball, Clerk, 45 Church Road, Barton Bendish, King's Lynn, Norfolk PE33 9GF (01366 347324)

Burnham Market

The Harold Moorhouse Charity

Eligibility: Individuals in need who live in Burnham Market in Norfolk only.

Types of grants: One-off grants are made ranging from £50 to £200 for heating, medical care and equipment, travel to and from hospital, education equipment and school educational trips.

Annual grant total: About £15,000 for educational and welfare purposes.

Applications: In writing to the correspondent. Applications should be submitted directly by the individual in any month.

Correspondent: Mrs V A Worship, 75 Gwyn Crescent, Fakenham, Norfolk NR21 8NE (email: mikeandjeanw@ hotmail.co.uk)

Buxton with Lammas

Picto Buxton Charity

Eligibility: People in need who live in the parish of Buxton with Lamas.

Types of grants: One-off and recurrent grants of £100 to £200 towards household bills, food, living expenses and so on.

Annual grant total: In 2008/09 the trust made seven grants totalling £600 to individuals.

Applications: In writing to the correspondent directly by the individual or a family member, or through a third party such as a social worker or teacher. Applications are considered at any time.

Correspondent: Dick W Smithson, Clerk, Avandix, Crown Road, Buxton, Norwich NR10 5EN (01603 279203)

Other information: Educational help for needy families is also available. Grants are also made to organisations or groups within the parish boundary.

Diss

The Diss Parochial Charities Poors Branch

Eligibility: People in need who live in the town and parish of Diss.

Types of grants: One-off grants ranging between £30 and £200 are made for a range of welfare purposes, including bereavement and funeral expenses.

Annual grant total: In 2009 the charity had an income of £21,000 and a total expenditure of £17,000. Previously the majority of grants have been welfare-related, with a couple of awards made for educational purposes.

Applications: In writing through DWP, Citizens Advice, Diss Health Centre, Diss Town Hall or directly to the correspondent. They are considered upon receipt.

Correspondent: Cyril Grace, 2 The Causeway, Victoria Road, Diss, Norfolk, IP22 4AW (01379 650630; email: cj.grace@ btinternet.com)

Other information: The charity also supports local organisations.

Downham Market and Downham West

Downham Aid in Sickness

Eligibility: People who are sick, convalescent or infirm and live in the district of Downham Market or the parish of Downham West.

Types of grants: One-off and recurrent grants according to need.

Annual grant total: Income and expenditure for the charity is around £1,000 per year. It gives grants to both individuals and organisations.

Applications: In writing to the correspondent for consideration in May and November. Applications can be submitted directly by the individual or through a social worker, Citizens Advice or other welfare agency.

Correspondent: Philip Reynolds, Clerk, 39 Bexwell Road, Downham Market, PE38 9LH (01366 383385; email: p. reynolds@fsbdial.co.uk)

The Hundred Acre Charity – Dolcoal

Eligibility: People in need who live in Downham Market, Downham West, Stow Bardolph and Wimbotsham.

Types of grants: Fuel and food vouchers of around £15.

Annual grant total: In 2009 the charity had an income of £7,200 and a total expenditure of £7,300.

Applications: In writing to the correspondent, after local advertisements are placed in shops in the village. Applications can be submitted directly by the individual and are usually considered at the end of November.

Correspondent: R W Stannard, Riverside Farm, Birchfield Road, Nordelph, Downham Market, Norfolk PE38 0BP (01366 324217)

East Dereham

The East Dereham Relief-in-Need Charity

Eligibility: People in need who live in East Dereham.

Types of grants: Recurrent grants ranging from £35 to £100 including payments of coal and clothing vouchers.

Annual grant total: Grants average around £11,000 a year.

Applications: On a form available from the correspondent, submitted either directly by the individual or through a social worker, Citizens Advice or other welfare agency. Applications are considered in December.

Correspondent: Derek Edwards, Lansdown House, 3 Breton Close, Dereham, Norfolk, NR19 1JH (01362 695835)

Other information: One-off grants are also made to organisations helping people in the community.

East Tuddenham

The East Tuddenham Charities

Eligibility: People in need who live in East Tuddenham.

Types of grants: Christmas grants for fuel and occasional one-off grants.

Annual grant total: Grants are usually awarded totalling £1,800 a year, mostly for welfare purposes.

Applications: In writing to the correspondent.

Correspondent: Mrs Janet Guy, 7 Mattishall Road, East Tuddenham, Dereham, Norfolk NR20 3LP (01603 880523)

Feltwell

The Edmund Atmere Charity

Eligibility: People, generally aged over 70, (except in special cases of dire need) who have lived in Feltwell for at least 10 years. Grants have been made to people with multiple sclerosis or a similar condition and children who are sick.

Types of grants: One-off grants in the range of £10 to £250.

Annual grant total: Grants usually total around £2,000 a year.

Applications: In writing to: G Broadwater, Treasurer, 16 Nightingale Lane, Feltwell, Norfolk IP26 4AR. Applications can be submitted between 1 October and 1 November either directly by the individual or through a relevant third party. Applications are considered in November.

Correspondent: Edmund Lambert, Hill Farm, Feltwell, Thetford, Norfolk IP26 4AB (01842 828156)

Sir Edmund Moundeford's Educational Foundation

Eligibility: Individuals in need who live in Feltwell.

Types of grants: Fuel grants.

Annual grant total: In 2009 welfare grants totalled £8,800, the majority of which was given in Christmas fuel payments (£8,500) and the rest paid for football kits (£300).

Applications: In writing to the correspondent.

Correspondent: B L Hawkins, The Estate Office, 15 Lynn Road, Downham Market, Norfolk PE38 9NL (01366 387180)

Foulden

The Foulden Parochial Charities

Eligibility: People in need who live in Foulden.

Types of grants: One-off and recurrent grants according to need.

Annual grant total: Grants usually total around £1,000 a year.

Applications: In writing to the correspondent, directly by the individual or through a welfare agency. Applications are considered when necessary.

Correspondent: Robin Mears, 88 School Road, Foulden, Thetford, Norfolk, IP26 5AA (01366 328745)

Garboldisham

The Garboldisham Parish Charities

Eligibility: People in need who live in the parish of Garboldisham. Generally, this is covered by the Relief-in-Need Fund, although widows and those over 65 who have lived in the parish of Garboldisham for over two years may qualify for allowances given by the Fuel Allotment Charity.

Types of grants: One-off and recurrent grants in the range of £30 to £600. Grants in kind are also made.

Annual grant total: Welfare grants usually total around £1,000 per year.

Applications: Applications can be submitted directly by the individual, including specific details of what the grant is required for. They are usually considered in July and December.

Correspondent: P Girling, Treasurer, Sandale, Smallworth Common, Garboldisham, Diss, Norfolk IP22 2QW (01953 681646)

Gayton

The Gayton Fuel Allotments

Eligibility: People in need or distress who live in the administrative parish of Gayton, which includes the village of Gayton Thorpe.

Types of grants: One-off and recurrent grants from £25 according to need.

Annual grant total: Grants usually total around £1,100 a year.

Applications: In writing to the correspondent. Applications should be submitted directly by the individual or a family member.

Correspondent: Annmarie Parker, Journeys End, Wormegay Road, Blackborough End, King's Lynn, Norfolk PE32 1SG (01553 841464; email: annmarieparker@pcoffice.freeserve. co.uk)

The Gayton Relief-in-Need Charity

Eligibility: People in need who live in the parish of Gayton.

Types of grants: One off grants usually ranging from £10 to £100.

Annual grant total: About £3,000 a year. Grants are given to both individuals and organisations.

Applications: In writing to the correspondent, or through the vicar of Gayton Church.

Correspondent: Barry Steer, 12 St. Marys Court, Gayton, Northampton, NN7 3HP (01604 858886)

Gaywood

The Gaywood Poors' Fuel Allotment Trust

Eligibility: Older people who are in need and live in the parish of Gaywood.

Types of grants: Grants to help with fuel costs.

Annual grant total: Grants usually total about £3,000 each year.

Applications: In writing to the correspondent through social services.

Correspondent: Mrs M Lillie, 'Edelweiss', Station Road, Hillington, King's Lynn, Norfolk PE31 6DE (01485 600615)

Harling

Harling Fuel Allotment Trust

Eligibility: People in need living in Harling. (In exceptional cases, grants may be made to people resident immediately outside the parish).

Types of grants: One-off grants to assist with the purchase of fuel.

Annual grant total: Grants average around £600 a year.

Applications: On a form available from the correspondent at any time from any source; a brief financial statement will also be required.

Correspondent: David Gee, Clerk, Hanworth House, Market Street, East Harling, Norwich NR16 2AD (01953 717652; email: gee@harlingpc.org.uk)

Hilgay

The Hilgay Feoffee Charity

Eligibility: People in need who live in the parish of Hilgay.

Types of grants: One-off and recurrent grants according to need, including fuel vouchers and help towards costs of apprenticeship or training.

Annual grant total: In 2008 the charity had an income of £35,000 and a total expenditure of £32,000. Grants to individuals totalled just under £2,000, with £1,500 distributed in apprenticeship grants and £470 made in general grants.

Applications: In writing to the correspondent, directly by the individual. Applications are considered in June each year.

Correspondent: Mrs P Golds, Reeve Cottage, Wards Chase, Stow Bridge, King's Lynn, Norfolk PE34 3NN

Other information: The charity also makes grants to local schools.

Horstead with Stanninghall

The Horstead Poor's Land

Eligibility: People in need who live in Horstead with Stanninghall.

Types of grants: One-off and recurrent grants for amounts up to a maximum of £2,000.

Annual grant total: In 2008/09 the trust had an income of £8,700 and a total expenditure of £9,600. Grants totalled around £9,000.

Applications: Applications, in writing to the correspondent, can be submitted directly by the individual, through a recognised referral agency (such as a social worker, doctor or Citizens Advice) or other third party, and are considered throughout the year.

Correspondent: W B Lloyd, Watermeadows, 7 Church Close, Horstead, Norwich NR12 7ET (01603 737632; email: chadlloyd@btopenworld.com)

Other information: This trust also makes grants for educational purposes and to support village amenities.

Little Dunham

The Little Dunham Relief-in-Need Charities

Eligibility: People in need who live in Little Dunham.

Types of grants: One-off grants according to need.

Annual grant total: Grants usually total around £2,500 per year.

Applications: The trustees usually depend on their local knowledge, but also consider direct approaches from village residents.

Correspondent: Mrs Linda A Wrighton, Candlestick Cottage, Burrows Hole Lane, King's Lynn, Norfolk PE32 2DP (01760 725406)

Other information: Grants may be given to the local primary school, church and community organisations.

Lyng

The Lyng Heath Charity

Eligibility: People in need who have lived in the parish of Lyng for at least one year.

Types of grants: One-off and recurrent grants between £30 and £40, primarily for fuel.

Annual grant total: Grants usually total around £500 per year.

Applications: On a form available from the correspondent or any member of the committee at any time. Applications can be submitted directly by the individual and are considered in November.

Correspondent: P L Dilloway, Woodstock, Etling Green, Dereham, Norfolk NR20 3EY (01362 691243)

Other information: Grants are occasionally made to village organisations.

Marham Village

The Marham Poor's Allotment

Eligibility: People of a pensionable age who are in need and live in Marham Village.

Types of grants: One-off vouchers of £35 for food and fuel, to be spent in local shops.

Annual grant total: In 2008/09 the allotment had assets of £89,000 and an income of £31,000. Grants were made totalling £21,000.

Applications: In writing to the correspondent. Applications are considered in October.

Correspondent: Wendy Steeles, Jungfrau, The Street, Marham, Kings Lynn, Norfolk PE33 9JQ (01760 337286)

Northwold

The Northwold Combined Charities and Edmund Atmere Charity

Eligibility: People in need who live in the parish of Northwold.

Types of grants: One-off grants according to need. Aids for disabled people are also loaned by the charity.

Annual grant total: In 2008 the charity had both an income and expenditure of £3,000.

Applications: In writing to the correspondent directly by the individual.

Correspondent: Mrs Beryl Quilter, Clerk to the Charity, Briars Moat, 3 Hovell's Lane, Northwold, Thetford, Norfolk, IP26 5NA (01366 727472)

Norwich

Benevolent Association for the Relief of Decayed Tradesmen, their Widows and Orphans

Eligibility: People who are in need and live in Norwich or the parishes of Costessey, Earlham, Hellesdon, Catton, Sprowston, Thorpe St Andrew, Trowse with Newton and Cringleford. Preference is given to those who have carried on a trade in the area of benefit and their dependants.

Types of grants: One-off and recurrent grants according to need.

Exclusions: The trust does not assist with bankruptcy fees.

Annual grant total: In 2008/09 the charity had an income of £6,100 and a total expenditure of £2,000.

Applications: In writing to the correspondent.

Correspondent: Nicholas Saffell, c/o Brown & Co, The Atrium, St George's Street, Norwich, Norfolk NR3 1AB (01603 629871; fax: 01603 760756; email: nick.saffell@brown-co.com)

Norwich Consolidated Charities

Eligibility: People on low incomes who are permanent residents of the city of Norwich. Grants are generally only made to those with dependants, unless the application is supported by a social worker. Applicants, if eligible, must have evidence that they have applied, and been rejected, for a Social Fund loan.

Types of grants: One-off grants for welfare in the range of £50 to £500. Grants given include those for carpets, cookers, beds, washing machines as well as childcare costs for low income, single parents. Some assistance is given towards medical items if supported by a doctor and social worker and all other avenues of help have been explored.

Annual grant total: In 2008 the charities had assets of £23 million and an income of £1.7 million. Grants were made totalling £12,000, with an additional £104,000 given to residents of the charities almshouses.

Applications: On a form available from the correspondent either through a social worker, Citizens Advice or other welfare agency or directly by the individual. Please ring or write to the office to confirm eligibility. Applications are considered by the trustees at five committee meetings each year.

Generally applicants will be asked to attend for an interview or they will be visited.

Correspondent: The Clerk, 1 Woolgate Court, St Benedicts Street, Norwich, NR2 4AP (01603 621023; email: david. walker@norwichcharitabletrusts.org.uk)

Other information: Grants are also made to charitable institutions within Norwich for welfare purposes.

Norwich Town Close Estate Charity

Eligibility: Freemen of Norwich and their families who are in need.

Types of grants: One-off grants, for example towards decorating costs, house repairs, carpets, spectacles and dental work. Grants are occasionally given for holiday costs. Small regular pensions have also been made to older people.

Annual grant total: In 2008/09 the charity made grants to individuals totalling £228,000, these were broken down as follows:

- pension: £122,000
- educational: £100,000
- TV licence: £3,400
- relief in need: £2,400

Applications: On a form available from the correspondent. Applications are considered throughout the year. Applicants living locally will usually be required to attend for interview.

Correspondent: David Walker, Clerk to the Trustees, 1 Woolgate Court, St. Benedicts Street, Norwich, NR2 4AP (01603 621023; email: david.walker@ norwichcharitabletrusts.org.uk)

Old Buckenham

The Old Buckenham United Eleemosynary Charity

Eligibility: People in need who live in Old Buckenham, Norfolk. Preference for pensioners (over 65) but others are considered.

Types of grants: Normally recurrent grants in coal or cash in lieu for those without coal fires. Grants are currently £50 or equivalent and distributed yearly in early December. Cases considered to be of exceptional need may be given more.

Annual grant total: Grants usually total about £2,000 each year.

Applications: New applicants should write to the correspondent following posted notices around the parish each autumn. Applications are usually considered in early November and can be submitted either directly by the individual, or through another third party such as any of the ten trustees. Any relevant evidence of need is helpful, but not essential.

Correspondent: Joan Jenkins, Priest Hill House, 49 Fen Street, Old Buckenham, Norfolk NR17 1SR (01953 452716; fax: 01953 452716; email: add.j@linelone. net)

Pentney

The Pentney Charity

Eligibility: People over 65 who have lived in the parish of Pentney for the last two years are eligible for fuel grants. Other people in need may also apply for help.

Types of grants: One-off grants of £50 to £150 for fuel costs, travel to and from hospital, funeral expenses, medical expenses, disability equipment, clothing and household bills.

Exclusions: No grants are given where help is available from the social services.

Annual grant total: In 2008/09 the charity had an income of £14,000 and a total expenditure of £16,000. Grants were made totalling about £15,000 and were given to both individuals and organisations.

Applications: In writing to the correspondent either directly by the individual; through a social worker, Citizens Advice or other welfare agency; or by a third party on behalf on the individual, for example a neighbour or relative. Applications are usually considered twice a year.

Correspondent: Susan Smalley, Falgate Farm, Narborough Road, Pentney, King's Lynn, Norfolk PE32 1JD (01760 337534)

Saham Toney

The Ella Roberts Memorial Charity for Saham Toney

Eligibility: People in need who are older, sick or who have disabilities and live in Saham Toney.

Types of grants: One-off cash grants to cover half the cost of dentures, glasses, physiotherapy or dental treatment, up to a maximum of £100 per application.

Annual grant total: About £1,000.

Applications: On a form available from the correspondent, to be submitted directly by the individual or a family member. Applications are considered on receipt.

Correspondent: Rosemary Benton, Treasurer, 36 Richmond Road, Saham Toney, Thetford, Norfolk IP25 7ER (01953 881844)

Saxlingham

The Saxlingham Relief in Sickness Fund

Eligibility: People who have medical needs who live in Saxlingham Nethergate and Saxlingham Thorpe.

Types of grants: One-off grants are given to eligible applicants for medical and other needs, including grants towards fuel at Christmas.

Annual grant total: In 2009/10 the fund had an income of £3,200 and a total expenditure of £5,200.

Applications: In writing to the correspondent, to be considered as they arrive.

Correspondent: Mrs Jane Helen Turner, 4 Pitts Hill Close, Saxlingham, Nethergate, Norwich NR15 1AZ (01508 499623)

The Saxlingham United Charities

Eligibility: People in need aged 70 or over who have lived in the village of Saxlingham Nethergate for five or more years.

Types of grants: Recurrent grants for coal and electricity of £50 to £100 and one-off grants for widows and widowers.

Annual grant total: In 2008/09 the charities had an income of £3,700 and an income of £4,800. Grants are made for welfare and educational purposes.

Applications: In writing to the correspondent. Applications can be submitted directly by the individual and are usually considered in October.

Correspondent: Mrs Jane Turner, 4 Pitts Hill Close, Saxlingham, Nethergate NR15 1AZ

Shipdham

The Shipdham Parochial & Fuel Allotment

Eligibility: People in need who live in Shipdham.

Types of grants: One-off grants generally ranging from £50 to £350.

Annual grant total: In 2009/10 the trust had an income of £12,000 and a total expenditure of £14,000. Grants were made totalling about £13,000.

Applications: On an application form available from the correspondent. Applications are usually considered quarterly.

Correspondent: Helen Crane, Meadow Bank, Carbrooke Lane, Shipdham, Thetford, Norfolk IP25 7RP (01362 821440; email: hscmeadowbank@ yahoo.co.uk)

Other information: The trust also makes grants to organisations.

South Creake

The South Creake Charities

Eligibility: People in need who live in South Creake.

Types of grants: Mostly recurrent annual grants towards fuel of between £35 and

£100 per year. No grants are given to people in work.

Annual grant total: In 2008/09 the charities had an income of £5,400 and a total expenditure of £4,800.

Applications: In writing to the correspondent. Applications should be submitted directly by the individual and are considered in November; they should be received before the end of October.

Correspondent: The Vicar, The Vicarage, 18 Front Street, South Creake, Fakenham, Norfolk NR21 9PE (01328 823433)

Other information: Grants can also be given to schools and playgroups.

Swaffham

Swaffham Relief In Need Charity

Eligibility: People in need who live in Swaffham.

Types of grants: Grants have been given for a number of reasons, for example for school uniforms, to provide disabled access facilities or mobility scooters, towards the installation of central heating, to relieve long term debt and to provide basic home start up facilities such as washing machines, fridges, cookers and so on.

Annual grant total: In 2008/09 the charity had an income of £20,000 and a total expenditure of £18,000.

Applications: In writing to the correspondent.

Correspondent: Richard Bishop, The Town Hall, Swaffham, Norfolk, PE37 7DQ (01760 722922; email: reliefinneed@ swaffhamtowncouncil.gov.uk)

Other information: Grants are also made to organisations.

Swanton Morley

Thomas Barrett's Charity

Eligibility: Older people in need who live in Swanton Morley.

Types of grants: One-off and recurrent grants according to need.

Annual grant total: Grants usually total around £2,000 a year.

Applications: In writing to the correspondent directly by the individual. Applications are considered in June and December.

Correspondent: Nicholas Saffell, Brown and Co, The Atrium, St George's Street, Norwich NR3 1AB (01603 629871)

Walpole

The Walpole St Peter Poor's Estate

Eligibility: Older people over 65 who are in need and live in the old parishes of Walpole St Peter, Walpole Highway and Walpole Marsh.

Types of grants: Annual Christmas grants of £10 to individuals over the age of 65, limited to one per household.

Annual grant total: The trust distributes about £1,500 a year in grants.

Applications: In writing to the correspondent. Applications should be submitted directly by the individual and are considered in November.

Correspondent: Peter Lambert, Holmleigh House, French's Road, Walpole St Andrew, Wisbech, Cambridgeshire, PE14 7JF (01945 780218)

Other information: Grants are also made to college or university students for books.

Watton

The Watton Relief-in-Need Charity

Eligibility: People in need who live in Watton.

Types of grants: One-off grants according to need. Recent grants have been given towards medical equipment, funeral expenses, clothing, carpets, kitchen and household expenses and to older people at Christmas time.

Annual grant total: Grants usually total about £2,000 each year.

Applications: In writing to the correspondent either directly by the individual or via a social worker, Citizens Advice, welfare agency or through a friend or neighbour. Applications are usually considered quarterly.

Correspondent: Derek I Smith, 39 Dereham Road, Watton, Norfolk IP25 6ER (01953 884044; email: derek@ frenzymail.co.uk)

Other information: Grants are also made to organisations with similar objects.

Welney

The Bishop's Land Charity

Eligibility: People in need (men over 65 years and women over 60 years) who live in the parish of Welney.

Types of grants: Grants of around £12 per person each year.

Annual grant total: This charity has an annual total expenditure of around £1,000.

Applications: Applications should be made by personal attendance or a signed note, to St Mary's Church – Welney on the second Saturday of December.

Correspondent: Mrs P Copeman, 1 Chestnut Avenue, Welney, Wisbech, Cambridgeshire PE14 9RG (01354 610226; email: g8sww@aol.com)

Other information: The charity owns approximately 12 acres of land which is let, and the income is used to make a payout to the elderly residents of the village at Christmas.

William Marshall's Charity

Eligibility: Widows in need who live in the parish of Welney.

Types of grants: Grants of £100 paid quarterly.

Annual grant total: In 2009 the charity had assets of £1.4 million and an income of £44,000. Quarterly payments to widows totalled £7,800.

Applications: In writing to the correspondent. The list of recipients is reviewed quarterly.

Correspondent: Lynda Clarke-Jones, The Barn, Main Street, Littleport, Cambridgeshire CB6 1PH (01353 860449; email: littleportpc@btconnect.com)

Other information: The local church receives an annual grant out of the net income from land rents.

West Walton

Poor's Estate (The West Walton Poors' Charity)

Eligibility: Older people in need who live in the parish of West Walton.

Types of grants: One-off grants are usually given at Christmas time.

Annual grant total: In 2008/09 the charity had both an income and total expenditure of £3,000.

Applications: The grants are advertised locally every year, giving a closing date for applications.

Correspondent: Mrs J E Johnson, Clerk, c/o Frasers Solicitors, 27–29 Old Market, Wisbech, Cambridgeshire PE13 1NB (01945 468700)

Wiveton

The Charities of Ralph Greenway

Eligibility: People in need who are over 60 and have lived in the village of Wiveton for at least three years. Preference is given to widows. Consideration is also given to other villagers who are in need and have lived in the parish for three years.

Types of grants: Small weekly pensions and one-off fuel grants. Other needs can also be considered.

Annual grant total: In 2008/09 the charities had an income of £2,700 and a total expenditure of £3,400. In previous years grants for welfare purposes have totalled around £1,000.

Applications: Applications, on a form available from the correspondent, should be submitted directly by the individual and are considered twice a year. However, if a need arises, a special meeting can be convened.

Correspondent: Mrs Margaret L Bennett, 4 The Cottages, Blakeney Road, Wiveton, Holt, Norfolk NR25 7TN (01263 741384)

Other information: Educational grants are also available from a subsidiary charity, for young people up to university age, including young people who are starting work.

Woodton

Woodton United Charities

Eligibility: People in need who live in the parish of Woodton.

Types of grants: One-off and recurrent grants of £20 to £300 according to need. Annual grants are made to older people and people who are disabled. Contributions are also made towards funeral expenses.

Annual grant total: In 2008/09 the charities had both an income and total expenditure of £3,000.

Applications: In writing to the correspondent directly by the individual, including details of the nature of the need. Applications can be submitted at any time.

Correspondent: P B Moore, 6 Triple Plea Road, Woodton, Bungay, Suffolk NR35 2NS (01508 482375)

Wretton

The Jane Forby Charity

Eligibility: People in need who live in the parish of Wretton.

Types of grants: One-off and recurrent grants according to need.

Annual grant total: Grants usually total around £2,000 per year.

Applications: In writing to the correspondent, directly by the individual or by a third party aware of the circumstances. Applications are considered in November.

Correspondent: Sarah Jane Scarrott, Warren House, Brandon Road, Methwold, Thetford, IP26 4RL (01366 728238; email: sjscarrott@tesco.net)

Other information: Recent accounts have not been filed with the Charity Commission.

Oxfordshire

The Appleton Trust (Abingdon)

Eligibility: People in need who live in Appleton or Eaton.

Types of grants: One-off and recurrent grants in the range of £50 to £100, towards needs such as fuel and bereavement costs.

Annual grant total: In 2009 the trust had an income of £5,200 and a total expenditure of £4,100.

Applications: In writing to the correspondent, either directly by the individual or through an appropriate third party.

Correspondent: David J Dymock, 73 Eaton Road, Appleton, Abingdon, Oxfordshire OX13 5JJ (01865 863709; email: appleton.trust@yahoo.co.uk)

Other information: Grants are also given to local organisations and for educational purposes to former pupils of Appleton Primary School.

The Bampton Welfare Trust

Eligibility: People who live in the parishes of Bampton, Aston, Lew and Shifford, of any occupation, who are in need. Preference is given to children, young people and older people.

Types of grants: One-off grants which can be repeated in subsequent years at the discretion of the trustees. Grants given include food vouchers for a family awaiting benefit payment, heating allowance for older people in need and assistance in purchasing a washing machine for a single parent with multiple sclerosis.

Annual grant total: In 2009 the trust had an income of £7,400 and a total expenditure of £6,300.

Applications: Applicants are advised to initially discuss their circumstances with the correspondent, who will advise the applicant on what steps to take. This initial contact can be made directly by the individual, or by any third party, at any time.

Correspondent: David Pullman, Mill Green Cottage, Bampton, Oxon OX18 2HF (01993 850589; email: david@dpullman. plus.com)

The Banbury Charities – Bridge Estate

Eligibility: People in need who live within the former Borough of Banbury.

Types of grants: One-off and recurrent grants towards living costs, household essentials and so on.

Annual grant total: In 2009 the charities had assets of £4.4 million and an income of £368,000. Grants were made to 434 individuals at an average of £277 per grant, totalling £120,000.

Applications: In writing to the correspondent. Applicants are encouraged to obtain a letter of support from their social worker, carer or other person in authority to give credence to their application. If this is not available, the trust will often arrange to visit the applicant.

Correspondent: Anthony Scott Andrews, Clerk, 36 West Bar, Banbury, Oxfordshire OX16 9RU (01295 251234)

Other information: The Banbury Charities is a group of six registered charities including Bridge Estate Charity, Countess of Arran's Charity (known as Lady Arran's Charity), Banbury Almshouse Charity, Banbury Sick Poor Fund, Banbury Arts and Educational Charity and Banbury Welfare Trust.

Cozens Bequest

Eligibility: People need who live in the parishes of Tetsworth, Thame, Great Haseley, Stoke Talmage, Wheatfield, Adwell, South Weston, Lewknor and Aston Rowant.

Types of grants: One-off grants according to need.

Annual grant total: Grants usually total around £1,500 per year.

Applications: In writing to the correspondent.

Correspondent: Mr A Martin, 26 Marsh End, Tetsworth, Thame, Oxfordshire OX9 7AU (01844 281202)

Other information: Grants are also made to organisations.

Ducklington & Hardwick with Yelford Charity

Eligibility: People in need or hardship who live in the villages of Ducklington, Hardwick and Yelford.

Types of grants: One-off grants in the range of £75 to £200. Grants given include those towards heating for older people, assistance with playgroup fees, furniture, funeral expenses, conversion of rooms for people who are older or disabled, provision of telephones, spectacles, school holiday assistance and assistance with rent arrears.

Annual grant total: Welfare grants usually total around £2,000 per year.

Applications: In writing to the correspondent. Applications are considered in March and November, but emergency cases can be dealt with at any time.

Correspondent: Mrs Joyce Parry, 16 Feilden Close, Ducklington, Witney, Oxfordshire OX29 7XB (01993 705121)

Other information: Grants are also made to organisations such as clubs, schools and so on.

The Faringdon United Charities

Eligibility: People in need who live in the parishes of Faringdon, Littleworth, Great and Little Coxwell, all in Oxfordshire.

Types of grants: One-off grants towards clergy expenses for visiting the sick, domestic appliances, holidays, travel expenses, medical and disability equipment, furniture and food and so on.

Exclusions: Grants cannot be given for nursing/retirement home fees or the supply of equipment that the state is obliged to provide.

Annual grant total: In 2008/09 the trust had an income of £21,000 and a total expenditure of £8,800.

Applications: In writing to the correspondent throughout the year. Applications can be submitted either through Citizens Advice, a social worker or other third party, directly by the individual or by a third party on their behalf for example a neighbour, parent or child.

Correspondent: Vivienne Checkley, Bunting & Co, 7 Market Place, Faringdon, Oxfordshire, SN7 7HL (01367 243789; fax: 01367 243789)

Other information: Grants are also made for educational purposes and to organisations helping people in need.

The Lockinge & Ardington Relief-in-Need Charity

Eligibility: People in need who live in the parish of Lockinge and Ardington.

Types of grants: One-off and recurrent grants between £30 and £60.

Annual grant total: Grants usually total around £5,000 a year.

Applications: In writing to the correspondent by the individual. Applications are considered in March, July and November although urgent cases can be considered at any time.

Correspondent: Mrs A Ackland, c/o Lockinge Estate Office, Ardington, Wantage, Oxfordshire OX12 8PP (01235 833200)

Ellen Rebe Spalding Memorial Fund

Eligibility: To help disadvantaged women and children to adjust more easily to the pressure of modern life, and to promote those conditions of society that will enable people of different cultures and faiths to understand and appreciate one another.

Types of grants: Grants are at the discretion of trustees and are administered monthly throughout the year. Grants are only distributed to those who intend to further the objectives of the trust.

Many grants have been given to enable graduate students to study comparative religion at academic institutions. Others have been for travel either to conferences or to study a religion in the country where it is practised.

Annual grant total: In 2008 grants totalled £56,000.

Applications: Applications should be made through Oxfordshire Social Services.

Correspondent: The Secretary, PO Box 85, Wetherden, Stowmarket, Suffolk IP14 3NY (website: www.spaldingtrust.org.uk)

The Thame Welfare Trust

Eligibility: People in need who live in Thame and immediately adjoining villages.

Types of grants: One-off grants of amounts up to £1,000, where help cannot be received from statutory organisations. Recent grants have been given towards a single parent's mortgage repayments and a wheelchair for a person who is disabled.

Annual grant total: In 2008/09 the trust had an income of £42,000 and made grants totalling £15,000. Grants are made to organisations and individuals for relief-in-need and education.

Applications: In writing to the correspondent mainly through social workers, probation officers, teachers, or a similar third party but also directly by the applicant.

Correspondent: J Gadd, 2 Cromwell Avenue, Thame, Oxfordshire, OX9 3TD (01844 212 564)

The Peter Ward Charitable Trust

Eligibility: People in need who live in Oxfordshire.

Types of grants: One-off and recurrent grants according to need.

Annual grant total: In 2008/09 the trust had assets of £994,000 and an income of £54,000. There was one grant made to an individual totalling £3,000.

Applications: In writing to the correspondent.

Correspondent: M D Stanford-Tuck, Trustee, A J Carter & Co, 22b High Street, Witney, Oxfordshire OX28 6RB (01993 703414; fax: 01993 778052)

Other information: Grants are also made to organisations (£81,000 in 2008/09). The trust has stated that: 'grants to individuals are not normally considered, and unsolicited applications are not encouraged'.

Bletchington

The Bletchington Charity

Eligibility: People in need who live in the parish of Bletchington, in particular people who are elderly or infirm.

Types of grants: Grants to people who are elderly and infirm at Christmas and Easter towards fuel bills and other needs. Help is given for travel, chiropody and television licences. Otherwise one-off grants for social welfare, education and relief-in-sickness according to need.

Annual grant total: In 2009 the charity had both an income and total expenditure of £10,000.

Applications: Generally as the trustees see a need, but applications can be made in writing to the correspondent by the individual or by a social worker, doctor or welfare agency.

Correspondent: John Smith, Quarry Bank House, Gibraltar Hill, Enslow, Oxon OX5 3AZ (01869 331307)

Other information: The charity also seeks to support any educational, medical and social needs that will benefit the village community as a whole.

Eynsham

The Eynsham Consolidated Charity

Eligibility: People in need who live in the ancient parish of Eynsham (which covers Eynsham and part of Freeland).

Types of grants: One-off grants ranging from £50 to £200.

Annual grant total: Grants to individuals generally total around £800 a year.

Applications: In writing to the correspondent including details of what the grant is for, the personal circumstances of the applicant and the cost involved. Applications can be submitted through a social worker, Citizens Advice or other welfare agency; or by the individual. They are considered quarterly, usually in January, April, August and October.

Correspondent: Robin Mitchell, 20 High Street, Eynsham, Witney, Oxfordshire OX29 4HB (01865 880665)

Other information: This charity also gives grants to organisations.

Great Rollright

The Great Rollright Charities

Eligibility: People who are in need and live in the ancient parish of Great Rollright.

Types of grants: One-off grants towards, for example, fuel payments and to older people at Christmas.

Exclusions: No grants are given for the relief of rates, taxes or other public funds.

Annual grant total: In 2008/09 the charities had an income of £11,000 and a total expenditure of £9,900.

Applications: In writing to the correspondent.

Correspondent: Paul Dingle, Tyte End Cottage, Tyte End, Great Rollright, Chipping Norton, Oxfordshire OX7 5RU (01608 737676)

Other information: The charities also give to local organisations.

Henley-on-Thames

The John Hodges Charitable Trust

Eligibility: People in need living in the Parish of St Mary the Virgin, Henley-On-Thames and the surrounding area.

Types of grants: One-off and recurrent grants towards, for example, white goods, carpets and flooring, clothing, mobility aids, bankruptcy fees and heating bills.

Annual grant total: In 2009/10 the trust had assets of £355,000 and an income of £18,000. Grants were made totalling £6,600

Applications: In writing to the correspondent.

Correspondent: Miss Julie Griffin, 3 Berkshire Road, Henley-On-Thames, RG9 1ND

Over Norton

The Over Norton Welfare Trust

Eligibility: People in need who live in the parish of Over Norton.

Types of grants: One-off grants for electricity stamps or coal vouchers to the value of £45 to £60.

Annual grant total: Grants usually total about £3,000 each year.

Applications: In writing to the correspondent.

Correspondent: Mrs B Thompson, 1 The Green, Over Norton, Chipping Norton, Oxfordshire OX7 5PT (01608 644438)

Oxford

The City of Oxford Charities

Eligibility: People in need who have lived in the city of Oxford for at least three years and who have a low income. Priority is given to children and people who are elderly, disabled or have a medical condition.

Types of grants: One-off grants of up to £600. Grants have been awarded for furniture to people moving home; washing machines; recuperation holidays for people with disabilities or medical problems and/or their carers; baby equipment; and wheelchairs and mobility scooters.

Annual grant total: In 2009 the charity made relief-in-need/sickness grants totalling £60,000.

Applications: Application forms are available from the correspondent or can be downloaded from the website. They should be submitted through a social worker, Citizens Advice or other welfare agency, but can be accepted from individuals. Applications are considered at meetings of the trustees which are held every six weeks. Applications should specify exactly what the money is for and the cost, as applications without exact costings will be delayed.

Correspondent: The Administrator, The Office, Stones Court, St Clements, Oxford, OX4 1AP (01865 553043; email: david@oxfordcitycharities.fsnet.co.uk; website: www.oxfordcitycharities.org)

Other information: Grants are also made to organisations.

The Stanton Ballard Charitable Trust

Eligibility: Individuals in need who live in the city of Oxford and the immediate area.

Types of grants: Small one-off grants according to need.

Annual grant total: In 2008/09 the trust had assets of £2.6 million and an income of £104,000. Grants to individuals totalled about £1,000.

Applications: On an application form available from the correspondent on receipt of an sae. Applications should be made through social services, probation officers or other bodies and are considered five times a year.

Correspondent: The Secretary, PO Box 81, Oxford OX4 4ZA (08707 605032)

Sibford Gower

The Town Estate Charity

Eligibility: People in need who live in the civil parish of Sibford Gower.

Types of grants: One-off and recurrent grants. The trust also provides free home chiropody treatment.

Annual grant total: In 2009 the charity made grants totalling £5,700 for general benefit and relief in need purposes.

Applications: In writing to the correspondent, to be considered at the twice-yearly trustees meeting.

Correspondent: Mrs Jean White, Whitts End, Sibford Gower, Banbury, Oxfordshire OX15 5RT (01295 780529)

Other information: Grants are also given to organisations.

Souldern

The Souldern United Charities

Eligibility: People in need who live in the parish of Souldern.

Types of grants: One-off and recurrent grants according to need.

Annual grant total: In 2009/10 the trust had an income of £8,000 and a total expenditure of £14,000.

Applications: In writing to the correspondent.

Correspondent: Mrs C Couzens, 2 Cotswold Court, Souldern, Bicester, Oxfordshire OX27 7LQ (01869 346694)

Steventon

The Steventon Allotments & Relief-in-Need Charity

Eligibility: People in need who live in Steventon.

Types of grants: One-off grants for the provision of food, fuel and personal items such as clothing, repair or replacement of faulty domestic equipment or furniture, loans of electric wheelchairs, provision of special equipment to chronically sick people and grants or loans for unforeseen difficulties. Large loans will need to be secured as a percentage of a second mortgage.

Annual grant total: In 2009 the charity made grants to 42 individuals totalling £19,000.

Applications: In writing to the correspondent. The trust advertises regularly in the local parish magazine. Applications should include full details of income and expenditure, and will be treated in strictest confidence.

Correspondent: Patrina Effer, 19 Lime Grove, Southmoor, Abingdon, Oxfordshire OX13 5DN (email: sarinc@patrina.co.uk)

Wallingford

The Wallingford Municipal & Relief-in-Need Charities

Eligibility: People in need who live in the former borough of Wallingford.

Types of grants: One-off grants for necessities including the payment of bills, shoes, cookers, fridges and so on. Payments are made to local suppliers, cash grants are not made directly to the individual.

Annual grant total: Grants total approximately £6,700 a year.

Applications: On a form available from the correspondent, submitted either directly by the individual or through a local organisation. Trustees meet about every three months, although emergency cases can be considered. Urgent cases may require a visit by a trustee.

Correspondent: A Rogers, Town Clerk, 9 St Martin's Street, Wallingford, Oxfordshire OX10 0AL

Suffolk

The Cranfield Charitable Trust

Eligibility: People who live in Suffolk and are in need.

Types of grants: One-off grants ranging from £100 to £1,500.

Annual grant total: In 2009/10 the trust had an income of £10,000 and a total expenditure of £18,000.

Applications: In writing to the correspondent.

Correspondent: Mrs S Price, Trustee, 22 Lucas Lane, Ashwell, Hertfordshire, SG7 5LN (01502 675278)

Other information: The charity also gives grants to organisations.

The Martineau Trust

Eligibility: 'Deserving people living in Suffolk who suffer directly or indirectly from an illness or disability and are in need.'

Types of grants: One-off grants up to £200 towards: clothing, including wigs, required following illness or surgery; bedding, including protective covers and special mattresses; travel for hospital appointments or visits; domestic appliances where the need arises through illness; mobility aids, scooters and 'riser chairs' not provided by the PCT or local authority; respite breaks for the sick and their carers; and, heating costs where the need arises specifically from illness.

Exclusions: No grants for: holidays and breaks for families; child care; alternative treatment therapies e.g. acupuncture; normal household running expenses; recurring grants; applications not relating to an illness or disability; and, equipment that should be provided by the PCT or local authority.

Annual grant total: The trust has an annual grant budget of around £20,000.

Applications: On a form available from the correspondent or to download from the website. Applications must be completed by a suitable third party, such as a social worker, health visitor, nurse or charity welfare officer.

Correspondent: Roger Lay, Clerk, 5 Princethorpe Road, Ipswich, Suffolk IP3 8NY (01473 724951; email: clerk@ martineautrust.org.uk; website: www. martineautrust.org.uk)

The Mills Charity

Eligibility: Individuals in need who live in Framlingham or are very closely associated with the town.

Types of grants: One-off grants towards hospital expenses, electrical goods, living costs, household bills, travel expenses, medical equipment, furniture and disability equipment.

Annual grant total: In 2008/09 the charity had assets of £6.7 million and an income of £358,000. Grants to individuals totalled £1,800.

Applications: In writing to the correspondent. Applications should outline the need and why it has arisen and preferably include a supporting letter from a professional or other suitable referee. They are considered every two months.

Correspondent: Chairman of the Trustees, PO Box 1703, Framlingham, Suffolk, IP13 9WW (01728 638038; email: info@ themillscharity.co.uk; website: www. themillscharity.co.uk)

Other information: Grants were also made to five organisations amounting to £33,000.

Aldeburgh

Aldeburgh United Charities

Eligibility: People in need who live in the town of Aldeburgh. The trust describes its current constituency of beneficiaries as including, 'senior citizens, people in specific sensitive situations, young and young minded people, and people in the development stage of life's experience'.

Types of grants: One-off and recurrent grants according to need.

Annual grant total: Grants are approximately £1,500 each year.

Applications: In writing to the correspondent.

Correspondent: Lindsay Lee, Administrator, Moot Hall, Market Cross Place, Aldeburgh, IP15 5DS (01728 452158; email: aldeburghtc@ moothall1.fsnet.co.uk)

Other information: The charity is a combination of various charities in Aldeburgh, some hundreds of years old.

Brockley

The Brockley Town & Poor Estate (Brockley Charities)

Eligibility: People in need who live in Brockley village.

Types of grants: In previous years recurrent grants of £65–£70 have been given, usually as rebates on electricity bills paid directly to the suppliers.

Annual grant total: In 2008 the trust had an income of £1,700 and a total expenditure of £1,500. Grants are made for educational and welfare purposes.

Applications: In writing to the correspondent, to be submitted directly by the individual or through relatives or family friends.

Correspondent: Jean English, Trustee, Old Shop Cottage, Mill Road, Brockley, Bury St. Edmunds, LP29 4AR (01284 830219)

Bungay

Bungay Charities

Eligibility: People in need who live in the parish of Bungay.

Types of grants: One-off grants averaging £200, to meet a wide range of needs. Older people, for example, can receive help with the costs of telephone installation, heating costs or travel to hospital, children from needy families can receive grants to pay for school trips or clothing and single parents can be given grants to help pay for furniture, washing machines and so on.

Annual grant total: About £1,500 a year.

Applications: In writing to the correspondent.

Correspondent: Peter Morrow, 11 Wharton Street, Bungay, Suffolk NR35 1EL (01986 893148)

Carlton and Calton Colville

The Carlton Colville Fuel & Poors' Allotment Charity

Eligibility: People in need who live in the ancient parish of Carlton Colville, with a preference for older people who only receive the basic state pension and have limited savings.

Types of grants: Recurrent grants for fuel and heating costs.

Annual grant total: In 2009 the charity had an income of £17,000 and a total expenditure of £13,000.

Applications: On a form available from the correspondent. Applications can be submitted directly by the individual or through a social worker, Citizens Advice or other welfare agency.

Correspondent: Keith Vincent, 23 Wannock Close, Carlton Colville, Lowestoft, Suffolk NR33 8DW (01493 852411)

Chediston

The Chediston United Charities, Town & Poors' Branch

Eligibility: People in need who live in the civil parish of Chediston.

Types of grants: One-off and recurrent grants according to need ranging from £5 to £100. Grants are given for alarm systems for older people, hospital transport, Christmas gifts, and to every child of school age or younger.

Annual grant total: About £2,000.

Applications: In writing to the correspondent. Applications are considered throughout the year, although mainly in November. The trust has no formal application procedure as requests are usually made personally to the trustees.

Correspondent: David Fossett, Clerk, Mount Pleasant Farm, Chediston, Halesworth, Suffolk, IP19 0BA (website: www.onesuffolk.co.uk)

Chelsworth

The Chelsworth Parochial Charity

Eligibility: People in need who live in the parish of Chelsworth.

Types of grants: One-off grants or payment for items, services and facilities that will reduce the person's need, hardship or distress.

Annual grant total: About £1,000.

Applications: In writing to the correspondent. The charity stated in early 2006 that it is 'solely for residents' and they will not accept any unsolicited applications.

Correspondent: Alison Russell, Tudor Cottage, 70 - 72 The Street, Chelsworth, Ipswich, Suffolk, IP7 7HU (01449 740438)

Corton

Corton Poors' Land Trust

Eligibility: People in need who live in the ancient parish of Corton.

Types of grants: Recent grants have included Christmas gifts for older people, funding for chiropody treatment, taxi fares to hospital and payment for home alarm installation and rent.

Annual grant total: In 2008/09 the trust had an income of £23,000 and a total expenditure of £17,000. Further details of beneficiaries were not available.

Applications: In writing to the correspondent. Applications can be submitted at any time directly by the individual or by an appropriate third party.

Correspondent: Ms C Murray, 48 Fallowfields, Lowestoft, NR32 4XN

Other information: Grants are also made to organisations which carry out the charity's aims within the area of benefit.

Dennington

The Dennington Consolidated Charities

Eligibility: People in need who live in the village of Dennington.

Types of grants: One-off and recurrent grants according to need including travel expenses for hospital visiting of relatives, telephone installation for emergency help calls for people who are elderly and infirm, and Christmas grants to older people. Grants range from £50 to £250.

Exclusions: The trust does not make loans, nor does it make grants where public funds are available unless they are considered inadequate.

Annual grant total: In 2009 the charities had an income of £14,000 and a total expenditure of £22,000. The charities give approximately £500 each year for educational purposes and £3,000 for welfare.

Applications: In writing to the correspondent. Applications are considered throughout the year and a simple means test questionnaire may be required by the applicant.

Grants are only made to people resident in Dennington (a small village with 500 inhabitants). The charities do not respond to applications made outside this specific geographical area.

Correspondent: W T F Blakeley, Clerk, Thorn House, Saxtead Road, Dennington, Woodbridge, Suffolk IP13 8AP (01728 638031)

Dunwich

The Dunwich Town Trust

Eligibility: People in need who live in the parish of Dunwich.

Types of grants: One-off grants are usually of around £250. Grants can be made for residents in temporary distress, helping with travel costs to and from hospital and bereavement. Other payments can be made for contact alarms for the elderly and infirm, fuel allowances and Christmas allowances and emergency relief for people in Dunwich.

Annual grant total: In 2009 grants to individuals for welfare purposes totalled £7,000.

Applications: Write to the correspondent requesting an application form.

Correspondent: John Cary, Black Pig Cottage, Monestary Hill, Dunwich, Suffolk, IP17 3DR (01728 648 927)

Other information: Formerly known as 'Dunwich Pension Fund'.

Earl Stonham

Earl Stonham Trust

Eligibility: People in need who live in the parish of Earl Stonham.

Types of grants: One-off grants up to a maximum of £200.

Annual grant total: In 2008/09 the trust had an income of £4,800 and a total expenditure of £6,100. Grants usually total around £3,000 overall, and can be made for both welfare and educational purposes.

Applications: In writing to the correspondent, to be submitted either by the individual or through a social worker, Citizens Advice or other third party. Applications are considered in March, June, September and December.

Correspondent: S R M Wilson, College Farm, Forward Green, Stowmarket, Suffolk IP14 5EH

Other information: Grants can also be made to organisations.

Framlingham

The Florence Pryke Charity

Eligibility: People in need who live in the ecclesiastical parish of Framlingham.

Types of grants: One-off grants ranging from £30 to £50 towards, for example, hospital travel costs and medical care.

Annual grant total: Grants total around £800 a year.

Applications: In writing to the correspondent either directly by the individual or through a relevant third person. Applications are considered monthly.

Correspondent: Sally Butcher, 90 Station Road, Framlingham, Woodbridge, IP13 9EE (01728 723365)

Gisleham

The Gisleham Relief in Need Charity

Eligibility: People in need who live in the parish of Gisleham.

Types of grants: One-off and recurrent grants according to need, but usually averaging about £50. Recent grants have been given for household bills, travel expenses and disability aids.

Annual grant total: In 2009/10 the charity had an income of £880 and a total expenditure of £2,500.

Applications: In writing to the correspondent: to be submitted directly by the individual. Applications are considered at any time.

Correspondent: Elizabeth Rivett, 2 Mill Villas, Black Street, Gisleham, Lowestoft, Suffolk NR33 8EJ (01502 743189; email: waveney.hospice@virgin.net)

Other information: A luncheon club for older people is held at the local school once a month during term time. Those that are deemed not able to pay are paid for by the trust.

Gislingham

The Gislingham United Charity

Eligibility: People in need who live in Gislingham.

Types of grants: Usually one-off grants according to need. For example, the cost of hospital travel for older people, playgroup fees or specific items or equipment.

Annual grant total: In 2009 the charity had both an income and total expenditure of £10,000.

Applications: In writing to the correspondent directly by the individual or verbally via a trustee.

Correspondent: R Moyes, 37 Broadfields Road, Gislingham, Eye, Suffolk IP23 8HX (01379 788105; email: moyes5@aol.com)

Other information: The charity also gives educational grants and supports village organisations and ecclesiastical causes.

Halesworth

The Halesworth United Charities

Eligibility: People in need who live in the ancient parish of Halesworth.

Types of grants: One-off grants according to need. Recent examples include travel abroad for educational purposes, medical equipment or tools needed for a trade.

Annual grant total: Grants usually total around £3,000.

Applications: In writing to the correspondent, directly by the individual or through a social worker, Citizens Advice or other welfare agency. Applications can be submitted at any time for consideration in January, July and December, or any other time if urgent.

Correspondent: Janet Staveley-Dick, Clerk, Hill Farm, Primes Lane, Blyford, Halesworth, Suffolk, IP19 9JT

Other information: Grants are also made to individuals for educational purposes.

Ipswich

The John Dorkin Charity

Eligibility: People in need who live in the ancient parish of St Clement's, Ipswich (broadly speaking the south-eastern sector of Ipswich bounded by Back Hamlet/ Foxhall Road and the River Orwell). Preference for the widows and children of seamen.

Types of grants: One-off cash grants of about £200 towards electrical goods, clothes, holidays, furniture and disability equipment.

Exclusions: No grants to applicants resident outside the beneficial area.

Annual grant total: Grants average around £6,000 a year.

Applications: In writing to the correspondent at any time, giving details of financial circumstances. Applications can be submitted through a third party such as a social worker, or through an organisation such as Citizens Advice or other welfare agency, and are considered twice a year.

Correspondent: G R Sutton, Kerseys Solicitors, 32 Lloyds Avenue, Ipswich, Suffolk IP1 3HD (01473 213311)

Mrs L D Rope's Third Charitable Settlement

Eligibility: People who are on a low income and live in the Ipswich area.

Types of grants: One-off grants according to need. Grants given include those for food, clothing and furnishings/furniture.

Exclusions: Grants are not given for new overseas projects, individuals working overseas, replacement of statutory funding, debt relief, health/palliative care or educational fees.

Annual grant total: In 2008/09 the settlement made grants to 806 individuals totalling £186,000.

Applications: In writing to the correspondent either directly by the individual or through a social worker, Citizens Advice or other welfare agency. Apply in a concise letter, saying what is needed and how the trust may be able to help. It helps to include details of household income (including benefits) and expenses, and a daytime telephone number.

Correspondent: C M Rope, Crag Farm, Boyton, Woodbridge, Suffolk IP12 3LH (01473 333288)

Other information: Grants are also made to organisations.

Kirkley

Kirkley Poor's Land Estate

Eligibility: Individuals in need who live in the parish of Kirkley.

Types of grants: One-off grants ranging from £50 to £300. Vouchers of £20 are also available to pensioners each winter to help towards the cost of groceries.

Annual grant total: In 2008/09 the charity had assets of £1.4 million and an income of £88,000. Grants were made totalling £40,000 and were distributed as follows:

Grants to individuals (welfare)	£60
Grants to individuals (education)	£1,900
Grocery voucher scheme	£15,000
Grants to organisations	£23,000

Applications: In writing to the correspondent.

Correspondent: Lucy Walker, 4 Station Road, Lowestoft, Suffolk NR32 4QF (01502 514964)

Lakenheath

The Charities of George Goward & John Evans

Eligibility: People in need who live in the parish of Lakenheath in Suffolk.

Types of grants: One-off grants of £25 to £300 according to need.

Exclusions: No help is given for the relief of public funds.

Annual grant total: In 2008 the charity had an income of £18,000 and a total expenditure of £14,000.

Applications: In writing to the correspondent. Applications can be submitted either directly by the individual or a family member, through a third party such as a social worker or teacher, or through an organisation such as Citizens Advice. They should be received by February and August for consideration in March and September respectively. Applications should include a brief financial situation and receipts are required for book grants.

Correspondent: Mrs Mary Crane, 3 Roughlands, Lakenheath, Brandon, Suffolk IP27 9HA (01842 860445)

Other information: Grants are also made to organisations and to individuals for welfare purposes.

Lowestoft

The Lowestoft Church and Town Relief in Need Charity

Eligibility: People in need who have lived in the area of the old borough of Lowestoft for at least three years.

Types of grants: On average ten one-off grants are made each year ranging from £50 to £500 for items and services such as furniture, clothing, childcare costs, help for disabled people, debt relief, help with funeral costs and so on.

Annual grant total: In 2008/09 the charity had an income of £9,000 and a total expenditure of £4,200.

Applications: In writing to the correspondent, directly by the individual. Applications are considered monthly.

Correspondent: John M Loftus, Clerk, Lowestoft Charity Board, 148 London Road North, Lowestoft, Suffolk NR32 1HF (01502 718700; fax: 01502 718709)

Other information: The charity also makes grants to local organisations.

The Lowestoft Fishermen's & Seafarers' Benevolent Society

Eligibility: Widows, children and dependants of fishermen and seamen lost at sea from Lowestoft vessels, who are in need.

Types of grants: Monthly payments and one-off grants.

Annual grant total: About £30,000 a year.

Applications: In writing to the correspondent.

Correspondent: H G Sims, Secretary, 10 Waveney Road, Lowestoft, Suffolk NR32 1BN (01502 574312)

The Lowestoft Maternity & District Nursing Association

Eligibility: People in a nursing or caring profession and retired nurses/carers who live/work in the borough of Lowestoft and either: (a) are retired and on a low income; (b) have a long-term disability; or (c) are experiencing short-term hardship, usually through illness.

Types of grants: On average 30 one-off and recurrent grants are made a year according to need, ranging from £25 to £250.

Annual grant total: Grants average around £1,500 a year.

Applications: In writing to the correspondent through community nurses or carers. Applications are usually considered in October.

Correspondent: Jennifer Grint, Trustee, 2 Hollow Lane, Carlton Colville, Lowestoft, NR33 8HP

Melton

The Melton Trust

Eligibility: People living in Melton who are in need, hardship or distress.

Types of grants: One-off and recurrent grants according to need. All pensioners in the parish can receive Christmas grants.

Annual grant total: Grants usually total about £2,500 per year.

Applications: Previous research suggested that the trust does not want people to apply, but they do 'try to give to everyone' (who is eligible).

Correspondent: Rev Michael Hatchett, Melton Rectory, Station Road, Melton, Woodbridge IP12 1PX (01394 380279; email: meltontrust.suffolk@googlemail.com)

Mendlesham

Mendlesham Town Estate Charity

Eligibility: People who are in need and live in the parish of Mendlesham, Suffolk.

Types of grants: One-off grants towards, for example, heating, hospital visiting and associated special needs, including bereavement.

Annual grant total: Grants to individuals usually total around £4,000 each year.

Applications: In writing to the correspondent. Applications can be submitted directly by the individual or through a third party such as a social worker or Citizens Advice.

Correspondent: Mrs S C Furze, Beggars Roost, Church Road, Mendlesham, Stowmarket, Suffolk IP14 5SF (01449 767770)

Other information: Grants are also made to the Church Estate Charity for the upkeep of St Mary's Church.

Mildenhall

The Mildenhall Parish Charities

Eligibility: Pensioners, widowers and widows in need who live in the parishes of Mildenhall and Beckrow.

Types of grants: The majority of the trust's giving is achieved through annual payments of £10 per person. One-off cash grants up to £500 towards travelling expenses to hospital, assistance to persons preparing to enter into a trade or profession and subscriptions to homes or hostels for infirm or homeless persons are also available.

Annual grant total: In 2008 the trust had an income of £15,000. Grants were made to over 1,300 residents totalling £13,000.

Applications: In writing to the correspondent either directly by the individual or through a recognised third party. Applications are considered three times a year.

Correspondent: Vincent Coomber, Clerk, 22 Lark Road, Mildenhall, Bury St. Edmunds, IP28 7LA (01638 718079)

Pakenham

The Pakenham Charities for the Poor

Eligibility: People in need who live in Pakenham.

Types of grants: One-off and recurrent grants of £20 to £1,250. Grants given include those for fuel, alarms for people who are elderly, disability equipment, medical equipment, hospital expenses, clothing and travel expenses.

Annual grant total: Grants usually total around £4,500 per year.

Applications: In writing to the correspondent either directly by the individual, through a third party such as a social worker, or through an organisation such Citizens Advice or other welfare agency. Applications are considered in early December and should be received by 30 November.

Correspondent: Christine Cohen, Clerk, 5 St Mary's View, Pakenham, Bury St Edmunds, Suffolk IP31 2ND (01359 232965)

Other information: Grants are also made to organisations which benefit the elderly, the sick or the poor of the parish.

Reydon

The Reydon Trust

Eligibility: People in need who live in the parish of Reydon.

Types of grants: One-off grants towards hospital expenses, clothing, food, travel costs and disability equipment. Vouchers are also given out at Christmas time.

Annual grant total: In 2008/09 the trust had assets of £473,000 and an income of £23,000. Grants were made totalling £6,900.

Applications: In writing to the correspondent. Applications can be submitted either directly by the individual, through a third party such as a social worker or via a doctor or health centre. They are considered upon receipt.

Correspondent: H C A Freeman, 22 Kingfisher Crescent, Reydon, Southwold, Suffolk IP18 6XL (01502 723746)

Risby

The Risby Fuel Allotment

Eligibility: People in need who live in the parish of Risby.

Types of grants: Annual grants, primarily to buy winter fuel, although also for other needs.

Annual grant total: Around £9,000, with £3,000 being given in fuel grants.

Applications: Applications made outside the specific area of interest (the parish of Risby) are not acknowledged.

Correspondent: Mrs P Wallis, 3 Woodland Close, Risby, Bury St Edmunds, Suffolk IP28 6QN

Rushbrooke

Lord Jermyn's Charity

Eligibility: People in need who are over 60 and live in the parish of Rushbrooke.

Types of grants: One-off grants according to need. Recent grants have been given for electricity, coal or other fuel, chiropody treatment, taxis for shopping and Christmas hampers.

Annual grant total: In 2008/09 the charity had an income of £6,700 and a total expenditure of £8,300.

Applications: In writing to the correspondent, either directly by the individual or through a third party.

Correspondent: Mrs W Cooper, Estate Office, Rushbrooke, Bury St Edmonds, Suffolk IP30 0EP (01284 386276)

Stanton

The Stanton Poors' Estate Charity

Eligibility: People in need who live in the parish of Stanton and are in receipt of means-tested benefits. Grants can be made in special cases of need or hardship outside these criteria at the trustees' discretion.

Types of grants: Grants generally range between £40 and £90, although larger applications may be considered.

Annual grant total: In 2009/10 the charity had an income of £3,800 and a total expenditure of £3,500.

Applications: In writing to the correspondent, for consideration in November.

Correspondent: Susan Buss, Treasurer, 3 Shepherds Grove Park, Stanton, Bury St Edmunds, Suffolk, IP31 2AY (01359 250388)

Stowmarket

The Stowmarket Relief Trust

Eligibility: People in need who live in the town of Stowmarket and its adjoining parishes including the parish of Old Newton with Dagworth.

Applicants must have approached all sources of statutory benefit. People on Income Support will normally qualify. People in full-time paid employment will not normally qualify for assistance, but there are possible exceptions. People with substantial capital funds are also ineligible.

Types of grants: Normally one-off, but recurrent grants have been given in special circumstances. Recent grants have been made for the purchase and repair of white goods; payment of modest arrears (rent, council tax, electricity, gas, water and telephone charges); repayments resulting from the overpayment of state benefits; carpets and floor coverings; beds, bedding and household furniture; electric wheelchairs and riser/recliner chairs; living/household expenses; car repairs; medical aids; and, clothing and footwear. Grants generally range from about £15 to £700, although in exceptional circumstances awards may exceed £1,000.

Annual grant total: In 2008/09 the trust had assets of £1.2 million and an income of £71,000. Grants were made to 187 individuals totalling £45,000. A further £25,000 was distributed to four institutions.

Applications: On a form available from the correspondent. Applications should be submitted through a third party such as a social worker, probation officer, Citizens Advice or doctor. Applications are considered at trustee meetings held three times a year, though urgent cases can be dealt with between meetings.

Correspondent: C Hawkins, Kiln House, 21 The Brickfields, Stowmarket, Suffolk IP14 1RZ (01449 674412; email: colinhawkins08@aol.com)

Stutton

The Charity of Joseph Catt

Eligibility: People in need who live in the parish of Sutton only.

Types of grants: One-off grants and loans to help with fuel, hospital travel expenses, convalescent holidays, household goods and clothing.

Annual grant total: In 2009 the trust had an income of £9,200 and a total expenditure of £7,500.

Applications: Applications can be submitted by the individual, or through a recognised referral agency (e.g. social worker, Citizens Advice or doctor) and are considered monthly. They can be submitted to the correspondent, or any of the trustees at any time, for consideration in May and November.

Correspondent: Keith R Bales, 34 Cattsfield, Stutton, Ipswich, Suffolk IP9 2SP (01473 328179)

Other information: The charity also supports local almshouses.

Sudbury

The Sudbury Municipal Charities

Eligibility: Older people (generally those over 70) who are in need and live in the borough of Sudbury.

Types of grants: Ascension Day and Christmas gifts, usually in the range of £10 to £30. Grants for special cases of hardship are also available.

Annual grant total: Grants usually total about £2,500 each year.

Applications: Grants are usually advertised in the local newspaper when they are available.

Correspondent: Adrian Walters, Clerk, Longstop Cottage, The Street, Lawshall, Bury St Edmunds IP29 4QA (01284 828 219; email: a.walters@sclc. entadsl.com)

Other information: The charities also make grants to organisations.

Walberswick

The Walberswick Common Lands

Eligibility: People in need who live in Walberswick.

Types of grants: Grants include quarterly payments to 17 individuals, towards gardening, telephone rental and television licence payments and Christmas cash and vouchers. One-off grants in the range of £35 to £1,200 are made for larger items and other emergencies.

Annual grant total: Welfare grants usually total around £6,000 per year.

Applications: In writing to the correspondent through a social worker, Citizens Advice or other welfare agency, or directly by the individual or through a relative or neighbour. Applications are considered in February, April, June, August, October and December.

Correspondent: Mrs Jayne Tibbles, Lima Cottage, Walberswick, Southwold, Suffolk IP18 6TN

Other information: Grants are also made to individuals for educational purposes and to organisations.

Surrey

The Banstead United Charities

Eligibility: People in need who live in the ancient parish of Banstead and Kingswood.

Types of grants: One-off grants, usually up to £500. Grants have been given towards funeral expenses, equipment for people who are disabled, travel for hospital treatment and rehabilitation, children's clothing and a small number of educational grants.

Annual grant total: Grants usually totalled around £1,500 a year.

Applications: In writing to the correspondent. Applications can be submitted directly by the individual or through a social worker, Citizens Advice or other welfare agency. They are considered throughout the year.

Correspondent: Michael Taylor, 6 Garratts Lane, Banstead, SM7 2DZ (01737 355827)

John Beane's Eleemosynary Charity (Guildford)

Eligibility: People in need living in the administrative county of Surrey.

Types of grants: One-off or recurrent grants according to need.

Annual grant total: In 2009/10 the charity made grants to 119 individuals totalling £27,000.

Applications: On a form available from the correspondent, submitted through a social worker, health visitor, Citizens Advice or other welfare agency.

Correspondent: B W France, 4 Henderson Avenue, Guildford GU2 9LP (01483 504180)

The Bookhams, Fetcham & Effingham Nursing Association Trust

Eligibility: People in need who are sick, convalescent, disabled or infirm who live in Great Bookham, Little Bookham, Fetcham and Effingham.

Types of grants: Grants of between £100 and £1,500 for items, services or facilities which will alleviate the discomfort or assist the recovery of such people, where these facilities are not available from any other sources.

Annual grant total: In 2008/09 the trust had an income of £9,300 and a total expenditure of £9,500. Grants to individuals and local organisations totalled around £9,000.

Applications: Applications should be referred through medical or social services, not directly from the public.

Correspondent: Margaret Blow, Secretary, 1a Howard Road, Great Bookham, Leatherhead, Surrey KT23 4PW (01372 452054)

Lady Noel Byron's Nursing Association

Eligibility: People in need of medical or welfare assistance who live in the parishes of East and West Horsley.

Types of grants: One-off or recurrent grants according to need for medical or welfare related purposes only. This has included grants towards holidays, equipment and such like.

Annual grant total: Grants total around £1,000 to individuals each year.

Applications: In writing to the correspondent. Applications can be made directly by the individual or through a social worker, other welfare agency or third party. They are considered at any time.

Correspondent: J R Miles, Postboys, Cranmore Lane, West Horsley, Leatherhead, Surrey KT24 6BX (01483 284141)

Other information: Grants are also made to organisations.

The Churt Welfare Trust

Eligibility: People in need who live in the parish of Churt and its neighbourhood.

Types of grants: One-off grants usually in the range of £10–£1,000.

Exclusions: The trust cannot commit to repeat or renew grants.

Annual grant total: In 2009 the trust had an income of £36,000 and a total expenditure of £54,000. Grants were made totalling £12,000.

Applications: In writing to the correspondent.

Correspondent: Mrs E Kilpatrick, Hearn Lodge, Spats Lane, Headley Down, Bordon, Hampshire GU35 8SU (01428 712238)

Other information: Grants are also given to organisations.

The Cranleigh & District Nursing Association

Eligibility: People in need who are sick and poor and live in the parishes of Cranleigh and Ewhurst.

Types of grants: One-off grants ranging from £25 to £500. Recent grants have been made towards carpets, phone rental, MedicAlert bracelets, chiropody, hospital visits and pavement vehicles.

Annual grant total: About £2,000 a year.

Applications: In writing to the correspondent through a social worker, Citizens Advice or other welfare agency.

Correspondent: Gill Bowles, 8 Mower Place, Cranleigh, GU6 7DE (01483 276213)

The Dempster Trust

Eligibility: People in need, hardship or distress who live in Farnham and the general neighbourhood.

Types of grants: One-off grants or help for limited periods only. Grants have in the past been given towards nursing requisites, to relieve sudden distress, travelling expenses, fuel, television and telephone bills, clothing, washing machines, televisions, radios, alarm systems and so on. Grants range from £50 to £500.

Exclusions: Help is not given towards rent, rates or house improvements.

Annual grant total: In 2008/09 the trust had an income of £14,000 and a total expenditure of £15,000.

Applications: On a form available from the correspondent to be submitted through a doctor, social worker, hospital, Citizens Advice or another welfare agency. Applications can be considered at any time.

Correspondent: Peter Jeans, Trustee, 21 Broomleaf Road, Farnham, GU9 8DG

The Ewell Parochial Trusts

Eligibility: People in need who live, work or are being educated in the ancient ecclesiastical parish of Ewell and the domain of Kingswood.

Types of grants: One-off or recurrent grants according to need.

Annual grant total: In 2009 the trust made grants to individuals totalling £24,000, distributed as follows:

Disadvantaged children	£6,600
Hardship awards	£5,000
Christmas grants	£4,600
Heating/living grants	£4,500
Pensions	£3,800

Applications: In writing to the correspondent. Applications which do not meet the eligibility criteria will not be acknowledged.

Correspondent: Miriam Massey, 19 Cheam Road, Ewell, Epsom, Surrey KT17 1ST (020 8394 0453; email: mirimas@globalnet.co.uk)

The Godstone United Charities

Eligibility: People in need who live in the old parish of Godstone (Blindley Heath, South Godstone and Godstone Village).

Types of grants: Food vouchers are usually given in December and March. One-off grants are also available.

Annual grant total: In 2008/09 the charities had an income of £6,500 and a total expenditure of £6,700.

Applications: In writing to the correspondent: either directly by the individual, through a relevant third party or via a social worker, Citizens Advice or other welfare agency. Applications should include relevant details of income,

outgoings, household composition and reason for request. All grants are paid directly to the supplier.

Correspondent: Mrs P Bamforth, Bassett Villa, Oxted Road, Godstone, Surrey RH9 8AD (01883 742625)

Other information: The charities also make grants to local organisations.

Oakdene Foundation

Eligibility: People in need who live in Greater London and Surrey.

Types of grants: One-off and recurrent grants according to need.

Annual grant total: In 2008/09 grants were made to both organisations and individuals totalling £18,000.

Applications: In writing to the correspondent. The foundation does not respond to unsolicited applications.

Correspondent: P A Tilley, Gastons Meadow, Oakdene Road, Bookham, Leatherhead, Surrey KT23 3HS (01372 453802; email: ptilley@nildram.co.uk)

The Henry Smith Charity (Eastbrook Estate)

Eligibility: Widows or people over 60 who are in need, of good character and have lived in the parishes of Long Ditton and Tolworth for the past five years.

Types of grants: Grants to be spent on heating fuel, clothing and electricity bills at named retailers.

Annual grant total: Grants usually total around £2,100 a year.

Applications: In writing to the correspondent. Applications are considered in December and January and must include details of the applicant's age and length of residence in the parish.

Correspondent: Ron Howard, Trustee, 4 Cholmley Terrace, Portsmouth Road, Thames Ditton, Surrey KT7 0XX (email: ron_286@yahoo.co.uk)

The Henry Smith Charity (Frimley)

Eligibility: People in need who live in the former parish of Frimley (Frimley, Frimley Green, Camberley and Mytchett).

Types of grants: One-off grants ranging from £100 to £200 towards clothing, bedding, furniture, disability equipment and electrical goods.

Annual grant total: Grants average around £600 a year.

Applications: In writing to the correspondent through a social worker, Citizens Advice or other welfare agency.

Correspondent: Derek McManus, Surrey Heath Borough Council, Surrey Heath House, Knoll Road, Camberley, Surrey

GU15 3HD (01276 707302; email: derek.mcmanus@surreyheath.gov.uk)

The Henry Smith Charity (I Wood Estate)

Eligibility: People over 60 who are in need and live in Chertsey, Addlestone, New Haw and Lyne, Surrey.

Types of grants: Recurrent fuel vouchers of £40, which can be used as part-payment of fuel bills.

Annual grant total: In 2008/09 the charity had an income of £21,000 and a total expenditure of £19,000.

Applications: In writing to the correspondent either through a social worker, Citizens Advice or other third party or directly by the individual. Applications can be considered at any time during the year.

Correspondent: Bernard Fleckney, c/o Committee Section, Civic Offices, Runnymede Borough Council, Station Road, Addlestone, Surrey KT15 2AH (01932 425620)

The Henry Smith Charity (Puttenham and Wanborough)

Eligibility: People in need who live in Puttenham and Wanborough parishes.

Types of grants: One-off grants for needy people who do not have an income other than pensions.

Exclusions: Grants are not given to people who are working or who own their house.

Annual grant total: The charity receives around £1,000 a year, allocated by Henry Smith's (General Estate) Charity, the majority of which is distributed in individual grants.

Applications: In writing to the correspondent, submitted in October for consideration in November.

Correspondent: David Knapp, No. 2 Old School House, School Hill, Seale, Surrey GU10 1HY (01483 887772; fax: 01483 887757; email: dsk@hartbrown.co.uk)

Other information: Grants are also given for the benefit of the parish as a whole.

The Henry Smith Charity (Richmond)

Eligibility: People experiencing hardship or distress who live in Richmond, Ham, Petersham and Kew.

Types of grants: One-off grants ranging up to £250. Recently the greatest number of grants have been made to unemployed single parents, towards children's clothing and fuel bills.

Annual grant total: Grants usually total around £2,000 per year.

Applications: In writing to the correspondent, from referring bodies such as social services, health authority or a Citizens Advice. Applications are considered at trustees' meetings in February, March, May, June, September, November and December.

Correspondent: Catherine Rumsey, The Richmond Charities, 8 The Green, Richmond, Surrey TW9 1PL (020 8948 4188; fax: 020 8948 6224; email: richmondcharities@ richmondcharities.org.uk)

The Henry Smith Charity (Send and Ripley)

Eligibility: People in need who live in Send and Ripley, and have done so for five years.

Types of grants: One-off annual grants of £30 a year to around 50 or 60 people in Send and a similar number in Ripley. Other grants are available from any remaining funds, and have included money towards a wheelchair for a disabled student.

Annual grant total: The annual income is about £4,500, all of which is available in grants.

Applications: In writing to the correspondent. Applications can be submitted directly by the individual, through a social worker, Citizens Advice or any other welfare agency or third party on behalf of the individual. Applications are considered as they arrive.

Correspondent: Geoffrey A Richardson, Emali, 2 Rose Lane, Ripley, Surrey GU23 6NE (01483 225322)

The Surrey Association for Visual Impairment

Eligibility: People who are blind or partially-sighted and who live in the administrative county of Surrey.

Types of grants: Small one-off grants are given when absolutely necessary. Grants are usually to help pay for equipment required to overcome a sight problem or a sudden domestic need.

Annual grant total: In 2009/10 the association had assets of £1.8 million and an income of £1.6 million. A budget of £5,000 is allocated for grants to individuals and to local clubs/classes. During the year £3,100 of this was distributed to individuals.

Applications: On a form available from the correspondent. Applications can be submitted at any time by the individual or through a social worker, welfare agency, club or any recognised organisation for blind or partially-sighted people.

Correspondent: Lance Clarke, Chief Executive, Rentwood, School Lane, Fetcham, Leatherhead, Surrey KT22 9JX (01372 377701; fax: 01372 360767; email: info@sa-vi.org.uk; website: www. surreywebsight.org.uk)

Other information: The association's main focus is the provision of services, advice and information for visually impaired people. It runs a resource centre equipped with a wide range of aids, equipment and media, some of which are provided free of charge. It also provides guidance on benefit claims and advice and support to young people and parents.

The Windlesham United & Poors Allotment Charities

Eligibility: Mainly elderly people and people with disabilities, who are in need and live in the parishes of Bagshot, Lightwater and Windlesham.

Types of grants: One-off grants mainly in the form of small heating grants.

Annual grant total: Grants usually total around £5,000 per year.

Applications: In writing to the correspondent at any time.

Correspondent: Mrs D V Christie, Clerk to the Trustees, 4 James Butler Almshouses, Meade Court, Bagshot, Surrey, GU19 5NH

The Witley Charitable Trust

Eligibility: Children and young people aged under 20 and older people aged over 60 who are in need and who live in the parishes of Witley and Milford.

Types of grants: One-off grants of £25 to £300, towards, for example, telephone, electricity and gas debts (up to about £150) usually paid via social services, and medical appliances not available through the Health Service. At Christmas about 40 food hampers are given.

Exclusions: The trust does not give loans or for items which should be provided by statutory services.

Annual grant total: Around £3,000 each year.

Applications: In writing to the correspondent, to be submitted through nurses, doctors, social workers, the clergy, Citizens Advice and so on but not directly by the individual. Applications are usually considered in early February and September, although emergency applications can be considered throughout the year.

Correspondent: Daphne O'Hanlon, Triados, Waggoners Way, Grayshott, Hindhead, Surrey GU26 6DX (01428 604679)

The Wonersh Charities

Eligibility: Older people and people with a disability who live in the parishes of Wonersh, Shamley Green and Blackheath.

Types of grants: A cash grant is given to each of the named people at Christmas. One-off grants are also available.

Annual grant total: In 2009/10 the trust had an income of £5,200 and a total expenditure of £2,100.

Applications: In writing to the correspondent preferably through a third party such as a Citizens Advice, trustee of the charity, local clergy or other organisation. Applications are usually considered in early July and early December.

Correspondent: Molly Howard, Pen Pell, Barnett Lane, Wonersh, Guildford GU5 0RZ (01483 893857)

Abinger

The Henry Smith Charity (Abinger)

Eligibility: People in need who live in the ancient parish of Abinger.

Types of grants: One-off or recurrent grants according to need.

Annual grant total: In 2008/09 the charity had an income of £11,000 and a total expenditure of £10,000. Grants are given to both individuals and organisations.

Applications: In writing to the correspondent.

Correspondent: Caroline Sack, The Rectory, Abinger Lane, Abinger Common, Dorking, Surrey RH5 6HZ (01306 737160)

Other information: The charity is also known as the 'Abinger Consolidated Charities'.

Ashford

Ashford Relief in Need Charities

Eligibility: People in need who live in the ancient parishes of Ashford and Laleham.

Types of grants: One-off grants according to need.

Annual grant total: In 2008/09 the charities had an income of £11,000 and a total expenditure of £7,000. Grants to individuals usually total around £3,000.

Applications: In writing to the correspondent. Applications can be made either directly by the individual, or through a third party such as a social worker, Citizens Advice or relative.

Correspondent: Peter G Harding, 8 Portland Road, Ashford, TW15 3BT (01784 252590; email: pjlr_2000@yahoo. co.uk)

Other information: Grants are also made to organisations.

Betchworth

Betchworth United Charities & Henry Smith Charity

Eligibility: People in need who live in the ancient parish of Betchworth.

Types of grants: One-off grants usually ranging from £60 to £250. The majority of funding is given for welfare purposes but a small amount is also available for educational needs under the Margaret Fenwick fund.

Annual grant total: Grants usually total around £9,000 per year.

Applications: In writing to the correspondent to be submitted by a third party, such as, a doctor, minister or social worker. Applications are considered at trustee meetings.

Correspondent: Mrs Sally Drayson, Hambledon, Blackbrook Road, Dorking, Surrey RH5 4DT (01306 888727)

Bisley

The Henry Smith Charity (Bisley)

Eligibility: People in need who live in Bisley.

Types of grants: Grants to assist with food costs are distributed twice a year.

Annual grant total: Grants total around £1,000 each year.

Applications: On a form available from the correspondent to be submitted directly by the individual.

Correspondent: Mrs Marjorie Tilbury, 267 Arethusa Way, Bisley, Woking, Surrey GU24 9BU (01483 489701; email: mjtilbury@btinternet.com)

Bletchingley

The Bletchingley United Charities

Eligibility: People in need, hardship or distress who live in the parish of Bletchingley.

Types of grants: One-off and recurrent grants in the range of £20 to £200 towards medical items, welfare support, gas and electricity and equipment such as cookers, fridges, freezers and so on.

Exclusions: Grants are not given for rates, taxes or other public funds.

Annual grant total: In 2008/09 the charities had an income of £10,000 and a total expenditure of £9,300.

Applications: In writing to the correspondent or to David Martin (94 High Street, Bletchingley, Surrey). Applications can be submitted either directly by the individual, through a third party such as a social worker, or through an organisation such as a Citizens Advice or other welfare agency. They are considered throughout the year.

Correspondent: Mrs C A Bolshaw, Cleves, Castle Street, Bletchingley, Surrey RH1 4QA (01883 743000; email: chrisbolshaw@hotmail.co.uk)

Other information: Care organisations working locally are also considered.

Bramley

The Henry Smith Charity (Bramley)

Eligibility: People in need who live in the parish of Bramley, Surrey.

Types of grants: One-off grants according to need.

Annual grant total: Grants usually total about £3,000 each year.

Applications: In writing to the correspondent; there are no application forms. The letter should contain as much information as possible about why support is required.

Correspondent: Rachael Hill, Bramley Village Hall, Hall Road, Bramley, Guildford GU5 0AX (01483 894138; email: bramleyparish@gmail.com; website: www.bramleyparish.co.uk)

Other information: This charity is also known as the 'Smiths Charity'.

Byfleet

The Byfleet United Charities

Eligibility: People in need who have lived in the ancient parish of Byfleet for at least a year.

Types of grants: Monthly pensions. One-off grants can also be given for items such as cookers, heaters, vacuum cleaners and nursery schools fees.

Annual grant total: In 2009 the charity had assets of £6 million and an income of £476,000. Grants were made to 89 individuals totalling £42,000 and a further £197,000 was paid in pensions.

Applications: By writing to, or telephoning, the correspondent. Applications can be made directly by the individual or through a third party such as a social worker, Citizens Advice, local GP or church. Applicants are usually visited and assessed.

Correspondent: Mrs C M Heath, Administrator, Stoop Court, Leisure Lane, West Byfleet, Surrey KT14 6HF (01932 340943)

Other information: The charity gives money to local organisations who work in a similar field (£27,000 in 2009). It also operates a sheltered housing complex of 24 flats, which are available to those in real need.

This charity is an amalgamation of smaller trusts, including the Byfleet Pensions Fund.

Capel

The Henry Smith Charity (Capel)

Eligibility: People in need who have lived in Beare Green, Capel and Coldharbour, usually for at least five years.

Types of grants: Mostly Christmas vouchers for older people redeemable at several local stores. The vouchers are £20 for couples and £15 for single people.

Annual grant total: Grants usually total about £2,000 each year.

Applications: In writing to the correspondent directly by the individual or a family member. Applications should be received by 1 November and are considered in December.

Correspondent: Mrs J Richards, Old School House, Coldharbour, Dorking, Surrey RH5 6HF (01306 711885)

Charlwood

John Bristow and Thomas Mason Trust

Eligibility: People who are in need who live in the parish of Charlwood as constituted on 17 February 1926, including Hookwood and Lowfield Heath.

Types of grants: One-off and recurrent grants and loans are given according to the need. Recent grants have been given for the annual service charge for community alarms for older people, riding lessons for individuals who are disabled, new shoes for a child and a holiday for a child with disabilities.

Annual grant total: In 2009 the trust had assets of £2.3 million and an income of £84,000. The trust made grants totalling £134,000, of which roughly £1,000 went to individuals.

Applications: On a form available from the correspondent or to download from the website. Applications can be submitted directly by the individual or through a third party. They will normally be considered within two weeks but can be dealt with more quickly in urgent cases.

Correspondent: Marie Singleton, Trust Secretary, 20 The Meadway, Horley, Surrey RH6 9AW (01293 883950; email: trust.secretary@jbtmt.org.uk; website: www.jbtmt.org.uk)

Other information: This trust is an amalgamation of the Thomas Alexander

Mason Trust and Revd John Bristow's Charity.

Smith & Earles Charity

Eligibility: People with disabilities or those over 65 and in need who have lived in the old parish of Charlwood for at least five years.

Types of grants: One-off and recurrent grants of up to £80.

Annual grant total: In 2008/09 the charities had an income of £6,100 and a total expenditure of £5,800. Grants to individuals for welfare purposes have previously totalled around £4,000.

Applications: On a form available from the correspondent. Applications for one-off (usually larger) grants should be submitted through a recognised referral agency (such as a social worker, Citizens Advice or other welfare agency). Applications for recurrent grants can be submitted directly by the individual. They are considered in November. Details of any disability or special need should be given.

Correspondent: Robin Pacey, Ivy Cottage, Russ Hill Road, Charlwood, Horley, Surrey RH6 0EJ (01293 863933)

Other information: Help is also given towards the hiring of halls for meetings for older people, hospices and school requirements.

Cheam

Cheam Consolidated Charities

Eligibility: People in need who live in Cheam. Preference is given to older people.

Types of grants: One-off and recurrent grants, of £50 to £200.

Annual grant total: Grants average around £3,600 a year. They are given to both individuals and organisations.

Applications: In writing to the correspondent, for consideration at the start of May and November. Applications can be made either directly by the individual, or via a social worker, Citizens Advice or other welfare agency.

Correspondent: Darren Miller, Trustee, The Rectory, 33 Mickleham Gardens, Sutton, SM3 8QJ (020 8641 4664)

Chertsey

The Chertsey Combined Charity

Eligibility: People in need who live in the electoral divisions of the former urban district of Chertsey.

Types of grants: Grants are given in the form of fuel vouchers, Christmas grants and one-off grants.

Annual grant total: In 2009/10 the charity had an income of £53,000 and a total expenditure of £58,000. Grants to individuals were made totalling £2,500.

Applications: On a form available from the correspondent.

Correspondent: M R O Sullivan, Secretary, PO Box 89, Weybridge, Surrey KT13 8HY

Other information: The charity also makes grants to organisations (£36,000 in 2009/10).

Chessington

Chessington Charities

Eligibility: People in need who live in the parish of St Mary the Virgin, Chessington. Applicants must have lived in the parish for at least one year.

Types of grants: Grants are usually one-off in the range of £30 to £250. Donations include those given to older people (with low income) at Christmas and for items such as special food, furniture, medical equipment, electrical goods and clothing.

Exclusions: Grants are not given 'as a dole' or to pay debts. Applicants must live in the Parish of St Mary the Virgin, which excludes those who live in the rest of the Chessington postal area.

Annual grant total: In 2008/09 the charities had an income of £4,300 and total expenditure of £6,600.

Applications: On a form available from the correspondent to be submitted either directly by the individual or through a social worker, Citizens Advice or other agency. Other applications are considered throughout the year. A home visit will be made by a trustee to ascertain details of income and expenditure and to look at the need. Applications for Christmas grants for older people must be received by 1 November and are distributed in this month.

Correspondent: The Clerk, 26 Bolton Road, Chessington, Surrey KT9 2JB (020 8397 4733)

Other information: Grants are also given to local organisations which help older people or people with disabilities such as Chessington Voluntary Care and Arthritis Care. Educational grants are also available for individuals.

Chobham

The Chobham Poor Allotment Charity

Eligibility: People in need who live in the ancient parish of Chobham, which includes the civil parishes of Chobham and West End.

Types of grants: The majority of grants are given in the form of vouchers, valuing

between £30 and £50, as payment towards goods in local shops. Awards were also made towards stair lifts, electric scooters and school trips and uniforms.

Annual grant total: In 2009/10 the charity had assets of £430,000 and an income of £41,000. Grants were made to 110 individuals totalling £9,400.

Applications: On a form available from the correspondent. Applications should be submitted directly by the individual for consideration at any time.

Correspondent: Mrs Elizabeth Thody, 46 Chertsey Road, Windlesham GU20 6EP

Other information: The trust also makes grants to organisations which benefit the local community (£25,000 in 2009/10) and manages an area of allotment land and almshouses.

Henry Smith Charity (Chobham)

Eligibility: People in need who live in the ancient parish of Chobham (roughly the current civil parishes of Chobham and West End) in Surrey.

Types of grants: One off grants, usually in the form of vouchers worth £20 to £30, to be used to purchase goods from local shops.

Annual grant total: In 2008/09 the charity had an income of £6,600 and a total expenditure of £6,400.

Applications: On a form available from the correspondent.

Correspondent: Jennifer Ellis, 6 Ashley Way, West End, Woking, Surrey GU24 9NJ (01483 475548)

Crowhurst

Crowhurst Relief-in-Need Charities

Eligibility: People in need who live in Crowhurst, Surrey.

Types of grants: One-off grants according to need. Recent grants of £100 to £250 have been given to help with fuel bills and travel to or from hospital.

Annual grant total: Grants usually total around £2,000 per year.

Applications: On a form available from the correspondent.

Correspondent: Mrs Edwards, 1 Lankester Square, Oxted, Surrey, RH8 0LJ (01883 712874)

East Horsley

Henry Smith's Charity (East Horsley)

Eligibility: People in need who have lived in East Horsley for at least two years and are disabled or in need.

Types of grants: One-off or recurrent grants according to need.

Annual grant total: Each year the trust receives about £1,000, allocated by Henry Smith's (General Estate) Charity which is divided according to need between welfare and educational grants.

Applications: In writing to the correspondent through a third party such as a social worker, teacher or vicar. Applications are considered in December.

Correspondent: Mr R Deighton, East Horsley Parish Council Office, Kingston Avenue, East Horsley, Surrey KT24 6QT (01483 281148; email: henrysmithcharity@ easthorsley.net)

Effingham

The Henry Smith Charity (Effingham)

Eligibility: People in need who live in Effingham.

Types of grants: One-off grants and gift vouchers, generally of £50 to £100; many grants are given at Christmas.

Annual grant total: Grants average about £3,000 a year, though the actual grant figure tends to fluctuate quite widely.

Applications: In writing to the correspondent. Applications are considered monthly.

Correspondent: The Clerk, Effingham Parish Council, The Parish Room, 3 Home Barn Court, The Street, Effingham, Surrey KT24 5LG (01372 454911)

Egham

The Egham United Charity

Eligibility: People in need who have lived in Egham, Englefield Green (West and East), Hythe, Virginia Water or the village of Stroude and St Ann's Heath for at least five years.

Types of grants: One-off grants according to need.

Annual grant total: Grants usually total around £9,000 a year.

Applications: On a form available from the correspondent: to be submitted through an appropriate third party such as a Citizens Advice or a social worker.

Correspondent: Max Walker, 33 Runnemede Road, Egham, Surrey TW20 9BE (01784 472742; email: eghamunicharity@aol.com)

Epsom

Epsom Parochial Charities

Eligibility: People in need who live in the ancient parish of Epsom.

Types of grants: One-off grants ranging from £100 to £500 according to need. Grants given include those for clothing, food, medical care and equipment and household appliances.

Annual grant total: In 2008 grants were made totalling £7,700.

Applications: On a form available from the correspondent. Applications can be submitted by the individual or through a social worker, Citizens Advice or other welfare agency. They are usually considered in March, June, September and December but should be submitted in the preceding month.

Correspondent: Patricia Vanstone-Walker, 42 Canons Lane, Tadworth, Surrey KT20 6DP (01737 361243; email: vanstonewalker@ntlworld.com)

Esher

The Henry Smith Charity (Esher)

Eligibility: People in need who live in the ancient parish of Esher.

Types of grants: Annual grants to a number of elderly/low income families to help with winter expenses; and emergency grants for furniture, white goods and so on. Grants are only to cover expenses not met by statutory authorities.

Annual grant total: The trust has an income of about £2,000, allocated by Henry Smith's (General Estate) Charity, all of which is given in grants.

Applications: In writing to the correspondent through a social worker, Citizens Advice or other third party. Details of the applicant's financial circumstances should be included. Annual grants are considered in December, emergency grants at any time.

Correspondent: Mrs G B Barnett, Clerk, 24 Pelhams Walk, Esher KT10 8QD (01372 465755; email: gill@gillmikebarnett. plus.com)

Gatton

The Henry Smith Charity (Gatton)

Eligibility: People in need who live in the parish of Gatton.

Types of grants: One-off grants for help with fuel costs, respite care, bedding, clothing, tools of the trade for apprentices and educational grants. Christmas bonuses are also available, traditionally in the form of food vouchers although this is being phased out due to a lack of stores who accept them.

Exclusions: Grants are not given for rates or taxes.

Annual grant total: The trust receives £2,300 income, allocated by Henry Smith's (Worth Estate) Charity.

Applications: In writing to the correspondent either directly or through a third party such as a doctor, minister of religion, councillor and so on. Applications are generally considered twice a year, but urgent applications can be considered within four weeks. The charity advertises before Christmas, whilst the trustees are well known within the community and know of people who are in need.

Correspondent: M S Blacker, Chair, 6a Orpin Road, Redhill, Merstham, Surrey RH1 3EZ

Guildford

The Guildford Poyle Charities

Eligibility: People in need who live in the borough of Guildford as constituted prior to 31 March 1974. A map showing the beneficial area can be viewed on the website.

Types of grants: Mainly one-off grants ranging between £100 and £300 for furniture, domestic appliances, flooring, decorating materials, children's clothing and so on. Christmas food vouchers are also available to families.

Annual grant total: In 2009 the charities had assets of £3.5 million, an income of £244,000 and a total expenditure of £152,000. Grants were made to 422 individuals totalling £42,000. A further £59,000 was given to organisations.

Applications: On a form available from the correspondent or to download from the website. Applications can be submitted at any time either directly by the individual or through a social worker, Citizens Advice or other welfare agency. They are considered every two to three weeks.

Correspondent: Janice Bennett, 208 High Street, Guildford, GU1 3JB (01483 303678; fax: 01483 303678; email: admin@ guildfordpoylecharities.org; website: www. guildfordpoylecharities.org)

Other information: The charities are also known as the Henry Smith's or The Poyle Charity.

The Mayor of Guildford's Christmas & Local Distress Fund

Eligibility: People in need who live in the borough of Guildford.

Types of grants: One-off grants of up to £150. There are no specific restrictions on what can be applied for and the purpose of the grant is defined in the application form. Grants are also made for Christmas events.

Annual grant total: In 2008/09 the trust had an income of £3,600 and a total expenditure of £13,000. Grants were made totalling about £12,000.

Applications: On a form available from the correspondent, to be submitted through a social worker, Citizens Advice, local GP or other relevant third party. Applications are usually considered in January, April, July and October.

Correspondent: Kate Walton, Guildford Borough Council, Millmead House, Millmead, Guildford, Surrey GU2 4BB (01483 444031)

Headley

The Henry Smith Charity

Eligibility: People in need who live in the parish of Headley.

Types of grants: One-off and recurrent grants are available to help with, for example, groceries and hospital travel.

Annual grant total: Grants usually total about £5,000 each year.

Applications: In writing to the correspondent or any trustee, giving the reasons for the application.

Correspondent: Anthony Vine-Lott, Broom Cottage, Crabtree Lane, Headley, Epsom KT18 6PS (01372 374728; email: tony.vinelott@btinternet.com)

Horley and Salfords

The Henry Smith Charity (Horley and Salfords)

Eligibility: Single people and married couples aged 75 or over and who have lived in the parish of Horley and Salfords for a minimum of 25 years.

Types of grants: Christmas bonuses are given as vouchers for local shops.

Annual grant total: Grants usually total around £5,000 each year.

Applications: On a form, to be collected from The Help Shop, Consort Way, Horley. Application forms are available from early November.

Correspondent: Miss A Middlecote, Clerk, Eton Chambers, 95 Victoria Road, Horley,

Surrey RH6 7QH (01293 782425; fax: 01293 775833)

Other information: Grants of £100 have also been given to first year students for books, usually to two or three students a year.

Horne

The Henry Smith Charity (Horne)

Eligibility: People in need who live in the ancient parish of Horne.

Types of grants: One-off grants are the norm, although recurrent grants can be considered.

Exclusions: Group applications are not accepted.

Annual grant total: Grants usually total about £4,000 each year.

Applications: On a form available from the correspondent. Applications can be submitted either directly by the individual or through a social worker and should include details of the applicant's level of income. They are normally considered twice a year (notices are posted around the parish).

Correspondent: Mrs Pam Bean, Hon. Secretary, Yew Tree Cottage, Smallfield Road, Horne, Horley, Surrey RH6 9JP (01342 843173)

Kingston-upon-Thames

The Charities of Ann Savage

Eligibility: People in need who live in the borough of Kingston-upon-Thames.

Types of grants: Mainly recurrent grants.

Annual grant total: Grants to individuals are generally around £1,000 a year. When funds allow, the trust donates half of its income to their local church.

Applications: The trustees usually support individuals known via their contacts at All Saints Parish Church in Kingston-upon-Thames. It is unlikely that grants would be available to support unsolicited applications.

Correspondent: Christopher Ault, Trustee, 18 Woodbines Avenue, Kingston-upon-Thames, KT1 2AY (020 8546 8155)

Leatherhead

The Leatherhead United Charities

Eligibility: People in need who live in the area of the former Leatherhead urban district council.

Types of grants: One-off grants in the range of £100 and £750 are given for the relief of need generally. Pensions are also given.

Annual grant total: In 2009 the charity had assets of £3.9 million and an income of £261,000. Grants were made to 58 individuals totalling £19,000.

Applications: On a form available from the correspondent and submitted through a recognised referral agency (e.g. social worker, Citizens Advice or doctor) giving details of income and the names of two referees. Applications are considered throughout the year.

Correspondent: David Matanle, Homefield, Fortyfoot Road, Leatherhead, Surrey KT22 8RP (01372 370073; email: luchar@btinternet.com)

Other information: The charity also makes grants to organisations (£2,100 in 2009).

Leigh

The Henry Smith Charity (Leigh)

Eligibility: People in need who live in Leigh, Surrey.

Types of grants: The trust has a list of all people over 65; each receives support at Christmas in the form of food vouchers, or help with household bills. Gifts may also be given at Easter in the years when the trust receives more income.

Annual grant total: In 2008/09 the trust had an income of £4,800 and a total expenditure of £4,600.

Applications: In writing or by telephone to the correspondent, or through a third party.

Correspondent: Mrs J Sturt, 12 Knoll Road, Dorking, RH4 3EW

Nutfield

Smith's Charity-Parish of Nutfield

Eligibility: People in need who live in the parish of Nutfield.

Types of grants: One-off and recurrent grants ranging from £35 to £45. Vouchers for local shops are given. The charity also makes some grants to village organisations.

Annual grant total: In 2008/09 the charity had an income of £4,800 and a total expenditure of £3,800.

Applications: In writing to the correspondent. Applications can be submitted either directly by the individual or by any of the four trustees and are considered in December.

Correspondent: Kenneth Rolaston, 7 Morris Road, South Nutfield, Redhill,

RH1 5SB (01737 823348; email: smithsnutfield@aol.com)

Ockley

Ockley United Charities (Henry Smith Charity)

Eligibility: People in need who live in Ockley (primarily older people living in sheltered accommodation provided by Ockley Housing Association or rented housing).

Types of grants: Recurrent annual cash gifts of £110.

Annual grant total: In 2008/09 the charities had both an income and expenditure of £9,100.

Applications: In writing to the correspondent. Applications should include details of income, housing and need. They are considered on a regular basis.

Correspondent: Timothy Pryke, Danesfield, Stane Street, Ockley, Dorking, Surrey RH5 5SY (01306 711511)

Other information: It also supports local organisations.

Oxted

The Oxted United Charities

Eligibility: People in need who live in the parish of Oxted.

Types of grants: One-off grants, generally in the range of £20 to £500. Recent grants have been given for clothing, food, education, utility bills, television licences, furniture and floor covering.

Annual grant total: In 2009/10 the charity had an income of £5,000 and a total expenditure of £4,500.

Applications: In writing to the correspondent. Applications are considered at any time and should be submitted directly by the individual or through a social worker, Citizens Advice or other welfare agency.

Correspondent: C J Berry, Trustee, Robinslade, Wilderness Road, Oxted, Surrey RH8 9HS (01883 714553)

Pirbright

The Pirbright Relief-in-Need Charity

Eligibility: People in need, hardship or distress who live in the parish of Pirbright.

Types of grants: One-off grants for a variety of items, services or facilities that will reduce the need, hardship or distress of the individual, including buying or renting medical equipment to use at home.

Exclusions: Grants will not be given for taxes, rates or any other public funds. The trustees must not commit themselves to repeating or renewing any grant.

Annual grant total: Grants total around £1,500 per year.

Applications: In writing to the correspondent or any of the trustees.

Correspondent: Philip Lawson, Stanemore, Rowe Lane, Pirbright, Surrey GU24 0LX (01483 472842)

Shottermill

Shottermill United Charities (Henry Smith and Others)

Eligibility: People in need who live in the parish of Shottermill, Surrey.

Types of grants: Grants usually ranging from £40 to £50 according to need. The charity distributes grocery vouchers at Christmas.

Annual grant total: About £1,000.

Applications: In writing to the correspondent. Applications can be submitted directly by the individual or through a social worker, Citizens Advice or other welfare agency or third party. They are considered at any time, but particularly at Christmas.

Correspondent: Hilary Bicknell, 7 Underwood Road, Haslemere, Surrey GU27 1JQ (01428 651276)

Staines

The Staines Parochial Charity

Eligibility: Older people over the age of 60 who live in the parish of Staines; people who are unable to work; people caring for a handicapped person and occasionally other people in need who live in the area of the former urban district of Staines.

Types of grants: One-off grants according to need for payment of gas or electricity bills. Grants usually range from £80 to £100.

Exclusions: No grants to individuals living outside the beneficial area.

Annual grant total: In 2008/09 the charity had an income of £5,200 and a total expenditure of £5,100.

Applications: On a form available from the correspondent including evidence of need, hardship or distress. Applications can be submitted either directly by the individual, through a social worker, Citizens Advice, welfare agency or other third party. The application must be sent via a trustee who must countersign the application. Applications are normally considered in September.

Correspondent: Carol Davies, Honorary Clerk to the Trustees, 191 Feltham Hill Road, Ashford, Middlesex, TW15 1HJ (01784 255432)

Other information: Eligibility for Housing Benefit or Income Support is taken as an indication of need.

Stoke D'Abernon

The Stoke D'Abernon Charities

Eligibility: People in need who live in the ancient parish of Stoke D'Abernon (which includes part of Oxshott).

Types of grants: One-off and recurrent grants according to need, ranging from £20 to £50. Usually 30 to 40 grants are awarded each year.

Annual grant total: Grants usually total around £1,000 per year.

Applications: In writing to the correspondent, directly by the individual or a family member, or through a third party such as a social worker, Citizens Advice or welfare organisation. They are considered at any time.

Correspondent: Mrs H C Lee, Beggars Roost, Blundel Lane, Stoke D'Abernon, Cobham, Surrey KT11 2SF (01932 863107)

Thorpe

The Thorpe Parochial Charities

Eligibility: People in need who live in the ancient parish of Thorpe, especially those over 60 years of age.

Types of grants: Grants of solid fuel or contributions to gas or electricity accounts and 'aids to the sick'. Grants range between £35 and £50. Educational grants are also available.

Annual grant total: About £2,000.

Applications: In writing to the correspondent by the end of October. Applications are usually considered in November.

Correspondent: Mrs D Jones, 9 Rosefield Gardens, Ottershaw, Chertsey, Surrey, KT16 0JH

Thursley

The Thursley Charities

Eligibility: People in need, including older people, single parents and bereaved young people, who live in the parish of Thursley in Surrey.

Types of grants: One-off and recurrent grants according to need ranging from £100 to £300.

Annual grant total: Grants usually total around £2,000 a year.

Applications: In writing to the correspondent. Applications can be submitted directly by the individual or through an organisation such as Citizens Advice, or through a third party such as a social worker. Applications are considered in November each year.

Correspondent: The Trustees, The Old Parsonage, Highfield Lane, Thursley, Godalming, GU8 6QQ (01252 702932; email: peter.muir@thursleychurch.org.uk)

Other information: The charities are the Charities of Anthony Smith and Henry Smith.

Walton-on-the-Hill

The Henry Smith Charity (Walton-on-the-Hill)

Eligibility: People in need who live within the parish of Walton-on-the-Hill.

Types of grants: One-off or recurrent grants according to need.

Annual grant total: The trust receives an income allocated by Henry Smith's (General Estate) Charity. Grants usually total around £2,000.

Applications: In writing to the correspondent.

Correspondent: Mrs J E Turnbull, Little Orchard, Egmont Park Road, Walton-on-the-Hill, Tadworth, Surrey KT20 7QG

West Clandon

The Henry Smith Charity (West Clandon)

Eligibility: People in need, mainly older people, who have lived in the parish of West Clandon for at least five years.

Types of grants: One-off cash grants of £45 to £100.

Annual grant total: Grants usually total about £2,500 a year.

Applications: In writing to the correspondent. The deadline for applications is 31 October. Grants are usually distributed during December.

Correspondent: Stephen Meredith, 11 Bennett Way, West Clandon, Guildford, GU4 7TN

West Horsley

The Henry Smith Charity (West Horsley)

Eligibility: People in need who live in West Horsley.

Types of grants: One-off or recurrent grants according to need.

Annual grant total: Grants usually total about £1,000 a year.

Applications: In writing to the correspondent. Please note, the charity has previously stated that resources are fully committed.

Correspondent: Mollie Lewendon, Trustee, Lansdowne, Silkmore Lane, West Horsley, Surrey KT24 6JB (01483 284167)

Weybridge

Weybridge Land Charity

Eligibility: People in need who live in Weybridge.

Types of grants:
- Emergency grants – individuals needing immediate help can receive supermarket vouchers or payments are made directly to suppliers of household essentials.
- Christmas grants – grants ranging from £50 to £240 distributed to 218 applicants.

Exclusions: No funding towards debt relief.

Annual grant total: In 2009 the charity had assets of £1.3 million and an income of £55,000. Grants to 241 individuals totalled £25,000.

Applications: Application forms for the emergency grants are available from Citizens Advice at Walton-on-Thames, the local GP surgery and from health and social workers throughout the year. Application forms for Christmas grants are available during September and October at the Weybridge Day Centre and Library and should be returned before 31 October for payments in first week in December.

Correspondent: Howard Turner, Little Knowle, Woodlands, Send, Surrey GU23 7LD (01483 211728)

Other information: Grants are also made to organisations.

Woking

The Henry Smith Charity (Woking)

Eligibility: People in need who live in the ancient parish of Woking.

Types of grants: One-off grants only.

Exclusions: Grants are not given for the relief of rates, taxes and other public funds.

Annual grant total: In 2009/10 the trust had both an income and a total expenditure of £5,800.

Applications: In writing to the vicar of the parish, either directly by the individual or through a social worker, Citizens Advice or other welfare agency.

Correspondent: David Bittleston, Pin Mill, Heathfield Road, Woking, Surrey GU22 7JJ (01483 828621)

Worplesdon

Worplesdon Parish Charities (including the Henry Smith Charity)

Eligibility: People in need who live in the parish of Worplesdon.

Types of grants: Vouchers to buy coal, clothing or groceries at Christmas.

Annual grant total: Grants usually total around £2,000 per year.

Applications: Apply when the distribution is advertised within the parish (normally in October/November each year). Emergency grants can be considered at any time.

Correspondent: Eric S Morgan, 21 St Michael's Avenue, Fairlands, Guildford, Surrey GU3 3LY (01483 233344)

Wotton

The Henry Smith Charity (Wotton)

Eligibility: People in need who live in the ancient parish of Wotton.

Types of grants: One-off grants ranging from £100 to £500. Grants have in the past been given to older people of the parish towards fuel and lighting bills and holidays, young people taking part in schemes such as The Duke of Edinburgh Award which will enhance their job prospects, and help towards the cost of independent projects or travel costs.

Annual grant total: Grants usually total around £5,000 each year.

Applications: In writing to the correspondent. Applications are considered in March and September. They can be submitted directly by the individual or through a third party.

Correspondent: Rosemary Wakeford, Secretary, 2 Brickyard Cottages, Hollow Lane, Wotton, Dorking, Surrey RH5 6QE (01306 730856)

West Sussex

Ashington, Wiston, Warminghurst Sick Poor Fund

Eligibility: People in need who live, firstly in the villages of Ashington, Wiston and Warminghurst, and secondly in West Sussex.

Types of grants: One-off grants according to need. Grants are given to provide or pay for items or services which will alleviate the need or assist the recovery of beneficiaries where assistance is not readily available from any other source.

Annual grant total: Grants to individuals usually total around £4,000.

Applications: On a form available from the correspondent. Applications can be submitted directly by the individual or a relevant third party.

Correspondent: Rod Shepherd, Sheen Stickland, 7 East Pallant, Chichester, West Sussex, PO19 1TR (01243 775966)

The West Sussex County Nursing Benevolent Fund

Eligibility: Nurses who are or have been engaged in community nursing in West Sussex and are in need. People in need who are in poor health, convalescent or who have disabilities and live in the administrative county of West Sussex may also qualify for assistance.

Types of grants: One-off and recurrent grants according to need. Recent grants include those towards wheelchairs, tricycles for children with disabilities and a respite holiday for a child with severe mental disabilities. Christmas gifts are also given.

Annual grant total: About £3,000.

Applications: On a form available from the correspondent. Applications can be submitted directly by the individual, or through a third party such as a social worker, Citizens Advice or other welfare agency.

Correspondent: Rod Shepherd, Sheen Stickland, 7 East Pallant, Chichester, West Sussex, PO19 1TR (01243 781255)

Horsham

The Suzanne Green Charitable Trust

Eligibility: Older people who are in need and live in West Sussex.

Types of grants: One-off and recurrent grants according to need.

Annual grant total: In 2008/09 the trust had assets of £276,000 and an income of £26,000. Grants were made totalling £90,000, of which £9,800 was given to individuals and £80,000 to organisations.

Applications: In writing to the correspondent. Applications can be submitted directly by the individual, a family member or the individual's representative. They are considered upon receipt and should include a profile of the applicant, the reason for the request and a statement of income and assets.

Correspondent: David Briffett, Secretary, 20 Glendale Close, Horsham, West Sussex RH12 4GR (01403 260876; email: davidbriffett@aol.com)

Other information: The trust has entered into a number of long-term support projects for older people in the district, therefore the amount available to individuals is limited.

The Innes Memorial Fund

Eligibility: People who are poor, sick and in need and who live in Horsham.

Types of grants: One-off grants given towards wheelchairs, cookers, alarms, domestic help, school uniforms, holidays, disability equipment, travel expenses and chiropody costs. On average 10 grants are made a year ranging between £100 and £250.

Annual grant total: In 2008/09 the trust had an income of £19,000. It made grants totalling £11,000, of which £7,000 went towards the chiropody service, £1,400 went to the Roffey Institute and £2,600 was paid in other donations.

Applications: In writing to the correspondent, to be submitted through a doctor or social worker.

Correspondent: Mrs P C Eastland, Administrator, 12 Coolhurst Lane, Horsham, West Sussex RH13 6DH (01403 263289)

Midhurst

The Midhurst Pest House Charity

Eligibility: People in need who live in the parish of Midhurst.

Types of grants: One-off grants in the range of £60 to £500. Recent awards have been given towards transport and holiday costs.

Annual grant total: In 2009 the charity had an income of £12,000 and a total expenditure of £4,800.

Applications: In writing to the correspondent either directly by the individual or through a social worker, Citizens Advice or other welfare agency. Applications are considered in April and October and should be received in the preceding month.

Correspondent: Tim Rudwick, Clerk, 31 Pretoria Avenue, Midhurst, West Sussex GU29 9PP (01730 812489; email: tim@rudwick.fsworld.co.uk)

Other information: Grants are also occasionally made to a local school.

Wisborough Green

The Elliott Charity

Eligibility: People who are older or who have disabilities, live in the parish Wisborough Green and are in need.

Types of grants: One-off or recurrent grants according to need, usually ranging between £200 and £500.

Annual grant total: Grants to individuals usually total around £500 a year.

Applications: In writing to the correspondent. Applications can be submitted directly by the individual or through a social worker, Citizens Advice or other welfare agency.

Correspondent: Mrs Patricia Ann Farmer, Old School Cottage, School Lane, Wilsborough Green, West Sussex RH14 0DU (01403 700492)

Other information: Grants are also made to community causes, including an annual donation to the Village Minibus Association.

9. LONDON

The Milly Apthorp Charitable Trust

Eligibility: People in need who live in the London borough of Barnet.

Types of grants: Grants are given for a range of needs, such as holidays for people (over nine years old) with physical disabilities and their carers/families, and holidays for young people (aged 14 to 25) towards adventurous expeditions and character building activities.

Annual grant total: In 2008/09 the trust had assets of £10 million and an income of £653,000. Grants totalled £620,000, of which £175,000 was given in grants to 315 individuals.

Applications: On a form available from the correspondent. Applications are usually considered in March, June, September and December and should be made through a registered charity in the preceding month. The trust does not invite applications, and will not reply to unsuccessful applicants.

Correspondent: Lawrence Fenton, Trustee, Iveco House, Station Road, Watford, WD17 1SR (01923 224411)

Arsenal Charitable Trust

Eligibility: People in need including those injured whilst playing sport, or their dependants who live in Greater London, with a preference for Islington and Hackney. The charity also supports the provision of recreational activities to those in need.

Types of grants: Grants and loans according to need.

Annual grant total: In 2008/09 the trust had assets of £1 million and an income of £129,000. Grants were made to three individuals totalling £3,200.

Applications: In writing to the correspondent.

Other information: The charity also provides relief to those affected by local or international disasters and operates in London, Israel and Sri Lanka.

Benevolent of Strangers' Friend Society

Eligibility: People in need, particularly 'strangers not entitled to parochial relief', that is people who have exhausted all other possible sources of funding. Beneficiaries must live in London, mainly inner London.

Types of grants: One-off and recurrent grants in the range of £50 and £150.

Annual grant total: Grants usually total about £1,000 a year.

Applications: Applications should not be made to the society since it does not make grants directly to individuals. It allocates funds to certain Methodist ministers living in most areas of inner London and some areas of outer London, who in turn distribute the funds to individuals in need of whom they become aware.

Correspondent: Chris Linford, Room 403, 1 Central Buildings, Westminster, London SW1H 9NH (020 7222 8010; fax: 020 7799 1452; email: chris.linford@ methodistlondon.org.uk)

Brentford & Chiswick Relief in Need and Sick Poor Persons Fund

Eligibility: People in need who live in Brentford and Chiswick.

Types of grants: One-off grants ranging from £50 to £200, which have recently been given towards a specialised computer, a special buggy for a child with disabilities, debts and a holiday for a person with disabilities.

Annual grant total: Grants average around £250 a year, though the actual grant figure tends to fluctuate quite widely.

Applications: In writing to the correspondent either directly by the individual or through a social worker, Citizens Advice or other welfare agency. Applications are considered at any time.

Correspondent: Julie Cadman, St Paul's Church Hall, St Paul's Road, Brentford, Middlesex, TW8 0PN (020 8568 7442)

Other information: The fund also makes grants to organisations.

Cripplegate Foundation

Eligibility: People in need who have lived or worked for more than 12 months in the ancient parish of St Giles, Cripplegate, the former parish of St Luke's, Old Street and the London borough of Islington. Asylum seekers and those who were previously homeless do not have to meet the one year residential qualification and can apply as soon as they move into the area. Applications are considered from people on a low income, with priority being given to those who are also coping with, for instance, illness, disability, debt, or family break-up.

Types of grants: One-off grants of up to £500 for household items, white goods, disability aids and adaptations and start-up packages for newly housed homeless people.

Exclusions: No grants are given towards housing costs, items already purchased, education or student expenses and wheelchairs. No repeat applications are considered within 2 years of the last approved grant award or within 12 months of the last unsuccessful grant application. This rule will only be waived in exceptional circumstances.

Annual grant total: In 2008 the foundation had assets of £26 million and an income of £2.5 million. Grants made to individuals totalled £208,000.

Applications: On a form available from the correspondent or on the website. Decisions are usually made within three weeks of receipt of the completed form. People who are unsure of whether they live in the beneficial area should telephone the trust before making an application.

Correspondent: Kristina Glenn, 76 Central Street, London EC1V 8AG (020 7549 8185; fax: 020 7549 8180; email: kristina.glenn@ cripplegate.org.uk; website: www. cripplegate.org)

Other information: Grants are also made to organisations.

The Isaac Davies Trust

Eligibility: People of the Jewish faith who live in London.

Types of grants: One-off grants according to need.

Exclusions: Grants are not given for educational study abroad.

Annual grant total: The trust's income is about £11,000 each year. Most of the income is given in grants to organisations, but around £2,000 is given to individuals, some of which is for educational purposes.

Applications: In writing to the correspondent.

Correspondent: The Secretary, United Synagogue, Adler House, 735 High Road, London N12 OUS (020 8343 8989)

The Edmonton Aid-in-Sickness & Nursing Fund

Eligibility: People in need who are in poor health and live in the old borough of Edmonton (mainly N9 and N18).

Types of grants: One-off grants usually up to £300. Recent grants have been made for clothing, furniture, household necessities, convalescence, household bills and debts and medical equipment not covered by NHS provision.

Exclusions: The trust will not subsidise public funds, therefore applicants should have sought help from all public sources before approaching the trust.

Annual grant total: In 2009 the fund had an income of £6,100 and a total expenditure of £5,200.

Applications: In writing to the correspondent either directly by the individual or through social services, Citizens Advice or other welfare agency. Applications can be received at any time.

Correspondent: David M Firth, Hon. Secretary, 9 Crossway, Bush Hill Park, Enfield, Middlesex EN1 2LA (020 8127 1949)

The Emanuel Hospital Charity

Eligibility: Members of the Church of England who are over 56 years old and have lived in the London boroughs of Kensington and Chelsea, Hillingdon or Westminster for at least two years.

Types of grants: Pensions of about £750 a year are paid in monthly instalments along with a Christmas 'bonus' of £60 per person. One-off grants are also available for essential household items.

Annual grant total: In 2008/09 the charity had assets of £1.3 million and an income of £74,000. Grants were made totalling £55,000, of which £53,000 was given in pensions to 64 beneficiaries and £1,700 in one-off grants to four individuals.

Applications: Application forms can be obtained from the correspondent and should be returned along with evidence of need, copies of birth certificate and baptism certificates. They should be submitted directly by the individual.

Correspondent: David Milnes, Town Clerk's Office, City of London, PO Box 270, London EC2P 2EJ (020 7332 1410)

Other information: The charity publicises its activities and details of pension vacancies in local papers, through welfare agencies and churches within the beneficial areas.

The Ronnie Gubbay Memorial Fund

Eligibility: Jewish women of Spanish and Portuguese origin who are in need. Preference is generally given to those living in the Greater London area.

Types of grants: One-off and recurrent grants according to need.

Annual grant total: In 2008/09 the fund had an income of £11,000 and a total expenditure of £3,000.

Applications: In writing to the correspondent.

Correspondent: The Secretary, 2 Ashworth Road, London W9 1JY (020 7289 2573)

Other information: This fund is one of the several trusts administered by the Spanish & Portuguese Jews Congregation and was established in 1944.

The Hampton Fuel Allotment Charity

Eligibility: People who are in poor health or financial need and live in the ancient parish of Hampton.

Types of grants: One-off grants averaging around £370 are given for heating costs, lifeline alarm systems and other essentials such as fridges, cookers, washing machines, wheelchairs and special medical equipment.

Exclusions: The charity is unlikely to support: private and further education; building adaptations; holidays, unless there is severe medical need; decorating costs, carpeting or central heating; anything which will replace statutory funds.

Annual grant total: In 2008/09 the charity had assets of £38 million, which generated an income of £2 million. Grants were made to over 2,100 individuals totalling £793,000 and were distributed as follows:

Fuel grants	1,700	£642,000
Essential equipment	380	£130,000
'Careline' telephone equipment	35	£21,000

Applications: On a form available from the correspondent or St Mary's, All Saints and St James's vicarages, the Greenwood Centre and Citizens Advice. Applications should be submitted by post either directly by the individual or through a third party. They are considered every two months, although decisions can be made more quickly in urgent cases.

Correspondent: Michael Ryder, 15 High Street, Hampton, Middlesex TW12 2SA

(020 8941 7866; fax: 020 8979 5555; website: www.hfac.co.uk)

Other information: Grants are also given to organisations which support people in need or provide community benefits in line with the charity's objects (£1 million in 2008/09).

The Hornsey Parochial Charities

Eligibility: People in need who live in the ancient parish of Hornsey in Haringey and Hackney, which comprises N8 and parts of N2, N4, N6, N10 and N16.

Types of grants: One-off grants for all kinds of need provided funding is not available from statutory or other sources, such as clothing, bedding or essential items and the costs of heating and lighting.

Annual grant total: In 2008 the Hornsey Parochial Charities made 113 welfare grants totalling £38,000. Grants averaged £400 each and ranged between £60 and £1,000.

Applications: Individuals can write requesting an application form which, on being returned, can usually be dealt with within a month.

Correspondent: Lorraine Fincham, Clerk to the Trustees, PO Box 22985, London N10 3XB (020 8352 1601; fax: 020 8352 1601; email: hornseypc@ blueyonder.co.uk)

Other information: Grants are also made for educational purposes.

Inner London Fund for the Blind and Disabled

Eligibility: People who are blind, partially sighted or disabled who live or are regularly employed in the borough of Greenwich, and people who are blind or partially sighted who live within the London area. Preference will be given to applicants who live alone.

Types of grants: Grants of £130 to £500 towards for example travel expenses, washing machines, wheelchairs, cookers, home improvements, holidays and redecorating expenses.

Exclusions: No grants towards rent arrears, rates, food, clothing/footwear, heating or lighting, except in exceptional circumstances. No application will be considered where an alternative statutory source of funding is available.

Annual grant total: In 2008/09 the fund had an income of £22,000 and a total expenditure of £93,000. Unfortunately, further details on its grant making activities were not available.

Applications: On a form available from the correspondent. Applications can be made directly by the individual or through a social worker. Details of income/ expenditure and charitable assistance received within the past year must be included.

Correspondent: Colin Brown, Chief Executive, c/o The Forum @ Greenwich, Trafalgar Road, Greenwich, London SE10 9EQ (email: admin@ blindindependencegreenwich.org.uk; website: www. blindindependencegreenwich.org.uk)

The Metropolitan Society for the Blind

Eligibility: Blind and partially sighted people who live on a permanent basis in one of the 12 central London boroughs or the City of London with a preference for registered blind people.

Types of grants: One-off grants up to £500 towards computer equipment and software, such as a large monitor or text-reading software; electronic text-magnification equipment; holidays and family visits; and, domestic equipment such as a talking microwave, fridges and other furniture. In exceptional circumstances, up to £1,000 may be available for low vision aids incorporating CCTV or computer assisted technology.

Exclusions: Awards are not normally made for the following: payment of outstanding debts, holidays outside the UK (although help with associated costs could be considered); payment of council tax/rent arrears; educational grants (although help with associated costs may be considered); installation of a telephone service where the applicant is in short-term or temporary accommodation.

Annual grant total: In 2009 the trust had assets of £4.7 million and an income of £583,000. Grants to 121 individuals totalled £30,000 and were broken down as follows:

General purpose	£24,000
Small grants	£4,800
Holiday grants	£420

Applications: On a form available from the correspondent. Applications should be made through a third party such as a social worker or through an organisation such as Citizens Advice or other welfare agency.

Applicants should first apply to the social fund whenever eligibility exists, and a check should be made to make sure that the applicant is in receipt of all the state benefits they are entitled to.

Correspondent: Roger Thurlow, Lantern House, 102 Bermondsey Street, London SE1 3UB (020 7403 6184; fax: 020 7234 0708; email: admin@msb.gb. com; website: www.msb.gb.com)

Other information: The society's primary function is as a full-time home-visiting agency on which it spends almost half its income; it also offers a small-scale escort service conducted by volunteer car drivers, normally in the London area. The society also supports organisations helping visually impaired people such as social clubs.

Mary Minet Trust

Eligibility: People who are living with a disability, sickness or infirmity and reside in the boroughs of Southwark or Lambeth.

Types of grants: One-off grants towards convalescence holidays, disability aids, medical equipment and household items such as washing machines, fridges, cookers, essential furniture, carpets, clothing, beds and bedding.

Annual grant total: In 2008/09 the trust had an income of £23,000 and a total expenditure of £29,000.

Applications: In writing to the correspondent either directly by the individual or through a social worker, Citizens Advice, welfare office or a third party such as a doctor, advice centre or victim support.

Correspondent: The Trustees, PO Box 53673, London, SE24 4AF (email: admin@ maryminettrust.org.uk)

Arthur and Rosa Oppenheimer Fund

Eligibility: Jewish people who are sick or disabled and live in London. Preference is given to older people.

Types of grants: One-off grants to those in need and recurrent grants over a longer period to cover nursing care for patients in their own homes. The charity also provides support for the provision of kosher food and other amenities.

Annual grant total: Grants usually total around £2,500 per year.

Applications: In writing to the correspondent, either directly by the individual, or via a social worker, Citizens Advice or other third party.

Correspondent: A Oppenheimer, Trustee, 9 Ashbourne Avenue, London NW11 0DP (20 8455 6066)

Other information: Organisations are also supported.

Port of London Authority Police Charity Fund

Eligibility: Former officers who have served in the port authority's police force, and their dependants.

Types of grants: One-off grants are given to help with unforeseen bills, household items, holidays and so on.

Annual grant total: In 2008/09 the fund had an income of £6,000 and a total expenditure of £10,000.

Applications: In writing to the correspondent, clearly stating the need for financial assistance. Applications are considered at quarterly meetings, or sooner if the need is urgent.

Correspondent: Andrew Masson, Chief Officer, Port Of Tilbury Police, Main Entrance, Tilbury Freeport, Tilbury, Essex RM18 7DU (01375 846781; email: andrew. masson@potll.com)

Positive East

Eligibility: People affected by HIV who live and/or receive treatment in East London and are in need of short term financial assistance to cover basic needs.

Types of grants: Grants of up to £25 each, up to a maximum of £50 in a year, with six months between each application. Each individual has a 'lifetime limit' of £150, after which access to the fund will be closed to them. Grants are given for one-off, HIV related expenses, child expenses such as school uniforms or medical treatment, utility bills, the cost of travel to an essential appointment and basic necessities such as food or clothing.

Exclusions: Grants are not given for:
- legal costs
- non-essential travel or travel outside of London
- funeral costs
- on-going non-HIV related treatment
- household goods
- credit card or other debts.

Annual grant total: Around £3,000 is allocated each year for emergency hardship grants.

Applications: On a form available from the correspondent. Applications can only be made through Positive East staff and are only available to registered members of the trust (new service users will need to fill in a registration form). Forms can be submitted at any time but applicants should note that the fund is a limited resource and will not be topped up again until the end of the financial year.

Before any grant is awarded proof will be required that the individual is not eligible for any other financial assistance. Equally, if the person has been the victim of a crime, a crime reference number should be included in the application.

Correspondent: Alastair Thomson, The Globe Centre, 159 Mile End Road, London E1 4AQ (020 7791 9307; email: info@ positiveeast.org.uk; website: www. positiveeast.org.uk)

Other information: Positive East is a new charity formed from the merger between the London East AIDS Network (LEAN) and the Globe Centre in 2005. The trust provides specialist advice on housing, welfare benefit and immigration issues. It also runs a range of support services including one-to-one counselling and training courses.

The Sheriffs' & Recorders' Fund

Eligibility: People on discharge from prison, and families of people imprisoned.

Applicants must live in the Metropolitan Police area or Greater London area.

Types of grants: One-off grants towards clothing, household items, furnishings, beds and bedding, white goods, carpets, baby needs and so on.

Annual grant total: In 2008/09 the fund had assets of £719,000 and an income of £382,000. Grants were made to 947 individuals totalling £133,000, around £110,000 of which was given in welfare grants.

Applications: On a form available from the correspondent, submitted through probation officers or social workers. They are considered throughout the year.

Correspondent: The Chair, c/o Central Criminal Court, Old Bailey, Warwick Square, London EC4M 7BS (020 7248 3277; email: secretary@srfund.net; website: www.srfund.org.uk)

Other information: Grants are also made for educational purposes and for special projects.

The Society for the Relief of Distress

Eligibility: People in need who live in the boroughs of Camden, Greenwich, Hackney, Hammersmith & Fulham, Islington, Kensington & Chelsea, Lambeth, Lewisham, Southwark, Tower Hamlets, Wandsworth, Westminster and the City of London.

Types of grants: One-off grants, usually of £25 to £100, for 'any cases of sufficient hardship or distress, whether mental or physical'. Grants may be given towards essential household items and clothing.

Exclusions: Grants are very rarely given towards holidays, funeral expenses or debts.

Annual grant total: In 2008 the society had an income of £17,000 and a total expenditure of £13,000.

Applications: Through a social worker, Citizens Advice, registered charity or church organisation only. Applications submitted by individuals will not be considered.

Correspondent: Caroline Armstrong, Trustee, 21 Hartswood Road, London, W12 9NE

The South London Relief-in-Sickness Fund

Eligibility: People in need through sickness, disability or infirmity who live in the boroughs of Lambeth and Wandsworth.

Types of grants: One-off grants up to £200, towards, for example, furniture, furnishings, clothing, holidays and medical equipment.

Exclusions: No grants towards taxes or debts.

Annual grant total: In 2009 the fund had an income of £12,000 and a total expenditure of £11,000.

Applications: In writing to the correspondent through a social worker, Citizens Advice or other welfare agency. Applications are considered quarterly (normally March, June, September and December). They should include details of the applicant's name, address, age, family composition, disability/illness, source of income and benefits, purpose of the grant, whether any other funding has been applied for and whether any applications have been made to the fund before.

Correspondent: Ozu Okere, Room 110, Wandsworth Town Hall, Wandsworth High Street, London SW18 2PU (020 8871 6035; fax: 020 8871 6036; email: ookere@wandsworth.gov.uk)

The Spanish Welfare Fund

Eligibility: People in need of Spanish nationality who live in London, and their dependants.

Types of grants: One-off and recurrent grants according to need.

Annual grant total: In 2009 the fund had n income of £6,100 and a total expenditure of £5,600.

Applications: In writing to the correspondent.

Correspondent: Robert Rouse, 9 Bridle Close, Surbiton Road, Kingston-Upon-Thames, Surrey, KT1 2JW

The St George Dragon Trust

Eligibility: People in need who live in Greater London and are moving, or have recently moved, from supported housing into independent accommodation.

Types of grants: One-off grants ranging from £100 to £400 for buying essential household equipment and furniture. Small grants of £50 to £100 are also available for the purchase of essential items following move-on. Applicants should not be eligible for a Community Care grant or support from the Social Fund and have only minimal resources. (A rare exception may be where a very low Community Care grant has been awarded – see Applications section.)

Exclusions: Grants are not made to students or to 'able young people'.

Annual grant total: In 2008/09 the trust had an income of £11,000 and a total expenditure of £9,700.

Applications: In writing, through a social, housing or welfare worker. Applications should be typed wherever possible and should be made on the headed notepaper of the organisation through which the application is being made.

The application should include: the name, age and sex of the applicant; the address of the applicant and time spent there; the address of new accommodation and date of move-on; the social history including history of homelessness and Case Plan; financial circumstances of the applicant detailing income sources and amounts, together with amounts of present outgoings plus those of the future as far as is possible; the applicant's eligibility for a Community Care Grant in relation to current need, and if a Community Care Grant was refused, the reason why, and whether the appeal process has been finalised; where a very low Community Care Grant has been awarded applications should include details of the amount granted, the purpose of the grant and how it has been spent; the amount requested from the trust and its purpose; help that has been obtained from other sources and details of other organisations approached; has the applying agency any funds of its own to make grants and if so, what grant is it making to the applicant or if it is not, why not; how long the referring worker has personally known the applicant and the worker's appraisal of this application; the name of the organisation to which any grant should be made payable; the signature of the applicant; and the signature of the referring worker and the work telephone number and address if different to that shown on the headed notepaper of the organisation.

It is the aim of the trustees to respond with the outcome together with the grant if applicable, within fifteen working days, or with the reason for and timescale of a deferment.

Correspondent: Nicki Vanham, 183 Blackhorse Road, London E17 6ND

Barking & Dagenham

The Dagenham United Charity

Eligibility: People in need who live in the ancient parish of Dagenham (as it was 1921 to 1924).

Types of grants: Gift vouchers at Christmas. In previous years, vouchers have been around £50 each, but this changes each year depending on the charity's income and the number of applicants.

Annual grant total: Grants average about £700 a year.

Applications: In writing to the correspondent either directly by the individual or through a social worker, Citizens Advice, other welfare agency or other third party. Details of any disability should be included if appropriate, along with information about the applicant's income, age and so on. Applications are considered in October/November.

Correspondent: Grants Officer, Corporate Finance Division, Civic Centre, Dagenham, Essex RM10 7BW (020 8227 2300)

Other information: This charity is an amalgamation of the William Ford & Dagenham United Charities.

Barnet

The Mayor of Barnet's Benevolent Fund

Eligibility: People who are on an income-related benefit and who live in the London borough of Barnet and have done so for at least six months.

Types of grants: One-off grants of up to £100 towards school uniforms and other children's clothing, essential household items, such as cookers, furniture and small one-off debts such as telephone bills.

Annual grant total: In 2008/09 the trust had an income of £6,000 and a total expenditure of £3,000.

Applications: Applications should preferably be submitted directly by the individual, but may also be made directly by a supporting agency. All requests should include a quotation for the items required.

Correspondent: The Grants Unit, London Borough of Barnet, North London Business Park, Oakleigh Road South, London, N11 1NP (020 8359 2020; fax: 020 8359 2685; email: ken.argent@ barnet.gov.uk)

Other information: Grants are also made for educational purposes.

The Finchley Charities

Eligibility: People in need who live in the former borough of Finchley.

Types of grants: One-off grants only.

Exclusions: No educational grants are made.

Annual grant total: In 2009 the charities had assets of £6.2 million, an income of £903,000 and a total expenditure of £985,000. A budget of about £25,000 a year is allocated for grants to organisations and individuals.

Applications: In writing to the correspondent either directly by the individual or through a social worker, Citizens Advice or welfare agency. Applications must include details of the amount being asked for and the reason for the application.

Correspondent: Jean Field, Manager, 41A Wilmot Close, East Finchley, London N2 8HP (020 8346 9464; fax: 020 8346 9466; email: info@ thefinchleycharities.org)

Other information: The trust's main concern is the provision of 156 flats for people in Finchley aged 60 and over, who have insufficient funds to purchase their own property.

Jesus Hospital Charity

Eligibility: People in need who live in the former district of Barnet, East Barnet and Friern Barnet.

Types of grants: One-off grants between £100 and £1,000 towards, for example, lifeline rentals, winter clothing, shoes, food vouchers, fridges/freezers, beds, gas cookers and utensils for single parent families and couples living on low incomes; and holidays for people with disabilities.

Annual grant total: In 2009 the charity had assets of £9 million and an income of £523,000. Grants to individuals totalled £14,000.

Applications: On a form available from the correspondent through a social worker, Citizens Advice, welfare agency, a minister or doctor. Applications should state whether the applicant is in receipt of Income Support or Housing Benefit and whether applications have been made to other charitable organisations. Applications are considered in January, March, May, July, September and November.

Correspondent: Mrs E Payne, Clerk to the Visitors, Ravenscroft Lodge, 37 Union Street, Barnet EN5 4HY (020 8440 4374; email: ravenscroft1679@onetel.com)

Other information: Support is mainly given to local organisations.

Eleanor Palmer Trust

Eligibility: People in need who live in the former urban districts of Barnet and East Barnet, This includes those living within the postal codes of EN4, EN5, N11 and N14.

Types of grants: One-off grants up to £1,000 towards, for example, carpets, furniture and clothing.

Exclusions: No grants available towards educational purposes, bankruptcy fees, medical costs, taxes or debts.

Annual grant total: In 2008/09 the trust had an income of £1.2 million and made grants totalling £30,000. These consisted of:

- grants for relief in need – £17,000
- amenities and grants to residents – £7,600
- lunch club for residents – £5,600.

Applications: In writing to the correspondent either directly or through an appropriate third party. Applications are considered every two months. They should include the names of any other charities to which applications have been made.

Correspondent: The Clerk to the Trustees, 106b Wood Street, Barnet, Hertfordshire EN5 4BY (020 8441 3222; fax: 020 8364 8279; email: info@ eleanorpalmertrust.org.uk; website: www. eleanorpalmertrust.org.uk)

Other information: The trust concentrates on running its own almshouses and a residential home for older people.

The Valentine Poole Charity

Eligibility: People in need who live in the former urban districts of Barnet and East Barnet (approximately the postal districts of EN4 and EN5).

Types of grants: One-off grants are given towards essential items such as household goods, children's clothing and food. Pensions are also made to older people.

Annual grant total: About £25,000 to individuals for welfare and education purposes.

Applications: On a form available from the correspondent for consideration in March, July and November. Applications should be submitted by a social worker, Citizens Advice or other third party or welfare agency, not directly by the individual.

Correspondent: The Clerk, The Forum Room, Ewen Hall, Wood Street, Barnet, Hertfordshire EN5 4BW (020 8441 6893; email: vpoole@btconnect.com)

Other information: Grants are also made to local organisations.

Bexley

The Bexley Mayor's Fund

Eligibility: People in need who live in the borough of Bexley.

Types of grants: Grants, usually in the range of £50 to £100, for a variety of needs (for example towards an electric wheelchair for an individual with disabilities and to buy new clothes for an older person whose home had been damaged in a fire). There can be an immediate response in emergency cases.

Annual grant total: Around £3,000 to individuals and organisations.

Applications: In writing to the correspondent. In practice, many applications are referred by the council's social services department who also vet all applications from individuals. Applications can be submitted at any time.

Correspondent: Dave Easton, London Borough of Bexley, Room 122, Civic Offices, Broadway, Bexleyheath, Kent DA6 7LB (020 8294 6150)

The Samuel Edward Cook Charity for the Poor

Eligibility: People in need who live in Bexleyheath.

Types of grants: One-off grants to individuals and families ranging from £50 to £300 for household essentials, holidays and so on.

Annual grant total: About £800.

Applications: In writing to the correspondent, directly by the individual. Allocation of the funds is at the discretion of the Minister of Trinity Baptist Church.

Correspondent: Revd T M Griffith, 75 Standard Road, Bexleyheath, Kent DA6 8DR (020 8303 5858)

The John Payne Charity

Eligibility: Older people who live in the ancient parish of East Wickham.

Types of grants: One-off grants of up to £100, mostly towards gas, electricity and water bills.

Annual grant total: Grants average around £2,000 each year, though the actual grant figure tends to fluctuate quite widely.

Applications: In writing to the correspondent, to be submitted through a social worker, Citizens Advice, Age Concern or a similar agency. They are considered in March and October. Financial details such as sources of income, rent and other bills are required.

Correspondent: Bill Price, Clerk, Foster's Primary School, Westbrooke Road, Welling, Kent DA16 1PN (020 8317 8142)

Other information: Grants are also made to the British Polio Fellowship to be given as grants for holiday relief for carers.

Brent

The Kingsbury Charity

Eligibility: People in need who live in the ancient parish of Kingsbury.

Types of grants: One-off grants according to need. Most of the charity's expenditure is on almshouses. Grants to individuals have previously included £100 towards the cost of a trip to Lourdes for a terminally-ill woman, and £100 to help a family with a six-year-old child with leukaemia.

Annual grant total: Grants to individuals usually total around £1,000.

Applications: In writing to the correspondent, either directly by the individual or through a social worker, Citizens Advice, other welfare agency or other third party. They are considered every six weeks.

Correspondent: Mrs Philomena Hughes, 29 Bowater Close, London NW9 0XD (020 8205 9712)

The Wembley Samaritan Fund

Eligibility: People in need who live in the electoral wards of Wembley (Tokyngton, Alperton, Sudbury, Sudbury Court and Wembley Central). The charity is particularly aimed at children.

Types of grants: One-off grants mostly for school uniforms, warm clothing, nursery equipment and the costs of school outings.

Annual grant total: Charitable expenditure averages around £5,000 each year.

Applications: By telephone or in writing to the correspondent.

Correspondent: Anne Lake, c/o Sudbury Neighbourhood Centre, 809 Harrow Road, Wembley, Middlesex HA0 2LP (020 8908 1220)

Other information: Grants are also made to local organisations.

Bromley

The Bromley Relief-in-Need Charity

Eligibility: People in need who live in the ancient borough of Bromley, though there is some discretion to make grants within the wider area of the modern borough of Bromley.

Types of grants: One-off grants of up to £150. Twice-yearly seasonal grants are also available.

Annual grant total: Grants generally total around £1,000 a year.

Applications: Only through social services or a similar welfare agency or a Citizens Advice, doctor, health worker, head teacher and so on.

Correspondent: M Cox, Clerk, Lavender House, 11 Alexandra Crescent, Bromley, Kent BR1 4ET (020 8460 5242)

Camden

Hampstead Wells & Campden Trust

Eligibility: People who are sick, convalescent, disabled, infirm or in conditions of need, hardship or distress and who live in the former metropolitan borough of Hampstead.

Types of grants: In addition to pensions, grants are given for a range of purposes including holidays, clothing, help with debts and medical purposes.

Annual grant total: In 2008/09 the trust had assets of £14 million and an income of £705,000. There were 2,868 grants made for welfare purposes which included grants for holidays, furniture and starter packs, fuel bills, pensions and help with debts totalling £190,000.

Applications: Applications should normally be sponsored by a statutory or voluntary organisation, or by a person familiar with the circumstances of the case e.g. a social worker, doctor or clergyman. Applications for pensions are made on a form available from the correspondent. Applications for one-off grants can be made in writing and should include the client's name, date of birth, occupation, address and telephone number, details of other household members, other agencies and charities applied to, result of any application to the Social Fund, household income, and details of any savings and why these savings cannot be used. Decisions are usually made within two weeks.

Correspondent: Mrs Sheila A Taylor, Clerk to the Trustees, 62 Rosslyn Hill, London NW3 1ND (020 7435 1570; email: grant@hwct.fsnet.co.uk; website: www.hwct.org.uk)

Other information: The trust also assists organisations or institutions providing services and facilities for the relief of need or distress. Grants are also made to individuals for educational purposes although this only makes up a small proportion of funding.

Charities Administered from the Guild Church of St Andrew Holborn – The Stafford Charity

Eligibility: People in need who have lived in the Holborn locality, centred on the ancient parish of St Andrew Holborn now comprising of the guild church of St Andrew Holborn and the parishes of St George the Martyr, Queen Square and St Alban the Martyr Holborn for at least three years.

Types of grants: Pensions of £600 per year for people in financial need who suffer from chronic medical problems and who are sick and disabled. One-off grants of up to £500 are also available to people on a low income for kitchen appliances, furnishings, carpets, medical equipment, clothing, redecoration costs and so on.

Annual grant total: In 2009 the charity had assets of £4.1 million and an income of £175,000. Annual awards totalled £61,000 and grants to individuals totalled £13,000.

Applications: On a form available from the correspondent, to be submitted either directly by the individual or through a social worker, Citizens Advice or other welfare agency. Applications can be submitted at any time. All applicants are visited by the grants officer.

Correspondent: The Grants Officer, St Andrew's Holborn, 5 St Andrew Street, London EC4A 3AB (020 7583 7394; fax: 020 7583 3488; email: charities@ standrewholborn.org.uk; website: www. standrewholborn.org.uk/charities)

St Andrew Holborn Charities

Eligibility: People in need resident in a defined area of Camden (applicants should call or check the website for confirmation of the beneficial area).

Types of grants: One-off grants up to £500 towards household appliances, clothing and so on. Pensions of £600 a year are available for the long term sick, older retired people, and people living with disabilities.

Annual grant total: In 2009 the trust had assets of £7.7 million and an income of £237,000. Grants were made to 148 individuals for welfare and educational purposes totalling £126,000. A further £154,000 was awarded to local organisations.

Applications: On a form available from the correspondent or to download from the trust's website. Once received, a home visit will be arranged and supporting documentary evidence will be requested.

Correspondent: The Grants Officer, St Andrew's Holborn, 5 St Andrew Street, London EC4A 3AB (020 7583 7394; fax: 020 7583 3488; email: info@ standrewholborn.org.uk; website: www. standrewholborn.org.uk)

Other information: This charity is the result of an amalgamation of three trusts: The City Foundation, The Isaac Duckett Charity and The William Williams Charity.

The St Pancras Welfare Trust

Eligibility: People in need or who are sick, convalescent, disabled or infirm who live in the old Metropolitan Borough of St Pancras (postal districts NW5, most of NW1, parts of N6, N19, NW3 and WC1). Applicants must have the support of a sponsoring agency. The trust does not accept direct applications.

Types of grants: One-off grants, usually between £100 and £300, for a wide range of needs. Grants can be cash or vouchers.

Exclusions: No grants are made for educational purposes, computers, utility bills, statutory payments or rent arrears.

Annual grant total: In 2008/09 the trust made 255 (215 cash and 40 vouchers) grants totalling £35,000.

Applications: The trustees will only consider applications made through statutory bodies such as social services or community organisations like Citizens Advice. Applications are considered in March, June, September and December and should be received two weeks prior to the meeting.

Correspondent: John Knights, Secretary to the Trustees, PO Box 51764, London, NW1 1EA (020 7267 8428; fax: 020 7267 8428; email: thesecretary@ spwt.org.uk; website: www.spwt.org.uk)

Other information: Occasional grants are given to organisations with similar objects.

City of London

The Aldgate Freedom Foundation

Eligibility: People over 65 who are in need who live in the parish of St Botolph's, Aldgate.

Types of grants: One-off and recurrent grants of £200 a year plus a £30 Christmas gift.

Annual grant total: About £15,000 per year.

Applications: On a form available from the correspondent, directly by the individual, through a social worker, Citizens Advice or through a councillor or an alderman. Details of income/capital/ expenditure and length of residence in the parish must be included. Applications are considered at any time.

Correspondent: Revd Dr Brian Lee, St Botolph's Church, St Botolph-without-Aldgate, Aldgate, London EC3N 1AB (020 7283 1670)

Other information: Grants are also given to hospitals within the city and St Botolph's church project.

The City Chapter & Percy Trentham Charity

Eligibility: Older people who are in need and have lived or worked in the City of London, including Glasshouse Yard.

Types of grants: One-off and recurrent grants according to need.

Annual grant total: In 2008/09 the charity had an income of £6,300 and a total expenditure of £5,300.

Applications: In writing to the correspondent via a local clergyman. Applications for regular grants are processed twice a year; all other applications are dealt with as they are received.

Correspondent: Andrew Gayler, 60 Hartley Down, Purley, Croydon, Surrey, CR8 4EA (020 8660 5562)

The Hyde Park Place Estate Charity (Civil Trustees)

Eligibility: People in need who are residents of the borough of Westminster.

Types of grants: One-off grants in the range of £50 and £500 to individuals and families for all kinds of need, including educational.

Exclusions: Refugees and asylum seekers are not eligible.

Annual grant total: In 2008/09 the civil trustees had an income of £458,000 and made grants totalling £149,000 of which £134,000 went to organisations and £15,000 to individuals.

Applications: All applications should be made through a recognised third party/ organisation and include a case history and the name, address and date of birth of the applicant. Applications are considered on an ongoing basis.

Correspondent: Shirley Vaughan, Clerk, St. George's Hanover Square Church, The Vestry, 2a Mill Street, London W1S 1FX (020 7629 0874)

The Mitchell City of London Charity

Eligibility: Men over 65 and women over 60 who are in need and who live or work, or have lived or worked, in the City of London for at least five years. Widows of men so qualified may also apply.

Types of grants: Pensions of £300 a year. One-off grants are also given at Christmas (£125) and on the Queen's birthday (£75).

Annual grant total: In 2009/10 the foundation had both an income and expenditure of £76,000. Pensions and grants usually total around £17,000.

Applications: On a form available from the correspondent including details of the applicant's income and expenditure. Applications can be submitted directly by the individual or through an organisation such as Citizens Advice. They are considered in March, June, September and November.

Correspondent: Margaret Keyte, Clerk, Fairway, Round Oak View, Tillington, Hereford HR4 8EQ (01432 760409; fax: 01432 760409)

The St John the Baptist Charitable Fund

Eligibility: People in need through poverty or sickness who live in the parish of St John the Baptist, Purley.

Types of grants: One-off grants, usually ranging from £100 to £500. Recent grants have been given towards trips to Lourdes and to support a disabled parishioner.

Annual grant total: Around £1,000 a year.

Applications: In writing to the correspondent, either directly by the individual or through the parish priest of St John the Baptist Church, a welfare agency or other third party. Applications are considered monthly.

Correspondent: P Bunce, 4 Highclere Close, Kenley, Surrey CR8 5JU (020 8660 7301; email: pmb.seacrest@ btconnect.com)

Ealing

Acton (Middlesex) Charities

Eligibility: People in need between the ages of 18 and 25 who have lived in the former ancient parish of Acton for at least five years.

Types of grants: One-off grants for the purchase of domestic items or other needs. Payments are made directly to suppliers.

Annual grant total: In 2008 the trust had an income of £9,500 and a total expenditure of £3,500.

Applications: On a form available from the correspondent, by referral from clergy, doctors, health visitors or other professional people.

Correspondent: Lorna Dodd, Clerk, c/o St Mary's Parish Office, 1 The Mount, Acton High Street, London W3 9NW (020 8992 8876; email: acton.charities@ virgin.net; website: actoncharities.co.uk/)

Other information: The trust also gives grants towards education and the arts, supporting individuals and local schools and carnivals.

The Ealing Aid-in-Sickness Trust

Eligibility: People in need, who live in the old metropolitan borough of Ealing (this includes Hanwell, Ealing, Greenford, Perivale and Northolt but not Southall or Acton), who are incurring extra expense due to long or short term illness.

Types of grants: One-off grants according to need.

Annual grant total: Grants average around £1,200 a year.

Applications: On a form available from the correspondent. Applications should be made through a third party such as a social worker or an organisation such as Citizens Advice.

Correspondent: Caroline Lumb, c/o William Hobbayne Community Centre, St. Dunstans Road, London, W7 2HB (020 8810 0277; email: hobbaynecharity@ btinternet.com)

The Eleemosynary Charity of William Hobbayne

Eligibility: People in need who live in the civil parish of Hanwell. Only in exceptional circumstances will grants be made to people who live outside of this area.

Types of grants: One-off grants, usually ranging between £50 and £600, for clothing, furniture and domestic appliances. Grants are paid directly to the sponsors or suppliers.

Annual grant total: In 2008/09 the charity had assets of £2.5 million, an income of £144,000 and a total expenditure of £94,000. Grants were made to 68 individuals totalling £13,000. A further £26,000 was distributed to local organisations.

Applications: On a form available from the correspondent: to be submitted through a sponsoring organisation such as a local health centre, church, outreach organisation or social services. Applications are considered on a monthly basis, though urgent cases can be dealt with more quickly.

Correspondent: Mrs Caroline Lumb, Clerk, The William Hobbayne Centre, St Dunstan's Road, London, W7 2HB (020 8810 0277; email: hobbaynecharity@ btinternet.com)

Enfield

The Old Enfield Charitable Trust

Eligibility: People in need, hardship or distress who live in the ancient parish of Enfield.

Types of grants: One-off grants can include help with unexpected expenses, help with clothing, replacing/providing household goods, beds, furniture and carpets, the special needs of people who are disabled or chronically ill, and exceptionally help with bills and debts and so on. Around 50 regular quarterly grants are also made to people on a low income in financial need.

Exclusions: No grants to people who are homeless or for items which the local or central government should provide.

Annual grant total: In 2008/09 the trust had an income of £545,000. A total of £216,000 was given in grants to individuals, of which £138,000 was given for welfare purposes. A further £13,000 was donated to organisations.

Applications: On a form available on request from the correspondent. Applications can be made either directly by the individual or through social services, probation service, hospitals, clinics or clergy. Applicants who write directly are visited and assessed. Grants are distributed either directly to individuals or through a welfare agency or suitable third party. Applications are considered on a monthly basis.

Correspondent: The Trust Administrator, The Old Vestry Office, 22 The Town,

Enfield, Middlesex EN2 6LT (020 8367 8941; email: enquiries@toect. org.uk; website: www.toect.org.uk)

Greenwich

The Charity of Sir Martin Bowes

Eligibility: People in need who live in the boroughs of Woolwich and Greenwich. Applicants must have lived in London for a minimum of ten years, and all statutory services must have been tried.

Types of grants: One-off grants according to need.

Annual grant total: In 2008/09 the charity had an income of £7,000 and a total expenditure of £8,000.

Applications: In writing to the correspondent.

Correspondent: Clerk of the Goldsmiths Company, Goldsmith's Hall, Foster Lane, London EC2V 6BN (020 7606 7010)

Other information: The charity also makes grants to organisations.

The Greenwich Charity

Eligibility: People in need who live in Greenwich.

Types of grants: One-off and recurrent grants according to need.

Annual grant total: In 2008/09 the charity had an income of £8,000 and a total expenditure of £14,000.

Applications: In writing to the correspondent.

Correspondent: Raymond Crudington, Grant Saw Solicitors, Norman House, 110–114 Norman Road, London SE10 9EH (020 8858 6971)

Other information: The charity also makes grants to organisations.

The Woolwich & Plumstead Relief-in-Sickness Fund

Eligibility: People in need who have a physical illness or disability and live in the parishes of Woolwich and Plumstead. When funds allow, applications may be accepted from people living in the borough of Greenwich.

Types of grants: On average 20 one-off grants are made a year ranging between £50 and £500 towards meeting a specific need or a contribution towards the total cost. Support for recurring items is not usually provided.

Exclusions: No grants to help with debts, utility bills, recurrent expenditure, structural works or rent.

Annual grant total: In 2009/10 the trust had both an income and total expenditure of approximately £10,000.

Applications: On a form available from the correspondent either directly by the individual or through a health visitor, district nurse, social services or other welfare agency. The application should include the applicant's income and expenditure; a supporting letter from a health professional confirming the diagnosis and the resulting problems; and the reason why a grant is needed. Applications can be dealt with as and when received.

Correspondent: Alan Mayes, Directorate of Finance, London Borough of Greenwich, Riverside House, Beresford Street, London SE18 6BU (020 8921 5264; email: alan.mayes@greenwich.gov.uk)

Hackney

Mr John Baker's Trust

Eligibility: Widows and unmarried women in need who are over 50 and have lived for at least five years in the parish of Christchurch, Spitalfields in the borough of Hackney.

Types of grants: Pensions normally amounting to about £90 per quarter.

Exclusions: People under 50 years of age are not eligible for support.

Annual grant total: Grants usually total about £5,000 each year.

Applications: An application form is available from the correspondent. The trust requires information regarding details of income, age and residency. Please note that the trust can only accept new beneficiaries when a vacancy occurs.

Correspondent: Diane Coyne, Brewers' Hall, Aldermanbury Square, London EC2V 7HR (020 7600 1801)

Hackney Benevolent Pension Society

Eligibility: People who are older and in need, and who have lived in Hackney for at least seven years.

Types of grants: Gifts of around £30 are given to pensioners at Christmas, on their birthday and at the society's annual general meeting in October.

Annual grant total: In 2008/09 the society had an income of £6,800 and a total expenditure of £5,600.

Applications: In writing to the correspondent.

Correspondent: Janet Cassell, Larch Corner, Coopers Lane, Crowborough, East Sussex TN6 1SN (01892 667416)

The Hackney District Nursing Association

Eligibility: Health care staff and residents who live in the London borough of Hackney and who are in need.

Types of grants: One-off grants, usually of £100 to £5,000, towards pensions and the provision of medical aids.

Annual grant total: In the 15 months from December 2007 to March 2009 trust had an income of £19,000 and a total expenditure of £279,000. No grants were made to individuals during the period.

Applications: An application form, available from the correspondent, should be submitted through an organisation such as a school or Citizens Advice by April for consideration in May.

Correspondent: Robin Sorrell, c/o Sorrells Solicitors, 157 High Street, Chipping Ongar, Essex, CM5 9JD (01277 365532; email: rsorrell@sorrells.org.uk)

Other information: Homes for nurses and midwives, clinics for child welfare and other relief and assistance can also be given to people in need in the area of benefit.

In 2008 the Hackney Parochial Charities took over the management and control of the Hackney District Nursing Association.

The Hackney Parochial Charities

Eligibility: People in need who live in the former metropolitan borough of Hackney (as it was before 1970).

Types of grants: The charities state that grants to individuals are usually made for the purchase of clothing and essential household equipment, although grants can be given for many other welfare purposes, such as bedding, furniture and medical and travel expenses for hospital visits. Grants have also been given for holidays for widows with small children and single parent families and for gifts at Christmas for children in need.

Grants are one-off, generally of £100 to £250, although individuals can apply annually.

Exclusions: No grants for statutory charges, rent, rates, gas, electricity or telephone charges.

Annual grant total: In 2009/10 the charities had assets of £3.7 million and an income of £491,000, of which £177,000 was distributed in grants mainly to organisations.

Applications: In writing to the correspondent. The trustees meet in March, June, September and November and as grants cannot be made between meetings it is advisable to make early contact with the correspondent.

Correspondent: Robin Sorrell, c/o Sorrells Solicitors, 157 High Street, Chipping Ongar, Essex CM5 9JD (01277 365532; email: rsorrell@sorrells.org.uk)

Hammersmith & Fulham

Dr Edwards' & Bishop King's Fulham Charity

Eligibility: People in need who are on low incomes and live in the old Metropolitan borough of Fulham.

Types of grants: One-off grants according to need are made towards essential items of daily living including kitchen appliances, beds, furniture and clothing (including school uniforms). Grants for other things such as, floor coverings, decorating materials, baby items, and disability aids are also considered.

Exclusions: Grants are not normally given to people who are homeowners. Arrears on utility bills are not paid, nor are grants given retrospectively.

Annual grant total: In 2008/09 grants were made for both educational and relief in need purposes totalling £136,000.

Applications: Application forms are available from the correspondent or on the charity's website. Applications must be submitted in hard copy either directly by the individual or through a third party. Though, it is important to note that individuals applying directly for a grant will be visited at home by the grants administrator.

The committee which considers relief-in-need applications, including educational grant applications, meets 10 times a year, roughly every four to five weeks. The charity suggests that applications be submitted around two to three weeks before the next meeting.

Correspondent: Marianne Harper, Grants Administrator, Percy Barton House, 33–35 Dawes Road, London SW6 7DT (020 7386 9387; fax: 020 7610 2856; email: clerk@debk.org.uk; website: www.debk.org.uk)

Other information: In April 2006 the activities, assets and liabilities of the Dr Edwards' & Bishop King's Fulham Charity (No. 247630) were transferred to the charitable company, of which it became a subsidiary and was renamed the Dr Edwards & Bishop King's Fulham Endowment Fund (No. 1113490 – 1). The fund continues to give money to both individuals and organisations, with its main responsibility being towards the relief of poverty rather than assisting students.

Fulham Benevolent Society

Eligibility: People in need living in the metropolitan borough of Fulham in need of temporary financial assistance.

Types of grants: One-off and recurrent grants according to need.

Annual grant total: In 2008/09 the society had an income of £7,000 and a total expenditure of £12,000.

Applications: In writing to the correspondent. Applications should be submitted through a third party such as, social services, Citizens Advice, general practitioner, or minister of religion.

Correspondent: Angela Rogers, 4 Maltings Place, London, SW6 2BT (020 7736 6128)

The Mayor of Hammersmith & Fulham's Appeal Fund

Eligibility: People in need who live in the borough of Hammersmith and Fulham.

Types of grants: Grants vary and are given for general relief-in-need.

Annual grant total: In 2008/09 the fund had an income of £8,700 and an unusually low total expenditure of £400 (£6,300 in 2007/08).

Applications: In writing to the correspondent either through a social worker, Citizens Advice or other third party.

Correspondent: I Hartzenberg, Mayor's Office, Room 201, Hammersmith Town Hall, London W6 9JU (020 8753 2013)

Haringey

The Tottenham District Charity

Eligibility: People in need, especially the elderly, who have lived in the urban district of Tottenham (as constituted on 28 February 1896, which is largely the postal districts of N15 and N17) for at least three years prior to applying.

Types of grants: One-off grants to people who are poor, elderly, sick or who have a disability to reduce need, hardship or distress. Grants are to help with clothes, carpets and essential household items and range from £50 to £500. Pensions of £10 a month are paid quarterly to elderly people and Christmas and Easter bonuses of £40 are also given.

Exclusions: No grants for education or debts.

Annual grant total: In 2008/09 the trust had assets of £2 million and an income of £107,000. Grants (£24,000) and pensions (£48,000) were made totalling £72,000.

Applications: On a form available from the correspondent, which can be submitted directly by the individual or through social services, Citizens Advice, other welfare agency or any other third party. Applications are considered on an ad hoc basis.

Correspondent: Carolyn Banks, Hon. Clerk, 7th Floor, River Park House, 225 High Road, London N22 8HQ (020 8489 2965)

The Wood Green (Urban District) Charity

Eligibility: People in need who have lived in the urban district of Wood Green (as constituted in 1896, roughly the present N22 postal area) for at least three years.

Types of grants: Pensions and small one-off grants ranging from, on average, £50 to £300. Grants have in the past been given towards household items such as beds, fridges and clothes.

Annual grant total: Previously about £7,000 for welfare and educational purposes.

Applications: On a form available from the correspondent, to be submitted directly by the individual or via a social worker, Citizens Advice or other welfare agency or third party. Applications are considered all year round.

Correspondent: Mrs Carolyn Banks, Clerk, c/o River Park House, High Road, Wood Green, London N22 8HQ (020 8489 2965)

Harrow

The Mayor of Harrow's Charity Fund

Eligibility: People in need who live in the borough of Harrow.

Types of grants: One-off grants usually up to a maximum of £150 are given for basic items such as beds, food, heating appliances, cookers, clothing and so on.

Annual grant total: In 2008/09 the fund had an income of £6,600 and a total expenditure of £7,000. Grants were made totalling about £3,500.

Applications: On a form available from the correspondent. Most applications come through a social worker, Citizens Advice or other welfare agency, although this does not preclude individuals from applying directly. Applications are considered at any time. Applicants must demonstrate that the individual/family is experiencing financial hardship and that the grant will alleviate ill health or poverty or improve essential living conditions. Grants are paid directly to the supplier or through a third party.

Correspondent: Hasina Shah, Finance Department, PO Box 21, Civic Centre, Harrow, Middlesex HA1 2UJ (020 8424 1573)

Other information: Grants are also given to local organisations and to schools for school trips.

Hillingdon

The Hillingdon Partnership Trust

Eligibility: People in need who live in the borough of Hillingdon.

Types of grants: Occasional one-off grants or gifts of equipment, furniture, clothes and toys.

Annual grant total: In 2008/09 the trust had an income of £487,000 and a total expenditure of £514,000. Grants to individuals have previously totalled around £30,000.

Applications: On a form available from the correspondent.

Correspondent: John Matthews, Chief Executive, Room 22–25, Building 219, Epsom Square, London Heathrow Airport, Hillingdon, Middlesex TW6 2BW, Middlesex TW6 2BW (020 8897 3611; fax: 020 8897 3613; email: john@ hillingdonpartnershiptrust.org.uk; website: www.hillingdonpartnershiptrust. org.uk)

Other information: The trust is a formal grouping of businesses and people in business who have come together as volunteers, either as representatives of local companies or as individuals. Essentially, the trust acts as a broker between business and the community and tries to match projects in need of funding with a company wishing to sponsor a local activity. As such, grant-making to individuals is only a small part of the trust's overall activities.

Uxbridge United Welfare Trusts

Eligibility: People in need who are physically or mentally disabled and people on low incomes (such as families with young children or people who are elderly) who live in the Uxbridge area (bordered by Harefield in the north, Ickenham in the east, Uxbridge in the west and Cowley/ Colham Green in the south).

Types of grants: One-off grants either in cash or for services or specific items such as furniture, equipment, clothing and help with fuel bills.

Exclusions: No grants are given for rent or rates.

Annual grant total: Between £40,000 and £50,000 a year; about £35,000 of this is given for welfare purposes.

Applications: On a form available from the correspondent. Applications can be submitted directly by the individual or through a social worker, Citizens Advice or other welfare agency. They are considered each month.

Correspondent: David W Routledge, Chair, Trustee Room, Woodbridge House, New Windsor Street, Uxbridge UB8 2TY (01895 232976)

Hounslow

The John Fielder Haden (Isleworth) Relief in Sickness Charity

Eligibility: People in need in the London borough of Hounslow.

Types of grants: One-off grants according to need.

Exclusions: No grants for educational or religious purposes or for funding animals or pets. Grants cannot be awarded for items which should be provided out of statutory funds. No repeat grants are made.

Annual grant total: Grants total around £2,000 each year.

Applications: Application and accompanying referral forms (to be completed by the referral agency) are available from the correspondent or to download from the website. Applications should be made through a recognised referral agency such as social services, Citizens Advice or other welfare organisation. Applications are considered six times year. Upcoming deadline dates can be found on the website.

Correspondent: Juliet Ames-Lewis, Executive Clerk's Office, Tolson Lodge, North Street, Old Isleworth, Middlesex TW7 6BY (020 8569 9200; fax: 020 8847 5514; email: info@iahcharity.org.uk; website: www.iahcharity.org.uk)

Other information: Grants are also made to organisations.

Islington

Lady Gould's Charity

Eligibility: People in need who live in Highgate (i.e. the N6 postal district and part of the N2, N8, N10 and N19 districts). This includes the temporary occupants of Beacon House and asylum seekers who can be said to be resident in the area. Most grantees are in receipt of income support and housing benefit, though the charity will also consider applications from people earning under £10,000 a year.

Types of grants: One-off grants generally ranging from £350 to £500, though more is available in exceptional circumstances. Grants are given for clothing, furniture, furnishings, baby necessities and white goods. Grants to help towards debts and

holidays are available but will only be given in very needy cases. It is possible that more than one grant will be awarded during the accounting year.

Annual grant total: In 2009 the charity had assets of £225,000 and an income of £96,000. Grants were made to 82 individuals totalling £30,000.

Applications: On a form available from the correspondent. Applications can be submitted directly by the individual or through a third party such as a social worker, Citizens Advice or other welfare agency. They are considered at any time.

Correspondent: G A Couch, Bircham Dyson Bell, 50 Broadway, Westminster, London SW1H 0BL (020 7783 3769; email: andycouch@bdb-law.co.uk)

Dame Alice Owen's Eleemosynary Charities

Eligibility: Widows in need who are over 50 and have lived in the parishes of St Mary, Islington and St James, Clerkenwell for at least seven years.

Types of grants: Recurrent grants including pensions.

Annual grant total: Grants are usually made totalling around £2,000 per year.

Applications: In writing to the correspondent.

Correspondent: The Clerk, The Worshipful Company of Brewers, Brewers' Hall, Aldermanbury Square, London EC2V 7HR (0207 600 1801)

Charity of Richard Cloudesley

Eligibility: People in need who are sick or disabled and live in the ancient parish of St Mary's Islington (roughly the modern borough, excluding the area south of the Pentonville and City Roads).

Types of grants: One-off grants, typically up to £200, to help with cases of sickness or disability only.

Annual grant total: In 2007/08 the charity had assets of £25 million and an income of £999,000. Grants to individuals totalled £187,000, and were broken down as follows:

Household items, clothing and bedding	£137,000
Holiday and respite care	£22,000
Personal equipment	£14,000
Therapy	£14,000

Applications: Applications should be made in writing to the correspondent through social services, a doctor, Citizens Advice or similar agency.

Correspondent: Keith Wallace, Clerk, 26th Floor, 20 Primrose Street, London, EC2A 2RS (020 3116 3624; email: kwallace@reedsmith.com)

Other information: Although submitted on time, 2008/09 accounts were not

available to view at the Charity Commission.

The St Sepulchre (Finsbury) United Charities

Eligibility: People over 60 who are in need who live in the parish of St Sepulchre, Islington (EC1 and N1).

Types of grants: Pensions and one-off grants ranging from around £100 to £300.

Annual grant total: In 2008/09 the charities made grants totalling £16,000 and quarterly pensions amounting to £15,000.

Applications: In writing to the correspondent either directly by the individual or through a social worker, Citizens Advice or other welfare agency.

Correspondent: Robin Harvey, 117 Charterhouse Street, London, EC1M 6AA (020 7253 3757)

Kensington & Chelsea

The Campden Charities

Eligibility: Individuals applying for funding must:

- be living in the former parish of Kensington
- have been living continuously in Kensington for two years or more,
- are a British or European citizen or have indefinite leave to remain in Britain
- be renting their home.

Working age members of the family must also in receipt of an out-of-work benefit (e.g. Income Support, Jobseeker's Allowance, Pension Credit Guarantee or Incapacity Benefit) or on a very low income.

Types of grants: The charity considers funding to all ages of applicant; however, it divides its funding into three basic categories:

- Young people (16–24)
- People of working age
- People of retirement age

The charity will give grants for:

- the costs associated with education or training courses that have a strong likelihood of leading to work
- the costs associated with moving from benefits to paid employment
- the costs associated with engaging in volunteer work or work experience that has a strong likelihood of leading to work
- goods or services that are related to education or work goals.

Exclusions: The charity will not give funding for:

- direct payment of council tax or rent
- debt repayments
- fines or court orders
- foreign travel or holidays
- career changes
- personal development courses
- post graduate studies
- computers
- individuals whose immediate goal is self-employment
- goods and services catered for by central government.

Annual grant total: In 2009/10 welfare grants totalled £423,000, the majority of which was given to over 400 pension age individuals totalling £362,000, with the remaining £61,000 given to 142 individuals and families of working age for child-care, fares, goods and services to assist them towards financial independence.

Applications: Preliminary telephone enquiries are welcomed. Specific application forms are available for social work organisations seeking pensions or charitable relief for individuals in the parish. Applications are considered by the case committee, the education committee or the board of trustees as appropriate. Each of these meets monthly (except during August).

Applicants should also be willing for a grants officer to visit them at home.

Correspondent: C Stannard, Clerk, 27a Pembridge Villas, London W11 3EP (020 7243 0551, Grants officer: 020 7313 3797; website: www. campdencharities.org.uk)

Other information: The charities also makes grants to organisations and individuals for educational purposes.

The Kensington and Chelsea District Nursing Trust

Eligibility: People who are older and frail and people who are physically or mentally ill who are in need and have lived for at least two years in the borough of Kensington and Chelsea.

Types of grants: One-off grants up to £1,000 for domestic appliances, medical and nursing aids and equipment, beds, bedding and other furniture and clothing. Up to 60 heating allowances of £100 are also made.

Exclusions: Grants are not given for payment of salaries, rents, court orders or fines.

Annual grant total: In 2008/09 the trust had assets of £1.1 million, which generated an income of £82,000. Grants totalled £32,000, £31,000 of which was given to 113 individuals and £500 was given in Christmas gifts.

Applications: On a form available from the correspondent. Applications must be submitted through a social worker, Citizens Advice or other welfare agency and are considered each month.

Correspondent: Margaret Rhodes, 13b Hewer Street, London W10 6DU (020 8969 8117; email: kcdnt@tiscali.co. uk)

Other information: There were 12 grants made to organisations totalling £16,000.

Kingston-upon-Thames

The Hampton Wick United Charity

Eligibility: People in need who live in Hampton Wick and most of South Teddington, within the parishes of St John the Baptist, Hampton Wick and St Mark, South Teddington.

Types of grants: One-off grants (with the possibility of future reapplication).

Annual grant total: Previously over £20,000 a year in educational and welfare grants. Recent information was not available.

Applications: In writing to the correspondent. The trustees normally meet three times a year to consider applications.

Correspondent: Roger Avins, 241 Kingston Road, Teddington, Middlesex TW11 9JJ

The Kingston-upon-Thames Association for the Blind

Eligibility: Blind and partially sighted people who live in the royal borough of Kingston-upon-Thames.

Types of grants: One-off grants of £50 to £2,000 have been given to help towards the cost of holidays, travel expenses, white goods, furniture, household repairs, computers and aids like 'Easy Reader'.

Annual grant total: In 2008/09 the association had assets of £134,000 and an income of £159,000. Grants were made totalling £3,300.

Applications: On a form available from the correspondent or the local Social Service Sensory Impairment Team (Tel: 020 8547 6600). If the applicant is not in receipt of income support, housing benefit, or family credit they will need to provide detailed financial circumstances. Applications are considered every other month from January onwards.

Correspondent: Della Murphy, Kingston Association for the Blind, Adams House, Dickerage Lane, New Malden, Surrey KT3 3SF (020 8605 0060;

email: kingstonassoc@btconnect.com; website: www.kingstonassociationforblind. org)

Other information: The association runs a home visiting scheme. Support is also given to satellite clubs for the blind and to talking newspapers.

William Nicholl's Charity

Eligibility: People in need who live in the former borough of Kingston-upon-Thames as constituted until 1964.

Types of grants: Recurrent pensions and fuel vouchers, ranging from £15 to £400.

Annual grant total: Grants usually total around £2,000 per year.

Applications: In writing to the correspondent. Applications can be submitted either directly by the individual or through a social worker, Citizens Advice, welfare agency or any other third party. Applications should be received in December and are considered in April.

Correspondent: Andrew Bessant, Royal Borough of Kingston-upon-Thames, The Guildhall, High Street, Kingston-upon-Thames, Surrey KT1 1EU (020 8547 4628; fax: 020 8547 5032; email: andrew. bessant@rbk-kingston.gov.uk; website: www.kingston.gov.uk)

Lambeth

The Clapham Relief Fund

Eligibility: People in need who live in Clapham.

Types of grants: One-off grants towards domestic appliances, beds and bedding, redecoration, clothing, convalescent holidays and so on.

Exclusions: No grants will be given where sufficient help is available from public sources. Support will only be given to permanent residents of Clapham. Grants are not usually given for debts and living expenses.

Annual grant total: In 2009 the fund had an income of £24,000 and a total expenditure of £26,000. Grants were made totalling around £13,000.

Applications: On a form available from the correspondent, including details of monthly income and outgoings and verification by a sponsor. Applications can be submitted either directly by the individual, through a welfare agency or by a third party such as a district nurse, charitable agency worker, parish priest or doctor. They are considered at trustee meetings held four times a year, although emergency grants of up to £300 can be awarded between meetings.

Correspondent: Shirley Cosgrave, Clerk to the Trustees, Holy Trinity Church,

Clapham Common North Side, London, SW4 0QZ (020 7627 0306; email: cosgraves@parliament.uk)

Lewisham

The Deptford Pension Society

Eligibility: Retired people in receipt of supplementary benefits who have lived in the former London borough of Deptford for at least seven years.

Types of grants: Pensions of £15 a month (£30 in December) to about 30 individuals.

Annual grant total: Grants usually total around £7,000 per year.

Applications: On a form available from the correspondent, for consideration bi-monthly. Applications can be submitted either directly by the individual or a family member, through a third party such as a social worker, or through an organisation such as a Citizens Advice or other welfare agency. The application form must be signed by the individual.

Correspondent: John Alan Dolding, 2 Hunts Mead Close, Chislehurst, BR7 5SE (020 8467 2335; email: jdolding@supanet.com)

Sir John Evelyn's Charity

Eligibility: People in need who are in receipt of state benefits and live in the ancient parish of St Nicholas, Deptford and St Luke, Deptford.

Types of grants: Grants for welfare purposes such as domestic equipment, holidays, outings and pensions.

Annual grant total: In 2009 the charity had assets of £2.3 million and an income of £62,000. Grants to individuals totalled £26,000, and were broken down as follows:

- Pension payments £8,300
- Pensioners' outings and holidays £11,000
- Miscellaneous grants to individuals £5,100
- Volunteer worker's expenses £1,700

Applications: On a form available from the correspondent. Applications are considered every two months.

Correspondent: Colette Saunders, Clerk's Office, Armada Court Hall, 21 McMillan Street, Deptford, London SE8 3EZ

The Lee Charity of William Hatcliffe

Eligibility: People in need, particularly people who are elderly or disabled, who have lived in the ancient parish of Lee in Lewisham for at least five years.

Types of grants: Regular allowances.

Annual grant total: In 2008 the trust had assets of £220,000 and an income of £55,000. Grants were made to 36 individuals totalling £22,000.

Applications: In writing to the correspondent.

Correspondent: Gordon Hillier, Oakroyd, Bowers Place, Crawley Down, Crawley, West Sussex, RH10 4HY (01342 713153; email: gandbhillier@tiscali.co.uk)

Other information: Grants are also made to organisations. During the year grants totalled £47,000.

Lewisham Relief in Need Charity

Eligibility: People in need, including those who are who are older, disadvantaged or who have disabilities and who live in the ancient parish of Lewisham, which does not include Deptford or Lee.

Types of grants: Small one-off grants for specific purposes rather than general need, including those for clothing, household bills, travel expenses, furniture, disabled equipment and legal fees. Christmas grants are also made to older people of £25 each.

Exclusions: No grants are made where statutory assistance is available.

Annual grant total: Around £1,000 a year is given in grants to individuals.

Applications: In writing to the correspondent either directly by the individual, through a third party such as a social worker, or through an organisation such as Citizens Advice or other welfare agency. Applications should include as much supporting information as possible to enable the trustees to make informed decisions about why the individual is in need. Applications are considered throughout the year.

Correspondent: Emily Roberts, Clerk's Office, Lloyd Court, Slagrove Place, London SE13 7LP (020 8690 8145)

Other information: The charity is primarily engaged in providing sheltered accommodation for the elderly at its almshouse, Lloyd Court. It also makes grants to small organisations aiding the people of Lewisham.

Merton

Wimbledon Guild of Social Welfare (Incorporated)

Eligibility: Individuals in need who live primarily in Wimbledon but also in the borough of Merton, with some preference for older people.

Types of grants: Small one-off grants according to need towards kitchen equipment, children's clothing, household bills and so on. The guild also distributes gifts in kind, including furniture, food and Christmas toys.

Annual grant total: In 2008/09 the guild had assets of £5.5 million and an income of £2.8 million. Grants were made to individuals totalling £43,000.

Applications: On a form available from the correspondent or to download from the website. Applications are considered every other month. Upcoming meeting dates can be found on the website. Applications must be received a week before the date of each meeting, except when applying for an emergency food grant.

Correspondent: Helen Marti, 30–32 Worple Road, Wimbledon, London SW19 4EF (020 8946 0735; fax: 020 8296 0042; email: info@ wimbledonguild.co.uk; website: www. wimbledonguild.co.uk)

Other information: The guild also runs clubs and classes, manages a care home and provides a counselling service.

Newham

The Mary Curtis' Maternity Charity

Eligibility: Pregnant women or mothers with children under one. Applicants must live in Newham and can be asylum seekers or pregnant underage.

Types of grants: One-off grants ranging from £150 to £100 towards, for instance, cots, pushchairs and baby clothes.

Annual grant total: In 2008/09 the charity had an income of £2,100 and a total expenditure of £2,900.

Applications: In writing to the correspondent, through a doctor, vicar, teacher, midwife or social worker. Applications are considered every month and should include details about the area in which the individual lives and how many children she is responsible for.

Correspondent: Geoffrey Wheeler, Durning Hall, Earlham Grove, Forest Gate, London E7 9AB (020 8536 3812; email: geoffrey.wheeler@aston-mansfield. org.uk)

Redbridge

The Ethel Baker Bequest

Eligibility: People in need who live in the parish of Woodford Baptist Church in the London borough of Redbridge.

Types of grants: One-off and recurrent grants according to need.

Annual grant total: In 2009/10 the bequest had an income of £1,700 and a total expenditure of £4,700.

Applications: In writing to the correspondent, although the trust states that its funds are already allocated.

Correspondent: K R Hawkins, Treasurer, 41 Bressey Grove, South Woodford, London E18 2HX (020 8989 7521)

Other information: Grants are also made to organisations.

Richmond-upon-Thames

The Barnes Relief-in-Need Charity and The Bailey & Bates Trust

Annual grant total: Please refer to the entry for 'The Richmond Parish Lands Charity', which is administered by the same office.

Correspondent: Jonathan Monckton, Director, c/o Richmond Parish Lands Charity, The Vestry House, 21 Paradise Road, Richmond, TW9 1SA (020 8948 5701; fax: 020 8332 6792; website: www.rplc.org.uk/Barnes.html)

The Barnes Workhouse Fund

Eligibility: People in need who live in the ancient parish of Barnes (in practice SW13).

Types of grants: Grants of up to £350, for example to provide items such as carpets, domestic appliances, children's clothing and school trips and assistance with the costs of medical needs not available from the National Health Service.

Exclusions: Grants are not generally made to people who are homeless, as the scheme requires applicants to be resident in Barnes.

Annual grant total: In 2008/09 the fund had assets of £7.4 million and an income of £500,000. Grants were made to 129 individuals to individuals, of which 103 grants totalling £26,000 were given for welfare purposes.

Applications: Applications can be submitted through a recognised referral agency (such as social worker, health visitor, Citizens Advice or doctor) on a form available from the correspondent. Applications are considered upon receipt.

Correspondent: Mrs M Ibbetson, PO Box 665, Richmond, Surrey TW10 6YL (0208 241 3994; email: mibbetson@ barnesworkhousefund.org.uk;

website: www.barnesworkhousefund. uk)

Other information: Grants are also made to organisations.

The Hampton and Hampton Hill Philanthropic Society

Eligibility: People in need in St Mary's and All Saints', Hampton and St James, Hampton Hill.

Types of grants: Grants of about £200 each are made to people who have suddenly come into financial need.

Annual grant total: Grants average around £2,000 a year. Priority is given to making grants to individuals, with any surplus funds left over donated to local organisations.

Applications: In writing to the correspondent.

Correspondent: Joan Barnett, Waverley, Old Farm Road, Hampton, Middlesex TW12 3RL (020 8979 0395)

The Petersham United Charities

Eligibility: People in need who live in the ecclesiastical parish of Petersham, Surrey.

Types of grants: Pensions and grants of £75 to £500, including Christmas and birthday gifts and grants towards heating and disability equipment.

Annual grant total: In 2008 the trust had an income of £7,000 and a total expenditure of £4,000.

Applications: In writing to the correspondent. Applications are considered in January, April, July and October and can be submitted either directly by the individual or through a social worker, Citizens Advice or other welfare agency.

Correspondent: The Clerk, The Vicarage, Bute Avenue, Richmond, TW10 7AX

Other information: Grants are also given for educational purposes.

The Richmond Aid-in-Sickness Fund

Eligibility: People in need who live in the borough of Richmond.

Types of grants: One-off grants ranging from £25 to £250 for bedding, fuel bills, recuperative holidays and other small cash grants for the relief of those in poor health.

Annual grant total: In 2009 the trust had an income of £4,700 and a total expenditure of £4,600, the majority of which was distributed in grants.

Applications: Applications should be submitted through a social worker, Citizens Advice or other welfare agency. They are considered on the first Wednesday of February, March, May, June, September, November and December.

Correspondent: Catherine Rumsey, The Richmond Charities, 8 The Green, Richmond, Surrey TW9 1PL (020 8948 4188; email: richmondcharities@ richmondcharities.org.uk)

The Richmond Parish Lands Charity

Eligibility: People who are in need and have lived in the TW9, TW10 or SW14 areas of Richmond for at least six months prior to application and have no other possible sources of help. Older people must be in receipt of a means tested benefit to qualify for a winter heating grant.

Types of grants: Crisis grants of up to £250, mostly for household goods, bills, debts, food and clothing. Grants of £50 towards heating bills are available to older people.

Annual grant total: In 2009/10 the charity made grants to over 1,000 individuals totalling £198,000 which were broken down into the following categories:

Crisis grants	298	62,000
Winter heating	650	33,000
Education and training	100	104,000

Applications: On a form available from the Clerk to the Education Committee, to be submitted directly by the individual. This includes details of current employment, income and expenditure, details of the course/expenses applied for and a statement in support of the application. Two references are required and applicants are usually asked to attend an interview. Applications should be based on financial need and parental income is taken into account up to the age of 25 years. There are two trusts which are also administered by the Richmond Parish Lands Charity:

The Barnes Relief in Need Charity (BRINC) – cc.no 200318
'BRINC small grant forms are available for existing RPLC small grants referral agencies. In addition some Mortlake based organisations will be invited to become referral agencies for individuals in need. Application forms for organisational and individual grants are available from the correspondent.'

The Bailey and Bates Trust – cc.no 312249
Grants are made for relief in need purposes for individuals living in the postcode area SW14. Please contact the correspondent for further details of how to apply. However, please note that charitable expenditure for this trust has been particularly low since 2005.

Correspondent: The Clerk to the Trustees, The Vestry House, 21 Paradise Road, Richmond, Surrey TW9 1SA (020 8948 5701; fax: 020 8332 6792; website: www.rplc.org.uk)

Other information: Grants are also made to organisations, which included 86 grants in the year totalling £664,000.

The Richmond Philanthropic Society

Eligibility: People in need who live in the borough of Richmond.

Types of grants: Small one-off grants up to a maximum of £250 including those for washing machines, cookers and fridges, prams, beds and bedding, TV licences, rent arrears and utility bills.

Exclusions: No grants are given for educational purposes or for the payment of council tax. There are no cash grants available.

Annual grant total: In 2008/09 the society had an income of £14,000 and made grants totalling £24,000.

Applications: Preferably through Citizens Advice, social services, district nurses, health visitors and so on.

Correspondent: Derrick Schauerman, Trustee, 29 Maze Road, Richmond, TW9 3DE (020 8940 0778)

Southwark

The Camberwell Consolidated Charities

Eligibility: Primarily older people in need who have lived in the former parish of Camberwell for at least two years. Priority is given to those whose income is on or around the minimum state pension.

Types of grants: Annual pensions of around £80. Hardship grants are also available for emergency items.

Annual grant total: In 2008/09 the charities had both an income and expenditure of £50,000. In past years pension payments were made to over 160 individuals totalling about £10,000.

Applications: On a form available from the correspondent. Vacancies are advertised in the local press and by social services, Age Concern and so on.

Correspondent: Mrs J McDonald, London Borough of Southwark, Town Hall, Peckham Road, London SE5 8UB (020 7525 7511)

The Christ Church United Charities

Eligibility: Older people in need who have lived in the former metropolitan borough of Southwark for at least five years.

Types of grants: One-off and recurrent grants according to need.

Annual grant total: In 2008 the charity had assets of £9.7 million and an income of £312,000. Grants were made totalling £30,000 and were distributed as follows:

Outdoor pensions	£17,000
Christmas parties	£3,400
Christmas parcels	£3,600
Summer holiday benefits	£6,100

Applications: In writing to the correspondent, either directly by the individual, via a third party or through a social worker, Citizens Advice or other welfare agency.

Correspondent: Clerk to the Trustees, Charities Office, 151–153 Walworth Road, London SE17 1RY (020 7525 2128/9)

Other information: The charity also maintains a number of almshouses for the benefit of older people over the age of 60 who are in financial difficulties, with preference given to single women.

The Joseph Collier Holiday Fund

Eligibility: People of pensionable age who live in the former metropolitan borough of Southwark (i.e. the northern part of the present borough of Southwark).

Types of grants: Yearly one-off grants towards the cost of recuperative holidays in the UK or travel expenses to visit a relative.

Exclusions: Homeowners are excluded, whether the house was bought by themselves or on their behalf.

Annual grant total: In 2008/09 the trust had an income of £12,000 and a total expenditure of £6,200. Grants totalled around £6,000.

Applications: Applicants should collect a form, in person from the office. Applications are considered all year round. Forms are not issued to any other party.

Correspondent: P E McSorley, Charities Section, Municipal Offices, 151–153 Walworth Road, London SE17 IRY (020 7525 2128; fax: 020 7525 2129)

The Peckham & Kent Road Pension Society

Eligibility: People who have lived in Peckham, SE15, for at least five years, receive Income Support and are over 60 (women) or 65 (men).

Types of grants: Monthly pensions.

Annual grant total: Grants usually total around £2,000 a year.

Applications: In writing to the correspondent.

Correspondent: Tim Reith, The Peckham Settlement, Goldsmith Road, London SE15 5TF (020 7639 1823)

Rotherhithe Consolidated Charities

Eligibility: Recurrent grants are made primarily to widows who are in need and have lived in the ancient parish of Rotherhithe for at least 10 years. Help is also given for the general benefit of those in need who live in the parish.

Types of grants: The trust pays an annual pension to widows in need. It also gives one-off grants and provides holidays.

Annual grant total: In 2008 the charity had assets of £3.3 million and an income of £136,000. Grants were made to 822 individuals totalling £82,000, and were distributed as follows:

Stipend grants	£40,000
Christmas donations	£3,300
Holidays	£39,000

Applications: In writing to the correspondent. Applications can be submitted directly by the individual or through a third party, and are considered at any time.

Correspondent: B D Claxton, Amwell House, 19 Amwell Street, Hoddesdon, Hertfordshire EN11 8TS (01992 444466; fax: 01992 447476; email: brian@ hbaccountants.co.uk)

Other information: Grants are also made to organisations (£4,700 in 2008).

The Mayor of Southwark's Common Good Trust (The Mayor's Charity)

Eligibility: People in need who live in the borough of Southwark and the immediate surrounding area.

Types of grants: One-off grants, averaging about £75 each, for medical equipment, clothing, domestic appliances, furniture and household items.

Annual grant total: In 2008/09 the trust had assets of £85,000 and an income of £10,000. Grants were made totalling £9,500.

Applications: In writing to the correspondent. Applications can be made either directly by the individual or through a social worker, Citizens Advice or other third party such as, a family member, MP or doctor. Applications should include full details of family/financial/health background and details of other sources of funds, including whether a previous application has been made to this trust.

Correspondent: Nancy Hammond, Secretary, 4th Floor, Southwark Town Hall, 31 Peckham Road, Southwark, London SE5 8UB (020 7525 5000)

Other information: The trust also makes grants to local community groups who provide services to the elderly, particularly at Christmas.

The United Charities of St George the Martyr

Eligibility: Older people in need in the parish of St George the Martyr (in north Southwark SE1).

Types of grants: One-off grants according to need, usually of up to £300, towards buying items such as kitchen equipment, furnishing and flooring, mobility aids, accompanied transport to medical and dental treatments, easy-fitting slippers and shoes and illuminated magnifying lenses. Pensions and Christmas parcels are also given.

Annual grant total: In 2008 the charity had assets of £5.7 million and an income of £371,000. Grants to individuals totalled £151,000, and were broken down as follows:

Pensions	£36,000
Christmas parcels and parties	£13,000
Pensioner holiday costs	£74,000
Pensioner day trips	£26,000
Purchases for pensioners	£1,100

Applications: In writing to the correspondent. The charity has previously stated that its grants and pensions are fully committed but that any new applications will be kept on file.

Correspondent: Clerk to the Trustees, Marshall House, 66 Newcomen Street, London SE1 IYT (020 7407 2994; email: stgeorge@marshalls.org.uk)

St Olave's United Charity, incorporating the St Thomas & St John Charities

Eligibility: People in need who live in Bermondsey (part SE1 and all SE16).

Types of grants: Individuals over the age of 70 can receive a birthday gift of £100 a year and a further grant towards holidays once every year or every two years. Depending on additional income, other one-off grants can be made for a wide variety of needs, including clothes, musical instruments and holidays.

Annual grant total: In 2008/09 the charity had assets of almost £9 million and an income of £398,000. Relief in need grants totalled £138,000 with a further £120,000 given for holidays.

Applications: Applications should be made in writing to the correspondent and are considered four times a year.

Correspondent: Angela O'Shaughnessy, 6–8 Druid Street, off Tooley Street, London SE1 2EU (020 7407 2530; email: st.olavescharity@btconnect.com)

Other information: Grants are also made to organisations and to individuals for education purposes.

The Emily Temple West Trust

Eligibility: People under 19, or their parents, who are in need and live in the metropolitan borough of Southwark.

Types of grants: One-off cash grants ranging from £150 to £500 towards, for example, clothing, food and toys.

Annual grant total: About £1,400 a year. Grants are given to both individuals and organisations.

Applications: On a form available from the correspondent. This can be completed by the individual or the individual's parents or through a third party such as a church, social services, advice centre and so on. Applications are considered in May and November.

Correspondent: The Administrator, Christ Church, 27 Blackfriars Road, London SE1 8NY (020 7928 4707; fax: 020 7928 1148; email: admin@christchurchsouthwark.org.uk)

Sutton

The Sutton Nursing Association

Eligibility: People who are in poor health and in need and live in the London borough of Sutton and the surrounding area.

Types of grants: One-off grants generally up to £500 for domestic items, furniture, respite care, carpets, disability aids and so on.

Exclusions: Recurrent grants and matters relating to ongoing liabilities are not considered.

Annual grant total: In 2008 the association had assets of £617,000 and an income of £26,000. Grants to individuals totalled £3,900.

Applications: Applications are usually made through a social worker, Citizens Advice or other welfare agency. They are considered bi-monthly and must include as much information as possible, such as the costs involved, funds available from other sources and the ability of the individual to contribute.

Correspondent: John Helps, 28 Southway, Carshalton, SM5 4HW (020 8770 1095; email: sna@skingle.co.uk)

Other information: The association also makes grants to the community nursing services, hospitals and local organisations.

Tower Hamlets

Bishopsgate Foundation

Eligibility: Pensioners over the age of 60 who live and work, or have lived or worked, in the parishes of St Botolph-without-Bishopsgate; Christchurch, Spitalfields; and St Leonard's, Shoreditch – all within the borough of Tower Hamlets.

Types of grants: Recurrent grants of around £180 per quarter plus a Christmas bonus.

Annual grant total: In 2008/09 the foundation had assets of £20 million and

an income of £2.3 million. Pensions were made totalling £43,000. Grants to local organisations totalled £35,000.

Applications: On a form available from the correspondent. Applications can be submitted either directly by the individual or through a social worker, Citizens Advice or other welfare agency. There are no deadlines and applications are considered as and when a vacancy arises.

Correspondent: Stephanie Dacres, Administration Manager, 230 Bishopsgate, London EC2M 4QH (020 7392 9200; fax: 020 7392 9250; email: enquiries@bishopsgate.org.uk; website: www.bishopsgate.org.uk)

The Henderson Charity

Eligibility: Older people who live in the hamlet of Ratcliff and the parish of St George's-in-the-East, Stepney. Applicants must be longstanding residents of the beneficial area and there is a maximum income requirement.

Types of grants: Small pensions of around £20 a month.

Annual grant total: In 2008/09 the charity had an income of £21,000 and a total expenditure of £33,000.

Applications: Vacancies are normally advertised locally through social services and appropriate welfare agencies. When a pension is available, application forms can be obtained from social services or the correspondent.

Correspondent: Jonathan Woodbridge, Ringley Park House, 59 Reigate Road, Reigate, Surrey RH2 0QT (01737 221911; fax: 01737 221677; email: jcw@paramount.uk.com)

The Trevor Huddleston Fund for Children

Eligibility: Children in need who live on the Isle of Dogs.

Types of grants: A number of one-off grants towards basic needs, particularly winter clothes and shoes.

Annual grant total: In 2008/09 the trust had an income of £5,800 and a total expenditure of £3,700.

Applications: In writing to the correspondent on behalf of the individual child by schools, social services, churches or other community agencies for consideration at any time. Applications made by individuals or their families are not considered.

Correspondent: David Longbottom, 87 Saunders Ness Road, London E14 3EB (020 7515 5388; email: huddlestonfund@aol.com)

The Ratcliff Charity for the Poor

Eligibility: Older people in financial need who live in the London borough of Tower

Hamlets, with a preference for the Stepney area.

Types of grants: One-off and recurrent grants according to need.

Annual grant total: In 2008/09 the trust had assets of £259,000 and an income of £48,000. Grants were made to 22 individuals totalling £12,000.

Applications: In writing to the correspondent.

Correspondent: Adrian Carroll, Clerk, Cooper's Hall, 13 Devonshire Square, London EC2M 4TH (020 7247 9577; fax: 020 7377 8061; email: clerk@coopers-hall.co.uk; website: www.coopers-hall.co.uk)

St Mildred's Relief-in-Need Charity

Eligibility: Families in need who live on the Isle of Dogs.

Types of grants: A number of one-off grants towards basic needs, particularly winter clothes and shoes.

Annual grant total: Grants usually total about £5,000 each year.

Applications: In writing to the correspondent on behalf of the individual child by schools, social services, churches or other community agencies for consideration at any time. Applications made by individuals or their families are not considered.

Correspondent: David Longbottom, 87 Saunders Ness Road, London E14 3EB (0207 515 5388; email: huddlestonfund@aol.com)

Stepney Relief-in-Need Charity

Eligibility: People in need who live within the old Metropolitan Borough of Stepney.

Types of grants: One-off grants of £100 to £500 will be considered for a variety of needs, including household items, clothing, holiday where individuals will benefit from a short break, convalescence costs following discharge from hospital, hospital travel, mobility aids and so on.

Exclusions: No grants are made towards the repayment of loans, rent, council tax or utility bills.

Annual grant total: In 2008/09 the charity had both an income and a total expenditure of £18,000. Grants are made for relief-in-need and educational purposes.

Applications: An application form is available from the correspondent and may be submitted either directly by the individual or through a relative, social worker or other welfare agency. The trustees usually meet four times a year, but some applications can be considered between meetings at the chair's discretion.

Correspondent: Mrs J Partleton, Clerk to the Trustees, Rectory Cottage, 5 White Horse Lane, Stepney, London E1 3NE (020 7790 3598)

Miss Vaughan's Spitalfields Charity

Eligibility: People in need who live in the ecclesiastical parishes of Christchurch with All Saints in Spitalfields, St Matthew in Bethnal Green and St Leonard, Shoreditch.

Types of grants: Originally clothing and support was given to poor mechanics and weavers in Spitalfields who were unable to work. Now grants are given to individuals and families who are convalescing, unemployed or disabled and also to large families on a low income.

Annual grant total: Total annual expenditure for this charity is between £500 and £1,200.

Applications: In writing to a member of the clergy from any of the eligible parishes.

Correspondent: Philip Whitehead, 45 Quilter Street, Bethnal Green, London E2 7BS (020 7729 2790)

Wandsworth

The Peace Memorial Fund

Eligibility: Children aged 16 or under who live in the borough of Wandsworth.

Types of grants: Grants of £40 to £75 towards holidays and school trips.

Annual grant total: About £7,000 a year, for welfare and education purposes

Applications: Through a welfare agency on a form available from the correspondent. Applications should be submitted in February/March and May/June.

Correspondent: Gareth Jones, Town Hall, Room 153, Wandsworth High Street, London SW18 2PU (020 8871 7520; email: garethjones@wandsworth.gov.uk)

The Wandsworth Combined Charity

Eligibility: Older people in need who have lived in the London borough of Wandsworth for at least three years.

Types of grants: Monthly pensions of about £20 and a small bonus payment at Christmas time. One-off grants are occasionally made but only when there is an exceptional need.

Annual grant total: In 2009/10 the charity had an income of £12,000 and a total expenditure of £14,000.

Applications: In writing to the correspondent, to be submitted either directly by the individual or through a

social worker, local church, Age Concern or similar third party.

Correspondent: R J Cooles, 179 Upper Richmond Road West, East Sheen, London SW14 8DU (020 8876 4478; fax: 020 8878 5686; email: rc@abbottcresswell.com)

Westminster

The St Marylebone Health Society

Eligibility: Families with children of school age and under who live in the former borough of St Marylebone in the city of Westminster i.e. east of Edgware Road and north of Oxford Street in NW8, NW1 or W1.

Types of grants: One-off grants for beds, bedding, household equipment, children's equipment, clothing and so on. Grants average between £300 and £400. Christmas grants are made in the form of grocery vouchers.

Holidays and outings for parents and their children are also supported. The applicant should have lived in the beneficial area for two years.

Exclusions: Overseas holidays and families without children cannot be funded. Grants are not given to adults not caring for children, to assist older people or to students. Cash grants are rarely given.

Annual grant total: In 2009 the society had an income of £14,000 and a total expenditure of £11,000.

Applications: Through a social worker, educational welfare officer or health visitor using the application form available from the correspondent. Holiday applications should be made by February if possible; other applications at any time.

Correspondent: David Dunbar, 31 Llanvanor Road, London NW2 2AR (0208 455 9612; email: dgldunbar@aol.com)

Strand Parishes Trust

Eligibility: People who live and/or work in the London borough of the City of Westminster, with preference for the parish of St Clement Danes and St Mary le Strand.

Types of grants: One-off grants and pensions.

Exclusions: No grants for expeditions, electives, non-residents of Westminster or asylum seekers.

Annual grant total: In 2008 the charity had assets of £4.2 million and an income of £203,000. Pensions were made to 82 individuals totalling £31,000 and a further

£26,000 was given in grants to 132 individuals.

At the time of writing (winter 2010) the charity's accounts for 2009 were overdue at the Charity Commission.

Applications: On a form available from the correspondent. Applications must be made through a sponsoring organisation i.e. social services or Citizens Advice.

Correspondent: Frank Brenchley-Brown, 169 Strand, London WC2R 2LS (020 7836 3205; fax: 020 7836 9850; email: sptwestminster@aol.com)

Other information: The Isaac Duckett's Charity, St Mary le Strand Charity and St Clement Danes Parochial Charities were amalgamated with other charities to form the Strand Parishes Trust.

The United Charities of St Paul's, Covent Garden

Eligibility: People in need who live in the city of Westminster.

Types of grants: One-off grants ranging from £50 to £120. Monthly payments are also made to several people. Grants can be paid directly or through hospitals, health authorities, family service units or an early intervention service.

Exclusions: Tuition fees and holidays are not funded.

Annual grant total: In 2008/09 the charities had an income of £6,400 and a total expenditure of £6,500. Approximately £4,000 is given annually in grants to individuals.

Applications: In writing to the correspondent.

Correspondent: C G Snart, Clerk, c/o 31 Manor Wood Road, Purley, Croydon CR8 4LG (020 8660 2786)

The Waterloo Parish Charity for the Poor

Eligibility: People in need who live in the parish of Waterloo, St John with St Andrew.

Types of grants: Small grants ranging from £25 to £100 for living expenses and domestic items.

Annual grant total: Grants average around £900 a year.

Applications: On a form available from the correspondent. Applications can be submitted either by the individual or through a social worker, Citizens Advice or similar third party. They are considered quarterly.

Correspondent: Parish Administrator, c/o St John's Vicarage, 1 Secker Street, London SE1 8UF (020 7450 4601; email: adminstjohnswaterloo@hotmail.co.uk)

The Westminster Almhouses Foundation

Eligibility: People in need who live in the London Borough of Westminster. Limited support is available to those living elsewhere in Greater London and to women living elsewhere in the UK.

Types of grants: One-off grants averaging around £250 for a variety of needs, for example, helping a previously homeless person set up home through the provision of white goods or basic furniture. Recurrent grants are also made.

Annual grant total: In 2009 the foundation had assets of £20 million and an income of £640,000. Pensions and welfare grants were made totalling £73,000.

Applications: In writing to the correspondent through a third party (i.e. social worker, GP or Citizens Advice worker) who can verify the circumstances.

Correspondent: Roy Sully, Clerk to the Trustees, 42 Rochester Row, London, SW1P 1BU (020 7828 3131; fax: 020 7828 3138; email: clerk@ westminsteralmshouses.com; website: www.westminsteralmshouses. com)

Other information: The foundation also makes educational grants.

The Westminster Amalgamated Charity

Eligibility: People in need who live, work or study in the old City of Westminster (the former Metropolitan Borough of Westminster) or those who have previously lived or worked in the area for a total of five years or more.

Note: the old City of Westminster is that area covered by Westminster Council which is situated south of Oxford Street.

Types of grants: One-off grants ranging from £100 to £350 towards: clothing; essential household items (furniture, white goods, kitchen equipment); holidays for individuals aged 60 and over (taken in the UK only); and decorating and flooring costs.

Exclusions: No grants for: TVs; CD/DVD players; mobile phones; computers/ software; educational needs; holidays abroad; debt repayment or fees.

Annual grant total: In 2009 the charity had assets of £5.9 million and an income of £238,000. Grants totalled £38,000 and were distributed as follows:

Holidays and fares	£2,800
Discretionary	£11,000
Household	£17,000
Clothing	£5,700
Other	£540

Applications: On a form available from the correspondent or to download from the website. Applications must be submitted through a recognised referral agency such as social services or Citizens Advice and be accompanied by a supporting statement. Applications will usually take four to six weeks to process.

Correspondent: Keith Rea, Clerk to the Trustees, School House, Drury Lane, London WC2B 5SU (020 7395 9460; fax: 020 7395 9479; email: wac@3chars.org.uk; website: www.w-a-c.org.uk)

Other information: The charity also makes grants to organisations (£98,000 in 2009).

ADVICE ORGANISATIONS

The following section lists the names and contact details of voluntary organisations that offer advice and support to individuals in need. The list is split into two sections: 'Welfare' and 'Illness and disability'. Each section begins with an index before listing the organisations by category.

The listings are a useful reference guide to organisations that individuals can contact to discuss their situation and receive advice and support. These organisations will have experience in tackling the sorts of problems that other individuals have faced, and will know the most effective and efficient ways of dealing them. They may also be able to arrange for people to meet others in a similar situation. As well as providing advice and support, many of the organisations will be happy to help individuals submit applications to the trusts included in this guide. They may also know of other sources of funding available.

Some organisations included in this list have their own financial resources available to individuals. We have marked these with an asterisk (*). This list should not be used as a quick way of identifying potential funding – the organisations will have criteria and policies that may mean they are unable to support all the needs under that category and the guide will include many more potential sources of funding than there are organisations here.

Some organisations have local branches, which are better placed to have a personal contact with the individual and have a greater local knowledge of the need. We have only included the headquarters of such organisations, which will be happy to provide details for the relevant branches.

It is helpful for the organisations listed if any request for information includes an sae.

This list is by no means comprehensive and should only be used as a starting point. It only contains organisations that have a national remit and does not include organisations that provide general advice and support solely to members of a particular religion, country or ethnic group. For further details of groups, look for charitable and voluntary organisations in your local phone book, or contact your local council for voluntary service (CVS) (sometimes called Voluntary Action) which should be listed in the phone book.

The following general welfare section includes 'Benefit and grants information' and 'Debt and financial advice', which may be of particular relevance during these difficult economic times.

There is also a separate section 'Service and regimental funds' (see page 107), which details where support and advice for ex-service men and women and their families in need can be sought.

Welfare

General   349
Benefit and grants information   350
Bereavement   350
   Children   350
   Parents   350
Carers   350
Children and young people   350
   Bullying   351
   Young people leaving care   351
Debt and financial advice   351
Families   351
Housing   351
Legal   351
LGBT   351
Men's Rights   351
Missing people   351
Offenders and ex-offenders   351
   Families of offenders   352
   Women offenders and ex-offenders   352
Older people   352
Parenting   352
   Abduction   352
   Adoption and fostering   352
   Childcare   352
   Divorce   352
   Expectant mothers   352
   Grandparents   353
   Mothers   353
   Single parents   353
Poverty   353
Refugees and asylum seekers   353
Relationships   353
Social isolation   353
Squatters   353
Victims of accidents and crimes   353
   Abuse   353
   Crime   353
   Disasters   353
   Domestic violence   353
   Medical accidents   354
   Rape   354
   Road accidents   354
Widows   354
Work issues   354
Women   354

General

Advice NI, 1 Rushfield Avenue, Belfast, BT7 3FP (tel: 028 9064 5919; email: info@adviceni.net; website: www.adviceni.net). For information on sources of advice and support in Northern Ireland.

National Association of Citizens Advice Bureaux (NACAB), Myddelton House, 115–123 Pentonville Road, London, N1 9LZ (tel: 020 7833 2181 [admin only]; email: info@nacab.org.uk; website: www.nacab.org.uk). For details of your local Citizens Advice office please see the website. Online advice is also available on a range of topics from the Citizens Adviceguide website: www.adviceguide.org.uk.

The Salvation Army, Territorial Headquarters, 101 Newington Causeway, London, SE1 6BN (tel: 0845 634 0101; email: info@salvationarmy.org.uk; website: www.salvationarmy.org.uk). Contact can also be made by completing an online enquiry form.

Samaritans, The Upper Mill, Kingston Road, Epsom, KT17 2AF (tel: 020 8394 8300; 24-hour helpline: 0845 790 9090; see phone book for local number; email: admin@samaritans.org (general) jo@samaritans.org (helpline); website: www.samaritans.org).

Benefit and grants information

The Association of Charity Officers (ACO), Central House, 14 Upper Woburn Place, London, WC1H 0NN (tel: 020 7255 4480; email: info@aco.uk.net; website: www.joblinks.org.uk)

Benevolence Today, (website: www.benevolencetoday.org)

Child Benefit, PO Box 1, Newcastle upon Tyne, NE88 1AA (helpline: 0845 302 1444 [8am–8pm daily]; textphone: 0845 302 1474; website: www.hmrc.gov.uk/childbenefit)

Child Support Agency, National helpline, PO Box 55, Brierly Hill, DY5 1YL (tel: 0845 7133 133 [Mon–Fri, 8am–8pm and Sat 9am–5pm]; textphone: 08457 138 924; website: www.csa.gov.uk). Contact can also be made by completing an online enquiry form.

Child Trust Fund, Child Trust Fund Office, Waterview Park, Mandarin Way, Washington, NE38 8QG (helpline: 0845 302 1470 [Mon–Fri, 8am–8pm and Sat 8am–4pm]; textphone: 0845 366 7870; website: www.childtrustfund.gov.uk). Contact can also be made by completing an online enquiry form.

Direct Gov, general information on money, tax and benefits (website: www.direct.gov.uk/en/ MoneyTaxAnd Benefits/index.htm).

Disability Benefits Helpline, Warbreck House, Warbreck Hill, Blackpool, Lancashire, FY2 0YE (tel: 08457 123 456 [Mon–Fri, 7.30am–6.30pm and Sat 9am–1pm]; textphone: 08457 224 433; email: DCPU.Customer-Services@dwp.gsi.gov.uk; website: www.direct.gov.uk/en/DisabledPeople/ index.htm)

Jobseekers (Benefit claim line: 0800 055 6688 [Mon–Fri, 8am–8pm]; textphone: 0800 023 4888; website: http://www.direct.gov.uk/en/ Employment/Jobseekers/index.htm).

Pension Credit Claim Line, (tel: 0800 99 1234 [Mon–Fri, 8am–8pm and Sat 9am–1pm]; textphone: 0800 169 0133; website: www.thepensionservice.gov.uk/pensioncredit/) See the website for information on local offices.

Tax Credits helpline, Tax Credit Office, Preston, PR1 0SB (tel: 0845 300 3900 [Mon–Fri, 8am–8pm]; textphone 0845 300 3909; website: www.hmrc.gov.uk/taxcredits)

Veterans Agency, SPVA, Norcross, Thornton Cleveleys, Lancashire, FY5 3WP (Veterans helpline: 0800 169 22 77 [Mon–Thurs, 8.15am–5.15pm and Fri 8.15am–4.30pm]; textphone: 0800 169 34 58; email: veterans.help@spva.gsi.gov.uk; website: www.veterans-uk.info)

Winter Fuel Payments (helpline: 0845 915 1515 [Mon–Fri, 8.30am–4.30pm]; textphone: 0845 601 5613; website: www.thepensionservice.gov.uk/ winterfuel/). Contact can also be made by completing an online enquiry form.

Bereavement

Cruse Bereavement Care, PO Box 800, Richmond-upon-Thames, Surrey, TW9 1RG (tel: 020 8939 9530; helpline: 0844 477 9400; email: info@cruse.org.uk or helpline@cruse.org.uk; website: www.crusebereavementcare.org.uk).

Natural Death Centre, In The Hill House, Watley Lane, Twyford, Winchester, SO21 1QX (tel: 01962 712 690; email: contact@naturaldeath.org.uk; website: www.naturaldeath.org.uk).

Survivors of Bereavement by Suicide (SOBS), The Flamsteed Centre, Albert Street, Ilkeston, Derbyshire, DE7 5GU (tel: 0115 944 1117; helpline: 0844 561 6855 [9am–9pm daily]; minicom: 01925 826204; Typetalk: 18002–01925 826204; email: sobs.admin@care4free.net; website: www.uk-sobs.org.uk).

Children

Child Bereavement Charity, The Saunderton Estate, Wycombe Road, Saunderton, Buckinghamshire, HP14 4BF (tel: 01494 568900; email: enquiries@childbereavement.org.uk or support@childbereavement.org.uk; website: www.childbereavement.org.uk)

Winston's Wish, 4th Floor, St James's House, St James Square, Cheltenham, Gloucestershire GL50 3PR; (tel: 01242 515 157; helpline: 0845 203 0405 [Mon–Fri, 9am–5pm]; email: info@winstonswish.org.uk; website: www.winstonswish.org.uk).

Parents

Child Death helpline, York House, 37 Queen Square, London, WC1N 3BH; (tel: 020 7813 8416 [admin]; helpline: 0800 282 986 [Mon, Thurs and Fri, 10am–1pm; Tues–Wed, 10am–4pm; and every evening 7pm–10pm]; email: contact@childdeath helpline.org; website: www.childdeath helpline.org.uk).

The Compassionate Friends, 53 North Street, Bristol, BS3 1EN (tel: 0845 120 3785; helpline: 0845 123 2304 [10am–4pm and 6.30pm–10.30pm daily]; email: info@tcf.org.uk or helpline@tcf.org.uk; website: www.tcf.org.uk).

Foundation for the Study of Infant Deaths, 11 Belgrave Road, London, SW1V 1RB (tel: 020 7802 3200; helpline: 080 8802 6868; email: office@fsid.org.uk or helpline@fsid.org.uk; website: www.sids.org.uk).

Stillbirth and Neonatal Death Society (SANDS), 28 Portland Place, London, W1B 1LY (tel: 020 7436 7940; helpline: 020 7436 5881 [Mon–Fri, 9.30am–5.30pm and Tues–Thurs, 6pm–10pm]; email: support@uk-sands.org [general information] or helpline@uk-sands.org; website: www.uk-sands.org).

Carers

Carers UK, 20 Great Dover Street, London, SE1 4LX; (tel: 020 7378 4999; CarersLine: 0808 808 7777 [Wed–Thurs, 10am–12pm and 2pm–4pm]; email: info@carersuk.org; website: www.carersuk.org).

Leonard Cheshire Disability, 66 South Lambeth Road, London, SW8 1RL; (tel: 020 3242 0200; email: info@LCDisability.org; website: www.lcdisability.org). Contact can also be made by completing an online enquiry form.

Children and young people

Action for Children, 3 The Boulevard, Ascot Road, Watford, WD18 8AG (tel: 01923 361500; email: ask.us@actionforchildren.org.uk; website: www.actionforchildren.org.uk).

Catch 22, Churchill House, 142–146 Old Street, London, EC1V 9BW (tel: 020 7336 4800; email: information@catch-22.org.uk; website: www.catch-22.org.uk)

ChildLine, 45 Folgate Street, London, E1 6GL (tel: 020 7650 3200; 24-hour advice helpline: 0800 1111; website: www.childline.org.uk). A personal inbox can be set up on the site which will allow you to send emails to Childline and save replies in similar way to a normal email service. Alternatively, send a message without signing in through the 'send Sam a message' function. You can also chat online with a ChildLine counsellor.

Children's Legal Centre, University of Essex, Wivenhoe Park, Colchester, Essex, CO4 3SQ (tel: 01206 877910; email: clc@essex.ac.uk; website: www.childrenslegalcentre.com).

The Children's Society, Edward Rudolf House, Margery Street, London, WC1X 0JL (tel: 0845 300 1128; email: supportercare@childrenssociety.org.uk; website: www.childrenssociety.org.uk).

Get Connected, PO Box 51719, London, NW1 5UH. (tel: 020 7009 2500; helpline: 0808 808 4994 [1pm–11pm daily]; email: admin@getconnected.org.uk [general enquiries]; website: www.getconnected.org.uk). The helpline can be contacted through an online enquiry form. There is also a Webchat service available between 4.30pm and 10.30pm every night accessible through the website.

National Youth Advocacy Service, Egerton House, Tower Road, Birkenhead, Wirral, CH41 1FN (tel: 0151 649 8700; helpline: 0800 616 101; email: info@nyas.net or help@nyas.net; or send a text message to 0777 333 4555; website: www.nyas.net)

NSPCC, Weston House, 42 Curtain Road, London, EC2A 3NH (tel: 020 7825 2500; helpline: 0808 800 5000; email: info@

nspcc.org.uk or help@nspcc.org.uk; website: www.nspcc.org.uk).

Save the Children UK, 1 St John's Lane, London, EC1M 4AR (tel: 020 7012 6400; email: supporter.care@savethechildren. org.uk; website: www.savethechildren.org. uk).

The Who Cares? Trust, Kemp House, 152–160 City Road, London, EC1V 2NP (tel: 020 7251 3117; email: mailbox@ thewhocarestrust.org.uk; website: www. thewhocarestrust.org.uk).

Youth Access, 1–2 Taylors Yard, 67 Alderbrook Road, London, SW12 8AD (tel: 020 8772 9900; email: admin@ youthaccess.org.uk; website: www. youthaccess.org.uk; for an online directory of information, advice and support services for young people).

Bullying

The Anti-bullying Alliance, National Children's Bureau, 8 Wakely Street, London, EC1V 7QE (tel: 020 7843 1901; email: aba@ncb.org.uk; website: www. anti-bullyingalliance.org; details of the regional offices are available on the website).

Kidscape Campaign for Children's Safety, 2 Grosvenor Gardens, London, SW1W 0DH (tel: 020 7730 3300; helpline: 0845 1205 204 [Mon–Thurs, 10am–4pm; please note the helpline is only for parents, guardians or friends who are concerned about a child being bullied]; email: webinfo@kidscape.org.uk; website: www.kidscape.org.uk).

Young people leaving care

National Leaving Care Advisory Service (NLCAS), 3rd Floor, Churchill House, 142–146 Old Street, London, EC1V 9BW (tel: 020 7336 4824; email: ncas@catch-22. org.uk; website: www.leavingcare.org).

Debt and financial advice

Age UK Money Matters, provides a range of advice on topics such as pensions, tax, financial management, consumer issues and benefits (website: www.ageuk.org. uk/money-matters).

Business Debtline, (tel: 0800 197 6026 [Mon–Fri, 9am–5.30pm]; website: www. bdl.org.uk). The debtline does not provide advice by letter or email.

Citizens Advice: Adviceguide, for online advice on a range of topics, including debt (website: www.adviceguide.org.uk). Details of your local Citizens Advice office can be found on the website.

The Consumer Credit Counselling Service (CCCS), Wade House, Merrion Centre, Leeds, LS2 8NG (helpline: 0800 138 1111 [8am–8pm weekdays]; website: www.cccs.co.uk). Contact can also be made by completing an online enquiry form.

Gamblers Anonymous (GANON), c/o CVS Building, 5 Trafford Court, off Trafford Way, Doncaster, DN1 1PN (helplines – London: 020 7384 3040; Manchester: 0161 976 5000; Sheffield: 0114 262 0026; Birmingham: 0121 233 1335; Glasgow: 0370 050 8881; Ulster: 0287 135 1329 [24 hours daily]; website: www.gamblersanonymous.org.uk).

IFA Promotions Ltd. 2nd Floor, 117 Farringdon Road, London, EC1R 3BX (email: contact@ifap.org.uk; website: www.unbiased.co.uk). IFA Promotions is the industry body responsible for promoting independent financial advice in the UK and provides help to individuals looking for a financial advisor.

National Debtline, Tricorn House, 51–53 Hagley Road, Edgbaston, Birmingham, B16 8TP (helpline: 0808 808 4000 [Mon–Fri, 9am–9pm and Sat 9.30am–1pm]; website: www.nationaldebtline.co.uk) Contact can also be made by completing an online enquiry form.

TaxAid, Linton House, Room 304, 164–180 Union Street, London, SE1 0LH (tel: 020 7803 4950 [advice agencies only]; helpline: 0845 120 3779 [Mon–Thurs, 10am–12pm]; email: mail@taxaid.org.uk; website: www.taxaid.org.uk). Contact can also be made by completing an online enquiry form.

TPAS (Pensions Advisory Service), 11 Belgrave Road, London, SW1V 1RB (tel: 020 7630 2250; pensions advice: 0845 6012 923; helpline for women: 0845 600 0806; helpline for self employed: 0845 602 7021; email: enquiries@pensionsadvisory service.org.uk; website: www. pensionsadvisoryservice.org.uk).

Families

Home-Start UK, Home-Start Centre, 8–10 West Walk, Leicester, LE1 7NA (tel: 0116 233 9955; freephone: 0800 068 6368; email: info@home-start.org.uk; website: www.home-start.org.uk).

Housing

Shelter, 88 Old Street, London, EC1V 9HU (tel: 0844 515 2000; helpline: 0808 800 4444 [Mon–Fri, 8am–8pm and Sat–Sun, 8am–5pm]; email: info@shelter. org.uk; website: www.shelter.org.uk).

Homes and Communities Agency, Arpley House, 110 Birchwood Boulevard, Birchwood, Warrington, WA3 7QH (tel: 0300 1234 500; email: mail@ homesandcommunities.co.uk; website: www.homesandcommunities.co.uk)

Legal

Advice Services Alliance (ASA), 6th Floor, 63 St Mary Axe, London, EC3A 8AA (tel: 020 7398 1470; email: admin@asauk.org.uk; website: www. asauk.org.uk).

Bar Pro Bono Unit, 48 Chancery Lane, London, WC2A 1JF (tel: 020 7092 3960; email: enquiries@barprobono.org.uk; website: www.barprobono.org.uk).

Community Legal Advice, (tel: 0800 0856 643; helpline: 0845 345 4345 [Mon–Fri, 9am–8pm and Sat 9am–12.30pm]; website: www.communitylegaladvice.org. uk). Contact can also be made by completing an online enquiry form.

Law Centres Federation, 22 Tudor Street, London, EC4Y 0AY (tel: 020 7842 0720; email: info@lawcentres.org.uk; website: www.lawcentres.org.uk). See the website for information on your local law centre.

LGBT

The Lesbian and Gay Foundation (LGF), 5 Richmond Street, Manchester, M1 3HF (tel: 0161 235 8035; helpline: 0845 330 3030 [6pm–10pm daily]; website: www. lgf.org.uk). Contact can also be made by completing an online enquiry form.

Stonewall, Tower Building, York Road, London, SE1 7NX (Office (admin): 020 7593 1850; Info Line: 08000 502 020 [Mon– Fri, 9.30am–5.30pm]; email: info@stonewall.org.uk; website: www. stonewall.org.uk)

Men's Rights

Mankind, Flook House, Belvedere Road, Taunton, Somerset, TA1 1BT (tel: 01823 334244; helpline: 01823 334244 [Mon–Fri, 10am–4pm and 7pm–9pm except Friday]; email: admin@mankind.org.uk; website: www.mankind.org.uk).

Missing people

Missing People, 284 Upper Richmond Road West, London, SW14 7JE; (tel: 020 8392 4590; helpline: 0500 700 700; email: info@missingpeople.org.uk [general]; or report@missingpeople.org.uk [to report a missing person]).

- *Runaway Helpline*, for young people who have run away from home or care (tel: 0808 800 7070; email: runaway@ missingpeople.org.uk).

- *Message Home Helpline*, for those wishing to send a confidential message home (tel: 0800 700 740; email: messagehome@missingpeople.org.uk)

Offenders and ex-offenders

APEX Trust, 7th Floor, No. 3 London Wall Buildings, London Wall, London, EC2M 5PD (tel: 020 7638 5931; helpline: 0870 608 4567 [Mon–Fri, 10am–5pm]; email: info@apextrust.com or jobcheck@ apextrust.com; website: www.apextrust. com).

National Association for the Care and Rehabilitation of Offenders (NACRO), Park Place, 10–12 Lawn Lane, London, SW8 1UD (tel: 020 7840 7200; Resettlement Plus helpline: 020 7840 6464 or freephone: 0800 0181 259 [Mon–Fri, 9am–5pm]; email: helpline@nacro.org.uk; website: www.nacro.org.uk).

Prisoners Abroad, 89–93 Fonthill Road, Finsbury Park, London, N4 3JH (tel: 020 7561 6820; helpline: 0808 172 0098; email: info@prisonersabroad.org.uk; website: www.prisonersabroad.org.uk).

UNLOCK, the National Association of Reformed Offenders, 35a High Street, Snodland, Kent, ME6 5AG (tel: 01634 247350; email: enquiries@unlock.org.uk; **website:** www.unlock.org.uk)

Families of offenders

Prisoners' Families helpline, (tel: 0808 808 2003 [Mon–Fri, 9am–5pm and Sat 10am–3pm]; email: info@prisonersfamilieshelpline.org.uk. Information sheets are available on request by post or can be downloaded from the website: www.prisonersfamilieshelpline.org.uk)

Partners of Prisoners and Families Support Group (POPS), Valentine House, 1079 Rochdale Road, Blackley, Manchester, M9 8AJ (tel: 0161 702 1000; email: mail@partnersofprisoners.co.uk; website: www.partnersofprisoners.co.uk).

Prisoners' Families and Friends Service, 20 Trinity Street, London, SE1 1DB (tel: 020 7403 4091; helpline: 0800 808 3444 [Mon–Fri, 10am–5pm]; email: info@pffs.org.uk; website: www.prisonersfamiliesandfriends.org.uk).

Women offenders and ex-offenders

Creative and Supportive Trust (CAST), 37–39 Kings Terrace, London, NW1 0JR (tel: 020 7383 5228, email: cast@castcamden.co.uk).

Older people

Friends of the Elderly, 40–42 Ebury Street, London, SW1W 0LZ (tel: 020 7730 8263; email: enquiries@fote.org.uk; website: www.fote.org.uk).

Age UK, York House 207–221 Pentonville Road, London, N1 9UZ (tel: 020 7278 1114; helpline: 0800 169 6565 [Mon–Fri, 9am–4pm]; email: contact@ageuk.org.uk; website: www.ageuk.org.uk).

Third Age Employment Network, 207–221 Pentonville Road, London, N1 9UZ (tel: 020 7843 1590; email: info@taen.org.uk; website: www.taen.org.uk).

Parenting

Home-Start UK, The Home-Start Centre, 8–10 West Walk, Leicester, LE1 7NA (tel: 0116 258 7900; freephone: 0800 068 6368; email: info@home-start.org.uk; website: www.home-start.org.uk).

Parentline Plus, CAN Mezzanine, 49–51 East Road, London, N1 6AH (tel: 020 7553 3080; 24-hour helpline: 0808 800 2222; website: www.parentlineplus.org.

uk) Contact can also be made by completing an online enquiry form.

Twins and Multiple Births Association (TAMBA), 2 The Willows, Gardener Road, Guilford, Surrey, GU1 4PG (tel: 01483 304 442; helpline: 0800 138 0509 [10am–1pm and 7pm–10pm daily]; email: asktwinline@tamba.org.uk; website: www.tamba.org.uk).

Abduction

Reunite (National Council for Abducted Children), P.O Box 7124, Leicester, LE1 7XX (tel: 0116 2555 345; Advice line: 0116 2556 234; email: reunite@dircon.co.uk; website: www.reunite.org).

Adoption and fostering

British Association for Adoption and Fostering (BAAF), Saffron House, 6–10 Kirby Street, London, EC1N 8TS (tel: 020 7421 2600; email: mail@baaf.org.uk; website: www.baaf.org.uk).

Adoption UK, 46 The Green, South Bar Street, Banbury, OX19 9AB (tel: 01295 752 240; helpline: 0844 848 7900 [Mon–Fri, 10am–4pm]; email: helpdesk@adoptionuk.org.uk; website: www.adoptionuk.org.uk).

After Adoption, Unit 5 Citygate, 5 Blantyre Street, Manchester, M15 4JJ (tel: 0161 839 4932; ActionLine: 0800 0568 578; TALKadoption: 0808 808 1234 [aimed at younger people]; email: information@afteradoption.org.uk; Text: 07818 594 201; website: www.afteradoption.org.uk).

Fostering Network, 87 Blackfriars Road, London, SE1 8HA (tel: 020 7620 6400; Fosterline: 0800 040 7675 [Wed–Fri, 12pm–3pm]; email: info@fostering.net; website: www.fostering.net).

National Association of Child Contact Centres, Minerva House, Spaniel Row, Nottingham, NG1 6EP (tel: 0845 4500 280 [call to for information of nearest centre]; email: contact@naccc.org.uk; website: www.naccc.org.uk).

National Organisation for Counselling Adoptees and Parents, 112 Church Road, Wheatley, Oxfordshire, OX33 1LU (tel: 01865 875000; email: enquiries@norcap.org; website: www.norcap.org.uk).

Post-Adoption Centre, 5 Torriano Mews, Torriano Avenue, London, NW5 2RZ (tel: 020 7284 0555; Advice line: 020 7284 5879 [Mon, Tues, Wed and Fri 10am–1pm and Thurs 5.30pm–7.30pm]; email: advice@postadoptioncentre.org.uk; website: www.postadoptioncentre.org.uk).

Childcare

Daycare Trust (National Childcare Campaign), 2nd Floor, Novas Contemporary Urban Centre, 73–81 Southwark Bridge Road, London, SE1 0NQ (tel: 020 7940 7510; helpline: 0845 872 6251 [Mon, Tues, Thurs and Fri 10am–1pm and Wed 2pm–5pm]; email:

info@daycaretrust.org.uk; website: www.daycaretrust.org.uk).

Family Rights Group, The Print House, 18 Ashwin Street, London, E8 3DL (tel: 020 7923 2628; advice line: 0800 801 0366 [Mon–Fri, 10am–3:30pm]; email: advice@frg.org.uk; website: www.frg.org.uk).

Divorce

Both Parents Forever, 39 Cloonmore Avenue, Orpington, Kent, BR6 9LE (helpline: 01689 854343 [8am–9pm daily]).

Families Need Fathers, 134 Curtain Road, London, EC2A 3AR (tel: 020 7613 5060 [9.30am–4.30pm Mon–Fri]; helpline: 0300 0300 363 [Mon–Fri, 6pm–10pm]; Email: fnf@fnf.org.uk; website: www.fnf.org.uk).

National Family Mediation, Margaret Jackson Centre, 4 Barnfield Hill, Exeter, Devon, EX1 1SR (tel: 0300 4000 636; email: general@nfm.org.uk; website: www.nfm.org.uk).

NCDS Trust (National Council for the Divorced and Separated Trust), PO Box 6, Kingswinsford, West Midlands, DY6 8YS (tel: 07041 478 120; email: info@ncds.org.uk; website: www.ncds.org.uk).

CAFCASS (Children and Family Court Advisory & Support Service), 6th Floor, Sanctuary Buildings, Great Smith Street, London, SW1P 3BT (tel: 0844 353 3350; email: webenquiries@cafcass.gsi.gov.uk; website: www.cafcass.gov.uk).

Expectant mothers

ARC (Antenatal Results and Choices), 73 Charlotte Street, London, W1T 4PN (tel: 020 7631 0280; helpline: 020 7631 0285 [Mon–Fri, 10am–5.30pm]; email: info@arc-uk.org; website: www.arc-uk.org).

British Pregnancy Advisory Service (BPAS), 20 Timothys Bridge Road, Stratford Enterprise Park, Stratford-upon-Avon, Warwickshire, CV37 9BF (tel: 0845 365 5050; Advice line: 0845 730 4030 [Mon–Fri, 8am–9pm; Sat 8:30am–6pm; Sun 9:30am–2:30pm]; email: info@bpas.org; website: www.bpas.org).

Brook (formerly Brook Advisory Centre), 421 Highgate Studios, 53–79 Highgate Road, London, NW5 1TL (tel: 020 7284 6040; helpline [for people under 25]: 0808 802 1234 [Mon–Fri, 9am–5pm]; email: admin@brook.org.uk; website: www.brook.org.uk).

Caesarean Support Network, 55 Cooil Drive, Douglas, Isle of Man, IM2 2HF (tel: 01624 661269 after 6pm and weekends).

Disability Pregnancy and Parenthood International (DPPI), National Centre for Disabled Parents, Unit F9, 89–93 Fonthill Road, London, N4 3JH (tel: 020 7263 3088; helpline: 0800 018 4730; email:

info@dppi.org.uk; website: www.dppi. org.uk).

National Childbirth Trust, Alexandra House, Oldham Terrace, London, W3 6NH (tel: 0844 243 6000; enquiries: 0300 33 00 770; breastfeeding line: 0300 330 0771 pregnancy and birth line: 0300 330 0772, postnatal line: 0300 330 0773 website: www.nctpregnancyandbabycare. com). Contact can also be made by completing an online enquiry form.

Grandparents

Grandparents Association, Moot House, The Stow, Harlow, Essex, CM20 3AG (tel: 01279 428040; helpline: 0845 4349585 [Mon–Fri, 10am–4pm]; email: info@ grandparents-association.org.uk; website: www.grandparents-association.org.uk).

Mothers

Meet-a-Mum-Association (MAMA), 7 Southcourt Road, Linslade, Leighton Buzzard, Bedfordshire, LU7 2QF (tel: 0845 120 6162; helpline: 0845 120 3746 [7pm–10pm weekdays]; email: meet_a_mum.assoc@btinternet.com; website: www.mama.co.uk).

Mothers Apart from their Children (MATCH), BM Box No. 6334, London, WC1N 3XX (email: enquiries@ matchmothers.org; website: www. matchmothers.org).

Single parents

Gingerbread, 255 Kentish Town Road, London, NW5 2LX (tel: 020 7428 5400; helpline: 0808 802 0925 [Mon–Fri, 9am–5pm and Wed 9am–8pm]; website: www. gingerbread.org.uk). Contact can also be made by completing an online enquiry form.

One Space, for information, advice and links to online support groups (website: www.onespace.org.uk).

Poverty

Care International, 10–13 Rushworth Street, London, SE1 0RB (tel: 020 7934 9334; website: www.careinternational.org. uk). Contact can also be made by completing an online enquiry form.

Counselling, 5 Pear Tree Walk, Wakefield, West Yorkshire, WF2 0HW (tel: 0800 321 32 45; website: www. counselling.ltd.uk).

Family Action 501–505 Kingsland Road, London, E8 4AU (tel: 020 7254 6251; grants service: 020 7241 7459 [Tues, Wed and Thurs 2pm–4pm]; website: www. family-action.org.uk). Contact can also be made by completing an online enquiry form.

The Law Centres Federation, 22 Tudor Street, London, EC4Y 0AY (tel: 020 7842 0721; email: info@lawcentres.org.uk; website: www.lawcentres.org.uk)

Refugees and asylum seekers

Asylum Aid, Asylum Aid, Club Union House, 253–254 Upper Street, London, N1 1RY (tel: 020 7354 9631; advice line: 020 7354 9264 [Mon 2pm–4:30pm and Thurs 10am–12:30pm]; email: info@ asylumaid.org.uk; website: www. asylumaid.org.uk).

Immigration Advisory Service, Third Floor, County House, 190 Great Dover Street, London SE1 4YB (tel: 020 7967 1330; website: www.iasuk.org). See the website for information on local offices.

Migrant helpline, Charlton House, Dour Street, Dover, Kent, CT16 1AT (tel: 01304 203977; email: mhl@migranthelpline.org; website: www.migranthelpline.org.uk).

Refugee Action, Head office, Third Floor, The Old Fire Station, 150 Waterloo Road, London, SE1 8SB (tel: 020 7654 7700; email: info@refugee-action.org.uk [for agency-wide matters only]; website: www. refugee-action.org.uk). See the website for a list of local offices.

Refugee Council, 240–250 Ferndale Road, Brixton, London, SW9 8BB; (tel: 020 7346 6700; advice lines – London: 020 7346 6777; Yorkshire and Humberside: 0113 386 2210; East of England: 01473 297 900; West Midlands: 0121 234 1971; Children's Panel: 0207 346 1134; website: www. refugeecouncil.org.uk).

Refugee Support Centre, 47 South Lambeth Road, London, SW8 1RH (tel: 020 7820 3606).

Relationships

Albany Trust Counselling, 239a Balham High Road, London, SW17 7BE (tel: 020 8767 1827; email: info@albanytrust.org; website: www.albanytrust.org.uk).

Family Planning Association, 50 Featherstone Street, London, EC1Y 8QU (tel: 020 7608 5240; helpline: 0845 122 8690 [Mon–Fri 9am–6pm]; email: general@fpa.org.uk; website: www. fpa.org.uk).

Relate (National Marriage Guidance) Premier House, Carolina Court, Lakeside, Doncaster, DN4 5RA (tel: 0300 100 1234; email: enquiries@relate.org.uk; website: www.relate.org.uk).

Social isolation

Meet-a-Mum-Association (MAMA), 7 Southcourt Road, Linslade, Leighton Buzzard, Bedfordshire, LU7 2QF (tel: 0845 120 6162; helpline: 0845 120 3746 [7pm–10pm weekdays]; email: meet_a_mum.assoc@btinternet.com; website: www.mama.co.uk).

Rural Stress helpline, Arthur Rank Centre, Stoneleigh Park, Kenilworth, Warwickshire, CV8 2LG (helpline: 0845 094 8286 [9am–5pm weekdays]; email:

help@ruralstresshelpline.co.uk website: www.ruralstresshelpline.co.uk).

Single Concern Group/Future Friends, P.O. Box 40, Minehead, TA24 5YS (tel: 01643 708008; helpline: 01643 708008 [Office Hours]).

Squatters

Advisory Service for Squatters (ASS), Angel Alley, 84b, Whitechapel High St, London, E1 7QX (tel: 020 3216 0099 or 0845 644 5814; email: advice@squatter. org.uk; website: www.squatter.org.uk).

Victims of accidents and crimes

Abuse

Childwatch, 7 Jarratt Street, Hull, HU1 3HB (helpline: 01482 325552; email: info@childwatch.org.uk; website: www. childwatch.org.uk).

National Society for the Prevention of Cruelty to Children (NSPCC), Weston House, 42 Curtain Road, London, EC2A 3NH (tel: 020 7825 2500; helpline: 0808 800 5000 [24 hour]; Childline: 0800 1111; email: help@nspcc.org.uk; website: www.nspcc.org.uk).

Action on Elder Abuse (AEA), 23–25 Mitcham Lane, Streatham, SW16 6LQ (tel: 020 8835 9280; helpline: 0808 808 8141; email: enquires@elderabuse.org.uk; website: www.elderabuse.org.uk).

Clinic for Boundaries (formerly Witness), 3rd Foor, 24–32 Stephenson Way, London, NW1 2HD (tel: 020 3468 4194; email: info@professional boundaries.org.uk website: www. professionalboundaries.org.uk).

Crime

Victim Support, Hallam House, 56–60 Hallam Street, London, W1W 6JL (tel: 020 7268 0200; Supportline: 0845 3030 900 [weekdays 9am–9pm and Sat–Sun, 9am–7pm]; email: supportline@ victimsupport.org.uk; website: www. victimsupport.org). For details on the regional offices please see the website.

Voice UK, Rooms 100–106, Kelvin House, RTC Business Centre, London Road, Derby, DE24 8UP (tel: 01332 291042; helpline: 0808 802 8686; helpline text number: 07797 800 642; email: voice@voiceuk.org.uk or helpline@ voiceuk.org.uk; website: www.voiceuk. org.uk).

Disasters

Disaster Action, No.4, 71 Upper Berkeley Street, London, W1H 7DB (tel: 01483 799 066; email: pameladix@disasteraction.org. uk; website: www.disasteraction.org.uk).

Domestic violence

Broken Rainbow, J414, Tower Bridge Business Complex, 100 Clements Rd, London, SE16 4DG (tel: 08452 60 55 60;

helpline: 0300 999 5428 [Mon 2pm–8pm, Wed 10am–1pm and Thurs 2pm–8pm]; email: mail@broken-rainbow.org.uk; website: www.broken-rainbow.org.uk).

Men's Advice Line and Enquiries (MALE), 1st Floor Downstream Building, 1 London Bridge, London, SE1 9BG (helpline: 0808 801 0327 [Mon–Fri, 10am–1pm and 2pm–5pm]; email: info@ mensadviceline.org.uk; website: www. mensadviceline.org.uk).

National Centre for Domestic Violence, 5 Riverview, Walnut Tree Close, Guildford, GU1 4UX (24-hour helpline: 0844 8044 999; minicom: 18001 08009 702070; text: 'NCDV' to 60777; email: office@ncdv.org.uk; website: www.ncdv. org.uk).

Women's Aid Federation, Head Office, PO BOX 391, Bristol, BS99 7WS (tel: 0117 944 44 11; national 24-hour helpline: 0808 2000 247; email: info@womensaid. org.uk or helpline@womensaid.org.uk; website: www.womensaid.org.uk). For details on the regional offices please see the website.

Medical accidents

Action for Victims of Medical Accidents (AVMA), 44 High Street, Croydon, London, CR0 1YB (tel: 020 8688 9555 [admin only]; helpline: 0845 123 2352; email: advice@avma.org.uk; website: www.avma.org.uk).

Rape

Rape Crisis centre, BCM Box 4444, London, WC1N 3XX (helpline: 0808 802 9999 [12pm–2.30pm and 7pm–9.30pm daily); email: info@rapecrisis.org.uk website: www.rapecrisis.co.uk). See website for contact information on local rape crisis centres.

Women Against Rape (WAR) and Black Women's Rape Action Project, Crossroads Women's Centre, 230a Kentish Town Road, NW5 2AB (tel: 020 7482 2496 [Mon–Fri, 1.30pm–4pm]; email: war@womenagainstrape.net or bwrap@dircon.co.uk; website: www. womenagainstrape.net).

Road accidents

RoadPeace, Shakespeare Business Centre, 245a Cold Harbour Lane, Brixton, London, SW9 8RR (tel: 020 7733 6103; helpline: 0845 4500 355; email: info@ roadpeace.org; website: www.roadpeace. org).

Widows

National Association of Widows, 48 Queens Road, Coventry, CV1 3EH (tel: 024 7663 4848; email: info@nawidows. org.uk; website: www.widows.uk.net).

Work issues

Employment Tribunals Enquiry Line, 3rd Floor, Alexandra House, 14–22, The Parsonage, Manchester, M3 2JA (Public Enquiry Line: 0845 795 9775; minicom: 0845 757 3722; email: manchesteret@ets. gsi.gov.uk; website: www. employmenttribunals.gov.uk). See website for the contact details of local employment tribunals.

Public Concern at Work, 3rd Floor, Bank Chambers, 6–10 Borough High Street, London, SE1 9QQ (tel: 020 7404 6609; email: helpline@pcaw.co.uk; website: www.pcaw.co.uk).

Women

Refuge, Fourth Floor, International House, 1 St Katharine's Way, London, E1W 1UN (tel: 020 7395 7700 (general); 24-hour helpline: 0808 2000 247; email: info@refuge.org.uk; website: www.refuge. org.uk).

Women and Girl's Network, PO Box 13095, London, W14 0FE (tel: 020 7610 4678; helpline: 020 7610 4345; email: info@wgn.org.uk; website: www.wgn.org. uk)

Women's Health Concern, 4–6 Eton Place, Marlow, Buckinghamshire, SL7 2QA (tel: 01628 478 473; email: pshervington@womens-health- concern. org; website: www.womens-health-concern.org). Contact can be made by completing an online enquiry form.

Illness and disability

Disability (general)   355
Addiction   356
Ageing   356
AIDS/HIV   356
Alcohol   356
Allergy   356
Alopecia areata and alopecia androgenetica   356
Alzheimer's disease   356
Angelmann syndrome   356
Ankylosing spondylitis   356
Arthritis/rheumatic diseases   356
Arthrogryposis   356
Asthma   356
Ataxia   356
Autism   357
Back pain   357
Behcet's syndrome   357
Blindness/partial sight   357
Bone marrow   357
Bowel disorders   357
Brain injury   357
Brittle bones   357
Burns   357
Cancer and leukaemia   357
Cerebral palsy   357
Chest/lungs   357
Child growth   357
Cleft lip/palate disorder   357
Charcot-Marie-Tooth disease   357
Coeliac disease   357
Colostomy   358
Cot death   358
Counselling   358
Craniosynostosis or craniostenosis   358
Crohn's disease   358
Crying/restless babies   358
Cystic fibrosis   358
Deafblind   358
Deafness/hearing difficulties   358
Dental health   358
Depression   358
Diabetes   358
Disfigurement   358
Down's syndrome   359
Drugs   359
Dyslexia   359
Dyspraxia   359
Dystonia   359
Eating disorders   359
Eczema   359

Endometriosis   359
Epidermolysis bullosa   359
Epilepsy   359
Feet   359
Gambling   359
Growth problems   359
Guillain Barré syndrome   359
Haemophilia   359
Head injury   359
Heart attacks/heart disease (general)   360
Hemiplegia   360
Herpes   360
Hodgkin's disease   360
Huntington's disease   360
Hyperactive children   360
Hypertension   360
Hypogammaglobulinaemia   360
Incontinence   360
Industrial diseases   360
Infantile hypercalcaemia   360
Infertility   360
Irritable bowel syndrome   360
Kidney disease   360
Limb disorder   360
Literacy/learning difficulties   360
Liver disease   360
Lupus   360
Marfan syndrome   360
Mastectomy   360
Ménière's disease   361
Meningitis   361
Menopause   361
Mental health   361
Metabolic disorders   361
Migraine   361
Miscarriage   361
Motor neurone disease   361
Multiple sclerosis   361
Muscular dystrophy   361
Myasthenia gravis   361
Myotonic dystrophy   361
Narcolepsy   361
Neurofibromatosis   361
Organ donors   361
Osteoporosis   361
Paget's disease   361
Parkinson's disease   361
Perthes' disease   361
Phobias   361
Pituitary disorders   362
Poliomyelitis   362
Post-natal   362
Prader-Willi syndrome   362
Pre-eclampsia   362
Psoriasis   362
Raynaud's disease   362

Retinitis pigmentosa   362
Rett syndrome   362
Reye's syndrome   362
Sacoidosis   362
Schizophrenia   362
Scoliosis   362
Seasonal affective disorder   362
Sickle cell disease   362
Sjögren's syndrome   362
Sleep disorders   362
Smoking   362
Solvent abuse   362
Speech & language difficulties   362
Spina bifida   362
Spinal injuries   362
Stress   363
Stroke   363
Thalassaemia   363
Thrombocytopenia with absent radii   363
Tinnitus   363
Tourette syndrome   363
Tracheo-oesophageal fistula   363
Tranquillizers   363
Tuberous sclerosis   363
Turner syndrome   363
Urostomy   363
Williams syndrome   363

Disability (general)

Action Medical Research, Vincent House, North Parade, Horsham, West Sussex, RH12 2DP (tel: 01403 210406; email: info@action.org.uk; website: www.action.org.uk).

Contact a Family, 209–211 City Road, London, EC1V 1JN (tel: 020 7608 8700; helpline: 0808 808 3555; textphone 0808 808 3556; email: info@cafamily.org.uk; website: www.cafamily.org.uk).

Disabled Living Foundation (DLF), 380–384 Harrow Road, London, W9 2HU (tel: 020 7289 6111; helpline: 0845 130 9177 [Mon–Fri, 10am–4pm]; email: helpline@dlf.org.uk; website: www.dlf.org.uk).

Disabled Parents' Network, Poynters House, Poynters Road, Dunstable, LU5 4TP (helpline and general enquiries: 0300 3300 639; email: information@disabledparentsnetwork.org.uk; website: www.disabledparentsnetwork.org.uk).

Disabilities Trust, First Floor, 32 Market Place, Burgess Hill, West Sussex, RH15 9NP (tel: 01444 239123; email: info@thedtgroup.org; website: www.disabilities-trust.org.uk).

Disability Alliance, Universal House, 88–94 Wentworth Street, London, E1 7SA (tel: 020 7247 8776; advice service: 0207 247 9342 [Mon–Fri, 10am–12pm – members only); email: office@disabilityalliance.org; website: www.disabilityalliance.org).

Disability Law Service (DLS), 39–45 Cavell Street, London, E1 2BP (tel: 020 7791 9800; minicom: 020 7791 9801; email: advice@dls.org.uk; website: www.dls.org.uk).

Disability Pregnancy and Parenthood International (DPPI), National Centre for Disabled Parents, Unit F9, 89–93 Fonthill Road, London, N4 3JH (tel: 020 7263 3088; helpline: 0800 018 4730; textphone: 0800 018 9949; email: info@dppi.org.uk; website: www.dppi.org.uk).

Invalid Children's Aid Nationwide (I CAN), 8 Wakley Street, London, EC1V 7QE (tel: 0845 225 4073; email: info@ican.org.uk; website: www.ican.org.uk).

* *Jewish Care*, Amélie House, Maurice and Vivienne Wohl Campus, 221 Golders Green Road, London, NW11 9DQ (tel: 020 8922 2000; helpline: 020 8922 2222 [Mon–Thurs, 8am–7pm and Fri 8am–2pm]; email: info@jcare.org; website: www.jewishcare.org).

Kids, National Office, 6 Aztec Row, Berners Road, London N1 0PW (tel: 020 7520 0405; email: enquiries@kids.org.uk; website: www.kids.org.uk).

Mobility Information Service, 20 Burton Close, Dawley, Telford, TF4 2BX (tel: 01743 340269; email: mis@nmcuk.freeserve.co.uk; website: www.mis.org.uk).

PHAB England, PHAB Centre, Summit House, 50 Wandle Road, Croydon, CR0 1DF (tel: 020 8667 9443; email: info@phab.org.uk; website: www.phab.org.uk).

Queen Elizabeth's Foundation (QEFD), Leatherhead Court, Woodlands Road, Leatherhead, Surrey, KT22 0BN (tel: 01372 841100; email: info@qef.org.uk; website: www.qefd.org.uk).

RESPOND, 3rd Floor, 24–32 Stephenson Way, London, NW1 2HD (tel: 020 7383 0700; helpline: 0808 808 0700; email: admin@respond.org.uk; website: www.respond.org.uk).

Royal Association for Disability & Rehabilitation (RADAR), Unit 12, City Forum, 250 City Road, London, EC1V 8AF (tel: 020 7250 3222; minicom: 020 7250 4119; email: radar@radar.org.uk; website: www.radar.org.uk).

Addiction

Addaction, 67–69 Cowcross Street, London, EC1M 6PU (tel: 020 7251 5860; email: info@addaction.org.uk; website: www.addaction.org.uk).

Tacade (Advisory Council on Alcohol and Drug Education), Old Exchange Building, 6 St Ann's Passage, King Street, Manchester, M2 6AD (tel: 0161 836 6850; email: ho@tacade.co.uk; website: www.tacade.com).

Ageing

Age UK, York House 207–221 Pentonville Road, London, N1 9UZ (tel: 020 7278 1114; helpline: 0800 169 6565 [Mon–Fri, 9am–4pm]; email: contact@ageuk.org.uk; website: www.ageuk.org.uk).

* *Counsel & Care*, Twyman House, 16 Bonny Street, London, NW1 9PG (tel: 020 7241 8555; helpline: 0845 300 7585 [Mon–Fri, 10am–4pm except Wed 10am–1pm]; email: advice@counselandcare.org.uk; website: www.counselandcare.org.uk).

AIDS/HIV

National Aids Trust, New City Cloisters, 196 Old Street, London, EC1V 9FR (tel: 020 7814 6767; email: info@nat.org.uk; website: www.nat.org.uk).

Terrence Higgins Trust, 314–320 Grays Inn Road, London, WC1X 8DP (tel: 020 7812 1600; advice & support: 0845 1221 200 [Mon–Fri, 10am–10pm and Sat–Sun, 12pm–6pm]; email: info@tht.org.uk; website: www.tht.org.uk).

Alcohol

Al-Anon Family Groups UK & Eire (AFG), 61 Great Dover Street, London, SE1 4YF (helpline: 020 7403 0888 [10am–10pm]; email: enquiries@al-anonuk.org.uk; website: www.al-anonuk.org.uk).

Alcohol Concern, 64 Leman Street, London, E1 8EU (tel: 020 7264 0510; email: contact@alcoholconcern.org.uk; website: www.alcoholconcern.org.uk).

Alcoholics Anonymous (AA), General Service Office, PO Box 1, 10 Toft Green, York, YO1 7NJ (tel: 01904 644 026; helpline: 0845 7697 555; email: help@alcoholics-anonymous.org.uk; website: www.alcoholics-anonymous.org.uk).

Drinkline, helpline: 0800 917 8282 [Mon–Fri, 9am–11pm].

Foundation 66, 7 Holyrood Street, London, SE1 2EL (tel: 020 7234 9940; email: info@foundation66.org.uk; website: www.foundation66.org.uk).

Turning Point, Standon House, 21 Mansell Street, London, E1 8AA (tel: 020 7481 7600; email: info@turning-point.co.uk; website: www.turning-point.co.uk).

Allergy

Action Against Allergy, PO Box 278, Twickenham, TW1 4QQ (tel: 020 8892 4949; helpline: 020 8892 2711; email: AAA@actionagainstallergy.freeserve.co.uk; website: www.actionagainstallergy.co.uk).

Allergy UK, Planwell House, LEFA Business Park, Edgington Way Sidcup, Kent, DA14 5BH (helpline: 01322 619898; email: info@allergyuk.org; website: www.allergyuk.org).

Alopecia areata and alopecia androgenetica

Alopecia UK, 5 Titchwell Road, London, SW18 3LW (tel: 0208 333 1661; email: info@alopeciaonline.org.uk; website: www.alopeciaonline.org.uk).

Hairline International, Lyons Court, 1668 High Street, Knowle, West Midlands, B93 0LY (website: www.hairlineinternational.co.uk).

Alzheimer's disease

* *Alzheimer's Society*, Devon House, 58 St Katharine's Way, London, E1W 1JX (tel: 020 7423 3500; helpline: 0845 300 0336 [Mon–Fri, 8.30am–6.30pm]; email: enquiries@alzheimers.org.uk; website: www.alzheimers.org.uk).

Angelmann syndrome

ASSERT (Angelman Syndrome Support Education and Research), PO Box 4962, Nuneaton, CV11 9FD (tel: 0300 999 0102; email info@angelmanuk.org; website: www.angelmanuk.org).

Ankylosing spondylitis

National Ankylosing Spondylitis Society (NASS), Unit 0.2, One Victoria Villas, Richmond, Surrey, TW9 2GW (tel: 020 8948 9117; email: admin@nass.co.uk; website: www.nass.co.uk).

Arthritis/rheumatic diseases

Arthritis Care, 18 Stephenson Way, London, NW1 2HD (tel: 020 7380 6500; helpline: 0808 800 4050 [Mon–Fri, 10am–4pm]; email: info@arthritiscare.org.uk; website: www.arthritiscare.org.uk).

Arthritis Research UK, Copeman House, St Mary's Gate, Chesterfield, S41 7TD (tel: 0300 790 0400; email: enquiries@arthritisresearchuk.org; website: www.arc.org.uk).

Arthrogryposis

Arthrogryposis Group (TAG), PO Box 5336, Stourport-on-Severn, Worcestershire, DY13 3BE (tel: 0800 028 4447; email: info@taguk.org.uk; website: www.tagonline.org.uk).

Asthma

Asthma UK, Summit House, 70 Wilson Street, London, EC2A 2DB (tel: 0800 121 62 55; Adviceline: 0800 121 6244; email: info@asthma.org.uk; website: www.asthma.org.uk).

Ataxia

* *Ataxia UK*, Lincoln House, Kennington Park, 1–3 Brixton Road, London, SW9 6DE (tel: 020 7582 1444; helpline: 0845 644 0606 [Mon–Thurs, 10.30am–

3.30pm and Fri 10am–1pm]; email: enquiries@ataxia.org.uk or helpline@ataxia.org.uk; website: www.ataxia.org.uk).

Autism

National Autistic Society (NAS), 393 City Road, London, EC1V 1NG (tel: 020 7833 2299; helpline: 0845 070 4004; email: nas@nas.org.uk; website: www.nas.org.uk).

Back pain

Back Care, 16 Elmtree Road, Teddington, Middlesex, TW11 8ST (tel: 020 8977 5474; helpline: 0845 130 2704; website: www.backcare.org.uk). Contact can also be made by completing a helpline enquiry form.

Behcet's syndrome

Behcet's Syndrome Society, 8 Abbey Gardens, Evesham, Worcester, WR11 4SP (tel: 0845 130 7328; helpline: 0845 130 7329; email: info@behcetsdisease.org.uk; website: www.behcets.org.uk).

Blindness/partial sight

British Retinitis Pigmentosa Society (BRPS), PO Box 350, Buckingham, MK18 5GZ (tel: 01280 821334; helpline: 0845 123 2354; email: info@brps.org.uk; website: www.brps.org.uk).

CALIBRE (Cassette Library of Recorded Books), Aylesbury, Buckinghamshire, HP22 5XQ (tel: 01296 432 339; website: www.calibre.org.uk). Contact can also be made by completing an online enquiry form.

International Glaucoma Association (IGA), Woodcote House, 15 Highpoint Business Village, Henwood, Ashford, Kent, TN24 8DH (tel: 01233 64 81 64; helpline: 01233 64 81 70; email: info@iga.org.uk; website: www.iga.org.uk).

Listening Books, 12 Lant Street, London, SE1 1QH (tel: 020 7407 9417; email: info@listening-books.org.uk; website: www.listening-books.org.uk).

National Federation of the Blind of the UK, Sir John Wilson House, 215 Kirkgate, Wakefield, WF1 1JG (tel: 01924 291313; email: nfbuk@nufbk.org; website: www.nfbuk.org).

Partially Sighted Society, 7/9 Bennetthorpe, Doncaster, DN2 6AA (tel: 0844 477 4966; email: info@partsight.org.uk; website: www.partsight.org.uk).

* *Royal National Institute for the Blind (RNIB)*, 105 Judd Street, London, WC1H 9NE (tel: 020 7388 1266; helpline: 0303 123 9999; email: helpline@rnib.org.uk; website: www.rnib.org.uk).

Voluntary Transcribers' Group, 8 Segbourne Road, Rubery, Birmingham, B45 9SX (tel: 0121 453 4268).

Bone marrow

Anthony Nolan Trust, Units 2–3, Heathgate Place, 75–87 Agincourt Road, London, NW3 2NU (tel: 0303 303 0303; email: info@anthonynolan.org; website: www.anthonynolan.org.uk).

Bowel disorders

National Advisory Service for Parents of Children with a Stoma (NASPCS), 51 Anderson Drive, Darvel, Ayrshire, KA17 0DE (tel: 01560 322024).

National Association for Colitis & Crohn's Disease (NACC), 4 Beaumont House, Sutton Road, St Albans, Hertfordshire, AL1 5HH (tel: 01727 844296; helpline: 0845 130 2233 [Mon–Fri, 10am–1pm]; email: info@CrohnsAndColitis.org.uk; website: www.nacc.org.uk).

Brain injury

British Institute for Brain-Injured Children (BIBIC), Knowle Hall, Bawdrip, Bridgwater, Somerset, TA7 8PJ (tel: 01278 684060; email: info@bibic.org.uk; website: www.bibic.org.uk).

Brittle bones

* *Brittle Bone Society*, Grant-Paterson House, 30 Guthrie Street, Dundee, DD1 5BS (tel: 01382 204446; helpline: 0800 028 2459; email: bbs@brittlebone.org; website: www.brittlebone.org).

Burns

British Burn Association, 35–43 Lincoln's Inn Fields, London, WC2A 3PE (tel: 020 7869 6923; Email: info@britishburnassociation.org; website: www.britishburnassociation.org).

Children's Fire and Burn Trust, 38 Buckingham Palace Road, London, SW1W 0RE (tel: 020 7233 8333; email: info@cbtrust.org.uk; website: www.cbtrust.org.uk).

Cancer and leukaemia

Action Cancer, 1 Marlborough Park South, Belfast, BT9 6XS (tel: 028 9080 3344; email: info@actioncancer.org; website: www.actioncancer.org).

* *CLIC Sargent Cancer Care for Children*, Griffin House, 161 Hammersmith Road, London, W6 8SG (tel: 020 8752 2800 [switchboard]; helpline: 0800 197 0068; email: helpline@clicsargent.org.uk; website: www.clicsargent.org.uk).

* *Leukaemia Care Society*, One Birch Court, Blackpole East, Worcester, WR3 8SG (tel: 01905 755 977; helpline: 0800 169 6680; email: care@leukaemiacare.org.uk; website: www.leukaemiacare.org.uk).

* *Macmillan Cancer Relief*, 89 Albert Embankment, London, SE1 7UQ (tel: 020 7840 7840; helpline: 0808 808 0000 [Mon–Fri, 9am–8pm]; textphone: 0808 808 0121; website: www.macmillan.org.uk). Contact can also be made by completing an online enquiry form.

Marie Curie Foundation, 89 Albert Embankment, London, SE1 7TP (tel: 0800 716 146; email: info@mariecurie.org.uk; website: www.mariecurie.org.uk).

Tak Tent Cancer Support, Flat 5, 30 Shelly Court, Gartnavel Complex, Glasgow, G12 0YN (tel: 0141 211 0122; email: tak.tent@care4free.net; website: www.taktent.org).

Tenovous Cancer Information Centre, 9th Floor, Gleider House, Ty Glas Road, Llanishen, Cardiff, CF14 5BD (tel: 029 2076 8850; helpline: 0808 808 1010; email: post@tenovus.com; website: www.tenovus.org.uk).

Cerebral palsy

SCOPE, 6 Market Road, London, N7 9PW (tel: 020 7619 7100; helpline: 0808 800 3333; email: response@scope.org.uk; website: www.scope.org.uk).

Chest/lungs

British Lung Foundation, 73–75 Goswell Road, London, EC1V 7ER (tel: 020 7688 5555; helpline: 08458 50 50 20; email: enquiries@blf-uk.org; website: www.lunguk.org).

Child growth

Child Growth Foundation, 2 Mayfield Avenue, Chiswick, London, W4 1PW (tel: 020 8995 0257; email: info@childgrowthfoundation.org; website: www.childgrowthfoundation.org).

Cleft lip/palate disorder

Cleft Lip & Palate Association (CLAPA), 1st Floor, Green Man Tower, 332B Goswell Road, London, EC1V 7LQ (tel: 020 7833 4883; email: info@clapa.com; website: www.clapa.com).

Charcot-Marie-Tooth disease

CMT International United Kingdom, 98 Broadway, Southbourne, Bournemouth, BH6 4EH (tel: 0800 652 6316; email: info@cmtuk.org.uk; website: www.cmt.org.uk).

Coeliac disease

Coeliac UK, 3rd Floor, Apollo Centre, Desborough Road, High Wycombe, HP11 2QW (tel: 01494 437278; helpline: 0845 305 2060; website: www.coeliac.org.uk). Contact can also be made by completing an online enquiry form.

Colostomy

Colostomy Association (CA), 2 London Court, East Street, Reading, RG1 4QL (tel: 0118 939 1537; 24hr helpline: 0800 328 4257; email: cass@colostomyassociation. org.uk; website: www.colostomy association.org.uk).

Cot death

Compassionate Friends, 53 North Street, Bristol, BS3 1EN (tel: 0117 966 5202; helpline: 0845 123 2304; email: info@tcf. org.uk; website: www.tcf.org.uk).

Foundation for the Study of Infant Deaths, 11 Belgrave Road, London, SW1V 1RB (tel: 020 7802 3200; helpline: 080 8802 6868; email: office@fsid.org.uk; website: fsid.org.uk).

Counselling

British Association for Counselling and Pychotherapy, 15 St John's Business Park, Lutterworth, LE17 4HB, (tel: 01455 883300; minicom: 01455 550307; email: enquiries@bacp.co.uk; website: www. bacp.co.uk).

Samaritans, The Upper Mill, Kingston Road, Ewell, Surrey, KT17 2AF (tel: 020 8394 8300; 24-hour helpline: 08457 90 90 90; see phone book for local number; email: admin@samaritans.org (general) jo@samaritans.org (helpline); website: www.samaritans.org).

SupportLine, PO Box 2860, Romford, Essex, RM7 1JA (tel: 01708 765222; helpline: 01708 765200; email: info@ supportline.org.uk; website: www. supportline.org.uk).

Craniosynostosis or craniostenosis

Headlines, 128 Beesmoor Road, Frampton, Cotterell, Bristol, BS36 2JP (tel: 01454 850557; email: info@headlines. org.uk; website: www.headlines.org.uk).

Crohn's disease

Crohn's in Childhood Research Association (CICRA), Parkgate House, 356 West Barnes Lane, Motspur Park, Surrey, KT3 6NB (tel: 020 8949 6209; email: support@cicra.org; website: www. cicra.org).

National Association for Colitis & Crohn's Disease (NACC), 4 Beaumont House, Sutton Road, St Albans, Hertfordshire, AL1 5HH (tel: 01727 830038; helpline: 0845 130 2233; email: info@CrohnsAndColitis.org.uk; website: www.nacc.org.uk).

Crying/restless babies

The CRY-SIS Helpline, BM Box CRY-SIS, London, WC1N 3XX (sae required); (helpline: 08451 228 669 [9am–10pm daily]; website: www.cry-sis.org.uk).

Cystic fibrosis

Butterfly Trust, Swanston Steading, 109/3B Swanston Road, Edinburgh, EH10 7DS (tel: 0131 445 5590; email: info@butterflytrust.org.uk; website: www. butterflytrust.org.uk).

* *Cystic Fibrosis Trust*, 11 London Road, Bromley, Kent, BR1 1BY (tel: 020 8464 7211; support helpline: 0300 373 1000; benefits helpline: 0300 373 1010; welfare helpline: 0300 373 1020; email: enquiries@cftrust.org.uk; website: www. cftrust.org.uk).

Deafblind

Deafblind UK, National Centre for Deafblindness, John & Lucille Van Geest Place, Cygnet Road, Hampton, Peterborough, PE7 8FD (tel: 01733 358100; helpline: 0800 132 320; email: info@deafblind.org.uk; website: www. deafblind.org.uk).

* *Sense*, 101 Pentonville Road, London, N1 9LG (tel: 0845 127 0060; textphone: 0845 127 0062; email: info@sense.org.uk; website: www.sense.org.uk).

Deafness/hearing difficulties

British Deaf Association (BDA), 10th Floor, Coventry Point, Market Way, Coventry, CV1 1EA (tel: 02476 550936; textphone: 02476 550393; email: bda@ bda.org.uk; website: www.bda.org.uk).

Guide Dogs for the Blind Association, Burghfield Common, Reading, RG7 3YG (tel: 0118 983 5555; email: guidedogs@ guidedogs.org.uk; website: www.gdba.org. uk).

Hearing Dogs for Deaf People, The Grange, Wycombe Road, Saunderton, Buckinghamshire, HP27 9NS (tel & minicom: 01844 348100; email: info@ hearingdogs.org.uk; website: www. hearingdogs.org.uk).

* *National Deaf Children's Society*, 15 Dufferin Street, London, EC1Y 8UR (tel: 020 7490 8656; minicom: 020 7490 8656; helpline: 0808 800 8880; email: ndcs@ndcs.org.uk or helpline@ndcs.org. uk; website: www.ndcs.org.uk).

Royal Association for Deaf People (RAD), 18 Westside Centre, London Road, Stanway, Colchester, Essex, CO3 8PH (tel: 0845 688 2525; minicom: 0845 688 2527; email: info@royaldeaf. uk; website: www.royaldeaf.org.uk).

Royal National Institute for the Deaf (RNID), 19–23 Featherstone Street, London, EC1Y 8SL (tel: 020 7296 8000; text: 020 7296 8001; information line: 0808 808 0123 [voice] 0808 808 9000 [text]; email: informationonline@rnid. org.uk; website: www.rnid.org.uk).

Dental health

British Dental Association, 64 Wimpole Street, London, W1G 8YS (tel: 020 7935 0875; email: enquiries@bda.org website: www.bda.org).

British Dental Health Foundation (BDHF), Smile House, 2 East Union Street, Rugby, Warwickshire, CV22 6AJ (tel: 0870 770 4000; helpline: 0845 063 1188; website: www.dentalhealth.org.uk). Contact can also be made by completing an online enquiry form.

Depression

Befrienders Worldwide, c/o The Samaritans, Upper Mill, Kingston Road, Ewell, Surrey, KT17 2AF (tel: 08457 909090; minicom: 08457 909192; website: www.befrienders.org).

Depression Alliance, 20 Great Dover Street, London, SE1 4LX (tel: 0845 123 2320; email: information@ depressionalliance.org; website: www. depressionalliance.org).

Depression UK, c/o Self Help Nottingham, Ormiston House, 32–36 Pelham Street, Nottingham, NG1 2EG (tel: 0191 239 9630; email: info@depressionuk.org; website: www. depressionuk.org).

MDF The Bipolar Organisation, Castleworks, 21 St. George's Road, London, SE1 6ES (tel: 020 7793 2600; email: mdf@mdf.org.uk; website: www. mdf.org.uk).

Samaritans, The Upper Mill, Kingston Road, Ewell, Surrey, KT17 2AF (tel: 020 8394 8300; 24-hour helpline: 08457 90 90 90; see phone book for local number; email: admin@samaritans.org [general] jo@samaritans.org [helpline]; website: www.samaritans.org).

Diabetes

Diabetes Foundation, Macleod House, 10 Parkway, London, NW1 7AA (tel: 020 7424 1000; website: www. diabetesfoundation.org.uk).

Diabetes UK, 10 Parkway, London, NW1 7AA (tel: 020 7424 1000; helpline: 0845 120 2960; email: info@diabetes.org. uk or careline@diabetes.org.uk; website: www.diabetes.org.uk).

Disfigurement

Disfigurement Guidance Centre, PO Box 7, Cupar, Fife, KY15 4PF (tel: 01337 870 281).

Let's Face It, Support Network for the Facially Disfigured c/o Christine Piff, 72 Victoria Avenue, Westgate-on-Sea, Kent, CT8 8BH (tel: 01843 833724; email: chrisletsfaceit@aol.com; website: www. lets-face-it.org.uk).

Down's syndrome

Down's Syndrome Association, The Langdon Down Centre, 2a Langdon Park, Teddington, TW11 9PS (helpline: 0845 230 0372 [Mon–Fri, 10am–4pm]; email: info@downs-syndrome.org.uk; website: www.downs-syndrome.org.uk).

Drugs

ADFAM National, 25 Corsham Street, London, N1 6DR (tel: 020 7553 7640; email: admin@adfam.org.uk; website: www.adfam.org.uk).

Cocaine Anonymous UK, PO Box 46920, London, E2 9WF (helpline: 0800 612 0225 [10am–10pm daily]; email: info@cauk.org.uk or helpline@cauk.org.uk; website: www.cauk.org.uk).

Daily Dose (part of the WIRED Initiative), no longer operating but the website contains extensive information and archives (website: www.dailydose.net).

DrugScope, Prince Consort House, Suite 204 (2nd Floor), 109/111 Farringdon Road, London, EC1R 3BW (tel: 020 7520 7550; email: info@drugscope.org.uk; website: www.drugscope.org.uk).

Early Break, 7211 Bury Road, Radcliffe, M26 2UG (Bury & Rochdale: 0161 762 2608; East Lancashire: 01282 604022; email: info@earlybreak.co.uk; website: www.earlybreak.co.uk).

Families Anonymous, Doddington and Rollo Community Association, Charlotte Despard Avenue, Battersea, London, SW11 5HD (helpline: 0845 1200 660; website: www.famanon.org.uk).

FRANK (National Drugs Helpline), (24-hour helpline: 0800 77 66 00; website: www.talktofrank.com). Contact can also be made by completing an online enquiry form.

Narcotics Anonymous (NA), 202 City Road, London, EC1V 2PH (tel: 020 7251 4007; helpline: 0300 999 1212; email: nahelpline@ukna.org; website: www.ukna.org).

Turning Point, Standon House, 21 Mansell Street, London, E1 8AA (tel: 020 7481 7600; email: info@turning-point.co.uk; website: www.turning-point.co.uk).

Dyslexia

British Dyslexia Association, Unit 8, Bracknell Beeches, Old Bracknell Lane, Bracknell, RG12 7BW (tel: 0845 251 9003; helpline: 0845 251 9002 [Mon–Fri, 10am–4pm and Tues–Wed, 5pm–7pm]; email: helpline@bdadyslexia.org.uk; website: www.bdadyslexia.org.uk).

Dyslexia Action, Egham Centre, Park House, Wick Road, Egham, Surrey TW20 0HH (tel: 01784 222300; email: info@dyslexiaaction.org.uk; website: www.dyslexiaaction.org.uk).

Dyspraxia

Dyspraxia Foundation, Administrator, 8 West Alley, Hitchin, Hertforshire, SG5 1EG (tel: 01462 455 016; helpline: 01462 454986 [Mon–Fri, 10am–1pm]; email: dyspraxia@dyspraxiafoundation.org.uk; website: www.dyspraxiafoundation.org.uk).

Dystonia

Dystonia Society, Second Floor, Camelford House, 89 Albert Embankment, London, SE1 7TP (tel: 0845 458 6211; helpline: 0845 458 6322; email: info@dystonia.org.uk; website: www.dystonia.org.uk).

Eating disorders

Eating Disorders Association (Beat), 103 Prince of Wales Road, Norwich, NR1 1DW (tel: 0300 123 3355; helpline: 0845 634 1414 [Mon– Fri, 10.30am–8.30pm and Sat 1.00pm–4.30pm]; Youth helpline: 0845 634 7650 [Mon–Fri, 4.30pm–8.30pm and Sat 1.00pm–4.30pm]; email: help@b-eat.co.uk or fyp@b-eat.co.uk (youth); website: www.b-eat.co.uk).

Eczema

National Eczema Society, Hill House, Highgate Hill, London, N19 5NA (tel: 020 7281 3553; helpline: 0800 089 1122; email: info@eczema.org; website: www.eczema.org).

Endometriosis

National Endometriosis Society, Suite 50, Westminster Palace Gardens, Artillery Row, London, SW1P 1RR (tel: 020 7222 2781; Crisis helpline: 0808 808 2227 [opening times vary depending on volunteer availability, see website for details]; Email: enquiries@endometriosis-uk.org; website: www.endo.org.uk).

Epidermolysis bullosa

Dystrophic Epidermolysis Bullosa Research Association (DEBRA), Debra House, 13 Wellington Business Park, Dukes Ride, Crowthorne, Berkshire, RG45 6LS (tel: 01344 771961; specialist helplines – Children's Nurse Consultant: Jackie Denyer 0207 829 7808; Specialist Paediatric Dietician: Lesley Haynes 020 7405 9200 ext 5761; Adult Nurse Consultant: Liz Pillay 020 8810 1265; email: debra@debra.org.uk; website: www.debra.org.uk).

Epilepsy

Epilepsy Action, New Anstey House, Gate Way Drive, Yeadon, Leeds, LS19 7XY (tel: 0113 210 8800; helpline: 0808 800 5050 [Mon–Thurs, 9am–4.30pm; Fri 9am–4pm]; email: epilepsy@epilepsy.org.uk or helpline@epilepsy.org.uk; website: www.epilepsy.org.uk).

The National Society for Epilepsy, Chesham Lane, Chalfont St Peter, Buckinghamshire, SL9 0RJ (tel: 01494 601300; helpline: 01494 601400 [Mon–Fri, 10am–4pm]; website: www.epilepsysociety.org.uk). Contact can also be made by completing an online enquiry form.

Feet

Sole-Mates, 46 Gordon Road, London, E4 6BU (tel: 020 8524 2423 [Mon, Tues, Thurs and Fri, 10am–3pm]. Send an sae for further information about sharing the cost of shoes for amputees and people with different sized feet.

Gambling

Gamblers Anonymous (GANON), c/o CVS Building, 5 Trafford Court, off Trafford Way, Doncaster, DN1 1PN (helplines – London: 020 7384 3040; Manchester: 0161 976 5000; Sheffield: 0114 262 0026; Birmingham: 0121 233 1335; Glasgow: 0370 050 8881; Ulster: 0287 135 1329 [24 hours daily]; website: www.gamblersanonymous.org.uk).

GamCare, 2nd Floor, 7–11 St John's Hill, London, SW11 1TR (tel: 020 7801 7000; helpline: 0845 6000 133 [8am–2am daily]; email: info@gamcare.org.uk; website: www.gamcare.org.uk).

Growth problems

Child Growth Foundation, 2 Mayfield Avenue, Chiswick, London, W4 1PW (tel: 020 8995 0257; email: info@childgrowthfoundation.org; website: www.childgrowthfoundation.org).

Restricted Growth Association (RGA), PO Box 15755, Solihull, B93 3FY (tel: 0300 111 1970; email: office@restrictedgrowth.co.uk; website: www.restrictedgrowth.co.uk).

Guillain Barré syndrome

Guillain Barré Syndrome Support Group (GBS), Ground Floor, Woodholme House, Heckington Business Park, Station Road, Heckington, Sleaford, NG34 9J (tel: 01529 469910; helpline: 0800 374 803; email: admin@gbs.org.uk; website: www.gbs.org.uk).

Haemophilia

* *Haemophilia Society*, First Floor, Petersham House, 57a Hatton Garden, London, EC1N 8JG (tel: 020 7831 1020; helpline: 0800 018 6068; email: info@haemophelia.org.uk; website: www.haemophilia.org.uk).

Head injury

Headway – National Head Injuries Association Ltd, Bradbury House, 190 Bagnall Road, Old Basford, Nottingham, Nottinghamshire, NG6 8SF (tel: 0115 924

0800; helpline: 0808 800 2244; email: enquiries@headway.org.uk or helpline@headway.org.uk; website: www.headway.org.uk).

Heart attacks/heart disease (general)

British Heart Foundation, Greater London House, 180 Hampstead Road, London, NW1 7AW (tel: 020 7554 0000; helpline: 0300 330 3311; website: www.bhf.org.uk). Contact can also be made by completing an online enquiry form.

HeartLine Association, PO Box 957, Camberley, Surrey, GU15 9FH (tel: 03300 224466; email: admin@heartline.org.uk; website: www.heartline.org.uk)

Hemiplegia

Hemi-Help, 6 Market Road, London, N7 9PW (tel: 0845 120 3713, helpline: 0845 123 2372 [Mon–Fri, 10am–1pm during term time]; email: info@hemihelp.org.uk; website: www.hemihelp.org.uk).

Herpes

Herpes Viruses Association (SPHERE), 41 North Road, London, N7 9DP (helpline: 0845 123 2305; email: info@herpes.org.uk; website: www.herpes.org.uk)

Hodgkin's disease

Hodgkin's Disease & Lymphoma Association, PO Box 386, Aylesbury, Buckinghamshire, HP20 2GA (tel: 01296 619040; helpline: 0808 808 5555 [Mon–Thurs, 9am–6pm and Fri 9am–5pm]; website: www.lymphoma.org.uk). Contact can also be made by completing an online enquiry form.

Huntington's disease

* *Huntington's Disease Association*, Neurosupport Centre, Norton Street, Liverpool, L3 8LR (tel: 0151 298 3298; email: info@hda.org.uk; website: www.hda.org.uk).

Hyperactive children

Hyperactive Children's Support Group, 71 Whyke Lane, Chichester, West Sussex, PO19 7PD (tel: 01243 539966; email: hacsg@hacsg.org.uk; website: www.hacsg.org.uk). If writing, the Group requests that you enclose a large sae.

Hypertension

Coronary Artery Disease Research Association (CORDA), Chelsea Square, London, SW3 6NP (tel: 020 7349 8686; email: info@corda.org.uk; website: www.corda.org.uk). Contact can also be made by completing an online enquiry form.

Hypogammaglobulinaemia

Primary Immunodificiency Association, Alliance House, 12 Caxton Street, London, SW1H 0QS (tel: 020 7976 7640; email: info@pia.org.uk; website: www.pia.org.uk).

Incontinence

Association for Continence Advice (ACA), c/o Fitwise Management Ltd, Drumcross Hall, Bathgate, West Lothian, EH48 4JT (tel: 01506 811077; email: aca@fitwise.co.uk; website: www.aca.uk.com).

Industrial diseases

Mesothelioma UK, Glenfield Hospital, Groby Road, Leicester, LE3 9QP (helpline: 0800 169 2409; email: mesothelioma.uk@uhl-tr.nhs.uk; website: www.mesothelioma.uk.com)

Repetitive Strain Injury Association (RSIA), c/o Keytools Ltd, Abacus House, 1 Spring Crescent, Southampton, SO17 2FZ (tel: 023 8029 4500; email: rsia@rsi.org.uk; website: www.rsi.org.uk).

Infantile hypercalcaemia

Williams Syndrome Foundation, 161 High Street, Tonbridge, Kent, TN9 1BX (tel: 01732 365152; website: www.williams-syndrome.org.uk).

Infertility

Infertility Network UK, Charter House, 43 St Leonards Road, Bexhill-on-Sea, East Sussex, TN40 1JA (Advice line: 0800 008 7464; email: admin@infertilitynetworkuk.com; website: www.infertilitynetworkuk.com).

Irritable bowel syndrome

The Gut Trust, Unit 5, 53 Mowbray Street, Sheffield, S3 8EN (tel: 0114 272 3253; email: info@theguttrust.org; website: www.theguttrust.org)

Kidney disease

* *British Kidney Patient Association (BKPA)*, 3 The Windmills, St Mary's Close, Turk Street, Alton, GU34 1EF (tel: 01420 541424; email: info@britishkidney-pa.co.uk; website: www.britishkidney-pa.co.uk).

National Kidney Federation, The Point, Coach Road, Shireoaks, Worksop, Notts, S81 8BW (tel: 01909 544 999; helpline: 0845 601 0209; email: nkf@kidney.org.uk; website: www.kidney.org.uk).

Limb disorder

British Limbless Ex-Servicemen's Association (BLESMA), 185–187 High Road, Chadwell Heath, Romford, RM6 6NA (tel: 020 8590 1124; email: headquarters@blesma.org; website: www.blesma.org).

Limbless Association, Jubilee House, 3 The Drive, Warley Hill, Brentwood, CM13 3FR (tel: 01277 725 182/4/6; email: enquiries@limbless-association.org; website: www.limbless-association.org).

Reach – The Association for Children with Hand or Arm Deficiency, PO Box 54, Helston, Cornwall, TR13 8WD (tel: 0845 130 6225; email: reach@reach.org.uk; website: www.reach.org.uk).

STEPS (A National Association for Families of Children with Congenital Abnormalities), Warrington Lane, Lymm, Cheshire, WA13 0SA (tel: 01925 750273; helpline: 01925 750271; email: info@steps-charity.org.uk; website: www.steps-charity.org.uk).

Literacy/learning difficulties

National Institute of Adult Continuing Education (NIACE), Renaissance House, 20 Princess Road West, Leicester, LE1 6TP (tel: 0116 204 4200; minicom: 0116 2556049; email: enquiries@niace.org.uk; website: www.niace.org.uk).

Liver disease

British Liver Trust, 2 Southampton Road, Ringwood, BH24 1HY (tel: 01425 481320; helpline: 0800 652 7330; email: info@britishlivertrust.org.uk; website: www.britishlivertrust.org.uk).

Lowe Syndrome Association (UK Contact Group) (LSA) 77 West Heath Road, London, NW3 7TH (tel: 020 7794 8858; email: lowetrust@gmail.com; website: www.lowetrust.com).

Lupus

Lupus UK, St James House, Eastern Road, Romford, RM1 3NH (tel: 01708 731251; email: headoffice@lupusuk.org.uk; website: www.lupusuk.com).

Raynaud's & Scleroderma Association, 112 Crewe Road, Alsager, Cheshire, ST7 2JA (tel: 01270 872776; freephone: 0800 9172494; email: info@raynauds.org.uk; website: www.raynauds.org.uk).

Marfan syndrome

Marfan Association UK, Rochester House, 5 Aldershot Road, Fleet, Hampshire, GU51 3NG (tel: 01252 810472; email: marfan@tinyonline.co.uk; website: www.marfan-friends-world.org.uk).

Mastectomy

Breast Cancer Care (BCC), 5–13 Great Suffolk Street, London, SE1 0NS (tel: 0845 092 0800; helpline: 0808 800 6000 [Mon–Fri, 9am–5pm and Sat 9am–2pm]; email: info@breastcancercare.org.uk; website: www.breastcancercare.org.uk).

Ménière's disease

Ménière's Society, The Rookery, Surrey Hills Business Park, Wotton, Dorking, Surrey, RH5 6QT (tel: 01306 876883; helpline: 0845 120 2975; email: info@menieres.org.uk; website: www.menieres.org.uk).

Meningitis

Meningitis Trust, Fern House, Bath Road, Stroud, Gloucestershire, GL5 3TJ (tel: 01453 768000; 24-hour helpline: 0800 028 18 28; children's helpline: 0808 801 0388; email: info@meningitis-trust.org; website: www.meningitis-trust.org).

Menopause

The Daisy Network Premature Menopause Support Group, PO Box 183, Rossendale, Lancashire, BB4 6WZ (email: daisy@daisynetwork.org.uk; website: www.daisynetwork.org.uk).

Mental health

CARE (Self Unlimited), 13 & 14 Nursery Court, Kibworth Business Park, Harborough Road, Leicester, LE8 0EX (tel: 0116 279 3225; email: info@selfunlimited.co.uk; website: www.selfunlimited.co.uk).

Mencap, Mencap National Centre, 123 Golden Lane, London, EC1Y 0RT (tel: 020 7454 0454; helpline: 0808 808 1111; Typetalk: 18001 0808 808 1111; email: help@mencap.org.uk; website: www.mencap.org.uk).

Mental Health Foundation, 9th Floor, Sea Containers House, 20 Upper Ground, London, SE1 9QB (tel: 020 7803 1100; email: mhf@mhf.org.uk; website: www.mentalhealth.org.uk).

Mind (National Association for Mental Health), 15–19 Broadway, Stratford, London, E15 4BQ (tel: 020 8519 2122; Mind information line: 0845 766 0163; email: info@mind.org.uk; website: www.mind.org.uk).

SANE (The Mental Health Charity), 1st Floor, Cityside House, 40 Adler Street, London, E1 1EE (tel: 020 7375 1002; helpline: 0845 767 8000; email: info@sane.org or sanemail@sane.org.uk (email support service); website: www.sane.org.uk).

Metabolic disorders

CLIMB (Research Trust for Metabolic Diseases in Children), Climb Building, 176 Nantwich Road, Crewe, CW2 6BG (tel: 0845 241 2173 or 0800 652 3181; email: adm.svcs@climb.org.uk; website: www.climb.org.uk).

Migraine

Migraine Action Association (formerly British Migraine Association), Forth Floor, 27 East Street, Leicester, LE1 6NB (tel: 0116 275 8317; website: www.migraine.org.uk). Contact can also be made by completing an online enquiry form.

Migraine Trust, 55–56 Russell Square, London, WC1B 4HP (tel: 020 7436 1336; email: info@migrainetrust.org; website: www.migrainetrust.org).

Miscarriage

The Miscarriage Association, c/o Clayton Hospital, Northgate, Wakefield, West Yorkshire, WF1 3JS (tel: 01924 200795; helpline: 01294 200799 [Mon–Fri, 9am–4pm]; email: info@miscarriageassociation.org.uk; website: www.miscarriageassociation.org.uk).

Tommy's, Nicholas House, 3 Laurence Pountney Hill, London, EC4R 0BB (tel: 020 7398 3400; Adviceline: 020 7398 3483; email: mailbox@tommys.org; website: www.tommys.org).

Motor neurone disease

* *Motor Neurone Disease Association (MND)* , PO Box 246, Northampton, NN1 2PR (tel: 01604 250505; helpline: 08457 626262; email: enquiries@mndassociation.org; website: www.mndassociation.org).

Multiple sclerosis

* *Multiple Sclerosis Society of Great Britain & Northern Ireland*, MS National Centre, 372 Edgware Road, London, NW2 6ND (tel: 020 8438 0700; helpline: 0808 800 8000 [Mon–Fri, 9am–9pm]; email: info@mssociety.org.uk or helpline@mssociety.org.uk (helpline); website: www.mssociety.org.uk).

Muscular dystrophy

Muscular Dystrophy Campaign, 61 Southwark Street, London, SE1 0HL (tel: 020 7803 4800; helpline: 0800 652 6352; email: info@muscular-dystrophy.org; website: www.muscular-dystrophy.org).

Myasthenia gravis

Myasthenia Gravis Association, The College Business Centre, Uttoxeter New Road, Derby, DE22 3WZ (tel: 01332 290219; helpline: 0800 919922; email: mg@mga-charity.org; website: www.mgauk.org.uk).

Myotonic dystrophy

Myotonic Dystrophy Support Group, 35a Carlton Hill, Carlton, Nottingham, NG4 1BG (tel: 0115 987 5869; helpline: 0115 987 0080; email: contact@mdsguk.org; website: www.mdsguk.org).

Narcolepsy

Narcolepsy Association (UK) (UKAN), PO Box 13842, Penicuik, EH26 8WX (tel: 0845 450 0394; email: info@narcolepsy.org.uk; website: www.narcolepsy.org.uk).

Neurofibromatosis

The Neurofibromatosis Association, Quayside House, 38 High Street, Kingston on Thames, Surrey, KT1 1HL (tel: 020 8439 1234; minicom: 020 8481 0492; email: info@nfauk.org; website: www.nfauk.org).

Organ donors

British Organ Donor Society (BODY), Balsham, Cambridge, CB21 4DL (tel: 01223 893636; email: body@argonet.co.uk; website: body.orpheusweb.co.uk).

Osteoporosis

National Osteoporosis Society, Camerton, Bath, BA2 0PJ (tel: 01761 471771; helpline: 0845 450 0230; email: info@nos.org.uk; website: www.nos.org.uk). Contact can also be made by completing an online helpline enquiry form.

Paget's disease

National Association for the Relief of Paget's Disease, 323 Manchester Road, Walkden, Worsley, Manchester, M28 3HH (tel: 0161 799 4646; email: director@paget.org.uk; website: www.paget.org.uk).

Parkinson's disease

* *Parkinson's Disease Society of the United Kingdom*, 215 Vauxhall Bridge Road, London, SW1V 1EJ (tel: 020 7931 8080; helpline: 0808 800 0303 [weekdays 9am–8pm and Saturdays 10am–2pm]; email: hello@parkinsons.org.uk; website: www.parkinsons.org.uk).

Perthes' disease

Perthes Association, PO Box 773, Guildford, GU1 1XN (tel: 01483 534431; helpline: 01483 306637; email: help@perthes.org.uk; website: www.perthes.org.uk). Contact can also be made by completing an online enquiry form.

Phobias

Anxiety UK (National Phobics Society), Zion Community Resource Centre, 339 Stretford Road, Hulme, Manchester, M15 4ZY (tel: 0161 226 7727: helpline: 08444 775 774; email: info@anxietyuk.org.uk; website: www.anxietyuk.org.uk).

First Steps to Freedom (FSTF), PO Box 476, Newquay, TR7 1WQ (tel: 0845 841 0619; helpline: 0845 120 2916; email: first.steps@btconnect.com; website: www.first-steps.org).

Pituitary disorders

Pituitary Foundation (PIT-PAT), PO Box 1944, Bristol, BS99 2UB (tel: 0845 450 0376; support line: 0845 450 0375; Endocrine Nurse helpline: 0845 450 0377 [Mondays 5.30pm–9.30pm and Thursdays 9am–1pm]; website: www. pituitary.org.uk). Contact can also be made by completing an online enquiry form.

Poliomyelitis

British Polio Fellowship, Eagle Office Centre, The Runway, South Ruislip, Middlesex, HA4 6SE (tel: 0800 018 0586; email: info@britishpolio.org.uk; website: www.britishpolio.org.uk).

Post-natal

Association for Post-Natal Illness, 145 Dawes Road, Fulham, London, SW6 7EB (tel: 020 7386 0868 [Mon–Fri, 10am–2pm]; email: info@apni.org; website: www.apni.org).

Prader-Willi syndrome

Prader-Willi Syndrome Association (UK), 125A London Road, Derby, DE1 2QQ (tel: 01332 365676 [Mon–Fri, 9.30am–3.30pm]; email: admin@pwsa.co. uk; website: pwsa.co.uk).

Pre-eclampsia

Pre-Eclampsia Society, c/o Dawn James, Rhianfa, Carmel, Caernarfon, LL54 7RL (tel: 01286 882685; email: dawnjames@ clara.co.uk; website: www.pre-eclampsia-society.org.uk).

Psoriasis

Psoriasis Association, Dick Coles House, 2 Queensbridge, Northampton, NN4 7BF (tel: 01604 251620; helpline: 0845 676 0076; email: mail@psoriasis-association. org.uk; website: www.psoriasis-association.org.uk).

Raynaud's disease

Raynaud's Scleroderma Association, 112 Crewe Road, Alsager, Cheshire, ST7 2JA (tel: 01270 872776; freephone: 0800 9172494; email: info@raynauds.org. uk; website: www.raynauds.org.uk).

Retinitis pigmentosa

British Retinitis Pigmentosa Society (BRPS), PO Box 350, Buckingham, MK18 1GZ (tel: 01280 821334; helpline: 0845 123 2354 [Mon–Fri, 9.30am–5pm and 6pm–9.30pm]; email: info@brps.org. uk or helpline@brps.org.uk; website: www.brps.org.uk).

Rett syndrome

Rett Syndrome Association UK, Langham House West, Mill Street, Luton, LU1 2NA (tel: 01582 798910; email: info@rettuk.org or support@rettuk.org; website: www. rettsyndrome.org.uk).

Reye's syndrome

National Reye's Syndrome Foundation of the UK (NRSF), 15 Nicholas Gardens, Pyrford, Woking, Surrey, GU22 8SD (tel: 01932 346843; email: g.denney@tiscali.co. uk; website: www.reyessyndrome.co.uk).

Sacoidosis

SILA (Sacoidosis and Interstitial Lung Association), c/o Department of Respiratory Medicine, 1st Floor, Cheyne Wing, King's College Hospital, Denmark Hill, SE5 9RS (tel: 020 7237 5912; email: info@sila.org.uk; website: www.sila.org. uk).

Schizophrenia

Rethink, 89 Albert Embankment, London, SE1 7TP (tel: 0845 456 0455; Advice Line: 020 7840 3188 [Mon–Fri, 10am–2pm]; email: info@rethink.org or advice@rethink.org; website: www. rethink.org).

Scoliosis

Scoliosis Association (UK) (SAUK), 4 Ivebury Court, 325 Latimer Road, London, W10 6RA (tel: 020 8964 5343; helpline: 020 8964 1166; email: info@ sauk.org.uk; website: www.sauk.org.uk).

Seasonal affective disorder

SAD Association (SADA), PO Box 989, Steyning, West Sussex, BN44 3HG (website: www.sada.org.uk). If writing, the Association asks that you include an sae.

Sickle cell disease

Sickle Cell Society (SCS), 54 Station Road, London, NW10 4UA (tel: 020 8961 7795; email: info@sicklecellsociety.org; website: www.sicklecellsociety.org). Contact can also be made by completing an online enquiry form.

Sjögren's syndrome

British Sjögren's Syndrome Association (BSSA), PO Box 15040, Birmingham, B31 3DP (tel: 0121 455 6532; helpline: 0121 455 6549 [Mon–Fri, 9.30am–4pm]; email: office@bssa.uk.net; website: www. bssa.uk.net).

Sleep disorders

British Snoring & Sleep Apnoea Association (BSSAA), Castle Court, 41 London Road, Reigate, RH2 9RJ (tel: 01737 245638; email: info@britishsnoring. co.uk; website: www.britishsnoring.co. uk).

Smoking

Fag Ends (Roy Castle Lung Cancer Foundation), The Roy Castle Centre, 4–6 Enterprise Way, Wavertree Tech Park, Liverpool, Merseyside, L13 1FB (helpline: 0800 195 2131 [Mon–Fri, 9.30am–8pm]; specialist pregnancy helpline: 0800 169 9169 [daily: 12.00pm–9.00pm]; website: www.stopsmoking.org.uk). Other language helplines are available; please see the website for details. Contact can also be made by completing an online enquiry form.

QUIT (National Society of Non-Smokers), 63 St Marys Axe, London, EC3A 8AA (tel: 020 7469 0400; helpline: 0800 00 22 00; email: info@quit.org.uk or email counselling: stopsmoking@quit.org. uk; website: www.quit.org.uk). Bengali, Urdu, Punjabi, Gujarati, Hindi, Turkish and Kurdish speaking counsellors are also available – please see the website for the individual helpline numbers and times.

Solvent abuse

Re-Solv, 30a High Street, Stone, Staffordshire, ST15 8AW (tel: 01785 817885; email: information@re-solv.org; website: www.re-solv.org).

Speech & language difficulties

Association for All Speech-Impaired Children (AFASIC), 1st Floor, 20 Bowling Green Lane, London, EC1R 0BD (tel: 020 7490 9410; helpline: 0845 355 5577 [Mon–Fri, 10.30am–2.30pm]; email: info@afasic.org.uk; website: www.afasic. org.uk). You can also contact the helpline by completing an online enquiry form.

British Stammering, 15 Old Ford Road, London, E2 9PJ (tel: 020 8983 1003; helpline: 020 8880 6590; email: mail@ stammering.org or info@stammering.org (helpline); website: www.stammering.org).

Royal Association in Aid of Deaf People (RAD), 18 Westside Centre, London Road, Stanway, Colchester, Essex, CO3 8PH (tel: 0845 688 2525; minicom: 0845 688 2527; email: info@royaldeaf.org. uk; website: www.royaldeaf.org.uk).

Speakability, 1 Royal Street, London, SE1 7LL (tel: 020 7261 9572; helpline: 080 8808 9572 [Mon–Fri, 10am–4pm]; email: speakability@speakability.org.uk; website: www.speakability.org.uk).

Spina bifida

Association for Spina Bifida and Hydrocephalus (ASBAH), 42 Park Road, Peterborough, PE1 2UQ (tel: 0845 450 7755; email: helpline@asbah.org; website: www.asbah.org).

Spinal injuries

Spinal Injuries Association, SIA House, 2 Trueman Place, Oldbrook, Milton

Keynes, MK6 2HH (tel: 0845 678 6633; counselling: 0800 980 0501 [Mon–Fri, 9.30am–4.30pm, closed 1pm–2pm]; email: sia@spinal.co.uk; website: www. spinal.co.uk).

Stress

The Coronary Artery Disease Research Association (CORDA), Chelsea Square, London, SW3 6NP (tel: 020 7349 8686; email: info@corda.org.uk; website: www. corda.org.uk).

Unwind Pain and Stress Management, Melrose, 3 Alderlea Close, Gilesgate, Durham, DH1 1DS (tel: 0191 384 2056 [Mon–Fri, 3pm–4pm]). If writing, please send a large (A5) stamped sae to receive an information leaflet and full list of resources, including prices.

Stroke

Stroke Association, Stroke House, 240 City Road, London, EC1V 2PR (tel: 020 7566 0300; helpline: 0303 303 3100; textphone: 020 7251 9096; email: info@ stroke.org.uk website: www.stroke.org. uk).

Thalassaemia

United Kingdom Thalassaemia Society (UKTS), 19 The Broadway, Southgate Circus, London, N14 6PH (tel: 020 8882 0011; email: office@ukts.org; website: www.ukts.org).

Thrombocytopenia with absent radii

TAR Syndrome Support Group, for further information please contact Susy Edwards (email: SusyEdwards@aol.com; website: www.ivh.se/TAR).

Tinnitus

British Tinnitus Association (BTA), Ground Floor, Unit 5, Acorn Business Park, Woodseats Close, Sheffield, S8 0TB (tel: 0114 250 9922; freephone: 0800 018 0527; minicom: 0114 258 5694; email: info@tinnitus.org.uk; website: www. tinnitus.org.uk).

Royal National Institute for the Deaf (RNID), 19–23 Featherstone Street, London, EC1Y 8SL (Voice: 020 7296 8000; textphone: 020 7296 8001; helpline: 0808 808 0123 [voice] 0808 808 9000 [text]; email: informationonline@rnid. org.uk; website: www.rnid.org.uk).

Tourette syndrome

Tourettes Action, Southbank House, Black Prince Road, London, SE1 7SJ (tel: 020 7793 2356; helpline: 0845 458 1252 or 020 7793 2357; Typetalk: 18001 0845 458 1252; email: help@tourettes-action.org. uk; website: www.tourettes-action.org. uk).

Tracheo-oesophageal fistula

Aid for Children with Tracheotomies (ACT), for further information please contact the secretary Amanda Saunders (tel: 01823 698398; email: support@ actfortrachykids.com; website: www. actfortrachykids.com).

Tracheo-Oesophageal Fistula Support Group (TOFS), St George's Centre, 91 Victoria Road, Netherfield, Nottingham, NG4 2NN (tel: 0115 961 3092; email: info@tofs.org.uk; website: www.tofs.org.uk).

Tranquillizers

First Steps to Freedom (FSTF), First Steps to Freedom, PO Box 476, Newquay, TR7 1WQ (tel: 0845 841 0619; helpline: 0845 120 2916; email: first.steps@ btconnect.com; website: www.first-steps. org).

Tranquilliser Anxiety Stress Help Association (TASHA), Alexandra House, 241 High Street, Brentford, Middlesex, TW8 0NE (tel: 020 8569 9933; helpline: 020 8560 6601 [Mon, Tues, 6pm–9pm and Sun–Wed, 5.30pm–8.30pm]; email: enquiries@tasha-foundation.org.uk; website: www.tasha-foundation.org.uk).

Tuberous sclerosis

Tuberous Sclerosis Association, PO Box 12979, Barnt Green, Birmingham, B45 5AN, England. (tel: 0121 445 6970; website: www.tuberous-sclerosis.org).

Turner syndrome

Turner Syndrome Support Society, 13 Simpson Court, 11 South Avenue, Clydebank Business Park, Clydebank, G81 2NR (tel: 0141 952 8006; helpline: 0845 230 7520; website: www.tss.org.uk).

Urostomy

Urostomy Association, 4 Demontfort Way, Uttoxeter, ST14 8XY (tel: 01889 563191; email: secretary.ua@classmail.co. uk; website: www.urostomyassociation. org.uk).

Williams syndrome

Williams Syndrome Foundation, 161 High Street, Tonbridge, Kent, TN9 1BX (tel: 01732 365152; email: enquiries@william–syndrome.org; website: www.williams-syndrome.org.uk).

INDEX

Note: Charities named after people are indexed under the *surname*.

1067 Trust Fund *283*

1930 Fund for District Nurses *83*

A

Abergwili Relief-in-Need Charity *166*

ABF The Soldiers' Charity (also known as The Army Benevolent Fund) *107*

ABTA Lifeline *103*

Accrington & District Helping Hands Fund *200*

Action for Blind People *48*

Active Foundation *26*

Acton (Middlesex) Charities *338*

Adamson Trust *139*

Addlethorpe Parochial Charity *221*

Age Sentinel Trust *32*

Aged Christian Friend Society of Scotland *139*

AIA Educational and Benevolent Trust *58*

Aid for the Aged in Distress (AFTAID) *32*

Aircrew Association Charitable Fund *108*

Airth Benefaction Trust *139*

Aitchison Trust (Christina) *169*

AJEX Charitable Foundation (formerly known as The Association of Jewish Ex-Servicemen & Women) *108*

AJR Charitable Trust *129*

Albrighton Relief in Need Charity *237*

Alchemy Foundation *17*

Aldbrough Poor Fields *174*

Aldeburgh United Charities *315*

Aldgate Freedom Foundation *337*

Aldo Trust *37*

Alexis Trust *123*

Alfreton Welfare Trust *213*

All Saints Relief-in-Need Charity *216*

Allan of Midbeltie Trust (James) *147*

Allen Charity (Mary Ellen) *214*

Al-Mizan Charitable Trust *17*

Almondsbury Charity *257*

Almshouse Charity *269*

Alveley Charity *236*

Alverstoke Trust *294*

Amalgamated Union Of Engineering Workers Fleet Street Branch Trust *73*

Ambleside Welfare Charity *195*

Ambulance Services Benevolent Fund *83*

Amersham United Charities *283*

Ancell Trust *286*

Anchor Society *256*

Anderson Bequest *151*

Anderson Charitable Foundation (Cole) *269*

Anderson Trust *150*

Anderson Trust (Andrew) *26*

Andrew Convalescent Trust (Frederick) *39*

Anglesey Society for the Welfare of Handicapped People *163*

Anglia Care Trust *277*

Anglian Water Assistance Fund (formerly The Anglian Water Trust Fund) *18*

Angus Council (Charities Administered by) *149*

Appleton Trust (Abingdon) *312*

Appleton Trust (Canterbury) *301*

Apthorp Charitable Trust (Milly) *331*

Argus Appeal *277*

Armchair *252*

Armenian Relief Society of Great Britain Trust *30*

Armstrong Charitable Trust (Elizabeth) *156*

Armstrong Trust (Nihal) *51*

Armthorpe Poors Estate Charity *179*

Arsenal Charitable Trust *331*

Arthritic Association *48*

Ashby-de-la-Zouch Relief-in-Sickness Fund *216*

Ashford Relief in Need Charities *322*

Ashington, Wiston, Warminghurst Sick Poor Fund *328*

Ashton Charity (including the Gift of Ellis Smethurst). (John) *186*

Ashton Keynes Charity *275*

ASPIRE (Association for Spinal Injury Research Rehabilitation and Reintegration) Human Needs Fund *43*

Assist Fund (formerly known as the Century Benevolent Fund) *68*

Associated Society of Locomotive Engineers & Firemen (ASLEF) Hardship Fund *92*

Association for the Relief of Incurables in Glasgow & the West of Scotland *155*

Association of Principals of Colleges Benevolent Fund *102*

Assyrian Charity and Relief Fund of UK *30*

Astley and Areley Kings Sick Fund *251*

Aston-cum-Aughton Charity Estate *178*

Atherton Trust *234*

Atmere Charity (Edmund) *308*

ATS & WRAC Benevolent Fund *108*

Attlee Foundation *18*

Auchray Trust *150*

Auto Cycle Union Benevolent Fund *100*

Auxiliary Fund of the Methodist Church *123*

Avenel Trust *139*

Avon & Somerset Constabulary Benevolent Fund *255*

Avon Local Medical Committee Benevolent Fund *255*

Avon Trust *244*

Axbridge Parochial Charities *273*

Axe (Non-Ecclesiastical Charity of Thomas) *267*

B

Backhouse Annuity Fund (Agnes) *195*

Backwell Foundation *256*

Badley Memorial Trust *244*

Bagri Foundation 18

Baines Charity 200

Baker Bequest (Ethel) 343

Balderton Parochial Charity 232

Ballance Trust (Freda & Howard) 247

Baltic Exchange Charitable Society 94

Bampton Welfare Trust 312

Banham Parochial Charities 307

Bankers Benevolent Fund 66

Banner Trust (Richard & Samuel) 247

Banstead United Charities 320

Barford Relief-in-Need Charity 242

Barham Benevolent Foundation 77

Barley Women's Institute 39

Barnes Charitable Trust (Ellen) 234

Barnes Relief-in-Need Charity and The Bailey & Bates Trust 344

Barnes Trust (William Clayton) 216

Barnes Workhouse Fund 344

Barnstaple & North Devon Dispensary Fund 261

Barnstaple Municipal Charities (The Poors Charity Section) 263

Barnwood House Trust 271

Barony Charitable Trust 18

Barrow Thornborrow Charity 194

Barrow's Charity (William) 302

Barton-upon-Humber Relief-in-Sickness Fund 222

Bath Clerical Families Fund (Archdeaconry of) 123

Bath Dispensary Charity 256

Battle Charities 290

Bauer Radio's Cash for Kids Charities 175

Baxter Charitable Trust (John Boyd) 139

Beacon Centre for the Blind 209

Beaminster Charities 269

Beasley Charitable Trust (Gertrude) 176

Beaumont (Charity of Letitia) 192

Beaumont & Jessop Relief-in-Need Charity 186

Beaumont Charity (Elizabeth) 266

Beckly Trust 255

Bedale Welfare Charity 175

Beeton, Barrick & Beck Relief-in-Need Charity 222

Beighton Relief-in-Need Charity 180

Belfast Association for the Blind 137

Belfast Sick Poor Fund 137

Bell Trust (Henry) 178

Benevolent Association for the Relief of Decayed Tradesmen, their Widows and Orphans 310

Benevolent Fund for Nurses in Scotland 139

Benevolent Fund of the Association of Her Majesty's Inspectors of Taxes 101

Berkshire Nurses & Relief-in-Sickness Trust 277

Berwick-upon-Tweed Nursing Amenities Fund 178

Betchworth United Charities & Henry Smith Charity 323

Bibby Bequest (Elizabeth) 140

Bideford Bridge Trust 261

Biggart Trust 140

Bilston Relief-in-Need Charity 246

Bilton Charity (Percy) 32

Bingham Trust 213

Bingham Trust Scheme 232

Bingham United Charities 232

Bingley Diamond Jubilee Relief-in-Sickness Charity 184

Birchington Convalescent Benefit Fund 44

Birkenhead Relief in Sickness Fund 205

Birmingham & Three Counties Trust for Nurses 209

Birmingham and District Butchers and Pork Butchers Association Benevolent Fund 244

Birmingham Jewish Community Care 245

Bishopsgate Foundation 346

Bisley (Ancient Charity of the Parish of) 272

Black Watch Association 108

Blackman Foundation (Isabel) 290

Blackpool, Fylde & Wyre Society for the Blind 200

Blackstock Trust 152

Blakeley-Marillier Charitable Fund (Mrs El) 169

Blakemore Foundation 245

Blakeney Twelve 306

Blakesley Parochial Charities 226

Blanchminster Trust 260

Bletchingley United Charities 323

Bletchington Charity 314

Blyth Benevolent Trust 140

BMA Charities Trust Fund 83

Boath & Milne Trust 140

Bolton & District Nursing Association 197

Bolton Poor Protection Society 197

Bond/Henry Welch Trust (James) 200

Book Trade Charity 67

Bookhams, Fetcham & Effingham Nursing Association Trust 320

Booth Charities 199

Bordon and Liphook Charity 294

Boston Green Trust 19

Botley (Charity of William) 276

Boughton Long Lawford Charity (Sir Edward) 240

Boveridge Charity 269

Bowcocks Trust Fund for Keighley 187

Bowes (Charity of Sir Martin) 338

Bowley Charity for Deprived Children 299

Bowness Trust 196

BP Benevolent Fund 89

Brackley United Feoffee Charity 226

Bradford & District Wool Association Benevolent Fund 183

Bradford Jewish Benevolent Fund 183

Brad's Cancer Foundation 50

Braintree United Charities 292

Bramhope Trust 187

Bramley Poor's Allotment Trust 180

Brampton Bierlow Welfare Trust 178

Bratton Fleming Relief-in-Need Charity 263

Braunston Town Lands Charity 226

Brecknock Association for the Welfare of the Blind 162

Brecknock Welfare Trust 162

Brentford & Chiswick Relief in Need and Sick Poor Persons Fund 331

Brentwood Charity 201

Brideoake (Charity of Miss Ann Farrar) 169

Bridge Trust 263

Bridgeland Charity 267

Bridgeman Charity Trust (Mary Dame) 248

Bridgnorth Parish Charity 236

Bridlington Charities 174

Brighton District Nursing Association Trust 290

Brighton Fund 290

Brisco Charity (Sarah) 291

Bristol Benevolent Institution 258

Bristol Charities 258

Bristol Corn Trade Guild 72

Bristow and Thomas Mason Trust (John) 323

British Association of Former United Nations Civil Servants Benevolent Fund 104

British Dental Association Benevolent Fund 84

British Fire Services Association Member's Fund 76

British Gas Energy Trust 19

British Jewellery, Giftware & Finishing Federation Benevolent Society 80

British Kidney Patient Association 55

British Motor Cycle Racing Club Benevolent Fund 100

British Office Supplies and Services Federation Benevolent Fund 101

British Polio Fellowship 54

British Racing Drivers Club (BRDC) Benevolent Fund 100

Brittle Bone Society 50

Brixton Feoffee Trust 264

Broadhempston Relief-in-Need Charity 264

Broadlands Home Trust 297

Broadway Cottages Trust 227

Brockley Town & Poor Estate (Brockley Charities) 315

Bromley Relief-in-Need Charity 336

Bromwich Charity (Thomas) 245

Brook Convalescent Fund (Charles) 186

Brooke Charity 216

Brooke Charity (Lizzie) 260

Broomfield United Charities 292

Brotherton Charity Fund 189

Broughton, Kirkby & District Good Samaritan Fund 175

Broughty Ferry Benevolent Fund 149

Brown Farnsfield Trust (John and Nellie) 229

Brown Habgood Hall and Higden Charity 271

Brownlow Charity (Lawrence) 196

Brownsdon & Tremayne Estate Charity (also known as the Nicholas Watts' Gift) 262

Brunts Charity 233

BT Benevolent Fund 103

Buchanan Society 140

Buckingham Trust 123

Budleigh Salterton Nursing Association 264

Bungay Charities 316

Buntingford Relief in Need Charity 299

Burma Star Association 108

Burton on Trent Nursing Endowment Fund 237

Burton-upon-Trent (Consolidated Charity of) 237

Bury Relief-in-Sickness Fund 197

Bushbury United Charities 248

Butterfield Trust 184

Buttle Trust (Frank) 27

Byfield Poors Allotment 227

Byfleet United Charities 323

C

Calderdale (Community Foundation for) 185

Calverton Apprenticing Charity 284

Camberwell Consolidated Charities 345

Cambridge Community Nursing Trust 286

Cameron Fund 84, 150

Campbell Trust (Norah Mavis) 279

Campden Charities 341

Cannington Combined Charity 273

Canterbury United Municipal Charities 302

Capital Charitable Trust 152

Card (also known as Draycott Charity) (Charity of John & Joseph) 273

Cardiff Caledonian Society 165

Cardiff Citizens Charity 166

Carlee Ltd 129

Carlisle Sick Poor Fund 195

Carlow Trust Fund (Leonora) 268

Carmen Benevolent Trust (Worshipful Company of) 92

Carnegie Hero Fund Trust 19

Carr Trust 238

Casselden Trust 303

Catenian Benevolent Association 36

Catharine House Trust 289

Catholic Clothing Guild 19

Catt (Charity of Joseph) 319

Cattle Trust (Joseph & Annie) 173

Caudwell Children (formerly The Caudwell Charitable Trust) 39

Central Exeter Relief-in-Need Fund 265

Ceramic Industry Welfare Society 68

Cerebra for Brain Injured Children and Young People 54

Chalker Trust (Henry & Ada) 189

Chalmers Trust (George, James & Alexander) 148

Champney Rest & Holiday Fund (Margaret) 26

Chance Trust 245

Chapel Allerton & Potternewton Relief-in-Need Charity (Leeds) 187

Chapman Charitable Trust (John William) 180

Charity Employees Benevolent Fund 104

Charlton Bequest & Dispensary Trust 183

Charlton Kings Relief in Need Charity 272

Chartered Institute of Building Benevolent Fund 67

Chartered Institute of Journalists Orphan Fund 82

Chartered Institute of Loss Adjusters Benevolent Fund 66

Chartered Institute of Management Accountants Benevolent Fund 58

Chasah Trust 123

Chasdei Tovim Me'oros 129

Chatham District Masonic Trust 303

Chatteris Feoffee Charity 286

Chauntry Estate 227

Cheam Consolidated Charities 324

Cheddington Town Lands Charity 284

Chelsworth Parochial Charity 316

Chertsey Combined Charity 324

Cheshire Provincial Fund of Benevolence 192

Chessington Charities 324

Chester Parochial Relief-in-Need Charity 193

Chesterfield General Charitable Fund 214

Chesterfield Municipal Charities 214

Cheyne Trust Fund (Gordon) 148

Children of the Clergy Trust 123

Children Today Charitable Trust 27

Chippenham Borough Lands Charity 275

Chipping Sodbury Town Lands 259

Chobham Poor Allotment Charity 324

Chownes Foundation 277

Christ Church Fund for Children 205

Christ Church United Charities 345

Christadelphian Benevolent Fund 124

Christie Bequest Fund (Robert) 152

Christie Fund 154

Christmas Gift Fund for the Old City of Canterbury 301

Chronicle Cinderella Fund 201

Church Eaton Relief-in-Need Charity 238

Church of England Pensions Board 124

Church School Masters and School Mistresses Benevolent Institution 102

Churt Welfare Trust 320

Cinema & Television Benevolent Fund 82

City Chapter & Percy Trentham Charity 337

City of London Linen and Furnishings Trades Association 70

Civil Service Benevolent Fund 69

Clackmannan District Charitable Trust 151

Clapham Relief Fund 342

Clarke Relief-in-Need Fund & The Wigston Relief-in-Need Fund (Elizabeth) 217

Clergy Rest Fund 124

Clevedon Forbes Fund 44

CLIC Sargent (formerly Sargent Cancer Care for Children) 50

Cliffe at Hoo Parochial Charity 305

Clophill United Charities 280

Closehelm Ltd 129

Clover Trust (Emily) 206

Coal Industry Benevolent Trust 71

Coal Trade Benevolent Association 71

Coalville and District Relief in Sickness Fund 217

Cockermouth Relief-in-Need Charity 196

Cockshot Foundation 191

Coddington United Charities 233

Coffey Charitable Trust 19

Colchester Catalyst Charity 291

Colchester Society for the Blind 291

Cole & Others (Charities of Susanna) 209

Coleman Trust (R V) 301

College of Optometrists and the Association of Optometrists (Benevolent Fund of the) 84

Collier Charitable Trust 124

Collier Holiday Fund (Joseph) 345

Colvile Charitable Trust (J I) 27

Colvill Charity 149

Colyton Parish Lands Charity 264

Combe Down Holiday Trust 258

Common Lands of Rotherham Charity 180

Community Foundation Serving Tyne & Wear and Northumberland 181

Community Shop Holiday Fund 187

Community Shop Trust 188

Confederation of Forest Industries 59

Congleton Town Trust 193

Conroy Trust 207

Conwy Welsh Church Acts Fund 163

Cook Charity for the Poor (Samuel Edward) 336

Cook Pensioners' Benevolent Fund (Thomas) 104

Coopers Liverymen Fund (William Alexander) 72

Cordwainers' Company Common Investment Fund 19

Corfe Castle Charities 270

Corkhill Trust (John Lloyd) 207

Corn Exchange Benevolent Society 73

Cornwall Community Foundation 260

Cornwall Retired Clergy, Widows of the Clergy and their Dependants Fund 260

Cornwallis Memorial Fund 301

Corporation of London Benevolent Association 91

Corporation of the Sons of the Clergy 124

Corwen College Pension Charity 162

Cottam Charities 202

Cotton Districts Convalescent Fund and the Barnes Samaritan Charity 191

Cotton Industry War Memorial Trust 70

Counsel & Care for the Elderly 33

County Durham Community Foundation 172

Coventry Nursing Trust 248

Cowbridge with Llanblethian United Charities 167

Cox Charity (George) 274

Cozens Bequest 313

Craigcrook Mortification 140

Cranbrook Charity 262

Cranfield Charitable Trust 315

Cranleigh & District Nursing Association 320

Crediton Relief-in-Need Charity 265

Crerar Trust for Single Poor (Alastair) 140

Cresswell Memorial (Eliza Ann) 214

Cricketers Association Charity 98

Cripplegate Foundation 331

Crisis Fund of Voluntary Service Aberdeen 148

Crohn's and Colitis UK 49

Crosby Ravensworth Relief-in-Need Charities 196

Crosland Fund 198

Crosthwaite Bequest (Lady) 181

Crowhurst Relief-in-Need Charities 324

Crusaid Hardship Fund 46

Culmstock Fuel Allotment Charity 265

Cumbria Constabulary Benevolent Fund 194

Cwmbran Trust 167

Cystic Fibrosis Trust 51

D

Dacorum Community Trust 300

Dagenham United Charity 334

Dahl Foundation (Roald) 51

Dargie Trust (Mrs Marie) 149

Datchet United Charities 282

Davenport Emergency Fund (Worcestershire) (Baron) 251

Davenport Emergency Grant (Leamington Spa, Kenilworth or Warwick) (Baron) 240

Davenport Emergency Grant (North Staffordshire) (Baron) 237

Davenport Emergency Grant (North Warwickshire) (Baron) 240

Davenport Emergency Grant (Nuneaton and Bedworth) (Baron) 240

Davenport Emergency Grant (Rugby) (Baron) 243

Davenport Emergency Grant (Warwickshire) (Baron) 241

Daventry Consolidated Charity 227

Davey (Charity of John) 261

Davies Trust (Isaac) 331

Dawber (Charity of John) 221

Deakin and Withers Fund 125

Deeping St James United Charities 222

Dempster Trust 321

Denham Nursing Fund 285

Dennington Consolidated Charities 316

Denny Care and Relief Fund (Brain Tumour UK) 49

Denton Relief in Sickness Charity 197

Deptford Pension Society 343

Derby City Charity 214

Derbyshire Annuity Fund (Lucy) 229

Desborough Town Welfare Committee 227

Devon County Association for the Blind 262

Dewsbury & District Sick Poor Fund 186

Diamond Charitable Fund (Gillian) 19

Dibden Allotments Charity 294

Dickinson Charity (Mary) 229

Dickinson Massey Underwood Charity 230

Dinas Powis Relief-in-Sickness Fund 168

Diss Parochial Charities Poors Branch 307

Dixon Pension Fund (Charles) 206

Dobson Trust 303

Dodbrooke Parish Charity 262

Dodgson Foundation (Derek & Eileen) 277

Dolphin Society 258

Donald Trust 148

Dorchester Relief-in-Need Charity 270

Dorkin Charity (John) 317

Dorrington Welfare Charity 223

Downham Aid in Sickness 307

Downham Feoffee Charity 287

Drake Fellowship (Francis) 98

Drexler Foundation (George) 71

Dronfield Relief-in-Need Charity 213

Drummond Trust (Kate) 305

Ducklington & Hardwick with Yelford Charity 313

Dudley Charity 249

Dudley Charity (Reginald Unwin) 249

Duffryn Trust 166

Dugdale Charity (Henry Percy) 187

Dundee Indigent Sick Society 149

Dunn Trust (W E) 210

Dunstable Welfare Trust 280

Dystonia Society 51

E

Ealing Aid-in-Sickness Trust 338

Earl Stonham Trust 317

Earley Charity 281

East Bergholt United Charities 292

East Dereham Relief-in-Need Charity 308

East Farndon (United Charities of) 227

East Knoyle Welfare Trust 275

East Tilbury Relief-in-Need Charity 293

East Tuddenham Charities 308

Eaton Fund for Artists, Nurses & Gentlewomen 39

ECAS (Access/Holiday Fund) 153

Eccles (Charity of Jane Patricia) 251

EDF Energy Trust 20

Edinburgh Merchant Company Endowment Trust 153

Edinburgh Royal Infirmary Samaritan Society 153

Edmett & Fisher Charity 305

Edmond Castle Educational Trust 195

Edmonton Aid-in-Sickness & Nursing Fund 332

Edridge Fund 91

Educational Institute of Scotland Benevolent Fund 141

Edwards Charity (Austin) 244

Egham United Charity 325

Egyptian Community Association in the United Kingdom 30

Eileen Trust 47

Elliot Bequest (Samuel) 156

Elliott Charity 329

Elliott Deceased (Charity of John McKie) 181

Eman Trust (Elizabeth) 284

Emanuel Hospital Charity 332

Emberton United Charity 285

Emmandjay Charitable Trust 185

EMMS International 154

Engineers Charitable Trust Fund (Worshipful Company of) 74

Engler Family Charitable Trust 129

English National Opera Benevolent Fund 63

Enville Village Trust 238

Environmental Health Officers Welfare Fund 76

Eos Foundation 278

Epsom Parochial Charities 325

Epworth Charities 180

Equipment for Independent Living 44

Equity Trust Fund 61

Essex Police Support Staff Benevolent Fund 291

Ewell Parochial Trusts 321

Exeter Dispensary & Aid-in-Sickness Fund 265

Exeter Relief-in-Need Charity 262

Exminster Feoffees 265

Exmouth Welfare Trust 266

Eynsham Consolidated Charity 314

Eyre Memorial Foundation (Monica) 33

F

Faculty of Advocates 1985 Charitable Trust 141

Falkirk Temperance Trust 151

Family Action (formerly Family Welfare Association) 20

Family Fund Trust 27

Family Holiday Association 31

Fareham Welfare Trust 297

Faringdon United Charities 313

Farnborough (Hampshire) Welfare Trust 294

Farndon Relief-in-Need Charity 233

Farriers Charitable Trust (Worshipful Company of) 76

Farthing Trust 286

Fawcett Johnston Charity 95

Featherstone Charity (Catherine) 286

Federation of Master Builders (Bristol Branch) Benevolent Fund 257

Feltmakers Charitable Foundation 70

Ferryhill Station, Mainsforth & Bishop Middleham Aid-in-Sickness Charity 172

Field Charity (Olive & Norman) 169

Fife Council (West Fife Area) (Charities Administered by) 151

Fifty Fund 230

Finchampstead & Barkham Relief-in-Sickness Fund 281

Finchley Charities 335

Finn Care (Elizabeth) 20

Finnart House School Trust 129

Fire Fighters Charity 76

Fisher (William) 179

Fisher Trust (Jane) 195

Fleming Bequest 152

Flintshire Welsh Church Acts Fund 164

Flitwick Town Lands Charity 280

Fluck Convalescent Fund 271

Fogelman Relief Trust (Isaac & Annie) 298

Fogwill Charitable Trust (David) 21

Folkestone Municipal Charities 303

Football Association Benevolent Fund 99

Footwear Benevolent Society (formerly The Boot Trade Benevolent Society) 70

Forbes Inverness Trust (Dr) 160

Forby Charity (Jane) 312

Fordath Foundation 249

Fordwich United Charities 303

Forester Trust (Lady) 234

Forsyth Family Trust (Clan) 21

Foster Charitable Trust (Stanley) 21

Foster Settlement (Alfred) 66

Foulden Parochial Charities 308

Fountain Nursing Trust 179

Four Winds Trust 125

Foxton Dispensary 201

Frampton Town Land & United Charities 223

Franklin Fund (Samuel) 287

French Memorial Trust (Anne) 306

Friends Hall Farm Street Trust 210

Friends of Home Nursing in Birmingham 247

Friends of the Animals 245

Friends of the Clergy Corporation 125

Friends of the Elderly 33

Frimley Fuel Allotments Charity 210

Friskney United Charities 223

Fritillary Trust 282

Frodsham Nursing Fund 193

Fryer Welfare and Recreational Trusts 264

Fudge Trust for Warminster (Ernest and Marjorie) 21

Fuel Allotment 286

Fulham Benevolent Society 339

Fund for Human Need 21

Fund For Nurses (Ethel Mary) 84

Furnishing Trades Benevolent Association 79

G

Gamekeepers Welfare Trust 59

Garboldisham Parish Charities 308

Garden Nicol Benevolent Fund 148

Gardening for the Disabled Trust 44

Gardner Trust (Grace) 177

Gargrave Poor's Land Charity 175

Garlthorpes Charity 174

Garrett Memorial Trust (Dr) 198

Gas Engineers Benevolent Fund (Institution of) 79

Gates Charitable Trust (Cyril and Margaret) 146

Gateshead Blind Trust Fund 182

Gateshead Relief-in-Sickness Fund 182

Gayton Fuel Allotments 308

Gayton Relief-in-Need Charity 308

Geest Charity (Gyles) 272

General Charities of the City of Coventry 248

Gent & Others (Charity of Priscilla) 241

George House Trust 191

George Trust (Ruby & Will) 72

German Society of Benevolence 31

Gibbons Charity 70

Gibson, Simpson & Brockbank Annuities Trust 203

Gilbert (Charity of Jane Kate) 247

Gild of Freemen of Haverfordwest 167

Gisleham Relief in Need Charity 317

Gislingham United Charity 317

Glasgow Bute Benevolent Society 156

Glasgow Dunbartonshire Benevolent Association 158

Glasgow Society of the Sons and Daughters of Ministers of the Church of Scotland 141

Glasspool Charity Trust (R L) 21

Glebe Charitable Trust 28

Gloucestershire Bowling Association Benevolent Fund 271

Gloucestershire Football Association Benevolent Fund 255

Godmersham Relief in Need Charity 303

Godson Charity (Edmund) 210

Godstone United Charities 321

Golborne Charities 198

Goldie (BBC) Trust Fund (Grace Wyndham) 82

Goodall Trust 186

Goodman Estate Charity (Valentine) 225

Goodwin Charity (Sir Stuart & Lady Florence) 180

Goore's Charity (John) 206

Gorsuch, Langley & Prynce Charity 236

Gourock Coal & Benevolent Fund 159

Gow Charitable Trust (Neil) 146

Goward & John Evans (Charities of George) 318

Gowland Trust (Ralph) 181

Gowthorpe Fund & Clergy Augmentation Fund (Charles Wright) 230

Grampian Police Diced Cap Charitable Fund 146

Grand Charitable Trust of the Order of Women Freemasons 36

Grand Charity (of Freemasons under the United Grand Lodge of England) 36

Grand Lodge of Antient, Free & Accepted Masons of Scotland 36

Grand Order of Water Rats Charities Fund 61

Grand Prix Mechanics Charitable Trust 100

Grandborough & Sutton Charities 242

Grant, Bagshaw, Rogers & Tidswell Fund 191

Grantchester Relief in Need Charity 287

Grantham Yorke Trust 245

Grateful Society 257

Great Glen Relief in Need Charity 218

Great Linford Relief in Need Charity 285

Great Torrington Town Lands Poors Charities 266

Green Charitable Trust (Suzanne) 329

Greenway (Charities of Ralph) 312

Greenway Benefaction Trust 251

Greenwich Charity 338

Greggs Foundation 169

Gregson Memorial Annuities 191

Griffiths Trust (I W) 126

Griffiths Trust (Megan and Trevor) 44

Grimsby Sailors and Fishing Charity 95

Grizzles Foundation 278

Groome Trust 296

Gubbay Memorial Fund (Ronnie) 332

Guild of Air Pilots Benevolent Fund 60

Guild of Benevolence of The Institute of Marine Engineering Science and Technology 74

Guild of Registered Tourist Guides Benevolent Fund 104

Guildford Poyle Charities 325

Guildry Incorporation of Perth 151

Gur Trust 130

Gurunanak 21

Gwalia Housing Trust 164

H

Hackney Benevolent Pension Society 339

Hackney District Nursing Association 339

Hackney Parochial Charities 339

Haden (Isleworth) Relief in Sickness Charity (John Fielder) 341

Haemophilia Society (The Tanner Fund) 52

Haendler Charity (Nathan and Adolphe) 130

Halesworth United Charities 317

Halifax Society for the Blind 185

Hall Charity (George & Clara Ann) 179

Hamilton Memorial Fund (Janet) 158

Hammersmith & Fulham's Appeal Fund (Mayor of) 340

Hampshire & Isle of Wight Military Aid Fund (1903) 109

Hampshire Ambulance Service Benevolent Fund 294

Hampshire Association for the Care of the Blind (HACB) 294

Hampshire Constabulary Welfare Fund 294

Hampshire Football Association Benevolent Fund 295

Hampstead Wells & Campden Trust 336

Hampton and Hampton Hill Philanthropic Society 344

Hampton Fuel Allotment Charity 332

Hampton Wick United Charity 342

Handsworth Charity 247

Harborne Parish Lands Charity 245

Hardwick Fund (Ben) 52

Harley Charity (formerly The Honourable Miss Frances Harley Charity) 165

Harling Fuel Allotment Trust 309

Harlow Community Chest 293

Harpenden Trust 300

Harpole Parochial Charities 227

Harris Charity 201

Harris Trust (James Edward) 165

Harrison & Potter Trust (incorporating Josias Jenkinson Relief-in-Need Charity) 184

Harrison Trust (Margaret) 213

Hart Charitable Trust 289

Hart Trust (Robert) 155

Hartley Memorial Trust (N & P) 45

Hatfield Broad Oak Non-Ecclesiastical Charities 300

Hatton Consolidated Charities 241

Hawley Almshouse & Relief-in-Need Charity 297

Hay Trust (Douglas) 141

Hayes (Kent) Trust 304

Hayward Trust (R S) 155

Head Award (Francis) 65

Headley-Pitt Charitable Trust 301

Heath Memorial Trust Fund 237

Heathcoat Trust 262

Help-in-Need Association (HINA) 292

Helston Welfare Trust 261

Henderson Charity 346

Henwood (Charity of Thomas) 261

Herd Memorial Trust (Anne) 141

Hereford Corn Exchange Fund 215

Hereford Municipal Charities 216

Hereford Society for Aiding the Industrious 215

Herefordshire Community Foundation 215

Herne Bay Parochial Charity 304

Heron (Eleemosynary Charity of Giles) 178

Hertfordshire Charity for Deprived Children 299

Hertfordshire Community Foundation 299

Hertfordshire Convalescent Trust 299

Herve Benevolent Institution (Peter) 257

Hewley Trust (Lady) 126

Heywood Relief-in-Need Trust Fund 199

High Wycombe Central Aid Society 285

Highweek Charities 266

Hilgay Feoffee Charity 309

Hill Charity (Christopher) 262

Hill Memorial And Benevolent Fund (Rowland) 90

Hill Trust (Mary) 252

Hillingdon Partnership Trust 340

Hills Charity (Helen Georgie) 304

Hilton Town Charity 287

Hindley Charitable Trust (Margaret Jeannie) 21

Hitcham Poor Lands Charity 285

Hobbayne (Eleemosynary Charity of William) 338

Hodnet Consolidated Eleemosynary Charities 236

Hodson Foundation Ltd (Frank) 234

Hogg Trust (George) 152

Holford Charity (John) 192

Holinsworth Fund of Help (CB & AB) 246

Hollands-Warren Charitable Trust 305

Holt (Charity of Ann) 186

Holywood Trust 156

Home Warmth for the Aged 33

Honiton United Charities 266

Honourable Company of Master Mariners 95

Hoper-Dixon Trust 22

Hopesay Parish Trust 236

Hordle District Nursing Association 297

Hornsby Professional Cricketers Fund Charity 98

Hornsey Parochial Charities 332

Horticultural Trades Association Benevolent Fund 80

Hospitality Action (formerly Hotel And Catering Benevolent Association) 80

Houghton Memorial Trust (Basil) 235

Houghton-Le-Spring Relief in Need Charity 182

Hounsfield Pension 126

Housing the Homeless Central Fund 32

Houston Charitable Trust 22

Hucknall Relief-in-Need Charity 233

Huddersfield Education Trust 187

Huddleston Fund for Children (Trevor) 346

Hugh Fraser Foundation (Emily Fraser Trust) 141

Hull Aid in Sickness Trust 173

Humberside Police Welfare and Benevolent Fund 173

Hume Trust (Elizabeth) 155

Hunstanton Convalescent Trust 278

Hunt Charitable Trust (Michael and Shirley) 38

Hunter Memorial Fund (John Routledge) 170

Hurst Will Trust (Arthur) 39

Husborne Crawley Charities of the Poor 280

Hutchinson Poors Charity (Joseph) 195

Hutchinson Trust (Gilling and Richmond) (Reverend Matthew) 176

Huyton with Roby Distress Fund 205

Hyde Park Place Estate Charity (Civil Trustees) 337

Hylton House Fund 170

I

Ibero-American Benevolent Society 29

Ickleton United Charities (Relief-in-Need Branch) 287

Ilchester Relief-in-Need and Educational Charity 273

Illston Town Land Charity 218

Incorporated Benevolent Association of the Chartered Institute of Patent Attorneys 89

Incorporation of Bakers of Glasgow 158

Independence at Home 45

IndependentAge (RUKBA) 34

India Welfare Society 31

Indian Police Benevolent Fund 89

Injured Jockeys Fund 100

Inner London Fund for the Blind and Disabled 332

Innes Memorial Fund 329

Institute of Clayworkers Benevolent Fund 69

Institute of Football Management & Administration Charity Trust 99

Institute of Healthcare Management Benevolent Fund 84

Institute of Physics Benevolent Fund 94

Institute of Quarrying Educational Development and Benevolent Fund 92

Institution of Engineering and Technology Benevolent Fund (IET Connect) 73

Institution of Materials, Minerals & Mining 87

Institution of Mechanical Engineers (Benevolent Fund of the) 75

Institution of Plant Engineers Benevolent Fund 75

Insurance Charities 67

Iprovision (formerly The Institute of Public Relations Benevolent Fund) 91

Iver Heath Sick Poor Fund 283

Iver United Charities 283

J

Jamieson Fund (George) 142

JAT 47

Jenkins Trust (Kay) 292

Jennifer Trust 55

Jesus Hospital Charity 335

Jewish Aged Needy Pension Society 130

Jewish Care 278

Jewish Care Scotland 142

John Hodges Charitable Trust 314

John Moore's Bequest 248

Johnson & the Green Charity (Christopher) 232

Johnson Bede & Lane Charitable Trust 287

Johnston Charity 149

Johnston Family Fund 22

Johnston Trust Fund (William) 22

Joicey Fund (Rose) 170

Joint Industrial Council & the Match Manufacturing Industry Charitable Fund 82

Jones Charity (Owen) 164

Jones Trust (William and John) 164

Jordison and Hossell Animal Welfare Charity 210

Journalists' Charity 82

K

Kay Fund (Louisa Alice) 197

Kelly Charitable Trust 171

Kempston Charities 280

Kenilworth Carnival Comforts Fund 242

Kenilworth United Charities 242

Kensington and Chelsea District Nursing Trust 342

Kent County Football Association Benevolent Fund 301

Kent Farmers Benevolent Fund 59

Kent Fund for Children 302

Kent Nursing Institution 302

Kesteven Children in Need 223

Kettering Charities (Fuel Grants) 228

Key Trust 142

Keyes Trust (Ursula) 192

Keyham Relief in Need Charity 218

Kidderminster Aid In Sickness Fund 252

Kilcreggan Trust 22

King Trust (Thomas) 298

King's Norton United Charities 249

Kingsbury Charity 336

Kingsclere Welfare Charities 295

Kingston Fund (Dr C S) 276

Kingston-upon-Thames Association for the Blind 342

Kirkby Lonsdale Relief-in-Need Charity 196

Kirkcaldy Charitable Trust 152

Kirke Charity 188

Kitchings General Charity 222

Knaresborough Relief-in-Need Charity 176

Knight Charitable Trust (H E) 126

Knox Fund (James and Jane) 159

Kroch Foundation (Heinz, Anna and Carol) 34

Kupath Gemach Chaim Bechesed Viznitz Trust 130

L

Lakeland Disability Support 195

Lamb Charity (John William) 230

Lancashire County Nursing Trust 201

Lancashire Football Association Benevolent Fund 201

Lancashire Infirm Secular Clergy Fund 192

Lancaster Charity 203

Lant Trust 246

LATCH (Llandough Aim to Treat Children with Cancer and Leukaemia with Hope) 161

Launderers Benevolent Trust (Worshipful Company of) 81

Lavender Trust 306

Law Society of Scotland Benevolent Fund 142

Leaders of Worship and Preachers Trust 126

League Managers Benevolent Trust 99

League of the Helping Hand 45

Leamington Relief-in-Sickness Fund 243

Leatherhead United Charities 326

Lee Charity of William Hatcliffe 343

Leeds Benevolent Society for Single Ladies 188

Leeds District Aid-in-Sickness Fund 188

Leeds Jewish Welfare Board 171

Lees Relief Trust (Sarah) 198

Leicester Aid-in-Sickness Fund 219

Leicester ARC (also known as Leicester and County Convalescent Homes Society) 217

Leicester Charity Link (formerly Leicester Charity Organisation Society) 217

Leicester Indigent Old Age Society 219

Leicestershire Coal Industry Welfare Trust Fund 217

Leicestershire County Nursing Association 217

Leigh United Charities 304

Leith Benevolent Association Ltd 154

Letchworth Civic Trust 300

Leukaemia Care Society 50

Leverington Town Lands Charity 286

Leveson Charity (Lady Katherine and Sir Richard) 239

Lewis (of Chigwell) Memorial Fund (George and Alfred) 292

Lewisham Relief in Need Charity 343

Licensed Trade Charity (Licensed Trade Support and Care) 77

Licensed Trade of Scotland (Benevolent Society of the) 78

Lichfield Municipal Charities 238

Lifeline 4 Kids 28

Lighthouse Club Benevolent Fund 68

Lincoln General Dispensary Fund 222

Lincoln Municipal Relief-in-Need Charities 224

Lincolnshire Police Charitable Fund 222

Lind Trust 126

Lindow Workhouse Trust 194

Lineham Charity (Henry & Elizabeth) 225

Linford Charitable Trust (Fred) 237

Lionheart (The Royal Institution of Chartered Surveyors Benevolent Fund) 68

Lipton Memorial Fund (Francis) 158

Liskeard (United Charities of) 261

Litchborough Parochial Charities 228

Litten Charitable Trust (Adelaide) 36

Little Charitable Trust (Andrew & Mary Elizabeth) 158

Little Dunham Relief-in-Need Charities 309

Littleborough Nursing Association Fund 203

Littledown Trust 302

Litton Cheney Relief-in-Need Trust 266

Liverpool Caledonian Association 204

Liverpool Corn Trade Guild 206

Liverpool Provision Trade Guild 204

Liverpool Queen Victoria District Nursing Association (LCSS) 204

Liverpool Queen Victoria Nursing Association (PSS) 204

Liverpool Wholesale Fresh Produce Benevolent Fund 206

Liversage Trust 214

Llandenny Charities 166

Llanidloes Relief-in-Need Charity 162

Lloyd Charitable Trust (Elaine & Angus) 278

Lloyd Trust (W M & B W) 202

Local Aid for Children & Community Special Needs 165

Lockerbie & District Sick Benevolent Association 157

Lockerbie Trust 157

Lockinge & Ardington Relief-in-Need Charity 313

London Metal Exchange Benevolent Fund 87

Londonderry Methodist City Mission 137

Long Bennington Charities 233

Loudoun Bequest 159

Loughborough Welfare Trusts 218

Lowestoft Church and Town Relief in Need Charity 318

Lowestoft Maternity & District Nursing Association 318

Lowton United Charity 203

Loxton Trust Fund (Harriet Louisa) 247

Lucas for the Poor & for Public Purposes (Charity of Robert) 281

Lund Holiday Grants (Lucy) 184

Luttrell Memorial Charity (J A F) 272

Lyall Bequest 126

Lyndhurst Welfare Charity 297

Lyng Heath Charity 309

M

MacAndrew Trust (B V) 279

Macclesfield Relief-in-Sickness Fund 193

Macdonald Bequest 152

MacDonald of Johannesburg Trust (Dr William) 248

MacDougall Trust 269

Macfarlane Trust 47

MacKenzie Trust (William) 160

Macleod Memorial Fund (Agnes) 142

Magic Circle Benevolent Fund 62

Maidstone Relief-in-Need Charities 305

Mair Robertson Benevolent Fund 150

Malam Convalescent Fund (Edward) 238

Malmesbury Community Trust 275

Manchester District Nursing Institution Fund 196

Manchester Jewish Federation 196

Manchester Jewish Soup Kitchen 197

Mann Trust (also known as The Wallsend Charitable Trust) (Victor) 183

Manor House Charitable Trust (incorporating The Charity of Lily Taylor) 230

Mantle Trust (William) 305

Manx Marine Society 200

Marine Society and Sea Cadets 95

Market Harborough & the Bowdens Charity 219

Market Overton Charity 219

Market Research Benevolent Association 82

Marshall's Charity (William) 312

Martin Trust (Douglas) 255

Martineau Trust 315

Masters Charity for Widows (Rev Robert) 287

Matthew Hall Staff Trust Fund 75

Matthew Trust 52

Maudlyn Lands Charity 263

Mayfield Charity 291

McCallum Memorial Fund (Catherine) 142

McKenna Charitable Trust 22

McKune Mortification (James) 157

McLaren Fund for Indigent Ladies 142

McLean Trust (George) 143

McLean Trust for the Elderly (Annie Ramsay) 143

Measures Charity (James Frederick & Ethel Anne) 246

Mellor Fund 197

Melton Mowbray Building Society Charitable Foundation 211

Melton Trust 318

Mendlesham Town Estate Charity 318

Meningitis Trust 52

Merchants House of Glasgow 155

Meriden United Charities 249

Merry Memorial Fund (Doctor) 290

Mersey Mission To Seafarers 204

Merseyside Jewish Community Care 205

Merthyr Mendicants 166

Metcalfe Smith Trust 189

Metropolitan Police Benevolent Fund 89

Metropolitan Police Civil Staff Welfare Fund 89

Metropolitan Society for the Blind 333

Micklegate Strays Charity 177

Middlesex Charitable Trust (Masonic Province of) 36

Middleton (Charity of Miss Eliza Clubley) 174

Middleton Relief-in-Need Charity 199

Middleton-on-the-Hill Parish Charity 216

Midgley Charity (William & Sarah) 187

Midhurst Pensions Trust 76

Mildenhall Parish Charities 318

Mills Charity 315

Minet Trust (Mary) 333

Mining Institute of Scotland Trust 88

Mitchell City of London Charity 337

Mobility Trust II 45

Molyneux Charity (Ann) 206

Monmouth Charity 166

Monmouth Relief-in-Need Charity 166

Monmouth Street Society, Bath 257

Monmouthshire Welsh Church Acts Fund 167

Montagu Neville Durnford & Saint Leo Cawthan Memorial Trust 298

Montgomery Welfare Fund 162

Moorhouse Charity (Harold) 307

Morar Trust 160

Morden College 34

Morgan Benevolent Fund (Junius S) 85

Morpeth Dispensary 178

Morris Beneficent Fund 40

Morrison Cox Fund (Mary) 148

Morval Foundation 129

Moser Benevolent Trust Fund 185

Motability 22

Motor Neurone Disease Association 53

Motoring Writers Benevolent Fund (Guild of) 82

Mottram St Andrew United Charities 193

Moulton (Non-Ecclesiastical Charity of William) 182

Mountsorrel Relief-in-Need Charity 220

Multiple Sclerosis Society of Great Britain and Northern Ireland 53

Municipal Charities 280

Municipal General Charities for the Poor 23

Murchie Charitable Trust (Maud Beattie) 207

Murdoch Trust (John) 94

Murray Trust (Matilda) 148

Musicians Benevolent Fund 63

Mylne Trust 127

N

NABS 59

Nafferton Feoffee Charity Trust 173

Nailsea Community Trust Ltd 259

Napton Charities 243

Nash Charity 109

Nash Will Trust (Mrs Alice Lilian) 40

National Association for the Care & Resettlement of Offenders (NACRO) 38

National Association of Master Bakers, Confectioners and Caterers Benevolent Fund 78

National Association of Schoolmasters Union of Women Teachers (NASUWT) Benevolent Fund 102

National Benevolent Institution 34

National Blind Children Society 48

National Caravan Council Benevolent Fund 68

National Federation of Fish Friers Benevolent Fund 78

National Federation of Retail Newsagents Convalescence Fund 88

National Federation of Sub-Postmasters Benevolent Fund 90

National Union of Journalists Provident Fund 83

Natlas Trust 23

Nautilus Welfare Fund (previously The NUMAST Welfare Fund) 95

Navenby Towns Farm Trust 224

Naysmyth Fund (Alexander) 143

Nazareth Trust Fund 127

NCDS (National Council for the Divorced & Separated Trust) 29

Neale Charity (Alex) 220

Neale Trust Fund for Poor Children 168

Nelson District Nursing Association Fund 203

New Appeals Organisation for the City & County of Nottingham 230

New Forest Keepers Widows Fund 298

New Masonic Samaritan Fund 37

Newbury & Thatcham Welfare Trust 282

Newcastle-under-Lyme United Charities 239

Newfield Charitable Trust 211

Newick Distress Trust 291

Newman Trust Homes 246

NewstrAid Benevolent Society 88

Newton on Derwent Charity 175

Newtownabbey Methodist Mission 137

Nicholl's Charity (William) 342

Nicholson Memorial Fund 218

Nightingale Aid-in-Sickness Trust (Florence) 45

Nimmo Charitable Trust (William Brown) 154

Nithsdale District Charities 157

Nitzrochim (Chevras Ezras) 130

Nivison Trust 157

NJD Charitable Trust 130

Norris Trust (Evelyn) 61

North East Area Miners Social Welfare Trust Fund 171

North of Scotland Quaker Trust 143

North Staffordshire Coalfield Miners Relief Fund 238

North Wales Association for Spina Bifida & Hydrocephalus 162

North Wales Police Benevolent Fund 162

North Wales Psychiatric Fund 163

North Wales Society for the Blind 161

North West Customs and Excise Benevolent Society 73

North West Police Benevolent Fund 192

Northampton Municipal Church Charities 228

Northcott Devon Foundation 263

Northern Ladies Annuity Society 171

Northwold Combined Charities and Edmund Atmere Charity 309

Norton Canon Parochial Charities 216

Norton Foundation 211

Norwich Consolidated Charities 310

Norwich Town Close Estate Charity 310

Norwood (formerly Norwood Ravenswood) 130

Nottingham Aged Persons' Trust 234

Nottingham Annuity Charity 230

Nottingham General Dispensary 231

Nottingham Gordon Memorial Trust for Boys & Girls 231

Nottinghamshire County Council Fund for Disabled People 231
Nuttall Trust 273

O

Oadby Educational Foundation 220
Oakdene Foundation 321
Ockley United Charities (Henry Smith Charity) 327
Ogilvie Charities 102
Old Buckenham United Eleemosynary Charity 310
Old Enfield Charitable Trust 338
Old Park Ward Old Age Pensioners Fund 214
Oldham United Charities 198
Oliver Will Trust (Ada) 50
Open House Darts League 215
Oppenheimer Fund (Arthur and Rosa) 333
Osborne Charitable Trust 23
Oswestry Dispensary Fund 235
Ottery Feoffee Charity 267
Ottringham Church Lands Charity 175
Over Norton Welfare Trust 314
Oxford Charities (City of) 314
Oxted United Charities 327

P

Padley Charity Fund (A L) 223
Page Fund 226
Paignton Parish Charity 267
Palling Burgess (United Charity of) 272
Palmer & Seabright Charity 250
Palmer Trust (Eleanor) 335
Pampisford Relief-in-Need Charity 288
Panton and Miss Anne Stirling Trust (Mrs Jeane) 143
Pargeter & Wand Trust 211
Parish Piece Charity 219
Parrott Trust Fund (Dorothy) 302
Pash Charitable Trust Fund (Albert Edward) 272
Paton Trust 127
Patrick Trust (Joseph) 54
Pattishall Parochial Charities 228
Pattullo Trust for Handicapped Boys (Gertrude Muriel) 147
Pattullo Trust for Handicapped Girls (Gertrude Muriel) 147
Pattullo Trust for the Elderly (Gertrude Muriel) 147

Payne Charity (John) 336
Peace Memorial Fund 347
Peckham & Kent Road Pension Society 345
Pedmore Sporting Club Trust Fund 211
Peel Legacy Trust (Lady) 127
Peirson Charitable Trust (Anne) 304
Pentney Charity 310
Penton Trust 295
Perennial 80
Perry Fund 40
Perry Trust Gift Fund 232
Persehouse Pensions Fund 211
Pershore United Charity 252
Pest House Charity (Midhurst) 329
Petersham United Charities 344
PGA European Tour Benevolent Trust 99
Pickles Memorial Benevolent Fund (H T) 88
Picto Buxton Charity 307
Pilkington Young Trust (Roger) 34
Pinn Charitable Trust (William Frank) 303
Pirate Trust 256
Pirbright Relief-in-Need Charity 327
Pitminster Charity 274
Pittis Charity for Widows (Mary) 297
Pitt-Rivers Charitable Trust 269
Plymouth & Cornwall Cancer Fund 256
Plymouth Charity Trust 267
Podde Trust 127
Polehampton Charity 281
Police Aided Clothing Scheme of Edinburgh 154
Poole Charity (Valentine) 335
Poor's Allotments Charity 284
Poppyscotland (The Earl Haig Fund Scotland) 143
Port of London Authority Police Charity Fund 333
Portishead Nautical Trust 259
Portsmouth Victoria Nursing Association 295
Positive East 333
Potter Charitable Trust (Margaret and Alick) 162
Pottery & Glass Trade Benevolent Fund (formerly the Pottery and Glass Trade Benevolent Institution) 91
Potton Consolidated Charities 281

Power Pleas Trust 251
Pratt Charity 197
Prestbury Charity (also known as The Prestbury United Charities) 271
Priestman Charity Trust (Sir John) 171
Prime Charitable Trust 97
Primrose Trust (John) 157
Princess Royal Trust for Carers 26
Prisoners of Conscience Appeal Fund 29
Pritt Fund 206
Professional Billiards & Snooker Players Benevolent Fund 101
Protestant Orphan Society for the Counties of Antrim & Down (Inc) 138
Provision Trade Charity 78
Provost Charities Fund, the D M Stevenson Fund & the Lethbridge Abell Fund (Lord) 158
Pryke Charity (Florence) 317
Public and Commercial Services Union Benevolent Fund 69
Purey Cust Fund 176
Puri Foundation 232
Pusinelli Convalescent & Holiday Home 29
Pyncombe Charity 127

Q

Quorn Town Lands Charity 220

R

Racing Welfare 100
Radio Forth Cash for Kids Appeal 144
Railway Benevolent Institution 92
Railway Housing Association & Benefit Fund 93
Rainy Day Trust (formerly Royal Metal Trades Benevolent Society) 87
Ramsay Foundation (Peggy) 65
Rank Benevolent Fund (Joseph) 174
Ratcliff Charity for the Poor 346
Rathbone Moral Aid Charity 215
Ravensden Town & Poor Estate 281
Rawlet Trust 239
Raygill Trust 177
React (Rapid Effective Assistance for Children with Potentially Terminal Illnesses) 46
Reading Dispensary Trust 281
Redcliffe Parish Charity 259
Rehoboth Trust 70

Reiss Trust for Old People (Florence) 34

Relief in Need Charity of Reverend William Smart 227

Relief in Need Charity of Simon Lord Digby and Others 242

REME Benevolent Fund 110

Removers Benevolent Association 93

Retail Trust (formerly Cottage Homes) 93

Retired Missionary Aid Fund 127

Reydon Trust 319

RFU Injured Players Foundation 55

Rhodesians Worldwide Assistance Fund 31

Rhona Reid Charitable Trust 23

Richard Cloudesley (Charity of) 341

Richmond Aid-in-Sickness Fund 344

Richmond Parish Lands Charity 344

Richmond Philanthropic Society 345

Rimpton Relief-in-Need Charities 274

Ringstead Gift 228

Ripple Trust (Ancient Parish of) 252

Risby Fuel Allotment 319

RMT (National Union of Rail, Maritime & Transport Workers) Orphan Fund 93

Road Haulage Association Benevolent Fund 93

Roade Feoffee and Chivall Charity 229

Roberts Charitable Trust (E C) 298

Roberts Home (Evan & Catherine) 163

Roberts Memorial Charity for Saham Toney (Ella) 310

Roberts Relief in Need Charity (Sir William) 244

Robinson Charity (Rebecca Guest) 179

Robinson Charity (Thomas) 205

Robinson Trust No. 3 (J C) 23

Rochdale Fund for Relief-in-Sickness 199

Rochdale United Charity 199

Roddam Charity 212

Rogers Charity (Porlock Branch) (Henry) 274

Rollright Charities (Great) 314

Ropner Centenary Trust 172

Ross Bequest (Mrs Esther) 158

Rosslyn Park Injury Trust Fund 55

Rotherhithe Consolidated Charities 345

Rowlandson & Eggleston Relief-in-Need Charity 176

Roxburghshire Landward Benevolent Trust 155

Royal Agricultural Benevolent Institution 59

Royal Air Force Benevolent Fund 111

Royal Air Forces Association 111

Royal Antediluvian Order of Buffaloes, Grand Lodge of England War Memorial Annuities 37

Royal Army Service Corps & Royal Corps of Transport Benevolent Fund 111

Royal Artillery Charitable Fund 111

Royal Ballet Benevolent Fund 62

Royal Belgian Benevolent Society 30

Royal Blind Society for the UK 49

Royal British Legion 111

Royal College of Midwives Trust 86

Royal College of Nursing Benevolent Fund 86

Royal Commonwealth Ex-Services League 112

Royal Institution of Naval Architects 88

Royal Literary Fund 65

Royal Masonic Benevolent Institution 37

Royal Medical Benevolent Fund 86

Royal Medical Foundation 86

Royal Military Police Central Benevolent Fund 112

Royal National Institute of Blind People 49

Royal National Mission to Deep Sea Fishermen 96

Royal Naval Benevolent Society for Officers 113

Royal Naval Benevolent Trust 113

Royal Naval Reserve (V) Benevolent Fund 113

Royal Observer Corps Benevolent Fund 113

Royal Opera House Benevolent Fund 61

Royal Scottish Corporation (also known as The Scottish Hospital of the Foundation of King Charles II) 144

Royal Signals Benevolent Fund 113

Royal Society (Scientific Relief Fund of the) 94

Royal Society for Home Relief to Incurables, Edinburgh (General Fund) 144

Royal Society for the Relief of Indigent Gentlewomen of Scotland 40

Royal Society of Chemistry Benevolent Fund 94

Royal Society of Musicians of Great Britain 64

Royal Theatrical Fund 64

Royal Ulster Constabulary Benevolent Fund 138

RTRA Benevolent Fund 73

Ruabon & District Relief-in-Need Charity 164

Rugby Football League Benevolent Fund 98

Rugby Relief in Need Charity 243

Rutland Dispensary 220

Rutland Trust 220

Ryde Sick Poor Fund (also known as Greater Ryde Benevolent Trust) 298

S

SACRO Trust 38

Saffron Walden United Charities 293

Saham Toney Fuel Allotment & Perkins Charity 306

Sailors' Society 96

Saint Giles Charity Estate 226

Saint Petrox Trust Lands 265

Salford Relief-in-Distress Fund (City of) 199

Salford Town Lands 283

Salisbury City Almshouse & Welfare Charities 275

Salter Trust (George & Thomas Henry) 250

Sandal Magna Relief-in-Need Charity 189

Sanders Charity (William) 167

Sandford Relief-in-Need Charity 267

Sands Cox Relief in Sickness Charity 247

Sandy Charities 279

Saunders Charity for the Relief of Indigent Gentry and Others (Mr William) 24

Saunders Relief-in-Sickness Charity (Florence) 288

Savage (Charities of Ann) 326

Sawley Charities 213

Saxlingham Relief in Sickness Fund 310

Saxlingham United Charities 311

Scaldwell Relief-in-Need Charity 229

Scale Charitable Trust Fund 295

Scarborough Municipal Charities 177

Scones Lethendy Mortifications 151

Scottish Cinematograph Trade Benevolent Fund 145

Scottish Hydro Electric Community Trust 145

Scottish National Institution for the War-Blinded 145

Scottish Nautical Welfare Society 145

Scottish Prison Service Benevolent Fund 146

Sedgefield District Relief-in-Need Charity 173

Semple Fund for Cancer Relief & Research (Mairi) 156

Sense, the National Deaf-Blind & Rubella Association 51

Severn Trent Water Charitable Trust Fund 24

sfgroup Charitable Fund for Disabled People 46

Shadwell Charity (William) 290

Shanks Bequest 151

Shaw Charities 202

Shaw-Stewart Memorial Fund (Lady Alice) 159

Shearer Bequest 157

Sheffield West Riding Charitable Society Trust 179

Shelroy Trust 306

Shepherd Charitable Trust (Eliza) 28

Sherburn House Charity 171

Shere & Others (Charity of John) 268

Sheriffs' & Recorders' Fund 333

Sherwood and Waudby Charity 175

Shetland Charitable Trust 160

Shipdham Parochial & Fuel Allotment 311

Shipman Charitable Trust (Thomas Stanley) 218

Shona Smile Foundation 50

Shottermill United Charities (Henry Smith and Others) 327

Show Business Benevolent Fund 62

Shrewsbury Municipal Charity 235

Shrewsbury Staff Welfare Society 235

Shropshire Football Association Benevolent Fund 235

Shropshire Welfare Trust 235

Sibthorpe Trust (Emily Ada) 280

Sidmouth Consolidated Charities 268

Siebel Charity (Mary Elizabeth) 233

Silversmiths and Jewellers Charity 81

Silverton Parochial Charity 268

Silverwood Trust 128

Simmons Pension Fund (Sydney) 71

Simpson Trust 148

Sister Agnes Benevolent Fund 114

Skelton Swindells Trust 202

Skerritt Trust 35

Slough and District Community Fund 282

Smisby Parochial Charity 220

Smith & Earles Charity 324

Smith Charity (Henry) 326

Smith Charity (Abinger) (Henry) 322

Smith Charity (Bedworth) (Henry) 242

Smith Charity (Bisley) (Henry) 323

Smith Charity (Bramley) (Henry) 323

Smith Charity (Capel) (Henry) 323

Smith Charity (Chobham) (Henry) 324

Smith Charity (Dovercourt) (Henry) 292

Smith Charity (Eastbrook Estate) (Henry) 321

Smith Charity (Effingham) (Henry) 325

Smith Charity (Esher) (Henry) 325

Smith Charity (Frimley) (Henry) 321

Smith Charity (Gatton) (Henry) 325

Smith Charity (Horley and Salfords) (Henry) 326

Smith Charity (Horne) (Henry) 326

Smith Charity (I Wood Estate) (Henry) 321

Smith Charity (Leigh) (Henry) 326

Smith Charity (Longnet Estate) (Henry) 260

Smith Charity (Newton St Loe) (Henry) 274

Smith Charity (Puttenham and Wanborough) (Henry) 321

Smith Charity (Richmond) (Henry) 321

Smith Charity (Send and Ripley) (Henry) 322

Smith Charity (UK) (Henry) 128

Smith Charity (Walton-on-the-Hill) (Henry) 328

Smith Charity (West Clandon) (Henry) 328

Smith Charity (West Horsley) (Henry) 328

Smith Charity (Westbury) (Henry) 276

Smith Charity (Woking) (Henry) 328

Smith Charity (Wotton) (Henry) 328

Smith Charity, Coventry (Samuel) 246

Smith Mair Bequest (Miss Annie) 157

Smorthwaite Charity 177

Snowball Trust 212

Society for Mucopolysaccharide Diseases 53

Society for Relief of Widows & Orphans of Medical Men 86

Society for the Assistance of Ladies in Reduced Circumstances 40

Society for the Orphans and Children of Ministers & Missionaries of the Presbyterian Church in Ireland 138

Society for the Relief of Distress 334

Society for the Relief of Poor Clergymen 128

Society of Authors Pension Fund 66

Society of Chiropodists (Benevolent Fund of the) 87

Society of Friends of Foreigners in Distress 29

Society of Motor Manufacturers & Traders Charitable Trust Fund 88

Society of Radiographers Benevolent Fund 87

Society of Schoolmasters and Schoolmistresses 103

Soham United Charities 288

Sollitt Memorial Trust (Herbert William) 224

Somerset Local Medical Benevolent Fund 273

Souldern United Charities 315

South Brent Parish Lands Charity 268

South Creake Charities 311

South London Relief-in-Sickness Fund 334

South Wales Police Benevolent Fund 165

South Warwickshire Welfare Trust 241

South West Peninsula Football League Benevolent Fund 263

Southampton (City Centre) Relief-in-Need Charity 298

Southampton and District Sick Poor Fund and Humane Society 299

Southampton Trust (Earl of) 295

Southery, Feltwell & Methwold Relief in Need Charity 307

Southport & Birkdale Provident Society 206

Sowton In Need Charity 268

Spalding Memorial Fund (Ellen Rebe) 313

Spalding Relief-in-Need Charity 224

Spanish Welfare Fund 334

Speccott Charity (Peter) 266

Special People Fund 268

Speed Trust (E D) 294

Speranza Trust 24

Sperring Charity (Ralph and Irma) 259

Spilsby Feoffees (Poorlands) Charities 224

Spittal Trust 151

Spondon Relief-in-Need Charity 215

Sponne & Bickerstaffe Charity 229

Springfield United Charities 293

SSAFA Forces Help 114

St Andrew Holborn Charities 337

St Andrews Welfare Trust 152

St Chad's and St Alkmund's Charity 235

St Cyrus Benevolent Fund 149

St George Dragon Trust 334

St George the Martyr (United Charities of) 345

St John the Baptist Charitable Fund 337

St Laurence Relief in Need Trust 282

St Leonards Hospital Charity 186

St Martin's Trust 269

St Marylebone Health Society 347

St Monica Trust Community Fund 256

St Pancras Welfare Trust 337

St Sepulchre (Finsbury) United Charities 341

St Vincent de Paul Society (England & Wales) 25

Staines Parochial Charity 327

Stanford Charitable Trust (Miss Doreen) 28

Stanton Ballard Charitable Trust 314

Stanton Charitable Trust 213

Starfish Trust 46

Stein Charitable Trust (Stanley) 35

Stephenson Memorial Trust (Paul) 38

Stepney Relief-in-Need Charity 347

Stetchworth Relief-in-Need Charity 288

Steventon Allotments & Relief-in-Need Charity 315

Stickford Relief-in-Need Charity 225

Stock Exchange Benevolent Fund 101

Stock Exchange Clerks Fund 101

Stockburn Memorial Trust Fund 228

Stockport Sick Poor Nursing Association 200

Stoddart Samaritan Fund 180

Stoke Mandeville & Other Parishes Charity 283

Stoke Poges United Charities 285

Storey (Foundation of Edward) 128

Stowmarket Relief Trust 319

Strain Nursing Charity (Edith) 272

Straits Settlement & Malay States Benevolent Society 35

Strand Charitable Trust (Mary) 25

Strand Parishes Trust 347

Strasser Foundation 238

Strathclyde Police Benevolent Fund 156

Strattons Bequest (Mrs Rona P) 103

Stroke Association 56

Sudbury Municipal Charities 320

Sunderland Guild of Help 181

Sunderland Orphanage & Educational Foundation 182

Sunderland Relief-in-Need Charity (Samuel) 184

Sunninghill Fuel Allotment Trust 283

Sunshine Society Fund 138

Sure Foundation 38

Surfleet United Charities 225

Surplus Fire Fund 154

Surrey Association for Visual Impairment 322

Sussex Police Charitable Trust 279

Sutterton Parochial Charity Trust 225

Sutton Coldfield Municipal Charities 250

Sutton Nursing Association 346

Sutton St James United Charities 225

Swaffham Bulbeck Relief-in-Need Charity 288

Swaffham Relief In Need Charity 311

Swallow & Others (Charities of Nicholas) 289

Swansea & District Friends of the Blind 167

Sway Welfare Aid Group 296

Sweet Charity 78

Swineshead Poor Charities 225

Swiss Benevolent Society 31

T

Tailors Benevolent Institute 71

Talisman Charitable Trust 25

Tamlin Charity 273

Tamworth Municipal Charity 239

Tansley Charity Trust 249

Tate Trust (Mrs A Lacy) 289

Taunton Aid in Sickness Fund 274

Taunton Town Charity 274

Tavistock, Whitchurch & District Nursing Association Trust Fund 263

Taylor Fund (Archibald) 157

Taylor Fund (H A) 220

Teesside Emergency Relief Fund 181

Temple West Trust (Emily) 346

Tenby Relief-in-Need & Pensions Charity 167

Tettenhall Relief-in-Need & Educational Charity 250

Textile Benevolent Association (1970) 71

Thame Welfare Trust 313

Thanet Charities 304

Thaxted Relief-in-Need Charities 293

The Dunwich Town Trust 316

The Pakenham Charities for the Poor 319

Theatrical Guild 65

Thomas Charity for Women & Girls (Lloyd) 32

Thompson Poors Rate Gift (Thomas) 182

Thompson Pritchard Trust 235

Thomson Trust (Hannah & Margaret) 150

Thornbury Consolidated Charities (administered by Thornbury Town Trust) 260

Thorngate Relief-in-Need and General Charity 297

Thornton Fund 128

Thorpe Parochial Charities 327

Thorpe Trust 234

Three Oaks Trust 25

Three Parishes Fund 296

Thursley Charities 327

Tile Hill & Westwood Charities for the Needy Sick 249

Timber Trades Benevolent Society 60

Tobacco Trade Benevolent Association 103

Todd (Charity of Edith Emily) 236

Todd Deceased (Charity of Edith Emily) 239

Todmorden War Memorial Fund 189

Tollard Trust 29

Toras Chesed (London) Trust 131

Torchbearer Trust Fund 128

Tottenham District Charity 340

Town Estate Charity 314

Town Moor Money Charity 183

Townend Charity (Ethel Maude) 174

Townrow Pensions Fund (Arthur) 128

Towries Charity (Robert) 174

Tracy Trust 282

Trades House of Glasgow 158

Trained Nurses Annuity Fund 87

Transport Benevolent Fund 92

Trant Goodwill Trust 296

Trinity House Maritime Charity 97

Tripp (Blue Coat) (Charity of John) 222

Troughton Charitable Trust (Mrs S H) 146

Tuberous Sclerosis Association Benevolent Fund 56

Turner Trust (Kathryn) 279

Tutbury General Charities 240

Twyford and District Nursing Association 296

Tyler Charity for the Poor 222

Tyringham Pension Fund for the Blind 284

U

UBA Benevolent Fund 66

UCTA Samaritan Benefit Fund Society 72

UNISON Welfare 91

UNITE the Union Benevolent Fund 67

United Charities of Saint Martin 252

United Law Clerks Society 81

United Utilities Trust Fund 192

Unity Fund for the Elderly 259

Universal Beneficent Society 35

Upwell (Cambridgeshire) Consolidated Charities 286

Ure Elder Fund for Widows 158

Uxbridge United Welfare Trusts 340

V

Vardy Foundation 26

Vawer's Charity (William) 167

Vegetarian Charity 38

Veterinary Benevolent Fund 104

Victoria Convalescent Trust 32

Victoria Homes Trust 138

Vincent Trust Fund (Eric W) 212

Vision Impaired West Glamorgan 165

Vokins Charitable Trust 279

Voluntary Service Aberdeen (Fuel Fund of) 149

W

Wake Charity (Bruce) 46

Walberswick Common Lands 320

Walker Benevolent Fund (Angus) 149

Wallingford Municipal & Relief-in-Need Charities 315

Walsh Fund (John) 180

Walsoken United Charities 289

Wandsworth Combined Charity 347

Wantage District Coronation Memorial & Nursing Amenities Fund 279

Wappenham Poors Land Charity 229

Warbleton Charity 291

Ward Charitable Trust (Peter) 313

Ware Charities 299

Warrington Sick & Disabled Trust 194

Warsop United Charities 234

Warwick Provident Dispensary 244

Warwick Relief in Need Charity 241

Warwickshire Constabulary Benevolent Fund 241

Watch and Clock Makers (National Benevolent Society of) 105

Waterloo Parish Charity for the Poor 348

Watford Health Trust 301

Watton Relief-in-Need Charity 311

Watts and The City of Rochester Almshouse Charities (Richard) 305

Webb Memorial Fund (Joanne) 246

Wellfield Trust 300

Welsh Rugby Charitable Trust 161

Welton Village Hall (formerly The Welton Town Lands Trust) 229

Wembley Samaritan Fund 336

West Gate Benevolent Trust 232

West Kirby Charity 207

West Sussex County Nursing Benevolent Fund 329

West Yorkshire Police (Employees) Benevolent Fund 184

Westminster Almhouses Foundation 348

Westminster Amalgamated Charity 348

Weston Memorial Fund (Harry) 249

Westward Trust 38

Westwood Charity (Chris) 250

Weybridge Land Charity 328

White (Ecclesiastical Charity of George) 293

Whittlesey Charity 289

Widows Fund 129

Widows, Orphans & Dependants Society of the Church in Wales 161

Williams Charities (Elizabeth) 163

Williams Charity (William) 269

Williamson Memorial Trust 35

Willingham & District Relief-in-Sickness Charity 222

Willis Trust (Henry & James) 252

Wilmington Parochial Charity 306

Wilmington Trust 175

Wilmslow Aid Trust 193

Wiltshire Ambulance Service Benevolent Fund 275

Wimbledon Guild of Social Welfare (Incorporated) 343

Winchester Rural District Welfare Trust 296

Winchester Welfare Charities 296

Windlesham United & Poors Allotment Charities 322

Wine Trade Foundation 79

Winham Foundation (Francis) 37

Winterscale's Charity (Robert) 177

Wireless for the Bedridden 35

Wirksworth and District Trust Fund 213

Witley Charitable Trust 322

Witting Trust (S C) 29

Witton Charity 307

Wokingham United Charities 282

Wonersh Charities 322

Wooburn, Bourne End & District Relief-in-Sickness Charity 284

Wood Bequest and the James Wood & Christina Shaw Bequests (James) 155

Wood Charity (John Theodore) 163

Wood Green (Urban District) Charity 340

Woodmancy Charitable Foundation (Christine) 263

Woodthorpe Relief-in-Need Charity 213

Woodton United Charities 312

Woolaston Walsall Charity (Blanch) 250

Woolwich & Plumstead Relief-in-Sickness Fund 338

Worcester Consolidated Municipal Charity 253

Worcestershire Cancer Aid Committee 252

Wormley Parochial Charity 301

Worplesdon Parish Charities (including the Henry Smith Charity) 328

Wraxall Parochial Charities 259

Wrenbury Consolidated Charities 193

Wrexham & District Relief in Need Charity 164

Wright (Charity of Jane) 177

Wright Funk Fund 172

WRNS Benevolent Trust 115

WRVS Benevolent Trust 41

Wybunbury United Charities 194

Wylde Memorial Charity (Anthony & Gwendoline) 212

Wylie Fund (Eliza Haldane) 146

Wymeswold Parochial Charities 221

Y

Yardley Great Trust 247

Yelvertoft & District Relief-in-Sickness Fund 226

Yonge Charity (Reverend Duke) 264

York City Charities 177

York Dispensary Charitable Trust 176

York Fund for Women & Girls 178

Yorkshire County Bowling Association Benevolent Fund 172

Yorkshire Water Community Trust 172

Young Memorial Trust (Jonathan) 212

Z

Zimbabwe Rhodesia Relief Fund 31

ZSV Trust 131